GW00494695

The Boulter Letters

The Boulter Letters

Kenneth Milne and Paddy McNally

EDITORS

FOUR COURTS PRESS

This book was set in 10.5 on 12.5 point Times New Roman by
Mark Heslington, Scarborough, North Yorkshire for
FOUR COURTS PRESS
7 Malpas Street, Dublin 8, Ireland
www.fourcourtspress.ie
and in North America for
FOUR COURTS PRESS
c/o ISBS, 920 N.E. 58th Avenue, Suite 300, Portland, OR 97213.

© Kenneth Milne, Paddy McNally and Four Courts Press 2016

A catalogue record for this title
is available from the British Library.

ISBN 978-1-84682-290-2

All rights reserved. No part of this publication may be reproduced,
stored in or introduced into a retrieval system, or transmitted,
in any form or by any means (electronic, mechanical,
photocopying, recording or otherwise), without the
prior written permission of both the copyright
owner and publisher of this book.

Printed in Great Britain
by CPI Antony Rowe, Chippenham, Wilts.

Contents

Acknowledgments

We have pleasure in acknowledging the very considerable assistance that we have received from the staffs of the Representative Church Body Library, the library of Trinity College Dublin and the National Library of Ireland. Other repositories whose staff and resources were consulted, and to whose custodians we wish to express our thanks were those of the British Library; the National Archives, Kew; the Parliamentary Archives, Westminster; the Public Record Office of Northern Ireland; the Bodleian Library, Oxford; the library of Christ Church College, Oxford; the library of Magdalen College, Oxford; the library of the University of Cambridge; the library of Trinity College, Cambridge; the Guildhall Library, London; Pearse Street Library, Dublin; University of St Andrews Library; Merchant Taylors' School; the Merchant Taylors' Company; the Worshipful Company of Coopers; London Metropolitan Archives; the Family Records Centre, London; Hampshire Record Office; and Southwark Local History Library. We are particularly grateful to Dr Stephen Maw of Oxford University Press and Judith Curthoys of Christ Church, Oxford, for their research on our behalf.

We thank Professor Toby Barnard, Professor Brendan Simms, Professor Nial Osborough, Professor Edward McParland, Dr Stuart Kinsella, Dr Caitríona Ní Dhúill and Mr Aonghus Dwane for their assistance at various stages and it is our wish to record our particular gratitude to Professor David Hayton of the Queen's University, Belfast, who has taken an interest in the project from the start, and whose considerable knowledge of the period in question has been most generously put at our disposal, especially where the biographical section of the work is concerned. While, needless to say, such errors and omissions that may remain are entirely the responsibility of the editors, they would have been much more numerous had not Professor Hayton's expertise been so readily available to us.

For permission to publish letters included in this volume we wish to thank the British Library Board and the controller of Her Majesty's Stationery Office. Letters from the Devonshire manuscripts are reproduced by permission of the duke of Devonshire and the Chatsworth House Trust.

Kenneth Milne wishes to record his gratitude to the late former provost of Oriel College, Oxford, Professor Ernest Nicholson, and Mrs Nicholson, for their kind hospitality.

We gladly acknowledge the permission granted by the board of Trinity College Dublin to reproduce the Bindon portrait of Archbishop Boulter on the cover and thank the Royalties Fund of the General Synod of the Church of Ireland for financial contributions towards publication.

The staff of Four Courts Press have shown exemplary patience and skill in bringing the book, first proposed in Dr Michael Adams' lifetime, to publication.

Bibliographical note

Kenneth Milne

There must be few studies of mid-eighteenth-century Ireland that do not at some point or other make reference to the printed editions of Primate Boulter's letters. Yet it is two and a half centuries since they first appeared, initially from the Clarendon Press in Oxford in 1769 as *Letters Written by His Excellency Hugh Boulter, DD, Lord Primate of All Ireland*, and a year later in Dublin, from George Faulkner. A new edition would seem to be timely, to put it mildly.

The 'advertisement' that prefaced both the Oxford and Dublin editions informed the reader that the letters had been collected by the archbishop's secretary, Ambrose Philips, and deposited by him in the library of Christ Church, Oxford, where Boulter had been dean from 1719 to 1724. With the exception of a few fair copies made by Philips, the 'advertisement' avers, all the originals were in Boulter's own hand. There is evidence in the accounts of the Oxford University Press that they were published 'at the expense of Dr Wall of Christ Church'.[1] Neither the archives of the press nor those of the college throw any light on this entry. Wall, who graduated in 1730, and died at the age of eighty-six in 1791, 'senior student of Christ Church and the eldest member of the university',[2] may have been motivated by simple *pietas* towards a former dean whose reputation no doubt lived after him. He would undoubtedly have received every encouragement in his endeavours from George Faulkner, the Dublin publisher. Many of the annotations to the Clarendon volumes can, as we know from the Dublin edition, be attributed to Faulkner, 'the most considerable bookseller-printer in eighteenth-century Ireland',[3] who was well known in literary, and to some extent political, circles in both Dublin and London. Clearly, Faulkner had a hand in the 1769 edition, and was cited on the title page as one from whom the Oxford edition might be purchased, along with such London booksellers as Daniel Price, manager of the Clarendon Press, and Robert Horsfield, treasurer of the Stationers Company.[4]

The *Letters* received a fair degree of attention from reviewers. *The Monthly Review or Literary Journal*, a publication very largely comprised of

---

1   Harry Carter, *A history of the Oxford University Press* (Oxford, 1975), i, p. 289.
2   Joseph Foster, *Alumni Oxoniensis, 1715–1886*, iv, p. 1489, *sub nom.* Wall, William.
3   M. Pollard, in W.J. McCormack (ed.), *Blackwell companion to modern Irish culture* (Oxford, 1999), *sub nom.* Faulkner, George.
4   John Nichols, *Literary anecdotes of the eighteenth century comprising biographical memoirs of William Bowyer, printer, FSA, and many of his learned friends*, 9 vols (London, 1813–15), iii, pp 426, 607.

book reviews, deemed the two volumes 'a valuable addition to the stock of materials for the history of Ireland', conceding, however, that they failed to 'display' Boulter's character 'as a divine', in which respect 'he was never, that we can recollect, greatly distinguished'.[5] Having described Boulter as a steady friend to the interests of Ireland, the reviewer, rather more surprisingly, claims that the archbishop always 'emphatically styled' Ireland as 'his country' from the time of his appointment to the primacy.[6] The reviewer also provides us with a pen portrait of the primate as being 'easy of access, affable and polite, and remarkable for a peculiar cheerfulness and sweetness of temper'.[7]

The Critical Review; or Annals of Literature by a Society of Gentlemen gave the *Letters* even more extensive treatment, deeming them 'the best evidences ever published of that extreme jealousy with which the English administration, under the two first princes of the Brunswick line, beheld the people of Ireland, and of the vast attention that was paid to the preservation of their dependency upon the crown of Great Britain!'[8] Providing some historical background to Boulter's role (when James Butler, 2nd duke of Ormond, was still alive and the Irish house of commons 'out of humour' with the English ministry), the reviewer claims that to all intents and purposes the primate was 'first minister' of Ireland. In fact, the *Review* contends, the *Letters* are those of 'a minister and a man of business' rather than of 'a pastor and a prelate'. His 'penetration' into every department of business is noted, though due account is taken of evidence, both in the letters and the footnotes, largely Faulkner's, that the primate was a generous giver. However, commenting on the 'naked' manner in which the letters are presented, the writer proceeds to supply some context. The primate's hostility to Archbishop King and Dean Swift is noted (as well as his 'closeness' to Philips, 'editor of the letters'). While maintaining that the *Letters* do indeed constitute 'the most authentic history of Ireland' for the period, *The Critical Review* attributes to Boulter a style marked by 'great force of expression, without violating, and, indeed without cultivating, any graces, either of elegance or delicacy'. Stylist or not, it says something for the merit of his correspondence that to this day the Boulter letters remain the authentic addition to the stock of materials for the history of Ireland that they were deemed to be over two hundred years ago.

5   *The Monthly Review or Literary Journal*, 42 (London, 1770), 287–8.
6   Ibid., 288.
7   Ibid., 289.
8   *The Critical Review; or Annals of Literature by a Society of Gentlemen*, 29 (London, 1770), 1827.

Hugh Boulter: a biographical sketch

Kenneth Milne

I

Hugh Boulter was born on 4 January 1672/3, a mere twelve years after the restoration of the Stuart line to the thrones of England, Scotland and Ireland. The city of London still bore marks of the devastation caused by the Great Fire of 1666, among these being the shells of burnt-out churches and the ruins of St Paul's cathedral. His father, John, was a parishioner of St Katharine Cree in Leadenhall Street, one of the few churches that survived the fire, and described by John Betjeman as 'the only Laudian church in London'.[1] The population of the parish in 1695 was about 1,600 and the number of inhabited houses 320. Disappointingly, the name Boulter does not figure on any of the monuments in the church, nor does it feature on the memorials in the tiny graveyard.[2] Parish baptismal records for the period 1663–93 are held in the Guildhall Library, London, but no entry for Hugh's baptism is to be found there.[3]

Lacking evidence from ecclesiastical sources, we are thrown back on the entry on Hugh Boulter in *Biographia Britannica*, where, according to 'memoirs communicated by one who was most intimate with Dr Boulter from his youth to his death' (possibly Joseph Wilcocks, bishop of Gloucester and then Rochester), the future primate of all Ireland was born in or near London of a 'reputable and estated family', the estates situated near Oxford, and ground rents drawn from London property in Bermondsey, Cripplegate

---

1 C.T. Robinson, *A register of the scholars admitted into Merchant Taylors' School from 1562 to 1874, compiled from authentic sources and edited with biographical notices*, 2 vols (Lewes, 1882), i, p. 315. I am grateful to J.G. Brown, archivist of the school, for his assistance. Eric de Maré, *Wren's London* (London, 1975), p. 87; John Betjeman (ed.), *Collins guide to English parish churches* (London, 1958), p. 253.

2 Anne Whiteman (ed.), *The Compton census of 1676: a critical edition* (London, 1976), p. 42. Noted by Kenneth Milne on a visit to the church on 11 Sept. 2001.

3 Guildhall Library, MS 78 89/1. Nor has a search of the vestry minute book of St Katharine Cree for the years 1639–78 and of the churchwardens' accounts for 1650–91 yielded any relevant information (MSS 1196 and 1198/1). Lists of parish residents for 1662 and 1664 (MSS 7689/1, 2) likewise proved unhelpful. Neither does John Boulter's name appear on the roll of members of the Company of Merchant Taylors, though it would have been usual for someone of his standing to belong both to a parish and a livery company (Peter Earle, *The making of the English middle class: business, society and family life in London, 1660–1730* (London, 1989), p. 252). I was advised by the Hon. Curator of the Worshipful Company of Coopers some years ago that many company records were destroyed in the Great Fire and that it is indeed possible that John Boulter belonged to such a company.

and Kensington.[4] His father, John, died in 1708 in the parish of St Olave, Southwark, possibly when staying with his son, who was rector. John Boulter's burial on 8 August 1708 is recorded in the register of St Katharine Cree and his will testifies to his landed assets.[5] The family's ownership of property is well documented, and Hugh's own will[6] lists substantial properties that tally with those bequeathed him by his father, who would seem to have belonged to an increasingly influential class in late seventeenth-century English society, possessing sufficient landed estates to give him social status, yet a man of business at a time when the Bank of England was newly founded and the activities of stock-jobbers were soon to be formalized as the stock exchange.

From 1678 to 1681, politicians and public opinion were much exercised with debating the prospect that should the king's brother James, duke of York, succeed to the throne, England would be faced with the first avowedly Catholic monarch since Mary Tudor. James' conversion to Roman Catholicism had already cost him his position as lord high admiral and periods of exile. The 'exclusion crisis' that ensued saw strenuous efforts on the part of some politicians (Whigs) to exclude James from the succession, while others (Tories) supported his cause, the two parties, whose rivalry was to lie at the heart of English politics for generations to come, deriving their nicknames from the derogatory terms attaching to Scottish and Irish rebels.

The revolution of 1688–9 that gave the crown to William III and Mary was bipartisan, but soon Whigs and Tories were again in deep conflict with one another. These were by no means monolithic political parties, indeed they were often divided among themselves. Yet whatever their passing internal divisions, the parties differed significantly on points of principle, Tories being more fervent than Whigs in their protectiveness of the prerogatives of the crown and of the established Church of England. Tories were especially alarmed by a Whig tendency towards the toleration of religious dissent. Moreover, some Tories, however much they might have wished to distance themselves from Jacobitism, were inhibited by their consciences from swearing loyalty to William and Mary. As an alumnus of Merchant Taylors' School, Hugh Boulter must surely have been aware that Ambrose

4   Andrew Kippis, *Biographia Britannica* (2nd ed. London, 1778–93), ii, p. 429 ff.; Joseph Wilcocks was a virtual contemporary at Merchant Taylors' and Magdalen (J.R. Bloxam, *A register of the presidents, fellows, demies ... and other members of Saint Mary Magdalen College in the University of Oxford from the foundation of the college to the present time* (Oxford and London, 1879), i, p. 120). Also, see *ODNB, sub nom.* Wilcocks, Joseph.
5   Guildhall Library, MS 7889/1; Family Records Centre (London), Prerogative Court of Canterbury, wills and administrations, 1701–99, 'John Boulter, Sept 1709' (Mic. A. Prob 6/85).
6   Copy of probate by decree of will of Hugh Boulter, archbishop of Armagh (NAI, T. 9643).

Bonwicke, who had followed the headmaster of his time there (John Hartcliffe), had been removed in 1691 for his nonjuring scruples.[7]

When seeking to understand Boulter's loyalties and politics in later life, it is essential to have in mind the political and ecclesiastical environment of his early years and to appreciate that whether viewed from the standpoint of parliament, church or academia the reigns of William III and Anne were among those periods of British history most riven by party faction. We cannot assume that the future primate's family was Whig rather than Tory, but it is likely to have been the former, the Tories tending to be identified with the special interests of landed property, while close ties existed between Whig magnates and the City, with bankers, manufacturers and overseas merchants being prominent on the Whig benches in parliament.[8]

On 11 September 1685, Hugh Boulter was admitted to Merchant Taylors' School, one of several London academies under the visitation or in the gift of city companies, and which had some link with the parish of St Katharine Cree. A 'merchant taylor' had funded the adornment of the church, and its roof was embellished with the company's arms. The school, whose statutes were framed in 1561,[9] could claim numerous distinguished alumni. Among them were several bishops, including Lancelot Andrewes (Winchester), Thomas Tenison (London, later Canterbury) and Matthew Wren (uncle to the architect of St Paul's, and who, as bishop of Ely, suffered great privations during the Cromwellian Protectorate). It has been calculated that 13.7 per cent of bishops appointed between 1689 and 1721 were alumni of Merchant Taylors' School. It boasted but one master and one usher in the 1660s, yet came to enjoy such a reputation that 2,357 boys were admitted in the years from 1700 to 1719, and it became one of London's biggest and most prestigious academies.[10] The school was credited with having a good library, provided by the Company of Merchant Taylors, which survived when the other school buildings fell victim to the Great Fire. St Katharine Cree was made available for use as a classroom on condition that a barrier was erected to keep the boys from running about the church. By the time Boulter was a pupil, new premises had been completed.[11]

7   *ODNB, sub nom.* Hartcliffe, John.
8   Geoffrey Holmes, *British politics in the age of Anne* (revised ed. London and Ronceverte, 1987), pp 151, 172, 182.
9   Robinson, *Register*, i, p. 315; P.J. Wallis, 'The Wase school collection: a neglected source in educational history' in *The Bodleian Library Record*, iv (1952–3), 78–104 at 80–1; E. Hatton, *A new view of London: or, an ample account of that city in eight sections* (London, 1708), i, pp 181–4; Nicholas Carlisle, *A concise description of the endowed grammar schools in England and Wales: ornamented with engravings*, 2 vols (London, 1818), ii, p. 59.
10 Geoffrey Holmes, *Augustan England: professions, state and society, 1680–1730* (London, 1982), pp 56–7.
11 Carlisle, ii, p. 67; D.R. Hirschberg, 'A social history of the Anglican episcopate, 1660–1760' (PhD, University of Michigan, 1976), p. 187. Like Boulter, 7.8 % were

Boulter matriculated at Christ Church, Oxford in 1687, aged fifteen, at a time when seventeen was more usual, his father designated 'pleb' in the college register, ranking below those of noble (or episcopal) lineage in a sharply stratified society, though the more well-to-do of the plebs went to Christ Church.[12] The following year, he was elected a demy of Magdalen, subsisting on one half of a fellow's income, eventually to return to Christ Church as dean in 1719.

Oxford colleges have never been strangers to politics, whether national or collegiate, but seldom have the two strands been more closely intertwined than in the second half of the seventeenth century. The alliance between church and state which underlay the foundations of the English *ancien régime* was reflected in the unreformed universities of Oxford and Cambridge, and the Magdalen to which Boulter transferred in 1688 was no exception.[13] A case in point was that of John Hough, president of the college, who had been chaplain to the duke of Ormond, lord lieutenant of Ireland, an advantageous position since chaplains to the lords lieutenant almost inevitably obtained preferment in the church.[14] Hough had been appointed head of house at Magdalen in 1687, but was removed by James II, who summoned the fellows to an audience at Christ Church and instructed them to appoint another president.[15] Hough was, however, restored in 1688, the year of Boulter's admission, and would secure further tokens of royal pleasure when he became in turn bishop of Oxford (a poor diocese, which he held *in commendam* with Magdalen), followed by translations to Lichfield and Coventry, and, eventually Worcester.[16]

Magdalen was particularly noted as a nursery of high-churchmanship, and while great numbers of the members of both universities were uneasy at the deposition of King James II, Oxford had a higher incidence of nonjurors than did Cambridge.[17] The most celebrated exponent of Oxford's Toryism

sons of merchants or 'in trade' (ibid., p. 176); W.A.L. Vincent, *The grammar schools: their continuing tradition, 1660–1714* (London, 1969), p. 127; K.E. Campbell, *St Katharine Cree Church: a brief history and account of St Katharine Cree Church* (revised ed. [London], 1999), not paginated; Robinson, *Register*, pp x–xi; Vincent, *Grammar schools*, p. 82.

12 Robinson, *Register*, i, p. 315; Bloxam, *Register*, iii, pp 60–1; Julian Hoppit, *A land of liberty: England, 1689–1727* (Oxford, 2000), p. 171; Lucy Sutherland, *The University of Oxford in the eighteenth century* ([Oxford], 1973), p. 5.

13 John Gascoigne, *Science, politics and universities in Europe, 1600–1800* (Aldershot, 1998), pp 401–2.

14 For examples of the preferment obtained by chaplains to the lord lieutenant, see Kenneth Milne (ed.), *Christ Church cathedral, Dublin: a history* (Dublin, 2000), pp 256–7.

15 *ODNB, sub nom.* James II and VII (W.A. Speck).

16 H.A. Wilson, *Magdalen College* (London, 1899), pp 211–12; 'Two presidents of Magdalen', *Temple Bar: a London Magazine*, 57 (1 Sept. – Dec. 1879), pp 63–79.

17 *Sermons and charges by the Rt Revd John Hough, D.D...to which is prefixed a memoir of his life by William Russell, B.D., fellow of Magdalen College* (Oxford, 1821); Gascoigne, *Science, politics and universities*, p. 404.

was Henry Sacheverell, who would be impeached by a Whig ministry in 1710, and who was more typical of the ethos of his college than were contemporaries such as Joseph Addison and Hugh Boulter. Thomas Gibson, bishop of London, another Magdalen contemporary of Boulter, both as demy and fellow, recalled Sacheverell as having been highly influential in the college, and much criticized by his Whig enemies.[18]

The foremost issues that preoccupied the politician, the ecclesiastic and the college don were facets of a common struggle to determine the political and religious character of the kingdom. The stances of the two major political parties, Tory and Whig, were reflected in similar partisanship engaged in by the 'high' and 'low' clergy of the Church of England. Tory high-churchmen were more sacerdotally and sacramentally inclined than were low-churchmen, having a higher regard for ecclesiastical hierarchy and church tradition. They saw themselves as 'the church party'. The low-church Whigs were more likely to evince a toleration of Dissent, even to the extent of making theological concessions in the interest of Protestant solidarity that were anathema to those who espoused high-churchmanship. There were, of course, exceptions to such generalizations. Some high-churchmen were eirenically inclined towards their Dissenting brethren, while by no means all low-churchmen were so disposed (as Boulter was to discover in Ireland). Similarly, there were exceptions to the general rule that high church went with Tory and low church with Whig. Nonetheless, in broad terms, that was how they cast their votes and the depth of animosity between church and Dissent contributed significantly to a widening of the gulf between Tory and Whig.[19] Party divisions in both church and state, in parliament and convocation (the Church of England's deliberative and legislative assemblies in Canterbury and York), were especially sharp during William's reign. Tories and high-churchmen were particularly incensed (and alarmed) that not only, under the terms of the Toleration Act of 1689, could Dissenters now meet legally to conduct their worship in their conventicles, but that public opinion was assailed by anti-Anglican and anticlerical publications in a manner that would have been unthinkable had not the Licensing Act been allowed to lapse in that same year. It was this sense of 'the church in danger' that lay behind the urgent Tory calls for convocation (prorogued since 1689) to be re-convened, reaching their climax in the furore created by Francis Atterbury's pamphlet of 1697 addressed to 'a convocation member', which attributed the growth of irreligion and other social ills to the 'suppression' of convocation, and which found a ready and turbulent response in the lower house. The bishops, mostly appointed by Whig ministries, dominated the

18 'Remarks on some of his contemporaries by Thomas Gibson' (Magdalen College Library, MS 434 C.1.2.13.).
19 Holmes, *Anne*, p. 47.

upper house of convocation while also comprising the lords spiritual at
Westminster. The lower house of convocation, particularly that of
Canterbury, provided a forum for the other clergy, which on occasion saw
passions rise to a frenzy. The reputation of the lower house of convocation
was such that William III, whose prerogative it was to convene it, hesitated
to do so. Nonetheless, when seeking to put together a ministry in 1700, and
beholden to Laurence Hyde, earl of Rochester to 'manage' this, the king
conceded the point and there was set in train a series of acrimonious
sessions. A similar intensity of debate was to recur at the time of
Sacheverell's trial and conviction and their aftermath in Queen Anne's reign.
Tories and high-churchmen were jubilant at the fall of the Whigs that
resulted, as they had been on the accession of the queen, whose devotion to
the interests of the Church of England was well attested. Whigs and low-
churchmen might persevere with their efforts to introduce reliefs for
Dissenters; it was to no avail. Similarly unavailing was a 'defiant front'
against the ministry, posed by Whig prelates, led by Archbishop Tenison
during the Whig period in opposition that was their lot for most of Anne's
reign.[20]

Boulter graduated BA in 1690, being ordained deacon that same year, and
thereby becoming eligible for election to fellowship, which he, together with
Sacheverell and Addison, obtained in 1696, their election being regarded
henceforth as 'the golden election' because of the distinction of the new
fellows.[21] The ministry of the church has been described as 'an overcrowded
profession' at this time. Clerical places were not easily obtained and fellowships were much sought after by men such as Boulter who lacked family
influence or patronage and could now have some expectation of
appointment to one of the many parishes to which the Oxford and
Cambridge colleges held the advowson.[22] Boulter took his MA in 1692 and
the degrees of bachelor and doctor in divinity were to follow (as, in 1730,
was an *ad eundem* doctorate from the University of Dublin, whose affairs
would occupy some of his time as primate of all Ireland). Throughout
Boulter's life, he retained a deep affection for Magdalen, which was to be a
major beneficiary under his will, and it has been suggested that he owed his
initial access to promotion to the good offices of the president, Hough, who
drew him to the attention of Sir Charles Hedges, one of the secretaries of
state (himself a Magdalen man), and who appointed Boulter his domestic
chaplain in 1700.

As with so many spheres of public life at the time, patronage was the key
to appointment to ecclesiastical office, and to subsequent promotion.

20 Ibid., pp 99, 400.
21 Peter Smithers, *The life of Joseph Addison* (2nd ed. Oxford, 1968), p. 13.
22 Geoffrey Holmes, *Augustan England: professions, state and society, 1680–1730*
    (London, 1982), pp 83–7, 93–4.

Chaplaincies such as Boulter's were a vital step on the ladder of preferment for those who lacked the necessary family connections to provide them with a parish living. 'London and the universities of Oxford and Cambridge were clerical labour exchanges where aspirant young clerics jostled "to catch the right eye or lawn sleeve", vying with one another for domestic chaplaincies in households possessed of good advowsons.'[23] Of bishops appointed between 1689 and 1721, 27.5 per cent had served as chaplains to the nobility and 23.5 per cent as bishops' chaplains. In the period from the Restoration of 1660 to 1760, no less than 22 per cent of bishops had themselves been bishops' chaplains, having in some cases assisted their patrons in the oversight of the diocese.[24] As the author of a contemporary pamphlet expressed it, 'merit alone will not raise you, though you have as much as any young man I know; but strong interest, fair opportunity and good recommendation will jostle all virtues, graces and accomplishments whatever ...'[25]

Hedges was secretary of state for the northern department when he appointed Boulter to be his chaplain, thus bringing the young cleric close to the corridors of power. A moderate Tory, Hedges was familiar not only with politics on the grand scale, but also with the political trauma that his old college had experienced under James II, when he had shown himself staunchly Anglican, thus highly commending himself to Queen Anne.[26] His enemies, such as the duchess of Marlborough, regarded him as a man of 'no capacity' for the position he held, 'nor ever could have been in that post but that, as everyone knows, My Lord Rochester cares for nothing so much as a man that he thinks will depend upon him', a man (Hedges) who 'voted very remarkable things that he might keep his place'.[27] His career suffered several vicissitudes, but under Anne he flourished, with intermittent disappointments, being regarded by other ministers as 'very zealous and industrious for his party'.[28]

The social standing of domestic chaplains would appear to have been somewhat ambiguous and the treatment they received varied according to the attitude of their patron. A series of essays published in 1700 (the year

23 Earle, *Making of English middle class*, pp 3–4, 64.
24 Hirschberg, 'Social history of the Anglican episcopate', pp 236 *et seq.*
25 *Advice to a young clergyman how to conduct himself in the common offices of life in a letter from a Right reverend Prelate* (London, 1741), p. 13.
26 Eveline Cruickshanks, Stuart Handley and D.W. Hayton, *The history of parliament: the house of commons*, 5 vols (Cambridge, 2002), iv, p. 318.
27 [Sarah Churchill], *An account of the conduct of the dowager duchess of Marlborough from her first coming to court to the year 1710 in a letter from herself to My Lord—* (London, 1712), pp 167–70.
28 *Memoirs of the secret services of John Macky, Esq., during the reigns of King William, Queen Anne and King George I published by his son Spring Macky* (London, 1733), p. 127.

when Boulter was taken into Hedges' household) included a dissertation on how a chaplain ought to be regarded.[29] For instance, his position in the dining room ought to be above that of the servants; rather, his office was 'to pray, bless and give absolution to those he is concerned with'. He is to counsel, exhort, and reprove the master of the family himself upon occasion (though with respect to his station), 'which offices are inconsistent with the condition of a servant ... He does not receive this commission from the master himself, or from any human authority, but from God himself, whose deputy he is in all things pertaining to religion'.[30] By Boulter's time, the status of chaplain had risen from what it had been for much of the seventeenth century and the appointment of scholars such as Boulter did much to enhance their prestige. Relations between patron and chaplain grew closer. There was 'a flowering of talent among those who wore chaplains' scarves' and patrons sought out men of literary talent to appoint to chaplaincies. Bishops increasingly delegated to them the examination of candidates for ordination.[31]

Hedges was experienced in ecclesiastical matters, having been chancellor and vicar general of the diocese of Rochester (a legal role) from 1686, and he recorded that, together with the bishop, dean and chapter of the diocese, he waited on King William as he passed through that city in 1695.[32] Archbishop William Tenison (1694 to 1715), wrote of how Hedges, as secretary of state, made recommendations to him where clerical appointments were concerned.[33] So it is scarcely surprising that Boulter shortly found himself at Lambeth Palace. Tenison was a scholar and promoted scholars. As rector of St Martin-in-the-Fields, he had established a library for young clergy who complained that they lacked access to books. He showed himself to be assiduous in making parochial visitations and in administering confirmation, on one occasion laying hands on 1,200 candidates in his cathedral at Canterbury, as well as preaching. Boulter may have gained insights into the established Church of Ireland during this period, for Tenison, with the active encouragement of Queen Mary, concerned himself with Irish appointments, serving on a commission set up by William III to deal with church affairs in Ireland, and maintaining that interest when the commission ceased to be active. For instance, he kept in touch with Irish matters through correspondence with Archbishop Narcissus Marsh of

---

29 Jeremy Collier, *Essays upon several moral subjects* (4th ed. London, 1700), pp 179–238.
30 Ibid., pp 199–200.
31 William Gibson, *A social history of the domestic chaplain, 1530–1840* (London and Washington, 1997), pp 39–42, 60–1, 66, 151.
32 Sir Charles Hedges to Sir William Trumbull, 11 Oct. 1695 (*Report on the manuscripts of the marquess of Downshire, preserved at Easthampstead Park, Berkshire* (HMC, 1924), i, p. 562).
33 Sir William Trumbull to bishop of Worcester, 8 July 1693 (ibid., p. 421).

Dublin, and the queen had hoped to persuade Tenison to move to Dublin when Francis Marsh (predecessor to Narcissus, thought to be no relation) died in 1693.[34]

Most bishops' chaplains (Canterbury's most of all) found themselves at the centre of ecclesiastical affairs and were particularly well placed for preferment. Among Tenison's chaplains who attained high office were Edmund Gibson, who held the see of London from 1723 to 1748, and William Wake, who eventually (via Lincoln) succeeded Tenison as archbishop. Boulter's chaplaincies were to reach their apogee some years later when he was called to court, and, as a chaplain to George I, became eligible for very high office indeed. But before that came about, he was to gain parochial experience, first as rector of St Olave's, Southwark, a crown advowson, and, for several years concurrently with that cure, as archdeacon of Surrey.

According to *Biographia Britannica* he owed the appointment to St Olave's to Charles Spencer, third earl of Sunderland, who had replaced Hedges as southern secretary in 1706, and had noticed the young chaplain on occasions when his duties had brought him to court.[35] It has also been conjectured that Addison, Boulter's contemporary at Magdalen, who had served as undersecretary with both Hedges and Sunderland, had assisted in promoting his cause.[36] Sunderland had succeeded to the title on the death of his father in 1702, and through his marriage in 1700 to Lady Ann Churchill, daughter of John Churchill, earl (later duke) of Marlborough, was well connected with the Whig politicians. Given the duchess of Marlborough's views on Hedges, already quoted, it was no doubt advantageous for Boulter that he now had in Sunderland a more politically acceptable patron where Whig ministers were concerned. Spencer, both before and after he came into the title, was regarded as cutting a good figure, both in the commons and subsequently in the lords. His high standing in Hanoverian eyes, which pre-dated their accession, assured him of favour when George I succeeded to the throne, and achieved for him in 1714 the lord lieutenancy of Ireland (which he declined to visit).[37]

Boulter (as was the custom) resigned his Magdalen fellowship on appointment to the living of St Olave's in 1708. According to the diocesan records of Winchester, he entered 'ad rectoriam S. Olavia per mortem ultima

34 Edward Carpenter, *Thomas Tenison, archbishop of Canterbury: his life and times* (London, 1948), pp 62–4.
35 *Biographia Britannica*, ii, 429. Bloxam (*Register*, vi, p. 62) claims that as a chaplain, Boulter 'necessarily appeared often at court, where his merit obtained for him the patronage of Spencer, earl of Sunderland, secretary of state, by whose interest he was advanced to the rectory of St Olave's in Southwark'.
36 Peter Smithers, *The life of Joseph Addison* (2nd ed. Oxford, 1968), p. 176.
37 Patrick McNally, *Parties, patriots and undertakers: parliamentary politics in early Hanoverian Ireland* (Dublin, 1997), p. 47.

incumbantis vacans'. He was presented by the queen, and all the required subscriptions had been made by 16 September 1708 in the following words:

> I, Hugh Boulter, D.D., before my institution to the rectory of St Olave's in the county of Surrey in the diocese of Winton [Winchester] do declare that I will conform to the liturgy of the Church of England as by law established, witness my hand this sixteenth day of September 1708. Hugh Boulter.[38]

Politically, Southwark was by no means safe either for Whigs or Tories, though a strong business interest (especially the brewing trade) and a large Dissenting population operated in favour of the Whigs.[39] Most elections were contested and could be turbulent, even riotous. Dr Sacheverell, who held a chaplaincy at St Saviour's in the borough, had at one stage appeared as a Tory champion and created such uproar that he had had to be escorted back to Oxford in order that the public peace might be maintained.[40]

Boulter attended his first vestry meeting at St Olave's on 25 November 1708,[41] and chaired the meetings regularly thereafter, while on occasion a curate presided. Vestry business was much what one would expect of an early eighteenth-century urban parish. Reports were received from the workhouse committee, and clothing allowances agreed for the boys there; churchwardens were elected; land was set aside for the building of a charity school; and arrangements were made for the maintenance of parish buildings, for fire precautions and for the care of tombstones in the churchyards.[42] In addition to making provision for such routine matters, consideration was given to preserving the health of parishioners in the face of such hazards as it was feared would be brought about by an influx of Palatine Protestants in 1710–11, indemnity being provided for any parochial officers who ran risks when attempting to stem the flood of such settlements.[43] Some thousand Palatines were given temporary accommodation in Southwark before being sent to Ireland and the colonies.[44] The parish was territorially small, if large in population, it being estimated that its fifty acres housed some thirty thousand inhabitants.[45] In 1724 (the year in which Boulter left for Ireland), the records show that 92 marriages were

38 Hampshire Record Office, 21 M65/E4/2/Winchester diocesan papers, institution registers 1697–1716 and subscription books, C1/f.17 v.
39 Cruickshanks et al., *History of parliament: the commons, 1690–1715*, pp 577–8.
40 Ibid., p. 591.
41 Southwark Local History Library. Loose handwritten note in St Olave's parish records (P.C 283. St. O I.; loc. cit., YJ 852 St. O).
42 Vestry book 1604–1724, 25 Nov. 1708, 3 Apr. 1711, 18 July 1716, 31 July 1717, 28 Nov. 1717.
43 Ibid., 18 Jan. 1710, 24 July 1715
44 Cruickshanks et al., *History of parliament: the commons, 1690–1715*, p. 592.
45 R. Ward (ed.), *Parson and parish in eighteenth century Surrey: replies to bishops' visitations*. Surrey Record Society (Guildford, 1994), p. ix.

performed in the parish, 622 baptisms and 933 burials.[46] While visitation responses for Boulter's incumbency do not survive, there is a reference in one of his sermons to a school at St Olave's with 60 girls, and to the fact that 45 girls had been apprenticed since the school's foundation.[47] Visitation records survive for the incumbency of Philip Ayerscough, Boulter's successor, and reveal the existence of a grammar school (62 scholars), a writing school (82 boys), two charity schools (one with 60 girls, the other with 54 boys) and many other kinds of charitable institutions.[48] Such returns suggest that St Olave's was educationally favoured, private enterprise supplementing endowments to a considerable degree. A description of a Southwark charity school, 'sixty boys clothed over a year with caps, bands, coats, stockings and shoes', and taught to spell, read English 'distinctly' and learn the catechism, could equally well have been written about similar institutions in Ireland that Boulter would do much to promote as primate.[49]

Boulter's enthusiasm for 'popular' education was to become especially apparent during his Irish primacy, but was already evident from his authorship of several pieces on education in the *Freethinker*, a short-lived but highly regarded journal founded by Ambrose Philips.[50] Philips was a noted, if minor, figure in both the political and literary worlds, who contributed much of the *Freethinker*'s content himself, and Boulter was one of its occasional contributors. Philips was secretary of the Kit-Kat Club in London, which has been variously described as 'a drinking society' and 'at its height … Britain's pre-eminent political society'.[51] Such institutions, indeed, were somewhat more than the social rendezvous that the former appellation might suggest. It was increasingly in these venues, and not at court, that art and literature were commissioned, business transacted, political plots laid, and the latest fashions put on display.[52]

Philips acknowledged in the first issue that in the title, 'freethinker' might appear to be a synonym for 'atheist'. On the contrary, it sought to awaken 'my countrymen' to the fact that popery is 'an absurd, superstitious, enthu-

---

46 Ibid., pp 57–61.
47 *A sermon preached in the parish of St Sepulchre's, May the 17th, 1722, being Thursday in Whitsun week, at the anniversary meeting of the children educated in the charity schools in and about the cities of London and Westminster by the Revd father in God, Hugh, lord bishop of Bristol* (London, 1722), p. 29.
48 Ibid., pp 57–61; Hampshire Record Office, Visitation returns 21M65/B4/1/3.
49 Ward, *Parson and parish*, p. xx; Hants. R.O., Trelawny MSS, 21M65/J9/7.
50 Nicholas Joost, 'The authorship of the *Freethinker*' in R.P. Bond (ed.), *Studies in early English periodicals* (Chapel Hill, 1957), p. 113.
51 Holmes, *Anne*, pp 21, 297; Ann Somerset, *Queen Anne: the politics of passion, a biography* (London, 2012), p. 529.
52 Robert Buckley and Newton King, *Early modern England, 1485–1714* (Oxford, 2004), p. 35. See also *The portraits of members of the Kit-Kat Club painted during the years 1700–1720 by Sir Godfrey Kneller for Jacob Tonson* (London, 1945) and Ophelia Field, *The Kit-Cat Club* (London, 2008).

siastic, idolatrous, cruel institution', while seeking to combat the deists and to show that Christianity need never be afraid to exercise its 'right of free thought'; hence the title.[53] Philips became a protégé of Boulter's, accompanying him to Ireland as secretary, and Philips' career there, which included a seat in the Irish parliament, was advanced by the future primate.

II

The political scene in England changed radically in 1714, the accession of George I initiating a lengthy period of Whig ascendancy during which Boulter would flourish, having given ample evidence of his loyalty to both church and crown in his sermons, such as when he preached at his friend Gibson's consecration as bishop of Norwich on 12 February 1716. It is the earliest of his sermons to have survived, and, coming but three years before his own consecration, it gives some indication of how he viewed the office of bishop, and of how he would exercise it himself.[54]

He took as his text 2 Timothy 1:6–7: 'Wherefore I put thee in remembrance that thou stir up the gift of God, which is in thee by the putting on of my hands. For God hath not given us the spirit of fear; but of power, and of love, and of a sound mind.' How, he asked rhetorically, is the gift of God to be stirred up? He replied that this would be by prayer, study of the scriptures and meditation. Above all, he emphasizes, it would be by experience: that is, by diligently discharging our duties as ministers of Christ. Paul's address to Timothy, might, he admits, at first glance seem inappropriate to an age when the church seemed secure and was heartily countenanced by the civil governors. But this was no guarantee against suffering grievously from the influence of its own corrupt members. Nor were external threats lacking: 'There have been several doctrines advanced making nearer approaches to popery … that bloody and superstitious religion', which can only lead people to disown most solemn oaths, 'and to throw off all allegiance and subjection to his rightful majesty King George'. As was to be clear from the earliest years of his Irish episcopate, Boulter still took the Jacobite threat seriously; understandably, within months of the rising of 1715. A conviction of the interdependence of church and state would run consistently through his entire episcopal ministry. But equally consistent, though prone to be overlooked in the context of his future eminence in Irish politics, was the sense of dependence on God for the strength to keep faith with both church and crown – 'that family which the providence of God and the laws of the land have set over us'.

In 1717, Boulter was made archdeacon of Surrey, which, like Southwark,

---

53 Smithers, *Addison*, p. 439; *The Freethinker*, 24 Mar. 1718. The library of Trinity College Dublin holds three bound volumes covering 1718–19.
54 Magdalen College Library, Oxford, MS a.18.16 (6).

lay in the diocese of Winchester. Now in his forty-fourth year, such recognition did not necessarily mark Boulter out as destined for greatness, since more than half of the bishops appointed between 1689 and 1721 had achieved such dignity by thirty-nine years of age.[55] His promotion was at least partly due to the advocacy of Edmund Gibson, who, writing to Archbishop Wake in 1716, expressed the hope that 'by the assistance of Your Grace and the bishop of Winchester, [Boulter] is to succeed in my archdeaconary ... a safe man'.[56]

It was customary for archdeacons to visit their archdeaconries once or twice a year and it would appear that Boulter very much modelled his conduct on the pattern established by Wake and Gibson, with which he would have been familiar.[57] Gibson set out the steps whereby he prepared for his first visitation of a parish by addressing the clergy and explaining to them that he was concerned to inspect churches, chancels and parsonages, and also to enquire into how they were carrying out their duties, their manners and their obedience to the canons of the church. It was Gibson's practice to give clergy notice of an impending visit, though not initially to give them precise dates. But it was not the clergy alone whose stewardship was examined at visitations: the churchwardens, who had responsibility for keeping the parish accounts, also came under scrutiny.[58]

Archdeacon Boulter was given further opportunity of personal service to the house of Hanover to which he expressed such unfailing devotion when he was appointed a chaplain to the crown in 1718. According to a description of the office of royal chaplain, published in 1720, and therefore almost contemporaneous with Boulter's tenure, the king's chaplains were forty-eight in number, four of them taking monthly terms of service.[59] When there were five Sundays in the month, the lord chamberlain appointed a preacher, the chaplaincies being regarded as in his gift,[60] though the monarch (or lord chamberlain) was open to recommendations as to who should be summoned to court. According to the memoir of an early eighteenth-century royal chaplain, they preached in the chapel royal on Sundays and church festivals, and before the household every morning. Twice daily, they read the divine

55 Hirschberg, 'Social history of the Anglican episcopate', p. 251.
56 Gibson to Wake, 24 Jan. 1716, Wake Letters, Christ Church Library, Oxford, 6, no. 91.
57 D.M. Owen, *Archives and the user*, i: *The records of the established Church in England* (London, 1970), p. 31.
58 Edmund Gibson, *Of visitations parochial and general: being the charges delivered to the clergy of the archdeaconry of Surrey by Edmund Gibson, DD, late archdeacon of Surrey and now bishop of Lincoln* (London, 1717), pp 1–3, 36; Charles Pendrill, *Old parish life in London* (Oxford, 1937), p. 93.
59 *The present state of the British court: or an account of the civil and military establishment of England* (London, 1720), p. 49.
60 Ibid., p. 50.

service before the king, out of chapel, and said grace before the king at dinner in the absence of the clerk of the closet. They came under the authority of the lord chamberlain, forming part of the staff of the chapel royal: dean, clerk of the closet, closet-keeper and chaplains, together with the gentlemen and boys of the choir.[61] 'Dr Boulter' appears on the rota for the month of May (most of those included had the title 'Dr'). The chaplains received no remuneration for their period of waiting at court, other than dinner, which was served to them on 'separate' tables.[62] Swift wrote to Stella (Esther Johnson) in October 1711 that he had never dined with the chaplains 'till to-day', and that their table was 'the worst provided table at court. We ate on pewter.'[63] The chaplains were, however, permitted by the Henrician statute governing pluralism to hold two 'incompetent' benefices, meaning benefices with the cure of souls, not *sine cures*.[64] It was therefore nothing out of the ordinary that Boulter should have been rector of St Olave's and archdeacon of Surrey while also at court.

The royal chaplains were well placed for promotion, 'being constantly in the king's eye for spiritual preferment, and being esteemed to merit from him by their attendance at court'. Indeed, their services being unremunerated, they considered themselves entitled to consideration. They were 'a class apart' in the contest for promotion, being in the succession of medieval court officials, who, in holy orders, had done much of the king's work, which in England (unlike Continental Europe), had not been the preserve of the aristocracy.[65] To be selected, as Boulter was, to accompany the early Hanoverian kings on their regular visits to Hanover bestowed 'a particular primacy in expectation of reward'.[66] The duke of Newcastle reportedly said, some years on, that 'the king's chaplain at Hanover has always set aside at all times other promises'.[67]

Hanover is the term generally used to describe the electorate of

---

61 Albert Hartstone (ed.), *Memoirs of a royal chaplain 1729–63: the correspondence of Edmund Pyle, DD, chaplain in ordinary to George II, with Samuel Kerrick, DD, vicar of Dersingham, rector of West Newton* (London, 1905), p. 263; J.M. Beattie, *The English court in the reign of George I* (Cambridge, 1967), pp 47–8, 280.

62 It would seem that at a later period an annual allowance replaced the board provided at court (David Baldwin, *The chapel royal: ancient and modern* (London, 1990), p. 261).

63 Jonathan Swift, *Journal to Stella*, 2 vols (Oxford, 1948), ii, p. 378.

64 21 Hen. VIII, c. 13.

65 *Present state of the British court*, p. 49; Norman Sykes, *Church and state in England in the eighteenth century* (rep. New York, 1975), pp 151–2.

66 Boulter's successor in the see of Bristol (Bradshaw) had also been a royal chaplain (C.E. Doble (ed.), *Remarks and collections of Thomas Hearne* (Oxford, 1906), viii, p. 263).

67 N. Sykes, 'The church in Johnson's England' in A.S. Turberville (ed.), *Johnson's England: an account of the life and manners of that age* (rep. Oxford, 1952), pp 15–38.

Brunswick-Lüneberg in the Holy Roman Empire. The ruling family was a
branch of the Guelf dynasty. Among the perquisites of this branch was
alternate succession to the bishopric of Osnabrück, where, during his
brother's possession of the see, George I was to die.[68] The connection
between the electorate of Hanover and the British kingdoms was an entirely
personal one, simply that of several states sharing the same monarch. It
came into being on the elector's succession to Queen Anne. When George I
first travelled to England as king, he brought with him a German chancery,
headed by Count von Bernstorff, to manage Hanoverian business, which
included foreign affairs. The interests of German officials did not necessarily coincide with those of George's English ministers (Sunderland, for
instance) and tensions were not uncommon. These were exacerbated by the
fact that – Hanover being something of a despotic state – more power
resided in the elector's hands than in the king's.[69] One author has described
George I as 'a true German prince of his time', who showed little regard for
the wishes of his people.[70] Both George I and George II visited Hanover for
several months every two years or so, where, basing themselves at the palace
of Herrenhausen on the outskirts of the city of Hanover, or at the electoral
spa of Pyrmont, they conducted tours of inspection of their German lands.
Particularly since the time of the Electress Sophia (George I's mother), the
court, despite the graciousness of its apartments and the splendour of its
gardens, was notably restrained, both in its way of life and its protocol, with
a seriousness of purpose that had been symbolized by Sophia's appointment
of the philosopher Leibnitz to be court librarian.[71] One particular point of
contrast between court life in Hanover and London was observed by John
Toland, 'a Donegal heretic',[72] the controversial, indeed notorious, religious
writer whose travels, sometimes necessitated by his own pamphleteering,
brought him to the Hanoverian court. He wrote to a Dutch politician:

> The clergy seldom appear at court either at Hanover or Berlin, and it would be
> no less scandalous for their characters to be seen soliciting there for prefer-
> ments, than if in your country they went to taverns or coffee-houses, which is

68 The following paragraphs describing Hanover are much indebted to R.M. Hatton,
   George I: elector and king (2nd ed. London, 2001); R.M. Hatton, *The Anglo-
   Hanoverian connection, 1714–60*. Creighton Trust Lectures (London, n.d.); Philip
   Konigs, *The Hanoverian kings and their homeland: a study of the personal union,
   1714–1837* (Sussex, 1993); Joyce Marlow, *The life and times of George I* (London,
   1973) and K.L. Ellis, 'The administrative connection between Britain and Hanover',
   Jn. Soc. Archiv., iii (1965–9), 546–66; Walter Graham (ed.), *The letters of Joseph
   Addison* (London, 1941), p. 140.
69 Derek McKay, 'The struggle for control of George I's northern policy 1718–19',
   Journal of Modern History, 45 (1973), 378; Marlow, *George I,* pp 21–2.
70 Konigs, *Hanoverian Kings*, pp 28–9
71 Ellis, 'Administrative connections', p. 553; Marlow, *George I,* pp 30–3.
72 J.G. Simms, 'John Toland (1670–1722), a Donegal heretic', *Irish Historical Studies*,
   16:63 (1969), 304–20.

as great a disgrace as if in England they frequented the theatre or other house of worse fame.[73]

There was usually at least one of the English chaplains serving at Herrenhausen when George I was there, and in 1719 that office was discharged by Hugh Boulter. The king's health was poor at the time, his doctors had insisted that he take the waters at Pyrmont and he had left England in May, much to the chagrin of his English ministers.[74]

Relations between the king and prince of Wales were notoriously bad. If anything this strengthened the monarch's determination to exert what he deemed to be his prerogatives where the upbringing of his grandson Frederick was concerned. While the prince and princess of Wales, Frederick's parents, resided in London, the young prince remained in Hanover as the elector's representative at court, and was educated there. Lady Mary Wortley Montagu waited on him in 1716, noting 'our young prince has all the accomplishments that it is possible to have at his age, with an air of sprightliness and understanding'.[75] Among these accomplishments may have been his command of the English tongue, doubtless part of the curriculum devised for him by Boulter, one of the tutors personally selected by the king for his grandson. Others were, it seems, recruited locally.[76] Addison, in one of his letters, alluded to the fact that 'His Grace [Boulter] had some share in teaching his highness English when he was a chaplain at Hanover'.[77] It can therefore be assumed that while George I was 'most solicitous for the advancement of his Hanover chaplains',[78] he would have been particularly well disposed towards Boulter's claims. Joseph Wilcocks, Boulter's contemporary at Magdalen, wrote that as a royal chaplain 'to the present king's grandfather' at Hanover, Boulter had frequent occasion to dine with Prince Frederick, 'who speaks English pretty well', but to what extent Boulter and the prince remained in contact is impossible to ascertain. However, when Frederick visited London in 1728, Boulter asked Bishop Gibson to present his humble duty, and to explain to the prince that but for matters of state in Ireland he would have waited on him himself.[79]

Opportunity for a sign of royal favour came while the monarch was out of England and Boulter was at hand in Hanover. News reached the king that

73 John Toland, *An account of the courts of Prussia and Hanover: sent to a minister of state in Holland* (London, 1714), p. 58.
74 Hatton, *George I*, p. 158.
75 Lady Mary Wortley Montagu to countess of Bristol, 25 Nov. 1716, in W.M. Thomas (ed.), *The letters and works of Lady Mary Wortley Montagu*, 2 vols (new ed. London, 1887), p. 135.
76 John Walters, *The royal griffin: Frederick prince of Wales, 1707–51* (London, 1972), pp 21–2, 27.
77 Walter Graham (ed.), *The letters of Joseph Addison* (London, 1941), p. 217.
78 Sykes, *Church and state*, p. 39.
79 Boulter to Gibson, 21 Dec. 1728.

George Smalridge, bishop of Bristol and dean of Christ Church, Oxford, had died on 27 September 1719. The two positions were offered to Boulter. He accepted the mitre, and it can be assumed that for the remainder of his assignment in Germany, the chaplain's mind was in a state of some excitement and anticipation.

Yet whatever his satisfaction on achieving episcopal rank, Boulter retained his living of St Olave's for some time to come, and this cannot but have been to the advantage of the parish as he now brought episcopal weight to its affairs. He already appeared in the vestry minutes as 'Mr Archdeacon', subsequent to his appointment to that rank in 1717, when, as befitted an archdeacon, he led his vestry in scrutinizing workmen's bills.[80] In 1720 (the year following his appointment to both Bristol and Christ Church, Oxford), there is a reference to Mr Barron, curate for the lord bishop of Bristol, who attended vestry meetings from then on, and, for instance, appointed church-wardens in the bishop's name.[81] Boulter remained on the parish committee that continued to press the commissioners for a new church. He also served on a committee established by the vestry to wait on parliament and the privy council in the hope of preventing amendments to a bill then before parliament to build a bridge over the River Thames.[82]

With the transformation of the political scene that took place with the accession of George I, Whig bishops such as Boulter came into their own. It was now to be the turn of the Whigs, in both church and state, to rejoice. Their triumph meant the ascendancy of the low-church clergy. Furthermore, in these early Hanoverian years, bishops' votes in the house of lords were crucial, and forming as they did a block of twenty-six votes, for the greater part of the eighteenth century they were under considerable pressure to attend.[83]

George I set foot in England at Gravesend on 14 November 1719, having been absent since 11 May. The warrant for the *congé d'élire* for the appointment of Boulter, 'one of our chaplains in ordinary' to the see of Bristol had been issued 'at our court at the Gohre' (one of the royal hunting seats at Hanover) on 15 October. Boulter had, 'on Thursday 12 [November], married Mrs Elizabeth Savage, with whom he had had £10,000 fortune'.[84]

80 Vestry book, e.g., 31 Mar. 1719.
81 Ibid., 19 Apr. 1720; e.g., 11 Apr. 1721.
82 Ibid., 16 Aug. 1720, 2 Dec. 1720, 11 Apr. 1721, 23 Jan. 1721.
83 W.A. Speck, *Stability and strife: England, 1714–1760* (London, 1977), p. 93; Holmes, *Anne*, pp 408–9.
84 F.M. Powicke and E.B. Fryde, *Handbook of British chronology* (2nd ed. London, 1961), p. 42. This was one of seven such periods of absence, and the king died in Germany on 11 June 1727 (ibid., p. 208); BL Add. MS 38,889, 'Precedent book', p. 84; John Le Neve, *Fasti ecclesiae Anglicanae, 1541–1857: Bristol, Gloucester, Oxford and Peterborough* (London, 1996), p. 12; Abel Boyer, *The political state of*

The ceremony took place in the parish of St Peter le Poer, Broad Street, in the city of London.

The lady is described in one report as 'daughter of Mr Savage, a packer'[85] in Mark Lane, where one of the earliest specialist exchanges, the Corn Exchange, was established in 1749 as part of the long-delayed rebuilding in an area demolished to prevent the spread of the Great Fire.[86] Somewhat less conventionally, she appears in a footnote to an edition of Swift's letters as 'a very fat, heavy woman' for whom horse riding was a recreation.[87] The terms of her will give some indication of the members of her family.[88] A sister, Ellen, was a beneficiary, as well as brothers Charles and Samuel. Charles would appear to have been father of another Elizabeth Savage, niece to Mrs Boulter, second wife to Walter Landor, whose son, Walter Savage Landor, a fairly minor literary figure, published some volumes of 'imaginary conversations'.[89] In one of these the interlocutors were Archbishop Boulter and Philip Savage, who was for many years chancellor of the Irish exchequer, and was member of parliament for Co. Wexford on three occasions. Despite his Tory associations, Philip Savage held office until 1717,[90] his patent being for 'good behaviour' rather than 'at pleasure', which caused the powers that be to hesitate, lest dismissing him might have seemed to be due to personal spite. Boulter, in the course of the 'imaginary conversation' says, 'My wife

Great Britain: being an impartial account of the most material occurrences ecclesiastical, civil and military (London, 1719), xviii, p. 464. He had been free to marry since resigning his Magdalen fellowship on 16 July 1709, the date of his institution at St Olave's (W.D. Macray, *A register of the members of St Mary Magdalen College, Oxford, from the foundation of the college* (new series, London, 1904), iv, p. 165).

85 Doble, *Remarks and collections*, vii, p. 70. Hearne is cited several times in the pages that follow, and, invaluable as his memoirs are in many respects, his prejudices must always be borne in mind, for, as the (old) *DNB* put it, he had no tenderness for the Hanoverians, having, it must be said, himself suffered greatly at the hands of prejudice in his potentially distinguished career. According to *OED*, a packer was middleman between vendor and vendee, charged with the supervision of exported goods liable to duty. Mark Lane was the address of substantial merchants and traders, and the story of a lady who was courted by 'a wealthy packer' is to be found in the memoirs of Mrs Laetitia Pilkington (*Memoirs of Mrs Laetitia Pilkington, wife to the Revd Mr Matthew Pilkington, written by herself*, 2 vols (Dublin, 1749), ii, p. 103).

86 David Kynaston, *The city of London: a world of its own, 1815–1819* (London, 1994), p. 10; Neil Hanson, *The dreadful judgement: the true story of the Great Fire of London in 1666* (London, 2001), p. 187.

87 Harold Williams, *The correspondence of Jonathan Swift* (Oxford, 1965), iv, p. 531. Revd Thomas Sheridan to Swift, 15 Sept. 1736.

88 PRO, Mic. 11/807/sig. 67.

89 W.S. Landor, *Imaginary conversations, with bibilographical and explanatory notes*, ed. G.C. Crumpt, 6 vols (London, 1891).

90 Ibid., ii, pp 352–61; *History of the Irish parliament, 1692–1800*, sub nom. Savage, Philip; see also C.I. McGrath, *The making of the eighteenth-century Irish constitution: government, parliament and the revenue, 1692–1714* (Dublin, 2000), esp. pp 229–31.

is impatient to embrace her sister',[91] the term not necessarily to be taken to denote a sibling, but possibly a relation by marriage. Items in Archbishop Boulter's accounts for January 1726 include the cost of one pound of tea for 'my lady'.[92] Another equally fleeting reference is to be found in an account of the life of John Barber, a Jacobite who was alderman and lord mayor of London for a spell. Barber, writing to Swift, refers to one of his chaplains, Matthew Pilkington (husband to the egregious Laetitia, noted for her somewhat revealing memoirs). The young chaplain was forever seeking patronage, and according to Barber was recommended by him to a certain Alderman Chapter, 'who got the Primate's wife's brother to write in his favour to the Primate'.[93] Swift had gained Matthew Pilkington's acquaintance through Dr Patrick Delany and his wife, and, owing to the scandals that came to be attached to both of the Pilkingtons came bitterly to regret that he had.[94]

While Boulter's published letters throw some light on his disposition and character, they tell little of his family life. As the title page to the eighteenth-century editions makes clear, they deal with 'the most interesting transactions which passed in Ireland from 1724 to 1738'. However, a letter of 3 August 1736 from the archbishop to the lord lieutenant (the duke of Dorset), refers to the fact that a brother-in-law, 'my wife's brother' had advised him on currency matters during a visit to Dublin. It is reasonable to assume that this is the relative described by Faulkner as a director of the Bank of England. Another brother-in-law, 'Mr Norris …who married a sister of my wife', sought the primate's good offices in seeking an interview in connection with a regimental vacancy.[95]

On Sunday 15 November 1719, Boulter was consecrated bishop for the see of Bristol at Lambeth Palace. Archbishop Wake was assisted at the ceremony by the bishops of Worcester (Hough), Salisbury (Talbot), Gloucester (Willis) and Lincoln (Gibson).[96] Henry Stephens, of Malden, Essex, former tutor and friend, for whom Boulter would persistently seek preferment, exhibiting thereby one of the most attractive facets of his character, preached on 2 Corinthians 6:8, 'By honour and dishonour, by evil report and good report: as deceivers and yet true …'[97] Such, he assured the

---

91 Landor, *Imaginary conversations*, ii, p. 352.
92 Trinity College Dublin library, 'Boulter account book', 29 Jan. 1726.
93 Charles A. Rivington, *Tyrant: the story of John Barber, Jacobite lord mayor of London, and printer and friend to Dr Swift* (London, 1989), p. 158.
94 Irvin Ehrenpreis, *Swift: the man, his works and the age* (London, 1983), iii, p. 868.
95 Boulter to Devonshire, 18 Apr. 1738.
96 E.H.W. Dunkin (ed.), *Index to act books of the archbishop of Canterbury, 1663–1859* (London, 1929); Christ Church, Oxford, MS 721, vi, p. 308.
97 Henry Stephens, *A sermon preached at the consecration of the Right Reverend father in God Hugh, lord bishop of Bristol, at Lambeth chapel on Sunday November 15, 1719* (London, 1719).

congregation, bishops must expect to encounter, especially at the hands of those 'who have a popish pretender at heart' (there had recently been an abortive attempt, in which the second duke of Ormond was implicated, to effect a Stuart restoration) for 'the disaffected will seek to sink the credit of those the greatest in power, who stand in their way'. It was a sermon that Boulter himself could have preached, touching as it did on the popish threat and the felicity of those fortunate enough to enjoy the spiritual and temporal benefits of English life under the house of Hanover. It cautioned against sins of presumption; for, though happily free from the errors and superstitions of popery, 'we are as ripe for judgment as they could be', ignoring the providence of God, and offending him by our 'profanity, pride and extravagance'. Stephens, while alerting his hearers to the perils of popery, was at the same time cautioning them against errors of another kind, such as were frequently referred to by preachers keen to promote the reformation of manners in their society, another preoccupation of Boulter's. On 4 April 1720, the new bishop was granted his heraldic arms.[98]

The king's happy return to England had been greeted by crowded streets, salvoes of guns, bonfires and illuminations as he proceeded by coach to London. Boulter's consecration had prevented the archbishop of Canterbury and others from attending at the chapel royal on Sunday 15 November. However, the newly consecrated bishop among them, they presented themselves on the following morning, congratulating the king on his safe arrival and on the success that had attended 'his gracious favour to poor Protestants in the Palatinate, Poland and Lithuania'.[99]

Hugh Boulter succeeded George Smalridge in the see of Bristol, and also succeeded him in the deanery of Christ Church, Oxford, an exceptional deanery that carried headship of both cathedral and college. And while episcopal rank brought great prestige (including a seat in the house of lords), it was the deanery that provided the bishop with the greater part of his income, Bristol being a poor diocese but Christ Church a rich college.[1] Boulter was fortunate in having George I for his patron, as it would appear

98 W.H. Rylands (ed.), *Grantees of arms named in dockets and patents between the years 1687 and 1898* (London, 1916), p. 40. Boulter's arms are described in *Burke's general armory of England, Scotland, Ireland and Wales* (London, 1884), p. 105.

99 Abel Boyer, *The political state of Great Britain: being an impartial account of the most material occurrences ecclesiastical, civil and military,* xviii (London, 1719), p. 410.

1 Rather precociously, while still Tenison's chaplain, Boulter had confided in Arthur Charlett, master of University College, Oxford, that Oxford (another poor diocese) 'is the bishopric of all England I should least desire to fix upon' (Norman Sykes, *Church and state in England in the eighteenth century* (rep. New York, 1975), p. 62). A similar situation existed in Dublin, for example, the emoluments of the bishop of Kildare being substantially enhanced by his income from the deanery of Christ Church in that city (Milne, *Christ Church cathedral*, p. 258).

that Archbishop Wake wanted the deanery to go to the bishop of Oxford and had lobbied the king to that effect through Sunderland (then also in Hanover). But Sunderland informed Wake that 'his majesty had already settled on Boulter for Bristol', and, 'considering the smallness of that bishopric, of [*sic*] making him also dean of Christ Church, which post requires a man of integrity and courage.'[2] The formal approval of Boulter's possession of both diocese and deanery is to be found in the archbishop of Canterbury's act book and runs as follows, dated 9 November 1719:

> Hugh Bo[u]lter, D.D., bishop of Bristol elect, having obtained his majesty's warrant directed to his grace for his dispensation that together with his bishopric he may retain and hold *in commendam* the deanery which he now holds of the cathedral church of Christ in the university of Oxford during his life and his incumbency in the said bishopric, and likewise, that together with the said bishopric he may retain (whole) *in commendam* the rectory which he now holds of St Olave's, Southwark, in the county of Surrey until the 29th day of September, which shall be in the year of Our Lord God 1722, with the fruits, profits and rights to the said deanery and rectory respectively belonging, petitioned his grace for his dispensation, etc, according to the tenour of the said royal warrant which was granted by fiat etc.[3]

The royal warrant was duly 'exhibited' to the archbishop, who directed that it be performed. Thus Boulter retained his rectory of St Olave's for a further three years, preaching his farewell sermon there on 8 November 1722, and assuring the congregation that:

> I am taking leave of a people amongst whom I have spent many years instructing and building them up in the knowledge of the Christian religion and for whom I shall always have a tender concern … being called by the providence of God to that inspection of other churches in a superior station.[4]

It should occasion no surprise that the new bishop held such a plurality of positions. Wake, en route to Canterbury, held a London parish while dean of Exeter and retained a parish *in commendam* for his first year as bishop of Lincoln.[5]

The see of Bristol was created in 1542 by Henry VIII out of the dioceses of Worcester, Gloucester, Bath and Wells, and Salisbury. Bishop Secker (1725–7) computed the income of the diocese at £360 per annum, out of which he paid £27 in tenths (tithes) and maintained a steward, and in 1762

2 Norman Sykes, *William Wake: archbishop of Canterbury, 1657–1737*, 2 vols (Cambridge, 1957), ii, p. 131.

3 Lambeth Palace Library, MS 721 vi, p. 308.

4 *A sermon preached in the parish church of St Olave, Southwark, on Sunday November 8th 1722 by the Rt. Revd father in God Hugh, lord bishop of Bristol, on the occasion of his leaving that parish. Published at the desire of the gentlemen of the vestry and other inhabitants of the aforesaid parish* (London, 1722), pp 6–7.

5 Sykes, *Wake*, i, pp 75, 159.

the bishop's emoluments were computed at £450. Bristol was described by Geoffrey Holmes, historian of Queen Anne's reign, as 'the most beggarly of all English sees',[6] and an account of it in 1816 shows that little had changed in the intervening decades:

> the least wealthy ecclesiastical promotion which confers the dignity of a mitre. In consequence of this comparative indigence the bishop of Bristol usually holds some valuable benefice in addition to the bishopric, or this see is conferred as a preliminary to an ecclesiastical promotion of equal dignity, with more ample revenues.[7]

Boulter was a case in point, on both scores. He held the deanery of Christ Church, Oxford, reckoned to be worth £800 *in commendam*, as Secker would hold the rectory of St James', Piccadilly, as well as a prebendal stall in Durham. Joseph Butler (1738–50) and Thomas Newton (1761–82) held the deanery of St Paul's *in commendam* with Bristol. Secker complained, as Boulter might well have done, of the expense of living in London while attending court and parliament, and yet maintaining hospitality in the diocese.[8] Furthermore, it was an awkward diocese to administer. On its creation it had been allocated Dorset rather than Gloucestershire or Somerset, thus 'effectively isolating the bishop from the clergy in his charge'.[9] There was no archdeacon of Bristol, the chancellor conducting visitations, and the archdeaconry of Dorset lay fifty miles from the episcopal seat. For all of these reasons the bishops of Bristol tended not to linger there, Butler and Newton being exceptional.[10] Likewise, most of the prebendaries (canons) of the Cathedral of the Holy and Undivided Trinity (which had until the creation of the diocese at the Reformation been an Augustinian abbey) were largely non-resident. The abbot's house had become the bishop's mansion, but had been greatly neglected and was much dilapidated.[11]

Yet the city of Bristol was growing. In 1660 there were eighteen parishes,

---

6   Elizabeth Ralph (ed.), 'Bishop Secker's diocesan book' in Patrick McGrath (ed.), *A Bristol miscellany* (Bristol, 1985), p. 24; John Walsh, Colin Haydon, Stephen Taylor (eds), *The Church of England c.1689–c.1833: from toleration to tractarianism* (Cambridge, 2002), p. 4; Geoffrey Holmes, *Augustan England: professions, state and society, 1680–1730* (London, 1982), pp 92–3.

7   John Evans, *The history of Bristol, civil and ecclesiastical, including biographical notices of eminent and distinguished natives*, 2 vols (Bristol, 1816), pp 146–7.

8   Holmes, *Augustan England*, pp 92–4.

9   Peter Virgin, *The church in an age of negligence* (Cambridge, 1989), p. 1. Bristol became part of the diocese of Gloucester and Bristol in 1836, reappearing in its own right in 1897.

10 Ralph, 'Bishop Secker's diocesan book', pp 23–4, 28.

11 Jonathan Barry, 'The parish in civic life: Bristol and its churches, 1640–1750' in S.J. Wright (ed.), *Parish, church and people: local studies in lay religion, 1350–1750* (London, 1988), p. 154; Joseph Bettey (ed.), *Records of Bristol Cathedral* (Bristol, 2007), p. 145.

nine of which were in the gift of the city corporation, serving a population of 15,000 which had risen to 20,000 in 1730 and 40,000 by 1750. The city's growing prosperity was due in no small measure to a vibrant slave trade for which Bristol was a major port at that time.[12] The diocese was not highly ranked among the sees of the established church, and the city itself cannot have held many attractions for Boulter, at least in political terms. It was counted third after London and Norwich among municipalities, and it was a largely open constituency with an electorate running into many hundreds of voters 'too difficult to manage by the usual methods of influence and patronage'.[13] Bristol had been a stronghold of Nonconformity since Dissenting congregations broke from the ecclesiastical establishment. For instance, there were proportionately more Quakers in Bristol than anywhere else in the kingdom, including some of the wealthiest congregations in the country, to the extent that there was a workhouse under Quaker auspices.[14] Whigs dominated the corporation and social elite, and Dissenters (largely, if not entirely, Whig voters) comprised one-third of the population.[15] Dissenters vied with the Church of England for influence in such important areas as the promotion of charity schools and the reformation of manners, Bristol in the 1690s having been one of the first cities to see the setting up of a Society for the Reformation of Manners.[16] The demise of that society was partly caused by religious tensions, influential figures in the established church regarding the somewhat pietistical approach of some who espoused that cause as tending to diminish the power of ecclesiastical authority.[17] The bishop is likely to have given close attention to the Society for the Reformation of Manners, as did his mentor Wake and his friend Gibson in their dioceses, emphasizing the prerogatives of the established church in such matters at a time when secular organizations tended to irritate by espousing the same objective from a non-theological perspective. Societies such as these were zealously supported by Whig bishops such as Boulter,

12 Ralph, 'Bishop Secker's diocesan book', p. 30; Barry, 'The parish in civic life', p. 152; David Richardson (ed.), *Bristol, Africa and the eighteenth-century slave trade to America*, i: *the years of expansion, 1698–1729* (Bristol, 1986).
13 Romney Sedgwick, *History of parliament: the commons, 1715–1754*, 2 vols (London, 1970), i, pp 244–5; J.H. Plumb, *The growth of political stability in England, 1675–1725* (London, 1967), pp 81–2.
14 Patrick McGrath (ed.), *Bristol in the eighteenth century* (Newton Abbot, 1977), p. 66; E.E. Butcher, *Bristol Corporation of the Poor, 1696–1898* (Bristol, 1972), p. 3; Lee Davison et al. (eds), *Stilling the grumbling hive: the response to social and economic problems in England, 1689–1750* (Stroud and New York, 1992), p. 122.
15 Geoffrey Holmes, *The Trial of Dr Sacheverell* (London, 1973), p. 37.
16 D.A. Spaeth, *The church in an age of danger: parsons and parishes, 1660–1740* (Cambridge, 2000), p. 227.
17 Barry, 'The parish in civic life', pp 169–70; M.E. Frissell, 'Societies for the reformation of manners' in Davison et al., *Stilling the grumbling hive*, p. 133.

though highly suspect in high-church circles, where they were regarded as tending to fraternize too closely with Dissenters.[18]

Likewise, one objective of the group (on whom the bishop is unlikely to have looked with favour) that founded the Corporation of the Poor, was to wrest such responsibilities from the hands of church vestries. It is noteworthy, however, that in the years 1708–22, and partly within Boulter's episcopate, many charity schools were set up in the poorer parishes.[19]

Boulter will have been aware of the need to ensure that his clergy used their not inconsiderable influence. Indeed, Dr Thomas Hearne, one of his sternest Christ Church critics, noted in his diary (at the time of Boulter's appointment to Armagh):

> The new metropolitan that is to be is returned from the west where he has been distressing all the clergy that agreed not with him in politics to the very utmost of his power, and is parting with them in the most provoking manner possible. One of them that was to preach before him took his text out of the 12th [chapter] of the Revelations and the 12th verse – 'the devil is come down unto you having great wrath because he knoweth that his time is but short.'[20]

As to how Boulter exercised his episcopate, we know scarcely anything at all. No visitation papers survive for the years prior to 1746. We do know that plurality was common as was its concomitant, non-residence, while, as has already been alluded to, the prebendaries of the cathedral were mainly non-resident.[21] A commentary on an edition of Bishop Newton's works described aspects of diocesan affairs quite bluntly: 'the bishops of Bristol were generally such birds of passage that they had little time to look into the value of their estates and (excepting Bishop Secker) scarce any of them have left any papers and memorandums behind them'.[22]

Some idea of how Boulter divided his time between his palace in Bristol and his deanery in Oxford may be gleaned from a letter of his (from Oxford, dated 10 July 1724) in which he informed his correspondent that 'on

18 G.V. Portus, *Caritas Anglicana, or, an historical inquiry into those philanthropical societies that flourished in England between the years 1678 and 1740* (London, 1912), pp 120–4; J.C.D. Clark, *Revolution and rebellion: state and society in England in the seventeenth and eighteenth centuries* (Cambridge, 1986), pp 395–6; Tina Isaacs, 'The Anglican hierarchy and the reformation of manners, 1688–1738', *Jn. Eccles. Hist.*, 33:3 (July 1982), 391–411 at 399; Craig Rose, 'Providence, Protestantism and godly reformation in the 1690s' in *Transactions of the Royal Historical Society*, sixth series (1993), 151–69 at 151. Also Craig Rose, *England in the 1690s: revolution, religion and war* (Oxford, 1999), pp 206–7.
19 Barry, *The parish in civil life*, pp 168–9.
20 A slight misquotation. The Authorized King James version reads: 'because he knoweth that he hath but a short time'.
21 Ralph, 'Bishop Secker's diocesan book', p. 29; Barry, 'Parish', p. 154.
22 *The works of the Right Reverend Thomas Newton, DD, late lord bishop of Bristol and dean of St Paul's, London, with some account of his life and anecdotes of several of his friends, written by himself*, 6 vols (London, 1787), p. 148.

Monday I design to set out on my visitation and shall be away from Oxford in Dorsetshire or at Bristol about seven weeks'.[23] Episcopal visitations, customary by the thirteenth century and continued after the Reformation, had become 'an institution for the maintenance of the Elizabethan religious settlement'.[24] Even those sees which held more financial attractions than Bristol had to accept the fact that episcopal oversight could be intermittent and brief, as bishops were expected to spend the greater part of autumn and winter attending court and parliament, and pastoral supervision was largely confined to intervals in the parliamentary sessions. Bishop Newton said that from the time of his consecration, he went to Bristol every summer and usually stayed there for three months.[25]

What we know of Boulter's tenure of the see is so fragmentary that it is impossible to assess his performance accurately. But knowing what we do about his devotion to duty both before and after Bristol, it seems not unreasonable to give him the benefit of the doubt. That he was not seen in retrospect as one of Bristol's outstanding bishops may, however, be inferred from his absence from a list of bishops whose episcopates feature in John Evans' *History of Bristol*, already cited. One of the few fragments that have come down to us suggests that he ran the diocese largely from Oxford. In a letter to Archbishop Wake, written from Christ Church and dated 26 September 1720,[26] he supported the candidature of a certain Mr Thornton, 'presently at Frome', for another living. Thornton made satisfactory provision for the cure of souls at Frome, 'attending when urgent cases arise'. Either he or his curate attended each Sunday, the curate having accommodation in an endowed chapel of ease there. Pastoral care was not neglected, though Boulter left it to Wake to determine whether or not Thornton should live in one or other of the parishes, but doubted if there was any precedent for a pluralist giving his bishop a bond obliging him to reside. He continued:

> I am much concerned at the shameful non-residence practised over the whole kingdom and till it can be more effectively remedied by some new laws should be very willing to go to the utmost of what the present laws permit to prevent [it] in my diocese if I could hope to be suffered by the importuning and solicitation of such as 'tis hard to deny.

Sermons preached by Boulter as bishop are entirely consistent with the sentiments he expressed before his elevation – loyalty to the Hanoverian dynasty and the Protestant cause, tempered with concern that his hearers might be found wanting and unworthy of God's favour. 'In the time of our health and prosperity we are apt to forget God, and neglect the concerns of

23 NA SP 35/50/77.
24 D.M. Owen, 'Episcopal visitation books', *History*, 49:166 (1964), 185–6.
25 Sykes, *Church and State*, ii, p. 167; Newton, *Works*, pp 124–5.
26 Lambeth Palace Library, Wake MSS, 14/8/no. 304.

another life,' were his appropriate words when the lords spiritual and temporal were assembled in Westminster Abbey on 16 December 1720, the day 'appointed by his majesty for a general fast and humiliation for obtaining the pardon of our sins, and averting God's heavy judgments', and at a time when the continent of Europe was afflicted by plague.[27] A similar admonitory note was struck by the bishop in 1722 when preaching before the Society for Promoting Christian Knowledge. Lauding the achievements of that society through its rapidly spreading charity schools, he expressed the hope that the trustees of the schools would see to it that the teachers 'instructed their scholars truly in the doctrines of our most excellent church without tincturing them at all with anything of those party quarrels and distinctions that so unhappily abound among us'.[28] When he preached before a kindred institution, the Society for the Propagation of the Gospel, and made reference to missionary work in the colonies, he again argued against complacency.

> Nor are those of our own people, who are settled there, to be left out of our regard, since in many places there, they had been for many years, and in some places more than one generation, without any ghostly teachers, so as to have retained little more than the name of Christians, till by the care and assistance of this society, that knowledge of the gospel has begun to be revived among them.[29]

With appointment to the episcopate came a seat on the bench of bishops in the house of lords, and Boulter was a good attender, his name seldom missing from the list of those present throughout the period of his occupancy of the see of Bristol. His parliamentary attendances, day after day and week after week throughout the parliamentary sessions from 23 November 1719 (within days of his consecration) to his final appearance on 22 April 1724, while evidence of the seriousness with which he took his parliamentary duties, also indicate the lengthy periods when he was away from his diocese and his deanery. On two occasions when he was unable to attend, he availed himself of the procedure whereby he could appoint a proxy, and in each case, as was to be expected, chose colleagues who shared his political views: William Fleetwood, bishop of Ely, and Lancelot Blackburne, bishop of

27 *A sermon preached before the lords spiritual and temporal in parliament assembled at the collegiate church of St Peter's, Westminster, on Friday December the 16th 1720 ... by the Right Reverend Father in God, Hugh, lord bishop of Bristol* (London, 1720).
28 W.B. and Edmund McClure, *Two hundred years: the history of the Society for Promoting Christian Knowledge, 1698–1898* (London, 1898), pp 145–6.
29 *A sermon preached before the Incorporated Society for the Propagation of the Gospel in foreign Parts at their anniversary meeting in the parish school of St Mary-le-Bow on Friday the 16th of February 1721. By the right Reverend Father in God, Hugh, lord bishop of Bristol* (London, 1722), pp 31–2.

Exeter (both in 1722).[30] Fleetwood was dubbed 'a great Whig' by Hearne[31] and Blackburne's political acceptability was attested to by his translation to York two years later. All English and Welsh archbishops and bishops were entitled to sit in the lords. They comprised one-sixth of the total membership, and, on occasion, their votes determined the outcome of divisions.[32] Frequently, however, Boulter was one of only eight or so bishops present, and once (on 20 October 1721) he was alone. He played his part on several committees to do with privileges and with 'perusing and perfecting' the journal, and was also put on a committee to consider how best to manage the custody of public records.[33] It should also be mentioned that convocation, which, as we have noted, was regarded by government as providing too convenient a platform for the expression of high-church Tory sentiments, was in suspension throughout this period. There were no sittings of that body from 1664–89, nor from 1717–1855, though a shadowy existence was preserved.[34]

Boulter was in the house when a number of significant issues were under consideration, three of which produced major debates: the Peerage Bill of 1719, the South Sea Bubble crisis and the deprivation and exiling of Bishop Francis Atterbury of Rochester. Boulter's name is attached to a rather insignificant piece of private legislation: 'a bill to facilitate debtors of Henry Colthurst', which is listed in the 'Proceedings at committees on bills and other matters'.[35] The bishop of Bristol is recorded as supporting the right of Quakers to 'affirm' rather than take an oath, a sign of his sympathetic attitude to any attempt by nonconformists to achieve concessions.[36] He did, appropriately enough, as head of an Oxford house, report to the lords from the committee on the act to enable Oxford Corporation to convey land for the building of the Radcliffe Camera, which in due course received the royal assent.[37]

The Peerage Bill, a cause célèbre in which the relationship between the king and the prince of Wales (then at a particularly low ebb) combined with

---

30 For a description of the workings of the proxy system, see J.C. Sainty, 'Proxy records of the house of lords, 1510–1733', *Parliamentary History*, 1 (1952), 161–5; parliamentary archives, proxy books, 1660–1733 (HL/PO/JO/13/1–8).

31 Quoted by John Moore in *ODNB, sub nom.* Fleetwood, William.

32 Andrew Swatland, *The house of lords in the reign of Charles II* (Cambridge, 1996), p. 275.

33 *Lords Jn.*, xxi, 166, 172 (23 Nov. 1719, 17 Jan. 1720).

34 White Kennett, *A history of the convocation of Canterbury ... 6 February 1700* (London, 1702); Norman Sykes, *From Sheldon to Secker* (Cambridge, 1959).

35 Parliamentary Archives, 'Lord bishop of Bristol: Colthurst bill', ff. 156–8.

36 [W. Cobbett], *The parliamentary history of England from the earliest period to the year 1803* (London, 1811), vii, col. 945 (17 Jan. 1723).

37 *Lords Jn.*, xxi, 536 (7 June 1721); L.S. Sutherland and L.G. Mitchell (eds), *The history of the University of Oxford*, v: *The eighteenth century* (Oxford, 1986), p. 733.

government ambitions to retain a majority of supporters in the lords through restricting the royal prerogative to create peers, fell in the commons and can scarcely have touched Boulter at all, though as part of a politically inspired 'reform' movement which also had the universities in its sights, he cannot have been indifferent.[38] The South Sea Bubble affair, which absorbed an inordinate amount of time in the lords, certainly touched Boulter in his pocket, something to which he referred in a letter to a Whitehall official with whom he was on very friendly terms, Charles Delafaye. In a letter to Delafaye from Oxford dated 17 October 1720, Boulter referred to the 'sad times you have had in London', as a result of which 'I have lost the little imagined wealth I took myself to be master of', a financial misfortune which he shared with many members of the Irish parliament who were virtually ruined in the black six weeks of August and September 1720, as indeed were many members of the British political classes.[39] Nonetheless, South Sea stock was among the assets distributed under the terms of his widow's will, though this may not have come to Mrs Boulter from the archbishop.[40]

Delafaye was a highly influential civil servant with whom Boulter is likely to have been well acquainted from the time when both men were at early stages in their distinguished careers. The future archbishop was chaplain to Secretary of State Sir Charles Hedges when Delafaye served as an undersecretary on Hedges' staff. Delafaye was chosen by the duke of Shrewsbury in 1713 to be his 'second' (private) secretary during his short-lived lord lieutenancy of Ireland, surviving to serve Shrewsbury's successor, Sunderland, and remaining in Ireland for three years. During this time, he secured a parliamentary seat for the borough of Belturbet, Co. Cavan, which he held until 1727. This gave him an insight into Irish politics that was to stand Boulter in good stead when he, in turn, found himself embroiled in Irish affairs. Back in England, and 'sustained throughout his career by powerful patrons',[41] not least the duke of Newcastle, Delafaye rose through the ranks and provided invaluable continuity 'at an intermediate level', not least when acting as secretary to the English lords justices who held office during royal absences in Hanover. It is clear from allusions made by Boulter in correspondence with Delafaye that the latter had shown him notable consideration at one time or another.

38 J.C.D. Clark, *English society, 1688–1832* (Cambridge, 1985), pp 155–6, 303.
39 Boulter to Delafaye (from Christ Church, Oxford), 17 Oct. 1720 (NA SP 35/23/93); Edith Mary Johnston-Liik, *History of the Irish parliament*, 6 vols (Belfast 2002), i, p. 97. He was the only bishop to vote (unsuccessfully) against a bill of 1721 to enable the South Sea Company to ingraft part of its capital stock (*Lords Jn.*, xxi, 465, 9 Mar. 1721).
40 Will of Elizabeth Boulter, née Savage, NA, Mic 11/807/sig. 67.
41 J.C. Sainty, *ODNB*. See also Sainty's 'A Huguenot civil servant: the career of Charles Delafaye, 1677–1762' in *Proc. Hug. Soc. London*, 5 (1975), 309–43 and Johnston-Liik, *History of the Irish parliament*, iv, pp 43–4.

The Atterbury affair not only pertained to the loyalty to the house of Hanover that was so frequently a theme of Boulter's sermons, but indeed involved him personally, if slightly.[42] Attterbury, bishop of Rochester, the talented leader of the high-church bishops, was a predecessor of Boulter's at Christ Church, and had surrendered that post for the deanery of Westminster, which became his on appointment to the see of Rochester. Atterbury deplored, as did Boulter, the growing acceptance of 'occasional conformity' by Dissenters and the spread of anticlerical, even atheistical, literature. But, unlike Boulter, Atterbury had scant confidence in the capacity of the Whigs to preserve the prerogatives of the church, and he became deeply implicated in a Jacobite conspiracy. Committed to the Tower of London, he endured great privations. When measures to punish him were before the commons he sought 'direction' from the lords as to whether or not to comply with an order to appear before the lower house, and in consequence was called to appear at the bar of the lords. Boulter was present on these occasions.[43] After each appearance, Atterbury was returned to the Tower, where his personal possessions were constantly searched, medical visits were made extremely difficult and his request to be allowed to receive Holy Communion was rejected. He did, however, gain some solace through visits from Francis Gastrell, who held a canonry at Christ Church *in commendam* with his bishopric of Chester. The Christ Church connection brought Boulter into the picture. In September 1722, Atterbury wrote to Secretary of State Townshend asking that he might be permitted to pray with his children, who had been kept away from him. On the following day, Townshend gave Atterbury permission to write to Boulter, as dean of Christ Church, and to his son's tutor there, about the matter; the result is unknown. Atterbury was exiled to the Continent, died in Paris in 1732 and his body was brought to England for a 'quiet' funeral at Westminster Abbey.[44]

Cardinal Wolsey's creation, Christ Church, had, from its inception, an intimate connection with the crown, the sovereign being visitor, and during the period of the Civil War when Oxford was the royalist capital, Christ Church was its citadel.[45] The chapter was drastically purged during the interregnum, but at the Restoration all was made well, and the college was very reluctant indeed to abandon the Stuarts for Hanover. Atterbury's political and ecclesiastical attitudes, already referred to, were typical, if in his case carried to extreme. But, nonetheless, dean and chapter were crown appointments, and they constituted the governing body of both cathedral and college, with the result that the complexion of both changed inexorably, if

42 For a treatment of this issue, see G.V. Bennett, *The Tory crisis in church and state, 1688–1730: the career of Francis Atterbury, bishop of Rochester* (Oxford, 1970).
43 *Lords Jn.*, xxii, e.g., 182 (6 May 1723).
44 Townshend to bishop of Rochester, 6 Sept. 1722 (NA SP 35/33/12); Bennett, *Tory crisis*, pp 305–7.
45 Hugh Trevor-Roper, *Christ Church, Oxford* (3rd ed. Oxford, 1989), p. 4.

slowly, in the course of time. Boulter's appointment has to be seen in this context, as should his subsequent appointment to Armagh: the entrusting of the interests of the Hanoverian succession and all that it entailed to a safe pair of hands.

Boulter had had no particular association with Christ Church (he had matriculated there but soon transferred to Magdalen), whereas his three immediate predecessors had held studentships (the Christ Church equivalent of fellowships).[46] Nor had he held a canonry there. But he was, to quote again his friend Edmund Gibson, 'a safe man'. As such, he was highly eligible for a deanery that called for integrity and courage, as Secretary of State Sunderland, then at Hanover with George I, had assured Archbishop Wake, who as has been already observed, favoured another candidate.[47]

Just as tensions in church and state reflected one another, so also were they reflected in the University of Oxford and its colleges. 'As an integral part of the church the university was subject to all the currents and cross-currents of political opinion, intellectual fashion and vested interest which characterized the eighteenth-century establishment.'[48] Furthermore, the situation was more complex than simply that of Whig versus Tory: there were strongly contrasting shades of opinion within the ranks of each, perhaps most clearly evident in the stance of Harleian Tories such as Canon William Stratford of Christ Church. These were regarded by some of their Tory brethren as scarcely orthodox, their policy one of moderation as they sought to avoid confrontation with the new political regime which regarded Oxford and its colleges, with scarcely an exception, as a 'nest of rebels', and the student body as 'notoriously disaffected'.

It is therefore hardly surprising that there would appear to have been a cool reception for the new dean in the light of both national and college politics, doubtless partially accounted for by the fact that his appointment was a departure from the Christ Church tradition that the deanery 'should come from inside'.[49] And, as is so often the case (especially with controversial appointments) unsympathetic commentators such as Thomas Hearne were quick to disparage. 'I am told that Dr Bolter [*sic*] is not a scholar, and that he is never reckoned good for any thing as to learning, unless it was scholastic divinity, and that he appeared very deficient even in that in his disputations, which he performed but meanly.'[50] Equally dismissive was Dr

46 E.G.W. Bill, *Education at Christ Church, Oxford, 1630–1800* (Oxford, 1988), pp 45–6.
47 See p. 23 above.
48 P. Langford, 'Tories and Jacobites, 1714–1751' in L.S. Sutherland and L.G. Mitchell (eds), *The history of the University of Oxford*, v: *The eighteenth century* (Oxford, 1986), pp 99–100, 105.
49 D.R. Hirschberg, 'The government and church patronage on England, 1660–1670', *Jn. Br. St.*, 20:1 (Fall 1980), 109–59.
50 Doble, *Remarks and collections*, vii, p. 64.

Stratford, who, disappointed in his expectation of the deanery,[51] gleefully reported on any shortcomings of the new incumbent, claiming that:

> Our new governor was recommended by the present ecclesiastical junto, whose recommendations only are regarded as to preferment, viz Norwich [Charles Trimnell], Sarum [i.e. Salisbury,William Talbot], Gloucester [Richard Willis], Lincoln [Edmund Gibson]. We are told he received orders to wait on those four bishops and thank them, and that he was expressly forbidden to take any notice of the archbishop of Canterbury [William Wake]. Accordingly, he never waited on the archbishop till the day before he came hither, when he could not avoid it in order to know the time of his consecration. It was said that the archbishop by way of rebuke told him he was surprised to see him, for that the public news had given him reason to think that he had gone to Oxford.[52]

Stratford's attitude to his dean hardened in the course of time and in 1722 he wrote to tell Edward Harley that 'our governor is as weary of us as we can be of him, and that he will leave us as soon as ever he can'.[53] Trimnell was a prominent member of a group of senior Whig churchmen and had been expected by some to succeed Tenison at Canterbury.[54] Willis had been one of the assisting bishops at Boulter's consecration in 1719. We have already encountered Gibson, Boulter's friend and patron for many years, a close associate of 'prime minister' Walpole; he has been described by a modern historian as 'someone for [whom], as for many Whig churchmen, the revolution had been, above all else, a providential intervention by God'.[55]

As to Boulter's impact on Christ Church in the university city with which he was so familiar, we have somewhat more contemporary evidence than for his incumbency of the see of Bristol. The chapter act books of Christ Church show that the dean made less use of proxies to represent him at meetings than did most of the other dignitaries, possibly because he had less need to augment his emoluments with extra-Oxford duties than they had, canons receiving about £300 per annum and the provision of residential accommodation being uncertain.[56] Boulter's diocese of Bristol may have ranked low in the league of bishoprics, but his college, Christ Church, made up for that by being among the largest by contemporary standards, and matriculating some twenty-five undergraduates in the year 1745/6. In addition, it was the wealthiest of the Oxford foundations, and according to at least one authority escaped the torpor that prevailed in so many of the colleges for much of the eighteenth century.[57]

51 Bill, *Education at Christ Church*, p. 42.
52 Stratford to Edward Harley, 11 Nov. 1719, *Portland MSS* (HMC, 1901), vii, p. 264.
53 Stratford to E. Harley, 18 Apr. 1722, ibid., p. 321.
54 W.M. Jacob in *ODNB*.
55 R.W. Davis (ed.), *Lords of parliament: studies, 1714–1914* (Stanford, 1995), p. 21.
56 Library of Christ Church College, Oxford, Act Book 41 (1713–54); undated letter from 'Hu: Bristol' (Bodleian Library, Tanner MSS, xxxv/70).
57 Lucy Sutherland, *The university of Oxford in the eighteenth century* (Oxford, 1973),

Boulter, as has already been mentioned, was regular in his attendance at chapter meetings where routine business such as admissions to the college was transacted. He appears to have taken advantage of his position to repay favours when he was able to do so. For instance, he wrote to Delafaye 'at my Lord [secretary of state] Stanhope's office' in April 1720 regretting that he was out when Delafaye had called on him, and acknowledging the pride that he would take in returning favours. He promised Delafaye to inform the subdean that it was his wish that a certain young man be admitted as a servitor of Christ Church as soon as a vacancy arose. (Servitors were among the lower echelons in a very class-conscious college society, and were, at least in theory, expected to make their way in college by performing menial duties.) Advocacy for this would seem to have been the purpose of Delafaye's visit.[58] Happily, a vacancy arose in time for the candidate in question to be admitted for the new academic year, and he was to come, bearing a note from Delafaye.[59] A more cryptic reference to what would seem to have been an undergraduate misdemeanour of some kind occurs in a letter of 10 July 1724 to a correspondent in Derry, expressing the hope that the escapade would teach the offender a lesson.[60] Chapter minutes contain frequent allusions to students infringing the rules by the frequenting of alehouses, riotous behaviour and generally perpetrating violent incidents.[61]

Involvement of the dean in more sedate aspects of university life was to be seen, for instance, in his recommendation in 1721 of Mr Whiteside of Christ Church for one of the Savile professorships, he being 'the best mathematician I know in Oxford and I believe very able to fill the place'.[62] He also had a part in the appointment of Thomas White to a lectorship in moral philosophy, corresponding with Gibson within weeks of the latter's translation from Lincoln to London in June 1724 (not long before his own translation to Armagh).[63] Slightly earlier, the two bishops had corresponded about the king's proposals for appointing to the two English universities professors of history who would have competence in modern languages.

p. 4; E.G.W. Bill and J.F.A. Mason, *Christ Church and reform, 1550–1867* (Oxford, 1970), p. 2; *The lives of Dr Edward Pococke by Dr Trellis, of Dr Zachariah Pearson and of Dr Thomas Newton by themselves, and of Rev. Philip Skelton by Mr Burdy*, 2 vols (London, 1816), ii, p. 12.

58 Boulter to Delafaye, 16 Apr. 1720 (NA SP 35/21/18).
59 Same to same, 17 Oct. 1720, (NA SP 35/23/93).
60 NA SP 35/50/77.
61 H.L. Thompson, *Christ Church* (London, 1998), p. 134.
62 Boulter to Wake, 9 Sept. 1721, Bodleian Library, Wake MSS, 16/no. 83. The earliest professorships in geometry and astronomy at Oxford were founded by Sir Henry Savile, fellow of Merton, provost of Eton, a formidable scholar who was the only layman among the translators of the King James Bible (Adam Nicolson, *Power and glory: Jacobean England and the making of the King James Bible* (London, 2003), pp 163–9).
63 Gibson to Boulter, 27 June 1724 (NA SP 35/30/45).

This royal bounty was not entirely motivated by academic considerations. According to Professor C.H. Firth, 'The country gentlemen were very generally Tories, and Whigs held it was largely due to their ignorance of the history of their own country.'[64] Boulter expressed disappointment with Oxford's lukewarm response to the offer, which he considered to be a generous one, and declared himself 'out of countenance', particularly since Cambridge had been more forthcoming.[65] Apart from such curricular (and political) issues, there were always those chapter meetings when stewardship of college property was on the agenda, such as that of July 1720. Presided over by 'the bishop of Bristol, dean', the chapter determined terms for a forthcoming leasing of Christ Church meadows.[66] One particularly unfortunate event relating to college property occurred in 1719–20, when the burning of Christmas decorations by the choristers on the eve of Candlemas caused damage to the hall estimated at £600.[67]

Stratford wrote to Harley on 10 April 1724 to say that 'the great ones above are dissatisfied with the management of our wise governor and wish to remove him', adding, some months later, 'I am amazed at the taste of the great men that can think Hugo [*sic*] fit to be primate.'[68] If, indeed, Boulter faced criticism, indeed hostility, both within the college and without, the deanery cannot have been a particularly comfortable billet. While it may well have been that his success in promoting the Whig interest in the college (and the university) fell short of what had been expected of him, Whigs made more progress at Christ Church than in the other colleges. Yet neither Smalridge, Boulter, nor their immediate successors established the kind of connections and relationships that were needed,[69] so that even by the 1730s the transformation had not been achieved. Lord Townshend may indeed (as Stratford alleged) have accused Boulter of slackness, and of having 'suffered the Tories to increase their power and numbers in that university',[70] but unsettled though he may have been it is difficult to reconcile such allegations of lethargy with what we know of Boulter's political conscientiousness before and after. Furthermore, it seems unlikely that such a record of failure would have brought Boulter the primacy of the Church of Ireland to which he was promoted.

64 C.H. Firth, 'Modern history in Oxford', *English Historical Review*, 125 (1917), 1–21.
65 Boulter to Gibson, 25 May 1724 (NA SP 35/49/70).
66 Christ Church Library, chapter act book 41 (1713–54).
67 Stratford to Harley, 2 Feb. 1720, *Portland MSS* (HMC, 1911), vii, pp xiv, 268.
68 Stratford to Harley, 10 Apr. 1724 and 25 July 1724 (*Portland MSS*, vii, pp 378, 381).
69 Langford, 'Tories and Jacobites', p. 114
70 Quoted in Bill, *Education at Christ Church*, pp 45–6.

III

Boulter received notice of his nomination to the see of Armagh while on a visitation of the Bristol diocese, and by some accounts, including his own, he was not overjoyed at the prospect of moving to Ireland.[71] Although lacking, so far as we know, any Irish family connections and never having previously set foot in the country, his previous career in England had led him into corridors of power where he must assuredly have gained insight into aspects of Irish political and ecclesiastical life. He may well have gleaned an impression of Ireland from his friend and contemporary Joseph Addison, who had been chief secretary of Ireland 1708–10 and 1714–15.[72] Boulter's chaplaincy with Secretary of State Hedges (who had appointed Addison),[73] and subsequently with Archbishop Tenison, who had much correspondence with Irish bishops, must also have given him an awareness of Irish issues. As has already been noted, the Irish church mattered to the crown, and Tenison was one of the commissioners appointed by William III 'to consider the best way of settling the Church of Ireland and promoting piety there' and particularly to consider what persons were fit to be made bishops.[74]

According to a letter from Secretary of State Townshend to Boulter, George I expressed himself well pleased when, however reluctantly, Boulter accepted the primacy.[75] Perhaps as an inducement, Townshend pointed out to Boulter that great sums of money would accrue to the new occupant of the

71 W.F. Hook, *An ecclesiastical biography* (London, 1847), iii, pp 3–7; Boulter to Newcastle, 4 Mar. 1725, where he refers to his contentment with what he had in England 'and my just expectations there …' *Biographia Britannia* (*sub nom.* Boulter) has it that he initially declined the offer of Armagh.

72 Addison's short term of office left some mark: his name survived in the dedication of a Dublin inn, 'Addison's Head' (Peter Somerville-Large, *Dublin* (London, 1979), p. 155) and 'Addison's Walk' is still a feature of Dublin's Botanic Gardens in Glasnevin, the neighbourhood in which he had a house, and where Addison Place, Addison Road and Addison Terrace survive.

73 For instance, at a time (1705) when Boulter was chaplain to Hedges, the secretary of state was receiving correspondence from the Irish chief secretary, Edward Southwell (who, confusingly, was simultaneously Irish secretary of state). In one letter in which Southwell described in some detail the balance of power between the Irish houses of parliament, he commented 'I never trouble you with what the house of lords do, because in truth they have hardly any business before them' (David Hayton, 'The beginnings of the "undertaker system"' in Thomas Bartlett and D.W. Hayton (eds), *Penal era and golden age: essays in Irish history, 1690–1800* (Belfast, 1979), p. 34).

74 *Cal. S.P. Dom., William & Mary, May 1690–Oct 1691*, p. 155; David Hayton, 'British Whig ministers and the Irish question, 1714–25' in Stephen Taylor, Richard Connors and Clyve Jones (ed.), *Hanoverian Britain and Empire: essays in memory of Philip Lawson* (Woodbridge, 1998), pp 37–64, at p. 63; Edward Carpenter, *Thomas Tenison, archbishop of Canterbury: his life and times* (London, 1948), p. 362. Tenison was urged to accept translation to Dublin (from Lincoln) on Archbishop Francis Marsh's death, but prudently waited another year for Canterbury (ibid., p. 364).

75 Townshend to Boulter, 27 July 1724 (NA SP 35/50/92).

Irish primacy from the renewal of leases 'upon your first coming in'. That Boulter had brought up the question of his future prospects and emoluments can be inferred from this, and from references to the deanery of St Paul's in the sentence that followed, suggesting that Boulter had raised the possibility of holding that deanery (perhaps *in commendam* with Bristol, as some successors were to do). But Townshend ruled out such an arrangement, partly because it depended on the life of the present dean, 'the duration of which is a thing uncertain', and furthermore because the king wished any appointment to St Paul's to be acceptable to the bishop of London (though that might not have been a problem, as Boulter's friend Gibson held London and perhaps put the idea into Boulter's head). So Townshend wrote, 'I therefore think your lordship has chosen the right [illegible] not to let slip this occasion of getting into a station where you will have great opportunity of doing a service to his Majesty and your country and to your own family, and I am sure I performed the duty of a friend and faithful servant in advancing it.'[76] As to what the emoluments of the office actually were, the rent roll of the archbishop of Armagh for 1724, Boulter's first year, shows an income of about £4,600 from rents (a year and a half's rent for a renewal of seven years), and a further income from fines at £1,000.[77]

There were those in Ireland who looked upon Boulter's appointment less favourably than did Townshend. Prominent among these was William King, the doughty archbishop of Dublin, whose initial reservations about Boulter's suitability developed into a deep personal animosity (amply reciprocated). As far back as the time of Boulter's preferment to Bristol and Christ Church, King had written to Dr Charlett, master of University College, that the death of the late bishop and dean (Smalridge) was a considerable loss to the church, and that he knew not what to make of his successor. 'I can remember never [having] heard his name before the *Gazette*. I wish the second temple may equal the first.'[78] When King learned of the death of Primate Lindsay of Armagh on his triennial visitation of Kildare in July 1724, he wrote to Bishop Gibson of London:

> It is of great moment to his Majesty's service as well as to this kingdom and church to have a person duly qualified in that station, and understanding that your lordship has exerted yourself in promoting the discipline and interest of the church which no man is better apprised of than your lordship, I judge it proper on this occasion to apply to your lordship's good offices with his Majesty's ministers who have influence in these affairs in order to procure us a good primate ... we have suffered much by the unhappy circumstances of his

76 Ibid.
77 PRONI, DIO 4/33/7. In addition there was a small number of 'petty copyholders', charged with 6*d.* and 3*d.* a piece for cabins and gardens, and whose obligations were observed by sending hens to the seneschal of the manor at Christmas (DIO 4/35/8).
78 King to Charlett, 7 Jan. 1719/20, Bodl., Rawl. D742.51b.

late grace of Armagh and it will require a person of spirit and knowledge to set things in order in that province and particularly in that diocese.[79]

King's own prospects can hardly have been bright. One historian has cited his inflexibility towards the Presbyterians of Ulster as the reason he was passed over, and his avowed reluctance to assume the responsibilities of a lord justice cannot have helped.[80] But quite apart from such considerations, King's general attitude to government must have ruled him out. He professed himself unwilling to be a candidate for Armagh, and had written accordingly to Marmaduke Coghill. Coghill has been described as 'one of the pillars of the Protestant establishment in early eighteenth-century Ireland' and 'a key figure in the political and social elite of early eighteenth-century Dublin'.[81] King had told him that only if he were convinced that his succession would be for the good of the church would he, 'lame as I am', travel to London to press his suit, opining that the Church of Ireland had sufficiently suffered from 'crazy, lame and superannuated primates'.[82]

Archbishop Wake would not have selected Boulter, though for different reasons. Canterbury's preferred candidate was Chandler of Lichfield, but Chandler was seen by government as too much under Wake's influence, and Wake was out of favour. Newcastle, secretary of state for the southern department, which dealt with Irish affairs, regarded the bishop of Lichfield as 'not for the king's service'. Gibson, who had replaced Wake in the ministry's confidence, and was, as we have already noted, Boulter's friend and patron, broke the news gently to Archbishop King:

> I shall always be ready to do what is in my power for the good of the Church of Ireland; and I took it for granted, that upon the primate's death, the chief government of it would have been put into the hands of some person upon the bench there. But I find things are like to take another turn here, and that the bishop of Bristol is intended for the primacy; who had indeed a good understanding, and is a worthy man. He is in his diocese [on a visitation]; and as he has not yet kissed the king's hand, the measure may still be changed, but this is what they intend at present.[83]

According to Bishop Nicolson of Derry, two of the lords justices then in residence in Dublin, Alan Brodrick, 1st viscount Midleton (lord chancellor of Ireland and head of one of the most influential political dynasties) and William Conolly (speaker of the house of commons and Midleton's rival),

---

79 King to Gibson, 14 July 1724 (Trinity College Dublin, King MSS, 2537/126–7).
80 Sykes, *Wake*, ii, pp 222–3; McNally, *Parties*, p. 48.
81 D.W. Hayton (ed.), *Letters of Marmaduke Coghill, 1722–1738* (Dublin, 2005), p. xi.
82 King to Coghill, 21 July 1724 (Trinity College Dublin, King MSS 2537/136–6).
83 Sykes, *Wake*, i, p. 145; Gibson to King, 30 July 1724 (Trinity College Dublin, MSS 1995–2008/2112).

had put forward the names of the archbishops of their respective provinces.[84] A month later, Nicolson wrote that the bishop of Peterborough, Richard Cumberland, had been talked of, but that he now heard that another had been chosen (Boulter presumably), reputedly, 'a person of good learning and excellent temper; and he has been exceedingly beloved in every one of his former stations'. This is one of those extremely rare occasions on which we get a reference, and even here it is second-hand, to the new primate's temperament, though not a reference that would have been endorsed by all the canons of Christ Church.

The royal nomination of the new primate was dated 12 August 1724, and the letters patent 31 August. To the members of the Irish establishment, Boulter was a largely unknown quantity.[85] 'We are all strangers to him', wrote Coghill to Edward Southwell, secretary of state for Ireland. Coghill presumed, however, that Southwell would be acquainted with Boulter because of the latter's Bristol connection (possibly having in mind Southwell's Gloucestershire estates). Coghill had a personal interest in the appointment since he held a life appointment under the primate, that of judge of the prerogative court, and looked to Southwell to commend him to the new archbishop.

Boulter arrived in Ireland on 3 November 1724, bringing with him Ambrose Philips, as secretary.[86] He wrote to Newcastle remarking on a long and tedious journey by land, but a short and easy passage by sea.[87] The lord lieutenant and most of the 'considerable persons' had sent him their compliments. The bishops of Meath, Henry Downes, and Kildare, Welbore Ellis, had been at the quayside to greet him, and the bishop of Dromore had called on him later that day. 'Tomorrow I shall make it my business to learn the

84 Nicholson to Wake, 31 July 1724 (Pearse Street Library, Dublin, Gilbert Coll., 27/177).
85 Coghill to Southwell, 21 Sept. 1727, Hayton, *Coghill letters*, p. 8.
86 See above for Philips' earlier career. Swift to Pope, 26 Nov. 1725 rather scathingly described Philips' status, as 'neither secretary nor gentleman usher, yet serves in both capacities' (David Woolley (ed.), *The correspondence of Jonathan Swift, DD*, 4 vols (Frankfurt am Main, 2001), ii, p. 623). Not surprisingly, the primate did what he could to promote his secretary's interests in Ireland, not always meeting with success. He exercised his patronage to have him returned to the Irish house of commons for the borough of Armagh in 1727. Philips retained this seat until 1749, there being no limitation on the length of Irish parliaments, other than the death of the monarch, until the Octennial Act of 1768. He was nominated for twenty-five parliamentary committees between 1727 and 1745, and was a founding member of the Dublin Society (Johnston-Liik, *History of the Irish parliament, 1692–1800*, vi, pp 62–3). Described by an early nineteenth-century critic as 'a man of integrity, but rather ludicrously solemn and pompous in his person and conversation' (Nathan Drake, *Essays, biographical, critical, and historical, illustrative of the Tatler, Spectator and Guardian*, 3 vols (London, 1805), iii, p. 269); he returned to London in 1748 and died there on 18 June of the following year.
87 Boulter to Newcastle, 3 Nov. 1724 (NA SP 63/382/173).

affairs of state here, and to transmit to your Grace what may be any ways worth knowing.' 'Very quickly', according to one biographer, he took his place on public bodies 'and gave weight and vigour to them'.[88] That he did not waste any time before exercising his prerogatives is borne out by a letter he wrote to Wake some weeks after his coming. He referred to 'the perpetual hurry I have been in here since my arrival with receiving and paying compliments' and trying 'to settle in the lodgings I am in, till I can find a house to fix in'. He excused his use of an amanuensis to write to his friends, since 'the weakening of my arm' required the employment of 'a third hand'. He continued: 'I miss little here but my friends and acquaintance', and his only complaint was that so many of his English colleagues were regarded as intruders.[89] Eventually he took up residence in Henrietta Street, Dublin, though he also had houses in Armagh and Drogheda.[90] In 1726 he sought the lord lieutenant's approval to use crown property at Chapelizod as a country house, 'as I cannot hope to make much use of my house at Drogheda'.[91] Henrietta Street was a highly fashionable address, the archbishop's residence, according to Maurice Craig, earning for that street the sobriquet of 'Primate's Hill'. A directory of 1738 showed that the archbishop of Armagh had as neighbours the master of the rolls, the clerk of the crown and king's bench and the cashier of the exchequer. Boulter's mansion replaced three recently built houses purchased by Luke Gardiner, who had developed the street. It was a large brick building with a frontage extending for ninety feet and was eventually purchased by the Society of King's Inns, which demolished it and built a library on the site.[92]

Historians have in recent years done much to provide us with evidence to show that the eighteenth-century Church of Ireland did not present quite such a dire image as had been somewhat uncritically accepted heretofore.[93]

88 A. Chalmers, *The general biographical dictionary*, 32 vols (London, 1812–17), *sub nom*. Boulter.
89 Boulter to Wake, 28 Nov. 1724.
90 Lindsay, Boulter's predecessor, lived on St Stephen's Green in Dublin (*Dublin Intelligence*, 15 July 1724), and Lindsay's predecessor, Narcissus Marsh, sometime archbishop of Dublin, had rented a house in town (Lambeth Palace Library, MS 929, f. 41). This source gives details of several episcopal residences in early eighteenth-century Ireland.
91 Boulter to Carteret, 26 Dec. 1726. According to John D'Alton, *The history of County Dublin* (Dublin, 1838, rep. Cork, 1976), p. 275. 'In 1726 Primate Boulter, while he filled the office of one of the lords justice, repaired the king's house here [Chapelizod], and occupied it as his personal dwelling.'
92 Maurice Craig, *Dublin, 1660–1860* (Dublin, 1980), pp 102–3; *Irish Builder*, 30:806–7 (1893), 161, 174, 177.
93 See, for instance, the work of T.C. Barnard, S.J. Connolly, D.W. Hayton, L.A. Landa and A.P.W. Malcomson. Connolly, for instance, makes the point that the negative picture of the clergy has been too much dependent on comments that cannot wholly be taken on trust (*Religion, law and power: the making of Protestant Ireland, 1660–1760* (Oxford, 1992), p. 182). Similarly, Andrew Sneddon writes that 'The Church of

While there can be little doubt that, even by the standards of the time, much fault could be found with the Irish ecclesiastical establishment, there has been too much reliance on the plethora of official enquiries into the state of the church (not least its educational provision) that poured forth from official commissions of one kind or another in the nineteenth century, and whose *raison d'être* was to highlight weakness and failure. Queen Mary's indictment ('everybody agrees that it is the worst in Christendom') has echoed, rarely challenged, down the ages.[94] A closer observer and equally stern critic, Narcissus Marsh, translated from Dublin to Armagh in 1703, wrote to Tenison in 1706 that he found the church in his new province in a better state than he had been led to expect.[95] Boulter, some twenty years later, closer by far than Marsh to the English establishment and acutely aware that it looked to him for results, could not take so sanguine a view.

As was to be expected, the primate had a leading part to play in national politics, which he relished. He is famed, if not notorious, for thoroughly deserving the confidence reposed in him by his political masters in London. But he was not another Richelieu or Mazarin, no major officer of state determining public policy and totally preoccupied with politics. Boulter saw himself as a spiritual leader, with all that that implied. While due acknowledgment has generally been given to his work to establish charitable foundations such as the clergy widows' houses in Drogheda, and his philanthropy at times of acute famine, nevertheless his works of charity have sometimes been perceived to be part of a political strategy, particularly in the case of his zeal for the ill-fated charter schools. Likewise, his unapologetic espousal of English as distinct from Irish interests (a distinction that he might have judged artificial) has, with other factors, combined to ensure that posterity has seen him more as a politician than a pastor. The historian W.E.H. Lecky, conceding that Boulter was of an unimpeachable private character, honest and well meaning, deemed him 'singularly devoid of all religious enthusiasm'.[96] Allowing for the fact that Lecky may have been using the term 'enthusiasm' in a sense rather different from that which it carries today (as indeed would Boulter's contemporaries), the remark can scarcely be regarded as a tribute to a churchman, however generously we interpret it, and was ill-deserved given what we know about the primate's pastoral conscientiousness.

Ireland in now seen as a relatively well-run institution in the sense of its ability to execute its pastoral duties ... It also possessed a core of bishops and influential reformers committed to raising clerical standards in the parishes' (*Witchcraft and Whigs: the life of Bishop Francis Hutchinson, 1660–1739* (Manchester, 2008), p. 137).

94 Carpenter, *Tenison*, pp 382–4.
95 Ibid.
96 W.E.H. Lecky, *A history of Ireland in the eighteenth century*, 5 vols (London 1892), i, p. 462.

Boulter came to Ireland at a time of very considerable political unrest, the turbulence created by the Wood's Halfpence affair showing little sign of abating. This controversy, in which Swift's *Drapier's Letters* played a significant role in inflaming public opinion, arose from the granting of a patent to William Wood to mint £100,800 worth of copper coin for Ireland, the patent allegedly having been purchased from the king's mistress, the duchess of Kendal. Critics maintained that the Irish currency would thereby be debased, quite apart from what was considered to be the impropriety of the transaction.

Boulter had, therefore, from the outset, to exercise his political skills in a determined manner. Although the established church was not shaken to the same extent as the political world by any such specific scandal, Nicolson of Derry expressed to Wake the view that whoever the new primate might be, he would need all the courage he could muster given the panic engendered by Wood's Halfpence.[97]

The established Church of Ireland lived in a state of almost continuous apprehension about the future, ever nervous that English Whig politicians, insufficiently aware of its precarious position and failing to attach sufficient importance to its crucial place in the 'Protestant constitution' would betray its (and, ultimately, their own) interests by ill-conceived concessions to Catholics and Dissenters. After two centuries, the Church of Ireland had made little headway in commending Protestantism (as the Anglican religious settlement was normally termed) to the greater part of the Irish population. Furthermore, in the north, where Protestants comprised much of the population, largely as the result of the Ulster Plantation and voluntary immigration, they frequently adhered to a Dissenting, mainly Presbyterian, tradition that was regarded by the established church as, if anything, a greater threat than popery. Boulter opened his heart in a long letter to Wake within eighteen months of arriving in Ireland.[98] He complained of serious irregularities of all kinds in the manner in which the Irish church conducted its business, which he was attempting to address, while at the same time contending with the behaviour of the archbishop of Dublin, some of whose aberrations Boulter believed he could not continue to tolerate without prejudicing the rights of his own successors.

Perhaps nothing better illustrates the sense of insecurity with which the Church of Ireland (and Boulter) viewed the Irish scene than the setting up of a committee of the house of lords in 1731 to investigate the state of popery in Ireland. Its findings were to bear out the worst fears of those who, like the primate, suspected that popery was resurgent rather than diminishing.

97 Nicolson to Wake, 21 Aug. 1724 (Pearse Street Library, Dublin, Gilbert Coll., 27/178).
98 Boulter to Wake, 21 May 1726.

Repeatedly, he wrote to England about the non-residence of the clergy and of the lack of churches, chapels and parsonages, which seriously undermined the capacity of the established church to fulfil its mission.[99] If things continued in this fashion, he warned, the Church of Ireland, rather than gaining ground, would lose even more.

Queen Mary's unflattering description of the Church of Ireland has already been quoted. Nor was the established church held in much greater esteem, at least as manifested in the eighteenth century, by the historian Lecky, whose assessment of it as beset with lethargy and paralysis was equally damning.[1] While the queen's opinion smacks of hyperbole and ignorance (she was scarcely in a position to draw comparisons with much of Christendom), Lecky's judgment is a more considered one, for, though he may have been out of sympathy with the church, he must as a former candidate for ordination have acquired some theological competence.[2]

Yet the pages that follow may give some indication that the Church of Ireland was rather more than a department of state, and that many of its luminaries (not least Boulter, so frequently identified as the quintessential erastian churchman) could discharge their pastoral and political responsibilities without experiencing any tension between the two spheres of duty. Philip O'Regan, biographer of Archbishop King, Boulter's bitter adversary on behalf of the Irish-born clergy, acknowledges that while the church had become more latitudinarian, more erastian and more Anglocentric under the influence of the English-born such as Boulter, there was an improvement in pastoral integrity.[1] Also worth bearing in mind is the fact that although many of the English were strangers to Ireland on arrival, their families stayed there after them. 'They might be *newcomers*; their descendants were natives.'[3]

Boulter's prestige stemmed in large measure from his appointment as one of the three lords justices of Ireland, who in the early Hanoverian period deputized for lords lieutenant, who were obliged to reside in Dublin only for the biennial parliamentary sessions. It was the lords justices who received instructions from London as to the conduct of Irish affairs (as well as a salary of £100 per month) and who headed the list of members of the Irish privy council, which met regularly, in and out of parliamentary sessions.[4] The office of lord justice was held by the archbishop of Armagh (customarily), the lord chancellor and the speaker of the house of commons. It was

---

99 Boulter to Wake, 13 Feb. 1728; Boulter to Newcastle, 7 Mar. 1728; J.A. Froude, *The English in Ireland in the eighteenth century*, 3 vols (London, 1872–4), i, p. 417.
1 Lecky, *Ireland*, i, p. 209.
2 Donal McCartney, *W.E.H. Lecky: historian and politician, 1838–1903* (Dublin, 1994), pp 12–17.
3 Philip O'Regan, *Archbishop William King of Dublin (1650–1729) and the constitution in church and state* (Dublin, 2000), p. 334.
4 F.G. James, *Lords of the ascendancy: the Irish house of lords and its members, 1600–1800* (Dublin, 1995), pp 148–9.

not unknown for a metropolitan other than Armagh to hold the office. Archbishop King held it during most of the archiepiscopate of Boulter's predecessor, Lindsay, but Lindsay was a high-church Tory. Once Boulter was in the saddle there was no thought of replacing him, and he held the position of lord justice on ten occasions.

The influence bestowed on Boulter by this high rank operated most obviously in the political sphere, but inevitably he could bring the weight of his dual office as primate and lord justice to bear on those matters of ecclesiastical policy and patronage where the lord lieutenant, and therefore the crown, had a say. For example, the lords justices signed the warrants for clerical appointments that were at the disposal of the monarch when sees were vacant. Travelling to England, the primate and his entourage took the royal yacht, when available, a privilege that was also, from time to time, enjoyed by other bishops.[5]

While it was the overall governance of Ireland that engaged his very considerable energies, there was a conspicuous ecclesiastical facet to that. His policy of promoting the English-born at the expense of the Irish-born is the aspect of his church strategy that has attracted most attention in the past and must be examined in some detail, if only in an attempt to ascertain what weight he gave to the suitability of candidates for ecclesiastical office in terms of their pastoral integrity as well as their origins and political allegiance. What emerges from a study of the primate's attitude to clerical appointments is not merely a policy governed by consistency of purpose (which few have ever questioned), but a total lack of cynicism. While making no attempt to conceal his primary objectives (in fact, he enunciated them clearly), he was concerned that those in whose appointment he was instrumental would serve not only the interests of church and state, but also of the people in their pastoral care. It might also be claimed, or at least postulated, that however biased he may have been in favour of the English-born, Boulter's policy did ensure that a breadth of ecclesiastical background and outlook was imported to the Irish church.[6] To quote the primate himself, writing to the archbishop of Canterbury, 'Your grace knows I have nothing to lose, but I may be made more or less capable of serving his Majesty, of doing good in the church, and of supporting the English interest, which labours under great disadvantages in this country, according as I have more or less countenance from England.'[7]

---

5   A note to this effect is to be found in the primate's accounts for 1724 (PRONI, DIO 2/35/7); NA SP 63/385/11; David Dickson, *New foundations: Ireland, 1660–1800* (2nd ed. Dublin, 2000), p. 87.
6   David Dickson has pointed out that there were eleven Irish-born and eleven English-born bishops at the beginning of George II's reign (*New foundations: Ireland, 1660–1860* (2nd ed. Dublin, 2000), p. 87).
7   Boulter to Wake, 30 June 1727.

When it came to patronage, the primate could sometimes find himself in contention with his fellow lords justices. Marmaduke Coghill wrote to Secretary of State Southwell in 1735 when the rich see of Derry was vacant ('a glorious preferment for anybody', worth £2,400 a year, besides tithes and patronage) that the lords justices could not agree on a candidate and that each was nominating his own man.[8]

The mention of preferment for an archbishop's son (though not realized on this occasion) as a consequence of Hoadley's departure from Ferns to Dublin, is a reminder of the pressures of a less political and more personal kind that frequently arose from family ambitions and obligations. Archbishop King once commented on the fact that the bishop of Waterford gave all livings of value to a brother and other relatives, and disposed of the vicar-generalship and registrarship of his diocese in similar fashion.[9] *Faulkner's Dublin Journal*, praising the chancellor of St Patrick's for ignoring the claims of a brother when making an appointment, opined that he was showing 'a rare and worthy example, to prefer the honour and service of God to the interest of his family'.[10] Edward Tenison (son of the archbishop of Canterbury) was a royal chaplain and became bishop of Ossory in 1730. He was succeeded there by Charles Este, one of Boulter's chaplains, whose promotion the primate had earnestly pressed for, persuading the lord lieutenant that Este was a man of great worth and learning.[11] When Edward Synge was made bishop of Clonfert in 1730, his father, the archbishop of Tuam, was the principal consecrating prelate and the sermon was preached by the new bishop's brother Nicholas, who would soon to be his father's archdeacon and eventually bishop of Killaloe. George Berkeley, bishop of Cloyne, presented his brother Robert to the parish of Midleton. The bishop of Killala and Achonry, Cary, made his son archdeacon of Killala. Robert Downes, son of the bishop of Derry, succeeded to two parishes in his father's diocese.[12]

Such an approach to ecclesiastical appointments, however unedifying it may appear to the modern mind, was part and parcel of the workings of government in the eighteenth century. The Irish church was not remarkable in Europe in this regard, nor is there much to suggest that, whatever about their mode of appointment, candidates for preferment in the Church of Ireland were any less appointable than has been the case in more open systems. It has been shown that all bishops who held Irish sees between 1692 and 1800 had attended university, only a couple failing to graduate,

---

8 Coghill to Southwell, 14 June 1735 (BL, Add. MSS, 21,122–3).
9 Richard Mant, *History of the Church of Ireland*, 2 vols (London, 1840), ii, p. 445.
10 *Faulkner's Dublin Journal*, 27–31 Jan. 1730/1.
11 Dorset to Newcastle, 2 Dec. 1735 (NA SP 63/398/90).
12 *Faulkner's Dublin Journal*, 30 May–2 June 1730; *Dublin News-Letter*, 26–30 Jan. 1743, 30 Jan.–2 Feb. 1742; *Faulkner's Dublin Journal*, 27–31 Jan. 1730.

and that a significant number owed their promotion to scholarship (Berkeley being a case in point).[13] As for what has come to be seen as the most characteristic feature of appointments during Boulter's term of office, the promotion of the English-born rather than the Irish-born, this policy was well under way, as F.G. James has pointed out, before Boulter's day, and the majority of bishops on the Irish bench were English by birth long before and long after Boulter's primacy.[14]

As a leading figure in the Irish house of lords, Boulter sought to manage parliamentary business. The bishops of the established church were significant figures in the upper chamber, as was that house in the constitution. Chief Secretary Southwell's comment to Secretary of State Hedges in 1705 that 'I never trouble you with what the house of lords do, because in truth they have hardly any business before them', would hardly have been appropriate when Boulter was primate.[15] Rather in the manner of a modern leader of the house or party whip (or, indeed of those 'undertakers' such as Speaker Conolly who managed the commons), the primate worked to ensure the safe passage of legislation that was often directed towards the welfare of the established church. Nor was his task as simple as might appear, for Tory sentiment was widespread among the bishops. Some measures were calculated to improve the management and efficiency of the church, while others aimed to strengthen its position by tightening the constraints on popery and Dissent. The parliamentary progress of such legislation, as recorded in the journals of the house of lords, gives little indication of the anxious days that Boulter spent on such matters, which are graphically illustrated by his correspondence. His concerns were by no means restricted to matters ecclesiastical, but these were of particular importance to him, a case in point being the enactment of laws addressing the high incidence of non-resident clergy, a perennial Achilles' heel of the Church of Ireland.

The new primate was introduced to the house of lords on 7 September 1725 with elaborate ceremony, and he scarcely missed a sitting from that day to the end of his life.[16] Within days of entering the house, legislation that was of the utmost significance to him was under discussion, the heads of a bill for building on church lands. The background against which he fought for the interests of the church was described in his letter to the bishop of London dated 11 January 1728.

> We are going on with some bills to mend the state of our church, by getting more glebes, churches, and chapels of ease, that we may in time have churches

13 F.G. James, *Lords of the ascendancy*, pp 141, 148.
14 F.G. James, 'The Church of Ireland in the early eighteenth century', *Historical Magazine of the Protestant Episcopal Church*, xlviii (1979), 433–51, at 442n.
15 Hayton, 'The beginnings of the "undertaker system"', p. 34.
16 *Lords' Jn. Ire.*, ii, 806 for an account of his introduction and volumes ii and iii for his attendances.

and resident ministers to answer our wants, for at present many of our people go off to the papists and presbyterians, for want of churches to repair to. Here is such a jealousy of increasing the wealth of the church, that what success our bills will have with the commons is uncertain.[17]

Under Poynings' Law (1494) Irish legislation was subject to scrutiny by the Irish and English (British from 1707) privy councils before coming before the two houses of parliament in Dublin.[18] In a series of letters to Archbishop Wake of Canterbury in 1728 (copied to Bishop Gibson of London), the Irish primate set out details of a raft of proposed legislation that could be regarded as a programme to meet the interlocking problems of non-residence, scarcity of churches and glebes, and tithe collection. Boulter claimed that these bills 'were of great consequence to religion in this country', and he sought Wake's assistance when they were discussed at the privy council in London.[19] The first bill was intended to 'explain and amend' earlier legislation by reducing the distance that must lie between a parish church and a newly formed chapel of ease, and dispensing with the need to have the consent of patron and incumbent (which had not been readily forthcoming in some cases). Only the Protestant inhabitants concerned were left with the right of consent ('as they must contribute towards building it'). Furthermore, 'at the insistence of the clergy we have likewise excluded such as live within two miles of a neighbouring church'.[20]

Another measure to come before the privy council in London was similarly to explain and amend earlier legislation in the light of experience.[21] The changes were intended to encourage landlords to make between fifteen and twenty acres of land available for a glebe on terms favourable to the clergy, and empowered the bishop to sequester any arrears of rent following the annual visitation. Boulter set out the matter baldly. 'Having endeavoured to provide glebes, we oblige all future incumbents having convenient glebes, to build. All are allowed three-fourths of what they lay out, but we see nothing but force will make them build.'[22]

He also mentioned two further bills being sent over to London at the same time. One was designed to facilitate the collection of tithes, and here he referred to one of the constant difficulties which was experienced by the church, and would continue to be for a further century or more. Similar legislation had twice fallen foul of the Irish house of commons, where so

17 Boulter to Gibson, 11 Jan. 1728.
18 10 Hen. VII, c. 4.
19 Boulter to Wake, 13 Feb. 1728.
20 6 Geo. I, c. 13, *An act for the better maintenance of curates within the Church of Ireland* (1719).
21 8 Geo. I, c. 12, *An act for the better enabling of the clergy having cure of souls to reside upon their respective benefices, and for the encouragement of Protestant schools within this kingdom of Ireland.*
22 Boulter to Wake, 13 Feb. 1728.

many of the members were landlords, and amendments had been made that were unpalatable to the church. Nor were the landed gentry the only obstacle he had to contend with. It appears that, for want of resident gentlemen, up to one-quarter of resident justices were clergy who might 'play the game into one another's hands', and so new legislation was intended to exclude clergy from being the justices before whom such causes might be tried. Several days later he wrote again about another three bills: 'to further help with the recovery of tithes', 'to further encourage the building of chapels of ease', and 'to enable archbishops and bishops to part with advowsons to other patrons so as to allow these to make better provision for clergy'.[23]

The primate's anxieties did not cease with the approval of the bills in London, for they still had to pass through both houses of the Irish parliament. He could by no means count on unanimity among the peers, even among the bishops, for, as he pointed out, Bolton, the bishop of Elphin, on occasion 'put himself at the head of those lords and others, who constantly oppose the government business here'.[24] The commons posed a greater challenge. Armagh told Canterbury: 'Our bench have been very busy with their friends in the house of commons, to pass our bills when returned, which if they do, we may hope by degrees to see somewhat of the face of religion in this country.'[25]

The attitude of the commons to the passage of such bills may well have stemmed, as Patrick McNally has suggested, from memories among the now-dominant Whig gentry of times when Anglican clergy supported their political enemies. Archbishop King, in a letter of 20 April 1715, commented that 'most of the clergy under the late management set themselves against the gentlemen, traversed them in their elections, endeavoured to turn them out of their boroughs, and in their convocation opposed the votes of the h[ouse] of commons by contrary votes'.[26] It also, inevitably, owed something to the natural resistance to paying taxes.

Boulter saw the interests of church and state as inseparable. Accordingly, his strategy was twofold: to reform and thereby reinvigorate the Irish Church while simultaneously working assiduously to protect its prerogatives as the established church of the kingdom. The latter policy involved him in endless vigilance where Catholicism and Protestant dissent were concerned, and, more positively, the promotion of the Protestant religion through education. He was haunted by the spectre of a resurgent Catholicism, which he believed

---

23 Same to same, 17 Feb. 1728.
24 Boulter to Townshend, 9 May 1728. Bolton was an Irish-born confidant of Carteret's and a constant thorn in Boulter's side. For more about their relationship see McNally, *Parties*, pp 80, 82, 99, 142, 192.
25 Boulter to Wake, 2 Apr. 1728.
26 McNally, 'Irish and English interests', p. 296; McNally, *Parties*, p. 152.

was already making steady progress not only, he suspected, through lacunae in the anti-popery laws, but also by the ineffectual manner in which such laws were executed. He was much alarmed by Catholic infiltration of the legal profession, believing that the practice of the law was mostly in the hands of so-called 'new converts', who were suspected of a mere outward conformity. He pushed for legislation to remedy the situation by requiring converts to have been so for five years before qualifying, and to bring up their children as Protestants.[27] But laws were of little avail unless enforced. A complaint had reached the house of lords 'of a very great increase in the number of popish priests and regulars and the present state of popery in this kingdom', and the house adopted a lengthy resolution which referred to the growing 'insolence' of Catholics building mass houses, and the need for judges to give directions to magistrates in the matter. The resolution was laid before the lord lieutenant, who informed the lord chancellor that he would so instruct the judges.[28] Such activity did not go unnoticed in Rome, where the pope had 'learned with sorrow about the artifices employed by that government not only to impede Catholicism there but to eliminate it, at least from the lives of the less educated section of the people', through Protestant schools. This was, indeed, one of Boulter's most fervent ambitions.[29]

The leaders of the established church, disturbed by rumours they were hearing, decided to set about collecting information on the activities of Catholic priests and regulars on a systematic basis. The lords set up a committee on the state of popery and reports were sought and received from the high sheriffs of Galway and Mayo and the mayor of Galway. On 4 December 1731, the primate reported to the house from that committee, and his report was ordered to be printed. Simultaneously, legislation was passed further strengthening the law concerning convert lawyers, the disarming of Catholics and annulling marriages between Protestants (or between Protestants and Catholics) by Catholic priests.[30] On 6 December 1731, a comprehensive document on the state of popery was presented to the house and ordered to be printed. In finding, that, for instance, 'several pretended popish archbishops, bishops and their officials, exercise ecclesiastical jurisdiction', it bore out Boulter's worst fears.[31]

---

27 3 Geo. II, c. 6 (1729), *An act for allowing further time to persons in offices to qualify themselves pursuant to an act entitled 'An act to prevent the further growth of popery'.*

28 *Lords Jn. Ire.*, iii, 99, 10 Nov. 1729; 111–12, 22 Dec. 1729; ibid., 114.

29 Cathaldus Giblin, OFM, 'Catalogue of material of Irish interest in the collection of Nunziatura di Fiandra, Vatican Archives' in *Collectanea Hibernica*, i (1958).

30 *Lords Jn. Ire.*, iii, 168 ff.; ibid., 161.

31 *Lords Jn. Ire.*, iii, 169–72. Also see *A report made by his grace the lord primate from the lords' committee to enquire into the present state of popery in the kingdom of Ireland* (Dublin, 1731).

Some years later, in 1747, this report was reprinted by the Incorporated Society for Promoting English Protestant Schools in Ireland in order to persuade its English supporters of the vital part played by its 'charter schools' in stemming the progress of Catholicism in Ireland. The Incorporated Society was a high priority of the primate, whose support for charity schools was manifest during his time at St Olave's, Southwark. He had confidence, in the face of evidence to the contrary, in the efficacy of elementary education of the Irish poor under the auspices of the established church as a powerful weapon against the spread of Catholicism. Several parliamentary measures intended to improve pastoral care in the parishes had provided for the 'encouragement of Protestant schools in the kingdom of Ireland', but the charter schools (so called because of their royal instrument of foundation) established by the Incorporated Society for Promoting English Protestant Schools in Ireland, were, at least in theory, a much more systematic scheme.[32] A network of boarding schools would instruct 'the children of the popish and other poor natives', boys and girls, not only in the English tongue and the principles of true religion and loyalty, but in husbandry and linen manufacture. The original plan was not Boulter's but that of Henry Maule, successively bishop of Cloyne and Dromore.[33] However, it had the wholehearted support of the primate. Boulter used his very considerable political and personal influence to promote the cause, even to the extent of paying for the parchment and engrossing of the petition to the king that set the process of incorporation in motion.[34] Not only did he assume the office of vice president and treasurer of the society (Dorset, the lord lieutenant, being president), but he also provided a school himself at Santry, Co. Dublin. The society became heavily indebted to him personally, and in 1742, the year of his death, he attended not only its meetings in Dublin, but also those of the corresponding society in London.[35] The schools never achieved their purposes, and after a century during which £1 million of public money was spent on them, had little to show for it other than a catalogue of corruption and abuse. This was scarcely Boulter's fault, and it is interesting to speculate as to whether or not much more would have been done to remedy matters, given his profound commitment to the purposes of

32 For example, 1 Geo. II, c. 15 and 3 Geo. II, c. 12; Milne, *Charter schools* (the charter is printed there in full: pp 337–44).
33 The archbishop of Cashel (William Palliser) presided at Maule's consecration (as protocol demanded, Cloyne lying in the province of Cashel). Boulter confided in Gibson how the archbishop of Dublin (King) could make difficulties for any other archbishop who might have hoped to carry out the rite in his province. 'To avoid a quarrel with his Grace of Dublin' Boulter held the ceremony in Dunboyne, diocese of Meath, the nearest parish to the province of Dublin (Boulter to Gibson, 13 Sept. 1726).
34 Boulter account book, 26 Mar. 1730.
35 Ibid., pp 28, 41.

the charter, had he been in office when the steady decline of the scheme into public opprobrium was signalled by successive public enquiries. A humane man, as is evident from his compassionate activity at times of famine and economic hardship, his zeal for the schools had been motivated not simply by what he described in a letter to the bishop of London as 'interest', but also by concern for the salvation 'of those poor creatures, who are our fellow subjects, to try all possible means to bring them and theirs over to the knowledge of the true religion'.[36]

Dissenters as well as Catholics were a worry to Boulter, and in some ways the established church regarded the former as a greater threat to its hegemony. Indeed, an issue on which the king's servants in Ireland and his ministers in England most frequently differed was that of the toleration of Dissent and the civic and political participation of Catholics. The British government thought that Protestant solidarity in Ireland in the face of the huge Catholic majority was self-evidently desirable. Boulter saw Dissenters as potentially undermining the Protestant constitution as he understood it. They were effectively barred from much political influence by the imposition of the sacramental test which required office holders and members of town corporations (though not of parliament) to certify having received Holy Communion according to the rites of the Church of Ireland. Successive British administrations attempted to remove this requirement, but in vain. In fact, defence of the sacramental test was one issue that drew Irish Whigs and Tories together.[37] An attempt to meet Presbyterian demands for the amelioration of the lot of Dissenters was afoot in the early 1730s, but Boulter, not averse to giving some relief to a manifestly loyal and industrious community, was realistic about the opposition building up in political circles in Ireland against such a move. Newcastle, having shown Boulter's communication to the king, replied that his majesty was greatly concerned that a measure that could so much strengthen the Protestant interest was being discouraged. However, Newcastle deferred to local advice, saying wistfully that it was an extraordinary situation in a country where no distinction should be kept up among Protestants.[38] Equally wistfully, the primate had written to Delafaye that the anti-popery feeling in the commons was not what it had been, and to Newcastle that he hoped the day would come when Protestants would be more inclined to unite.[39]

Presbyterian representations for repeal of the test continued, the *Dublin Evening Post* reporting in 1733 that large numbers of Dissenting teachers had come to town to lobby for it. It was being said that Dorset, the lord lieutenant, had given signs that some concession would be made, though

36 Boulter to Gibson, 5 May 1730.
37 McNally, *Parties*, pp 45–6, 138.
38 Newcastle to Boulter, 5 Feb. 1732.
39 Boulter to Delafaye, 4 Jan. 1732; Boulter to Newcastle, 19 Feb. 1732.

Boulter believed it would be folly to proceed when there was so little chance of success in parliament.[40] He anticipated a two-to-one vote against such a measure in the lords and three-to-two in the commons, commenting that opposition was being stoked up by pamphlets written by Archbishop Synge of Tuam and Dean Swift. He rather feared that the Dissenters' agents 'mistook civil answers for promises', and believed that the more prudent among the Dissenting laity saw the impracticability of introducing a bill on the matter in such a political climate.[41] Some fifty years were to pass before the sacramental test was removed, though its rigours were in some degree abated by the use of an indemnity act whereby transgressors were retrospectively excused.[42]

Outside the political sphere, however, the lot of the Dissenters was infinitely happier than that of the Catholics. While under no circumstances conceding the theological correctness of Dissent, Boulter had little hesitation in providing a Huguenot minister for the de Joncourt linen workers in Dundalk (in his diocese) and was prepared to receive 'kindly' the Calvinistic evangelical preacher, George Whitefield.[43] Even when the *Dublin Intelligencer* reported that the pastor of the Presbyterian meeting house in Eustace Street, Dublin, had appeared in a black gown, 'in imitation of our Protestant ministers',[44] there was no outraged cry of 'insolence' such as was so frequently levelled at Catholics perceived to have exceeded the bounds of seemly behaviour. Boulter was capable of showing compassion to individual Dissenting ministers where he discerned no threat to Anglican ascendancy. A letter of 31 March 1729 to Walpole conveys, sympathetically, solicitations on behalf of Presbyterian ministers for resumption in the payment of the *regium donum*, the royal bounty granted to Presbyterian ministers since the reign of Charles II, which had been interrupted due to the king's death. The primate argued that they were in sore need of the money, though properly 'sensible there is nothing due to them'.[45]

Boulter's involvement in the legislative process was by no means restricted to parliamentary procedure in the house of lords. He also included what he described as 'preparing bills for [the privy] council'.[46] Such political work was not only concerned with matters of church order and finance, but also with issues of public morality. He regularly voiced his anxiety that much more energy needed to be put into 'the reform of public manners', an element that we have already encountered in his preaching. He attributed

40 *Dublin Evening Post*, 29 Sept. to 2 Oct. 1733; Boulter to Newcastle, 18 Dec. 1733.
41 Boulter to Gibson, 20 Dec. 1733.
42 19–20 Geo. III, c. 6.
43 Milne, *Charter schools*, p. 352n; *NHI*, iv, 687–8.
44 *Dublin Intelligencer*, 21 Oct. 1730.
45 Boulter to Walpole, 31 Mar. 1729
46 Boulter to Gibson, 10 Feb. 1738.

much of what he saw as a decline in standards of behaviour to the inroads of unbelief. While in some measure 'latitudinarian' in that he held views such as a tolerance towards Dissent, a hallmark of many 'latitudinarian' bishops of the time (at least in England), like his mentor Gibson, Boulter deplored some of the tendencies of the time. Perhaps unexpectedly, given his own Anglocentric outlook, Boulter praised the work of John Richardson, a clergyman of the established church who laboured to bring the Book of Common Prayer to the Irish in their native language, the archbishop going so far as to seek preferment for Richardson to ease his circumstances.[47] He also recognized Dr Delany of St Werburgh's, a high-churchman and one of Swift's circle, subsequently dean of Down, whom he otherwise criticized for the pursuit of gain as TCD's 'greatest pupil-monger'.[48] Delany, he conceded, was a strong defender of 'our most holy cause against the present audacious insults of unbelievers'. Boulter asked the bishop of London to look favourably on Delany's wish to have something he had written examined with candour.[49] The primate went so far as to suggest that the sending of missionaries abroad from Ireland might well be suspended until needs nearer home were met, though he was sympathetic to the needs of continental Protestants, supporting, for instance, a collection in aid of those in Lithuania, then part of the Polish-Lithuanian Commonwealth.[50]

Some critics of the church pointed the finger of blame for low standards in high places at the clergy themselves. One such, James Read, published an open letter to the primate in 1737 in which he severely criticized those bishops who left the examination of candidates for ordination almost entirely to archdeacons, 'so that here the bishop hath little more to do than barely to perform the ceremony', while the preparation of the candidates was 'entirely thrown upon the parochial minister'. Visitations, Read remarked, were of as little trouble to the bishop as they were of advantage to the church.[51]

Yet visitations were by no means mere matters of form, at least where Boulter was concerned, and in an age when other means of communication were difficult, they provided almost the only kind of regular inspection and accountability.[52] When Boulter wrote to Gibson in July 1726 that annual

47 Boulter to Dorset, 3 Sept. 1730.
48 Boulter to Newcastle, 12 Oct. 1725.
49 Boulter to Gibson, 12 Aug. 1731.
50 Boulter to Dorset, 29 May 1731; Boulter to Wake, 3 Dec. 1728.
51 James Read, *An essay on the simony and sacrilege of the bishops of Ireland, together with some proposals for redressing the same ... with a prefatory letter to the lord primate of Ireland* (London, 1737), pp 107, 109–10.
52 One of many instances that could be cited is that of Archbishop King receiving the (unwelcome) news of Boulter's appointment to Armagh when holding his triennial provincial visitation (King to Gibson, 14 July 1724 (Trinity College Dublin, King MSS 2537/126)).

diocesan visitations were the practice in Ireland, he had already completed several such expeditions, customarily in July. Triennial visitations of his province as distinct from his diocese were also part of his routine. The diocesan visitations lasted some two to three weeks, while provincial visitations took him away from Dublin for up to five weeks. These were held, of necessity, during the summer when parliament was not sitting and political life had slowed down. But a major consideration must also have been the fact that the roads were comparatively passable in the summer months.[53]

A remarkable printed document relating to Boulter's visitation practices survives in the library of Trinity College Dublin.[54] It is headed '*The procedure of his Grace HUGH, Lord Archbishop of Armagh, Primate and Metropolitan of all Ireland. In the course of his ordinary visitation of the diocese of Armagh, and his triennial visitation of the several dioceses in the province of Armagh in the year of Our Lord 1730*'. It shows that he travelled to Trim on Monday 29 June, conducted the visitation of the diocese of Meath there on Tuesday and Wednesday, proceeding thence to Longford (for the visitation of Ardagh), followed in due course by Kilmore and Clogher, finally returning from Magheralin (Dromore) to Armagh on 28 July. After that strenuous progress, he held the visitation of the lower part of his own diocese at Dundalk on 29–30 July, and of the upper part at Drogheda on July 31. It may be added that there was a social aspect, at least where some visitations were concerned, the innkeeper at Armagh receiving £17 7s. 11½d. for the visitation dinner in 1734 and £29 9s. 3d. in 1738.[55]

Eighteenth-century bishops attached great importance to the 'charge' that they delivered to their clergy when on visitation, and Boulter was no exception. Neither was he an exception from the common practice of having these charges printed. As he remarked after a visitation in 1725, 'As some think it may be of some service to the government, at least by giving me the more weight among the well-affected, when they see my sentiments in print I have thoughts of speedily putting it in the press ...'[56] The substance of his charges was very much in line with what he had said in former times to the clergy of Bristol, though in his first address to the clergy of Armagh he struck a personal note, admitting that coming as a stranger he had yet to identify the specific needs of the diocese. However, he impressed on them that all clergy were obliged to remember that they were ambassadors of Christ, stewards of his household, watchmen and guides. He had hopes that Dissenters would be drawn to the church by policies of 'charity and sweetness', and that kindness should be shown to Catholics who gave signs

---

53 Boulter to Gibson, 30 July 1726; *Dublin Gazette*, 27–30 June 1730.
54 Trinity College Dublin, Press A.7.5.
55 Boulter account book, 2 Aug. 1734, 17 Aug. 1738.
56 Boulter to Newcastle, 3 Aug. 1725.

of being prepared to forsake their errors. Indeed, in his view it was a rebuke to Protestants that there had been so few conversions to the established church.[57]

His provincial charges carried a similar message, putting it to the clergy that when 'common Christians' fell short of the standards that they ought to maintain, they confirmed the unbeliever in error and shook the faith of those of weak profession. How much more culpable were the clergy if ever they set an example of vice and impiety?[58] The impiety of youth he attributed to a lack of grounding in the faith. Six years later, he was still lamenting the 'gross ignorance' of doctrine still apparent despite the length of time since the Reformation, and deprecating the great number of people who remained in 'the darkness and dregs of popery'. He urged the necessity of sermons that would advance the truth, enforcing it by proofs of scripture. Above all, the catechizing of children must not be neglected, and, with some insight into the child mind, he confessed to a fear that 'too great a part of our sermons is lost upon them, and never so much as enters into their understandings'. Even more perceptive was his admonition that the young should be instructed in the catechism, 'not barely to say it by heart, but really to take the meaning of it'.[59] He proceeded to make the point (so evident in his hopes for the charter schools) that bringing up children to be diligent at work protected them from idleness and so from vice. When Boulter visited the diocese of Dromore, the bishop, Maule, appeared 'in a new suit of lawns spun by the girls of [Dundalk] charter school'.[60] Above all, the clergy must lead holy and irreproachable lives, and so the primate's concern with education was not confined to the elementary school work of the Incorporated Society, but also embraced the well-being of the University of Dublin, whence came so many of the ordained.

The primate was no stranger to university and college politics. His years as an undergraduate at Magdalen and as dean of Christ Church, Oxford equipped him to operate, albeit initially without a formal role, at Trinity College Dublin. He had, after all, enormous standing as the first of the lords justices on whom the college waited with compliments at Dublin Castle on their reappointment in 1738 during the interregnum of Devonshire's

57 *The charge given by Hugh, lord archbishop and primate of all Ireland to his clergy at his primary visitation of his diocese, begun at Drogheda, July 16 and continued at Armagh, July 22, 1725* (Dublin, 1725), pp 5, 16–17.

58 *The charge given by Hugh, lord archbishop of Armagh and primate of all Ireland at the triennial visitation of his province, begun at Trim, June 30, 1730* (Dublin, 1730), pp 10–11. This is the charge delivered on the visitation of June/July 1730 described above.

59 *The charge given by Hugh, lord archbishop of Armagh and primate of all Ireland at the triennial visitation of the clergy of his province, begun at Drogheda, June 15, 1736* (Dublin, 1736), pp 6–7, 14.

60 Milne, *Charter schools*, p. 43.

viceroyalty.[61] He was far from confident that the college was in safe political hands, as he made clear in 1729.[62] Believing there to be an undue 'Irish-born' influence there, he suggested that changes in the charter were desirable to make the primate a visitor (the vice chancellor and archbishop of Dublin being *ex officio* visitors as things stood).[63] According to Lecky, bias in favour of the English-born in ministerial circles had led to a strong anti-government spirit in Trinity, and consequently Boulter reputedly hated it as a Tory influence and 'a seminary of Jacobitism'.[64] In fact, Boulter did not say precisely that, but rather stressed the difficulty of keeping the college from becoming such a threat.[65] Certainly, Provost Baldwin, who held office throughout Boulter's primacy and whom the primate strenuously supported, was no Jacobite. He has been described as being possessed of a 'narrow and Whig orthodoxy', which drove several of the fellows, such as Patrick Delany, into a futile opposition, as already alluded to. The primate, writing to Newcastle in 1724–5, referred to a sermon supposedly preached in the college by Delany in a manner unhelpful to the provost.[66]

But not all his considerations relating to Trinity were political. He argued that Dr John Whitcombe, a fellow, should not receive royal dispensation to hold his fellowship as well as the living of Louth, maintaining that not only would it block promotion in the college, but could also be used as a precedent for retaining fellowship with a preferment possibly greater than Whitcombe's. He also believed it inadvisable for the crown to get involved in such a matter.[67] Whitcombe was, however, tutor at Trinity to the lord lieutenant's son, Lord George Sackville, and had such contacts in higher circles that he became bishop of Clonfert within a year and eventually archbishop of Cashel (1752–3).[68] In Whitcombe's case, Boulter argued to no avail, but had, no doubt, been encouraged to take the line he did by an earlier success, when he had prevented Dr Delany from retaining his fellowship when appointed to St John's parish in Dublin. The arguments that Boulter had put forward in Delany's instance were, however, more political (perhaps even personal) than academic. He feared that Delany, whom he described as

---

61 *Dublin News-Letter*, 28 Mar.–1 Apr. 1738.
62 Boulter to Newcastle, 20 Feb. 1729.
63 R.B. McDowell and D.A. Webb, *Trinity College Dublin, 1592–1952: an academic history* (Cambridge, 1982), p. 96.
64 Lecky, *Ireland*, i, p. 422.
65 Boulter to Wake, 6 July 1727.
66 McDowell and Webb, *Trinity College Dublin*, p. 38; Boulter to Newcastle, 9 Mar. 1725.
67 Boulter to Dorset, 14 Jan. 1735; same to same, 13 Mar. 1735.
68 Timothy Godwin was translated from Kilmore to Cashel in 1727 and died in 1729. He replaced William Nicolson (Derry) who was nominated for Cashel in January 1727 but died before taking up office there. John Whitcombe, translated from Down to Cashel in 1752 died the following year.

a great Tory, would never be tempted to leave the capital for richer pastures if he could draw an income in Dublin from both college and parish.[69]

Where the plight of individual clergymen was concerned, Boulter was well informed and prepared to provide redress in difficult situations. In 1724, a curate, Thomas Dawson, on 'behalf of himself and all the curates of the Church of Ireland' prepared a petition to parliament which claimed that they were badly paid (since legislation to improve their condition had been ignored)[70] and 'that they can neither furnish themselves with books, nor procure the necessaries of life'.[71] The men in question were in all likelihood the 'perpetual curates' who occupied a precarious position at the bottom of the ecclesiastical ladder.[72] Whether or not parliament received the petition, it is clear that Boulter needed no persuading that many clergy were in dire straits, be they curates or incumbents with small livings. Swift and others might fulminate against the higher clergy, claiming that they took little thought for their more impecunious brethren when they promoted legislation for parochial reform and including residency that obliged them to build glebe houses, but such disregard is certainly not borne out by Boulter's attitude as set out in a circular letter to the bishops of his province within months of his coming to Ireland.[73] At a meeting of the trustees of the Board of First Fruits, which dispensed relief to impecunious clergy, held on 15 December 1724 with an attendance that included the primate, the lord chancellor, the lord chief justice, the solicitor general and six bishops, it was decided to send to all archbishops and bishops a letter asking for a list of every small living 'as well parsonages as vicarages', which either lacked glebe houses altogether or had inadequate ones, so that 'a full knowledge of the wants of the Church of Ireland' might be obtained.[74] The fund for augmenting the incomes of the poorer clergy, Queen Anne's Bounty, was in debt, and, with the support of the archbishop of Dublin and several other bishops, Boulter recommended that the bishops should make an annual donation for three years out of their own incomes, and that other clergy with incomes of £50 or more also subscribe. The scheme was to be entirely voluntary, and there is no evidence to suggest that it succeeded, though Nicolson of Derry (the see nearest in wealth to Armagh) told Wake that the bishops of the northern province gladly agreed to support Boulter's proposal, and that they would give it more detailed consideration when they

---

69 Boulter to Newcastle, 12 Oct. 1725.
70 2 Geo. 1, c. 13.
71 Draft copy in PRONI, DIO 4/5/3/81.
72 D.H. Akenson, *The Church of Ireland: ecclesiastical reform and revolution, 1800–1885* (New Haven and London, 1971), p. 55.
73 Jonathan Swift, *Irish tracts*, ed. Herbert Davis (Oxford, 1971), p. xxxv; 'Circular letter to the lord primate's suffragan bishops', 24 Dec. 1724.
74 PRONI, DIO 4/11/2/2.

next met at the approaching session of parliament.[75] There is no evidence
that they did so.

The primate did his best for those clergy for whom he felt a responsibility.
The preferment of his Irish chaplains was fairly easily achieved, though they
were not always as appreciative of his efforts as he would have wished. Dr
Skerrett, who came with him to Ireland, was one of his nominees for the see
of Cloyne when it became vacant in 1726. The primate heard (via the bishop
of London) that Skerrett was displeased not to have been Boulter's sole
nominee, and when the former chaplain turned up his nose at further
proposals, Boulter gave him £100 to defray his travel expenses, and had
done with him.[76] Charles Este, already mentioned, who had held a
studentship at Christ Church, Oxford, was, on Boulter's nomination, made
bishop of Ossory in 1736. The primate could persevere in the interests of a
deserving case, and did so to a remarkable extent on behalf of Dr Henry
Stephens, his tutor when he first entered Christ Church as an undergraduate,
subsequently vicar of Malden in Surrey, who preached at his consecration as
bishop of Bristol and had been a fellow contributor to *The Freethinker* in
earlier times.[77] Stephens was a scholar for whom Boulter persistently sought
at least a canonry at Christ Church, making the point to Sir Robert Walpole
that Stephens, now approaching sixty years of age, was 'the only clergyman
in England I have or shall recommend to the ministry for anything there'.[78]
Eventually, through the good offices of Gibson, Stephens was in 1733 made
a prebendary of Winchester.[79] When pleading the case of one Blennerhassett,
a former chaplain of his at Bristol, Boulter told Canterbury that a doctorate
from him would help greatly in finding a suitable living in Ireland. 'I have
not yet heard whether my predecessors have claimed a right of giving
degrees, but if they have, in the present ferment here against the English, it
would be very unpopular in me to exercise such a power in favour of one of
my countrymen.'[80] Charles Morgan, who came to Ireland from Bristol with
the primate, stayed in archiepiscopal service until his death in 1738, and it
is clear that Boulter acted as a conscientious executor of his will. As the

75 Nicolson to Wake, 6 June 1725 (Pearse Street Library, Dublin, Gilbert MSS, 27, 185).
   Nicolson's sturdy support for Boulter's scheme was put forward as a reason why the
   archbishop recommended him for the archbishopric of Cashel in 1727. The bishop
   was reluctant to move, and, in fact, though nominated for Cashel, died before moving
   (Clyve Jones and Geoffrey Holmes (eds), *The London diaries of William Nicolson,
   bishop of Carlisle, 1702–1718* (Oxford, 1985), pp 61, 172). For a detailed account of
   the origins of the Queen's Bounty, see Akenson, *Church of Ireland*, pp 113–14.
76 Boulter to Carteret, 28 June 1726; Boulter to Gibson, 30 July 1726; same to same, 18
   Mar. 1727.
77 Boulter to Townshend, 28 Sept. 1727; Joost, 'The authors of the *Freethinker*', p. 117.
78 Boulter to Walpole, 3 Feb. 1730.
79 Boulter to Gibson, 1 Nov. 1733.
80 Boulter to Wake, 28 Nov. 1724.

primate himself was to do, Morgan made bequests to both Magdalen and Christ Church, and Boulter, writing to Butler, president of Magdalen, to inform him of the death of 'our old friend' asked the president to find out where Morgan's sister lived so that she might learn of her inheritance.[81]

Archbishop Boulter's philanthropy has never been denied, even by those who have regarded him as politician rather than churchman. Best known of his charitable acts is his contribution to famine relief in the 1740s, but with the other lords justices he had moved earlier in 1728 to have the export of corn prohibited, and received a vote of thanks from the house of commons for his distribution of corn throughout the kingdom at that time.[82] This caused Downes of Derry, writing to Gibson, to opine as the primate set out on his triennial visitation in 1730, 'that excellent prelate must have great satisfaction in his travelling through the north, which he was greatly instrumental in preserving from the utmost distress through want of bread last year …'[83] The lords justices proclaimed a day of fasting and humiliation on 4 February 1741, a year of famine and consequent epidemics, and sermons to support the poor were preached in all Dublin churches ('which were never so much crowded') the lords justices themselves attending Christ Church Cathedral.[84] The building of almshouses and their endowment at Armagh and Drogheda (where his principal diocesan residence was situated) are credited to him, and he funded Armagh's market house at a cost of £1,000. Boulter supported Dr Steevens' Hospital in Dublin, where he furnished a ward, and King Charles II's foundation, the King's Hospital, Dublin, for boys and old men.[85] He was the first president of the Dublin Society and though one of its historians found no evidence that he did more than lend his name to the newly founded society,[86] the eulogistic poem, 'Boulter's Monument', was written by Samuel Madden, famous for the premiums scheme which was adopted by what came to be known as the Royal Dublin Society. Boulter's personal interest in the Dublin workhouse was demonstrated when he, with others, moved to reduce pressure on it by providing a daily meal for every deserving case deemed worthy by the governors. The governors of Mercer's Hospital met at the primate's house on at least one occasion to examine the accounts, and in 1741 he gave 'a considerable sum of money' for the support of unemployed weavers.[87] He encouraged industry

81 Boulter to Dr Butler, 29 Apr. 1738.
82 Boulter to Newcastle, 17 Dec. 1728; Walter Harris, *The whole works of Sir James Ware concerning Ireland revised and improved*, 2 vols (Dublin, 1764), i, p. 133.
83 Downes to Gibson, 28 June 1730 (University of St Andrews Library, Gibson MSS).
84 *Faulkner's Dublin Journal*, 10–13 Jan. 1741, 3–7 Feb. 1741/2.
85 A. Chalmers, *The general biographical directory*, 32 vols (London, 1812–17), *sub nom.* Boulter; Harris, *Ware*, i, p. 133.
86 Terence de Vere White, *The story of the Royal Dublin Society* (Tralee, 1955), p. 15.
87 *Dublin News-Letter*, 30 Dec. 1740–3 Jan. 1741, 22–6 Feb. 1737, 30 June–4 July 1741.

on a somewhat larger scale, financially and otherwise, by supporting the construction of the Newry Canal, which was intended to promote trade in the northern counties by bringing coal from Tyrone to Dublin via Newry. The canal opened for traffic in 1742, shortly before the primate's death, and the collier *Boulter*, which had been launched in 1740, arrived in Dublin with a cargo of coal.[88]

The primate was a wealthy man and a detailed picture of his business affairs in the diocese of Armagh is presented by the surviving account book kept by his agent Richard Morgan, covering the entire period during which he was archbishop. The income from his estates for his first six months in office totalled £2,303, though after Morgan had met the primate's various obligations, Boulter received only £813.[89] While there was some variation in rental income between 1724 and 1742, it was generally in the range of £2,000 to £2,500 per half-year. Many charges on the income were for charitable works, such as payments to poor widows, to the poor in general and to an apothecary on behalf of 'the poor about Armagh'. He paid the debts of some of the prisoners in Armagh gaol and helped a widow to send her son to sea. There were payments to certain clergy (to enhance their salaries or pay their debts, presumably), and to the charter-school master at Armagh, as well as grants towards the repair of churches and towards the building of the market house. He provided the salary (£20 per annum) of the sovereign, chief magistrate of the corporation of Armagh, over which the primate had considerable sway both by charter and by custom.[90]

Attention has already been drawn to the fact that the published letters of Archbishop Boulter (and such unpublished ones as have survived and are included in this edition) relate to his correspondence with government ministers, containing, as the title page of the eighteenth-century editions asserts, 'an account of the most interesting transactions which passed in Ireland from 1724 to 1738'. We have scarcely any material of a personal nature (other than the detail that he used spectacles, at least towards the end of his life).[91] However, by virtue of his high offices in church and state, Boulter was constantly involved with matters legal and constitutional, and he must have quickly learned to take them in his stride. In his first primatial year, for instance, he was embroiled personally in a case involving the crown (through the attorney general, as defendant). This was over a matter of patronage in his own diocese, where the deanery and rectory, in the gift of

---

88 *Faulkner's Dublin Journal,* 27–30 Sept. 1740; *Dublin News-Letter,* 30 Mar. 1742.
89 Trinity College Dublin, 'Book of accounts with his grace the lord primate', MS 6399, pp 4–14.
90 *Report of the commissioners of municipal corporations in Ireland, 1835–6,* xxviii, p. 672.
91 'Spectacles and cases for your Grace' figure in his accounts (Trinity College Dublin, 'Book of accounts', 19 Feb. 1741).

the crown and the archbishop respectively, had come to be held by the one person. Boulter pleaded (successfully, the British house of lords determining in his favour) in defence of his own prerogatives.[92] But we do have evidence of another issue that arose after 1738, which proved less tractable and more troublesome, and which must have preoccupied the primate to quite a considerable extent in his declining years.[93]

Its origins lay in legislation of Henry VIII which granted jurisdiction of the court of prerogative royal and the court of faculties in Ireland to the archbishop of Armagh and his successors forever. Charles I empowered the archbishop and his successors to appoint deputies or commissaries 'for the term of their natural lives or during good behaviour'. Marmaduke Coghill had been appointed commissary of the prerogative court in 1699 in succession to his father, but as his health deteriorated during Boulter's primacy, he became 'peevish, indecisive and racked with gout',[94] and he decided to relinquish the position. Being precluded from himself appointing a deputy, he recommended to the primate that Nathaniel Bland should take his place. Boulter and Bland entered into a bond under a penalty of £10,000, whereby Bland would resign on Coghill's death, which occurred on 9 March 1739. Within days, Boulter demanded Bland's resignation, which the latter refused to give, claiming that he was guiltless of 'any neglect or misbehaviour in the execution of the said office'. The dispute went to court, with much examination of witnesses as to what precisely the bond entailed. Eventually, the primate was vindicated and though legal proceedings continued for over a year, Bland's final appeal was dismissed. This long-running episode must have imposed some strain on the aging archbishop. There were costs in financial terms also, legal expenses (including journeys to London, solicitors' fees and other related matters) totalling some £500 in the years 1739–41.[95]

Boulter was by no means immune to the mental and physical discomfort that resulted from the stresses of political life. He admitted as much to Dorset at a time of currency crisis in 1738, writing: 'I have had a great share of suffering on this account, as far as the most virulent papers, and the curses of a deluded and enraged multitude could go: but God be thanked I am got

---

92 King's Inns Library, Dublin, House of Lords Appeals, vol. 7, no. 295. I am indebted to Professor Nial Osborough for this reference and for much advice where legal matters are concerned.

93 The account that follows is based on James Brown, *Report of cases upon appeals and writs of error in the high court of parliament for the year 1701 to the year 1779*, 4 vols (London, 1781), to which source I was introduced by Professor Osborough. See also PRONI, DIO 4/5/8 and DIO 4/7/1–13.

94 Hayton, *Ruling Ireland*, p. 253.

95 Trinity College Dublin 'Book of accounts'. The penultimate entry is a payment to the sub-sheriff 'for taking Dr Bland'.

safe through all.'[96] 'The poor primate', wrote Lord George Sackville to his father the duke of Dorset, who had until very recently been lord lieutenant:

> has been greatly threatened by anonymous letters, so that he has been obliged to have a corporal and six men lie in his house every night for this month past to rescue him from any insult. The other day at the lord mayor's feast the dean [Swift] before all the company tackled [him] against low[ering] the gold and told the primate that had it not been for him he would have been torn to pieces by the mob, and that if he [Swift] held up his finger he could make them do it that instant.[97]

Laetitia Pilkington heard about that confrontation between primate and dean and was told that Swift 'quitted his hold of the archbishop's cassock when the lord lieutenant arrived'.[98] A venomous verse-squib of Swift's was equally threatening, however jocular its tone:

> It's a pity a prelate should die without law;
> But if I say the word – take care of Armagh[99]

The first inklings that Boulter had a health problem are touched on in the press in mid-1740. *Faulkner's Dublin Journal* reported that the primate had recovered from an indisposition and would be sworn in as first lord justice 'next week'.[1] This took place on 13 May, the other two lords justices having been sworn in some weeks earlier.[2] The *Dublin Newsletter* reported in July that Boulter had attended at the Castle 'for the first time since his indisposition'.[3] This explains why Boulter, a most assiduous attender at the house of lords, only took his seat on eight out of sixty-nine days between 17 November 1739 and his death three years later, and was absent on major occasions, such as when the lord lieutenant was present. From a letter written by the lord lieutenant, Devonshire, to Newcastle, in May 1742, we learn that Boulter had begged royal permission to go to England 'on account of his health and some offices of his own'.[4] Maule of Dromore reported several days later that 'my lord primate with ten thousand blessings of the inhabitants of this island embarks in the [royal] yacht for England next week, may providence send him safe to us again'.[5] By the end of the month

96 Boulter to Dorset, 11 Feb. 1738.
97 Sackville to Dorset, 6 Oct. 1737, HMC *Stopford-Sackville*, i, 166–7. Sackville, a graduate of Trinity College Dublin, had been appointed clerk to the council in April 1737, and would be chief secretary, 1750–5.
98 A.C. Elias Jnr (ed.), *Memoirs of Laetitia Pilkington*, 2 vols (Athens and London, 1997), ii, p. 709.
99 Ehrenpreis, *Swift*, iii, p. 862.
1   *Faulkner's Dublin Journal*, 6–10 May 1740.
2   *NHI*, 'Maps, genealogies, lists' (Oxford, 1984), ix, p. 497, n. 94.
3   *Dublin News-Letter*, 1–5 July 1740.
4   Devonshire to Newcastle, 13 May 1742 (NA SP 63/405/43).
5   NA SP 63/405/45.

he had set out on what was to prove his last journey to England, attended to the quayside by the other lords justices, the lord chancellor and the speaker of the house of commons, the streets being lined with regiments of foot.[6] The July news-sheets claimed that he was 'in a very good state of health' (possibly a sign that economy with the truth on such occasions is no modern phenomenon in politics) and would return to Ireland in September.[7] When September came, reports that he was very ill in London were denied and attributed to an incident in which he broke the skin on his leg when entering his coach. Another report in early October claimed that he had left London for Ireland 'in very good health', but a few days later the same journal reported his death at his house in London after two days' illness.[8] Boulter died without issue on 27 September 1742. His widow survived him by twelve years, dying on 3 March 1754, her jointure of £20,000 'by his Grace's will' bequeathed to the poor of Ireland.[9]

Generations would pass before reforming zeal such as that evinced by Boulter would manifest itself again, as it did in the persons of Archbishop Stuart of Armagh (1800–22) and archbishops Agar (1779–1801) and Brodrick (1801–22), prelates with Boulter's determination to compel the church to do its duty while at the same time seeking to provide it with a clear field of action.[10] Brodrick in particular, like Boulter, saw evangelization through schools as central to the mandate of the established church. Like Boulter, Brodrick too was to be frustrated by the apparent inability of so many within the church, lay and clerical, to share his vision and effectively to exercise that mandate. Boulter had written to Wake three years after arriving in Ireland, describing the predicament of the established church, whose members were outnumbered five to one by Catholics, having 800 clergy to the Catholics' 3,000. Many of the Protestant clergy were without parsonages and glebe land to build them on and there was a consequently high incidence of non-residence. Reformers of the late eighteenth and early nineteenth centuries found much the same dispiriting situation as had confronted Boulter (though there were areas, such as parts of his own diocese of Armagh, where much had been achieved). A survey conducted by the Revd Dr Daniel Beaufort, rector of Navan, Co. Meath, and a celebrated

---

6 *Faulkner's Dublin Journal,* 29 May–1 June 1742; *Dublin News-Letter,* 29 May–July 1742, 1 June 1742; *Dublin Mercury,* May 1742.

7 *Faulkner's Dublin Journal,* 17–20 July 1742.

8 *Dublin News-Letter,* 31 Aug.–4 Sept. 1742; 2–5 Oct. 1742; 9–12 Oct. 1742.

9 *New Oxford DNB, sub nom.* Boulter, Hugh; *Gentleman's Magazine,* 1754, p. 142.

10 See A.P.W. Malcomson, *Archbishop Charles Agar: churchmanship and politics in Ireland, 1760–1810* (Dublin, 2002); Kenneth Milne, 'Principle or pragmatism: archbishop Brodrick and church education policy' in Alan Ford, James McGuire and Kenneth Milne (eds), *As by law established: the Church of Ireland since the Reformation* (Dublin, 1995), pp 187–94.

cartologist, revealed that in 1787 only one-third of the clergy of the established church of Ireland had houses to live in.[11]

So far as Boulter's apprehensions about the growth of popery were concerned, there was, likewise, little comfort for later bishops such as Richard Woodward of Cloyne, whose *Present state of the Church of Ireland* was first published in 1787. Fifty years on, Woodward, like Boulter, was an active promoter of humanitarian causes, but unlike him he displayed a toleration of Catholics that even extended to granting them limited political rights. Yet Woodward's determination to resist any infringements of the prerogatives of the established church equalled Boulter's, as did his dismay at the lack of support for the clergy forthcoming from the laity, and the theological indifference of the landed class.[12] Woodward's constant stressing of the vital part played by the Church of Ireland in maintaining the Protestant constitution of the state, and its precarious position in the face of Catholicism and Dissent, is reminiscent of much of what Boulter believed. It also suggests that both men were unrealistic in their calculation of what the Church of Ireland could accomplish, as it became increasingly clear to English politicians that the established church was not the effective agent for the reconciliation of the population of Ireland to the religious and political establishments that it claimed as its prerogative.

11 Akenson, *Church of Ireland*, p. 324.
12 *NHI,* 'Eighteenth-century Ireland' (Oxford, 1986), iv, p. 88.

Boulter and his letters

Paddy McNally

Today academics and students take for granted instant electronic access to a range of eighteenth-century published material comparable to the collections of the world's leading research libraries. It is perhaps worth emphasizing, therefore, just how significant *Letters Written by His Excellency Hugh Boulter, DD, Lord Primate of All Ireland* has been to successive generations of scholars and students of eighteenth-century Ireland. I first became aware of Hugh Boulter in the mid-1980s, in conversations with a select group of fellow students at Queen's University Belfast who were studying the 'special subject' on early to mid-eighteenth-century Ireland taught by A.T.Q. Stewart. Published contemporary sources relevant to the politics of Ireland in this period were few and far between at that time, and students were expected to study Boulter's correspondence in some detail. When I subsequently embarked on my doctoral research on the politics of early Hanoverian Ireland, the letters of Hugh Boulter were one of the first sources to which I turned my attention. Even today it is hard to think of a collection of published correspondence relevant to the political history of Ireland in this period which equals that of Boulter in extent and significance.[1]

Before examining the core themes of the *Letters*, however, it is perhaps worth commenting upon some of their limitations. One might expect that the letters of the primate of the Church of Ireland would be an invaluable resource for students of Irish Protestantism and the history of eighteenth-century religion more generally. However, Boulter appears to have been largely uninterested in the theological controversies which exercised so many of his contemporaries. References to the established church are almost wholly related to practical, institutional matters such as the repair of church buildings, parochial structures and providing the clergy with a viable

---

1 For modern surveys of the civil and ecclesiastical history of Ireland in the early Hanoverian period see D.W. Hayton, *Ruling Ireland, 1685–1742: politics, politicians and parties* (Woodbridge, 2004); S.J. Connolly, *Religion, law and power: the making of Protestant Ireland, 1660–1760* (Oxford, 1992); idem, *Divided kingdom: Ireland, 1630–1800* (Oxford, 2008); Toby Barnard, *A new anatomy of Ireland: the Irish Protestants, 1649–1770* (London, 2003); Ian McBride, *Eighteenth-century Ireland: the isle of slaves* (Dublin, 2009); Paddy McNally, *Parties, patriots and undertakers: parliamentary politics in early Hanoverian Ireland* (Dublin, 1997); Eoin Magennis, *The Irish political system, 1740–1765: the golden age of the undertakers* (Dublin, 2000); Alan Ford et al. (eds), *As by law established: the Church of Ireland since the Reformation* (Dublin, 1995); Christopher Fauske (ed.), *Archbishop William King and the Anglican Irish context, 1688–1729* (Dublin, 2004).

income.[2] True, Boulter often related this concern for the physical state of the church and the material well-being of the clergy to a desire to encourage clerical residence and thereby the promotion of Protestantism and his active efforts to sponsor the charter-school movement in the 1730s could be interpreted as evidence of an enthusiasm for proselytism. On the whole, however, his correspondence demonstrates no genuine, sustained personal zeal for converting either Catholics or Protestant dissenters to the established church. Rather, his ambition appears to have been essentially the consolidation of the Church of Ireland and the elimination of its most glaring deficiencies. In this, as in all other aspects of Boulter's career, he comes across as a pragmatic, thorough and determined administrator.

Boulter's private views on Catholicism and Protestant dissent are elusive. He clearly regarded Catholicism as a political threat, commenting on the 'insolence' of the 'papists' at times of diplomatic tension in Europe, for instance, and reporting rumours of any suspicious activity on their part.[3] He also exercised himself about perceived loopholes in penal legislation, particularly the laws designed to prevent Catholics from practising the law. In the main, however, Boulter appears to have been relatively relaxed about the 'Catholic question'. This is not entirely surprising. The bulk of the penal laws affecting Irish Catholics had been introduced long before his arrival in Ireland. Legislation in the 1720s and 1730s was normally designed to clarify previous acts, and eliminate loopholes which permitted Catholics to evade their consequences.[4] In spite of occasional outbursts of anti-Catholic feeling in reaction to events in Europe (the execution in 1724 of at least ten Protestants in the Polish town of Thorn being a notable example), like the majority of his contemporaries in Protestant Ireland, Boulter appears to have been content that the internal Catholic threat had largely been contained.[5] The primate's time in Ireland coincided with an unusually lengthy period of peace in Europe, which effectively removed the prospect of any intervention on the part of Continental Catholic powers in support of the Jacobite cause. On the other hand, Boulter remained alert to any prospect of tampering with the revolution settlement, warning the government of the dangers which would accompany any hint of questioning the land settlement which followed the Williamite war.[6]

With regard to Protestant dissent too, Boulter's concerns were political and institutional and we gain no real insight into his personal views on the theological differences between the respective Protestant churches. Even in

2   Boulter to Wake, 13 Feb. 1728.
3   Boulter to Newcastle, 19 May 1726; same to same, 11 June 1726.
4   Boulter to Newcastle, 4 Dec. 1731.
5   McBride, *Eighteenth-century Ireland*, p. 206.
6   Boulter to Newcastle, 30 Mar. 1727; same to same, 18 Apr. 1735; same to same, 9 Feb. 1736.

respect of the appropriate role which Protestant dissenters might be permitted to enjoy under the Hanoverian regime, Boulter's private views are frustratingly elusive. Certainly he forcefully advised the ministry against sponsoring the attempts of Protestant dissenters to achieve a repeal of the sacramental test in the early 1730s, but, characteristically, his arguments on these occasions were on grounds of political pragmatism rather than principle. At no point in his correspondence with ministers on this subject did Boulter express a personal opinion as to the desirability of either the continuation or repeal of the test. Rather, Boulter contented himself with warning that any attempt to secure repeal would cause serious political diffi- culties in Ireland and would, in any case, certainly fail to pass either house of the Dublin parliament. In this respect, he may well have been employing a strategy commonly used by Irish parliamentary managers or 'undertakers' when asked by the British government to support measures of which they privately disapproved. By stressing the political impracticability of securing such legislation such men were enabled to withhold their support while avoiding an overt breach with the ministry. Thus, while Boulter assured the duke of Newcastle that he considered it regrettable that there continued to be divisions between the Protestant communities in Ireland, he advised that nothing could be done to remedy this in the present circumstances.[7]

There are some indications, however, that Boulter's attitude towards Protestant dissent was less hostile than that of many of his fellow bishops, especially those who were Irish. In a letter to Newcastle in July 1725 referring to his first visitation to his diocese, Boulter commented that his charge to the Anglican clergy (which he had printed shortly afterwards) 'had made the Protestant Dissenters in those parts easy'.[8] While instructing the clergy that their ambition certainly should be the conversion of Protestant dissenters to the established church, Boulter advocated that nonconformists be treated with due respect and civility:

> To this end, we should, as occasion offers, try to remove their Ignorance by proper Instructions, and their Errors by sound Arguments. But, whatever we attempt of this nature, must be done with all Meekness and gentleness, with all Expressions of Kindness and good will to them, attended with a Readiness to do them all good Offices.
>
> ... many of them declare, that they do not separate from the church, because they look upon Conformity to it as absolutely unlawful, but because they esteem their own way more pure and more edifying. And wherever the like Disposition is found in any Dissenters of this Nation, Kindness and Gentleness, and the unblameable Conversation of the Clergy, will go a great way towards drawing them over to our Communion.[9]

7 Same to same, 15 Jan. 1732; same to same, 18 Jan. 1732; same to same, 19 Feb. 1732.
8 Same to same, 3 July 1725.
9 *The charge given by Hugh, lord archbishop of Ardmagh and primate of all Ireland, to his clergy ...* (Dublin, 1725), pp 15–16.

Such a stance towards Protestant dissent was in marked contrast to that of his predecessor as primate, the high Tory and possibly Jacobite Thomas Lindsay. It was also very different from the position of William King, archbishop of Dublin and effectively head of the Church of Ireland since the death of Queen Anne, who was a committed and consistent opponent of Protestant nonconformity.

Boulter's response to a memorial from Dissenting ministers in 1729, however, indicates that his more tolerant attitude towards Dissent had clear limits. The memorial had asserted that one of the key reasons leading to the emigration at that time of numerous northern Dissenters to the American colonies was the burden of paying tithes to the Anglican clergy. In terms very similar to those articulated by Archbishop King some years before, Boulter rejected this claim and alleged that the high level of rents imposed by landlords was the true burden.[10] It is clear that when it came to the rights and property of the established church the episcopate spoke with a unified voice. In the same month, on the other hand, Boulter wrote to Sir Robert Walpole in support of a request for the continuation of an annual payment of £800 from the king for the support of Irish Dissenting ministers.[11]

In terms of Boulter's correspondents, the most significant were the duke of Newcastle, and successive lords lieutenant (Carteret, Dorset and Devonshire). Others with whom he communicated less frequently were Archbishop William Wake of Canterbury, Bishop Edmund Gibson of London, Sir Robert Walpole and Charles Delafaye.[12] For the first eight years of his career in Ireland it is clear that his relationship with Newcastle was the critical one. While the letters between the two men are formal and, on Boulter's part in particular, deferential in tone, they suggest that the relationship between the two was characterized by mutual trust and respect. Newcastle certainly entrusted Boulter with the management of affairs that required secrecy or delicacy. When in 1728 it seemed possible that the notorious Jacobite-supporting former chief minister of Spain, the duke de Ripperda, might be forced to land in Ireland en route to England, Newcastle instructed Boulter to aid him in any way necessary but 'to take care to do this in as private a manner as possible'.[13]

10 King to Wake, 2 June 1719 (BL, Add. MS 6117, fos. 58–9); Boulter to Gibson, 13 Mar. 1729.
11 Boulter to Walpole, 31 Mar. 1729.
12 Thomas Pelham Holles, 1st duke of Newcastle, secretary of state for the Southern Department, 1724–48; John Carteret, 2nd earl of Granville, lord lieutenant of Ireland, 1724–30; Lionel Cranfield Sackville, 1st duke of Dorset, lord lieutenant of Ireland, 1730–7; William Cavendish, 3rd duke of Devonshire, lord lieutenant of Ireland, 1737–44; William Wake, archbishop of Canterbury, 1716–37; Edmund Gibson, bishop of London, 1723–48; Sir Robert Walpole, first lord of the treasury, 1721–42; Charles Delafaye, MP for Belturbet, 1715–27, Undersecretary to the secretary of state for the Southern Department, 1724–34.
13 Newcastle to Boulter, 3 Oct. 1728.

More controversial was Newcastle's instruction to the primate in 1730 secretly to facilitate the activities of French recruitment officers in Ireland. The king had refused a French request for a formal licence to raise recruits but had promised 'that provided the officers behaved themselves well, they should be suffered to raise their recruits'.[14] Newcastle asked Boulter to ensure that if any of them were to be arrested on account of their activities they should be released from custody as soon as practicable. Clearly alarmed at the possible consequences of such an irregular way of proceeding, Boulter immediately consulted with his fellow lords justices. Their opinion was that without an express order from the king they were powerless to act in the matter. Moreover, Boulter warned of the impact on Irish opinion of it being known that the ministry was conniving at the recruitment of Irish Catholics for the service of France. In the end, public outcry over this episode both in Britain and in Ireland led to the French officers being ordered to leave the country.[15]

Letters between Boulter and Newcastle were less frequent after 1732. It is not entirely clear why this was the case. It coincided with the duke of Dorset's arrival in Ireland as viceroy for the first time, but it is also the case that in early 1732 there had been a difficult exchange between the primate and Newcastle over the ministry's desire to attempt a repeal of the sacramental test in Ireland. Newcastle's response to Boulter's advice that such a measure was totally impracticable certainly displays the displeasure of the king and the ministry.

> His Majesty was greatly concerned, that what must so evidently contribute to the strengthening of the Protestant Interest there should be so much discouraged … It is indeed very extraordinary, that such a clause should be liable to meet with difficulties in either House, in a Country where no distinctions should be kept up among Protestants, which might be an occasion of disuniting them, considering the great disproportion in number, that there is between them and the Papists.[16]

In the many years of the correspondence between the two men this is the closest to a formal ministerial rebuke of Boulter's conduct that can be found. The following year, Newcastle refused to intercede with a senior army officer to support a patronage request from Boulter.[17] Thereafter the relationship between the two men evidently became even more distant. In 1737 Boulter responded to a request from Mrs Wall to intercede with Newcastle to help secure for her son a place at the law faculty at Christ Church, Oxford, by explaining that 'There has for some time been very little

14 Same to same, 26 Sept. 1730.
15 Boulter to Newcastle, 14 Oct. 1730; Boulter to Dorset, 8 Dec. 1730.
16 Newcastle to Boulter, 5 Feb. 1732.
17 Boulter to Newcastle, 3 May 1733; Newcastle to Boulter, 19 May 1733. For the primate's rather terse response, see Boulter to Newcastle, 7 June 1733.

correspondence between the Duke of Newcastle and me, so that I did not think it proper to write to him on this occasion.'[18]

Having worked with Dorset during the parliamentary session of 1731–2, Boulter's communication to the ministry thereafter tended to go through the lord lieutenant. It certainly seems that his relationship with Dorset was more open than it had been with his predecessor. Boulter's relationship with Carteret appears to have been quite distant and at times strained due to the latter's unpopularity with the Walpole ministry and his close partnership with the speaker of the Irish house of commons, William Conolly. Several letters contain evidence of the tensions between the primate and the viceroy, particularly over the disposal of patronage.[19] Carteret's desire to appease opinion in the Irish house of commons (and his alleged favouritism towards those with Tory backgrounds) could easily conflict with Boulter's ambition to secure and enhance the 'English interest' in Ireland. Informing Boulter of Dorset's appointment as viceroy, Newcastle was keen to reassure him that his influence with the ministry would be in no way diminished. He implied, moreover, that the primate's relationship with the new viceroy should be of a different nature from that which he had had with Carteret:

> Your Grace will therefore be pleased to behave, and write to the Duke of Dorset, without any reserve, and in the same free and open manner as you have been so good as to do to me or any other of the King's servants here; and you may depend upon my Lord Duke having the same regard for you and treating you with the same confidence and distinction. As for my part, I shall always make it my business, both out of the personal respect I have for your Grace, and out of zeal for the King's service, to see that your credit and influence, which have been of such great use to the ease and success of the administration in Ireland, may never suffer the least diminution and I will be answerable for the Duke of Dorset's being in the same sentiments.[20]

The initial exchange of correspondence between the duke of Devonshire and Boulter, on the other hand, indicated the prospect of a more distant and formal relationship. Upon his appointment as lord lieutenant in 1737, Devonshire wrote to the Irish lords justices requesting detailed information about the civil and military establishments and instructing them to communicate with him via his chief secretary, Edward Walpole.[21] Learning of Devonshire's appointment Boulter had confided to Dorset's secretary, Walter Cary, that he feared that he would thereby lose influence. 'We all talk of an exchange of places between the Dukes of Dorset and Devonshire. I

---

18 Boulter to Mrs Wall, 17 May 1737.
19 See, for example, Boulter to Newcastle, 19 May 1726; Boulter to Carteret, 19 May 1726; Boulter to Newcastle, 26 July 1726; Boulter to Gibson, 30 July 1726; Boulter to Carteret, 7 Mar. 1727; Boulter to Wake, 23 May 1727.
20 Newcastle to Boulter, 20 June 1730.
21 Devonshire to lords justices, 18 Apr. 1737.

hope it is to the satisfaction of our present Lord Lieutenant; but I fear I shall be a loser in my interest at the Castle by the exchange.'[22]

An illustration of the apparent decline in Boulter's influence with the British ministry after 1737 came two years later following the sudden resignation as lord chancellor of Thomas Wyndham. Having consulted with the latter and the speaker of the commons, Henry Boyle, the primate wrote to the viceroy, the duke of Newcastle and Sir Robert Walpole recommending either the chief justice of the Common Pleas, Sir James Reynolds, or the solicitor general, John Bowes, as the most suitable candidates to be Wyndham's successor. Boulter pointed out to Devonshire that 'I rather think, the longer service of the Lord Chief Justice, and his superior station will make his promotion less invidious.'[23] In the past Boulter may have felt confident that a joint recommendation from the Irish lords justices would carry very significant weight in London. On this occasion, however, he appeared less assured. He certainly expressed apprehensions about the possibility of a successor being sent from England.

> If it be thought proper to send us a Chancellor from England, I must entreat it may be one of an unblemished character, a man of skill in his profession, and who has been always firm in his affection for his Majesty's family. Your Lordship cannot but be sensible, what uneasiness may be created here by one barely suspected of other principles, and that if he really be such, he will probably be tempted to put himself at the head of a party, that with his countenance may greatly embarrass affairs. And though I should be glad he should be one of proper courage, yet I should be sorry to see one sent hither who could think nothing done right in which he did not dictate.
>
> But considering how near the session of parliament is, I should think it cannot be hoped that one sent from England should either have a sufficient knowledge of our forms, or make those friendships with any of the Lay Lords here, as to promise his presiding in the house of lords with any great weight or success.

Boulter concluded his letter with a comment which would prove prophetic. 'I hope your Grace will endeavour to prevent the opinion of any in England, unacquainted with us and our affairs, being of greater weight as to the characters of persons living and acting amongst us, than our judgment who live on the spot.'[24] In the event, neither Reynolds nor Bowes was appointed, the position being given to the attorney general, Robert Jocelyn, apparently due to the recommendation of Jocelyn's old patron the British lord chancellor, Lord Hardwicke. It may well also be of some significance that Jocelyn had sat since 1727 as a member of parliament for Newtown, a borough controlled by the Ponsonby family. In July 1739, William Ponsonby

22 Boulter to Walter Cary, 26 Mar. 1737.
23 Boulter to Devonshire, 7 Aug. 1739; Boulter to Newcastle, 7 Aug. 1739.
24 Boulter to Devonshire, 7 Aug. 1739.

had married Lady Caroline Cavendish, the viceroy's eldest daughter. Later in the year, Devonshire appointed his son-in-law as his private secretary. John Ponsonby, a future speaker of the Irish house of commons, succeeded Jocelyn as member for Newtown and four years later would marry another of Devonshire's daughters. Having such intimate connections with an Irish family with significant parliamentary influence could only serve to complicate the viceroy's relationship with the Irish political establishment in general.[25]

Traditionally Boulter has been regarded as the personification of the 'English interest' in Ireland. Such a representation is not unjust as he certainly displayed a consistent determination to uphold the power and influence of the British government over Irish affairs. Shortly after his arrival in Ireland the primate urged Newcastle to 'use your interest to have none but *Englishmen* put into the great places here for the future, that by degrees things may be put into such a way, as may be most for his Majesty's service, and the ease of his Ministry'.[26] On the other hand, Boulter's approach to the government and administration of Ireland was not crude, displaying a pragmatism and subtlety which easily can be underestimated. Specifically, Boulter was only too aware of the need to be sensitive to Irish opinion and to avoid the impression of an overweening English domination of public affairs. One of the most commonly cited of Boulter's letters is the very first in the original edition. Written shortly after his arrival in Ireland, the primate complained to the archbishop of Canterbury that 'too many of our own original esteem us Englishmen, as intruders'. In the same letter, however, Boulter explained that 'in the present ferment here against the English' he feels it would be unwise of him to confer a doctorate on his former chaplain to strengthen the latter's credentials to obtain a post in the Church of Ireland.[27] This is just the first example of many instances when Boulter recognized the delicate nature of his position and the need to attend to Irish opinion.

On occasion the foremost defender of the English interest in Ireland employed arguments which are more often associated with the Irish 'patriot' tradition. Expressing his concern to Newcastle about a bill then being introduced in the British house of commons relating to Irish land ownership, Boulter strongly argued that the Westminster legislature should not interfere in concerns purely relating to Ireland.

> On this occasion I must beg leave to observe to your Grace, that it must be dangerous to give way to passing bills originally in *England* relating to private property in *Ireland,* where the interest of England and his Majesty's service no

25 E.M. Johnston-Liik, *History of the Irish parliament, 1692–1800,* 6 vols (Belfast, 2002), ii, pp 224–5; iv, pp 488–90; xi, p. 89.
26 Boulter to Newcastle, 29 Apr. 1725.
27 Boulter to Wake, 28 Nov. 1724.

ways call for it, where the legislature are no way acquainted with the laws, and the reason of enacting them ... If this be often practised it must needs create great uncertainty in our property here, and give great and just cause of uneasiness without the least service to the Crown, or benefit to *England*.[28]

Any suggestion that the primate may have 'gone native' after ten years' residence in Ireland, however, would be misguided, for he was perfectly capable of reversing this stance as circumstances required. In 1737 Boulter wrote to Robert Walpole, in what reads like a last ditch effort to reverse the resolution of the Irish house of commons in 1736, that the tithe of agistment on 'dry and barren cattle' was illegal. The primate warned that the associations lately formed in Ireland to oppose the payment of the tithe represented a dangerous precedent and that a similar strategy could be employed in the future to oppose the execution of laws passed by the British parliament. He also employed an argument similar to that used (with more success) fifty years later when the tithe issue was once more a subject of national debate, that is, that the established church was an indispensible pillar of the Anglo-Irish connection.

I need not on this occasion observe what a support the Bishops with the weight of their estates and power are to the crown, both here and in England; but I must observe that they are of more immediate consequence here, to keep up the just dependence of this nation on the crown and kingdom of England, which too many here are disposed, if possible, to throw off, daily complaining of it as an almost insupportable burthen.[29]

Boulter's apparently contradictory statements on these two occasions regarding the Anglo-Irish constitutional relationship might well be an illustration of the pragmatism which characterized his entire political career. Possibly fearing adverse political consequences in Ireland due to any suggestion that the Westminster parliament might tamper with the Irish land settlement, Boulter urged the ministry to act with discretion. However, when the property rights of the Church of Ireland were threatened by the actions of the Irish house of commons the primate was perfectly capable of arguing for Ireland's dependency upon Great Britain.

The tone of Boulter's correspondence is almost always temperate, measured and thoughtful. Occasionally, however, he allowed his passion to show through. Between 1724 and 1733 Boulter was involved in a drawn out saga as he attempted to secure an appointment for his friend Mr Henry Stephens. Prior to his departure for Ireland, Boulter had apparently been promised that Stephens would be appointed to the first vacant canonry at Christ Church, Oxford. This agreement was not honoured, however, and Boulter was forced to remind his various correspondents in England of the

28 Boulter to Newcastle, 18 Apr. 1735.
29 Boulter to Walpole, 9 Aug. 1737.

undertaking for nearly ten years before Stephens was finally appointed to a post.[30] This issue was clearly very close to his heart, and his frustration and anger over what he termed his 'ill usage' over this affair is revealed in a number of letters, but most notably in the one written in June 1725 to his successor as bishop of Bristol and dean of Christ Church, William Bradshaw.

> I cannot but think myself very ill used by your lordship, by the violent pushes you have been pleased to make against Mr Stephens coming to Christ Church upon a vacancy, when you know very well I had a positive promise of the next canonry there for him … I find if my friend Mr Stephens suffers in this point, it lies wholly at your door; and I hope though I am on this side of the water, I am not without friends, that may on a proper occasion remember any ill usage to me.[31]

In terms of the content of Boulter's letters, by far the most significant theme is the disposal of patronage. From the beginning of his career in Ireland Boulter made clear his determination that episcopal and judicial appointments in particular should be managed systematically to enhance the control of the British government over Irish affairs. Thereafter he set out methodically to preserve and if possible extend the presence of Englishmen in the church, judiciary and privy council. This proved to be no straight-forward matter, however. Although it is clear that Boulter's views were taken very seriously by the ministry, he did not always get his own way.[32] Boulter also recognized that there were limits to what practically could be achieved in this regard. This was especially the case when posts fell vacant while the Dublin parliament was in session. In September 1725, for instance, when it appeared that the archbishopric of Cashel might soon fall vacant, Boulter wrote to the duke of Newcastle that it was advisable 'the better to prevent any uneasiness in either house of parliament, to fill his place with some Englishman that is already on the bench here'.[33] This comment is illus-trative of one of the subtleties of the patronage system in that Irish opinion was apparently less offended by the promotion of an English-born candidate already resident in the country than the appointment of a candidate from over the water. This attitude appears to have applied to judicial as well as episcopal appointments. Partly this may have been because such promotions from within did not necessarily increase the proportion of Englishmen on the episcopal or judicial benches but it may also be reflective of a more positive perception of men who were already known and respected in Ireland as opposed to strangers. It is also the case, of course, that the promotion of a

30 Boulter to Gibson, 1 Nov. 1733.
31 Boulter to Bradshaw, 12 June 1725.
32 For examples see Boulter to Dorset, 14 Jan. 1735, 31 Jan. 1735, 20 Feb. 1735, 13 Mar. 1735.
33 Boulter to Newcastle, 11 Sept. 1725.

man who was already resident in Ireland created a vacancy which, in turn, could make possible a whole series of promotions further down the line, from which Irish candidates could hope to benefit.

While Boulter was clear in his ambition to increase the proportion of English-born bishops in Ireland he was also adamant that only men of good character and of sound political credentials should be appointed. The primate repeatedly warned correspondents of the negative consequences of sending over unsuitable men. Prematurely speculating on the possible death of Archbishop King in 1725, for instance, Boulter made clear his ambition 'gradually to get as many English on the bench here as can decently be sent hither; but that I think being on the English bench alone, is not a sufficient qualification for coming to the best promotions here; and that an imprudent person may easily be tempted by Irish flattery, to set himself at the head of the Archbishop of Dublin's party, in opposition to me'.[34] Discussing the possible translations within the episcopate following the death of the archbishop of Cashel in 1727, Boulter advised Newcastle, 'If it be thought proper to send some Bishop from England to Cashel, Derry, or Meath, I should be sorry if any should be sent because of his little worth or trouble-someness there, for such a one will do the English interest a great deal of mischief here, and I hope it will be considered whether he be one that is likely to agree with me.'[35]

Boulter had suffered the consequences of the appointment of an eminently unsuitable candidate early on in his Irish career when he had agreed to a request from Lord Townshend to appoint one Thomas Power to a church living in Ireland.[36] It transpired, however, that Power had been engaged by the government as an *agent provocateur* in order to obtain information against the notorious 'Waltham Blacks', the generic term applied to gangs of men engaged in smuggling and deer poaching in various forests in Hampshire and Berkshire who were also suspected of involvement in Jacobite conspiracy. Power was subsequently arrested for his involvement, and eventually pardoned.[37] Only five months after notifying Townshend of Power's appointment to a living in Co. Tyrone, Boulter felt it necessary to have his secretary write to the latter expressing his grave displeasure at his disreputable conduct.

> You are presented as a person who have neither discretion in your words and conversation, nor proper decency in your actions and conduct, nor a due regard to the offices of your function ... I am ordered to acquaint you, that my Lord

34 Same to same, 4 Mar. 1725.
35 Same to same, 2 Jan. 1727.
36 Boulter to Townshend, 24 Sept. 1725.
37 For Power's role in the affair of the Waltham Blacks, see Pat Rogers, 'The Waltham Blacks and the Black Act', *Historical Journal*, 17:3 (1974), 465–6; E.P. Thompson, *Whigs and Hunters: the origin of the Black Act* (London, 1990), pp 68–78, 221–2.

is very much troubled to have so indifferent a character of a clergyman, whom, he has promoted; and that he will not rest satisfied with such a behaviour as brings a scandal on religion, and a disrepute on himself.[38]

This episode was clearly a major embarrassment to the primate and apparently led to a furious exchange with Archbishop King, which, according to one account, 'did occasion such resentments as are not to be made up'.[39] Understandably, Boulter was keen to avoid a repetition of any such scenario. The appointment of Thomas Rundle to the lucrative bishopric of Derry in 1735, therefore, caused him a degree of anxiety. This vacancy had been anticipated for some time due to the ill health of the previous incumbent, Henry Downes, and Boulter seems to have felt that he had secured a firm agreement as to who should succeed. Informing Dorset of the death of the bishop, Boulter reminded the viceroy of their understanding: 'As your Grace was pleased to settle it with my Lord Chancellor, the Archbishop of *Dublin*, and me, that in this case the Bishop of *Kilmore* should be translated to *Derry*, and the Bishop of *Killala* to *Kilmore*, the Speaker is come into that recommendation in our publick letter'.[40] It was almost unimaginable that a recommendation which had the support of the viceroy, primate, lord chancellor, speaker and archbishop of Dublin would not succeed, and Boulter must have been confident that his view would prevail. Circumstances in England, however, intervened to lead to a different outcome. Rundle had been recommended for the bishopric of Gloucester by Lord Chancellor Charles Talbot. It seems that he was on the verge of official confirmation of his appointment when Bishop Gibson of London intervened to prevent it. Rundle was an admirer of the Arian theology of Samuel Clarke, and his acquaintance with the deist Thomas Chubb resulted in speculation and rumour. The eventual compromise to the dispute in London was that Rundle would be appointed to Derry instead. Learning of this turn of events, Boulter wrote to Dorset, 'I confess I am very sorry to hear that the publick service has made it necessary to give the bishoprick of Derry to Dr Rundle, because your Grace cannot but be sensible it will give a handle to some clamour here. But to be sure our affairs must give way to the more weighty concerns in England.'[41] In the event, Boulter's fears over the possible consequences of Rundle's appointment appear to have been unfounded.[42]

Broader political considerations on occasion led Boulter to moderate his ambitions to enhance the English presence in Ireland. Perhaps the most

38 Ambrose Philips to Rev Mr Power, 24 Feb. 1726.
39 Marmaduke Coghill to Edward Southwell, 23 Dec. 1725, in D.W. Hayton (ed.), *Letters of Marmaduke Coghill, 1722–1738* (Dublin, 2005), p. 33.
40 Boulter to Dorset, 14 Jan. 1735.
41 Same to same, 20 Feb. 1735.
42 See entry for Rundle in *Oxford dictionary of national biography* (www.oxforddnb.com).

striking example of this came in 1729 following the death of William Conolly, speaker of the commons and the government's chief parliamentary manager or 'undertaker'. Two years before, Boulter had considered it necessary to exert his influence to the full in order to block an attempt by Carteret and Conolly to have Theophilus Bolton appointed to the archbishopric of Cashel. On that occasion, Boulter had written with an unusual degree of frankness to the bishop of London. He refuted the claim apparently made by Conolly that the house of commons would be 'very much disobliged' if Bolton were not promoted, and asserted that 'every Englishman of consequence' in Dublin believed that such an appointment would be 'a great blow to the English interest' in Ireland. Boulter pointedly concluded by desiring 'the ministry to consider who is the proper person to recommend to bishopricks here, an Irish Speaker or an English Primate'.[43] The following month the primate described Bolton as, 'as dangerous an Irishman as any on the bench',[44] and informed Newcastle that 'If it be designed I should have that weight with the Bishops as to dispose them to unite in his Majesty's service here, I think my recommendation ought to be regarded on this occasion'.[45] In the event, Boulter's view prevailed, a powerful and public demonstration of his influence with the ministry, and, by implication, a blow to the prestige of Lord Carteret.

Two years later, however, the situation was different. There was a great deal of political uncertainty following the recent death of Conolly and 'uneasiness' within the house of commons. Moreover, Archbishop King of Dublin had died in May and his successor had not yet been appointed. There had apparently been a dispute as to who should succeed to Dublin and the ministry had adopted the common practice of delaying naming a successor to such a key post until the parliamentary session had concluded. Consequently both archbishoprics were simultaneously vacant. Initially Boulter recommended that Richard Smallbrooke, the bishop of St David's, be appointed to Dublin and the bishop of Ferns, John Hoadly, to Cashel. He added, however, if it be thought unwise to appoint two Englishmen to the posts, that of the possible Irish candidates, the archbishop of Tuam, Edward Synge, was 'the most proper person to remove to Cashel'.[46] Evidently, therefore, Boulter remained convinced that Bolton should not be entrusted with such an important position. The next day, however, having consulted with Carteret and Lord Chancellor Wyndham, Boulter reported to the bishop of London that 'in the present uneasy state of the house of commons, I think it will be too bold a step at one and the same time to give two Englishmen the two best posts in the church, next to the primacy'. They had agreed,

43 Boulter to Gibson, 25 Apr. 1727.
44 Boulter to Wake, 23 May 1727.
45 Boulter to Newcastle, 20 May 1727.
46 Same to same, 13 Dec. 1729.

therefore, that the English-born Hoadly should indeed be appointed to Dublin, the more senior of the archbishoprics. Choosing his words carefully, Boulter went on to report 'it is thought proper to remove the Bishop of Elphin to Cashel ... This is a scheme I should not project, if we were not in a troubled state here, but circumstances considered, is what I hope will most conduce to keep things quiet in this country.'[47] The primate's discomfiture over this recommendation is easy to imagine and Bolton's promotion can be regarded, at least in part, as Carteret's revenge for his own humiliation two years previously.

A common practice of Boulter when posts fell vacant was to present the ministry with a variety of recommendations.[48] He would normally make clear his preferred option but, recognizing that objections might easily arise in London, he would often suggest alternatives. Given possible delays in communications between London and Dublin and the possibility of being outmanoeuvred by rivals in England this was a self-evidently intelligent strategy. Thus in June 1726 Boulter wrote to Newcastle, the bishop of London and Carteret recommending his chaplain, Dr Skirret to succeed to the bishopric of Cloyne. It seems clear, however, that Boulter feared that Skirret's appointment might be objected to in London and he indicated to all three correspondents that if this indeed proved to be the case that he recommended Dr Maule, dean of Cloyne, instead. The situation was further complicated when Boulter and his fellow lords justices wrote a joint letter to Carteret suggesting three possible candidates for the post, including Maule but not Skirret.[49] In the end, Maule was appointed to the position, with Boulter receiving an assurance that Skirret would be provided for 'upon a proper occasion'.[50] A consequence, however, was that Boulter received an angry letter from Skirret complaining that he had not been recommended singly. The bishop of London had apparently shown him Boulter's letter which had recommended Skirret in the following terms:

> I must beg the favour of your Lordship to learn on what terms Dr Skirret stands with the ministry: if he is acceptable to them, I would willingly recommend him for a successor to the Bishop deceased; and if your Lordship finds they are prejudiced against him, I think Dean Maule, who is Dean of Cloyne, would be one of the most proper of this nation to succeed.[51]

It is easy to see how Skirret might have regarded this as a half-hearted recommendation on the primate's part, but as Boulter subsequently explained to Gibson:

---

47 Boulter to Gibson, 14 Dec. 1729; Boulter to Newcastle, 14 Dec. 1729.
48 See Boulter to Carteret, 2 Jan. 1727, for example.
49 Boulter to Newcastle, 30 June 1726.
50 Newcastle to Boulter, 9 July 1726.
51 Boulter to Gibson, 28 June 1726.

I thank your Lordship for the account you give me of Dr Skirret's uneasiness for not being named singly in my recommendation, and am glad you think I was in the right; indeed what I proceeded upon was, that if I had named him singly, and that nomination was not hearkened to, I did not doubt but the bishoprick would be filled before I could have time to send over another recommendation. I own if I had been upon the spot to recommend by word of mouth, I need not have named a second, till I had found the first I named was objected to, but in so remote a situation as I am in, I could not hope for time for a second nomination.[52]

The breach between Boulter and his chaplain proved to be permanent. Six months later Boulter recommended Skirret for the bishopric of Killala, but this apparently did not satisfy the latter.[53] In a letter to Gibson, the primate made clear his displeasure: 'Upon Dr Skirret's making a jest of my having recommended him to Killala, I sent him word that I thought myself discharged from recommending him any more; and I have since given him 100 *l.* to make amends for his two journies hither; so that I have now done with him.'[54]

A major preoccupation of Boulter during his time in Ireland was the state of the economy. Boulter commented upon various perceived weaknesses in the Irish economy (supporting bills to encourage tillage, for example) and he repeatedly displayed a genuine concern for the plight of the poor.[55] He had a particular and consistent obsession, however, with the state of the country's currency. This issue, of course, had been at the forefront of public attention when he arrived in Ireland at the height of the Wood's Halfpence controversy.[56] Although Irish opposition to the plan to coin £100,800 worth of copper halfpence (later reduced to £40,000) eventually forced the ministry to withdraw the patent, even opponents of Wood's halfpence admitted that the currency situation in the country was far from satisfactory.[57] Boulter first mentioned this issue in October 1725 in relation to the value of Portuguese gold coins. From late 1726, he embarked on a drawn-out and extremely vexatious campaign to reform the Irish currency. Boulter repeatedly complained about the adverse consequences on trade of the want of small denomination silver coinage. This, he argued, was due to the

52 Same to same, 30 July 1726.
53 Boulter to Newcastle, 2 Jan. 1727.
54 Boulter to Gibson, 18 Mar. 1727.
55 Boulter to Wake, 13 Feb. 1729; Boulter to Newcastle, 13 Mar. 1729; Boulter to Dorset, 21 Apr. 1731.
56 For this episode see D.W. Hayton, 'British Whig ministers and the Irish question, 1714–25' in D.W. Hayton, *Ruling Ireland*; P. McNally, 'Wood's halfpence, Carteret and the government of Ireland, 1723–26', *Irish Historical Studies*, 30:119 (May 1997).
57 Marmaduke Coghill to Edward Southwell, 2 Feb. 1725, in Hayton, *Letters of Marmaduke Coghill*, pp 15–20.

disparity in valuation of English silver specie between England and Ireland, which encouraged Irish bankers and merchants to export silver and import gold in exchange. According to Boulter, the bankers themselves admitted that they made a 2 per cent profit on such currency transactions.[58] Boulter first attempted to address this issue in December 1726 when he tried to obtain the approval of the Irish privy council for a scheme to put 'gold coins and English silver on the current bottom they pass for in England, so as to leave no temptation to any trader to carry out English silver from hence, or import gold hither preferably to silver'.[59] At that time, however, 'the apprehensions of a war and the interest of the bankers here with some in the council' prevented any progress.[60] Boulter renewed his attempt in June 1728 with the apparent support of Carteret. Coincidentally William Conolly was temporarily absent from Dublin at the time due to illness, and the primate noted that 'his absence will rob the bankers of one to whom they formerly applied, and on whom they could make some impressions'. He also agreed that it would be desirable to have a quantity of new copper coins minted but, in light of the furore raised by Wood's halfpence, understandably thought that this should only be done with the consent of the Irish parliament.[61] Nothing was achieved, however, and the following April, Boulter, again with Carteret's support, tried once more to have the privy council approve his plan.[62] On this occasion the council initially approved a scheme to lower the value of gold, only to reverse the decision shortly afterwards. It appears that in the interim, Irish bankers, supported by Conolly, had mobilized opposition to the proposal, and in the face of such opposition, the council backed down. Boulter noted that his opponents 'have universally possessed the people that the scheme is an English project, formed in England, and carried on by my Lord Chancellor, myself, and other English here, with a design to drain this kingdom of their gold, as they are already drained of their silver'.[63]

The following year, Boulter became convinced that nothing could be achieved through the council and asked that the revaluation be carried out by royal proclamation.[64] In the same month, he suggested to Carteret the possibility of having £15,000 worth of copper currency coined for Ireland at the British mint. Once again, however, nothing was achieved due to a combination of Irish opposition and apparent indifference in Britain. Boulter recommended the minting of copper coinage once more in 1732, entreating

58 Boulter to Carteret, 10 Apr. 1729.
59 Same to same, 21 Dec. 1726.
60 Boulter to Newcastle, 25 June 1728.
61 Boulter to Carteret, 11 July 1728.
62 Same to same, 10 Apr. 1729.
63 Same to same, 13 May 1729.
64 Boulter to Newcastle, 2 May 1730.

the duke of Newcastle 'to forward an affair very necessary here, and where my reputation is entirely at stake'.[65] Despite his efforts, it would be another five years before the primate eventually achieved approval for the minting of the copper currency and the new coins began to arrive in Ireland.[66] In September of that year, apparently weary of the public abuse he had suffered (from Jonathan Swift among others) over his currency revaluation scheme, Boulter raised the possibility of his retiring.[67] Finally, in early 1738 Boulter prevailed, although his letter to the duke of Dorset strongly suggests that this hard-fought victory was accompanied by a very bitter taste.

> I take this occasion to thank your Lordship in my own name, and that of every honest and understanding person in this nation, for having at last brought about the lowering [of] our gold here. Your Grace has no doubt been fully informed of the clamours raised against it, and the insult on the government by Dean Swift on that occasion; together with the petitions of the house of commons, and the warm debates there on that subject.
>
> I have had a great share of suffering on this account, as far as the most virulent papers and the cursers of a deluded and enraged multitude could go: but God be thanked, I am got safe through all. There had been no such usage of me, or opposition to so necessary a step, or insult of the populace, if those joined in power had acted with the courage that became governors ...
>
> The effect of this alteration is already felt in having guineas, half-guineas, and pistoles very common, instead of 4 *l.* pieces: and silver is in much greater plenty than it was; and the clamour that had been raised is very near over.[68]

The barbed comment about the lack of courage of Ireland's governors primarily relates to Boulter's fellow lords justices, and Lord Chancellor Thomas Wyndham in particular.[69] Since the resignation of Alan Brodrick, Viscount Midleton, in 1725, the ministry, in part at least in response to Boulter's constant urging, had ensured that only English-born candidates occupied this key post.[70] Consequently, from 1725 onwards, two of the three lords justices who deputized for the viceroy in his absence (the majority of the time) were English-born, a marked contrast to the situation between 1714 and 1725 when all three lords justices were usually Irishmen.[71] The intention clearly was that the government of Ireland, in the absence of the

65 Same to same, 25 July 1732.
66 Boulter to Walter Cary, 26 Mar. 1737.
67 Boulter to Newcastle, 29 Sept. 1737. For Swift's opposition to the currency revaluation scheme see Irvin Ehrenpreis, *Swift: the man, his works, and the age* (London,
   1983), iii, pp 840–3, 859–62.
68 Boulter to Dorset, 11 Feb. 1738.
69 See same to same, 17 Oct. 1732; same to same, 6 Mar. 1733.
70 Richard West (1725–6), Thomas Wyndham (1726–39) and Robert Jocelyn
   (1739–56).
71 The one exception was when lords Grafton and Galway were appointed as lords
   justices to manage the parliamentary session of 1715–16 due to the resignation of the
   earl of Sunderland as lord lieutenant in August 1715.

viceroy, should be very firmly in the control of the English interest. In practice, however, Boulter found that he could not always rely on the support of Wyndham, who he occasionally accused of being afraid of offending Irish opinion, or of being unhealthily influenced by speakers of the house of commons.[72]

Boulter's correspondence sheds some interesting light onto the perennially vexed question of the penal or 'popery' laws, particularly into the tortuous Irish legislative process through which such laws were passed and the manner in which 'conversion' was practised to undermine their impact. Boulter was especially exercised by what he regarded as the unhealthy extent to which the prohibition on Catholics practising law was being evaded. In 1728, he recommended to the duke of Newcastle a bill tightening the rules on converts entering the legal profession claiming that 'The practice of the law, from the top to the bottom, is at present mostly in the hands of new converts … Things are at present so bad with us, that if about six should be removed from the bar to the bench here, there will not be a barrister of note left that is not a convert.'[73] A chief object of the bill was to ensure that converts raised as Protestants those of their children who were under fourteen years of age at the time of their conversion. Boulter explained that they were obliged to add an apparently unnecessary clause requiring Protestants also to raise their children within the established church. 'The occasion of this latter clause is, that the sons of some converts breed their children papists, and reckon they do not incur the penalties appointed for converts educating their children papists, because say they, our fathers were indeed converts, but we are original Protestants.'[74] Demonstrating his own expertise in splitting legislative hairs, Boulter commented, 'I should flatter myself, that as in this bill we have not meddled with the papists, but only with persons professing themselves Protestants, the foreign ministers cannot with any reason or decency make any application to his Majesty against this bill.'[75] Like other English-born bishops in early Hanoverian Ireland, Boulter could be baffled and frustrated by the apparent reluctance of some Irish parliamentarians (especially in the Lords) to legislate on the Catholic question. In raising once more the issue of the excessive number of converts from Catholicism who were practising the law, Boulter commented to Carteret, 'your Lordship has likewise seen, that nothing can be moved about papists or converts in either house but what is at last so clogged as to come to nothing'.[76]

Boulter's letters on occasion offer some fascinating insights into the

72 See, for example, Boulter to Dorset, 6 Mar. 1733.
73 Boulter to Newcastle, 7 Mar. 1728.
74 Boulter to Gibson, 7 Mar. 1728.
75 Boulter to Newcastle, 7 Mar. 1728.
76 Boulter to Carteret, 20 July 1727.

relationship between patronage and politics in the Hanoverian state, and contemporary concepts of honour and dependency. In May 1732, for instance, he wrote to the duke of Dorset in the following terms recommending that the son-in-law of the MP for Tuam, Agmondisham Vesey, be appointed to the deanery of Ardfert. Vesey had apparently had friends intercede on his behalf with Boulter and the speaker of the commons, Sir Ralph Gore.

> Mr Agmondisham Vesey is father-in-law to Mr Meredith, and he came to me with him, and took occasion to assure me of his readiness to concur in all measures the government could desire next session, which a man of honour could possibly join in. I told him I was sure the government would never desire any thing a man of honour could not comply with, and assured him I would write to your Grace in behalf of his son.
>
> As your Grace had been mentioning Mr Vesey, as one proper to be gained, I was glad of his applying on this occasion: since the boon he asks is not great, if he should fly off. But I hope this may open a way to fix him against another session.[77]

More commonly, however, Boulter concerned himself with the management of the upper house. In October 1732 he wrote to the lord lieutenant seeking the king's favour for Lord Mount Alexander, who he claimed 'has nothing at all to subsist upon, and is ready on all occasions to attend his Majesty's service at the house of lords'.[78] Four days later, Boulter requested a favour for another Irish peer, Lord Cavan, who had requested that he be appointed to the vacant position of master of the Royal Hospital, Kilmainham.

> Your Grace very well knows he is the only Lay-Lord that is a man of business in the house of lords, where he is never wanting to serve the government ... And if he has this preferment, he will always be at hand to assist in the Privy-council. He is very willing, if this provision be made for him, to drop the pension he at present enjoys of 400 *l. per ann.* which will be an ease to our establishment, and that your Grace knows is of some consequence here.[79]

At the beginning of the following year, Boulter wrote on behalf of Lord Altham, who was already in receipt of a pension of £200 per annum. Boulter explained that Altham was indebted and 'has a lady and three children alive, and one coming every year, it will be very hard for him to carry the year about with his present pension ... He is at present reduced to such necessities, as it is a pity a peer of this kingdom, and who may possibly be a peer of Great Britain, should be reduced to.'[80] The following year, Boulter was

77 Boulter to Dorset, 11 May 1732.
78 Same to same, 28 Oct. 1732.
79 Same to same, 2 Nov. 1732. Cavan's application was unsuccessful, Dorset appointing one of his own dependants instead.
80 Same to same, 11 Jan. 1733.

obliged to remind Dorset of Altham's situation, explaining that his current pension 'is too little for him to subsist upon, though he were a better manager than he is. You Grace knows he never was wanting to attend the king's service at the house of lords.'[81]

Of the wide range of other themes which arise in Boulter's correspondence, a few more are, perhaps, worthy of mention. The governance of Trinity College was clearly a concern in the 1720s, with Boulter apparently anxious to weaken the influence of Toryism there.[82] The letters also provide information on the origins of the well-intentioned but ultimately ill-fated charter-school scheme designed 'to teach the children of the papists the *English* tongue, and the principles of the Christian religion'.[83] Boulter also offers an insight into one of the most celebrated trials of the eighteenth century, that of Lord Santry for murder in 1739. Following the peer's conviction and sentence to death, Boulter advised the lord lieutenant that the lords tryers who had convicted him 'are all very desirous to have his life saved. But those of them, who are very much his friends, rather wish that the present terrors he lies under should not be too soon removed, even by a farther reprieve.'[84] Finally, there is evidence of the continued active role played by the monarch in political affairs. Newcastle continually assured Boulter of the notice taken of his advice by the king and the latter's gratitude for the care he took to promote his service in Ireland. Even allowing for the inevitable degree of flattery on Newcastle's part, this does appear to have been genuine.[85] Interestingly, Boulter believed that it was easier to have Irish business attended to in London when the king was in Hanover, implying that foreign and British domestic affairs were given priority when the king was in England.[86]

In relation to the affairs of the Church of Ireland, Boulter's chief concern was with improving the material infrastructure of the church, encouraging clerical residence and providing the clergy with an appropriate income. After the failure of a scheme which he advocated shortly after his arrival in Ireland to raise funds to purchase glebes and tithe impropriations through an augmentation of the Fund of First Fruits, in subsequent years he successfully

81 Same to same, 14 Aug. 1734. For details of Altham's colourful career ('kidnapper and bigamist') see his entry in *Oxford dictionary of national biography* (www.oxforddnb.com).
82 Newcastle to Boulter, 27 Apr. 1725.
83 Boulter to Gibson, 5 May 1730; Boulter to Dorset, 1 Feb. 1735; Boulter to Rundle, 19 Feb. 1737. Kenneth Milne, *The Irish charter schools, 1730–1830* (Dublin, 1996).
84 Boulter to Devonshire, 3 May 1739. On the Santry trial see Neal Garnham, 'The trials of James Cotter and Henry, baron of Santry: two case studies in the administration of criminal justice in early eighteenth-century Ireland', *Irish Historical Studies*, 31:123 (May 1999), 328–42.
85 Newcastle to Boulter, 21 June 1726; same to same, 5 Dec. 1728.
86 Boulter to Walter Cary, 11 Nov. 1736.

promoted a series of acts of parliament with the objective of improving the structure of the established church.[87] In 1736, however, the church suffered a major blow when the Irish house of commons declared that the tithe of agistment (that paid on 'dry and barren' cattle) was illegal. In December 1735, the commons had received a petition from several individuals 'in behalf of themselves and the Rest of the Farmers, Grasiers of Ireland, setting forth, That several of the Petitioners have been of late, and now are sued for the Tythes of the Agistment of dry and barren Cattle'. The petition claimed that such tithes were a very recent innovation, never having been demanded before.[88] The petition was apparently a response to recent resorts to law by the clergy to enforce their payment, notably by Bishop Edward Synge of Ferns and Leighlin.[89] A committee appointed to look into the matter quickly reported in favour of the petitioners and, following the receipt of another petition on the matter in March 1736, the house resolved:

> That the Allotments, Glebes, and known Tythes, with other ecclesiastical Emoluments, ascertained before this new Demand of Tythe Of Agistment for dry and barren Cattle, are an honourable and plentiful Provision for the Clergy of this Kingdom.
>
> That the Demand of Tythe Agistment for dry and barren Cattle is new, grievous, and burdensome to the Landlords and tenants of this Kingdom ... That all legal Ways and Means ought to be made Use of to oppose all Attempts that shall hereafter be framed to carry Demands of Tythe Agistment into Execution, until a proper Remedy can be provided by the Legislature.[90]

The effective abolition of this (admittedly disputed) source of the church's income by a simple resolution of the house of commons clearly represented a worrying and dangerous precedent. Given the potentially grave consequences of this assault on ecclesiastical property rights the muted response of Boulter and his fellow bishops is, on the face of it, surprising. However, the extent of anticlerical feeling raised by the issue appears to have been extensive. Boulter later commented that 'I was told by some of sense that went the circuits, that there was a rage stirred up against clergy, that they thought equalled anything they had seen against the popish priests, in the most dangerous times they remembered.'[91] Given such a level of opposition

---

87 'Circular letter to the lord primate's suffragan bishops', 24 Dec. 1724.
88 *Journals of the house of commons of the Kingdom of Ireland* ... (Dublin, 1796), iv, 184.
89 Maurice J. Bric, 'The tithe system in eighteenth-century Ireland', *Proceedings of the Royal Irish Academy*, section C, vol. 86C (1986), 275–6; D.W. Hayton and Stephen Karian, 'Select document: the division in the Irish house of commons on the "tithe of agistment", 18 Mar. 1736, and Swift's "Character ... of the Legion Club"', (forthcoming). I am very grateful to Professor Hayton for the opportunity to consult this paper in advance of publication.
90 *Commons Journals, Ireland*, iv, pp 199, 219.
91 Boulter to Anglesey, 8 Jan. 1737.

to payment of this tithe throughout the country, Boulter apparently advised the clergy to avoid confrontation over the issue, and to rely on the assurances from some MPs that the matter would be addressed in the next session of parliament. The commons' resolution, indeed, had suggested that the legislature would seek to provide a 'proper Remedy' at a future point. By the beginning of the following year, however, Boulter was gloomy about such prospects, declaring, 'I expect nothing from them.' If anything, he appears to have feared further attacks on the tithe system, with the tithes on flax and potatoes being the next targets.[92]

This attack on the church also needs to be seen within the broader context of lay-clerical relations in Britain and Ireland by the mid-1730s. The possible repeal of the sacramental test had repeatedly been raised in both countries since the early 1730s and it appeared that the Walpole administration was not entirely hostile to the prospect. Moreover, in Britain at least, there had been an increasing climate of anticlericalism both in parliament and in print, which came to a head in the parliamentary session of 1736, when the bishops succeeded in defeating a government-sponsored Quakers' tithe bill in the house of lords. This resulted in a permanent breach between Walpole and Bishop Gibson of London, hitherto regarded as the prime minister's 'pope'.[93] Boulter's response to the actions of the Irish commons in 1736, therefore, must be seen in a context in which the established church in both countries felt somewhat besieged. A letter to Edmund Gibson written some weeks after the commons' resolution on the tithe of agistment certainly suggests that Boulter's confidence had suffered a serious blow.

> The clergy here have been attacked in a violent manner, in relation to tythe of agistment, and associations over a great part of Ireland have been entered into against paying it. We intended to have applied to your Lordship and our other friends in England for proper help on this occasion; but to our great surprise, we find the clergy of England, and the Bishops in particular, in a worse state than we are yet come to ... I see very little more to be done by us, than endeavouring to discharge our several duties consistently, and recommending ourselves and the cause of religion, to the divine protection.[94]

Boulter's correspondence in 1736 and 1737 relating to the tithe dispute indicates that, although he continued to lobby on the church's behalf over the issue, from an early stage he was essentially resigned to defeat.[95] Furthermore, the content of some of his letters in this period suggests a more general attitude of disconsolation on his part. The combined effects of the attack on church property rights, his apprehension of a loss of influence

92 Ibid.
93 Stephen Taylor, 'Sir Robert Walpole, the Church of England, and the Quakers' tithe bill of 1736', *Historical Journal*, 28:1 (1985), 51–77.
94 Boulter to Gibson, 18 May 1736.
95 Boulter to Walpole, 9 Aug. 1737.

under Devonshire's viceroyalty and the wearisome battle to reform the Irish currency seem to have drained the energy of the primate. Boulter was also depressed about what he saw as unhealthy developments in political and societal attitudes, a reflection of the concern of many in the 1730s about the spread of freethinking and immorality. In January 1737, Boulter had speculated about the causes of the recent attacks on the church:

> We generally suppose this ferment is encouraged from England, as are our great outcries for a common-wealth. What things will end in God only knows, but I am very much surprized to hear from England, that the young noblemen that travel abroad, come back zealous for a common-wealth, as some of our young noblemen here shew themselves to be. I cannot but think by the experiment that has been made formerly, the nobility have very little reason to hope they shall keep their ground, if monarchy be once ruined.[96]

Indeed, in March 1738, a committee of the Irish house of lords had presented a report 'into the Causes of the present notorious Immorality and Profaneness', focusing particularly on the phenomenon of devil worship allegedly practised by the society known as the Blasters.[97] Commenting to Bishop Gibson on the outcome of the dispute over the tithe of agistment, Boulter had expressed the view that 'I cannot help thinking that one great occasion of this rancour against the clergy, is the growth of atheism, profaneness, and immorality.'[98] The clear vision, vigour and determination which had characterized the activity of the administrator-politician of the 1720s seems by the latter half of the 1730s to have been transformed into a melancholic and weary pessimism.

96 Boulter to Anglesey, 8 Jan. 1737.
97 *Journals of the house of lords* (Dublin, 1779), iii, 413–14.
98 Boulter to Gibson, 18 May 1736.

A note on the text

Paddy McNally

We have endeavoured as far as is practicable to reproduce the previously published correspondence in the original format, with the exception of correcting errors in the dating of several letters. There was some inconsistency in the dating of a number of letters in the original editions compared with the manuscript letters in the state papers. Where these have been identified, the date of the state-papers version has been provided. In one case, the printed version of a letter (Boulter to Newcastle, 19 January 1735/6) has been replaced by a slightly fuller version from the state papers. In the original published version of the *Letters*, old-style dating was employed. In this edition, both old-style and new-style dates have been provided, to avoid confusion and because this was the normal practice in the manuscript letters.

In terms of the unpublished correspondence, it was decided partially to modernize the content to aid comprehension (as indeed was done in the original edition). Our intention was to render the text as accessible and fluent as possible to the reader while retaining the essential characteristics of the original manuscript letters. Thus, ampersands and thorns have been replaced, some capitalization has been standardized following the practice of the original edition ('House of Commons'), and (particularly in the case of draft versions of letters) abbreviations have been extended ('wch' to 'which', 'Majty.' to 'Majesty'). Where it does not impair comprehension, original spellings have been retained ('Bishoprick'). In some cases where the original texts lack consistency, the most commonly employed version has been adopted (Bishop 'Synge' rather than 'Syng'). Punctuation has largely been retained, the most significant exception being the replacement of most colons and semi-colons with full stops and commas, respectively. Other inconsistencies in the manuscripts (mainly relating to capitalization) have been reproduced as in the original letters. Although not always indicated in the originals, it appears that Boulter wrote all of these letters while in Dublin.

The unpublished correspondence has been inserted in chronological order amongst the original letters. The former can be distinguished by the relevant archival reference.

Apart from those relating to previously unpublished letters, footnotes are reproduced from the 1770 edition of the *Letters*.

The responsibility for any errors or omissions in the presentation of the additional manuscript letters is entirely mine.

Abbreviations:
NA – National Archives (formerly Public Record Office), London
PRONI – Public Record Office of Northern Ireland, Belfast
BL – British Library, London

The Boulter Letters

To his Grace the Archbishop of Canterbury.

Dublin, Nov. 28, 1724.

My Lord,

Your Grace will have the goodness to excuse my not writing sooner, considering the perpetual hurry I have been in here since my arrival, with receiving and paying compliments, and trying to settle a little in the lodgings I am in, 'till I can find a house to fix in. I had, I thank God, a very good journey and a quick passage hither, and can complain of no inconveniency I suffered, but the weakening of my arm, which obliges me to use another hand to write to my friends. My family have had their health very well here, and the weather has been what I should have counted good in England. I miss little here but my friends and acquaintance; and I have little to complain of but that too many of our own original esteem us Englishmen, as intruders.

At my coming away from England, I was very much straitened in my time, or I had crossed to Lambeth to take leave of your Grace, when I should have recommended to your favour Mr. Blenner-Hasset for his Doctor's degree, I have known him for many years to be well-affected to his Majesty's family, and he was my chaplain all the time I was Bishop of Bristol, and his circumstances and family are such that a good living here will make him easier than any thing he has hopes of in England: and as I have given him hopes of doing somewhat for him, he thinks he shall command the more respect if he comes over a Doctor. I have not yet heard whether my predecessors have claimed a right of giving degrees; but if they have, in the present ferment here against the English, it would be very unpopular in me to exercise such a power in favour of one of my countrymen, nor would it answer the end he proposes. He will speedily wait upon your Grace in hopes of obtaining this favour at your hands. I am glad to find, by the King's speech and the addresses of both houses, which is the last news we have had, that you are likely to have a quiet sessions in England, and wish, when our turn comes, we may have as easy a one here. I shall always be proud of receiving your Grace's commands, and am, my Lord,

Your Grace's most humble, and
Most obedient Servant,
Hu. Armagh.

To the Duke of Newcastle, Secretary of State.

Dublin, Dec. 3, 1724.

My Lord,

It was Sunday last before I had the honour of your Grace's of the 17th past: I am very glad to find his Majesty's affairs go so smoothly in the Parliament in England; I could heartily wish every thing was so easy here.

I have not troubled your Grace with an account of the behaviour of the old grand jury, and the presentment of the new; because I did not question your having an immediate account of both from better hands.

We are at present in a very bad state, and the people so poisoned with apprehensions of Wood's halfpence, that I do not see there can be any hopes of justice against any person for seditious writings, if he does but mix somewhat about Wood[1] in them. I must do the better sort of people here, the justice to say, they speak with great concern of the imprudence of the grand juries, and the ill stop to justice: but those who would hinder it now are unable. But all sorts here are determinately set against Wood's halfpence, and look upon their estates as half sunk in their value, whenever they shall pass upon the nation.

Our pamphlets, and the discourses of some people of weight, run very much upon the independency of this kingdom; and, in our present state, that is a very popular notion. But others, (who possibly have had a hand in raising this ferment at first) declare publickly against all such notions, professing the utmost loyalty to his Majesty; and are very uneasy at the ill humour, and insolent behaviour of the people. I am satisfied, many here think ten or fifteen thousand pounds worth of halfpence would be of service; but they dare not say so to any Irishman; nor at present does there seem to be any way of composing matters; all fearing or pretending to fear, the parliament; and except things cool a little, I am apt to think the parliament would fear the madness of the people. Though all people are equally set against Wood here, yet many of the present madnesses are supposed to come from Papists, mixing with, and setting on others, with whom they formerly had no manner of correspondence.

I have been in such an unsettled state, that I have been less able to learn how things go, than I hope to do in some time. As I gain more knowledge myself, I shall take care to give your Grace the best information I can; and shall always be ready to receive your Grace's commands.

I am, my Lord,
Your Grace's most humble,
And most obedient Servant,
Hu. Armagh.

---

1   Dr Swift, D. S. P. D. overthrew this pernicious scheme by writing the Drapier's letters, and other papers against this base coin. See Swift's works, vol. 4. printed by George Faulkner.

Circular Letter to the Lord Primate's Suffragan Bishops

Dublin, Dec. 24, 1724.

My Lord,

As I am very desirous to serve the Church,[2] to which it has pleased God to call me; I have, since my arrival, been enquiring into the wants of the Clergy here, and the produce of the fund given to supply those wants. And finding, that the fund will, probably raise but 300l. per annum, communibus annis; and, that this scanty fund is about 1500l. in debt; I have been talking with my brethren, the bishops, about encouraging a subscription among them and the inferior clergy, to bring the fund out of debt, and make a small beginning of a larger supply to the wants of the Church; in hopes, that we may (after having done somewhat ourselves) with the better grace apply to the laity for their assistance.

And the proposal at last agreed upon by the Archbishop of Dublin, the Bishops of Meath, Dromore, Elphin, Clonfert, and myself, to be communicated to our brethren the bishops; and (if approved by them) to be, by them, recommended to the inferior clergy in their respective dioceses, for their concurrence, is this: That every archbishop and bishop would be pleased to subscribe, at the rate of 2 per cent. per annum, for three years, out of his yearly income, to be rated by himself, deductis oneribus: and (in like manner, and for the same term) that every clergyman, possest of above 100l. per annum, subscribe at the rate of 1 per cent. And, that every clergyman, possest of preferment from 50 to 100l. per annum, subscribe Ten Shillings. Any one, notwithstanding, to be at liberty to subscribe a larger proportion if he thinks fit.

This is designed to be employed in aid of the fund of first-fruits: the money so gathered, to be lodged in the hands of Dr. Coghill;[3] and to be laid out in purchasing glebes, or impropriations, as the bishops shall direct. Several of the clergy, who have been talked with here, have expressed a readiness to come into the design, if the bishops would subscribe a double proportion of what the clergy were desired to subscribe, on this occasion. The whole is desired to be entirely voluntary. I have reason to believe the Archbishops of Cashel[4] and Tuam[5] will chearfully come into the design.

I DOUBT not of your Lordship's readiness to concur with any thing, that may be of service to religion: but I must desire your opinion concerning this proposal; as being satisfied, you are a better judge of what may be done, in

2   His Grace left the whole of his fortune, which was very considerable, except some few legacies, to the charitable uses proposed in this letter.
3   The right honourable Marmaduke Coghill, a civilian, and afterwards a commissioner of the revenue.
4   Dr. Palliser.
5   Dr. Synge.

prudence to advance the worship of God and the protestant religion, in this
nation, than myself, who am so newly arrived here.

I am, my Lord,
Your Lordship's very affectionate
Brother, and humble Servant,
Hu. Armagh.

Letter to the Bishop of Waterford.[6]

Dublin, Jan. 19, 1724/5.

My Lord,

I have received your Lordship's of the 13th instant, and I am very much
surprised at the account it encloses. I do not remember to have heard of any
case like it in England. The Dean seems to me not to have behaved himself
with the respect due to his Diocesan: and I could wish your Lordship had put
him more in the wrong, by shewing a little more patience and temper on
your side. But, what provocations were first given by the Dean; or, what was
the full state of the dispute in the morning, on which the quarrel in the
afternoon was grounded, does not appear by the account your Lordship has
enclosed.

I am not yet enough acquainted with the laws and constitutions of this
church, to be able to advise what is proper to be done by your Lordship in a
legal way: but I could heartily wish, that (for the prevention of scandal)
some method could be found of adjusting the differences, between your
Lordship and the Dean, (of which, I hear, this is but one branch) by an
amicable arbitration.

If, upon talking with others, I meet with any advice, worth transmitting to
your Lordship, you shall not fail of hearing from, my Lord,
Your Lordship's affectionate
Brother, and humble Servant,
Hu.Armagh.

To the Duke of Newcastle, &c.

Dublin, Jan. 19, 1724/5.

My Lord,

It is now some weeks since I had the honour of writing to your Grace, as
I was desirous to learn as much as I could from all hands, before I gave your

6   Dr. Mills.

Grace the trouble of another letter: I have in the mean time, made it my business to talk with several of the most leading men in parliament; and have employed others to pick up what they could learn from a variety of people: and I find by my own and others enquiries, that the people of every religion, country, and party here, are alike set against Wood's halfpence, and that their agreement in this has had a very unhappy influence on the state of this nation, by bringing on intimacies, between Papists and Jacobites, and the Whigs, who before had no correspondence with them: so that 'tis questioned, whether (if there were occasion) justices of the peace could be found, who would be strict in disarming Papists.

The apprehension of the loss they shall suffer if these halfpence are introduced, has too much cooled the zeal of numbers, that were before very well affected; and it has appeared by some occurrences since my arrival, of which your Grace had (no doubt) a particular account at the time they happened: and I fear on any new occasion, it would still more appear, that the uneasiness against the halfpence is a protection for any sedition, uttered or published, that has any thing against the halfpence intermixed with it. So that it is impossible for the government, in our present state, to have justice against any such delinquents, nor do I believe, that any witnesses in such a prosecution, could be safe in their persons.

That there has been a great deal of art used to spread this general infection, and that the Papists and Jacobites have been very industrious in this affair for very bad ends, I find most of the men of sense here will allow. It is likewise certain, that some foolish and other ill-meaning people, have taken this opportunity of propagating a notion of the independency of this kingdom on that of England; but I must, at the same time, do justice to those of the best sense and estates here, that they abhor any such notion; and that they esteem the great security of all they have here, to lie in their dependency on the kingdom as well as King of England. And I hope the folly of some, and the wickedness of others, in spreading such pernicious principles, will not provoke any on the other side of the water, to take any angry steps, to distress a nation, where the Protestants are generally well affected to his Majesty; and where the title to their estates is visibly interwoven with that of his Majesty to the Crown; and where no great damage can be done them, without sensibly hurting England: and I the rather hope so, because there are other methods of preventing any ill consequence of such notions, which are very obvious, and of which I shall, if desired, speak more particularly another time.

At present I shall only proceed to acquaint your Grace, what are the apprehensions people generally have here, of what shall certainly suffer by the new halfpence being introduced, and which keep a spirit of uneasiness in them 'till the patent is absolutely sunk; for whilst that subsists, though not pushed into execution, 'tis considered here as a storm, that will some day break over their heads.

By the best computations or conjectures here, the current coin of this nation, in gold, silver, and copper, is thought not to exceed 400,000 l. The addition of 40,000 l. in new copper, to the present copper-money, will make the copper-money of this nation, at least, one-eighth of their whole specie. They think where the copper-money is so considerable part of the whole specie, it is impossible to keep it from making a sensible part in all payments, whether of rents, debts, or the purchase of goods: that if it be once admitted to have a currency it will the more work its way into all payments; as men of substance in trade will be tempted by a premium (from the patentee) of 20, 30, or 40 per cent. to force it's currency among the meaner people; and they again can only pay their landlords and others, in such as they receive: that (when, instead of serving for change, it enters into all payments) it will be impossible to hinder the Dutch and others, from pouring in large quantities of counterfeit copper: that the consequence of this must be the loss of our silver and gold,, to the ruin of our trade and manufactures, and the sinking the rent of all the estates here.

This is the substance of what the men of sense and estates here, are fully possest with. And when I tell them the copper-money of England is considerably short of the intrinsic worth of what it goes for; and that yet I never could hear of any surmise of the Dutch pouring in any counterfeit copper there; nor, was it ever attempted to make payments in copper there: what they answer is, that probably all the copper-money there, in being at once, seldom exceeds one hundredth part of the whole specie of money; and so is kept barely for use of change.

I have been talking with them, whether there could not be room for admitting from 10 to 20,000 l. in copper? which I have reason to believe they want; or at least, that it would be a kindness to the nation if they had it. But they all agree, in the present ferment, it is impossible to admit any: and they all express a jealousy, that the admitting any new copper would open a door for such a quantity, as would prove ruinous to this nation.

These are the present notions of people here, which 'tis in vain to try to remove: and as long as the fear of the new halfpence lasts, there is no hope of any peace and quiet in people's minds: and much less of any so much as decent proceedings, if a parliament were to sit. This has made me talk further with the same persons, what compromise can be offered to have Wood's patent sunk. I have told them there can be no doubt but Wood must have been a very great sufferer by the obstructions he has already met with; and must be still a much greater, if his patent be resigned: that I did not find any body in England doubted of the legality of the grant: that where the patentee was not proved to have contravened the conditions of the grant, it could not in justice be revoked; [to this they unanimously reply, that he has uttered worse than his patent allows] that Wood could not be supposed willing to resign it, without a proper compensation; and that the seditious and clamorous behaviour of too many here, must rather tend to provoke his Majesty and his ministry to support the patent, than to take any extraordinary steps to sink it; and that therefore the most proper way seemed to be, the proposing some reasonable amends to Mr. Wood, in order to his resigning the patent.

What those of sense and interest in parliament, and that are well affected, all agree in, is, that, while the fear of these halfpence hangs over this nation, it is impossible to have things easy here, but that they dare not offer any expedient, nor make any such proposals to those on the other side of the water, for fear of being fallen on, as undertaking for the parliament: but that if the ministry will please to make a computation of what it may be reasonable to give Mr. Wood for resigning his patent, and for his past losses, and to send an order from his Majesty to pay any body (really in trust for Mr. Wood, but without mentioning his name in the order) such a sum per annum for such a term of years, as they judge a reasonable equivalent, they do not doubt being able in parliament, to provide for such a payment (if his patent has been first resigned) whatever suspicions there may be, that the payment is to Mr. Wood; or whatever opposition is made to it in the house. And if the nation is gratified in this, they do not question, but by degrees publick justice will again flourish, and the former zeal for his Majesty and his family revive. And I cannot but say that without doing something like this, there is no prospect of any end of our present hearts and animosities.

Your Grace will have the goodness to excuse the length and freedom of this letter, which nothing should have drawn from me but my concern for his Majesty's service, and a desire that your Grace should know the true state of affairs here.

The Archbishop of Dublin[7] has of late been very ill, so that his life was almost despaired off: but his illness has since ended in a regular and painful fit of the gout, so that I do not apprehend he is in any present danger. Your Grace had heard from me sooner on this subject, if I had known his condition before the worst was over: all that I shall say now is, that I think his Majesty's service absolutely requires, that whenever he drops, the place be filled with an Englishman, and one with whom I may hope to have a very good agreement. But of this I shall write further another time, as your Grace shall give me encouragement.

I am, &c.

7   Dr. King.

To the same.

Dublin, Mar. 4, 1724/5.

My Lord,

It is now above a month ago, since I troubled your Grace with a very long letter, relating to the affairs of this nation: and I should not have written again on any of the subjects therein mentioned, till after receiving your Grace's commands, if there were not repeated advices from England, that upon the report of the Archbishop of Dublin's illness, there was a very great canvass on the bench about his successor, without the least regard to what might be represented from hence, as of service to his Majesty. Your Grace knows very well that I was very content with what I had in England, and my just expectations there; and that it was purely in obedience to his Majesty's pleasure, that I came hither: and now I am here, the only thing that can make me uneasy, is, if I should not be enabled to carry on his Majesty's service here; the prospect of doing which is the greatest comfort I have in my present station. But if the Bishopricks here, are to be disposed of elsewhere, without leaving me room for any thing more, than (as it may happen) objecting against a person, who may be sent over to the best promotions here, when I have done so; and if I be not allowed to form proper dependencies here, to break the present Dublin faction on the bench, it will be impossible for me to serve his Majesty further than in my single capacity. I do not speak this, as if I did not think there are some on the English bench, that would do very well in Dublin, and would heartily join with me in promoting his Majesty's measures; or that I do not esteem it wise gradually to get as many English on the bench here as can be decently sent hither; but that I think being on the English bench alone, is not a sufficient qualification for coming to the best promotions here; and that an imprudent person may easily be tempted by Irish flattery, to set himself at the head of the Archbishop of Dublin's party, in opposition to me. And besides, as there is a majority of the Bishops here that are natives, they are not to be disobliged at once.

I hope I shall never behave myself so as to be thought unfit to take care of his Majesty's interest on the bench here, and beg that, till it be found I am, I may be effectually supported in that authority and dependence, which I can assure your Grace I desire for no other end, than to be the more able to serve his Majesty.

I am, &c.

To the same.

Dublin, Mar. 9, 1724/5.

My Lord,

There has been a great deal of heat here, about an affair that has lately happened in the College, of which I had written sooner to your Grace, but that I hoped it might have been terminated here, as the statutes of the College direct, without giving any trouble at London. But as I hear from all hands, that very partial accounts of it have been sent over to England, and a great deal has been talked of it there among the Lords, and that great endeavours are using there to bring the matter before the Council, I think I should be wanting in my duty to his Majesty, if I did not give your Grace a short information of the case, which may prevent any hasty measures being taken through surprize.

Two Under-graduates of the College, one of them a scholar of the house, had company at their chambers till about an hour after the keys of the College were carried, according to custom, to the Provost:[8] when their company was willing to go, upon finding the College gates shut, and being told the keys were carried to the Provost, the Scholars went to the Provost's lodgings, and knocked there in an outrageous manner. Upon the Provost's man coming to the door to see what was the matter, they told him they came for the keys to let out their friends, and would have them, or they would break open the gates: he assured them the keys were carried to his master, and that he durst not awake him to get them, and then the man withdrew: upon their coming again to knock with great violence at the Provost's door he was forced to rise, and came down and told them, they should not have the keys, and bid his man and the porter take notice who they were: The next day he called the two Deans to his assistance, as their statutes require, and sent for the lads to his lodgings; the scholar of the house came, but not the other; to him they proposed his making a submission for his fault in the hall, and being publicly admonished there. This he made a difficulty of doing, and upon their proceeding to the hall, when he came out of the lodgings, he put on his hat before the Provost, and walked off. The Provost and Deans went on to the hall; and, after waiting there some time, to see whether he would come and submit, they expelled them both.

It seems the Scholar's name is Annesly, and he is a remote relation of my Lord Anglesey's, the depending on whose interest and support has, I believe, given encouragement to the great ferment and bustle there is in this town, about this affair; in which my Lord Lieutenant and the two Visitors of the College have been applied to, to get the Scholar restored, who have all by messages or letter, intimated to the Provost, their desire that he would restore

8 Dr. Baldwin.

the lad: nor am I against it, upon the intercession of those great men; if the lad be obliged to make a full submission, and the Provost have some satisfaction made him for being abused to his face, in a sermon at the College chapel by one of the senior fellows,[9] who is at the head of all our present stir in this place.

What is said here, to be endeavouring on the other side of the water, is the reducing of the power given the Provost by the statutes, and sharing it with the seniors. As this is a Royal foundation, and the Provost is made by the Crown, I suppose it will scarce be thought adviseable to strip him of that power which his Majesty's predecessors have thought fit to trust him with; and besides, if I may believe the universal voice of all here, who I am sure are well-affected to his Majesty, nothing but the hearty steadiness of the Provost, supported by the power vested in him by the statutes, can give a check to that ill spirit in the College, which grew up there in the latter part of her late Majesty's reign. I am certain of this, if the Provost is driven to admit the lad without a proper submission, there is an end of his power, and of all discipline in the College.

If your Grace desires a more particular account of this affair, and the statutes relating to it, I shall get it from the proper hands, and transmit it: but in the mean time I thought it necessary to send this account to your Grace, as I shall always esteem myself the common patron of all the King's friends here in the Church and University.

I am, &c.

Newcastle to Boulter

Whitehall, Apr. 1. 1725.
(NA. SP. 63/385/80)

My Lord,

I am to acknowledge the honour of your Grace's letter concerning the expulsion of one of the scholars of Dublin College, and I acquainted the King with the contents of it, who took great notice of your care and zeal in every thing wherein his service and the public good is concerned. I have not heard of any such application here about it, as your Grace mentions, and if any should be made you may be assured that nothing will be done that might prejudice the rights or lessen the power of the Provost, who by the character you give him does on the contrary deserve his Majesty's favour and countenance. I return your Grace many thanks for having informed me of this transaction, and I desire you will be so good as to acquaint me with any thing that shall happen, which you may judge worth the notice of his Majesty or

9   Supposed to mean Dr. Delany.

his servants here, who you may be assured will always have a particular regard for your opinion.

I am with great truth and respect
My Lord
Your Grace's
Most obedient humble servant
Holles Newcastle.

To the Duke of Newcastle, &c.

Dublin, Apr. 20, 1725.

My Lord,

I had the honour of your Grace's of the first instant, and am very much obliged to you for making a favourable representation to his Majesty of the advice I sent relating to the College; I am sure I shall always endeavour to shew the greatest care and zeal about his service, and I hope his Majesty will never find me negligent in any thing of that nature.

The stand the Provost has made, has brought others to reason; and the lad, after having made such submission, as the Provost thinks reasonable will be re-elected; and one of the senior fellows is to make the Provost satisfaction for abusing him in a sermon at the College chapel: I hope these two steps will secure the Provost's authority for the future. I shall always make it my business to send your Grace whatever information I think may be of service to his Majesty, and shall use my endeavours not to be mistaken in the characters of any persons I have occasion to mention.

I must again recommend Mr. Stephens to your Grace's protection; I would hope that (as he will certainly be a promoter of polite learning) if he is sent to Christ-Church, and is willing to take the Treasury there, and employ under him a proper person, for whom he will be answerable, (which is as much as half the Treasurers there since the Restoration have done) that my successor cannot with justice complain, if he is made Canon there: But if it be thought for his Majesty's service to have a more active person there than the misfortune of his eyes will permit him to be, I must entreat your Grace that he may be provided for by somewhat that is near an equivalent in some other Church, whenever a vacancy happens at Christ-Church; he is the only friend I have in England that I shall trouble the Ministry about there, and your Grace's kind care of him in this affair, shall always be esteemed the highest obligation by,

My Lord, &c.

To Lord Townshend, Secretary of State.

Dublin, Apr. 29, 1725.

My Lord,

I am sensible that I have been guilty of a very great omission, in not having sooner returned your Lordship my most hearty thanks, for recommending me to his Majesty for so great a post, both for dignity and profit; I can assure your Lordship it has not been owing to want of either gratitude or duty to your Lordship: But whatever my post is here, the only thing that can make it agreeable to me (who would have been very well content with a less station in my own country) is, if I may be enabled to serve his Majesty and my country here, which it will be impossible for me to do according to my wishes, if the English interest be not thoroughly supported from the other side. When I left England, I did not doubt but your Lordship was sufficiently sensible how much this had been neglected for many years, and of the necessity there was of taking other measures for the future; but those of us from England, whose hearts are still with our country, fear all this is forgotten, when we hear that the Mastership of the Rolls (which as it is for life, is one of the greatest places in the law here) is permitted to be sold to a native[10] of this place; as I believe the thing is past revoking, I shall trouble your Lordship no further about this affair. We should likewise be very much alarmed (if we took it for any other than an idle report) that our Attorney-General is to be made Lord Chancellor here; against whom the English here have nothing to object, but that they think the only way to keep things quiet here and make them easy to the ministry, is by filling the great places with natives of England; and all we would beg is, where there is any doubt with your Lordship about the consequence of a place here, that you would have the goodness to write hither to know its weight, before it be disposed of. None of us desire to recommend to any such places; but we would entreat that in filling them up, a strict regard may be had to the English interest; which if it be neglected in some more instances of consequence, though I am effectually pinned down here, yet others (who are very able and thoroughly disposed to serve their country) will think of returning thither again. I will only add, that (as all accounts from England are positive we are to have a new Chancellor) I heartily wish we had one sent as soon as may be, that he may have time to look a little about him, and know somewhat of things and persons here before the next session of parliament is opened.

Your Lordship will have the goodness to excuse these lines, which I have

10 Thomas Carter, Esq; who had also the King's-Bench office, and who was made a Privy-counsellor, on his being Master of the Rolls, which he purchased from the Earl of Berkely. He was deprived of the last employment in the year 1754, and soon after made Secretary of State for Ireland.

taken the freedom to trouble you with, purely out of my zeal for his Majesty and his service here.

I am, &c.

Newcastle to Boulter (draft).

Whitehall, Apr. 27, 1725.
(NA. SP. 63/385/88–9)

My Lord,

I have received the honour of your Grace's letter of the 20th of this month and laid it before the King, who very much approved the countenance and encouragement you gave to the Provost of Dublin College and the pains you took to maintain his authority as the most effectual means to preserve good order and discipline in that society and to keep under that spirit of sedition and disaffection that has of late years prevailed too much among them. His Majesty is very sensible of the zeal and care for his service which you showed upon this occasion and ordered me to return you his particular thanks for it. And as I had the honour to write to you in my letter of the 13th of the last month your Grace may always depend upon his Majesty's support for enabling you to carry on the public service and upon the endeavours of his Majesty's servants here to contribute all they can to your ease and satisfaction.

I beg your Grace will be assured that we are not unmindful of Mr. Stevens, and that as for myself in particular, I shall employ my best offices to have some provision made for him, and shall constantly with great pleasure make use of every opportunity of doing what may be agreeable to you and of showing the very great [illegible] and sincerity with which I am etc.

My Lord
Your Grace's
Most humble and obedient servant

To the Duke of Newcastle, &c.

Dublin, Apr. 29, 1725.

My Lord,

I have by this post, at the desire of some of his Majesty's hearty friends here, written to my Lord Townshend what a blow we think is given to the English interest, by the creation of a new Master of the Rolls, and the uneasiness we are under at the report that a native of this place is like to be made Lord Chancellor. I must request of your Grace, as I have of his

Lordship, that you would both use your interest to have none but Englishmen put into the great places here for the future, that by degrees things may be put into such a way, as may be most for his Majesty's service, and the ease of his Ministry. Your Grace will be so good as to excuse this freedom from,

My Lord, &c.

To the same.

Dublin, May 1, 1725.

My Lord,

As I did myself the honour to write to your Grace the last post, I should not have given you the trouble of another letter so soon, but that I since understand our Lord Chancellor[11] has desired leave to resign his place, and that the Lord Chief Baron here is recommended to succeed him: Lord Chief Baron Hale is a worthy man, and heartily in the English interest, and I believe very capable of filling that post; but I must entreat, in the name of all of us here, that if he is thought of, a proper person from England may be sent to succeed him in his present post, or the English interest will go very much backward here, but as there has been so long a talk of a new Chancellor here, I almost take it for granted that the Ministry must have settled who is to fill that place from England, and all that I have to say on that supposition is, that as there is a deficiency of 100,000l. to be supplied by the parliament, I should think it most adviseable, if there has been a necessity of promising an addition to the salary, to tempt a man of worth over, which has been much talked of here, the order should come over after the parliament is up, to pay him such addition from the date of his patent. I cannot help suggesting on this occasion, that one reason of our deficiency here, is the fall of the Customs by vast quantities of goods being run here from the Isle of Man, which is the great magazine of goods intended to be run, and from whence they are, as opportunity offers, transported hither in small vessels. I can hardly question but the Customs in England must suffer more this way than ours do in Ireland: And the only remedy we talk of here for this evil, is, if his Majesty were to buy the island of the Earl of Derby, and afterwards he may command the proper measures to prevent goods being lodged there for running.[12] I thought it my duty to mention this, though I do not question but your Grace knows more of the affair than I do.

I am, &c.

---

11 Allen Broderick, Lord Viscount Middleton.
12 This scheme was at last adopted, after about 40 Years deliberation.

To the same.

Dublin, May 8, 1725.

My Lord,

By some letters from Limerick by yesterday's post, news is brought that the Bishop of Limerick is dead: on this occasion I find the Lord Lieutenant recommends his first Chaplain, Dr. Buscough, to succeed in that See. As Dr. Buscough is of some standing, and has supported a very good character, and is well affected to his Majesty and his family, and I am assured he will constantly concur with me in supporting his Majesty's interest here, I make bold likewise to recommend him to your Grace for his Majesty's favour for the said Bishoprick.

I am, my Lord, &c.

Newcastle to Boulter.

Whitehall, May 11, 1725.
(NA. SP. 63/385/111)

My Lord,

I had the honour of your Grace's letters of the 29th past and 1st instant, and laid them before the King, who observed with great satisfaction your zeal and concern for his service, and for bringing things upon a right foot where you are, and your care in suggesting what occurs to you that may contribute to it. Your Grace may be assured that the intimations you give will always be very well received by the King, and of very great weight with his Majesty and his servants here and that care will be taken to send such a person from hence to supply the vacancy of a Lord Chancellor, as will be entirely agreeable to your Grace, and concur with you in the measures for attaining those good ends you have in view. Your hint with relation to the ill use that is made of the present constitution of the Isle of Man, in running goods from thence into England and Ireland, is a very right one, and due attention will be given to it in a proper time.

I am with great truth and respect.

My Lord, etc.

Holles Newcastle.

To Lord Carteret.[13]

Dublin, May 12, 1725.

My Lord,

I Heartily beg your Excellency's pardon that I have not sooner returned my thanks for the many favours and civilities received from your Lordship in this kingdom. I endeavour to go on as well as I can in the post your Excellency has left me in, and hope by degrees to grow so much master of the affairs of this nation, as to be able to give you a better account of things than I can at present.

By the last mail we have sent your Excellency an account of the several persons recommended for the chapel of Rings-End.

Mr. Samson is the person his Grace of Dublin, I believe, most wishes to succeed out of the three mentioned in his memorial; and I have that character of his diligence in his present curacy, which is a very great one, and which he has served about sixteen years, as well as his good life and conversation, that I have no objection to him.

Your Excellency has a memorial in your packet in behalf of Mr. Vaughan, curate of St. John's, and he will do very well if your Excellency thinks proper.

Mr. Whitcomb, fellow of the College, is another candidate, who has a very good character for morals, learning, and the affection to his Majesty, and as this preferment is consistent with his fellowship, it would be of more value to him than a living of perhaps double the value. The only objection I know against him is, that he must reside in the College, and either of the other two will go and live at Ring's-End; as I think they are obliged to do by the foundation, which requires that the curate there should not be absent from the place above sixty days in the year.

We have not yet got an account from the Commissioners of the arrears at Lady-day in the hands of the Collectors, or then standing out; as soon as we have we will transmit that to your Excellency, with an account of what the government then owed.

As we have this day received orders for sending four Battalions to England, we shall take the best measures we can to have it done with speed. And I find people are now sensible to the difficulty the government would have been under on this occasion, if you have not contrived to take off a year's arrears of the army from the current service.

The army are mightily pleased with the enlargement of their subsistence, as are all the tradesmen who have dealings with the officers.

We have had strong rumours that Sir J. St. Leger[14] is to be turned out, and

---

13 John, Lord Carteret, afterwards Earl of Granville in right of his mother.
14 A Baron of the Exchequer.

Mr. Nutley to succeed him; I have every where affirmed it is impossible to be true; since your Excellency and every one in the service here knows how abnoxious the latter is to all of this country who wish well to his Majesty, and that I believed no such thing would be done without, at least, consulting you before hand.

I shall trouble your Excellency no further at present, but beg leave to subscribe myself,

My Lord, &c.

To the Archbishop of Canterbury.

Dublin, May 22, 1725.

My Lord,

Mr. Blenner-Hasset is very much obliged to your Grace for your great kindness to him in relation to his living in Sussex, and as I know his circumstances, I was very well disposed to second your Grace's good intentions, by letting my living lapse, not doubting by your Grace's interest, if mine failed, of securing a presentation from my Lord Lieutenant. But we have since been so continually alarmed with news of changes from England, that he was unwilling to run the hazard of a new Lord Lieutenant with a needy chaplain.

Your Grace will before this have heard that the Bishop of Limerick is dead, and that Dr. Buscough is recommended to succeed him: I have likewise added my recommendations, but with what success I have not yet heard. Considering the good character he has had for many years, and the little success he has had in England, I should think it hard if they refuse him his promotion in England.

Since my arrival here I have met with a practice in the Church, that to me seemed very odd, having heard of nothing like it in England, which is of Presbyters holding a second or third benefice in commendam, instead of having a faculty: the practise I believe was owing to my predecessor refusing a faculty where it might be thought reasonable, which made them look out for some stratagem to compass the same thing; and what they have pitched upon and practised here, has been by granting the broad seal to hold a second or third, without institution or induction. That your Grace may the better understand the nature of this new tenure, I have here sent you the copy of a fiat of this sort:

This fiat containeth his Majesty's grant and donation of the Deanery of the Cathedral Church of Kilmacduach, &c. now void and in his Majesty's disposal, by the death of Stephen Handcock, late Dean thereof unto Charles Northcote, Clerk, Master of Arts, to have and to hold the said Deanery in commendam to him the said Charles Northcote, together with the Prebend of Kilmacdonough, the Rectory and Vicarage of Kilmaghan, the entire

Rectory of Boughillane, and the Vicarage of Clonfert, alias Sanctae Trinitatis Christ Church Newmarket, in the Diocese of Cloyne, which he now holds and enjoys; and also to enter into the said Deanery without institution, installation, or other solemnity; and is done according to his Grace's warrant, bearing date The 19th day of Nov. 1719.

I have enquired whether there is any act of parliament here, that gives the crown any such power, and am assured there is none, so that I think it stands on the same bottom as a Bishop taking a commendam after consecration. I have discoursed with my Lord Lieutenant of the illegality, as I conceive it, of this practise, and of the dangerous consequences of it, since I can apprehend it to be no other than a sequestration of a benefice, granted by lay-powers, without being accountable for the profits received, and without being charged with the cure of souls; and I do not see but in time they may proceed to make such grants of benefices to laymen. I told his Excellency if he pleased to give the several persons concerned in these extraordinary grants, which are, as far as I can learn, about half a dozen, legal grants of the same preferments they now possess, I will readily grant them faculties for the holding them, that things may be brought into the legal way, and farther abuses may be prevented. His Excellency seemed very much surprized at this method of granting commendams to Presbyters, and is very ready to put this affair into the right channel. But before I proceed any further in this matter, I shall be obliged to your Grace for your opinion, whether what has been done already is legal, that I may occasion no needless disturbance here, and I am sure your Grace's opinion of this matter will thoroughly satisfy his Excellency.

I thank your Grace for your kind hints relating to the power I claim to grant faculties, and other extra-episcopal powers, and I find it stands upon a grant made by King James I. to the then Archbishop of Armagh, and his successors for ever, in virtue of a clause in one of our Irish acts of parliament, which they assure me is a legal grant, and sufficiently confirmed by above one hundred years possession.

I thank your Grace for your kind prayers, and hope I shall always make it my endeavour to promote the good of this Church, though I fear I shall not always meet with the ready concurrence I could wish for here.[15] However, upon the encouragement your Grace gives me of your friendship, and your abilities to direct in any difficult case, I shall take the liberty to consult your Grace where I am in the least doubtful whether I am going upon sure grounds or not.

I am, &c.

---

15 His Grace's scheme, recommended in his third letter, had then failed.

To the Duke of Newcastle, &c.

Dublin, June 3, 1725.

My Lord,

By the letters this day we have an account that my Lord Chief Baron Hale is to be removed to the Bench in England; I could heartily wish, if it could have been without damage to him, who is a very deserving gentleman, that he might have continued here till Michaelmas term next, to have assisted at the next sessions of parliament. Your Grace is sensible we have a new Chancellor[16] wholly unacquainted with Irish affairs, and my Lord Chief Justice Windham and myself, have not been long enough here, not to stand in need of information on several occasions; and I can assure your Grace, it is very hard to rely on what those of this country advise in any difficult case. But whatever can be done in that affair, I do not question his Majesty's sending us a proper person from England to succeed him.

Your Grace and the rest of the ministry were sufficiently sensible (when I left England) of the necessity of filling the great posts here with English; and if the same measures be not followed, we that are here shall have a bad time of it, and it must prove of great prejudice to his Majesty's service. And on the other hand, if we are continued to be supported, I do not fear but affairs will by degrees be brought to that state which the ministry desire. I am so fully satisfied of the ministry's prudent resolution of this point, that I shall trouble your Grace no further, but to subscribe myself,

My Lord, &c.

To the Bishop of Bristol.

Dublin, June 12, 1725.

My Lord,

Since your Lordship has not been pleased to write to me, as you promised my Lord Bishop of London some months ago, I think it proper to trouble your Lordship with a few lines. I cannot but think myself very ill used by your Lordship, by the violent pushes you have been pleased to make against Mr. Stephens coming to Christ Church upon a vacancy, when you know very well I had a positive promise of the next canonry there for him, some months before there were any thoughts of my removing hither: his merit for learning, and his affection to his Majesty and his family, you are no stranger to; and as I know the state of the College as well as your Lordship, I know his coming there can be of no disservice to his Majesty, or any ways distress the business of the College, since he is willing to be Treasurer. I find already

---

16 Mr West, who married a daughter of Dr. Gilbert Burnet, Bishop of Sarum.

you have been pleased to say that it is settled that Dr. Faulkes shall be Treasurer, and no doubt if Dr. Terry continues Sub-Dean, Dr. Foulkes is a very proper person, and then there will be no want of Mr. Stephens having any office at all; if Dr. Terry does not, Dr. Foulkes is a very proper Sub-Dean, and Mr. Stephens will discharge the office of Treasurer: and you cannot but know that if he supplies that office by a deputy at his own hazard, he does as much as most Treasurers there have done.

I understand you give out, that in the push you make against Mr. Stephens, you only consult your Majesty's service, but I know your only aim is serving a friend of your own; which I am not against your doing, wherever any preferment is fairly open; but I desire it may not be at the expense of a friend of mine, who has had a positive promise of what you are labouring to get.

My behaviour to your Lordship in relation to your first coming to the College, and your being afterwards thought of for the Deanery, as well as upon your settling in the College, does not deserve such injurious treatment of me as you have been pleased to shew on this occasion. I find if my friend Mr. Stephens suffers in this point, it lies wholly at your door; and I hope though I am on this side of the water, I am not without friends, that may on a proper occasion remember any ill usage to me. I understand you have given out the Canons are against his coming thither: I know those on whose support you must very much depend, have that good opinion of his worth, and know my friendship for him so well, that they are far from being against his coming amongst them. I hope you will consider calmly whether you are using me and my friend as you would be willing to have others use you, or a friend of yours.

I am, &c.

Newcastle to Boulter.

Whitehall, June 22, 1725.
(NA. SP. 63/385/147)

My Lord,

I had the honour of your Grace's letter of the 3rd instant, and will not fail to acquaint the King with your constant attention to his service. My Lord Chancellor of Ireland will be setting out in a very short time for that kingdom, and will have his Majesty's particular directions to join with your Grace in support of the English Interest where you are.

The favour that his Majesty designs for my Lord Chief Baron Hale, is in return to his faithful services during his stay in Ireland, but as his Majesty has not yet resolved upon a proper person to succeed him as Chief Baron, all that I can as yet write to your Grace upon that head is, that you may be assured that his successor will be such a one as you shall approve of, and I may venture to repeat to you in the strongest manner his Majesty's resolution, that you shall have all the support that you can possibly desire with regard to affairs both in church and state. I beg the continuance of your Grace's correspondence, and that you will believe me to be with great truth and respect

My Lord etc.
Holles Newcastle.

To the Duke of Newcastle.

Dublin, Aug. 3, 1725.

My Lord,

Since the honour of your Grace's of June 29, I have been employed on a visitation of my diocese, where I have by my charge to the clergy, made the Protestant Dissenters in those parts easy, and have, I hope, given some courage to his Majesty's friends. I met with all the civility I could desire, both from the gentry and the clergy; and as the latter desired me to print my charge, and as some others think it may be of some service to the government, at least by giving me the more weight among the well-affected, when they see my sentiments in print, I have thoughts of speedily putting it to the press. I am sensible how much I am obliged to your Grace for favourably representing to his Majesty my attention to his service.

My Lord Chancellor arrived here in my absence, but as I have been here now three or four days, we have had some conferences, and I am sure we shall both concur to the utmost of our power in promoting his Majesty's service. I am glad to find by him that we are to have a good Lord Chief Baron here; and it is somewhat the greater pleasure to me that I had some knowledge of Mr. Dalton in England.

I am the more encouraged to continue any diligence I have hitherto used by the repeated assurances your Grace is pleased to give me of his Majesty's gracious intention to support me here, and can promise his Majesty and assure your Grace that I shall make no other use of what support he is pleased to give me, than to maintain his interest in this Kingdom.

As the sessions of parliament is now drawing near, I hope my Lord Lieutenant will be impowered in his speech to speak clearly as to the business of the half-pence, and thoroughly rid this nation of their fear on that head: I should hope if this is done, we shall have a pretty easy session; the manner that is most proper I submit to your Grace and others in the ministry, who are best judges how his Majesty's honour may be best preserved, and this nation at the same time made easy.

As by examining into Pratt's[17] accounts, it appears the nation is run above

17 Deputy Vice Treasurer of Ireland, which place he lost, and was succeeded by Luke Gardiner, Esq;

100,000l. in debt, besides the 50,000l. for the interest of which provision is made, it must be expected that we shall have some grumbling speeches in both houses; but if the dread of Wood's half-pence is effectually removed, I hardly doubt of a good issue of the sessions.

I am now come to continue at Dublin for the rest of the year, and shall be proud of receiving your commands.

I am, &c.

Lord Chancellor Richard West to Newcastle.

Dublin, Aug. 6, 1725.
(NA. SP. 63/386/9–10)

My Lord,

I gave your Grace the trouble of a letter upon the 26th of last month, to which I have nothing to add from any thing I have yet heard. But it still continues to be the universal notion, that the copper halfpence is the affair, that can in any wise embroil the approaching sessions of parliament. Since that time My Lord Lieutenant has done me the honour to show me a letter from your Grace to his Excellency, wherein he is desired to send over his opinion as to what is proper to be done in relation to that copper patent. His Excellency has also been pleased to communicate to me, the answer which he intends to write to your Grace upon that head, and has also commanded me to trouble your Grace upon the same occasion.

Your Grace will perceive by my Lord Carteret's letter, that he has heard it rumoured as if Mr. Wood's patent was to be surrendered, and he has mentioned it to me in such terms, that I am pretty sure he believes the fact to be so. And it is upon that foundation, that the alternative expedient, he mentions is proposed. By conversing with my Lord Primate, I find his Grace to be of the same opinion with myself, that something or other for the satisfaction of the people here, should be said at the first opening of the parliament, and my Lord Lieutenant as your Grace will see by his letter, seems to think some mention of it should be made in his speech. But considering that a surrender, is more properly the act of the patentee than of the Crown, I submit to your Grace's consideration, whether that should not be done in such general terms as not to particularize the manner in which the affair is transacted. The other method which my Lord Carteret mentions, is that of a message from the Crown to the Houses of parliament. The end proposed by both these ways of proceeding is the same, to put an end to this unhappy affair of the halfpence, and as the general opinion is if that be done, that the business of this parliament will be tolerably easy, I ask pardon of your Grace if I suggest, that in my poor opinion, the sending of a message (whatever it may be in law) is yet in the opinion of the world, more peculiarly the act of the King and of his ministers in England, than the other way of proceeding can possibly be understood to be. Not but at the same time, I think some general words, may be also very properly inserted in his Excellency's speech.

Upon review of what I have written, I begin to fear that my zeal may be looked upon to be presumption, I therefore humbly ask pardon for what ever may be amiss in this letter, since I am sure my intention in writing it is sincere and upright.

I am with the greatest submission and respect
My Lord
Your Grace's
Most obedient and
most humble servant
R. West

My Lord,
My Lord Chancellor having communicated this letter to me, as I troubled your Grace by the last post, I think I need not give your Grace a fresh trouble, but only declare that I concur with my Lord Chancellor's opinion.
I am,
My Lord
your Grace's
most obedient and most humble servant
Hu. Armagh

To the Duke of Newcastle.

Dublin, Aug. 14, 1725.
My Lord,
After having wrote so lately to your Grace, I should not have given you the trouble of these lines, if it were not out of the great concern I have that his Majesty's service may go on as smoothly as possible in the approaching parliament; and this I would hope may be done, if my Lord Lieutenant is enabled to put an end to all fears about the half-pence in his speech: if he is not, there will certainly be a great heat in both houses, which it will be impossible to keep within any bounds of decency; and this may give an advantage to those that will be glad of making a disturbance about Captain Pratt's affair, or would appear some way considerable by raising a clamour. And I wish what favour his Majesty shall please to shew us about the half-pence, be not afterwards taken as an effect of their noise rather than his Majesty's goodness. But the whole I have written is submitted to your Grace's superior prudence.

My Lord Lieutenant and our new Lord Chancellor went yesterday to Drogheda to see the place of the action on the Boyne;[18] at their return the proper preparations will be making for a good session, but most will depend on what instructions your Grace shall transmit.

I am, &c.

To Lord Townshend.

Dublin, Sept. 4, 1725.

My Lord,

As I have been visiting my diocese this summer, and have been persuaded to print my charge to the clergy, in hopes it may be of some service here, I have made bold to send your Lordship some copies; Mr. Edgecombe was so kind as to undertake to deliver them to Sir Robert Walpole, with a desire to forward them to your Lordship: I must beg of your Lordship to present one to Prince Frederick[19] with my most humble duty, to accept of another yourself, and to dispose of the remaining four as your Lordship pleases.

I cannot omit taking this opportunity of thanking your Lordship for all favours, and assuring your Lordship I shall make the best use I can of the great post you have procured me, to his Majesty's service in this place; and I am sure in so doing I shall best answer your Lordship's expectation. I must likewise acknowledge the obligations we all lie under here for your procuring so great an instance of his Majesty's goodness, as the revoking Wood's patent; I cannot say every body here is as thankful as they ought to be on this occasion, but do not doubt but both houses will make the most profound return of gratitude to his Majesty.

I am glad it has lain in my power to provide for Mr. Power the clergyman, to his satisfaction, whom your Lordship was pleased to recommend to my care, before I left England; I have given him a living of about 150l. per ann. I shall trouble your Lordship no longer, but beg leave to subscribe myself,

My Lord, &c.

18 On the first of July, 1690, a great battle was fought at this place between the armies of King William III. and James II. in which the former was victorious. In honour of which success, there is one of the finest obelisks in the world erected there to commemorate this event.
19 Eldest Son of George, Prince of Wales, afterwards George II. who was succeeded in the principality of Wales, by the said prince Frederick, who died March 20, 1751. His present Majesty George III. is the eldest son of his Royal Highness.

To the Duke of Newcastle.

Dublin, Sept. 9, 1725.

My Lord,

I have had the honour of your Grace's of the 26th ult. I can assure your Grace that it was with the greatest pleasure I saw the exemplification of the surrender of Mr. Wood's patent at the council, because I am sure it will make his Majesty's business go on smoothly in parliament, and quiet the minds of all his Majesty's well-affected subjects here. His Majesty's enemies, and those who want to be considerable by making an opposition to his Majesty's business in parliament, could not disguise their looks enough not to shew their great disappointment by this great instance of his Majesty's goodness and condescension to this nation. And though some have laboured to disguise the fact and given out that the patent was surrendered to my Lord Abercorn,[20] yet when the sessions open on Tuesday se'nnight, there will be no more room for deceiving the people as to the fact, and I am satisfied his Majesty will then receive the utmost returns of gratitude from both houses, which will be no other than the sense and voice of all the people of this nation, that do not wish for disturbances. I have discoursed with several members of parliament, who all express the utmost thankfulness for this single instance of his Majesty's favour, and give the greatest assurances, of an easy sessions. I am sensible I have had no other hand in this affair than representing the true state of this nation to the ministry, and am very glad his Majesty employs such as are willing to be informed of the truth, which I shall always make it my endeavour to acquaint them with.

There is a perfect agreement betwixt me and my Lord Chancellor, and I dare say will continue, not only on account of our old friendship, but out of the earnest desire we both have of promoting his Majesty's service; and I am thoroughly sensible of what assistance he will be to me in so doing, and I shall not be wanting in my endeavours to assist him in the same.

I must beg your Grace's acceptance of one of my charges, which I trouble Mr. Edgecombe to take with him to your Grace; and likewise the favour of sending a small parcel to my Lord Townshend at Hanover.

I am, &c.

To the same.

Dublin, Sept. 11, 1725.

My Lord,

As I had the honour of writing to your Grace by the last post, I should not so soon have given you a new trouble, but for an accident that has since

20 A Scotch Earl, and Lord Viscount Strabane in Ireland.

happened to the Archbishop of Cashel. Whilst his lady was bathing his leg with brandy or spirits, they unfortunately took fire, and his leg is so hurt by it, that his life is thought to be in great danger. As his post is the third in this Church, and has a good income belonging to it, I thought it my duty to give your Grace immediate notice of the danger he is in.

As soon as there is any decisive turn in his illness, I shall inform your Grace of it; in the mean time I would suggest, that if he dies, as the parliament is now just opening, I should rather think it most adviseable for his Majesty's service, the better to prevent any uneasiness in either house of parliament, to fill his place with some Englishman that is already on the bench here. And I must entreat that no measures may be taken on the other side of the water in this affair, so as not to leave full room for advice or a representation from hence.

There has been some time ago a great discourse here of a design to remove the Provost of this College to a Bishoprick, not so much out of good will to him, as to make way for another to succeed him; but as the person who it is suspected will push for being his successor, is one that in the opinion of his Majesty's friends here would be a very dangerous man in that station, I cannot but take this opportunity of begging, that your Grace and the rest of his Majesty's servants would be upon your guard against any hasty promise being obtained from his Majesty relating to the Provostship here. The present Provost is a very good man, but it is of the last consequence here who succeeds him, by whatever means there happens a vacancy in his place. I shall trouble your Grace no more at present, but subscribe myself,

My Lord, &c.

To the same.

Dublin, Sept. 21, 1725.

My Lord,

I have had a pretty laborious day of it in the House of Lords, where my Lord Lieutenant opened the sessions with a very good speech. Things went very well in the House of Commons, where they came to a proper resolution for an address without any thing worth calling opposition; but in our House we fought through a resolution for an address with great opposition from the Archbishops of Dublin and Tuam, my Lord Middleton and others, and upon a division they carried the words great wisdom to be added to his Majesty's goodness and condescension, for which we were to thank his Majesty, in putting an end to Wood's patent; but as this is no doubt meant as a reflection on what is past, or an insinuation of the weight of our clamours, I hope with my Lord Lieutenant's assistance to throw those words out, either in the committee, or when the address is reported to the House.

By the best account I can get, the Archbishop of Cashel has got over his late hurt, so that I shall trouble your Grace no more on that head, but subscribe myself,

Your Grace's, &c.

To the same.

Dublin, Sept. 23, 1725.

My Lord,

We this day reported to the house the address to his Majesty, and after a long debate, threw out the words great wisdom before the words royal favour and condescension, so that when the address comes over to England, your Grace will see where it was to have come in, and will better judge of the impropriety of it, and that a reflection was designed by it on the ministry, as some of them plainly shewed in the debate it was intended for.

There were 21 against those words standing part of the address, and 12 for it. I am satisfied one thing aimed at by this push was to slur an English administration: but I hope by this majority we have pretty well discouraged all attempts of that kind, or any other to make an uneasy session.

I cannot help mentioning to your Grace that my Lord Forbes has been one of the most active and I think most peevish Lords here, after his Grace of Dublin and my Lord Middleton, of any concerned in this push. I must on the other side, do my Lord Lieutenant the justice to acquaint your Grace that he has been very industrious these two days to bring the Lords to a proper temper. As I have nothing farther to acquaint your Grace with, I shall beg leave to subscribe myself,

My Lord, &c.

To the Archbishop of Canterbury.

Dublin, Sept. 24, 1725.

My Lord,

As there is a perfect recess from business in England, and we are just entering upon it, by our session of parliament opening last Tuesday, I thought it might not be unacceptable to give your Grace some short account of what has passed here.

My Lord Lieutenant was pleased to appoint me to be the mover of an address to his Majesty upon his speech, and to prepare proper heads on that occasion; accordingly after his Excellency's speech from the throne, I proposed an address, and in a short speech run through the several heads I thought proper, and then gave in a written resolution to be an instruction to the committee, that were to draw up the address: upon reading the resolution, after some opposition to the offering such a resolution in writing, his Grace of Dublin proposed an amendment to the resolution, by inserting the words great wisdom, so that the part where they stood would have run thus, and to express the grateful sense they have of his Majesty's great wisdom, royal favour and condescension, in putting so effectual an end to the patent formerly granted Mr. Wood, &c. And the reason he gave was in effect, that the ministry had been the authors of that patent, but that his Majesty had been wise enough to see the ill consequences of it, and so had revoked it. This I opposed, as declared to be intended as a reflection on the ministry, and so a debate ensued; but several of the house thinking it a compliment to his Majesty to own his wisdom, and not seeing the impropriety of it, where we were thanking him for what we ought to ascribe to nothing but his goodness, his amendment was carried.

On Wednesday I brought into the committee an address somewhat differing in form from the resolution of the house, and without the words great wisdom, but they insisting that the committee were bound down to those words as having been upon debate settled by the house, I was forced to add them, but as it appeared more in the committee that they were intended to reflect on the ministry, yesterday a motion was made in the house upon the report, to leave them out of the address, and after a long debate (in which my Lord Middleton laboured to revive the former heat about Wood's patent, and where he and others evidently shewed those words were intended as a reflection) they were thrown out by 21 against 12.

I have in these debates done my part according to my abilities, to support his Majesty's service. I am sensible one thing that in part disposed some to be peevish, was the seeing an English Primate[21] here. My Lord Lieutenant was under great concern about this affair, that there should be an attempt against thanking his Majesty in the most decent manner, and spoke to several of the Lay Lords to bring them to temper, without which we had been worsted.

The words great wisdom were to have stood in the address immediately before the words royal favour. I have sent your Grace one of my Lord Lieutenant's speeches, and shall send you this address and that to his Excellency as soon as they are printed; we presented his Excellency with both to day. The Commons have gone on with great temper and unanimity. Your Grace will excuse this long letter.

I am, my Lord, &c.

---

21 This must be an invidious reflection, as most of the Primates of Ireland, since the reformation have been from England. February 1770.

Newcastle to Boulter (draft).

Whitehall, Sept. 30. 1725.
(NA. SP. 63/386/146)

My Lord,

I give your Grace many thanks for the honour of your letters of the 21st and 23nd instant and for the great share you have had in getting so dutiful and loyal an Address passed in the House of Lords of Ireland as [illegible] my Lord Lieutenant has transmitted hither, in which you have performed a service to his Majesty that I am sure will meet with the most gracious acceptance. I thought I could not [illegible] recommend it to the King than by transmitting to my Lord Townsend copies of your Grace's letters to me.

I hope now the discontented have tried their strength, to so little purpose the session will go on smoothly and the issue of it will be such as may prove entirely to his Majesty's service and satisfaction. It is a great pleasure to me to see your Grace so successfully at the head of his Majesty's friends and servants in the House of Lords of Ireland.

I am very much obliged to your Grace for the particular account you have been pleased to give me of what passed upon this occasion; and I beg you will continue to take the trouble of informing me of what shall occur in either House that may be worth communicating to me here.

I am with the greatest sincerity and respect etc.

To the Duke of Newcastle &c.

Dublin, Oct. 2, 1725.

My Lord,

I received your Grace's obliging letter of the 23rd past, and before this your Grace will have received two of mine, giving an account of what happened in the House of Lords last week; since which nothing has past worth notice, except our ordering an impudent poem[22] on those debates to be burned, and the printer to be taken into custody.

I find every body judges that the difficulty of the session is over in our house, by our having had a fair trial of our strength there; and that the malecontents of the House of Commons will be less enterprizing now they see so little prospect of any disturbance in our house.

I can still assure your Grace the generality here are very sensible of his Majesty's goodness in procuring the surrender of Wood's patent. I thank your Grace for transmitting a copy of my last letter to Hanover, and am obliged to you for your approbation of what I proposed.

22 Entitled, On Wisdom's Defeat, In a learned debate, &c.

The Archbishop of Cashel is in a declining condition still, and probably will scarce outlive many months; whenever he drops I shall immediately acquaint your Grace with it, and with what removes I apprehend may be most for his Majesty's service. I am very sensible of the great obligations I lye under to his Majesty's ministers both in England and Hanover, both before and since my translation hither, and shall on all occasions shew that the zeal for his Majesty's service as may most recommend me to the continuance of their esteem and friendship.

I must take this occasion of reminding your Grace of a paper sent from the Council here just before his Majesty left England, relating to the new gold species of Portugal: what we desired was that they might be put on the same foot with guineas, in proportion to their weight and fineness; the want of having their value settled by a proclamation is a great hindrance to trade here, and leaves room for their being counterfeited with impunity. If there has been no report yet made from the mint relating to them, I would beg your Grace to call for one; if there has, I must entreat that we may have the necessary orders sent us for publishing a proclamation here.

I am, &c.

To the same.

Dublin, Oct. 12, 1725.

My Lord,

I had the honour of your Grace's of the 30th of the last, and am very well pleased that your Grace approves of what I did at the opening of the session, in the business of the address, and that you think it will be graciously accepted by his Majesty. I thank your Grace for transmitting a favourable account of my actions to Hanover.

I believe the struggle in the House of Lords is pretty well over; but I find there will be some contention in the House of Commons about paying the debts of the nation; but as the management of that affair is put into the hands of the speaker and the rest of his Majesty's hearty friends, I do not doubt but that all will end well.

There are great endeavours used to mislead the country gentlemen, but there will be equal pains taken to set them right. When any thing material occurs here, I shall take the liberty to acquaint your Grace with it.

By the promotion of Dean Percival to the rectory of St. Michan's in this city, the parish of St. John's (in this city too) is become vacant; and the chapter of Christ Church (who are the patrons) have presented Dr. Delany[23] to it; he is one of the senior fellows of the College here, and their greatest

---

23 Afterwards preferred to the profitable Deanry of Downe.

pupil-monger: what with his fellowship and pupils, he is thought to have six or seven hundred pounds per ann. He is a great tory, and has a great influence in these parts; and it were to be wished for his Majesty's service, that he might be tempted by some good country living to quit the College; but if he has St. John's with his fellowship, there can be no hopes of his removal: but I am informed, that without a royal dispensation, he cannot keep his fellowship with this new living; I must therefore desire your Grace, that if any application be made on the other side of the water, for his Majesty's dispensing with the statute of the College relating to the value of a living that may be held with a fellowship, that your Grace would get it stopt.

    I am, &c.

Boulter to Newcastle.

Oct. 16, 1725.
(NA. SP. 63/386/196)

My Lord,

    Your Grace will have the goodness to excuse my troubling you in behalf of an old friend, the Reverend Mr. Stephens of Maulden in Surrey. Your Lordship may be pleased to remember I made application for his having the next vacant Canonry of Christ Church, when there was no likelihood of my quitting that Deanery in haste: and that, it appearing then that Dr. Foulkes had by the recommendation of the present Archbishop of York obtained a promise of the first Canonry that fell there, your Grace and my Lord Townshend were so good as to promise me the second vacancy in that church for Mr. Stephens, upon my desisting from all opposition to Dr. Foulkes. As Dr. Foulkes has since succeeded in the place of the present Dean, your Lordships were so kind as to renew the promise made about Mr. Stephens before I left England. I am very sensible what opposition has been made to the performance of this promise by my successor. But as the only material objection made by him has been removed by Mr. Stephens's offering to be chosen Treasurer there, and to get the office performed at his own expense and hazard, I must beg of your Grace to support my friend in his just pretensions to a specific performance of the promise made and repeated to me. I don't hear of any likelihood of an immediate vacancy there, but I would willingly guard against any measures being hastily taken, if a vacancy should happen, to the prejudice of the promise made to me. Mr. Stephens has no friend to rely on in this affair but myself and I must throw myself wholly on your Grace's friendship for the support of my just pretensions in his favour; and I shall always esteem it as a very great obligation laid on,

My Lord
your Grace's
most obedient and most humble servant
Hu. Armagh

Newcastle to Boulter.

Whitehall, Oct. 21. 1725.
(NA. SP. 63/386/202–03)

My Lord,

I have received the honour of your Grace's letter of the 12th instant, and I am very glad to find by it, that the King's affairs on your side are in so prosperous a situation that the struggle in the House of Lords is over, and the business of the House of Commons is in so good hands, that there is no reason to doubt, but it will be managed with equal success, and all will end well.

My Lord Lieutenant having transmitted Dr. Delany's petition, for a dispensation to hold the living of St. John's, to Mr. Delafaye, to be laid before the Lords Justices, I acquainted their Excellencies with the purports of your Grace's letter upon that head. They thereupon ordered an answer to be written to the Lord Lieutenant, that they had not granted, what the Doctor desires, his petition being too general, not setting forth the statute, which he desires may be dispensed with, the value of the living, nor what has been the usage in those cases. This answer may indeed give room for a further application from Dr. Delany, but if he makes any, your Grace may be assured, care will be taken to disappoint him. I return your Grace many thanks for this instance of your constant attention, to every circumstance that can occur, in which the King's service and the public good may be concerned, and I am etc.

Holles Newcastle.

To the Duke of Newcastle &c.

Dublin, Oct. 28, 1725.

My Lord,

I have received the honour of your Grace's of the 14th and 21st instant, and am very glad to find my endeavours to serve his Majesty, and to make the sessions easy in our house are so well accepted: I shall always continue the same diligence, and as the affair of the debts of the nation and providing for them, has taken a different turn in the House of Commons from what was hoped, I perceive we must be the more vigilant in our house, for fear the success they have had in the commons should give new spirit to those who want to make disturbances. The tories have pushed very unanimously with the discontented whigs on this occasion, and I fear his Majesty's friends have not been so diligent in undeceiving the country gentlemen as might have been expected from them; but I hope in another session the debts may be provided for; though in the mean time great numbers must suffer very much by the slowness of the payments.

I have nothing new to send about the Archbishop of Cashel, besides my acknowledgments for your kind assurances on that head.

I thank your Grace for pressing the treasury for a report upon the Portugal coin, and hope we shall in a little time receive the necessary orders from England.

I likewise thank your Grace for the care you have already taken, and design for the future to take in Dr. Delany's affair, which his Majesty's friends here look upon as a piece of service to the government.

I am, &c.

To Lord Townshend.

Dublin, Nov. 4, 1725.

My Lord,

I have had the honour of your Lordship's of the 15th of the last, and am very glad that my behaviour in the House of Lords, at the opening of the sessions was acceptable to his Majesty, and approved by your Lordship: I shall always esteem it my duty to serve his Majesty with the greatest zeal, and to the utmost of my abilities on all occasions that offer here; and shall do it with more cheerfulness, as I find his Majesty is willing I should do so.

I am sensible of the hurry your Lordship must have been in upon removing to the Gohrde,[24] and shall never impute any delay in your Lordship's answers, but to want of leisure.

As soon as any vacancy happens in the Church here, I shall upon your Lordship's encouragement, trouble you with my opinion what may be most for his Majesty's service.

I thank your Lordship for your kind acceptance of my charge, and your trouble in distributing those I sent you. I am, with the greatest sincerity and respect,

My Lord, &c.

---

24 A hunting seat of the King's at Hanover.

Newcastle to Boulter.

Whitehall, Nov. 4, 1725.
(NA. SP. 63/386/250–51)

My Lord,

I have received the honour of your Grace's letters of the 16th and 20th of the last month, and was very sorry to find by that of the 20th, that notwithstanding the fair appearance we had at the opening of your session of Parliament, and their Loyal and Dutiful Addresses, so ill a return should be made, for the very extraordinary mark of grace and favour, they have so lately received from the Crown; a favour, which, if credit might be given to what some of themselves advanced, they would have purchased at a considerable rate, though now they scruple to make the necessary provision for the support of the Establishment. However I hope, that since the discontented Whigs joined with the Tories have been able to make so small a majority, your Grace and the rest of his Majesty's servants and friends will be able to get the better of this confederacy, and that by opening the eyes of honest well meaning Country Gentlemen, who may have been misled, this affair may be retrieved, and the session be brought to a better issue, than this last transaction seems to promise.

Dr. Delany has presented a new petition with those particulars mentioned in it, that were wanting in the former, and My Lord Lieutenant of course transmitted it hither. The Lords Justices had so much business this day, that they could not enter upon the consideration of Dr. Delany's affair, which gives at least a week's delay; and when they do, as I have already written to your Grace, I will endeavour to find some way to put him off.

Your Grace may be assured, that when a vacancy happens at Christ Church, I shall not be unmindful of your recommendation of Mr. Stephens, nor shall my best endeavours be wanting to contribute all that is in my power towards his success. I have discoursed with the Bishop of London upon that affair, who is very desirous your Grace's friend should be served in a manner, that may be agreeable to you, but as my Lord Bishop has mentioned to Mr. Stephens his accepting of some other preferment, in lieu of the Canonry of Christ's Church, we should be glad to know, whether you should like any such agreement should be made with Mr. Stephens, and your Grace may be assured there is no thoughts of doing anything in it, but with your approbation. I shall ever gladly embrace every opportunity of demonstrating the zeal and regard, with which I am

My Lord etc.
Holles Newcastle

To the Duke of Newcastle, &c.

Dublin, Nov. 11, 1725.

My Lord,

I have had the honour of your Grace's of the 4th instant, and am concerned as well as your Grace, at the ungrateful return here made to his Majesty's late signal favour to us; but I hope all will end well, as the discontented party seem every day to lose ground in the House of Commons: and I can assure your Grace no endeavours are wanting in his Majesty's friends and servants to open the eyes of the honest and well-meaning country gentlemen, who had been very much prepossessed by those that want to embarrass affairs here.

As to Dr. Delany's affair; when I was in England, and belonged to the University, I was always against persons holding any tolerable preferments with their fellowships, as being a hindrance to succession in Colleges, and excluding some or other, that may want that help in their education, from getting upon a foundation; and though a power is reserved to the crown to dispense with the statutes of the College here, yet I would hope it will not be done merely for being asked for, where there is not some very good motive beside: whereas in this case, his Majesty's friends here think it is certainly for his Majesty's interest, that the Dr. should not be permitted to hold a preferment with his fellowship that will put him above the temptation of accepting a country living, in some one of which they heartily wish he was settled.

I heartily thank your Grace for your promise not to forget Mr. Stephens, upon a vacancy at Christ Church, and as the only thing that has been in earnest proposed by way of equivalent, is scarce of half the value or dignity of a Canonry of Christ Church, I should desire a specifick performance of the first engagement, and must in that as well as I shall on all other occasions, depend upon your Grace's friendship and support. I am with the greatest sincerity and regard,

My Lord, &c.

Newcastle to Boulter.

Whitehall, Nov. 13, 1725.
(NA. SP. 63/386/280)

My Lord,

A letter from my Lord Lieutenant of Ireland, was this day laid before the Lords Justices, with a second petition enclosed from Dr. Delany, for a dispensation to hold the Prebend of St John's together with his Fellowship, supplying in some measure, in this paper the defects of his former petition.

However their Excellencies had that regard for your Grace's opinion, that notwithstanding diverse precedents, which the Doctor quoted of like dispensations, yet they have refused to grant what he desires. This, being in a case where the same favour has seldom been refused, may convince your Grace of the great deference that is paid here to your advice, and I hope it will have the good effect you propose by it, of establishing and supporting the interest of the King's friends in the College, which must be of so great consequence with you.

I am very glad I could on this occasion give a mark of my particular care and concern for whatever comes recommended from your Grace, which you may always depend on, being with the greatest truth and respect etc.

Holles Newcastle

To the Duke of Newcastle.

Dublin, Nov. 16, 1725.

My Lord,

I am very sorry that I must send your Grace word that yesterday the discontented carried every thing before them, and have falsely stated the debt of the nation, and (in effect) closed the committee of supply; and I am the more troubled at this behaviour of the Commons, because it is so unworthy a return to his Majesty's late goodness to us. The army is like to be in great distress by what they have done, to prevent which they talk of doing a most unjust and unreasonable thing, the voting that the payments on the civil lift shall be postponed, to supply the exigencies of the army. Great pains have been taken by my Lord Lieutenant, and by all his Majesty's servants and friends of consequence, to bring the members to reason, and much has been said in the house in debates on these occasions, on the side of his Majesty's service; but it was only saying, that the carrying such a question would bring on new taxes, and the question however true or reasonable in itself, was sure of being lost.

My Lord, I must take the liberty to acquaint your Lordship, that the ill success his Majesty's affairs have met with, is owing to the indefatigable industry and art of two leading men in the House of Commons: the interest of the first of them must every day decrease, as the father[25] is now out of post, and upon retiring to England; and as the son[26] himself is far from being beloved here: the other has no personal interest; and if he has not the support of a new place, or new countenance, will soon sink in his weight.

Whatever uneasiness is created here by any turbulent or designing

25 Lord Viscount Midleton.
26 The hon. St. John Broderick.

persons, whilst his Majesty and his ministers think proper any ways to employ me in the public service, will at least light as heavy upon me as any body here: but I am very willing to undergo my share of any such trouble at any time, if no new encouragement is given to such doings, by buying off any discontented persons here; for if any body is bought off, there will always arise a succession of people to make a disturbance every session; and there wants no accident here to furnish a bottom of popularity, every one having it always in his power to grow popular, by setting up for the Irish, in opposition to the English interest. And there is no doubt but some occasion of things going as they have, has been an unwillingness in too many to see an English administration well established here; and an intention to make all the English already here, uneasy; and to deter others from coming hither. But if those who have places here, and yet have joined in the late measures, are remembered after the sessions; and if nobody finds his account in having headed the opposition made now to his Majesty's service, I do not doubt but the face of affairs will here gradually alter, and we may hope that the next sessions will be more easy and successful.

I am, &c.

To the Duke of Newcastle.

Dublin, Nov. 20, 1725.

My Lord,

I had yesterday the honour of your Grace's of the 13th instant, with advice that their Excellencies the Lords Justices[27] were pleased to refuse the favour desired by Dr. Delany. I can assure your Grace, the opposition I made to it was not from any pique to the Dr. but that I thought myself, and found his Majesty's friends here, were of opinion, that it was not for his Majesty's service that the Dr. should have a parish in this city.

By his petition I perceive your Grace might apprehend that it was only a dignity, of the nature of a sine cure, that he desired to hold with his fellowship, as is the case of prebends in England; but this prebend, as most other dignities here, has a parish with cure of souls annexed to it.

I am very sensible of the great regard shewn to me on this occasion by their Excellencies; and hope by degrees, with the assistance I have from his Majesty's ministers, to support and encrease his Majesty's friends in the College: I am sure it is my settled purpose, and shall always be my endeavour to make no other use of the countenance I meet with from your Grace and the rest of the ministers, than the advancing his Majesty's service here.

27 In England.

I humbly thank your Grace for the particular care and concern you have been pleased to shew on this, as well as all other occasions, for my representations and requests.

I am, my Lord, &c.

To the Bishop of London.

Dublin, Nov. 30, 1725.

My Lord,

The prints, as well as private letters, by the last mail, inform us that the Bishop of Chester is dead: as this makes a vacancy at Christ Church that was not so soon reckoned upon, I must apply to your Lordship for your assistance to get that canonry for Mr. Stephens. It is probable before long there will be another vacancy, to answer the schemes of some other persons, which may make them less active on this occasion to oppose me: and as your Lordship was an early witness of the promises made me in favour of Mr. Stephens, upon my dropping all opposition to Dr. Foulkes; you are best able to be my solicitor in this affair; and the many proofs I have formerly had of your friendship make me not doubt but you will give me this further instance of your kindness, by heartily serving my friend Mr. Stephens on this occasion. I can assure your Lordship I shall always esteem it one of the greatest obligations laid on,

My Lord, &c.

To the Duke of Newcastle, &c.

Dublin, Nov. 30, 1725.

My Lord,

Since I troubled your Grace last, the prints inform us that the Bishop of Chester is dead, by which there is a canonry of Christ Church become vacant: I would hope as there is still a probability of another vacancy before long by the death of Dr. Burton, that those who have been forming schemes for some friends of theirs against that vacancy should happen, may be content to stay for it, and that the promise made me that Mr. Henry Stephens, Vicar of Malden in Surrey, should have the first canonry that fell, may be performed. It is a favour I have often troubled your Grace about, and your supporting my just pretensions on this occasion, will always be acknowledged as one of the greatest obligations, by

My Lord, &c.

To The Archbishop of Canterbury.

Dublin, Dec. 8, 1725.

My Lord,

I am obliged to your Grace for your favour of the 17th ult. but it came not to hand till almost a fortnight afterwards, nor have we had any mail since that which brought the 25th ult.

I am very much obliged to your Grace and the other Lords Justices, for rejecting Dr. Delany's request for a faculty to hold a living with his fellowship. I can assure your Grace it was not out of any ill will to the person that I opposed it, but that his Majesty's friends here think it would be very much for his Majesty's service, if he were removed from the College to some other part of the Kingdom, instead of having a living here in town, and such an addition to his fellowship, as may put him beyond any temptation but that of a wife, to quit it. This was my reason then, and stills continues so, but I am now a little surprized with what I did not then know, that his application was not to be dispensed with from the obligation of any statute, but of an oath he had taken never to hold such a benefice: this, where there is not an express clause in the oath, nisi tecum aliter dispensatum fuerit, seems to me altogether new.

I can assure your Grace, whatever weight you and others in power on that side of the water are pleased to give to any representations of mine, I shall make no other use of it than for the service of his Majesty, and the peace and quiet of the country I am placed in.

I am sorry to hear your Grace has been disordered with a cold, and hope it may be quite gone off before this. Now the Bishop of Chester is gone off, the Bishop of Bristol, will, I hope, have an easy time of it at Christ Church.

If there had been any thing particular in our bills, especially relating to the Church, I should have given your Grace advice of it. We suppose here that the money bill has been some days at Holyhead, and shall be glad to see it, because without it some of the duties expire at Christmas. I shall in a little time have occasion to give your Grace an account of a bill now drawing up relating to parsonage-houses.

I hope his Majesty may be safe landed in his dominions before this comes to your hands. I last week removed to a new house here, where I propose, God willing, to spend the rest of my days. I am, with the greatest respect,

My Lord, &c.

Newcastle to Boulter.

Whitehall, Dec. 16, 1725.
(NA. SP. 63/386/352)

My Lord,

My absence in the country is the occasion of my acknowledging at once the honour of your Grace's letters of the 11th, 16th, 20th and 30th of the last month.

It is very unfortunate that the endeavours of your Grace and the rest of the King's friends and servants in Ireland have had no better success. I take the business of the sessions there to be so far over, that there is little possibility of retrieving what has been done there to the disservice of the government, and indeed of the nation itself. The reflections your Grace makes upon it are very judicious and I doubt not but those measures will be followed that you propose, which seem indeed the most proper to subdue that spirit of opposition, which is too prevalent in that country.

The late Bishop of Chester's preferments will not be disposed of, as I believe, till his Majesty's return. Your Grace may depend upon my doing all I can to procure the Canonry of Christ Church for Mr. Stephens as I shall always with the greatest pleasure and readiness endeavour, to the utmost of my power, to show the sincerity and respect with which I am etc.

Holles Newcastle

P.S. If the Canonry of Christ Church should go with the Bishopric of Chester, your Grace I am sure will not in that case think that inconsistent with the promise that has been made to you for Mr. Stephens.

To the Duke of Newcastle.

Dublin, Dec. 23, 1725.

My Lord,

As we are in hopes his Majesty may now be upon the point of landing in England, and as probably the bishoprick of Chester and canonry of Christ Church may be disposed of soon after his arrival, your Grace will have the goodness to excuse my putting you in mind of Mr. Stephens of Malden, for the canonry. After what I have already wrote on this occasion, I need say nothing farther than that in serving my friend, you will lay the greatest obligation on,

My Lord, &c.

To the same.

Dublin, Dec. 30, 1725.

My Lord,

I have lately had the honour of your Grace's of the 16th, and am glad my several dates of the last month have come safe to your hands. I am very sorry the endeavours of his Majesty's servants and friends have had no better success here, this session of parliament, and that the people have so little consulted their own true interest. I would hope the reports we have here are groundless, that a certain Lord, who acted with as much peevishness as any body in our house, and had a great hand in animating the commons to their behaviour, is likely to be sent in a great post to the West Indies.

I shall always be ready to do my part in pursuing those measures, which shall be thought proper by my superiors, to break that spirit of opposition, which has of late exerted itself so much here.

I must beg leave to put your Grace in mind of the letter from the council here, relating to the new species of Portugal gold. I must own we deserve no favour here,[28] but as the parts of England we trade with, would find their advantage in having the value of those species settled by proclamation, as well as we of this nation; and, as every body here must be sensible, that under our present behaviour, the granting us this favour must be owing to the application of the English from hence, I would hope that the settling of that affair would be of some service to his Majesty.

I thank your Grace for your kind promises to use your best endeavours to procure the canonry of Christ Church, now vacant, for my friend Mr. Stephens. If his Majesty's service requires the making any person Bishop of Chester, who must have that canonry to support his bishoprick, I must beg of your Grace, that at the same time, it may be settled, that Mr. Stephens shall succeed to the next vacancy there, by whatever means it shall happen.

I have nothing to trouble your Grace with further at present, than my sincere wishes that you may enjoy a great many years with the same health and happiness as you have gone through this, I am, with the greatest sincerity and respect.

My Lord, &c.

To the same.

Dublin, Jan. 10, 1725/6.

My Lord,

I am sorry to find by a letter I have received from the Bishop of London that there has been a necessity of putting my friend Mr. Stephens by the

28 Is not this most rash, with regard to Ireland?

vacant canonry of Christ Church; however I learn by the Bishop and others, that I was very much obliged to your Grace's friendship on that occasion, and that you have obtained an absolute promise of the next vacancy that shall happen there for my friend. I must still depend on your friendship for the performance of this new promise.

I hope our bills that we have sent from hence will meet with all convenient dispatch at the council, that our sessions may be brought to a conclusion. I do not despair of seeing a vote of credit carried in the House of Commons at our next meeting, which will make things pretty easy. The poor opposition that was made here on occasion of the last address to his Majesty by Mr. Brodrick and his friends, has given a new spirit to the Whigs, and Mr. Speaker and others have assured me, they will omit nothing in their power that may bring a good appearance of his Majesty's friends together against the 17th of this month.

The general report is, that Dean Swift designs for England in a little time; and we do not question his endeavours to misrepresent his Majesty's friends here, wherever he finds an opportunity: but he is so well known, as well as the disturbances he has been the fomenter of in this kingdom, that we are under no fear of his being able to disserve any of his Majesty's faithful servants, by any thing that is known to come from him: but we could wish some eye were had to what he shall be attempting on your side of the water.

I am, &c.

Boulter to Charles Delafaye.

Feb. 22, 1726.
(NA. SP. 63/387/50–1)

Sir,

I have received yours of the 15th, 17th instant with the papers enclosed and am very much obliged to you for furnishing me with a perfect knowledge of the grounds and design, as well as the justice, of the late Hanover Treaty. I must own, before I saw those papers, I did not so well understand, how we could insist with the Emperor that he should not grant his subjects what privileges he thought fit, in trade, however prejudicial they might be to us. But I see now, that by former Treaties the subjects of Flanders were restrained from trading to the E. Indies. I am very glad to hear, that the debates in both Houses, on Thursday last, ended so well. If anything can prevent a war, it must be the zeal and heartiness of an English Parliament in supporting his Majesty's measures. I am surprised, that anybody, in either House, should think it unreasonable to assist his Majesty in the defence of his German dominions, when they are exposed to insults purely for his Majesty's endeavours to secure the trade of England. Thursday next will be our great day, here, in the House of Commons where the friends of the Government will endeavour to carry a vote of credit for interest, at the rate of 7 percent. for a year's pay, that is due to the army, and half a year's pay, due to the Half-pay Officers, making together about sixty two thousand pounds. The interest is proposed to be for two years and comes to about nine thousand, four hundred pounds. By the end of the 2 years, if their calculation of the Revenue holds true, the principal will be paid. My Lord Lieutenant has been indefatigable, on this occasion, to bring the members to a sense of the necessity of this step, both out of justice to the creditors of the Government, and to put the army upon such a foot, as to be of any use in case of an emergency. For, at present, our Treasury is in so low a condition, that we can neither march 3 or 4 thousand men across the country, nor embark 3 or 4 Regiments if his Majesty should send for them. As the Speaker, and other friends of the government have likewise been very active, during our recess, I have hopes that things will succeed well, on Thursday. But, as the enemies of the Government are very industrious too, and very fruitful in finding out lies, adapted to the several capacities of the Country Gentlemen; and, as there is a wrong-headedness in too many, who mean well, there is no answering for anything, till it is over. I should be very glad of your continuing the favour of imparting to me what may be of consequence.

I am, Sir, with very great truth, your faithful friend and very humble servant,

Hu. Armagh.

To the Archbishop of Canterbury.

Dublin, Feb. 24, 1725/6.

My Lord,

As our bills arrived here on Tuesday, the parliament met, according to their adjournment, on this day, to proceed on business, and the first thing done in both houses, was acquainting them with his Majesty's answers to their several addresses; in our house nothing happened, as nothing was expected: but in the House of Commons (as his Majesty in his answer expressed his hopes that they would take care to put the army in a condition for service, if there should be occasion) there came on a debate of several hours. What was designed to be carried there was an address to his Majesty, to apply so much of the money given this session of parliament as might pay two years interest at seven per cent. of the arrears of the army from Midsummer 1724, to Midsummer 1725; and likewise two years interest of the arrears due to the half-pay officers, from Christmas 1724, to Midsummer 1725. The arrears of the army for the time mentioned, amount to about

51,000 pounds; the arrears due to the half-pay officers for the six months, amount to about 11,000 pounds, and there would then have been left due near nine months to both of them. But after great debates, it was found it would be but by a small majority things could be carried in that way, and that much the same thing could be compassed in another way, into which the house came at last without a division; which was to address his Majesty to apply 10,000 pounds for the use of the army in what manner he shall think proper; so that what is understood here is, that their several debentures for the time mentioned, will be struck so as to carry interest for two years; and there is no doubt but the officers will then be able to part with them as ready money. I think they have likewise engaged to provide for these 10,000 pounds, together with the arrears themselves that shall be found then standing out, at the next sessions of parliament.

I was willing to send your Grace an account of this, as being the best thing that has passed in the house this sessions, though with as ill a grace, and with as perverse an opposition, as such a thing could be done with.

As the house sat late on this occasion, and I have the account of what passed only by word of mouth, it is not so nicely exact as I could have wished to have sent it to your Grace. I am glad to find by the publick papers, that things go in your parliament with such zeal and affection to his Majesty, as we hope here will intimidate his enemies both at home and abroad. I am, with the truest respect,

my Lord,

Your Grace's, &c.

To the Reverend Mr. Power.

Dublin, Feb. 24, 1725/6.

Sir,

I received yours of the 24th of November, in answer to mine of the 20th, and delivered your present, which was kindly received.

What I write to you now is by the express orders of my Lord Primate, to inform you that his Grace hears from persons of credit such things of you as are highly displeasing to him. You are represented as a person who have neither discretion in your words and conversation, nor proper decency in your actions and conduct, nor a due regard to the offices of your function; and that the result of your whole behaviour has given such offence to the generality of your parishioners, that your congregation falls off daily from you. I am ordered to acquaint you, that my Lord is very much troubled to have so indifferent a character of a clergyman, whom he has promoted; and that he will not rest satisfied with such a behaviour as brings a scandal on religion, and a disrepute on himself.

I am, Sir,
Your very humble servent,
AMBR. PHILIPS.

To the Duke of Newcastle.

Dublin, Mar. 22, 1725/6.

My Lord,

I had the favour of your Grace's of the 10th instant, and am very much obliged to you for your kind congratulations on my being made one of the Lord Justices: I can assure your Grace I shall in that station, as I have in what I already enjoy here by his Majesty's favour, most faithfully endeavour to promote his Majesty's service.

I am very sensible of the great hurry of important business there has been in England, so as to hinder your regularly corresponding about our small affairs.

We have indeed at last put a pretty good end to a troublesome session of parliament; but without somewhat done to shew that the opposing his Majesty's service here, is not the way to make court in England, we can hardly fail of having as uneasy a sessions the next.

In obedience to his Majesty's letter upon the address of the Commons here, my Lord Lieutenant is issuing the debentures of the army for one year, and of the half-pay officers for six months, so as to carry quarterly payments of interest for two years from Christmas last, till the parliament meets again to pay off the principal; and I hope those arrears will by this method be circulated for two years, whilst the current service is answered by the revenue coming in in the mean time.

But I cannot but observe that those who have made the great disturbance in parliament, are as busy now in frightning the bankers and other monied men from having any thing to do with these warrants, and advancing any money upon them, as they were in hindering the payment of our debts in the house: I hope it will be without any effect, but I think their past and present behaviour requires that the government should shew their resentment of such proceedings; and the more so, because one of the arts by which they have drawn too many well-meaning members to join with them in parliament, has been telling them that by their opposition they were making court on the other side of the water. I am very sensible that by the language some from hence, who talked in that way, have met with at their arrival in England from the ministry, they know the contrary. But the country gentlemen here will never be persuaded of this, but by seeing those men turned out of our privy council. And I would hope that the disobliging two or three members of the House of Commons in England, will not be thought of greater consequence than the keeping things quiet here, by shewing a just displeasure against those who would embroil this Kingdom.

There is another thing I must beg leave to mention, and on which subject I shall speak my sentiments very freely to the ministry, when I have the honour to wait upon them in England; and that is the granting places for more than one life, or the reversion of places now full. I see plainly so far as it has prevailed, or shall hereafter prevail, it tends to loosen that small hold the crown still retains in this nation; as I shall therefore always oppose any applications of that nature from hence, so I hope the ministry will have the goodness to discourage all sollicitations of the like kind on the other side of the water.

Here have been great complaints of the amendments and defalcations made in our bills by the Attorney General: I must own I could wish he would have consulted my Lord Chief Baron Gilbert or Baron Hale, before he had determined things to be provided for by law here, which our judges assure us are not provided for; but on this subject I may possibly trouble your Grace some other time.

I have formerly wrote about Mr. Carter, and I hope when the judges return from their circuits, to be able to point out such a way of dealing with him, as will make his opposition in future sessions of little weight: I am sure the rudeness with which he has, in his speeches in parliament, treated the English ministry, not to say the whole nation, as well as those of us who are settled here, deserve that he should be made an example of.

Your Grace will have the goodness to excuse the liberty I have taken in this letter, in which I can assure you I have no other view than in the best manner I can, to promote the interest of England and his Majesty's service in this country.

I am very glad to find by your Grace's letter that things have so good an aspect both at home and abroad, and heartily wish they may go on with success.

I am, &c.

Boulter to Charles Delafaye.

Apr. 9, 1726.
(NA. SP. 63/387/130–1)

Sir,

I have received yours, with your kind congratulation upon my being appointed one of the Lords Justices. I am now entered on my office, having been sworn, this day sennight, and shall endeavour to discharge it, the best I can, for his Majesty's service. Our Parliament made a pretty good conclusion, especially, as my Lord Lieutenant has made that use of their

Address, as to take off 60 thousand pounds of the arrears from burdening the current service, at which, those, who were at the head of the uneasiness in Parliament, expressed a great deal of dissatisfaction. And, I very much apprehend, that if the Ministry do not show them some public mark of their resentment, the same persons will be able to make a disturbance the next session. I am very glad to hear, the Hanover Treaty meets with so good success abroad, as well as so hearty a support at home, and I heartily wish this may prevent a rupture. As you have been in this Kingdom, and know the thirst we have after news from England, you can best judge how charitable it will be in you to send an account of anything material, that passes on your side of the water.

I am, Sir,

your faithful friend and humble servant,

Hu. Armagh.

To the Duke of Newcastle.

Dublin, Apr. 5, 1726.

My Lord,

His Excellency the Lord Lieutenant left the castle about four in the afternoon last Friday, and after some stay in the bay of Dublin, set sail about ten that night: as the wind continued very fair that night and the next day, we had no doubt here but that on Saturday in the afternoon his Lordship must be landed at Hyle-Lake. It was then thought proper to have the commission for the Lords Justices sealed that night, when we were sworn in council. Yesterday we received the ceremonious compliments of the city and university in the presence chamber: what farther compliments are to be made on this occasion are to be received in the closet. I do not question but there will be a good agreement amongst us; but if by any accident there be not, I shall endeavour to take care that it may not be through any fault of mine. When any thing of consequence occurs here, I shall be sure to acquaint your Grace with it; in the mean time I beg leave to subscribe myself,

My Lord, &c.

To Lord Carteret.

Dublin, Apr. 16, 1726.

My Lord,

The bearer is wife to Mr. Cassel; he is the person who gave from time to time the best accounts of the popish priests, and what was doing amongst that party: he tells me his wife will have occasion to wait on your

Excellency, to sollicit an affair of his, and desired I would give her a few lines to introduce her. I hope your Lordship will be so good as to excuse this trouble, since it was a favour I could not well deny him.

I am, my Lord, &c.

To the Duke of Newcastle.

Dublin, May 14, 1726.

My Lord,

We have from time to time transmitted to his Excellency the Lord Lieutenant an account of all we have learnt relating to the ship Patience seized at Killybeg's, and by this mail have sent the copy of a letter to one Deaz, a Jew, that probably discovers the truth of the captain's design.

I find the papists are in several parts here employed in fasting and prayers, by an order from the pope, as they say, and a promise of indulgences, but on what occasion they do not own.

There seem likewise to be men listing in several parts, but whether from France or Spain is uncertain, though they pretend for the former: but by the laws here it is capital to list or be listed in any foreign service, without leave from the crown.

We have had strong reports that Mr. Nutley is going to be made a judge here, but as he has had very severe censures past on him by the House of Commons, at the beginning of his Majesty's reign, and is counted one most in the secrets of the tories, I have ventured to say that I was sure there could be nothing in it.

Since my Lord Lieutenant's arrival at London nothing has happened that has required my writing to your Grace, nor should I give you any trouble at present, only to assure your Grace that as any thing of consequence happens, I shall be sure to inform your Grace of it.

I rely on your Grace's goodness for Mr. Stephens, whenever a canonry shall fall at Christ Church.

I am, &c.

To the same.

Dublin, May 19, 1726.

My Lord,

In my last I gave your Grace a hint that numbers were listing here for foreign service. We have daily new accounts from several parts that the lusty young fellows are quitting the country, on pretence that they are going to England for work. Such as have occasion to employ many hands, begin to feel the effects of this desertion, and nobody here questions but that all these really are going into foreign service.

We shall not be wanting in our endeavours to keep every thing quiet here: but as accounts from all hands seem to forebode some mischievous designs among the papists, I am very apprehensive that before some months are past, there will be a necessity of putting the militia here in good order, to prevent any surprize, especially since six regiments have been drawn from hence. But of this affair I have not yet had an opportunity of talking with the other Lords Justices; nor shall we attempt any thing of that nature till the designs of the papists here clear up farther, and we are able to make a proper representation of the state of this nation, and receive his Majesty's commands what he will please to have done.

We have given all possible dispatch to the transportation of the forces, and in whatever else occurs, shall use our best endeavours to serve his Majesty, and secure the peace of this Kingdom.

I am, in duty to his Majesty, obliged to acquaint your Grace that the new list of privy counsellors has very much offended several that are best affected to his Majesty here; and that we of the English nation think by this increase our weight will grow less in the council than it was: and besides, we think it very much lessens that authority we imagine it is designed we should have here, to have a thing of this moment settled and finished, without our being in the least consulted[29] whether we were of opinion it would be for his Majesty's service to admit such a number and such persons.

I am confident we shall serve his Majesty here to the utmost of our power, but that power must every day grow less, if it appears that things of the greatest consequence are fixed on the other side of the water without our privity.

I am, &c.

To Lord Carteret.

Dublin, May 19, 1726.

My Lord,

I think it my duty to acquaint your Excellency, that every day fresh accounts come in to us that there are great numbers listing here for foreign service; the word given out in these parts is, that they are going over to England to work. Complaints come in daily from such as employ numbers of hands, that the lusty young fellows are quitting them upon this pretence. There are likewise accounts from several parts that unusual fastings and

---

29 My Lord Lieutenant had no regard to the Primate and the other Lords Justices in this instance.

devotions are set on foot among the papists, and very seditious sermons preached amongst them.

We have given the necessary orders to all custom-house officers to have a watchful eye on all who attempt to leave the kingdom: and shall as new informations come in, go on giving the best orders we can.

But by the best judgment I can make, in some time we shall be under a necessity of putting the militia here in order, to prevent any surprize. But of this we have not yet had time to consider maturely; and as whenever it is done, it may cause some alarm, we shall do nothing of that nature, without first laying the state of affairs here before his Majesty, and receiving his commands.

I am very sorry, my Lord, to be forced to acquaint your Lordship, that the new increase of our privy council has given very great uneasiness to several well-affected to his Majesty here, on account of the characters of several of the persons. And I cannot but say that the English think it is a great weakening to that weight we had in the privy council before.

When General Macartney arrives in England, I am confident he will report that we have used all possible diligence in expediting the transport of the forces, which we hope, if the wind permits, will sail from Cork the middle of next week.

When we are masters of any regular examinations relating to what is transacting among the papists here, we shall transmit them to your Excellency, to be laid before his Majesty. In the mean time I thought it proper to let your Lordship know in general what is doing here.

I am, &c.

To the Archbishop of Canterbury.

Dublin, May 21, 1726.

My Lord,

The encouragement your Grace has been pleased to give me, to ask your advice in any difficulty I meet with here, occasions my giving you this trouble. I find myself very much aggrieved by the Archbishop of Dublin in some points, the which are of such a nature, that I cannot (without prejudice to my successors) suffer them to go on, without looking out for some remedy. But I am unwilling to take any step, before I have the favour of your opinion and advice, as to what measures are most proper to be taken by me, or rather by the crown, which is, I think, at least as much concerned as I am, in the case I shall now lay before you.

The power the Archbishop of Armagh claims of granting licences for marriages, at uncanonical hours and places, is as follows:

In the 28th of Hen. VIII. there was a statute past here, entitled, the Act of

Faculties; which for the bulk of it, is only a recital of the English statute of the 25th of Hen. VIII. concerning peter-pence and dispensations; with an application at the end to the kingdom of Ireland. There is likewise another statute past here 2do. Eliz. entitled, an act for restoring to the crown the ancient jurisdiction over the estate ecclesiastical and spiritual, and abolishing all foreign authority repugnant to the same; which act is almost verbatim the same with the English statute 10mo Eliz. of the same title, as to the general part; and as to the repealing and reviving part, repeals or revives such statutes of Phil. and Mary, or Hen.VIII. as were thought proper to be repealed or revived. And in both these acts, there is a power lodged in the crown, to authorize such person or persons as the crown shall think proper to exercise the several powers therein mentioned in this kingdom.

In virtue of these two statutes (which in the beginning of the grant are mentioned as the foundation of the several powers therein granted) King James the first, by letters patent to Christ. Hampton, Archbishop of Armagh, (dated April 10. anno regni of England 20. and of Scotland 55.) did among other things, grant full power, authority, and jurisdiction to him the said Christ. Hampton and his successors Archbishops of Armagh for ever, from time to time and at all times requisite, to give, grant, and dispose of all manner of such licenses, dispensations, compositions, faculties, grants, rescripts, delegacies, instruments, and all other writings (of what kind, nature, or quality soever they be) as by force of the said Act of Parliament may be given and granted, in the most large and ample manner: and did likewise by the same letters patent, enable Christ. Hampton and his successors, &c. to appoint a commissary or commissaries, under them. In virtue of these letters patent, my predecessors have from time to time appointed commissaries, who as occasion has offered, have granted faculties for marriages at uncanonical hours and places, which are here usually termed prerogative licenses.

The authority of these licenses never has (that I can learn) been disputed, nor is it now; but his Grace of Dublin is pleased to set up his licenses as of equal force with the prerogative licenses; which licenses of his differ no farther from the common episcopal licenses in England, than what neces- sarily follows from their being directed here, to the clergyman who is to marry the parties; whereas in England, they are directed to the parties to be married. The canons indeed here are very severe against any clergyman marrying in uncanonical places or hours: the 52d. canon here punishing the so doing in a beneficed clergyman, with deprivation; in a non-beneficed clergyman, by degradation: whereas by the English canon, the punishment is only suspension per triennium.

But to give a currency to the common episcopal licenses (which are all his Grace of Dublin even pretends to grant) he has been pleased (both in private conversation, and at his publick visitations) to encourage his clergy to marry at any hour, and in private houses, purely in virtue of one of his licenses; assuring them they need not be afraid of the canon, since he is the only person who can call them to account for breach of the canon, and that (they may depend upon it) he never will call them to such account.

The use the Archbishop of Dublin makes of his licenses in this way (by making them serve for marrying at uncanonical hours and places) is usurping a power, which no ways belongs to him by any law or custom. As as the power I claim entirely depends on the supremacy given to the crown in spiritual matters by these acts of parliament, and is derived to me (and my successors) from the crown; I take this proceeding of his Grace to be a direct invasion of the authority of the crown, as well as an injury to me. And therefore I think the crown as much concerned to stop these irregular proceedings as I am.

Now what I desire of your Grace is, to inform me, which is the most proper method for either the crown or myself, or both, to put a stop to this illegal practice: and likewise which is the best and easiest way of convicting and punishing any clergyman in the diocese of Dublin, who breaks the canon in this manner, though his proper ordinary will not meddle with him.

And as the ignorance I have observed in the most eminent common lawyers of England in ecclesiastical matters, persuades me that I can have very little help from consulting the lawyers of this country, who are much inferior to those of England for skill and experience, I am the most desirous to have your Grace's advice in this matter: and the grievance I labour under on this head, is the greater here, because the people are more vain than in England; and those of moderate fortunes in this country, think it beneath them to be married at the regular time and place. And in the way his Grace of Dublin has put this affair, the breaches of the canon relating to marriages, and the invasions of that power granted by the crown to the Archbishops of Armagh, are more numerous here than they would be, if any bishop made the like attempt in England.

I shall in a post or two send a copy of this case to the Bishop of London, to desire his opinion likewise: for I have a troublesome and perverse opponent to deal with; and cannot have too much assistance. I hope his lordship will wait upon your Grace to discourse over the subject with you, that upon any difficulties which either may offer, I may have your joint sense, or if opportunity should not offer of your consulting together, I shall be very thankful for your Grace's advice singly.

I am, my Lord, &c.

To the Duke of Newcastle.

Dublin, June 11, 1726.

My Lord,

As we had some disturbance in this town last night, I thought it my duty to give your Grace a short account of it, to prevent its being taken for an affair of greater consequence than it proved.

As there had been various reports spread about the town, that the papists intended to make a rising about the 10th of June, though we had no reason to apprehend any such thing would be attempted, yet we thought ourselves obliged in prudence to give the proper directions to the forces here to be in readiness, if any thing should happen either on Thursday night, yesterday, or last night. All things were quiet till yesterday in the evening, when a very numerous rabble assembled in Stephen's Green, as they usually have done on the 10th of June, and between eight and nine (upon a message to the Lord Mayor from some of the inhabitants of the Green, complaining of such a riotous assembly) the Lord Mayor, Sheriffs, and some aldermen, attended with a number of constables, came on the Green to disperse the rabble, but meeting with opposition, and being assaulted with stones, bricks, and dirt, the Lord Mayor sent for assistance to the forces, and had first a detachment of about 40 foot, and afterwards about the like number of horse; at first the rabble would not disperse, but upon some of the foot firing with ball, and wounding three or four of them, and the horse appearing soon after, they dispersed, and about 30 of them are taken and imprisoned. They will very speedily be examined; and we are not without hopes of finding out some gentlemen, who by some circumstances are thought to have had a hand in occasioning this disturbance. If we are able to come at any design of importance, we shall send advice of it; but at present I do not find that there was much in it than the popish rabble coming down to fight the whig mob, as they used to do on that day, only that upon the prospect of a war, the papists are better in heart, and so might come in greater numbers.

We have given the necessary orders without any noise or shew, to have every thing ready to prevent the prisoners being rescued, if any such attempt should be made. I am, with great sincerity and respect,

My Lord, &c.

To the Bishop of London.

Dublin, June 11, 1726.

My Lord,

The bearer (Hugh Tillam) is a servitor-batchelor of Trinity College in Dublin, and is disposed to take orders and go to the West Indies. I have a

certificate of his sobriety and studiousness from his tutor, Dr. Delany; he
tells me he takes with him some recommendations to your Lordship, to
which he desires I would add mine in this letter: your Lordship, upon examination, will be best able to judge whether he has learning sufficient; if he
has, and you think it proper, I would recommend him to your Lordship to
find some way of employing him in the Church in the West Indies.

I am &c.

To Lord Carteret.

Dublin, June 16, 1726.

My Lord,

I have received the honour of your Excellency's of the 19th past, and am
very much obliged to your Lordship for the kind account I find you have
been pleased to give his Majesty of my behaviour. It will always be a great
pleasure to me, if I have been any ways useful in assisting you to promote
the King's service, which you have always at heart.

I have taken what opportunities offered thoroughly to contradict the
reports spread here relating to Sir J. St. Leger and Mr. Nutley, as I shall all
others which tend to disserve his Majesty.

I am afraid the hurry of business has made your Excellency forget my
Lord Roscommon's case. As there are King's letters for giving a pension to
some other Lords, I was in hopes we should have received one for
encreasing his pension, which is less than what is allowed to others, and half
of it goes to his brother's widow, as I am informed.

Mr. Philips is extremely pleased with the honour you do him of so kindly
remembering him.

Dr. Wye of Drogheda, has wrote to me to recommend one of his sons to
your Excellency, for your interest for a commission, if ten new regiments are
raised, as has been rumoured.

I am, &c.

Newcastle to Boulter.

Whitehall, June. 21, 1726.
(NA. SP. 63/387/212–3)

My Lord,

I have received the honour of your Grace's letter of the 11th instant, and
I hope you will be so good as to excuse, on account of the hurry of business
we have been in, my returning you thanks at the same time for that, and
some former letters you have taken the trouble to write to me, which I have

constantly laid before the King, who always read with pleasure the perfect accounts and the judicious observations, you send with relation to what relates to His service in Ireland, for the promoting of which, and of the public welfare in that country. His Majesty has great dependence upon your zeal, capacity and diligence.

The King very much approved and commended the conduct of the Lords Justices in the affair of the riot, that happened on the 16th June in Stephen's Green. As to the Privy Councillors that have lately been made, his Majesty was concerned to find, that that promotion was contrary to the inclinations of those in Ireland, who are best disposed to serve him, but indeed my Lord Lieutenant, engaged probably by promises made whilst he was there, represented it in so strong a manner as necessary to be done, that it was complied with in pure deference to his opinion; and I can with great truth assure your Grace, that, except my Lord Southwell, who had a promise of it of a long standing, whenever any should be made, there is not one of them but what were entirely recommended and named by his Excellency. Since the thing is over and not to be recalled, I doubt not but your Grace will endeavour to make the matter as easy as possible, and if you can put me in a way of contributing to it, you may be assured, that your advice and opinion, as it is of great weight with the King's servants here, will always meet with the greatest regard from me, who am with the utmost sincerity and respect,

My Lord etc.

Holles Newcastle

To the Duke of Newcastle.

Dublin, June 25, 1726.

My Lord,

I have just now received the honour of your Grace's of the 21st , and am thoroughly sensible of the hurry you and the rest of his Majesty's servants must have been in, on account of the great affairs now transacting.

It is a great satisfaction to me that what I endeavour to do for his Majesty's service is well taken. Every thing here has been very quiet since the 10th of June.

As to the affairs of the privy counsellors, your Grace may depend on my endeavouring to make that and whatever else is once over, as easy as I can; and that on all occasions I shall be ready to suggest what I think may be most for the King's interest.

By letters that came to town yesterday, there is advice that the Bishop of Cloyne is in a very dangerous way; as soon as there is any farther advice about him, I shall communicate it to your Grace; but I thought proper to acquaint you with this at present, to prevent any surprise in naming his successor, for some here are not without fears that interest may be made for a tory on this side, to succeed to that or the next vacancy on the bench.

I am, &c.

To the same.

Dublin, June 28, 1726.

My Lord,

I have this day seen a letter from a good hand, that gives advice of the death of the Bishop of Cloyne: I have by this post wrote to his Excellency on this affair about a successor.

The person I would recommend, if he is acceptable to your Grace and the ministry, is Dr. Skirret, who has attended me hither as chaplain; but if your Lordship thinks he is not so fit, I would recommend Dr. Maule, Dean of Cloyne, to succeed to the bishoprick; he is counted one well affected to his Majesty, and is very diligent in the discharge of the cures he has at present, and has the honour of being known to several Bishops in England.

I shall trouble your Grace with no more at present, but subscribe myself,

My Lord, &c.

To the Bishop of London.

Dublin, June 28, 1726.

My Lord,

Since my last there is advice come by a good hand, that the Bishop of Cloyne is dead. I have by this post wrote to the Duke of Newcastle and my Lord Lieutenant about this affair.

I must beg the favour of your Lordship to learn on what terms Dr. Skirret stands with the ministry: if he is acceptable to them, I would willingly recommend him for a successor to the Bishop deceased; if your Lordship finds they are prejudiced against him, I think Dean Maule, who is Dean of Cloyne, would be one of the most proper of this nation to succeed.

As I am not present to talk with the ministry, I cannot put the management of this affair into better hands than your Lordship's, who I am sure will be for what you think most for the good of the Church, his Majesty's service, and my reputation.

I am, &c.

To Lord Carteret.

Dublin, June 28, 1726.

My Lord,

There is advice in town that the Bishop of Cloyne is dead, which by the accounts of last Friday is very likely to be true. On this occasion I must desire of your Excellency to recommend Dr. Skirret for his successor, if he be any ways acceptable to the ministry: and in that case, as your Excellency knows the great incumbrances on that bishoprick, I must beg the favour of your Excellency to reserve for him the other preferments in the gift of the crown, enjoyed by the late Bishop, that the Dr. may not be ruined by taking that bishoprick.

If Dr. Skirret is one the ministry are set against, I should willingly recommend Dean Maule for that bishoprick, who as I am assured is one well-affected to his Majesty, and is very diligent in the discharge of his present cures.

I have had the honour of your Excellency's of the 11th. I am,

My Lord, &c.

To the Duke of Newcastle.

Dublin, June 30, 1726.

My Lord,

Yesterday the Lords Justices met, and we wrote a common letter to my Lord Lieutenant relating to a successor to the late Bishop of Cloyne, in which three persons are named: Dr. Maule, Dean of Cloyne, Dr. Howard, Dean of Ardagh, and Mr. Gore,[30] Dean of Down. I have already wrote to your Grace my sentiments about Dean Maule, and give you this farther trouble only to do justice to the other two gentlemen, that Dean Howard is accounted well affected to his Majesty, as is Dean Gore; but Dean Maule is senior to them both.

I am, &c.

To the Bishop of London.

Dublin, June 30, 1726.

My Lord,

Upon the Lords Justices meeting yesterday, we joined in a letter to my Lord Lieutenant, naming three candidates for the bishoprick of Cloyne;

30 Chaplain to the House of Commons, and brother to Sir Ralph Gore, Bart.

Dean Maule, Dean Howard of Ardagh, and Dean Gore of Down: the last two are counted well affected to his Majesty, but are juniors to Dean Maule: and the last is not, that I can hear, in circumstances to afford to take the bishoprick of Cloyne, which has a burthen of about 2500l. on it; so that I make no change in my recommendation by the last.

I am, &c.

To Lord Carteret.

Dublin, July 2, 1726.

My Lord,

Since the last trouble I gave your Excellency, I have received a letter from Dr. Wye of Drogheda (whom your Lordship was so kind as to make your chaplain, and to encourage him to hope for somewhat in the church) to desire that if Dean Howard should be made Bishop of Cloyne, your Excellency would be pleased to bestow on him the deanery of Ardagh, and chantership of Christ Church: he has been a great many years minister of Drogheda, which is a considerable cure.

I have likewise had a letter from the Bishop of Meath, the which I send enclosed to your Excellency: I suppose it is to desire you would be pleased to send an order to present his son to the living of Moynet, about which there may possibly be a lawsuit with Mr. Carter, who pretends to be patron of it. I shall in the mean time endeavour to learn what I can of the title of the crown, and what will be the best method to maintain it.

I am, &c.

P. S. Mr. Daniel Pulteney arrived here yesterday, and was admitted clerk of the council this day.

To Lord Townshend.

Dublin, July 2, 1726.

My Lord,

Dr. Rowan fellow of the college here designs to wait on your Lordship with a petition to his Majesty, to appoint him Professor of the Law of Nature and Nations in this University, with a power of taking such gentlemen for pupils as are willing to put themselves under his care, and he will oblige himself to read such a number of lectures in a term as shall be thought proper, without any salary from the crown for the same, only on condition of enjoying his fellowship with all its emoluments, and the like privileges as are already granted to the professors established in this college.

He has always been well affected to his Majesty and his family, and is of abilities to fill the professorship he asks for with reputation. And I think it can be of no disservice to the College, that he should enjoy the same privileges as other professors enjoy; and hope that his being encouraged to continue in the college, may help to keep up there a good affection to his Majesty. I therefore take the liberty to recommend him to your Lordship for your favour in promoting his request. I am,

My Lord, &c.

To Lord Carteret.

Dublin, July 6, 1726.

My Lord,

I have the honour of your Excellency's of the 28th of the last, and humbly thank you for remembering the Earl of Roscommon, and hope to hear after your Lordship's return to London, that his Majesty is graciously pleased to make an addition to his former pension.

The present vacancy of the bishoprick of Cloyne, as it occasions no doubt, very numerous applications to your Lordship, so it brings some upon me.

Mr. Abbadie, Dean of Killaloo, has been with me to desire my recommendations to your Excellency to be thought of for some deanery which he supposes may happen to be vacant by promotion on this occasion. He represents (and has shewn me papers from former governors here confirming) that he had a promise in King William's time; of the first considerable preferment that fell, (which happened to be the deanery of St. Patrick's) but that deanery being thought improper for one who could speak no English, he was put off with that of Killaloo, with a farther promise of making him amends in somewhat better, which has never been performed. But his great uneasiness, is that many years ago, when there was an extreme scarcity of money here, he was obliged to let all his preferment's during his incumbency for about 120l. per ann. though now they would let for about 300l. per ann. he would be glad to take a preferment of 200, or 250l. per ann. for what he has, (which is the deanery of Killaloo, with four sine cures, all in the gift of the crown united by an episcopal union pro hac vice.) Your Lordship knows him to have the character of a man of learning, and one well affected to his Majesty.

I have likewise received a letter from Dr. Dongworth, who would be thankful for either of Dean Howard's preferments in Dublin, if he should be removed to Cloyne; and another from Dr. Tisdale to the same purpose, who I perceive has wrote to your Excellency on this occasion. Your Lordship knows them both, and will have the goodness to excuse my giving you this trouble.

We had signed an order for paying the pensions recommended to me by your Excellency before the receipt of yours, and I shall every quarter take care of their speedy payment. I am, my Lord, with the greatest respect and sincerity,

Your Excellency's, &c.

Newcastle to Boulter.

Whitehall, July 9, 1726.
(NA. SP. 63/387/224)

My Lord,

I have received the honour of your Grace's letter of the 30th of last month, with a former one upon the subject of the vacancy of the see of Cloyne, which you will forgive my not acknowledging sooner; and having laid them before the King, his Majesty has determined to give the Bishopric to Deane Maule finding it would be agreeable to your Grace. My Lord Lieutenant of Ireland is out of town, and I have not yet heard from him concerning this matter, however your Grace may look upon this promotion of Dean Maule as fixed. As to your Chaplain his Majesty will be very willing to do something for him upon a proper occasion. I cannot finish this letter without repeating my thanks to your Grace for the frequent accounts I have received from you of the state of affairs where you are, and your judicious observations upon them, of which I must beg the continuance as being very much for his Majesty's service.

I am etc.

Holles Newcastle

To the Archbishop of Canterbury.

Dublin, July 12, 1726.

My Lord,

I have received your Grace's answer to mine about marriage licenses, but I find I have expressed myself so obscurely in the case as to be misunderstood. The Archbishop of Dublin does not pretend to have power to grant any other than episcopal licenses, nor does he grant any other; but what I complain of is, that he encourages his clergy to marry at uncanoncial hours and in uncanonical places, though their license contains no such power. I shall follow your Grace's kind advice in not being too hasty to engage with so litigious and obstinate a person, whatever my grievance may be.

On occasion of what your Lordship writes to me about my apparitor-general's patent, I have enquired of my commissary how that affair stands, who tells me that my apparitor-general has nothing to do in, nor fee out of, the prerogative court, for any wills proved there. That the officer there answering to the apparitor, is called the marshal of the court, and has twelve-pence fee for every will proved there, as the apparitor-general has for every will proved in the consistory court: but that the two jurisdictions are kept as distinct as they could be if they resided in two different persons. As this is the case of my apparitor-general, I think it can be of no service in the contro-versy depending before your Grace, to have a copy of the patent of my apparitor-general; but if you think it may, I shall as soon as you are pleased to intimate it, send a copy of his patent.

My commissary likewise tells me, he cannot by any writings now extant (though he has made a most diligent search) trace the least foot-steps of any extra-episcopal power relating to faculties, grounded on prescription, but that all such power rests here on the King's commission; so that either the pope had more fully swallowed up all metropolitical power here, than he was able to do in England, or those antient records, in which somewhat would have appeared to the contrary, have been destroyed in the wars.

I am, &c.

To the Duke of Newcastle.

Dublin, July 12, 1726.

My Lord,

I understand Sir Hans Sloan, has waited upon your Grace to desire your favour in introducing Dr. Welsted to the King, with a book he has dedicated to his Majesty. As I believe Sir Hans has read the book, he will be able to give you an account of the nature and design of it.

I can assure your Grace there are few in the kingdom of more learning than Dr. Welsted; and I believe but very few who have greater skill in physic than he has; and as I have intimately known him almost from the time of our first going to the university of Oxford, I can assure your Grace on my personal knowledge, that he has been all along a hearty friend to, and advocate for, the revolution, and a steady adherent to the interests of the house of Hanover in the worst times, for which I am satisfied he has been distressed in his business by the disaffected. After what I have with the greatest truth said, it will be but a slight recommendation of him to your Grace, that he is one of the oldest and heartiest of my friends, and that whatever countenance you give him, or favour you are pleased to shew him on this or any other occasion, will be esteemed a very particular obligation laid on me, who am with the greatest respect and sincerity,[31]

My Lord, &c.

31 The reader hath already observed with pleasure, what a steady friend his Grace shewed himself to be to Mr. Stephens; to Dr. Welsted he was still more so, for that

To Lord Carteret.

Dublin, July 14, 1726.

My Lord,

Whilst your Excellency was in this kingdom, I delivered you a petition from Mrs. Pepper, widow to General Pepper. I remember your Excellency was then of opinion, as the General had sold out of the army, and died in good circumstances, she could not without very great favour, obtain any pension as his widow: this makes me rather discourage her from going to England to sollicit for a pension, which would engage her in a certain expence, upon a very uncertain prospect; but as the General has left a son behind him, for whom he made no provision, she is very desirous somewhat may be done for him in regard to his father's services: I find, as he is in very indigent circumstances, he would be very glad to serve his Majesty in any capacity. His mother says he is very sober and very well-affected to his Majesty.

As he waits upon you personally with this, he can best satisfy your Lordship as to his own character, and what he would be thankful for. I take the liberty to recommend him to your Excellency's favour to put him in some way fit for a gentleman, if you shall find him such as Mrs. Pepper has represented him to me.

I am, my Lord, &c.

To the Duke of Newcastle.

Dublin, July 26, 1726.

My Lord,

I have had the honour of your Grace's of the 9th, with the account of his Majesty's having determined to give the bishoprick of Cloyne to Dean Maule, and am very thankful to his Majesty for having that regard to my

worthy gentleman having fallen into decay in the latter part of his life, my Lord Primate, though he was no relation, gave him two hundred pounds a year at the least, during his life; nor was his friendship wanting to the Doctor's family after his decease; the Primate then maintained a son of the Doctor's as a commoner at Hart hall in Oxford, with an intent of effectually providing for him, but the poor young gentleman died before he had taken a degree. Dr. Welsted was one of the editors of the Oxford Pindar, and esteemed an excellent Greek scholar; he had been chosen immediately after the revolution, together with the Primate, Dr. Wilcocks Bishop of Rochester, Dr. Sacheverell, and the incomparable Mr. Addison, a demy or fellow of Magdalen college, Oxford; and this went by the name of the golden election many years afterwards in that college: the most worthy Dr Hough was President of Magdalen college at this time, and was the cause of my Lord Primate's promotion afterwards, by recommending him to be chaplain to Sir Charles Hedges, then Secretary of State.

recommendation, and for his gracious intention to do something for my chaplain, Dr. Skirret, on a proper occasion. We have been expecting the two or three last mails to receive his Majesty's commands by my Lord Lieutenant, about that bishoprick, but we have not yet heard any thing from his Excellency.[32]

I am very much obliged to your Grace for taking in good part, the accounts I send you of affairs here, and my opinion of them; I am sure they are by me entirely designed for his Majesty's service.

The middle of next week I intend to set out for the north upon my visitation, which will occasion my absence from Dublin for about a fortnight.

I am, &c.

To the Bishop of London.

Dublin, July 30, 1726.

My Lord,

I am very much obliged to your Lordship for the very distinct advice you give me relating to the practice of the clergy of this city, in marrying at uncanonical hours and places, in virtue of the common licenses: though it is a direct breach of the canon, without any pretence to support it, yet I shall follow your advice, not to begin any information against any offender, till I have thoroughly mooted the point here. My Lord Chancellor is entirely of your Lordship's opinion, as to the course to be taken in this affair.

I had answered your letter relating to the bishoprick of Cloyne sooner, but that I have been every day expecting that we should receive his Majesty's commands about it; but they are not yet arrived, which (as I have had a letter from the Duke of Newcastle with the same advice as your Lordship sent me) I am a little surprized at, and suppose my Lord Lieutenant must have kept the order till at his arrival in London he could endeavour to get it altered.

I understand his Lordship came to London the end of last week, so that I suppose we shall very speedily receive orders one way or another.

I am glad to find your Lordship has the same good opinion of Dean Maule that I have; and am obliged to you for the good advice you give me about my future recommendations. I have followed your Lordship's directions, and said nothing of what you wrote about the bishoprick, still waiting his Majesty's orders, and Dean Maule has still continued in the country.

I thank your Lordship for the account you give me of Dr. Skirret's uneasiness for not being named singly in my recommendation, and am glad

---

32 His Excellency perhaps was not in haste to give an account of a transaction he did not like.

you think I was in the right; indeed what I proceeded upon was, that if I had named him singly, and that nomination was not hearkened to, I did not doubt but the bishoprick would be filled before I could have time to send over another recommendation. I own if I had been upon the spot to recommend by word of mouth, I need not have named a second, till I had found the first I named was objected to, but in so remote a situation as I am in, I could not hope for time for a second nomination. I find by an angry letter I received from the Doctor, that you were pleased to shew him mine, which I could rather wish had not been done.

As Bishops hold annual visitations here, next Wednesday I intend to go on the visitation of my diocese, and shall be absent from Dublin about a fortnight.

I am, my Lord, &c.

To Lord Carteret.

Dublin, Aug. 20, 1726.

My Lord,

I had not the honour of your Excellency's of the 26th past, till I was upon my visitation, which has been the occasion I have answered it no sooner. I have a very good opinion of Dean Howard, as likewise of Mr. Synge and Mr. Ward; and shall be glad to see the first advanced, and the other two well provided for. Upon the receipt of your Lordship's, I wrote to have an account sent you of Dean Maule's preferments, which I did not know, but Mr. Lingen[33] has, I am told, upon my writing, sent your Lordship their several denominations. The living of Mourn Abbey has I believe, usually gone with the deanery of Cloyne, which induced Dr. Maule to build a house there. The living of Cork is by act of parliament, upon the first vacancy, to be divided into the two parishes of St. Mary Shandon, and of St. Paul: the first will upon the division be left worth better than 200l. per ann. the latter worth near 100l. the dean is not yet come to town, but on his arrival, if Mr. Lingen's account is any ways wrong, I will send a better. I find there is likewise fallen the deanery of Clonfert, about which the Lords Justices have written in my absence. The Bishop of Clonfert has desired I would recommend Mr. Forbes to your Excellency for that deanery, as one who would be of great service to him in the government of that diocese.

The late Dean of Clonfert held two or three little things in the diocese of Kildare, concerning which I find your Excellency has transmitted to you the Bishop of Kildare's memorial, to desire they may be disposed of to one who may reside on them personally. I should be glad if your Excellency would

---

33 William Lingen, Esq; one of the secretaries to the Lords Justices.

by them, or by St. Paul's at Cork, at present provide bread for poor Mr. Horner.

There has been a great mistake committed in the King's letter relating to Dean Maule, by ordering him the same commendams his predecessor held; this is contrary to what is practised commonly, which is where a bishoprick wants a commendam, to find it in the preferments of the person promoted; and besides, I do not hear from any body that the crown has any pretence to the provostship of Tuam. But of this I shall write farther to your Excellency when Dean Maule comes to town. The affair of Youghall was over before my arrival, but I think it has gone as my Lord Burlington desired. I humbly thank your Excellency for your care of my Lord Roscommon's affair. I am,

Your Excellency's, &c.

To the Bishop of London.

Dublin, Sept. 6, 1726.

My Lord,

The bearer is Mr. Abbadie, Dean of Killaloo, one who for many years has made a figure in the world, by the writings he has published: I find upon enquiry, he was by King William recommended to the government here for somewhat considerable, and would have had the deanery of St. Patrick's, which fell soon after, but that having no knowledge of our language, it was thought improper to place him in the greatest preferment in this city: However it was then fixed that he should have the next deanery that fell, which happened to be that of Killaloo, which was given him with one or two little things to make him amends for its falling short of the other deanery, and with those helps he had but about half the value of what had been designed him. At first he made about 240 l per ann. of his preferment, but afterwards, upon a great scarcity of money here, was obliged to let his preferments during incumbency for about 120 l. per ann. which I find was a pretty common case at that time with a great many other clergymen. He had afterwards repeated promises of having somewhat farther done for him, but nothing beyond promises. As this is but a small income, and now he grows old he finds he wants an amanuensis to assist him in his studies, he would gladly have somewhat better either here or in England. He has firmly adhered to his Majesty's family here in the day of trial, and is every way a worthy man. I shall do my endeavour to serve him here, but as opportunities may not offer here so soon, he desired I would recommend him to your Lordship, in hopes somewhat might be done for him in England.

He would hope, if that consideration may be of service to him, that as his preferments are all in the gift of the government, they might easily be obtained for some friend of your Lordship's, if the Dean had somewhat given him in England.

I take the liberty to recommend him to your Lordship's favour and countenance, and if it shall lie in your way to help him to somewhat in England that may be an honourable subsistence for him, the small remainder of life he is likely to live, you will do a kindness to a person of merit, and very much oblige,

My Lord, &c.

To the same.

Dublin, Sept. 13. 1726.

My Lord,

I have before me your Lordship's of the 10th past, which I had answered sooner, if we had any thing stirring here worth writing about.

I am glad the ministry were so unanimous in supporting the nomination of Dean Maule to the bishoprick of Cloyne. His instruments were passed last week, and he was last Sunday consecrated by myself (at the desire of the Archbishop of Cashel) and the Bishops of Kildare and Fernes. We are on these occasions forced to go to Dunboyne, the first parish in my province, to avoid a quarrel with his Grace of Dublin, who expects any Archbishop that consecrates in this town, should take a formal licence under hand and seal for so doing.

There has been a mistake in granting a commendam to the Bishop of Cloyne. As they followed the pattern of the grant to the late Bishop of Cloyne at the secretary's office, they have made the provostship of Tuam part of his commendam, which we have no reason as yet to believe to be in the King's gift.

I find by your Lordship's account that Dr. Skirret must have placed himself so as to overlook that part of my letter which your Lordship did not read to him, which I am sure was exceedingly rude in him. I thank your Lordship for your kind advice.

I have lately received a letter from Mr. Pope, (whom I recommended to your Lordship just before I left England) to desire I would remind you of him, for fear he should be forgotten through the multiplicity of your business. As his behaviour deserves, and when your Lordship shall find a proper occasion, I should be obliged to your Lordship to think of him.

I am, &c.

P.S. I have lately heard from Mr. Stephens, who is full of his Acknowledgments of your Lordship's great civility, and the encouragement you give him.

To the Duke of Newcastle.

Dublin, Nov. 12, 1726.
My Lord,

Having by a mail this day heard from England, that Dr. Gilbert is likely to be removed from Christ Church to the deanery of Exeter, I must beg leave to put your Grace in mind of Mr. Stephens: as he was put by that very canonry to prefer one just returned from serving at Hanover, I hope if this vacancy should happen, his Majesty will be graciously pleased to bestow on him what has been so long promised me on his account. I wholly depend on your Grace's friendship on this occasion, and am, my Lord, in all sincerity,
    Your Grace's, &c.

To the same.

Dublin, Nov. 26, 1726.
My Lord,

We continue so very quiet here, except on account of the recruits for foreign service, that I should have nothing to inform your Grace of, if it were not for the present indisposition of my Lord Chancellor:[34] he has been ill for four or five days with a great cold and fever; he was blistered last night with little or no success, but is so much mended upon the blister running very well this afternoon, that he is thought to be out of danger. I hope your Grace has received mine of the 12th instant, about Mr. Stephens.
    I am, my Lord, &c.

Boulter to Newcastle.

Nov. 28, 1726.
(NA. SP. 63/388/95)
My Lord,

Since I wrote to your Grace on Saturday, things have taken an unhappy turn with my Lord Chancellor, and it is very uncertain whether he will live. I thought it my duty to give you this advice, and am,
    My Lord,
    Your Grace's,
    most dutiful and
    most obedient servant
    Hu. Armagh

34 West.

Boulter to Newcastle.

Nov. 29, 1726.
(NA. SP. 63/388/97)

My Lord,

I wrote a letter yesterday to your Grace, with a melancholy account of my Lord Chancellor. I have this day talked with his physician, who tells me he rested pretty well last night, and that his blisters run well, and his head was this morning easy and clear, so that he thinks there is a good prospect of his doing well. I am very glad that I can send your Grace this agreeable news, and am

My Lord,
Your Grace's,
most obedient and
most humble servant
Hu. Armagh

To Lord Carteret.

Dublin, Dec. 3, 1726.

My Lord,

After about twelve days illness of a fever, my Lord Chancellor died this day about two in the afternoon: his death is very much lamented here by all, but especially by the lawyers, whose good will and esteem he had entirely gained by his patience, civility, and great abilities. As he was an old friend and acquaintance of mine, I am very much troubled at this loss, as well as I am heartily concerned for the terrible blow it is to his family.

I earnestly wish his place may be filled by one that may give the same satisfaction he has given.

I take it for granted his successor will be an Englishman; but I cannot help suggesting that I think it would be of service, and especially against the next session of parliament, if either the Lord Chief Justice Windham, or Lord Chief Baron Dalton were advanced to that station, and their vacant places supplied from England.

They have both established a very good character here, and are well skilled in the affairs of Ireland, beyond what a new comer can hope for under a year at least; and I think such a promotion would be an encouragement to a person of some worth to come over in one of their places, where they saw it was a step to the highest post in this country.

I am, &c.

To the Duke of Newcastle.

Dublin, Dec. 3, 1726.

My Lord,

The uncertain accounts I have sent your Grace of the health of my Lord Chancellor, have been owing to the various accounts we got here from his physicians, and the turns in his distemper; but he this day died about two o'clock in the afternoon: he had by his abilities and humanity gained a general esteem here, and especially among the lawyers, with whom he was most concerned.

I heartily wish his place may be filled with one that may give equal satisfaction. I take it for granted that his successor will be a native of England, who, besides his being duly qualified as a lawyer, must be one of an undoubted whiggish character, or it will give great uneasiness in this country.

I cannot help suggesting on this occasion that I think it might be for his Majesty's service to advance either the Lord Chief Justice Wyndham, or my Lord Chief Baron Dalton to that post. They have both a very good character, and are very well liked here: they both know the country, and the business very well, and are both very well known: so that either of them will be capable of doing more service to his Majesty next session of parliament among the members of both houses, than a new comer will be capable of doing: and I would hope it may be an inducement to some person of worth to be willing to succeed either of them from England, when they see the rightly behaving themselves as Judges a step to the highest post in the law here. They have both discharged their places with that reputation, that I have no other reason for recommending my Lord Chief Justice Wyndham first, but his being the senior of the two. If either of them be thought of for Lord Chancellor, we may soon have the place filled.

Your Grace will excuse what I have said, as proceeding not so much from friendship for those gentlemen, as a desire most effectually and speedily to promote his Majesty's service here.

I am, &c.

To Lord Townshend.

Dublin, Dec. 3, 1726.

My Lord,

This afternoon, about two o'clock, we lost my Lord Chancellor, after about twelve days illness. He has left behind him a very good character, and his death is very much regretted here.

I have no doubt but his place will be filled up with some Englishman: but whoever is thought of for it, besides a proper knowledge in his profession, ought to be one that has always been attached to the revolution and Hanover succession, or it will create great uneasiness here.

I hope your Lordship will have the goodness to forgive my suggesting what I think would be for his Majesty's service on this occasion, which is the advancing either my Lord Chief Justice Wyndham, or Lord Chief Baron Dalton to the chancellorship. They have already acquired a very great reputation by an able and impartial discharge of their offices, and are very well beloved for their great civility to all who have had any affairs with them. They have a good knowledge of Irish affairs, and are acquainted with a great number of both houses of parliament. Nor do I think that it will be possible for any new comer either to establish so good a character, or gain so much esteem as they have, before next session of parliament; much less will such an one have that knowledge, either of persons or things here, against that season as they have.

Of the two, as my Lord Chief Justice Wyndham has been here longest, I rather think him the most proper.[35]

If it be thought advisable to advance one of them, I hope his place will be supplied from England: and I should think that the preferring one of them to be Chancellor, will not only be an encouragement to English judges here to acquit themselves well, but be an inducement to persons of worth to come over hither, when they see a judge's place a step towards the highest station in the law here. But all this is submitted to your Lordship's better judgement, by

My Lord, &c.

To the Duke of Newcastle.

Dublin, Dec. 6, 1726.

My Lord,

In my last to your Grace, I gave you an account of the death of my Lord Chancellor, and what I thought might be for his Majesty's service on this unhappy occasion. I give your Lordship this farther trouble, to desire your interest with his successor, to make Mr. Philips[36] his secretary: he is one who has always been hearty in his Majesty's interest, and that of his family: he has the honour to be known to your Grace, as having been secretary to the Hanover club in the Queen's time. He is at present with me in my family,

---

35 He was soon after this recommendation appointed.
36 Notwithstanding Mr. Pope hath said, that Still to one Bishop Philips seems a wit, and in another place, – Ambrose Philips be preferr'd for wit: I do not find he is ever recommended on that account in these letters; he is recommended in this, for qualities Mr. Pope could not well have been recommended for, viz. that he had been always in his Majesty's interest, and that of his family.

and might officiate as secretary to the Lord Chancellor without leaving me. What service your Grace shall please to do him in this affair, will be esteemed a very great obligation laid on,

My Lord, &c.

Newcastle to Boulter.

Whitehall, Dec. 13, 1726.
(NA. SP. 63/388/103)

My Lord,

I am indebted to your Grace for the honour of several letters you have been so good to write to me, and hope you will so far make allowance for the continual hurry of an employment like mine, as to forgive my not having regularly acknowledged them.

As soon as I received yours of the 3rd Instant, acquainting me with the death of Lord Chancellor West, in whom the King has lost a very useful servant, a friend, and the country where he resided an officer whose abilities were every way equal to his high station, I immediately laid it before his Majesty, who, without any hesitation, made choice of the person your Grace proposed to be his successor, of whom you give so good a character, that I doubt not but he will supply the want of that assistance, which you always had, with so much pleasure and satisfaction, from the late Lord Chancellor in everything that related to his Majesty's Service.

As to what your Grace has mentioned of Mr. Stephens, there has not of late happened any vacancy at Christ Church, but when there does, you may depend upon my using my best endeavours to serve him, or that he may be otherwise provided for to his satisfaction, and I hope you will do me the justice to be persuaded of the great regard I shall always have to your recommendation, being with the utmost sincerity and respect,

My Lord etc.
Holles Newcastle

To the Duke of Newcastle.

Dublin, Dec. 20, 1726.

My Lord,

I have just now received the honour of your Grace's of the 13th. I am too sensible of the great hurry of your station, to expect an answer to every letter I trouble you with.

I am very glad to find the affair of giving us a new Lord Chancellor, has met with that dispatch; and I can assure your Grace he is one who by his behaviour here has made himself very acceptable, and that his promotion will be very much liked; and he has on all occasions been very diligent at the council to advance his Majesty's service there. And he and I have always had a perfect agreement together. We are to have a council to-morrow, against which time his patent will be got ready, and we shall there deliver him the seals.

Since the arrival of this news my Lord Chief Justice Whitshed has been with me, to desire he may be recommended to succeed Lord Chief Justice Wyndham in the Common Pleas. He complains, that he finds the business of his present station very fatiguing as he advances in life, and says the two stations are about the same value; but the Common Pleas is a place of less trouble: he represents that he has with great zeal and fidelity served his Majesty, and made himself many enemies by so doing, and would hope for this favour as a reward of his services.

I must do him the justice to say, that he has certainly served his Majesty with great zeal and affection, and has drawn on himself the anger of the Jacobites by so doing, and the malice of other discontented persons here, by discountenancing seditious writings in the affair of the half-pence: and if we may have another person of worth from England to succeed him, I think he may deserve the favour he desires. But I hope the filling up two of the Chief Justices places with persons from England, is a point that will not be departed from notwithstanding.

I thank your Lordship for the kind assurances you give me of supporting Mr. Stephens in the promise made me on his behalf.

I am, &c.

To Lord Carteret.

Dublin, Dec. 21, 1726.

My Lord,

We have at last gone through the affair of the coin, and sent our desire to his Majesty, which we hope will somewhat alleviate our present calamity.

The substance is, putting gold coins and English silver on the current bottom they pass for in England, so as to leave no temptation to any trader to carry out English silver from hence, or import gold hither preferably to silver. As to the advance made on foreign silver, it is but one half-penny in a piece of eight, above its current value in English money, and can be of no consequence to any in England, but to such as want to buy it up as bullion for exportation, and to them it will be no great matter. It has been with some difficulty that we have been able to manage things so well, and to keep off meddling with English silver, and trying to get the advantage of England; as likewise to prevent the addressing for a mint to be established here. We have avoided any calculations, both to prevent our request being sent to the officers of the mint, and running a length of time there; and because we were satisfied no calculation of ours could give any light or be of any weight on your side of the water. If in this particular we have not complied with the very words of your Excellency's letter to us, I am sure we have done our best to answer your intentions, which were to assign the most proper methods to remove the great want of silver here that were likely to be granted us from England.

Your Excellency knows very well the great scarcity of silver here, when you left us, and I can assure you it has gone on increasing to the great detriment of trade, among the lower people and manufacturers, and to the putting all degrees under great difficulties to find money for common marketing; and without some speedy remedy the evil will be of dangerous consequence here. We must therefore beg of your Excellency, out of your tender regard to this kingdom, to press for a speedy relief: your known goodness and your particular knowledge of our case, make it needless to add any thing farther, on this occasion. I am, with the greatest and most sincere respect,

My Lord, &c.

To the same.

Dublin, Dec. 22, 1726.

My Lord,

I have received the honour of your Excellency's of the 13th, and am very glad his Majesty has made so good a choice of a new Chancellor, and do not doubt the public business being perfectly well carried on by him. I had great hopes when I wrote on that occasion, that my sentiments agreed with your Lordship's, as your Lordship had for so long been an eye witness of my Lord Chief Justice's behaviour, and of the satisfaction he gave here. He was yesterday admitted Lord Chancellor in council.

Since the arrival of the messenger, my Lord Chief Justice Whitshed has been with me, and desired I would write in his behalf, that he might succeed Lord Chief Justice Wyndham in the Common Pleas; he thinks his present place is about the same value, but complains of the great fatigue of it, as he advances in years; and he pleads his faithful services to the crown: your Lordship knows better than I that he has served his Majesty very faithfully, and that in some very troublesome affairs; and that he has by so doing made himself many enemies here; and if he could be made easy, so that we had an Englishman of worth to succeed him, it would be very well; and what he desires is a reasonable compensation of his past services. But I hope it will be a point still kept up to have two English chiefs amongst the judges: the whole I submit to your Lordship's better judgement.

I have this day seen my Lord Chief Baron, who thanks your Excellency for your kind remembrance of him on the late remove, but is disposed to keep in his present post.

It is talked here that there is one solliciting for an advancement on this occasion, whose success would not be pleasing here. I have this day seen the Attorney General, and find if there were to be a vacancy in the King's Bench, he would not care to remove thither.

I shall speedily answer your Excellency's of the 17th.

I am, &c.

To the same.

Dublin, Dec. 26, 1726.

My Lord,

On Thursday last the messenger brought me the honour of your Excellency's of the 17th, and I think not only myself but the generality here are very well pleased with the choice his Majesty has made of a Chancellor and Lord Justice. I believe Mr. Wyndham will give great satisfaction in both posts, and from the experience I have had of him already in public business, I am satisfied we shall act with a perfect agreement.

I am obliged to your Lordship for setting the least value upon my friendship, and shall always esteem it one of the happinesses of my life to continue in your Lordship's good graces.

I have been to wait on Mrs. West, to assure her of your Excellency's kind intentions to procure her some favour from his Majesty: but as she sees nobody, I was not admitted, but I have taken care to let her know how kind your Excellency is to her. We were all sworn Lords Justices on Friday last. Mr. Conolly is gone into the country for the holidays.

As Chappel-izod[37] is now at liberty, I have thoughts, with your Excellency's good liking, to borrow it for a country-house, as I cannot hope to make much use of my house at Drogheda. I heartily wish your Excellency a happy new year, and many of them. I am, my Lord, with the utmost truth and respect,

Your Excellency's &c.

37 A palace belonging to the King, adjoining to the Phoenix park near Dublin.

To the Duke of Newcastle.

Dublin, Jan. 2, 1726/7.

My Lord,

The Archbishop of Cashel died this morning, about five o'clock, after a few days indisposition from a cold. The person I would recommend to succeed to Cashel, and who is willing to remove is the Bishop of Derry;[38] to whose bishoprick I would recommend the Bishop of Meath[39] as a successor; and to his bishoprick the bishop of Dromore; and to his Dr. Cobb, Bishop of Killala. If the scheme goes on thus far, I would recommend Dr. Skirret for the bishoprick of Killalla; and if he is not pitched upon, Dr. Howard, Dean of Ardagh.

If it be thought proper to send some Bishop from England to Cashel, Derry, or Meath, I should be sorry if any should be sent because of his little worth or troublesomeness there, for such an one will do the English interest a great deal of mischief here, and I hope it will be considered whether he be one that is likely to agree with me.

I am, &c.

P. S. I have reason to believe the Bishop of Derry will not be fond of removing to Cashel, if the Bishop of Meath be not thought of for his successor; and in that case the Bishop of Kilmore and Ardagh[40] is a very proper person to remove to Cashel; and either the Bishop of Dromore or Fernes, to Kilmore; or in that case, Kilmore and Ardagh is worth the acceptance of an English Bishop, being reckoned at better than 2000l. per annum.

To Lord Carteret.

Dublin, Jan. 2, 1726/7.

My Lord,

Yesterday morning died the Archbishop of Cashel, after a few days indisposition from a cold. Last winter I had the honour of talking over with your Excellency what removes on the Bench might be proper, in case of his death. As all then mentioned were approved by your Lordship, and are still alive, I would still recommend for the translations then talked of; the Bishop of Derry to the Archbishoprick of Cashel, the Bishop of Meath to the bishoprick of Derry; the Bishop of Dromore to the bishoprick of Meath; and

38 Dr. Nicholson.
39 Dr. Downes.
40 Dr. Godwin; he was soon afterwards appointed, another vacancy having happened, by the unexpected death of Archbishop Nicholson.

the Bishop of Killala to the bishoprick of Dromore. If the scheme goes on this far, I would recommend Dr. Skirret to succeed to the bishoprick of Killala; and if he is not pitched upon, Dean Howard; and if he has Killalla, I hope your Excellency will remember Mr. Synge for part of the Dean's preferments.

If it be thought proper to break this scheme, by sending some Bishop from the Bench in England to Cashel, Derry, or Meath; I hope we shall not have one sent for being troublesome or good for nothing there; and I hope, regard will be had to his being likely or unlikely to agree with me. I remember I have in conversation mentioned two that I should not desire to see here; one for the restlessness of his temper, the other for the great liberties he was pleased to take with my character upon my being made Primate.

If it should not be thought proper to remove the Bishop of Meath to Derry, I am satisfied the Bishop of Derry had rather continue where he is; and in that case the Bishop of Kilmore is a proper person to remove to Cashel; and either the Bishop of Dromore or Fernes to Kilmore; and the Bishop of Killalla to Dromore or Fernes: I must own I think it would keep things more easy here, if the Archbishoprick should be bestowed on a Bishop here.

I heartily wish your Excellency many happy new years, and am,
My Lord, &c.

To Lord Carteret.

Dublin, Jan. 3, 1726/7.

My Lord,

I this day received your Excellency's of the 20th of December, and am entirely of your Lordship's opinion, that what his Majesty is graciously pleased to do for Mr. West's family should be in trust for his widow and children: Mrs. West's conduct since my Lord Chancellor's death, has so far given countenance to some whispers which went about before, that though his Lordship's death was very much lamented, it is not so popular here to do much for his widow. His son I believe is pretty well secured by the marriage settlement, and by a voluntary settlement the late Chancellor told me his father had made on him and the grandson after his decease; but I fear no provision at all is made for the daughter. I shall talk with some others about the quantum, and the best method of doing it: and shall afterwards acquaint your Lordship with the result of their sentiments.

Colonel Cornwallis this day brought your Excellency's orders relating to the embarkation of the two regiments for Gibraltar, and we immediately gave all the necessary orders on that occasion, and have dispatched an express to Colonel Parker, with his orders and a letter of credit. We are now expecting General Macartney with the orders relating to the other four regiments, till whose arrival we can do nothing more than we have done, which is stopping the ordinary payments in the treasury, that we may have money to clear the several regiments to be embarked, and answer what other disbursements this service may call for. As soon as he comes, we shall hasten all the proper orders.

The Archbishop of Cashel dying last Sunday morning, we have by a messenger yesterday, sent your Excellency what recommendations we thought proper on that occasion; and I trouble you with a letter in particular.

To the same.

Dublin, Jan. 5, 1726/7.

My Lord,

Since I had the honour of writing last to your Excellency, Mr. Proby a clergyman is dead, and the living of Loughcrew in the diocese of Meath, being in the King's gift, is at the disposal of your Excellency. My Lord Chancellor has a relation here a clergyman, one Mr. John Willoughby, in recommending whom we shall join next Saturday. But as your Excellency might in the mean time have a letter from some other hand, I give you the trouble of this, to prevent the effects of a more early application than we can make jointly.

I am, &c.

To the Duke of Newcastle,

Dublin, Jan. 5, 1726/7.

My Lord,

As we talk here that some new regiments will be raised, Colonel Cavalier[41] was with me today, to desire I would recommend him to be put in commission on this occasion. I told him it was wholly out of my way to recommend to the army, but as he had very much distinguished himself abroad in the last war, I would venture to take the liberty to acquaint your Grace that he is alive, and very willing to serve his Majesty if a war comes on.

I am, &c.

41 He was a French officer, who wrote his own Memoirs, and the History of the Civil Wars, in the Cevennes, in the reign of Lewis XIV.

Newcastle to Boulter.

Whitehall, Jan. 12, 1726/7.
(NA. SP. 63/388/160)

My Lord,

I have received the honour of your Grace's letter of the 2nd Instant, and laid it before the King, and your Grace will find of what weight your opinion and recommendation is with his Majesty and His servants, by the list of promotions on the Bishop's Bench in Ireland upon the death of the Archbishop of Cashel, which is exactly what you proposed.

I mentioned Dr. Skirret to My Lord Lieutenant for the Deanery of Ardagh, which will become vacant by Dr. Howard's succeeding to the Bishoprick of Killala, but his Excellency seemed to have some other intentions. I shall be glad to serve Dr. Skirret upon a proper occasion, and I shall endeavour to approve myself with great truth and regard.

My Lord etc.
Holles Newcastle

To Lord Carteret.

Dublin, Jan. 16, 1726.

My Lord,

I have had the honour of your Excellency's of the 7th, and I hope that if my Lord Chief Justice Whitshed is removed to the Common Pleas, we shall have one from England sent to the King's Bench.

I am glad the Bishops are likely to be made according to the scheme settled with your Excellency when you was here. I am obliged to your Excellency for your kind manner of granting me the use of Chappel-izod.

We have given the necessary orders for making the computation for filling the army, and shall return it with all possible speed.

Mr. Williams[42] was with me last night from Mrs. West, to desire me to write to your Excellency to forward the settling some pension on her and her children. I am pretty well satisfied all the effects Mr. West has left, will do little more than answer his debts on both sides of the water. But as I am settled here, I do not care to meddle in any thing of a pension, that I apprehend will not be so popular as I could wish, for the sake of my deceased friend. As your Lordship cannot but be sensible of the clamours that will be raised upon the English here, if any of his Irish creditors should go unpaid, I could wish the trustees of the pension may have a power of

42 Secretary to the late Chancellor West.

applying part of the pension to pay those debts, if there should be any fear of those creditors being neglected.

I am, my Lord, &c.

To the same.

Dublin, Jan. 17, 1726/7.

My Lord,

As we are likely to have thirty-four new companies raised upon this establishment, I take this opportunity to put your Lordship in mind of Mr. Hayward, whom I recommended formerly to your Lordship for a lieutenant's or captain's commission. I know the new companies are to be supplied with officers out of the half-pay list here: but as several on that list are too old to serve, there may be room for him on this occasion: if there be, I shall take it as a great obligation if your Lordship will be so kind as to remember him.

I am, my Lord, &c.

To the Duke of Newcastle.

Dublin, Jan. 21, 1726/7.

My Lord,

I have had the honour of your Grace's of the 12th, and am extremely obliged to his Majesty and the ministry for the weight they have been pleased to give my recommendations with his Majesty upon the vacancy of the Archbishoprick of Cashel. I can assure your Grace I had no other view in the several parts of that scheme, than promoting his Majesty's service, by obliging a number of persons that are all very well affected, and will, I doubt not fill their respective new stations, to the satisfaction of his Majesty's friends here.

I thank your Grace for recommending Dr. Skirret to my Lord Lieutenant for the deanery of Ardagh; but nothing here that is not considerably better than what he enjoys in England can be of service to him, since by the laws of this country, he must quit whatever he has in England, to be capable of taking any thing here.

I am, &c.

To Lord Carteret.

Dublin, Jan. 21, 1726/7.

My Lord,

There is one Lieutenant John Cunningham, in Colonel Haye's regiment, who was recommended to me by the Bishop of Fernes, to be my gentleman usher: I find he has been eighteen years a lieutenant, and has on all occasions shewn his zeal for his Majesty and his family: he is gone to Gibraltar with his regiment; but as there are two companies to be added to that and the other regiments of foot left on our establishment, if the list of captains on the half-pay here should not furnish out captains enough that are proper for the thirty-four additional companies, I should be obliged to your Excellency to think of him for a captain's commission, in some of them, and his place may be filled by some lieutenant on the half-pay.

To the Archbishop of Canterbury.

Dublin, Jan. 24, 1726/7.

My Lord,

I thank your Grace for your opinion about matrimonial cases, which I had done sooner, but that your letter has been mislaid.

I find by the King's speech and addresses of both houses, with the other accounts of things, that it is very probable we shall have a war, since there seems to be nothing wanting on the part of our adversaries, but money. I must own I am not so angry on this occasion with the King of Spain for his breach of faith, as with the Emperor, who on account of the services done him in person and his family, lies under the greatest obligations possible to the kingdom of England.

As it is possible the present prospect of affairs may bring on a publick fast in England, which will likewise be attended with a fast here, I should be very glad in such a case to have the same form of prayer used here as in England, as has been generally practised; but then it will be of some consequence to have that form as soon as may be, that we may print it here, and have our fast as near the day appointed in England as we can.

I must on this occasion desire the favour of your Grace to furnish me with such a form, if there should be a fast, and to let me know before-hand in what time after the fast is once fixed, I may hope to receive it. As what is particular on such occasions is only proper psalms, lessons, collects, gospel and epistle, with some few responses, an account of them may be easily transmitted with a letter, as soon as they are fixed in England, without staying for a printed copy.

I am, &c.

To the Duke of Newcastle.

Dublin, Jan. 26, 1726/7.

My Lord,

As his Grace of Dublin[43] has of late been pretty much out of order, though I cannot hear for certain that he is in any great danger, several letters may go from hence representing him as dying. That such accounts may not occasion any hasty measures being taken, I must beg leave to suggest, that the archbishoprick is a place of very great importance, and a good agreement betwixt the Primate and the Archbishop is of great consequence to the English interest here; I would therefore humbly intreat that no steps may be taken about appointing his successor, upon any rumours of his death, till my representations on that subject are considered, which I shall not fail to be speedy in sending, whenever it pleases God to remove his Grace. I am,

Your Grace's, &c.

To Lord Carteret.

Dublin, Jan. 26, 1726/7.

My Lord,

I have had the honour of your Excellency's of the 21st, and as far as I can hear, the late promotions on the Bishop's bench are very agreeable to the generality; I have not heard of any who has found fault with them but the Archbishop of Dublin. As his Grace is at present very ill, it is possible there may be occasion for speedily thinking of a successor for him. If it pleases God to remove him, your Excellency shall have my thoughts by the first opportunity. I shall take the first time that offers to tell the new Bishop of Meath what your Excellency says: I believe he is very sensible how very much he is obliged to your Lordship for his translation, and that if the recommendations or wishes of some in power here could have prevailed, that bishoprick had gone another way.

I can guess at the solicitations your Lordship must have about Dean Howard's preferments, by the share I have had here to get me to write to your Excellency about them.

I have enquired about St. Werburg's, and am told the value of it is about 250l. per ann. and St. Audoen's, which Mr. Synge now has, is near 200l. per ann. But though the removing to St. Werburg's without Finglass, will be no great advancement in point of profit, yet as it is a more creditable post, and has been usually a step to a bishoprick, and as Mr. Synge is engaged in a great quarrel with his present parishioners, I believe he will hardly refuse to

43 Dr. King.

remove to St. Werburg's alone; and as your Excellency observes, he may have it made up another time: as to his living of St. Audoen, by his promotion it will come to the disposal of the Archbishop of Dublin, and whether he will give it to Mr. Ward I cannot tell; indeed if his Grace should drop, and Mr. Synge be removed during the vacancy, St. Audoen's will come to your Excellency's disposal.

I have not had an opportunity of enquiring of the Bishop of Fernes about Mr. Saurin, whom I do not know, but have heard much of his brother at the Hague.

I know Mr. Mitchel very well, and take him to be a worthy gentleman, and think as he does, that some other trustee would be more proper than Mr. Williams.

I am sorry Mr. West's circumstances come out so bad; that his widow and children do certainly want some help; but as we reckon he must have received above 6000l. by his being Lord Chancellor, it is hardly believed here that he could worst his circumstances by coming hither.

Beside the parish of Drogheda, Dr. Wye who is lately dead, was possessed of the parish of Dunleer in that neighbourhood, and of two or three little parishes that were supposed to be united to Dunleer, which is in the gift of one Mr. Tenison, who derives his title from the Lord Dartmouth: upon Dr. Wye's death it comes out that my Lord Dartmouth had only a grant of the patronage of Dunleer from the crown, and that the patronage of some or all the other parishes does not appear to have been granted away by the crown, in whom it was by the forfeiture of the old patrons; that Dr. Wye was presented to Dunleer by my lord Dartmouth, before he parted with the estate there, that the Dr. having no competitor, took the other parishes, which had been enjoyed by his predecessor, and held them till death: but as it does not appear that those parishes have ever been united as the law directs, or that the right of the crown, if any union was, has been considered and settled by having a proper share of turns, a caveat is entered with me, to institute nobody either to Dunleer or the supposed union, till enquiry is made what is the true state of this affair: and I would beg of your Excellency not to make any promise of the King's turn to the whole or any part of that supposed union, till the affair is better understood. As this discovery is made by Dr. Wye's family, who has left eight or nine children unprovided for, and one of them a clergyman of sober life and good character, (who was his father's curate at Dunleer) your Excellency will be pleased to consider how far it may be proper to do somewhat for him, if those livings or some of them should appear to be in the gift of the crown.

I am, &c.

To the Duke of Newcastle.

Dublin, Feb. 2, 1726/7.

My Lord,

Since I had the honour of giving your Grace an account of the Archbishop of Dublin's illness, he has been for some days thought past recovery, but is now looked upon by all to be out of danger for the present; if any alteration should happen, I will give your Grace advice of it.

I am sorry that we had occasion to send off a flying packet last night to my Lord Lieutenant, with an account that the men of war and transports designed for Gibraltar are driven back to Cork, and that two of the transports are missing, and one of the men of war disabled for present service: I would hope by the news from England this day, that those forces will not be wanted at Gibraltar so soon as was apprehended.

I am, my Lord, &c.

To Lord Townshend.

Dublin, Feb. 2, 1726/7.

My Lord,

It is a great pleasure to all his Majesty's friends here to hear what vigour and resolution both houses of parliament shew in defence of his Majesty, and the support of those wise measures he has taken in the perplexed state of affairs into which the union betwixt the Emperor and Spain has brought all Europe.

I am too sensible of the great load of business your Lordship must have on your hands at such a juncture, to trouble you about so small an affair as is the subject of this letter, without first begging your pardon; but I hope the concern I have for my friend will be thought a just excuse.

I have advices from several hands, that some are forming schemes to put Mr. Stephens by the next canonry of Christ Church which may become vacant, under the specious pretence of an equivalent.

As the first promise was made me for him near three years ago, upon my giving way to Dr. Foulkes having the next turn there, which he has since had, and was again renewed to me before I left England, I must put myself under your Lordship's care for having a specifick performance of the canonry promised Mr. Stephens.

Whoever they are that make a push for their friends in opposition to him, I am sure they cannot have a greater zeal for his Majesty's service than I have; and I question whether they are in posts where they have greater opportunities of serving his Majesty than the station his Majesty has been graciously pleased to bestow on me; and I hope I have not been behind them in the success I have had in my endeavours to promote his Majesty's service here. Mr. Stephens is the only clergyman I shall desire to be provided for in England by his Majesty's favour; and I intreat your Lordship to support the promise you was so good as to make me.

I am, &c.

To Lord Carteret.

Dublin, Feb. 9, 1726/7.

My Lord,

I received your Excellency's kind letter of the 2d instant, and am very much obliged to your Lordship for your friendship in relation to the filling up of the archbishoprick of Dublin whenever it happens to be vacant: your Lordship was very good in the discourse you had with one of the ministers, and I hope they will consider what you represented, that it will be for his Majesty's service to appoint such an Archbishop as I can depend upon for acting in concert with me. I am entirely of opinion that the new Archbishop ought to be an Englishman, either already on the bench here, or in England: as for a native of this country, I can hardly doubt but whatever his behaviour has been or his promises may be, when he is once in that station, he will put himself at he head of the Irish interest in the church at least; and he will naturally carry with him the college and most of the clergy here. I am satisfied the person Mr. Conolly wants to have in that station, is the Bishop of Elphin, whom your Excellency knows as well as I do. As for one on the bench in England, I hope the ministry will never think of sending any body hither, because he is restless there, since his restlessness there will have no consequence to the publick, but he may here be sure of a dissatisfied party to head.

His Grace of Dublin tells every body the bishop of Bristol has a promise of being his successor, which I should be very sorry to find true.

Since the Archbishop's illness I have talked with the new Bishop of Derry,[44] and acquainted him what your Excellency had told me formerly of your kind intentions in relation to him, for which he expressed the greatest thankfulness, but said, he was by his late translation made so very easy, that he should desire to be excused from any farther remove; which I find were your Lordship's thoughts about him.

About ten days ago I wrote to a Bishop in England, and another in Ireland, to know their thoughts about removing to Dublin, if a vacancy should happen, but have not yet received any answer from either of them: what I

---

44 Dr. Downes, father of Dr. Downes, late Bishop of Raphoe, a son who even did honour to such a father.

proposed to myself was to be able to lay down two schemes, either for one of the bench here or one in England to have Dublin, as soon as I could have settled upon receiving their answers, and to leave it to the ministry to judge which they thought most proper: as soon as I hear from them, I shall be able to write more explicitly to your Excellency, and do in the mean time desire your friendship, that nobody may be pitched upon who may make me uneasy, since that cannot be done without disserving his Majesty.

His Grace is rather better than he has been; but it is very uncertain whether he may ever come abroad again.

I am satisfied there will be a good deal of murmuring here to see the archbishoprick filled with an Englishman, but I think it is a post of that consequence, as to be worth filling aright, though it should occasion murmuring.

I thank your Lordship for keeping yourself on the reserve about Dunleer, till that affair is better cleared up, and your disposition to consider young Wye if there be room for it.

We have a report here that Mr. Saurin is to have the chancellorship of St. Patrick's, which as it is either inseperably annexed to St. Werburg's, or will leave St. Werburg's not worth Mr. Synge's removing to, if it can be separated from it, I suspect to be a mistake for the chantorship of Christ Church.

I had yesterday a letter from Mrs. West,[45] that she hears from London, that the pension to be granted her is likely to be only during pleasure; she is very willing to take it so, rather than have the affair delayed for any length of time, but would be very glad if it might be obtained, as was at first proposed, for a certain term of years; and seems very apprehensive that upon her death, without a fresh application of friends, it might drop in the new way; I sent her word, that a great many pensions on this establishment, granted only during pleasure, were paid as regularly for many years, as if they had been first granted for a certain term; and that as the pension was to be vested in trustees, her death I thought would make no change if the children were then living, but that I would write to your Excellency in her behalf, to get the most advantageous grant for her.

I must before I conclude, beg pardon of your Excellency for giving you the trouble of so long a letter, and am, with the greatest respect and truth,

My Lord, &c.

P. S. I had forgot to mention to your Excellency that as the Bishop of Derry's patent was not past till this week, I believe he cannot receive the Candlemas rents of that bishoprick without a letter from the treasury in England on his behalf; I remember I had such a letter at my coming hither for the Lammas rents of the primacy: as they amount to near 600l. which is a sum of conse-

---

45 Widow of the late Chancellor of that name.

quence to his Lordship, I beg leave to recommend his case to your Excellency for obtaining this favour for him. In England there is a clause of course in the patent for the restitution of temporalities to any Bishop giving him the profits or rent that became due during the vacancy.

To the Archbishop of Canterbury.

Dublin, Feb. 16, 1726/7.

My Lord,

I have received your Grace's favour of the 7th, and thank you for your kind promise of sending me a copy of the prayers for a fast in MS. as soon as the thing is fixed. I do not wonder that we at this distance are unable to judge whether we are to have peace or war, when those at the helm, who know all that passes, are at a loss to know which we shall have. The reasons of the conduct of Great-Britain are reprinted here, and have given great satisfaction to his Majesty's friends: as for others nothing can satisfy them.

Our late promotions on the bench have been generally well approved of, and the more as two natives of this country have been considered in them.

His Grace of Dublin has been very ill, but seems now to have got over the present shock. I wish his place may be well filled, whenever it pleases God to remove him. I am sorry to hear your Grace has been out of order this winter, but hope the approaching spring will entirely set you up. I thank you for your kind wishes, and am with the greatest sincerity and respect,

My Lord, &c.

To the Duke of Newcastle.

Dublin, Feb. 18, 1726/7.

My Lord,

We were yesterday surprized with the melancholy news that the new Archbishop of Cashel,[46] on Tuesday morning last died of an apoplexy at the palace at Londonderry. I am very sorry we have lost so learned and worthy a man.

We have been very much teased with applications on this occasion: the Bishop of Kildare, who is the oldest Bishop on the bench here, except the Archbishop of Dublin, would willingly remove thither; I must do him the justice to say, he is an hearty Englishman, and I believe a thorough enemy

46 Dr. William Nicholson, author of an English, Scotch and Irish Historical Library. He was translated from Carlisle to Derry, and from thence to Cashel, and died the month following.

to the pretender, his only fault is, that he is rather counted a tory here: if he were thought of, the bishoprick[47] of Kildare and deanery of Christ Church will come to be disposed of: if he is not thought of, and the archbishoprick of Cashel be filled from hence, I should recommend the Bishop of Kilmore[48] for Cashel, the Bishop of Fernes[49] for Kilmore, and the Bishop of Clonfert for Fernes; and out of consideration of his brother Sir Ralph Gore, Chancellor of the Exchequer, the Dean of Down for the bishoprick of Clonfert.

But as we are now but nine English Bishops on the bench here out of two and twenty; I must inform your Grace that I think it would be for his Majesty's service to fill Cashel from the bench in England, or to send one from England to the bishoprick vacant by any translations made here: if the first is done I hope nobody will be sent hither from the bench in England for being restless or good for nothing there, or who is not likely to agree with me, since this will certainly weaken the English interest here. If the latter method be taken, I hope a divine of some character will be sent hither, since the encouragement is not contemptible, Kildare and Christ Church being worth 1600l. per ann. and Clonfert worth better than 1200l. per ann.

I hope likewise that whatever recommendations go from hence, none but a native of England will be thought of for Cashel.

I am, my Lord, &c.

To Lord Carteret.

Dublin, Feb. 18, 1726/7.

My Lord,

We had yesterday the melancholy news that the Archbishop of Cashel died of an apoplexy on Tuesday morning last at Londonderry. I am afraid his family will lose about 500l. by his late translation.

Upon this vacancy of the Archbishoprick, the Bishop of Kildare has been with me and the other Lords Justices, and desires to be considered as being the oldest bishop on the bench except his Grace of Dublin: he is upon all occasions a most hearty Englishman, and I believe an enemy to the pretender; but your Excellency knows he is rather a tory.

The Bishop of Kilmore is the next Englishman, that may be thought of, and I scarce doubt but he would take Cashel, though he is not here to be asked the question.

---

47 Dr. Welbore Ellis.
48 Dr. Timothy Godwin.
49 Dr. Josiah Hort.

The Bishop of Fernes would either take Cashel, if the Bishop of Kilmore should be unwilling to remove, or take Kilmore if he accepts Cashel.

The Bishop of Clonfert would be very glad to succeed the Bishop of Fernes, though he will hardly gain any thing by the remove; but as he has the rectory of Louth in commendam, which whenever he leaves it, will fall into the vicarage, and not come to the government to dispose of, he would desire to keep that, without having the commendam the present Bishop of Fernes enjoys: and in this case there will be a benefice of 290l. per ann. to be given either as a commendam to the new Bishop of Clonfert, or as your Excellency shall judge proper.

For the bishoprick of Clonfert there are several who would gladly succeed to it. Dean Daniel, Dean Dobbins, Dean Cross, but as Sir Ralph Gore has been with the Lords Justices to recommend his brother the Dean of Down to the bishoprick that shall be left vacant upon other translations, and answers for his brother's behaviour: I think it will be most adviseable to gratify Sir Ralph Gore.

But if the Bishop of Kildare should be translated to Cashel, I could wish some Englishman were to succeed him; and if it were one that would be a proper person to succeed to Dublin upon a vacancy it would be the less invidious, but in that view it ought to be one from the bench in England, which it may very well be, since Kildare and Christ Church are a good 1600l. per annum.

Though the Bishop of Elphin is mentioned in our common letter, and probably Mr. Conolly may write in his behalf, yet I believe your Excellency will be of my opinion, that it will be too dangerous a step to trust him in that post.

My Lord Chancellor and I have been computing, that if some person be not now brought over from England to the bench, there will be thirteen Irish[50] to nine English Bishops here, which we think will be a dangerous situation.

Upon the encouragement your Excellency has given me, I take the liberty to acquaint you, that the oldest friend I have on the bench in England, is Dr. Smalbroke, Bishop of St. David's, and that I should be very glad to see him here; he has heard very ill reports of the air of Dublin, and been frighted with

50 February,1770. At this time there are but two archbishops, natives of Ireland, Dr. Arthur Smith of Dublin, and Dr. Michael Cox of Cashel. The six suffragan bishops, are, the honourable and right reverend Dr. Henry Maxwell, of Meath, Dr. Jemmet Browne, of Cork, Dr. Nicholas Synge, of Killaloo, Dr. James Leslie, of Limerick, Dr. William Gore, of Elphin, and Dr. Charles Agar, of Cloyne. There was at one time in the Houses of Lords of Ireland, a majority of native bishops; all of whom were gentlemen of good families, of the greatest charity, piety and learning, among which were five, who had been fellows of the university, to wit, Dr. Howard of Elphin, Dr. Edward Synge, of Clonfert, Dr. Clayton, of Cork, Dr. Whetcombe, Archbishop of Cashel, and Dr. Berkeley, Bishop of Cloyne.

paying down 2000l. for buildings on that archbishoprick. But possibly he may not be afraid of Cashel, which is most certainly in a good air, and where there is nothing to pay. I shall by this post write to him, to wait on your Excellency to deliver his own sentiments.

I should be satisfied if the Bishop of Glocester or Bangor were sent hither either on this occasion, or to Dublin when it falls, but I have formerly mentioned two[51] on the bench to your Lordship, whom I should be sorry to see here.

I am, &c.

To the Bishop of London.

Dublin, Feb. 18, 1726/7.

My Lord,

I am sorry that I have occasion to acquaint your Lordship, that your very good friend the Archbishop of Cashel, was on Tuesday morning last found dead on the floor in his room at Londonderry: we have lost a very worthy man, and I fear his family will lose 500l. by his late translation. The scheme I would recommend if the Archbishoprick of Cashel is to be filled up from hence, is the Bishop of Kilmore to have Cashel, the Bishop of Fernes to have Kilmore, and the Bishop of Clonfert to have Fernes, and on account of the worth and interest of his brother Sir Ralph Gore, Chancellor of the Exchequer here, the Dean of Down to have the bishoprick of Clonfert.

But I must own as by the death of Archbishop Nicholson there are but nine English Bishops on the bench here, and by this scheme there will be thirteen Irish, I cannot but think it will be most for his Majesty's service either to send one from the bench in England to Cashel or Kilmore, (which latter is worth about 2000l. per ann.) or else to put an Englishman into Clonfert, that the English interest may not decrease here. Your Lordship knows the oldest friend I have on the bench is the Bishop of St. David's, whom I should be glad to see here; but I hope if he is not sent, no person will be sent hither for being restless and uneasy there, or good for nothing, or that is not likely to agree with me.

The Bishop of Kildare would gladly go to Cashel, who is the senior on the bench, except the Archbishop of Dublin; he is a hearty Englishman, and I believe an utter enemy to the pretender, but he is counted a tory here. If he should be translated to Cashel, his bishoprick and the deanery of Christ Church are worth an Englishman's coming for, being a good 1600l. per ann.

Mr. Saul, formerly of Magdalen College, and in your Lordship's former diocese of Lincoln, would I do not question willingly take the bishoprick of

51 The Bishop of Bristol was certainly one of the two.

Clonfert, which is better than 1200l. per ann. or Kildare and Christ Church; your Lordship knows him very well, but I should be sorry to have some weak person sent hither.

As I do not know but very pressing instances may be made from hence, to have the Bishop of Elphin[52] translated to Cashel, I must acquaint your Lordship that he is an enterprizing man, and I do not doubt but he would soon set himself, if he had that station, at the head of the Irish interest here.[53] I am,

My Lord, &c.

To Lord Carteret.

Dublin, Mar. 7, 1726/7.

My Lord,

I had this day the honour of two of your Excellency's, one of the 21st, the other of the 25th of February last.

Since I wrote to your Lordship about Mr. Wye, Mr. Prime Serjeant has been with me, in favour of a brother of his, who has a living of about 100l. per ann. in my gift, which he would willingly quit for Dunleer, if it be in the gift of the crown. It is not for the advantage in point of profit that he would make the exchange, but that he would come nearer Drogheda, where he was born, and where some of his relations live; he is an elderly batchelor in very good circumstances, and I hope has generosity enough to be persuaded to build a parsonage house at Dunleer, if he had that living.

As I know the regard your Excellency has for the Prime Serjeant, and as I should be willing myself to oblige both him and his brother, and as in this scheme Mr. Wye will have a living with a parsonage house upon it, as there is on Mr. Singleton's present living, I did not discourage the Prime Serjeant from writing to your Lordship in favour of his brother; and if I see Mr. Wye before I know your farther pleasure, I will tell him I have heard from your Excellency, that if Dunleer is in the gift of the crown, some provision shall be made for him.

The Crown-sollicitor has been ordered to attend me, to have instructions from me what enquiries he is to make in the offices, to know whether the crown has a right to Dunleer or not: but he has not yet come near me; I shall endeavour to quicken him, and as soon as we know any thing certain in this affair, we shall acquaint your Lordship with it.

I think his Majesty's grant to Mrs. West is very kind, and though it be

---

52 Dr. Theophilus Bolton, a man of great learning, and vast abilities.
53 He did so when he was afterwards made Archbishop of Cashel, to his great honour, and the benefit of his country.

during pleasure, will probably be continued as long as she lives, or her children can be supposed to want it; and I fear if it had been for a certain term of years, and had not been vested in proper trustees, it had soon been sold for ready money.

As to a memorial from the Bishop of Derry,[54] I remember I had the quarter due in the vacancy granted me, without a memorial. We shall to-morrow acquaint your Lordship with the vacancy of the living in that diocese, of which I thought we had wrote by the same post as the Bishop.

I am very much obliged to your Lordship for the kind discourse you had with the Bishop of St. David's, and find him not so much afraid of Ireland as he was before; when I have sent him some particulars about the archbishoprick of Dublin, which he wants to know, I believe he will be very well satisfied about taking Dublin if he can, when it falls; and I shall be very much obliged to your Excellency for your kind concurrence on that occasion.

I find[55] your Lordship of different sentiments from what I have about filling Cashel; I should have been very glad if it had fallen at any time when I could have had a personal conference with you on that subject. I rather think the Bishop of Elphin should be kept longer in a state of probation; I am satisfied his great friend is Mr. Conolly, and that most of those who sollicited here for him, were set on by him; but it is with great satisfaction that I find you think it is not convenient to place him in the see of Dublin; and indeed I think none but a native of England ought to be in that station.

I shall cheerfully shew what countenance I can to the gentlemen you are pleased to name for the Bishop of Killala's preferments, particularly to Mr. Saurin, who as being a stranger, will most want it. We shall to-morrow give the necessary orders about dispatching their instruments. I am,

Your Excellency's, &c.

To Lord Carteret.

Dublin, Mar. 11, 1726/7.

My Lord,

The occasion of my troubling your Excellency at this time, is to put you in mind that it is generally the custom for the Bishop of Meath to be one of the Privy Council here, which if your Lordship approves of, a warrant might soon be sent to admit the new Bishop.

I have lately had some discourse with some officers here, who are under great apprehensions of the difficulty there will be of raising in England the additional men designed for the several companies here, after the English

---

54 Dr. Henry Downs, who was translated from Meath to this Bishoprick.
55 My Lord Primate's opinion prevailed at this time.

levies are made, and the summer is come on: and they think if care was taken to admit none into the service but protestants, who are the sons of protestants, it might be very easy to raise the number wanted in the north of this kingdom, out of persons very well affected to his Majesty. As our foot is now reduced to eleven battalions, and there can be no doubt but the emissaries of Spain are at work here to dispose the papists to make a disturbance; if this method were approved of, we might soon have our battalions full, to our greater security.

I am, my Lord, &c.

To the Duke of Newcastle.

Dublin, Mar. 11, 1726/7.

My Lord,

I have of late been talking with several officers of the army, who are very apprehensive, that considering the great levies of men now making in England, and that the summer comes on apace, it will be very difficult to raise the number of men with which our companies are to be augmented, if they are allowed to beat up for volunteers only in Great Britain: and they humbly think that if leave were given to raise men in this country, and none to be admitted but such as can have good certificates of their being protestants themselves, and that their parents were likewise protestants, it would be easy in a short time to raise the number wanted here, in the north of this kingdom, of men hearty and zealous for his Majesty and his family.

As we have no more than eleven battalions of foot left in this kingdom, it would be of service towards keeping things quiet here, to have our companies augmented as soon as may be; and it would likewise discourage the papists from too hastily listening to the emissaries of Spain, who are no doubt at present very busy amongst them, and giving them hopes of some disturbance here.

I thought it my duty to transmit to your Grace what is suggested here, as proper for his Majesty's service, but with an entire submission to better judges.

I am, my Lord, &c.

To the Bishop of London.

Dublin, Mar. 16, 1726/7.

My Lord,

I have troubled your Lordship but with one letter about the archbishoprick of Cashel, because I supposed that affair would have been soon settled; but as it runs into some length, and we have various reports about it, I shall venture sending this letter, though it may possibly come too late to signify any thing.

All the English here think it will be a dangerous step to make the Bishop of Elphin Archbishop. As to another scheme wrote from England, of sending one from thence either to Kilmore or Fernes, as it will be one who is not on the bench in England, I think he may very well begin with Clonfert, which is worth 1500l. per ann. and hardly 100l. per ann. less than Fernes, and then three on the bench will be obliged here.

I have by me a letter of your Lordship's, which I shall speedily answer.

I am, &c.

To the same.

Dublin, Mar. 18, 1726/7.

My Lord,

Upon Dr. Skirret's making a jest of my having recommended him to Killala, I sent him word that I thought myself discharged from recommending him any more; and I have since given him 100l. to make him amends for his two journies hither; so that I have now done with him.

I do not find we have yet had a new application in form about Mr. Monroe's children; when we have I shall serve them what I can on account of your Lordship's recommendation.

I do not know any thing of the present patent here for printing common prayer books: there is one edition in folio here, that is at least equal to the best in England. If any such application is made as your Lordship mentions, I shall be ready to do any thing that is fair and reasonable for one whom you are pleased to concern yourself for.

We are in great expectation here of what the Commons did last Monday about the Emperor's memorial.

I was in hopes to have heard before this from your Lordship, what is doing about the archbishoprick of Cashel.

I am, &c.

To the Duke of Newcastle.

Dublin, Mar. 30, 1727.

My Lord,

We have lately received his Majesty's commands about augmenting the eleven battalions here, and have given all the necessary orders on that occasion, and have the money ready to advance to the recruiting officers.

By the reports we have here, I am afraid Serjeant Birch will not come hither, but I hope my Lord Chancellor will send us one in his room that is thoroughly well affected.

I was in hopes we should have known his Majesty's pleasure about the Archbishoprick of Cashel before this. As there must have been some rubs in that affair, I could wish your Grace had been at leisure to let me know them, and I might possibly have cleared up any difficulty. I should guess by the flying accounts we have, that the Bishop of Kilmore will be removed to that Archbishoprick: he is the best beloved by his Majesty's friends of any that have been mentioned from England, as standing here in competition for that see, as well as much senior to the others, which used to be a consideration of weight in England; and the English here think it of great consequence that it should be given to an Englishman.

Every thing here is very quiet, except that in spight of all our endeavours, recruits are still going off for Spain as well as France.

A Bill that is going on in England for reversing an outlawry here,[56] gives very great uneasiness, both as it will affect the possessions of several who have been fair purchasers under the faith of an act of parliament here; and as it is looked on as a leading case to others of the same nature, which may shake the property of many hundreds in this nation.

I am, &c.

To Lord Carteret.

Dublin, Mar. 30, 1727.

My Lord,

I had this day the honour of your Excellency's of the 25th; I am sorry I should be guilty of such a neglect as not to date my letter.

I am now pretty well master of what title the crown has to Dunleer, which the Attorney General is persuaded is a very good one. When the Prime Serjeant returns from the circuit, I will talk with him about it, and if his brother is willing to support the title of the crown, as I believe he will, I shall immediately give your Lordship advice of it, in order to receive your commands; and I shall take care of Mr. Wye. When the Attorney General arrives, he will talk with your Lordship about this affair.

Mr. Gardiner has the money ordered for the new levies, ready to advance to the officers, and likewise a month's subsistence for April, part of which will go for levy money.

We have signed the proper orders relating to the pay of the four regiments, from Christmas to Lady-day; and likewise to place a serjeant, corporal,

56 Supposed to be that of Lord Clancarty.

drummer, and twenty-five private men in each company on the military establishment, from Lady-day last.

We have been frequently pressing Mr. Gardiner to get the publick accounts ready to be audited as soon as possible; and he this day told me the remainder of Mr. Prat's accounts, from Christmas, 1724, to the time of his being dismissed, are now engrossing; and that his clerks have almost finished the accounts from thence to Christmas, 1725, which he will soon order to be engrossed; but he thinks that it would save a great deal of trouble, and 300l. to the government, if the accounts from Christmas, 1725, to Lady-day, 1727, were audited at once, and not broke into two audits: but as your Lordship has intimated formerly, you would have them passed from Christmas, 1725, to Lady-day, 1726, and then from Lady-day, 1726, to Lady-day, 1727, we shall make no alteration in that method, without knowing your pleasure. My Lord Chief Baron will set about auditing the remainder of Mr. Prat's accounts as soon as the Barons return from their circuits; and will afterwards make all possible dispatch that the approaching term will allow in auditing the rest of the accounts to Lady-day last.

I am glad to find an alteration is made as to the height of the men required in former levies; since it was thought it would have been pretty difficult to raise the number wanted, if that size had been insisted on.

As the chief reason why a general officer viewed all the recruits as they arrived from England, was to see that they answered that standard, your Excellency will be the best judge, whether there will now be any occasion for sending a general officer to Cork to view the new levies as they arrive there.

I am sorry to hear it reported that Serjeant Birch refuses to come hither, but I hope we shall have another sent us that is thoroughly well affected.

I am, &c.

To the Archbishop of Canterbury.

Dublin, Apr. 1, 1727.

My Lord,

On Monday last Mr. Saurin[57] came to me with your Grace's letter of the 7th past; I recommended him to the Bishop of Kildare, who installed him on Thursday in the chantorship of Christ Church, and is ready to do him what service lies in his power. I am glad to hear so good a character of this gentleman from your Grace, and hope he may be of service in this church. I shall very readily shew him what favour I can.

I fear, notwithstanding some accounts from England flatter us with the

---

57 He was a very worthy French refugee.

hopes of a peace, we shall have a war. The Emperor seems by his carriage to be bent on it, and the Spaniards have now money to carry it on for some time. Whenever a war is declared, and a day of fasting settled in England, I shall expect to be favoured with the form of prayer from your Grace.

What has kept the disposal of the archbishoprick of Cashel so long in suspense I cannot tell: I hope as some accounts suggest, it will be given to the Bishop of Kilmore, who is very well beloved here, and many years senior to those who are talked of as his competitors. We have lost a very valuable and useful person in the late Archbishop of Cashel.[58]

God preserve his Majesty if he commands abroad, and give him good success!

I hope your Grace will recover your strength as the warm weather comes on, and I heartily wish you all health and happiness. I am,

My Lord, &c.

To the Bishop of London,

Dublin, Apr. 1, 1727.

My Lord,

I have received your Lordship's of the 11th past, by Mr. Saurin, and am glad to find he is a gentleman of so good a character; I have recommended him to the Bishop of Kildare, who is ready to do him any service in his power, and has installed him last Thursday in his chantorship. I shall be always ready to shew him what countenance I can.

I hope the Bishop of Kilmore is to go to Cashel, as our most authentick accounts run here; there is not one on the bench better beloved by the King's friends here, and he is several years senior to all who are talked of as his competitors. I should have been glad to have heard from your Lordship pretty early how things were likely to go, but I suppose the uncertainty of what was designed might hinder you from writing.

We a little impatiently expect some news from Gibraltar, though the officers here that have been at that place, give such accounts of it, that we are not apprehensive the Spaniards can take it.

I must desire your Lordship's friendship to Mr. Stephens, in whose behalf I some time since wrote a very pressing Letter to my Lord Townshend.

I am, &c.

---

58 Nicholson.

To Lord Carteret.

Dublin, Apr. 1, 1727.

My Lord,

Though we have in common this day put your Excellency in mind of our being without any guard against Spanish privateers, yet I cannot help farther suggesting, that there is no doubt but that we have too many here who neither want the disposition nor opportunity to give an account of our nakedness to Spain, and that it may be a temptation to the enemy, if it be only for the disgrace of the thing, to come and insult us in the very harbour of Dublin.

I am, &c.

To the Bishop of London.

Dublin, Apr. 25, 1727.

My Lord,

As I have heard nothing from your Lordship since mine of the first instant, and as we have not yet had any orders about the archbishoprick of Cashel, I cannot help writing a line or two more on that subject, though it may possibly come too late.

It is reported here that our Speaker has wrote that the House of Commons will be very much disobliged if the Bishop of Elphin has not Cashel. I am on the contrary assured, that among the whigs of that house, setting aside the Speaker's creatures and dependants, there is hardly one who will not be better pleased to have the Bishop of Kilmore made Archbishop than the Bishop of Elphin.

I must likewise inform you, that I have discoursed with every Englishman of consequence in this town, whether clergy or laity, and can assure you that there is not one who is not of opinion that the giving the archbishoprick to Bishop Bolton will be a very great blow to the English interest in this kingdom. I would beg of your Lordship if the affair be not over, to represent this to the ministry.

I shall likewise write a letter to the Duke of Newcastle, to desire the ministry to consider who is the proper person to recommend to bishopricks here, an Irish Speaker or an English Primate.[59] I shall trouble your Grace no farther at present, and am,

My Lord, &c.

---

59 Bishop Bolton was at this time set aside, and Dr. Godwin, Bishop of Kilmore appointed; but afterwards the necessity of affairs required, as the Primate thought, that Bishop Bolton should be appointed, and it was accordingly done; but the government had reason afterwards to repent of what they then did.

To Lord Carteret.

Dublin, Apr. 27, 1727.

My Lord,

Since the Prime Serjeant[60] is returned from the circuit, he has been looking over the title of the crown to the living of Dunleer and the other parishes that are, or are supposed to be united to it; and is desirous to have a presentation to them for his brother John Singleton. As we are not well able to settle whether they are rectories or vicarages, or which are one which the other, he thinks it will be safest if your Excellency pleases to direct that Mr. John Singleton be presented to the parishes of Dunleer, Capoche, Disert, Moylare, Drumcarre, and Monasterboys, and against the patent is drawn, we will take care to give every parish its proper title of rectory or vicarage.

I begin now to be pressed by the clerk presented by Mr. Tenison, who has this day brought his presentation; and, would willingly have a presentation from the crown to oppose to theirs, as soon as may be. I have still very good reason to believe the title to all to be in the crown, or at least this turn, if there has been a valid union; and if not, all are certainly in the crown, except Dunleer. I am,

My Lord, &c.

To the Duke of Newcastle.

Dublin, Apr. 29, 1727.

My Lord,

The bearer colonel Cavallier[61] desired I would favour him with a letter to introduce him to your Grace; if there had been occasion to raise any new regiments, he would have been glad to have served his Majesty at this juncture in the new levies.

As there has been lately a promotion of general officers, and some of his juniors have been made brigadiers, he comes over to England in hopes that it was purely his being out of the way that made him be forgotten. The figure he made, and the faithfulness and the courage with which he served the crown in the last war, are the occasion of my recommending him to your Grace's favour and protection in this affair, though it be so much out of my sphere.

I am,

Your Grace's, &c.

60 Singleton.
61 N. B. This is that colonel Cavallier who made so great a figure in the Cevennes, against the powerful armies of France; he was in some respects the Paoli of those days.

To Lord Townshend.

Dublin, May 9, 1727.

My Lord,

We were for two or three posts here under a very great concern upon the news we received of the dangerous state of health Sir Robert Walpole was in: his death will at any time be a very great loss, but we could not but esteem it a more than ordinary stroke, if it had happened at this critical conjuncture. As our repeated accounts from England now give us assurance that he is out of all danger, I cannot omit congratulating your Lordship on the happy occasion of his recovery, which must be a great satisfaction to you, both on account of the private relation and friendship between you,[62] and your Lordship's concern for the publick interest.

I am, &c.

To Lord Carteret.

Dublin, May 9, 1727.

My Lord,

We had this morning advice that Mr. Forbes is dead: he was Vicar of Dunboyne cum Kilbride, and minister of Ballymaglessan, both in the diocese of Meath: the former is reputed to be worth 150 or 160l. per ann. and is undoubtedly in the gift of the crown: the latter is worth about 60l. per ann. and is supposed to be in the gift of the crown, but is claimed by the Bishop of Meath, as being in his patronage. As we do not meet till tomorrow, I was willing to give your Excellency the earliest advice I could of this vacancy.

The Bishop of Meath[63] has been with me to desire I would recommend Dr. Philip Whittingham for the vicarage of Dunboyne cum Kilbride: if he is preferred to it, he must quit the parish of Moylisker in West Meath, worth from 80 to 100l. per ann. which is likewise in the gift of the crown, to which the Bishop would willingly recommend Mr. Hugh Vaughan, whom we have formerly recommended to your Excellency for some small living.

I know Dr. Whittingham to be a very worthy man, who has a wife and several children; and Mr. Vaughan is one of a good character. The Chancellor of the Exchequer and Dr. Coghill have been with me likewise to recommend Mr. Rogers, Fellow of the College, to the living of Ballymaglessan;[64] (he is one of a very fair character) if that living be in the gift of the crown.

---

62 These two friends and brothers-in-law unhappily differed afterwards. Lord Townshend retired into the country, and was the greatest improver of Land ever known in Norfolk; he introduced the cultivation of turnips.
63 Dr. Ralph Lambert.
64 My Lord Primate provided for this gentleman afterwards with one of his own livings: he was esteemed much.

This evening Mr. Dean Winter has been with me, to apply for Mr. Horner to succeed to the living of Dunboyne, and himself to succeed to the living of Clayne, which Mr. Horner now has. Dunboyne is better than Clayne, and beside there is a powerful popish gentleman in Clayne parish, that gives Mr. Horner a great deal of trouble, and whom the Dean will be better able to deal with, as he is a native, and one of a good estate.

As for the Dean and Mr. Horner, your Excellency knows them both so well, that I need say nothing of them. I am,

My Lord, &c.

To the same.

Dublin, May 13, 1727.

My Lord,

I had the honour of your Excellency's of the 6th, and we have likewise had your order about Mr. Singleton's presentation. I have been for near three months pressing the proper officers to get the papers out of the Rolls office, that will shew whether Mr. Tenison has any title to Dunleer, or whether it is in the crown: but partly with the assizes intervening and partly the natural laziness of people here, I have not yet compassed it; but on Wednesday next am promised this affair shall come before the Attorney-General in form, and if he reports the patronage to be in the crown, we shall present Mr. Singleton to it. I shall take care of Mr. Wye on this occasion, according to my promise.

We have spared no pressing to get Mr. Pratt's affairs ended, and hope in a little time to sell his estate. There shall be nothing wanting on our parts to finish his matters, and to have Mr. Gardiner's[65] account passed to Lady-day last, before your Excellency's arrival here.

Your Lordship will by this post receive an account of what recruits are arrived here already; and we shall still send fresh accounts every fortnight according to your order.

I am, &c.

To the Duke of Newcastle.

Dublin, May 20, 1727.

My Lord,

I have so long forborn troubling your Grace about the archbishoprick of Cashel, in expectation of our speedily receiving his Majesty's commands about it; but as no orders are yet come, and the reports we have here about

65 Mr. Gardiner succeeded Mr. Pratt; the first named perhaps the best; the last the worst Deputy Vice-Treasurer that ever was in Ireland.

what is intended are various, and his Majesty's speedy going abroad must occasion some determination in that affair very soon, your Grace will excuse my giving you this trouble to renew my recommendations of Dr. Godwin, Bishop of Kilmore, to the archbishoprick of Cashel, and of Dr. Hort, Bishop of Fernes, to the bishopricks of Kilmore and Ardagh.

The present Bishop of Kilmore has been some years longer on the bench than any that have been talked of for the archbishoprick; and is, I may safely say, the best beloved by his Majesty's friends here, of any English Bishop: the Bishop of Fernes is senior to the Bishop of Elphin.

If it be designed I should have that weight with the Bishops as to dispose them to unite in his Majesty's service here, I think my recommendation ought to be regarded on this occasion; and I can assure your Grace, it is not any particular friendship to the Bishop of Kilmore, but a regard to his worth, and to the most likely method of keeping up a good understanding among his Majesty's friends on the bench, that makes me so hearty in recommending him. I hope I may depend on your Grace's friendship to support me in this affair, and shall always remain,

My Lord, &c.

To the same.

Dublin, May, 23, 1727.

My Lord,

I should sooner have acknowledged the receipt of your Grace's recommendation of the 11th inst. but that upon speaking to my Lord Chancellor about the Lady Tyrconnel's[66] affair, he told me he had lately increased the number of delegates in her cause, and that he would immediately acquaint your Grace with it. As the affair lay wholly in my Chancellor's power, and was over before your Grace's writing, I had not an opportunity of shewing my readiness to comply with your recommendations on this occasion, but when I have, I shall always shew that.

I am, &c.

To the Archbishop of Canterbury.

Dublin, May 23, 1727.

My Lord,

I had the honour of your Grace's of the 25th past; and am of your opinion that it would have been better to have held a fast at the beginning of the

66 Relict of the Duke of Tyrconnel, who succeeded Lord Clarendon as Lord Lieutenant of Ireland in the reign of James II. Her Grace was a sister to Sarah, Dutchess of Marlborough.

sessions: but I suppose the ministry might fear that such a step would have been interpreted a sure prognostick of a war, and might have given a shock to publick credit. I am sorry that the blame of this omission is unjustly thrown on your Grace.

I find by the King's speech, it is still uncertain whether we shall have peace or war; if the latter, I depend on your goodness to send me the form of prayer for the fast.

We have yet no orders about Cashel, and I am sorry that my Lord Lieutenant[67] should insist so much for one, who is much a junior, and as dangerous an Irishman as any on the bench.

I have heard your Grace has been out of order of late, but at the same time I had the satisfaction to be informed that you was pretty well again. I heartily wish your Grace all health and happiness, and am,

My Lord, &c.

To Lord Carteret.

Dublin, May 30, 1727.

My Lord,

Last Saturday we sent your Excellency a memorial relating to the living of Cahirconglish in the diocese of Cashel, fallen to the crown by the vacancy of the archbishoprick. Mr. Hugh Vaughan, whom your Excellency named to Mr. Samson's living in Cork, if it had been in the gift of the crown, has been with me this evening to desire me to recommend him for this living, and will to-morrow deliver in a memorial on that subject, which we shall transmit to your Lordship; but as he hears the former memorialist is gone for England to solicit for it, he was desirous another post might not be lost.

I understand we shall have a third memorial from Mr. Gregory, who has been curate there for some years, which we shall likewise send your Excellency. I hear the living is worth from 160 to 200l. per ann,

I am, &c.

To Lord Carteret.

Dublin, June 4, 1727.

My Lord,

Yesterday we had advice that Mr. Justice Parnell[68] was dead at his house in the country. Mr. Prime Serjeant, the Attorney and Sollicitor-General, have

---

67 N. B. The Lord Lieutenant did not then carry his point against the Primate, though he had the assistance of the Speaker to back his recommendation; Bishop Bolton was a high tory, and a great friend of Dean Swift's, and was undoubtedly a man of abilities; more need not be said, as his true character may be easily drawn from these letters.

68 He was brother to the Rev. Dr. Parnell the celebrated poet.

made no application about succeeding to his place: but I hear they have not made very positive declarations against accepting it. Mr. Dixon, who has a very good character both for his abilities and for his affection to his Majesty, has made some application to be recommended; and the Lords Justices are disposed to recommend him, if those above-mentioned are not for removing; which, I find, as the session of parliament is coming on, it is rather wished they may not desire. But I find we all think, as term is over, and considering the present circumstances, it may be better to keep that place open for some time.

My Lord Chancellor will write more fully on this subject to your Excellency. I am,

My Lord, &c.

To the Duke of Newcastle.

Dublin, June 6, 1727.

My Lord,

I am sensible of the trouble I have lately given your Grace with repeated letters relating to the archbishoprick of Cashel, at a time you was over much pressed with business of much greater consequence to the publick; and I do not wonder that your Lordship could not find leisure to return any answer: but by his Majesty's letters we received yesterday relating to that affair, I find I was not forgot; I most humbly thank your Grace for supporting my recommendations on this occasion, which I can assure you had no other intention than his Majesty's service, and the strengthening the English interest here.

I am, &c.

Newcastle to Boulter.

Whitehall, June 6, 1727.
(NA. SP. 63/388/227)

My Lord,

I have not had so much time as to return your Grace my thanks for the honour of your several letters. I hope however you will have seen by what has been done here, that the disposition of the vacant sees in Ireland is made agreeable to your own recommendation and I can assure your Grace, the King has the greatest regard imaginable for your opinion, and is desirous on all occasions to do what may best support your Grace's credit amongst the clergy. As to the promotion of Dr. Hoadley, he being brother to our good Bishop of Salisbury, who has so well deserved of the Government, and even very lately, his Majesty thought the moment application was made for him, he could do no less than give him the vacant Bishoprick, as he is an extraordinary good sort of man, I do not doubt but your Grace will think this Instance of his Majesty's favour well bestowed upon him.

I am etc.

Holles Newcastle

To the Bishop of London.

Dublin, June 8, 1727.

My Lord,

I have been applied to by Mr. Amy of Camberwell, who has the honour of being known to your Lordship, to recommend his nephew Mr. Amy, of the Church of Windsor, to your Lordship for a small prebend of St. Paul's: I remember your Lordship had occasion to enquire into his character when I was in England, and seemed well disposed to have done somewhat for him in the King's Chapel on a fair occasion; but that view is at an end, by his having a little living given him in the neighbourhood of Windsor by that Church; but still as he has a needy mother and sister to support, he stands in need of some farther help, which if it suits with your Lordship's conveniency, I would recommend him for. I am,

My Lord, &c.

To Lord Carteret.

Dublin, June 10, 1727.

My Lord,

I have just now received your Excellency's of the 6th, and hope you will please to remember Mr. Vaughan on some other occasion, since your Lordship was at this time pre-engaged in favour of Mr. Massey.

I am glad to hear his Majesty is probably landed in Holland after an easy passage.

The accounts had been some time ago passed to Lady-day was twelve-month, had they not been stopped for a letter that is expected from England, at the application of Mr. Edgecomb,[69] not to bring on Mr. Pratt's balance on the new account, which must be done according to the methods of auditing accounts here, if no such order comes: but Mr. Gardiner assures me the account to Lady-day last is preparing as fast as it can, so that no time shall be lost by the aforesaid delay: and I hope the account will be passed to Lady-

69 One of the Vice Treasurers of Ireland, afterwards created Lord Edgecomb.

day last before your Excellency's arrival here, There shall no endeavours be wanting on my part to compass it. Mr. Pratt's estate is now selling, but the sale goes on but slowly that I can find.

On Monday I set out on my provincial visitation, and shall be absent from Dublin near five weeks, but as we have a peace now, I shall hardly be wanted for that time.

I am, &c.

To the Duke of Newcastle.

Dublin, June 10, 1727.

My Lord,

I am so very sensible that in the great hurry of business there has been in England, my recommendations have not been forgot, that I have already returned your Grace my hearty thanks, as I do again by this, for your kind support of me in the disposition of Cashel.

I have a great value and friendship for the Bishop of Salisbury,[70] and in part know the services he has done the government both formerly and of late, and I am very well acquainted with Dr. Hoadley his brother, and know his affection to his Majesty, and that he has spirit to help to keep up the English interest here; so that I am very well satisfied with his promotion to the bishoprick of Fernes; and I have the more reason to be so, because in my first letter on the vacancy of the archbishoprick, I hinted that I thought it would be for his Majesty's service here, after some translations to fill up the last bishoprick from England, since the English grew the less number on the bench here.

Next Monday I intend to set out on the visitation of my province, which will take me up near five weeks time. I am glad the certainty of a peace gives me an opportunity of quitting Dublin to look after my province this summer, which otherwise I should have been unwilling to do, if the war had gone on.

I hope before this the news of his Majesty's landing in Holland is arrived at London. I am,

Your Grace's, &c.

To Lord Carteret.

Dublin, June 29, 1727.

My Lord,

I most heartily condole with your Excellency upon the sudden and unexpected death of his late Majesty: I was engaged in the visitation of my

70 Dr. Hoadley, afterwards Bishop of Winchester.

province when the melancholy news overtook me, and had some thoughts of going on, since his Majesty would be proclaimed, and all the usual orders given before I could possibly reach Dublin, but upon finding the other Lords Justices were uneasy at my absence, I returned hither last night.

Every body is extremely pleased with his Majesty's happy and quiet accession to the throne, and with his most gracious declaration in council; and they do not doubt but his Majesty will pursue those wise measures which will make him as great as his father, and his people as easy as they were under him.

As a new parliament must be called here, and a session come on as soon as possible, I must take the liberty to represent to your Excellency how much it would be for his Majesty's service, by giving them courage to exert themselves, and a weight with others, if my Lord Chancellor and Lord Chief Baron had new patents speedily for their places, as likewise the other judges; I mention only the two first in particular, because the present doubtful tenure they have of their places must be a great weakening to the English interest, and of ill consequence in the elections, and at the session of parliament.

There is another thing I cannot but suggest to your Excellency, though I am under no fear of the experiment being made, that any thing which looks like bringing[71] the tories into power here, must cause the utmost uneasiness in this kingdom, by raising the spirits of the papists of this country, and exasperating the whigs, who your Lordship knows, are vastly superior among the gentlemen of estates here.

I find Mr. Broderick has declared he will stand for Speaker against Mr. Conolly, and uses his utmost efforts to secure as many as he can among the new members. The whole kingdom is in the utmost ferment about the coming elections; but I hope this will have no worse consequences than are usual on such occasions.

I can safely appeal to your Excellency for my having to the best of my power served his late Majesty, and supported the English interest here; and I shall always serve his present Majesty as faithfully; but to be able to do it with the good effect I desire, I hope I shall be as well supported as I have been: your Excellency knows I have nothing to ask; and I believe Princes have seldom over many that are disposed to serve them as faithfully on so easy terms.

It would put a good spirit into the King's friends here, and particularly the English, if they knew by your Excellency's means what they had to depend on. I beg your Lordship's pardon for the freedom and length of this letter, and am,

My Lord, &c.

---

71 This was no bad admonition to Lord Carteret, who appeared to have been much inclined to favour them.

To the Archbishop of Canterbury.

Dublin, June 30, 1727.

My Lord,

I heartily condole with your Grace upon the unexpected death of his late Majesty,[72] and at the same time congratulate you on the happy and peaceable accession of his present Majesty to the crown.

I was engaged in the visitation of my province when the news overtook me, and found myself obliged to return to Dublin, by the importunity of my friends here, though I had not got through half my work. This my absence has occasioned my not writing sooner to your Grace.

The signing of the preliminaries before the late King was taken from us, has I hope procured us that peace, which I fear we should have been otherwise very uncertain of till next summer.

Every thing here is as quiet as in England, excepting the heats attending the election of a new parliament, which must come on immediately with us, as the former parliament is dissolved by the King's death, and the funds will expire at Christmas next. His Majesty's most gracious declaration in council has given universal satisfaction here.

But your Grace will easily see there is great room for people's hopes and fears, till things are a little better settled, and it is seen what ministry is to be England, and who are to keep or lose their places here.

Your Grace knows I have nothing to lose, but I may be made more or less capable of serving his Majesty, of doing good in the Church, and of supporting the English interest, which labours under great disadvantages in this country, according as I have more or less countenance from England. I have in particular done my endeavours here to serve his late Majesty with the greatest faithfulness, and shall serve our present Sovereign with the same fidelity; but the services I can do will be much lessened, if I am not supported in my station; and as I am satisfied your Grace will come in for a great share of power under the King, I must beg the favour of you to give me your support here upon proper occasions.

It would certainly be of great service against our approaching parliament, if my Lord Chancellor and my Lord Chief Baron had their places speedily confirmed by new patents; and till that is done they can neither have courage, nor a proper weight. For matters abroad we have his Majesty's declaration, but what measures are likely to be pursued at home are so variously wrote over hither, that the King's best friends know not how to act. If your Grace shall think it any ways proper, I should be glad to know a little of what we are to depend upon.

---

72 George I. who died almost suddenly at Osnabrug, the palace of his brother the Bishop of that district, in his way to Hanover, by eating a melon.

I am sensible I have very much trespassed on your Grace's time and patience, but the great kindness I have formerly met with from your Lordship, encourages me to give you this trouble.

I am, My Lord, &c.

To Lord Townshend.

Dublin, July 1, 1727.

My Lord,

I was engaged in the triennial visitation of my province, when the melancholy news of the King's death overtook me, and the importunity of my friends here brought me back to Dublin before I had half finished my visitation.

I most heartily condole with your Lordship upon this great and unexpected loss, and at the same time congratulate your Lordship on the quiet and peaceable accession of his present Majesty to the throne of his father.

We have no other bustle among us than what arises from the warm canvass going on in all parts about the election of members for the ensuing parliament.

His Majesty's most gracious declaration in council has given great satisfaction here.

I am sensible of the great hurry your Lordship must be in at this juncture, and should not have interrupted your more weighty affairs, if I had not thought myself obliged to take the first opportunity to thank your Lordship for all favours, and particularly for the support I have found from your Lordship to enable me the better to serve his Majesty in this country; and I desire the continuance of the same from your Lordship on all proper occasions.

I am, &c.

To the Duke of Newcastle.

Dublin, July 1, 1727.

My Lord,

I most heartily condole with your Grace upon the unexpected loss of his late Majesty, and at the same time congratulate you on the peaceable accession of his present Majesty to the crown.

I was engaged in the visitation of my province when this news overtook me, and returned to Dublin but last Wednesday.

Every thing here is very quiet, and all are very well pleased with his Majesty's most gracious declaration in council.

It is very happy that the preliminaries were signed before this fatal stroke, since otherwise it seems very probable the Emperor would have taken till next spring to consider whether it were getter for him to have peace or war.

I take this opportunity to thank your Grace for the support you have given me since my coming hither, and to desire the continuance of your favour on all proper occasions.

I am, &c.

To the Bishop of London.

Dublin, July 4, 1727.

My Lord,

I yesterday received your Lordship's of the 29th past, and most heartily condole with you on the unexpected death of his late Majesty: the news overtook me in the middle of the visitation of my province, and the importunity of friends has brought me back to Dublin.

I am glad to hear things are likely to go in the state pretty near as they were, and hardly think they will mend by changing in the Church; however, I remember when I was in England, it was thought other persons would come into play in the Church upon the change which has now happened.

I have been particularly concerned for Mr. Stephens's ill luck on this occasion, and will follow your Lordship's advice to try what my old friends can or will undertake for him.

The priest your Lordship mentions has been several times with me, and I do not find any of my brethren object to his sincerity; but most of the priests here are so ignorant, and there is so much hazard in trusting them in our church, that it is very hard to put them in any way here of getting their bread. If O Hara could be put into some little business in the West Indies, I believe it would be better for him; but I have not yet talked with him whether he is willing to go thither, nor shall I, till I know whether your Lordship would be willing to send him.

By the change that your Lordship thinks will happen in the church affairs, I shall be greatly at a loss for your friendship; but hope still for your assistance as it shall lye in your way, and shall on all occasions hope for the continuance of your good advice, as often as I find reason to have recourse to it.

It is very likely Dr. L-l will look out for some other way to push, as things now stand.

I am, &c.

To the Archbishop of Canterbury.

Dublin, July 6, 1727.

My Lord,

As Dr. Baldwin, Provost of the College here, goes now for London, to wait upon his Majesty with an address, and to know his pleasure about their chancellorship, which he had whilst he was Prince; I have given him this my letter, to introduce him to your protection as there may be occasion. He is a very worthy gentleman, a man of learning, and extremely well affected to his Majesty and his family, and shewed himself to be so in the latter end of the Queen's time, when he was Vice-Provost.

There has lately been an election of a fellow in the College which has occasioned a quarrel there, in which he has been very much misrepresented and abused: and he has been threatened with their preferring a petition to the King, and having the power given him by the statutes reduced. The power he has is indeed beyond any thing any Head of a College has in Oxford, but is all little enough to keep the college here from being a seminary of jacobitism:[73] through the strength of a faction in the College against him.

I would beg leave of your Grace that he may have the liberty to lay his case before you, as there may be occasion, and that you would give him your protection as far as he wants it, and your Grace shall think it reasonable.

I am, my Lord, &c.

To the Archbishop of Canterbury.

Dublin, July 8, 1727.

My Lord,

I have had the honour of your Grace's, with the King's speech enclosed, which is truly gracious and condescending, and gives the utmost satisfaction to his Majesty's subjects here; and we do not doubt but his Majesty speaks his sincere sentiments and intentions.

I thank your Grace for the favour you intend me of sending the prayers as soon as possible, when that affair is once settled; and I think your Lordship is very much in the right on that occasion, to implore the divine blessing on his Majesty's endeavours for a happy and lasting peace.

I am sorry to hear your Grace is obliged to keep close at Lambeth during the present hurry, and pray God to give you better health for the good of the Church and service of his Majesty. We have since seen the address of both

73 His Grace must be very much mistaken, or to speak in the softest terms, he was grosly imposed upon by some ignorant malicious people, as the fellows of the university of Dublin, have been as remarkable for charity, piety, religion, learning and loyalty, as any other College in Europe, since the reign of Queen Elizabeth.

Lords and Commons to the King, and are all pleased to find them so hearty and loyal. The last day of June I wrote to your Grace to desire your friendship and support in my station upon this turn, which I again request. I likewise recommended my Lord Chancellor and Lord Chief Baron to have their commissions renewed speedily, and must desire your Grace to speak to my Lord Lieutenant and the ministry to this purpose, as an opportunity offers; they have both discharged their offices with great diligence and abilities, and very much to the satisfaction of the people here; and have both heartily concurred with me in the council and elsewhere, in whatever might promote the English interest here.

I have no apprehensions but that my Lord Lieutenant and the ministry desire to continue them in their places, but it would give them more courage and more weight in our present circumstances, if they were presently confirmed in their employments.

I am, my Lord, &c.

To the Duke of Newcastle.

Dublin, July 8, 1727.

My Lord,

As by his late Majesty's demise all commissions here expire of course, within six months, I take the liberty to put your Grace in mind that I think it would be for his Majesty's service, as we are in a ferment over the whole nation about elections, that the commissions of consequence which are designed to be renewed, were renewed with all convenient expedition.

And in particular I think it would be of service in the present juncture, if my Lord Chancellor and Lord Chief Baron had speedily new grants of their places. They have both attended their courts with the greatest diligence, and have given an unusual dispatch to the business of their courts, to the general satisfaction of the country, on account of their abilities and impartiality. They have always most heartily joined with me in whatever might be for his Majesty's service, and the support of the English interest here; and the speedy renewing of their commissions would enable them to act with more courage and with greater weight than they can do whilst others may imagine their places are doubtful. My Lord Lieutenant knows their behaviour, and the character they have gained here so well, that I do not doubt but his Excellency is for their continuing here; and indeed a change in their places would very much weaken the government now the session of a new parliament is so near.

I take this affair to be of such consequence, that I shall write to my Lord Townshend on the same subject.

I hope your Grace will not forget my friend Mr. Stephens, if a vacancy should happen in Christ Church.

I am, my Lord, &c.

To Lord Townshend.

Dublin, July 8, 1727.

My Lord,

As all commissions here are only held precariously for six months at present, I beg leave to put your Lordship in mind that I think it would be very much for his Majesty's service if such commissions (especially those of note) as are thought proper to be renewed, were renewed speedily.

And I must in particular recommend to your Lordship our Lord Chancellor and Lord Chief Baron to have new commissions for their places, with all convenient expedition. They have both attended their courts with a diligence unusual in this country, and administered justice with great abilities and impartiality, to the satisfaction of the country, where they have both gained the greatest esteem and love; and they have on all occasions chearfully concurred with me in whatever was for his Majesty's service, and the English interest in this kingdom. It would be a great encouragement to his Majesty's servants here, and would give me as well as them the more courage in our serving his Majesty, to see those who have so well behaved themselves in two of the greatest posts here, distinguished by having their new commissions speedily granted. They are known to my Lord Lieutenant to have given that general content here, that I do not question his Excellency's being for their continuance here.

I am, my Lord, &c.

To Lord Carteret.

Dublin, July 11, 1727.

My Lord,

I had yesterday a memorial delivered me from Mrs. West, which she desired I would transmit to your Excellency. I have enquired into the fact whether she has no other provision than 250l. per annum during the father's life, and by a paper drawn up by Mr. Mitchel with the words of the marriage settlement, am satisfied she has no other provision made for her, and that in the opinion of the lawyers both in England and here, neither she nor her daughter, till the son is dead without issue, can be entitled to any part of the thirds of old Mr. West's real or personal estate. I find it was taken for granted in drawing up the settlement that Mr. West the father would die before his son. As these are circumstances I did not know before, and that makes Mrs. West's case very deplorable, I cannot but most earnestly recommend her and her children to your Excellency's favour to obtain the renewal of the annuity granted them by his late Majesty.

Mr. Mitchel[74] will be able to give your Excellency full satisfaction that this is truly her case and the case of her daughter. I am,

Your Excellency's, &c.

To the same.

Dublin, July 15, 1727.

My Lord,

I am very much obliged to your Excellency for the honour of yours of the 8th instant: if I had the honour of any share in his late Majesty's affection, I am sure it must have been very much owing to your kind representations of my services.

And I am sensible of your goodness in acquainting his present Majesty, that the supporting of me here will be for his interest; and I desire the continuance of your good offices with the King.

I am glad we are not likely to have any alterations in Ireland, and that the commissions here will be renewed immediately upon the renewal of those in England.

We are obliged to your Lordship for the early care you took of us English here; and every body here is sensible of what advantage it will be to his Majesty's service that we have had a Governor of your Excellency's abilities long enough amongst us to know as much of this country as any native.

While the same measures are pursued as were in the last reign, we shall be all easy here; and it must be left to his Majesty to judge what persons are most proper to be employed in his service. The assurances your Lordship gives me in these affairs are a great satisfaction to me.

I hear there is a clause in an English bill, which speaks of the chancellorship of the University here as most certainly vacant by the King's accession to the crown, but here it is thought at the most to be only dubious. We are giving what dispatch we can to the bills that are to be sent over to England, in order to have a new parliament, and hope we shall send such as will be approved there, and will meet with little opposition here.

I am, &c.

---

74 Brother-in-law to Mrs. West; he had married her sister: both the ladies were daughters of Dr. Burnet, Bishop of Salisbury.

To the same.

Dublin, July 20, 1727.

My Lord,

I have had the honour of your Excellency's of the 13th, and before the receipt of this your Lordship will receive the two lists of officers which are of importance in our present state, and with all possible speed an account of all other patents for places.

We have been in such a hurry with getting the bills ready to be sent to England, that I have not had time to draw up a short account of the Bishop of Cloyne's case for your information, but will do it by the first opportunity. My Lord Chancellor has written so fully about the bills we have sent, that I have little to add.

The whole council were satisfied it was our duty to transmit a money bill, but we think if your Excellency is here early enough it will be better to make no use of it; as to the corn and tillage bill, the great damage to this kingdom by landlords tying up their tenants from ploughing, the throwing so many families out of work that might be employed by tillage, and the terrible scarcity next to a famine that a great part of the kingdom now labours under by the corn not yielding well last year, and to which we are liable upon any the least accident in our harvest, make us all very desirous of having it past; and as it is only five acres out of an hundred that are to be tilled, and that every farmer has till Michaelmas come two years to lay out his schemes of ploughing, we hope it will not be counted any hardship to force them to plough so small a proportion of their land.

The want of such a provision as is made in the bill about mending bridges, has often occasioned 50 or 100l. expence to the county, where 5 or 10l. would have done at first.

The indemnifying bill speaks for itself.

As to the bill requiring some years conversion in papists before they practise the law, your Lordship knows the bad case we are in here with new converts practising, and the dangerous consequence it may have in length of time; your Lordship has likewise seen, that nothing can be moved about papists or converts in either house but what is at last so clogged as to come to nothing; which made us willing to send over a bill to this one point; if there are political reasons on the other side of the water for dropping it, the crown is under no difficulty, because we have sent bills enough without it; but I believe if it is returned, it will certainly pass here.

I hear this day, that the address yesterday presented by some Roman Catholicks, occasions great heats and divisions among those of that religion here.

I am, &c.

To the Archbishop of Canterbury.

Dublin, Aug. 10, 1727.

My Lord,

I have had the honour of your Grace's of the 12th and 19th past. I believe the behaviour of the parliament to the King, in relation to the civil list, and the King's most gracious speech at the end of the sessions; have universally pleased all honest men.

I am sorry to hear your Grace complain so much of your infirmities, and hope you may find benefit by the Tunbridge waters; and I heartily wish your Grace may have strength to serve the Church and our country for many years yet to come; and I desire your Grace's protection on all proper occasions.

His Majesty has been graciously pleased to renew his grants to all in place here, except to Mr. Medlicott, one of the commissioners of the revenue, in whose place he has put my Lord Pembroke's second son,[75] whom we expect here very speedily.

The changes made in places in England, are such as I believe give no uneasiness, except to the particular friends of those turned out, since those are all left in who will have the direction of affairs.

I am very much afraid by your Grace's account and the hurry they seem to be in about court, that we shall scarce have a day of prayer and thanksgiving, as has been proposed by your Grace.

I thank your Lordship for your kind reception of Dr. Baldwin, and your intention to support him, if there be occasion.

I find my Lord Lieutenant is likely to come hither later in the year than we could wish, for the easy dispatch of business in the parliament.

We have had a greater run of hot weather together, than there has been since I came to this country. I am,

Your Grace's, &c.

To Lord Carteret.

Dublin, Aug. 24, 1727.

My Lord,

We have been in great expectation of Mr. Stern's[76] return with the bills, and his Majesty's orders for issuing the writs for a new parliament, but hear nothing of him or his motions by the mail that came in this day and brought the letters of Saturday last.

I am sorry to hear two of our bills are lost on the other side, and particularly the corn bill, which is very much wanted here.

75 Honourable Mr. Herbert.
76 Clerk of the parliament.

It is thought here that elections will generally go well.

The Bishop of Fernes[77] and his family are arrived here to-day, after being at sea four days.

I have here sent your Lordship enough of the Bishop of Cloyne's case to make it understood what he desires, with a copy of the private bill his predecessor obtained in England, relating to the lands of Donaghmore. If I had more large materials your Excellency should have had a more distinct account of his case.

I shall leave it to your Excellency what change you will think proper to make in the list of privy-councellors here; your Excellency knows as well as any body, who of the present list are enemies to England, and oppose the King's business on all occasions.

I shall submit it to your Excellency whether it may be proper for the strengthening of the English interest here, to have the present Archbishop of Cashel inserted in the new list.

I am sorry to hear your Lordship has had a fit of the gout so early in life. I am, &c.

The CASE of
The present Bishop of CLOYNE,[78]
On which he applies for relief.

By an act passed the second session 1 reg. Anne c. 21. the forfeited estates in this kingdom, unsold or undisposed of, were vested in the Queen, her heirs and successors; and the money arising from them to be brought into the Exchequer in Ireland, and there to be kept apart from her Majesty's other revenues, to be applied as the parliament of England shall direct.

By an act 2 & 3 reg. Anne c. 10. the money remaining in the treasury of England from the sale of forfeited estates here, Lord Bophin's 25000l. and other rents, arrears, &c. were to go towards paying a year's interest on the debentures. Since which, no other disposal has been made by the parliament of England of these forfeitures, except in the late Bishop of Cloyne's bill: the state of which is this:

The late Bishop of Cloyne understanding that the lands and manor of Donaghmore had once belonged to the see of Cloyne, had probably by some agent bid 4020l. for the said lands, and paid down 1340l. as one third of the purchase money. After which he applied to the parliament of England, and obtained an act of parliament there, by which the other two thirds of the purchase money were remitted. The lands and the manor of Donaghmore were for ever united to the see of Cloyne.

77 Dr. Hoadley; he was afterwards Archbishop of Dublin, and succeeded Dr. Boulter in the primacy.
78 Dr. Henry Maule.

But in order to reimburse him the 1340l. he had advanced, he was to be repaid that sum out of the undisposed forfeitures here. And because that fund might prove deficient, his executors, &c. were to keep the estate of Donaghmore upon his death, &c. till the whole 1340l. or what part of it remained unpaid, with interest from the time of his death, was answered out of the rents of the lands of Donaghmore.

The part of that private act relating to this, I have sent a copy of.

Now it seems some of these undisposed estates, and some money from arrears &c. are still in the hands of the commissioners of the revenue here.

Whether the late Bishop of Cloyne applied to the commissioners to be paid the 1340l. I cannot learn; but the whole sum remains unpaid, and in virtue of the act last mentioned, the late Bishop's executors keep the lands of Donaghmore from the present Bishop.

And his application to the government is, that pursuant to the act of parliament, the 1340l. may be paid out of the undisposed forfeited estates.

By what I have heard the commissioners here say, those estates are indebted to the revenue here for the recovery of them near 900l. and some body has been made receiver of those rents at a salary of near half or a third part of the rents. But a thorough knowledge of the state of those forfeited estates can scarce be had till your Excellency in person makes those enquiries, which we cannot so well push on.

To Lord Carteret.

Dublin, Aug. 26, 1727.

My Lord,

Early this morning died the Lord Chief Justice Whitshed, very much lamented for his great abilities and zeal for the service of the publick.

I must take this occasion to press your Excellency that his place may be filled from England.[79] I can assure your Lordship we have by experience found the want of two English Judges in the privy council, since the removal of my Lord Chancellor to his present post; and I am confident where there is the least shew of an affair between England and Ireland, or where there is need of impartiality between any contending parties, that may be before the council, we shall be in the last distress, if this vacancy be not filled from England: I do not speak this that I want to have the place filled immediately, since I rather think it will be of service to have it kept uncertain who shall succeed till the approaching sessions of parliament is pretty well over.

But I would prevent any surprise by an early application from hence for

---

79 An Englishman (Mr. Reynolds) was sent, as is requested in this letter.

the present vacancy, or for a removal from the King's bench, as was done before.

I am, &c.

To the Duke of Newcastle.

Dublin, Aug. 26, 1727.

My Lord,

This morning died my Lord Chief Justice Whitshed, by which the place of Lord Chief Justice in the Common Pleas is become vacant.

I must beg leave on this occasion to acquaint your Grace that it is of the utmost consequence to have this vacancy filled from England.

We have found by experience since the Lord Chief Baron has been the only Englishman among the three chief Judges, that things have gone very heavy in the privy council here.

When any thing is transacting in council that can be thought to be for the advantage of England, or where any persons of consideration here may be offended, the best we can hope for from a native of this place is, that he will stay away from council instead of promoting the King's service by his presence and debating.

I must likewise take the liberty to caution against suffering the present Lord Chief Justice[80] of the King's Bench to remove to the Common Pleas, which was the game played last time, with an intent to keep off a person from England, and played with success. There will be no difficulty in finding a lawyer of worth in England to come over to the Common Pleas, which is almost a sine-cure; but it was then found, and will again be found difficult to get a person of any worth to come over to be Lord Chief Justice of the King's Bench.

I am apt to think it may be for the King's service not to fill this place before the main business of our parliament is over; but must represent it as the joint sense of the English here, that it ought to be filled from England.

There are so many Irish in the council, and many of them more opposite to England than any one there ought to be, that it is of the last importance to us to have two of the Judges, who shall always be in the interest of England.

I am, &c.

80 Rogerson, formerly Recorder of Dublin.

To the same.

Dublin, Aug. 31, 1727.

My Lord,

What I was apprehensive of in the letter I lately wrote to your Grace, has accordingly happened, for Lord Chief Justice Rogerson has applied to be removed to the Common Pleas, and pleads for it the precedent of Lord Chief Justice Whitshed being favoured with such a removal.

I cannot but observe the cases are extremely different; Lord Chief Justice Whitshed had really broke his health by ten or twelve years service in the King's Bench, and had brought on himself a great storm of malice by his faithfully serving his Majesty in that post; and if it was thought proper to fill the place of Lord Chief Justice of the Common Pleas at that time from this side of the water, he could hardly have been denied his request; though the grant has been of little benefit to him, and it is thought his uneasiness upon some affronts he met with[81] since his removal, helped to shorten his days. But Lord Chief Justice Rogerson is so far from being worn out in the King's service, that he has not yet once sat in the King's Bench; and as he pleads the late precedent in his favour, I hope care will be taken not to suffer a second precedent, for fear it should by degrees be thought so much the right of a Lord Chief Justice of the King's Bench to remove to the Common Pleas if he thinks fit, that it may be reckoned a hardship to put him by: and as the post of Lord Chief Justice of the Common Pleas is one of the most easy stations among the Judges here, I hope things will be so managed as to keep it free at least to be disposed of to some English lawyer of worth.

And I must again represent to your Grace, that I think it is of consequence to his Majesty's service here that the present vacancy in the Common Pleas should be filled from England, as well as every other vacancy hereafter, in the same post.

My Lord Chief Baron Dalton thinks he may be of more service to the King and the country where he is, and therefore does not desire to remove to the Common Pleas, though it is attended with much less trouble than his present post.

I am, my Lord, &c.

---

81 From Dean Swift, and several others, for dissolving a Grand Jury who would not find bills of indictment against the author and printer of the Drapier's fourth letter to the whole people of Ireland. See Swift's Works, Vol. IV.

To Lord Carteret.

Dublin, Aug. 31, 1727.

My Lord,

Since I had the honour of writing to your Excellency, Lord Chief Justice Rogerson has made application to be recommended to the Common Pleas. There was a great deal to be said why the Lord Chief Justice Whitshed, who had been worn out in the King's service in the King's Bench should be considered and made easy in a place of less trouble than the post he then held: but this is an application from one in good health, and who has not so much as sat in the King's Bench as yet; and as he pleads the late precedent, we all think it is the more necessary not to make a second precedent; which if repeated, will almost rob the crown of the disposal of the most easy place among the Judges in this kingdom. I mention this in particular against the removal of Lord Chief Justice Rogerson to the Common Pleas, but must still continue of opinion that it is most for his Majesty's service that the place should be filled from England.

I am, &c.

To the same.

Dublin, Sept. 18, 1727.

My Lord,

Yesterday Dr. Travers, minister of the round Church (alias St. Andrews) died. That parish is by act of parliament to be divided into two parishes, and the gift of it is in seven trustees, of which the Archbishop of Dublin is one, and has as is said, a negative on the rest. But beside this the Dr. had the chancellorship of Christ Church, which is in your Excellency's gift; some tell me the chancellorship is worth 80l. per ann. others at least 120l. I shall mention the several persons that have applied to me to be recommended to your Lordship for this promotion, in the order they applied.

Dr. St. Paul was the first, who says that your Excellency was pleased to promise to do somewhat for him, and that the chancellorship has no cure of souls, and is very convenient for his following his school here.

The next that applied was Mr. Manley,[82] in behalf of his son Mr. Holt; he appears for the round Church, and if he succeeds there Mr. Manley will be satisfied. But as Mr. Doogat the Archbishop's nephew likewise appears, and it is supposed the Archbishop will exert his negative and agree to no other presentation but that of his nephew, if that should be the case, and there is

---

82 Deputy Postmaster General of Ireland, whose daughter was married to the Rev. Mr. Holt.

no prospect of Mr. Holt's succeeding to the living, Mr. Manley would be very thankful if his son might succeed to the chancellorship of Christ Church.

This morning Mr. Synge was with me, and represented that in the last removal your Excellency favoured him with, he bettered himself but 30l. per annum, and that in tythes instead of a rate on houses, and he is desirous to succeed to the chancellorship.

As your Lordship knows all the candidates and their characters, I only lay their pretensions before you.

My Lord Santry has been with me to desire I would acquaint your Lordship that it is his request that his nephew Mr. Keating, who is one of the clerks assistant of the House of Lords, might be put on a level with the other clerk assistant: I know his nephew is diligent in his present business, and if what he desires is not to the detriment of another, which I shall endeavour to enquire, I would join in his request to your Excellency.

I believe several of our elections will be over this week, and it is thought they will generally go well.

I am,
My Lord, &c.

To the same.

Dublin, Sept. 23, 1727.

My Lord,

I had yesterday the honour of your Excellency's of the 14th, and am glad to hear that it is intended that the Lord Chief Justice's place shall be filled from England, and should hope people here will be satisfied with the puny Judge's place being filled from this country, but hope neither will be done till the session of parliament is over.

We generally think the session will be easy, though I find there are some very busy in giving out that a land-tax is designed, with what views it is easy to guess.

The Archbishop of Cashel[83] is not yet come, but we suppose he is now at Holyhead, and will be here to-morrow.

I think[84] the reasons for dropping our two bills are not very strong. We shall do whatever lies in our power to have every thing ready against the opening of the parliament.

I have lately received a letter from Mrs. West, complaining of the coldness

---

83 Dr. Thomas Godwin.
84 The corn bill was passed afterwards in another session, and so was the other, if it was the popery bill as it seems to be.

of Mr. Mitchel to her, on the account as she says, that she paid the Irish creditors preferably to what was due to him from Mr. West, on account of some bargain about stocks; and as she fears that Mr. Mitchel for this reason may sollicit her affair but coolly, she desires I would put your Excellency in mind of being so kind to her as to get her pension renewed.

I have formerly transmitted her memorial to your Lordship, and should be sorry if she should suffer for having paid the Irish creditors preferably to others, since it was what myself and the rest of the English here all advised, for the credit of our nation, and to prevent applications to have her pension when granted, stopped, to pay them. I very much fear that without the pension being renewed, Mrs. West and her daughter will be wholly destitute at the death of old Mr. West. I am,
My Lord, &c.

To Lord Townshend.

Dublin, Sept. 28, 1727.
My Lord,

Having lately had an account from England, that Dr. Burton,[85] Canon of Christ Church, has been out of order, I beg leave to put your Lordship in mind of your promises in favour of Mr. Stephens, that he should succeed to the first vacancy in that Church. He is the only friend in England I shall trouble your Lordship about, and your supporting his pretensions to that canonry, whenever it falls, will always be esteemed the greatest obligation laid on me.

I am, my Lord, &c.

To Lord Carteret.

Dublin, Oct. 3, 1727.
My Lord,

I had this day the honour of your Excellency's of the 28th past. Dr. St. Paul was with me this morning, and I told him your Lordship did not intend to dispose of the chancellorship till your arrival here.

I am very sorry that things have so fallen out as to detain your Lordship so long in England, that I fear there will hardly be time to settle the operations of the parliament in the best manner before they meet.

We are pretty much alarmed here at an article in the English news, that

85 Dr. Burton had been tutor to the Primate, when he was entered of Christ Church in Oxford.

Alan Brodrick, son to the late Lord Chancellor of Ireland, is made one of the Commissioners of the Customs; and we are apprehensive it may give too much spirit to the Brodricks here, and be made use of by them to engage others to obstruct the King's business in parliament.

I am,

My Lord, &c.

To the Duke of Newcastle.

Dublin, Oct. 3, 1727.

My Lord,

Looking over the English news this day, we find this article, that Alan Brodrick, son to the late Lord Chancellor of Ireland, is made one of the Commissioners of the Customs. As the whole opposition the King's affairs met with last session in the House of Commons, came from the Brodricks, we are somewhat apprehensive that any thing which looks as if that family was in favour in England, may give them spirit, and engage others to join with them in perplexing matters the approaching sessions of parliament. I am,

Your Grace's, &c.

To the Bishop of London.

Dublin, Jan. 11, 1727/8.

My Lord,

I am sensible it is a great while since I last wrote to your Lordship, but it has not been owing to my having a less desire of the continuance of your Lordship's friendship, but for want of matter to write about; your Lordship is in the busy scene of life, and I in a kingdom where little happens worth communicating to any abroad: and I must own as nothing but a disturbance can make room for affairs of consequence passing here, I most heartily wish we may still continue of as little concern to others as we are at present.

The difficulties that might have been apprehended in our session are pretty well over; the accounts are adjusted, and the usual supply voted, and a bill ordered to be brought in accordingly. We had an attempt made in our House to call for the accounts of the nation, which as it was new here, might have occasioned a quarrel with the House of Commons, and probably was intended so to do, but it was overruled by about 28 to 11.

We are going on with some bills to mend the state of our Church, by getting more glebes, Churches, and Chapels of Ease, that we may in time have Churches and resident ministers to answer our wants, for at present many of our people go off to the papists or Presbyterians, for want of Churches to repair to.

Here is such a jealousy of increasing the wealth of the Church, that what success our bills will have with the Commons is uncertain.

I hope for your Lordship's support of them in the council when they come there, against which time I shall send you a proper account of them.

I must again recommend Mr. Stephens to your Lordship's protection, as to the promise made him of a canonry of Christ Church.

I find the peace is still uncertain, though we hope for the best.

The Bishop of Cloyne will I believe apply for a bill in England, relating to his bishoprick, of which I shall give your Lordship a larger account another time.

I heartily wish your Lordship many happy new years, and am,

My Lord, &c.

To the Archbishop of Canterbury.

Dublin, Jan. 13, 1727/8.

My Lord,

It is a great while since I had the honour of a letter from your Grace, which I have not answered sooner, because I had nothing new to write from hence; what little this country now affords is, that our session goes on very quietly, and the usual supplies are voted, and a bill going on accordingly.

I find by my Lord Lieutenant the ministry are not desirous that a convocation should sit here; nor do I desire it, except they had some useful business to do, and I was thoroughly certain they would confine themselves to that.

I have had no great occasion or leisure to enquire into the nature of our convocation here, but as it is made up of the clergy of four provinces, I find some of our bench question whether they have ever been settled in such a regular method of being called, as to make a truly legal assembly.

I am glad to find things have gone so very well in England since his Majesty's accession, and that the late King's friends (who most certainly are so to his present Majesty) have no cause of complaint.

My Lord Lieutenant has made no change in any place here.

We were some time ago more certain of a speedy peace here by all accounts than we seem to be at present, but I hope all will end well.

I most heartily wish your Grace many happy new years, and am very much obliged to your Lordship for your readiness to assist me on occasion with your interest. I am sure the steady attachment of your Grace to his Majesty's family and person will always make you have a weight at court.

I believe the Bishop of Cloyne will have occasion to apply for a bill in

England, relating to an incumbrance on his bishoprick; when it is certain that he must apply I shall trouble your Grace with the particulars of his case.

I am, my Lord, &c.

To the Duke of Newcastle.

Dublin, Jan. 16, 1727/8.

My Lord,

It is now a great while since I did myself the honour to write to your Grace; the great hurry of business your Lordship must have been engaged in, and the peaceable state we have been in here, without any particular accidents that required writing about, have been the occasion of so long a silence.

The difficulties that were in part apprehended in the sessions of parliament are now pretty well over: the publick accounts have been stated to the satisfaction of the Commons, and the usual money bill will be ready for the council next Monday. As the accounts have been now audited by the Commissioners of Accounts to Lady-day last, and will whilst the English have any power here, be regularly audited every year, it will not be so easy to embroil a session as it was the last time the parliament sat, when Prat's accounts were in such confusion, for want of being regularly audited for some years.

I hope it has not contributed a little towards things passing easy here, that since the government has been pretty much in English hands, things have gone with greater impartiality, and every body of consequence has been treated with more regard than they have been formerly

My Lord Chancellor and Lord Chief Baron have been very diligent in the affair of the accounts; and it has not been without great pressing that we could get the several officers to have the accounts ready to be audited before the parliament met: and I must do them both the justice to say, that they give great content in their respective courts.

Our new Lord Chief Justice[86] landed on Saturday, was sworn into his place yesterday, and was this day sworn of the privy council; I hear that good character of him, that I do not question but by his abilities and integrity he will be a great strengthening of the English interest.

Your Grace will be so good as to excuse my again recommending Mr. Stephens to your protection for the promise formerly made me, that he should have the next canonry of Christ Church that happened to be void. I am,

My Lord, &c

86 Reynolds.

To the Archbishop of Canterbury.

Dublin, Feb. 13, 1727/8.

My Lord,

As we are sending over some bills to England, which are of great consequence to religion in this country, and in the supporting of which at council
I must beg your Lordship's assistance, I give you this trouble to let you know
what is our case, and what are our views in them.

There are probably in this kingdom five papists at least to one protestant:
we have incumbents and curates to the number of about 800, whilst there are
near 3000 popish priests of all sorts here. A great part of our clergy have no
parsonage houses, nor glebes to build them on: we have many parishes eight
and ten, twelve and fourteen miles long, with it may be only one Church in
them, and that often at one end of the parish: we have few market towns that
supply convenient food for the neighbourhood, nor farmers that can supply
the common necessaries of life, which may be had at most farmers in
England; so that all agree no clergyman in the country can live without a
moderate glebe in his hands: and as there can be no hopes of getting ground
of the papists without more Churches or Chapels, and more resident
clergymen, we have been framing two bills, one for explaining and
amending an act for the better maintenance of curates in the Church of
Ireland, 6° Georgii. By that act a Bishop was enabled to cause one or two
Chapels of Ease to be erected in any parish where a number of Protestants
lived six miles from the Church, and that was understood to mean six
country miles, which are at least nine measured miles, and in many places
twelve: we have reduced that distance to five measured miles, the incumbents and patrons consent we have omitted, as what we fear will render the
bill useless: the consents we have made necessary are such protestant inhabitants as may want a Chapel exclusive of those of the Mother-church, or on
the other side of it, as they must contribute towards building it: at the
instance of the clergy we have likewise excluded such as live within two
miles of a neighbouring Church: the Bishop has the same power of
appointing a salary for these new curates as that act allowed.

We have likewise there provided for the building of Chapels of Ease in
cities and towns corporate.

The other is an act to explain an act for the better enabling of the clergy
having the cure of souls to reside on their respective benefices, &c. 8° Georg.
c.12 There is by the old act a power of giving land under 40 acres for a glebe,
at half the improved rent or more; but as most of the estates here are under
settlements, it has little effect: and there are now three or four gentlemen that
would grant 15 or 20 acres for glebes if they were at liberty. This act therefore
is to empower those under settlements to give a glebe at the full improved
rent, to be settled by a jury, on condition of building and improving.

Beside the benefit of distress for arrears of rent, the bishop is impowered to sequester the whole living upon complaint to pay such arrears. And that the successor may not have an unreasonable arrear come upon him, the Bishop is obliged to enquire at every annual visitation which we hold here, whether the rent is paid, and to sequester and see it paid. The same power of giving a glebe is extended to perpetual curacies in livings appropriate or impropriate.

Having endeavoured to provide glebes, we oblige all future incumbents having convenient glebes to build. All are allowed three-fourths of what they lay out, but we see nothing but force will make them build.

As there are several schools of whose endowments I am trustee, that have some no house, others inconvenient little ones, without land near them, the same encouragement is given to them to build as to the clergy, and they are impowered to exchange some land for a convenient demesne, under proper inspection.

We have likewise sent over a bill about the recovering of tythes and other ecclesiastical dues, under 40s. We had the English act before us, but have altered some things to please the Commons, who have twice thrown out a bill of the same nature; oblations and obventions are omitted to please them. We have likewise excluded clergymen from being the Justices before whom such causes may be tried, that they might not play the game into one another's hands; for in many places here one fourth or fifth of the resident justices are clergymen, for want of resident gentlemen.

The bill is exceedingly necessary here, since the recovery of little dues costs more than they are worth, and the justices will not help. People stand contempt and excommunication, and the taking up costs too much, and beside most of them must be absolutely ruined if taken up.

There is likewise another bill coming which has been in force seven years already, by which the incumbent that has been a wrong clerk is accountable for the profits received, after such allowances made for serving the cure. The laity in both houses are very eager for it, and the English Bishops are for it, there having been formerly very extraordinary things done here by Bishops, in putting clerks in possession that scarce had the shadow of a title.[87]

I am,

Your Grace's, &c.

To the same.

Dublin, Feb. 17, 1727/8.

My Lord,

I lately troubled your Grace with an account of three bills we are sending from hence; I shall now trouble you with an account of two or three more, in the passing of which in England I must desire your Grace's assistance.

---

87 This and the two following letters were copied and sent to the Bishop of London also.

The first relates to the more easy recovery of tythes and other ecclesiastical dues of small value. The value settled in the bill is not exceeding 40s. We had the English act before us, but have altered some things in it, partly because of the different case we are in from those in England, and partly to please the Commons, who have twice thrown out a bill of the same nature. In the first place, instead of small tythes in the English act, we have substituted tythes under 40s. per ann. The occasion of this change is, that in a great part of this kingdom the bulk of the farmers have but four, six, eight or ten acres, and a farmer of twenty acres is a great farmer, which makes it very troublesome and expensive to recover tythes either in a spiritual court or in the exchequer.

The usual way of suing for tythes here is in the spiritual courts; and for the small portion most people are to pay here, it will not often be worth while to go into the exchequer. Now when one of these sorry wretches is put into the spiritual court, he usually incurs contempt for non-appearance, and afterwards falls under the sentence of excommunication, which he does not regard; if a clergyman should then be at the expense of taking out a writ de excommunicato capiendo, and take the defendant up, the costs of the suit and tythes recovered, would absolutely beggar the poor wretch; so that these causes are seldom carried through: but when the fellow is found not to be frighted with excommunication, (which considering the number of papists and dissenters here, is most generally the case) it is dropped.

There is indeed an English statute 27° Hen. 8. c. 20. an act for tythes to be paid throughout this realm, which was plainly intended to affect Ireland as much as England, by which two justices of the peace, upon non-appearance in the spiritual court, might oblige the defendant to appear and to give security to abide the sentence of the court; but as Ireland though at first mentioned, is not afterwards repeated, the judges and justices here seem to be of opinion that the justices cannot act here in virtue of that statute; and the justices will not assist the spiritual courts and the Commons will not hear of an act for the justices to help the ecclesiastical judge, so that this act about recovering tythes, &c. would be of great service to the clergy here.

The words oblations and obventions have been omitted as having been formerly objected against by the Commons. And to remove any jealousy that the clergy might try all these causes before one another, we have excluded the clergy from acting as justices in the execution of this act; which is the more reasonable here, because in many counties one fourth or fifth part of the residing justices are of the clergy; since otherwise many tracts of lands of ten or fifteen miles every way would have no resident justice.

We shall likewise send over an act to impower Archbishops, &c. to part with the advowson of benefices under 30l. per ann. or more. My brethren the bishops consented to this bill before it was offered. And that your Grace may the better understand the expediency of this bill, it will be proper to inform you, that in many parts of this kingdom, by means of impropriations, there are vicarages or curacies worth but 5, 10l. &c. per ann. that in several places the Bishops let the same person enjoy three or four on to seven or eight of these, which possibly all together make but 60, 80 or 100l. per ann. or little more: and there is it may be but one or two Churches on all the denominations, which is the name we give these parishes: that the patronage of the greatest part of these is either in the Crown or the Bishops; that there might be difficulties raised as to the Crown parting with its right, but we think there can be no objection to suffer Bishops to part with their right for the good of the Church, and procuring additional clergymen; and we have the more reason to try what effect this temptation of the sole patronage to a lay benefactor may have, since the act of King Charles I. by which any one who restored tythes to the Church was to have a turn with the old patron in proportion to the value of tythes given, in respect of the old income of the Church, has had very little effect. We have in the same bill encouraged people to build and endow Chapels of Ease by giving them and their heirs the nomination to such Chapels.

Your Grace will see that in this act we had before us the act passed in England 1° Georg. I. Only that we have no fund to help such benefactors as there is in England; and as there are trustees of the first fruits here for buying glebes or tythes for small livings, we have in this act made them the repositories of the authentick value of small livings, and of all augmentations in virtue of this act, that there may be some to see that the grants are such as they ought to be for value and validity.

In this kingdom the clergy paid the 20th, not the 10th to the Crown, as in England, and first fruits; but the 20ths were given off by Queen Anne, and the first fruits are the only fund the trustees have, which communibus annis, rises no higher than from 3 to 400l. per ann. deducting charges, without a power to receive any benefactions. I hope it may please God in time to dispose the parliament to permit these trustees to receive benefactions for so good purposes; since what we are now doing in our Church bills seems to be very well liked; though when I first came hither, the laity would not have heard with patience the least proposal of what we are now attempting.

The clause in this bill by which the patron of a Chapel of Ease may nominate, if the Chapel be not actually filled then, though the nomination be then lapsed to the Bishop or Crown, is taken from the English bill. There was this day added to the said bill a clause to impower Bishops, &c. to encourage their tenants by a proper lease to enclose and preserve copse wood, which will be of service to all parties.

I must beg your Grace's assistance in the council, that our good designs may not be there sunk and prevented.

I am, my Lord, &c.

To the same.

Dublin, Feb. 24, 1727/8.

My Lord,

I have troubled your Grace with two long letters already, and must beg leave to trouble you with a third, about some other bills we are sending over, in getting which returned hither I must beg your Grace's assistance at the council.

As many of the parishes here are very large and intermixed with other parishes, and others of too little income to subsist by themselves, and little enough for extent to be united to some other parish or part of a parish, there was an act passed in the 14° and 15° of King Charles the second, by which parishes might be divided or united for conveniency's sake, with proper consents and the approbation of the chief governor and the council. As that act was expired, a new act was passed 2° Georgii, for the real union and division of parishes, in which was a proviso, that no union made in virtue of the former act of King Charles the second should be capable of being dissolved, nor any part of such union be united to any other parish, unless the parish Church of such united parish does lye three country miles from some part of such parish, &c.

Now as three country miles are often five or six measured miles; and as several of those unions were made without regard to the conveniency of the people, but purely to make a rich benefice; as we are now endeavouring to make it possible to have the worship of God celebrated in all parts of this kingdom, we find it necessary to repeal this clause, and to lay such parishes open to a division as well as other old parishes.

There is another clause added to that bill, which relates to the removing of the site of Churches. By the act 2° Georgii, for the real union and division of parishes, it is enacted that the site of an inconvenient Church may be changed for one more convenient with the consent of the patron, &c.

Now with us many Churches stand at the end of a long parish, or on the wrong side of a bog or river, in respect of the greatest part of the parishioners, or at least protestants; so that it would be very convenient to change such situation of the Church; but where the King is patron, as his consent is to be had, the expence of having a letter from England to give his Majesty's consent under the broad seal here to such a change, and passing a patent for it, is so great, as to discourage these removals: and I can assure your Grace 10l. is harder to be raised here upon a country parish than 100l. is in England upon a parish of the same extent, and our gentry part with money on such occasions as unwillingly as the peasantry.

It is therefore provided in the same bill, that the chief governor, &c, may consent for the King where the King is patron; and as the King's patronage cannot be hurt by such a change of the site of a Church, but the parish will probably prove of better value; and as the taking off of this expence may occasion the building several more convenient Churches, we hope the bill will be returned to us: And I can assure your Grace there are instances in two or three acts already where the chief governor, &c. is impowered to consent for the King.

These two clauses make up an act, entitled, an act, for repealing a clause in an act for the real union and division of parishes; and to enable the chief governor, &c. to consent for the crown, &c.

There is part of another bill which will go over, that is of great consequence to this kingdom; the title of the act is, I think, an act to prevent frauds. &c. in buying corn, &c. and to encourage tillage.

It is the latter part of this bill about tillage that is of great moment here, The bill does not encourage tillage by allowing any premium to the exporters of corn, but barely obliges every person occupying 100 acres or more (meadows, parks, bogs, &c. excepted) to till five acres out of every 100; and so in proportion for every greater quantity of land they occupy. And to make the law have some force, it sets the tenant at liberty to do this, notwithstanding any clause in his lease to the contrary. We have taken care to provide in the bill, that the tenant shall not be able to burn-beat any ground in virtue of this act; and since he is tied up from that, and from ploughing meadows, &c. the people skilled in husbandry say, he cannot hurt the land though he should go round the 100 acres in 20 years.

I find my Lord Trevor objected to a bill we sent from council, that this was a breaking of private contracts, and invading property: but I think that nothing, since the lessor receives no damage by it, and the publick is very much benefitted; and this is no more than what is done every session in England, where rivers are made navigable or commons inclosed; and in many road bills.

I shall now acquaint your grace with the great want we are in of this bill: our present tillage falls very short of answering the demands of this nation, which occasions our importing corn from England and other places; and whilst our poor have bread to eat, we do not complain of this; but by tilling so little, if our crop fails, or yields indifferently, our poor have not money to buy bread. This was the case in 1725, and last year, and without a prodigious crop, will be more so this year. When I went my visitation last year, barley in some inland places, sold for 6s. a bushel, to make the bread of; and oatmeal (which is the bread of the north) sold for twice or thrice the usual price: and we met all the roads full of whole families that had left their homes to beg abroad, since their neighbours had nothing to relieve them with. And as the winter subsistance of the poor is chiefly potatoes, this scarcity drove the poor to begin with their potatoes before they were full grown, so that they have lost half the benefit of them, and have spent their stock about two months sooner than usual; and oatmeal is at this distance from harvest, in many parts of this kingdom three times the customary price; so that this summer must be more fatal to us than the last; when I fear many hundreds perished by famine.

Now the occasion of this evil is, that many persons have hired large tracts of land, on to 3 or 4000 acres, and have stocked them with cattle, and have no other inhabitants on their land than so many cottiers as are necessary to look after their sheep and black cattle; so that in some of the finest counties, in many places there is neither house nor corn field to be seen in 10 or 15 miles travelling: and daily in some counties, many gentlemen (as their leases fall into their hands) tye up their tenants from tillage: and this in one of the main causes why so many venture to go into foreign service at the hazard of their lives, if taken, because they can get no land to till at home. And if some stop be not put to this evil, we must daily decrease in the numbers of our people.

But we hope if this tillage bill takes place, to keep our youth at home, to employ our poor, and not be in danger of a famine among the poor upon any little miscarriage in our harvest. And I hope these are things of greater consequence than the breaking through a lease, so far as concerns ploughing five acres in an hundred.

I shall trouble your Grace no more at present, but am,

My Lord, &c.

To the Duke of Newcastle.

Dublin, Mar. 7, 1727/8.

My Lord,

As we are now very nigh got through our several bills at the council, I shall beg leave to give your Grace an account of some few of them, in the returning of which from the council of England, I would beg your Grace's assistance.

We have in this kingdom but about 600 incumbents, and I fear 3000 popish priests, and the bulk of our clergy have neither parsonage-houses nor glebes: and yet till we can get more Churches or Chapels and more resident clergymen, instead of getting ground of the papists, we must lose to them, as in fact we do in many places, the descendants of many of Cromwell's officers and soldiers here being gone off to popery.

To remedy this evil, we have sent over a bill for the better maintenance of curates, by which Bishops are enabled with the consent of the protestant parishioners, to have one or more Chapels built in large parishes, and to oblige the incumbent to pay for serving them.

By another bill to enable the clergy to reside, we have empowered persons under settlements, and all Bishops and other ecclesiastical persons, to grant a glebe where wanted, not exceeding 40 acres at the full improved rent; and oblige all future incumbents that have a convenient glebe, and a living not less than 150l. per ann. to build a parsonage-house; of which expence they are to be reimbursed three fourths by their successor, the next to be reimbursed two, and the following incumbent one fourth.

There is a third bill to encourage benefactors to increase our poor livings, (many of which have so small an income, that in some parts of the kingdom, the same person enjoys four, five, and sometimes on to eight or nine of them, and yet has not 100l. per ann.) by enabling Archbishops, Bishops, and other ecclesiastical persons to part with the advowson of livings under 30l. per ann. to such benefactor as will endow such small living with 30l. per ann. or more; and by giving the patronage of a Chapel to any one who shall build a Chapel and endow it with 30l. per ann. or more. In this act we had before us, one to the same purpose past in England in the first year of his late Majesty.

In a bill to repeal a clause in a former bill, about the real union and division of parishes, there is a clause that the chief governor may, where the King is patron, consent for the King, to the removing the site of a Church to a more convenient place in the parish. Our parishes here are exceeding poor, and the addition of 16 or 20l. in the fees, prevents building a Church in a convenient part of the parish, where the old Church stands it may be at one end of a very large parish; and we hope as the King's patronage cannot be hurt, but rather improved by such a change, that this clause will be granted us.

As these are in some sort Church bills, I have not troubled your Grace with a very particular account of them, but have sent a more large account of them to the Bishop of London, who will be able to inform your Grace more fully of their nature and design, as well as of the following bills, if your Grace desires it.

There is another bill gone over, part of which is for the encouragement of tillage; it is to the same purpose as one that went from the council to England at his Majesty's happy accession. It gives no premium to the exporter of corn, but obliges every person occupying 100 acres or more, to plough five for every 100 acres he possesses, excepting meadows and other pasture lands; and as the landlords in some parts here tye up their tenants from ploughing, it releases the tenant from such articles as far as five acres in 100; but that the landlord may be no sufferer, the tenant is not at liberty to burn-beat the land. For want of tillage our young fellows have no employment at home, and go into foreign service; and upon any accident in our harvest, we are in danger of a famine.

Since I came here in the year 1725, there was almost a famine among the poor; last year the dearness of corn was such that thousands of families quitted their habitations to seek bread elsewhere, and many hundreds perished; this year the poor had consumed their potatoes, which is their winter subsistance, near two months sooner than ordinary, and are already through the dearness of corn, in that want, that in some places they begin already to quit their habitations. I hope we shall meet with so much compassion at the council, as to let us have this bill returned, that the inconveniencies we are at present so frequently exposed to, may be gradually removed.

There is another bill gone over, to regulate the admission of barristers, attornies, six-clerks, sollicitors, sub-sheriffs, deputy officers, &c. which is of the last consequence to this kingdom.

The practice of the law, from the top to the bottom, is at present mostly in the hands of new converts, who give no farther security on this account, than producing a certificate of their having received the sacrament in the Church of England or Ireland, which several of them who were papists at London, obtain on the road hither, and demand to be admitted barrister in virtue of it, at their arrival; and several of them have popish wives and mass said in their houses, and breed up their children papists.

Things are at present so bad with us, that if about six should be removed from the bar to the bench here, there will not be a barrister of note left that is not a convert.

To put some stop to this evil, this bill endeavours to obtain some farther security of the sincerity of these converts: 1. by obliging all that come to the bar hereafter, or practise as attornies or sollicitors, &c. or act as sub-sheriffs, sheriffs clerks, or deputy officers in the courts, to make a declaration against popery, and take the oath of abjuration before they are admitted or practice: 2. that every convert shall have been so five years before his admission, or so practising or acting: 3. that he breed up all his children under 14, as well those born before his conversion, as those after, in the protestant religion: and 4. that whoever fails in any of these points, shall incur the penalties and disabilities to which those relapsing from the protestant religion to popery are liable.

Every body here is sensible of the terrible effects of this growing evil, and both Lords and Commons are most eagerly desirous of this bill.

We have likewise by this bill inflicted the same penalties on every convert or protestant who shall breed up any child a papist. But if the latter part be thought too severe, or have too strong a party against it, I hope, however that what relates to lawyers, attornies, sollicitors, sub-sheriffs, &c. will be granted us, or the protestant interest must suffer extremely here.

I should flatter myself, that as in this bill we have not meddled with the papists, but only with persons professing themselves protestants, the foreign ministers cannot with any reason or decency make any application to his Majesty against this bill.

We have this week had before us a bill, in which the value of several goods that pay custom, that were before unsettled, is fixed. By a letter that we shall send with it from the council, I hope it will appear that we have acted with a due sense of our duty to his Majesty; and I can assure your Grace that the altering a rate sent up by the Commons, was done with that gentleness and tenderness, that some very warm men of that house, have thanked my Lord Chancellor and myself for the tenderness we shewed on that occasion to the subject, and have assured us they do not question the Commons readily acquiescing in what is done.

As I must have tired your Grace by this time, I shall conclude with subscribing myself,

My Lord, &c.

To the Bishop of London.

Dublin, Mar. 7, 1727/8.

My Lord,

After the great trouble I have already given your Lordship about our bills, I must desire your farther assistance at the council about one bill more.

It is an act for regulating the admission of barristers, attornies, six-clerks, &c. As the laws stand already these several persons ought to be protestants, but they give no further security of their being so, than that, if they are born of popish parents, they must produce a certificate of their having received the sacrament in the Church of England or Ireland; and must educate their children under 14 years of age at their conversion in the protestant religion. But as the law stands at present, a man may the day after his real or pretended conversion, be admitted a barrister, attorney, &c. and practise as a sollicitor, or be a deputy officer or sub-sheriff, &c. and we have had several who were papists, and on the road from London hither have taken the sacrament and obtained a certificate, and at their arrival here have been admitted to the bar. They likewise pretend that the children born after their conversion are not included in that clause about educating their children protestants, because they were not under 14 at the time of their conversion; so that many of these converts have a popish wife who has mass said in the family, and the children are brought up papists.

Now this grievance is the greater here, because the business of the law from top to bottom is almost in the hands of these converts; when eight or ten protestants are set aside, the rest of the bar are all converts; much the greatest part of attornies, sollicitors, deputy officers, sub-sheriffs, sheriffs clerks, are new converts; and the old protestants are every day more and more working out of the business of the law, which must end in our ruin.

This makes us attempt to remedy this evil by this bill, for the success of which both Lords and Commons are equally sollicitous. In this bill the farther securities we require of all these people are: 1. that for the future, all taking to the law shall make the declarations, and take and subscribe to the oath required in the act to prevent the farther growth of popery, 2° Annae reg. the declaration is against several of the errors of popery; the oath is that of abjuration: 2. that nobody shall be admitted a barrister, &c. till five years after his conversion, and continuing in the Church of Ireland: 3. that they breed up the post nati as well as the ante nati under 14, protestants: 4. that he who offends in any of these points shall fall under the disabilities, &c. to which one relapsing from the protestant to the popish religion is subject.

This is what we tried originally to push at, but were forced to take in all converts educating their children papists, and subject them to the like incapacities, and likewise protestants so offending: the occasion of this latter clause is, that the sons of some converts breed their children papists, and reckon they do not incur the penalties appointed for converts educating their children papists, because say they, our fathers were indeed converts, but we are original protestants.

I find there are great hopes here among the papists, that the bringing in all converts makes such a strength against the bill, that it will be sunk in England. If there be any danger of that, or what relates to all converts be thought too severe, I would beg we may have so much returned to us of the bill as relates to all in any branch of the law; for we must be undone here if that profession gets into the hands of converts, where it is almost already got, and where it every day gets more and more.

I have referred his Grace of Newcastle, to whom I have wrote about some of our bills, to your Lordship, to be more fully informed than I could inform his Lordship in the compass of a letter: the bills he is most likely to enquire after are, the clause about the chief governor consenting for the King to the change of the site of a Church, the tillage bill, and the bill about lawyers, but your Lordship will be so good as beside talking to him on those, to inform him of any of the others he wants to understand more distinctly.

I shall trouble your Lordship no more at present, but subscribe myself,
My Lord, &c.

To the Archbishop of Canterbury.

Dublin, Apr. 2, 1728.

My Lord,

I have received the honour of your Grace's of the 19th past, and am very glad to have it under your Lordship's hand that you are out of danger, and daily recovering strength, and pray God to raise you up again for the good of the Church.

I am very much obliged to you for the care you took of our Church bills, under so great weakness, by recommending the care of them to so able a person and so good a friend of the Church as my Lord Privy Seal.[88] I find most of them are gone through the committee of council, and hope as my Lord was fully instructed in our wants, that he has struck out an alteration made by the Attorney-general in our bill for the residence of clergymen, which if it has stood, will defeat the chief intention of the bill.

Our bench have been very busy with their friends in the House of Commons, to pass our bills when returned, which if they do, we may hope by degrees to see somewhat of the face of religion in this country.

I have been enquiring about the value of Mr. Horner's living, and believe it to be about 160l. per ann. I believe he has been under great difficulties, as he was very bare of money when he first took it, and was kept out of part of the tythes of the first year, and has had but slow payments of the tythes of the second harvest, since it is generally counted good payment if a clergyman gets half his tythes paid him the Candlemas after they were due. His uneasiness is not owing to his temper, but to very great rudenesses he has met with from a popish gentleman of a good estate in his parish, whose tenants most of the parishioners are, as they are likewise papists. And I do not find he has given any other offence than preaching against popery, and talking with some of his parishioners to bring them over to our Church. As Mr. Horner is one who has a sense of his duty, I hope he may be of service here, and after some time he may be removed to somewhat better.

I am glad the affair of a prolocutor, and the meeting of a convocation are gone off so easily, and hope things will daily come to a better temper in England.

Colonel Valon, who came hither with the Marquiss of Montandre,[89] has been with me, and brought me an account of the kind care you had taken of our Church bills, and of the fair way of recovery your Grace was in, before I had the honour of your last.

I shall trouble your Grace no more at present, but conclude with my best wishes for your health and happiness, and subscribe myself,

My Lord, &c.

To the Bishop of London.

Dublin, Apr. 13, 1728.

My Lord,

I most heartily thank your Lordship for the trouble you have been at, and the care you have taken about our Church bills; I am very well satisfied with the words or Churches being kept in, and the reasons you give for it; and in

88 Thomas Lord Trevor.
89 Master of the Ordnance in Ireland.

the main have very little fear of any Bishops giving away the estates of their sees to augment livings, though by that clause they are impowered to do it.

I could heartily wish the powers desired for persons under settlements to grant 40 acres for a glebe had been granted us.[90] Another time we must try for 20 acres, without which we cannot compass parsonage-houses here. But about this I shall trouble your Lordship no more at present.

Our curates bill has passed the Commons, and there appears a disposition in them to pass our other Church bills; though one of them, viz. the tythe bill, has had a petition preferred against it by the quakers, who are to be heard by council against it on Tuesday next. I think their petition will do the bill no hurt, since it was resented by the Commons as a shameful piece of ingratitude to the Bishops, without whom their bill about their affirmation could not have passed.

Another sessions, if it please God that I live, I shall endeavour after your Lordship's advice, to make the affair of our Church bills more easy to your Lordship.

My Lord Lieutenant hopes our parliament will have done time enough for him to set out for England about the 9th of next month. We shall do our part in the House of Lords to let him be at liberty by that time. On Monday will be the warmest day this session in the House of Commons about the privilege bill, which meets with so great opposition there, that the success is doubtful.

I am, my Lord, &c.

To the Archbishop of Canterbury.

Dublin, Apr. 18, 1728.

My Lord,

I have had with me Sir Thomas Taylour, a very worthy gentleman of this country, to desire I would write to some of my friends in the House of Lords in England to attend a cause he had depending there, in which John Cahill and William Donellan are appellants, and Sir Thomas defendant.

I find they trump up against him a lease made in the year 1680, which they never made any claim upon till 1720, after he by laying out above 1000l. per ann. on the estate had raised the rent about 100l. per ann. If such old leases are once allowed (considering how easy it is to get people here to swear to any thing) the protestant possessors here will have but precarious estates where they have been fair purchasers, and have laid out great sums in improving estates.

But the merits of the cause your Lordship will best know from what is

90 A bill did pass afterwards.

proved at the bar. The only favour I desire is that you would be pleased to attend at the hearing of the cause, which will very much oblige,

Your Grace's, &c.

To the Duke of Newcastle.

Dublin, Apr. 25, 1728.

My Lord,

Though your Grace in the great hurry of business has not found leisure to honour me with a letter, yet by the success of our bills in the council, I find your Lordship has not forgot the request I made to you about them. I have great hopes they will prove of great service here to strengthen the protestant interest, and will prove useful both in Church and state.

As I was known to be a hearty sollicitor for them, their being returned us has given me some additional weight here, which I need not tell your Grace, with whatever else lies in my power, shall always be employed for his Majesty's service here.

To-morrow the fate of the privilege bill, which has already past the Commons, will be determined in our House; and I think it will be there carried to the great benefit of this kingdom.

I am, my Lord, &c.

To the same.

Dublin, Apr. 30, 1728.

My Lord,

On Friday last came on the debate in our House, about the privilege bill, which was carried 25 against 19: there was one proxy among the 25, and seven among the 19. Several of our Lords who are very much in debt, and value themselves upon paying nobody, were from the first very much against the bill; but the great opposition made on this occasion, was formed and managed by the Bishop of Elphin,[91] who put himself at the head of those Lords, and drew in some others, with a view of making himself considerable by being at the head of a party of lay Lords against the bench of Bishops. All the lay Lords that oppose the government in whatever they can, joined against the bill. There was no Bishop against it but the Bishop of Elphin, and of Waterford, for whom he was proxy. The Lord Middleton was the first who spoke against the bill, and that very prolixly and to little purpose: he was very well answered by the Archbishop of Tuam.[92] After this the Bishop of

91 Dr. Bolton.
92 Dr. Synge.

Elphin made a speech with very false reasonings, and some inflaming passages against England: though in the close of his speech, he was rather as circumstances now stand, for the passing the bill: he has very much lost himself with both sides by his shuffling speech on this occasion. As his speech did no hurt to the bill, we let the debate drop without answering him.

I hope it will not be thought proper, when a vacancy happens of an Archbishoprick, to reward one with it who has endeavoured to form a conspiracy of lay Lords against the Bishops here, who are the persons on whom the government must depend for doing the publick business.

We shall probably conclude our sessions next Monday, when more truly useful bills will have passed, than have passed for many sessions put together.

I must again thank your Grace for your kind care of our bills at the council.

I am, my Lord, &c.

Newcastle to Boulter.

Whitehall, May 7, 1728.
(NA. SP. 63/390/87)

My Lord,

I am to return my thanks to your Grace, for several letters I had the honour to receive from you, the last being dated the 30th of April, and I hope you will be so good as to forgive my not having troubled you with particular acknowledgements of them, considering the continual hurry we have been in here during the session of Parliament.

I have informed the King from time to time, of the very useful hints I received from your Grace, and I can assure you, that his Majesty is very sensible of your zeal for His service, and pays great regard on all occasions to your advice. The letter your Grace sent me whilst the Bills from Ireland were before the Council, was particularly of use to the Attorney General, and his Majesty's servants here have had the greatest attention to it, as your Grace will have found by the return of the Bills therein mentioned.

Your last contains a very instructive account of the debates in the House of Lords upon the Priviledge Bill, and gives a good deal of light into the particular disposition of some members of that House. I laid it before the King, and his Majesty took particular notice of the contents of it.

I heartily wish your Grace joy of the happy conclusion of your session of Parliament, in which you have had the satisfaction of seeing so many good Bills brought to perfection, and beg leave to assure you of the very truth and respect with which I am

etc.

Holles Newcastle

To Lord Townshend.

Dubin, May 9, 1728.

My Lord,

It is with great pleasure that I hear from all hands, that I may now congratulate your Lordship upon your recovery from a long and dangerous illness, and I heartily wish you may continue many years in a state of health for the service of his Majesty and your country.

On Monday our session ended, which has gone on with more quiet and unanimity than usual; and in which more useful bills[93] have passed than for many sessions together before. And I hope both gentry and clergy will use those powers now given them gradually to plant religion and civility in this country.

I must on this occasion own the great obligations I lie under to your Lordship, and the rest of the privy council, for the regard shewn to my accounts and recommendations of several of our bills.

The chief opposition that was made here to any of our bills, was to the privilege bill, and the greatest stand against it was in the House of Lords. Several of our Lords that are embarrassed in their circumstances, might naturally be supposed to be against it: but the greatness of the opposition was owing to the management of the Bishop of Elphin, who put himself at the head of those Lords and others who constantly oppose the government business here, and by misrepresentations drew in some other Lords of no ill intentions to engage their word and honour to each other to throw out the bill. His view no doubt was to make himself considerable enough by being at the head of this strength to be bought off. One part of the push he now made was to get all the lay Lords here to confederate against the Bishops, who must always be depended upon for doing the King's business. But as he has miscarried in his attempt, and has offended all sides, so as to be in no danger of appearing again at the head of so many Lords as he did now, I hope his behaviour will be remembered, when he or his friends push for the archbishoprick of Dublin for him.

As your Lordship was so good as to promise me before I left England that Mr. Stephens should have the next canonry of Christ Church, and as Dr. Burton cannot probably hold our long, I must again recommend Mr. Stephens to your Lordship's protection and favour on that occasion; and your support of his pretensions will be esteemed the greatest obligation by,

My Lord, &c.

---

93 His Grace was the framer of most, if not of all these bills.

To the Duke of Newcastle.

Dublin, May 25, 1728.

My Lord,

I had the honour of your Grace's of the 7th inst. I am sensible of the great hurry you was in during the sessions of parliament, and am the more obliged to your Lordship for the great care you was pleased, in the midst of so much business of greater consequence, to take of our bills, and can assure your Grace the returning of all our publick bills was very gratefully taken here. I am satisfied we have in some of them laid a very foundation for gradually strengthening the protestant interest here, and civilizing this country.

The great distress the poor are in, through a great part of this country, has raised a resolution in many of the gentry to put the tillage bill in execution, which I hope will in a few years prevent our suffering little less than a famine almost every other year.

I am very glad to hear that any accounts I sent of our bills were of service to the Attorney-General when he had them under consideration; and make my humblest acknowledgments for the regard shewn by your Grace and the other ministers, to what I suggested on that occasion.

I am very much obliged to your Grace for your favourably representing my endeavours to serve his Majesty.

As at the latter end of the sessions a scheme was formed by a Bishop to raise a party that might on occasion oppose the service of his Majesty in the House of Lords, I thought it my duty to acquaint your Grace with it at the first appearance. But I hope we shall easily defeat any future attempts of the same nature.

As my Lord Lieutenant did his part towards procuring a quiet session of parliament here, so I must do that justice to the rest of the English in power here, to say that we were not in the least wanting in our several stations to promote the same good end.

As the want of silver grows every day greater here, to the great prejudice of our manufactures, and the retail trade, I shall in a little time draw up a memorial on that subject, containing the true causes of our distress and the proper remedies, which I should be glad to have communicated to the Chancellor of the Exchequer,[94] if he can find leisure to have it considered. I am,

My Lord, &c.

94 Sir Robert Walpole.

To the same.

Dublin, May 31, 1728.

My Lord,

Mr. Manley, our Post-master here, having occasion to go to England to sollicit a continuance of his pension of 200l. per ann. which dropt by the death of his late Majesty; I was willing to give him what assistance I could, by recommending him to your Grace for your kind help. He is one who has behaved himself well in his post, and is well affected to his Majesty, and has always distinguished himself by his zeal for the illustrious House of Hanover, in the worst times. The pleas he has for having his pension continued he will inform your Grace of; but your assistance of him on this occasion will be counted an obligation by,

My Lord, &c.

To Lord Carteret.

Dublin, June 6, 1728.

My Lord,

It was with great satisfaction I heard that your Excellency was safely arrived at London. I was in hopes we should this day have answered your Excellency's two letters relating to the Caesar, but as we differed among ourselves, and likewise the council (whom we summoned upon this occasion) differed about the sense of your Lordship's last letter, whether we were left at liberty to let that ship go free, if we thought proper, considering all circumstances, it will be another post before we can acquaint your Lordship with what we have done. Some here applied the King's approbation (mentioned in your letter) to your having put the Caesar under quarantine; and other of us thought his Majesty approved of the directions you was pleased to give us in yours of the 25th past, viz. to act as we thought proper. I am,

My Lord, &c.

To the same.

Dublin, June 20, 1728.

My Lord,

I have had the honour of your Excellency's of the 13th instant.

We have since examined more strictly into the case of the ship Caesar, and find she has nothing on board beside corn, which is not reckoned very liable to take or keep infection; however what we have at last agreed on, is to discharge her at the end of forty days from her first being under the care of Captain Rowley. We shall be very careful never to depart from the general rules without very good reason, and the utmost caution.

We yesterday received Mr. Twell's resignation, and elected Mr. Ellis chaplain to the hospital, pursuant to your Lordship's recommendation. There was some little grumbling in favour of Mr. Hawkins the reader, but in the end all matters were accommodated.

Since your Lordship left us, Dr. Coghill has made some alterations in the paper about the Delegates, which my Lord Chancellor is satisfied with, and which we shall, when fully settled, transmit to your Excellency. I thank your Lordship for having the affair of the coin in your thoughts, to talk with the ministry about it when you see a proper opportunity.

Lord Justice Conolly has been pretty much out of order ever since the 10th of this month, and still continues weak and low-spirited. As Mr. Medlicott is now arrived, he designs to retire to Mr. Pearson's for some time, to try to recover himself.

We shall on Saturday have a council to swear in the Lords Anglesea, Shannon, and Forbes.[95]

I am, My Lord, &c.

To the Duke of Newcastle.

Dublin, June 25, 1728.

My Lord,

In mine of the 25th past, I acquainted your Grace that I hoped in a little time to send you a memorial relating to the want we are in of silver, with the true cause of our distress, and the proper remedies to be applied to this evil, which I desired to be communicated to Sir Robert Walpole.

I have here sent it with an account of the present value of our coins; and the favour I have to desire of Sir Robert Walpole is to look it over, and see whether the scheme there proposed is rational, and what he will intercede with his Majesty to grant us, if we apply for it from the council here.

We had this affair before the council, upon a letter from my Lord Lieutenant in the year 1726, and had made all our calculations of the value intended for gold and silver coins in a new proclamation upon the scheme here proposed; and had almost finished the affair, but the apprehensions of a war and the interest of the bankers here with some of the council, hung up the affair then, and it has slept ever since. But as the want of silver every day increases upon us, and loudly calls for some relief, I have sent over this memorial, that the ministry may be apprized of what we would push at here,

95 Privy Counsellors.

and if the scheme, which I take to be rational, and in respect of England, unexceptionable, be approved of by Sir Robert Walpole, I have no doubt but the Lord Chancellor and myself shall be able to bring it to bear in spight of all the interest of the bankers in the council, where it is greater than it ought to be.

I must recommend the deplorable condition of this kingdom for want of silver to your Grace and the Chancellor of the Exchequer, and I must the more earnestly intreat your assistance, because I have engaged that if they will concur here in what is right, I will answer for the success on the other side of the water.

I should be glad to hear how the scheme is approved of by Sir Robert Walpole as soon as he has leisure to consider it, because we forbear setting it in motion, till we know his judgment of it. I am,

Your Grace's, &c.

To Lord Carteret.

Dublin, July 11, 1728.

My Lord,

I have had the honour of your Lordship's of the 2nd instant, which I communicated to my brethren; and we are all very sensible how much we are obliged to his Majesty for his kind disposition in regard to this kingdom, and to your Excellency for your care of us on this and all other occasions. And we agree entirely in our sentiments on this affair, that two proper remedies for our present want of silver, are the lowering the value of gold, and raising the price of foreign silver. As to the having any silver coined here, on the account of this nation, at the mint in the tower, we think it is an affair that requires and will admit of farther deliberation. As to the coining of copper half-pence, we are all of opinion that it is a thing not to be meddled with but by the parliament, and that if his Majesty will favour the nation with such a coinage on account of the publick, it will be a thing proper for your Excellency, if we have the happiness of seeing your Lordship here another parliament, as I hope we shall, to make an offer of it to the parliament from his Majesty.

Before I had the honour of your Excellency's, I discoursed with my Lord Anglesea on the scheme we had projected two years ago to help our want of silver, who approves entirely of both parts of it, and has since acquainted me that he opened it to my Lord Forbes,[96] who he says is a man of numbers and calculations, who likewise entirely approves it; and my Lord has promised

96 The late Earl of Granard.

me that upon notice, he will come up out of the country to push it on in council.

Upon the encouragement your Lordship gives in your Letter that we may venture to raise the foreign silver, so as not to exceed the middle price of silver bullion in England, which is 5s. 5d. per ounce, I have had a calculation made upon the bottom of 5s. 4½d. which my Lord Chancellor very much approves of, and which being one half-penny under the middle market price in England, will I hope meet with no obstruction there, and as it is one half-penny per ounce higher than the foot formerly calculated upon, will more certainly help us to some foreign silver.

I am at present employed in going round and discoursing the privy counsellors separately, to prepare them for their concurrence, and if I find them favourably disposed, we will endeavour to push the thing before the judges go their circuits. We keep the affair as secret as we can, and I am satisfied it will be of service if it can be pushed through before it is much talked of.

In order to facilitate this matter as much as I could on the other side of the water, I drew up a paper on this subject, of about two sheets, which I sent to the Duke of Newcastle, to be communicated to the Chancellor of the Exchequer, whose approbation this alteration of our coin must have, before it can be passed. It is wholly on the short scheme I gave in to your Lordship, but as it is for the use of persons who know nothing of our coins, it is worked out into a greater length. I shall by the next mail send your Excellency a copy of it, such as it is.

If we have sense enough here to come into this alteration of our coin, and your Excellency can get it approved of in England, I am sure it will set our coin on so reasonable a footing, and be of that advantage to this nation, that your government will be always remembered in this country with esteem.[97]

As soon as we take any step in this affair, I shall send your Excellency word. Mr. Conolly is retired for some time into the country for his health, where I hear he grows better. I believe his indisposition will prevent my visiting my diocese this summer; but as his absence will rob the bankers of one to whom they formerly applied, and on whom they could make some impressions, I believe we shall get the easier through this business for his being out of the way.

I am, &c.

97 My Lord Primate himself was the first and most steady promoter of this scheme.

To the same.

Dublin, July 15, 1728.

My Lord,

I have by this mail sent your Excellency a copy of the paper I lately sent the Duke of Newcastle, relating to our want of silver. And as this contains a full and distinct account of the state of our coin, and the occasions and remedies of our want of silver, I think we may be the shorter in the letter from the council to your Lordship. If possible we will bring on this affair before the Judges go their circuits.

Your Lordship was pleased to give some hopes of giving an ensign's place to my Lord Mayor's[98] son, if it suits with your Lordship's conveniency, my Lord Chancellor and myself should be glad if the present vacancy were bestowed on him.

I am, &c.

To the Duke of Newcastle.

Dublin, July 16, 1728.

My Lord,

In my last I sent to your Grace a memorial relating to our want of silver in this nation, which I desired might be communicated to Sir Robert Walpole. Soon after the English prints informed us that Sir Robert was gone for a fortnight into the country. As his absence when my letter arrived must have occasioned my paper being laid aside for a while, I trouble your Grace with this to desire it may not be forgotten at his return.

Our want of silver here is such, that it is common to give six-pence for the change of a moidore, and to take a guinea or pistole for part of the change. And I know some in Dublin, who have occasion to pay workmen every Saturday night, that are obliged to pay four-pence for every twenty shillings in silver they procure.

We have hundreds of families (all protestants) removing out of the north to America; and the least obstruction in the linen-manufacture, by which the north subsists, must occasion greater numbers following, and the want of silver increasing, will prove a terrible blow to that manufacture, as there will not be money to pay the poor for their small parcels of yarn.

Since I drew up that memorial I have a certain account that the middle price of silver bullion in England[99] for ten years last past, has been 5s. 5d.

98 Sir Nathaniel Whitwell.
99 The bankers had told his Grace so, but it appears afterwards in these letters that they had imposed upon him.

English per ounce, which makes me desirous (for the more certain procuring of some foreign silver here) to put our silver at the rate of 5s. 4½d. English per ounce, which is indeed one halfpenny higher than the price proposed in that paper, but is still one halfpenny under the middle price of silver bullion in England.

If silver grows more scarce with us, our rents must certainly fall, not only to our prejudice who live here, but to the damage of the noblemen and gentlemen of England, who have estates here, and of those others who spend their rents in England.

I should be glad to know Sir Robert Walpole's opinion as soon as he has leisure: and hope we shall be gratified in an affair of so much consequence to us, and of no damage to England.

I am, &c.

To the Bishop of London.

Dublin, Aug. 20, 1728.

My Lord,

It is now a great while since I had the favour of one from your Lordship; I hope it has not been any continuance of the illness that hung about you in the spring that has occasioned so long a silence. I should have been glad to have heard from one so likely to know, whether peace or war be more probable, about which we at this distance are still uncertain. I hear there is a great noise about a sermon preached by the Bishop of Glocester, but have not yet seen it. I should be sorry to find that he had given any just occasion of offence.

I have lately heard from Mr. Sparke, whom your Lordship was pleased to recommend as an interim schoolmaster at Chigwell. He complains of unjust and hard usage from the governors there, and tells me that he and they shall soon appear before your Lordship: I do not reckon that I know what the case is, as I have my account only from one side, nor do I farther recommend him to your Lordship than to be protected from oppression, if that be his case.

We have had a rumour here that the Duke of Newcastle is dead, I hope there is nothing in the report.

The ill state of health of Lord Justice Conolly has confined me to Dublin the whole summer, though he is better than he has been.

I am, &c.

To Lord Carteret.

Dublin, Sept. 3, 1728.

My Lord,

By the mails that came in last night, we had advice of Thomas Clements's death, and I have had two or three gentlemen with me to day to desire my recommendation in favour of his brother Nathaniel Clements, to succeed him as agent to the pensioners. I have not seen either of my brethren since this news came, but was however willing to give your Excellency advice of this application.

I am, my Lord, &c.

To Sir Robert Walpole.

Dublin, Sept. 14, 1728.

Sir,

I some time ago troubled his Grace of Newcastle with a memorial relating to our want of silver in this kingdom, with the causes and cures of this want, which I desired might be communicated to you for your consideration: that if you approved of the scheme as reasonable and not prejudicial to England, we might set the affair going in council in order to make a regular application to his Majesty, for leave to publish a proclamation here.

I was willing, Sir, to know your sentiments, whether we might hope for his Majesty's compliance with our request, before my Lord Chancellor and I make any push in council for an application to his Majesty, since we have the whole interest of the bankers, which is very great here, against reducing the value of gold; and we are unwilling to go through a violent contest here to carry a point, except we had hopes our application would not afterwards be rejected in England.

The bankers here own that by the different proportion of gold to silver here, from what it bears in England, they get 2 per cent. in remittances to England, and the popular argument they use against this reduction is, that as things now stand, all gentlemen enjoying estates, pensions, or places, who draw off their money to England, lose 2 per cent. of what they draw off to the benefit of this kingdom.

In the year 1726, upon a letter from my Lord Lieutenant, we had made a great progress in this affair; and had in a committee of council, settled the designed value of foreign gold upon the bottom proposed in the memorial Mr. Delafaye has delivered you from the Duke of Newcastle; and we had the several species of foreign silver assayed, and had settled their intended value upon the bottom of 5s. 4d. per ounce sterling, but the talk of a war, with the interest of the bankers, put a stop to our proceedings at that time. But, as the want of silver is since increased upon us, so that in many places of this kingdom 8d. is a common premium for changing a moidore, and 4d. for procuring 20 shillings in silver is what is paid in Dublin, if some remedy be not applied speedily, our manufactures must be ruined.

I have given several people of fashion here hopes, that as we desire nothing but putting gold and English silver on the same bottom as they stand on in England, I could obtain this favour on the other side of the water. If I succeed in this application, it will give me some weight here, which I am sure shall always be employed in the service of his Majesty.

This makes me a most earnest suitor in behalf of this kingdom, whose manufactures must daily decay, and rents sink, unless the favour of altering the present currency of gold and silver be granted us; whilst the whole profit of the present inequality of gold and silver, will rest in the bankers hands.

All the encouragement I at present want, is an assurance that if we go on with this affair in council, and that if we apply in form from hence to his Majesty, we may hope to have our request granted.

In the memorial I mention putting foreign silver at 5s. 4d. English per ounce sterling, but as I am since informed that the middle price of silver bullion for ten years past has been 5s. 5d. English per ounce at London, I should rather desire to put foreign silver at 5s. 4¼d. English per ounce here, and have accordingly ordered a calculation to be made: but for that I am not so earnest as for the rest of the scheme, without which we are gradually undoing here.

The occasion of my giving you this trouble is that the Duke of Newcastle has for some time been out of town, and that though I find my memorial has been delivered to you, I cannot learn that my letters were communicated to you, to acquaint you with what I desired.

I hope, Sir, you will be so good as to favour me with an answer at your leisure.

I am, &c.

To Lord Carteret.

Dublin, Sept. 17, 1728.

My Lord,

The Lord Mayor has been with me, and desired I would transmit the inclosed to your Excellency: he told me it was in behalf of his son, that you would be pleased to bestow on him the Lieutenant's place he was formerly mentioned for by my Lord Chancellor and myself. I must again take this opportunity of recommending him to your Lordship's favour, if you are not otherwise engaged. I am,

My Lord, &c.

To the Archbishop of Canterbury.

Dublin, Oct. 1, 1728.

My Lord,

On Sunday I had the favour of your Grace's of the 22nd past, with the occasional offices revised and published by authority. I thank your Grace for your kindness in sending them so early, and shall endeavour to have them ordered here against November 5.

I hope your visitation, and the spending of some time at Tunbridge, may have confirmed your health, and recovered your strength, which I most heartily wish for the publick good.

Our accounts from England give us great hopes of a peace or a truce.

I must again thank your Grace for the service you did our Church bills in England last winter. As I find the lawyers are against a tenant in tail granting a glebe, we must e'en acquiesce.

I am, &c.

Newcastle to Boulter.

Windsor Castle, Oct. 3, 1728.
(NA. SP. 63/390/159)

My Lord,

The King being informed that the Duke de Ripperda having sailed from the coast of Portugal in order to come into England, had been drove into Cork in Ireland, his Majesty has commanded me to acquaint your Grace, that in case the Duke should be still at Cork or in any other part of Ireland, you should take an opportunity of letting him know, that you have received the King's commands to furnish him with whatever may be necessary for his voyage and even to supply him with what money may be wanting for that purpose. Your Grace will take care to do this in as private a manner as possible, that at the same time that the Duke may be convinced of his Majesty's good intentions towards him it may be done in such a manner as to give as little offence as possible. Sir Robert Walpole will write to Mr. Conolly to furnish your Grace with £500 for this purpose. If before you receive this letter you should have had notice that the Duke is gone from the coast of Ireland, as it is probable, your Grace will take no notice of your having received these orders from his Majesty.

I am etc.

Holles Newcastle

To the Duke of Newcastle.

Dublin, Oct. 14, 1728.

My Lord,

I this day had the honour of your Grace's of the 3rd. instant, and should have most cheerfully obeyed his Majesty's commands relating to the Duke de Ripperda,[1] but as the Duke left Cork several days ago, and by the accounts in the English prints, is landed in the west of England, there is no room for any thing more in this affair, than keeping his Majesty's orders a secret.

I am, &c.

To the Archbishop of Canterbury.

Dublin, Nov. 9, 1728.

My Lord,

I am very much obliged to your Grace for sending me the occasional services amended, and the account of an alteration relating to that for the 5th of November, which was forgotten in the first account. I have since looked the several alterations over, and think they are very right, and in a great measure necessary: I was unwilling to publish them here till some Bishops came to town, that I might have their approbation; but shall take care to have them published by authority, before the 30th of January.

I am glad to hear your Grace has perfectly recovered the weakness occasioned by your last fit of sickness, and most heartily wish you all health and happiness.

We are under great trouble here about a frenzy that has taken hold of very great numbers, to leave this country for the West Indies; and we are endeavouring to learn what may be the reasons of it; and the proper remedies; which as soon as we are able, we shall lay before the government in England. I am,

My Lord, &c.

1 There did not in the present century appear a more extraordinary man than this Duke de Ripperda; he was born and bred a merchant in Holland; had great abilities; was by the States General sent Ambassador to Spain; turned Roman Catholic; was created a Baron, then a Duke and Grandee, by his most Catholic Majesty; became a principal Favourite and Minister of State; had an illicit correspondence with the ministry in England; was taken into custody, and imprisoned; made an escape, by the means of a fair Castillian woman, to England, where he was protected; after some residence there, he went to Muly Abdalla, Emperor of Fez and Morocco, turned Mahometan, was circumcised and made Bashaw and Prime Minister to that Prince. See his Memoirs from 1715 to 1736, which have been translated into most European languages.

To the Duke of Newcastle.

Dublin, Nov. 23, 1728.

My Lord,

I am very sorry I am obliged to give your Grace so melancholy an account of the state of this kingdom, as I shall in this letter, but I thought it my duty to let his Majesty know our present condition in the north. For we have had three bad harvests together there, which has made oatmeal, which is their great subsistance, much dearer than ordinary, and as our farmers here are very poor, and obliged as soon as they have their corn, to sell it for ready money to pay their rents, it is more in the power of those who have a little money to engross corn here, and make advantage of its scarceness, than in England.

We have had for several years some agents from the colonies in America, and several masters of ships that have gone about the country, and deluded the people with stories of great plenty and estates to be had for going for in those parts of the world: and they have been the better able to seduce people, by reason of the necessities of the poor of late.

The people that go from hence make great complaints of the oppressions they suffer here not from the government, but from their fellow subjects of one kind or another, as well as of the dearness of provision, and say these oppressions are one reason of their going.

But whatever occasions their going, it is certain that above 4200 men, women, and children have been shipped off from hence for the West Indies within three years, and of these above 3100 this last summer. Of these possibly one in ten may be a man of substance, and may do well enough abroad, but the case of the rest is deplorable, the rest either hire themselves to those of substance for their passage, or contract with the masters of ships for four years servitude when they come thither, or if they make a shift to pay for their passage, will be under a necessity of selling themselves for servants for four years for their subsistance when they come there.

The whole north is in a ferment at present, and people every day engaging one another to go next year to the West Indies. The humour has spread like a contagious distemper, and the people will hardly hear any body that tries to cure them of their madness. The worst is that it affects only protestants, and reigns chiefly in the north, which is the seat of our linen manufacture.

This unsettled state puts almost a stop to trade, and the more so as several who were in good credit before have taken up parcels of goods on trust and disposed of them, and are gone off with the money, so that there is no trade there but for ready money.

We have had it under our consideration how to put some stop to this growing evil: we think by some old laws we can hinder money being carried abroad, and stop all but merchants, that have not a license, from going out of the kingdom.

By this post we have sent my Lord Lieutenant the representation of the gentlemen of the north, and the opinion of our lawyers what can be done by law to hinder people going abroad; but these are matters we shall do nothing in without directions from his Majesty. But whatever can be done by law, I fear it may be dangerous forcibly to hinder a number of needy people from quitting us.

There is one method that can do no hurt, and we hope may do good, which is keeping corn at a reasonable price till next harvest, that so dearness of bread may drive none from us. And to compass this we are subscribing for a sum of money to buy corn where it can be had the cheapest, and to sell it to loss in the north, to keep the markets down there; and I believe we shall have good success in our subscription.

But I fear except leave be given to prohibit by proclamation the exportation of corn from hence, we shall fail even in this project.

I was just willing to give your Grace an account of our present difficulties, and fear I shall have occasion to trouble you more on this subject.

I am, &c.

To Lord Carteret.

Dublin, Nov. 28, 1728.

My Lord,

Mr. Cassell has been often with me to press me to put your Excellency in mind of his memorial: your Lordship knows his case and pretensions very well; and his great concern is for a provision for his wife, if she survives him.

All I shall add is, that if somewhat is not soon done in his affair, it is unlikely he will live to see it.

I could not well refuse him putting your Excellency again in mind of his request. I am,

My Lord, &c.

To the Duke of Newcastle.

Dublin, Dec. 3, 1728.

My Lord,

I have by the mail that came this day from England, received letters from two of my brothers in law, Mr. Savage[2] and Mr. Merrett,[3] both merchants in

2   A Director of the Bank of England.
3   Whose only daughter married my Lord Cunningham, of the kingdom of Ireland.

London, and very well affected to his Majesty, to desire me to trouble your Grace in behalf of Mr. William Ball, a merchant at Alicant.

I find by them that Mr. Barker, late consul of Alicant, is dead, and they are desirous Mr. Ball, who has been a merchant at Alicant about eight years, may succeed to that employment. I am confident they would not trouble me to write to your Grace on this occasion, except they knew Mr. Ball to be every way qualified for that post.

If your Grace is not otherwise engaged already your favouring Mr. Ball in his affair, would be esteemed a great obligation by,

My Lord, &c.

To the Archbishop of Canterbury.

Dublin, Dec. 3, 1728.

My Lord,

I have had the favour of your Grace's of the 21st past, and am very much obliged to you for sending us the occasional offices as altered, for you guessed right, that we use the same offices here with the alterations necessary for this country; and I hope to have these offices settled here before the 30th of January.

We are endeavouring here by a subscription, to provide against one reason given here for people leaving us, which is the dearness of provision, by having three bad harvests together; and we have consulted the ministry, to know what other measures that are in our power, may be proper to be taken.

The keeping of people here by force, will I fear, have bad consequences, the numbers that are infected with this humour, being very great; but the putting some difficulties in people's way, and obliging fraudulent debtors to pay their creditors, may probably do some good.

I am very sorry for the terrible calamity that has befallen those of Copenhagen, and heartily wish them a good collection in England, but a collection here will turn to little if any account. We had since I came hither, a collection for the protestant Churches in Lithuania, about which I spoke to several bishops at parliament, and afterwards wrote a circular letter to my suffragans, and to every clergyman in my diocese, to promote the collection, and yet there was not gathered 300l. in the kingdom, and of that about 100l. came out of my diocese. But at present with the desertion of our people in the north, and the want of corn there, little can be expected from even thence, where protestants are most numerous; and Munster and Connaught are mostly papists, and his Grace of Dublin is against all collections for foreigners in his province of Leinster.

I thought proper just to acquaint your Grace with what may probably be the success of a collection here, if his Majesty should please to order one.

I wish your Grace all health and happiness, and am,
My Lord, &c.

To Sir Robert Walpole.

Dublin, Dec. 4, 1728.
Sir,
Mr. Nuttal, the Sollicitor to the Commissioners of the Revenue here, has so misbehaved himself, that he is as I hear, dismissed his office. The place I understand is in the disposal of the Commissioners in England, which occasions my giving you this trouble, to recommend for his employment one Mr. Richard Morgan,[4] who is my agent here: he is well affected to his Majesty, and has been brought up an attorney, and is very diligent and understanding in business, and has the character of a very honest man; I am sure I have always found him to be so.

I am sensible, Sir, I am going out of my immediate province, in meddling in this affair, but I hope, from your goodness, Sir, whatever you please to do in it, you will at least excuse this trouble from,

Sir, your humble servant.

Newcastle to Boulter.

Whitehall, Dec. 5, 1728.
(NA. SP. 63/390/181)
My Lord,
I have received the honour of your Grace's letter of the 23rd of last month, relating to the infatuation that has of late prevailed among the common people in the North of Ireland, of removing from thence to the Plantations; and I have laid it before the King, who extremely commended your zeal, and is very sensible of the great pains your Grace takes for the promoting his Majesty's service and the good of His Kingdom, in the Government of which you have now so great a share. His Majesty has ordered the consideration of this matter to be referred to a Committee of Council, and every thing will be done in it that is possible.

I am etc.

Holles Newcastle

4   This gentleman was also agent to Dr. Hoadly, when Archbishop of Dublin, as also
    when Primate.

To Lord Carteret.

Dublin, Dec. 14, 1728.

My Lord,

I had yesterday the honour of your Excellency's of the 3d. instant, and am glad to find the consideration of the proclamation about corn is likely to come on in a cabinet council so soon. We had this day a great many gentlemen with us at the castle, complaining of the accounts of the exportation of corn in several parts, and the great distress we are likely to be under, except a speedy stop be put to it; and we could scarce pacify them though we assured them your Lordship had acquainted the King with that affair, and that his Majesty had ordered a cabinet council to consider it, and that we did not question receiving his Majesty's commands in a post or two.

The want of such a proclamation is at least made use of as a pretence by the gentlemen of the north, for not coming into the subscription we mentioned in our letter, without which I fear some thousands will perish before next harvest.

I am glad your Lordship is so kind as to think of the affair of our coin. If we had an enlivening letter from your Excellency, I hope we might make some advance here towards an application to the King from the council: but as our brother Conolly is pretty much in with the bankers, and they think they shall lose 2 per cent. in their remittances, if gold should be reduced, he now talks that at this unhappy juncture in the north, he is afraid that it would be unreasonable: so that I fear if it were to be moved in council, he would encourage several underhand to oppose it. On the contrary, I think in this very juncture, the getting or keeping of silver, as it would promote the little retail business, would be of service to us: and if we had any hint after it has been considered in a cabinet council, that upon application, our desire to have our money altered, would be granted, I believe, with a word from your Lordship to help us, my Lord Chancellor and I could secure the point in council.

I have nothing farther to add to my memorial on that subject, but that upon considering that in the scheme formerly proposed, foreign silver is set at the lowest price it is ever sold for in England, and that our people are afraid, if the Mexico piece of eight were set at 5s. Irish, we should go too high: I have thought of a middle way, which is setting the Mexico piece of 17 pwts. 4 grs. at 5s. Irish, on which supposition foreign silver would go at 5s. 9d. 3 qrs. Irish per ounce: whereas in the old scheme the Mexico piece is but 17 pwts. bare, and on that supposition silver will go at 5s. 9d. Irish per ounce, so that the difference will not be quite one halfpenny per ounce, and yet that advance will make it more worth while to keep silver here: and this can be done because the full weight of the Mexico piece is 17 pwts. 12 grs.

I shall by the next post send your Excellency a calculation of the foreign silver coins upon this new supposition.

I am, &c.

To the Duke of Newcastle.

Dublin, Dec. 17, 1728.

My Lord,

Last Friday I had the honour of your Grace's of the 5th instant, and thank you for laying our melancholy state before his Majesty: I hope we shall speedily know his Royal pleasure about a proclamation, prohibiting the exportation of corn from hence. On Saturday we had a great number of the principal gentry here, who pressed somewhat rudely for such a proclamation, and were hardly satisfied with our assuring them the affair was already laid before his Majesty, and that we expected his Majesty's pleasure by one of the next mails. It is certain we had a very bad crop of corn last year, and that commissions are come to buy up great quantities here, so that it is to be feared we shall before spring suffer extremely by its dearness. But I do not doubt, but we shall receive his Majesty's commands in that affair before this comes to your Grace's hands. As we hope in due time to know what he pleases to order relating to the people going to the West Indies; the infatuation still spreads, and the dearness of provisions must needs increase it, if not prevented.

I am greatly obliged to his Majesty for the good opinion he is pleased to entertain of my zeal for his service, and hope I shall never give him reason to alter it.

I am,
My Lord, &c.

To the Bishop of London.

Dublin, Dec. 21, 1728.

My Lord,

We are very much rejoiced here at the arrival of Prince Frederick[5] at St. James's as I find by the accounts from England all friends to the government are there. As I am confined here by being in the government, and by my Lord Justice Conolly's weakness, I must desire the favour of your Lordship when you next wait upon his Royal Highness to present my most humble duty to

5   Prince of Wales, eldest son of George II. His Grace had some share in teaching his Highness English, when he was a Chaplain at Hanover.

him, and to assure him that nothing but my being detained here by his Majesty's service should hinder me from having the honour of waiting on him, and paying him my most dutiful respects in person on so happy an occasion.

This cold weather has pretty much pinched his Grace of Dublin, not that he is apprehended to be in any immediate danger, but as reports may be spread in England that he is dead, and pushes made for naming a successor to him, I beg the favour of you to wait on the ministry, and desire they would not fix on a successor upon any rumours of his death. It is a matter of great consequence to his Majesty's service, and the English interest here, and I hope that no native will be thought of for the place, nor an Englishman be fixed upon too hastily.

I am,

My Lord, &c.

To Lord Carteret.

Dublin, Jan. 4, 1728/9.

My Lord,

I understand by his Grace of Canterbury there were some small changes made in the occasional offices of the Church in England, which he was so kind as to send me. As the 30th of January is now coming on, I have thoughts of having the like alterations made here, as likewise ordering the office of the King's inauguration day to be used here, but I thought it improper to speak to the Lords Justices or the privy council about it, till I had your Excellency's approbation of the design. I heartily wish your Lordship many happy new years.

I am, &c.

To the same.

Dublin, Jan. 15, 1728/9.

My Lord,

The Rev. Mr. John Quarterman died here yesterday, by whose death the union of Burn-church, consisting of Burn-church, alias Kiltranine vicarage or parish, Dunfort vicarage, Kilfaragh whole rectory, and the monastery or rectory of Gerpoint, with all its members and dependencies in the diocese of Ossory, is become vacant, and in the gift of your Excellency.

As your Lordship was pleased to promise me the disposal of the first living I desired, upon my relinquishing a living in the diocese of Clogher, to Dr. Delany, I make it my request to your Lordship, that you would be pleased to order the said union to be given to the Rev. Mr. John Richardson, on whom I did intend to have bestowed the living I then relinquished. I am,

Your Excellency's, &c.

To Lord Townshend.

Dublin, Jan. 16, 1728/9.

My Lord,

The age and frequent returns of illness the Archbishop of Dublin has laboured under the greatest part of this winter (though I do not apprehend that he is in any immediate danger of dying) have made me think it proper to write a few lines to your Lordship about a successor to him, if he should fall, that there may be no surprise.

It is certain that it is of the last consequence to the King's service that he be an Englishman; whether it will be thought best to send one from the Bishops bench in England, or to remove one from the bench here to that post, I submit to your Lordship's wisdom: if the former be thought of, the person I should be most desirous to see here, as being one of the oldest friends I have on the bench there, that would be willing to come, is the Bishop of St. David's, of whose behaviour your Lordship must have some knowledge, as he has been in the house about five years: if the latter be judged best, I think the Bishop of Fernes is the most proper that can be thought of here; he behaved himself very well last sessions of parliament here; he is one of courage, and very hearty for the English interest, and is a good speaker; and I am satisfied he is one that would concur with me in promoting his Majesty's service; he is very well liked of here for an Englishman.

But I must beg to speak freely that I hope nobody will be sent hither, because he is troublesome or uneasy elsewhere. It is of great consequence that there be a good agreement between the Primate and the Archbishop of Dublin; and one in that post who would set up himself against the Primate, would be sure of being caressed, flattered, and followed by the Irish interest here.

I cannot on this occasion omit my thanks to your Lordship for your supporting me here ever since I came, as you gave me hopes you would, and I hope the good effects of it have appeared. And I think the English interest is at present on that good footing, headed by my Lord Chancellor and myself, that the continuance of the same support, promises a pretty quiet state of things for the future.

I should hardly have given your Lordship this trouble before-hand, if we had not reports from time to time that endeavours are using to secure this post either for some dangerous person here, or not very promising on the other side.[6]

I am, &c.

To Lord Carteret.

Dublin, Jan. 25, 1728/9.

My Lord,

On the 23d instant I had the honour of your Excellency's of the 11th, which I this day communicated to the Lords Justices, and upon advising with Lord Chief Justice Rogerson, who happened to be at the castle, and the Prime Serjeant with the Attorney and Sollicitor-general, we find it proper to have his Majesty's commands for what alterations are to be made in the occasional offices, as likewise for the late alterations in relation to the Royal family which his Majesty has been pleased lately to order in council in England; and we find that in the several proclamations issued on the like occasions, mention is made of our having received his Majesty's commands.

I shall look over the alterations made in the occasional offices in England, and likewise see what alterations may be necessary to be made in the occasional office for the 23d of October, which is not observed in England, and transmit them to your Excellency by the next post, together with a copy of the letter your Excellency was pleased to send us, relating to the alterations made in the prayers for the Royal Family at his Majesty's accession; that so your Lordship may see what form was then used to signify his Majesty's pleasure to us; and as soon as we receive his Majesty's commands, we shall issue a proclamation accordingly.

I shall by this post write to England for the form of prayer appointed for the inauguration day, to see whether there is any thing in it that need be changed here; and shall after perusing it, acquaint your Excellency whether it will require any change, or be proper as it stands in England, that we may accordingly receive his Majesty's commands.

I am, My Lord, &c.

To the same.

Dublin, Jan. 28, 1728/9.

My Lord,

In mine of Saturday last I promised your Excellency by this post, on account of what alterations would be proper to be made in the several

6   His Grace seems to place his chief confidence in my Lord Townshend.

occasional offices, pursuant to what has been done in England, and I had accordingly drawn them up.

But as your Lordship hinted in yours that it should be done in the best manner which you thought I knew, I went on at the same time with an enquiry at the council and the secretaries office, into what method was pursued when those forms of prayer were last altered, which was in the year 1715: and by the books in the secretary's office I found things then took a longer train than any body was able to inform me of, which I shall communicate to the other Lords Justices to-morrow, that we may pursue the same method again, and when things are settled with them, shall send your Lordship an account of it.

As the time is too short to make any such alteration against the 30th of January now approaching, there will be time enough to have that affair pursued in the way formerly observed, before the 29th of May, and care shall be taken accordingly.

But the alterations his Majesty has been pleased to order lately in relation to the Royal Family, can be enforced here as soon as your Excellency pleases to send us his Majesty's commands about them.

And I have here sent your Excellency an extract of your letter of the 16th of June 1727, in which you sent us his Majesty's first commands on that subject, in pursuance of which we then issued a proclamation, as we shall now, so soon as we receive the like orders.

I am, my Lord, &c.

To the same.

Dublin, Feb. 1, 1728/9.

My Lord,

I humbly thank your Excellency for your kind order to have Mr. Richardson presented to the union of Burn-church; but as there is some reason to apprehend that the Crown and the Bishop of Ossory[7] present alternately to that union, and that this is the Bishop's turn, the last turn having been filled by the Crown, we have ordered enquiry to be made in the several offices, to learn how that affair stands, before we make a presentation, which we fear can be of no effect; as soon as we can learn any thing certain in this business, I shall acquaint your Lordship with it.

I am, &c.

7   Sir Thomas Vesey, Bart.

To the same.

Dublin, Feb. 13, 1728/9.

My Lord,

I have lately received a letter from Mr. Ratcliff, in which he acquaints me that he has made application to your Excellency for the new professorship in the oriental tongues, and desires me to give your Lordship a character of him. As I do not know how those professorships are to be bestowed, whether on those who are actually of the College, or indifferently on any who are qualified for them, I cannot tell what to say on this occasion: but I must do him the justice to acquaint your Excellency that I have heard him spoken of as one that understands the oriental tongues the best of any body in this country.

I am, my Lord, &c.

To the Archbishop of Canterbury.

Dublin, Feb. 13, 1728/9.

My Lord,

I am glad to hear your Grace is mended, and still likely to mend in your health, which I heartily wish a continuance of.

We are endeavouring by a subscription[8] to raise money and buy corn, to supply the necessities of the north, and have hitherto kept the markets there from rising unreasonably, and hope to do so till next harvest. We think this will put some stop to the great desertion we have been threatened with there: and so far as they may be concerned in it, I hope the landlords will do their part by remitting some arrears or making some abatement of their rents. As bad as things have been here, I am satisfied the bulk of these adventurers worst themselves by removing to America, and hope the frenzy will gradually abate.

I have lately received a letter from your Grace relating to one Mr. Carol, a convert, which I had answered sooner, but that I staid till I had an opportunity of talking with my Lord Chief Baron about his case, who tells me he has an extraordinary bad character, whatever his religion may be, that he has been convicted of endeavouring to suborn witnesses, and that a prosecution

8   There is no doubt but his Grace contributed largely to this subscription; but what he did in the year 1739–40, in the great frost, almost exceeds belief; there was not a poor distressed person in the great city of Dublin who applied, that was not daily relieved to the full, and chiefly by his bounty: the House of Commons took this so well, that they voted him very justly their thanks on this very remarkable instance of his goodness. The sums he then expended must have been very great indeed, yet when he hath been complimented on this and frequent other occasions of the like sort, his usual answer was, that he should die shamefully rich.

has been ordered against him in the Exchequer for making a rasure in a record; so that he thinks Carol will hardly venture into this kingdom.

I shall always be ready to support any real protestant here who suffers from the malice of the papists, so far as lies in my power, and still the more upon your Grace's recommendation; but I submit it to your Grace whether there be a possibility of shewing any countenance to one who has so bad a character. I am,

My Lord, &c.

To the Duke of Newcastle.

Dublin, Feb. 18, 1728/9.

My Lord,

The occasion of my troubling your Grace at present, is that it is generally talked here, that the affair of the new professorships is just settling, and the professors going to be named. I find that business has been wholly managed with Dr. Coghill, without acquainting my Lord Chancellor or me with what has been doing.[9] Dr. Coghill has indeed had some discourse with me about what lectures it might be proper to oblige the professors to read, and under what penalties; but we have neither of us been let into the secret who are designed for the new professors. I could therefore wish that before the persons are settled, we might be acquainted who they are to be, that your Grace may be informed whether they are such as the King's friends here wish were put in.

I cannot omit mentioning on this occasion, that we the Lords Justices here were somewhat surprized that Dr. Coghill was rather employed than the Lords Justices, to acquaint the College that it would be agreeable to the court, if the Prince of Wales[10] were to be elected Chancellor of this University. I hope you will excuse this trouble. I am,

Your Grace's, &c.

To the same.

Dublin, Feb. 20, 1728/9.

My Lord,

I troubled your Grace but last post with somewhat relating to the College here. But as I have since learned somewhat more of what is transacting there, I think myself obliged to give you some farther informations.

9   It is to be feared that Lord Carteret played the Primate, a slippery trick in this case as well as in some others; he says himself in one of his letters to Dean Swift, when people ask me how I governed Ireland, I say that I pleased Dr. Swift.

10   His Royal Highness was accordingly elected.

As it may happen that the Vice-Chancellor[11] may be sick at the time of the commencement, when degrees are to be given, of which they have two in a year, one just before Lent, the other at the time of the Cambridge commencement, it was the custom for the Vice-Chancellor to name a Pro-Vice -Chancellor, to officiate in case of the Vice-Chancellor's sickness or absence; but upon the last who was named Pro-Vice-Chancellor coming to be sworn before Lord Chancellor Middleton, it appeared the statutes did not give any power to the Vice-Chancellor to name a deputy, upon which there has been no such deputy here for some years.

I am informed that to prevent any accident of that nature, it has been proposed to have an additional statute or clause to the charter, made by the King, to give such a power to the Vice-Chancellor, which I think is reasonable. But I am informed likewise, that this affair is taking another turn in England, and that they are for appointing three Vice-Chancellors, with equal power, viz. the Bishop of Clogher, the present Vice-Chancellor; the Bishop of Raphoe,[12] who never comes to town but in parliament time; and Dr. Coghill, one of the representatives for the University in parliament, and always in town.

What seems pretty much aimed at in this affair, is to give Dr. Coghill a greater weight and authority in the College than he has already. And as he is the person with whom the affair of the professorships has been settled, as well as who are to be professors, I think his weight is already pretty great.

He is a person of abilities, and of a fair character, but as determined a supporter of the Irish against the English interest here, as any body, though with more prudence than many others, and therefore I hope it will be considered whether it be so proper to give him so much authority as seems now putting into his hands by these schemes.

There is one thing I must suggest on this occasion, which is, that as the Chancellor, Vice-Chancellor, and Archbishop of Dublin are the present Visitors of the College, it is possible one thing designed by making three Vice-Chancellors (who probably may all three become Visitors) may be the rendering useless the power of the Archbishop of Dublin in a visitation of the College, if he should ever be an Englishman.

I cannot help saying I think it would have been for the King's service here, if what has been lately transacting in relation to the Professors, and what is now doing, had been concerted with some of the English here, and not wholly with the natives, and that after a secret manner, that the College might have thought it their interest to have some dependance on the English.

And here I cannot help suggesting, whether if any alteration is made in the charter with relation to the Vice-Chancellor's power, it may not be proper at

11 Dr. Sterne, Bishop of Clogher.
12 Dr. Nicholas Forster, was a senior Fellow of the University of Dublin, afterwards
     Bishop of Killaloe, from whence he was translated to Raphoe.

the same time to add to the present Visitors, the Lord Primate and the Lord Chancellor of Ireland, for the time being; whom his Majesty shall please from time to time to place in eminent stations here; but hitherto all these College affairs have been kept a secret from my Lord Chancellor and me.

I hope your Grace will have the goodness to excuse the trouble of this long letter.

I am, &c.

To Lord Carteret.

Dublin, Mar. 8, 1728/9.

My Lord,

I thank your Excellency for your kind order to present Mr. Richardson to the union of Burn-church; but before we could actually pass his patent for it, I procured a copy of the act of union from the Register of Ossory, that in the council-office being burnt; upon perusal of which the Attorney-general says, there is no doubt but that the Crown and Bishop of Ossory[13] are to present alternately to that union, and that as the Crown presented the last turn, the Bishop is to present this turn; so that it is to no purpose to take any farther step in that affair.

We have had several tumults in Cork, Waterford, Limerick, and other places in the south, on pretence that corn was exported thence to England; though if we may believe the merchants here, little has been attempted to be exported of late, but to the north of Ireland; and by all accounts there is great plenty in those parts, and corn at a very reasonable price.

We have wrote to the several magistrates in those parts to be diligent in preserving the peace, and have ordered the officers of the army to assist the civil magistrates on occasion, wherever we have been applied to for it.

We have by this post sent your Excellency the memorial delivered to us by the dissenting ministers here, from the letters of their friends in the north: we objected against two heads of it, as we have acquainted your Excellency; but there is another part relating to the grievances about tythes, which is very far from being true. I do not doubt but some persons in the north may have been oppressed by the farmers of tythes. But I have at every visitation I have held had as great complaints from the clergy of the hardships put upon them by the people, in coming at their just dues, as the people can make of being any ways oppressed by the clergy or their tythe farmers, and I believe with as much reason. As to the expensiveness of the spiritual courts which they

13 Sir Thomas Vesey, Bart. son of Dr. John Vesey, Archbishop of Tuam, and Vice-Chancellor of the University of Dublin, and three times one of the Lords Justices of Ireland.

complain of, that will be very much avoided by the act passed last sessions for the more easy recovery of tythes of small value. And indeed the gentlemen have ever since I came hither, been putting it into the heads of their tenants, that it was not their rents, but the paying of the tythes that made them find it hard to live on their farms. And it is easy to see that this was a notion that would readily take with Scotch presbyterians.

We shall in time make some farther remarks on that memorial. I am, My Lord, &c.

To the Duke of Newcastle.

Dublin, Mar. 13, 1728/9.

My Lord,

As we are in a very bad way here, I think myself obliged to give your Grace some account of it.

The scarcity and dearness of provision still increases in the north; many have eaten the oats they should have sowed their land with; and except the landlords will have the good sense to furnish them with seed, a great deal of land will lye waste this year.

There has been set on foot a subscription here in Dublin, to buy corn from Munster, where it has been very cheap, to send it to the north, in order to keep the markets down; but though we have bought about 3000l. worth of oats, oatmeal, and potatoes there, yet first by the continuance of easterly winds for three weeks, and since by the insurrections of the mob in those parts, not one boat load is yet arrived in the north; which is a great increase to their distress.

There have been tumults at Limerick, Cork, Waterford, Clonmel, and other places, to prevent the corn we have bought from going to the north. Those at Limerick and Cork have been the worst, where they have broken open ware-houses and cellars, and set what price they pleased on provisions; but I hope we shall hardly hear of any more riots, having given the necessary orders both to the civil and military officers in those parts to take care to prevent or suppress all riots. There is no doubt but the buying of corn there has raised their markets; but still as we are assured from thence, there is great plenty in the country; and provisions are in some places as cheap again as in the north; but where dearest, at least one third part cheaper. There is one reflection these poor wretches have not made, that by their riots the country are deterred from bringing them in provisions, which will make things dearer in those places than the exportation they are so angry at.

We have given orders to the several magistrates and the judges of assize to have the rioters prosecuted and severely punished.

The humour of going to America still continues, and the scarcity of provisions certainly makes many quit us: there are now seven ships at Belfast that are carrying off about 1000 passengers thither; and if we knew how to stop them, as most of them can neither get victuals nor work at home, it would be cruel to do it.

We have sent for 2400 quarters of rye from Coningsbery; when they arrive which will probably be about the middle of May, we hope the price of things will fall considerably in the north, and we suppose they will mend pretty much when our supplies arrive from Munster.

The dissenting ministers here have lately delivered in a memorial representing the grievances their brethren have assigned as the causes in their apprehension of the great desertion in the north: as one of those causes related to the ecclesiastical courts here, and as it is generally reported here that the Irish gentlemen at London are for throwing the whole occasion of this desertion on the severity of tythes, I have by this post written to the Bishop of London a very long letter on that subject, and have desired him to wait on the ministry and discourse with them on that head.

I shall get a copy of this memorial and send your Grace my thoughts on some other parts of it.

I am,

My Lord, &c.

To the Bishop of London.

Dublin, Mar. 13, 1728/9.

My Lord,

As we have had reports here that the Irish gentlemen in London would have the great burthen of tythes thought one of the chief grievances that occasion such numbers of the people of the north going to America, I have for some time designed to write to your Lordship on that subject.

But a memorial lately delivered in here by the dissenting ministers of this place, containing the causes of this desertion, as represented to them by the letters of their brethren in the north, (which memorial we have lately sent over to my Lord Lieutenant,) mentioning the oppression of the ecclesiastical courts about tythes as one of their greatest grievances: I found myself under a necessity of troubling your Lordship to discourse with the ministry about it.

The gentlemen of this country have ever since I came hither been talking to others, and persuading their tenants who complained of the excessiveness of their rents, that it was not the paying too much rent, but too much tythe that impoverished them: and the notion soon took among Scotch presbyterians, as a great part of the protestants in the north are, who it may easily be supposed do not pay tythes with great chearfulness. And indeed I make no doubt but the landlords in England might with great ease raise a cry amongst their tenants of the great oppression they lie under by paying tythes.

What the gentlemen want to be at is that they may go on raising their rents, and that the clergy should still receive their old payments for their tythe. But as things have happened otherwise, and they are very angry with the clergy, without considering that it could not happen otherwise than it has, since if a clergyman saw a farm raised in its rent e.g. from 10 to 20l. per ann. he might be sure his tythe was certainly worth double what he formerly took for it. Not that I believe the clergy have made a proportionable advancement in their composition for their tythes, to what the gentlemen have made in their rents. And yet it is upon this rise of the value of tythes that they would persuade the people to throw their distress.

In a conference I had with the dissenting ministers here some weeks ago, they mentioned the raising the value of tythes beyond what had been formerly paid, as a proof that the people were oppressed in the article of tythes. To which I told them, that the raising the value of tythes did not prove any oppression, except it were proved that the value was greater than they were really worth; and that even then the farmer had his remedy by letting the clergy take it in kind.

And there is the less in this argument, because the fact is, that about the years 1694 and 1695, the lands here were almost waste and unsettled, and the clergy in the last distress for tenants for their tythes, when great numbers of them were glad to lett their tythes at a very low value, and that during incumbency, for few would take them on other terms; and as the country has since settled and improved as those incumbents have dropt off, the tythe of those parishes has been considerably advanced without the least oppression, but I believe your Lordship will think not without some grumbling. The same no doubt has happened where there have been careless or needy incumbents, and others of a different character that have succeeded them.

I need not mention to your Lordship what I have been forced to talk to several here, that if a landlord takes too great a portion of the profits of a farm for his share by way of rent, (as the tythe will light on the tenants share) the tenant will be impoverished: but then it is not the tythe but the increased rent that undoes the farmer. And indeed in this country, where I fear the tenant hardly ever has more than one third of the profits he makes of his farm for his share, and too often but a fourth or perhaps a fifth part, as the tenant's share is charged with the tythe, his case is no doubt hard, but it is plain from what side the hardship arises.

Nor need I take notice to your Lordship of what I have been forced to talk very fully here, that if the lands were freed from payment of tythe, the tenant would not be the better for it, but the landlord, who would in that case raise his rent accordingly, and would probably receive 15 or 20s. for additional rent, where the clergyman now receives 10s. for tythe; and that it would be the same in proportion if the tythes were fixed to some modus below their real value, which I am apprehensive the gentlemen may attempt to do by a bill next sessions.

As for the complaints of the oppressions in the ecclesiastical courts, your Lordship knows the dilatoriness and expensiveness of suits there. And yet till within seven or eight years all suits for tythes, &c. were there; since that time by degrees the clergy have sued in cases of consequence in the Exchequer; but for dues of small value, they still are sued for there. But in the main no body sues in those courts that can by fair means get any thing near his due; since, when the clergy have put persons into those courts the defendants either give them all the delay and trouble they can, or else stand under contempt for never appearing, and let things go to the last extremity, and stand excommunicated, and possibly when a writ de excommunicato capiendo is taken out, and they find they have 7 or 8l. to pay, they run away: for the greatest part of the occupiers of the land here are so poor, that an extraordinary stroke of 8 or 10l. falling on them, is certain ruin to them.

I can assure your Lordship that at every visitation I have held here, which is annually, the clergy have made as great complaints of the hardships put upon them by the people in getting in their tythes, especially their small dues, as the people can of any oppression from the clergy. And to my knowledge many of them have chose rather to lose their small dues, than to be at a certain great expence in getting them, and at an uncertainty whether the farmer would not at last run away without paying any thing. And I can affirm to your Lordship that the laiety here are as troublesome and vexatious as they can be in England, and from time to time fight a cause of no great value through the Bishop's court, then through the Archbishop's, and thence to the Delegates, where the clergy sue for what is most evidently their due.

I would not be understood by this to deny that any clergyman or farmer of tythes ever did a hard thing by the people, but that there is not frequent occasion of complaint against them.

However last sessions we passed a bill here for the more easy recovery of small tythes, &c. which I believe will remove this cause of complaint, since I believe very few will spend some pounds to recover that in a spiritual court, which may be recovered for some shillings in another way.

Upon occasion of the conference I had some weeks ago with the dissenting ministers here, I have enquired of several of the clergy, that are understanding and fair men, who have assured me, that as far as their knowledge reaches, they believe that generally the farmers do not pay more than two thirds of the real value of their tythes.

Another thing they complain of in their memorial is, the trouble that has been given them about their marriages and their school-masters. As to this I told them, that for some time they had not been molested about their marriages, and that as to their school-masters I was sure they had met with very little trouble on that head, since I had never heard any such grievance so much as mentioned till I saw it in their memorial.

Another matter complained of is the sacramental test, in relation to which I told them, the laws were the same in England.

As for other grievances they mention, such as raising the rents unreasonably, the oppression of Justices of the Peace, seneschals, and other officers in the country, as they are no ways of an ecclesiastical nature, I shall not trouble your Lordship with an account of them; but must desire your Lordship to talk with the ministry on the subject I have now wrote about, and endeavour to prevent their being prepossessed with any unjust opinion of the clergy, or being disposed, if any attempt should be made from hence, to suffer us to be stript of our just rights.[14]

I am, &c.

To Sir Robert Walpole.

Dublin, Mar. 31, 1729.

Sir,

The dissenting ministers of this place having applied to me to recommend their case and that of their brethren to your kind patronage, I have made bold to trouble you with this letter by Mr. Craghead, one of their number, and their sollicitor on this occasion. They inform me that his late Majesty was graciously pleased to give out of his privy purse to the ministers of the north 400l. per ann. and the like sum to those of the south, to be distributed to those ministers who had no share of the 1200l.[15] on the establishment here; and that his present Majesty has graciously continued this allowance to them: that by his late Majesty's death they apprehend they lost two years, what they hoped to have otherwise received. They are sensible there is nothing due to them, nor do they make any such claim: but as the calamities of this kingdom are at present very great, and by the desertion of many of their people to America, and the poverty of the greatest part of the rest, their contributions, particularly in the north, are very much fallen off, it would be a great instance of his Majesty's goodness, if he would consider their present distress.

Sir, it is certain they are under very great difficulties at present, on the accounts they mention; and I am assured from good hands, that several of them who have had 50l. per ann. from their flock do not receive 15l. It is but

---

14 His Grace does not shew in this letter any partiality to the dissenters, with which he used to be charged by the few tory enemies he had; and he had no others:—The truth is, that he was naturally a very moderate and impartial man, but very steady in the pursuit of those measures he thought just and right, and for the service of the cause he was engaged to support.

15 It does not appear from the manuscript whether it is 120 or 1200l.

doing them justice to affirm, that they are very well affected to his Majesty and his Royal Family, and by the best enquiries I could make, do their endeavours to keep their congregations from deserting the country; not more than one or two of the younger ministers having any ways encouraged the humour now prevailing here. And his Majesty's goodness in giving them some extraordinary relief on this occasion of their present great distress, would undoubtedly make them more active to retain their people here.

I cannot help mentioning on this occasion that what with scarceness of corn in the north, and the loss of all credit there, by the numbers that go or talk of going to America, and with the disturbances in the south, this kingdom is at present in a deplorable condition. But I hope we shall be able to keep every thing pretty quiet, and that if it please God to send us a good harvest, things will gradually mend.

I am, &c.

To Lord Carteret.

Dublin, Apr. 10, 1729.

My Lord,

I had this day the honour of your Excellency's of the 5th instant, and have since talked with my Lord Chancellor about altering the value of our coin, which we shall endeavour to give all possible expedition to.

But we are both of opinion that nothing can be moved in the council about it, till the return of the Judges; for the bankers here are all against it, for a plain reason which they themselves told me, which is that they get 2 per cent. in the exchange by the present inequality of gold and silver, and your Lordship knows what strength they have in the council.

We are very much obliged to his Majesty for his kind disposition to this country; and I am sure we ought not to be insensible that the favourable representations your Excellency has been pleased to make of our attachment to his Royal Family, have very much contributed to this.

I shall take a proper opportunity of talking with the Lords Justices of a copper coinage, and as soon as I know their sentiments, I will write to your Excellency on that subject.

I am, &c.

To the same.

Dublin, Apr. 24, 1729.

My Lord,

As we find we have two new privy counsellors made here, we cannot forbear putting your Excellency in mind of my Lord Cavan.[16] We both applied to your Lordship when you was here, that he might be made a privy counsellor, and you were pleased to promise us, that you would recommend him to his Majesty the first opportunity, to be made a member of that right honourable board. By what has happened we apprehend your Excellency may have forgotten him; and we beg leave again to recommend him to be made a privy counsellor, as being one of a very antient noble family here, and firmly attached to his Majesty, and who on all occasions, has been of great service to the government in the House of Lords; and we doubt not but he would be equally serviceable in the council. We are,

My Lord, &c.

To the same.

Dublin, Apr. 26, 1729.

My Lord,

I thought your Excellency might be pleased to hear by the first opportunity, that on Thursday last we communicated your Lordship's letter, and the other papers transmitted with it, relating to the coin, to the privy council, and that we then appointed a committee to take the affair into consideration; since which the committee met last night, and reduced the value of gold to what it goes for in England; and this night they settled the value of foreign silver agreeably to the paper your Excellency sent over, in which the piece of eight of 17 pwts. 4 grs. is valued at 5s. Irish. As Mr. Conolly went out of town yesterday and does not return till Tuesday, we cannot have a council till Wednesday, when I hope we shall finish this affair.

Several attended to oppose the reducing of the value if gold, but were able to say little in the committee, and will be less able to stand a debate in the council.

I am, my Lord, &c.

16 This must be a joint letter from the Lords Justices Boulter and Wyndham.

To the same.

Dublin, May 1, 1729.

My Lord,

Since I wrote last to your Excellency, the committee have drawn up and delivered in their report to the council, relating to the coins here current, which council was held yesterday; but as a petition was then given in by several merchants and others, against lowering the gold, desiring to be heard on that subject, we thought proper to order them to be heard by themselves, not by council, next Monday, when I hope we shall one way or another conclude that affair.

The bankers have bestirred themselves to the utmost on this occasion, and appear to have that influence over the traders and others of this place, that those who are most satisfied that what the council are doing, is for the benefit of this nation, dare not publickly own their sentiments. They are setting about petitions against this reduction, and playing the whole game of Wood's half-pence.

I rather think we shall carry the affair in the council, and when our letter to your Excellency on this subject is once gone over I believe they will gradually cool.

At present hardly any are capable of hearing reason, but if they should come to temper, so that there are any hopes that arguments may work upon them, I would willingly know your Excellency's pleasure, whether you would give leave to have the memorial presented to your Lordship printed. Among other things they are pleased to give out, one is, that the memorial was written by Mr. Conduit, and is designed to ruin this nation.

As the bankers have behaved themselves with great insolence to the government on this occasion, and are visibly sacrificing the good of the publick to their private advantage, and plainly appear to have a greater power than it is proper they should have, when this affair is a little blown over, I have a proposal to make to your Excellency which has been suggested to me by some in trade, and which I rather think may be of service to the nation, and will considerably take down the insolence of the bankers.

I am, &c.

To the Duke of Newcastle.

Dublin, May 8, 1729.

My Lord,

As the Archbishop of Dublin has been out of order for four or five days, and is now apprehended to be in very great danger, I think it proper to acquaint your Grace with it, that there may be no surprise in disposing of a place of so great consequence, upon any report of his death from other hands. By the next post I shall inform your Grace what is the event of his sickness.

I am, &c.

N. B. The same intelligence was likewise sent to Lord Carteret.

To Lord Carteret.

Dublin, May 9, 1729.

My Lord,

Upon occasion of the vacancy here by the death of the Archbishop of Dublin, I beg leave to mention to your Excellency, that if his Majesty should fill that see from England, I would desire your Lordship to use your interest for the Bishop of St. David's, whom I formerly mentioned to you; but if from hence, I think the Bishop of Fernes the most proper person.

I am, &c.

To Lord Townshend.

Dublin, May 9, 1729.

My Lord,

Yesterday in the evening died his Grace the Archbishop of Dublin. As in January last I troubled your Lordship with a letter about filling this archbishoprick, whenever it should happen to be vacant, and declared my opinion that for the support of the English interest here, it was absolutely necessary that it should be bestowed on a native of England, I shall not now repeat what I then wrote: but shall just renew my recommendations at that time, that if his Majesty is pleased to send one from the bench of England, the Bishop of St. David's is my oldest friend there: if he is pleased to fill it from hence, the Bishop of Fernes is the most proper person.

The filling this place with an able man is of great consequence to his Majesty's service here, and I therefore hope nobody will be thought of in England to be sent hither, because he is troublesome or good for nothing there.

I must beg leave on this occasion to recommend to your Lordship's protection Mr. Stephens, that he may have a specifick performance of the promise made me of bestowing on him the next canonry vacant at Christ Church. I am,

My Lord, &c.

To the Duke of Newcastle.

Dublin, May 9, 1729.

My Lord,

Yesterday in the evening died the Archbishop of Dublin, after a few days indisposition. I have formerly written of the consequence of filling this post well, and for the support of the English interest here, it is necessary it should be an Englishman. If it be filled from the bench in England, the oldest friend I have there is the Bishop of St. David's: if from the bench here, the Bishop of Fernes[17] is I think much the most proper person. I am,

Your Grace's, &c.

Boulter to Newcastle.

May 12, 1729.
(NA. SP. 63/391/55)

My Lord,

Having by accident an opportunity of sending a letter this day, I beg leave to add to what your Grace will receive from me by Saturday's mail last, that I hope your Lordship will be so good as to remember what I have formerly wrote of the necessity of filling the See of Dublin with an Englishman; and the person I would recommend to succeed to Fernes, if Bishop Hoadley be made Archbishop, is the Bishop of Clonfert, who is a very honest sensible person.

I am, with the greatest truth and respect,

My Lord,

Your Grace's

most humble and

most obedient servant

Hu. Armagh

To Lord Carteret.

Dublin, May 13, 1729.

My Lord,

I am sorry I can give your Excellency no better an account of the success of our endeavouring to mend the state of our coin here. However I think myself obliged to acquaint you with what has passed on this occasion.

Upon the receipt of your Excellency's letter, and the papers transmitted

17 Dr. Hoadley succeeded Dr. King in the Archbishoprick of Dublin.

with it, we ordered a council to meet, and communicated your Lordship's letter and the papers to them. As the affair had been fully considered in the year 1726, and there was no alteration proposed to be made to what the committee of council had then agreed upon, except raising the foreign silver from 5s. 4d. to 5s. 4½d. English per ounce, I would fain have had a committee withdraw immediately and make us a report, that we might before we parted have done the business, and transmitted it to your Excellency, before it made any noise; but this was opposed as being too precipitate, and what might perhaps be called a job-work; so the matter was referred to a committee in the common way, who on Friday was fortnight went through the gold coins, and the next day the silver; and if Mr. Conolly had not gone out of town then we could have finished the affair on Monday following; but he not returning till Tuesday night, we could not have a council till Wednesday, against which time, the merchants at the instigation of the bankers and other remitters and their dependants, had a petition ready against the scheme. They pretended not to be ready to speak then, and we gave them till Monday to prepare, I must own against my advice.

When we met on Monday was se'nnight to hear them, we had a petition from the Lord Mayor and common-council of Dublin, the grand-jury of the county and of the city of Dublin, and from the city of Cork, against what the council were doing. The merchants who appeared were persons all concerned in remittances, and one Bindon,[18] a broken merchant of Limerick. I and some of the council answered what they said, but in the end they pretended they were not quite ready; and so they were indulged to be heard again as last Monday, and to offer what they thought proper.

When we met last Monday we had a petition from the merchants of Londonderry to the same purpose with the others; and the merchants offered a scheme, the substance of which was, raising the English shilling to 13½d. and finding some fault with the proportions of the several pieces of gold and silver in our scheme; in which if there are any errors, they will best be corrected by the master of the mint in England.

On this occasion as there was a great assembly in the council-chamber, in a speech I made, I endeavoured to shew the necessity of doing what we proposed; the perniciousness of raising English silver, what the nation lost by our present inequality of gold and silver, who were the gainers by it, and answered their objections; and desired all to remember who had hindered the removing of our present evil, if the ferment that had been raised among the people should make it adviseable not to proceed any farther in the affair.

When the petitioners retired, the prevailing opinion in the council was,

18 David Bindon, Esq; a very eminent merchant, of exceeding good family, of great knowledge in trade, suffered much in the South Sea Scheme, in 1720, and was a member of parliament in the reign of George II.

that though the thing proposed by the committee was most certainly for the advantage of the kingdom, yet considering the present clamour and uneasiness of the people against it, it was most prudent to let the affair rest.

For the better understanding of this I must acquaint your Lordship that they have universally possessed the people that the scheme is an English project, formed in England, and carried on by my Lord Chancellor, myself, and other English here, with a design to drain this kingdom of their gold, as they are already drained of their silver.

As I found this had been industriously spread among the people, in my speech[19] on Monday, I gave them an account what applications had been made to your Excellency on this subject when you was here the first time, what had been done in it in the year 1726, in council and out of it, and shewed that at present England got 2½ per cent. in all goods they bought here, which advantage they would lose by this reduction, so that the scheme could not come from thence.

I am sorry his Majesty's gracious intentions and your Excellency's kind endeavour to save this nation from a certain, though slow ruin, should meet with no better a return here; but I hope those things have been said on this occasion, that with an increase of our sufferings here, will by degrees, open the eyes of men of sense, and that a time may come, when petitions will be offered in behalf of the reduction proposed.

I am, &c.

To the Duke of Newcastle.

Dublin, May 17, 1729.

My Lord,

I have already troubled your Grace with two letters on the occasion of the death of the Archbishop of Dublin, with an account who I think may be most proper to fill that see, and to succeed the Bishop of Fernes if he should be promoted to Dublin. If the Bishop of Clonfert should succeed to Fernes, I think either Dean Alcock, or Essex Edgworth Chancellor of Ardagh, will be very proper to succeed to the bishoprick of Clonfert.

By our last mail from England we learn that Dr. Stratford, Canon of Christ Church, is dead; and I must upon this intelligence beg the favour of your Grace to support the interest of Mr. Stephens, for whom before I left

19 My Lord Primate was said upon great provocation from Eaton Stannard, Esq; Recorder of Dublin, to have been a little off his guard at this time, and for this once to have spoken some hasty words; but the Recorder suffered for his temerity all his life time afterwards, the government would never make him a Judge, though he was a good lawyer and an honest man; it appears indeed in Swift's letters, that he had been chosen Recorder by his interest.

England, I had a promise of the next vacancy in that church: which I did not insist on upon the former vacancy, but let it go in favour of Dr. Gibert, but I hope Mr. Stephens will not meet with a second disappointment; and your Grace's favour to him in the present vacancy, will be esteemed a very great obligation by him who is,

My Lord, &c.

To Lord Carteret.

Dublin, May 17, 1729.

My Lord,

I have lately troubled your Excellency with two or three letters in particular, as well as our common letters, on occasion of the archbishoprick of Dublin being vacant. I have only this to mention farther to your Lordship, that if things end in a vacancy of a bishoprick here, which Dean Gore is not willing to take, I should willingly recommend to your favour either Dean Alcock, or Essex Edgworth Chancellor of Ardagh, to succeed. I am,

Your Excellency's, &c.

To the same.

Dublin, May 20, 1729.

My Lord,

I have received the honour of your Excellency's of the 13th inst. and I hope you have received mine of the same date, giving an account of what has passed in council in relation to the coin.

Your Lordship might justly suppose after the applications made to you on that head, that the regulation proposed in relation to the gold would have passed to the universal satisfaction of the kingdom, as it is undoubtedly for its benefit. But your Excellency rightly observes, that you are acquainted with the humour of the people here, and so are less surprised at the opposition given to it: and indeed except what opposition was owing to the bankers, all the rest turned upon their being unwilling to be served by Englishmen, and it was not any argument against the thing that weighed with those who made loud clamours against it, but its being proposed and supported by Englishmen; and this was the popular argument to prove there was somewhat amiss in it.

We have proceeded with as much prudence and caution in this affair as we could. And we chose to hear the merchants speak to the subject, rather than barely receive their memorial, that we might have an opportunity of undeceiving the people by what we could say against them in publick, whereas the people could have known nothing of what passed in a debate in the council.

As the memorial was sent to your Excellency I thought it would be wrong to print it without your leave; but I have no thoughts of printing that or any thing else on the subject, till the people are grown cool, and my Lord Chancellor thinks it advisable; and then it shall be such a one as he approves of, but we will carefully avoid doing any thing in this matter that may enflame the nation.

What has been hinted to me, as a thing that would oblige the bankers to keep more cash by them than they do, and would probably by degrees bring the merchants to keep their own cash is, if the officers of the revenue were strictly enjoined to take only cash, and not bankers notes for payments in the revenue, the greatest part of which are at present made in bankers notes: besides it would have another great advantage, which is, that as things now stand, if any run should happen upon the bankers, the government has not one penny of money to go on with; but in the other case, they would have some money at command. But I do not speak of this as a thing any ways proper to be done at present; since I fear in our present distress, if the government were to refuse taking the notes of bankers, it would cause an immediate run upon them; which as our circumstances now stand, would put a stop to all trade and payments amongst us: but I mention it as a thing worth your Excellency's consideration, when we have the happiness of your presence with us.

As every thing is very quiet here, and we hope likely to continue so, I cannot apprehend that there is any necessity of your Lordship's coming hither before September; whenever I can learn that there is occasion for it, I will not fail giving your Excellency advice of it.

Since we sent to your Lordship Mr. Espin's and Mr. Vaughan's memorials, I have learned that Mr. Espin has already about 200l. per ann. in the church, and as much temporal estate; whereas Mr. Vaughan has nothing but a curacy, so that the vicarage given to him, will be bestowed on one who very much wants it.

I am, &c.

To the same.

Dublin, June 5, 1729.
My Lord,

I have the honour of your Excellency's of the 29th past, and thank your Lordship for your kindness to the Bishop of St. David's, in the affair of the archbishoprick of Dublin, with which he acquainted me with great acknowledgments of the obligations you had laid on him.

I am sorry that affair is likely to be kept long in suspense, since I think it would rather be for his Majesty's service, that the new Archbishop whomsoever his Majesty pleases to pitch upon, were well settled in his station before the parliament meets.

Several here seem sensible of the folly of the clamour raised against regulating our coin, but all that is left to be done at present, is staying till the greatness of the evil makes them importunate for a remedy.

I am glad your Excellency approves of the persons I mentioned as proper to fill some vacancy, if there should be any removes here.

I am, my Lord, &c.

To the Duke of Newcastle.

Dublin, June 10, 1729.

My Lord,

I have lately troubled your Grace with two or three letters on occasion of the death of the Archbishop of Dublin, with my opinion whom I thought most proper to succeed to that see, according as his Majesty should please to pitch upon one on the bench in England or here.

I am sensible his Majesty was in such a hurry, as he was just then going abroad, when the first advice of his Grace's death came, that it could not be expected that affair should be settled before his departure: but I am sorry to hear that it is generally talked at London, that the archbishoprick is not likely to be disposed of till his Majesty's return.

As our parliament will probably meet in September, or the beginning of October, I cannot but think it would be for his Majesty's service here if a successor were settled in the archbishoprick time enough for him to form some acquaintance and interest here before the parliament is opened, and to let the disappointments of some who are seeking for that station, be a little digested before that time; for I very much fear, that notwithstanding all precautions, we are in danger of having a troublesome session, as the debts of the nation are very much increased within a few years.

I thought it my duty to his Majesty humbly to make this representation. I am,

My Lord, &c.

To the Bishop of London.

Dublin, June 12, 1729.

My Lord,

I have been favoured with your Lordship's of the 3d instant.

I am glad that those who make an unjust clamour about tythes here, have had more modesty than to think they could persuade people on your side of the water to believe that to be one of the causes of protestants going hence to America.

I thank your Lordship for designing to attend when the cause Mr. Horan is concerned in comes before the Lords; it is a cause of some consequence to this country.

There had been formerly some objection made to Mr. Stephens being Canon of Christ Church, on account of there being a want of persons to bear office there: but I hoped it had been removed by his offering to be treasurer, and finding one to act under him, for whose honesty he would be security. I believe half the treasurers there have transacted their business by one of their servants, (and possibly the Bishop of Oxford did so) without being security for them.

I cannot but think I am hardly used in this affair, to have a stop put to a promise made me some years ago and since renewed, to gratify the opposition made by my successor, who neither had done, nor is capable (if I may say so without vanity) of doing that service to the crown which I have done here and at Oxford.

I thank your Lordship for the service you have done Mr. Stephens in this affair, and recommend him to your farther protection.

Your Lordship I dare say, does not doubt of my friendship to the Bishop of St. David's, and I am thoroughly satisfied of his being a good church-man, and as fast a friend to that branch of our constitution as any man. And I did not set up a rival against him, but your Lordship knows in all recom-mendations on these occasions I have thought it prudent to mention two persons; since if one should prove less acceptable, I am not present to recommend a second. And I have reason to believe that great interest has been formed for the Bishop of Fernes on the other side of the water two years ago, and since often renewed there for the post now vacant. For this reason I thought proper to name him with the Bishop of St. David's; since it is very much for his Majesty's service that there should be a good under-standing between the new archbishop and myself; as I am sure there will be, whether his Majesty pitches upon the Bishop of St. David's or the Bishop of Fernes; and as to the latter, I can assure your Lordship he has given here no occasion to be thought no friend to the Church, and is allowed by every body to be a good speaker in the House of Lords, and consequently will be so in the council: and I must inform your Lordship that is of no small consequence to the support of his Majesty's service and the English interest here.

I am very sorry to find the choice is likely to be put off for so long a time, since it is of moment to our affairs here, that the new Archbishop should be settled and have time to look about him, if possible, before our parliament meets, which will be the latter end of September or beginning of October. But there is one thing I must beg of your Lordship to guard against, that under a notion of not offending the friends of either of the present candidates, a new person may not be clapt upon us.

I can easily see and no one here doubts, but there is such a person in view, who will neither be acceptable here, nor of service to the English interest. I hope, after what I have written in many letters before, I need not again urge the necessity of the see not being filled with a native of this country.

I am sorry peace and war continue still so uncertain: and fear the Spaniards are trifling with us, so as to lose the time of action for this year, which if they should do it will light heavy on the ministry.

I am,

My Lord, &c.

To Sir Robert Walpole.

Dublin, June 14, 1729.

Sir,

The repeated accounts we have here that the archbishoprick of Dublin is not likely to be disposed of till his Majesty's return, are the occasion of my giving you this trouble.

If things are not already fixed otherwise, I would beg leave to represent that I think it would be for his Majesty's service here to have that affair settled as soon as it conveniently can. The session of our parliament will come on in September or October; and I could wish that those here who may be displeased that they are not considered on this occasion, or that the post is bestowed on an Englishman, may have time to cool before the meeting of the parliament.

If his Majesty shall please to send us an Archbishop from England, it would be of service to the King's affairs here that he should be settled and form some acquaintance, and begin to have weight against the session. Or if his Majesty shall please to fill that station with one from the bench here, I think it would be best to have the consequent removes over by that time.

I have so often before the vacancy happened, wrote of the necessity of filling the place with an Englishman, that I hope I need not make any new representation on that head.

It is likewise of some consequence that the person pitched upon be one whom I may depend upon for there being a good agreement betwixt him and me, which I am sure will be the case, if either the Bishop of St. David's or the Bishop of Fernes be the person.

And I should be very sorry if the effect of this delay should be the bringing on the stage some other candidate, which is what is by many here apprehended to be in some measure aimed at, by deferring this matter for so long a time.

Whether any such thing be designed you are best able to judge, and I beg leave to recommend it to you to prevent any such use being made of it.

I am, &c.

To the Archbishop of Canterbury.

Dublin, July 3, 1729.

My Lord,

Since I had the honour of your Grace's relating to Mr. Bury of Finglass; Mr. Baron Pocklington has given me a very good character of him; and Sir Ralph Gore, a person of distinction here, has introduced him to me, and confirmed what Mr. Baron had said of him. I shall upon your Grace's recommendation have a regard to him, and endeavour on a proper occasion to help him to somewhat in the Church.

I am, my Lord, &c.

To Sir Robert Walpole.

Dublin, July 8, 1729.

Sir,

As I troubled you with a letter not long ago, relating to the Archbishoprick of Dublin, I should not so soon have given you a new trouble, but that we are informed, that great endeavours are used and much art to bring into play on this occasion, some new person on this side of the water. I can assure you, so far as I may be supposed capable of judging, there is nobody on the bench here so able to do his Majesty service in this country, nor I think of those who would willingly take the archbishoprick, any so acceptable to the well affected of this kingdom, nor can I depend so firmly on being assisted in all publick affairs by any one here, as the Bishop of Fernes. I beg leave to lay these things plainly before you, and to desire your help, that some other person here may not be worked in, who may be of little or no service, (and perhaps disservice) where all possible help is little enough.

I am, &c.

To the same.

Dublin, Aug. 12, 1729.

Sir,

I had sooner answered the letter you honoured me with of the 19th past, but that I received it when I was upon my visitation, from which I am lately returned.

I am very much obliged to you for the kind opinion you are pleased to express of my endeavours to support the King's interest here, and I can assure you they shall never be wanting. And I am sensible how much I am indebted to you for the personal regard you are pleased to honour me with.

I am glad to hear the affair of the archbishoprick continues in so good a way; I could heartily wish that the two Bishops in England who oppose one another in this business, could be brought to agree, they are both my very good friends, as are the Bishops of St. David's and Fernes, and I hope the competition betwixt them, will not make way for some third person to be let into the archbishoprick that may be less acceptable, and with whom I cannot promise myself to have the same good correspondence as with either of them.

I should have been glad that this affair had been settled before my Lord Lieutenant's arrival here; but am very easy, as you give me hopes the delay will be of no prejudice.

I beg leave to take this opportunity to thank you for the support you have given me on this and all other occasions since my coming hither.

I am, Sir, &c.

To Lord Carteret.

Dublin, Aug. 12, 1729.

My Lord,

Upon my return from my visitation I had the pleasure of receiving one of Lady Disert's[20] favours, for which I beg leave to trouble your Excellency to make my compliments, with my most sincere congratulations to the bride and bridegroom, for in that light they appear yet to me at this distance: as it is a marriage which has the approbation of your Excellency and my Lady Carteret, I question not but it will prove happy, which are my most hearty wishes.

We begin now to look with some pleasure at the near prospect of seeing your Lordship amongst us, and I doubt not but your presence will by degrees

20 One of the daughters of Lord Carteret, who was married to the Earl of Disert, a Scotch nobleman.

remove those difficulties we at present apprehend in the next session of parliament.

This city is not so free from tumults as it ought to be, and as we hoped the proclamation published some time ago would have made it; but if it be possible to awaken the magistrates out of their present lethargy, we shall endeavour to have all things quiet here against your Lordship's arrival.

I am,

My Lord, &c.

To the Bishop of London.

Dublin, Aug. 28, 1729.

My Lord,

In my last to your Lordship I could not help expressing myself with some resentment that the opposition made by my successor against Mr. Stephens, should have met with such success; but I was then sensible how much I was obliged to your Lordship for preventing the canonry of Christ Church from being actually given away to another. I still retain the same sense of my obligations to your Lordship, and as you are best able to judge of what can or cannot be done for my friend Mr. Stephens, I again recommend him to your Lordship's protection, and leave it entirely to your Lordship's goodness and prudence to manage that vacancy so that he may be put into possession of somewhat reasonable before that is given away.

We are still here under an uncertainty who is to be Archbishop of Dublin, and I take it for granted shall continue so till his Majesty's return. Your Lordship knows the Bishops of St. David's and Fernes are both old acquaintance and friends of mine, and as I have wrote to your Lordship, so have I wrote to the ministry, that I shall be easy on whomsoever of them the choice shall fall since I have no doubt of agreeing very well with either of them, but it will be otherwise if some third person should be put into that post: and I am the more concerned that it should not be another because it is generally understood here that I am a friend to both of them; but it will be clear that if another be made Archbishop, my recommendation has been of no significancy, which opinion, I am sure, must have an ill effect on the bench here. I must therefore beg of your Lordship, who are upon the spot, if possible, to hinder such a disgrace from happening to me.

I can assure your Lordship that if one has Dublin, and the other be made sure of Cashel, Derry, or Kilmore, the first that falls, I believe the person who has this promise kept to him, will rather be a gainer as to providing for a family.

We have a fine crop of corn on the ground, and have had above three weeks very fine weather to get it in, and though we have now some wet, yet if it please God not to continue it for a long time, it will for the most part be got in very well.

I hope in a little time all the doubts written to us from London about the peace will be cleared up. I am,

My Lord, &c.

To the Duke of Newcastle.

Dublin, Sept. 9, 1729.

My Lord,

I have so often troubled your Grace on Mr. Stephens's account, that if I could avoid it I would not give you the additional trouble of this letter. Your Grace knows I had the promise of the next canonry of Christ Church for him: and that there has been one vacant for some time by the death of Dr. Stratford, and that it was not filled before his Majesty went abroad, that Mr. Stephens might be provided with somewhat else in the King's gift, before that was given away: your Grace has frequently renewed the promise of securing an equivalent for Mr. Stephens, if he should fail of the canonry of Christ Church promised him. I must therefore again recommend him to your Grace's protection, and intreat that the present vacancy at Christ Church may not be filled up till Mr. Stephens is actually provided for. This favour, if your Grace will please to obtain it for him, will be some security for his being taken care of, but if the vacant canonry be given away first, he will only rest upon a general promise, and be rather in a worse case than he has been in for some years past.

Your Grace's kind support of his pretensions on this occasion, will be esteemed the greatest obligation by,

My Lord, &c.

To Sir Robert Walpole.

Dublin, Sept. 9, 1729.

Sir,

As I have made bold to trouble you in affairs of greater consequence, I hope you will excuse this trouble in a matter of less importance, but in which my friendship for the person concerned makes me very solicitous.

Before I left England I obtained a promise of the next canonry of Christ Church for Mr. Stephens, of Malden in Surrey, and have since been frequently promised that he should have that or an equivalent.

When a canonry fell there by the death of Dr. Stratford, a little before his Majesty went abroad, I renewed my application for Mr. Stephens, but found that upon some objections made to Mr. Stephens on account of the misfortune of his eyes, it was rather designed to give that canonry to Dr. Knipe, and to give some other equivalent to Mr. Stephens; but the better to secure the performance to Mr. Stephens, it was thought proper to keep that canonry open till he was actually provided for.

Now as his Majesty is upon his return, and it is probable Dr. Knipe will be very desirous to be put in possession of the canonry intended for him, the favour I have to ask of you, Sir, is that Dr. Knipe may not be made Canon, till Mr. Stephens, who had a prior promise of that preferment, is otherwise provided for. This I hope will be some real security for his being speedily taken care of, but if the present vacancy be once filled up, and instead of a canonry Mr. Stephens has only a promise of some other preferment, from what has happened to him already in this affair, I am afraid his future expectations may be very uncertain.

As he always supported the character of an ingenious man and a good scholar at the University, and was thoroughly well affected to the succession in his Majesty's family in the worst times, and has been an old and intimate acquaintance of mine almost from my first admission at Oxford, I most earnestly recommend him and his interest in this affair to your favour and protection.

I am, &c.

To the Bishop of London.

Dublin, Sept. 13, 1729.

My Lord,

Upon the receipt of your Lordship's of the 4th instant, I immediately wrote to the Duke of Newcastle, Sir Robert Walpole, and the Speaker, according to your advice. I have this day received another from your Lordship on the same subject, and I am very much obliged to you for your kindness on this occasion to Mr. Stephens, and beg the continuance of your good offices for him, that the canonry may not be actually filled till he is provided for: and hope by your kind assistance he may get somewhat on this occasion.

I am sorry to hear my Lord Townshend has declared he will have no concern in Church matters.

I cannot learn whether any thing is yet fixed about the archbishoprick of Dublin, and hope after all it will go either to the Bishop of St. David's or Bishop of Fernes; and think if the former should fail now, it may be worth his while to have an eye to some other bishoprick that may fall here; and I cannot but think either Cashel, Derry, or Kilmore would be rather more beneficial for his family than Dublin.

I am sorry my conduct in this affair has been disagreeable to your Lordship, whom I should be very unwilling to offend; and I believe if the Bishop of St. David's knew the true state of affairs here, he would excuse the part I have acted since the death of the late Archbishop.

I am glad to find the quarrel with Prussia is blown over, and that the King is so soon expected in London.

My Lord Lieutenant[21] landed here this day, and will I believe open the parliament Tuesday come se'nnight, when I heartily wish we may have an easy session. I am,

My Lord, &c.

To the same.

Dublin, Oct. 7, 1729.

My Lord,

As the session of our parliament is begun, we are thinking of some necessary bills; and as most of our clergy have neither house nor glebe, we are for trying to help them to some. We attempted last session to have a bill to impower a tenant in tail, to make a grant of 40 acres, at the full improved value for a glebe, which was disapproved in England. We would now attempt to impower such tenant to grant a glebe of 20, or rather than fail, of 10 acres, on the same conditions as before. But we would first willingly know what would be allowed of in England. We think 10 acres cannot be thought any great damage to the remainder man; and without such an help, as most of our estates are under settlements, there is scarce any coming at glebes.

We were told my Lord Trevor very much opposed our last bill, I should be obliged to your Lordship, if you would talk the matter over with him, and any others your Lordship shall judge proper, and let me know what success may be hoped for, if we send over such a bill.

I am, &c.

Newcastle to Boulter.

Kensington, Oct. 14, 1729.
(NA. SP. 63/391/157–8)

My Lord,

I am almost ashamed to write to your Grace after having so long omitted to return my thanks for the several letters I have had the honour of receiving

---

21 John, Lord Carteret, the third time of his being here, which was a great advantage to this kingdom, as it made him well acquainted with all the affairs thereof.

from you which I hope your Grace will be so good as not to impute to neglect or want of attention to the intimations you have been pleased to favour me with. The chief reason indeed that induced me to delay writing to your Grace was, that there was nothing yet determined about the disposal of the Archbishoprick of Dublin; and you will have heard from Sir Robert Walpole, that his Majesty does not intend to fill that See, 'till the session of your Parliament is over. I have learnt with the greatest pleasure, that in all appearance their proceedings will be to the King's satisfaction. His Majesty and his servants are very sensible how much your abilities and unwearied application have contributed to the ease and success of his Majesty's service in Ireland. If I durst ask the favour, after having been myself so faulty, I would desire your Grace's continuing at your leisure to honour me with your commands, and with an account of the state of affairs with you and your observations upon them.

I beg that your Grace will do me the justice to be persuaded of my inclination to serve Mr. Stephens. You have, I believe been informed of the objections that were made to his having a Canonry at Christ Church, on account of his infirmity. That, which was lately given to Dr. Knipe the Chaplain attending his Majesty at Hanover, though it might before have been intended him, was disposed of abroad, and the Warrant signed there, before it was known to any body here. I shall not fail continuing on all proper opportunities to represent Mr. Stephen's case, and your Grace's recommendation of him, to his Majesty and His servants, and shall gladly obey your commands on all occasions, being with the greatest sincerity
     etc.
Holles Newcastle

To the Duke of Newcastle.

Dublin, Oct. 23, 1729.
My Lord,
I have had the honour of your Grace's of the 14th instant, and am too sensible of the hurry of business in England to expect a regular correspondence from one in your Grace's station. I have the best proofs of my not being neglected by your Lordship and others in the ministry by my having been hitherto supported here.

As the session of our parliament is now opened, I think his Majesty does very right in not filling the archbishoprick of Dublin till our parliament rises, and shall say nothing farther on that subject at present, than that I hope it will at last be filled with an Englishman.

Your Grace has no doubt had an account of Mr. Conolly's illness, and quitting the chair, and Sir Ralph Gore being chosen in his room. It is likely

Mr. Conolly will not live many days.

The session has opened very well, and most of the members seem disposed and promise to provide some fund to pay interest for about 200,000l. of our debts, till we are able to pay them. And indeed without such a provision, the wheels of the government will be so clogged here, that in case of any accident, we shall hardly be able to send a regiment abroad, if called for. But at the same time there is a very bad spirit, I fear, artfully spread among all degrees of men amongst us, and the utmost grumbling against England, as getting all our money from us either by trade or otherwise.

And this spirit has been heightened by a book[22] lately published here about the absentees, who according to the calculation of that author, draw from us about 62,000l.[23] per. ann. It is certain the sum of his calculations are wrong, since according to them, about 440,000l. per. ann. would be paid by us as as our ballance of trade, &c. which if true, would in about three years have left us without money.

And I believe among less intelligent persons, they are for taxing the absentees 4s. in the pound; but I am satisfied the men of sense in either house are too wise to make an attempt of that nature, which they know could only exasperate England, without ever having such a bill returned to us.

We are no doubt in a miserable condition, by having had three or four bad harvests together, and if God had not blessed us with a plentiful crop this harvest, we had been ruined for some years, but I hope we shall pick up by degrees.

But there is an evil spirit here, that instead of owning whence our calamities really came, would throw all upon England.

The absentees spending their money there, the restraints upon our wool and woollen manufactures, the encrease of the establishment pensions, though we tell them his present Majesty has granted none, and our regiments being at Gibraltar, though we tell them the common defence of England and Ireland required it, are the great topics of complaint. On Tuesday they went into a committee on the state of the nation, where these heads were opened with some others, and on Monday they are to sit again. Whether they will, as some propose, draw up a memorial to be presented to his Majesty, setting forth their misery to no purpose; or whether they will, as the wisest amongst them are disposed, content themselves to redress such evils as they can, is hard to judge. I rather hope things will end the latter way, after the warm men have been permitted to discharge their fire.

God be thanked the government is not concerned in these heats, nor the administration fallen on. And I may venture to say there has not been any

22 Wrote by Thomas Prior, Esq;
23 Supposed to be paid to pensioners on the establishment of Ireland.

such impartial administration here since the revolution, as has been for the five years last past, that the government has been in English hands.

If I can judge any thing in the matter, there is a necessity of continuing to support the English interest here, or what things may in time come to, I shall leave to others to think.

There is no doubt but Mr. Conolly's illness and impossibility of ever acting again, has made things worse than usual, as it must be some time before the several clans that united under him, can settle under a new director. But steadiness in England, will, I doubt not, by degrees settle us again here.

I am very glad to find my endeavours here are accepted by his Majesty, and favourably thought of by the ministry. I shall continue to promote his Majesty's service here to the utmost of my power. I cannot tell but the rights of the clergy may be attacked this session: if we cannot make a stand here, as I hope we shall, I must in the behalf of all my brethren, implore his Majesty's protection on the other side of the water.

The Bishop of London has acquainted me how things have passed in relation to Mr. Stephens, and I am very much obliged to your Grace for being so kind as to promise to take him under your protection. I must beg leave to acquaint your Grace he begins to advance towards 60, so that he cannot afford to be long postponed. I am,

Your Grace's, &c.

To the Bishop of London.

Dublin, Oct. 29, 1729.

My Lord,

The bearer Mr. John Fulton, Master of Arts, of Trinity College in Dublin, is desirous to go to the West Indies, where he has some relations; and has applied to me to be recommended to your Lordship to be ordained and sent thither. Besides the testimonials he has to produce to your Lordship, I have enquired about the character he bears in the College, and am assured he hath behaved himself very well there, and supports a good character.

If your Lordship can dispose of him to America, so as to have some employment there, it will be an addition to the favour to give him what dispatch your Lordship can, as he does not abound in money. And your Lordship's kind assistance of him, as far as your Lordship shall find him to deserve it, will be esteemed an obligation, by

My Lord, &c.

To the Duke of Newcastle.

Dublin, Oct. 30, 1729.

My Lord,

I am very sorry I must acquaint your Grace that the ill spirit I mentioned in my last still increases, or at least seems to intimidate those who are better disposed in the House of Commons.

The privy council was attacked on Saturday last about the overdrawing of the concordatum for the two last years; but the Committee then broke up without any conclusion, by its being carried that the chairman should leave the chair. On Monday they seemed to have dropped the farther pursuit of that affair; but on Tuesday it was, through non-attendance of some, and ill-concerted measures of those present, carried without withdrawing, that the over-drawings of the concordatum would be of ill consequence to the kingdom.

To-morrow it is expected that there will be a report to the house from the committee, when we are promised that the house will disagree with the committee. If gentlemen will attend and unite in their measures it may easily be done; but hitherto there has been very little agreement, nor any well concerted management in that house. There is no doubt but Mr. Conolly's illness has been one occasion of this disjointedness, and it will require time to bring the several clans which united in him to centre in another.

After his death being expected for several days, Mr. Conolly died this morning about one o'clock. He has left behind him a very great fortune, some talk of 17,000l. per ann.

As his death makes a vacancy among the commissioners of the revenue, my Lord Chancellor and I have been talking with my Lord Lieutenant on that subject, and we all agree it will be for his Majesty's service that a native succeed him: and as Sir Ralph Gore, the new speaker, does not care to quit the post of Chancellor of the Exchequer, which he is already possessed of, and which by an addition made to the place by his late Majesty is worth better than 800l. per ann. and is for life, to be made one of the commissioners, we join in our opinion that the most proper person here to succeed Mr. Conolly is Dr. Coghill,[24] who is already a person of weight, and has done service in the parliament; and we think by this addition will be more capable of serving his Majesty both in and out of the house.

I am, &c.

24 Right Hon. Marmaduke Coghill was accordingly appointed.

Newcastle to Boulter (draft).

Whitehall, Nov. 11, 1729.
(NA. SP. 63/391/200)

My Lord,

I have received the honour of your Grace's letters of the 27th and 30th of the last month which I laid before the King who is very sensible of your constant attention to his Majesty's service, and of the great advantage that his Majesty's affairs in Ireland receive from it.

The King was extremely concerned for the loss of so great and good a man, and who had so much zeal for the interest of his Majesty and of his country as Mr. Conolly had, and very readily consented to what was proposed by my Lord Lieutenant and recommended by your Grace as the unanimous opinion of his Majesty's servants in Ireland, that Dr. Coghill should succeed Mr. Conolly as a Commissioner of the Revenue; and the King hopes, that this gentleman's interest, joined with Sir Ralph Gore's, and the diligence and activity of those who wish well to the public will be able to overcome that evil spirit, which his Majesty, with concern, found, by your letters, has arisen and seems to gain ground in the House of Commons. The account which your Grace has given of the situation of affairs there, must as you will easily imagine have made his Majesty desirous to know what turn they will take, and I hope your Grace will therefore favour me with frequent and particular accounts of what passes during the session.

To the Duke of Newcastle.

Dublin, Nov. 13, 1729.

My Lord,

In my last I gave your Grace an account of a resolution passed in the committee of accounts, relating to the overdrawings of the concordatum. When the committee came to make their report, it was unanimously agreed to have that resolution expunged. There were likewise in the same committee great heats about over-drawing the military contingencies, but without coming to any resolution about it.

As these two articles are the only branches of payment that can be charged with any unforeseen expence, or be used in case of any emergency, upon talking with several members of the necessity of some such fund to have recourse to on occasion, they were brought to drop their first heat.

Almost every day this week has been spent in the committee of ways and means; about granting the usual additional duties there has been no dispute, but about providing for the interest of 200,000l. debt owing by the publick, whether it should be in the grand bill of supply, or in a bill by itself; and the last being agreed on, whether only for two years, or till the debts are paid, it is carried only for two years. The fund for the payment of the interest is an additional duty upon wines and brandies, and 4s. in the pound upon absent officers, civil or military; in the latter, all under field officers are excepted, and such of both are excused as shall obtain his Majesty's sign manual.

The two bills are now drawing up, and I hope in a few days will be before the council here.

The house has not yet been in another committee on the state of the nation; and there is no guessing what measures they will take there. As the warm men have had success in some divisions in the house, I do not expect any thing of temper when they are in the committee.

When they have done any thing I shall acquaint your Grace with it. I am, Your Grace's, &c.

To the same.

Dublin, Nov. 22, 1729.

My Lord,

I this day had the honour of your Grace's of the 11th instant: Dr. Coghill's being made commissioner in the room of Mr. Conolly is very acceptable here; and I hope he and Sir Ralph Gore will by degrees get together the friends of Mr. Conolly and others well disposed, to join heartily in his Majesty's service; but this is more than they will be able to effect this session: however the King's business is now over, though it has met with great rubs and delays, and has been done with an ill grace; and our two money bills were sent off on Thursday last; the first is the usual tax-bill; the other is made up of several little taxes, by which it is proposed to pay the interest of 6 per cent. for 200,000l. of our debts, for two years, and if more is raised than 12000l. per ann. to sink part of the principal. It was attempted to give this fund till the debt was sunk, but that was rejected by a majority of five voices. There was afterwards a motion made that it should be inserted in the bill, that at the end of two years either the principal should be repaid or interest continued; but this was opposed and dropped, though it was declared to be the sense of the house. As the act for the additional duties of the first bill granted last session, expires on Christmas day, and the new duties of the second bill begin from that day, we hope they will be returned us soon enough to be passed before that time.

The committee on the state of the nation is still open, but if I may believe some of the discontented members, there will hardly any thing be done there, except settling a better proportion betwixt our gold and silver, than there is at present. And I very much fear that the weight of the bankers is so great here, that it may be carried to raise our silver, instead of lowering our gold; as a guinea passes here for 23s. Irish, which is 3d. more than it passes for in England; and a moidore for 30s. Irish, which is 9d. the bankers and remitters have had the benefit of carrying out all our silver, and bringing back gold for it; and now they want by raising the English shilling an half-penny, to have the benefit of carrying out all our gold, and bringing back English silver. My Lord Chancellor, myself, and several others, are doing what we can to prevent this mischief, but are uncertain of the success.

If the bankers prevail, I shall send over a short memorial against what the Commons may address for, if I cannot get either the House of Lords or privy council to join with me;[25] for such a raising of the silver will undo us here.

I am, &c.

To the same.

Dublin, Dec. 11, 1729.

My Lord,

The dangerous conditions in which the Archbishop of Cashel now lies, is the occasion of my giving your Grace this trouble, humbly to desire that no measures may be taken to dispose of that Archbishoprick, till I have an opportunity of acquainting your Lordship that it is actually vacant.

I am,

My Lord, &c.

To the same.

Dublin, Dec. 13, 1729.

My Lord,

This morning died Dr. Godwin, Archbishop of Cashel: I have just time to acquaint your Grace, that this may be a means of compromising the dispute about the archbishoprick of Dublin, by removing the Bishop of St. David's to Dublin, and the Bishop of Fernes to Cashel;[26] but if this be done, I should think it would be better to defer doing it till after the parliament is up. If it be apprehended that it may give too much offence to bestow at the same time the two best posts in the Church, after the primacy, on Englishmen, I must say that I think the most proper person to remove to Cashel, will be Dr. Synge, Archbishop of Tuam. I am,

My Lord, &c.

25 This resolution was a very spirited one, and very consistent with his Grace's usual courage, and conduct.
26 It appears clearly by this letter, that the Bishop of London had no reason for charging my Lord Primate with a partiality to the Bishop of Fernes, which it seems his Lordship misapprehending the thing, had done.

Boulter to Newcastle.

Dec. 14, 1729.
(NA. SP. 63/391/262)

My Lord,

Yesterday morning after some days illness died Dr. Goodwin Archbishop of Cashel, very much beloved and lamented here. By his death there is a second Archbishoprick vacant here and I should have been very ready to lay hold of this opportunity to compromise the dispute about the Archbishoprick of Dublin; but I fear it is too much at one and the same time to give two of the best posts in the Church next to the primacy to two Englishmen.

My Lord Chancellor and I have on this occasion had a conference with my Lord Lieutenant, and we think as circumstances now stand with the uneasiness among the Commons here, that the best scheme for keeping things quiet is, that Dr. Hoadley Bishop of Fernes be transferred to Dublin, that the Bishop of Clonfert be translated to Fernes, and, if there be a disposition in England to bestow a Bishoprick on Dr. Clayton, that he have Clonfert. That the Archbishoprick of Cashel be bestowed on the Bishop of Elphin, that the Bishop of Killala be removed to Elphin, and that Dr. Synge son to the Archbishop of Tuam be promoted to Killala.

This is the scheme we agreed upon as most for his Majesty's service in the present circumstances of this Kingdom.

I am, with the greatest truth & respect,
My Lord,
your Grace's
most humble &
most obedient servant.
Hu. Armagh

To the Bishop of London.

Dublin, Dec. 14, 1729.

My Lord,

Yesterday died, after some days illness, the Archbishop of Cashel,[27] very much lamented here. I should at another time have thought this vacancy might have compromised matters as to the archbishoprick of Dublin, but in the present uneasy state of the House of Commons, I think it will be too bold a step at one and the same time to give two Englishmen the two best posts in the Church, next to the primacy.

The scheme pitched on with my Lord Lieutenant and Lord Chancellor,

---

27 Dr. Timothy Godwin, who was translated to the See from Kilmore and Ardagh.

considering the present circumstances of the kingdom is, that the Bishop of Fernes[28] be translated to Dublin, the Bishop of Clonfert to Fernes; and if there be a disposition in England to make Dr. Clayton Bishop here, as we are assured there is, I have nothing to say against his being promoted to Clonfert. As to the archbishoprick of Cashel, it is thought proper to remove the Bishop of Elphin to Cashel, the Bishop of Killalla to Elphin, and Dr. Synge son to the Archbishop of Tuam, to Killalla.

This is a scheme I should not project, if we were not in a troubled state here, but circumstances considered, is what I hope will most conduce to keep things quiet in this country.

I am, &c.

To the Duke of Newcastle.

Dublin, Dec. 16, 1729.

My Lord,

Since I had the honour to write to your Grace about the affairs of parliament, the Commons have voted that the moidore shall go for 30s.[29] and seem disposed to raise all other coins answerably to that value.

As their votes are not laws, I do not apprehend any thing they can vote can do us any more mischief than putting off the necessary reduction of our gold till another session of parliament. Though if others of the council were of my sentiments, as we are undone without a reduction of our gold, we would with his Majesty's leave set things to rights before their next meeting: and I am satisfied the good effects of the alterations proposed in council would be so sensibly felt before that time, that there would be no grumbling about it when the parliament meets next.

If they go on farther in the money affair, and address his Majesty to do any thing wrong in it, I shall trouble your Grace with a memorial against any such destructive measures.

The Commons and several others without doors, are in a great heat about the alterations made by the council in England to our lesser money bill. I believe a great many will be for losing the bill rather than agree to the alterations. They are by all who know what they are, allowed to be for the better, but the point insisted upon is, that no alteration whatsoever shall be made either in the English or Irish council, to a money bill. It is certain the law here is against these warm men, and so are the precedents: and it is hoped that the majority of the house will be sensible of the bad consequences of rejecting that bill, which will run this nation much deeper in debt, and may

28 Dr. John Hoadly, translated to Dublin, and after the death of Dr. Boulter to the primacy of Ireland.
29 His Grace foretold this surprizing event in a former letter.

end in a dissolution; and that they will take care that the bill passes; but it cannot be without much heat and opposition. On Thursday the fate of this bill will be decided.

I yesterday wrote to your Grace about the vacancy on the death of the Archbishop of Cashel.

I am, &c.

To the same.

Dublin, Dec. 20, 1729.

My Lord,

In mine of the 16th I gave your Grace an account of the great ferment we were in here about the alterations made in our little money-bill by the council in England. Yesterday came on the debate about it in the House of Commons, and after about four hours debate, it was carried in favour of the bill, by 124 against 62. There have been other divisions since upon every step of the bill, with greater inequality; but the first was the great trial.

To-day the bill was sent up to the Lords, and we suppose both the money-bills will receive the Royal assent on Monday. As far as I can find, if the debate had come on before there had been time to talk with the members, the bill had been lost, the warmth against the alterations was at first so great. And I am of opinion the bill had not been carried by so great a majority, if it had not been for fear of a dissolution of the parliament, as the greatest part of our commoners are not willing to be at the expense of a new election.

The King's business is now done, of which I am glad, though I could wish it had been done with a better grace.

I cannot but look on this as a very good session, considering the greatest part of the debts of the nation is put in a method of payment, which will certainly be pursued the next session.

Whether now the commons are got right in one point, and are very much broken among themselves, they may not be brought to think likewise right about the affair of our coin, I cannot yet guess.

I am, My Lord, &c.

Newcastle to Boulter (draft).

Whitehall, Dec. 30, 1729.
(NA. SP. 63/391/296)

My Lord,

I ordered Mr. Delafaye to acknowledge the honour I have received of your Grace's letters of the 14th and 16th instant; and though I can not yet inform you who the person is, that is to have the Bishoprick of Clonfert, yet I would not delay my thanks for your Grace's letter of the 20th and my congratulations on the new Money Bills having passed your House of Commons by so great a majority. The King is very sensible of the great share which your Grace's conduct and application have in the good success that attends his Majesty's service in Ireland, and you may be assured that as all imaginable regard is always had to whatever comes from your Grace. What you have represented with relation to the regulating of the value of Guineas and of foreign coins will have its due weight here. I am extremely obliged to your Grace for your goodness in continuing to favour me with your correspondence, though the business of my office will not suffer me to be as punctual as I could wish in acknowledging it; and I beg leave to assure you of the sincere respect with which I am etc.

To the Duke of Newcastle.

Dublin, Jan. 1, 1729/30.

My Lord,

I this day received a letter from Mr. Delafaye, by your Grace's order. I am very sensible of the great hurry your Lordship must be in upon the change made in the other office, and the approach of the session of parliament in England, where I doubt not things will go easy, since a peace is concluded with Spain.

I am very much obliged to the ministry for the regard that has been shewn to my recommendations in the late promotions on the bench here. Dr. Synge is a very worthy man, but may very well stay till another opportunity.

I am very glad to hear Clonfert is designed for an Englishman, since there are but nine English on the bench, and twelve Irish, and it may be very proper to give some more strength to the English there. But I hope the person to be sent from England will be a person of some worth, and who is likely to join with us that are here already.

I think there can be no grumbling here if Clonfert be bestowed on an Englishman, but it may easily be kept open till the season of grumbling is over.

As far as I can find many among the commons that were concerned in voting to keep up the moidore to its present value begin to doubt whether they have done right in it; and the whole affair of our coin seems to rest there.

We shall consider whether it may not be proper to take that affair into consideration in the House of Lords after the recess, and endeavour to rectify the mistake of the commons.

I have formerly acquainted your Grace that the lesser money bill was carried, and passed in due time. I think there can hardly be any squabble in either house now that can much concern his Majesty. We have a great many bills now before the council from the commons, to which we shall give all possible dispatch.

I beg leave to wish your Lordship many happy years, and am,

My Lord, &c.

To the Bishop of London.

Dublin, Jan. 2, 1729/30.

My Lord,

On the 15th past I troubled your Lordship with an account of the scheme about the vacant archbishopricks, that was thought most adviseable in our present turbulent condition. We yesterday received his Majesty's orders in pursuance of those applications, except that Dr. Clayton is sent to Killalla, and that Clonfert is reserved for some Englishman.

I cannot but say we want some help on the bench here, where at present we have but nine English Bishops out of 22. The person we are told is not fixed upon, and I should be obliged to your Lordship if you would endeavour that it may be some worthy person. I do not well know whether Mr. Saul would be willing to come hither, if he would, I should think him a very proper person for our bench. Of the English here, the only person I know is Dr. Longworth, who is also known to your Lordship, and who has behaved himself very well on his living in the north.

I am sorry there has been any misunderstanding betwixt your Lordship and me on account of the archbishoprick of Dublin; and should have been for compromising matters in favour of the Bishop of St. David's on the vacancy of Cashel, if your Lordship had not assured me he would think of nothing here if he failed of Dublin, and we had not been in a very uneasy situation in the House of Commons. But I hope things will again settle, since I desire still, and hope it is a favour you will grant me, that I may trouble you to discourse with the ministry about what I apprehend to be for his Majesty's service in the promotions here.

I have read the Bishop of St. David's book with a great deal of pleasure, and am glad to hear it takes well in England.

We shall very speedily send over some bills from hence, and among the rest the glebe bill; the number of acres mentioned in the bill is 20, but rather than fail, we should be glad of 10.

We have had a popery bill brought into our house, partly for registering a number of secular priests, and partly more effectually to drive out the regulars from hence; but it was this day rejected in the house. I must own I think it is better letting them alone, whatever may otherwise be proper, till after the congress at Soissons[30] is over.

We have had a very uneasy session here, but I hope, as the peace with Spain is settled, you will have an easy one in England. I heartily wish your Lordship many happy new years, and am.

My Lord, &c.

To the same.

Dublin, Jan. 10, 1729/30.

My Lord,

I have had the honour of your Grace's of the 30th past, and had before received an account of the promotions on our bench from Mr. Delafaye, by your Grace's orders.

I am very glad things have ended so well in the House of Commons as they have, and shall not be wanting in my endeavours to promote his Majesty's service there and elsewhere to the utmost of my power. It is not certain that they will attempt any thing farther there about our coin, if they do I shall trouble your Lordship with a memorial on that subject. I am obliged to your Grace for the regard you are pleased to express for my representations, and desire they should have no farther weight than the reasons with which I shall upon occasion support them, may deserve.

The Bishop of Cork is at present very ill, and there have been reports, though false, that he was dead. If he should die, as any Englishman would rather chose Cork than Clonfert, I think Dr. Synge,[31] (if his Majesty pleases) may have Clonfert bestowed on him, where his father the Archbishop of Tuam had rather see him, on account of its neighbourhood to Tuam, than in any other bishoprick; and Cork may be bestowed on an Englishman.

I was willing just to mention this, that Clonfert may not be given away till it is known whether Cork will be vacant or no.

As any thing occurs here, worth your Grace's notice, I shall not fail to acquaint you with it.

I am, my Lord, &c.

---

30 For a general peace among the principal powers of Europe.
31 Edward Synge, eldest son of the Archbishop. His other brother Nicholas, was advanced to the see of Killaloe in 1745, by the Earl of Chesterfield, then Lord Lieutenant of Ireland.

To the Bishop of London.

Dublin, Jan. 10, 1729/30.

My Lord,

I have received your Lordship's of the 30th past, and am sorry the Bishop of St. David's has done with all thoughts of Ireland, since he might still fare better here than he may do in haste in England.

In mine of the 2d instant to your Lordship, I took notice of Clonfert being in our last promotions reserved for an Englishman, and mentioned two for it, if it was not engaged, one in England, one here: I find Dean Cross[32] would be willing to take it, whom your Lordship knows.

This week we had a report for two or three days that the Bishop of Cork[33] was dead; but by letters from Cork that came in yesterday, he was not dead but still ill. If he dies, Dr. Synge may be gratified with Clonfert, where his father the Archbishop of Tuam, on account of its neighbourhood to Tuam, had rather see him than in any other bishoprick, and Cork may be reserved for an Englishman. And I am sure any Englishman would rather chuse Cork than Clonfert. I only mention this that Clonfert may not be disposed of till it is known in England whether Cork is like to be vacant or no.

I have this week received a letter from Dr. Jenney, relating to the deanery of Clogher, in which he acquainted me he had written to your Lordship about it.

Dr. Jenney is a very worthy man, but as my Lord Lieutenant in his first commission, had the disposal of deaneries here, and that we think it was a little hard to have them taken from him in his second commission,[34] I do not care to oppose his recommendation on the other side of the water. I am,

My Lord, &c.

---

32 Rector of St. Mary's, Dublin, who had been chaplain to the English factory in Turkey.
33 Dr Peter Brown, was educated in the university of Dublin, was a Senior Fellow and Provost. He was promoted to the sees of Cork and Ross in the year 1709, and died at Cork in August, 1735. He was a prelate of great piety, charity and abilities; a most eminent preacher; two volumes of his sermons were published some time after his death. He also wrote other tracts, one of which was against drinking to the memory of the dead. He was succeeded by Dr. Robert Clayton, from Killalla, who was afterwards translated to Clogher.
34 This was generous in the Primate. But there was some reason for taking away that power, my Lord Lieutenant had given away three out of four deaneries to high tories, who were Gentlemen of learning, great abilities, fortune, and good character: but the Primate wanted to have the sole appointment of all ecclesiastical preferments.

To the Duke of Newcastle.

Dublin, Jan. 17, 1729/30.

My Lord,

In my last to your Grace, I mentioned that the general report here was, that the Bishop of Cork was dead or dying. I do not find that report confirmed this week, so that I rather suppose he may be out of danger: as soon as I hear any thing to the contrary, I will acquaint your Grace with it.

We have sent over to England a bill to make more effectual an act to encourage the draining and improving of bogs and unprofitable low grounds, &c. which act was passed in the second year of his late Majesty. The former act proposed draining bogs &c. by voluntary undertakers, but as no such have since offered themselves, this act provides a fund for doing it, which is computed at about 4000l. per ann. and is likewise designed for the encouragement of tillage here.

Last year we found the terrible effects of the want of tillage, by a want of corn little short of a famine; and when we endeavoured to cure this want by buying corn by subscription, and sending it to the several parts of the north to be sold there at a reasonable price, we found the land carriage of the corn, for want of some rivers being made navigable, (that it was hoped would have been so by the act of the second of his late Majesty) to come to a much greater sum than there was occasion to abate in the price given for our corn. So that the intention of this act is to prevent our falling into the like calamity again, by a miscarriage of one or two harvests here, And this act is what the whole nation with reason apprehend to be much for their common interest, that I most humbly entreat it may be sent us back.

I am, my Lord, &c.

To Sir Robert Walpole.

Dublin, Jan, 22, 1729/30.

Sir,

I have been applied to by a person of weight in this country to write in behalf of Mr. Foulk, who has lately been removed from the place of Examinator to the Collector in the Port of Dublin.

As it is an affair wholly out of my province, I shall meddle no farther in it than to inform you that upon enquiry into his character, I find from good hands, that he has been in the service of the revenue for 29 years, and has for his diligence and honesty, been advanced from some of the meanest posts, by one step after another, to this of Collector in Dublin, which is the most considerable post of that nature in this kingdom, and requires a thoroughly able and honest person in it. Having said this, I shall wholly submit it to your pleasure whether you shall think fit to let him continue in this post, in which the commissioners here have lately placed him, or to appoint some other to that employment.

I am, My Lord, &c.

To the same.

Dublin, Feb. 3, 1729/30.

Sir,

I beg your patience whilst I lay before you the case of a particular friend of mine in England, Mr. Stephens, Vicar of Malden in Surrey, and desire your kind interposition in his favour.

He was formerly Fellow of Merton College in Oxford, and was for some years Chaplain to the English factory at Oporto, where he suffered very much in his eyes. He was always reckoned a good scholar, and a very ingenious man in the University; particularly he was valued for his skill in the classics, and polite learning: he has always been a person of good morals, and to my knowledge one well affected to the revolution, and to the succession in his Majesty's family in the worst times.

When I was Dean of Christ Church, I made application to my Lord Townshend and the Duke of Newcastle, to have him preferred to a canonry of Christ Church, where he might be of service notwithstanding his bad eyes, by encouraging polite learning among the youth of the College; and I obtained a promise in his favour on the next vacancy by death.

Some time after, when his late Majesty was pleased to remove me to the primacy here, I renewed my applications to the ministry for him, and had a promise that he should be taken care of the next vacancy by death there, and that he should not suffer by my removing to Ireland. Since my coming hither I have frequently put the ministry in mind of him, and have had repeated assurances that he should have the next vacant canonry of Christ Church, or an equivalent. Particularly upon the death of Dr. Gastrel, late Bishop of Chester, I renewed my applications for him again, but as that happened just when Dr. Gilbert returned from attending his late Majesty at Hanover, and it was thought proper to reward him for that service with some immediate preferment, I desisted, upon repeated assurances that he should certainly have the next vacancy or an equivalent.

Here things rested till the death of Dr. Stratford, when I renewed my applications again, and with the intervention of the Bishop of London, who has been so kind as to appear for him, it was settled that Dr. Knipe should have the canonry then vacant, but that he should not be put in possession of it till Mr. Stephens had some equivalent given him. And upon this foot that affair stood, when Dr. Knipe went to Hanover with his present Majesty, who was pleased to send orders from Hanover that Dr. Knipe's patent for the canonry then vacant, should immediately pass, which was accordingly done, and Mr. Stephens had nothing done for him, as had been before intended.

The request I have to make to you is that you would lay the case of this deserving, but unhappy clergyman before her Majesty, and favour his pretensions with your interest. The misfortune of his eyes has made it so, that he could not be put in the usual methods of advancement, by being made Chaplain to the King.

His character I answer for, his pretensions I have laid before you; and I must add, that as he advances apace towards sixty, there is not much time left to do any thing for him.

My Lord Bishop of London knows him, and all that has been transacted in his affair, and I am sure is disposed to assist him in his application for some dignity.

He is the only clergyman in England I have or shall recommend to the ministry for any thing there, and your kind patronage of him in his just pretensions to their Majesty's favour, will always be esteemed a very great obligation laid on,

Sir, your humble servant,

To the Bishop of London.

Dublin, Feb. 3, 1729/30.

My Lord,

I have received your Lordship's of the 15th past, and thank your Lordship for your readiness to do any service to the general state of the Church of Ireland, and have hopes your Lordship will reconsider the affair of promotions here, and will at the least for the good of his Majesty's service here, be willing to be concerned with me in recommending to vacancies here. Your Lordship is too sensible of the ill effects of throwing the great preferments of the Church into a scramble, and I shall be very sorry to be under a necessity of applying to the ministry by any other hand than your Lordship; and I still flatter myself the long friendship I have had with your Lordship, will on farther consideration, prevail with your Lordship to re-assume the kind part you have hitherto acted on that occasion.

I some time ago mentioned to your Lordship that Dean Cross had applied here for the bishoprick of Clonfert.[35] What is settled about that bishoprick I do not know: if it be still at liberty, I have no objection to Dean Cross having it; he is an hearty Englishman and we begin to grow weak on the bench.

35 This see was filled up by Dr. Arthur Price, soon after translated to the united
   bishoprick of Leighlin and Fernes; and to the see of Meath in 1733.

I have by this post written a letter to Sir Robert Walpole in pursuance of your directions to be laid before her Majesty, relating to Mr. Stephen's affair; and I hope, as your Lordship is so kind as heartily to espouse his interest, that he will at last meet with better success than he has hitherto.

It was with great pleasure I yesterday read your Lordship's of the 27th ult. with an account that our glebe bill was passed as we sent it over, and I thank your Lordship for your kind assistance in that affair. I am,

My Lord, &c.

To the Duke of Newcastle.

Dublin, Mar. 10, 1729/30.

My Lord,

Our session advances towards a conclusion, and I hope will last but a short time after the rest of our bills come from England. But there is still a turbulent spirit in too many of the House of Commons: it is rather expected that they will next week take some farther wrong step about our coin, but what it will be we cannot yet learn. We are generally very thankful here for the favour intended us in taking off the duty on wool and yarn exported from hence to England; I am fully satisfied it is the only effectual way to prevent the running of Irish wool to France.

We have a very strong report that there is an addition likely to be made to the privy council here: as they are already 60, we find it pretty difficult to carry on the King's service there as we could wish, and if the number be increased, it will be still more difficult. I am afraid the weight and power of the privy council is not sufficiently understood in England, which makes me beg leave to acquaint your Grace, that the approving or rejecting of the magistrates of all the considerable towns in this kingdom is in the council here; and that as the correcting or rejecting of any bills from either House of Parliament is in them, if they are increased much more, the privy council of England may have more trouble from a session of parliament here than they have at present.

I can assure your Grace the English interest was much stronger at the board four years ago than it is now.[36] I must at the least beg the favour that no addition be made to the council here, till my Lord Chancellor and I are acquainted who are designed to be added, and have time to give our sentiments about them: though it will be less invidious to make no addition at all.

I wish there may not be a necessity before many years are over of

---

36 His Grace was much in the right to desire this of the Duke of Newcastle, and had the more reason for it, as Lord Carteret had used him but scurvily in the appointment of privy counsellors, without any participation of such nomination with his Lordship.

reducing the number of the present members. I do not write barely my own sense but that of others of his Majesty's faithful servants here. I am,
  My Lord, &c.

To the same.

Dublin, Mar. 19, 1729/30.

My Lord,

On Monday last the Lords sent down to the Commons, the bill for preventing riots in the city of Dublin and liberties adjoining, where after a first reading, the question was put for a second reading; when after most furious speeches, it was carried by 93 against 54, that it should not be read a second time. Though the bill in our present circumstances, as we have suffered very much from riots and tumults last summer, and even during the present sitting of the parliament, would be of great service, if it be not absolutely necessary to the keeping of the peace of this city, yet I should hardly have troubled your Grace with an account of the miscarriage of this bill, if the chief argument made use of to inflame the House against the bill had not been such as I think myself obliged to acquaint the ministry with, which is its arising originally in the privy council here: a thing common to many bills from time to time, and to which the council have an unquestionable right.

It is very common in debates in the Commons to abuse the privy council, but this is the first time since my coming hither, that a bill has been in plain defiance of our constitution, thrown out for rising in the privy council.

I shall, as soon as the parliament rises, give your Grace an account of the right and power of the privy council here, and of the consequence it is of to his Majesty's service here, to have their authority supported; as likewise of the present disposition of the House of Commons, that the ministry may take it into their consideration what will be the most proper method effectually to support the privy council.

We had yesterday a motion made in the House of Lords by the Earl of Barrimore, for a bill to enable his Majesty to re-assume all pensions granted by the crown from Lady-day 1702 to Lady-day 1727; the consideration of which motion is put off for a fortnight, and will from thence be adjourned till the parliament rises, by a majority of about five to one. I am,
  Your Grace's, &c.

To the Duke of Dorset.

Dublin, Apr. 6, 1730.

My Lord,

It is with great pleasure that I hear from Mr. Gardiner,[37] that the money due to Messrs. Lawman and Hoburg to Lady-day 1730, is actually remitted to London. I am sorry that affair met with so great delays, but considering the very low estate of our treasury, we have at last made a good handsome recompence for its being put off so long.

I am, my Lord,

Your Grace's most humble, and

Most obedient Servant,

Hu. ARMAGH.

To the Duke of Newcastle.

Dublin, Apr. 21, 1730.

My Lord,

His Excellency[38] the Lord Lieutenant embarked yesterday morning for England: as the wind has not been very favourable since, we believe he can hardly reach Park-gate before this night. There is a misunderstanding between his Excellency and the Bishop of Clonfert, whom his Majesty has been pleased to name to the bishoprick of Fernes, about a commendam. The Bishop is very thankful to his Majesty for the bishoprick of Fernes, and designs to take it, but hopes nothing will be decided against him about the commendam, or any stop put to his having the bishoprick of Fernes, till he has an opportunity of laying his case before his Majesty, to whose pleasure about the commendam, he will most chearfully submit. I am,

My Lord, &c.

To Lord Carteret.

Dublin, Apr. 25, 1730.

My Lord,

Since your Excellency left us, I have done what I could to bring the council to declare their opinion about the reducing of gold, but though much the greater part think it is what ought to be done, yet they are so afraid of the House of Commons, that I have not been able to bring them to say as much.

37 Luke Gardiner, Esq; Deputy Vice Treasurer of Ireland, and soon after sworn a Privy Counsellor.

38 Lord Carteret, afterwards Earl of Granville in Right of his Mother.

My brother justices are both against the council giving their opinion in the matter; so that at the council held to day on that subject, it was to no purpose to press it; it was almost with difficulty that we got the affair recommitted in order to draw up a letter to your Excellency with an historical narration of what has passed in council relating to the coin, since the year 1711, with particular orders to insert the resolutions of the committee 1729, relating to gold and silver coins, that the whole may be laid before his Majesty.

Sir Ralph Gore[39] would fain have the game of last summer played over again, by hearing the merchants and receiving petitions, but my Lord Chancellor[40] and I are resolved not to permit it.

The committee are to meet on Monday, and my Lord Chancellor has promised to have a council, and send away those resolutions with a letter by Tuesday's post.

I find by Sir Ralph Gore's proposal to day, that the merchants are now as some of them last year were, for raising foreign silver, though nothing be done about the gold; but as the whole view of this is to carry on their present gainful trade of importing gold and carrying out silver, by the help of foreign silver, now the trade begins to fail for want of English silver, my Lord Chancellor and I shall take care to prevent any such application from the council.

I am sorry I can give no better account of this affair, but my endeavours have not been wanting to make things go better.

I am, &c.

To the same.

Dublin, Apr. 30, 1730.

My Lord,

I am sorry to inform your Excellency that the affair of the coin meets with such difficulties in the council, that the letter we shall, I suppose, agree to-morrow to send to your Excellency, will come to just nothing. Those of the House of Commons in the council seem backward to agree to any thing contrary to the vote of their House; but I lay the whole miscarriage at the door of others; one[41] of which is wrong in his notions about the coin, and the other,[42] I think, at least as much afraid of the House of Commons as any commoner there. Had the last of these shewn any spirit, all would have gone right, and I believe most of the commoners would have had courage to do

39 Then one of the Lords Justices, and Speaker of the House of Commons of Ireland.
40 Thomas Lord Wyndham, who died some Years after in England, by whose Death the Title became extinct.
41 Sir Ralph Gore.
42 Lord Chancellor Wyndham.

what they think is right. But when they see their governors afraid of the House of Commons, how can we expect courage in the members of that House? The Lords in council have courage to do the right thing, but it is to no purpose to push at what two of the Lords Justices will not sign.

I gave your Excellency a hint of this before you left us, and then foreboded what I now am more certain of, the difficulties the government here will lye under, if any accident should happen that requires a little courage.

I think we shall send your Lordship the resolution of the committee of the council about the alterations proposed last summer, without daring so much as to desire your Excellency to lay them before his Majesty.

The warm men of the House are as noisy about town against the reduction of gold, as they were in the house. But I have had several others of fashion to beg it may be done to save us from ruin.

All the hopes now left us are, that your Excellency will from the resolutions of both Houses, and the papers sent from the council (though without any resolution, or so much as desiring your Excellency to lay them before his Majesty) take occasion to move his Majesty to refer the matter to the officers of the mint, and to order what he shall judge proper upon their report.

Your Excellency knows our distress, and the genuine remedy, and except you have the goodness to represent our case truly to his Majesty, and obtain relief from his goodness, we want either sense or honesty, or courage enough so much as to ask for a cure of our evils from hence.

I am, &c.

To the Duke of Newcastle.[43]

Dublin, May 2, 1730.

My Lord,

I have formerly troubled your Grace with some accounts of the distress we are in here for want of silver, and the proper remedy of this evil, by a reduction of our gold to the value it obtains in England, and raising the foreign silver to near the middle price it bears in England.

The privy council here have more than once had this affair under consideration, and a committee of council last summer had settled the value they proposed gold and silver should pass for here, if approved by his Majesty: but as our bankers and other remitters find their advantage in the present disproportionate value of our gold and silver, they raised a great opposition to any reduction of gold here, and set on foot petitions against it. As we were

43 Henry Holles Pelham, then Secretary of State.

at that time in a state of famine, and nobody could tell how our harvest might prove, it was thought proper to defer proceeding in that affair, lest any misfortune of any other kind might be imputed to such reduction. But much the greatest part of the council were then of opinion, that the alterations drawn up by the committee, were the proper remedy for our evil.

This affair has since been taken up by the commons, but the weight of the bankers in that house is such, that very early in the sessions they carried a vote that the moidore[44] should not be reduced: the carrying of that vote hindered their doing any thing farther for a great while, because the house were sensible they had been wrong in that step.

About a day before the parliament rose, the Lords passed a resolution, that our want of silver was occasioned by our gold and silver not bearing a proportionable value to what they bear in England; and to desire the Lord Lieutenant to get this evil cured in the proper method. What was the opinion of the Lords, was, that the gold was over-rated; but they avoided saying so much, because the commons had already voted that a moidore should not be reduced.

When the commons met the last day of our session, they fell into a great heat about the Lords resolutions, and talked of laying the key of the house on the table, in order not to be interrupted by a message from my Lord Lieutenant, and passed a vote in that heat against lowering the gold at all. The warmth of the house was such, that though most of the members who know any thing of the subject of coins, thought the house were voting wrong; yet they found it to no purpose to make any opposition.

Things being in this case, my Lord Lieutenant acquainted the council with the resolution of the Lords and Commons, and desired their advice in the matter; which, I think, I may say they promised to give: I am sure it is their duty to give it: but upon our holding a council after my Lord's departure, on this subject, too many of the council expressed a fear of offending the commons, though one great business of the council is to be a check upon both Lords and Commons, and did not care to give their opinion. All they could be brought to was, to send over to my Lord Lieutenant an account of what has passed in the council since the year 1711, relating to the coin, and the resolutions of the committee of council in 1729, about settling their value. But both in that account, and in their letter to my Lord Lieutenant, they shew they lean to the opinion of reducing the gold, though they had not courage to speak out.

As this is our present case, through the influence of the bankers and remitters on the House of Commons, and the timidity of the council, the only

44 At this time a moidore passed for thirty shillings, Irish money, a guinea for one pound three shillings, French and Spanish pistoles for eighteen shillings and six pence, and all other gold coins large and small, in the same proportion.

remedy remaining for our evil is, if his Majesty will be pleased to refer the resolutions of the committee of council 1729, transmitted to my Lord Lieutenant, to his officers of the mint, and if upon their report these resolutions are thought reasonable, to send his orders hither for a proclamation to issue accordingly.

I have had several worthy men both Lords and Commoners with me, begging that I would go on with this affair, notwithstanding the heats about it, since our manufactures and retail trade are under the last distress for want of silver. The lowest price of changing a moidore in most parts being 8d. and often 1s. or more.

The resolutions of that committee 1729, are to be seen in a printed vindication of the alterations intended to be made by the council in the value of the coins current in this kingdom, which I understand was sent your Grace.

Whether foreign silver be raised or not, as in that scheme, is not of that great consequence, though the raising of it will be of some service to us, but the lowering of the gold, as is there proposed, is of the last consequence to us.

If his Majesty would be graciously pleased to order such a proclamation, the bankers who have made all the disturbances and opposition to this reduction, are the very people that would labour to keep every thing quiet, because any disturbance on such a proclamation, will end in a run on themselves.

And the certainty of our having silver, and the benefit to our trade by it will so soon appear, that I am sure before another session of parliament, the face of affairs will be so altered, that every honest man in or out of the House of Commons, will be thankful for the change.

If I did not think this an affair of the last importance to the welfare of this kingdom, and consequently to his Majesty's service here, I should be for holding my peace (as is the behaviour of some other of his Majesty's servants here) and let the nation labour under its present distress, till they come to a better mind.[45] I am,

Your Grace's, &c.

To the Bishop of London.[46]

Dublin, May 5, 1730.

My Lord,

In pursuance of the last letter I was favoured with by your Lordship, I desired my brethren on the bench not to send over any more missionaries for

---

45 In this letter his Grace shews great ability, resolution, and honesty.
46 This letter was copied and sent likewise to the Archbishop of Canterbury.

the West Indies from hence, till we heard from your Lordship that a supply was wanting. Some time before the receipt of that letter, one or two had been very well recommended to me for that service, but I shall not now trouble your Lordship about them, till farther advice.

The great numbers of papists in this kingdom, and the obstinacy with which they adhere to their own religion, occasions our trying what may be done with their children to bring them over to our church; and the good success the corporation established in Scotland for the instruction of the ignorant and barbarous part of that nation has met with, encourages us to hope if we were incorporated for that purpose here, that we might likewise have some success in our attempts to teach the children of the papists the English tongue, and the principles of the Christian religion;[47] and several gentlemen here have promised subscriptions for maintaining schools for that purpose, if we were once formed into a corporate body. This has set the principal nobility, gentry, and clergy here on presenting an address to his Majesty to erect such persons as he pleases into a corporation here for that purpose, which we have sent over by the Lord Lieutenant, to be laid before his Majesty: the copy of this address I have here sent your Lordship, in which you will in some measure see the melancholy state of religion in this kingdom. And I do in my own name and that of the rest of my brethren, beg the favour of your Lordship to give it your countenance. I can assure you the papists are here so numerous that it highly concerns us in point of interest, as well as out of concern for the salvation of those poor creatures, who are our fellow subjects, to try all possible means to bring them and theirs over to the knowledge of the true religion.

And one of the most likely methods we can think of is, if possible, instructing and converting the young generation; for instead of converting those that are adult, we are daily losing many of our meaner people who go off to popery.

I am sure your Lordship will be glad of any opportunity of advancing the glory of God, and promoting his service and worship among those who at present are strangers to it.

I thank your Lordship for your second pastoral letter, I hope it will do great service to religion in England; and we hope it may be of service to us here, though irreligion does not shew itself so barefaced amongst us; I have therefore encouraged its printing here. I am,

My Lord, &c.

---

47 Dr. Maul Bishop of Cloyne, afterwards Bishop of Meath, being a gentleman of good family and fortune, expended a great part of his estate, to establish this foundation, which is now supported by Parliament, and voluntary contributions. His Grace the Lord Primate had also great merit in promoting this charity, of the Protestant charter schools in Ireland.

To the Duke of Newcastle.

Dublin, May 7, 1730.

My Lord,

The number of papists in this kingdom is so great, that it is of the utmost consequence to the protestant interest here to bring them over by all Christian methods to the Church of Ireland. In order to do this, we are labouring to increase the number of Churches and of parsonage houses, for the benefit of resident incumbents; and have passed some acts the three last sessions, to come at glebes for the clergy to live on, the greatest part of the livings here having neither house nor land belonging to them.

But the ignorance and obstinacy of the adult papists is such, that there is not much hope of converting them. But we have hopes if we could erect a number of schools to teach their children the English tongue, and the principles of the Christian religion, that we could do some good among the generation that is growing up. And as we find this design has been carried on with good success in Scotland, under the conduct of a corporation erected in that country by his late Majesty, we hope we may have the same success under a like corporation in this kingdom: and great numbers of nobility and gentry have expressed a willingness to come into subscriptions for that end, if there were a corporation established here to take on them the management of schools for instructing the popish youth.

This has been the occasion that the principal nobility, gentry, and clergy here have joined in an address to his Majesty, to erect such a corporation here, in such manner as his Majesty shall judge proper, which we desired the Lord Lieutenant to lay before his Majesty. A copy of this address I have herewith sent your Grace, by which you will see the bad state the protestant religion is in here.

And I make it my request to your Grace in my own name, and that of my brethren the Bishops, that you would be pleased to give your countenance to our address, that we may obtain the charter we desire.[48]

I am, my Lord, &c.

To Lord Carteret.

Dublin, May 20, 1730.

My Lord,

I have received the honour of your Excellency's of the 14th inst. and thank your Excellency for your great kindness to this nation in obtaining of his Majesty that the papers transmitted by the privy council be referred to the

48 It was granted.

officers of the mint, in order to lay a foundation for such orders as may put a stop to the present calamity we lye under. And I must renew my request to your Excellency that you would complete our deliverance, which I find those here who know well enough the method of compassing it have not the courage to attempt, without some orders from England.

Upon the least encouragement from your Excellency, I think I could bring the privy council to join in an application to his Majesty for the coining of 15,000l. in copper at the mint, since in private conversation, the most[49] timorous of them own to me, that they do not think the resolution of Lords and Commons inconsistent with one another.

I most gratefully acknowledge your kindness in those favourable representations your Lordship has been pleased to make of my conduct for the service of his Majesty, and I shall continue to endeavour not to give any just cause of complaint against me. I am,

My Lord, &c.

To the same.

Dublin, May 28, 1730.

My Lord,

By some letters which have been shewn me here, I find his Majesty and your Excellency have been very much solicited in behalf of Mr. Daniel Kimberly,[50] but that your Excellency was of the same opinion as we were of here, that the crime was so common in this country, as well as so heinous in itself, that there was no room for mercy.

We have had a great deal of trouble here in this affair, by giving way to Sir Ralph Gore's desire to reprieve him from Wednesday to Saturday last week: upon which Mr. Kimberly got an opinion from an obscure lawyer, that by his being reprieved, the sheriff could not lawfully execute him, till there was a new rule of court made about him, the day being lapsed on which he ought to have been executed by the first order of court. The sheriff was at a stand upon this, but advised with Mr. Justice Bernard[51] and some other lawyers, who assured him the reprieve did not cancel the order, but only suspended it for so many days. On Saturday last we had the Judges, the

---

49 He certainly means Chancellor Wyndham, if not Sir Ralph Gore also.
50 Daniel Kimberly was an Attorney, and some Way aiding and assisting in the Marriage of Mr. Brad. Mead with Miss Reading, who was an Heiress in Right of her Mother, which Marriage, by Acts of Parliament, was contrary to Law, without Consent of Parents, or Guardians; upon which Warrants were issued against Mr. Mead and Mr. Kimberly who made their Escape; the first to Holland, and the other to London, where he was taken, brought to Ireland, was tried, found guilty, and executed.
51 A Judge of the Common Pleas, a very eminent Lawyer, and Person of large Fortune, having purchased a great Part of the Earl of Cloncarty's Estate.

Prime Serjeant, Sollicitor, and Mr. Serjeant Bowes[52] to consult with, who were all of the opinion that the sheriff could execute him on the day to which he was reprieved. But some of them saying they had not thoroughly studied the point, we thought fit to reprieve him till yesterday, and sent to the Prime Serjeant, Attorney, Sollicitor, and Mr. Bowes, to have their opinion in writing on this subject, which they gave in on Tuesday, agreeing that he might be executed at the expiration of the reprieve, without any new order. Upon this, since the prerogative was deeply concerned, that the granting of a reprieve for a few days should not be carried to reprieve a male factor till next term, and since such a precedent must probably have raised scruples in every sheriff in Ireland, whether after any reprieve they could without a new order from the Judge execute a criminal, we thought fit to give no farther reprieve, and he was executed yesterday.

I must own I was very much surprized at this difficulty being raised here, having not heard the least hint of any such thing in England; but I think the affair is now so settled, that for some time at least no attempt of this nature is likely to be made on the prerogative here.

I thought it my duty to give your Excellency this short account of an affair, that has given us more trouble than I think it need have done.

Sir Ralph Gore went into the country last Monday morning. I am,
My Lord, &c.

To Sir Robert Walpole.

Dublin, June 4, 1730.

Sir,

The gentleman that waits upon you with this, is Mr. Dobbs,[53] one of the members of our House of Commons, where he on all occasions endeavours to promote his Majesty's service.

He is a person of good sense, and has for some time applied his thoughts to the improvement of the trade of Great Britain and Ireland, and to the making our colonies in America of more advantage than they have hitherto been[54] and has written his thoughts on these subjects, which he is desirous to offer to your consideration.

As he has not the honour to be known to you, he applied to me to open a way for his waiting on you.

I need say nothing of what his thoughts are on those subjects, since he will

---

52 Afterwards Lord Chancellor of Ireland, and was created a Peer of that Realm. The Title is extinct, his Lordship having no issue.
53 Arthur Dobbs, Esq Author of the North-West Passage to India.
54 He was afterwards made Governor of North Carolina.

be better able to explain them, and you are more capable of judging of them than I can be.

I presume no farther than to recommend him for an audience at leisure, and to do afterwards in the affair as you shall think most proper.

I am, &c.

To Lord Carteret.

Dublin, June 6, 1730.

My Lord,

Your Excellency by the last mail will receive two applications about some livings vacant by the death of Mr. Martin; one from Mr. Gardiner, in behalf of his nephew; the other from another gentleman for the vicarages of Erk and Claragh.

I have been able to meet with nobody that can give a distinct account of what livings Mr. Martin had, and whether the living Mr. Gardiner applies for is either the living of Erk or Claragh; if it be, he applies for it by some other name.

I need say nothing in favour of Mr. Gardiner's petition, since I am sure he wants no recommendation to your Lordship's favour.

I have since received a letter from the Bishop of Ossory, in favour of Mr. John Read, to whom he has lately given the Church of St. Mary in Kilkenny, which he says is a most laborious cure, and not worth above 60l. per ann. and he desires that your Excellency would be pleased to give Mr. Read the rectory of Claragh, not worth above 30l. per ann. which is contiguous to St. Mary's, and has no Church, but the parishioners constantly resort to St. Mary's. Claragh, his Lordship says, has often been given to the Minister of St. Mary's, to help him out; and this he assures me is the true case of these parishes.

I thought proper to send your Excellency this representation of the Bishop of Ossory, that we may know your Excellency's pleasure.

I am informed the present Bishop of Clonfert had the provostship of Galway worth about 150l. per ann. which I do not find is held in commendam by his Lordship, or disposed of to any body else. I should be obliged to your Excellency if you would be pleased to bestow it on Mr. John Richardson, Minister of Belturbet, whom I designed to have named to the College for the living of Derivoilan in the diocese of Clogher, but quitted my recommendation that Dr. Delany might have it, which accordingly he had. I am,

My Lord, &c.

To the same.

Dublin, June 11, 1730.

My Lord,

I have had the honour of your Excellency's of the 4th inst. and am glad to find our conduct relating to Kimberly is approved by your Lordship.

I hope as applications on this occasion were discouraged on your side of the water, so they will always be, or there must be a dangerous obstruction of justice here.

I thank your Lordship for putting the affair of our coin in so hopeful a way, and shall be very well pleased to receive his Majesty's commands on that subject.

I was ready to have granted Dr. Delany[55] the faculty your Excellency desired, but upon consulting with the learned, he thought his business might be done without one. I am,

My Lord, &c.

Newcastle to Boulter (draft).

Windsor Castle, June 20, 1730.
(NA. SP. 63/392/142)

My Lord,

As I know your Grace will be informed from other hands of the King's intention to appoint the Duke of Dorset Lord Lieutenant of Ireland, I forbore acquainting you with it, till his Majesty had actually declared it, which was done yesterday in Council, and you may be assured that this alteration is made entirely with the approbation of your friends here, and by their advice; and that the Duke of Dorset and Lord Wilmington are with us in the most perfect concert and union imaginable. Your Grace will therefore be pleased to behave, and write to the Duke of Dorset, without any reserve, and in the same free and open manner as you have been so good as to do to me or any other of the King's servants here; and you may depend upon my Lord Duke having the same regard for you and treating you with the same confidence and distinction. As for my part, I shall always make it my business, both out of the personal respect I have for your Grace, and out of zeal for the King's service, to see that your credit and influence, which have been of such great use to the ease and success of the administration in Ireland, may never suffer the least diminution and I will be answerable for the Duke of Dorset's being in the same sentiments. I hope your Grace will continue to honour me

---

55 Dr. Delany in the latter part of the Primate's time, made as much court to him as ever he had done before to Dean Swift.

sometimes with your commands, and I beg that you will ever be fully persuaded, of the sincere and unalterable respect with which I am,

To the Duke of Newcastle.

Dublin, June 24, 1730.

My Lord,

I am sorry I am to acquaint your Grace that my Lord Chief Baron Dalton died yesterday, after a short confinement.

His Majesty had not a servant here of greater abilities or courage, nor that served him with more zeal and fidelity. He has been directly worn down in the diligent attendance on his business; and I rather believe has worsted his circumstances by coming hither.

I have this day joined with my Lord Chancellor in a letter to your Lordship, representing who we think is the fittest person to succeed him, if his place be filled from this side of the water. But I most humbly represent, that it will, we both think, be of service to his Majesty here, if an able person be sent us from England for that employment. And I do not question but some may be found there of the profession of great skill in the law, and proper to stand a debate in the privy council, who will not think much of coming to Ireland for 12 or 1300l. per ann.

But all this is most humbly submitted to his Majesty's pleasure. I am,
My Lord, &c.

To Sir Robert Walpole.

Dublin, June 24, 1730.

Sir,

Yesterday died here, after a short indisposition, Lord Chief Baron Dalton; he has rather been declining in his health for some time, and has been directly worn down by his great attention to business.

His Majesty had not a servant here that served him with greater abilities, diligence, and zeal, than he did. I believe his family has rather suffered by his coming hither.

My Lord Chancellor and myself have by this post acquainted my Lord Lieutenant and the Duke of Newcastle, what removes we judge most proper for his Majesty's service on this occasion, if the place be filled from hence.

But by what has been already done for three successions in that post, we think it is most likely to be filled from England. And we cannot but think that it will be of great service to have a worthy person sent over. The Lord Chief Baron is one of the council here, where a good man will be very useful.

I believe there may be some at the bar in England of great worth, that may think it worth while to come hither for 12 or 1300l. per ann.

I hope, Sir, you will excuse my giving you this trouble, since it is a matter of great concern to his Majesty's service here.

I am, &c.

To the Duke of Dorset.

Dublin, June 27, 1730.

My Lord,

We yesterday received the agreeable news we have been long in expectation of here, that his Majesty had been pleased to declare your Grace our Lord Lieutenant. I can assure you, my Lord, that those who are best affected to his Majesty, are very well pleased with it.

I should have taken the liberty from the little acquaintance I have had the honour to have with your Grace, and the character you have always borne, to write on any occasion freely to your grace what I apprehended might be for his Majesty's service.

But it is a great pleasure to me, that I have received the Duke of Newcastle's assurances, that I may write at all times to you without any reserve, and that I may depend on having (as he is pleased to express it) your Grace's having the same regard for me, and treating me with the same confidence and distinction that I have constantly met with from the ministry ever since my coming hither.

I most heartily wish your Grace's government may prove easy and successful, and do assure your Lordship nothing shall be wanting on my part to contribute to its being so.

Sir Ralph Gore is this evening returned from the north, and on Monday I set out on the visitation of my province, which will take me up about five weeks: but any commands your Grace shall honour me with, directed to Dublin, will be forwarded to me. I am,

My Lord, &c.

To the Duke of Newcastle.

Dublin, June 27, 1730.

My Lord,

I have been honoured with your Grace's of the 20th inst. I am very glad to hear that the alteration which has been made in the government here, has been by the advice of your Grace and the other ministers, and that there is so perfect an union between the ministry and the Duke of Dorset and Lord

Wilmington;[56] and doubt not but this conjunction will very much contribute to his Majesty's service, and defeat the efforts of the discontented.

I did indeed hope from the good character of the Duke of Dorset, that I might write to him what I thought might be for his Majesty's service. But it is with great pleasure that I receive those encouragements from your Grace to write to him with the same freedom and openness, that your Lordship has permitted me to use to yourself. And I desire to meet with no greater regard or confidence from him, than I have met with from the ministers ever since they were pleased to send me hither. And I take this opportunity to return my most humble thanks to your Grace and the other ministers for all the favour and countenance I have now for some years constantly received from them: and shall always endeavour to make that return which I am sure will be most acceptable to them, the promoting of his Majesty's service to the utmost of my power.

I thank your Grace for giving me leave to do myself the honour of troubling you on occasion with a letter, and for assuring me of the continuance of your friendship and protection.

As my Lord Lieutenant is a stranger to the affair of our coin, I beg leave to desire that his Majesty's orders, if he shall please to send us any, may not be transmitted hither till my return from my triennial visitation, on which I set out next Monday, and shall not return till about the 5th of August. For I believe that the lords Justices will not care to do any thing in the affair till we are all together: and I am satisfied it will be of great service, that whatever shall be ordered may be immediately executed, without allowing time to the bankers and remitters here to sow any uneasiness in the minds of the people about that affair. I am,

My Lord, &c.

To Lord Carteret.

Dublin, June 28, 1730.

My Lord,

We this day received the honour of your lordship's of the 23d. As I am to set out tomorrow on my visitation, I shall miss of the opportunity of joining with my brethren in those just acknowledgments they will no doubt make of the many services you have done this kingdom during your administration; and it is with great pleasure I find the zeal any of us have under your Lordship's conduct, shewn for his Majesty's service, is approved by your

56 Spencer Compton, Speaker of the British House of Commons, afterwards Earl of Wilmington.

Lordship, and that we have had the happiness to satisfy you that we had a sincere regard for your Lordship.

I thank your Lordship for retaining so great a concern for Ireland, and am glad this kingdom has a friend, who will on all occasions be able to serve it.

I heartily wish your Lordship all health and prosperity, and if you should at any time honour me with any commands here, I shall receive them with the greatest pleasure and satisfaction. I am,

My Lord, &c.

To the Duke of Newcastle.

Dublin, Aug. 6, 1730.

My Lord,

I had the honour of your Grace's letter about Mr. Cresset when I was upon my visitation, from which I returned last Tuesday. I have enquired since and find Mr. Cresset's instruments were passed in my absence. He has been with me since my arrival at Dublin, and I acquainted him with the recommendations your Grace had given of him, and my readiness to shew him any favour on your account.

The Lord Bishop of Ossory died to-day, and we shall in our letter to my Lord Lieutenant, mention such as may be proper to be promoted to that see; but I must beg leave to inform your Grace that I think it will be very much for his Majesty's service to fill that see with a worthy person from England.[57] I am,

My Lord &c.

To the Duke of Dorset.

Dublin, Aug. 7, 1730.

My Lord,

I had the honour of your Grace's upon my visitation, which kept me from Dublin till Tuesday last.

I am very much obliged to your Grace for the encouragement you give me to write to you with the utmost freedom, and I assure you, my Lord, I shall never offer you any advice but what I think will be for his Majesty's service, and your Grace's honour.

Since my return the Bishop of Ossory is dead, and we have this day joined in a letter to your Grace, mentioning the most proper persons here to be promoted to that see. But I must beg leave to assure your Grace that I think

---

57 It was done accordingly, and Dr. Tenifon was appointed.

it is of great importance to the English interest, and consequently to his Majesty's service here, that some worthy person should be sent us from England to fill this vacancy. If any person here should be thought of, I take the promotion most for the King's service here, will be the making Dr. Baldwin Bishop, and Dr. Gilbert Provost[58] in his room.

I am, &c.

To the same.

Dublin, Aug. 22, 1730.

My Lord,

I have the honour of your Grace's on the 15th inst. I am glad to hear of the promotion of Dr. Edward Tenison to the bishoprick of Ossory, and thank your Grace for the news. He is an old acquaintance of mine, and I have always known him to be heartily attached to his Majesty's family: and I remember his often speaking of the countenance your Lordship was pleased to give him. I make no doubt but he will behave himself here, so as to make himself agreeable to his Majesty's friends. I am,

My Lord, &c.

To the same.

Dublin, Sept. 3, 1730.

My Lord,

The deanery of Duach or Kilmacduach, I know not which they call it, is now vacant by the death of Dr. Northcote, worth about 120 or 140l. per ann.

I should be very much obliged to your Grace if you would be pleased to bestow it on Mr. John Richardson, Rector of Belturbet; he is a worthy person and well affected to his Majesty, and was many years ago concerned in a design to translate the Bible and Common Prayer into Irish, in order the better to bring about the conversion of the natives; but he met at that time with great opposition, not to say oppression here, instead of either thanks or assistance; and suffered the loss of several hundred pounds expended in printing the Common Prayer book, and other necessary charges he was at in that undertaking.

I should be very glad, I could contribute somewhat to make him a little

---

58 Revd. Dr. Claudius Gilbert. a Gentleman of great learning and abilities, who purchased a large and fine Collection of Books at different Times, which he bequeathed to the University of Dublin, of which he was one of the Fellows.

easy in his circumstances, and procure him by your Grace's favour, some dignity in the Church.

I am, my Lord, &c.

Newcastle to Boulter.

Windsor Castle, Sept. 26, 1730.
(NA. SP. 63/393/4–5)[59]

My Lord,

As I take the liberty sometimes to trouble your Grace upon what relates to his Majesty's service, I am persuaded you will forgive my doing it upon this occasion. You know, My Lord, that the King is daily receiving applications from the French Ambassador in the behalf of officers in the French service, that are taken up in Ireland, for raising recruits there for the Irish Regiments that are kept up in France. The French Court, some time ago, applied to the King that his Majesty would be pleased to grant His Licence for their raising recruits in Ireland, engaging, in the strongest manner, that the officers so employed should behave themselves with so much decency and discretion, with regard to the Government, that there should not be the least occasion of complaint on their account; and the King did not think fit to give an authority in form for it, yet his Majesty was pleased to promise, that provided the officers behaved themselves well, they should be suffered to raise their recruits, as you will find by the enclosed copy of what his Majesty commanded me to declare in His name to Count Broglie. The King, at the same time, insisted upon knowing the names of the officers to be employed, and the number of recruits that was wanting, which I also send herewith; but this leave is to subsist only three months from the time of your Grace's receiving this letter. The King has that dependence upon your Grace's prudent management of this affair, that his Majesty leaves it to you to take such measures as you shall think proper, that the officers in the French service may not be molested, during that time, in raising, and sending over to France, the number of men specified in the enclosed paper, and no more. But as they go to Ireland upon this assurance, if any of them should be apprehended within that time, you will take care that they be discharged as soon as possible, and that none of them may suffer upon this occasion. My Lord Lieutenant of Ireland will write also to your Grace to this purpose.

I shall give the chief of these officers a letter to your Grace, to make him known to you. It was proposed by the French Ambassador that he should reside in Dublin, to be at hand to receive the pleasure of the Lords Justices

59 For a copy of this letter in French, see NA. SP. 63/393/156–7.

upon any incident that might happen, but, in my opinion, this would not be proper by any means. It will be sufficient that he leaves with you a direction, by which you may, on occasion, send to him in the country. Your Grace will take no further notice of this letter than you shall find absolutely necessary for the performance of his Majesty's commands.

I am etc.

Holles Newcastle.

To the Duke of Dorset.

Dublin, Oct. 1, 1730.

My Lord,

I have had the honour of your Grace's of the 19th past, and most humbly thank your Lordship for your kind intention to bestow the deanery of Duach on Mr. Richardson, upon your receiving the usual notification of the vacancy from the Lords Justices.

Mr. Richardson has since delivered a memorial on that occasion, which we have transmitted to your Grace with our recommendation.

I am sensible how much I am obliged to your Grace for the readiness you have shewn in this affair to comply with my request.

I am, &c.

To the Duke of Newcastle.

Dublin, Oct. 14, 1730.

My Lord,

On Friday last Lieutenant Colonel Hennecy brought me your Grace's of the 26th past; I told him as we were several mails behind-hand, by the packet-boats being all on this side, I had not received the letter your Grace referred to, but that upon the recommendations your Lordship gave of him, I should afford him all the protection I could; and I directed him to call upon me after the arrival of the next packets.

As he acquainted me with the business he came about, I took occasion to sound the Lords Justices the next day on the subject of his errand, and found there would be a necessity of laying before them what commands I received from your Grace, to be able to do any thing in the affair.

And as the mails arrived yesterday morning, by which I received the honour of your Grace's other letter of the 26th past, with the other papers you was pleased to send me, I have since discoursed with the other Lords Justices on the subject, and find they apprehend there will be greater difficulties in this affair than at first offered.

If we encourage the French officers to set about raising their recruits, upon assurances that we will take no notice of it, they will be liable to great molestations, since every Justice can take examinations against them and commit them, nor can we release them, but by due course of law, or by granting them a pardon. And whether they may not be the more busy in disturbing those levies, if they find them rather countenanced by the government, we cannot answer.

What has happened to several of them formerly when they were raising recruits here in a clandestine way (though as we knew his Majesty's intentions, we slighted, and as far as we well could discouraged complaints on that head) your Grace very well knows from the several applications made to your Lordship from the French Embassador. And what spirit may by artful men be raised among his Majesty's subjects when they hear some hundred recruits are raising in this kingdom for France, and how it may set magistrates every where on distressing the officers employed in this service, no one can tell.

To what excesses of heat people are capable of running here, when they once take a thing right or wrong into their heads, the ferments raised here about[60] Wood's half-pence is too plain demonstration.

And I must beg leave to hint to your Grace that all recruits raised here for France or Spain, are generally considered as persons that may some time or other pay a visit to this country as enemies. That all who are listed here in those services, hope and wish to do so, there is no doubt.

There is without controversy a power in his Majesty to grant leave to any persons to levy men here under his sign manual, by an act passed 8°. Georg. I. c. 9. and by the same act the government here can grant such a licence under their hands; but I find that without his Majesty's express orders for it, nobody here dares venture to grant a licence to the French officers to raise the intended recruits, since no one can answer what heats that may possibly occasion at present as well as at the next meeting of parliament.

I should be very glad if I knew how to manage this affair to his Majesty's satisfaction, and am very much obliged to his Majesty for having so good an opinion of me as your Grace is pleased to assure me in your letter.

I am sure it will be always my greatest ambition to promote his Majesty's service. But I am sorry I cannot give a more promising account of the success of this affair, since I perceive nothing can be done in it till his Majesty is pleased directly to signify his pleasure. However effectual care shall be taken that none of the officers who are come hither, suffer on this account.

Lieutenant Colonel Hennecy called on me this morning, and I directed him and his officers to appear as little as may be in publick, and to wait till

---

60 See the Drapier's Letters on this occasion, wrote by the Rev. Dr. Swift.

we are further instructed in his Majesty's pleasure, since at present there were some difficulties in the way.

I have communicated your Grace's letter to none but the Lords Justices, to whom I found it necessary so to do, and shall take all the care I can, that no other person knows any thing of it. But I find by some of the prints published here this day, that some[61] accounts are come from England that a number of recruits for the Irish regiments in the French service is to be raised here by his Majesty's leave, and that the French officers employed in that service are arrived here.

I am, &c.

To the Duke of Dorset.

Dublin, Oct. 15, 1730.

My Lord,

I had the honour of your Grace's of the 29th past, at the same time that I received one from the Duke of Newcastle; which I have communicated to my brethren, without whom nothing could be done in that affair; and as there appeared great difficulties in the management of that business, I have sent an account of them to the Duke of Newcastle, that we may receive his Majesty's commands.

I am sure I shall on this and all other occasions with the utmost zeal and diligence, promote his Majesty's service. I am,

My Lord, &c.

To the same.

Dublin, Nov. 17, 1730.

My Lord,

I did not receive the honour of your Grace's of the 20th past, till the 8th instant, and I deferred answering it since, in hopes I might bring things to bear to your Grace's satisfaction. But though I have taken what pains I could in the matter and have desired my brethren to concur with what your Lordship proposes, by drawing up the directing clause of the warrant agreeably to what has been settled to be the meaning of his Majesty's letters, yet I have not been able as yet to prevail with them.

They seem chiefly to insist on its being wrong to sign a warrant pursuant to letters in which part is not agreeable to act of parliament, and are appre-

61 See Swift's Works, vol. 9.

hensive, that as those letters of course are before the House of Commons every session, it may furnish a handle for raising some heats there.

And on the other side, they make a difficulty of explaining the sense of his Majesty's letters in the directing clause of the warrant, though it is putting no other sense on the King's letters, than what is settled with your Grace, as we suppose with the knowledge of the rest of the ministry.

I have on this occasion given them such hints as I thought I might, that I heard if the letters were returned, we should receive new ones, that would put the affair of excusing these pensions from the tax out of all dispute as to the whole sums: and that I was satisfied the pensions were in favour of such persons, as that they would not be sunk by their being returned to England.

But I have hitherto had no success; I shall make another effort, and if nothing can be done, I think it will be more adviseable to have the letters called back to England, than to lie unexecuted here.

I am sorry to find the affair of the Irish recruits makes such a noise in England, since I hardly doubt but near the same number, as there is a disposition to allow of this year, have been clandestinely raised here annually for some years past. There is a great ferment here on the same account.

This kingdom is very much obliged to your Grace for your kind intentions to endeavour, on all proper occasions, to lessen any weight that may be laid on us. And I shall not be wanting in acquainting the gentlemen of this nation, how much we are indebted to your Lordship for this your good disposition in our favour.

I am, your Grace's, &c.

To the same.

Dublin, Dec. 5, 1730.

My Lord,

I yesterday received the honour of your Grace's of the 28th past, and shall do what I can to get warrants signed upon Lawman's and Hoburg's letters, that the ministry may not have any new trouble about them.

And we this day have referred the consideration of that affair to the Prime-serjeant, Attorney and Sollicitor-general: and I likewise gave them the two draughts your Grace sent me, to see whether they might not either follow them, or from thence take some hint of somewhat that they thought would do.

I told them as from myself what your Grace suggested about the acts of 1727 and 1729, and that the late act could not refer to the first, but only to the last; so that our lawyers have now the whole affair before them.

I shall do what I can to dispatch this affair to your Lordship's mind, but find I cannot answer for the event. I am,

My Lord, &c.

To the same.

Dublin, Dec. 8, 1730.

My Lord,

I yesterday received the honour of your Grace's of the first inst. and it is with great pleasure I find by your Lordship's that the French officers will soon be recalled from hence: since that affair of the recruits makes a great noise here, and as far as I understand, a much greater at London. They have met with no rudeness here, and I believe will meet with none at their going off. They should be treated more civilly than they have been, if I had not found myself clamoured at here, and fallen upon in the papers of England, for a civility I did not shew them: and if there should be any apprehensions of their being insulted, we shall take what care we can to prevent it. I am,

My Lord, &c.

To the same.

Dublin, Dec. 26, 1730.

My Lord,

I hope we shall put the desired end to the affair of Mr. Lawman and Hoburg, by signing the usual order, upon his Majesty's letters in their favour, as soon as Sir Ralph Gore comes to town, who is gone into the country for the holidays, the Prime-serjeant, Attorney and Sollicitor-general having agreed in a favourable report; but they think the surest way to prevent any canvassing of that affair in parliament will be to have their agent make no difficulty of letting the taxes be deducted till Christmas 1729, since which time there is no doubt but they are legally excused from the 4 s. in the pound on their pensions.[62] And this I think is what agrees with your Grace's sentiments in this affair. When we have signed their warrants, I shall make it my business to help them to some money, as soon as our treasury can furnish any.

Colonel Hennecy called on me two or three days ago, and acquainted me that he and the officers with him had orders to leave this kingdom; and that as soon as two or three of them who were gone to see their friends in the country were returned (which would be in eight or ten days) they would embark for England,

I must do the Colonel the justice to acquaint your Grace that I have not

---

62 This Tax dropped at the Expiration of the Act, but was again renewed by Parliament in 1757. See a most excellent Pamphlet, entitled, a List of the Absentees of Ireland, and an Estimate of the yearly value of their Estates and Incomes, spent abroad, two Editions of which were printed in 1767, and 1769.

heard any complaint of his or the other officers behaviour whilst they have been here.[63]

I am, my Lord, &c.

To the Duke of Newcastle.

Dublin, Dec. 31, 1730.

My Lord,

Last week Colonel Hennecy called upon me to acquaint me that he had received orders to quit this kingdom, with the other officers who followed him, and that he hoped if he staid a few days, till he could call some of the officers to Dublin that were then in the country visiting their friends, to take them over with him, it would not be taken ill, which I told him I thought it could not. He has since been with me to acquaint me that he shall go off with the yacht which is expected to sail every day for England.

As he desires I would give your Grace an account of his behaviour here, he waits upon his Lordship with this letter, to inform you that he has behaved himself with great prudence during his stay here, and has kept himself and his officers from appearing in any publick places, or giving any offence; and has from time to time called upon me to know whether I had any orders to give him, that he might punctually observe them; and he has readily complied with any directions I thought it might be proper to give him.

I am glad this affair is at last happily concluded, after having been the occasion of so great a noise here, and of a much greater in England.

I am, my Lord, &c.

To the Duke of Dorset.

Dublin, Jan. 9, 1730/1.

My Lord,

As probably an affair that has lately happened here may make a greater figure in the English papers than it justly deserves, I think it my duty to give your Grace an account of it.

On Tuesday last just before midnight Sir Robert Echlin called upon me, to tell me that there was a fellow came to the horse guards here, giving an account that a French officer had sent him over with a horse to Bullock, a

63 Sir Robert Walpole, the most frank and ingenuous man in the world confessed, (which few ministers are apt to do) that he had been wrong in this measure, and immediately advised the recalling of the officers; convinced perhaps more by the reasons in the letter, Pag.25, than by all the clamours of the Craftsman, &c.

place about five miles from hence, where he endeavoured to persuade him to go over to France with him, offering him money, which he refused, that there were four or five French officers there, and about 60 men listed in the pretender's service, who lay there to go on board a sloop for France. I was very much surprized at Sir Robert's chusing to come to me about such an affair at such a time of night. But as I have been but ill used both in the prints here and in England about the French recruits, I thought I could not refuse taking notice of his information; and the rather because Colonel Hennecy had assured me that none of the officers who came with him had raised any recruits here.

Accordingly I directed Sir Robert to have the fellow carried before the Lord Mayor to be examined upon oath, and I sent by him a letter to the Lord Mayor, acquainting him what Sir Robert had told me, and desiring him to examine the informant on oath, and according as the examinations came out, to send to the Town Major and acquaint him with the case. Upon examination, the substance of what Sir Robert had told me came out, only that there was nothing sworn about the Pretender, and that there were but about 40 men. Upon taking those examinations the Lord Mayor sent them to the town Major, who immediately waited upon the[64] General, who ordered 50 foot and four dragoons to march to Bullock, and either seize or disperse those people. When they came there on Wednesday, they found there had been about forty men listed for abroad, and four or five French officers with them, but that they went on board a sloop about eleven o' clock the night before.

I am, my Lord, &c.

To the same.

Dublin, Jan. 12, 1730/1.

My Lord,

I have just now received the honour of your Grace's of the 7th inst. We expect Sir Ralph Gore in town on Saturday, and shall I believe the first opportunity afterwards, sign the warrants for Lawman and Hoburg, since as we have a favourable opinion from the lawyers, Sir Ralph cannot well make any difficulty about it, and my Lord Chancellor now makes none.

I mentioned the affair of the taxes before Christmas 1729, at the desire of others, since I thought your Grace had spoken very plain in that affair. As soon as the warrants are dispatched I shall make it my business to get them some money as fast as our treasury can supply it, consistently with the services absolutely necessary.

64 Thomas Pearce, General and Commander in Chief of the Forces in Ireland.

I believe Colonel Hennecy and the other officers went off in the yacht to day, since he told me they were to go in it.

There is a clergyman, a man of worth, one Mr. Horner, a native of Switzerland, recommended hither by his Grace of Canterbury, to whom Lord Carteret gave the rectory of Clane, in the diocese of Kildare; he has been very ill treated, and is made very uneasy there by a popish gentleman, to whom the greatest part of that parish belongs; and as he is a stranger, is but ill supported by the neighbouring protestants: he has had his stack of fuel fired in the night, and I think part of his house burnt down by it, and is daily threatened to be served so again. I have now an opportunity of removing him to a protestant neighbourhood in my diocese, where I hope he will be very useful, if your Grace will be pleased to bestow the rectory of Clane upon his resigning it, on Mr. Hoskins, that I may be able to provide for a clergyman who lies on my hands, by giving him the living that Mr. Hoskins now enjoys; which I shall acknowledge a great favour.

I am, &c.

To the same.

Dublin, Jan. 26, 1730/1.

My Lord,

On the 12th instant I did myself the honour to acquaint your Grace that I believed the first opportunity after Sir Ralph Gore's arrival in town, we should sign the warrants for Lawman and Hoberg, since as we have a favourable opinion from the lawyers in that affair, Sir Ralph Gore could not well make any difficulty about it; and my Lord Chancellor them declared, he made none, as we had the opinion of the lawyers to justify us. But since then, my Lord Chancellor is pleased to declare, he is of different sentiments in that affair; and Sir Ralph Gore joins with him. We are to have another conference on that subject; and have as good as agreed to send a letter to your Excellency, to let you know what canvass that affair may possibly go through in the House of Commons; but that as we have the opinion of the lawyers in the point, if your Grace after our representing what may happen in the House of Commons, shall direct us to sign those warrants, we shall do it. This was our sense, when last together; but after the unexpected turns this affair has taken, I will not answer what may be our sense to-morrow.

I am, my Lord, &c.

To the same.

Dublin, Feb. 6, 1730/1.

My Lord,

I have had the honour of your Grace's of the 23d past, and am very well pleased with your approbation of my conduct upon Sir Robert Echlin's information.

I am very much obliged to your grace for coming into the scheme about the rectory of Clane, and will take care to have the resignation ready against you are pleased to give orders for bestowing that rectory on Mr. Hoskins, upon Mr. Horner's giving in his resignation of it.

We have troubled you, my Lord, with a letter relating to Messrs. Lawman and Hoburg's affair; and I shall, according to your Grace orders, forward that affair immediately, and get as large a payment on those warrants, as our treasury can admit of.

I am, my Lord, &c.

To Mrs. Wall.

Feb. 13, 1730/1.

Madam,

I have received yours of the 9th of January and the 1st inst. but the last came not to hand till Thursday last. I am very sorry to hear of the death of my cousin Tomes. I have gradually broken the matter to her son, and hope he will behave himself under this loss like a good Christian. I am sorry to find you are so much dejected, as you appear to be by both letters; and hope you will get over March better than you expect. I am very glad to hear your son goes on well with his studies; and the best thing he can do, is to pursue his learning at the University for three or four years more, without thinking of any ramble, either here or any where else. My spouse and I give our service to you and your family. Pray my service to my cousin Tomes, and let him know I am very much concerned for his great loss.

I am, Madam, &c.

To the Duke of Dorset.

Dublin, Feb. 20, 1730/1.

My Lord,

On the 8th inst. Mr. Brandreth[65] brought me the honour of your Grace's of the 10th past. We have since dispatched his instruments agreeably to your

65 Mr. Brandreth had been tutor to Lord Middlefex, his Grace's eldest son.

Grace's directions. I found he did not want a faculty to hold the two prefer-ments, else I was ready to have granted one, as I shall be to give him my favour and protection on all occasions. He seems to be a sensible gentleman, and very well behaved; and I doubt not but he will give general satisfaction here.

I am, my Lord, &c.

To the same.

Dublin, Feb. 27, 1730/1.

My Lord,

I have the honour of your Grace's of the 20th, and return my thanks for the directions you intend to send about the living of Clane.

We are very well pleased with the two new letters of his Majesty relating to Messrs. Lawman and Hoburg, and hope to satisfy your Grace upon your arrival here, that it will be of some service to your Grace's administration here, that they did not pass in the old form. I shall endeavour to get a very handsome payment upon them: but it could be larger, if your Grace thinks we may stay till after Lady-day for it, that it may not appear in the account to be laid before the Commons next session of parliament. I should be glad to receive your Grace's directions in this point as soon as may be. I am,

Your Grace's, &c.

To the Duke of Newcastle.

Dublin, Mar. 1, 1730/1.

My Lord,

The affair of the French recruits is blown over without any thing farther than uncertain rumours here of some letter from somebody to encourage the officers in their levies.

But as there are two or three persons likely to be tried the approaching assize in the country, I thought proper to write to your Grace, to know what his Majesty will please to have done, if they should happen to be convicted. I rather fancy it will happen, as it has happened on most of the like occasions, that the evidence on which they have been committed will fall short at the trial, so that they may be acquitted. But for fear of the worst, I should be glad to know what is to be done, if it should prove otherwise. For I find on account of the noise that has been made in England and here about that affair, the Lords Justices will not interpose without his Majesty's commands.

If I am not much mistaken, when Mr. West[66] Mr. Connolly[67] and myself were in the government in his late Majesty's reign, his Majesty was pleased to order us not to permit any to be executed for listing in foreign service, till we knew the King's pleasure.

The officers who are supposed to have enlisted them are got off. I am, My Lord, &c.

To the Duke of Dorset.

Dublin, Mar. 23, 1730/1.

My Lord,

I have had the honour of your Grace's of the 13th instant: and I have since spoke to Mr. Gardiner to provide money for a good handsome payment upon Messrs. Lawman and Hoburg's pension; and intend tomorrow to get an order to him for it as soon as may be after Lady-day. Money is very low in our treasury, but we will strain as far as possible.

To the Duke of Dorset.

Dublin, Apr. 21, 1731.

My Lord,

The terrible distress we are under in this nation, upon account of the disproportionate value of our gold and silver coins, to what they bear in England, and the want of silver consequent upon it, is what your Grace has probably heard of, and what I shall take the liberty to write more to your Lordship about, if I am encouraged by your Grace to do it.

But beside the want of silver, the ordinary people here are under the last distress for want of copper money; of this I met with complaints last year at every place in the visitation of my province; and it is what is every day complained of in this town. Tradesmen that retail, and poor people are forced to pay for getting their little silver changed into copper, and are forced to take raps or counterfeit half-pence, of little more than a quarter of the value of an English half-penny, which has encouraged several such coiners, and must end in the great loss of the poor, whenever they pass no longer; and the farther that time is put off, the greater the loss will be.

As we have long laboured under this calamity, the House of Lords towards the close of the last sessions, applied to the then Lord Lieutenant, to

66 Lord High Chancellor, and one of the Lords Justices of Ireland.
67 William Conolly, another of the Lord Justices, Speaker of the House of Commons, and a Commissioner of his Majesty's Revenue in Ireland.

desire his Majesty to let us have 15,000l. coined in farthings and half-pence, of the same fineness as the English copper money, at the rate of 26d. the pound of copper, as we then thought that 24d. were coined in England out of a pound of copper, the English had 24d. upon the bottom of two shillings English going for 26d. here, and that what profit arose from this coinage might go to the use of the publick here.

I was the person that moved for this address, and added the latter part, upon an assurance I had from my Lord Carteret that his Majesty had promised to grant us as much, if we desired it.

There was likewise a resolution passed in the House of Commons, probably on occasion of this address of the House of Lords, that it would be for the benefit of the nation to have a mint erected here, without any mention of any copper, silver, or gold coinage.

What my Lord Carteret did at his return to England in this affair, I know not, as he never sent us any letter about it.

And thus things have rested, till some time ago, when my Lord Forbes[68] made application to me, that considering the deplorable condition the poor were in for want of copper money, it would be of the greatest service to get some; and that by some discourse he had had with Mr. Conduit, Warden of the Mint, he fancied we might buy a quantity from the mint, for this nation, and that he and many others would readily advance a sum of money, if I thought proper, and would join in it. I told him how sensible I was of the great distress the poor were in here for want of copper, and that I would join in any such undertaking. He then promised to write to Mr. Conduit on this subject, to know whether we might be private purchasers, or must apply to his majesty for leave to have some copper coined, since we wanted copper in another proportion to the English shilling than what it bears in England. He sometime after received an answer from Mr. Conduit, that nothing could be done for us without his Majesty's leave, and sent an estimate of the coinage as in England, and as would be proper for us, a copy of which I have here sent your Grace, with what he apprehended would be the gain upon it.

Upon Lord Forbes's communicating this to me I talked with my brethren the Lords Justices on the subject, who concurred with me in opinion that such a copper coinage was both exceedingly useful and necessary, and that it would be of service to have it as soon as possible, considering our present distress, since though the parliament should come into proper measures about it, it could not be brought to bear in less than nine or twelve months, but in this way it could be brought to bear in three months.

We have since sounded some of the council about this affair, who concur with our sentiments, and we had in part resolved upon having a council, in order to apply to your Grace about this affair, but we have since considered

68 Son of the Earl of Granard.

that we would not directly apply to your Grace with the weight of the council, till we had previously acquainted your Grace with the matter, and in part knew how your were disposed; and besides, if it were once known that such an application was made to your Grace, it would give some obstruction to the circulation of raps, which though it must happen at last, we would not have happen without a remedy of better money following as soon after as may be.

In Mr. Conduit's scheme we find that only 23d. halfp. are coined out of a pound weight of copper, so that to keep our copper money as near in intrinsic value to the English copper as may be, we propose coining only 25d. halfp. out of a pound weight of copper.

If your Grace gives us leave to apply, we think of applying only for 50 tuns, which will make 11,900l. Irish, but we have no doubt but we shall be pressed to apply for more soon; nor do I think that less than 150 or 200 tuns will answer the occasion; but we are willing to be petitioned for more when the goodness of these and the want of more is seen by every body.

Mr. Conduit tells us about 1000l. will set the affair a going, which we shall raise here, without desiring any interest or other profit by it. We propose paying the money advanced into Mr. Gardiner's hands, and to make the first payment and let him receive the copper money as it is sent hither, and dispose of it, and with the produce answer any subsequent payments, till the whole is disposed of. So your Grace or the parliament may have a Crown officer to examine about the gains, if you shall think proper.

As to the gains, Mr. Conduit does not allow for deductions which must be made, which will strike off above half the profit he computes, as your Grace will see by the scheme, No. II. inclosed. Indeed, if the exchange should prove but 10 per cent. which it possibly may prove very soon, the profit will be on Mr. Conduit's quantity 202l. greater, and on ours 101l.

The resolution of the Lords relating to a copper coinage, and that of the Commons about a mint, were twice considered in council, whilst my Lord Carteret was Lord Lieutenant, and it was the opinion of every body that they were no ways inconsistent, since it might be for the good of the nation to have a mint, but as it would be long before that could be established and brought to work, it might at the same time be very proper to afford a more speedy remedy to our present sufferings, which was what the Lords proposed.

I think it my duty at the same time that I acquaint you what was and still is, as far as I can learn, the sense of the privy council, to acquaint your Grace likewise, that by what I have been told, the view of some warm men in the House of Commons in moving that resolution about a mint, was, that as they are very zealous for a mint here, they were against coining even copper at the tower, lest it should mark out a way for coining gold and silver for us, if there were occasion, and it should appear by a plain experiment with how much greater expedition, ease, and cheapness we might have any money coined at the Tower, than it can be coined here.

I have now informed your Grace of our present wants of copper money, and the readiest remedy for this evil, and likewise what are the views of those who possibly intended to hinder the address of the House of Lords being complied with, for an immediate coinage of copper: and your Grace will be the best judge whether you ought to encourage our immediate application for the coinage of 50 tuns of copper at the Tower, or will leave that affair to take what turn may happen to be given it in parliament.

And here I must inform your Grace that some of the most understanding men of the Commons tell me their opinion is, that their House will be able when they sit, to agree upon no present remedy for our evil.

As your Grace designs to honour us with your company in a few months, if it be thought proper to do any thing in this affair, there is no time to be lost. And if your Grace pleases to send for Mr. Conduit, he can best inform you in what time a good quantity of copper money can be coined for our use.

As your Grace will see I have wrote with the utmost confidence in your Grace, I hope my letter will be kept a secret.

I am, my Lord, &c.

Number I.

Mr. Conduit's Scheme.

Formerly the mint gave 18d. a pound for all the copper they coined; but the English Copper Company having contracted to furnish the mint with 100 tuns of copper at 13¼ d. a pound, they find themselves losers by it, and declare they will furnish no more under 15d. a pound.

The reason why more is given than the market price is, that they must deliver it in bars of the exact size of the species to be coined, and take back and work over again what is amiss, which is usually 2/5 of the whole.

A pound avoirdupois of copper is
coined into 23d. in England, which
is - 0 1 11

If the pound of copper cost 0 1 1 ¼
And the coinage - - - - - - - 0 0 4 ¾
                  ——— 0 1 6

Remains gain on the coinage   0 0 5 ½

It is offered to coin at the mint in England, copper for Ireland, 26d. in the pound avoirdupois ⅙ farthings, and ¾ halfpence, for 5d. a pound, all charges included except 20s. a tun to be given to the Comptroller.

26d. a pound is - - - - - - - - - - - - - - 0 2 2
So that if the pound of
     copper comes - - - - 0 1 3
And the coinage - - - - - - - - 0 0 5
               ————— 0 1 8
Remains profit on the coinage   0 0 6

Which on 100 tuns comes to 5,600l. out of which deduct 20s. a tun to be paid to a Comptroller, there remains 5,500l. neat profit.

Number II.

Observations on the calculation of profit to be made by the coinage of 100 tuns of copper in Mr. Conduit's scheme.

As we propose coining but 25½d. a pound instead of 26d. a pound of copper, there will be a profit of 5½d. so that instead of 56l. profit on a tun, deducting a half-penny a pound (which comes to 4l, 13s. 4d. a tun) there will remain but 51l. 6s. 8d. profit on a tun, out of which deduct 20s. a tun to the Comptroller, the remainder is 5033l. 6s. 8d.

Again, as there must 20d. a pound be paid in England for copper and coinage, that will amount to 186l. 13s. 4d. a tun to be paid in England, this on 100 tuns will amount to 18,666l. 13s. 4d. to which add 100l. the Comptroller's fee, the total to be paid in England will amount to 18,766l. 13s. 4d. If we suppose to be paid more in England for agency, casks, packing carriage, and shipping, at the rate of 3 per cent. on the above sum, that will amount to better than 561l. to be answered there, the total will be 20, 254l. 3s. 4d. to be paid there.

As the middle exchange here is 11 per cent. the return will cost better than 2123l.

Suppose then the total gain on 100
     tuns to be - - - - - - - - - - - - 5033 6 8
Deduct from this
     agency, &c.- - - - - 561 0 0
Charge of remittance - - - 2123 2 0
              ————— 2684 0 0

Remains still of profit   2349 6 8

Out of which, when freight, landing,
and other expences here are answered,
probably the remaining profit may be
from 2100l. to - - - - - - - - - - - - - 2200 0 0

And as we propose to begin with
but 50 tuns of copper, probably
the profit may be from 1050l. to   1100 0 0

To the Duke of Newcastle.

Dublin, Apr. 24, 1731.

My Lord,

On Wednesday I was honoured with your Grace's of the 14th instant. I wish our treasury had been in a better condition, but as it is, I have taken care to have a year's pension paid in to Mrs. Spence's agent, which clears her to Christmas last inclusive, and a bill is remitted accordingly to-day. It is with a great deal of pleasure that I received your Grace's commands, which have given me a small opportunity of shewing my readiness on all occasions to own the many obligations you have been pleased to lay on me.

I am, &c.

To the Bishop of London.

Dublin, May 11, 1731.

My Lord,

It has been a very great surprise to me this winter to hear of the attacks made on the rights of the clergy by two bills brought into the House of Commons, one relating to tythes, the other to the fines for renewal of Church leases.

I find that what always used to be of weight in both houses, that these were manifest attempts on the undoubted right and property of the clergy, was with too many of no weight at present.

I am very glad the storm is blown over for this season, and I hope the open declarations their Majesties were pleased to make in favour of the rights of the clergy, may prevent any new attack being hastily made on them.

If I am not misinformed, your Lordship has been very usefully employed in publishing a short but full vindication of the rights of the clergy as to tythe. To which I have seen an answer, published, as the title says, by a member of parliament. I think we of the clergy are very much obliged to that author, since he speaks pretty plain, that in his opinion the nation ought to pay nothing to the clergy except they please, and that the fewer the clergy are reduced to, the better for the nation.

The rights of a free people seem to be carried a great length by some people in England in their writings. In several pamphlets one of their rights has been asserted to be, to publish what they please about religion, and another to publish the same about all affairs of state; and this author has now started a third, which is, to be eased from the burthen of tythes. I wish the landed gentlemen would reflect, whether the next privilege of a free-born Englishman may not be to be excused from the burthen of rents, since the tenants of England do almost as much out number the landlords, as the laiety do the clergy. I must own it is with great grief that I see daily such things published, and those liberties taken with persons in power, and such a disregard to all the rights and properties of the subject, as I think must by degrees end in some publick disturbance.

As to the clergy in particular, I believe there never has been a time, when there has been less reason to complain of any oppressions from the spiritual courts, or disaffection to the constitution than at present; and I cannot but think by what I am informed, that one cause of these attacks made on them, is from those who are very uneasy to see so great a strength on the bench of Bishops supporting his Majesty and his ministry; but of this your Lordship is a better judge.

But at the same time I cannot but believe that if there were fewer pluralities, and more of the clergy discharged their duty on their livings, it would take off a great deal of that envy and malice which seems to be raised.

It is very happy for us of the clergy here, that our brethren in England are able to stand their ground, for if you are once borne down, all that may pass in England against the clergy, will seem to be acts of calmness and temper, in respect of those warm attacks that would soon be made on us here.

I most heartily wish our brethren in England good success in maintaining their rights, and congratulate their having a person so knowing and prudent as your Lordship to assist and conduct them in the defence they are obliged to make of their property, against so unjust and so unreasonable attempts.

I am, &c.

To the Duke of Newcastle.

Dublin, May 27, 1731.

My Lord,

I am very much obliged to your Grace for taking in so good part the late small return made by me for the many favours received of your Grace; and shall always set the highest value on the continuance of your favour and friendship.

I must likewise desire your Grace to acquaint the Dutchess of Newcastle how much I am obliged to her for the honour of her acknowledgments of my having befriended Mrs. Spence.

I am glad the session of parliament is ended so well in England, and heartily wish ours may succeed as well.

We are very much obliged to your Grace for your zeal in the promoting of the act for explaining the naturalization act, in which as you rightly observe, the interests of England and Ireland, and the honour of his Majesty's government are highly concerned. But we are apprehensive here that three clauses which were added to that bill, as sent up by the Commons, will do some mischief here.

As to the Irish yarn bill, which was thrown out in the House of Lords, I can assure your Grace, that I am fully satisfied the part you acted in that affair, was not out of any disregard to Ireland, but purely that you thought the rejecting of it at present, was for the service of England.[69] But at the same time I must beg leave to inform your Grace, that it is my opinion upon conversing with gentlemen of those parts of Ireland where most wool is run, that the passing of that bill would have more effectually prevented the running of wool from hence to France, than all the laws besides, which you in England or we in Ireland can devise, to prevent that clandestine trade; since it would have made it the general interest of the landed gentlemen, and of the poor people, every where to have endeavoured to hinder any wool being carried off from hence to France; and I believe the gentry in those parts would have done their utmost to prevent it.

But at present, as you have done nothing in England to set us an example of what you would expect from us, unless my Lord Lieutenant comes over with instructions what it is that is desired of us, I believe we shall be put to it, to find out what method to take to hinder the running of wool. And after we have taken in the former sessions, one step to encourage carrying our yarn to England by taking off a duty amounting to 12,000l. per ann. which must be made good by some new duties, and after nothing has been done on the other side agreeable to our hopes, not to say to the promises made us, I wish the sessions may prove as easy as all his Majesty's servants here wish, and will use their utmost endeavours to make it.

I am, &c.

To the Duke of Dorset.

Dublin, May 29, 1731.

My Lord,

Since your Grace was so good as to send orders to have Mr. Hoskins presented to the rectory of Clane, upon Mr. Horner's resigning it, Mr. Horner has resigned that living, and I have collated him to a living in my diocese. But before any thing farther is done about Clane, I would beg the favour of your Grace to let Mr. Daniel of Killybegs be presented to the rectory of Clane, upon Mr. Hoskins being presented to Killybegs, which I doubt not obtaining from the Bishop of Rapho, who is patron of Killybegs.

---

69 The Primate seems to argue like an Irish Patriot in this letter, but in truth he argues like a true friend to both England and Ireland, whose interests, as he thought were inseparable.

It will be for the conveniency of those two clergymen to make that exchange; and I hope your Grace will be so good as to permit it.

I am, &c.

To the same.

Dublin, June 22, 1731.

My Lord,

The lady that waits upon your Grace with these is relict of Lord Roche, as he was commonly called, whose ancestor was attainted and lost his title and a large estate about the rebellion of 1641. His late Majesty was pleased to give him a pension here during his life: I think it was 200l. per ann. which I believe was the only support of him and his family. Since his death, his widow being destitute of support, made application to his present Majesty for a pension for the maintenance of herself; and as I understood by her, my Lord Carteret gave her hopes that his Majesty would grant her request; but as nothing is yet done in it, she thought proper to go over to England to solicit in person. I believe she has some friends there who will assist her with their interest, but as your Grace's good will must be of the greatest service to her, I humbly recommend her to your Grace to help her to somewhat that may be a subsistence for her, since I am fully persuaded she is at present without one. As for the particulars of her case, I refer your Grace to her own relation. I am,

My Lord, &c.

To Lord Carteret.

Dublin, June 24, 1731.

My Lord,

Mr. Mansfield has lately brought me the honour of your Lordship's of the 26th of April, recommending him to my protection here. If your Lordship is so good as to speak for him to my Lord Lieutenant,[70] I shall be very ready to do him what good offices I can with his Grace, as occasions offer. I am,

My Lord, &c.

70 Lionel, Duke of Dorset.

To the Duke of Dorset.

Dublin, June 26, 1731.

My Lord,

I have the honour of your Grace's of the 17th inst. and I shall be obliged to your Grace if you please by the first opportunity to send an order for presenting Mr. Daniel to the rectory of Clane, that there may be no squabble about tythes, as harvest is just coming on now.

I had to-day some talk with my Lord Chancellor about the copper coinage, and we are both of opinion that it is now too late to do any thing in that affair till we have the opportunity of discoursing with your Grace in person on that subject.

As to purchasing in the raps,[71] we are both of opinion that it will be very wrong to do it; nor have either of us heard any body here suggest that such a thing would be proper: and we would both beg that there never may be the least hint dropt of any such intention, since it may occasion the coining of some thousands of pounds more of raps, the loss of which will be heavy enough on the poor, as things stand already.

Sir Ralph Gore is in the country at present, so that I could not have his sentiments on this subject.

I am, &c.

To the Same.

Dublin, Aug. 3, 1731.

My Lord,

I had designed not to have troubled your Grace about an affair of no greater importance than is the subject of this letter till I had the honour of seeing your Grace at Dublin; but as your Grace may then be in a great hurry, and I am informed you have already fixed several of your chaplains, I take the liberty to recommend to your Grace's favour, to be put in that list, Dr. Essex Edgworth, Chancellor of the diocese of Ardagh, a bishoprick held by the Bishop of Kilmore. I should not recommend him on this occasion, if did not know him to be every way a most worthy clergyman.

I am, &c.

71 A base sort of half-pence.

To the Bishop of London.

Dublin, Aug. 12, 1731.

My Lord,

The person who waits upon you with this, is Dr. Delany, minister of one of the principal[72] Churches in this city, and one of our most celebrated preachers. He has of late employed his thoughts and pen in the vindication of our most holy Religion, and has some thoughts of printing what he has written,[73] if it shall be thought to be of service. I knew of no person to whose judgment it was more proper to submit his performances than your Lordship, who have so happily engaged yourself in the controversy, and seem to have the conduct of the defence of our most holy cause against the present most audacious insults of unbelievers. He comes over with a disposition to submit his writings, and the printing of them, to your Lordship's opinion.

I am, &c.

To the Duke of Newcastle.

Dublin, Dec. 4, 1731.

My Lord,

I hope your Grace will have the goodness to excuse my giving you this trouble on account of one of the bills now sent over to be laid before the privy council in England, for rendering more effectual an act for the better securing of the government by disarming papists; since the papists here declare publickly, that they have employed agents on the other side of the water to have the bill sunk there.

That your Grace may the better understand the case, I must beg leave to acquaint you that in the 7th of King William an act was passed here, entitled, an act for the better securing the government by disarming papists. The intent of which was not only to take away the arms then in the hands of papists, but constantly to keep them and their successors disarmed; and it has been the opinion of the Judges from time to time, that the law had forbid all papists at any time to keep or carry arms. But upon a papist being indicted last summer assizes in the county of Galway upon that act, for carrying arms, though it was not disputed either that he was a papist, or carried arms, yet the jury were pleased to acquit him. Upon this it has been understood by the papists every where, that the said act only concerned the papists then living, and the arms they had in their possession at the time that act was

72 St.Werburgh's Parish.
73 Revelation examined with Candour; the Life of King David, and many other Pieces, with a Volume of Sermons.

passed; and upon talking with the Judges, we find that act was drawn up so ill, that there is too much room for such an opinion. This occasioned the House of Lords to bring in heads of a bill to render that act more effectual, and this new act is very little more than the old one corrected to what it was originally designed for; only this being thought more prudent than to bring in a bill, which by its very title should have owned the first act to be grossly defective.

The power given in the old act to the government to license such papists to bear arms as they thought proper, is here continued, with a power of revoking such licenses, when they shall think fit, which was forgot in the former act. The chief additions to this new bill are, that no protestant servant to a papist shall have any arms whilst he is in that service; for this was one way of eluding the act, whilst it was thought to be in force, to keep a protestant servant, who pretended to be the proprietor of all arms found in the house of his popish master. That the proof of a person being commonly reputed a papist, shall be sufficient to convict such person offending against this act, except he prove himself a protestant, for on some trials it was found very difficult to prove a man to be a papist, though the whole country knew him to be so.

And another is, that no papist shall be on the jury in any trial upon this act.

My Lord,

As what has happened has in a manner repealed the act of the 7th of King William, so far as relates to the disarming of papists; and as the papists in Dublin have upon it put on swords, and those in the country in Conaught at least travel publickly with swords and fire-arms, we cannot think ourselves nor the government here safe, unless the act we now send over be passed. The papists by the most modest computation, are about five to one protestant, but others think they cannot be less than seven to one. And what use they have formerly made of their arms in this kingdom, our histories give too melancholy an account of.

And I can assure your Grace, that the papists in the country, before the defects of this act were discovered, were so formidable, that scarce any magistrate durst put any of the laws against regulars, &c. in execution, for fear of being murthered, or having his houses fired in the night. And if our present bill miscarries, they will grow much more formidable and insolent; nor have the papists scrupled often giving threats against every magistrate that was more active on any occasion than his neighbours.

They had found out several evasions of the act of the seventh of King William, which we would willingly have prevented, but as some difficulties arose in drawing up proper clauses for that purpose, and too many in the House of Commons shew a disposition to favour the papists more than is consistent with the protestant interest here; we have omitted all such clauses, and confined our selves to what was the undoubted intention of that act, and to some new clauses which nobody can well object to, to make it in some measure effectual.

And I must beg of your Grace to use your interest with the council, to return us this bill without any ways weakening it; since without this bill his Majesty's government will be in great danger here if any unhappy occasion abroad should give the papists a little more boldness than they have at present, and the protestants will not be safe in their persons.

I am, my Lord, &c.

Boulter to Charles Delafaye.

Jan. 4, 1731/2.
(NA. SP. 63/395/17–18)

Sir,

I thank you for your kind letter of 23rd past. I am very glad to find my letter was not useless by the Duke of Newcastle's being out of town and that it has been communicated to those I believed might see it. We are very much obliged to you for your zeal for our safety on this occasion. And I thank you for being at the trouble of extracting those passages out of my letter, which might be of use to the Council for the Bill, since you had no better brief. If the bill comes back as we sent it, I have no doubt of its passing both Houses, the clause, which some of the Commons were offended at, being left out in Council. But this is more than they, who were not of the Council, know. The clause objected to by the Attorney General (by which reputed papists to avoid the penalties of the Act were to prove themselves to be protestants) would have met with no great difficulty here. But, if it be struck out in England, as being too hard, it will not spoil the bill. I had answered your letter sooner, but that I thought whatever might be determined about this bill, would be over before you could receive mine. But, by what I have heard to day, I believe matters will hardly be over before this comes to your hands. I am this day informed, that there is a design to tack to this bill a clause for repealing the Sacramental Test in favour of the Dissenters. The thought is indeed very just and natural, that as that Test was first established here by an additional clause put into a popery bill in England, it should be taken away in the same method. But, I must observe, that there is great difference in the times. There was then a very great spirit against popery amongst the Commons, which I fear I cannot say now, and that made them willing to submit to what they did not otherwise like, rather than lose their Bill against popery: and even the Dissenters then in the House begged them to take it with that clog. But at present, we have too many young giddy members in the House, under no direction, and full of a false patriotism, who are too likely even to throw out a thing they liked, merely for it's coming from England. And, as this bill is necessary to secure the peace of this Kingdom, we have endeavoured to send it over to England so framed, and we hope it will return so to us, that there may be only one question about it in the House of Commons. Whether they are for disarming papists, or not.

I am very glad to hear from you what we hope for from the public papers, that there will be a general peace among all Christian Princes. I am, Sir your most faithful friend and servant.

Hu. Armagh.

Newcastle to Boulter.

Whitehall, Jan. 6, 1731/2.
(NA. SP. 63/395/1–2)

My Lord,

At my return from Sussex, I found here the letter with which your Grace has been pleased to favour me concerning the Popery Bill now lying before the Privy Council. According to the general directions I had left, it was laid before the King and communicated to his Majesty's servants, and has been of great use in giving a perfect and clear notion of that matter, and I can assure your Grace that whatever endeavours the papists may have used to obstruct the Bills being approved here in Council, who have sent over an agent to solicit against it, they have been very unsuccessful, as you may be persuaded that any application from that quarter would be but of little weight here. Every body wishes the Bill may pass, and the alterations that will be made to it, as it was sent over, will be but few, and not intended in the least to lessen the force and effect of it, but only to make it less liable to objections, which from a passage in your Grace's letter and from common report there is but too much reason to apprehend may be made to it when it goes back to be passed by the two Houses of your Parliament. The reason of it's not being sent with the other Bills, as I presume your Grace will have heard, is that the Presbyterians of Ireland have thought this a proper opportunity to apply for the repeal of the Test, which was imposed upon them by a clause added here to a Bill of that nature in the latter part of Queen Anne's reign, with what view you will easily guess, and whether that clause shall be repealed by adding one in like manner to this Bill, is the matter now under consideration. They have represented that the doing this would not be disagreeable to your Grace, nor to most of the Lords spiritual and temporal or to any who truly understood and have at heart the real interest of their country; and indeed considering the great disproportion there is between the papists and the Protestants of Ireland, it does not seem consistent with good policy to lay so many of those last under disabilities that render them less useful to the public service, and to that of the Protestant cause in particular than they would otherwise be. I heartily thank your Grace for the lights you have given us into the state of this affair, and desire you will be assured that whatever comes from you will always be most graciously received by the King and have great weight with his Majesty's servants, and in particular with me who am with much truth and respect, etc.

Boulter to Newcastle.

Jan. 15, 1731/2.
(NA. SP. 63/395/3–4)

My Lord,

I am obliged to your Grace for the honour of yours of the 6th instant, and am very glad that my former letter about the bill for disarming the Papists was of any use to give a notion of that matter. I hope the alterations that may be made will be such as not to weaken the Bill. Most of the objections it was liable to here were removed in Council, that it might pass the easier. I am glad to hear the papists met with so little encouragement on this occasion; and the rather because we think here, that they have been guilty of a great rudeness to my Lord Lieutenant and the privy Council at least, in not preferring a petition here against it, if they had any thing reasonable to object, and if they had been rejected here, it had then been time enough to apply on the other side.

I had heard somewhat, before I received your Grace's, of the application of the Presbyterians for a repeal of the Test, as you will perceive by a letter I wrote to Mr. Delafaye on that subject, since I had heard your Grace was not then in town. As they had published here a little pamphlet on that subject, it had occasioned some discourse whether such a Bill could be obtained here, which made me the more able to write on that subject as soon as I heard what was doing at London. But there was no suspicion here of the thing being done by inserting any additional clause in a Bill from hence of quite another nature. But since I wrote to Mr. Delafaye, I have made it my business to enquire of some of the Lords, and of some who best know the disposition of the House of Commons, and I have reason to believe that, if the repealing the Test were to be attempted originally either in the House of Lords or Commons, it would miscarry; but that, if it comes over from England added to some Irish Bill, it is still more certain of miscarrying, since I find, they call such an addition tacking, and most that set up for patriots will on that very account reject it.

I am very apprehensive, that on the Bench of Bishops a majority will be against it and I don't doubt but a great majority of the lay Lords will oppose it. And if the first trial is made in our House, some who might be for it, if it were not to stand a trial afterwards in another place, will ever make themselves obnoxious, without hopes of succeeding. As to the calculations made by some of the Dissenters here about their strength in the House of Commons on this occasion, some reckon they have about 50 sure, others that they have a third part of the House, and they hope the weight of the government would give them a majority. But this I very much doubt, since in this and the last session many who have places under the Crown have voted wrong, where the Crown was directly concerned. And I am assured, that when this very thing was attempted under the Duke of Bolton, after being recommended to the parliament from the King, not above 10 out of 50 in places voted for the repeal of the Test, but instead of it the parliament then gave the Dissenters a toleration, which they had not before. And yet there were then several leading men in the House of Commons, who at the time of laying on the Test had in a manner promised to take it off the first opportunity, who are since dead.

I am pretty well satisfied, that if such a clause be sent us over, it will give a certain prelate an opportunity of setting himself at the head of a great party of Lay Lords in our House, and of the inferior clergy through the whole nation.

The Bishops here, who are for letting the Dissenters live unmolested, have at present that weight with their clergy, as to keep them from any unreasonable warmth against Dissenters in their sermons; but, if those Bishops can once be run upon as persons who would bring Dissenters into power, they will soon lose their present weight, and both they and the Dissenters will be the subject of angry discourses from the pulpit. Nor do I believe those heats will be confined to the clergy. I find Dean Swift has begun all ready to sound the alarm.

I am pretty well satisfied, that the Dissenters have very much magnified their importance here. Their strength is principally in the North, where indeed they are numerous, but not proprietors of much land or wealth. I have been assured, that, if the Test were taken off, there are not 20 persons amongst them qualified for substance to be justices of the peace. As we are now tolerably quiet, and the sending us this Bill will probably raise great heats here without succeeding, I cannot but represent it as my humble opinion, that it is most for his Majesty's service not to send it over; and that, if any attempt in favour of the Dissenters be thought proper, they should be directed to make the best interest they can against another session; and, if they meet with encouragement, try for a Bill in the House of Commons.

I beg your Grace's pardon for troubling you with so long a letter, but I thought the duty I owe his Majesty laid me under an indispensable obligation to let your Grace know what I think to be the disposition of both Houses in relation to repealing the Test, and what may be the most probable

consequences of an attempt of that nature, that I may give the best light I can
to the Ministry to judge what is most expedient for his Majesty's service.

I am, with the greatest sincerity and respect,

My Lord,

Your Grace's

most humble and

most obedient servant

Hu. Armagh

Boulter to Newcastle.

Jan. 18, 1731/2.

(NA. SP. 63/395/5–6)

My Lord,

Having by the last post written so long a letter to your Grace about the
affair of repealing the Sacramental Test, I shall be the shorter in this.

As my Lord Lieutenant came to town on Saturday in the evening, my Lord
Chancellor and I waited on his Grace on Sunday morning by agreement, and
the Speaker came in a little after, and we acquainted him what was the report
about town relating to the Sacramental Test, and what we found to be the
disposition of the parliament in relation to that affair. And we assured his
Grace, that upon trying people upon that head, we were morally certain it
could not succeed in the House of Commons. The Speaker in particular said,
that he found many whom he hoped would have been for it, were very warm
against it, and that, if it was brought on there would in their House be nothing
like a show in its favour. He gave likewise an account of what had been
attempted in favour of the Dissenters the 2nd and sixth of his late Majesty, and
that all ended in giving them a toleration, which they had not before; though
in the last attempt the affair had been twice recommended from the King. But
I shall not enter into those particulars, because I believe my Lord Lieutenant
will give an exact account of them. And the Speaker said, the opposition was
now much stronger than ever it had been. The Archbishop of Dublin was
likewise called in who said he was fully satisfied, the thing could not be
carried. And we were all of opinion, that the warmth against it was such, that
it would sink any bill it came over with. We then agreed to talk with some of
the Dissenters, and desire them, if they thought the same, or upon enquiry
found it to be so, that they would write over to their friends in England what
they found to be the disposition of the parliament. And yesterday, some of us
talked with some of them, and others with others, and found them fully
persuaded the thing could not be done, now at least, and some of them
promised to acquaint their friends at London with it.

My Lord Lieutenant has talked with several others, who give him the same account as we have done. And we are all of opinion, upon the several conferences we have had with our friends, that nothing of that nature can be done now and that the very attempt will occasion very great heats in Parliament, and indeed over the whole nation. We likewise find, that many letters are sent into the country to fetch up the absent Lords and Commoners. So that we all think it is for his Majesty's service that this affair should not be stirred this session.

I am, with the greatest respect and sincerity,

My Lord,

Your Grace's

most humble and

most obedient servant,

Hu. Armagh

Newcastle to Boulter

Whitehall, Feb. 5, 1731/2.
(NA. SP. 63/395/7–8)

My Lord,

I have been favoured with your Grace's letters of the 15th, 18th and 25th of last month, and laid them before the King, and his Majesty was very well pleased with the attention you showed for His service, in giving so full and distinct an account of the general disposition of the members of both Houses in Ireland, with relation to the taking off the Test. His Majesty was greatly concerned, that what must so evidently contribute to the strengthening of the Protestant Interest there should be so much discouraged, but since your Grace, as well as my Lord Lieutenant, and the rest of the King's servants in that Kingdom, and even the Dissenters themselves, appear to be fully persuaded, that the adding a clause, for that purpose to any of the Bills against Popery depending before the Council here, would have made it miscarry in your Parliament; though that was the manner in which the Test was established in Ireland; His Majesty has been pleased to lay aside the thoughts of it for the present. It is indeed very extraordinary, that such a clause should be liable to meet with difficulties in either House, in a Country where no distinctions should be kept up among Protestants, which might be an occasion of disuniting them, considering the great disproportion in number, that there is between them and the Papists.

The two Bills against Popery, which are looked upon to be the most material, For rendering more effectual the Act for disarming Papists, and For the Amendment of the Law in relation to Popish Solicitors, have accordingly been passed here in Council without any alterations, but such as were thought necessary to explain and make them more effectual towards answering the ends proposed, and will, it is hoped, be the less liable to exception, when they are laid before the two Houses in Ireland. As to the other three Bills relating to the Roman Catholics, it being more difficult to adjust and settle some clauses in them, they are under consideration. But considering that those other Bills upon the same subject, which are of such importance have already been agreed to, I look upon it to be very uncertain, whether these three will be passed in this session.

I am

etc.

Holles Newcastle

Boulter to Newcastle.

Feb. 9, 1731/2.
(NA. SP. 63/395/50–1)

My Lord,

I must acquaint your Grace with the melancholy news of the sudden death of Dr. Lambert Bishop of Meath on Sunday last. He had broken his arm about ten days before, but that seemed to be in so good a way of healing, that it is hardly apprehended that his death was occasioned by that accident.

My Lord Lieutenant has been pleased to consult with the Lord Chancellor, the Archbishop of Dublin and me, who might be a proper person to fill that Bishoprick, and what other removes might be for his Majesty's service on this occasion. And we were all of opinion, that, all things considered, the most proper person to succeed to Meath was Dr. Ellis Bishop of Kildare. He is by his present Bishoprick the second Bishop in Ireland, as the Bishop of Meath is the first. He has been many years longer on the Bench than any other Bishop, and is old. He has rather been a Tory, but I will answer for his being heartily well affected to his Majesty and his family. And there is not a Bishop on the Bench that has on all occasions shown a greater readiness to serve the government in the House of Lords and elsewhere, than he has to my knowledge ever since my arrival here, nor is there one more thoroughly in the interest of England than he is. And I must in particular own my obligations to him for giving me from time to time the best advice from his long knowledge of this country, and whatever informations he thought might be of use to me or for his Majesty's service. And my Lord Chancellor and the Archbishop of Dublin have met with the same kind usage from him, and entertain the same good opinion of his prudence that I have. And we all three think it will be for his Majesty's service to have this mark of his Royal favour bestowed on him.

To succeed him in his Bishoprick and Deanery of Christ Church (which always goes with the Bishoprick of Kildare) we think Dr. Cobb Bishop of

Dromore a very proper person: and for his successor we think of Dr. Maule Bishop of Cloyne: for a successor to him we think of Dr. Synge Bishop of Clonfert, who will rather lose by the remove, but would be glad of it, because he has an estate in that neighbourhood: and for Clonfert we think my Lord Lieutenant's first Chaplain Dr. Cary will be a very proper person.

There is no body on the bench that desires to remove to Cloyne or Clonfert, nor do I know any beside the Bishop of Cloyne that desires to remove to Dromore, and the present Bishop by removing thither from Killalla was a loser.

All these several persons would be very thankful to his Majesty for these removes and we are of opinion that it will be for his Majesty's service to make these several promotions, and that as soon as his Majesty shall think proper. What I have here wrote about these several promotions is what my Lord Lieutenant has been pleased to approve.

The Bishop of Kilmore does not desire to remove to Meath. And I hope no encouragement will be given to any to neglect their duty and attendance here, by faring the better for soliciting in person for preferments as they fall. If a door be once opened that way, we shall have the example soon followed by too many, and his Majesty's servants here will not be able to answer for his Majesty's service being as effectually carried on as they all desire and endeavour it should be.

I am, with the greatest truth and respect,
My Lord,
Your Grace's,
most humble and
most obedient servant,
Hu. Armagh

P.S. Since the writing of this, I have waited upon my Lord Lieutenant, and find that, as Dr. Cary is likely to be taken care of otherwise in this scheme, he will by this post recommend Dean Daniel for the Deanery of Down. He is one who has in the worst of times distinguished himself by his zeal for the Hanover succession, and has probably spent 1500 l in supporting the title of the crown to the Rectory of Armagh, and was thought to have been somewhat hardly used in the House of Lords in that affair. And I believe his promotion to that Deanery will be acceptable to the friends of the Government here. If Dean Daniel is removed to Down, I believe his Grace will recommend his second chaplain Mr. Blandret to the Deanery of Armagh, which is worth but about 70 l per annum. Mr. Blandret bears a very good character.

My Lord, I would have wrote this letter over fair, if the going off of the mail had allowed me time.
H.A.

Boulter to Newcastle.

Feb. 19, 1731/2.
(NA. SP. 63/395/60)

My Lord,

I have the honour of your Grace's of the 5th instant, but it came later to hand than usual by reason of contrary winds.

I am very sensible of the great honour his Majesty does me in being pleased with my attention to his service, which I promise I shall never be wanting in. There is no doubt but it would be a strengthening of the protestant interest here, if those of all denominations could unite, but they are not at present in a disposition to do it. But I hope some other time they may be in a better temper, since the papists here are so much superior to the protestants in number. The 2 bills his Majesty has been graciously pleased to return us are here esteemed of more consequence than those not returned. We are in the House of Lords very well satisfied with the disarming bill as amended. But I hear there is some grumbling among the Commons, that the bill against popish solicitors is too much weakened by the alterations made in England.

I hope, when they consider it more maturely, they may find themselves mistaken. As for the other 3 bills, if there remain several difficulties to be adjusted in some of the clauses, I believe the session is so near an end that it cannot be expected to have them returned at this time.

I am, with the greatest truth and respect,
My Lord,
Your Grace's,
most humble and
most obedient servant,
Hu. Armagh

Newcastle to Boulter.

Whitehall, Feb. 19, 1731/2.
(NA. SP. 63/395/62)

My Lord,

I have received the letter your Grace favoured me with of the 9th Instant, concerning the promotions, which my Lord Lieutenant has proposed upon the occasion of the Bishop of Meath's death, and I have laid it before the King.

The reasons given for it, and the unanimous concurrence of his Majesty's servants, with my Lord Lieutenant's opinion in a matter of this importance, could not but have the greatest weight with the King, and be very agreeable to his Majesty. Accordingly the King's Letters, for the translations to the several Bishopricks, and for the making of Dr. Cary Bishop of Clonfert, are signed, as also those for bestowing the Deanery of Down upon Mr. Daniel, and that of Armagh upon Mr. Brandreth.

I am with the greatest truth and respect etc.

Holles Newcastle

Boulter to Newcastle.

Feb. 29, 1731/2.
(NA. SP. 63/395/70)

My Lord,

I am very glad his Majesty has been graciously pleased to approve of the several recommendations made by my Lord Lieutenant with the unanimous concurrence of his Majesty's servants here, and the reasons for them. The regard his Majesty has condescended to show on this occasion to their opinion, and the quick dispatch of this affair, will, I doubt not, be of service here, as it will give strength to his Majesty's servants, when it is seen that his Majesty gives such attention to their joint recommendation. The several persons promoted are very thankful for their respective shares of his Majesty's favour.

I am, with the greatest truth and respect,

My Lord,

Your Grace's,

most humble and most obedient servant,

Hu. Armagh

To the Duke of Dorset.

Dublin, Mar. 20, 1731/2.

My Lord,

I have had the honour of your Grace's of the 11th instant, and am very much obliged to your Grace for your answer to mine of the 21st past.

What my Lord Carteret had done with the resolutions of the House of Lords and Commons, which he took over with him, we had no account of before. But judging it probable they were referred to the Commissioners of the Treasury, we were for serving the nation in their present extreme want of copper money, by a method that might avoid any enquiry into so complicated an affair, as the setting the value of the gold and silver coins current here, and the considering whether it were more proper to have a mint erected here, or to have leave given us to have copper money to such a quantity, coined at the tower; which method was, by an address from the Lords Justices and Privy-council for leave to have fifty tuns of copper coined at the tower, without any relation to any thing done either by the Lords or Commons here. Whereby all that would have been brought before the Treasury had been, whether his Majesty would please to let us have fifty tuns of copper coined at the tower, at such a rate as answers to the English copper coinage, and to permit the gain made by it to come to the use of the publick.

And I can assure your Excellency that I have never heard of any application made by any but the privy-council here to the King on any occasions relating to the coin, till last session. And so far were the House of Commons from thinking it a point belonging to them, that Mr. Conolly acquainted my Lord Chancellor and me that a few years before I came hither there had been a committee appointed by the House of Commons, to consider at what value gold and silver coins ought to pass here; but after some time spent in it , they dropped making any report to the House of what resolutions they had come to in the committee, as thinking that an affair wholly belonging to his Majesty's prerogative. Nor had they meddled with it last sessions but that the remitters and merchants of Cork thought it more to their advantage to have things continue in their present bad state, than have them reformed according to the rational scheme designed by the privy council: and they were the persons who engaged some members in that house to drive them to the resolutions they came to: and the resolutions of the House of Lords[74] were designed only as a ballance against the hasty resolutions of the other house.

After these hints, I shall rest the affair with your Grace. I am, My Lord, &c.

To the same.

Dublin, May 4, 1732.

My Lord,

After the difficulties and dangers your Grace met with in your first attempt for England, it was a great pleasure to hear to-day, that your second voyage proved so favourable.

By the accounts we have from England there is no doubt of your Grace's having time to lay before his Majesty what you shall judge proper for the service of this country before he sets out for Hanover; and we are all satisfied we cannot desire a better sollicitor.

---

74 Those resolutions were framed by his Grace, and supported by him in the House of Lords.

I take this opportunity to make my acknowledgments to your Grace for all the favours I received from you here, and desire I may be honoured with the continuance of them. I am,

My Lord, &c.

To the Same.

Dublin, May 11, 1732.

My Lord,

We have wrote to your Grace by this mail, recommending Mr. Meredith for the deanery of Ardfert. The deanery is of little value, and is rather desired for the dignity than the profit of it.

Mr. Agmondesham Vesey is father-in-law to Mr. Meredith, and he came to me with him, and took occasion to assure me of his readiness to concur in all measures the government could desire next session, which a man of honour could possibly join in. I told him I was very sure the government would never desire any thing a man of honour could not comply with, and assured him I would write to your Grace in behalf of his son.

As your Grace had been mentioning Mr. Vesey, as one proper to be gained, I was glad of his applying on this occasion: since the boon he asks is not great, if he should fly off. But I hope this may open a way to fix him against another session.

He has given the same assurances to other friends, whom he employed to speak to Sir Ralph Gore and me. As this is the state of this affair, I must desire your Grace to be so good as to recommend Mr. Meredith to his Majesty for the said deanery. I am,

My Lord, &c.

To the Same.

Dublin, May 27, 1732.

My Lord,

It was with very great pleasure I received the account from your Grace, of your family being all arrived at London in good health.

I am sensible the loss of time your Grace suffered by your troublesome passage, must have hindered your knowing his Majesty's pleasure about some of our Irish affairs; but the distress we are in for want of copper money, and the ready concurrence that affair was likely to meet with from the ministry, make me hope your Grace has found an opportunity of consulting his Majesty about the copper coinage. I am,

Your Grace's, &c.

A MEMORIAL TO His Grace the DUKE of DORSET.

May it please your Grace,

   The want of copper money is so great in this kingdom, as to put the more ordinary sort of people, particularly the soldiers, under the greatest difficulties in all their little transactions: obliging them to pay for the exchange of silver, and to take raps that are not of a fourth part of the value of an English half-penny. And their necessities have encouraged several wicked people to make counterfeit copper money at this time, which must end in the great loss of this nation.

   We therefore think it would be of great service to his Majesty, and of great advantage to his good subjects here; if a quantity of good copper money were, as soon as conveniently may be, coined for the use of this kingdom. And we desire your Grace will be pleased to obtain his Majesty's permission, that we may have fifty tuns of copper coined at the mint, of the same fineness as the English half-pence are coined of, part in half-pence, and part in farthings; and that as the English shilling passes with us for 13d. and out of a pound of copper is coined at the mint 23_d. English, we may be permitted to coin out of a pound of copper 25½d. that our copper money may be as near as may be of the same proportionable value as the copper money of England: and that no private person may make any advantage of this coinage, we desire that his Majesty may be pleased to order that after the expence of the copper, coinage, exchange for remittance, carriage, and other necessary expences, the remaining profit may go to the use of the publick here.

   It is proposed that this copper money should have his Majesty's head on one side, and the Irish harp and crown on the other. The sum of copper money that will arise out of 50 tuns coined after this proposal, will amount to 11,900l. Irish. The money that may be necessary to set this coinage a going, will be little more than 1000l. which is proposed to be advanced here without any profit to those who advance it.

   As our present calamity for want of good copper money is very great, and grows every day greater, and as the design will take up some time in executing, after his Majesty has graciously given us the permission we desire, we humbly beg your Grace will take the first opportunity to obtain his Majesty's leave, that we may immediately set about an affair that will be of so great service to the ordinary people of this kingdom.

   The House of Lords, &c.

Boulter to Newcastle.

June 24, 1732.
(NA. SP. 63/395/140)

My Lord,

I am sorry I am obliged to trouble your Grace about an affair I formerly gave your Lordship a great deal of trouble about. It is [illegible] to Mr. Stephens Vicar of Maulden in Surrey, for whom I had obtained a promise from the Ministry of a Canonry of Christ Church in Oxford before I left England. But since his Majesty's happy accession, it was settled that, when Dr. Burton or some other Canon made a vacancy at Christ Church, Mr. Cross prebend of Winchester should be removed to Christ Church and Mr. Stephens should succeed to Mr. Cross's prebend at Winchester. Though this was much to Mr. Stephens' disadvantage, yet it was acquiesced in.

But I now understand that Mr. Cross is lately dead and this scheme over. I therefore most earnestly recommend Mr. Stephens to your Grace's protection, that he may be effectually provided for the next vacancy at Christ Church, in some way to be settled with my Lord Bishop of London.

Mr. Stephens is, as I have formerly assured your Grace, a most deserving person, and was always a friend to the revolution, and to the House of Hanover, and is the only friend about whom I have troubled the Ministry in England and as he is towards sixty, whatever is done for him must be done speedily.

The experience I have already had of your Grace's friendship on other occasions, and your readiness to help Mr. Stephens in the former scheme, make me entirely depend on your goodness for fixing this affair to his advantage.

I am with the greatest truth and respect,
My Lord
your Grace's
most obedient and most humble servant,
Hu. Armagh

To the Duke of Dorset.

Dublin, July 22, 1732.

My Lord,

I was in hopes to have given your Grace the trouble of a letter relating to the copper coinage sooner, but it was not before Thursday last that we could finish the affair, and sign a letter. I am sorry it is in so perplexed a manner, with so much regard to what passed in the two houses two sessions ago: but your Grace will see that in the opinion of the council, our necessities require such a coinage, and that speedily. I first opened the affair upon receipt of Mr. Cary's[75] letter, in council, on Wednesday the 12th instant, when we appointed a committee to consider the matter and make a report. My Lord Chancellor seemed to have a little courage then, Sir Ralph Gore was not then returned out of the country, last Saturday we received the report from the committee, when my Lord Chancellor expressed great fears of offending the House of Commons, and the affair was re-committed. Sir Ralph Gore spoke very plainly that he had last sessions talked with several members about what was designed, that except Mr. Stevenson, who wanted to have the coinage himself, every one approved the design; and thought it best to be done by the council, for fear of any unreasonable addition, if the affair was moved in the House of Commons. I likewise assured them I had promised some members to get the thing done, if they would keep it out of the house, which was accordingly done. However, my Lord Chancellor insisted on not concluding till the Lord Chief Justice and Lord Chief Baron returned from the country; and that notice should be taken of the resolutions of the House of Lords and the Commons two sessions ago. Against Wednesday the 19th the committee had the report ready agreeably to my Lord Chancellor's desire. In the debates we had, every body allowed it was the most reasonable scheme as to the goodness of the half-pence, and most advantageous, as the publick was to have the profit: that the necessities of the nation required a speedy remedy, and this was the only one; but as some few were afraid of offending the Commons, I put them in mind that we were to act for the King's interest, without regard to the sense of either house; and that though the Commons, in a sudden heat had come to a resolution, yet as they had sate since for four or five months, and never meddled with that affair, it was a tacit retractation. Several of the members in town, that usually are in the opposition, have been spoke to, and highly approve of the affair.

I must beg that we may be favoured with leave to have 50 tuns coined at the mint, of the same fineness as the English copper coin, at 25½d. per pound avoirdupois, and that the profit may go to the publick here.

We are not sure whether we should in our letter desire your Grace to apply to his or her Majesty, but we mean to have it obtained as soon as may be. The want of good change is so great, that the sooner we may set about it the better. As 1000 or 1500l. may be wanted to set the affair a-going, care will be taken to provide it: there is no doubt but we shall want about 100 tuns more.

About letting the old half-pence circulate, I believe there wants no order from England, but if your Grace approves it, as it is necessary, and is a sort of condition of the new coinage, we can do it by proper orders to the Vice-Treasurer. I am,

My Lord, &c.

75 Secretary to his Grace the Lord Lieutenant of Ireland.

Boulter to Newcastle.

July 25, 1732.
(NA. SP. 63/395/150–51)

My Lord,

The assistance I have on all occasions met with from your Grace makes me apply to you at present in an affair where the interest of this kingdom and his Majesty's service here is very much concerned, without any possibility of damage to England. We have for 3 or 4 years last past been under the greatest distress in carrying our manufactures and all the lower business of trade for want of copper change. This has encouraged ill-disposed persons to make counterfeit halfpence, which we call raps, and as these meet with some currency from the necessity the poor are under of having some kind of change, they still go on multiplying, and the loss by them will grow every day greater. To remedy these evils, we last week came to a resolution in Council to apply by my Lord Lieutenant to his Majesty for leave to have 50 tuns of copper, of the same fineness as the English halfpence are made of, to be coined at the Mint, part in halfpence, part in farthings, at the rate of twenty five pence and a halfpenny out of a pound of copper avoir du pois weight. And to desire, that the profit arising from this coinage may go to the public here.

By the coinage being carried on in this way, we avoid all the inconveniencies apprehended from Wood's halfpence. We are sure our copper will not be baser than is proposed, and that no more can be coined for us than what the Government find necessary to apply for, and there can be no clamour at any private person's being a gainer by it.

The reason of coining 25½ out of a pound of copper, is that at the mint they coin 23½ d out of a pound for the use of England; and as an English shilling passes here for 13 d this will make our copper money proportionately as good as that in England.

We propose on the reverse of the coin to have a Crown and Irish harp to distinguish this from the English copper money. As such copper money is extremely wanted here, the people being forced in many places to take little notes instead of change to be able to carry on their manufactures, and as the English here have in a great measure answered for the success of this application, I shall hope we shall meet with favour and dispatch.

We shall, no doubt, have occasion to apply for 50 or 100 tuns, before we have done: but we are desirous to begin by showing them a pattern of good halfpence and farthings, and convincing them, that they may be had in a way very beneficial to this kingdom.

And yet with all this care, I am satisfied, we shall have some find fault here. But persons of sense, who have any candour, do own that this is the most rational as well as most beneficial scheme to the public, that was ever started here about a copper coinage.

I must on this occasion beg your Grace's assistance and the rest of his Majesty's servants to forward an affair very necessary here, and where my reputation is entirely at stake.

I am, with the greatest truth and sincerity,
My Lord,
Your Grace's,
most humble and most obedient servant,
Hu. Armagh

To the Duke of Dorset.

Dublin, Aug. 15, 1732.

My Lord,

I had some time ago a memorial transmitted me by Mr. Cary, that had been laid before your Grace by the Bishop of Meath, relating to the archdeaconry of Kells granted to him in commendam, in order to have part of the endowment of it annexed to the bishoprick in lieu of several impropriations he is willing to give up, to the several parishes they are in, desiring to know my sentiments of the matter.

As I know how poorly those parishes are provided for at present, I cannot but approve the design, as do my brethren the Lords Justices.

But to prevent any misunderstandings or exceptions, I desired the Bishop of Meath to deliver in a memorial to the Lords Justices, that we might in common consider the matter, and recommend it jointly to your Grace; but as my brethren have been lately out of town at Sir Ralph Gore's, and I am going this week on my visitation, where I shall be absent for a fortnight, nothing can well be done in it till my return. However I promised the Bishop of Meath, that I would in the mean time acquaint your Grace with my approbation of it, and would give it all possible dispatch at my return; with which he was well satisfied. And I hope at my return to Dublin, we shall jointly recommend it to your Grace. He proposes by your Grace's assistance to have the affair settled by an English act of parliament next session; but it is necessary he should have the archdeaconry in commendan in the mean time, that it may not lapse. When the affair is settled in better form, I shall trouble your Grace with a more particular account of it. I am,

My Lord, &c.

To the same.

Dublin, Sept. 27, 1732.

My Lord,

The bearer, Mr. Horan, is a gentleman whom I presented to your Grace in this kingdom, when he gave you a memorial of his case.

He is the person who had a trial here with a descendant of one of those who went to France upon the surrender of Limerick, and afterwards followed the cause to the House of Lords in England; and was encouraged by those in power here to solicit an application of the 7° and 10 of Queen Anne, by a new act in England, so as to secure protestant purchasers against the descendants of those who chose to go and serve France, rather than stay in their own country.

On this occasion he has taken several journies to England, and been at very great expences, and has certainly been a considerable loser, the estate of which he had been a purchaser, not making him amends for his expences. He therefore hopes that as he has stood the expence of a law-suit here, and an appeal in England, and been at great trouble and expence in soliciting an affair, the well settling of which is of consequence to the protestant interest of this kingdom, your Grace would be so kind as to recommend him to his Majesty's favour for some place in this kingdom.

Most of the facts he mentions since 1724, I know to be true, and I am thoroughly sensible he must have been a sufferer in this affair, which I think it is a pity he should be, and therefore I recommend him to your Grace's favour.

I am, my Lord, &c.

To the same.

Dublin, Oct. 17, 1732.

My Lord,

I had owned the honour of your Grace's sooner but that I found by it there were very little hopes of any thing being done in the affair of our copper coinage, till his Majesty's arrival brought the several great officers to town. As that is now done, and the hurry of compliments on that occasion is now over, I must beg of your Grace to forward that affair as much as you can. I hope what is so reasonable in itself, so necessary for us, and of no damage to England, will meet with no difficulty on your side of the water.

Your Grace most justly thought it could have met with no objections here, especially after what you had heard on that subject from so many of the principal persons here. Nor had there been any obstacle here, but for the timorousness of one person.[76]

But as the thing is so much wanted, and the method proposed for doing it, in itself so reasonable and just, I make no doubt but when it is once well executed every body will applaud it.

I am, my Lord, &c.

To the same.

Dublin, Oct. 28, 1732.

My Lord,

Since I came to town to settle, there have been with me my Lord Mount Alexander and Lord Strangford, to desire I would put your Grace in mind of them, now upon his Majesty's return.

The case of the first your Grace knows is that he has nothing at all to subsist upon, and is ready on all occasions to attend his Majesty's service at the House of Lords. The case of the latter is, that there is a pension granted for the maintenance of my Lord and his mother; but as he is now of age and learning fit for the University, he would willingly prosecute his studies at the college here, but without an additional pension from his Majesty's bounty, he is unable to be at the expence. I am told he is a good scholar, and soberly disposed; and I should think it is a pity he should not be encouraged to go on and improve himself.

As this is their case, I take the liberty to recommend them to your Grace for your intercession with his Majesty, that he may be pleased to grant to each of them some mark of favour out of his royal bounty.[77] I am,

My Lord, &c.

To the same.

Dublin, Nov. 2, 1732.

My Lord,

Since we wrote yesterday to acquaint your Grace with the death of General Stern,[78] my Lord Cavan is come to town, and has delivered in his memorial relating to the mastership of the hospital. I believe there is no one applies on this occasion, that has been longer in the service than his Lordship, and that more constantly attended his duty whilst he was in the

76 Lord Chancellor Wyndham.
77 The Primate's request was granted.
78 Governor of the Royal Hospital, or invalid Soldiers at Kilmainham near Dublin, and much on the same Foundation as that of Chelsea near London.

army. Your Grace very well knows he is the only Lay-Lord that is a man of business in the House of Lords, where he is never wanting to serve the government: and I should hope it will not be thought amiss to consider one of that house, for a post now vacant. And if he has this preferment, he will always be at hand to assist in the Privy-council. He is very willing, if this provision be made for him, to drop the pension he at present enjoys of 400l. per ann. which will be an ease to our establishment, and that your Grace knows is of some consequence here. On these considerations I cannot but heartily recommend him to your Grace, for his Majesty's favour on this vacancy.

I am, my Lord, &c.

To the same.

Dublin, Dec. 7, 1732.

My Lord,

As we have not yet had any intimations of his Majesty's pleasure about the mastership of the hospital here, I just take the liberty to put your Grace again in mind of my Lord Cavan, as I cannot but think, if the place is disposed of to any person here, it would be of service to his Majesty in the House of Lords, to bestow it on his Lordship. I am,

My Lord, &c.

To the same.

Dublin, Jan. 11, 1732/3.

My Lord,

I had the honour of your Grace's of Dec. 28, last Sunday.

I do not question but there were good reasons why my Lord Cavan could not be provided for at present; but I hope some care will be taken of him on another opportunity. We shall to morrow have a meeting of the governors of the hospital, when we shall take care to appoint Colonel Bragg[79] master of the hospital, whom I heartily wish joy of this promotion.

My Lord Altham[80] has within this post or two written to your Grace to have somewhat farther done for him by his Majesty, and I promised him to write to your Grace on his behalf. His present pension is 200l. per ann.

---

79 Supposed to be the natural Son to the late E. of D. and Brother to his G. the D. of D. then L. L. of I——d.

80 Nephew to Arthur Earl of Anglesea, and presumptive Heir to that Title and Estate, who died before his Uncle. He was succeeded in both Titles and Estate by his Brother James.

which I fear is pretty much anticipated by debts he had contracted for his subsistence, before his Majesty was pleased to grant it him. But if it be not anticipated, as he has a lady and three children alive, and one coming every year, it will be very hard for him to carry the year about with his present pension. If your Grace could prevail on his Majesty to make some addition to what he has at present, it would be a very seasonable relief to one who I am certain is at present reduced to such necessities as it is a pity a peer of this kingdom, and who may possibly be a peer of Great Britain, should be reduced to.

I am, &c.

To the same.

Dublin, Jan. 25, 1732/3.

My Lord,

I am very sorry I am obliged to trouble your Grace on an occasion so melancholy to myself. My wife's breast has been very bad for some time, but of late is grown much worse, which makes me very desirous to carry her over to England, to see whether I can meet with better advice there than here. But I am sensible, as I am in the government here, I cannot stir without his Majesty's leave, whether by his letter, or by signifying his pleasure to the government here by your Grace, I cannot tell. I must therefore beg of your Grace to obtain his Majesty's leave for my coming to England, as soon as may be, for I am under apprehensions, that if my wife is not removed soon, her breast may be so bad, that it may be dangerous for her to travel.

I think there will be no difficulty in letting the government stand as it does, or that an order from his Majesty may be lodged here to grant a commission to my Lord Chancellor and Sir Ralph Gore to act jointly or separately, in case either of them should be taken ill. I do not speak this upon my own account, since I shall not reckon myself entitled to any salary from the day I leave Ireland, I have communicated this affair to my Lord Chancellor, but no farther and I can assure your Grace I shall not stay needlessly in England, if his Majesty pleases to give me his gracious leave to take this journey. And it may happen, that after leave obtained, I may find it impracticable to stir.

Your kind and speedy interposition with his Majesty on this occasion, will be a very great obligation to,

My Lord, &c.

To the same.

Dublin, Feb. 12, 1732/3.

My Lord,

I humbly thank your Grace for procuring me his Majesty's leave to come to England. I hope by the next mail to receive his Majesty's letter in due form.

If I had been apprehensive of their wanting a form at the secretary's office, which I fear has occasioned some delay in my affair, I should at first have sent them the King's letter, granted to his late Grace of Dublin, on a like occasion, but it was not suggested to me till late, and I sent it to Mr. Delafaye,[81] this day fe'nnight. But I hope they will have found a form before that comes to hand.

As soon as his Majesty's letter comes, I shall make what haste I can to London, if my spouse is able to undertake the journey; when I hope to have the honour to wait on your Grace.

I am, your Grace's, &c.

To the same.

Dublin, Feb. 24, 1732/3.

My Lord,

Your Grace so well knew Sir Ralph Gore, and the deserved esteem he had, that I need say nothing of his character, or the loss the publick will have by his death. For my own particular, it has put me in my present circumstances, under the greatest distress.

I thank your Lordship for obtaining for me his Majesty's leave to come over to England, and his Majesty's letter to alter the quorum here to make my absence the less inconvenient. When the letter came, Sir Ralph was in a very bad way so that if the new commission had passed, there was I believe a necessity of passing it before his death, which would have made it the more practicable for me to go the England though he died; not that I would have done it, without first knowing his Majesty's pleasure. But as the government was in danger of being in a case unforeseen when that letter was granted, and your grace enjoining me not to produce that letter except my journey was certain, I did not think myself sufficiently authorized to have a new commission passed, and accordingly nothing was done it, and I believe now nothing can be done in virtue of that letter.

As Sir Ralph Gore is dead, there seems to be an opportunity, without any offence, of putting the General[82] in as the third person in the commission,[83]

81 One of the Under Secretaries of State.
82 Of the Army.
83 Of Lords Justices.

who I remember your Grace thought was the proper person, and that it was inconvenient and even dangerous to let the government keep on too long with the office of the speaker.

My Lord Chancellor and I shall very soon trouble your grace with our opinion, whom we think it will be most for his Majesty's service to recommend for speaker.

As I cannot but wish that I may be at liberty, if her health will permit it, to carry my wife over to England, for advice, I would humbly offer, that if my Lord Shannon[84] be added to the commission of Lords Justices, and the clause for enabling one Lord Justice to act in the absence or sickness of the others, though my Lord Shannon could not be here so soon, yet, as one of this country would actually be in the commission, and might be expected here in a little time, I might be able to go to England in less than three weeks, if my wife should not by that time be too ill to travel. But if my journey at this time be thought prejudicial to his Majesty's service here, I entirely submit.

The point is a matter of great moment to the peace of this kingdom, not only during your Grace's administration, but probably under several successors to your Grace; and I hope will not therefore be too hastily determined.

I am, my Lord, &c.

Boulter to Newcastle.

Mar. 6, 1732/3.
(NA. SP. 63/396/15)

My Lord,

The Lord Chancellor and I, by the last mail, wrote to my Lord Lieutenant our sentiments of the most proper person to be recommended by the Government to the office of Speaker, now vacant by the death of Sir Ralph Gore, a person of weight in this kingdom, and a faithful servant of his Majesty. But as it is an affair in which not only the ease of the administration of the present Lord Lieutenant, but his Majesty's service in this kingdom under his Grace's successors is very much concerned, we both thought proper to communicate our thoughts to the Ministry, which I hope will make your Grace excuse my giving you the trouble of these lines.

Mr. Henry Boyle (of a younger branch of the Burlington family) had before written to us to recommend him to my Lord Lieutenant for his favour, and has, we find by the letters come in by yesterday's post, begun to solicit

84 —— Boyle, Lord Viscount Shannon, general and commander in chief of the forces in Ireland, whose daughter married the Earl of Middlesex, eldest son to Lionel Duke of Dorset.

the interest of his friends for obtaining the chair. He has of himself a very good interest among the members and we think, in our present circumstances, it will be most for his Majesty's service, and for the good of the common interest of England and Ireland, that he should be supported by the Government in this affair.

I cannot omit taking this occasion of mentioning it as my sense, that the present condition we are in furnishes a proper occasion of appointing a Lord Justice who is not speaker of the House of Commons, since it may in time be of ill consequence to the Crown to have it thought here, that a speaker by virtue of that station is entitled to be one of the Lords Justices.

I am, with the greatest respect and truth,

My Lord,

your Grace's,

most humble and most obedient servant,

Hu. Armagh

To the Duke of Dorset.

Dublin, March 6, 1732/3.

My Lord,

In the letter from the council to your Grace, notice is taken that no answer is come to their former application for the currency of the old copper money for some time: and it is apprehended that without some order on that head there may, upon issuing out the new species, be such a stagnation of the old copper, as may occasion great distress, if not some disturbance among the meaner people. It was therefore the opinion of the council that his Majesty should be desired to give such orders as he shall in his wisdom judge proper in that affair, to prevent a sudden stop to the currency of the old species. The raps were by all thought to be out of the question. And this was so much the sense of the council, that till somewhat of this nature be done, I am satisfied my Lord Chancellor will not advance one step in this affair.

I have since talked with the commissioners on that subject, whose opinion is, that as in England the collectors are not obliged to receive more than 5¾d. in any one payment in copper, as 6d. is there the least piece of common silver money; so here, where 6½d. is our least piece of silver coin, they should not be obliged to receive more than 6d. in copper in any one payment; though they may be left at liberty to receive more, if they please.

But I cannot but think it will be necessary to put some restraint upon that liberty, so that they may not e.g. at the most take more than one shilling in the pound in copper in one payment, to prevent as much as may be, the fraud of collectors.

There is another trouble I must give your Grace in this affair: I think the directions your Grace sent us in your letter, to give what orders were proper in this affair, were sufficient to authorize us to appoint an agent, or take any other necessary step; but my Lord Chancellor is grown so much more scrupulous since the death of Sir Ralph Gore, that at first he talked of appointing no agent, except such agent would be security to indemnify him in case of any accident or mismanagement: but I have since brought him, upon the advice of my Lord Chief Justice Rogerson, io consent to appoint an agent, and set the work a-going, if your Grace will signify to us that it is his Majesty's pleasure that we should appoint an agent in this affair: I think it would not be amiss if it were expressed such an agent or agents as we shall judge proper either here or in England.

Mr. Gardiner is willing to undertake the agency of this affair, and will answer the calls for money out of his own cash; and as the bankers here stand obliged to him for his favour on many occasions, he hopes to engage some of them to get a correspondent of theirs in London, to negociate the contract, and do what else is necessary there, without being paid for agency. He was even willing to have indemnified my Lord Chancellor, but that I thought was too much.

I should be glad if we had his Majesty's pleasure signified to us to those two points, as soon as may be conveniently, because I fear no material step will be taken here till that is done.

Mr. Gardiner will in the mean time write to a proper person in London to enquire about the price of copper, and prepare matters there but till his Majesty's pleasure be signified, we shall not be able to advance farther here.

I am very sorry your Grace should have so much trouble in an affair that every body allows to be even necessary for carrying on all smaller transactions here. And if it were in my power, I would save your Grace this trouble. I am,

My Lord, &c.

To the same.

Dublin, March 15, 1732/3.

My Lord,

We received the honour of your Grace's letter of the 10th instant, and write again in the same manner, that what passed on this occasion, may as far as in us lie, be a secret to all persons here.

In our last we represented to your Grace our thoughts concerning the several candidates, and that Mr. Boyle appeared to us to have by much the best personal interest, and such as could not without difficulty be opposed, if he persisted in his pretensions. If this was not the case of one of the candidates, it might be adviseable to wait for such accidents as time may throw in the way, before his Majesty favoured either of them with his recommendation; but as it is a thing hardly to be expected that any number of persons should keep themselves disengaged for so long a time as six months, and as there may not be wanting those who may endeavour to persuade Mr. Boyle that he has not been kindly used by the government's taking no favourable notice of his applications, we are very apprehensive that such delay may give room to the forming some party, which may raise a dangerous opposition to so late a recommendation as your Grace proposes. We should be very unwilling to disoblige either of the candidates, as being persons for whom we have a great regard, but we beg leave to observe, that since such declaration must be made before the election, the effects of any resentment on that account may be worn out the sooner it is made, especially if it be in favour of one, who it is generally thought cannot fail of success. It may be proper to take notice that it is almost a general notion, that if Mr. Boyle was once recommended by the government, all other opposition would be at an end.

People have not been wanting to surmise here that Mr. Boyle's standing was only in order to transfer his interest at a proper time to some other. The effect of this has been, that Mr. Boyle has by his friends, discountenanced any such suggestion, and many of his friends have declared against any such transfer.

We assure your Grace we continue in the same opinion we were of when your Grace was here as to the filling up the third place in the government and this seems a favourable opportunity for putting that scheme in execution.

Your Grace must be sensible that 500l. a session cannot be a sufficient provision for the expence of a speaker, and therefore he will be apt to expect some other support from the government. Whether the chancellorship of the Exchequer be a post proper for a speaker not otherwise provided for, is a matter we shall not presume to meddle with; but we cannot help taking notice, that from the nature and duties of that office, it may be for his Majesty's service that it should be given to some person of weight, who usually resides here.

We shall use our best interest and endeavours to keep the friends of the government disengaged till his Majesty's further pleasure is known.

Your Grace will excuse us for being so particular in an affair wherein his Majesty's service, the ease and honour of your Grace's administration, and the quiet of this kingdom, are highly concerned.[85]

We are, my Lord, &c.

85 The two principal candidates were Mr. Prime-serjeant Singleton, (afterwards Chief Justice of the Common Pleas, which he resigned; and was in a short Time after appointed Master of the Rolls in the Room of Mr Carter who was deprived of that office) and Mr. Boyle, who was created Earl of Shannon; and it was generally thought

To Mr. Walter Cary, Secretary to the Lord Lieutenant.

Dublin, Apr. 7, 1733.

Sir,

I have received yours of the 24th past, and hoped to have answered it sooner, but that we are still starting difficulty after difficulty in the matter of the copper coinage, which made me willing to see them all through if I could, before I give you any farther trouble: and I hope we shall upon the return of the Judges from the circuit, be able to settle them all. As for money, I had taken care about that, but I find now it is doubted whether any private person may advance it with safety, though he desires to get nothing by doing so. However in whatever way the money is advanced, there can never be more than about 2000l. paid before hand. I thought all was over when my Lord Lieutenant was pleased to signify to us that it was his Majesty's pleasure we should name an agent, but I find myself mistaken. I have begged hard that all may be thought of at once, and as there will be a necessity of a King's letter for keeping on the circulation of the old half-pence, and circulating the new, and as the Commissioners answer to what was referred to them is now come to our hands, I flatter myself we shall draw up the form of a King's letter, that will contain all the powers we fancy we want, and set this affair a going at last. I must beg the favour of your assistance to expedite the passing of the King's letter, when we send it over. I shall then trouble you again on this subject. In the mean time I thank you for putting my Lord Lieutenant in mind of Mr. Warren's affair; and I shall by this post thank his Grace for his favour on that occasion. I am,

Sir, your humble servant,

To the Duke of Dorset.

Dublin, Apr. 7, 1733.

My Lord,

I humbly thank your Grace for your favour in giving leave to Mr. Digby to resign his place of Porter to the Castle in favour of Mr. Warren. But though I was desirous to serve Mr. Warren, yet had I known what Mr. Cary has informed me of, viz. the solicitations Mr. Digby had used not long ago to get into that place, I should have staid for some other opportunity to have served Mr. Warren. I am,

Your Grace's, &c.

that the Primate turned the scale in favour of Mr. Boyle, who was chosen speaker. Mr. Boyle was a stanch whig, and a steady friend to the House of Hanover, and ever acted in perfect harmony with the Primate.

To the Duke of Newcastle.

Dublin, May 3, 1733.

My Lord,

I hope your Grace will have the goodness to excuse my giving you this trouble. One Mr. Godly is chaplain to Brigadier General Dormer's regiment on our establishment, and I am disposed to bestow on him a parsonage in my gift, but as I have several of the clergy here on my hands, I must at the same time make some provision for one to whom I lye under a promise of preferment, his name is John Richardson, Dean of Kilmacduagh; so that the removal of Mr. Godly depends upon the Brigadier General being so good as to permit Mr. Godly to resign his chaplainship in favour of Mr. Richardson. I am sensible there is usually upon these occasions a present to the Colonel for his consent, but as the chaplain who quits cannot well make any such present, and the person I propose to succeed him, is too poor to make it, I must beg the favour of Mr. Dormer to permit the resignation without any present. He will have one advantage by the change, that Mr. Richardson is at least 25 years older than Mr. Godly. As I have not the happiness to be acquainted with the General, I cannot apply to him myself for this favour, but I am assured your Grace's kind solicitation in this affair will obtain what I desire. I therefore make it my request to your Grace, that you would interest yourself for me in this exchange, and add this to the many obligations I already lye under. As the living I design for Mr. Godly is already vacant, I should be glad the sooner the resignation were agreed to.

I am, &c.

To the Duke of Dorset.

Dublin, May 25, 1733.

My Lord,

As the summer is advancing apace, I cannot but beg leave to renew my application to your Grace for obtaining the King's letter relating to our copper coinage; though it will be impossible to finish it before the parliament meets, yet as we may easily have 2 or 3000l. worth of copper coin over before that time, I think the surest way to prevent any wrong votes about that affair, is to let the nation see what good copper they are to have, and to let it appear by the King's letter, that the publick and not any private person is to have the benefit of the coinage. And I am fully persuaded that the determining this affair by the King's letter, and putting it in part in execution, is the most likely way to prevent what probably may otherwise be voted, an address to his Majesty for erecting a mint here; and I can assure your Grace several members of parliament with whom I have discoursed, think with me in this affair.

I have by this post wrote to Sir Robert Walpole, to desire his assistance in dispatching the King's letter.

I have lately received the honour of your Grace's letter recommending Sir Daniel McDonald, to whom I shall be ready to shew all proper favour.

I shall be obliged to your Grace, if your will please when you see a proper occasion, to remember Mr. Moland,[86] one of my family, for a pair of colours.

I am, my Lord, &c.

To Sir Robert Walpole.

Dublin, May 25, 1733.

Sir,

After his Majesty had been graciously pleased to give us leave to coin what copper we wanted at the Tower, and to issue his warrant to the master of the mint to coin for us, I was in hopes we should immediately have set about a copper coinage, but I find that it is still apprehended here, that his Majesty's letter to the government is wanting to authorize us to name an agent for carrying on that coinage, and for circulating it here, and providing for a proper circulation of the copper now current here, that has been coined under former patents.

I have sent my Lord Lieutenant, who I hope will apply to you on this occasion, a draught of such a letter as we want, as well drawn up as we could get it done here, though I do not question but in point of form it is very deficient, but by it will however appear, what are the things we apprehend we want to receive his Majesty's commands for, and in the Treasury it may easily be put into a right form, and any thing else added, that shall be thought necessary there. As the summer is now advancing, I think it would be of service to have such a letter dispatched soon, that we may have a quantity of the new copper coin over here, before the meeting of parliament, that it may be seen how much better it is than any that has yet been coined, and that by such letter it may appear no private person is to have any benefit by this coinage. And I am the more desirous to have the matter settled and in part executed before the parliament meets, because it will be the most effectual way to prevent any votes about a coinage in the House of Commons, where I think, and I find others that know the House very well, are of the same opinion, they are very likely, if this affair be not first fixed by such a letter, and in part put in execution, to vote an address to his Majesty for erecting a

86 Mr. Moland was his Grace's gentleman, but a man of good family, who had an Estate left to him some Time after.

mint here, which though it may appear a very idle project in itself, yet is a very popular thing here.

I must own it would have been better if the whole copper coinage could have been over by this time; but it is so much wanted and so much enquired after by all people in business here, that it is to be wished it may now be dispatched as soon as may be.

I should have troubled you sooner on this account, but the hurry of affairs in England, made me unwilling to interrupt any thing of greater consequence.

But I hope you will be able in a little time to find leisure to cast a thought on the wants of this kingdom, and I am sure the distress the trading people here are under for want of copper money is so great, that we shall be very much obliged to you if you will be so kind as to give some dispatch to the King's letter, without which we can make no farther advance in the affair of our copper coinage.

I am, Sir, &c.

To the Duke of Newcastle.

Dublin, June 7, 1733.

My Lord,

I thank your Grace for the honour of your's of the 19th past. I am sorry I should have occasion to apply to your Grace for your kind assistance, at a time when your Lordship cannot well ask Major General Dormer for the leave I desired, since I make no doubt of your readiness to comply with any request of mine, that may not happen to be improper.

I am, my Lord, &c.

To the Bishop of London.

Dublin, June 21, 1733.

My Lord,

The bearer is Mr. Lafont, who was educated in this College, where he took his master's degree five years ago, and was two years ago admitted ad eundem in Oxford. I am assured from very good hands, that he is a good scholar, and one of a sober life and conversation. As he has some relations at London from whom he has some expectations, he is going to settle there, and designs for orders. On this occasion he desired me to recommend him to your Lordship for your countenance; which from the good character I have of him, I believe he will very well deserve.

I am, my Lord, &c.

To Sir Robert Walpole.

Dublin, Aug. 25, 1733.

Sir,

I make bold to trouble you in behalf of Mr. Ambrose Philips, a gentleman who came over to this kingdom with me, and for whom I have not been able hitherto to make any provision. He is member of parliament for Armagh, and very zealously affected to his Majesty. As there is now a Collector's place vacant at Maryburrow, in the Queen's county, by the death of the late Collector, I would beg the favour of you to name him for the said collectorship[87] to his Majesty's Commissioners here, which will be a great addition to the many favours I have already received from you. I am,

Sir, your humble servant, &c.

To the Bishop of London.

Dublin, Nov. 1, 1733.

My Lord,

I heartily thank your Lordship for the effectual care you have taken of Mr. Stephens,[88] upon the death of Dr. Burton. He has in his letters to me expressed his grateful sense of the obligations he lies under to your lordship on this occasion.

I am obliged to your lordship for sending me an account of the amendments designed in the bill about ecclesiastical jurisdiction, and I think you was putting things upon a right foot; but I do not wonder that the officers of the spiritual courts were against it.

Since the opening of our parliament several dissenting ministers are come from the north to solicit the repeal of the test; they are rather sanguine in their hopes of success, if the government here lay its whole weight to it. But by the best information I can get, the success in the House of Commons will be very doubtful with all the help that can be given them: and if it be brought in, whatever be the event of the bill, it will throw the whole country into very great heats.

Our sessions, as far as it has gone, has been pretty uneasy, though I hope all will end well. I have no doubt but yours will be very warm; nor will the people be suffered to cool till the new election is over. I hear the success the applications from without doors had last sessions will bring on petitions to the Commons about reducing the army, &c. except the present state of

87 Mr. Philips was not provided for on this occasion, but his Grace made him ample amends afterwards, by giving him a considerable place in his own gift, which was that of Judge of the Prerogative Court.
88 He was made a Prebendary of Winchester.

Europe prevents it. We here look upon a war as unavoidable, which may possibly make things more quiet at home.

I am, &c.

To the Duke of Newcastle.

Dublin, Dec. 18, 1733.

My Lord,

As an affair of great consequence is just over with us, I mean the push for repealing the test in favour of the Dissenters, I thought it my duty to acquaint your Grace how that affair stands.

When my Lord lieutenant first came hither this time, he let the Dissenters and others know, that he had instructions, if it could be done, to get the test repealed; and he has since spoke to all any ways dependant on the government, as well as to others, whom he could hope to influence, to dispose them to concur with the design, and so have others done that have the honour to be in his Majesty's service.

But it was unanimously agreed, that it was not proper to bring that affair into either house of parliament till the supply was secured. However as the design could not be kept secret, and as the Dissenters sent up agents from the north to solicit the affair among the members of parliament, it soon occasioned a great ferment both in the two houses and out of them, and brought a greater number of members to town than is usual. There came likewise many of the clergy from the several parts of the kingdom to oppose the design; and a pamphlet war was carried on for and against repealing the test, in which those who wrote for it shewed the greatest temper.

And thus the persons who came to town to oppose it, by degrees heated one another, and visibly gained ground, and the members of the House of Commons were, by adjourned calls of the House, kept in town.

There were daily reports spread, that the bill would be brought in such or such a day; and some in the opposition gave out, they would move for it, that the point might be decided one way or another: till at length, after much impatience shewn on the occasion, on this day se'nnight, a very unusual, and I think unparliamentary motion was made, that after the next Friday the House would neither receive bills nor heads of bills, for repealing any part of the acts to prevent the growth of popery, in one of which the sacramental test is enacted. There was some opposition made to the shortness of the time, and the next Monday moved for, but the warmth of the House, which was a very full one, against any farther delay, and indeed against any repeal of the test, appeared so great and so general, that it was thought most prudent not to divide about that resolution.

And upon considering what then appeared to be the sense of much the greater part of the House, and what was found to be the disposition of the members by talking with them, it was concluded at a meeting at the Castle on Wednesday morning, and another on Thursday morning, where some of the agents for the Dissenters were present, to be most for the credit of the government and the peace of the kingdom, not to push for a thing which plainly appeared impracticable: and it was thought a very dangerous step to unite a majority of the House in an opposition to the intentions of the government, since it was not so certain when such an union might be dissolved.

And at a meeting of several members of the House of Commons, who were disposed to repeal the test, it was agreed that in the present state of affairs, it would be wrong to push for a thing that would certainly miscarry.

Whilst this affair has been depending, there have been great heats in the House of Commons, and a more than usual obstruction of publick business; and the House of Lords has had their share in their coming to some resolutions, though not on this subject, which would scarce have been carried or moved at another time. And I am fully of opinion that though the repeal had passed in the Commons, it would have miscarried among the Lords. But I hope now this uneasiness and handle of discontent is over, things will gradually cool, and return to their former course.

I find some of the Dissenters now say, the thing ought to have been tried sooner in the session. But, as I mentioned before, it was the opinion of his Majesty's servants that the supplies ought to be secured before any danger was run of raising heats in the House: and besides, in the method of our parliament, no bill can be carried by surprize, because though the heads of a bill may be carried on a sudden, yet there is a time for a party to be gathered against it by that time a bill can pass the council here, and be returned from England, when it is again to pass through both Houses for their approbation before it can pass into a law.

What has happened here will probably the less surprize your Grace, because the Archbishop of Dublin in London acquainted the ministry that he thought such a repeal could not pass here: which has been my opinion from the beginning of the session.

What representation the Dissenters here may make of this affair I cannot tell: but I believe their agents from the north had at first met with either such encouragement or such general civil answers, that they had given greater hopes of success to their friends in the country than there was just reason for. And some of them at the meeting at the Castle[89] last Thursday, were for pushing the affair at all adventures, urging that they thought they should not

---

89 The Castle meant here is the King's palace in Dublin, where in the absence of the Lord Lieutenants the Lords Justices meet, have their levies, and do the publick business.

lose the cause very dishonourably, though upon what passed there they seemed to have little hopes of its succeeding, in which I think they looked more at their own honour than his Majesty's service. But this I am sure of, that all present in the service of the crown, were of opinion, that the push ought to be made, where there was no probability of success.

I am, &c.

To the Bishop of London.

Dublin, Dec. 20, 1733.

My Lord,

The affair of repealing the test is now over with us: whilst it was carrying on it occasioned very great heats in the Commons: and your Lordship will easily guess that many of the[90] Clergy were not wanting in their zeal to raise what opposition they could against it. I am apt to think that there were near three to two against it among the Commons; and the majority was so clear, that I question whether many who were for it would not have absented themselves or have voted against it, if it had come to a division, to avoid marking themselves to no purpose. And I am fully satisfied that in the House of Lords, there would have been at least two to one against it.

My Lord Lieutenant was not wanting in his endeavours to dispose those in the service of the government, or whom he could any ways influence, to promote the repeal. But for two days before the day fixed in the House of Commons for bringing it in, if at all, there was a meeting at the Castle of those of distinction in his Majesty's service, and at the second meeting the principal agents for the Dissenters from the north were present, when it was the unanimous opinion of those in his Majesty's service, that the repeal could not be carried in the House of Commons, and that therefore no such bill ought to be brought in, since a fruitless attempt would be to the dishonour of the government and would probably bring about such an union among opposite parties as might not soon be dissolved. Some of the agents of the Dissenters there present, seemed satisfied, but one or two of them were for having the thing hazarded, insisting it would not be lost by a dishonourable majority. I hear some among the Dissenters, especially among their ministers, are very angry on this occasion.

I am apt to think one reason of it may be, that when they first canvassed among the members, they mistook civil answers for promises, and wrote to their friends in the north with greater hopes of success than they had reason

---

90 Dr. Synge Archbishop of Tuam, Dr. Swift, Dr. Tisdell, and many other Gentlemen of great Abilities wrote several excellent Pamphlets on this occasion. Besides, the Ministry and Clergy of England were violently against it.

for; and now do not care to own that they were mistaken in their calculations. Though besides I am satisfied they were mistaken in their numbers, because several who had promised them at first, upon seeing such a heat raised by it, fell off.

Another reason given by them to several for pushing it, when it seemed desperate, was that their friends in England instructed them to push it at all adventures.

The heat among the churchmen here will, I think be soon over; but I do not hear of much disposition to temper among the Dissenters. It is certain their preachers are drawing up a memorial to send over to their friends in England to throw the blame of the miscarriage on my Lord Lieutenant, though unjustly, since he was not wanting in his endeavours to serve the Dissenters, but really it was not at all practicable, at least at this time. But some of their laity, those especially of more temper and prudence, are endeavouring to hinder it, but with what success is not yet known.

As this is an affair of some consequence, I thought proper to give your Lordship a short account of it.

I am,

My Lord, &c.

To the Duke of Newcastle.

Dublin, Jan. 6, 1733/4.

My Lord,

On New-year's day died Dr. Ellis,[91] Bishop of Meath. As that Bishop by his station, is the first Bishop in Ireland, and usually a privy counsellor, the person thought most proper to fill that see by my Lord Lieutenant, my Lord Chancellor, the Archbishop of Dublin and me, is Dr. Price,[92] the present Bishop of Fernes; and the person most proper to succeed him is thought to be Dr. Synge, the present Bishop of Cloyne; they are both firmly attached to his Majesty, and of great service in the House of Lords, and I think they are both in the English interest: I would therefore most humbly recommend them to his Majesty's favour for the said translations.

As to a successor to the bishoprick of Cloyne, my Lord Lieutenant looks upon it as settled in England that Dean Berkeley[93] is to be made Bishop here the first occasion. I have therefore nothing to say on that head, but that I

91 Dr. Welbore Ellis, who had been chaplain to James Butler the last Duke of Ormond.
92 Dr. Price had been chaplain to Mr. Conolly, and Dr. Synge, was a son of the Archbishop of Tuam.
93 Dr. George Berkeley, Dean of Derry, author of the Minute Philosopher, and many other learned Works, among which were Queries relative to Ireland, and other useful Papers on that Occasion, published by George Faulkner.

wish the Dean's promotion may answer the expectation of his friends in England. I am,

My Lord, &c.

To the same.

Dublin, Feb. 25, 1733/4.

My Lord,

Among other bills sent over for passing the privy council in England, is one for the relief of the creditors of Ben. Burton and Francis Harrison, &c. which I must beg leave to recommend particularly to your Grace's care, that it may return to us. The several bankers mentioned in the title of the bill, continued the same bank without interruption with great credit; but as appears at last, had drawn off unreasonable dividends, and Ben. Burton and Fr. Harrison had bought great estates, so that the bank was worth nothing at the time of Harrison's death, but the succeeding banks paid off the former bank with the money of the new creditors, till at last payment was stopped. The equity of the bill is founded on the first bankers having had their debts of the bank paid with the later creditors monies; and an act 8 Georg. I. by which the unsettled estate of any banker is liable at the time of his death to all the bank debts; so that when Harrison died his estate was liable to pay all the debts of the bank as well as Burton's, since they were answerable jointly and severally. His estate is since got into the hands of strangers, from whence it could be long and expensive suits be fetched out by the 8 Georg. I. but as this would be very tedious and expensive, and no little creditor could have any benefit that way, this act vests the estates of the several bankers in trustees, who are to determine all claims in a summary way, and to sell as much as will pay the debts of the several banks; but as to Harrison they are not to sell more than will answer the debts of the bank at the time of his death; and if by such sale he has paid more than his share of those debts, it is to be made good out of the unsold estates of the other bankers, or the remaining debts and securities belonging to the bank; since that is not an affair between the creditors and the bankers, but between the bankers themselves to adjust their several proportions.

When this bank stopped payment last June, it had very nigh overturned all our paper credit here, and if this bill miscarries, it is not doubted but our bankers will all be blown up. And at the same time, we have so little specie here, probably at the most not above 500,000l. that without paper credit, our trade cannot be carried on, nor our rents paid.

Your Grace may have seen my name in the votes, as a petitioner for this bill, but there is little more than 200l. owing to me on my own account, and I can assure your Grace that it is not any regard to my own concern in the bank, which is a mere trifle, but a regard to the publick credit of this kingdom, which is in danger of being sunk if this bill should miscarry, that occasions my pressing your Grace to get us this bill returned.

I am, &c.

To the same.

Dublin, Mar. 2, 1733/4.

My Lord,

The traders in silks and stuffs here have been with me to desire I would write in behalf of a bill gone from hence to prohibit the wear of East India goods in this kingdom. They assure me the silk weavers and others at London will solicit for the bill before the privy council, as what will be of advantage both to the English and Irish manufacturers.

I do not pretend to be a very good judge in the matter, but must refer your Grace to what the manufacturers in England have undertaken to make out; and if it is probable the bill may be of service to both nations, I heartily recommend it to your Grace's countenance. I am,

My Lord, &c.

To Sir Robert Walpole.

Dublin, Mar. 28, 1734.

Sir,

By the last two mails are come several private letters that talk doubtfully of the success of Burton's[94] bill, and insinuate that there have been letters from great persons in Ireland representing that the passing it would be of great detriment to this kingdom.

That the Lord Chief Justice Rogerson should have written against that bill is not strange, since whatever is taken from Harrison's estate towards paying the debts of the bank is taken from Mr. Creighton who married the Lord Chief Justice's daughter; so that the Chief Justice's letter is not from an indifferent hand.

But the truth of our case, and what every man of sense here knows, is, that if this bill miscarries, it must put an end to our paper credit here, by an immediate run upon the bankers or gradual forbearing to lodge money there: and it is certain we have not cash enough in the nation to carry on our common trade or pay our rent or taxes: and I very much question whether if

94 For the Relief of the Creditors of Benjamin Burton, Francis Harrison, Charles Burton, and Daniel Falkiner, Esqrs, Bankers in Dublin, which Bill was passed into Law.

our paper credit fails, it would not be with the utmost difficulty that our army could be subsisted. And as this is the opinion of every body here, the miscarriage of this bill cannot but make a great disturbance in both Houses of Parliament.

It is likewise reported that the bankers bill is likely to be lost. If there is any hardship in it, it was by the consent of the bankers here; and all new in it is, that they cannot settle any part of their estate upon a marriage, &c.

There was a clause offered in the council, that their estates should be discharged from the debts of the bank within a term of years after the death of a banker, or his giving notice that he was quitting the business; but it was thought, considering that if this had been a law at the time of Mr. Harrison's death, the creditors of the bank would have lost about 40 per cent. it was there apprehended that if such a clause passed, the first banker that died or gave notice of his designing to quit the business, would occasion all the notes of that bank being called for, and that might bring a run on the others, so it was not thought safe to venture such a clause.

The banker's bill will please, and yet gives no such great security to the creditors more than before; but if it is lost it may do mischief.

I am, my Lord, &c.

To the Duke of Dorset.

Dublin, June 4, 1734.

My Lord,

Mr. Dean Marsh, Dean of Kilmore, died yesterday morning: his deanery is reckoned worth 300l. per ann. As I have not had an opportunity of talking with the other Lords Justices about a proper person to recommend to your Grace for this deanery, I shall not mention any till we meet at the castle next Friday. But only desire the favour of your Grace not to engage for any body till we can write about it.

I take this occasion to put your Grace in mind of the kind promise you was pleased to make me of providing for Mr. Robert Moland in the army.

I am, my Lord, &c.

To the same.

Dublin, June 11, 1734.

My Lord,

Last week we troubled your Grace with a recommendation of Mr. White to the deanery of Kilmore upon the request of Mr. Justice Gore. As nobody else applied, we recommended him for the deanery, though Mr. Justice would have been very well satisfied if some other person had had the deanery, who might have left some other thing to provide for Mr. White with. I have since had a letter from Mr. John Richardson, Dean of Kilmacduagh, that he would be very thankful if I could get him the deanery of Kilmore, which is within two or three miles of his parish of Belturbet, for the deanery of Kilmacduagh. As this would be a very advantageous change to him, and as he at present lies a very heavy burthen upon me, till he has somewhat better than the deanery of Kilmacduagh, which your Grace was so kind as to give him on my recommendation, it would be a very great obligation laid on me, if your Grace would be pleased to obtain the deanery of Kilmore for Mr. Richardson, and the deanery of Kilmacduagh for Mr. White.

I am, my Lord, &c.

To the same.

Dublin, Aug. 14, 1734.

My Lord,

I had the honour of your Grace's with an account of your having taken care of Mr. Moland. I have lately been to visit my diocese, or I had sooner returned my thanks to your Lordship for obtaining his commission, which is since arrived here; and I do not question but he will behave himself well in his post, if any occasion offers.

I thank your Grace likewise for remembering the Bishop of Kildare, who has since taken his place in council. As for the deanery of Kilmore, if Dr. Witcomb has it, or it is any ways disposed of for his service, I shall not any ways desire to break any such scheme.

I must beg leave to put your Grace in mind of my Lord Altham, that he may have an addition made to his pension, since what he has at present is too little for him to subsist upon, though he were a better manager than he is. Your Grace knows he never was wanting to attend the King's service at the House of Lords.

The Bishop of Derry continues much in the same way as formerly, only that he must be weaker than he was. I hope as to the translations that may be proper, whenever it pleases God to remove him, they continue as your Grace was pleased to settle them when you was here; though I find by what is said here from good hands, there have been some endeavours used to alter them, but I would flatter myself, without success, since I think it cannot be done without creating a general discontent on the bench of Bishops. I am,

My Lord, &c.

To the Bishop of London.

Dublin, Sept. 9, 1734.

My Lord,

Mr. Auchmuty[95] has every way answered the good character your Lordship was pleased to give of him. He has had the misfortune to be taken ill, as he was spending some time among his friends in the north. It is possible this climate did not agree so well with him, after having been so long in a much warmer. I find by him Mr. Shaw, a[96] fellow of Queen's, is publishing his travels, which are likely to be curious, and that your Lordship gives the author your countenance on that occasion. I have taken some of Mr. Shaw's receipts, and shall endeavour to dispose of them here, but we are very little given to promote subscriptions here, and especially for what is going on in England.

We are here very uneasy about the superiority of the French arms, and I can assure your Lordship the papists here are more than ordinarily insolent on that occasion. I have no doubt but the government are doing what is most prudent in the present situation of affairs. I am,

My Lord, &c.

To the Duke of Dorset.

Dublin, Oct. 14, 1734.

My Lord,

As my Lord Altham is by the advice of some of his friends in England going thither, to solicit an addition to his pension, and as his principal hopes are in your Grace's recommending his case heartily to his Majesty, he desired me to give him a letter to your Lordship on this occasion. Your Grace may remember he was by the House of Lords recommended to his Majesty for some farther provision; and your Grace knows he has on all occasions constantly attended at the House of Lords to carry on his Majesty's service. He has a wife and several children, and is likely to have more; and his present pension of 200l. per ann. is what, with the best management must be a very scanty maintenance for a nobleman. I would therefore humbly beg of your Grace, that you would recommend his Lordship to his Majesty for some other provision. It ought not to be forgot, that at the death of my Lord Anglesea, he will be a peer of Great-Britain, whether he be able to succeed to his Lordship's estate or not.

I am, &c.

95 Had been Chaplain to the army and garrison at the island of Minorca.
96 He was afterwards King's Professor of Greek in Oxford, and a Head of a House there.

To the same.

Dublin, Dec. 28, 1734.

My Lord,

I was in hopes your Grace had perfected the affair of removing Ensign Pepper in Colonel Hamilton's regiment, to Lieutenant's half-pay, and bringing Mr. Wye into his room; but I have lately heard from the Colonel, that it is not yet done: I must therefore renew my most earnest request to your Grace that you would bring that affair about in favour of a son of a deceased clergyman of my diocese, and one who it is believed by those who know him, will make a very good and diligent officer in his Majesty's service: the doing of which will be esteemed a great favour, by

My Lord, &c.

To the same.

Dublin, Jan. 7, 1734/5.

My Lord,

Inclosed I take the liberty to send your Grace the memorial of the bearer Lieutenant Cunningham, in which he desires on account of his long standing in the army, and his constant zeal for the House of Hanover, to be advanced to a Captain's commission upon a proper occasion. I believe what he affirms of his zeal for the present family, and the dangers he ran on that account in Queen Anne's time, to be true; and do make bold to recommend him to your Grace for a better commission, when your Grace shall meet with a convenient opportunity,

I am, my Lord, &c.

To the same.

Dublin, Jan. 14, 1734/5.

My Lord,

This morning died the Bishop of Derry after five or six days extreme pain and weakness.

As your grace was pleased to settle it with my Lord Chancellor, the Archbishop of Dublin, and me, that in this case the Bishop of Kilmore should be translated to Derry, and the Bishop of Killalla[97] to Kilmore, the

97 This was that Dr. Clayton who soon afterwards removed to Cork, and some time after to Clogher, afterwards made such a noise in the world, by his Essay on Spirit, and who actually sickened and died upon being informed that he would certainly be attacked in the House of Lords in Ireland on account of that book. London Edition.

Speaker is come into that recommendation in our publick letter; and the Lord Chancellor and I shall by this post write to Sir Robert Walpole to promote those translations. And I hope as there can be little more than 200l. per ann. difference between those bishopricks, neither Mrs. Clayton nor any other person will be for removing the Bishop of Killalla directly to Derry, which considering his years, and how few juniors he has on the bench, must certainly create great uneasiness among the other Bishops.

As to the bishoprick of Killalla, we have in our publick letter, named three for it, whom we all think to be well affected to his Majesty. But I cannot but think with my Lord Chancellor and the Archbishop of Dublin, that it will be very dangerous to let the majority of natives, who are already twelve on the bench, grow greater: and we cannot but be apprehensive that as they grow stronger there, they will grow more untractable. I have therefore by this post wrote to Sir Robert Walpole. And I make it my earnest request to your Grace, that some prudent English divine of good character, may be thought of to be sent amongst us; since we have not any Englishman here at present of that age, prudence, and good character, as to avoid a clamour if he were made a Bishop.

I think I am obliged to tell your Grace that the affair of Dr. Whitcomb's[98] having a royal dispensation to hold his fellowship with the living of Lowth, begins to make a great noise here; and so far as I can see, is likely to make a much greater, as hindering the succession in the college, and opening a door to farther dispensations, when they say, as the living is probably better than 500l. per ann. he has no occasion for such a favour.

I hope your Grace will excuse my taking this liberty to let you know what I take to be for his Majesty's service in the present juncture.

I am, my Lord, &c.

To Sir Robert Walpole.

Dublin, Jan. 14, 1734/5.

Sir,

Early this morning died the Bishop of Derry: his death has been long expected; so that when the Lord Lieutenant was here, upon the translation of the Bishop of Fernes to Meath, and the Bishop of Cloyne to Fernes, the Lord Chancellor, and the Archbishop of Dublin, and I agreed with his Grace, that if he would come into those translations, we would very readily join with him in recommending Dr. Hort, Bishop of Kilmore to be translated to the bishoprick of Derry; and Dr. Clayton, Bishop of Killalla to the bishoprick of Kilmore: and we have accordingly this day, with the Speaker, sent such a

98 College Tutor to Lord George Sackville.

recommendation. We have had some reports here, that a push is making at London to pass by the Bishop of Kilmore, and remove the Bishop of Killalla directly to Derry. As the Bishop of Killalla is very young for a Bishop, and has but four juniors on the bench, I am satisfied it will create a great uneasiness, if he should be translated to the best bishoprick in this kingdom. And as there can be but about 200l. per ann. difference in the two bishopricks, I would hope Mrs. Clayton,[99] if she were talked to, would not make a push for a point that may very much distress us here.

As for those we have recommended to succeed to the bishoprick of Killalla, I think them all to be well affected to his Majesty's service; but as there are already twelve of this country on the bench, I must beg leave to represent it as a thing of very great consequence, that the last in the remove should be an Englishman, that by degrees we may at least be an equality on the bench, for I fear if the majority increases on the other side, we shall soon find them unmanageable. I could therefore most heartily wish that a prudent person of good character were sought for in England to be sent over for the bishoprick of Killalla; as the bishoprick is worth full 1100l.per ann, it is no contemptible thing in this country. But I would at the same time beg that we may not have one sent over who may be a burthen or a disgrace to us. You will have the goodness to excuse this freedom, which I take to be wholly for his Majesty's service. I am,

My Lord, &c.

To the Duke of Dorset.

Dublin, Jan. 31, 1734/5.

My Lord,

As by the death of the Lord Santry the government of Londonderry is become vacant, I cannot but take this occasion to recommend the Earl of Cavan to succeed him.

Your Grace knows very well of what service he has been in the House of Lords, and how necessary he is to carry on his Majesty's service there: when he was put by the Mastership of the Hospital, your Lordship seemed disposed to remember him upon Lord Santry's death; and I think as it was the only government possessed by a Lord, it may occasion an uneasiness among the Lords, if this post should be given to a Commoner.

I find my Lord Cavan is willing to quit his present pension of 400l. per ann. from the crown, if he may have this government, and a pension of 200l. per ann. for his son Lord Lambert, to enable the father to bestow a proper education on him.

---

99 A very favourite Lady of the Bed Chamber to Queen Caroline, Consort of George II.

I cannot but represent it as a thing highly for his Majesty's service, that his Lordship should have this government. I am,

My Lord, &c.

To the same.

Dublin, Feb. 1, 1734/5.

My Lord,

The bearer is Mr. Hansard, Secretary to the Charter Society of Protestant Schools in this kingdom. As there is a much greater spirit in London towards promoting any good and pious design, and they are much abler to do it than we are in this country, we have sent him to London to promote subscriptions for carrying on our good designs, and we are the more encouraged to do so, because we find the like society in Scotland have in a few years got about 3000l. in London for the like charity in Scotland. And we hope as we have the same established church as England, and are of the same blood, we may reasonably expect greater assistance than has been given to the Scotch society. And besides, we have a particular claim on the noblemen and gentlemen of this country that live in England; who we think ought to contribute to any good design that is carrying on in their country.

We have on this occasion directed our secretary to wait on your Grace, to receive any commands you shall please to give him, and in hope of your Lordship's countenance.

The greatest part of our society are for applying to his Majesty for his bounty to our corporation, as he was pleased to give the Scotch society 2 or 3000l. per ann. But I have differed from them in my sentiments as to applying to his Majesty at present, and have told them both in private and publick, my reasons for it, That as the nation is at present very much in debt, I do not know but if his Majesty should give us a grant of a handsome annuity it may occasion some clamour and uneasiness in the House of Commons; and besides that I am desirous we should by repeated trials, come to such a method of educating the children of poor papists and others in Christian knowledge and honest labour, as to be able boldly to say, that we only want a greater fund to be able to make so useful a design more general. And I hope in two or three years we shall make those experiments, and meet with that good success, as to pitch upon a settled method of instructing and usefully employing the poor children.

But this whole affair I entirely submit to your Grace's better Judgment. Your Lordship will likewise be the best judge whether it may be proper at this time to apply to the[1] Queen and the rest of the Royal Family for their

1 Caroline.

bounty, or stay till a farther season. And if your Grace shall judge it proper to apply now, we must entirely depend on your Grace's directions in what manner it is best to be done, and on your assistance in doing it. I am,

My Lord, &c.

To the same.

Dublin, Feb. 20, 1734/5.

My Lord,

I have had the honour of your Grace's of Jan. 23. and Feb. 13. I am obliged to your Lordship for your kind information, that there was room for accidents in England, in relation to the bishoprick of Derry, which otherwise was likely to go as was desired from hence. But till you knew somewhat certain, I thought there was no occasion to trouble your Grace with another letter. I hope your Grace will be so good as to forward the removes in Colonel Hamilton's regiment, as soon as there is a Secretary of War settled.

I confess I am very sorry to hear that the publick service has made it necessary to give the bishoprick of Derry to Dr. Rundle,[2] because your Grace cannot but be sensible it will give a handle to some clamour here. But to be sure our affairs must give way to the more weighty concerns in England. I hope however the new Bishop will soon come, and settle amongst us.

There is a favour I have to ask of your Grace, which is that if, by procuring a resignation, I can make a vacancy in the entire rectories of Killorglin, Knockane, Killtallogh, Killgarrinlander, and the rectory of Currens, worth about 200l. per ann. in the present possession of Mr. Elias Debuts, in the diocese of Ardfert and Aghede, in the county of Kerry, all in the gift of the Crown, your Grace would be pleased to order Mr. George Palmer to be presented to the said rectories. Mr. Palmer is a clergyman of a very fair character in my diocese, and was born in that neighbourhood, or he

---

2   Notwithstanding what my Lord Primate mentions in this place, when he came to be personally acquainted with the Bishop, he entertained the highest esteem for him, and the good Bishop was by no means behind his Grace in his affection towards him. Dr. Rundle, as Mr. Pope says, had a heart; and he shewed it much to one of my Lord Primate's relations, when his Grace was deceased, and incapable of making him any return: this good man had been most abominably abused, and my Lord of London, the Primate's old friend, had given too much ear to that abuse, so that it may easily be imagined, that his Grace was prejudiced against the Bishop of Derry at the first; but my Lord Chancellor Talbot, who was perhaps not only the best, but also the most able and discerning person of his time, could never have recommended an improper person; and it was a pity that my Lord of London, who certainly meant well, had not taken the Chancellor's recommendation in that light. Dr. Rundle would undoubtedly have made as good a Bishop of Gloucester as he afterwards did a Bishop of Derry, where to his own honour, and to that of those who promoted him, he obtained the well merited applause of all good men.

would hardly have the courage to think of removing into Kerry. The granting this request will be esteemed an obligation by him, who is,

My Lord, &c.

To the same.

Dublin, Mar. 13, 1734/5.

My Lord,

I should have been glad if it had been thought most consistent with his Majesty's service to have bestowed the government of Derry on my Lord Cavan, because I fear we may have some occasion for his help in the House of Lords, except he is made some way easy, which I hope from what your Grace is pleased to say, will not be forgot, if an opportunity offers.

I have had the honour of your Grace's letter of the 20th past, and had answered it sooner but that I was willing to make the best enquiries I could relating to Dr. Whitcomb's affair, before I wrote to your Lordship. And I must beg leave to acquaint your Grace, that as far as I can learn, the apprehension of his holding the living of Louth creates much uneasiness, as it at present will stop a succession in the College, and may probably be used as a precedent for holding any the greatest preferment with a fellowship for the future; and if the dispensation be granted, is likely to raise so much clamour, that I cannot but think it most adviseable not to interpose his Majesty's authority in his favour at present: and I hope your Grace will have it in your power on some other occasion, to make him amends for this disappointment.

On Tuesday the Visitors cited the Provost, Fellows, &c. to a visitation of the College, to be held on the 20th instant. There have been such difficulties started from the College, and so much listened to by their Vice-Chancellor, the Bishop of Clogher,[3] that I fear the visitation will not prove such as will answer expectation. I have taken all opportunities of desiring the fellows and their friends to avoid all needless disputes and oppositions for fear of their falling into the hands of worse Visitors next session of parliament. I hope and wish the best, but things do not promise very well. I am,

Your Grace's, &c.

To the same.

Dublin, Mar. 14, 1734/5.

My Lord,

Since I wrote to your Grace yesterday, I have received a letter from Mr. Cary, expressing your Lordship's readiness to present Mr. George Palmer to

3   Dr. Stern.

the entire rectories of Killorglin, Knockane, Killtallogh, Killgarrinlander, and the rectory of Currens, now possessed by Mr. Elias Debuts, and in the gift of the Crown, upon Mr. Debuts resigning them. I most humbly thank your Grace for this favour; and I shall by to-morrow's post write to Mr. Debuts to resign them immediately: and if your Lordship please to signify your pleasure to the Lords Justices to present Mr. George Palmer to the said rectories, upon such resignation, I believe your Grace's order and the resignation will arrive at Dublin near the same time. I am,

My Lord, &c.

To the Bishop of London.

Dublin, Mar. 20, 1734/5.

My Lord,

I thank your Lordship for your kind and patient attendance on my Lord Doneraile's cause, I am glad things went so unanimously in the House. Mr. Horner, whom your Lordship mentions, is since dead at London. I esteemed him a very good man, and had removed him from another diocese into mine. If he had lived, your Lordship's good opinion of him would have been an addition to what I had before conceived of him.

Though the prints tell us that France seems to come into our plan of pacification, I can hardly believe a peace so near at hand.

I am glad to hear things go so well in parliament in the main. There is no doubt but the committee of elections will increase the majority: I hope as your Lordship does, that the strong opposition which has been made, will keep people in some reasonable bounds. It is to us here a melancholy consideration, that there seems to be so great a disposition to attack the most eminent persons in the Church; and to strip them all of their just rights. But I think the same spirit prevails against all governors alike, and indeed against every thing that is serious and orderly.

I am glad the Dissenters are disposed to be quiet this session; what may be the state of affairs another year, God only knows.

I find your House has pretty well got through the affair of the petition of the Scotch Lords, only we have not yet heard what is done upon the protest made in Scotland.

If your Lordship can find leisure, it will be very obliging if you would now and then send an account of what passes.

I am, &c.

To the Duke of Dorset.

Dublin, Apr. 8, 1735.

My Lord,

I thank your grace for your orders to present Mr. Palmer to Mr. Debuts's livings, upon his resignation, which I expect every day from Limerick. Your Lordship will be so good as to excuse my putting you in mind again of Dillon Wye's affair.

Mrs. Humphreys the housekeeper of the Castle and Chappel-Izzod has some time ago delivered in a memorial about rebuilding the gardener's house at Chappel-Izzod, which is so ruinous that Sir Edward Pearce (in whose time Carter the gardener applied either to have it repaired or rebuilt) and Mr. Dobbs[4] have both reported that they thought it not worth while to repair it, because there were those cracks in it, that they could not answer for its standing when repaired.

It is proposed making it a little better than it need have been, if the house-keeper did not design to live in it: but as by her patent she is to have lodgings there as well as in the Castle, it may not be thought amiss to be at a small expence more for her convenience than a meer gardener would have required.

There has been a scheme drawn of the intended building, and a calculation of the expence, which Mr. Dobbs's clerk assures us will not exceed the computation, which we shall speedily transmit to your Grace: for as the expence will amount to 280l. we are unwilling to do any thing in it without directions from your Grace. I should not have given you the trouble of this, but that Mrs. Humphreys is now in London, as well as Mr. Dobbs, who has seen the house, and knows the affair, so as to be able to inform your Grace fully of the matter; and Mr. Humphreys is afraid Mr. Dobbs may leave London before our letter can wait upon your Grace, as we shall not meet this week: I submit the whole affair to your Grace's pleasure, and am,

My Lord, &c.

To the Duke of Newcastle.

Dublin, Apr. 18, 1735.

My Lord,

The occasion of my troubling your Grace at present is, that we have this week learned that there is a bill brought into the House of Commons with a

4   Arthur Dobbs, Esqr who succeeded Sir Edward Lovet Pearse, Master of the King's Works, who was the Designer and Architect of that superb Structure the Parliament House in Dublin.

specious title, that it is apprehended here may be of great prejudice. The title of the bill is, A bill for securing the title of Protestants, &c.

On this occasion I must beg leave to observe to your Grace, that it must be dangerous to give way to passing bills originally in England relating to private property in Ireland, where the interest of England and his Majesty's service no ways calls for it, where the legislature are wholly unacquainted with the laws, and the reason of enacting them. And it can hardly be supposed, that such bills are not moved for with some private views, which the persons concerned in promoting such bills know would be immediately discovered here, but cannot easily be guessed at there.

And the time of bringing in this bill is the more suspicious, as it must needs be hurried through now towards the latter end of a session, before there is sufficient time, for those who are likely to suffer by it here to know that any thing is going on in parliament, that may affect their property, or having time to make a proper opposition to it. If this be often practised it must needs create great uncertainty in our property here, and give great and just cause of uneasiness without the least service to the Crown, or benefit to England.[5]

I have sent your Grace inclosed a copy of some particular remarks, by some of our ablest lawyers here, of the particular inconveniencies that will follow from it; but they are what only offer themselves at first view to them, having but just received a copy of the bill this week.

I must beg of your Grace that if this bill be not dropped in the House of Commons, it may be effectually opposed in the House of Lords, as it will overturn the property of many protestants here. I have heard of one this very afternoon that will be stripped of an estate of 2000 l. per ann. if this bill passes into a law.

I am, &c.

To the Bishop of London.

Dublin, May 20, 1735.

My Lord,

I am obliged to your Lordship for your late letter, and am glad that the best pieces against popery, written in King James's time, are designed to be reprinted. I think it is much better than what was intended here some years ago, to reprint all that was then published.

I shall very cheerfully promote subscriptions here, into which I think the Bishops will generally come, and several of the clergy, and some few of the College. I think I cannot fail of getting forty or fifty subscriptions, but little can be done in it till the parliament brings people to town in the winter. We

5   The Primate shews himself in this letter to be a true friend to Ireland, and to the proper distribution of justice to all parties.

are very much troubled with popery here, and the book cannot but be very useful, but we are not over-much given to buy or to read books.

I thank your Lordship for the assistance and encouragement you are pleased to give Mr. Hansard, in getting subscriptions for carrying on protestant working schools here: I am sure we can hardly hope to get any ground of the papists without them.

I am glad to hear from your Lordship that those attackers of all Church establishments, are less regarded than formerly. I am very sure if the notions every day printed about liberty, can get much ground among the people of England, things will not continue quiet many years.

The Persian Traveller is reprinted here, but I do not hear any great character of the performance, but scandal sells the best of any thing with us, as well as in England. We think that if the quarrel between Spain and Portugal goes on, England must be drawn in.

I find by yesterday's mail that your session is over: I heartily wish you may have the next session as easy. I am,

My Lord, &c.

To the Duke of Newcastle.

Dublin, Nov. 2, 1735

My Lord,

I humbly thank your Grace for the kind compliments you were pleased to make me by my Lord Lieutenant: I am truly sensible of your favourable regard at all times to any requests or representations I have had occasion to make from hence, and promise myself the continuance of your protection and countenance.

It was with a great deal of pleasure that I heard from his Grace your good dispositions in favour of Mr. Elte,[6] my chaplain: as the poor Bishop of Ossory died here last Saturday, there is now an opening for him on the bench of Bishops, and my Lord Lieutenant is so kind to him as to recommend him for successor to the late Bishop. I most heartily concur with the recommendation, and do assure your Grace that Mr. Elte is one heartily well affected to his Majesty and his family, and who has by his behaviour here gained a general love and esteem. I must beg your Lordship's kind concurrence and assistance in this recommendation, which will be owned as a new obligation laid on,

My Lord, &c.

6 Mr. Elte had been a Student of Christ Church in Oxford, and succeeded to the bishoprick as then recommended.

To the same.

Dublin, Dec. 27. 1735

My Lord,

In the last transmits of bills we have sent over one entitled, "An act for rendering more effectual an act to amend and explain an act to encourage the building of houses, and making other improvements on Church lands, and to prevent dilapidations."

As what is enacted in this act, and those referred to in it, is wholly different from any law in England, I must recommend it to your Grace's protection, that it may not be thrown out by the gentlemen of the law on your side, by reason of their not knowing the necessity and use of it here.

By the wars in this country in 1641 and 1688, most of the Bishop's palaces and the parsonage-houses were destroyed; and as it was found that people were unable or unwilling to rebuild them, where the whole expence was to light on the builder, there was an act passed in the 10th of King William, to encourage the rebuilding of houses, and making other improvements on Church lands, in which the encouragement was to divide the expence or loss equally among three successive incumbents, so that the builder or his executors should recover two thirds of his expences of his next and immediate successor, and that successor one third of the original expence of his immediate successor, and so the affair stopped.

As this encouragement had not much of the desired effect, and few parsonage-houses had been then built, farther encouragement was given by a new act passed the 12th of George I, by which the loss was divided among four successive incumbents, and the builder or his executors, &c. Were to receive three-fourths of the original expense of his immediate successor; and such successor two-fourths of his successor; and such successor one-fourth from his successor; and there the affair stopped.

In thus distributing the expense this bill makes no change, but endeavours the better to secure to the builder or his successors, such money as they were by that act designed to be reimbursed. Now by the former act, the builder or other person entitled to a payment from the successor, had no remedy but against his immediate successor, nor could that next successor sue his successor, except he had entirely paid his successor; so that whenever the successor proved insolvent, the builder, &c. lost all the money he or his executors were not paid. By this act the builder, &c. may come upon the second successor for what was unpaid by the first, so that it do not exceed what the first successor could have demanded of him, if he had made his entire payment to the builder, &c. and if the successor to the builder had paid more than he was to lose, he is allowed likewise to sue the second successor for what he had paid more than he was to lose. And because it sometimes happens that an incumbent dies before he has received so much of the profits of his living as may at all assist him to pay his successor, this act enacts, That no incumbent shall be deemed a next successor for the purpose of paying to his predecessors, for any buildings or improvements made in virtue of those acts, who was not before his death or removal, entitled to a year's profits of the benefice, but that the first person so entitled, shall for this purpose only, be reckoned the next successor.

There is then a clause to make the act of a piece, that as it cannot be seen till the end of a year, who is the next successor as to payments, it allows even in case of the death of the builder, &c. which was not allowed before, a year for the payment of half what was due, and the rest to be paid the year following in two half yearly payments.

The next clause relates to an omission that may have been made in the Bishop's certificate settling what was bona fide laid out, of an account of the clear yearly value of the benefice on which the building or improvement was made, and allows the time of two years to rectify such omissions by an additional certificate, containing an account of the clear yearly value of the benefice.

There is another clause that enacts, that though all account of the intended building had not been given in to the Bishop three months before it was actually begun, yet this omission shall not invalidate any certificate and for the future enacts only a fortnight as necessary to deliver in an account of the intended building.

There is another clause for security's sake, and to cut off subterfuges for not building; which enacts, that bishopricks that have usually gone together, shall be reckoned but as one preferment for the purpose of settling the two years income, beyond which no person by the 12th of George I. can certify for any building or improvement on Church-lands.

As these several things were settled by the unanimous consent of the Bishops in town before the bill was brought into the House of Lords, as necessary to encourage the building on Church-lands, I must beg of your Grace that the bill may be returned without any alteration that may defeat the intention of any of the clauses. I am,

My Lord &c.

Boulter to Newcastle.

Jan. 19, 1735/6.
(NA. SP. 63/399/5–6)[7]

My Lord,

In several parts of this Kingdom the parishes are very large, and run to a great length without a proportionable breadth, so that it is found convenient to divide many parishes, and to erect new ones out of parts, it may be, of 2 or 3 old parishes, and to this purpose we have an Act for real Union and Division of parishes. But upon going to put that bill in execution by erecting a new parish out of part of 3 parishes, a difficulty was started, whether, where any such parish is erected, there could be any presentation to such new parish, till all the several parts of which such parish is constituted were void, and it appeared most probable that there could be no presentation. The effect of which would be, that though such a new parish could be erected, yet it might require a course of many years, before any incumbent could be put in possession of such new parish. As this is a great discouragement to the erecting new parishes, how much soever they may be wanted for promoting the service of God we have past here a Bill for explaining an Act for real Union and Division of parishes. Which is wholly designed to enable patrons, where new parishes have been enacted, out of parts of old parishes, to present upon any one part becoming vacant, and the Bill directs how such Clerk is to be inducted etc. still saving to the surviving incumbents of the other old parishes all the rights and profits they enjoyed before, during their respective incumbencies.

And as no Union or division can be made without the consent of the patrons, and it has been found that the consent of his Majesty on such occasions, where he is patron, either under his sign manual or the great seal, is both troublesome and chargeable to get, and till a new parish can be presented to, which cannot be done till after an Union already made takes place, there is no person to be at that trouble and expence. By this Act, the Lord Lieutenant, chief governor or governors for the time being are empowered to consent for his Majesty, who can be no loser by such Union or division, because the patronage continues, after every Union or division, where it was before.

As this Act will be of great service in this country, where more churches and parochial ministers are very much wanted to make the better stand against popery, if the Bill should meet with any difficulty, which I can hardly apprehend it will, I must desire your Grace's favour and protection that it may be returned to us.

---

7   The original Boulter Letters contains an abbreviated version of this letter dated 20 January.

I am, with the greatest truth and respect,
My Lord,
your Grace's,
most humble and most obedient servant,
Hu. Armagh.

Newcastle to Boulter.

Whitehall, Feb. 5, 1735/6.
(NA. SP 63/399/21)

My Lord,
This letter will be delivered to Your Grace by Messrs. Ioncour, two brothers, of the principal family at St. Quintin in France, concerned in the linen manufacture there. They are Protestants, and go with a design, if they meet with proper encouragement, to settle themselves in Ireland, not only with a view, of teaching the Irish to whiten their linen to the greatest perfection, but also of improving the growth of flax in that country. As your Grace will see at large, by the enclosed memorial, which Messrs. Ioncour have put into my hands, and of which I have transmitted a copy to the Lord Lieutenant of Ireland,[8] with his Majesty's directions to His Grace, to give them all manner of support, and encouragement in the prosecution of an undertaking which may prove so beneficial to his Majesty's subjects, in Great Britain, and Ireland.

Your Grace will so easily be convinced of the usefulness of this design, that I am persuaded, I need say very little to engage you to give these gentlemen your countenance and protection upon this occasion.
I am, etc.
Holles Newcastle

To the Bishop of London.

Dublin, Feb. 9, 1735/6.

My Lord,
The bearer is the Rev. Mr. Cox, one of a very good family here, and of a fair character. He goes over to England to oppose the reversing of the Lord Clancarty's attainder, if any such thing should be attempted this session: he is in possession of 400 l. per ann. part of the Clancarty estate, which his father bought under the faith of two English acts of parliament, the Irish trustee act, and a particular act obtained by the Hollow-Sword-Blade

8 For this copy of the memorial see NA SP. 63/399/25.

Company, who had bought great estates here of the trustees, to make good the titles of those who purchased under them. He will be best able to give your Lordship an account of these several acts. But as not only he, but great numbers of protestant purchasers, who have improved the Clancarty estate to near 60,000l. per ann. think they may be affected by such a reversal, I need not tell your Lordship what a ferment the discourse of it has occasioned in those parts where the estate lies. But I must farther add, that as probably two-thirds of the estates of protestants here were popish forfeitures origi-nally, the uneasiness is universal; since they think if the attainder of any family be reversed now, another family may at another time obtain the same favour, and another at another season, so that no possessor of such forfeited estate can tell how long he or his may continue in the quiet enjoyment of what they have bought under the faith of English acts of parliament, and on the improvement of which they have laid out their substance. The House of Commons here have represented their sense of this matter to his Majesty, as the House of Lords did two or three sessions ago, to which they then received a most gracious answer, which was the reason they did not address now.

As a step of this nature would give great uneasiness to his Majesty's protestant subjects here, I desire your Lordship would, where you shall judge it proper, represent the importance of the case.

I have wrote a letter on this subject to his Grace the Duke of Newcastle, and sent it by the same hand.

I am, my Lord, &c.

To the Duke of Newcastle.

Dublin, Feb. 10, 1735/6.

My Lord,

The bearer is the Rev. Mr. Cox,[9] one of a very good family here, and of a good character.The occasion of his going to England now is, the appre-hension he is under of the attainder of the late Lord Clancarty being reversed. He is in possession of about 400l. per ann. bought by his father from the Hollow-Sword-Blade Company, who had bought great estates here of the Irish trustees, which they afterwards sold, and obtained a particular act in England to secure the titles of those who purchased under them; so that his title is under the faith of two English acts of parliament, the Irish trustee act, and the act obtained by the Hollow-Sword-Blade Company.

But the purchasers under either or both acts are very much alarmed here at the talk of the Lord Clancarty's attainder being reversed; since they do not

9   The present Archbishop of Cashel, formerly of Christ Church, Oxford.

know how far it may affect their titles, who are thought to possess amongst them to the value of 60,000l. per ann. as they have improved their estates. Nor are they the only people alarmed here, but all that are the purchasers of forfeited estates, apprehend that if one attainder is reversed, other forfeiting families may from time to time, obtain the like favour, which may affect above half the estates now enjoyed by protestants. The House of Commons have made an address on this occasion to his Majesty, and the like about two sessions ago was made by the House of Lords, which they did not repeat now, because his Majesty then gave them a very gracious answer, and nothing has been since done of that nature.

I can assure your Lordship any thing of this nature will be a great blow to the protestant interest here, and will very much shake the security protestants think they now have of the enjoyment of their estates under his Majesty and his Royal family. As for either the general case, or his case in particular, Mr. Cox will be able fully to inform your Lordship: and I think the affair of the last importance to the protestant interest here, which makes me take the liberty to lay the case before you.

I am, &c.

To the Bishop of London.

Dublin, May 18, 1736.

My Lord,

The clergy here have been attacked in a violent manner, in relation to tythe of agiftment, and associations over a great part of Ireland have been entered into against paying it. We intended to have applied to your Lordship and our other friends in England for proper help on this occasion; but to our great surprise we find the clergy of England, and the Bishops in particular, in a worse state than we are yet come to. I am sorry they have been so ill supported by those from whom they might so justly expect help, and whose interest it was to have given it them.

But I cannot help thinking that one great occasion of this rancour against the clergy, is the growth of atheism, profaneness, and immorality. God in his good time put a stop to it.

I see very little more to be done by us, than endeavouring to discharge our several duties consistently, and recommending ourselves and the cause of religion, to the divine protection.

I am sorry to hear your Lordship has had so great a share in what abuses have passed on the Bishops. I have, I think, disposed of most of the receipts your Lordship sent, me for the subscriptions, and received most of the money: as soon as I can settle those accounts with one or two that have undertaken to dispose of some of the receipts, I will send your Lordship an account of it, with the persons who are to be called on for the second payment, and shall be ready to pay the money received.

I am, my Lord, &c.

P.S. My Lord Lieutenant embarked yesterday for England.

To Sir Robert Walpole.

Dublin, May 25, 1736.

Sir,

My Lord Lieutenant takes over with him an application from the government and council here for lowering the gold made current here, by proclamation, and raising the foreign silver.

My Lord Carteret has formerly talked with you about the distress we were then under for want of silver, and some steps were then taken to lay that evil and the remedy before his Majesty; but the opposition then made by the bankers, and the change of the Lord Lieutenant, was the occasion of the design dropping at that time. But as the evil has since increased, and has been by some of the best understanding and most disinterested persons fully laid before my Lord Duke of Dorset, he has been so kind as to join with the privy council here, in a representation of our deplorable case for want of silver, and what we apprehend to be the proper remedies for our present calamity.

It is certain that silver is so scarce with us, that the lowest price usually paid for 20s. in silver, is 4d. premium; but it is more commonly in the north (which is the seat of our linen manufacture) 6d. and 7d. in the pound. And the occasion of this want of silver is, that our several species of gold made current here by proclamation, pass for more silver here than they do in England, e.g. a guinea passes here where an English shilling goes for 13d. at 23s. Irish, or 21s. English and 3d.

A moidore, which is worth about 27s. in England, passes here for 30s. Irish, or 27s. English, and 9d. and the rest of our gold is in the main proportion to the value of the moidore. And whilst this is our case, no man in trade will carry a moidore from hence, to instance in one piece of gold, if he can get silver, when he loses 9d. by the moidore as soon as he lands at Chester; nor will he bring from Chester 27s. English, when he can gain 9d. by bringing a moidore.

And to express this in greater numbers; if a merchant brings with him 100l. from London; if he brings it over in English silver, that will be 108l. 6s. 8d. here, which arises from the shilling passing here for 13d. but still that is the same money under another name: if he brings it in guineas, he will put them off at 109l. 10s. 4d. Irish, if in moidores or other Portugal gold, he will put it off at 111l. 2s. 2d. So that by bringing over what is only 100l. in England, in guineas he will gain 1l. 3s. 8d. and by bringing it over in moidores, &c. he will gain 2l. 15s. 6d. and on the contrary by taking over guineas to pay 100l. English on the other side of the water, he will lose 1l. 3s. 8d. and by taking over moidores, &c. to pay 100l. there, he will lose 2l. 15s. 6d. And as the merchant in all his importations and exportations will mind his gain, the effect of this is, that no trader will take gold out of his country if he can help it, but silver; nor moidores, &c. if he can get guineas.

So that in our present state our silver daily decreases, and the gold grows upon us. And the distress the want of silver must occasion to our manufacturers, labourers, small retailers, and all the lesser transactions of trade and business, I need not expatiate upon.

But this is not our only calamity, but unfortunately the value of the new species of Portugal gold has been so settled here, that there is 2d. profit in bringing over a 4l. piece, as we call the larger pieces of Portugal gold, rather than two 40s. pieces, and 2d. profit in bringing over a 40s. piece, rather than two 20s. pieces; and so on with respect of the silver pieces of that species; besides which, as the least want of weight in the foreign pieces of gold, or even their not turning the scale, carries an abatement of 2d. a piece, there may be a loss of 2d. on every lesser piece on that account, and consequently so much greater as the number of smaller pieces is to make up a greater of the same value, e.g. upon eight, 10s. pieces, there may be a loss of eight 2d. if the 4l. pieces do not turn the scale: so that it is to the profit of the merchant to import the larger pieces of gold rather than the smaller; and they have gone on in using this advantage, till half the money we have at least is in 4l. pieces, which are of no service at the market, and in all lesser transactions of trade; and the next species with us is the 40s. piece; and to be sure above three quarters of our money is in those two species, and without some remedy we shall in two or three years have scarce any money but 4l. pieces.

And there is another inconvenience that follows from our scarcity of silver, that we suffer from 2 to 2½ per cent. in the exchange, and are really paid so much less in the price of what we sell to foreign merchants, and lose so much in paying for what goods we buy from abroad.

And it is certain that all the noblemen and gentlemen of this country, who live in England, lose from 2 to 2½ per cent. in the remittances of their money to England, which is used as a popular argument against the proposed reduction, that the absentees will get so much per cent. by it; whilst they will not consider that the nation at present loses five times as much in the export and imports of goods, and the absentees will gain by this reduction of the exchange.

Now the remedy we propose in our representation to his Majesty, is a very easy and obvious one, that we may have leave to reduce our gold, to go for as much English silver as it is worth, in proportion to the guinea going for 21s. English; and accordingly we have calculated what we reckon the several species of gold ought to go for, according to their weight and fineness, in Irish money valuing an English shilling at 13d. Irish; and to get rid as much as we can of the larger pieces of foreign gold, we have set the lesser pieces about a penny a piece above their value in respect of the larger piece above them. And this reduction of the gold is the more reasonable, because gold has in effect reduced itself the 6d. in the pound we propose in our scheme, since 6d. is about the middle price that is paid to get 20s. in silver.

There is no doubt but it would be absolutely right when we are reducing, to reduce the English shilling to 12d. which it went for here before the recoining of the silver in King William's time; but as the shilling is in effect the measure of all payments, and as the English shilling has gone so long for 13d. we think that cannot be done without an act of parliament to settle an answerable reduction in the rents and debts.

Our bankers and remitters here continue to make great opposition to this reduction, since our present inequality of gold and silver is an article of great profit to those through whose hands all the money of this nation passes; and we make no doubt but they will, by their partners and correspondents in England, make what opposition they can to the scheme proposed by the council, and we apprehend they may think it worth their while to advance money, if they can find persons to take it among the number thro' whose hands this affair must pass, to obstruct it; and that many merchants who deal in Ireland will join with them, to keep up the advantage they have by the exchange being always from 2 to 2½ per cent. against us.

But as we are almost on the brink of ruin, by the present unhappy state of our money, and as by the farther want of silver, and the increase of our larger pieces of gold, our linen manufacture must soon decay, and our inland trade be at a stand; I most earnestly beg of you to give us your utmost assistance on this occasion to have our gold reduced, and put us in a possibility of carrying on our trade and manufactures, by having a tolerable proportion of silver, without which we must soon be a ruined nation.

I have now explained our reasons and views in the scheme we proposed for reducing gold, but if we have been any ways mistaken in our calculations, those errors will be easily corrected by the abler hands this affair must pass through in England.

In relation to the other branch of our scheme, about raising the price of foreign silver, I believe there will be great room for amendment. It was a scheme more come into to gratify the bankers and merchant remitters, who clamoured for it, and by what I can learn, they have misinformed us about the price of foreign bullion, which they affirmed to be 5s. 4½d. English per ounce; whereas I have been since told it has not been above 5s. 3d. per ounce for two years past; but this will be before those who know how the fact is.

The great thing we want is, the reduction of our gold, which I beg we may obtain leave to do by your powerful intervention.

The importance of the affair to this nation, and your goodness, will I hope, excuse the length of this letter.[10] I am,

My Lord, &c.

To Lord Anglesea.

Dublin, May 27, 1736.

My Lord,

The knowledge your Lordship has of the want of silver in this country for some years, the causes of it, and the attempts made to remedy the evil in my Lord Carteret's time, your Lordship is so well acquainted with, that I need not repeat them; all that I need inform your Lordship of is, that the evil has gone increasing as it could not but do, but with one unhappy circumstance that was not apprehended when I talked with your Lordship on that subject, which is, that one half of our money here at least, is in 4l. pieces, some think three quarters; but by the best accounts I think there can be little less than three quarters in them and 40s. pieces, so that the bulk of our money is useless at markets, and for paying all the manufacturers; 4d. is the lowest price that is paid for 20s. silver, and very often 2s. 8d. and 2s.10d. is given for changing a 4l. piece into all silver.

The occasion of our money running into the larger pieces is, that as the not turning the scale loses 2d. in the piece, that loss is but single upon a larger, but is repeated in the number of lesser pieces that make up the same value, e.g. it can be but 2d. on 4l. but it may be 8d. on four 20s. and 16d. on eight 10s. pieces. We have lessened this loss in our scheme by proposing to make use of the half quarter, and allowing 1d. for that, so that where the loss used to be 2d. for not turning the scale, it will be but 1d. for the future.

And besides, our new species of Portugal gold has been so unhappily settled, that there is 2d. profit by bringing over a 4l. piece, rather than two 40s. pieces, and so on in that line; so that if some remedy be not applied, in two or three years more we shall scarce have any species but 40s. pieces.

This has been so effectually represented to my Lord Lieutenant, that he has joined with the council in a representation to his Majesty of our calamity,

---

10 This letter in some time produced the desired effect, which was looked upon by the Lord Primate and his friends, as the most useful, and therefore the most important transaction of his life. It is scare conceivable, considering the clearness of the case, what a bitter opposition was made by Dean Swift and others; and how poorly the Primate was assisted, nay he was even opposed by some who ought to have been his supporters from reason, from interest, and from the duty they owed to their country, and to government. London edition.

and the remedy we desire to be applied to it: which is setting the foreign gold at the proportional value that the guinea has to the shilling in England, agreeably to the scheme formerly intended in the council, only that to obviate an inconvenience not observed before, we propose giving about a penny advantage to every lower piece of gold, in respect to the piece immediately above it.

The bankers and remitters have raised the same clamour as formerly against it, and the most popular plea against it is, that this reduction of the gold will fall the exchange at least 2 per cent. which will turn to the advantage of the absentees. I have endeavoured to satisfy them that if the absentees get 2 per cent, by this reduction, the nation will get 2 per cent. in all their exports and imports, which will be four or five times as much as the absentees will gain by this reduction: but all arguments are nothing against the prepossessions of the bankers.

As I know your Lordship's concern for the good of this kingdom, and your sense of our distress and the proper remedy, I thought proper to acquaint your Lordship in what posture this affair stands, that as we have got the matter on the other side of the water, whither I could never get it before, your Lordship may be pleased to solicit our having orders for issuing a proclamation to reduce gold, &c. I am but little solicitous about the raising of foreign silver, and am rather apprehensive of the bankers having misrepresented things to us, in affirming silver bullion sells usually at 5s. 4½d. English; whereas several tell me it has not for two years past sold for 5s. 3d. And if silver bullion is over-rated here, the bankers will in time carry our gold out, and we shall be over-run with foreign silver; but that will be a much less evil than what we labour under at present, but what has been the price of silver bullion in England for some time can easily be known there. I take the liberty to recommend this affair of our coin to your Lordship, as of the utmost consequence to this kingdom.

I am, my Lord, &c.

Newcastle to Boulter.

Whitehall, May 29, 1736.
(NA. SP 63/399/104)

My Lord,

M. Dillon by whom you will receive this letter, being called to Ireland by his private affairs, M. Chavigny, the French Minister here, has desired me to recommend him to the Lords Justices of Ireland, as you will see by the enclosed note which M. Chavigny gave me.[11] M. Dillon during his stay in

---

11 For enclosed note (in French) see NA. SP. 63/399/106

England, has, by his behaviour, acquired the regard and esteem of all those that have been acquainted with him. I therefore take the liberty to beg that Your Grace will favour him with your good offices upon any proper occasions during his stay in Ireland, by which you will very particularly oblige

My Lord
Your Grace's
Most Obedient
Servant

To the Duke of Newcastle.

Dublin, May 31, 1736.

My Lord,

His Grace the Lord Lieutenant has taken over with him a representation to his Majesty from the government and privy council here, giving an account of the deplorable condition we of this kingdom are in through the want of silver, and the method we apprehend will relieve us; which is, the lowering of gold to pass here for what it is worth in England, at the rate of 21s. English, or 1l. 2s. 9d. Irish, where a shilling passes for 13d. for as gold is over-rated with us at present, whoever brings over foreign gold hither, gets 2½ per cent. and whoever carries out gold from hence, loses 2½ per cent. and whilst this is our case, we must every day grow worse: and indeed by some particular advantages attending the 4l. pieces of Portugal gold, above half our money is run into those pieces, and in a little time we shall hardly have any other money. If we continue in this case, our linen manufacture must decline, and our inland trade every day sink.

It already costs from 4d. to 8d. or 9d. in the pound to get silver, so that what we desire to reduce gold to by proclamation, is in reality already done.

I shall not run through the particulars, because they are sufficiently explained in our memorial, and the remedies. But I must beg your Grace to help us to have orders for the proclamation, or we must be a ruined people soon. I am,

My Lord. &c.

To the Duke of Dorset.

Dublin, June 1, 1736.

My Lord,

I thought it my duty to acquaint your Lordship that it is supposed Mr. Harrison the commissioner is past recovery: how far it may be proper, if he dies, to send over some Englishman that understands business, and has spirit enough not to be too much over-awed here, I leave to your Grace's consideration.

I am, my Lord, &c.

To Sir Robert Walpole.

Dublin, June 4, 1736.

Sir,

I take the liberty on occasion of the death of Mr. Harrison, to represent to you the absolute necessity there is, if a successor to him be sent from England, to send one that has a good skill in the affairs of the revenue, and that is a man of application and courage; the more weight he is of in himself the better.

If one be appointed to succeed him that fails either in skill or diligence, the revenue, which is at present rather in a declining condition, will most certainly fall still more, and this will draw on a deficiency in the provision made for the establishment here: and increase our debts, which cannot but make every following session of parliament more uneasy. You will be so good as to forgive the freedom I take. I am,

Sir, your humble servant, &c.

To the Duke of Dorset.

Dublin, June 4, 1736.

My Lord,

I am very glad to hear of your Grace's safe arrival at London, but could have wished his Majesty had staid a little longer, that the affair of our coin might have been put in some method before his departure; but I hope the same thing may be done under her Majesty. My Lord Granard gives me great hopes from the discourse he had with some of the great men, that if the affair be pushed it will certainly be granted. I am afraid the bankers have over-reached us in the value of foreign silver: I shall trouble your Grace with a particular letter on that subject before I go on my visitation, which will be in about ten days.

Mr. Harrison died yesterday, and the only person that has applied to us to succeed him is Dr. Trotter,[12] whom I think the fittest man in this kingdom for that post; but as I take it for granted some person will be sent from England for that employment, I beg your Grace would be pleased to represent the necessity that the person they send be one well versed in the business, and a

12 Thomas Trotter, Esq, a Civilian, Vicar-General of the Diocese of Dublin, and
   Member of Parliament.

man of probity, courage, and application: if they send us a weak or indolent man, the revenue here will certainly fall, and your Lordship knows better then any body the trouble a Lord Lieutenant has with a parliament upon the increase of our debts.

I am, my Lord, &c.

To the Duke of Dorset.

Dublin, June 10, 1736.

My Lord,

Before your Grace left this kingdom, I acquainted your Lordship that I feared the bankers had misinformed the council about what was the middle price of bullion in England, which they affirmed was 5s. 4½d. English per ounce; but I am since assured that for two or three years past, it has hardly reached 5s. 2½d. per ounce; and if this be the case, I must beg leave to desire that the reduction of the gold may go on without any alteration of the present proclamation price of foreign silver, or that at the highest it may not be set higher than at 5s. 2½d. per ounce, or 5s. 3d. English at most.

To state this matter in a tolerable light, I must observe, that the reason of thinking at all of raising the price of foreign silver was, that by setting it at a price that might make it worth while to utter it as money here, we might have some of it as it was brought in, circulate here as money; whereas whilst the proclamation price is less than the bullion price, it will still be carried into England or Holland as a commodity: and if 5s. 4½d. were that price, though it was sometimes as low as 5s. 3d. yet if at other times it sold for 5s. 6d. there was no fear of our being over-run by it, for though it might be imported here at 5s. 4½d. English as long as it bore a less price at other markets, yet when the price came to 5s. 5d. or more, our bankers would pick it up, and send it where it bore a better price than that given by proclamation.

But if things are so altered that in England it seldom is above 5s. 2½d. and or at most 5s. 3d. English per ounce, there will always be a gain of three half-pence for carrying it to England, and often a 2d. per ounce: the effect of which will be that the bankers will change all our gold when reduced into foreign silver; for in that case by buying up foreign silver at 5s. 3d. with gold from hence they will gain 2l. 7s. and near 2d. per cent. If they can buy it at 5s. 2½d. they will make 3l. 4s. per cent. profit, and this is gain enough to carry out all our gold, and furnish us with only foreign silver. This evil indeed will not be so detrimental to our trade and all the lesser transactions of life, as our present case is, but is an inconvenience worth our guarding against.

Your Grace knows the original intention here was only lowering the gold, but that as some of their petitions against that pressed for raising foreign silver, it was thought it could do no hurt to gratify them in that point, if it was set at the middle market price in England; but in that the merchants here have deceived us, representing it at 5s. 4½d. English, when it is really but 5s. 3d. at highest.

I have with this sent your Grace two calculations of the several pieces of silver mentioned in the memorial sent by the council, one upon the bottom of an ounce of silver passing for 5s. 2½d. English, or 5s. 7d. Irish; the other at 5s. 3d. English, or 5s. 8¼d. Irish.

In the memorial the Maximilian, Leopold, Holland, Bear, Cross, Danish and Lion dollar, are left at the old proclamation price, because as they are below standard, they are more liable to be counterfeited, and therefore the council did not like to give any encouragement to their importation.

If any thing is done about raising the price of foreign silver, I would hope it may not be set above 5s. 3d. English, at the highest; but I think it would be better if it were left at the present proclamation price: but if we are not permitted to reduce our gold, we shall soon have none but great pieces of gold, which are entirely useless in all lesser commerce.

I am, your Grace's, &c.

To the same.

Dublin, July 31, 1736.

My Lord,

I have been often thinking that Mr. Gardiner would be a very useful person in the privy council here, but I questioned whether any in his station had ever been of that body; but as I now understand that Sir William Robinson,[13] who was in the same station, was at the same time a privy councellor, that difficulty is removed: and as we now hardly know when the government is secure of a question, I apprehend it would be for his Majesty's service, if he were made a privy councellor. As Mr. Tighe is dead, this would not increase the number of the council, and I think he stands upon a bottom that few others could plead for being admitted to the council. But I submit all to your Grace's better consideration, and am,

My Lord, &c.

To the same.

Dublin, Aug. 3, 1736.

My Lord,

I am very glad to hear from your Grace that our affair of reducing the gold is likely to go on, which I hope will be done very speedily, since Sir Robert

13 Deputy Vice-Treasurer.

Walpole, according to the prints, is returned to London, and that the affair of the rate foreign silver ought to be set at, will at the same time be taken into consideration. I understand by my wife's[14] brother, who has been here to see me, that for six or seven years foreign silver has seldom risen to 5s. 3d. per ounce in London.

I must beg of your Lordship to press this affair to the utmost: at the same time I must likewise beg of your Grace to give Mr. Gardiner leave to go on with the copper coinage, which wants no reference, and only a compliment to be made to her Majesty[15] for leave to go on with what has been already granted. I can assure your Lordship the distress in the north for want of silver and copper, is inconceivable, people for want of better small money, taking pieces of copper not worth a half-penny, and promissory notes on cards for 3d. or 4d. that are issued to the value of some hundred pounds, by persons worth nothing, and that will certainly run away when they are called upon to change them.

Sir Marmaduke Wyvil[16] brought me a recommendation from your Grace, on which account I will shew him all the respect I can.

Since we wrote to your Lordship about the death of Mr. Vesey, my Lord Cavan has wrote to the Lords Justices singly about succeeding to the Hospital, and is willing to quit his pension of 400l. per ann, for it, which will be a saving to the nation. I have nothing new to add to what I formerly wrote to your Grace on the like occasion.

Colonel Tichbourn has likewise desired the same post, by which the government of Charlemont fort would be vacant. I am,
My Lord, &c.

To the same.

Dublin, Aug. 28, 1736.

My Lord,

I have had the honour of your Grace's of the 15th instant, and am glad to hear our representation is gone to the Treasury, though at present it cannot be hoped it can be very much expedited; but I would beg of your Grace to direct Mr. Cary[17] to forward it as much as may be.

As Mr. Gardiner has your Grace's leave to proceed in the affair of the copper, I believe he will make what dispatch he can, for our want of it is very great.

14 Mr. Savage, an eminent Merchant in London.
15 Queen Caroline, Consort of George II.
16 Deputy Post-Master General in Ireland.
17 Secretary to the Duke of Dorset, then Lord Lieutenant of Ireland.

As to his being admitted of the privy council, I am glad your Grace thinks the same of his usefulness there as I do, and I hope your Lordship will find a way to let him in, and yet keep the door shut against the numbers that have asked for that favour; and in that view I must acquaint your Grace, that by the deaths of Mr. Parry,[18] Mr. Tighe[19] and Sir T. Taylour,[20] who were always at hand to make a number at the council, we are now hardly able to get a council, especially when the Chief Judges are on their circuits, so that there will be a necessity of making two or three privy councellors that always live at Dublin.

I am sensible of your Grace's constant regard to the low circumstances of this kingdom, and do not doubt but what additions are ordered to the powder magazine, were thought necessary upon advising with the proper officers. And as for any thoughts of a citadel, the barrack with the regiments quartered there, without any offence or grumbling, is another sort of a citadel than this can ever be represented to be. I hope I shall manage it so, as that your Grace may hear no more of that affair.

I am, my Lord, &c.

To the Duke of Newcastle.

Dublin, Sep. 28, 1736.

My Lord,

Mr. Dillon has brought me the favour of your Grace's. I am glad to hear he has behaved himself so much to the satisfaction of all who knew him in England; and doubt not but his behaviour here will be answerable: and as your Lordship is pleased to recommend him, I shall most readily favour him with my good offices on all proper occasions. I am with the greatest truth and respect.

My Lord, &c.

To the Duke of Dorset.

Dublin, Nov. 11, 1736.

My Lord,

Since I had the honour of your Grace's last commands, the building of the magazine has not been stopped for want of money. But of late one of the arches has fallen in, which they are endeavouring, as I hear, to repair, so that

18 Publick Register of deeds and wills. He was a Welshman.
19 Right Honourable Richard Tighe.
20 Sir Thomas Taylour, Bart.

what was intended to be finished against the winter, will yet take up some time.

I must again renew my request that the affair of our coin may be forwarded as much as possible, that it may be over before his Majesty's return, when greater affairs will call for the attendance of the ministry and council. I understand our representation is referred to the officers of the mint, and that they have a copy of the letter I troubled your Lordship with on that subject, but that Mr. Conduit is doubtful whether they can take any notice of it, because it is not referred to them. I rather think that in their report no particular notice need be taken of it; but if they will have such regard as they shall think proper to what is there suggested, it is all that can be desired, since it may be taken very ill here, if the report of the officers of the mint, which has usually been sent hither with his Majesty's commands on such occasions, it shall appear that a particular member of the council made a different representation from that of the board, though it should be founded on our having been deceived in our former accounts of the value of silver bullion.

Every thing here is very quiet, but the Lords Justices have a troublesome business to come on, that of appointing sheriffs. I am,

My Lord, &c.

To Mr. Walter Cary.

Dublin, Nov. 11, 1736.

Sir,

I am very glad to hear our copper coin is at last set a going, but at the same time I find it is likely to proceed so slowly, that it will drive us to great extremities in the mean time, as the currency of all raps, if not of other true half-pence will be stopped by it. To prevent the latter, we have indeed orders to order the taking the old patent half-pence in the revenue; which I think will keep them current, and accordingly as soon as the new half-pence are upon arriving, we shall give orders accordingly. But still, if the copper company could supply a greater quantity than one tun per week, and the mint could coin them, it would be better for us. I shall write to Mr. Bowes about the former, and if the company can perform their part, I must desire you to prevail on the mint to do theirs. I could heartily wish that 50 tuns at least were coined some time before the parliament met, if a second fifty were not then going on, though I should be more glad of the latter: and indeed I am fully satisfied, that less than 150 or 200 tuns will not make things easy here, and that it is of great consequence to have them with all possible dispatch.

The Sollicitor-general gave me a copy of a letter from Mr. Conduit, relating to our gold and silver coins; on which I would beg leave to make the following remarks.

1. If there be no objection to that part which relates to the reduction of gold, I wish they would report that clearly.

2. As to my letter, I do not apprehend there is any occasion to take notice of it in their report, and it is only to put them in mind that we in our representation went upon a supposition that silver bore such a price, which afterwards I learned was greater than it really bore; and indeed in our representation, we mention that we suppose silver to bear such a rate, but at the mint they could not but know it was the true middle price of it.

3. That though 5s. 4½d. may be the middle price of silver in bars, yet if foreign silver coin has for some years sold but for 5s. 2d. to 5s. 3½d. per ounce, that ought to regulate the price intended to be given to the value of foreign coins here, because it is their value, and not that of silver in bars which is to be settled.

4. That the settling such a price on old pieces of eight, and another on new, will produce confusion here, where the ordinary people will not soon learn the difference betwixt the one and the other.

5. That I am sensible the value of the Mexico piece and the French crown in the old proclamations, is less than they will sell for as a commodity, that value having been fixed by the advice, as I have reason to believe, of the bankers, on the bottom of the English silver coin, at the rate of 5s. 2d. English per ounce, the effect of which has been, that by getting the gold raised, they are all carried out of the kingdom.

6. As to the weight of the Mexico, Seville, and Pillar pieces of eight, and of the Portugal gold, we have set them at the weight the generality of those had that came amongst us; and as the weight of those pieces both of silver and gold is reckoned higher in England than we have fixed them at in our proclamations, it is plain we have set each piece at a higher value than it bears in England.

7. In distinguishing the Pillar and Peru pieces of eight, we follow the former proclamations.

8. As to the Maximilian, Leopold, &c. dollars, or ducatoons of Spain, they may well enough be omitted, if they are scarce in England, for they are all vanished from hence.

9. I am sensible it is a disadvantage to have foreign coins current as money by weight, but absolute ruin to have them current by tale; and therefore could wish we had as little of them as may be.

In our case, foreign gold is necessary, but I would gladly prevent foreign silver from being set at such a price as to make it worth our bankers while to exchange our gold for foreign silver, by raising it, as they have already changed all our silver for gold, by raising that.

As for the affair of a coinage of silver at the tower, for the use of this country, it is what will require mature consideration, and is more than I shall pretend to speak to on so short a warning.

As you know our present distress for want of change, I must beg of you to press the reduction of our gold, if possible, before his Majesty's return, after which it will not be easy to get the council to attend to Irish affairs: and if our silver is raised, I beg it may not exceed the middle value of foreign silver coin; but I could heartily wish the foreign silver were left as it is, and then a small pittance of English silver money with the copper would answer our purpose.

I am, Sir, &c.

Newcastle to Boulter (rough draft).

Whitehall, Nov. 23, 1736.
(NA. SP 63/399/148)

My Lord,

I give your Grace the trouble of this letter, at the request of Mr Herbert [illegible] that Mr John Markham of Kingstown may be appointed High Sheriff of the County of Kerry for the year ensuing. As Mr Markham is represented to be a gentleman of a very good character, I have ventured to promise Mr. Herbert that he will have the Honour of Your Grace's favour and [illegible] upon this occasion, which will very much oblige

My Lord etc.

[I] am persuaded you will be so good as to grant my request, and [illegible] of which I hope there can be no objection

I am

N

To the Duke of Dorset.

Nov. 25, 1736.

My Lord,

When your Grace was in Ireland, I delivered your Lordship a petition, including her case, from the Widow Feilding relict of Col. Feilding,[21] and sister to the late Lord Santry. I have been since very much importuned by her and several of her friends to remind your Grace of her application. I am satisfied she is in a very poor and miserable condition, and in danger of

21 Governor of the Royal Hospital near Dublin for invalid Soldiers.

being arrested by some of her creditors. I shall say nothing farther on this occasion, but submit the whole to your consideration.

I am,

MyLord, &c.

To the Earl of Granard.

Dublin, Nov. 29, 1736.

My Lord,

As your Lordship thoroughly knows the distress we are in for want of silver, and the advantage the bankers make of the inequality of our gold and silver; and as the representation of the council here is now before the officers of the mint, I must beg of your Lordship to follow this affair close with Mr. Conduit, and get a report from the mint, and afterwards to forward that business before the committee of council, that if possible, we may receive the necessary orders before his Majesty's return; after which, I fear we must expect but little dispatch in any Irish affair from the ministry, till the session of parliament is over in England.

By what I can learn, they have no difficulty at all at the mint about the reduction of gold, but about the silver they seem at a loss how to take any notice of a letter I sent to my Lord Lieutenant on that subject, to shew that we had over-rated foreign silver in our representation, and rather to wish nothing was done about the silver coins; which letter my Lord Lieutenant has communicated to them, but it was not referred to them by the council. As to that, I would observe, that I do not apprehend there is any occasion of any notice being taken of that letter in their report from the mint; but if that suggests any hints to them that may be of use, they may make use of them as of any other knowledge they have in that affair: and there is the more room for it, because in our representation we observe, that in our calculations we reckoned 5s. 4½d. English as the middle price of foreign silver, but refer ourselves to the mint as knowing that better than we do.

I find likewise that it is suggested on the other side that 5s. 4½d. is the middle price of silver in bars, but that of late, because of their being somewhat baser than formerly, the price of pieces of eight has been from 5s. 2d. to 5s. 3½d. per ounce, and that therefore there ought to be a distinction between old and new pieces of eight, and that the old at least may be set at 5s. 4½d. per ounce.

To this I observe, that we shall not easily bring the people here to know the old from the new pieces of eight, and that we are not fixing the price of silver in bars, but of foreign silver coin.

They say they do not find any calculation of the[22] Leopold, Maximilian,

22 German Silver Coins.

&c. dollars, among any of Sir Isaac Newton's calculations, and therefore think they are not to be met with in England. On this I observe, that we have none of them now in Ireland, and if they have none of them in England, they may very safely be omitted, for we only put them in because they were in former proclamations here, when they were more common.

What your Lordship and I both think is, that it were to be wished that by degrees the gold and silver current here, was chiefly gold and silver English coin: that if our gold was reduced we might hope to get rid of our present inundation of foreign gold; and that there is a necessity of not over-valuing foreign silver coins, which will make it worth the bankers while to carry out our gold and over-run us with silver coins from abroad. And the surest way of preventing that would be by leaving the foreign silver coins at their present value here; but if somewhat must be done about them, I hope they will not be set higher than at the rate of 5s. 2½d. or 5s. 2¾d. English per ounce, which I hope would not hurt us.

I should not have troubled your Lordship with so long a letter, but that I know your heart is thoroughly set on redressing our present deplorable estate; and if by your Lordship's diligent sollicitation of this affair, it can be brought to bear whilst the ministry is at leisure before his Majesty's return, your Lordship will do one of the greatest pieces of service to this nation.

Our copper coinage is I believe before this, actually begun at the mint; all I could wish about it is, that it could receive greater dispatch than I fear it is likely to meet with. I am,

My Lord, &c.

Article relative to the gold, delivered to Lord Granard.

We desired it might be reduced according to the value of the English guinea.

We desired that the lesser species of each sort of gold might have about half a grain advantage allowed to make it worth while rather to import the lesser pieces than the greater pieces.

But if it be considered that the least want of full weight causes a deduction of a grain according to the present way of allowing for a grain, and half a grain according to what we proposed in our application to his Majesty, it is possible a little more should be allowed; since to exemplify in the 4l. piece, though the 40s. piece be set half a grain lower than half the weight of the 4l. piece, yet this does little more than answer the allowance of half a grain for any want of weight in a 4l. piece, and of two half grains for the least want of weight in two 4s. pieces; and so of the other lesser pieces in that and other species.

But at the same time, if too much be allowed for the small pieces, they will be imported instead of silver.

Article relative to the silver species, delivered to the same.

We have from the representation of the merchants and bankers, and from what was the middle price of foreign silver or bullion at London, when we were endeavouring to make application before, desired to set foreign silver at 5s. 4d. per ounce English; but I have since learned that foreign silver in England since the year 1728, has seldom been higher than 5s. 2½d. English per ounce, and never higher than 5s. 3d. English per ounce.

But if foreign silver be worth at the highest but 5s. 3d. English per ounce, and we have made our calculations upon 5s. 4d. there will be a profit of 1l. 5s. 4d. &c. decimals in importing 100l. English in foreign silver.

If foreign silver be worth but 5s. 2½d. English per ounce, there will be a profit of 2l. 2 decimals per cent. by importing it.

And in either case it will be worth the bankers while to change our reduced foreign gold into foreign silver so advanced.

We have indeed referred this matter to the consideration of the mint, who can best tell what is the middle price of foreign silver at London.

I have since our representation sent to my Lord Lieutenant a full state of this matter, desiring that if there are difficulties in this matter of settling the price of foreign silver, they would drop this part of our application relating to foreign silver, and only order the reduction of foreign gold as desired.

To the Duke of Dorset.

Dublin, Dec. 13, 1736.

My Lord,

We this day troubled your Grace about a living in the diocese of Ossory, vacant by the promotion of Mr. Tisdall: it consists of three denominations, the rectory of Gaulskill, and vicarages of Dunkit and Kilcollum, worth about 100l. per ann.

Of the three persons we recommended, I cannot but wish your Grace would bestow it on Mr. Samuel Henry, who was recommended to your Grace by the Bishop of Kilmore and myself, when your Grace was last in Ireland; he came over from the Dissenters to the Church some years ago, and has hitherto got nothing but a curacy of 40l. per ann. and that rather precarious. He is one of a good life and conversation, and a most diligent curate: he is about 60 years old, and has a son and two daughters on his hands to maintain, and has been obliged to sell a small paternal estate he had for their support, so that his necessities are very pressing: but I submit the whole to your Grace's judgment. I am,

My Lord, &c.

To the Duke of Newcastle.

Dublin, Dec. 23, 1736.

My Lord,

I have had the honour of your Grace's of the 22d past, but it did not come to hand till last week; and we had long before appointed one Mr. Herbert Sheriff for Kerry; and as this gentleman was formerly in a pressing manner recommended by Mr. Herbert of England for that office, but was then put by for reasons that have now ceased, I doubt not but Mr. Herbert will be as well satisfied with his name-sake being made Sheriff, as if Mr. Markham had been so.

Had there been room I should have been on this, as I shall, on all other occasions be, very forward to acknowledge the obligations I lye under to your Lordship.

I cannot conclude without pressing your Grace to get the affair of lowering the gold here expedited, for want of which we are in the last distress in this country. I am with the greatest truth and respect,

My Lord, &c.

To the Duke of Dorset.

Dublin, Dec. 29, 1736.

My Lord,

The bearer is Mr. Wye, who has had an affair long depending in the army about removing one Mr. Pepper out of the army into the room of one upon half-pay, and putting him into commission in Mr. Pepper's place, in Col. Hamilton's regiment: the particulars of the case he will inform your Grace of. The business had probably been done two years ago, but for the ill state of health Sir William Strickland, then Secretary of War was in. As the person in half-pay may chance to die, if the affair is still depending, which will raise new difficulties, and as Mr. Wye has long ago done all on his part, I must intreat your Grace to bring the affair about as soon as it can conveniently be done, or Mr. Wye will be in danger of being ruined. I am very sorry I have been obliged to give your grace so much trouble in this matter both here and in England. I am,

My Lord, &c.

To the Earl of Granard.[23]

Dublin, Jan. 2, 1736/7.

My Lord,

I learn from London that the representation of the council has been some time before the officers of the mint, and that as to the reduction of the gold, they seem to make no difficulty, and I believe they are not against reporting as to the silver, agreeably to the representation; but as in a letter I wrote to the Lord Lieutenant on that subject, which they have before them, they are at some loss what notice they can take of it, as it has not been referred to them by the council, I think they need not in their report take any notice of it, but only attend to what it suggests.

They say silver bullion is about the price of 5s. 4½d. but pieces of eight about three half-pence lower. I have wrote to Mr. Cary that it would be a difficulty here to distinguish between the old and new pieces of eight; that we are settling the price of foreign money not bullion; that if we over-rate it, the bankers will change away our gold for foreign silver.

My Lord,

I must beg of your Lordship, as you know the case, and have the interest of this nation at heart, which is in the last distress for want of silver, that you would follow this affair close with Mr. Conduit, that if possible, it may be done before his Majesty's return,[24] when there will be such a hurry of English business, that it will be in vain to hope for any thing till the session of parliament is over.

I am, my Lord, &c.

To the Duke of Dorset.

Dublin, Jan. 8, 1736/7.

My Lord,

As Major Don in Sir James Wood's regiment is lately dead, and there may probably be several removes in the regiment on this occasion, I shall be much obliged to your Grace if you would please to bestow a first lieutenancy on Robert Moland, at present a second Lieutenant in the said regiment by your Grace's favour. I am,

My Lord, &c.

23 This Nobleman was an Admiral in the English Fleet, of great Experience and Bravery; a Privy Counsellor in Ireland; a British Member of parliament; an Embassador to the Court of Russia; and Governor of the Counties of Westmeath and Longford.
24 King George II. who frequently made Journies to Hanover, his native Country, as did also his Father George I.

To the Earl of Anglesea.

Dublin, Jan. 8, 1736/7.

My Lord,

I am very much obliged to your Lordship for your kind letter, and the concern you express both for this kingdom in relation to our coin, and for the rights of the clergy.

I am sorry my letter did not come to your hands till you was in the country, since I make no doubt but your Lordship's representations would have a good effect both with my Lord Lieutenant and the ministry.

I have not been wanting in my endeavours to get our evil remedied, and the memorial of the council is referred to the officers of the mint: and I hear those in power seem all convinced that we are in a very bad way, and that our gold ought to be lowered; but nothing is yet done, and I hear my Lord Lieutenant is too much disposed to make the reduction at twice, which will defeat the cure; for there will be above 1 per cent. to be got by importing gold upon a half reduction, so that it will help us to no silver, and the bankers are so much masters of the House of Commons, that I apprehend if the affair be not quite over first, they will get some idle votes to prevent any farther reduction.

I shall represent this to my Lord Lieutenant as soon as I have an answer to my last letter to him on that subject.

I have sent your Lordship the resolutions of the House of Commons, in relation to agiftment, but there were some other votes ready to have been passed, one particularly to fall on the Barons of the Exchequer on that subject, which though they were stopped by some of the House that were wiser, yet seem to have intimidated that court almost as much as if they had passed. After these votes were over, associations were entered into by most of the Lay-lords and Commoners, to join against agiftment; and the like associations were sent down to most counties against the assizes, and signed in most counties, though refused in some. In some places they went so far as to talk of chusing a country treasurer, and supporting any law-suit on that subject against the clergy by a common purse.

I was told by some of sense that went the circuits, that there was a rage stirred up against the clergy, that they thought equalled any thing they had seen against the popish priests, in the most dangerous times they remembered.

I could not forbear telling my Lord Lieutenant on occasion of these associations, that though the rights of the clergy were in particular attacked at present, yet this method was of most dangerous consequence to the government, since by the same method that was now taken to distress the clergy, the execution of any law or act of parliament might be effectually obstructed.

As some that were more prudent than others amongst them, said they would endeavour to settle things another session in some reasonable way, and hoped the clergy would let things rest in the mean time, and as the latter part of the last resolution seems to promise somewhat of that nature, the Bishops thought it most adviseable to persuade the clergy to be quiet till next sessions, that it might not be said things would have been amicably settled if it had not been for the heat of the clergy. I expect nothing from them, but the clergy have behaved themselves with a temper that has surprized their enemies. I believe they will bring in a bill next sessions, that will half ruin the clergy here, which there will be no possibility of stopping here but I hope the friends to the constitution in Church and State, will sink such bills in the council in England.

We generally suppose this ferment is encouraged from England, as are our great out-cries for a common-wealth. What things will end in God only knows, but I am very much surprized to hear from England that the young noblemen that travel abroad, come back zealous for a common-wealth, as some of our young noblemen here shew themselves to be. I cannot but think by the experiment that has been made formerly, the nobility have very little reason to hope they shall keep their ground, if monarchy be once ruined.

I have likewise sent your Lordship the covenants Lord Piesly[25] has inserted in the pieces lately made on his father's estate, which if followed, must disable the clergy from gathering their dues, or having more, for them than the tenant is pleased to pay.

There was likewise a paper delivered by Lord Piesly among his tenants, which though strictly legal, will, considering the number of tenants concerned, in small pieces of ground, very much distress the clergy.

I shall not be wanting to write to our other friends in England to support us there, for here no stand can be made.

What has been already done, is but the beginning of what is intended, for several of them speak out, that the present claims of the clergy, even those about the legality of which there is no dispute, are matter of frequent controversy, and breed quarrels between the clergy and laity, and which ought to be taken away, and they mention in particular small dues, tythe of flax, and potatoes, the last at least to be reduced.

All we desire is, that we may be upon the bottom of other subjects as to our dues, and enjoy the like benefit of the courts of justice as others do, for the recovery of our just rights.

I must beg of your Lordship to forgive the length of this letter, and to continue the same good friend to the clergy both of England and Ireland that you have hitherto been.

I am, my Lord, &c.

---

25 Eldest son to the Earl of Abercorn in Scotland, and Lord Visc. Strabane in Ireland.

To Mr. Walter Cary.

Dublin, Jan. 13, 1736/7.

Sir,

Yesterday I received yours of the 4th instant, and the intended report, together with nine mails more, I am sorry to hear you have been so much out of order, and are not yet quite well, but I hope as the spring advances, your health will improve.

I am glad the affair of our coin is in so good a way, and that no time may be lost, have returned my observations on the report and memorandums of Mr. Conduit, by which you will see I am very well satisfied with this report, and desire little or no change to be made, and what I do I submit to him. I have likewise returned the report and paper annexed, as his Grace intimated.

I shall communicate the affair to none but such as I can absolutely trust, and hardly to them. I hope it may be pushed on as fast as may be, on the return of the report, that the good effects of the reduction may be sensibly felt before the end of the summer.

I am sorry any accident has happened about the copper coinage; I should be glad if the mint and the company could furnish us with a greater quantity per week than has been hitherto talked of.

My Lord Chancellor[26] is not yet come, but expected from Chester the first fair wind.

I heartily return your good wishes, and many happy new years, and am, Sir, your humble servant.

To the Duke of Dorset.

Dublin, Jan. 13, 1736/7.

My Lord,

I had not the honour of your grace's of the 1st instant till yesterday, when we received the mails together.

I am glad to find the affair of our coin is in so good a way, and think Mr. Conduit has dropt the business of foreign silver in a very decent manner. And I cannot desire he should speak more fully of the necessity of reducing our gold than he has.

As to any difference in their valuation of the gold coin and ours, I am very easy about it since though I had ours from the best hands here, I make no doubt but they of the mint are better skilled in that matter, and have more frequent opportunities of examining the weight and intrinsic worth of foreign gold coins than any here can have.

26 Lord Wyndham.

I have drawn some few remarks on the memorandums, at the bottom of the valuation paper, which I have sent to Mr. Cary, to be communicated to Mr. Conduit, which will make no difficulty in the affair, let him judge as he thinks proper.

My Lord Chancellor is not yet arrived and the wind at present is against him.

I shall endeavour to have the magazine finished as your Grace desires, and hope it may be done without giving your Grace any farther trouble.

I thank your Grace for your kind intentions to Mr. Henry.

I thank your Lordship for your kind wishes, and am sure nobody can with greater sincerity and heartiness, wish your Grace many happy new years than,

My Lord, &c.

To the Bishop of Down.[27]

Dublin, Jan. 15, 1736/7.

My Lord,

Mr. Oneal has called upon me with your Lordship's letter and the certificate of several clergymen. I know not what to say to what they have testified, but I must acquaint your Lordship that for several reasons your brethren on the bench here think, if you have any regard to your character and the notions every body has of the occasions of your original design, you will certainly drop it. And I must assure your Lordship, that I so far concur with them, that I declare to your Lordship, if you go on with it, no part of the blame or clamour shall directly or indirectly lye on me.

I am, my Lord, &c.

To the Bishop of Rochester.[28]

Dublin, Jan. 25, 1736/7.

My Lord,

I have had application made to me in behalf of James Shiell, at Westminster school, lately removed with great credit as I am informed into the fifth form. I am assured he is a very good lad and a good scholar; he wants to get upon the foundation[29] the approaching election, but fears

---

27 Dr. Hutchinson, author of a book on witches, and an almanack.
28 Dr. Wilcocks.
29 He did get on the foundation, and was afterwards Student of Christ Church, and now is an eminent Lawyer, a King's Council, and one of the Commissioners of appeal in Ireland. (February 1770)

without some friend appearing for him he may be postponed. His father is proctor of the prerogative court here, of a very fair character, and very desirous his son may have the advantage of being educated under his good discipline. If the lad answers the character I have of him, I heartily desire your favour in his behalf, that he may be brought into the college next election.

I am, my Lord, &c.

To the Bishop of Elphin.

Dublin, Jan. 27, 1736/7.

My Lord,

We had this day a navigation board, where we were informed your Lordship must by this time be at Bath.

As we have dismissed Mr. Cassel[30] from that work, and are making enquiries about a proper person from England that has been concerned in works of the like nature, and is able and willing to undertake the conduct of that affair, I was desired by the board to prevail with your Lordship to discourse with Mr. Allen,[31] who made the Bath river navigable, whether he can recommend a proper person for that undertaking, and on what terms such person or persons would be willing to come. Mr. Lucas's brother has had some discourse on that subject with Mr. Allen, but as your Lordship has usually been present at those boards, you will be better able to talk with Mr. Allen; and the account you send us will be more satisfactory. And as Mr. Allen is very understanding in those matters, whatever lights you can get from him, which I find he is not backward to communicate, may be of service to us.

Your Lordship can conclude nothing with Mr. Allen, but only get the best lights you can: for we are at the same time making two other enquiries of the same nature, and intend to employ him whom we apprehend to be most capable of executing the work, and who will come on the most reasonable terms.

As I know how much your Lordship has the interest of this kingdom, and in particular the success of the work at heart, I need not press you to undertake the trouble we desire you to be at.

It will be of service to us to have an answer with all convenient speed, that

---

30 One of the greatest Architects in Europe, who designed that noble Edifice of Leinster House in Dublin; the Lying-in-Hospital; the Musick-Hall, and many other superb Structures in Ireland. He was born in Germany, and made the grand Tour, which gave him the most elegant taste.

31 This is the celebrated Ralph Allen, Esq; of Pryor-Park, near Bath.

we may be able to determine on somewhat before the season advances too far.

I am,

My Lord, &c.

To Sir William Chapman.[32]

Dublin, Feb. 19, 1736/7.

Sir,

I am almost ashamed to write to you so long after the receipt of the letter you favoured me with, together with the resolutions of our corresponding society, in favour of Mr. Hansard.[33] But I was then in the country, and unfortunately mislaid your letter, and have but lately found it: the resolutions I immediately communicated to the society, where, though they were of weight, yet they had not all the success I heartily wished they might have had in his favour. For my part I did him all the service I could.

We are very much obliged to you and the other gentlemen of the society for so heartily espousing our interest; I am sure what our charter society are labouring after, is the most rational push that has been made for establishing the protestant religion more universally in this kingdom, than it has hitherto been. And I hope that through the blessing of God, and the assistance of charitable persons in England, joined with our endeavours here, there will be a sensible change made here in a course of some years.

I am very glad of this opportunity of renewing a correspondence with so worthy a gentleman, whom I had the happiness to know in England.

I must beg of you and the other gentlemen who are so kind as to correspond with us in our design, to promote as much as in you lies, the contributions of well disposed persons in England, that we may make our views the more extensive. And I have no doubt but if we are once able to set on foot about 20 working schools, in the several distant parts of the kingdom, and put them into a right method, we shall meet with support and encouragement here from the legislature.

I am, &c.

32 Merchant in London.
33 Was Agent for the Protestant Charter Schools in Ireland, sent to England to solicit Subscriptions for this most religious and useful Undertaking, and was very successful therein.

To the Bishop of Derry.[34]

Dublin, Feb. 19, 1736/7.

My Lord,

At our last meeting of the charter society we had before us the minutes of the last meeting of our corresponding members in London, with an account of their having appointed Mr. Cole[35] a salary of 80l. per ann. for officiating as secretary, and solliciting for us. There is no doubt that what they did was pursuant to a desire we formerly made to them to chuse such a secretary as they thought proper, and to appoint him what salary they judged reasonable, to be paid out of the monies collected in England. However as we had given our secretary here but 50l. per ann. it occasioned some heat amongst us. I said what I could to pacify them, that we were very much obliged to the gentlemen there for their kind assistance; that if we had any misunderstanding with them it would very much obstruct our subscriptions there, and that what they had done would oblige them in honour to be the more diligent in raising contributions for our aid, since 80l. would make a very large deduction out of 220l. annual subscriptions that Mr. Hansard had obtained in England before his return, and which we did not find had been yet enlarged: so that upon the whole I prevented their coming to any rash resolution, and especially upon my promising to write to your Lordship upon the subject.

I could heartily wish they had made the secretary a less appointment, but I much fear it would be a dangerous step to desire our correspondents to make an alteration in what they have done.

And though some here were of opinion that one commissioned by us to make collections at London would want no other help to obtain large contributions, yet I am fully persuaded, that without being recommended or introduced by some gentlemen of weight, and having the way first prepared for him, such a person would not so easily obtain admission, nor meet with the same encouragement. And besides, gentlemen among their acquaintance have those frequent opportunities of opening the nature and probable good effects of our design, that a meer secretary at a single audience could not possibly promise himself. As this is the case, I think it absolutely necessary to court the assistance of those gentlemen, and to get as many more as are willing to join with them, and think we must avoid whatever may offend those who have already engaged to assist us.

I have told your Lordship what others have said, and what are my sentiments in this affair: your Lordship who is on the spot will best judge what is most proper to be done, and will accordingly either wholly conceal what has

34 Dr. Rundle.
35 Another Agent, for the Protestant Charter Schools, who resided in London.

happened here, or communicate so much as you think may be without damage to our design communicated. And you will be so kind as afterwards to write me such a letter on the occasion, as I may lay before the society here.

Your Lordship knows how ignorant we are here of what passes in London, that I should be thankful for a little intelligence from thence.

I am, my Lord, &c.

To the London Society.

Dublin, Mar. 8, 1736/7.

Gentlemen,

I have been favoured with your letter relating to the disputed election[36] at Londonderry, and think you are acting very honourably in endeavouring to support your rights and privileges there, and was in hopes that I might have had interest enough in the council to have both elections declared void, that the citizens and Freeholders of Derry might have proceeded to another election, when they fully understood what was your sense about that affair; but I found there was such a number of privy councellors come prepossessed about that election, that there was no room for opposing so great a torrent. And I rather think your surest way of supporting your privileges, will be by due course of law, if things should take a wrong turn at another election.

I can assure you I have always had a disposition to serve you, and maintain your privileges to the utmost of my power; and shall on all proper occasions shew that I am so disposed.

I am, &c.

To the Archbishop of Canterbury.[37]

Dublin, Mar. 8, 1736/7.

My Lord,

Though I am late in my congratulations on your Grace's promotion to the see of Canterbury, yet I am behind none in my heartiness and sincerity. I am glad to hear from England that your character, learning, and prudence has made all parties well pleased with your advancement. And I question not but your caution and temper will be of great service to the Church, at a time when she seems to be so violently attacked on all sides. I pray God to direct you in that high station, and grant that you may long enjoy it to the benefit both of Church and State.

I am, my Lord, &c.

36 Of Magistrates for the City.
37 Dr. Potter.

To the Duke of Dorset.

Dublin, Mar. 17, 1736/7.

My Lord,

I have lately received a letter from Lord Cavan, renewing his application for the government of Derry upon the present vacancy, with the condition of giving up 400l. per ann. of his present pension. Your Grace remembers what then past, and knows how serviceable he is in the House of Lords.

How the affair of the Hospital stands I do not know, but if Colonel Tichbourn be thought of for it, I believe the several candidates on the late vacancies might all be made easy; and I cannot but wish my Lord Cavan were considered, or we may find the want of him in the session of parliament. I am,

My Lord, &c.

To Mr. Walter Cary.

Dublin, Mar. 26, 1737.

Sir,

I received yours of the 8th, and am glad to hear Mr. Conduit has delivered in to the Lords of the Treasury his report. Your postscript about his relapse, has somewhat alarmed me, but I hope the account we have since had in the prints, that he is recovered, will hold true.

Two tuns of our copper half-pence are arrived here, and four tun more has been shipped some time, which we hope speedily to receive; and since that a tun and half more. As soon as we have received about 2000 pounds worth, which we compute will answer the wants of Dublin, we shall issue a proclamation about their circulating. Dean Swift has raised some ferment about them here, but people of sense are very well satisfied of the want and goodness of them. I must beg the continuance of your good offices both as to the silver and gold, and to push on coining the copper as fast as may be.

We all talk of an exchange of places between the Dukes of Dorset and Devonshire. I hope it is to the satisfaction of our present Lord Lieutenant; but I fear I shall be a loser in my interest at the Castle by the exchange.

I thank you for your kind compliments, and in return wish you all health and happiness, and shall, as you give me leave, trouble you on occasion, for what may be of service to this country. I am,

Sir, your humble servant, &c.

To the Duke of Dorset.

Dublin, Apr. 9, 1737.

My Lord,

I have the honour of your Grace's of the 2d instant; and as his Majesty has thought fit to ease you of the fatigue of our government, I am glad he has been pleased to restore you to your former station.

I have heard from others a very good character of the Duke of Devonshire, but it is a great satisfaction to me to hear it so fully confirmed by your Grace.

I have not the honour to be personally known to our new Lord Lieutenant, and shall therefore be obliged to your Lordship, if you will please to speak to him about me as you shall think proper; and his Grace may depend on my poor assistance in whatever may promote his Majesty's service here, and the true interest of this kingdom.

We are very much obliged to your Grace that you quit us with an intention still to promote our good by your interest on the other side of the water: and I am sure we want from time to time such powerful patrons to help and protect us.

I return your Grace my most hearty thanks for the many civilities and favours I have met with from you, in the course of your government; and shall always own it as a great addition to them, that you are pleased to give me leave to continue a correspondence with your Grace, and to apply to you for your assistance on proper occasions.

I am, your Grace's, &c.

P.S. I find Mr. Dillon Wye's affair is not yet completed. If, as I fear, it cannot be done before your Grace entirely quits the management of Irish affairs, I should be glad your Grace would recommend it to our new Lord Lieutenant, and, if you shall think proper, recommend him at the same time to be a gentleman at large to his Grace the Duke of Devonshire, that he may have the better chance to be remembered.

To the Lords Justices of Ireland.

Piccadilly, Apr. 18, 1737.

My Lords,

His majesty having been graciously pleased by letters patent under the great seal of Great Britain, dated the 9th instant, to appoint me Lord Lieutenant of his kingdom of Ireland, I take this opportunity to acquaint your Excellencies therewith, and that there is inserted in the said letters patent, a clause continuing your Excellencies to be Lords Justices of that kingdom, during my absence, with the same powers and privileges, as were granted by letters patent under the great seal of Ireland, appointing you to be Lords justices in the absence of the late Lord Lieutenant.

It is a sensible pleasure to me that your Excellencies are continued in the government of Ireland, as during your former administration, your Excellencies conducted the affairs of that kingdom with ability and integrity, and with zeal and affection to his Majesty's person and government: I assure myself that the honour and interest of his Majesty, and the welfare and prosperity of his subjects, will be the constant care and concern of your Excellencies, and I shall on all occasions make a faithful representation to his Majesty of your zeal and regard for his service.

I desire to hear frequently from your Excellencies concerning all matters relating to his Majesty's service, and that you will order the proper officers to lay before you, as soon as may be, the following particulars, viz.

I. An account of the present state of the revenue, and of the expence of the management thereof, each distinguished under its proper head.

II. The establishment both civil and military of the expence of his Majesty's government, as it now stands, with the particular dates, as far as the same can be collected, of the time when every particular charge was brought upon the establishment.

III. A list of the officers both civil and military, in his Majesty's service, with the dates of their respective patents, (distinguishing those that are for life or lives, during good behaviour, and during pleasure) Warrants and Commissions.

IV. A list of all the officers upon the establishment of half-pay, with the dates of their commissions, and an account also, as far as the same can be collected, of their ages and places of residence.

V. A state of his Majesty's regiments of foot, horse, and dragoons in Ireland, with their complements; a state of the cloathing, off-reckonings, effectives, &c. together with a list of the present quarters of the army.

VI. A list or lists of the governors and custodes rotulorum of the several counties of Ireland, of the justices of the peace, deputy lieutenants, and officers of the militia, together with a list of the independent companies and troops of militia.

All which several accounts and lists I desire your Excellencies will be pleased to transmit to me as soon as conveniently you can.

Having appointed Mr. Edward Walpole[38] to be my chief secretary, I desire your Excellencies will favour him with your correspondence on all proper occasions.

I am, my Lords,

38 Second Son of Sir Robert Walpole Knight of the Garter, who was many Years first Minister of State in England. Mr. Edward Walpole was afterwards made a Knight of the Bath.

With great truth,
Your Excellencies,
Most faithful humble servant,
Devonshire.

To the Duke of Dorset.

Dublin, Apr. 28, 1737.
My Lord,

I have the honour of your Grace's of the 25th past, by Mr. De Ioncourt; and since his arrival we have had a linnen board, and have furnished him and his brother with money to go with their workmen to Dundalk, where we have fixed this new manufacture,[39] which I hope will turn to good account to this nation, and deserve our further encouragement. I shall still be ready to give them what further support may be necessary upon your Grace's recommendation, and shall always be proud to receive your Grace's commands.

I am, my Lord, &c.

To Horace Walpole, Esq;

Dublin, Apr. 28, 1737.
Sir,

Mr. De Ioncourt has lately brought me the favour of yours of the 4th instant. On account of your former recommendation, I did him what service I could at the linnen board, where we agreed with him and his brother on the terms for which they are to carry on the cambrick manufacture; and gave one of the brothers money to go to France and bring over skilful workmen. Before his return we had fixed upon Dundalk for the place to settle that manufacture in, with the approbation of his brother, and since his return we have advanced money to send the workmen thither to begin their business.

And whatever support I can give them at the board shall not be wanting. And I have great hopes this manufacture will turn out well to the great advantage of this kingdom, which must in the end be to the advantage of England. I am,

My Lord, &c.

39 This manufactory was established by a voluntary subscription of 30,000l. at Dundalk, on the estate of lord viscount Limerick, afterwards earl of Clanbrassille, and is now a thriving manufacture. February 1770.

To the Duke of Devonshire.

Dublin, Apr. 28, 1737.

My Lord,

It was with great pleasure that I saw your Grace's letter to the Lords Justices, notifying his Majesty's having appointed you Lord Lieutenant of Ireland.

The great character your Grace has from every body, satisfies me we shall be happy under your administration, if it be not our own fault.

I have made it my endeavour to serve his Majesty faithfully here, and shall always labour to promote his interest and honour, and the prosperity of his subjects; and am glad that I and the other Lords Justices have been rightly represented to your Grace on that head: and I dare answer for them as well as myself, that we shall do our utmost to make your administration here easy.

Beside those publick letters you are pleased to encourage us to write, there will be occasions when it may be for the service of his Majesty and the good of this kingdom, that I should give your Grace an account of my particular sense of affairs, which I hope you will allow me the liberty to write to your Grace. I can promise that I will never knowingly mislead you, and your Grace will always be judge of what I propose.[40]

I am glad your Grace has appointed Mr. Edward Walpole your secretary, whom, beside the universal good character he supports, I have had the pleasure of knowing here.[41]

I shall always be very proud of receiving your Grace's commands, and beg leave to subscribe myself,

My Lord, &c.

40 His Grace's administration was the happiest, the longest, and perhaps the most useful that was ever known in Ireland, since the House of Hanover came to the crown, which was greatly owing to the confidence he placed (advised so to do by his good friend Sir Robert Walpole) in my Lord Primate. My Lord Primate died in this administration, but had gone through three sessions of parliament, without losing as it best remembered, a single government question; but at the same time this is observed, be it also recollected, that his Grace of Devonshire did greatly strengthen his own hands, and by that means those of the government, by a double alliance in marriage with the powerful family of Ponsonby, who then had great weight, and now are of still greater consequence in that kingdom. This alliance, no doubt, contributed much to making things go easy then, as it did afterwards during the short administration of that amiable, most worthy, and truly noble personage, the last Duke of Devonshire.

41 Mr. Walpole being in a very bad state of health, came to Ireland to drink Goats Whey at mountains of Moran, by which he perfectly recovered.

To the Duke of Dorset.

Dublin, May 7, 1737.

My Lord,

I heartily thank your Grace for your favourable recommendation of me to the Duke of Devonshire. I think I may venture to say he will never find me aiming at any job-work, and that he may depend on my always promoting his Majesty's service, and the ease of his Grace's administration, to the utmost of my power.

I am likewise obliged to your Lordship for your kindness to Mr. Dillon Wye, and hope somewhat may offer to be done in his favour by my Lord Lieutenant.

It is very kind in your Grace, and agreeable to the treatment I have always met with from you to give me leave to apply to you on proper occasions.

I cannot help acquainting your Grace, that we yesterday signed a proclamation for giving currency to the new half-pence, after a most tedious course of delays and difficulties; from what quarter you may easily guess: and I hope this affair will very much sink the popularity of Dean Swift in this city, where he openly set himself in opposition to what the government was doing. I am,

My Lord, &c.

To the Bishop of London.

Dublin, May 10, 1737.

My Lord,

I have been several times asked by some of the subscribers to the poetry tracts, when they would be published, and as I hear nothing about them this May, when your Lordship in your last seemed to think they would be published, I must again enquire of you when we may hope for them.

I did intend to have waited on your Lordship and my other friends in England this spring, but it was so late before our new Lord Lieutenant was declared, that I must lay aside all thoughts of such a journey this year.

I shall be ready to encourage the buying Mr. Serce's book here so far as I can; but we are less given to buy books here than can be imagined.

We have endeavoured during the interval of parliament, to keep our clergy quiet about agistment, in hopes some reasonable composition might have been thought of, but I cannot find that any of the laity have troubled themselves about it, or are disposed to come into any thing which we might propose as reasonable. And I fear if we should propose any thing, it would create the same ferment as they raised last sessions, so that I am very apprehensive the parliament may push at some bill which may strip the clergy of a great part of their legal dues: and I do not see any possibility of making a stand here; so that our whole hope is in the protection of his Majesty, by throwing out any unreasonable bill in the council of England. For my part I shall do what I can to prevent any bill of that nature coming into either house, but with what success I cannot tell.

If we are attacked, we must beg the hearty assistance of our friends in England; every body gives us a very good character of our new Lord Lieutenant, so that I hope we shall live easy under his administration. I am,
My Lord, &c.

To the Bishop of Litchfield.[42]

Dublin, May 10, 1737.

My Lord,
It was with great pleasure that I received your Lordship's. I am very much obliged to you for your civilities to the Bishop of Elphin, and am satisfied if he had staid longer in town, your Lordship would have had more full proofs of his being a person of learning.

I am very glad your Lordship is willing to throw a vail over any misunderstandings that have happened betwixt us formerly.[43] I can assure you that I have all along been so sensible that in that affair all appearances have been so much against me, that I have never had the least anger or resentment on account of any warmth you may have expressed on that occasion, and I shall be very glad to have a correspondence renewed between two old friends.

I was in hopes I should have had an opportunity of waiting upon you in person this spring at London, but the appointing a new Lord Lieutenant, was delayed so long, that I have laid aside all thoughts of that journey at present.

I thank your Lordship for your excellent charge, and am sorry to find that you are infested with popish emissaries in England as we are in Ireland.

My spouse gives her duty to your Lordship, and both of us our service to your good lady.
I am, &c.

To the Duke of Dorset.

Dublin, May 16, 1737.

My Lord,
I have been honoured with your Grace's of the 5th instant, and have written by this post to the Duke of Devonshire on the two points your Grace directed.

---

42 Dr. Smallbrooke, who had been removed from St. David's.
43 See the Primate's former letters of recommendation, where he always names the Bishop of St. David's first for the fee of Dublin.

I have desired the favour of him to make Mr. Gardiner a privy counsellor, and given him the just character he deserves, and for further information have referred to your Grace. As I could not tell but the King's letter on this occasion might be kept to be brought over by his Grace, I desired it might be sent over as soon as his Grace pleases, if he complies with my request; particularly that he might be of service if any dispute should arise about a proclamation for lowering our gold.

On which subject I have likewise written to his Grace, telling him how forward that affair is on the other side of the water, and desiring it may be dispatched as soon as he pleases, that the ruffle which such a reduction must cause, whenever it is done, may be quite over before the session of our parliament draws near. I have likewise desired his Grace that his Majesty's orders on that head may be very clear and express, that we may not be troubled with any delays or difficulties here. I have no doubt but your Grace is sensible why I desire this, from many things that have happened under your Grace's administration.

I have referred the Duke of Devonshire to your Grace to be fully informed how this affair of the coin stands, and what has been done in England about it, and where it now rests. If your Grace would be so good as to order Mr. Cary to give his Lordship a copy of the memorial to his Majesty on that head, I think his Grace would sufficiently understand the merits of the cause.

I am very much obliged to your Grace, and most heartily thank you for beginning a correspondence between my Lord Lieutenant and me, and your kind intentions to cultivate it: and I hope my behaviour to my Lord Lieutenant will be such as to answer what you are pleased to represent to him he may expect from me.

I cannot conclude without acquainting your Grace, that notwithstanding all the opposition and clamour of Dean Swift, the papifts, and other discontented or whimsical persons, our new copper half-pence circulate, and indeed are most greedily received.

I am, my Lord, &c.

To the Duke of Devonshire.

Dublin, May 16, 1737.

My Lord,

Your Grace will be so good as to excuse my putting you in mind of an affair now depending in the Treasury, relating to the reduction of our gold. We are in the last distress for want of silver in all the lower parts of business, there being a profit of 2½ per cent. by bringing Portugal gold here rather than silver, and the same loss by carrying gold from hence rather than silver, so that what silver we had has been still exporting, and the return of our exports have been still made in gold: this our condition we represented to his Majesty from the government and council, when his grace the Duke of Dorset was here last, and our representation was referred to the council, and from thence to the Treasury, and so to the officers of the mint, where it has rested by the sickness of Mr. Conduit; but as he is now well, as I am told, and has a report ready when called for, I must desire of your Grace to set that affair on foot again, and to get the Treasury to call for that report, and make the report to the council, that we may receive his Majesty's orders for a proclamation for such reduction as he shall please to fix upon.

This is an affair of great consequence to this nation, and the sooner it is done before the session of our parliament, that the little ferment such a reduction must cause whenever it is made, may be quite over, I think the better. If your Grace will be so good as to enquire of the Duke of Dorset, he will acquaint you how this affair stands, and of what importance it is to this nation to have it soon settled. I must beg that his Majesty's commands on this occasion, be very express and positive, that there may be no difficulty or delay here when they are sent us.[44]

There is another affair which I formerly troubled the Duke of Dorset about, and which I beg leave to lay before your Grace, which is the making Mr. Gardiner a privy counsellor. He is deputy to the Vice-Treasurers of this kingdom, and one of the most useful of his Majesty's servants here; as your Grace will be fully satisfied, when you do us the honour to be with us.

There is nobody here more against increasing the number of privy-counsellors than I am, who think they are by much too numerous; but it is because many have been brought in there without any knowledge of business, or particular attachment to his Majesty's service, merely for being members of either House of Parliament; but we want such an one as Mr. Gardiner there, to help to keep others in order, as he is most zealously attached to his Majesty by affection as well as by interest, and is a thorough man of business, and of great weight in this country; and I find he will not be the first in his post of deputy that has been a member of the privy council. And if your Grace pleases, I should be glad the King's letter were sent as soon as you think proper, for his admission, that he may be of the council when the reduction of the gold comes on; though I think, if his Majesty's commands are very express on that occasion, none will presume to make the least opposition.

I have formerly troubled the Duke of Dorset about Mr. Gardiner's affair, and to his Grace I refer your Lordship to be more fully informed of Mr. Gardiner's character, and of what service he may be to his Majesty in the council.

---

44 His Grace of Devonshire had the honour of carrying this most desirable scheme into execution.

I beg pardon for having trespassed so long on your Grace's patience, but I hope from your own goodness and from my sincere intention to serve his Majesty in what I have written, I may obtain your Grace's excuse. I am,
My Lord, &c.

To Mrs. Wall.

Dublin, May 17, 1737.
Madam,

I have received yours of the 10th, and have by this post written to the Bishop of Peterborough,[45] to secure his favour for your son.[46] There has for some time been very little correspondence between the Duke of Newcastle and me, so that I did not think it proper to write to him on this occasion. I heartily wish your son good success. I am glad to hear your daughter is better than she has been. My spouse and I are well, God be thanked, and give our service to you and your family.

I am, Madam, &c.

To the Duke of Dorset.

Dublin, May 24, 1737.
My Lord,

As your Grace was pleased to honour us with your presence at the first opening of our charter society, and accept of being our president, and encourage us by your generous benefaction, you will pardon my desiring one favour more of your Grace, which is to recommend us to the favour and protection of our new Lord Lieutenant, and to join with his Grace in recommending us to his Majesty's bounty. His Lordship has already been spoke to on that subject, and is well disposed to assist us, but your Grace's interposition with him will have a weight much superior to any application that has already been made to him. And your joint recommendations to his Majesty cannot fail of procuring us his bounty.

His Majesty has been formerly acquainted with our intentions, and expressed his approbation of our design. Her Majesty has likewise been applied to, and is disposed to assist us with her bounty, but as I am informed, is willing rather to follow his Majesty's example than to be before hand with

---

45 Dr. Clavering, at the same time Canon of Christ Church.
46 This was a Law Faculty Place in Christ Church, Oxford. This Gentleman is supposed to have been a Master in Chancery in Ireland some time after this date, which employment he sold, and returned to England.

him. And there are several persons of quality and worth about the court, who have expressed their readiness to follow the royal example.

Your Grace most thoroughly knows the unhappy ignorance and bigotry to popery under which the greatest part of this nation labours; and the excessive idleness they are addicted to. And I am sure the push now made by this society in erecting working schools for the education of the children of poor papists, as well as of the meanest of the protestants, both in christian knowledge and some useful business, is the most rational method that has yet been attempted to bring about any reformation in this nation.

And we find that as our design is more known here and our fund increases, gentlemen from the several parts of the kingdom are daily making proposals of giving us land and other assistance to settle such working schools on their estates.

And I make no doubt but when we are once fallen into a well settled method of managing these schools, and have so far multiplied them that the good effects of them are visible in the several parts of the kingdom, the Commons here will very readily assist the good design with an annual fund.

But this must be a work of time, and will require the assistance of voluntary contributions to bring about, which cannot be better promoted than by his Majesty's gracious example; which I hope will not be wanting upon your Grace's and our new Lord Lieutenant's intercession.

We are printing an account of our proceedings from our first establishment, which as soon as finished shall wait on your Grace. I am,

My Lord, &c.

To the Duke of Devonshire.

Dublin, Jun. 7, 1737.

My Lord,

I have had the honour of your Grace's of the 14th past, encouraging me to give your Lordship my particular sense of any affair that may occur here.

I am very much obliged to your Grace for this liberty, which I assure your Grace I shall not make use of but in what I apprehend may be for his Majesty's service, and for your Grace's ease and honour. Upon the assurances his Grace the Duke of Dorset gave me, that your Lordship would not be offended, if I offered my best advice on occasion, I made bold to trouble your Grace about Mr. Gardiner's being made privy counsellor here, and about obtaining his Majesty's commands relating to the lowering the value of the gold coins here current, which I hope your Grace will think of when you find a proper season.

I have been applied to by Dr. St. George who was chaplain to the Duke of Dorset, to serve in the same capacity to your Grace. He has always been well affected to his Majesty and his family. And I hope your Grace will not fill up the list of chaplains before your arrival here, that there may be room for him and several other worthy clergymen who have not yet applied, but I am confident will, when we have the pleasure to see your Grace here.

We have in a publick letter given your Grace an account how the affair of Mr. Nugent[47] and Capt. Macguire stands. As for the latter, I believe things may be so managed as to prevent any farther proceedings against him, but the papists here have for some time been so insolent, and there is so general a disposition among protestants and papists to insult magistrates for doing their duty, that we think it proper for preserving the peace of the country, to prosecute any persons indifferently that demand satisfaction of any magistrate for putting the laws in execution. I am,

My Lord, &c.

To the Duke of Devonshire.

Dublin, Jun. 18, 1737.

My Lord,

I have had the honour of your Grace's of the 7th past, and thank your Lordship for your enquiry about our coin, and recommending it to Sir Robert Walpole. As the speaker is now in the country, and I find my Lord Chancellor is unwilling to do any thing in that affair without Mr. Boyle's name being to it as well as ours, if his Majesty's commands on that subject come to us a little after the middle of next month, it will be time enough; for it will be of service to have a proclamation issued here at once, without giving the disaffected any previous time for clamour.

I thank your Grace likewise for your kindness to Mr. Gardiner. I am,

My Lord, &c.

To the Duke of Newcastle.

Dublin, Jun. 18, 1737.

My Lord,

It is always with great pleasure that I have the honour of your Grace's commands. We here were very well pleased with the Duke of Dorset for our governor, upon repeated experience of his behaviour amongst us: but we receive from all hands so good a character of the Duke of Devonshire, whom his Majesty has pleased to appoint to succeed him, that we have no doubt of

47 These Gentlemen being Roman Catholicks, were indicted at the assizes for wearing swords contrary to law.

our being equally happy under his administration: and I am the more confirmed in it by your Grace's authority from your personal knowledge of his Lordship.

I am very much obliged to your Lordship for the good impressions you and other my friends in England have been pleased to make on his Grace in my favour. And I can undertake to assure your Grace, that whatever assurances you may have given his Lordship of my hearty zeal for his Majesty's service, and readiness to make his administration here easy, by the best advice and assistance I can give him, shall be fully answered to the utmost of my power. And it is a great pleasure to me to know on what footing I stand with our new governor.

I lye under those repeated obligations to your Grace, that it is the utmost satisfaction to me that you are pleased to think that I have constantly acted here for his Majesty's service and the publick good, since I am sure it would give your Grace a great deal of uneasiness if I failed of my duty in those points; and there is no person by whom I more desire my conduct here should be approved than by your Grace. I am,

My Lord, &c.

To the Duke of Devonshire.

Dublin, July 22, 1737.

My Lord,

When Dunleer, &c. was last vacant, I took the liberty to recommend for it, Dr. St. Paul, a very worthy man of learning, and well affected to his Majesty, and of some standing in the Church. It was then bestowed on Mr. Molloy,[48] who is since dead. I beg leave to renew my recommendations in favour of Dr. St. Paul, whom if your Excellency shall prefer, it will make a vacancy in the vicarage of Carlingford, which is in my gift, and which I am ready to bestow as your Grace pleases to command. But if it be not taking too much upon me, I would in that case recommend for the vicarage of Carlingford Mr. Hanover Sterling, who is tutor to the Master of Rolls children,[49] and one whom he would gladly provide for, and who is a young man of worth and good principles. Your Grace's favour on this occasion, will be esteemed a great obligation on,

My Lord, &c.

48 Mr. Edward Molloy, a gentleman of exceeding good character and great learning, was a Fellow of the University of Dublin, and preceptor to Lord George Sackville, third son of the Duke of Dorset.
49 The Rt. Hon. Thomas Carter, displaced in the Year 1754.

P. S. I think it proper to acquaint your Grace that Mr. Molloy was possessed of the treasurership of Christ Church as well as Dunleer, yet they have no relation to one another, and probably never were possessed by the same person before.

To the Reverend Mr. Bowes.

Dublin, July 23, 1737.

Sir,

Whereas Mr. Woolsey[50] informs me his person is in danger in the neighbourhood of Dundalk, where he is obliged to go to let his tythes, I desire you would to the utmost of your power protect his person, whilst he behaves himself harmlessly and prudently.

I am, Sir, &c.

To Sir Robert Walpole.

Dublin, Aug. 9, 1737.

Sir,

I am very sorry for the occasion I have to trouble you. But as it is what the King's interest and the peace of the publick here are very much concerned in, I doubt not of your excuse for my so doing.

You have heard from others of the warmth of the House of Commons last session against the demands made by the clergy of agistment, and probably may have read the votes passed there on that occasion.

Several of the clergy had sued for agistment, and the courts of justice here had determined in their favour, and the claim in general was so established, that the only controversy in the several suits for some time, had been about the number of cattle, and the quota to be paid for them: it has been decided to be due by common law; it has indeed been said on the other side, that the claim is new, and so it is in some parts of the kingdom, but has been regularly paid in the north, where things have been best and soonest settled. But the case of the clergy here is very different from that in England, which has been the very antient usage is hard to say; but since the reformation, whilst the lands were mostly in popish hands, the clergy took what they could get thankfully, and very few ever went near their livings to do duty. That I do not look upon law to have had a free course here till since the reformation, and from thence to have gradually come to the knowledge of people. Without this tythe there are whole parishes where there is no provision for

50 This gentleman was thought to be a little crazy at some certain periods.

the minister: but we do not desire to be judges, but that our rights may stand on the same bottom as those of other subjects, and the judges not be intimidated by votes of either House of Parliament from doing us justice, if we seek for it.

As a great part of the gentry entered into associations not to pay for agistment to the clergy, and to make a common purse in each county to support any one there that should be sued for agistment, and were understood by the common people every where to be ready to distress the clergy all manner of ways, in their other rights, if they offered to sue for agistment, it was thought adviseable to hinder as much as we Bishops could, any of the clergy from carrying on or commencing any suits on that head for a time; and the more so, as several persons among the Commons of more wisdom and temper, promised to think of some reasonable accommodation in this affair against another session.

But though the clergy have been quiet, and behaved themselves during this interval with a temper that has surprised their adversaries, yet I cannot find any of the laity have thought of any the least reasonable method of compounding matters, but the bulk of them reckon they have by the votes made last session carried this point, and are thereby animated to make new attacks on other rights of the clergy. I have in vain represented to several of them that in the south and west of Ireland by destroying the tithe of agistment, they naturally discourage tillage, and thereby lessen the number of people, and raise the price of provisions, and render those provinces incapable of carrying on the linnen manufacture, for which they so much envy the north of this kingdom.

It is certain that by running into cattle the numbers of people are decreasing in those parts, and most of their youth out of business, and disposed to list in foreign service for bread, as there is no employment for them at home, where two or three hands can look after some hundreds of acres stocked with cattle, and by this means a great part of our churches are neglected, in many places five, six, or seven parishes (denominations we commonly call them) bestowed on one incumbent, who perhaps with all his tithes scarce gets an hundred a year.

I must on this occasion not only observe the illegality of these associations, but the danger of them to the government, and especially to any acts of parliament passed in England relating to this country, which may be esteemed hardships here, since I do not well see, if this humour goes on, how such acts can be put in execution here. And how far and to what other purposes such associations may in time extend, I do not pretend to judge, but I find in some counties they already begin to form associations against what they own due to the clergy, but they are encouraged by the success of this first attempt to go on to further steps. The humour of clans and confederacies is neither so well understood nor felt in England as it is here.

But by discourses dropt among people and by some papers handed about, there are other undoubted rights of the clergy, that are designed to be voted away one after another, or taken away by new laws, if they are permitted to go on, and I find we Bishops are threatened to have our fines if not part of our estates taken from us. I need not on this occasion observe what a support the Bishops with the weight of their estates and power are to the crown, both here and in England; but I must observe that they are of more immediate consequence here, to keep up the just dependence of this nation on the crown and kingdom of England, which too many here are disposed, if possible, to throw off, daily complaining of it as an almost insupportable burthen.

I cannot accuse the bulk of the protestants except the Scots in the north here, of being enemies to episcopacy and the established clergy as such, but some gentlemen have let their lands so high, that without robbing the clergy of their just dues, they are satisfied their rents can hardly be paid; and others fall in with them, that they may be able to raise their lands as high; and the controversy here is, not whether the farmer shall be eased of an unreasonable burthen, but whether the parson shall have his due, or the landlord a greater rent. Some hope they might come in for plunder, if the Bishops were stripped, and most of the needy gentry here envy to see the Bishops by a proper frugality, though not without a decent hospitality easy in their circumstances.

Against any attacks of this nature we shall prepare to make as good a provision for defence as we can; we shall not be wanting in our endeavours with those of weight in the House, and that are capable of any moderation, to prevent any new attempts on the rights of the clergy, without bringing on an attack by hastily raising a clamour that we are going to be attacked. But our great and only powerful defence under the divine providence, is from the protection of his Majesty, from whose goodness we would hope to be defended in our just rights in common with our fellow subjects.

And I would hope that if some discouragement from the crown were given to what is so unreasonable and unjust itself, and must raise the greatest heats and animosities amongst us, and give the utmost encouragement to the papists to see protestants so violently attacking their own clergy; and that passing the next sessions quietly would with such discountenances very much cool and balk the designs of the ill intentioned, I cannot but make it my request, that you would be so kind as to recommend us to his Majesty's protection, which he has graciously declared in his speeches to parliament he would afford our brethren of England, and that when my Lord Lieutenant comes to receive his instructions from his Majesty before his setting out for his government here, he may be directed by his Majesty to signify in what way shall be thought most proper, that the clergy may enjoy their legal rights, and that his Majesty will be graciously disposed to protect them therein from all unjust attacks.

By a paper of queries handed about it looks as if some gentlemen designed to have a committee appointed to examine into the behaviour of the Bishops and clergy in their pastoral cures: I must own we are not saints, nor are we the greatest of sinners; but what a committee set on foot by such as have the views there is reason to fear too many have, may vote concerning our conduct, is easily guessed in general; and I hope will make no bad impression against us with the unprejudiced. But at the same time I cannot but heartily wish that these measures may be prevented, which I have great reason to believe are set on foot from England, and designed to be followed there, if they meet with success and encouragement here. I am,

Sir, your humble servant, &c.

To the Archbishop of Canterbury.

Dublin, Aug. 9, 1737.

My Lord,

I am satisfied there is no occasion of suggesting to your Grace, that the Church of England and Ireland are so interwoven in point of interest, that one cannot suffer, but the other will soon fall into the same distress. Your own goodness and concern for a sister church, would sufficiently engage you to help us in our distress, though we were sure the example would not be followed on your side of the water.

This makes me apply to your Lordship in our present and our apprehended distress. The House of Commons here attacked the tithe of agistment last session, and by their votes have so far intimidated the Judges and the Clergy, that they have carried on no suits since, and especially to prevent any further ill consequences; as the gentry here have almost universally entered into an association to support any person sued on that account by a common purse in every county; and as they threatened to distress the clergy in all their other rights, if they offered to sue for agistment. But though some were for venturing all this, and suing for what in the courts here has been declared to be their right, yet as some grave men in that House promised to think of some temper to reconcile the laity and clergy on that point by some reasonable composition to be enacted this session, we prevailed on all the clergy to sit quiet. But instead of any such proposal, the generality of the laity are encouraged to make farther attempts on the rights of the clergy; and several in their discourses and some queries that are handed about in writing seem to design taking away some undoubted rights of the clergy, supposing the tithe of agistment not due in some parts of the kingdom where it has not been demanded till lately, and among other things they seem to design taking away from Bishops, if not part of their lands, yet at least all fines. How much the crown would suffer, if such things go on, by losing the weight the

Bishops must have, by their estates and authority at present, I need only suggest; what I have to desire in behalf of myself and brethren, both on the bench and off of it, is that you would represent our present state to his Majesty and the ministry, that, my Lord Lieutenant when he comes soon to receive his instructions from his Majesty before his coming hither, may be directed to let it be known here to his Majesty's servants and others, that it is his Majesty's intention to support the clergy in their just rights, as he has been graciously pleased to intimate in some of his speeches in England, and that he will take it ill of those who shall attempt to raise heats and animosities here between the laity and the clergy. I have wrote to the same purpose to Sir Robert Walpole, but I make no doubt but your Grace's representations on our behalf will have a much greater weight than any suggestions of mine.

My Lord Lieutenant will come to London soon after the 20th instant, to receive his Majesty's instructions. I am,

My Lord, &c.

To the Duke of Newcastle.

Dublin, Aug. 16, 1737.

My Lord,

The countenance and friendship I have met with from your Grace ever since I came hither, makes me give you this new trouble.

The clergy here were last session of parliament attacked in their rights by the House of Commons, who passed several votes against them and their right to tithe of agistment. At the same time several serious men of that House gave us hopes that against the next session some temper might be found out to make that affair easy between the clergy and laity; but instead of any hopes of doing so, evil intentioned persons have raised a worse spirit against the clergy than had been raised then; and if one may guess by some words dropt by some persons, and by a paper privately handed about, some of them are disposed to strip the Bishops of some of their lands, and the rest if not all the clergy, of several of their uncontroverted rights. And till this spirit is laid, it is impossible to hope for any compromise about the affair of agistment. I am sure the oppressing the Bishops and Clergy here, will be very much to the damage of the Crown, and we hope it is his Majesty's intention to defend us and our rights as well as our brethren in England. And though I hope it will not be found so easy a work here to run down the Clergy, as some imagine, yet I must own their great security, next under the Divine Providence, to be in his Majesty's protection; but it would be much better to prevent any such attempts and the heats they must occasion, than finally to defeat them.

I wrote to Sir Robert Walpole on this subject, and desired that our Lord Lieutenant might be instructed to let it be known here that it was his Majesty's full intention to protect the Clergy here in their present just rights, and that he should be offended with such as attempted to invade them. My request to your Grace is that you would join with Sir Robert Walpole in representing these matters to his Majesty, and obtaining such instructions to my Lord Lieutenant; and that you would in virtue of your particular friendship with my Lord Lieutenant, dispose him to be the patron of the Clergy here in their present unhappy situation, and engage him to let me from time to time apply to him in their behalf, as things shall occur. I can assure your Grace I shall make no other use of such liberty and encouragement than to promote peace and quiet, and his Majesty's service in this kingdom.

I am, my Lord, &c.

To the Duke of Newcastle.

Dublin, Sept. 29, 1737.

My Lord,

I have had the honour of your Grace's letter relating to the address to his Majesty delivered by the Lord Mayor and city of Dublin. I communicated the matter to my Lord Chancellor and Mr. Speaker, who agreed that it was most proper for my Lord Lieutenant to acquaint them that you had been so kind as immediately to deliver their address to the King, and that his Majesty received it very graciously, since we had sent it as the government, and that we could not now return the answer in that capacity. I therefore delivered your Lordship's letter to my Lord Lieutenant, who sent for the Lord Mayor and Sheriffs, and acquainted them with the contents of your Grace's letter, of which probably he may have sent your Grace advice.

The affair of reducing the gold has by the management of the bankers and remitters, and the whole popish party here, occasioned a great deal of heat. The former are very unwilling to part with so considerable a part of their profit, though it visibly tended to the ruin of the country, by running all our money into 4l. pieces.[51] I have in a particular manner been ill used on this occasion, and monstrous stories have been spread about to enrage the people.

It is possible some discontented people may endeavour to bring the affair into parliament, and make some reflecting votes on the council here, which

---

51 Which then passed in England as they do now for 3l. 12s. and the other Portuguese Gold coins in the same Proportion, to which Standard the Currency was reduced in Ireland, which is now 3l. 17s. 8d.

by our constitution has a power to check the proceedings of both Lords and Commons. I think they will not be able to carry any vote on that point; but if they do, I am sure the only check here on their heat at any time will be taken away, except his Majesty is pleased to support the council. In the whole affair I am satisfied, the aim of several is to depress the English interest here, which the more some labour to depress, the more necessary will it be to support it here by his Majesty's authority.

As for myself, I make no difficulty of retiring if it may be of any use, and indeed have of late been so ill used in this affair, that nothing but his Majesty's service should hinder me from retiring.

The heats in this town begin to cool, and would have been over by this time, if they had not been artfully kept up for a handle in another place.[52]

I am, my Lord, &c.

To the Bishop of London.

Dublin, Feb. 10, 1737/8.

My Lord,

I heartily beg your Lordship's pardon for not having answered your Lordship's last favour sooner, but I have for some weeks been so constantly employed about our bills here, to prepare them for the council in England, or reject them in our council, that it has put all other business out of my head. I am very glad the popery tracts are at last finished, and as I had 50 receipts for the first payment of the subscriptions, I thought it most proper to return the money to your Lordship to pay the booksellers, and accordingly I have here sent you a bill on my brother Mr. Savage for 52l. 10s. I believe there are about 15l. of the money I have not received, though I have given out the receipts, but that is an affair I am to look after. It is expected here that the books should be sent to some correspondent of the booksellers in Dublin, where they may be had by the subscribers, on delivering in their receipts and the other guinea; and I guess no subscriber will fail taking out his book, as many of them have been very earnestly enquiring after the books.

I took care to have Dr. Jenney made one of the Lord Lieutenant's chaplains, and shall serve him according to your Lordship's desire as occasion offers.

52 Such a spirit of opposition had been raised on this occasion by Dean Swift and the bankers, that it was thought proper to lodge at the Primate's house an extraordinary guard of soldiers; but truth soon got the better of this delusion, and the people returned again to their senses. Dean Swift not long after this feeble effort, this *telum imbelle fine ictu*, became one of his own *meer* doting Struldbrugs; an event which he was always apprehensive of, in his more melancholy moments; and this way of thinking was the principal motive to that noble charity, which to his great honour he founded in Dublin for lunatics and idiots. London Edition.

We have got pretty well through the attacks on the Church here in bills; but I cannot answer but the Commons may make some angry votes before their rising, particularly about agistment, on occasion of a clergyman having imprudently given notice to his parishioners to pay it on pain of being prosecuted. He is sensible of his error in not staying till the session was over, before giving notice; but the affair having made a noise, may probably produce some votes.

I am satisfied our people are set on here by some correspondents in England; we shall defend ourselves here as well as we can, but our last dependence is on the King and council in England.

We entertain great hopes here of an accommodation being concluded with you.

I heartily wish the Church may escape all attacks this session; for I think every day it must be seen, that the Church is not attacked purely on its own account.

I am, my Lord, &c.

To the Duke of Dorset.

Dublin, Feb. 11, 1737/8.

My Lord,

I have very lately received your Grace's commands in favour of Mr. Darcey, to whom I shall very readily do all good offices in my power.

I take this occasion to thank your Lordship in my own name, and that of every honest and understanding person in this nation, for having at last brought about the lowering our gold here. Your Grace has no doubt been fully informed of the clamours raised against it, and the insult on the government by Dean Swift[53] on that occasion; together with the petitions of the House of Commons, and the warm debates there on that subject.

I have had a great share of suffering on this account, as far as the most virulent papers, and the curses of a deluded and enraged multitude could go: but God be thanked, I am got safe through all. There had been no such usage of me, or opposition to so necessary a step, or insult of the populace, if those joined in power had acted with that courage that became governors. Though I must do them justice, that when it came to be debated in the House of Commons, they were not wanting in engaging their friends to stand by what the government had done.

The effect of this alteration is already felt in having guineas, half-guineas, and pistoles very common, instead of 4l. pieces: and silver is in much greater plenty than it was; and the clamour that had been raised is very near over.

---

53 On this occasion a black flag was displayed on the top of St. Patrick's, and a dumb peal as they call it, was rung, with the clappers of the bells muffled.

I cannot conclude without thanking your Lordship for all the favours received during your government, and of still recommending myself to your protection.

I am, my Lord, &c.

To the Bishop of London.

Dublin, Apr. 12, 1738.

My Lord,

The bearer is Mr. Strain, who has served two cures in my diocese; in the first I found him placed by my predecessor, the second I removed him to. He behaved himself very well in both cures, without any reproach either as to his morals or prudence; but as there were reports spread about the country that he was not in priest's orders, and as when called upon he was not able to give a satisfactory proof of his having been ordained by a deprived Bishop in Scotland, as he asserted he was, and that the instrument he produced of his being so ordained was not sufficiently supported, there was a necessity of dismissing him from his cure.

But he says, one Mr. Cockbourn, who was a non-juror, but since has taken the oaths, was present at his ordination, and can prove it, if at London; or if not, yet he thinks he can find those at London, that by their correspondence at Edinburgh, will be able to attest those proofs he can have from Edinburgh.

As he has thoughts of seeking his fortune in the West Indies, and is positive he can clear the imputation he lies under here, he begged me to write to your Lordship to give him an opportunity of vindicating his innocency before your Lordship; and if he does so, to recommend him to your Lordship to put him in a way of getting bread in some of our plantations. And as he has no crime laid to his charge, but pretending falsely to be in orders, if he is able to prove he is unjustly accused on that head, I cannot but in compassion desire your Lordship to be assistant to him. I am very tender of giving your Lordship any trouble of this nature, but as the case is uncommon, I hope you will have the goodness to excuse my writing to your Lordship in his behalf, if he appears innocent.

I am, my Lord, &c.

To the Duke of Devonshire.

Dublin, Apr. 18, 1738.

My Lord,

The bearer is Mr. Norris, who married a sister of my wife's;[54] he is agent to Sir James Wood, and comes over to wait upon your Grace to solicit about a vacancy in Sir James Wood's regiment. I do not take upon me to meddle in that affair, but desire your Grace will be pleased to give him a favourable reception, and to do what you shall think most proper.

I am, my Lord, &c.

To Dr. Butler.[55]

Dublin, Apr. 29, 1738.

Sir,

Our old friend Mr. Morgan was taken ill with a dozing this day se'nnight, and continued pretty much so till he died on Wednesday night. Last night he was buried. He left a scrap of a will written in his own hand, by which he leaves to his sister Catharine Wynn, alias Gunn, living near Henley in Oxfordshire, 100 guineas, to her heirs 100 guineas; for new casting two bells at Christ Church 100l. to the new buildings at Magdalen college 100l.

As I know nothing where his sister lives, I desire you would be so kind as to learn where she lives, and acquaint her with it. But besides what he has left her in this will, as I never heard him talk of any other relation he had, she will be entitled, I suppose, to the rest of his estate; which in the whole may amount to 1200l. or better.

His papers have not yet been searched, when they have I shall acquaint you whether any other will is found: and send you a more exact account of his effects.

I shall take care to dispose of what few effects in goods he has left. What cloaths he has I believe may be given to the servants that attended him, if his sister thinks proper.

His funeral expences, doctor, surgeon, apothecary, &c. I shall discharge out of his effects, and any thing that appears due from him, which can be very little. I believe it will not be worth while to come over hither about his effects, since I shall take care to have his affairs as well looked after as any one from England can do; and the ballance shall be faithfully returned.

54 Miss Savage, a Lady of Fortune.
55 President of Magdalen college, Oxford, and a Member of Parliament for that University.

Any thing his sister thinks proper to order on this occasion, had better be sent to Mr. Philips[56] under cover to me.

I am, Sir, &c.

To the Bishop of London.

Dublin, Apr. 28, 1738.

My Lord,

The trouble I give your Lordship is in favour of the bearer, Mr. Norris, a Batchelor of Arts, of this college. It seems he went over to England in expectation of some preferment, but has met with a disappointment; but could, if he was ordained, be provided with a chaplainship in one of the men of war designed for the West Indies, which he is willing to accept of. But as he is wholly a stranger to any of the Bishops of England, and to any one there to recommend him for orders, he has wrote to his friends here to obtain a letter, setting forth his character, that he may have the favour of being ordained. His tutor, Mr. Cartwright,[57] who is a person of worth and honour, gives the following account of him under his hand:

Mr. Norris was my pupil, he has taken the degree of Bachelor, and has a testimonium to certify it: he behaved himself with diligence and virtue, during his residence in the college: and since he left it, I am well assured his life has been innocent and industrious.

I find it is not many months since he left the college, and as his character is so well supported, and if he misses this opportunity, it may possibly be a long time before he finds any employment, I take the liberty to recommend him to your Lordship for orders, if you think it proper, and find him as well qualified as I believe you will.

I am, my Lord, &c.

To the Duke of Devonshire.

Dublin, May 1, 1738.

My Lord,

As it is taken for granted here that Col. Pyot is dying or dead, Capt. Vernon is very desirous that if the Major of the regiment is made Lieutenant Colonel, and the eldest Captain is made Major, he may succeed to the troop that will become vacant. I am very tender in meddling with affairs so much out of my province, but I beg leave just to hint to your Grace how hearty he

56 Ambrose Philips, Esq. Secretary to his Grace.
57 A Senior Fellow of the University of Dublin.

has shewn himself on all occasions for his Majesty's family, and how much he is attached to your Grace: and such a post I believe would fix him amongst us to spend his pay and his own estate in this country. But I submit the whole to your Lordship's pleasure. I am,

My Lord, &c.

To the Earl of Granard.

Dublin, May 4, 1738.

My Lord,

I most heartily congratulate your Lordship on your new government,[58] and make no doubt but it is on those honourable terms as make it agreeable to your Lordship. I thought I could hardly have had occasion to trouble your Lordship about any thing in so remote a part of the world; but it happens that my Chaplain Mr. Congreve, who is of a good family in Staffordshire, has an uncle in New York, in the service of the government, whose circumstances are somewhat particular. The person is Capt. Charles Congreve, who about thirty years ago was going for New York, Lieutenant and Adjutant, with his wife, family, and all his effects, and a number of recruits and a brevet for a Captain's commission in one of the independent companies. In their passage they met a privateer, whom they engaged, and hoped to have got off in the night, but were betrayed by the master of the ship, who had insured the vessel. In the engagement the Captain lost his arm, and was obliged at his return to New York, by the expences of supporting, himself, his family, and recruits, and other misfortunes to sell his commissions of Lieutenant and Adjutant, by which he lost the benefit of his brevet, and remained there without any commission till eight or nine years ago, when he was made Lieutenant by the recommendation of the Earl of Essex, and is now upon duty in a very remote part of that province.

The favour I have to beg of your Lordship is that you would shew him your countenance, and as your Lordship shall find it consistent with the service, to remove him to a more comfortable situation.

I am, My Lord, &c.

To Mrs. Wall.

Dublin, Dec. 19, 1738.

Madam,

I am glad to hear your son has behaved himself so well at the college as to have so many votes for a faculty place.

---

58 Governor of the Counties of Westmeath and Longford.

I am pretty well satisfied I am not so much behind hand in answering your letters as you seem to think in your last; and I believe few or none of your letters have miscarried. I last week sent a bill to Mr. Gell for your use. I am sorry to hear you are in so indifferent a state of health, and that your husband is as unkind as ever. It is with great pleasure that I hear your son minds his studies. I understand by you and others, that Mrs. Sparks is returned safe to London, but neither I nor any of my family have heard from her since she left this place.

My service with my spouse's to you and your family, wishing you all a happy Christmas.

I am, Madam, &c

Boulter to Duke of Devonshire.

(Devonshire MSS, Chatsworth, CS1/242.4; PRONI. T.3158/82)
Apr. 28, 1739.

My Lord,

Count Taaff called upon me this week, and showed me a letter from your Grace recommending him to the favour and protection of the Lords Justices, which he may most certainly depend on. But he has not yet been to wait on the Government in form, because yesterday, which is one of our days of meeting, was employed in the trial of Lord Santry. When he was found guilty by the unanimous opinion of twenty three peers, who attended as Lords Tryers. At their desire the Lord High Steward fixed this day two months for the day of his execution. I hope it will very greatly contribute to the peace and quiet of the Kingdom, that by this instance it will appear that no man's quality can entitle him to destroy his fellow subjects with impunity.

I this day understand that a petition, signed by the greatest part of the peers who found him guilty, recommending him to his Majesty's mercy will be presented to the Lords Justices on Monday to be transmitted to your Grace. I was willing to give your grace the earliest information I could of this matter.

As to this unhappy Lord's character and behaviour heretofore I shall say nothing, since your Grace is as well acquainted with them as any person here in Dublin.

I must on this occasion observe to your Grace, that my Lord Chancellor has exerted the utmost care and diligence to have the whole affair managed with the greatest order and exactness, as it will serve for a pattern to future times; and that the success of his labours has been such, that I question whether any trial proceeded with greater solemnity, order, decency and quiet than this has.

I am, with the greatest truth and respect,

My Lord,
your Grace's,
most humble and most obedient servant,
Hu. Armagh

Boulter to Duke of Devonshire.

May 3, 1739.
(Devonshire MSS, Chatsworth, CS1/242.4; PRONI. T.3158/82)
My Lord,

Last post we sent your Grace copies of the late Lord Santry's petition to the Lords Justices, and the representation of the Lords of the Tryers. By talking with them, I find they are all very desirous to have his life saved. But those of them, who are very much his friends, rather wish that the present terrors he lies under should not be too soon removed, even by a farther reprieve. And I should guess, that so his life be secured, several of them would be glad to have him, by imprisonment, or a removal out of this country for some years, kept from being in the way of doing farther mischief here, and that his estate, which for his life is now in the Crown, may be by a new grant so limited, as to tie him up from further extravagancies.

I thought it my duty to acquaint your Grace what are their present sentiments here.

I am, with the greatest truth and respect,
My Lord,
your Grace's,
most humble and most obedient servant,
Hu. Armagh

Boulter to Duke of Devonshire.

Aug. 7, 1739.
(Devonshire MSS, Chatsworth, CS1/242.4; PRONI. T.3158/97)
My Lord,

I was to have been out a fortnight longer on my Triennial Visitation, but upon receiving a letter from my Lord Chancellor, that he had wrote for leave to resign his post, I immediately came to Dublin, to consult with my Brother Justices, who might be recommended from hence as most likely to promote his Majesty's service in that great post.

In our public letter we have mentioned the most eminent in the law as able to fill that station. But I find we agree in our sentiments, that the most proper are, the Lord Chief Justice Reynolds, and Mr. Bowes the Solicitor General, both of them Englishmen and most thoroughly well-affected to his Majesty and Family. The first has with abilities presided in the court of Common Pleas above twelve years. The other, as your Grace knows, besides discharging his post with great abilities, has with courage and zeal for his Majesty's service distinguished himself in the House of Commons, though he has not been supported there as he ought to have been by others of his Majesty's servants. But I rather think, the longer service of the Lord Chief Justice, and his superior station will make his promotion less invidious.

Your Grace knows my sentiments, and I think I have had your Lordship concurring with me, that the Lord Chancellor should always be a native of England, and one who continues thoroughly attached to the interest of England.

If it be thought proper to send us a Chancellor from England, I must entreat it may be one of an unblemished character, a man of skill in his profession, and who has been always firm in his affection for his Majesty's family. Your Lordship cannot but be sensible, what uneasiness may be created here by one barely suspected of other principles, and that if he really be such, he will probably be tempted to put himself at the head of a party, that with his countenance may greatly embarrass affairs. And though I should be glad he should be one of proper courage, yet I should be sorry to see one sent hither who could think nothing done right in which he did not dictate.

But considering how near the session of parliament is, I should think it cannot be hoped that one sent from England should either have a sufficient knowledge of our forms, or make those friendships with any of the Lay Lords here, as to promise his presiding in the House of Lords with any great weight or success.

I hope your Grace will endeavour to prevent the opinion of any in England, unacquainted with us and our affairs, being of greater weight as to the characters of persons living and acting amongst us, than our judgement who live on the spot.

Your Lordship will pardon my freedom on this occasion, since it is a point of the last consequence to his Majesty's service here, that a proper person be appointed Lord Chancellor.

I am, with the greatest truth and respect,
My Lord,
your Grace's,
most humble and most obedient servant,
Hu. Armagh

Boulter to Newcastle.

Aug. 7, 1739.
(BL. Add. MS. 32,692, fol. 210)

My Lord,

It is now a great while since I troubled your Grace about any affairs here, as nothing has happened of consequence enough to engage your Lordship's interposition. But at present, as my Lord Chancellor is about leaving us, there is an affair of great importance depending, which is the appointing his successor.

It is of the utmost consequence to the English interest here, that the Lord Chancellor be an Englishman, free from any family attachments in this country.

Of those recommended by the speaker and me, in our public letter to my Lord Lieutenant, as able to fill the place, the most proper and the only Englishmen, I think, are the Lord Chief Justice Reynolds, and the Solicitor General Mr. Bowes. The first has with dignity filled the place of Lord Chief Justice of the Common Pleas, and has been very useful and diligent in the privy council. The latter has for several years discharged the place of Solicitor General with reputation, and has been very useful and active in his Majesty's service in the House of Commons. Either of them are very fit for the place, but the first has the advantage of a superior station and longer service.

If any person be thought of in England, I must entreat, he may be one of a good character, of skill in his profession, and one always attached to the House of Hanover. The least tendency another way or even the suspicion of it, will embarrass affairs here very much.

Though I rather think, that, as the session of Parliament here is so nigh, it will hardly be possible for one fresh sent from England to preside in the House of Lords with authority and success.

I am my Lord,
your Lordship's,
most humble and most
obedient servant,
Hu. Armagh

I have wrote to the same purpose to my Lord Lieutenant and Sir Robert Walpole.

Boulter to Newcastle.

Mar. 4, 1741/2.
(NA. SP 63/405/29)

My Lord,

   As it is said there will be ten new regiments of marines raised, I take this
opportunity of again recommending to your Grace for a commission in the
new levies, Mr. John Hayward. He was formerly a Lieutenant, and had
agreed for a Captain's commission, in order to pay for which he sold his
Lieutenancy, and before he had paid for the Captain's commission, there
came an order from the late King forbidding the selling commissions, by
which unforeseen accident he was thrown out of the army, and has continued
so ever since. His father was a messenger in the Secretary's office and had
his senses impaired, and his life shortened by a blow he received in the
discharge of his office, which, I think, is a circumstance pleading in favour
of the son. And as Mr. Hayward has been in the service already, he can
certainly be of more immediate use in the army than a mere stranger in that
business. As I know him to me well affected to his Majesty and family, and
to be in great distress by being so long out of all employment, I most heartily
recommend to your Grace to get him a proper commission, the doing which
will be esteemed a great favour by him, who is with great truth and respect

   My Lord
   your Grace's,
   most humble and most obedient servant
   Hu. Armagh

Index

REDBRIDGE LIE

To renew this item please teleph

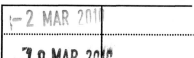

~ 2 MAR 2010

7 0 MAR 20

CH00662854

WHEN
STARS
COLLIDE

PAUL WESTRAN

30108   026495445

First published by O Books, 2006
O Books is an imprint of John Hunt Publishing Ltd., The Bothy,
Deershot Lodge, Park Lane, Ropley, Hants, SO24 0BE, UK
office1@o-books.net
www.o-books.net

Distribution in:

UK and Europe
Orca Book Services
orders@orcabookservices.co.uk
Tel: 01202 665432 Fax: 01202 666219 Int. code (44)

USA and Canada
NBN
custserv@nbnbooks.com
Tel: 1 800 462 6420 Fax: 1 800 338 4550

Australia
Brumby Books
sales@brumbybooks.com
Tel: 61 3 9761 5535 Fax: 61 3 9761 7095

New Zealand
Peaceful Living
books@peaceful-living.co.nz
Tel: 64 7 57 18105 Fax: 64 7 57 18513

Singapore
STP
davidbuckland@tlp.com.sg
Tel: 65 6276 Fax: 65 6276 7119

South Africa
Alternative Books
altbook@peterhyde.co.za
Tel: 021 447 5300 Fax: 021 447 1430

Text copyright Paul Westran 2006

Design: Stuart Davies

ISBN-13: 978 1 905047 74 1
ISBN-10: 1 905047 74 6

All rights reserved. Except for brief quotations in critical articles or
reviews, no part of this book may be reproduced in any manner without
prior written permission from the publishers.

The rights of Paul Westran as author have been asserted in accordance
with the Copyright, Designs and Patents Act 1988.

A CIP catalogue record for this book is available from the British Library.

Printed in the USA by Maple Vail Press

WHEN
STARS
COLLIDE

PAUL WESTRAN

BOOKS

Winchester, UK
Washington, USA

LONDON BOROUGH OF REDBRIDGE	
3010 802649544	
HJ	13-Nov-2009
133.583	£16.99
REDILF	

CONTENTS

Underneath the stars I'll meet you
Underneath the stars I'll greet you
And there beneath the stars I'll leave you
Before you go of your own free will
Go gently…
Kate Rusby *'Underneath the Stars'*

Foreword

My association with astrology began in 1984. I met a girl who believed in astrology and who would give compatibility readings for friends. She based her readings on a book by Linda Goodman called *Love Signs* and on one occasion I borrowed this book. It was the first astrology book I read. I didn't actually read all of it (it is almost 1200 pages long) just the bits of it that were relevant to me. I was seeing a 'Virgo' at the time, so I looked at the combination of Scorpio (my own 'Sun Sign') and Virgo, hoping to find true insight into the relationship I was in. I guess I was curious and perhaps like most people who read books like this, I wanted some validation that I was in a good relationship and the author provided it. One thing I did notice though was that this particular author was far more enthusiastic about Scorpio and Pisces or Scorpio and Cancer as couples than she was about Scorpio and Virgo. I wondered why.

About a year later a strange series of coincidences caused me to begin a personal study of astrology. I learned how to cast a birth chart. At some point I also learned how to progress a birth chart (or move it forward in time) and about synastry, or the comparison of two birth charts. In the late 1990s I put two principles of progressions and synastry together and started to study the new subject which is known variously as progressed synastry, temporal synastry or synastric progressions[i]. The result of this study is this book.

[i] The term synastric progressions was coined by Robert Blaschke. The term temporal synastry was suggested by Dennis Elwell.

Introduction

When Stars Collide is a unique book in that it looks at relationship astrology from a new and different perspective. In the pages that follow I will introduce the idea that human compatibility changes and that this change is reflected in astrology in profound and remarkable ways.

This is a book about forming intimate relationships and their subsequent changes. It shows how astrological factors mark out times of relationship change and upheaval: the beginnings and endings; the highs and lows. Because the techniques used here involve observing the *changes* in *planetary connections* through time, it is possible to demonstrate using simple graphs how astrology relates to relationship formation and change. Put simply: *Why we love who we love when we love them.*

You might think that the horoscope is a fixed and unchanging entity. I prefer to regard it as a dynamic, moving and changing entity; albeit one that has a very firm foundation. Astrology is the study of the meaning inherent in time and no two moments in time and space are the same. Essentially I see the 'birth' chart (or 'natal' horoscope) as the foundation of a process, in the same way that an acorn is the foundation of an oak tree. The birth horoscope is therefore a map of potentiality.

I recognise that astrology is not a science in the modern sense, but I do believe that it is a valid system of knowledge and understanding, and is appreciable as such, especially if we adjust our expectations of it in subtle ways. Astrology is the attempt to extract meaning from time. Science is subject to time, but time is not necessarily subject to science. If it were vice versa, Galileo would not have had to wait 200 years for the publication of his *Dialogue on the Two Chief Systems of the World*

I have sought to answer the question: *How should the horoscope work?* The answer is simple: *"Because astrology is the study of meaning applied to time, it should work as a four-dimensional 'moving and growing' concept,* **not** *solely as a three dimensional 'fixed and static' concept."* I believe we can gain a better understanding of astrology from this small leap. People change – so do horoscopes.

To show how astrology in its dynamic form plays a role in relationships, this book uses 'secondary progressed charts'. Basically, planets in the natal chart play a role in whom we attract and who we are attracted to, and planets in the secondary progressed chart, which is concerned with inner psychological change, show us when these attractions will happen. Here are a couple of examples:

When the late Paula Yates began a relationship with the punk rocker Bob Geldof in 1977 the Sun's position in her secondary progressed horoscope was 119 degrees 0 minutes of arc from Venus' position in Bob's secondary progressed chart. When they married in 1986 this distance was 119 degrees and 25 minutes, when they separated in 1995, the distance was 119 degrees 0 minutes once again. These two 'virtual' planets never quite reached the angle of 120 degrees, a very important angle in astrology, but were at their closest when the couple married in 1986. When Paula left Bob she entered a relationship with Australian rock star Michael Hutchence. When this relationship began, Michael's 'progressed' Venus position was 118 degrees away from Paula's 'progressed' Sun position and was closing in rapidly towards 120 degrees, much more rapidly than the 18 year journey of Paula and Bob's progressing Sun and Venus.

When Diana Spencer's relationship with Prince Charles began in 1980, the Sun's position in her secondary progressed chart was 118 degrees away from the Venus position in Prince Charles' secondary progressed chart. By 1995 these two symbolic planetary positions had moved through four degrees, and were just over 122 degrees apart when they divorced. In 1987 this 120-degree angle became exact. Curiously, in 1986 Camilla Parker-Bowles' progressing Venus was 117.5 degrees away from Charles' progressing Sun. By 1997, the year Charles hosted her fiftieth birthday party, this angle had closed in to be exactly 120 degrees.

Astrology aside, it can easily be seen that all four cases cite the same angle between the same two planets and so signify an interesting coincidence. For those with an idea what the 120 degree distance between two planets in any horoscope or between two horoscopes means, the two preceding paragraphs will be very interesting indeed. Because these readers may be in the minority, I will take some time in the pages of this book to firmly establish in simple terms the astrological meaning of this angle, known to astrologers as a *trine*, and its significance.

The best way to demonstrate how progressions work in synastry is to produce real examples. Better still produce real historical examples that are well known. Two examples won't be enough to convince you. I have used hundreds here and have many hundreds more, all from the public record. You can easily find more yourself, and work out how it applies to you and your relationships.

The symbols for the zodiac signs used in astrology are set out at the foot of each page for ease of reference:

♈	♉	♊	♋	♌	♍	♎	♏	♐	♑	♒	♓
Aries	Taurus	Gemini	Cancer	Leo	Virgo	Libra	Scorpio	Sagittarius	Capricorn	Aquarius	Pisces

I must also introduce a word that might be unfamiliar to many readers, this word is *Ephemeris*. An Ephemeris is a table of planetary positions and it is used by astrologers to find the positions of the planets on a particular day and time.

PW. Perth, Western Australia, June 2005

For Sarah Louise

Acknowledgements

As is the case with all books that contain biographical information, this one owes much to the work of others. I have read over a hundred biographical books and hundreds of biographies published in other formats to gain the necessary authority to comment upon the timing of the relationships in this book. As such I have to mention several authors, living and departed, whose work, in a very different area to my own, has allowed me to elucidate what I believe to be one of the hidden facets of the human condition.

Donald Spoto, James Spada, Sheridan Morley, Jane Ellen Wayne, Carol Matthau, Tina Turner, Elaine Feinstein, Barry Norman, Edward Epstein, Frances Farmer, Roman Polanski, Martin Gottfried, Nigel Cawthorne, Kenneth S Lynn, Roger Lewis, Graham McCann, Cheryl Crane, Artie Shaw, Patrick Garland, Penny Junor, Fred Lawrence Guiles, Lord Olivier, Martin Seymour-Smith, Marianne Gray, Roger Vadim, Brigitte Bardot, Bob Geldof, Ellis Amburn, Leonard Mosley, Shirley Maclaine, Belinda Jack, Stewart Granger, Robert Lacey, Peter Manso, C. David Heymann, Christopher Andersen, Gerry Agar, Joan Collins, Tim Ewbank, Stafford Hildred, Mia Farrow, Peter Harry Brown, Pat H. Broeske, J. Randall Taraborrelli, Michael Burn, Alison Weir, Graham Lord, Eddie Fisher, Leonard Maltin, Michael Todd Jr. and Evelyn Keyes.

I would like to acknowledge the American Federation of Astrologers for permission to quote from Lois Haines Sargent's work *How to Handle your Human Relationships,* copies of which can be obtained from www.astrologers.com. I would also like to thank Jodie and Steven Forrest for permission to quote from their book *Skymates,* copies of which can be obtained from www.sevenpawspress.com.

Eric Francis, author of www.planetwaves.net, was kind enough to allow me to use a long piece from his web site about fractals and secondary progressions. Thanks also to David Plant for permission to quote from his work about Johannes Kepler and to Neil Spencer for permission to quote from his excellent book *True as the Stars Above.*

All of the books and sources used are noted in the bibliography section at the end of *When Stars Collide.*

Thank you to Alois Trendl and his team at Astrodienst for their ephemeris, which is used in the construction of synastry matrices. To David Cochrane at Cosmic Patterns software (www.patterns.com) for producing the Kepler program, used throughout this research study for calculations and the generation of control groups, and to Pat Taglilatelo at www.astro-databank.com for allowing me to reproduce birth data from the most important astrology research product on Earth.

Thanks also to Sumeet Srivastava at Solaris Solutions in Bangalore.

Acknowledgements and thanks to David McCann and Rob Hand for information about Placidus de Titus and the origin of secondary progressions; Jim Crawford, Jenny Crawford, Jon Crawford, Shelley Von Strunckel, David Laws, Julian Hilton, Nan Geary, Kim Maynard, Clare Martin, Peter Williams, Mick O'Neill and Dennis Elwell for their help, encouragement and interest along the way and the following initials belong to some of the people I have encountered in my work as a professional astrologer: PM, RS, SCL, SC, AS, SS, BKR, JF, KP, SP, SV and MM: they know who they are.

In order to find out about celebrity and historical relationships, the web site IMDB.com has been of great service in pointing me in the direction of who I should be looking at. The Internet Movie Database contains lists of celebrity couples, together with dates of marriage. Without this source, tracking down 'who loved who and when they loved them' would have been a more onerous task and as such I acknowledge and thank the authors of this web site.

Because this study deals with celebrity relationships, it has been important for me to keep up to speed with developments in current and recent high-profile relationships. I have used a number of sources to do this.

I have found myself becoming a reader of *Hello* and *OK* magazines over the past three years.

Thanks and love to my sister Ann Marie and my brothers Terry and Tony. I have utilized Tony's historical knowledge and his current address book at times while writing this book. Thanks also to my sister-in-law Gini Newton, for her contribution to my quest for accurate historical information.

Special thanks to Kate Rusby for allowing me to reproduce the first verse from her breathtakingly beautiful song, *Underneath the Stars*. This song can be heard in full on the album *Underneath the Stars* released by Compass Records (www.compassrecords.com). If you go to www.katerusby.com you can find out lots more information about Kate and her music. My thanks also go to Steve Rusby at Pure Records.

John Anthony West's book *The Case for Astrology* set me upon a path of research into astrology and his suggestion that Carl Jung had overlooked some important issues in his famous experiment into astrology contributed the method that has been used in this survey of relationships. My thanks go to John for permission to quote from his book.

The fact that this study became a book owes a great deal to astrologer and author Garry Phillipson. The idea crystallised on the night Garry introduced Sarah and I to modern jazz at a Paul Motian concert in Bradford on Avon. Garry has also made some suggestions that have, I believe, improved the readability of this book, in particular the idea that a graph could be used to illustrate the collision of individuals in relationships.

Adam Fronteras, my literary agent and director of Esoteric Entertainments has worked very hard to place this book with the right publisher. I therefore offer sincere thanks and appreciation of the fact that he has shared my vision from our first contact in 2004.

Special thanks to John Hunt, the publisher of this and many other 'O' books and to designer Stuart Davies for his patience in typesetting the book.

Part One

The Changing Horoscope

One

Cosmic Thingummys

There are certain moments when our cosmic thingummys don't fuse properly
Private Lives (1931 Film Version)
Noel Coward, Hans Kraly and Richard Schayer

If all the various cosmic thingummys fuse at the same moment, and the right spark is struck, there's no knowing what one mightn't do
Private Lives (1930 Stage Version)
Noel Coward

In the stage version of *Private Lives*, Noel Coward uses the phrase 'Cosmic Thingummys' to describe the unknown forces that bring people together in relationships.[i] In the first film version of the same play, made by MGM in 1931, screenwriters Hans Kraly and Richard Schayer changed the use of the phrase to describe a 'blip' in a relationship. Until now there has actually been no good astrological explanation for this off-the-cuff-one-liner. That is: there really are certain moments when we don't see eye to eye with our loved ones but our cosmic thingummys and their complex relationship with our partner's cosmic thingummys don't change. So there must be an interruption from some third-party cosmic thingummys, then?

Perhaps not…

If you look at an old photograph of yourself, what do you see? It's certainly you, but it's not the *current* you.

♈	♉	♊	♋	♌	♍	♎	♏	♐	♑	♒	♓
Aries	Taurus	Gemini	Cancer	Leo	Virgo	Libra	Scorpio	Sagittarius	Capricorn	Aquarius	Pisces

Astrology is like this: your 'birth chart' is a bit like that old photograph, it is a picture of you, but there is another *you* that is constantly changing, from day to day, month to month, year to year.

So what does astrology have to do with change? I guess you think you'll always be a warm hearted and sensitive Cancerian or a direct and forthright Aries. Well, you'd be right, but you would also be missing some of the subtleties that make astrology so exciting and interesting. One of these subtleties involves how we change in reference to our relationships.

Have you ever wondered why some relationships last a lifetime while others peter out after a few months or why some people grow apart after a few good years?

It is true that everyone has a horoscope or birth chart. It is also true that everyone's horoscope stays the same for life. But people change: their tastes change; the style of clothing they choose to wear is often dictated by fashions that change, circumstances change and social, political and economic structures evolve; seeking to harness new developments in order to improve the way that we, as human beings, live our lives. Life moves on. Our response, in the main, is ideally to move with it, ever onward, living life as a series of events that hopefully, as a collective process, moves humanity towards a better world, and as individuals towards a greater level of peace, harmony and wisdom through the acquisition of knowledge and understanding born from experience.

In short, every day has a different flavor. Our earliest memories gradually become a distant dream; it feels as if our earlier self or selves become distant acquaintances whom we once knew quite well. They are people who, if we could send them a letter or share a conversation, we are likely to impress or baffle by our tales of what the world has become, what technologies are now available, the wonders of internet shopping and text messaging or, if we're older, possibly even penicillin and television.

We might ask our younger self what they had hoped from their future, especially if their notions of what they may become are dreams that we

♈	♉	♊	♋	♌	♍	♎	♏	♐	♑	♒	♓
Aries	Taurus	Gemini	Cancer	Leo	Virgo	Libra	Scorpio	Sagittarius	Capricorn	Aquarius	Pisces

have forgotten in the passage of time. Our younger selves might be impressed at our personal achievements, but in the main, and particularly if we're not in therapy at the time, it is *they* who would be asking the questions and *we* who would be providing the answers.

But they are we. We are they. They share the same DNA as us, they have the same name and in some cases the same address. And, of course, they also have the same horoscope… Well, that's almost, but not 100%, true. They share our *natal* horoscope (our birth chart), but their progressed horoscope is different to the one we have now. The further back in time we must travel to see them in our memories, the more their progressed horoscopes will differ from ours.

Relationship Change

Relationships change as much as anything else. We all know this. Most people who have had a close personal and sexual relationship will have also experienced that their feelings towards their partner, after a period of time, undergo certain changes. Passion can wither like a rose on the bower. In the majority of cases, our efforts to preserve it are doomed to failure. At the outset of love, the brain secretes larger doses of phenylethylamine (PEA), a natural form of amphetamine. The effect of this chemical lasts only between six months and three years, after which couples begin to view each other in less idealistic terms. The result of this experience is often summed up as: 'We both changed and as a result we grew apart', or more optimistically: 'We took our relationship to another level'. Some might seek to revisit this feeling of desire by choosing another partner, and so as one relationship ends another begins. They might be described as 'in love with being in love'. Others whose emphasis is, let's say, less sensation-oriented remain constant and faithful because their attachment and compatibility with each other transcends their outlet for desire and passion – they allow their relationship to move onto this other level. While others still – and they would appear to be the minority in celebrity circles –

♈	♉	♊	♋	♌	♍	♎	♏	♐	♑	♒	♓
Aries	Taurus	Gemini	Cancer	Leo	Virgo	Libra	Scorpio	Sagittarius	Capricorn	Aquarius	Pisces

remain passionately in love for life and possibly beyond that.

No one knows what triggers PEA secretion between specific individuals. Love at first sight happens even though no one really knows what 'sight' has got to do with it. With astrology it is clearer: when two people meet they share a kind of resonant musical vibration. If this vibration is at a specific frequency, love in its many guises can happen.

Progressed Charts - Fractals of Life

Astrology has described attraction and compatibility for thousands of years. Popular relationship astrology doesn't go much further than judging the potential conflicts and compatibilities between two people, and for some people this fact is one of the problems of astrology – after all, what use is it if it just tells you about the 'potential you'? What about the 'actual you'?

One way of describing the *secondary progressed horoscope* is as follows: the *natal horoscope* or *birth chart* we are all born with is not fixed. It is not 'set in stone'. It changes throughout life. The birth chart is a layer of potential that we can access more fully through a process of unfolding. At birth the secondary progressed horoscope is identical to the natal horoscope, but it changes slowly from the first moment of life until a point about four months after our birth, each day after birth relates to a year, so, depending on how long we live, but certainly after a maximum of 125 days, it ceases to have any relevance to our earthly lives. This progressed horoscope maps out the way that we change as individuals on an internal, psychological level. This is important to relationships, because what changes us *on the inside* is reflected in our behavior and personal preferences are influenced by our internal condition.

To unfold the birth chart, we must move away from the collective real-time approach provided by planetary transits towards a personal measure of change in the horoscope: away from real-time astrology and towards virtual-time astrology.

Real-time astrology is the observation of planetary motions and their

♈	♉	♊	♋	♌	♍	♎	♏	♐	♑	♒	♓
Aries	Taurus	Gemini	Cancer	Leo	Virgo	Libra	Scorpio	Sagittarius	Capricorn	Aquarius	Pisces

effect on the horoscopes of individuals as seen in the *transits* of the Sun, Moon and planets. This method could also be called the 'day for a day' method of astrology because one day in the ephemeris (or table of planetary movements) equals one day in an individual's life. This type of astrology is applied most commonly by astrologers who work with large groups, for example those who make daily forecasts in newspaper columns using the Sun's position in the twelve signs of the zodiac. The day-for-a-day (or day-by-day) movements of planets in this respect are interpreted for each of the twelve zodiac signs. Each sign is given a different forecast based on these planetary transits, but each forecast relates to roughly a twelfth of the astrologer's readership. Transits are therefore an exteriorised influence: they happen to everyone and have a different effect depending upon the time, date and place of birth of the individual concerned.

Virtual time astrology, on the other hand, increases our magnification of an issue and delves more deeply into changes and events in the lives of individuals as opposed to large groups.While transits can be applied to individuals, they can also be applied to everyone; progressions, on the other hand, are much more focused upon individuals. They are similar in principle to the concept of fractals in mathematics. A fractal is an image or object wherein a fraction of the image can be seen to embody the principles of the greater whole.

So, whereas the astrology we are most used to witnessing can be termed 'a day for a day', the most common predictive technique used by astrologers since the seventeenth century is termed 'a day for a year'. The astrologer takes every day after the birth of a person or thing to be equal to a year in the life of that person or thing. This system is also termed *secondary pro-gressions*. Secondary progressions are used by the majority of western astrologers because they constitute a set of extremely accurate and exact forecasting tools. Secondary progressions open the horoscope up in slow motion, and allow a sharply magnified glimpse at the astrological process.

It follows in many cases that an astrologer who is seeing a client will

♈	♉	♊	♋	♌	♍	♎	♏	♐	♑	♒	♓
Aries	Taurus	Gemini	Cancer	Leo	Virgo	Libra	Scorpio	Sagittarius	Capricorn	Aquarius	Pisces

have at least three charts to compare. The *birth chart*, which is a fixed device and describes the subject's potential; the *transiting chart*: the chart that includes the positions of the planets at any given moment and a *progressed chart* which is the fine-tuning device that allows us to see how the birth chart has unfolded to the moment in time under discussion.

The secondary progressed chart shows accurately how we change through life. And more, it also shows who we will be attracted to and when.

This makes the secondary progressed horoscope the most likely one to be amenable to certain types of scientific testing.

The Geometry of Love

In *Love Signs*, Linda Goodman used a common and useful geometric technique to describe how different signs of the Zodiac connect with each other. Her main focus was on Sun signs (commonly known as Star signs) and their compatibility. That is, she described how – say – Geminis get along with – say – Leos in close relationships.[ii] The interpretations given are based on the angles between the signs in question. For example, those signs opposite each other in the Zodiacal circle have a different relationship to those signs next to each other. Linda also mentioned that elements in the birth horoscope or natal chart other than the Sun also play a major role in relationships. Here I mean to show how one of these elements – the planet Venus – plays the most obvious role in bringing people together in relationships.

The approach I take is a combination of two simple astrological ideas. First, that planetary positions in the birth chart play a role in our personality, our internal condition and therefore our outward behaviour, the result of which is that they somehow signify who we attract, who we conflict with and who we are attracted to. Second, the idea that the symbolic progression of planetary positions (or opening up the birth chart) from the date of birth can show how the potential in the birth chart will manifest internally and dynamically: that is they show how we change through life.

♈	♉	♊	♋	♌	♍	♎	♏	♐	♑	♒	♓
Aries	Taurus	Gemini	Cancer	Leo	Virgo	Libra	Scorpio	Sagittarius	Capricorn	Aquarius	Pisces

Astrology, in any of its many guises, always asserts that certain combinations of planets in people's birth charts are more harmonious than others. The planets in the chart occupy positions around the 360 degrees of the circle (the Zodiac). If we measure the geometric distances in degrees, minutes and seconds from one planet to another around this circle we can determine whether their principles or energies will combine with similarity, harmony, ambivalence, competitiveness or conflict. In a birth chart, these contacts or *aspects* can often tell us about a person's potential. In relationships all we do is measure these same geometric angles, but instead of the planets being in the same chart, we look at two separate birth charts, measuring the angles between planets to find out how two individuals will get along in different circumstances. This is what is meant by the *geometry of relationships*. If we add the two progressed charts for a particular year to the two natal charts, we can then determine if the dynamics of the relationship will be subject to major change, and if so, when these changes are likely to take effect.

The Sun and Synastry

Although 'Sun sign' contacts (connections between the Sun in different horoscopes), play a role in relationship astrology, they do not play a very romantic role. The Sun in astrology is masculine, assertive and competitive and as such – in isolation – it is more suited to bringing friends, team mates and business partners together than lovers. It should also be mentioned that the Moon's position in the natal chart and its aspects to another person's planets (particularly the Sun and Venus) plays an important and common role in the quality of our relationships, but this quality of emotional attraction and support, nurture, security and day-to-day compatibility is not the subject of this book.

Venus and Synastry

Venus, on the other hand, is the prime mover in romantic relationships and

♈	♉	♊	♋	♌	♍	♎	♏	♐	♑	♒	♓
Aries	Taurus	Gemini	Cancer	Leo	Virgo	Libra	Scorpio	Sagittarius	Capricorn	Aquarius	Pisces

therefore the most important element in the synastry of lovers.

I will show that serious and intimate relationships, although obviously the product of free will, can be shown in the *majority of cases in this study*[iii] to have the astrological significators (also called indicators or influences) astrologers would expect to find in intimate partnerships. Often these significators or indicators are present by progression (and therefore subject to change) rather than present in the birth charts (and therefore fixed for life).

Intimate relationships are more likely to occur when Venus in one person's *fixed birth chart* or in their *secondary progressed chart at the time the relationship began* comes into a close aspect or geometric angle of:

0 degrees *(this is called a conjunction and in this book a conjunction is measured as being relevant when two planets are between 0 and 2 degrees apart),*

-or-

120 degrees *(this is one third of an equilateral triangle and is called a trine; in this book a trine is measured as being relevant when two planets are between 118 and 122 degrees apart)*

-or-

180 degrees *(this is when two planets sit opposite each other and, naturally this is called an opposition; in this book an opposition is measured as being relevant if it lies between 178 and 180 degrees)* **with either the Sun, Venus or Mars in the *fixed birth chart*, -or- in the *secondary progressed chart* of a second person *at the time their relationship began*.**

From a quantitative point of view, I have divided the major aspect types (0, 30, 60, 90, 120, 150 and 180 degrees), into 147 styles (natal, natal-progressed, progressed-natal where appropriate, and progressed-progressed). I have then calculated the prevalence of two-degree aspects across these styles between the natal and progressed charts of 1300

♈	♉	♊	♋	♌	♍	♎	♏	♐	♑	♒	♓
Aries	Taurus	Gemini	Cancer	Leo	Virgo	Libra	Scorpio	Sagittarius	Capricorn	Aquarius	Pisces

relationships. In doing so I have found that the 33 styles that include Venus in 120 degree *trine*, 0 degree *conjunction* and 180 degree *opposition,* occur either proportionately more often than the other major aspects involving Venus and those planetary combinations that do not include Venus. Or, if they do not occur significantly more often than some aspects, a level of independent influence[iv] upon the relationship can be ascribed to them. This book is, however, mostly based upon the qualitative viewpoint that these Venus aspects allow us to take. Counting aspects just provides us with a pointer that shows us where to look to find qualitative significance in the relationships under scrutiny. We are therefore able to home in on the factors in relationships that play a role in the initial attraction of couples.

Results suggest that more relationships begin when Sun and Venus '*or*' Venus and Mars '*or*' Venus and Venus are about **0, 120** or **180 degrees** apart than when these planets are **60, 90, 150** or **30** degrees apart. The two degree orb is applied rather than a one degree orb, simply because when assessing planetary aspects between birth charts, where no time of birth is available, an error of about one degree can occur. These figures and statistics will be looked at in detail later on in the book.

The subject of this enquiry begins with the start date of the relationship – the relationship seen as an event.

Progressed synastry suggests that if two people meet at the right time, when certain of the planets in their progressed and natal charts are lined up in these certain geometric patterns, then they can quite possibly engage in a specific type of relationship. If one of these planets is Venus and the couple are disposed towards a relationship, then the likelihood of it being a close intimate loving relationship is increased. Here's a personal example:

In 1997, a few months after my partner Sarah and I began our relationship, I first encountered evidence that progressions may play a role in synastry. Our *progressing-Venuses* (which were in fact travelling in different directions) were exactly 120 degrees apart for a few months in 1997 and,

♈	♉	♊	♋	♌	♍	♎	♏	♐	♑	♒	♓
Aries	Taurus	Gemini	Cancer	Leo	Virgo	Libra	Scorpio	Sagittarius	Capricorn	Aquarius	Pisces

when this is placed into the perspective of our whole lives, it became evident that a very short window of opportunity was open for us to meet and start a relationship. Sarah had decided to leave the city in which we both lived at the time. We lived together for a few months (July to September 1997) before she left town. Our progressing-Venus trine reached exactly 120 degrees on 20 July 1997 and then began to separate. Venus trines such as this help to facilitate the start of relationships, but more often, Venus in both charts will be moving forward making roughly the same progress. In our case, the likely foundation of the relationship is limited to a short window of time. Of course, this would only appear to be relevant to someone who believes in astrology and understands the significance of such an angle between Venus across two horoscopes.

It seemed to me like a collision had taken place that changed both our lives. A year later we were living together 200 miles away. It struck me that this 'window of opportunity' created by Venus might be relevant in other people's relationships and I assumed that this factor would have been encountered by and commented on by many other astrologers.[v]

Displaying Progressed and Natal Data

To begin with, in order for the reader to grasp the information being presented here, it is necessary for me to display data in two ways. First the raw data is shown using a four tier matrix like **Fig. 1** then the data is shown graphically, which results in a graph like **Fig. 2**. I will give a taste of what is to come in the next few pages, but in order to interpret this information the next few chapters will be written to accommodate those readers who have not yet become accustomed to what is basically astrological shorthand. Without this shorthand, you will appreciate, this book would be much longer and, I believe, much more difficult to follow.

♈	♉	♊	♋	♌	♍	♎	♏	♐	♑	♒	♓
Aries	Taurus	Gemini	Cancer	Leo	Virgo	Libra	Scorpio	Sagittarius	Capricorn	Aquarius	Pisces

Natal and Progressed Synastry Matrix

		1	2	3	4	5	6	7	8	9
A	Day		S.Time	Sun	Moon	Mercury	Venus	Mars		
B		8	3:26	15 ♏ 08'	12 ♍ 39'	03 ♐ 07'	14 ♏ 53'	15 ♍ 29'	1966	paul
C		31	14:39	10 ♈ 11'	07 ♍ 01'	01 ♈ 16'	23 ♈ 36'	12 ♐ 41'	1997	sarah
D		9	5:29	16 ♐ 28'	05 ♏ 56'	26 ♏ 35'	23 ♐ 49'	02 ♎ 38'	1997	paul
E		3	12:48	12 ♓ 19'	28 ♌ 56'	16 ♒ 42'	22 ♈ 34'	02 ♐ 34'	1969	sarah

Fig.1, Matrix showing the natal planetary positions for Paul and Sarah together with their progressed planetary positions for the year 1997. Progressed-Venus', 120 degrees apart in 1997, forming a trine between the signs Aries and Sagittarius, are shown highlighted with a double-boxed line.

Collision Graph

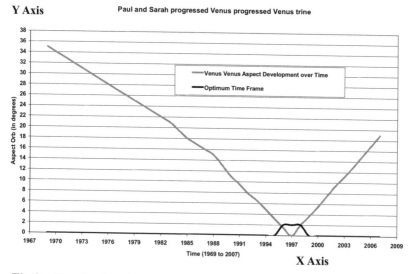

Y Axis

Paul and Sarah progressed Venus progressed Venus trine

Venus Venus Aspect Development over Time
Optimum Time Frame

X Axis

Fig.2. Graph showing the conjectured window of opportunity occurring in 1997 the result of progressing direct Venus in trine to progressing retrograde Venus

This is what such a collision looks like when plotted on a graph. The X

♈	♉	♊	♋	♌	♍	♎	♏	♐	♑	♒	♓
Aries	Taurus	Gemini	Cancer	Leo	Virgo	Libra	Scorpio	Sagittarius	Capricorn	Aquarius	Pisces

(horizontal) axis is the time from Sarah's birth in 1969 to the year 2007 (still a few years away, at the time of writing) and the Y (Vertical) axis shows the number of degrees the two progressing planets are from being in this highly significant aspect: the 120 degree trine.

This type of graph depicts the perfection of an angle between two planets. The grey line labelled "Venus-Venus Aspect Development over Time" shows the 'trajectory' of the progressed aspect from 158 degrees in 1969, the year Sarah was born, to 120 degrees in July 1997. It actually depicts the "orb" or the distance to and from exactness of the aspect over a number of years and as such the label "Aspect Orb" is used on most of the collision graphs in this book. The black line labelled "Optimum Time Frame" represents the time period when this aspect is within two degrees. This happened in 1996. Our first date was on 7 May 1997. This time period is also referred to as the "Window of Opportunity" or "Optimum Time Period".

For progressed-Venus-synastry generally, the most powerful period of attraction seems to occur inside this window of opportunity in the two degrees before the aspect reaches exactness. The two degrees after the aspect has achieved exactness are relevant, but relationships that begin when the Venus aspect is separating (or post-exactitude) may differ in some ways from those that begin when the Venus aspect is applying (or is pre-exactitude). When we refer to an aspect *applying*, we consider it to be very intense, powerful and it creates an atmosphere of expectation. When an aspect is referred to as *separating* it is still noticeable, but less intense, and there may be a feeling of relief, satisfaction or security depending on the type of aspect involved. A separating aspect of harmony might leave a feeling of emptiness, whereas a separating aspect of conflict creates a feeling of relief. As such we would expect relationships to begin more often under applying harmonious aspects such as the trine which should bring couples together, or sometimes under separating difficult aspects such as the 90 degree square, which may keep people apart when they are applying.

♈	♉	♊	♋	♌	♍	♎	♏	♐	♑	♒	♓
Aries	Taurus	Gemini	Cancer	Leo	Virgo	Libra	Scorpio	Sagittarius	Capricorn	Aquarius	Pisces

Method

My method has been simple. I have looked for examples of real intimate relationships based on the idea that the feelings experienced by people who fall in love, or just fall in lust, contain common elements. I have trawled through the internet, references books, encyclopaedia, biographies, magazines, newspapers, astrological, genealogical and biographical databases and come up with more than 1300 examples of intimate relationships where both birth dates and the start date of relationship are known. If I had used a sample of non-celebrities, this information would not necessarily have been available. I then calculated the positions of the Sun, Venus and Mars in both the birth charts of each couple and their progressed charts for the year they either met or married (depending on the information available). I have then measured the angles between the Sun, Venus and Mars in all combinations carefully noting the appearance of seven different types of angle between these planets.

These angles between planets, all of which are astrologically important, are:

0 degrees: 30 degrees: 60 degrees: 90 degrees: 120 degrees: 150 degrees: 180 degrees

In my case, the 'relationship indicator' was a trine between Venus in my secondary progressed chart and Venus in my partner's secondary progressed chart. This is not the most common of the relationship indicators. Here is an example that includes the most common 'relationship indicator' and which is also one of the best known relationships in modern history.

Prince Charles and Diana, Princess of Wales

Basically Diana's natal-Venus at 24 degrees Taurus (cell B6 in the matrix below) opposes Charles' natal-Sun at 22 degrees Scorpio (D3), although it is just outside the two degree limit I have imposed for my study, it is still relevant in that this relationship was one of attraction, but his will

♈	♉	♊	♋	♌	♍	♎	♏	♐	♑	♒	♓
Aries	Taurus	Gemini	Cancer	Leo	Virgo	Libra	Scorpio	Sagittarius	Capricorn	Aquarius	Pisces

(symbolized by the Sun in Scorpio) opposed her idea of what relationship should be (symbolized by Venus in Taurus). The primary relationship indicator is his progressing-Venus (C6) being in a 120-degree trine aspect to her progressing-Sun (D3). This means he was enchanted by her at first and the relationship was forged, if out of Royal necessity, also because she found him attractive. There is also a trine between Diana's progressing-Venus (D6) and Charles' natal-Venus (E6) giving a romantic context. This aspect became exact in 1982 and after this point the romance of their situation will have lessened considerably. This aspect can be said to demarcate the short honeymoon period of their relationship.

Many people will remember the newly engaged couple on British TV in 1981, asked if they were in love, Diana replied 'Of course' while Charles said 'Whatever "in love" means'.

	1	2	3	4	5	6	7	8	9
A	Day	S.Time	Sun	Moon	Mercury	Venus	Mars		
B	1	14:23	09 ♋ 42'	25 ♒ 39'	03 ♋ 10'	24 ♉ 26'	01 ♍ 40'	1961	diana
C	17	2:59	25 ♐ 52'	15 ♋ 18'	28 ♐ 42'	26 ♏ 59'	16 ♏ 04'	1981	charles
D	21	15:42	28 ♋ 46'	08 ♏ 55'	08 ♋ 45'	15 ♊ 42'	13 ♍ 41'	1981	diana
E	14	0:49	22 ♏ 25'	00 ♉ 25'	06 ♏ 57'	16 ♏ 23'	20 ♐ 56'	1948	charles
F	1	14:23	09 ♋ 42'	25 ♒ 39'	03 ♋ 10'	24 ♉ 26'	01 ♍ 40'	1961	diana
G	22	3:19	00 ♒ 57'	26 ♏ 37'	06 ♒ 40'	03 ♐ 12'	19 ♑ 57'	1986	charles
H	26	16:02	03 ♌ 33'	19 ♑ 20'	15 ♋ 24'	21 ♊ 14'	16 ♍ 45'	1986	diana
I	14	0:49	22 ♏ 25'	00 ♉ 25'	06 ♏ 57'	16 ♎ 23'	20 ♐ 56'	1948	charles
J	1	14:23	09 ♋ 42'	25 ♒ 39'	03 ♋ 10'	24 ♉ 26'	01 ♍ 40'	1961	diana
K	28	3:42	07 ♑ 04'	18 ♐ 45'	16 ♑ 19'	10 ♐ 40'	24 ♑ 37'	1992	charles
L	1	16:25	09 ♌ 17'	18 ♈ 13'	25 ♋ 41'	27 ♊ 56'	20 ♍ 27'	1992	diana
M	14	0:49	22 ♏ 25'	00 ♉ 25'	06 ♏ 57'	16 ♎ 23'	20 ♐ 56'	1948	charles

Fig. 3 Prince Charles and Diana, Princess of Wales natal and progressed planetary positions 1981, 1986 and 1992: Charles progressed-Venus is moving more quickly than Diana's progressed-Sun

The trine aspect is a connection of vision, sympathy, co-operation and harmony. When the Sun and Venus form a trine between two horoscopes, it is often indicative of powerful attraction, but this attraction is consummate

♈	♉	♊	♋	♌	♍	♎	♏	♐	♑	♒	♓
Aries	Taurus	Gemini	Cancer	Leo	Virgo	Libra	Scorpio	Sagittarius	Capricorn	Aquarius	Pisces

rather than purely sexual.

The progressed-Sun-Venus trine never left this couple throughout their marriage, but after it reached exactness in 1987 their marriage effectively ended, in fact, earlier than this in 1985 a destructive progressing-Venus (H6) natal-Mars (I7) square aspect became exact and this probably involved them becoming more remote as intimate partners as their ideas about their relationship began to conflict seriously. This is of course symbolic of a matter coming to a head and in the previous few years the behavior of one or both is highlighted by this aspect. By 1992, Diana's progressed-Mars (L7) squares Charles' natal-Mars (M7), signifying 'differing methods' and she goes public with their different approaches to their relationship, they separate and their marriage ends officially in 1995. By this time their progressed-Sun (L3) progressed-Venus (K6) trine is receding and the window of their relationship is closing. There you have it - the royal marriage in a progressed-synastry nutshell.

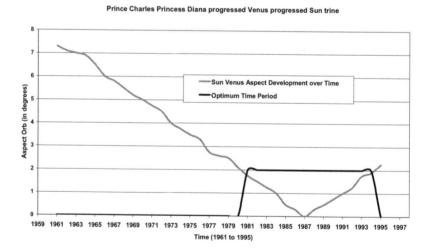

Fig.4 Graph showing the two degree window of opportunity 1981 to 1995 created by Charles and Diana's progressed-Sun-Venus trine

♈	♉	♊	♋	♌	♍	♎	♏	♐	♑	♒	♓
Aries	Taurus	Gemini	Cancer	Leo	Virgo	Libra	Scorpio	Sagittarius	Capricorn	Aquarius	Pisces

This graph shows the collision of Charles' progressing-Venus with Diana's progressing-Sun. For this couple the years when this aspect was within *two* degrees of being exact is the period of their marriage. The point at which this trine aspect began to separate (1987) marked the effective end of their relationship. An aspect such as this is at its most powerful as it applies (i.e. becomes exact) and is substantially weakened as it separates. If this particular aspect is the main attracting factor in a relationship, then changes are likely to take place in the way the couple relate as the aspect perfects and separates.

Prince Charles and Camilla Parker-Bowles

In order to illustrate the fact that the patterns I am calling attention to recur with significant regularity, here is another significant relationship of the heir to the British throne.

Although this relationship is a little difficult to accurately time, here is how it panned out over the years:

Charles met Camilla Shand in summer 1970 at this time she was seeing Andrew Parker-Bowles. By summer 1972 Charles and Camilla had started seeing each other. Charles left the UK in December 1972 to take up a commission on HMS *Minerva* and was out of the country for most of 1973. By July 1973 Camilla had married Andrew Parker-Bowles.

Although Camilla's role in Charles' life is well documented, it is uncertain how intimate they were until some time in 1986, when their close relationship was once again re-kindled. It is suggested that Charles sought Camilla's advice on marrying Diana Spencer. The first argument of Charles and Diana's relationship may have concerned the gift of a bracelet presented to Camilla by Charles two days before his marriage to Diana in 1981.

In February 1989, Diana is supposed to have confronted Camilla about her relationship with Charles. Later the same year telephone conversations between Charles and Camilla were intercepted and taped. Excerpts were

♈	♉	♊	♋	♌	♍	♎	♏	♐	♑	♒	♓
Aries	Taurus	Gemini	Cancer	Leo	Virgo	Libra	Scorpio	Sagittarius	Capricorn	Aquarius	Pisces

published in 1992. A complete transcript was published in 1993.

Charles and Diana agreed to separate in 1992 and in 1996 they divorced.

In 1997 Charles hosted a 50th birthday party for Camilla, less than two months later Diana died.

Charles gradually placed the idea into the public consciousness that he and Camilla were a couple. Slowly the Royal family and the British public became more accepting of their relationship. Charles and Camilla were married in 2005.

The natal synastry of this couple is interesting. Born with a natal-Sun (B3) Sun (E3) trine, they will always see eye to eye in broad terms. Because they were also born just over a year apart, their progressed-Sun's (C3 and D3) are also in a permanent 120-degree trine as the progressed-Sun moves at a regular rate of about 1 degree per year. Had they born a few more years apart (judging by the distance of the Sun-Sun trine, anything over two years), then their progressed-Sun's would never be in this aspect.

	1	2	3	4	5	6	7	8	9
A	Day	S.Time							
B	17	0:46	23 ♋ 47'	10 ♋ 02'	19 ♋ 55'	10 ♋ 34'	11 ♊ 16'	1947	camilla
C	8	2:24	16 ♐ 43'	19 ♓ 59'	14 ♐ 31'	15 ♏ 49'	09 ♑ 08'	1972	charles
D	11	2:25	17 ♌ 41'	05 ♊ 08'	00 ♌ 45'	11 ♌ 17'	28 ♊ 13'	1972	camilla
E	14	2:35	22 ♏ 29'	01 ♉ 20'	07 ♏ 04'	16 ♎ 28'	21 ♐ 00'	1948	charles

Fig. 5 Matrix showing the relative planetary positions for Charles and Camilla's natal horoscopes together with progressed planetary positions for the year 1972

In 1972, Charles' progressing-Mars (C7) in Capricorn is briefly applying to oppose Camilla's natal-Venus (B6) in Cancer. This aspect had reached exact by 1974. There is also a progressed-Venus (Charles C6) progressed-Sun (Camilla D3) 90 degree square aspect that seems to have sabotaged their relationship, at least in the 1970s. This aspect is quite long lived; it is applying within 2 degrees in 1972, and will become exact in 1980 to 1981

♈	♉	♊	♋	♌	♍	♎	♏	♐	♑	♒	♓
Aries	Taurus	Gemini	Cancer	Leo	Virgo	Libra	Scorpio	Sagittarius	Capricorn	Aquarius	Pisces

(the time of Charles' courtship and marriage to Diana) it then begins to separate beyond 2 degrees and therefore becomes weaker by 1986.

1986 is the year we are informed that their romance was once again re-kindled.

In 1986 another more fluid and harmonious aspect is forming, this time between Camilla's progressing-Venus (D6) and Charles' progressing-Sun (C3).

This aspect is the same one that Charles shared with Diana. It slowly formed outside the strict two-degree barrier in 1986, and came into orb probably around late 1987. A long protracted aspect, the Sun moving slightly more slowly than Venus. Eventually this aspect achieved perfection by becoming exact. And it did so …in 1997.

	1	2	3	4	5	6	7	8	9
A	Day	S.Time	Sun	Moon	Mercury	Venus	Mars		
B	17	0:46	23 ♋ 47'	10 ♋ 02'	19 ♋ 55'	10 ♋ 34'	11 ♊ 16'	1947	camilla
C	22	3:19	00 ♑ 57'	26 ♍ 37'	06 ♑ 40'	03 ♐ 12'	19 ♑ 57'	1986	charles
D	25	3:20	01 ♍ 09'	19 ♐ 55'	27 ♌ 12'	28 ♌ 36'	07 ♋ 22'	1986	camilla
E	14	2:35	22 ♏ 29'	01 ♉ 20'	07 ♏ 04'	16 ♎ 28'	21 ♐ 00'	1948	charles

Fig 6. Matrix showing the relative planetary positions for Charles and Camilla's natal horoscopes together with progressed planetary positions for the year 1986. Venus in Camilla's progressed chart is beginning to form a trine to the Sun in Charles' progressed chart

When we delve into the patterns of progressed synastry, a hidden solution to astrological synastry appears to emerge. Of course, we know that Charles and Camilla had a brief relationship in 1972, we also know that Charles' progressing-Venus and Camilla's progressing-Sun were squared then – that is, they were 'star crossed' – we know that this 'cross' aspect became exact in 1980 – 81, at the time that Charles married Diana. When Venus and the Sun are 'crossed' or squared, there is often an external (perhaps previous life choices) rather than an internal (personal feelings) influence at work,

♈	♉	♊	♋	♌	♍	♎	♏	♐	♑	♒	♓
Aries	Taurus	Gemini	Cancer	Leo	Virgo	Libra	Scorpio	Sagittarius	Capricorn	Aquarius	Pisces

Prince Charles Camilla Parker-Bowles progressed Sun progressed Venus trine

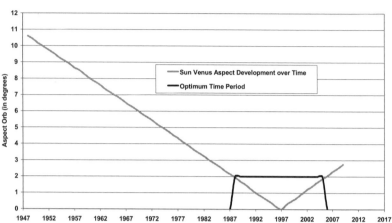

Fig. 7 Graph Showing the two degree window of opportunity 1987 to 2006 created by Charles and Camilla's progressed-Sun-Venus trine

which keeps a couple apart. In the most famous case of 'stars being crossed' – Romeo and Juliet's – it was the enmity of their families that prevented the two lovers from being together.[vi]

We also know that Charles married Diana, a woman whose progressing-Sun was in an applying trine aspect to his progressing-Venus (a contrast to the square between his Venus and the then-married Camilla's Sun). This trine aspect was in a two degree cycle, beginning in 1980 completing to be exact in 1987 and separating beyond two degrees in 1995. We can also see that the year that Charles and Diana's progressed trine started to separate, 1987, is almost coterminous with both the resumption of Charles and Camilla's relationship, (which, according to biographers took place at an unspecified point in 1986) and the entry of a second progressed-Sun-Venus trine to within two degrees. This aspect became more powerful as time went by and achieved exactness in 1997, the year that Prince Charles hosted a party for Camilla's 50th birthday.

♈	♉	♊	♋	♌	♍	♎	♏	♐	♑	♒	♓
Aries	Taurus	Gemini	Cancer	Leo	Virgo	Libra	Scorpio	Sagittarius	Capricorn	Aquarius	Pisces

The long road to the perfection of this aspect began in 1948, at Charles birth, it was then nearly eleven degrees from being exact, but it slowly closed in at a rate of about a quarter of a degree per year, eventually setting the backdrop that drew this couple back together. (The rate of progress here is similar to the rate of progress of a conjunction of the same two planets shared by the Duke and Duchess of Windsor, mentioned in Chapter nine.)

You may think it odd that the same person would have the same (or at least a similar) progression in two relationships and that this progression can be seen to coincide with both relationships. It is odd. But we must remember that in the case of Charles and Diana, it was *his* Venus and *her* Sun in a trine aspect and in the case of Charles and Camilla, *her* Venus and *his* Sun in trine. This is significant, in that it is often easier for the woman to play the Venus (passive) role and the man to play the Sun (directive) role in a relationship.

For someone to abandon their partner after a progressed-Sun-Venus trine has run its course, and then take up with a new partner who shares the same aspect is not a unique event, as we will observe in Chapter thirteen.

Of course, this isn't always what happens, but the astrology as I practice it, fits the facts as I know them. Essentially the *progressed Sun*, Venus and Mars symbolize our changing views of respectively: our life path and goals (Sun); our relationships and tastes (Venus) and our physical expression (Mars), whereas our *natal Sun*, Venus and Mars are an unchanging template of primarily these factors.

Of course there are many other ideas or principles that these planets individually symbolize and we will explore these as the book develops.

I began to collect the *celebrity* relationship data that led to this book in May 2001; one more example is the first such relationship I examined, the relationship of two British celebrities: Chris Evans and Billie Piper.

This couple, who met when Billie Piper (at the time a teenage singing star, and who is now carving a niche as an award winning actress) appeared on Chris Evans' radio show at Christmas 2000, were married in May 2001

♈	♉	♊	♋	♌	♍	♎	♏	♐	♑	♒	♓
Aries	Taurus	Gemini	Cancer	Leo	Virgo	Libra	Scorpio	Sagittarius	Capricorn	Aquarius	Pisces

in Las Vegas. Chris Evans is a media tycoon and, at the time, the owner of the British radio station Virgin Radio, he had pursued Billie and bought her a Ferrari (even though she couldn't yet drive), which he had filled with flowers. They hit it off and their relationship worked.

I looked at the planetary positions for their birth charts and found nothing remarkable or 'close' in the angular relationships between the Sun, Venus and Mars. There is an inconjunct aspect (or an angle of 150 degrees) between Billie's natal-Venus, which is situated at about 18 degrees Virgo (at grid ref C6 in **Fig 8**) and Chris's natal-Mars, which is situated at about 18 degrees Aries (at grid ref B7 in **Fig 8**).

	1	2	3	4	5	6	7	8	9
A	Day	S.Time	Sun	Moon	Mercury	Venus	Mars		
B	1	0:37	11 ♈ 18'	16 ♌ 09'	23 ♓ 04'	25 ♒ 01'	17 ♈ 39'	1966	evans
C	22	12:04	29 ♍ 09'	29 ♏ 44'	17 ♎ 00'	18 ♍ 05'	01 ♐ 40'	1982	piper

Fig.8 Chris Evans and Billie Piper natal planetary positions Sun to Mars

I then added their progressed planets to the birth chart planets and found a number of close and relevant planetary contacts between the couple.

For their relationship I constructed a four-tier matrix that allowed me to see their progressed and natal planetary positions next to each other. This is what the final Evans-Piper grid matrix looks like:

	1	2	3	4	5	6	7	8	9
A	Day	S.Time	Sun	Moon	Mercury	Venus	Mars		
B	1	0:37	11 ♈ 18'	16 ♌ 09'	23 ♓ 04'	25 ♒ 01'	17 ♈ 39'	1966	evans
C	10	13:15	16 ♎ 51'	23 ♋ 42'	02 ♎ 27'	10 ♎ 31'	14 ♐ 18'	2001	piper
D	5	2:51	14 ♉ 32'	22 ♏ 37'	23 ♈ 04'	00 ♈ 20'	13 ♉ 04'	2001	evans
E	22	12:04	29 ♍ 09'	29 ♏ 44'	17 ♎ 00'	18 ♍ 05'	01 ♐ 40'	1982	piper

Fig.9. Chris Evans and Billie Piper natal planets together with progressed planetary positions for 2000

Chris Evans was born on 1 April 1966. The time used here is 12:00hrs

♈	♉	♊	♋	♌	♍	♎	♏	♐	♑	♒	♓
Aries	Taurus	Gemini	Cancer	Leo	Virgo	Libra	Scorpio	Sagittarius	Capricorn	Aquarius	Pisces

GMT. His progressed planets for 2001, his thirty-sixth year, are the positions of the planets 36 days after he was born – 5 May 1966.

Billie Piper was born on 22 September 1982. The time used here is 12:00hrs GMT. Her progressed planets for her nineteenth year are taken from the positions of planets on 10 October 1982, 19 days after she was born.

I use a grid reference system to navigate this matrix, so the date 1966 is at grid reference B8. Line A contains at grid ref A1 the *Day* in the ephemeris that the line was taken from, A2 holds the sidereal time or *S.Time* for that day at Noon in London, A3 contains the symbol for the Sun, A4 the Moon, A5 Mercury, A6 Venus and A7 Mars.

Row B includes information for Chris Evan's day of birth 1 April 1966. His Sun in Aries (B3), Moon (B4), Mercury (B5), Venus (B6), Mars (B7), the year 1966 (B8) and his identifier Evans (B9).

Row E includes information for Billie Piper's day of birth 22 September 1982. Her Sun in Virgo (E3), Moon (E4), Mercury (E5), Venus (E6), Mars (E7), the year 1982 (E8) and her identifier Piper (E9)

Row C contains Billie Piper's progressed planetary positions for the year 2001. Her Sun has progressed into Libra (C3), Moon (C4), Mercury (C5), Venus (C6), Mars (C7), the year 2001 (C8) and her identifier Piper (C9)

Row D contains Chris Evan's progressed planetary positions for the year 2001. His Sun has progressed into Taurus (D3), Moon (D4). Mercury (D5), Venus (D6), Mars (D7), the year 2001 (D8) and his identifier Evans (D9)

Most notably Billie's progressing-Venus at grid reference C6 in Fig. 9 was almost exactly opposite Chris's natal-Sun at grid reference B3 in Fig. 9. Also Chris's progressing-Venus was in a trine aspect (that is it was almost exactly 120 degrees) to Billie's natal-Mars (E7). Both of these aspects are 'applying', which is another word for 'waxing' or 'becoming exact'.

Astrologers might have expected to find these types of aspect in the

♈	♉	♊	♋	♌	♍	♎	♏	♐	♑	♒	♓
Aries	Taurus	Gemini	Cancer	Leo	Virgo	Libra	Scorpio	Sagittarius	Capricorn	Aquarius	Pisces

natal chart, but because the progressed chart is a model of how we are at the moment in question, it makes sense to speculate that these progressed planetary contacts play a role in relationships. What is exciting about this is that most of the textbooks that mention progressed planetary aspects or contacts emphasise the fact that they are only noticeable if they are near to being exact. If we look at the motion over time of the development of these two aspects we can see that there is only a short window of time for them to take advantage of these progressed aspects. Here is a graph showing how this window opened in late 1999 and closed in 2002:

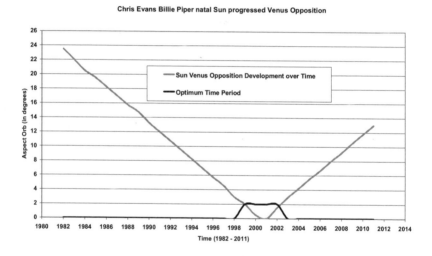

Fig.10. Possible window of opportunity (1999 to 2003) created by Evans-Piper Sun-Venus opposition

Chris and Billie's Sun-Venus opposition is accompanied by a second progressed aspect that is also a strong indicator of a close intimate relationship – their progressed-Venus natal-Mars trine (D6 – E7). Below is a graph showing the window of opportunity for this aspect to take place. It should be noted that the most intense and powerful point of any aspect is just before it becomes exact. An opposition between the Sun and Venus, as

♈	♉	♊	♋	♌	♍	♎	♏	♐	♑	♒	♓
Aries	Taurus	Gemini	Cancer	Leo	Virgo	Libra	Scorpio	Sagittarius	Capricorn	Aquarius	Pisces

will become clear during the course of this text, is an intensely *attracting* aspect, whereas the trine aspect between Venus and Mars, as well as being a physically attracting and satisfying exchange, is also an intensely *supportive* aspect where both feel equitably treated by each other.

Although their dates of birth are available, Chris and Billie's times of birth are not in the public domain at this time. It is therefore important to note that their window of opportunity is based upon them both being born at Noon. Using their actual birth times would not affect this graph too drastically as the motion of the progressed-Sun, Venus and Mars is never much more than a degree a year. The window is therefore at its most powerful between 2000 and 2001 (when the aspect was waxing, or applying) regardless of their times of birth. The Venus-Mars trine aspect begins to tail off from 2002 – 2004.

It was announced in September 2004 that Chris and Billie were to separate.

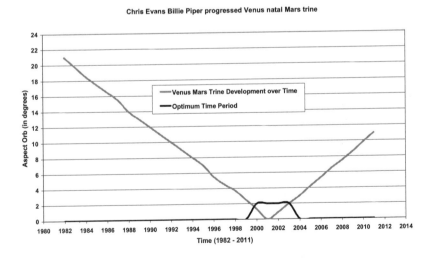

Chris Evans Billie Piper progressed Venus natal Mars trine

Fig.11. Graph showing a second window (2000 to 2004) created by Evans-Piper progressing-Venus - natal-Mars trine

♈	♉	♊	♋	♌	♍	♎	♏	♐	♑	♒	♓
Aries	Taurus	Gemini	Cancer	Leo	Virgo	Libra	Scorpio	Sagittarius	Capricorn	Aquarius	Pisces

If progressed planetary aspects really do play a role in relationships, surely this intervention will happen often and to a much greater degree of accuracy than the regular natal contacts that 'Love Sign' astrology describes. It occurred to me that if these types of aspect happen by progression they may show up as the astrological ingredients or catalysts that bring people together in the first instance and may also explain some fleeting relationships or the changes that happen internally to people in relationships that means their relationship has to change or end.

I went on to collect the birth dates of as many celebrity couples as I could, together with their marriage date or the year their relationship began. I have spent four years carefully checking their planetary connections. I have been aided in this venture by Cosmic Patterns *Kepler* software; by the *Astrodienst* ephemeris and by *Astrodatabank*, a collection of over 30,000 individual horoscopes.[vii]

I eventually discovered that the case of Evans and Piper was not unique and, indeed, you will find as this book progresses that the patterns displayed in these matrices and graphs are good examples of a phenomenon that I have found to take place in a significant number of the relationships.

I believe that these connections between Venus in one person's horoscope and other planets in their partner's charts create a favorable harmonic resonance that makes attraction more likely. Subtle differences between the type of aspect and the planets involved in the aspect dictate the manner of the courtship, the relationship and the dynamics that exist between the couple. An opposition of Mars and Venus is intensely sexual as it involves the masculine planet of physical love (Mars) facing the feminine planet of receptive love (Venus), a trine of Venus is wonderfully romantic as it combines the relationship planet of both partners, while a conjunction of the Sun and Venus creates a feeling of synoptic and similar relationship and life-choice ideas because it mixes the similarity of the conjunction with the ideals (Sun) of one partner with the aesthetic beauty and values (Venus)

♈	♉	♊	♋	♌	♍	♎	♏	♐	♑	♒	♓
Aries	Taurus	Gemini	Cancer	Leo	Virgo	Libra	Scorpio	Sagittarius	Capricorn	Aquarius	Pisces

of the other partner. The result is appreciation and respect. When these aspects are transient via the progressed chart, these effects change, dissipate or wear off.

So that's how progressed and natal synastry works. Often it is not easy to put your finger on exactly what it is you like or dislike about someone, astrology turns the whole process of defining these difficult questions into one of geometry and harmonics: basically mathematics with meaning. It makes sense to say: "I like him because he is kind and attractive", but it is also a subjective statement. To say, "I like him because his Venus is in Cancer and his Sun trines my Venus" is nonsense to most, but it is also an objective, mathematical statement that holds within it a lot of admittedly arcane, but actually tangible and *graspable* information.

As you may have already observed, trying to communicate complex concepts in an uncommon language such as astrology is no cakewalk. I have therefore taken pains to establish a step-by-step guide in the following chapters so that hopefully any reader can begin at the beginning and grasp the implications of this subject.

This book is not meant as a guidebook for those seeking the perfect relationship; (precisely because many of the relationships herein were not ideal relationships) more it is a book that explains the symbolic role certain planets and aspects play in relationship astrology.

Ideally and at most, it can help individuals who have been in love gain insight into why, how and when changes manifest; how others have dealt with change in relationships. It should be remembered that just one element or factor related to relationships is being revealed, the one that is common to most – what makes us attracted to someone. There is much more involved in the personal interaction of people and couples than just the role played by Venus.

The subjects selected for inclusion in this book have, in the main, been those famous people who have had a lot of romantic involvements with other famous people. From Chapter six onwards I will use a number of

♈	♉	♊	♋	♌	♍	♎	♏	♐	♑	♒	♓
Aries	Taurus	Gemini	Cancer	Leo	Virgo	Libra	Scorpio	Sagittarius	Capricorn	Aquarius	Pisces

different examples of relationships to illustrate my theories. Despite the fact that any book of this nature requires the author to be selective as to the relative merits of those cases included, I have tried to be unselective

How to Read Progressed Synastry Matrices: Cary Grant and Dyan Cannon

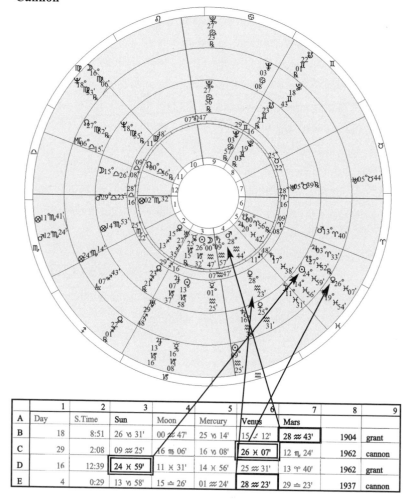

	1	2	3	4	5	6	7	8	9
			S.Time	Sun	Moon	Mercury	Venus	Mars	
A	Day	8:51	26 ♑ 31'	00 ♒ 47'	25 ♑ 14'	15 ♐ 12'	28 ♒ 43'	1904	grant
B	18	2:08	09 ♒ 25'	16 ♍ 06'	16 ♑ 08'	26 ♓ 07'	12 ♏ 24'	1962	cannon
C	29	12:39	24 ♓ 59'	11 ♓ 31'	14 ♓ 56'	25 ♒ 31'	13 ♈ 40'	1962	grant
D	16	0:29	13 ♑ 58'	15 ♎ 26'	01 ♒ 24'	28 ♒ 23'	29 ♎ 23'	1937	cannon
E	4								

Fig.12. Cary Grant and Dyan Cannon – "Quadwheel" Chart including their natal charts together with progressed charts for 1 January 1962

♈	♉	♊	♋	♌	♍	♎	♏	♐	♑	♒	♓
Aries	Taurus	Gemini	Cancer	Leo	Virgo	Libra	Scorpio	Sagittarius	Capricorn	Aquarius	Pisces

wherever possible and this is most notably the case where there are a series of relationships involving one individual or group that supports my theory I have also included any that do not directly support my theory. I have been spoiled for choice when it came to selecting examples for this book, which is always a good sign for any theory.

Cary Grant's natal chart is the innermost chart wheel and corresponds with row B in the matrix. This is followed by Dyan Cannon's natal chart in the inner middle wheel, which corresponds with row E. The next wheel, the outer middle wheel, is Cary's progressed chart and corresponds to Row D, while the outer most chart wheel (and Row C) is Dyan Cannon's progressed chart. Both progressed charts show the couple's progressed planetary positions for 1 January 1962. Cary and Dyan share a natal-Venus-Mars conjunction (the planetary zodiacal positions are highlighted with a single black border in the matrix) and a progressed-Sun-Venus conjunction (the planetary zodiacal positions are highlighted using a double lined border).

This picture illustrates the relationship between the progressed synastry grids used throughout this book and their relationship to the astrological charts. In this case, the picture is of the natal charts of Cary Grant and Dyan Cannon and their progressed charts for the year 1962, the year their relationship began. They met in 1961, married in 1965 and separated in 1968.

Quick Glossary

Synastry is the comparison of astrology charts, it is another word for relationship astrology

Progressions are the symbolic unfolding of the planet's positions in the birth chart. The type used in this book are calculated by moving the natal chart forward by one day for every year of life – the progressed planetary positions for your thirtieth year correspond with the planet's positions thirty days after you were born

The **zodiac** is the circle through which we measure planetary positions,

♈	♉	♊	♋	♌	♍	♎	♏	♐	♑	♒	♓
Aries	Taurus	Gemini	Cancer	Leo	Virgo	Libra	Scorpio	Sagittarius	Capricorn	Aquarius	Pisces

it is divided into twelve signs each occupying 30 degrees of this circle

The **natal chart** is another word for the birth chart or horoscope

An **aspect** is a geometric angle between two planets measured in degrees, minutes and seconds around the zodiacal circle

An **orb** is the geometric distance of inexactness we allow before we conclude that an aspect is of less value, this is also measured in degrees, minutes and seconds

A **conjunction** happens when two planets are very close together in the natal chart separated by no more than an 'orb' of two degrees

A **square** is formed when two planets are 90 degrees from each other around the zodiacal circle we allow a square from 88 to 92 degrees

A **trine** is formed when two planets are 120 degrees from each other around the zodiacal circle we allow a trine from 118 to 122 degrees

An **opposition** is formed by two planets directly opposite each other (or 180 degrees apart) around the zodiacal circle we allow an opposition from 178 to 180 degrees

An **inconjunct** (also called a quincunx) is formed when two planets are separated by a distance of 148 to 152 degrees

A **sextile** is formed when two planets are separated by a geometric distance of 58 to 62 degrees

A **semi-sextile** is formed when two planets are separated by a geometric distance of 28 to 32 degrees

Transits are the real-time (rather than symbolic) motions of the planets and their contacts with planets in the natal and progressed charts are delineated to establish things that *happen to you* rather than *change that takes place within you*

The **Sun** is the planet of will and aspirations – it negotiates our deals

Venus is the planet of love, attraction, romance and values – it makes our compromises

Mars is the planet of aggression, sex and desire – it asserts our desires

♈	♉	♊	♋	♌	♍	♎	♏	♐	♑	♒	♓
Aries	Taurus	Gemini	Cancer	Leo	Virgo	Libra	Scorpio	Sagittarius	Capricorn	Aquarius	Pisces

Two

Relationship Astrology or Synastry

That day the solar system married us, whether we knew it or not...
Ted Hughes

Natal Synastry (or relationship astrology) is the comparison of two birth charts in an attempt to discern the type of social, spiritual, physical, aspirational and intellectual connection two people will make with each other. Natal synastry involves the comparison of the planetary positions in both birth charts in order for the astrologer to assess what the manner of these connections are and which will be most noticeable in a couple's relationship. Many factors are taken into consideration, but in the case of intimate relationships (the subject of this book) those that relate to harmony and attraction are the most important, at least initially. Many other factors also play a role in natal synastry; from which planets are in which signs to how many contacts or angles are formed between the planets.

Interpreting the effects of different planetary mixes is in itself a little bit like interpreting soup. If synastry is a fact of life, then all the planets are involved in the mix and as anyone who has tasted soup will tell you, some flavors are more subtle than others. What this study of progressed and natal synastry seems to reveal is that at the beginning of an intimate relationship, more often than not, some of these planetary flavors are more noticeable than others. The study also suggests that all we need is one harmonious pattern or flavor to make us believe that 'this soup' is the best we've ever

♈	♉	♊	♋	♌	♍	♎	♏	♐	♑	♒	♓
Aries	Taurus	Gemini	Cancer	Leo	Virgo	Libra	Scorpio	Sagittarius	Capricorn	Aquarius	Pisces

tasted. Again this is because the resonance caused by a single harmonious astrological connection has the effect of 'music', which somehow limits or overrides the surrounding 'noise'.

What is Attraction?

To attract is to draw by some winning influence: charm, allure, to entice, to win. So says the dictionary used by Lois Haines Sargent on page 10 of her book about relationship astrology *How to Handle your Human Relationships.* She continues:

> *'If you are attracted to another person, you are interested, curious, have a friendly feeling, and are disposed to look for favor upon that other person. You will pursue and encourage the acquaintanceship. An attraction felt between members of the same sex creates friendship. When two persons of the opposite sex are strongly attracted and feel the pull of animal magnetism, or what can be termed the polarity of opposites, we have the basis for romance.* 'viii

Sargent was writing the 1950s and as such, her views of same-sex relationships are colored by her time, but she makes some important points and her short book is generally considered to be of great value to relationship astrologers.

> *'Sometimes such an attraction is superficial or temporary. Many a person has been attracted to another person of the opposite sex for a brief period and afterward wondered exactly what he or she had seen in that person* 'ix

Sargent does not give a reason for fleeting attraction, but she does give astrological reasons for attraction. I can neither totally agree nor disagree with her views on what attracts individuals to each other from an astrological perspective. Her views are these:

> *'If real love is to develop, the attraction should be more than a superficial one. In comparing horoscopes we analyze various factors,*

♈	♉	♊	♋	♌	♍	♎	♏	♐	♑	♒	♓
Aries	Taurus	Gemini	Cancer	Leo	Virgo	Libra	Scorpio	Sagittarius	Capricorn	Aquarius	Pisces

and the greater the number of aspects of attraction, the stronger will be the attraction ...A comparison based on planets alone, without an Ascendant for either party would be inadequate, and judgement must be rendered with many reservations. **Most important in judging attraction is the aspect between the Ascendant of one chart and the planets of the other** *[Sargent's emphasis].* [x]

She continues:

'Unless the Ascendant or Descendant of one horoscope combines with the planets of the other by sign, it is doubtful that the attraction would result in marriage. [Sargent's emphasis]' [xi]

I don't know how much experimentation Lois Sargent did to arrive at this conclusion, but it is certain that in the 1950s she did not consider the idea that progressing planets play a role in attraction. She emphasises that the Sun, Moon, Venus and Mars are of major importance, but that Mercury and Jupiter are also important, but less indicative of emotional appeal. I agree with her on these points

I have seen some examples of successful relationships that do not include progressed or natal-Venus aspects but which include aspects of either the Sun or Venus and the Descendant. Sargent's view may be correct, but my view, supported by evidence, is that Venus is the prime mover in attraction. My study is not exclusively arrived at through looking at couples whose time of birth is known, but their date of birth and (crucially) the date of their relationship is available. This means that while I can neither agree nor disagree that all of Sargent's views are correct or not, I do contend and will evidence the fact that planetary aspects are more important to attraction than she believed when writing in 1958.

What is a Relationship?

A relationship in the context of this book is an intimate union of two

♈	♉	♊	♋	♌	♍	♎	♏	♐	♑	♒	♓
Aries	Taurus	Gemini	Cancer	Leo	Virgo	Libra	Scorpio	Sagittarius	Capricorn	Aquarius	Pisces

people whose ideal purpose is to provide mutual support and love, the result
being a commitment of time, attention, love and dedication, whether that be
for one night or for sixty years. The union is usually accompanied by some
level of sexual attraction and activity. Notwithstanding this, the actual
purpose of the union can be self-satisfaction and the actual result can be
possessiveness, jealousy, indifference or hatred. When I use the term
conventional intimate relationship I do not necessarily mean *gender-
conventional*, I mean *emotionally conventional*. There is no difference,
astrologically, between the feelings of attraction and love that same-sex
partners have for each other than those between partners of different sexes.
Examples of unconventional relationships include those entered by force,
arranged marriages, marriages of convenience, relationships with *strong*
sado-masochistic elements, ménage a trois, relationships where one
individual seeks to have overwhelming control over their partner, relationships which begin and continue through threats and violence and
politically-motivated or (on occasion) some royal and aristocratic
marriages.

What is Love?

There are different kinds of intimate love described by psychology and
sociology. Psychology sees two types of love, *passionate love* (longing
accompanied by physiological arousal) and *companionate love* (positive
regard, affection and intimacy not accompanied by physical arousal).

Robert Sternberg's *Triangular Theory of Love* suggests three elements
of love: intimacy, passion and commitment in different combinations cause
different types of love. Intimacy in isolation accounts for *liking* or friendship, *limerance* or infatuation is the result of passion without intimacy or
commitment. *Empty love* is caused by commitment without passion or
intimacy. *Romantic love* is a combination of intimacy and passion without
committment while *companionate love* is the result of intimacy and
commitment minus passion. The whirlwind romance or *fatuous love* is

♈	♉	♊	♋	♌	♍	♎	♏	♐	♑	♒	♓
Aries	Taurus	Gemini	Cancer	Leo	Virgo	Libra	Scorpio	Sagittarius	Capricorn	Aquarius	Pisces

caused by passion and commitment, but is not necessarily accompanied by any knowledge or intimacy, while the highest form of love in this theory, *consummate love*, is the combination of passion, intimacy and commitment.

There are other theories, notably the three phases of love: lust, attraction and attachment. Scientists believe that the brain's state when in love is similar to a form of mental illness. Love, it appears, has an effect something akin to drugs.

At the opposite end of the spectrum to astrology stand authors such as Garth Fletcher, whose concern is in understanding loving relationships from a scientific perspective, related mainly to genetics and evolutionary theory. He writes:

'The warp and woof of human love illustrate two key points. First that evolution works by tinkering with what already exists, so that evolved adaptations often have a ramshackle quality about them. Human love is like this. It consists of a hotchpotch of cognitions, emotions and behaviors that obviously have a genetic basis, but which unfold in a flexible fashion depending on the cultural and social environment and the goals of the individual. Second, striking universalities or strong cross-cultural similarities indeed suggest that love and related emotions represent specific adaptations that have associated functions in humans.[xii]

Of course, this book tries to shed light on what Fletcher describes as striking universalities.

Often relationships begin with the hope that both parties will share ideals, support each other in ways that satisfy both people, and that they will be physically matched in both aesthetic attraction and in terms of levels of gentleness, tactility and communication.

Certainly among many people today, conventionally speaking, the first level of compatibility is often but not always, physical attraction, followed by intellectual compatibility, through to aspirational, emotional, communicational and participative factors. Similar social, educational,

♈	♉	♊	♋	♌	♍	♎	♏	♐	♑	♒	♓
Aries	Taurus	Gemini	Cancer	Leo	Virgo	Libra	Scorpio	Sagittarius	Capricorn	Aquarius	Pisces

cultural and religious backgrounds are also said to play a part in compatibility. Occasionally people compromise heavily in one area in order to achieve a level of compatibility with their partner for reasons such as wealth and status or the comfort of companionship to avert loneliness and solitude. In short-lived relationships the compromise is usually heavily in favour of physical and sexual attraction and compatibility.

Astrological factors (Venus, Sun, Mars in harmonious aspect) should reflect conventional compatibility, but not necessarily artificial or compromised compatibility as there are other factors involved here that may outweigh these conventional compatibility factors.

Just as we have many processes supporting our life, for example, we breathe air, this is linked to the taking in of oxygen, which enters the bloodstream and is pumped by the heart around the body and to the brain. These processes are all relevant and connected but they are separate processes all the same. The same thing can be said of aspects in the progressed chart. Each aspect highlights a dynamic of behavior: when a planet's position connects with the planetary position of someone else's birth chart or progressed chart (at the time), then the aspect formed relates to an element of their relationship.

Astrological theory (such as it is) can be understood simply if we say that the planets act like connectors and receptors: like blocks of different shapes and sizes that try to find a fit. If this fit is a 90-degree square, the relationship may be conflicting, remote, businesslike or requiring lots of hard work depending on which planets are making the fit. If the fit is a triangle or trine, then the connection may be easy going, naturally flowing and spontaneous. If there are many different fits, squares, triangles, circles (conjunctions and oppositions) and pentagons (quintiles) there may be a relationship full of different dynamics, the success of which depends on the context of the relationship. This is the case with most relationships. Also where there is no connection between planets, there may be no relationship after the initial meeting, or, in a relationship the planets that do not

♈	♉	♊	♋	♌	♍	♎	♏	♐	♑	♒	♓
Aries	Taurus	Gemini	Cancer	Leo	Virgo	Libra	Scorpio	Sagittarius	Capricorn	Aquarius	Pisces

connect[xiii] symbolize activities and interests that are kept separate. The aspects between the planets in the two (or four) charts are basically connectivity protocols.

The Sun in one chart is the part of one individual that attempts to negotiate deals with other individuals. The planet Venus is the part of the chart that seeks to reach compromise. Essentially what is taking place in the first instance is a process of striking a deal. If the Sun and Venus connect by favorable or harmonious aspect in a potentially intimate relationship, then the likelihood of a deal being struck is higher than if the the Sun and Venus don't connect harmoniously or do not connect at all. The 120-degree trine, the same-degree conjunction and the 180-degree opposition provide the most heightened or most conventionally attractively shaped connections and their effect is probably the most influential factor in relationship astrology. This does not guarantee quality, just heightened feelings of ease, attraction and harmony. In contrast to the Sun, Mars asserts physicality and Venus often admires this trait, the result is basically 'physical cooperation caused by sexual attraction'. When Venus in one chart meets Venus in another chart, there can be a soft, romantic and sentimental attraction...and lots of gushy poetry.

Often what happens in the celebrity relationships I have studied is that the harmonious or good aspects that are present at the beginning of the relationship appear to hide or play down any difficult issues that are also present. This could be termed a *Rose-Colored Scenario*. People can often put up with areas of incompatibility because their attention is diverted by, say, good sex; the pure romance of their situation or the 'magnetic' attraction the couple feel. In essence people wear 'rose colored spectacles' and ignore negativity at the outset of relationships. The temptation is to believe that conflicts or incompatibilities can be either lived-with or that they may be able to change the other person in some way. It would appear that in cases where progressed synastry is the main attracting factor that this acceptance doesn't last forever. Although when the progressing factor that

♈	♉	♊	♋	♌	♍	♎	♏	♐	♑	♒	♓
Aries	Taurus	Gemini	Cancer	Leo	Virgo	Libra	Scorpio	Sagittarius	Capricorn	Aquarius	Pisces

brought a couple together passes, it may be replaced by some situation or progressing aspect that is actually better.

I have seen examples that suggest to me that occasionally, negative or disharmonious progressed aspects keep people apart and when they start to separate, the floor is cleared for a relationship to begin. This is the *Romeo-Juliet* or *Star-Crossed* scenario mentioned previously and created by *separating* or *waning* square aspects to Venus.

Astrology books that make comments about planetary synastry tend to suggest that a mixture of harmonious and disharmonious aspects is good in a relationship, the idea being that the harmonious aspects are like undiluted aspects of joy and disharmonious aspects are like undiluted aspects of conflict. A mixture of both waters down the effect of each aspect and creates a balance in the relationship that can be seen to have a character of its own. This character is, of course, ideally functional rather than dysfunctional.

With natal to natal contacts for example, someone whose natal-Sun is at 1 degree Leo (people born on around 25 July will have this Sun position) will always have some kind of harmonious affinity with those people who have their natal-Sun at 1 degree Aries (people born around 21 March) and 1 degree Sagittarius (people born around 23 November). Of course, if their natal Moon is at 1 degree Cancer, then not only do they have a Sun-Moon square in their own chart, it will color the way they get along with their 1 degree Aries pals more sharply than their 1 degree Sagittarian pals simply because 1 degree Cancer is a more difficult aspect for 1 degree Aries than it is for 1 degree Sagittarius.

Not that square aspects are all bad, in fact they are often constructive. The problem with them in relationships is that most people are conventionally accustomed to expect harmony and ease rather than conflict and friction in close personal relationships. Square aspects in the natal chart deliver the capacity for hard work in individual personalities; they do so by creating a conflict situation that requires resolution. This is the case with

♈	♉	♊	♋	♌	♍	♎	♏	♐	♑	♒	♓
Aries	Taurus	Gemini	Cancer	Leo	Virgo	Libra	Scorpio	Sagittarius	Capricorn	Aquarius	Pisces

relationships, with a Sun square it may not be that you do not find your partner attractive; you may even have 'psychic' moments. The problem can be external constraints that come between you, for example parenthood, fame, distance, poverty or imprisonment. As with all astrology, being such a complex of unique connections, conventions are just that, conventions; they are not constants. But as I hope to show, understanding these conventions can be useful in attempting to uncover the hidden patterns that underpin relationship astrology.

All practising astrologers know that the birth chart is a dynamic rather than a static entity, it is something that changes from day to day, month to month, year to year, their only problem is that they have no consensus as to how to measure these changes. There is also disagreement on how much emphasis should be placed on planets in the progressed chart. There are a number of different ways to track the changes in a birth chart and by far the most popular is the method I have employed: *the Day for a Year* method. This method is described in detail in Chapter three, but basically the astrologer takes the day of your birth and counts forward one day for every year of your life. A chart can be erected for each day after the day of your birth and these charts correspond directly with each year after your birth, showing how you change. So if you want to know about yourself aged 40 you count forty days after your birth and erect a chart for that day. As the planets move at different speeds, certain areas of personality change at different rates. The Sun and the Moon are the most constant of these planets. The Sun moves one degree per year. It would therefore take the Sun 360 years to move through all the signs whereas the Moon moves around the whole chart in about 28 years.

All of the planets apart from the Sun and the Moon undergo an astronomical anomaly which means that they appear to travel backwards through the sky (from our point of view) this is termed retrogradation, the upshot of this is that their positions relative to Earth and therefore their apparent speed of motion, changes. This means that for some people

♈	♉	♊	♋	♌	♍	♎	♏	♐	♑	♒	♓
Aries	Taurus	Gemini	Cancer	Leo	Virgo	Libra	Scorpio	Sagittarius	Capricorn	Aquarius	Pisces

(depending on when they are born) Venus will move forwards quickly (just faster than the Sun), for others it will move backwards slowly while for some it may slow down, stop, then start to move slowly backwards or forwards through the zodiac sign it occupies. Mercury moves more quickly than the Sun, but it also appears to move backwards more often than Venus and Mars. Mars moves more slowly than Venus and appears to move backwards less often.

Goodman Classifications

Linda Goodman wrote her book *Love Signs* in the 1970s, this book took eight years to complete and details the relationship dynamics between all the Sun Signs. It uses a code to describe the angles between the signs.

Linda Goodman's Sun Sign Pattern Classifications

Same sign relationships are called	1:1	This corresponds with the Conjunction
Adjoining sign relationships are called	2:12	This corresponds with the Semi-sextile
Signs separated by one sign are called	3:11	This corresponds with the Sextile
Signs separated by two signs are called	4:10	This corresponds with the Square
Signs separated by three signs are called	5:9	This corresponds with the Trine
Signs separated by four signs are called	6:8	This corresponds with the Inconjunct
Signs opposite each other are called	7:7	This corresponds with the Opposition

Although in principle I agree with the poetic interpretations given by Linda in *Love Signs*, I can also say that if you were to use her book as the basis for a scientific experiment into whether more Aries people were happily married to Leos than to Cancerians, I would not expect positive results. This is because although the Sun is important in astrology, on its own it does not symbolize the principles at work in close intimate relationships. It is a part of the relationship dynamic in the conventional sense, but we do not compare the Sun position in one chart with the Sun position in another to signify attraction. Often people with a close

♈	♉	♊	♋	♌	♍	♎	♏	♐	♑	♒	♓
Aries	Taurus	Gemini	Cancer	Leo	Virgo	Libra	Scorpio	Sagittarius	Capricorn	Aquarius	Pisces

positive Sun-Sun link get along well, but there is more to a relationship than this.

Compatibility in Astrology

More often we look at the Sun in one chart and Venus in another for attraction, the Sun and the Moon for marriage and emotional support, Sun-Mars and Venus-Mars for physical and sexual compatibility, then secondarily, Venus-Venus for romantic appreciation, Mars-Mars for working together or physical and methodological interraction and Sun-Sun for compromise required (Venus-Venus, Sun-Venus and Mars-Venus for willingness to compromise). We would also include Mercury for intellectual matching and ability to mentally understand and communicate with each other. For example if I were to look at a set of couples who use a lot of verbal communication in their lovemaking I might look at their Mercury-Mars, Mercury-Venus or Mercury-Pluto contacts, depending on the content of their bedroom discussions. Essentially though, to investigate whether relationship astrology has any validity, it would be folly to just use Sun-Sun contacts.

Carl Jung carried out a famous and inconclusive experiment with marriage astrology. He used the Sun, the Moon and the Ascendant/Descendant axis (this axis, also referred to as the cusp of the 1st house - the Ascendant and 7th house - the Descendant, are the degrees of the zodiac opposite each other on the horizon at the moment of birth), as his significators. He also worked with wide 'orbs' or wide aspects, this means that a conjunction between the Sun and the Moon would still be valid when these two celestial bodies are eight degrees apart. Many astrologers would say this is not a particularly relevant distance for the Sun and Moon. He only used the conjunction (0 to 8 degrees) and opposition (172 - 180 degrees) aspects, ignoring completely the most theoretically powerful   conventional relationship aspect, the trine (120 degrees).

♈	♉	♊	♋	♌	♍	♎	♏	♐	♑	♒	♓
Aries	Taurus	Gemini	Cancer	Leo	Virgo	Libra	Scorpio	Sagittarius	Capricorn	Aquarius	Pisces

Synastry or Human Relationship Astrology

There are many different ways of seeing how astrology works. Astrologers tend towards the following ideas about the role of Mars and Venus and the Sun and Moon in synastry.

Firstly, the role of these planets is gender-dependent. I take a different but complimentary view.

Ronald Davison writes:

'...*Venus shows by its sign and position and aspectual strength, the native capacity to create and maintain harmony... in a male horoscope, the Moon and Venus are the significators of the feminine side of the native's nature and, by extension, of the type of woman he is likely to be attracted.* 'xiv

'...*In a female horoscope the Sun and Mars represent the masculine side of the nature and, by extension, the type of man to whom the native is likely to be attracted.* 'xv

Dependent on many internal and external factors (and there are many) people exhibit and conduct themselves with differing levels of what you might call their 'masculine and feminine sides'; some women are more controlling, assertive and outgoing than others and often this is influenced by the behavior of their partners past and present. The same goes for men. Trying to pin down which gender responds most to their inner Mars or inner Venus is difficult. It is better just to observe the connections between these planets and assess from them which person takes which role in the relationship. The Sun and Mars are usually more active and the Moon and Venus more passive. Gender is relevant, but only in an archetypal way, so limiting astrology to Mars and Sun = Man *and* Moon and Venus = Woman would probably lead to confusion and impasse. I suspect that some relationships that fail have 'their planets the wrong way around', and the role reversal is a contributing factor, but it is by no means the case for all such relationships.

♈	♉	♊	♋	♌	♍	♎	♏	♐	♑	♒	♓
Aries	Taurus	Gemini	Cancer	Leo	Virgo	Libra	Scorpio	Sagittarius	Capricorn	Aquarius	Pisces

Three

Dynamic Astrology

Ch ch ch changes...
David Bowie

Ptolemy, the Greek-Egyptian astronomer who lived in the second century, describes five astrological aspects: the conjunction, which happens when two or more planets are in the same place in the zodiac, the 60 degree sextile or one sixth of a hexagon, the 90 degree square, one quarter of an actual square, the 120 degree trine, or one third of a triangle and the 180 degree opposition, where two planets are directly opposite each other.

The sixteenth-century astronomer-astrologer Johannes Kepler rejected the basis on which Ptolemy made his distinction between aspects: that they were based upon the ideas that the signs in which the planets fell when making these aspects were either in elemental harmony or in conflict (Earth and Water mixed well, Fire and Water did not). But he did use Ptolemy's analogy of the aspects in astrology being similar to the notes in the musical scale.

David Plant writes:

Pythagoras discovered that the pitch of a musical note depends upon the length of the string which produces it. This allowed him to correlate the intervals of the musical scale with simple numerical ratios. When a musician plays a string stopped exactly half-way along its length an octave is produced. The octave has the same quality of sound as the note produced by the unstopped string but, as it vibrates at twice the frequency, it is heard at a higher pitch. The mathematical relationship between the keynote and its octave is expressed as a 'frequency ratio' of

♈	♉	♊	♋	♌	♍	♎	♏	♐	♑	♒	♓
Aries	Taurus	Gemini	Cancer	Leo	Virgo	Libra	Scorpio	Sagittarius	Capricorn	Aquarius	Pisces

1:2. In every type of musical scale, the notes progress in a series of intervals from a keynote to the octave above or below. Notes separated by intervals of a perfect fifth (ratio 2:3) and a perfect fourth (3:4) have always been the most important 'consonances' in western music. In recognising these ratios, Pythagoras had discovered the mathematical basis of musical harmony.

The key to Kepler's proposed reform is his approach to the aspects. Traditional astrology recognises five significant relationships, based upon the twelvefold division of the zodiac signs. Ptolemy taught that their significance was derived by analogy with the ratios of the musical scale. The conjunction is equivalent to the same two notes played in unison. The opposition divides the circle in the ratio 1:2, which corresponds to the octave. The sextile (5:6) corresponds to a minor third, the square (3:4) to a perfect fourth and the trine (2:3) to a perfect fifth. By placing less emphasis upon the zodiac signs, however, Kepler was free to explore additional aspect relationships in his pursuit of the Pythagorean synthesis of music, geometry and astronomy.[xvi]

Kepler collected and studied at least 800 birth charts and concluded that when planets formed angles equivalent to particular harmonic ratios a resonance was set up, both in the archetypal Earth Soul and in the souls of individuals born under those configurations: "in the vital power of the human being that is ignited at birth there glows that remembered image..."

The geometric-harmonic imprint constitutes "the music that impels the listener to dance" as the movements of the planets, by transit and direction (or progression), echo and re-echo the natal theme.[xvii]

This musical explanation of astrology relates well to the idea that people are attracted to each other based on frequencies and resonances inherent in their birth charts in the same way that we can be attracted to a piece of music or a work of art, we are actually responding to its frequency or its

♈	♉	♊	♋	♌	♍	♎	♏	♐	♑	♒	♓
Aries	Taurus	Gemini	Cancer	Leo	Virgo	Libra	Scorpio	Sagittarius	Capricorn	Aquarius	Pisces

number rather than its literalness.

John Anthony West explains:

'In the [world] where Mozart moves us, it is frequency rather than magnitude that is significant. Magnitude may or may not play a role (as in rock music). But there is no known modern scientific way to judge the significance of frequency, even though it can be measured very precisely. The secret of quality (in music, art, architecture, and to a lesser extent in poetry and literature) resides in frequency, harmony and rhythm and our inherent ability to respond. What is involved is the phenomenon of Resonance. When we deal with frequency, harmony and rhythm, or Resonance, what we are actually dealing with is Number, and the interplay of principles; the same principles upon which astrology is based.'[xviii]

David Plant continues:

In addition to the Ptolemaic aspects, Kepler proposed the quintile (72°), bi-quintile (144°) and sesqui-quadrate (135°). Extending the analogy of the musical scale, the quintile, a division of the circle by five, is equivalent to an interval of a major third (4:5), the sesqui-quadrate to a minor sixth (5:8) and the bi-quintile to a major sixth (3:5).[xix]

Secondary Progressions

Change on the internal psychological level is discerned in astrology by expanding out the birth chart, this is done by *progressing* the planet's positions in the chart. I should reiterate that this process should not be confused with transits, which are effectively the positions of the planets moving through the zodiac on any given day. The relationship between transiting planets and planets in your birth chart is unique, but their positions (roughly equating to the theme of the moment) are constant, meaning that one pattern affects everyone's different birth chart in different

♈	♉	♊	♋	♌	♍	♎	♏	♐	♑	♒	♓
Aries	Taurus	Gemini	Cancer	Leo	Virgo	Libra	Scorpio	Sagittarius	Capricorn	Aquarius	Pisces

ways. Implicit in this is that the transiting chart is thematic, but our response to it is varied.

Progressions take one time frame (in the case of secondary progressions, a day) and use it to symbolically explain another time frame (a year)

In the foreword to Nancy Hastings book *Secondary Progressions* Rob Hand writes:

'One of the most widely used predictive techniques in astrology is secondary directions, or progressions as they are also called. The basis of this technique is simple, although a bit mind-bending to those not used to the ways of astrology. One simply substitutes one day for each year of life after birth. If an individual is 30 years old a chart is erected for 30 days after birth, examined both in its own right and compared to the natal chart as well.'

He goes on to say:

'Secondaries are among the most widespread and useful predictive techniques in the astrologers toolbox.'

'..the inherent problem with secondaries is that they have no plausible rationale, at least none that is given in astrological literature. The noted author and metaphysical theorist Arthur Young[xx] has commented in private correspondence that secondaries, and in fact all systems of directions, are the most revolutionary techniques in astrology...Only a symbolic world-view in which symbolism has the same level of reality that science gives to energy and matter can serve to explain secondaries and other kinds of direction.' [xxi]

Bernadette Brady writes in *Predictive Astrology The Eagle and the Lark*:

'...One of the first considerations is to look at how progressions differ from transits and the additional information they yield...All transits and progressions will start to express their energy, or effect, at the deep

♈	♉	♊	♋	♌	♍	♎	♏	♐	♑	♒	♓
Aries	Taurus	Gemini	Cancer	Leo	Virgo	Libra	Scorpio	Sagittarius	Capricorn	Aquarius	Pisces

levels of the unconscious. The first indications of this may occur in the dream world as ideas and energy bubble up to levels of consciousness. However, it is here that transits and progressions go separate ways. The transit being a new piece of energy, is considered so alien by the conscious mind that it is rapidly projected onto the outside world so it can be viewed safely by the conscious mind...The progression, however, is not alien. It has been recorded at the time of infancy and meticulously collected piece by piece by the individual in the first 90 odd days of life. [xxii]

Stephen Arroyo writes on the subject:

'*There are at least a dozen methods of progressions currently used by astrologers...As far as I have been able to determine, the secondary progressions are best for understanding psychological developments and periods of unfoldment and intensive growth, although they often correspond with specific events and major experiences as well.*'[xxiii]

Charles E. O. Carter stated that nothing can come to pass by progression that is not indicated in the natal chart.[xxiv]

Robert Blaschke interprets this as:

'*Carter believed that the natal chart limits the operation of progressions inexorably; the natal chart shows what is likely to happen and the progressions, when.*' [xxv]

Martin Freeman writes:

'*...progressions are an entirely personal forecasting indicator, unlike transits, which are collective.*' [xxvi]

Eric Francis mentions the narrow orbs of secondary progressions along with the ideas of them leading up to the culmination of an event:

♈	♉	♊	♋	♌	♍	♎	♏	♐	♑	♒	♓
Aries	Taurus	Gemini	Cancer	Leo	Virgo	Libra	Scorpio	Sagittarius	Capricorn	Aquarius	Pisces

'There is no special trick to reading progressions except to say that you must look at the chart very carefully. You look carefully at the degrees, and exactly what happened last, and what is about to happen next. Well, that's the whole trick. One must be extremely precise and not miss much. Really, one puts the chart under a microscope and looks at every little subtle movement. Tradition holds that when using progressions you work with extremely small orbs, within one degree on either side of an aspect. As the aspect applies or forms, some kind of development or experience is approaching; as the aspect is perfected, the experience is in full strength; as the aspect separates, the experience wanes and gives way to the next one. Progressions train an astrologer to look at the chart very carefully. That is a fine habit and it only supports intuition.' [xxvii]

Dane Rudhyar writes:

'On the one hand we have the radical birth chart, which gives us the symbolical pattern or hieroglyph, of the individual being – a spatial figure. On the other hand we have what are called progressions or directions which aim at determining the unfoldment of the individual being throughout the span of his Earthly life – a time element' [xxviii]

Laurie Efrein says on the difference between transits and progressions:

'Technically the difference between transits and progressions is that transits show what happens to you, and progressions show how one gradually changes and develops.' [xxix]

First used by Placidus de Titus circa 1657,[xxx] but possibly postulated by Johannes Kepler about fifty years before,[xxxi] secondary progressions are one of the most widely used predictive or forecasting tools in astrology.

In practical terms, the day-for-a-year system requires the astrologer to treat a day in the ephemeris (table of planetary positions) as symbolic of a

♈	♉	♊	♋	♌	♍	♎	♏	♐	♑	♒	♓
Aries	Taurus	Gemini	Cancer	Leo	Virgo	Libra	Scorpio	Sagittarius	Capricorn	Aquarius	Pisces

year of life counted from the day of birth. This means that there is an astrological relationship between the planets and the moment of birth and the planets which relate to the current moment. So the line of planets in the ephemeris thirty days after the date of birth relate directly to the thirtieth year of life. Most astrologers believe the planets show how we change. *Implicit* in this view is the idea that in some way we *become* our progressed chart or that our actual birth chart changes in line with the potentials in the natal chart. This philosophy has not been widely explored, but as can be seen from Charles Carter's comment, the natal chart puts limits on the extent of expression that progressions can achieve.

If progressions 'work' in relationship astrology then it seems logical to assume that their influence will be present for a limited period of time and present only for the duration of the orb of the aspect.[xxxii] The modern Western use of progressed aspects, described above by Eric Francis, demands that they have a limited influence in terms of time. This is where progressed aspects differ in astrology from natal aspects where a much larger orb is allowed and no time limit is inferred. Many Western astrologers use progressions to calibrate or rectify individual horoscopes this is because progressions are the astrological equivalent of a fine-tuning device.

Secondary progressions (along with other systems including profections, solar arc, primary, minor and tertiary progressions) are a symbolic system, which in the view of some stands outside the literal/astronomical cause and effect scenario of the natal chart and as Hand observes, there is no scientific rationale for this. Indeed, to some people who do not do astrology, they are an absurdity: an idea that is patently unscientific because it involves a symbolic relationship between planets and people rather than an actual relationship (the planets positions at birth). My view is that this is a good reason to take progressions seriously.

♈	♉	♊	♋	♌	♍	♎	♏	♐	♑	♒	♓
Aries	Taurus	Gemini	Cancer	Leo	Virgo	Libra	Scorpio	Sagittarius	Capricorn	Aquarius	Pisces

How Can Progressions Work?

In order to realise how congruent the idea of symbolic progressions might be, we have to drop the idea that some kind of gravitational ray or force causes astrological correspondences. Just because the natal chart is a real-time event this does not prove anything about astrology or the means by which astrology works. It is therefore no massive philosophical leap towards accepting the idea of symbolic progressions.

As mentioned at the beginning of this book, systems of progression have been likened to mathematical fractals. Eric Francis says the following:

'Anyone familiar with the concept of a fractal will recognise how this concept relates to progressions. A fractal is an image of a pattern in nature. The idea was developed by an IBM research scientist named Benoit Mandelbrot who in the 1970s was working on graphic representation of complex geometric patterns. The work had the potential of helping discover a method for how to store extremely complex images in very small amounts of disk drive space. What scientists soon discovered as a result of Mandelbrot's work is that nature is entirely a phenomenon of patterns. Even the most seemingly chaotic movements of nature — the bubbles under a waterfall, the millions of twigs in a tree, or the shape of a coast line — exist in distinct patterns.

Essentially, if you look at a small piece of the whole — a sample of the tree's branch system, for example — you can use a computer and predict the shape of the tree. Studying the patterns in small samples of a shoreline will tell you something about the shape of the whole coast. There are no truly chaotic patterns in nature; they all reveal an underlying order if you know how to look for it, or rather, let yourself see it. This is called fractal geometry. A fractal is an image of a chaos pattern.

This phenomenon extends to the study of astrology. Applying fractal theory to the progressed horoscope, we have a basis for the idea that a small sample of life (the first 90 days) is going to tell us something

♈	♉	♊	♋	♌	♍	♎	♏	♐	♑	♒	♓
Aries	Taurus	Gemini	Cancer	Leo	Virgo	Libra	Scorpio	Sagittarius	Capricorn	Aquarius	Pisces

about the whole pattern of experience (the first 90 years). I believe that the progressed horoscope represents the first use of the concept of fractal theory even though it was discovered centuries before fractals were discovered. 'xxxiii

Synastric Progressions

Progressing planets are like cars driving along a highway. They mostly travel at different speeds, and sometimes in different directions. Often we find one vehicle is driving alongside another vehicle doing about the same speed. When faster moving cars approach they are only alongside for a short time and before long they are away and out of sight. This is similar to the way synastric progressions work. Sometimes though, driving on a long country road, when you arrive at a crossroads in the middle of nowhere, you find that the only other car for miles around has arrived at the same crossroads at exactly the same time. This is also a bit like a serendipitous synastric progression, and, according to my observations, this happens quite often.

Progressed *aspects* (angular relationships between two planets) are different to aspects in the natal horoscope in that we allow tight orbs or narrow leeway for progressed planetary aspects (usually a maximum of one degree 'applying' and one degree after becoming exact or 'separating') these aspects show the culmination of changes in our lives, whereas we allow larger orbs for natal charts where the aspects describe psychological characteristics. It therefore follows that if progressions are relevant in synastry they:

(a) Pertain to the phenomenon of the relationship: the fact that a relationship takes place might be accompanied by progressed aspects from the inner planets to each other and from the inner planets to the natal chart

(b) These aspects would not be relevant if they were out of orb and so they would be both easier to see and more defined: they may be more

♈	♉	♊	♋	♌	♍	♎	♏	♐	♑	♒	♓
Aries	Taurus	Gemini	Cancer	Leo	Virgo	Libra	Scorpio	Sagittarius	Capricorn	Aquarius	Pisces

exact than natal synastry

(c) Because natal astrological compatibility is relevant to the psychological make up and elemental balance of the chart, it is also relevant in terms of whole signs rather than exact aspects, whereas the secondary progressions of the Sun, Venus and Mars which are more concerned with how our personal lives slowly change, may provide some statistical relevancy because they are only effective when near to being exact.

Progressions signify how we change, they also seem to often regulate or operate with great relevancy at the beginning of an intimate relationship. Sometimes to those who can understand the meaning of progressed planetary aspects, their efficacy appears undeniable. Most of the time they provide merely a partial view of what happened to make a relationship begin, change or end because for most people relationships are something more than just their Sun, Venus and Mars. Indeed the Moon's position, (symbolising how we respond emotionally to another individual) and aspect is much more relevant to relationships and compatibility than any Mars – Mars aspect, which symbolizes among other things the way two people 'work' together: i.e. their physical methods. The progressed Moon moves quickly in comparison to the other planets in the progressed chart and although aspects to the natal Moon are of paramount importance, in order to accurately analyse either the natal or progressed Moon accurate times of birth must be recorded. For the Sun, Venus and Mars an accurate date of birth and year of relationship are all that are needed in order to establish an aspect, because all three of these planets move at a maximum speed of about $<=$ one degree of arc per day, give or take about 15 minutes of arc (a quarter of a degree).

Dynamic Models of Astrology

It is a mistake to look at astrology as a static system; that you are a nothing

♈	♉	♊	♋	♌	♍	♎	♏	♐	♑	♒	♓
Aries	Taurus	Gemini	Cancer	Leo	Virgo	Libra	Scorpio	Sagittarius	Capricorn	Aquarius	Pisces

more than a set of factors decided upon at the moment of birth. I have heard sceptics liken astrology to bigotry and racism claiming that to compartmentlise the population into 12 is to encourage prejudice based on astrology, with the possibility that – say – insurance companies will make risk decisions based on sun signs. The mistake here is that astrology seeks to compartmentalise, when it actually does the antithesis of this. Astrology is, and always has been, a study of unique moments in time and space, and, by extension, what makes us unique as individuals. People, however, do try to compartmentalise their surroundings and astrologers are people, often with a particular desire or compunction to compartmentalise. Astrology as a subject might be seen from the outside as a tool for ordering and simplifying life and this might attract certain types of people who wish to do this, but from a philosophical and practical point of view, it appears that astrology does not lend itself well to sweeping generalisations... not ones that stand up to scrutiny. When we observe change we can do it either from the singular perspective or from the collective perspective. We collectivise astrology because mass communication demands it.

Astrology is a study of discrete moments in time and as no moment in time happens more than once in an epoch we are forced to always work with unique configurations. What we do try and achieve is the application of rules that are based upon previous configurations i.e. what happens to one person when transiting Saturn opposes their natal-Venus might have relevance to everyone who experiences this opposition, so if they experience doubts about their relationship at the same time as the aspect happens, then because the two planets symbolize doubt (Saturn) and relationships (Venus) then this is a signature that might repeat itself. To say that all Aquarians are liable to have a difficult time in relationships because Saturn is in Leo for the next two and a half years is a sweeping broad generalisation, because not all Sun Aquarians will have Venus in Aquarius. Many Sun Aquarians (people born in late January through early to mid February) will know they are Aquarians, but most will not know which sign

♈	♉	♊	♋	♌	♍	♎	♏	♐	♑	♒	♓
Aries	Taurus	Gemini	Cancer	Leo	Virgo	Libra	Scorpio	Sagittarius	Capricorn	Aquarius	Pisces

'their Venus' is in. In actual fact many Aquarians *will* have Venus in the same sign as the Sun simply because Venus is never more than 48 degrees from the Sun in the natal chart and so the generalisation might be made and it might actually apply in a good number of cases. And so when one astrologer is communicating with many people, she/he is required to generalise and will often do so with reasonable level of success despite the incongruence of astrology's unique-moment-time status and the science-like-compartmentalism of generalised sun sign astrology.

Serious astrologers are at pains to tell you that you're not just a zodiac sign. Your horoscope or birth chart is a unique map. It is as unique to you as an email address or a personnel number, in fact, it's as if the universe presented you with a tracking device when you were born: it knows where you are and furthermore it knows more or less what potentials you have. If we live in a universe where both time and our conscious perception of it are linked by some collective holographic constant then we also live in a universe where astrology is more likely to be true.

The only factor that makes you truly unique in the universe is the place and time you were born, the horoscope is a map of that moment. But natal (birth chart) astrology is not just that horoscope, it is much more: *progressions are part and parcel of natal astrology.*

The difference between the natal chart and the progressed chart

The natal chart is a map of potentiality, the planets positions and interrelationships are symbolic significators of different elements of an individuals psyche. Which sign they fall in gives clues as to how the planets meaning will manifest in a person's personality and psyche. Which *house* of the horoscope governs in what area of life this planet will have most influence, and the angles between the planets describe the different ways we can utilise the attributes symbolized by the planets and use them to achieve our potential. This chart is, as we have already noted, fixed. The

♈	♉	♊	♋	♌	♍	♎	♏	♐	♑	♒	♓
Aries	Taurus	Gemini	Cancer	Leo	Virgo	Libra	Scorpio	Sagittarius	Capricorn	Aquarius	Pisces

progressed chart starts its progress at the moment of birth, and at that moment it is identical to the natal chart.

In order to progress a chart we have to move the positions of the planets forward (or backwards if you are using a technique known as converse progressions) at a specific rate that will correspond with a discrete measure of time, for example *secondary progressions* = a day for a year. This means that the positions of the planets ten days after you were born correspond with your personality and potentials for your tenth year. In progressed synastry (the combination of progressions with relationship astrology) the positions of the Sun, Venus and Mars, relate to your developing aspirations, aesthetic tastes, ideas about relationships, attractiveness, sexual needs or proclivities, and types of attraction. Other planets relate to other issues and of course there are many other elements in intimate relationships that are also symbolized by these other planets.

The differences between the way natal and progressed planets affect our personalities is not clear in astrology, although the effect of natal planets is given more scope than those of progressed planets which are much more finely focused. The idea that we have two charts (and if you consider the other systems of progression, many more than two), is not an easy concept to grasp. You might ask which one is relevant. The answer will always be both (or all) are relevant, but that the birth horoscope is more important because it is consistent. The progressed chart is constantly changing and so it is useful to look at it in other ways. It is probable that an applying progressed trine, conjunction or opposition involving Venus with Venus, Mars or the Sun will be far more intensely felt than an identical natal aspect involving the same planets.

An analogy to use is again with music: the horoscope or horoscopes create a vibrating cacophony of sound: each planet in the natal chart plays a consistent bass line: this is a repetitive reiteration of your potential in music; while the same planet in the progressed chart plays a melody that is constantly changing. When this progressing planet changes sign or house,

♈	♉	♊	♋	♌	♍	♎	♏	♐	♑	♒	♓
Aries	Taurus	Gemini	Cancer	Leo	Virgo	Libra	Scorpio	Sagittarius	Capricorn	Aquarius	Pisces

it either plays the same melody on a different instrument or a different melody on a different instrument. You can choose to listen to either the bass line or the melody, but when this sign change takes place and the melody changes, the bass line remains the same, steady and sure.

Interruptions to the many bass lines and melodies in the horoscope arrive in the form of transits from planets, which create augmentations, interruptions, distortions, diminishment or amplification of these consistent bass lines and changing melodies. These interruptions are external measures of change and can be either obvious or hardly noticeable. Basically transits *happen to you* while progressions *change you from the inside.*

Adrian Duncan writes on this issue:

'To take a musical parallel, progressions show modulations in the basic tone of the birth horoscope, while transits show outer disturbances which either harmonise with the basic tone, or not. Transits come and go and may or may not create lasting structural changes in our lives. Progressions are a slow ripening process – often less dramatic in effect, yet more far reaching.'[xxxiv]

So while the horoscope changes, it's important to remember that it does so within its own context.

♈	♉	♊	♋	♌	♍	♎	♏	♐	♑	♒	♓
Aries	Taurus	Gemini	Cancer	Leo	Virgo	Libra	Scorpio	Sagittarius	Capricorn	Aquarius	Pisces

Four

Relationship Planets in Signs

*What's your sign? Do you know? Let me guess,
you're Scorpio...
Des'ree 'What's your Sign?'*

Nothing of value in this book requires the presence of the twelve signs of
the zodiac in any particular order. They are useful reference points, not least
because they allow us to measure angles easily by giving us a scale of
reference (360 degrees divided into twelve sectors). This chapter explores
their meanings.

Zodiac Signs

Signs of the Zodiac can be subdivided into different groupings that help to
explain and differentiate their underlying astrological meanings.

The twelve signs are Aries, Taurus, Gemini, Cancer, Leo, Virgo, Libra,
Scorpio, Sagittarius, Capricorn, Aquarius and Pisces. They are always
listed in this order.

The first subdivision is by quality. The three qualilties are Cardinal,
Fixed and Mutable. Each of these divisions contains four signs.

The Cardinal Signs are Aries, Cancer, Libra and Capricorn

The Cardinal signs embody discrete principles, but all have the urge to *act*
and *do* in common.

♈	♉	♊	♋	♌	♍	♎	♏	♐	♑	♒	♓
Aries	Taurus	Gemini	Cancer	Leo	Virgo	Libra	Scorpio	Sagittarius	Capricorn	Aquarius	Pisces

With Aries the urge to act is to assert the identity and this is often to the exclusion of the feelings of others

With Cancer the urge to act is to protect the identity, this is often to the exclusion of association with others

With Libra the urge is to harmonise with others, this is often to the exclusion of decision making

With Capricorn the urge is to assert the status or position in society often to the exclusion of the aspirations of others

The Fixed Signs are Taurus, Leo, Scorpio and Aquarius

The Fixed signs embody discrete principles, but have the urge to *maintain* in common

For Taurus the urge is to maintain possessions and values, stubbornness and lack of adaptability is a possible result

For Leo the urge is to maintain the creative will; the inability to value other people's contributions is a possible result

For Scorpio the urge is to maintain secrecy and mystery, a consequence can be loneliness

For Aquarius the urge is to maintain freedom of expression, occasionally this can alienate them from society

The Mutable signs are Gemini, Virgo, Sagittarius and Pisces

The Mutable signs embody discrete principles, but all have the urge to *adapt* in common

With Gemini the urge to adapt is through the gathering and exchange of information, a consequence is procrastination by focus on trivialities

With Virgo the urge to adapt is through structured analysis, a consequence is procrastination through attention to details

With Sagittarius the urge is to adapt through exploration, a consequence

♈	♉	♊	♋	♌	♍	♎	♏	♐	♑	♒	♓
Aries	Taurus	Gemini	Cancer	Leo	Virgo	Libra	Scorpio	Sagittarius	Capricorn	Aquarius	Pisces

is procrastination due to avoidance of responsibilities

With Pisces the urge is to adapt through imagination and vision, a consequence is procrastination through dillusion and lack of focus

The second subdivision is by element. The four elements are Fire, Earth, Air and Water. Each of these divisions contains three signs.

The Fire signs are Aries, Leo and Sagittarius

The Fire signs embody common principles, therefore they mix well. They all have a different quality and so bring different perspectives to the same core element. Fire symbolizes creativity, inspiration and courage.

Fire signs, collectively speaking, are those among us whose infectious enthusiasm seeks to create and inspire. They prefer inspiration that can be followed up on. They are great motivators, although the extent of their leadership qualities varies between the three signs. They like to initiate projects.

The Earth signs are Taurus, Virgo and Capricorn

The Earth signs embody common principles, therefore they mix well. They all have a different quality and so bring different perspectives to the same core element. Earth symbolizes structure, practicality and construction.

Farming, engineering and building are all archetypal Earthy pastimes.

The Air signs are Gemini, Libra and Aquarius

The Air signs embody common principles, therefore they mix well. They all have a different quality and so bring different perspectives to the same core element. Air symbolizes mentality, intellect and balance.

The detached qualities of the Air signs lend themselves to activities that require balance and give a feeling of freedom. Gliding, parachuting, water skiing, snowboarding, skateboarding and surfing are some of the leisure activities that relate to the laid-back Air triplicity.

♈	♉	♊	♋	♌	♍	♎	♏	♐	♑	♒	♓
Aries	Taurus	Gemini	Cancer	Leo	Virgo	Libra	Scorpio	Sagittarius	Capricorn	Aquarius	Pisces

The Water signs are Cancer, Scorpio and Pisces

The Water signs embody common principles, therefore they mix well. They all have a different quality and so bring different perspectives to the same core element. Water symbolizes emotion, sensitivity and power.

The Water triplicity is joined by watery qualities. Sometimes their calling is a little too fey to be highly regarded by all of society, but jobs that require intuition, sympathy and guile are all favorites for the three Water signs. Investigative work, psychotherapy, nursing and any function that requires an element of sensitivity is embodied within the principle of this triplicity. Understanding how other people react is also a useful trait that is related to watery intuition.

The third subdivision is by polarity. The two polarities are Positive, or Masculine and Negative or Feminine.

The positive signs are Aries, Gemini, Leo, Libra, Sagittarius and Aquarius

The Positive signs embody complimentary principles, they generally mix well. Air and Fire are objective principles in astrology. Problems can arise with opposite signs of the same quality, but generally speaking they will enhance each other. Well-used adages include Fire helps Air to rise up, Air helps Fire to Grow. Too much Air puts Fire out and too much Fire consumes Air.

The negative signs are Taurus, Cancer, Virgo, Scorpio, Capricorn and Pisces

The Negative signs embody complimentary principles, they generally mix well. Earth and Water are subjective principles in astrology. Problems can arise with opposite signs of the same quality, but generally speaking they will enhance each other. Adages include: Water can help Earth to become fertile and Earth can help channel Water. Too much Earth soaks up Water and too much Water mixed with too little Earth produces mud.

♈	♉	♊	♋	♌	♍	♎	♏	♐	♑	♒	♓
Aries	Taurus	Gemini	Cancer	Leo	Virgo	Libra	Scorpio	Sagittarius	Capricorn	Aquarius	Pisces

Earth and Fire find it hard to find common ground when on the one hand the Earth principle is to be practical while the Fire principle is to be creative, they follow their own path to enlightenment, as do Earth and Air, Air being objective and Earth being subjective. Water and Fire have a hard time basically because Water puts out Fires light or Fire evaporates Water. Air and Water have discrete objectives and together they either kick up a storm at sea or become becalmed in the doldrums.

TWO PLANETS ARE IN TRINE IF THEY ARE 120 DEGREES APART (around the same degree FOUR ZODIAC SIGNS APART)

	♈	♉	♊	♋	♌	♍	♎	♏	♐	♑	♒	♓
Fire Trine	♈	♉	♊	♋	♌	♍	♎	♏	♐	♑	♒	♓
	Ari				Leo				Sag			
Earth Trine	♈	♉	♊	♋	♌	♍	♎	♏	♐	♑	♒	♓
		Tau				Vir				Cap		
Air Trine	♈	♉	♊	♋	♌	♍	♎	♏	♐	♑	♒	♓
			Gem				Lib				Aqu	
Water Trine	♈	♉	♊	♋	♌	♍	♎	♏	♐	♑	♒	♓
				Can				Sco				Pis

Fig.13 The Fire Trine includes Aries, Leo and Sagittarius; the Earth trine, Taurus, Virgo and Capricorn. The Air trine includes Gemini, Libra and Aquarius and the Water trine includes Cancer, Scorpio and Pisces.

TWO PLANETS FORM A SQUARE IF THEY ARE 90 DEGREES (around the same degree THREE ZODIAC SIGNS APART)

	♈	♉	♊	♋	♌	♍	♎	♏	♐	♑	♒	♓
Cardinal Square	♈	♉	♊	♋	♌	♍	♎	♏	♐	♑	♒	♓
	Ari			Can			Lib			Cap		
Fixed Square	♈	♉	♊	♋	♌	♍	♎	♏	♐	♑	♒	♓
		Tau			Leo			Sco			Aqu	
Mutable Square	♈	♉	♊	♋	♌	♍	♎	♏	♐	♑	♒	♓
			Gem			Vir			Sag			Pis

Fig.14 The Cardinal square includes Aries opposite Libra crossing Cancer opposite Capricorn. The Fixed square includes Taurus opposite Scorpio crossing Leo opposite Aquarius. The Mutable square includes Gemini opposite Sagittarius crossing Virgo opposite Pisces

♈	♉	♊	♋	♌	♍	♎	♏	♐	♑	♒	♓
Aries	Taurus	Gemini	Cancer	Leo	Virgo	Libra	Scorpio	Sagittarius	Capricorn	Aquarius	Pisces

TWO PLANETS FORM AN OPPOSITION IF THEY ARE 180
DEGREES (or around the same degree SIX ZODIAC SIGNS APART)

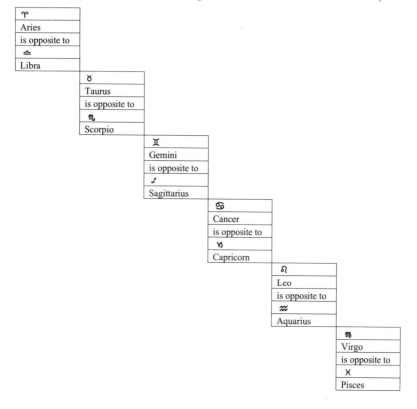

Fig.15 Table of opposite signs

TWO PLANETS ARE IN CONJUNCTION IF THEY ARE CLOSE
TOGETHER, USUALLY IN THE SAME ZODIAC SIGN.

Planets in ♈	Aries can conjunct (or conjoin) planets in	♈ Aries
Planets in ♉	Taurus can conjunct (or conjoin) planets in	♉ Taurus
Planets in ♊	Gemini can conjunct (or conjoin) planets in	♊ Gemini
Planets in ♋	Cancer can conjunct (or conjoin) planets in	♋ Cancer
Planets in ♌	Leo can conjunct (or conjoin) planets in	♌ Leo

♈	♉	♊	♋	♌	♍	♎	♏	♐	♑	♒	♓
Aries	Taurus	Gemini	Cancer	Leo	Virgo	Libra	Scorpio	Sagittarius	Capricorn	Aquarius	Pisces

Planets in ♍	Virgo can conjunct (or conjoin) planets in	♍ Virgo
Planets in ♎	Libra can conjunct (or conjoin) planets in	♎ Libra
Planets in ♏	Scorpio can conjunct (or conjoin) planets in	♏ Scorpio
Planets in ♐	Sagittarius can conjunct (or conjoin) planets in	♐ Sagittarius
Planets in ♑	Capricorn can conjunct (or conjoin) planets in	♑ Capricorn
Planets in ♒	Aquarius can conjunct (or conjoin) planets in	♒ Aquarius
Planets in ♓	Pisces can conjunct (or conjoin) planets in	♓ Pisces

Fig.16 Table of Conjunctions

Aries Archetype
Sun in Aries

Aries tends to rush headlong into things. The archetypal Aries will write their own script to life, which means ignoring the judgement of others and often being a law unto themselves. They like a fight and are often described as warlike, though they enjoy politics, drama and science just as much.

Aries traditionally rules the head and face.

A markedly positive sign, Aries women are go-getters who like to get their own way or do their own thing.

The Sun in Aries tends to produce dynamic woman and hard men capable of making quick decisions although they are not always the best decisions. The Sun here has a strong combative flavour, it also likes fast cars, clear goals and to be admired for achievements. These people are fast thinking, fast living and inclined to be carefree, courageous and often political. Head injuries and scars to the face are common with Aries.

Clyde Barrow, Vincent van Gogh, Flavio Briatore, Rene Descartes, Marvin Gaye, Henri II of France, Warren Beatty, Craig Breedlove, Dodi Al Fayed, Russell Crowe, Diana Ross, Maya Angelou, Jayne Mansfield, Joan Crawford, Bette Davis, John Wayne Bobbitt and Françoise Dorleac.

The Aries outlook is childlike and simple; focussing on their own point of view without great thought for the feelings of others or the consequences

♈	♉	♊	♋	♌	♍	♎	♏	♐	♑	♒	♓
Aries	Taurus	Gemini	Cancer	Leo	Virgo	Libra	Scorpio	Sagittarius	Capricorn	Aquarius	Pisces

of sharing their point of view. This is often a good thing, for without great single-minded initiators with high self-regard and belief in simple concepts, progress in science and art would be limited. Aries is all about engaging with the life-process itself and the simplest way of understanding the Aries principle is *being*. Some time between birth and the 30th birthday, Aries Sun will progress into Taurus. This is a cue to bring form to the impulse of action and activity. Taurus slows Aries down and urges Aries to become logical and careful. Whenever a Fire Sun progresses into an Earth sign it is tempered and has to become disciplined. For Aries this can translate to slowing down. Earth always urges Fire to become responsible and structured; the creativity and activity of Aries is quite childlike and self-oriented. Taurus still has an element of self-centredness, but the concern is more to do with the subject's possessions and values rather than their identity, which Aries tends to project with pride. Later on the Aries Sun may progress into Gemini where it is encouraged to engage, write and teach.

Venus in Aries

Being in Aries is not a natural state for Venus as it is opposite one of its rulerships, Libra. Traditionally it is said to be weak in Aries, but actually this is a poor descriptive term. Venus in Aries tends to result in the masculinisation of a principle that is at its conventional-best in Libra or Taurus. Sex can be rushed independent of gender, conquest can be a part of the romantic act and same-sex relationships are not unknown. Other factors can come into play to underplay the Venus-Aries principle, but there is often a difficulty in coming to terms with romantic love, even if this doesn't manifest as hurried foreplay or an inability to consider one's partner. Venus in Aries can sometimes manifest in the use of colorful and abusive language; occasionally in controversial or bad taste; often in unhappy love affairs and occasionally in unconventional sexual experimentation. People with Venus in Aries include:

Marilyn Monroe, Jayne Mansfield, Jean Harlow, Melissa Etheridge,

♈	♉	♊	♋	♌	♍	♎	♏	♐	♑	♒	♓
Aries	Taurus	Gemini	Cancer	Leo	Virgo	Libra	Scorpio	Sagittarius	Capricorn	Aquarius	Pisces

Nigel Hawthorne, Jim Jones, Marshall Applewhite, Eddie Murphy, Laurence Olivier, Daphne Du Maurier, Lana Turner, Jack Nicholson, George Clooney, Anne Heche, Mia Farrow, Leslie Grantham, Michelangelo, Robespierre and Charles Baudelaire.

Venus in Aries need not have a problem though, for what many people term the love life is often different to the sex-life, whereas Venus in Aries makes little or no differentiation. It's a question of perspective.

Mars in Aries...

...On the other hand, is completely at home here. These people really do love a fight and in many cases they are proud of their physical prowess; as both lovers and fighters. They are ambitious but thoughtful to a point. Mars in Aries often has a charitable side and likes to look after those less fortunate. There is often a noticeable facial scar, a head scar or a broken nose for Mars in Aries. Often the face is striking. Sex is important.

Russell Crowe, Jim Clark, Gianni Agnelli, Yvette Mimieux, Kevin Costner, Paul Newman, Anthony Quinn, Oliver Reed, Franco Nero, Lance Reventlow, Moshe Dayan, Molly Ringwald, Paloma Picasso, Prince Aly Khan and Tycho Brahe are all examples of people with natal-Mars in Aries.

Taurus Archetype
Sun in Taurus

Taureans are practical, down-to-earth, pragmatists who know the value of possessions and are fond of good living. Often with an outdoor lifestyle, they are fond of ideas of self-sufficiency and value useful ideas and things. Many Taureans are sceptical of astrology and other esoteric subjects, mainly because they favor materialist viewpoints and question the practical application of such ideas. Taurus is the natural sign of the gardener, the builder and through the sign's rulership of the throat and voice it is also the home of the singer. There is a stubborn and persistent quality in their make-up that can imbue them with patience to cope with

♈	♉	♊	♋	♌	♍	♎	♏	♐	♑	♒	♓
Aries	Taurus	Gemini	Cancer	Leo	Virgo	Libra	Scorpio	Sagittarius	Capricorn	Aquarius	Pisces

frustration well.

Sun in Taurus is a lover not a fighter, a singer more than an actor. These people are fond of money, possessions and often their value system (typically unswerving and practical) is a salient part of their make up. Meaning and values are immutably bound together in the Taurean paradigm. The softness of Venus ruled Taurus is found in the art of Dante Rossetti, the ballet of Fonteyn and the music of Menuhin; its fixed opinions and tendency to static belief in the ideas of David Icke, Marshall Applewhite and the last Russian Tsar Nicholas II and its tendency to sublimely soft beauty in the faces of Audrey Hepburn, Joanna Lumley and Penelope Cruz. Singers known for their unique singing voice are often a product of Taurus: Donovan, Roy Orbison, Bing Crosby, Engelbert Humperdinck, Willie Nelson, Bobby Darin, Barbara Streisand, Tammy Wynette, Stevie Wonder, Billy Joel, Enrique Iglesias, Sheena Easton, Bobby Vee, Frankie Valli, Richie Valens, Joe Cocker, Rita Coolidge, Dame Nellie Melba, Steve Winwood, Eric Burdon, Glen Campbell, Cher... all singers whose voices are immediately recognisable and often mimicked, and, coincidentally all born with the Sun in Taurus

Other Sun Taureans include:

Oliver Cromwell, Adolph Hitler, Krishnamurti, Soeren Kierkegaard, The Ayatollah Khomeini, Pope John Paul II, Glenda Jackson, Candice Bergen, Thomas Huxley, Shirley Maclaine, Queen Elizabeth II. Did I mention fixed opinions?

Some time between birth and the 30th birthday, the Taurus Sun will progress into Gemini. The lesson to be learned from this is that change is good and diversification will not always hurt. Taurus learns to socialise and to step out of its box, often becoming open to other people's ideas and opinions or to publishing their own ideas. In one tragic case it found the gift of oratory and mobilised a nation on a path to destruction, this was when Hitler's progressed-Sun entered the sign of Gemini in 1920. Later in life the Taurus Sun may progress into Cancer where it will start to want to

♈	♉	♊	♋	♌	♍	♎	♏	♐	♑	♒	♓
Aries	Taurus	Gemini	Cancer	Leo	Virgo	Libra	Scorpio	Sagittarius	Capricorn	Aquarius	Pisces

actively make progress and possibly stand up for or protect the interests of others.

Venus in Taurus...

...is a good place for those who wish to accumulate wealth or value. Being in its rulership (Venus is said to rule Taurus and Libra), Venus has two main functions, as lover and provider. It symbolizes our capacity for romantic love and for accumulation of wealth. In Taurus, the accumulation of wealth is more pronounced. Partnership is less important to those with Venus in Taurus than the experience of romantic love. This is not the case with Libra where partnership is of paramount importance.

Warren Beatty, Charles Chaplin, Johnny Depp, Adolph Hitler, Paul McCartney, Prince, Sid Vicious, Mark Wahlberg, Jane Russell, Jean Anouilh, Alanis Morrisette and Ann-Margret all have Venus in Taurus.

Mars in Taurus

Mars is weaker here, being in the sign that is opposite its other 'rulership', Scorpio. As such it distorts its own principles. Mars clearly relates to the physical sex act, physical work and also to ambition. Mars is in Venus-ruled sign here and is therefore slowed down. This either feminises Mars, or it distorts the physical expression so that physical sexuality can become unnecessary, softened or covert.

Pier Angeli, Charles Chaplin, Dirk Bogarde, Mick Jagger, Robert De Niro, Liberace, Shirley Maclaine, Adolph Hitler, Johnny Ray, Ginger Rogers, Joan Sutherland and Madonna.

Gemini Archetype
Sun in Gemini

Gemini people are talkers and writers. Sometimes they are skilled musicians. If I was writing in the usual astrological style I would say that they are extremely good communicators. More accurately they are

♈	♉	♊	♋	♌	♍	♎	♏	♐	♑	♒	♓
Aries	Taurus	Gemini	Cancer	Leo	Virgo	Libra	Scorpio	Sagittarius	Capricorn	Aquarius	Pisces

characterised by their method of communication. Therefore, if you come across someone who speaks rarely it is mistake to dismiss them as not Geminian simply because the most noticeable thing about them is their method of communication (or lack of it), though it is important to note that there is likely to be an astrological factor, such as an unaspected Mercury or Saturn opposite or conjunct Mercury which may be responsible for the quiet, undemonstrative Gemini. Naturally many Geminians like to talk and to write, often gravitating into sales, literature and journalism. It's interesting to note that another of Gemini's characteristics being an Air sign is its ability to detach itself from emotional involvement in issues. From this characteristic stems the trait of unbiased reporting and uncaring tabloid intrusion. Expressive hand gestures are a common trait.

Sun in Gemini tends to bring forth a creative wordsmith or a writer for whom ideas take on a life of their own. The theme is communicating ideas without necessarily associating. This tends toward mass-marketing and 'throwing ideas out into the wind to see what comes back'. These people include Salman Rushdie, Ian Fleming, Bob Dylan, Francoise Sagan, Jean-Paul Sartre, Walt Whitman, Erich Segal, the Marquis de Sade, Thomas Mann, John Masefield, Ben Jonson, Thomas Hardy, Ralph Waldo Emerson, Anne Frank, Gwendolyn Brooks, Lord Bulwer-Lytton, Allen Ginsberg, Omar Khayyam (perhaps), Pierre Salinger and William Butler Yeats.

Gemini is also associated with sales and marketing. It's useful in such a role to be fond of and good at communicating with others, although it is more pertinent for a salesperson to be born with Mercury in Gemini, many Sun Gemini's are born with this Mercury position anyway.

Some time between birth and the 30th birthday, the Gemini Sun will progress into Cancer. This is often the time when Gemini looks to becoming a parent or teacher, but in all events Gemini usually moves away from focussing on the trivialities of life towards more important and serious issues (obviously this is the case for most people as they grow, but Gemini is a fun-loving, sign with a youthful outlook). Cancer is the sign of

♈	♉	♊	♋	♌	♍	♎	♏	♐	♑	♒	♓
Aries	Taurus	Gemini	Cancer	Leo	Virgo	Libra	Scorpio	Sagittarius	Capricorn	Aquarius	Pisces

the nurturer and the protector. Cancer also coaches, teaches and acts on behalf of others. Cancer is the sign of the home and Gemini may progress into staying at home or studying or working from home. Cancer is the second Cardinal sign and therefore needs to act and do. Gemini has been doing an awful lot of thinking and talking and must now put that into action.

Later on the Gemini Sun may progress into Leo, where the urge will be to become creative, possibly through writing, art and design or theatre work. Geminis naturally like to use their hands so sculpture and modelling is a favorite outlet during this phase.

Venus in Gemini...

...likes to have more than one partner, or it likes to have two sides to its love-making. Bi-sexuality is possible (though by no means certain) under this sign; in theory so are extra-marital love affairs as Venus and Gemini together implies 'two-loves', although that could also be interpreted as 'two marriages'. It is also common for Venus in Gemini to be unemotional about love and sex, although they do not want their partners to two-time them, they often don't consider their partner's feelings when out and about on their own. This can come across as double standards, but it's really just emotional detachment and the need for variety, at least during early life. This trait is shared to differing degrees by Libra (less) and Aquarius (more). Venus in Gemini is as capable of faith and love as any other Venus position, problems arise only when their propensity to intellectualise love and relationships causes them to detach emotionally. Mormon leader Brigham Young, who is said to have married 52 times, was born with Venus is Gemini.

Music, particularly the appreciation of music, is common with this Venus placement.

Venus in Gemini people include: Clara Bow, Leslie Caron, Cher, Bette Davis, Joan Collins, Enrique Iglesias, George Michael, Al Pacino, Gregory

♈	♉	♊	♋	♌	♍	♎	♏	♐	♑	♒	♓
Aries	Taurus	Gemini	Cancer	Leo	Virgo	Libra	Scorpio	Sagittarius	Capricorn	Aquarius	Pisces

Peck, Mary Pickford, Tyrone Power and Bob Dylan.

Mars in Gemini

The principle at work here is the adoption of adaptability and diversification of the personal physical drive and adaptable personal ambition. These people take on different types of work in order to make ends meet (or they might hold down two jobs). There is also a lot of tactility in intimate relationships. They also have the ability to take ideas and put them into action, consequently this should be a good position for film producers and directors. Jean-Jacques Annaud, Luc Besson, Claude Berri, Cecil B Demille, Daniel Gelin, Sergio Leone, Akira Kurosawa, Dennis Hopper, Rennie Harlin, Sydney Pollack, Tim Robbins, Roberto Rossellini, Don Simpson, Preston Sturges, William Wyler, Lina Wertmuller, Anna Maria Tato, Jacques Deray, Alessandro Blasetti, Harry Shearer and Sean Penn all share this Mars position.

Also with Mars in Gemini are Meryl Streep, David Soul, O J Simpson, Jean Simmons, Diana Ross, Pola Negri, Steve Martin, Peter Lorre, Lilian Gish, David Duchovny, Sean Connery and Loni Anderson.

Cancer Archetype
Sun in Cancer

The underlying principle for the sign of the crab is protection, of themselves, of their families, of their people. Consequently a good number of this sign enter politics, usually as conservatives, but often just because they wish to protect the interests of those people with whom they have an affinity. Edward Heath, Alex Douglas-Home, Emmeline Pankhurst, John Quincy Adams, Bob Dole, George McGovern, Ross Perot, Georges Pompidou, Nelson Rockerfeller, Donald Rumsfeld, Kenneth Starr, David Owen, Nelson Mandela, Pierre Laval, Lionel Jospin, Calvin Coolidge, George W Bush and Lamar Alexander are all Sun Cancerians. Every once in a while you come across a person whose mannerisms reflect their Sun

♈	♉	♊	♋	♌	♍	♎	♏	♐	♑	♒	♓
Aries	Taurus	Gemini	Cancer	Leo	Virgo	Libra	Scorpio	Sagittarius	Capricorn	Aquarius	Pisces

sign. With Cancer you will often find that they walk sideways defensively, stand with their shoulder facing you as they speak and clutch pieces of paper to their chest in case you see the obviously important information on the document they are holding. Sun in Cancer also describes someone for whom nurturing and mothering are practical issues. This was most noticeable in the life of Diana Princess of Wales.

Some time between birth and the 30th birthday Cancer Sun will move into Leo where it will seek the limelight, at least for a time. Many famous actors and actresses (which is one of the things Leo urges people to become) are born with the Sun in Cancer, but take to their profession when their Sun progresses into Leo.

Natalie Wood, Sly Stallone, Milton Berle, Neile Adams, Isabelle Adjani, Annabella, Sally Blane, Gary Busey, James Cagney, Jackie Chan, Yul Brynner, Tom Cruise, Bill Cosby, Willem Dafoe, Harrison Ford, Charlotte Gainsbourg, David Hasselhoff, Farley Granger, Angelica Huston, Kris Kristofferson, Bonnie Langford, Janet Leigh, Gina Lollobrigida, Peter Lorre, Tobey Maguire, Jean Marsh, Jean Murat, Freddie Prinze, Corin Redgrave, Diana Rigg, Richard Roundtree, Eva Marie Saint, Jenny Seagrove, Terrance Stamp, Barbara Stanwyck, Patrick Stewart, Meryl Streep, Donald Sutherland, Lupe Velez, Lindsey Wagner and Robin Williams are examples of this.

Sun Cancer must move away from self-protection towards self-proclamation. Later on Cancer may move into Virgo, here the security conscious crab whose film career has begun to pay dividends may want to perfect their art in fringe theatre or count their pennies in some form of business or financial management. Virgo also likes to work behind the scenes, so producing or directing might also be a preferred option, at least for Cancerian actors.

Venus in Cancer

Venus here is mothering, protective and cautious. She is cautious in love

♈	♉	♊	♋	♌	♍	♎	♏	♐	♑	♒	♓
Aries	Taurus	Gemini	Cancer	Leo	Virgo	Libra	Scorpio	Sagittarius	Capricorn	Aquarius	Pisces

and relationships. It is vitally important for the welfare of such people to find an exclusive and genuine partner who will love and nurture their relationship potential; otherwise a retreat in to their shell is a likely consequence. Venus in Cancer is sometimes assertive, but generally only when it comes to its relationship needs being met. Cancer Venus will give their whole for the security of a partner's love. They will sometimes allow themselves to be controlled and can cling to their partners. An early marriage is often on the cards, so these people tend not to be in the relationship market for too long until later life and then only if their relationship fails or ends.

The following are all Cancer Venuses: Eva Peron, Keanu Reeves, Pier Angeli, Eva Marie Saint, Arnold Schwarzenegger, Jimmy Stewart, Mae West, Raquel Welch, Yul Brynner, James Cagney, Pauline Collins, Judy Garland, Cameron Diaz and Olivia de Haviland

Mars in Cancer

Women with this placement want to stand by their man, particularly if he's faithful to them. Cancer is not the favorite position for forthright Mars whose principle is action. The Cancerian principle is caution and as such this can be a dissonant place for Mars to act, being constantly held back by security considerations. Cautious action can sometimes be a good indicator of good judgement, but Cancer is an emotional sign and Mars an assertive planet. Men with this position have great poise; are caring individuals, but are not particularly dynamic; women with this position are receptive sexually, but often forego their own needs for those of their partner...at least for a while.

People born with this Mars position include: Richard Gere, Frank Capra, Jean Marais, Liza Minelli, William Shatner, Don Ameche, Ingrid Bergman, Halle Berry, Coretta Scott-King, Patsy Cline, Tammy Wynette, Vivien Leigh, Mary Martin, Emma Thompson, Kenneth Branagh and Jean Cocteau.

♈	♉	♊	♋	♌	♍	♎	♏	♐	♑	♒	♓
Aries	Taurus	Gemini	Cancer	Leo	Virgo	Libra	Scorpio	Sagittarius	Capricorn	Aquarius	Pisces

Leo Archetype
Sun in Leo

This sign is easy to spot, like Aries, because the Sun is such an important part of their lives and as we all know when Leo birthdays are (between July and August) it is often possible to guess a Leo Sun person because they like to dominate, be the centre of attention, they like to entertain and they are extremely creative artists, thinkers and actors. (Their hairstyle is sometimes a giveaway as well.) This is the sign of the stage – the spotlight and the big film – where the TV spotlight falls more archetypally on their opposite sign Aquarius. Leo is symbolized by the Lion, the king of the jungle and like the big pussy cats they are they like to be stroked, tickled and allowed out through the cat flap to go and get on with their own thing (which sometimes, but not always, involves terrorising those smaller and weaker than themselves)...until it's time to eat and go to bed, of course. Sun Leo's often come across as sun-worshippers and often sport suntans. Leo women have the ability to bring home the bacon (or the Gazelle). Leo men should avoid being caught napping.

Ben Affleck, Antonio Banderas, Tony Bennett, Clara Bow, Dino de Laurentiis, Geri Halliwell, Robert de Niro, Dustin Hoffman, George Hamilton, Madonna Ciccone, Mick Jagger, Peter O'Toole, Rosanna Arquette, Matthew Perry, Robert Plant, Andy Warhol, Patrick Swayze, Arnold Schwarzenegger, Sean Penn, Roman Polanski, Kevin Dillon, Delores Del Rio and Norma Shearer all share this Sun Leo position.

Some time between birth and 30th birthday, the Leo Sun will progress into Virgo. Fire without form is a bit like a loose cannon. As we saw with Aries, when fire progresses into an Earth sign it is given structure and reason. The key lessons here for Leo is that being the centre of attention is easier if you are technically proficient at something. This is where creative Leo learns his or her craft. Long hours in dance, acting or singing classes pay off as Leo becomes technically adept at their chosen method of self-publicity. Later on the Leo Sun will progress into Libra and so will begin to

♈	♉	♊	♋	♌	♍	♎	♏	♐	♑	♒	♓
Aries	Taurus	Gemini	Cancer	Leo	Virgo	Libra	Scorpio	Sagittarius	Capricorn	Aquarius	Pisces

recognise others as important and also learn lessons of justice, fairness and reciprocity.

Venus in Leo...

...likes to sing. Its placement here is all about demonstrating its creativity; singing is one obvious way that Venus manifests through its rulership of Taurus, which in turn rules the throat and voice.

Whitney Houston, Paula Abdul, Eddie Fisher, Nicole Kidman, Jenny Lind, Harry Secombe, Gwyneth Paltrow, Madonna Ciccone, Barry Manilow, Van Morrison and Olivia Newton-John all have Venus in Leo.

Venus in Leo is also a charming and romantic lover, they aren't too bothered about the setting because their imagination is quite well developed and so a picnic in a country meadow will do as well as a meal at a top restaurant. Love is important to them, and they are self-aware and so giving them adoration is the greatest gift you could give (of course, something made of 18 carat gold would also go down a treat as well).

Mars in Leo

The tendency for Leo to be generous and giving is only really apt if they can get something in return. Mars, symbolising the subject's sexuality, is self-oriented. That's not to say Leo is not capable of altruism, because this is a position that allows Leo's creative projects to tackle issues that help others. But the creativity that is inherent in helping others is part and parcel of the expression of self that Leo needs. Leo likes to be thanked and praised, but actually seeing the results of their altruism is often enough for this giant of creative thought and action.

Mars is in Leo in the charts of these people: Brigitte Bardot, John Quincy Adams, Sting, Fyodor Dostoevsky, Rudy Giuliani, Bruce Springsteen, Niels Bohr, Robert Graves, Benjamin Disraeli, Thomas Jefferson, Bette Midler, Helen Keller, Andrew Lloyd-Webber, Shimon Peres, Sylvia Plath, Ann Widdecombe, Sophia Loren, Gina Lollobrigida

♈	♉	♊	♋	♌	♍	♎	♏	♐	♑	♒	♓
Aries	Taurus	Gemini	Cancer	Leo	Virgo	Libra	Scorpio	Sagittarius	Capricorn	Aquarius	Pisces

and over 200 professional astrologers (many of whom had progressed-Mars in Virgo when they took up astrology).

Virgo Archetype
Sun in Virgo

Virgo often takes a back seat. Virgo actors tend to be stylistically odd or supporting players. This is the sign of service, analysis, technique and criticism. Virgo likes to play the supporting structural role and as such many fine Virgoan technicians scaffold the careers of the more creative and outstanding characters in history and public life. Virgo is critical, hardworking, reclusive and analytical.

The front line – above the titles – Virgo actors include Sean Connery, Peter Sellers, Jeremy Irons, Lauren Bacall, Richard Basehart, Ingrid Bergman, Greta Garbo, Cameron Diaz, Elliott Gould, Sophia Loren, Roddy McDowall, Raquel Welch, Hugh Grant and Lily Tomlin. Below the titles come Jack Warren, Tuesday Weld, Catherine Oxenberg, Ricki Lake, Mark Harmon, Ed Begley and Barbara Bach.

Virgo often comes into its own in science, and being an Earth sign they are often sceptical of astrology. Here are some of the great contributors to Science from this practical, analytical and structured sign:

Al Biruni, Ancel, Cuvier, Fizeau, Flamsteed, Frechet, Huygens, Eugene Houseman, Lavoisier, Frederick Robbins, Donald Glaser and Stephen Jay Gould...

...of course, if what I say is true about Virgo, there will be many other major contributors to science who did not become famous because their Virgo nature encouraged them to maintain a low profile...

At some point between birth and the 30th birthday, Sun Virgo will progress into Libra, here the technically expert, attention to detail that perfectionist Virgo has spent their tenure in their home sign perfecting, is opened up and given direction and purpose by Cardinal Libra. Libra brings balance and harmony to strait-laced Virgo and also introduces the

♈	♉	♊	♋	♌	♍	♎	♏	♐	♑	♒	♓
Aries	Taurus	Gemini	Cancer	Leo	Virgo	Libra	Scorpio	Sagittarius	Capricorn	Aquarius	Pisces

stay-at-home Virgo to the pleasures of association, and if this is age-appropriate, of intimate relationships too. Virgo tends to work in supporting roles, but the transition into Cardinal Libra brings the opportunity for prominence, an example of this is that of Rania Al-Yasin who was working in a bank, then as her progressed-Sun moved into Libra, she met and married Prince Abdullah of Jordan. She is now Queen Rania of Jordan. Later on, Virgo will progress into Scorpio where mundane detail, structure and balance are replaced by questions of life, death and taxes.

Venus in Virgo...

...is quite a practical placement. Often there are complaints that people with this placement are calculating or structured in their lovemaking. Their practical attitudes can manifest as apparent coldness in relationships and sometimes sparse and minimalistic tastes in decoration and clothing. Practicality is the keyword and often people with this placement can be found doing something other than having sex for its own sake. They are not slaves to the whim of their desires, especially not in later life.

Anne Bancroft, Brigitte Bardot, Ingrid Bergman, Bryan Ferry, Carrie Fisher, Angelica Huston, Chrissie Hynde, Deborah Kerr, Sean Penn, Patrick Swayze, Martin Balsam and Julio Iglesias

Mars in Virgo

This is a technical sign position. Mars in Virgo makes for technically gifted lovers who hone their skill over years of practice. They have to do this because they are not particularly passionate people and as such make a point of making a good impression in order to not appear too boring. In life the principle they live by is 'will it work?' mainly because the underlying symbolism is practical, detailed, action. This is not the most aggressively competitive sign placement, but it can be a good placement for a team player. This is a useful sign placement for engineers and systems analysts.

Bill Wyman, Midge Ure, Bing Crosby, Bob Champion, Princess Diana,

♈	♉	♊	♋	♌	♍	♎	♏	♐	♑	♒	♓
Aries	Taurus	Gemini	Cancer	Leo	Virgo	Libra	Scorpio	Sagittarius	Capricorn	Aquarius	Pisces

Nigel Havers, Bob Hope, Andre Blondel, Ernest Hemingway, Gene Wilder, Ed Moses, Raquel Welch, Sylvester Stallone, Yves Montand, Michael Landon, Bob Geldof, Peter Frampton, Isaac Hayes, Clark Gable and Olivia De Havilland all share this sign position.

Libra Archetype
Sun in Libra

According to traditional astrology, if the Sun is strong in Aries – its *Exaltation* – it must be weak in Libra, which is called its *Fall*. The idea being that certain planets sit more comfortably in some signs than others is part and parcel of our understanding of astrology and must be taken seriously or much of the interpretive foundation of astrology is ignored. Libra is the home of Venus and the planet most comfortable here is Saturn. The Sun, being a masculine principle that symbolizes our ego, is separated into two here. Libra divides in order to balance and in doing so halves the power of the Sun. Decision making is difficult because they have to see both sides of the argument and this can cause vacillation and oscillation. Positively speaking this can also translate into passive resistance; Mohandas K Gandhi was a Sun Libran. Libra is also based on the idea of association in that it is the 7th sign and therefore signifies 'other people'. It is the first sign in the twelve where the Sun is urged to look outside of itself and encounter other people and external considerations. The Libra archetype is very concerned with *relating*.

The cardinal nature of Libra invites the person to become political, but the politics of Libra is different from the protective policies of Cancer. Libra is interested in justice; negatively, Libra justice can sometimes be simplistic justice, either paying too much, or completely lacking in, attention to the grey areas in society.

Margaret Thatcher, Edwina Currie, Michael Collins, Georges Clemenceau, Dwight D Eisenhower, Eamon DeValera, Vaclav Havel, Jesse Jackson, Benjamin Netanyahu, Juan Peron, Vladimir Putin, Pierre Trudeau,

♈	♉	♊	♋	♌	♍	♎	♏	♐	♑	♒	♓
Aries	Taurus	Gemini	Cancer	Leo	Virgo	Libra	Scorpio	Sagittarius	Capricorn	Aquarius	Pisces

Ann Widdecombe, John Profumo, John Lennon, Silvio Berlusconi, David Ben Gurion, Chester Arthur, Jimmy Carter, Bob Geldof, Sting, Charlton Heston, Robert Muldoon and Sandro Pertini were all born with a Libra Sun.

Sometime between birth and the 30th birthday, Libra Sun will progress into Scorpio. This is a time when Libra begins to see the world as a place where justice and fairness are not always present. Often when the Libran is older (born towards the beginning of the sign), this change will appear more obviously than when the change takes place during early life. The usual result is that thoughts and ideas that the young Libran took for granted are challenged by the deprivation and depravity that exists in the world. This is typically the recognition that 'life's not fair'; Bob Geldof and Sting are good examples. Later in life the Sun might progress into Sagittarius, this happens between their early thirties and early sixties, they are then challenged to educate, explore and to develop their ideals. Sometimes this is a time when Libra becomes close to their god through their chosen religion, or alternatively they can become philosophical in their outlook.

Venus in Libra...

... is seldom out of a relationship. This is the planetary position for those who love to be in love and whose very persona can on occasion become synonymous with relationships and intimate associations. Harmony is vitally important for this person who will retreat away from noise and aggression. They like to have equilibrium in their relationships and are acutely aware if they are being treated unfairly. Their Achilles heel is an attraction to Aries people who aren't the quietest people in the world and as such they have their work cut out when this type of relationship arises in their lives. They are capable of compromise. Just as well really.

Rita Hayworth, Grace Kelly, Madame du Barry, May Pang, Lord Alfred Douglas, Freddie Mercury, Oscar Wilde, Pablo Picasso, Bo Derek, Cheryl Tiegs, Claudia Schiffer, Tanya Tucker, Angie Dickinson, Calista Flockhart, Lauren Hutton, Elke Sommer, Joan Blondell, Britt Ekland, Vivien Leigh,

♈	♉	♊	♋	♌	♍	♎	♏	♐	♑	♒	♓
Aries	Taurus	Gemini	Cancer	Leo	Virgo	Libra	Scorpio	Sagittarius	Capricorn	Aquarius	Pisces

Woody Allen, Marlee Matlin, Loretta Swit and the New York Statue of Liberty.

Mars in Libra...

...often gives way to extremeties. Similar to Mars being in Taurus or Venus being in Aries, Mars makes mistakes here, usually because there is a slight imbalance between what Libra Mars person projects and what the person feels. Libra is concerned with 'other people' generally and Mars as concerned with self-fulfillment. Consequently give and take can occasionally be erratic. Size matters more to Mars in Libra than it does to any of the other placements of Mars. The good news is that this placement can compromise and arbitrate like no other Mars position: this is useful in relationships. Mars in Libra can sometimes be passive to the point of uncompetitiveness, but as far as spiritual development is concerned, there can be fewer better placements for Mars.

Some members of this group include: Pamela Anderson, Candy Barr, Maria Callas, Barbara Bach, Anais Nin, Heather Locklear, Britt Ekland, Morgan Fairchild, Whoopi Goldberg, Kiefer Sutherland, David Carradine, Roman Polanski, John Malkovich, Barry Gibb and Eminem.

Scorpio Archetype
Sun in Scorpio

The essence of this sign is *plumbing the depths in order to find the secret of life*. Scorpio is in some senses the darkest place in the zodiac and as such the people born under this sign are often the most mysterious. This is the arctic region of the zodiac, so here we have an extreme mixture of daylight and darkness.

Some Scorpio principles include the idea of shared property (or other people's assets). Scorpions make good investment bankers and creative accountants. Often we find the solvers of mysteries among the eighth sign.

Many prolific female Scorpios are associated with sexuality and power

♈	♉	♊	♋	♌	♍	♎	♏	♐	♑	♒	♓
Aries	Taurus	Gemini	Cancer	Leo	Virgo	Libra	Scorpio	Sagittarius	Capricorn	Aquarius	Pisces

in all its senses, Marie Curie, Bjork, Linda Evans, Bo Derek, Barbara Boxer, Calista Flockhart, Grace Kelly, Barbara Hutton, Hedy Lamarr, Vivien Leigh, Jayne Mansfield, Melina Mercouri, Demi Moore, Indira Gandhi, Sylvia Plath, Winona Ryder, Loretta Swit and Sophie Marceau.

Sometime between birth and the 30th birthday, Scorpio Sun will progress into Sagittarius. This is a time when Scorpio begins to explore new ideas with versatility and optimism. Often when the Scorpio is older (born towards the beginning of the sign in October), this change will appear more obviously than if it happens when they are young (born mid November). The usual result is that thoughts and ideas that were mysterious to the young Scorpio become the subject of their higher education or of their propensity for solving mysteries. Later in life the Sun might progress into Capricorn, this happens between their early thirties and early sixties; they are then challenged to bring structure and success to their investigations, adventures and studies. This is when some Scorpios can become a force in their field.

Venus in Scorpio

Similar in effect to Venus in Aries, this placement suffers from unhappiness in love at least in early life. This position is prone to sentimental poetry and heartbreak. Food, love and beauty are all issues for Venus in Scorpio and often these people will comfort eat after their unhappy love affairs. Scorpio can be obsessive and when Venus is in Mars/Pluto ruled Scorpio the obsession can be love or sex. Scorpio also often allows people to lift the lid on their partner's indiscretions and so faithfulness is key for Venus in Scorpio; finding a faithful match is particularly important in young adulthood, this Venus position tends to repel those with a free and easy take on life because it comes with bags of jealousy and possessiveness. Later on, however, the older more philosophical Scorpio Venus will have set their partner free and found that they have returned. This is a key lesson for Scorpio Venus to learn. So, *if you love someone set them free* is a real issue

♈	♉	♊	♋	♌	♍	♎	♏	♐	♑	♒	♓
Aries	Taurus	Gemini	Cancer	Leo	Virgo	Libra	Scorpio	Sagittarius	Capricorn	Aquarius	Pisces

in this corner of the zodiac. Occasionally the extremes of Scorpio can cause individuals to become very unhappy and unable to cope with their feelings, sometimes with difficult and unwelcome consequences in regard to their values and their desire to express their emotions.

Montgomery Clift, Ted Bundy, Larry Flynt, Charles Manson, Dennis Nilsen, Diana Dors, Gianni Versace, Ava Gardner, Lillie Langtry, Eric Edwards, Richard Pryor, Winona Ryder and Mama Cass Eliot all share this position.

Mars in Scorpio...

...is a great position for people who want to do their own thing because it allows individuals to use executive power to great effect. Passionate, deep and intensely physical, there is a self-knowledge opportunity to be gained here. Sex is a fundamental no-brainer with these guys. They don't get mad, but they like to get even. Joseph P. Kennedy, the man who coined this phrase, was born with Mars in Scorpio.

Clara Bow, Sammy Davis Jnr, Leonardo Di Caprio, Linda Evans, Sally Field, Mel Gibson, Grace Kelly, Jeremy Irons, Barbara Hutton, T.E Lawrence, J.R.R Tolkien, Douglas Adams, Stefanie Powers, Vanessa Redgrave, Edward G. Robinson and Frank Zappa.

Sagittarius Archetype
Sun in Sagittarius

Sagittarius is the sign of the zodiac most concerned with discovery and adventure. This sign has bags of optimism and versatility. Sagittarius is the sign of the Archer; there are many strings to this Archer's bow, including religion, higher education, law, foreign travel, adventure, gambling, luck, exploration and above all, the ability to get to the crux of the issue at hand. While opposite sign Gemini is concerned with everyday issues, Sagittarius has big, collective ideas, like those of religion and philosophy. Sagittarius is a big thinking sign and is most at home when in a tent in a little-explored

♈	♉	♊	♋	♌	♍	♎	♏	♐	♑	♒	♓
Aries	Taurus	Gemini	Cancer	Leo	Virgo	Libra	Scorpio	Sagittarius	Capricorn	Aquarius	Pisces

part of the world. This sign loves freedom to act and hates to be tied down by becoming a wage-slave. This is the archetypal sign of the sportsperson and besides having great aim they often diversify and play more than one sport. Successful Sagittarian sportspeople may be characterised by their ability to shoot, pitch, score baskets and hit targets. This sign is the University of the Zodiac and as such, its students often keep odd hours, up until 5am, sleeping until 2pm. Well, students will be students. Most Sagittarians really enjoy having fun, the one exception that comes to mind is Woody Allen, who has the Sun, Mercury and Jupiter in Sagittarius, usually a sign of great optimism but, unfortunately for Woody all of these planets are squared (90 degrees away) from the heavy leaden planet Saturn in Pisces. His chart ruler is the comedy planet Mercury and the Ascendant is Virgo so he has built his act on self-effacing, pessimistic humour in an anhedonic style.

Famous people with a Sagittarian Sun include: Uri Geller, Bruce Lee, Kenneth Branagh, David Carradine, Sir Winston Churchill, Sammy Davis Jr, Joe DiMaggio, Walt Disney, Chris Evert, John Paul Getty, Betty Grable, Bette Midler, Edith Piaf, Bhagwan Shree Rajneesh, Charles Schultz, Britney Spears, Tommy Steele, Jean-Louis Trintignant and Sir Laurens Van der Post.

Some time between birth and the 30th birthday, the Sagittarius Sun will progress into Capricorn. The Sagittarian will then take on some of the characteristics of the following sign: this is symbolically the point when the adolescent adventurer starts to grow up. He leaves university/higher education and goes to work. The challenge is for Sagittarius to make practical use of some of the things they learned while traversing the sign of religion, philosophy, law and higher knowledge. Later they may progress into the unconventional realms of Aquarius. Here they become less concerned with their own quests and try to become sympathetic to the plight of and development of others.

♈	♉	♊	♋	♌	♍	♎	♏	♐	♑	♒	♓
Aries	Taurus	Gemini	Cancer	Leo	Virgo	Libra	Scorpio	Sagittarius	Capricorn	Aquarius	Pisces

Venus in Sagittarius

Venus here makes a person broad-minded with regard to love and relation-ships. These people tend not to be judgmental, and although all the signs need security in a relationship as much as any other, Venus here makes them less hidebound to traditional ideas of what makes a relationship work. Some people with this Venus position prefer not to be tied down in a relationship simply because it means tying them down geographically and they do like to wander. Having said that they are still quite passionate and prone to giving their all (at least for a while) in pursuit of their dream partner; they are, however, equally philosophical about setting their loved one free. Later in life depending on the direction of Venus' progression they can either become settled or they try hard to work at their relationship.

Kim Basinger, David Bowie, Kevin Costner, Gerard Depardieu, Jamie Lee Curtis, Hedy Lamarr, Jean Marais, Vanessa Paradis, Roger Vadim, Tina Turner, Maria Shriver and Jimi Hendrix all share this Venus position.

Mars in Sagittarius

This is a dynamic position for Mars and can lead to poised and driven individuals whose physical prowess is an important part of their lives. They are versatile lovers whose big ideas of what sex should be often translate into bedroom games. The core theme in this placement is adventurous activity, which leads to a kind of aggressive dynamism. The mutable (or changeable) part of the exchange of principles between Mars and Sagittarius (Sag being one of the four mutable signs) means that there isn't always a whole lot of focus in their physical activities unless they play sport. There are good and bad ways of expressing yourself physically and often Mars in Sagittarius likes to be combative and aggressive.

Warren Beatty, Cyd Charisse, Fritjof Capra, Faye Dunaway, Ellen Degeneres, Lesley Anne Down, Rita Hayworth, Sylvia Kristal, Pier Paolo Pasolini, John Travolta and W.C. Fields share this Mars position.

♈	♉	♊	♋	♌	♍	♎	♏	♐	♑	♒	♓
Aries	Taurus	Gemini	Cancer	Leo	Virgo	Libra	Scorpio	Sagittarius	Capricorn	Aquarius	Pisces

Capricorn Archetype
Sun in Capricorn

There never was a sign more stoic in their outlook than Capricorn. Being an Earth sign, Capricorn likes structure and is practical. The difference between the other two Earth signs Virgo and Taurus is that Capricorn is ambitious and has a great desire to get to the top of their profession or field. There is a great need to 'do' something about their situation and being ruled by the planet Saturn can have its drawbacks as Capricorn can often become morose and negative in their outlook. Capricorn knows what it wants and the Sun here means that a person's goals; their life-path, is closely linked to achieving respect and status. They also know that the safest way to achieve this is by being conventional and stable. Their ability to have fun is often limited by their desire to make something of themselves so they will work hard and save playtime til later. Their personal qualities include the ability to design and build structures, both physically and mentally. They are pragmatic about life and will only do something 'alternative' if it is also useful. Capricorn artists and writers often construct images or personas that have tangibility enabling them to use their work as a vehicle for their ideas. They are serious and controlled individuals with a wry, dry sense of humour. Actors with this position often play serious roles and depression, sadness and melancholy is often a problem for Capricorn, though this is seldom part of their public persona. When Capricorn makes it to the top, they have a tendency to stay there.

Elvis Presley, David Bowie, Rod Stewart, Dolly Parton, Johnny Ray, Sissy Spacek, Donna Summer, Richard Widmark, Jane Wyman, Loretta Young, Telly Savalas, Anthony Hopkins, Frank Langella, David Lynch, Diane Keaton, James Earl Jones, Mel Gibson, Robert Duvall, John Denver, Kevin Costner, Nicolas Cage and Muhammad Ali.

Some time between birth and the 30th birthday the Capricorn Sun will progress into Aquarius where it will be challenged to stop working for its own status and begin to work for the good of others. Capricorn has to come

♈	♉	♊	♋	♌	♍	♎	♏	♐	♑	♒	♓
Aries	Taurus	Gemini	Cancer	Leo	Virgo	Libra	Scorpio	Sagittarius	Capricorn	Aquarius	Pisces

to terms with the detachment of Aquarius and to rise above its earthbound perspective to get an overview of situations. Structure will always play a role in Capricorn's life, but the free-form approach of the Air sign Aquarius is a challenge in itself. New, unconventional ideas and approaches are utilized by the Capricorn who often appears to be an innovator. Later in life Capricorn may progress into Pisces and must come to terms with the intangible and unstructured lessons of intuition and inspiration that Pisces is prone to present. The pragmatist's spiritual journey begins here.

Venus in Capricorn

The principle here is serious love, a consequence is that they prefer not to engage in one-night-stands and prefer long-term relationships and liaisons with substance. Venus is controlled here and can wait for the right person to turn up. Another consequence is that the people who have Venus in Capricorn can be either early or late starters in relationships. This apparent contradiction depends on whether they imagine themselves to be older than they actually are, or whether they prefer to concentrate on work rather than play. This controlled seriousness can also manifest as structure in art or creative work. There is a preference for work over play (a Capricorn theme) and there is likely to be a little disappointment in relationships due to the Saturn rulership of this sign. There could also be a fear of intimacy and a dislike of too much proximity.

Noel Coward, Walt Disney, James Dean, Clark Gable, Elvis Presley, Britney Spears, Justin Timberlake, Jane Wyman, Dolly Parton, Edith Piaf, Juliet Mills and Bjork all have Venus in Capricorn.

Mars in Capricorn

Mars is happy in this sign because it is brings structure to the dynamic activity that Mars likes to have. Capricorn is a Cardinal sign and so needs to 'do'; to 'act', but it does so with practicality rather than caution (which is the way Cancer likes to express itself). People with this Mars position

♈	♉	♊	♋	♌	♍	♎	♏	♐	♑	♒	♓
Aries	Taurus	Gemini	Cancer	Leo	Virgo	Libra	Scorpio	Sagittarius	Capricorn	Aquarius	Pisces

like to get things done, but they usually adopt the correct amount of reservation and forward thrust to bring about cogent change. In their sexual liaisons there is skill and poise, if there is sometimes a little lack of confidence to start with. Capricorn strives to achieve and like Virgo it knows that to achieve it is a good idea to be technically proficient at anything you do. This is the case with sex and physical intimacy; Mars in Capricorn likes to practice, then when the serious relationship comes along they have achieved good technical virtuosity.

Woody Allen, Drew Barrymore, David Bowie, Marlon Brando, Marlene Dietrich, Mia Farrow, Gene Hackman, Michael Hutchence, Ali McGraw, Merle Oberon, Eartha Kitt and David Frost share this sign position of Mars.

Aquarius Archetype
Sun in Aquarius

This is the most unconventional sign of the zodiac. This is the organising innovator who looks at problems from a slightly different perspective. Aquarians are motivated by a need to express their individuality and as such (like their opposite sign Leo) they often become performance artists of some sort. Aquarius is also the sign of technology, revolution, upheaval and change and the Sun here invites an individual to have a go at being different and to live on the cutting edge. This is an interesting place for a fixed sign, because they tend to become stubbornly different and occasionally get into trouble because their view of the world is not the same as that of other people (and particularly the establishment) a consequence of this is that as they stubbornly cling to their unusual world view they can become vilified and shunned. Often though, they are feted as free thinkers and humanitarians. They are good at organising group activities and facilitating discussions. Aquarius is one of the more charitable signs of the zodiac whose love of freedom is similar to the Libran's love of justice and the Gemini love of truth. They share good balance with Gemini and Libra and often take up technical sports such as water-skiing, snowboarding,

♈	♉	♊	♋	♌	♍	♎	♏	♐	♑	♒	♓
Aries	Taurus	Gemini	Cancer	Leo	Virgo	Libra	Scorpio	Sagittarius	Capricorn	Aquarius	Pisces

skateboarding, flying, driving or windsurfing. Aquarius (and to some extent Gemini and Libra) sometimes has a hard time speaking with sincerity; this is just because they are detached and objective thinkers and communicators.

Stan Collymore, Sonny Bono, Bobby Brown, Phil Collins, James Dean, Ellen Degeneres, Mia Farrow, Clark Gable, Zsa Zsa Gabor, Michael Hutchence, Holly Johnson, Terry Jones, Jeanne Moreau, Roger Vadim, Mozart, Ronald Reagan, Oprah Winfrey, Tallulah Bankhead, Linda Blair, Geena Davis, Sascha Distel, Farrah Fawcett and Juliette Greco.

Some time between birth and the 30th birthday, Aquarius will progress into Pisces. This is a cue for the Aquarians stubborn unconventionality to give way to sensitivity to others and while not reining in the spark of genius that may be wholly part of the Aquarian nature, it does mean that intuition and inspiration take the place of objective detachment. Later the Sun may progress into Aries, this is a call for Aquarius to stop just *thinking* differently but to start *acting* decisively.

Venus in Aquarius

The core theme here is freedom in relationships. Often this sign position brings people who prefer to sleep alone. Although they do like to be intimate it is often difficult for them to retain interest in the conventional types of relationship that most of the other signs prefer to have. This is the sign position for the open relationship and there is often something unusual about this sign-position's intimate union. Venus in Aquarius will in the past often have been the first to flout convention and cross-racial barriers because humanitarian Aquarius sees the person not the skin-color. There is little emotional baggage with Venus in Aquarius, what heartbreak Aquarius encounters is either put down to experience or quickly forgotten. It is sometimes hard for Venus in Aquarius to settle down because, like their fellow Air sign Gemini, Aquarius can intellectualise love and is fond of association with others. There can be a tendency towards libertarianism.

♈	♉	♊	♋	♌	♍	♎	♏	♐	♑	♒	♓
Aries	Taurus	Gemini	Cancer	Leo	Virgo	Libra	Scorpio	Sagittarius	Capricorn	Aquarius	Pisces

Joseph Smith, founder of the Mormon religion was born with Venus in Aquarius.

Nicolas Cage, Simone de Beauvoir, William Burroughs, Cyrano de Bergerac, Christine Keeler, Oliver Reed, Sharon Tate, Ted Danson, Yoko Ono, Kim Novak, Loretta Young, Sharon Tate, Sissy Spacek, Pola Negri, Leslie Neilson, Akira Kurosawa, Eddie Izzard and Phil Collins.

Mars in Aquarius

The principle here is individualistic action. As we have noted, Aquarius is unorthodox and can often shake established traditions through anything from mild unusualness to outright revolutionary behavior. Mars here seeks detachment and freedom of expression. The style of Aquarius Mars is to shock and surprise and at the physical level, as with all the Air signs, Aquarius can have an open-minded attitude to sex (Hugh Hefner has Mars in Aquarius; not to mention John Major whose affaire with Edwina Currie shocked a nation). Mars in Aquarius assures that they do it their way and to hell with convention.

Tom Baker, Winona Ryder, Enzo Ferrari, Jack Brabham, Howard Hughes, Audie Murphy, Burgess Meredith, Cary Grant, Jane Fonda, Bridget Fonda, Farrah Fawcett, John Cleese, Julie Christie, John Bon Jovi and Tallulah Bankhead.

Pisces Archetype
Sun in Pisces

This is a most confusing life-plan to have. Pisces is a mutable (adaptable) water (emotional) sign. Tears can be shed over anything and often are. Pisces Sun is the final sign for the Sun and signifies the old portion of life that many of us spend institutionalised in homes or hospitals. Pisces is the sign of the completely selfless person and this can translate as so-adapt-able-they-become-almost-identity-less. This is the price you pay for being the wisest and most intuitive sign of the zodiac. The problem

♈	♉	♊	♋	♌	♍	♎	♏	♐	♑	♒	♓
Aries	Taurus	Gemini	Cancer	Leo	Virgo	Libra	Scorpio	Sagittarius	Capricorn	Aquarius	Pisces

they face is that intuition and illusion have close proximity and that is why Pisces has often been depicted as both the saint who has a divine vision and the deluded individual. There is an empathic gentleness inherent in Pisces that comes, some say, from many lifetimes, others because Pisces is so sensitive to the plight of others. The life-path is closely related to the fine line between delusion and vision. The underlying principle of this archetype is *belief* and this opposes the idea of analysis or reductionism, which is Virgo's forte. It is no accident that the symbol of the fish is a strong collective religious symbol. Pisces is also strongly associated with Jupiter, so optimism in the face of despair is another Pisces trait. Pisces is associated with dance and rhythm and Cyd Charisse, Liane Dayde-Giraud, Sandy Duncan, Yorg Lanner, Rudolph Nureyev and Vaslav Nijinsky were all Sun Pisces. Many Pisceans have gifted imaginations some whose fantasies can become either intricate and interesting or somewhat tiresome and affected. Pisceans include: Douglas Adams, Edgar Cayce, Cyrano de Bergerac, Charlotte Church, Kurt Cobain, Buffalo Bill Cody, Nicolaus Copernicus, Albert Einstein, Galileo Galilei, Henrik Ibsen, Steve Jobs, Jack Kerouac, Urban Leverrier, Josef Mengele, Michelangelo, Boris Pasternak, FDR, Robert Wadlow, Sir Ranulph Fiennes, Christine Keeler, Anais Nin, Pier Paolo Pasolini, Rudolph Steiner, George Harrison, Tammy Faye Bakker, Frederic Chopin, Ivana Trump and – possibly – Osama Bin-Laden.

Some time between birth and the 30th birthday the Pisces Sun will progress into Aries. Here the many different strings to the Piscean identity begin to merge and the result is a push for independence and direction. The move from Water to Fire always means the subject must work off a little steam, while the move from mutable to cardinal changes the path from one of adaptability and contemplation to one of direction, action and possibly aggression. Later on the Sun may progress into Taurus where Pisces is challenged to find structure and foundation in the world.

♈	♉	♊	♋	♌	♍	♎	♏	♐	♑	♒	♓
Aries	Taurus	Gemini	Cancer	Leo	Virgo	Libra	Scorpio	Sagittarius	Capricorn	Aquarius	Pisces

Venus in Pisces

Venus is capable of such selfless and undying love in Pisces that it is difficult to verbalise the pain and heartache that someone with this sign position must endure when they lose their love. While being sentimental, they are not overly so and as time goes by and relationships develop, Pisces is shrewd if not a little lucky in finding someone who shares their outlook. Venus in Pisces prefers a long-term intimate relationship, but, being adaptable, they will often take their time to find the right match. Love is a mystical and karmic business for this Venus position and often Pisces will find their mate 'after searching for ten thousand lifetimes'.

Tammy Wynette, John Travolta, Barbara Streisand, Betty Ford, Edgar Cayce, Emanuel Swedenborg, Joanne Woodward, Ron Howard, Charlotte Church, Geena Davis, Celine Dion, Michelle Pfieffer, Michael Wilding, Sonny Bono, Kurt Cobain, Alice Cooper and Serge Gainsbourg.

Mars in Pisces

Mars here is governed by the principle of dissolving action. Pisces dissolves and dissipates while Mars wants to act and create. Pisces is the sign of imagination while Mars is the planet of sex. As such, people with this sign position of Mars often bring fantasy into the bedroom. This is a prime position for love on the beach, aboard ship, in the sea etc. etc. Sometimes, usually early in adulthood, Pisces Mars can be promiscuous or easily led by others who seek to control them. This changes as time goes by, but lessons are sometimes hard-learned. There is often a high degree of morality masked by a cool or hip projected image.

Jim Bakker, Che Guevarra, Charles Lindbergh, Chris Rock, Steve McQueen, Marilyn Monroe, Eva Marie Saint, Rob Lowe, Tina Turner, Lupe Velez, Errol Flynn, Eric Clapton, Patrick Duffy, Lana Turner, Elizabeth Taylor and LL Cool J.

Although the Sun is an important indicator of what you want to get from life, the Sun impulse does change as it progresses. Likewise Mars shows

♈	♉	♊	♋	♌	♍	♎	♏	♐	♑	♒	♓
Aries	Taurus	Gemini	Cancer	Leo	Virgo	Libra	Scorpio	Sagittarius	Capricorn	Aquarius	Pisces

how you assert yourself and how you perform sexually. Mars can also show up in your manner and methods. Other important indicators are the Moon which describes how we adapt emotionally; how supportive we can be and in what ways we support and nurture our partners. The chart ruler: the planet that rules the sign on the Ascendant often shows up clearly in the personality and therefore is a strong indicator for the types of people who will like us. But no other planet has the impact on who we attract, or who attracts us, than the astrological Venus.

♈	♉	♊	♋	♌	♍	♎	♏	♐	♑	♒	♓
Aries	Taurus	Gemini	Cancer	Leo	Virgo	Libra	Scorpio	Sagittarius	Capricorn	Aquarius	Pisces

Five

Symbols and Aspects in Astrology

My evenings are taken up largely with astrology. I make horoscopic calculations in order to find a clue to the core of psychological truth...
Carl Jung (from a letter to Sigmund Freud)

The Planets

The planetary symbols are as follows:

☉	☽	☿	♀	♂
The Sun	**The Moon**	**Mercury**	**Venus**	**Mars**

Because this book is mainly about the Sun, Venus and Mars, and includes some mention of the Moon I will concentrate on the following three symbols:

The Sun
Keywords and concepts for the Sun include:

The will, pride, arrogance, creative power, desire to be special, character, individuality, power, authority, ones level of influence, negotiation, hope, courage, aspirations or wishes for one's life, honour, innermost being, central force around which all else revolves, the masculine part of one's nature, the extent to which one can be assertive, the father-figure.

♈	♉	♊	♋	♌	♍	♎	♏	♐	♑	♒	♓
Aries	Taurus	Gemini	Cancer	Leo	Virgo	Libra	Scorpio	Sagittarius	Capricorn	Aquarius	Pisces

Venus
Keywords and concepts for Venus include:

Love, art, physical attraction, aesthetic taste, harmony, beauty, romance, satisfaction through emotional involvement, charm, appreciation of luxury, compromise, appreciation of values, that voluntary force which draws and bonds people together in relationships[XXXV], pleasure, hedonism, receptivity to love, wallowing in a sty of luxuries.

Mars
Keywords and concepts for Mars include:

Energy, activity, aggression, physicality and physical sexuality, courage, active energy, determination, the enjoyment of or appreciation of work, the means by which we pursue a goal, the ability to compete, survival energy, self-motivation and self-seeking effort.

Multi-Planet Meanings

The way that planetary meanings intermingle and meld into new and different concepts is through their angles to each other, these angles are created in space as the planets pass through a seemingly random, but essentially predictable path and their angular relationships to one another change, creating ever-changing geometric patterns. These angular relationships are called *aspects*.

The Aspects
Conjunction (0 Degrees)

Conjunctions are all about similarity and commonality. They emphasize, they underline, they embolden and they draw parallels. The Conjunction in

♈	♉	♊	♋	♌	♍	♎	♏	♐	♑	♒	♓
Aries	Taurus	Gemini	Cancer	Leo	Virgo	Libra	Scorpio	Sagittarius	Capricorn	Aquarius	Pisces

relationship astrology is best seen as a couple holding hands and walking forward together. They have recognized themselves in each other. They are *together*, but see the world from a *slightly* different perspective. They go to work, do their own thing and then share their experiences and offload on each other at home. Similarity in relationships is good, but it is not always complimentary and sometimes the intensity of the conjunction becomes wearying and burdensome. It works well for some, but not for others and it largely depends on your expectations and temperament whether this will be indefinitely harmonious. When Venus is involved, there are often only subtle differences between the effects of the conjunction and the opposition.

Semi-Sextile (30 Degrees)

The semi-sextile aspect in the relationship chart denotes the teacher and the pupil, it denotes also the individual and their property and it therefore signifies a relationship which is not close; not a union of desire, passion and unconditional love, but one of practicality and utility; where both parties use each other for a concrete purpose: to learn, to finance, to provide faith and esteem in each other or where one party treats the other as their property. This union is no better and no worse than any other, it's just not what most individuals conventionally aspire to, but it is one that many become involved in at some time in their lives. The semi-sextile can be visualized as a couple one of whom is teaching; the other learning.

Sextile (60 Degrees)

In the natural zodiac, the two Air signs Gemini and Aquarius are a sextile away from the beginning of Aries. In the Equal House chart, the first degree of both the 3rd and 11th houses is a sextile away from the Ascendant. It is described by Rael and Rudhyar as useful in offering 'integrative solutions to bi-polar problems'. This is because the sextile aspect can provide a link between an opposition (a 180 degree bi-polar problem) and a trine (a 120

♈	♉	♊	♋	♌	♍	♎	♏	♐	♑	♒	♓
Aries	Taurus	Gemini	Cancer	Leo	Virgo	Libra	Scorpio	Sagittarius	Capricorn	Aquarius	Pisces

degree aspect of vision, understanding and solution).

It can therefore theoretically provide a compatibility link between those areas of two people's personalities that are not in harmony.

More often, though, this aspect is one that provides lines of communication. The sign of Aquarius is an associative sign, it manifests as a propensity for group-work, membership of clubs and organizations and staid humanitarian campaigning. Gemini denotes neighbors and all sorts of communicational activities, from *semaphore* to *texting*. The 11th house is where you keep your friends and the 3rd is where you keep your neighbors and siblings. Theoretically, sextile aspects should bring together people who have known each other as friends or associates before they got involved as lovers, as such there may be a genuine liking with this aspect, but there will always be something *external* in common like bird-watching or Amnesty International rather than something *internal* like insatiable attraction or desire. Of course, this aspect will not give you anything more or less than it promises and often it provides just what a lot of people want in a relationship which is a friend they make love to and – in general – this kind of relationship works. The Sextile can be visualized as a couple talking and socializing.

One of the most talked about relationships in modern times (especially in Europe) is that of David and Victoria Beckham. The closest planetary factor in their relationship is a sextile aspect between her natal-Venus and his natal-Sun. Five of Howard Hughes' relationships involved this aspect – natally – between the Sun and Venus.

The sextile inclines two principles, which are complimentary, to communicate and co-operate.

Square (90 Degrees)

The 90-degree aspect is an aspect of invigoration, excitement and incendiary, it is also one of work. The square is an aspect that creates a need for action and this is often felt as conflict, but it is just as easily understood

♈	♉	♊	♋	♌	♍	♎	♏	♐	♑	♒	♓
Aries	Taurus	Gemini	Cancer	Leo	Virgo	Libra	Scorpio	Sagittarius	Capricorn	Aquarius	Pisces

by considering the difference between business and pleasure. The square in relationship astrology often manifests as a businesslike relationship where common patterns of behavior are limited by the matter at hand. If the relationship becomes less businesslike and more sociable, it is then that differences become apparent. Often there are tuts of disapproval between 'squared' people; this can lead to greater areas of conflict. Different standards, ideals and behavior are the main reason for disharmony, depending on the planet involved. Sometimes you do get a really bad square that turns into a dangerous situation this often involves Mars and Saturn. With the usual relationship planets (Sun Moon Venus), there is generally less serious conflict and instead this becomes disagreement or dissatisfaction.

The square can be visualized as a couple working together...often on different projects – or – two people 'squaring' up to each other.

The square inclines the two principles to excitable action because they are radically different and work in radically different ways.

Trine (120 Degrees)

Trines are aspects of natural vision and complimentarity. In the birth chart they provide resources that can be used easily, so easily in fact that people often waste trines by using them to dodge working hard. Trines are aspects of opportunity and compatibility of principles that integrate to form a productive mingling of planetary dynamics. This aspect is the cornerstone of relationship astrology, simply because in the modern age where we have increased choice of partner, more people choose easy relationships and natural attraction.

Trines in relationships exhibit themselves as mutual understanding, success and compatibility. They can also signal complacency. It's a common human problem to waste talent and to squander resources when they appear to be in abundance. The same goes for love.

The trine can be visualized as a couple embracing.

♈	♉	♊	♋	♌	♍	♎	♏	♐	♑	♒	♓
Aries	Taurus	Gemini	Cancer	Leo	Virgo	Libra	Scorpio	Sagittarius	Capricorn	Aquarius	Pisces

Inconjunct or Quincunx (150 Degrees)

This is not always ideal in human relationships and under this aspect we often find a feudal relationship where one individual is master while the other is their servant or it can be a relationship of investment where one planet lends and the other borrows. Alternatively this aspect could also depict a therapist-client relationship. The aspect is between signs that 'do not behold each other', I take this to mean that the planets do not really see or regard each other and this can translate to ambivalence.

The inconjunct can be visualized as a couple where one is preparing dinner while the other has paid for the food. The inconjunct aspect between the Sun and Venus is common in relationships, but it is not the factor that gets the relationship started in the first instance.

Opposition (180 Degrees)

The Opposition is an anomaly in relationship astrology in that the two planets involved are in conflict with each other, but the aspect is still popular in relationships. Depending on the planets involved, oppositions can symbolize conflicts of opinions, opposing views and stand-up fights. They also have the potential for intense magnetic attraction and passionate behavior. This is often because planets in opposite signs are not actually in incompatible elements and the 7th house cusp (the point opposite the beginning of the chart) is closely related to relationships. There is open communication with an opposition. Some types of opposition are not good for relationships, for example a Mars Saturn opposition between a couple's natal charts may end in fear, mistrust or tears if not in physical aggression and violence. Others involving the Sun and Venus, Venus and Venus, Mars and Venus and especially the Sun and Moon are often good indicators of balance in a relationship. With oppositions both partners have a role to fulfill that cannot be done by the other. The sign opposite your Sun often embodies *what you are not* and many people seek fulfillment by allowing their opposite number to give them perspective, love and physical passion.

♈	♉	♊	♋	♌	♍	♎	♏	♐	♑	♒	♓
Aries	Taurus	Gemini	Cancer	Leo	Virgo	Libra	Scorpio	Sagittarius	Capricorn	Aquarius	Pisces

The opposition can be visualized as a couple dancing. Often this is *dirty* dancing, as it were.

Before giving my own interpretation of the combinations of the Sun, Venus and Mars and in order to show the consistency of meaning adopted by astrologers, these interpretations are preceded by excerpts from Lois Haines Sargent's *How to Handle Your Human Relationships,*[xxxvi] which includes comparative planetary aspect interpretations. Interpretations from the following works are also paraphrased in some places: Ron Davison's *Synastry,*[xxxvii] Frances Sakoian and Louis S Acker's *The Astrology of Human Relationships*[xxxviii] and Stephen Arroyo's *Relationships and Life Cycles.*[xxxix]

The Sun with the Sun

If, in the words of the Bard, all the world really is a stage and we are merely poor [method] actors then the Sun is our *motivation*.

Sun Conjunct Sun

Sargent writes:

> *Creative power urges combine, individuals will either be unusually compatible or will irritate each other.*[xl]

The other astrologers agree that this is not a particularly exhilarating combination and that there are no connotations of love in this type of connection.

Sun Opposite Sun

Sargent writes:

> *Creative power urges will either oppose or balance each other. Sometimes they attract, sometimes they repel.*[xli]

♈	♉	♊	♋	♌	♍	♎	♏	♐	♑	♒	♓
Aries	Taurus	Gemini	Cancer	Leo	Virgo	Libra	Scorpio	Sagittarius	Capricorn	Aquarius	Pisces

The other astrologers suggest that the individuals involved are able to balance each other out and compliment each other's deficiencies. One astrologer, Davison, believes that opposite Suns can occasionally cause 'love at first sight'.[xlii] This is a common belief among some practitioners. Arroyo writes:

> With Sun opposite Sun there is some kind of stimulation and complimentary energy flow...There's an attraction, and you're also pulling in opposite directions.[xliii]

Sun Trine Sun

Sargent writes:

> Creative power urges harmonize easily.[xliv]

The other astrologers believe that the Sun in trine aspect to the Sun establishes a supportive tie born from mutual respect allowing both to support each other's creative self-expression.

Sun Square Sun

Sargent writes:

> Creative and power urges can clash.[xlv]

The other astrologers believe that the Sun square Sun combination is not good, resistance, resentment and a clash of wills is the result.

Sun aspects with the Sun result in shared, conflicting or tangential aspirations and wishes. In relationships, because the Sun is a masculine symbol it is competitive and dynamic. When two Suns aspect each other the consequence is varying degrees of admiration or contempt. There is often a Sun-Sun connection in obvious power struggles, especially in business. Sun aspecting Sun is also common in friendships and family relationships, but it does not have much bearing on the initial attraction that begins a relationship.

♈	♉	♊	♋	♌	♍	♎	♏	♐	♑	♒	♓
Aries	Taurus	Gemini	Cancer	Leo	Virgo	Libra	Scorpio	Sagittarius	Capricorn	Aquarius	Pisces

♀ ♀
Venus with Venus
Venus Conjunct Venus

Sargent writes:

Individuals express affection in the same way.[xlvi]

The other astrologers concur with this suggesting emotional sympathy and common tastes. Davison cites an example of a married couple who both had Venus in Taurus in the 7th house, who when their marriage entered difficulties, they both left it to the other to take the initiative of re-establishing harmony, he says that as Venus in Taurus is one of the least likely indicators of positive action, the 'discords were left to multiply, finally resulting in divorce'.[xlvii]

David Niven and his first wife Primula Rollo (known as Primmie) shared a natal-Venus conjunction in Aquarius. Niven spotted Primmie in a nightclub just after the outbreak of WWII. She was dressed in a WAAF (Women's Auxiliary Air Force) uniform. He did not approach her but thought she was the most beautiful person he had ever seen. In his autobiography he alludes to the fact that he spent the next few weeks thinking about her and trying to find her in wartime London (a time when many people were in uniform).

Eventually he bumped into her again and this time he engaged her in a conversation. They were married a few weeks later. Niven's biographer Sheridan Morley remarks that they were patently very much in love if somewhat vague about each other's backgrounds, characters and interests.[xlviii]

Theirs was a happy marriage, but it was punctuated by war and separation. On Niven's return to Hollywood after the war, Primmie suffered a serious head injury during a party game at Tyrone Power's house and died a few days later.

♈	♉	♊	♋	♌	♍	♎	♏	♐	♑	♒	♓
Aries	Taurus	Gemini	Cancer	Leo	Virgo	Libra	Scorpio	Sagittarius	Capricorn	Aquarius	Pisces

	1	2	3	4	5	6	7	8	9
A	Day	S.Time	Sun	Moon	Mercury	Venus	Mars		
B	21	22:02	02 ♓ 03'	13 ♋ 08'	16 ♒ 54'	14 ♒ 26'	01 ♎ 04'	1918	rollo
C	31	0:31	09 ♈ 53'	11 ♐ 21'	04 ♈ 17'	26 ♒ 13'	10 ♊ 34'	1940	niven
D	15	23:29	24 ♓ 05'	01 ♉ 58'	26 ♓ 24'	15 ♒ 45'	23 ♏ 47'	1940	rollo
E	1	22:33	10 ♓ 02'	09 ♏ 12'	15 ♓ 04'	15 ♒ 22'	22 ♉ 11'	1910	niven

Fig.17. Matrix showing the natal planetary positions of David Niven and Primula Rollo, together with their progressed planetary positions for the year 1940

As can be seen in this matrix, the romantic nature of the natal-Venus conjunction (B6 and E6) is accompanied by Primmie's progressing-Venus (D6) exactly conjoining David's natal-Venus in 1940, the year of their brief courtship and marriage. The amplification of feelings influenced by the progressed-Venus conjunction is well attested in many cases: it's as if the world stops for everyone except the two people involved and a lifetime is lived in two weeks. The progressing aspect places the natal aspect in a temporal context: the time was right. By the time of Primmie's death six years later, her progressing-Venus has moved from 15 to 18 degrees Aquarius.[xlix]

Venus Opposite Venus

Sargent writes (Sargent links Venus oppositions with Venus squares, whereas I would distance the two aspects):

Minor differences of taste, moral sentiment and attitude towards social life, beauty and culture.[1]

The other astrologers suggest romantic attraction, the result of which is dependent upon the condition of Venus in both charts (which basically means that if you can relate to others, the opposition isn't a problem, but if you can't, it is.)

The opposition can work out well.

♈	♉	♊	♋	♌	♍	♎	♏	♐	♑	♒	♓
Aries	Taurus	Gemini	Cancer	Leo	Virgo	Libra	Scorpio	Sagittarius	Capricorn	Aquarius	Pisces

	1	2	3	4	5	6	7	8	9
A	Day	S.Time	Sun	Moon	Mercury	Venus	Mars		
B	15	19:36	24 ♑ 41'	04 ♒ 15'	23 ♑ 23'	20 ♐ 36'	28 ♓ 29'	1592	jahan
C	14	3:28	23 ♉ 26'	14 ♏ 09'	14 ♊ 04'	08 ♋ 46'	16 ♎ 07'	1612	mahal
D	4	20:55	14 ♒ 59'	04 ♏ 11'	28 ♒ 16'	01 ♑ 08'	12 ♈ 43'	1612	jahan
E	25	2:13	05 ♉ 05'	24 ♒ 02'	07 ♉ 37'	19 ♊ 20'	04 ♒ 31'	1593	mahal

Fig.18 Matrix showing the natal planetary positions of Shah Jahan I and Mumtaz Mahal, together with their progressed planetary positions for the year of their marriage: 1612.

In this example, Shah Jahan I and Mumtaz Mahal shared nineteen years in a blissful opposition of Venus. Jahan built the Taj Mahal as a memorial to Mumtaz, the love of his life.[li]

Venus Trine Venus

Sargent writes:

There are similar attitudes in love and friendship.[lii]

The other astrologers suggest emotional rapport and few clashes of taste.

This aspect is central to the synastry of Gwyneth Paltrow and Chris Martin. A natal-Venus trine (B6 – E6) is amplified by an accompanying progression (C6) in 2003.

	1	2	3	4	5	6	7	8	9
A	Day	S.Time	Sun	Moon	Mercury	Venus	Mars		
B	27	0:52	04 ♎ 58'	11 ♊ 33'	11 ♎ 25'	21 ♌ 41'	28 ♍ 05'	1972	paltrow
C	28	0:23	07 ♈ 41'	14 ♋ 02'	19 ♈ 56'	21 ♈ 27'	06 ♓ 33'	2003	martin
D	28	2:54	05 ♏ 40'	03 ♌ 28'	27 ♏ 46'	27 ♍ 44'	18 ♎ 12'	2003	paltrow
E	2	22:40	11 ♓ 47'	01 ♌ 23'	00 ♓ 16'	21 ♈ 09'	16 ♒ 16'	1977	martin

Fig.19 Matrix showing the natal planetary positions of Gwyneth Paltrow and Chris Martin, together with their progressed planetary positions for the year 2003.

♈	♉	♊	♋	♌	♍	♎	♏	♐	♑	♒	♓
Aries	Taurus	Gemini	Cancer	Leo	Virgo	Libra	Scorpio	Sagittarius	Capricorn	Aquarius	Pisces

Mia Farrow reports a conversation in her book *What Falls Away*, between director Roman Polanski and actor John Cassevetes.

'One work day, while we were waiting to shoot, Roman was discoursing about the impossibility of long-term monogamy given the brevity of a man's sexual attraction for any one woman. An impassioned John Cassevetes responded that Roman knew nothing about women, or relationships, and that he, John, was more attracted than ever to his wife Gena Rowlands. Roman stared at him and blinked a few times, and for once he had no reply.' [liii]

John Cassevetes and Gena Rowlands shared a *natal-Venus-Venus* trine. Twenty two years later, and incidentally a few months after the death of John Cassevetes, Roman Polanski married Emmanual Seigner, a woman with whom he shares the same natal-Venus-Venus trine aspect, and to whom, to date, he has been happily married for nearly seventeen years.

Venus Square Venus

Sargent writes:

Affection is not expressed in the same way. [liv]

The other astrologers suggest incompatible temperaments, shared self-indulgent habits and a possessive, cloying relationship.

	1	2	3	4	5	6	7	8	9
			Sun	Moon	Mercury	Venus	Mars		
	Day	S.Time	Sun	Moon	Mercury	Venus	Mars		
A	Day	S.Time	Sun	Moon	Mercury	Venus	Mars		
B	9	11:00	17 ♍ 29'	29 ♓ 41'	14 ♍ 14'	15 ♒ 53'	28 ♓ 34'	1908	simone
C	15	14:08	22 ♋ 33'	11 ♍ 39'	13 ♌ 40'	07 ♊ 11'	13 ♏ 14'	1929	sartre
D	30	12:22	08 ♒ 52'	24 ♈ 05'	19 ♒ 44'	11 ♓ 46'	13 ♈ 18'	1929	simone
E	21	12:34	29 ♊ 40'	25 ♒ 41'	26 ♊ 24'	14 ♉ 57'	08 ♏ 27'	1905	sartre

Fig.20 Matrix showing the natal planetary positions of Jean Paul Sartre and Simone de Beauvoir together with theior progressed planetary positions for 1929.

♈	♉	♊	♋	♌	♍	♎	♏	♐	♑	♒	♓
Aries	Taurus	Gemini	Cancer	Leo	Virgo	Libra	Scorpio	Sagittarius	Capricorn	Aquarius	Pisces

Jean Paul Sartre and Simone de Beauvoir shared a long, but non-exclusive, relationship for over 50 years. While at the beginning of the relationship in 1929 we can observe two progressed-Venus trines, and they also share a wide natal-Sun-Venus trine, the manner of their attitude to relationships is dictated by their natal-Venus positions (B6 – E6). Sartre was a practical sensualist and Beauvoir a free-thinking experimentalist. The fact that they did not demand exclusivity contributed to the success of their companionship, but this is not a conventional relationship.

Venus in aspect to Venus symbolizes shared, conflicting or tangential approaches to harmony, art, love and romance. In relationships this is an important aspect symbolising mutual love and attraction, but because Venus is a feminine symbol, she often needs a more dynamic planet to activate a relationship, otherwise there is likely to be mutual attraction, but no real impetus to get the relationship off the starting blocks. Harmonious aspects including the trine, conjunction and opposition signify that a couple has similar or complimentary aesthetic taste. There is sharing of love, respect and ideas about relationships generally. Difficult aspects including the Square and Inconjunct signify that the couple want different things from relationships. This indicator often means that the couple spend time apart either physically or emotionally.

Mars with Mars
Mars Conjunct Mars

Sargent writes:

Desires are often similar or in agreement.[lv]

Aggressiveness, impulsive behavior or passionate sex attraction are some qualities noted by the other astrologers on the subject of Mars conjunct Mars.

♈	♉	♊	♋	♌	♍	♎	♏	♐	♑	♒	♓
Aries	Taurus	Gemini	Cancer	Leo	Virgo	Libra	Scorpio	Sagittarius	Capricorn	Aquarius	Pisces

Mars Opposite Mars

Sargent writes:

In marriage this aspect can cause tensions, since the desire natures conflict; or, if they are in agreement, individuals will not want what they want at the same time.[lvi]

Irritation, reaction and coercion are all words used by the other astrologers to describe the relationship that includes this aspect.

Arroyo writes:

...Very stimulating, very activating, but can you live with the other person? Sextiles, conjunctions and trines...are excellent for harnessing your mutual energies. Mars opposition Mars and Mars square Mars show a problematical thing in terms of getting things done.[lvii]

Mars Trine Mars

Sargent writes:

Unity of desire, energy, action. Helpful in marriage for sexual compatibility.[lviii]

The other astrologers suggest work, drive and aims are compatible under this combination.

Mars Square Mars

Sargent writes:

See Mars opposite Mars.

The other astrologers suggest friction, temper and occasionally violence can ensue under this combination. A 'clash of wills' ensues.

Mars in aspect to Mars symbolizes shared, conflicting or tangential approaches to passion, sport, work, and active recreation. In relationships, Mars aspects can reveal how sexually compatible a pair are. This in itself

♈	♉	♊	♋	♌	♍	♎	♏	♐	♑	♒	♓
Aries	Taurus	Gemini	Cancer	Leo	Virgo	Libra	Scorpio	Sagittarius	Capricorn	Aquarius	Pisces

does not tend to begin relationships, it can often help prolong them, but in the final analysis continuation and love are not born from such contacts. Harmonious Mars – Mars aspects by trine and sextile in isolation are nice, but are possibly secondary indicators in relationships. Squares and oppositions can lead to heated, possibly violent arguments.

Research suggests Mars seems to prefer the harder, more dynamic aspects of square and opposition to the softer and easier aspect of trine and conjunction; in the same way Venus prefers harmony. Mars in isolation embodies basic masculine principles. In many of the relationships in this study Mars positions relate directly to the methods employed by partners and how they harmonise in the 'task management' part of their relationship.

The Sun with Venus

This is the most important connection in relationship astrology bar none. We will encounter this connection in many of the relationships in this book and so a detailed explanation of the interaction of these two planets is key to the understanding of why they play such a vital role so often in relationships. Apart from blending the ideals (the Sun) with aesthetic beauty (Venus), there is also the mingling of the ideals or goals (Sun) of one with the values (Venus) of the other that makes this interaction symbolically valid as well as actually valid. Respect is the best word to sum up the natural outcome of this two-planet interaction, but this is an involved and loving type of respect.

Sun Conjunct Venus

Sargent writes:

Magnetic attraction.[lix]

The other astrologers emphasise attraction, fun and affection. Davison goes

♈	♉	♊	♋	♌	♍	♎	♏	♐	♑	♒	♓
Aries	Taurus	Gemini	Cancer	Leo	Virgo	Libra	Scorpio	Sagittarius	Capricorn	Aquarius	Pisces

on to suggest that the arrival of the Sun by progression at the conjunction of Venus, when this planet is aspected by the other person's Sun may signal the beginning of a significant relationship between them.[lx]

	1	2	3	4	5	6	7	8	9
A	Day	S.Time	Sun	Moon	Mercury	Venus	Mars		
B	25	17:18	02 ♎ 40'	15 ♏ 50'	28 ♎ 16'	28 ♎ 47'	02 ♍ 28'	1968	smith
C	14	13:29	20 ♎ 28'	27 ♌ 51'	24 ♎ 39'	03 ♏ 10'	19 ♒ 19'	1997	jada
D	24	19:12	01 ♏ 21'	10 ♐ 12'	15 ♎ 42'	04 ♐ 15'	20 ♍ 29'	1997	smith
E	18	11:47	24 ♍ 55'	12 ♍ 45'	09 ♍ 03'	00 ♎ 48'	12 ♒ 25'	1971	jada

Fig.21 Matrix showing the natal planetary positions of Will Smith and Jada Pinkett, together with their progressed planetary positions for the year 1997.

...and in the case of Will Smith and Jada Pinkett, the type of double conjunction referred to by Ronald Davison, where a natal-Sun-Venus conjunction is amplified by a progressed conjunction of the same two planets, did exactly what he said it would do: it began a highly significant relationship. This combination is also present in the following relationships: Omar Sharif and Faten Hamama, Andre Agassi and Steffi Graf, Edward Norton and Courtney Love, Luc Besson and Maiwen Le Besco, Dennis Hopper and Brooke Hayward, Rip Torn and Anne Wedgeworth and Steven Soderbergh and Jules Asner.

Sun Opposite Venus

Sargent writes:

Very strong aspect for attraction, can be favorable for marriage.[lxi]

The other astrologers suggest fondness for each other's company and romantic attraction, but suggest that the Sun person can occasionally overpower the Venus person

The double Sun-Venus opposition also occurs frequently, but in some senses it is less successful in relationships and occurs in some notable

♈	♉	♊	♋	♌	♍	♎	♏	♐	♑	♒	♓
Aries	Taurus	Gemini	Cancer	Leo	Virgo	Libra	Scorpio	Sagittarius	Capricorn	Aquarius	Pisces

extra-marital affairs. The relationship of Darryl Zanuck and Virginia Fox, and that of Danny Kaye and Sylvia Fine were two of Hollywood's most enduring marriages, both of which shared a natal-Sun-Venus opposition together with a progressed-Sun-Venus opposition at the outset of the relationship, but despite the fact that these marriages lasted so long (both were circa fifty years), the truth was that the couples separated often. Kaye and Fine were reunited quickly, but Fox and Zanuck spent almost twenty years apart as Zanuck indulged his creative passions in a long European adventure.

	1	2	3	4	5	6	7	8	9
A	Day	S.Time	Sun	Moon	Mercury	Venus	Mars		
B	5	10:54	11 ♍ 58'	22 ♎ 24'	02 ♎ 07'	20 ♌ 24'	00 ♌ 33'	1902	zanuck
C	11	3:13	19 ♉ 50'	09 ♋ 40'	03 ♊ 56'	04 ♈ 23'	10 ♉ 26'	1924	fox
D	27	12:21	03 ♎ 26'	10 ♌ 21'	29 ♎ 19'	17 ♍ 33'	14 ♌ 14'	1924	zanuck
E	19	1:46	28 ♈ 29'	21 ♍ 00'	18 ♈ 09'	12 ♓ 27'	24 ♈ 01'	1902	fox

Fig.22. Matrix showing the natal planetary positions of Darryl Zanuck and Virginia Fox, together with their progressed planetary positions for the year 1924.

Sun Trine Venus

Sargent writes:

> *Magnetic attraction. Individuals are mutually inspiring, encouraging and cooperative.*[lxii]

The other astrologers concur, suggesting that this is a good combination for harmony, romantic and sexual attraction and the feeling that the couple were 'made for each other'.

A large number of relationships happen to people who not only share a Sun – Venus trine natally, but also by progression when the relationship began. This double Sun-Venus trine is somewhat revealing in one case. At the time of their marriage Michael Jackson and Lisa Marie Presley were thought to be engaging in an elaborate publicity stunt, but Lisa Marie has

♈	♉	♊	♋	♌	♍	♎	♏	♐	♑	♒	♓
Aries	Taurus	Gemini	Cancer	Leo	Virgo	Libra	Scorpio	Sagittarius	Capricorn	Aquarius	Pisces

since claimed this was a love match. Their progressed and natal synastry conforms to an ideal and conventional exchange of feelings.

	1	2	3	4	5	6	7	8	9
A	Day	S.Time	Sun	Moon	Mercury	Venus	Mars		
B	29	4:24	06 ♏ 21'	17 ♓ 36'	25 ♌ 19'	17 ♌ 20'	22 ♉ 08'	1958	jackson
C	27	9:28	08 ♓ 25'	04 ♓ 30'	17 ♒ 06'	09 ♒ 32'	08 ♈ 15'	1994	presley
D	4	6:46	11 ♎ 29'	02 ♋ 01'	11 ♎ 16'	01 ♎ 55'	02 ♊ 20'	1994	jackson
E	1	7:45	12 ♒ 09'	21 ♓ 51'	00 ♓ 20'	07 ♑ 36'	18 ♓ 18'	1968	presley

Fig.23. Matrix showing the natal planetary positions of Michael Jackson and Lisa Marie Presley, together with their progressed planetary positions for the year 1994.

Sun Square Venus

Sargent writes:

Power or creative urges conflict with social or love urge.[lxiii]

The other astrologers posit disharmony, they do not suggest that this is insurmountable disharmony. There are hurt feelings and emotional disappointments and also temporary separations that actually strengthen the relationship.

The Sun-Venus square is less popular than the Sun-Venus trine, although this is no guarantee of a bad relationship, such unions often entail compromise. This suits some, but it cannot be categorised as a conventionally desirable element in a relationship. I consider the Sun-Venus square aspect to be the archetype for the relationships that have come to be known as star-crossed. This means that close applying Sun-Venus squares may keep couples apart while separating Sun-Venus squares may sometimes signal external pressure receding.

Love, values and aspirations… how one person's aspirations and life-goals fit in with another person's capacity to love and how the Sun person's ability to provide practical security and support fits in with the Venus person's appreciation of love and beauty. In relationships

♈	♉	♊	♋	♌	♍	♎	♏	♐	♑	♒	♓
Aries	Taurus	Gemini	Cancer	Leo	Virgo	Libra	Scorpio	Sagittarius	Capricorn	Aquarius	Pisces

the favorable aspects between Sun and Venus are the most prevalent indicators drawing couples into relationships.

The 'Sun person' will be the dynamic force – the attracted – the Venus person says 'OK, impress me'. This is also the aspect of the Sultan and Scherherezade. Venus tempts, flaunts, lures and entices passively while the Sun is drawn to her, drives, calls, badgers and ultimately becomes the dynamic drive in the relationship.

Where there is a favorable aspect or link between Venus and the Sun, the Sun will protect and Venus returns this compliment with love. The mingling of these two principles does not mean that Venus is not attracted to the Sun. She sees the Sun person as the dynamic embodiment of her principles, someone who will allow her to thrive and flourish, while the Sun person sees the Venus person as the aesthetic embodiment of their ideal.

When the aspect between these two planets is a Square this can cause the two to be repulsed or sometimes their union will be lived in excess. The square aspect is difficult to deal with and as such the mingling of the principles will cause too much conflict for Venus and she will avoid the Sun person. The Sun person likewise may come to see the Venus person as the antithesis of their ideals. Inconjuncts produce a utiltarian relationship, possibly like the banker-borrower, therapist-client or master-servant situation. Venus being the passive planet is always the borrower, client or servant. Semi-sextiles tend towards ambivalence or a detached relationship; often the Sun person is the teacher and the Venus person the pupil. Relationships where the man is the Venus person are common, but not everyone regards this as an ideal situation and it depends on one's background and temperament for this type of relationship to work out regardless of the aspect. There is, however, always a good chance that a relationship will begin with harmonious Sun-Venus aspects regardless of gender.

♈	♉	♊	♋	♌	♍	♎	♏	♐	♑	♒	♓
Aries	Taurus	Gemini	Cancer	Leo	Virgo	Libra	Scorpio	Sagittarius	Capricorn	Aquarius	Pisces

The Sun with Mars
Sun Conjunct Mars

Sargent writes:

> *This aspect stimulates the aggressive spirit and ambitions of both parties.*[lxiv]

The other astrologers suggest that if the partners respect each other's independence this can be useful. There is sometimes rivalry.

Sun Opposite Mars

Sargent writes:

> *Power urge opposes aggressive urge...this [can be] a very conflicting aspect...there can be jealousy, rivalry. They may be impatient with each other and even vindictive.*[lxv]

The other astrologers suggest differences stem from reaction between the Mars person's impulsiveness and aggressivness, contrasting with the authoritarianism of the Sun person.

Sun Trine Mars

Sargent writes:

> *Power urge harmonizes with aggressive urge. Each individual simulates self-confidence, energy, ambition, enthusiasm, initiative, courage...agreement in working towards a common goal.*[lxvi]

This combination promotes co-operation and supportive effort leading to self-improvement according to the other astrologers. The Sun provides the strategy, Mars the drive to achieve. The trine provides the creative means.

♈	♉	♊	♋	♌	♍	♎	♏	♐	♑	♒	♓
Aries	Taurus	Gemini	Cancer	Leo	Virgo	Libra	Scorpio	Sagittarius	Capricorn	Aquarius	Pisces

Sun Square Mars

Sargent writes:

The ambitions of the two individuals will conflict...hostility is easily aroused. They 'lock horns'.[lxvii]

The other astrologers suggest this is a very difficult aspect producing violent conflicts, clashes of wills and disagreements. A power struggle ensues.

Mars aspects with the Sun symbolize Sex and Security... how one person's aspirations and life-goals fit in with another person's sexual needs and how the Mars person's sexuality will compliment the aspirations of the Sun person's.

In relationships harmonious aspects between these two planets are good for sex. This is often to do with varying degrees of sexual, but not emotional, compatibility. Both planets embody masculine principles, and so a couple with these planets in positive aspect will enable them to work together well. The Sun person has a goal and the Mars person the means to help them reach it. In sexual relationships, this aspect can encourage the use of aggression and forthright physical contact. There is also a likely conflict if either partner tries to control the other, which is a trait of both Mars and the Sun. The Sun is wilful and controlling, Mars is aggressive and controlling. There is little emotional contact in this aspect as both planets represent pragmatic principles, but there is much desire and this is the underlying key word for this contact.

Venus with Mars

This planetary connection is probably the next most important after the Sun with Venus. The co-mingling of these two principles is essentially love and sex. Also though, it is the mixing of the values (as opposed to ideals) of one with the activities of another.

♈	♉	♊	♋	♌	♍	♎	♏	♐	♑	♒	♓
Aries	Taurus	Gemini	Cancer	Leo	Virgo	Libra	Scorpio	Sagittarius	Capricorn	Aquarius	Pisces

Venus Conjunct Mars

Sargent writes:

> *The desire nature of Mars stimulates the love nature of Venus. This is a strong aspect of attraction between the sexes.*[lxviii]

Sakoian and Acker suggest that this aspect is *'perhaps the strongest single comparative aspect for sexual attraction...much passion and excitement'.*[lxix]

Davison states that contact between Venus and Mars is the *'primary indicator of compatibility at the physical level'* (this does not imply that the conjunction is the primary aspect of compatibility), Mars representing the desire nature and Venus the desired, so that in a romantic relationship, Mars is apt to take the initiative and Venus to invite that initiative. For this reason it has been suggested that it is desirable for the male Mars to be in aspect with the female Venus, but he states, there is no real ground for questioning the desirability of the male Venus to be in aspect to the female Mars.[lxx]

I don't believe that these two planets in a conjunction provide the *strongest* single comparative aspect for sexual attraction, but I do believe that the conjunction is a very effective aspect for conventional sexual compatibility.

	1	2	3	4	5	6	7	8	9
A	Day	S.Time	Sun	Moon	Mercury	Venus	Mars		
B	15	1:31	24 ♈ 46'	15 ♋ 23'	01 ♈ 08'	00 ♊ 44'	02 ♋ 51'	1959	thompson
C	7	23:58	17 ♑ 10'	19 ♍ 28'	18 ♑ 13'	02 ♓ 52'	05 ♋ 35'	1988	branagh
D	14	3:25	22 ♉ 56'	06 ♌ 59'	02 ♉ 45'	04 ♋ 21'	19 ♋ 35'	1988	thompson
E	10	22:07	18 ♐ 38'	10 ♍ 49'	04 ♐ 26'	00 ♒ 24'	15 ♋ 50'	1960	branagh

Fig.24. Matrix showing the natal planetary positions of Kenneth Branagh and Emma Thompson, together with their progressed planetary positions for the year 1988.

Kenneth Branagh and Emma Thompson shared a progressed-Venus-Mars

♈	♉	♊	♋	♌	♍	♎	♏	♐	♑	♒	♓
Aries	Taurus	Gemini	Cancer	Leo	Virgo	Libra	Scorpio	Sagittarius	Capricorn	Aquarius	Pisces

conjunction (D6 - C7) that was active between 1987 and 1990. Other coupling aspects are present including a natal-Venus – natal-Venus trine (B6 – E6) and Branagh's progressing-Venus (C6) is in an exact trine with Thompson's natal-Mars (B7) in 1988. They were married in 1989.

Venus Opposite Mars

Sargent writes:

Similar to the conjunction, but with more disturbing emotional reactions. Sometimes there is resistance and the attraction will not always be felt by both parties. Jealousy will often raise its head.[lxxi]

The other astrologers speak of intense sexual and romantic attraction, but no guarantee of an enduring relationship.

Getting the balance right is all-important for this opposition, a high proportion of relationships with this contact burn out, and not always through lack of compatibility, but through exhaustion. Progressed-Venus opposite Natal-Mars is the most significant contact, but the progressed version of this opposition features in some of the most memorable of historical relationships. Errol Flynn and Lili Damita, Russell Crowe and Meg Ryan, Richard Burton and ElizabethTaylor, Lana Turner and Johnny Stomponato, DH Lawrence and Frieda Weekley, Mick Jagger and Jerry Hall, Rita Hayworth and Orson Welles and Mick Jagger and Marianne Faithfull all share this aspect in one of its four forms within two degrees.

Venus Trine Mars

Sargent writes:

Similar to the conjunction, but without the tendency to emotional excesses and jealousy...A very favorable aspect to be found in the charts of marriage partners. [lxxii]

Sakoian and Acker suggest 'this is perhaps the best comparative aspect for

♈	♉	♊	♋	♌	♍	♎	♏	♐	♑	♒	♓
Aries	Taurus	Gemini	Cancer	Leo	Virgo	Libra	Scorpio	Sagittarius	Capricorn	Aquarius	Pisces

sexual compatibility...strong romantic attraction.[lxxiii] Davison, more conservatively notes that Mars-Venus does not guarantee a good marriage, but often one with a strong physical element.[lxxiv]

	1	2	3	4	5	6	7	8	9
	Day	S.Time	Sun	Moon	Mercury	Venus	Mars		
A									
B	10	7:33	19 ♑ 24'	28 ♏ 05'	26 ♐ 06'	04 ♓ 46'	03 ♑ 08'	1945	stewart
C	8	2:26	14 ♏ 55'	05 ♏ 54'	01 ♏ 25'	12 ♏ 47'	04 ♏ 03'	1975	ekland
D	9	9:31	19 ♒ 53'	01 ♑ 32'	05 ♒ 38'	06 ♈ 37'	25 ♑ 51'	1975	stewart
E	6	0:15	12 ♎ 04'	21 ♌ 11'	22 ♎ 42'	01 ♎ 28'	12 ♎ 05'	1942	ekland

Fig.25. Matrix showing the natal planetary positions of Rod Stewart and Britt Ekland, together with their progressed planetary positions for the year 1975.

Rod Stewart and Britt Ekland share two Venus-Mars aspects, one a trine at its most powerful in 1975 (B6-C7), shows why they got together, the other is a natal square (B7-E6) and could be one reason why they were fundamentally unsuited.

Venus Square Mars

Sargent writes:

See Venus Opposite Mars

The other astrologers see the strong sexual attraction in this combination, but do not see a depth of emotional compatibility. Davison suggests this is the sort of aspect found in casual love affairs. I have found that close *trine* aspects between progressed-Venus and progressed-Mars are the most frequently found Venus-Mars aspect in casual love affairs.

The Venus-Mars square is not an unsexy aspect, but its presence in the Stewart - Ekland relationship as well as other volatile relationships such as Ava Gardner and Frank Sinatra (aka the Battling Sinatras), Lana Turner and Lex Barker, Vivien Leigh and Laurence Olivier and Jackie and John F. Kennedy illustrate the fact that it is not a passive 'hearts and flowers'

♈	♉	♊	♋	♌	♍	♎	♏	♐	♑	♒	♓
Aries	Taurus	Gemini	Cancer	Leo	Virgo	Libra	Scorpio	Sagittarius	Capricorn	Aquarius	Pisces

contact. Other aspects of Venus and Mars are more conventionally ideal. With the square we find the actions of one are fundamentally at odds with the values and ideas about relationships, of the other.

Sex, the enjoyment of the physical act of love, passion and desire, aesthetic appreciation of the physical human form. In relationships this contact is primarily a connection between the principle of love and the outlet for the energy that love causes. In practice Mars-Venus aspects cause deep attraction that is a primary cause of relationships. There are many examples of this contact by favorable aspect in some of the most passionate relationships. Venus-Mars is a conventional aspect for deeply physical relationships and again sees a masculine idea (Mars) being paired with a feminine idea (Venus) and as such we again find Venus combing her hair on a rock by the sea or in a woodland glade when along rides Mars. He dismounts, approaches, is entranced and overcome by desire he takes Venus in his arms and carries her off to his castle. The type of aspect formed between these two planets is again important. If it is trine or conjunction, then the likelihood is Venus doesn't mind being carried off, if it is an Opposition, she might be intrigued by Mars, will often find him extremely attractive, but on occasion may want to consider her options. With the Square, she might be unimpressed. Inconjunct and Semi-sextile are not favorable in this case as these aspects promote ambivalence and Mars may not even get off his horse in these cases and if he does it will be because he needs some shirts ironing.

Shared Experience

In his 1979 book, *Relationships and Life Cycles*, Stephen Arroyo writes about aspect comparisons in relationships. He states that inter-aspects signify shared experiences.

> *'If you have a real close aspect – say within two degrees – between one of your planets and one of the other person's planets, you'll then often have what is sometimes called "shared experience". This is*

♈	♉	♊	♋	♌	♍	♎	♏	♐	♑	♒	♓
Aries	Taurus	Gemini	Cancer	Leo	Virgo	Libra	Scorpio	Sagittarius	Capricorn	Aquarius	Pisces

particularly true of the close conjunctions and oppositions. In other words, all this means is that transits will simultaneously activate both of your planets, and therefore whatever that close aspect indicates in the relationship will be activated. ˙lxxv

With this in mind, it is worth mentioning that if a couple share a semi- sextile between the Sun and Venus, any transiting planet that makes a square aspect to the Sun in this relationship will make a trine or a sextile aspect to their partner's Venus. This means that when the Sun person is 'down', the Venus person might be 'up'. It is possible to see that this type of synastry could help a couple in that they are not both 'down' at the same time. If a long-term outer-planet transit were involved, however, it could also mean differences of experience that might weigh heavily on the relationship.

Progressed aspects create **windows of opportunity**, in which people can establish worthwhile bonds by making them either temporarily *very* compatible with others or allowing them to change and grow and while doing this introducing them to other people who are at a similar stage in their growth.

The Three Styles of Relationship Aspect
Natal – Natal

This style of aspects takes place when a planet/s in the <u>birth</u> chart of one individual correspond in one of the several geometric relationships already described with a planet/s in a second individual's <u>birth</u> chart.

Natal – Progressed

When the planets in an individual's <u>progressed</u> chart correspond to one of the geometric relationships with the planets in a second individual's <u>birth</u> chart, this is a Natal – Progressed (or Progressed – Natal) aspect. This aspect will have a limited duration. With the Sun, Venus and Mars, such a

♈	♉	♊	♋	♌	♍	♎	♏	♐	♑	♒	♓
Aries	Taurus	Gemini	Cancer	Leo	Virgo	Libra	Scorpio	Sagittarius	Capricorn	Aquarius	Pisces

progression will usually last a maximum of five years, and often less, though there will be occasions when a planet reaches its station (it appears to stand still prior to turning retrograde) when the aspect may last a while longer than five years. Of course the length of the aspect depends on how much leeway we allow. Two degrees either side of exact is the maximum we can safely apply to a relationship progression.

Progressed - Progressed

When a planet in one person's <u>progressed</u> chart makes an aspect to a planet in another person's <u>progressed</u> chart, this is what is meant by progressed - progressed aspects. The planets involved are often moving at similar speeds in the same direction and can therefore progress quite happily in step for a lifetime, sometimes though, one changes direction and the two planets separate from aspect, or they may have been travelling in different directions to start with and only briefly come together in aspect. Often Venus moves a little quicker than the Sun or Mars and the aspect can last from as little as five years.

When Venus moving backwards in the progressed chart makes an aspect to the progressing-Sun in another's chart, and a relationship ensues, because the Sun only ever moves forward, the relative speed of the two planets is doubled. In this instance there may be less time to enjoy the honeymoon period of the relationship.

The Difference between Progressed and Natal

There are conjectural differences between the way progressed and natal aspects manifest in synastry. Any progressed planet is in motion while any natal planet is fixed. It is worth noting, however, that while a progressed-Venus trine, conjunction or opposition will have a definite lifespan and will probably have a significant role to play in a close relationship, it will never dictate the fate of the relationship.

The most important difference between natal and progressed trines,

♈	♉	♊	♋	♌	♍	♎	♏	♐	♑	♒	♓
Aries	Taurus	Gemini	Cancer	Leo	Virgo	Libra	Scorpio	Sagittarius	Capricorn	Aquarius	Pisces

conjunctions and oppositions of Venus appears to be their intensity. Progressed relationship aspects appear to be much more intensely felt by those experiencing them than their equivalent natal aspects.

The Wrong-Chart Problem: Ronald Colman and Benita Hume

When I first looked into Ronald Colman's relationship with Benita Hume, I used 1938 – the year of their marriage – as the start-year of their relationship. This produces a progressed synastry chart with no close conventional natal or progressed aspects other than natal-Mars (B7) opposite progressing-Mars (C7). Mars on its own is not a good indicator of attraction and therefore it is not often the vital factor at the beginning of a relationship. Mars oppositions are also not particularly romantic aspects. They pitch your drive and energy against that of your partner and so in an established relationship there can be anything from heated arguments to 'bedroom Olympics'.

	1	2	3	4	5	6	7	8	9
			Sun	Moon	Mercury	Venus	Mars		
A	Day	S.Time	Sun	Moon	Mercury	Venus	Mars		
B	9	3:18	20 ≈ 44'	00 ♓ 10'	25 ♑ 19'	04 ♑ 02'	10 ♈ 40'	1891	colman
C	15	15:34	22 ♏ 13'	10 ♏ 03'	14 ♐ 01'	14 ♐ 03'	10 ♎ 11'	1938	hume
D	28	6:23	07 ♈ 46'	13 ♏ 39'	12 ♈ 41'	25 ≈ 14'	14 ♉ 25'	1938	colman
E	14	13:28	20 ♎ 13'	04 ♍ 57'	03 ♏ 53'	03 ♐ 51'	20 ♍ 09'	1906	hume

Fig.26. Matrix showing the natal planetary positions of Ronald Colman and Benita Hume, together with their progressed planetary positions for the year 1938.

Upon reading about the pair, it transpired that Colman and Hume became an item in 1934 and uncharacteristically for 1930s Hollywood, they did not marry for four years. Barry Norman writes:

'According to Bessie Love when Colman finally met Benita Hume he "did a nose dive. He really didn't make much sense he was so misty –eyed". [lxxvi]

♈	♉	♊	♋	♌	♍	♎	♏	♐	♑	♒	♓
Aries	Taurus	Gemini	Cancer	Leo	Virgo	Libra	Scorpio	Sagittarius	Capricorn	Aquarius	Pisces

This description is typical of a Sun – Venus trine and in 1934 Ronald Colman and Benita Hume actually experienced two of these by progression. By the time of their marriage these aspects were further apart and therefore less intense, but they had provided the window of opportunity that brought two people together who fell and remained in love until Colman's death in 1958. They also had an exact Sun – Sun trine (B3 – E3) meaning that their birthdays were about 120 days apart, this suggests they found much common ground after the intense passion of the window of opportunity had passed.

	1	2	3	4	5	6	7	8	9
			Sun	Moon	Mercury	Venus	Mars		
A	Day	S.Time	Sun	Moon	Mercury	Venus	Mars		
B	9	3:18	20 ≈ 44'	00 ♓ 10'	25 ♑ 19'	04 ♑ 02'	10 ♈ 40'	1891	colman
C	11	15:18	18 ♏ 11'	12 ♍ 58'	10 ♐ 58'	14 ♐ 40'	07 ♎ 41'	1934	hume
D	24	6:07	03 ♈ 49'	25 ♍ 01'	04 ♈ 32'	20 ≈ 38'	11 ♉ 36'	1934	colman
E	14	13:28	20 ♎ 13'	04 ♍ 57'	03 ♏ 53'	03 ♐ 51'	20 ♍ 09'	1906	hume

Fig.27. Matrix showing the natal planetary positions of Ronald Colman and Benita Hume, together with their progressed planetary positions for the year 1934.

♈	♉	♊	♋	♌	♍	♎	♏	♐	♑	≈	♓
Aries	Taurus	Gemini	Cancer	Leo	Virgo	Libra	Scorpio	Sagittarius	Capricorn	Aquarius	Pisces

Part Two

The
Relationships

Six

George Sand

The old woman I shall become will be quite different from the woman I am now. Another I is beginning
George Sand

The late eighteenth century brought a number of major changes to society which still reverberate through life today, not least the idea that the common people could take control, not only of their own lives, but also the control of the lands in which they lived. France and the US are two early examples of this move towards freedom and liberty that was also accompanied by the discovery of a new planet – Uranus, named after the Sky god. This discovery in 1781 also presaged the first balloon flight by Pilâtre de Rozier and Marquis d'Arlandes in a balloon built by the Mongolfier brothers, another example of humankind breaking free from the boundaries of limitation previously defined by the astrological Saturn.

Among the plethora of new ideas that this new freedom gave birth to were those put forward by Mary Wollestonecraft, mother of Mary Shelley, who was the pioneer of feminism. Her book, *A Vindication of the Rights of Women,* became the first feminist treatise, in it she sought to:

> *'persuade women to endeavour to acquire strength, both of mind and body, and to convince them that the soft phrases, susceptibility of heart, delicacy of sentiment, and refinement of taste, are almost synonymous with epithets of weakness '*lxxvii

In writing this work, published in 1792, she foreshadowed by a few decades

♈	♉	♊	♋	♌	♍	♎	♏	♐	♑	♒	♓
Aries	Taurus	Gemini	Cancer	Leo	Virgo	Libra	Scorpio	Sagittarius	Capricorn	Aquarius	Pisces

the career of a most remarkable of feminist woman: Aurore Dupin, born in 1804 and who became better known to the world as George Sand.

Sand was a free spirit, a liberal reformist, and after leaving her first husband, Baron Casimir Dudevant, in 1830, she took a man's name as her pseudonym and struck at the heart of the nineteenth-century societal conventions that forced women such as herself into unhappy marriages with books such as *Valentine* (1832). Sand was as famous for her lifestyle as for her writing. She had married Baron Dudevant in 1822 when she was eighteen, this is described by her biographers as a marriage of convenience and it is clear she did not marry for love. She began a number of high profile affairs in 1831, the first with novelist Jules Sandeau, from whom she took her pen name.

There is nothing remarkable in Sand and Dudevant's natal or progressed synastry for 1822. Dudevant's Mars is close to being in a conjunction with Sand's Sun and as such, their physical relationship would have had an air of unthreatening familiarity about it.

Casimir Dudevant

	1	2	3	4	5	6	7	8	9
A	Day	S.Time	Sun	Moon	Mercury	Venus	Mars		
B	1	17:00	09 ♋ 44'	26 ♈ 37'	18 ♊ 30'	17 ♌ 15'	22 ♉ 56'	1804	sand
C	1	8:40	09 ♌ 05'	17 ♒ 19'	29 ♋ 53'	19 ♋ 04'	29 ♋ 53'	1822	dudevant
D	19	18:10	26 ♋ 54'	24 ♐ 37'	15 ♋ 14'	19 ♌ 04'	05 ♊ 33'	1822	sand
E	5	6:53	13 ♋ 18'	21 ♒ 08'	07 ♌ 51'	16 ♊ 23'	12 ♋ 19'	1795	dudevant

Fig.28 Matrix showing the natal planetary positions of Baron Casimir Dudevant and Aurore Dupin (George Sand), together with their progressed planetary positions for 1822, the year if their 'convenient' marriage.

The sextile between their natal-Venus' is friendly but not much more. Sand's Mercury can for a time identify with Dudevant's detached Gemini Venus. Mercury agrees in principle to the intellectualisation of love.

♈	♉	♊	♋	♌	♍	♎	♏	♐	♑	♒	♓
Aries	Taurus	Gemini	Cancer	Leo	Virgo	Libra	Scorpio	Sagittarius	Capricorn	Aquarius	Pisces

Mercury can always be overruled by other factors.[lxxviii]

Belinda Jack notes that marriage to Casimir was acceptable to Sand because of Casimir's fraternal manner and the 'relative asexuality' of their friendship.[lxxix]

Sand herself notes:

> *'He never talks of love and confesses himself little disposed to passion. He speaks of an unfailing friendship, and compares the calm domestic happiness of our hosts [the Roettiers] with what he believes he can provide'*[lxxx]

Jack describes Casimir Dudevant as unsentimental and unromantic. The continuation of their relationship was because Aurore (Sand) rationalised it and denied her desire to break free and live like the characters she created. This rationalisation equated to a form of compromise that was unlikely to last.[lxxxi]

In June 1823, Aurore gave birth to a baby boy; they named him Maurice.

In Dudevant we see the detachment and lack of passion that Venus in the intellectual sign of Gemini can manifest. In Sand's natal chart, Venus is in Leo a position of passion, creativity and, if there were ever a sign position of Venus symbolic of the desire to be adored, then Leo is that sign. And Sand's marriage to Dudevant is characterised by his lack of attentiveness to her.

> *'I continue to live a solitary life, if it is possible to believe oneself to be alone when in the company of a husband whom one adores. While he hunts I play with my little Maurice, or I read.'*[lxxxii]

And so their relationship continued. There were financial disagreements as the years passed and Aurore's intellectualisation of her marriage had long since dissipated. By 1829 Casimir had openly taken a mistress; while this is something of a French tradition, Aurore Dudevant was determined to seek

♈	♉	♊	♋	♌	♍	♎	♏	♐	♑	♒	♓
Aries	Taurus	Gemini	Cancer	Leo	Virgo	Libra	Scorpio	Sagittarius	Capricorn	Aquarius	Pisces

life and love elsewhere and in doing so she was to become George Sand.

Aurore met the novelist Jules Sandeau on 30 July 1830. It was from his surname that she took her new identity. She fell in love with Sandeau's youthfulness (he was just nineteen years old), his timidity and his awkwardness. She was living in Paris. This was a time of freedom and creativity: a chance to make good use of her rebellious nature and channel her beliefs into the written word. She collaborated with Sandeau on a novel *Rose et Blanches*. She describes Sandeau in correspondence with Dr Emile Regnault as:

'*..adorable as a hummingbird of fragrant savannahs* '[lxxxiii]

The beginning of their relationship seems to have involved a game of hide and seek, where the couple would take turns to hide and watch each other, unseen.

This liaison became love:

'*If you only knew how much I love him, the poor child! How, from the first day, his expressive look, his sudden and candid movements, his timid gaucheness wih me, made me want to see him, to examine him. I do not know the nature of my curiosity, but each day it became greater.* '[lxxxiv]

…and then as it starts to wane she begins to see him in a different light:

It is possible that Sandeau was unfaithful, but their relationship seems to have ended in June 1833, when her last correspondence on the subject of Sandeau is dated.

Their synastry is based around a slowly applying progressed-Sun-Venus opposition. In 1830, the polarity of Sand's progressed-Sun in Leo and Sandeau's progressing-Venus in Aquarius is an agent of gentle, passionate rebellion. The motion of this opposition is very slow. Venus makes up just ten minutes of arc in two years. It would become exact, but not until 1854. Too long a wait for most relationships.

♈	♉	♊	♋	♌	♍	♎	♏	♐	♑	♒	♓
Aries	Taurus	Gemini	Cancer	Leo	Virgo	Libra	Scorpio	Sagittarius	Capricorn	Aquarius	Pisces

Jules Sandeau

	1	2	3	4	5	6	7	8	9
A	Day	S.Time	Sun	Moon	Mercury	Venus	Mars		
B	1	17:00	09 ♋ 44'	26 ♈ 37'	18 ♊ 30'	17 ♌ 15'	22 ♉ 56'	1804	sand
C	10	17:59	18 ♓ 50'	19 ♍ 00'	24 ♒ 46'	02 ♒ 13'	01 ♐ 16'	1830	sandeau
D	27	18:42	04 ♌ 33'	09 ♈ 17'	01 ♌ 49'	15 ♌ 59'	11 ♊ 01'	1830	sand
E	19	16:44	29 ♒ 46'	05 ♑ 19'	03 ♒ 51'	14 ♑ 44'	23 ♏ 30'	1811	sandeau

Fig.29. Matrix showing the natal planetary positions of George Sand and Jules Sandeau, together with their progressed planetary positions for the year 1830.

	1	2	3	4	5	6	7	8	9
A	Day	S.Time	Sun	Moon	Mercury	Venus	Mars		
B	1	17:00	09 ♋ 44'	26 ♈ 37'	18 ♊ 30'	17 ♌ 15'	22 ♉ 56'	1804	sand
C	13	18:11	21 ♓ 49'	25 ♎ 32'	29 ♒ 06'	05 ♒ 15'	02 ♐ 19'	1833	sandeau
D	30	18:54	07 ♌ 25'	21 ♉ 43'	08 ♌ 06'	14 ♌ 20'	13 ♊ 03'	1833	sand
E	19	16:44	29 ♒ 46'	05 ♑ 19'	03 ♒ 51'	14 ♑ 44'	23 ♏ 30'	1811	sandeau

Fig.30. Matrix showing the natal planetary positions of George Sand and Jules Sandeau, together with their progressed planetary positions for the year 1833.

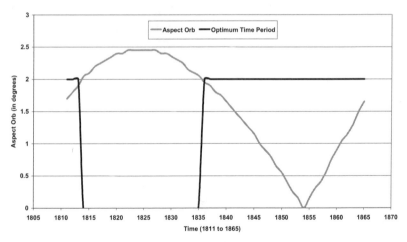

Fig.31. Graph showing the trajectory of Sand and Sandeau's Sun-Venus opposition: it was exact in 1854, long after their relationship ended

♈	♉	♊	♋	♌	♍	♎	♏	♐	♑	♒	♓
Aries	Taurus	Gemini	Cancer	Leo	Virgo	Libra	Scorpio	Sagittarius	Capricorn	Aquarius	Pisces

Marie Dorval

It is said that Sand's most desperate love was her love for Marie Dorval, the most celebrated actress in Paris at the time. They met in January 1833 and despite warnings from Gustave Planche that Marie was a lesbian, Sand sought her out for a meeting.

Belinda Jack comments that the letters exchanged between Sand and Dorval that survive are testament to their *'strength of feeling, and to the respect, admiration and, above all, mutual curiosity which they felt. From the moment of their first meeting in mid January 1833, they felt an extraordinary sympathy...* 'lxxxv

Their relationship created a scandal and was detailed by the writer Arsene Houssaye fifty years later in a dramatic version of events that reflects the facts in the same way that a Hollywood epic about the Roman Empire does: virtually, possibly, but not certainly.

Dorval was with Alfred de Vigny at the time and Sand was with Jules Sandeau, but it appears de Vigny recognized Sand as a rival in as much as his description of her as a seductress, but also because he described her as *like a man.*

Belinda Jack reproduces some of Sand's sentimental and emotional writing to Dorval, emphasising that this type of close familiarity was not unusual in letters of the time, but at the same time she says that Sand's letters to Dorval including lines such as:

'For my part I feel I love you with a heart brought back to life and rejuvenated by you. 'lxxxvi

...are quite unlike her letters to other women friends.

It is probable that Sand and Dorval shared an intimate relationship, what is debated is their roles in this relationship. Judging by the fact that there is a close applying trine between Dorval's progressing-Mars and Sand's natal-Venus in 1833, it would appear that this is a relationship where Dorval is the director.lxxxvii

♈	♉	♊	♋	♌	♍	♎	♏	♐	♑	♒	♓
Aries	Taurus	Gemini	Cancer	Leo	Virgo	Libra	Scorpio	Sagittarius	Capricorn	Aquarius	Pisces

	1	2	3	4	5	6	7	8	9
A	Day	S.Time	Sun	Moon	Mercury	Venus	Mars		
B	1	17:00	09 ♋ 44'	26 ♈ 37'	18 ♊ 30'	17 ♌ 15'	22 ♉ 56'	1804	sand
C	10	5:37	22 ♒ 25'	27 ♐ 40'	29 ♑ 01'	01 ♈ 13'	16 ♐ 38'	1833	dorval
D	30	18:54	07 ♌ 25'	21 ♉ 06'	08 ♌ 06'	14 ♌ 20'	13 ♊ 03'	1833	sand
E	6	3:19	16 ♑ 52'	14 ♍ 26'	04 ♒ 45'	04 ♓ 01'	23 ♏ 52'	1798	dorval

Fig.32. Matrix showing the natal planetary positions of George Sand and Marie Dorval, together with their progressed planetary positions for the year 1833.

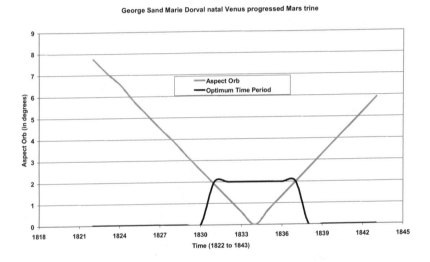

Fig.33. Graph showing the two degree window of opportunity 1831 to 1838 created by Dorval and Sand's progressed-Mars natal-Venus trine.

Prosper Merimee

For a short while in April 1833, Sand was taken by Prosper Merimee, famous as the author of *Carmen*.

'*The strength of his vision fascinated me for eight days. I thought he knew the secret to happiness*'.[lxxxviii] She goes on to say that she found in him nothing but coldness and bitter jesting. Their Sun-Venus trine, often a useful relationship indicator is obviously overshadowed by their

♈	♉	♊	♋	♌	♍	♎	♏	♐	♑	♒	♓
Aries	Taurus	Gemini	Cancer	Leo	Virgo	Libra	Scorpio	Sagittarius	Capricorn	Aquarius	Pisces

progressed-Mars – Venus squares and the fact that Merimee's natal-Venus is in detached Libra while Sand's Sun is in emotional Cancer.

	1	2	3	4	5	6	7	8	9
	Day	S.Time	Sun	Moon	Mercury	Venus	Mars		
A									
B	1	17:00	09 ♋ 44'	26 ♈ 37'	18 ♊ 30'	17 ♌ 15'	22 ♉ 56'	1804	sand
C	28	0:16	04 ♏ 32'	13 ♈ 35'	25 ♎ 13'	08 ♏ 12'	16 ♏ 11'	1833	merimee
D	30	18:54	07 ♌ 25'	21 ♉ 43'	08 ♌ 06'	14 ♌ 20'	13 ♊ 03'	1833	sand
E	28	22:17	04 ♎ 47'	05 ♓ 21'	00 ♏ 23'	00 ♎ 40'	25 ♎ 33'	1803	merimee

Fig.34. Matrix showing the natal planetary positions of George Sand and Prosper Merimee, together with their progressed planetary positions for the year 1833.

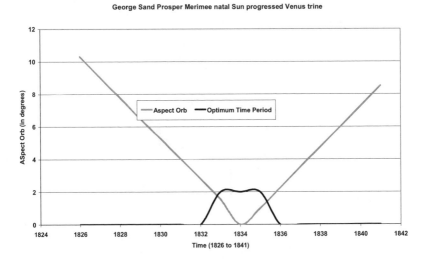

George Sand Prosper Merimee natal Sun progressed Venus trine

Fig.35 Graph showing the two degree window of opportunity 1833 to 1835 created by Sand and Merimee's progressed-Venus natal-Sun trine

Merimee was certain that Sand's lack of sexual fulfilment and her dissatisfaction in this regard was due to her choice of lovers. He tried to convince Sand that he could deliver a different kind of sexual experience to the ones she had so far had. She hoped he possessed a deep understanding of life, but was disappointed by him.

♈	♉	♊	♋	♌	♍	♎	♏	♐	♑	♒	♓
Aries	Taurus	Gemini	Cancer	Leo	Virgo	Libra	Scorpio	Sagittarius	Capricorn	Aquarius	Pisces

Sand is said to have commented to Marie Dorval: *'last night I had Merimee, it was nothing out of the ordinary.*'lxxxix

Marie repeated these words to Alexandre Dumas who in turn told everyone else and before long Sand's words were preceding echoes of laughter all over Paris.

This particular eight-day period happened to be at a point (1833) when their progressed-Sun-Venus trine was at its most powerful: the point just prior to it becoming exact.

Alfred de Musset

In Musset, Sand found a lover with whom she could experience great passion. He was a flirt and she described him as a 'great dandy' with whom she would not be suited. She later found herself sitting next to him at a dinner at the Freres Provencaux. She invited him to call on her.

He soon wrote to her:

'My dear George, I have something silly and ridiculous to tell you. I am foolishly writing instead of telling you, as I ought to have done, after our walk. I am heartbroken tonight that I did not tell you. You will laugh at me and you will take me for a man who simply talks nonsense. You will show me the door, and fancy that I am not speaking the truth…I am in love with you.'xc

Sand declared in August 1833 that she had fallen in love with Alfred de Musset.

They visited Italy together the following year and quickly fell out of love, declaring as much to each other.

Their synastry includes a natal-Sun (E3) Venus (B6) trine in fire signs. This type of aspect, seen throughout this book is enough to make any couple feel love. The fact that eternal love is not guaranteed is probably a matter for, on one level, other astrological factors and on another, higher level, the collective content of a person's life and character up to that point

♈	♉	♊	♋	♌	♍	♎	♏	♐	♑	♒	♓
Aries	Taurus	Gemini	Cancer	Leo	Virgo	Libra	Scorpio	Sagittarius	Capricorn	Aquarius	Pisces

in time. Sand and Musset have many favorable connections between their natal charts: her Mars in Taurus gets along well with his Venus in Capricorn, her Sun in Cancer is less than five degrees from opposing his Capricorn Venus. Her Moon in Aries is not badly disposed to Musset's Sun in Sagittarius. So where is the problem?

	1	2	3	4	5	6	7	8	9
A	Day	S.Time	Sun	Moon	Mercury	Venus	Mars		
B	1	17:00	09 ♋ 44'	26 ♈ 37'	18 ♊ 30'	17 ♌ 15'	22 ♉ 56'	1804	sand
C	3	17:40	12 ♑ 14'	00 ♉ 50'	26 ♑ 26'	03 ♎ 41'	29 ♎ 35'	1833	de musset
D	30	18:54	07 ♌ 25'	21 ♉ 43'	08 ♌ 06'	14 ♌ 20'	13 ♊ 03'	1833	sand
E	11	16:09	18 ♐ 48'	24 ♊ 50'	19 ♐ 40'	14 ♑ 23'	16 ♎ 28'	1810	de musset

Fig.36. Matrix showing the natal planetary positions of George Sand and Alfred de Musset, together with their progressed planetary positions for the year 1833.

Different people want different things and just because people find that they prefer to have Venus harmony to Venus conflict, it is impossible to get the *full* picture of a couple's synastry purely from the positions that two planets occupy in their birth charts. What it does give is a head start.

As an epitaph for their relationship, Belinda Jack writes:

'By 6 March 1835 the passionate affair with the mysterious Musset was, in the conventional sense, over. For both, however, it was a relationship whose depths of passion and anguish, of exhilaration and despair, of mutual understanding and mutual incomprehension, would feed their writing for years to come. [xci]

Michel De Bourges

Sand met Louis Chrysostome-Michel, known as Michel of Bourges, on 9 April 1835. After their initial meeting, during which Michel paid great attention to every word Sand uttered, Michel embarked on a campaign of letter writing in order to win Sand's heart.

♈	♉	♊	♋	♌	♍	♎	♏	♐	♑	♒	♓
Aries	Taurus	Gemini	Cancer	Leo	Virgo	Libra	Scorpio	Sagittarius	Capricorn	Aquarius	Pisces

'His letters followed with a rapidity without time for replies. This ardent soul has resolved to take hold of mine.' [xcii]

De Bourges was the lawyer who sued for divorce on behalf of Sand from the Baron Dudevant in 1835. She became his mistress, but Sand being Sand, this statement could as well be written in reverse. It has been said that Sand wrote an unpublished novel *Engelwald the Bald Person* about De Bourges, the manuscript was burned in 1864.

I found a comment on a web page[xciii] translated from French to English by Google that suggests *'He could have been the most satisfying lover Sand ever had.'* This comment is not qualified, but that her less satisfying relationships were with those people whom she dominated synastrically; that is: those whose Venus aspected one of her masculine planets. Her relationship with Musset was initially quite successful and was driven by Musset's natal-Sun in trine to Sand's Venus along with the case of Dorval, where Sand's Venus met Dorval's Mars seems to have been much more satisfying than those with Sandeau and Merimee. In the case of De Bourges, his progressing-Sun is aspecting her Venus. This means that for a short period of time from 1835 to perhaps 1837 and post-Dorval she experimented for once with the female role in a relationship.

	1	2	3	4	5	6	7	8	9
			Sun	Moon	Mercury	**Venus**	Mars		
A	Day	S.Time	Sun	Moon	Mercury	Venus	Mars		
B	1	17:00	09 ♋ 44'	26 ♈ 37'	18 ♊ 30'	17 ♌ 15'	22 ♉ 56'	1804	sand
C	7	17:06	15 ♐ 57'	00 ♌ 22'	17 ♐ 08'	01 ♒ 17'	04 ♏ 11'	1835	de bourges
D	1	19:02	09 ♌ 20'	20 ♊ 21'	12 ♌ 12'	13 ♌ 08'	14 ♊ 23'	1835	sand
E	30	14:37	07 ♏ 34'	08 ♓ 04'	19 ♎ 04'	16 ♐ 42'	09 ♎ 41'	1797	de bourges

Fig.37. Matrix showing the natal planetary positions of George Sand and Michel de Bourges, together with their progressed planetary positions for the year 1835.

Things were to change later though and she again fell into a relationship with a man who must have reminded her a little of Sandeau.

♈	♉	♊	♋	♌	♍	♎	♏	♐	♑	♒	♓
Aries	Taurus	Gemini	Cancer	Leo	Virgo	Libra	Scorpio	Sagittarius	Capricorn	Aquarius	Pisces

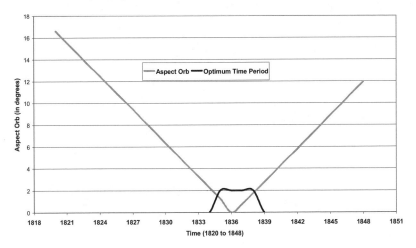

George Sand Michel de Bourges natal Venus progressed Sun trine

Fig.38. Graph showing the two degree window of opportunity 1834 to 1838 created by Bourges' and Sand's progressed-Sun natal-Venus trine

Fredric Chopin

Like Sandeau, Chopin was a delicate man. He was twenty-seven when he encountered Sand (through Franz Lizst, as it happened). According to Liszt, it appears that Chopin was a little nervous about meeting Sand and put off their meeting. Chopin was wary of women writers and Sand was as Liszt puts it:

'…*feared as a sylph'*.

Sand made the first advances as in the case of her relationship with Sandeau and it is easy to see both anecdotally and astrologically that she dominated both relationships.

March and McEvers comment on this relationship as follows:

'*Chopin attracted the vivacious, high-spirited George Sand. Their relationship was extremely intense and dynamic while it lasted, but in some respects it was as if her energy burned up his vitality.'* [xciv]

♈	♉	♊	♋	♌	♍	♎	♏	♐	♑	♒	♓
Aries	Taurus	Gemini	Cancer	Leo	Virgo	Libra	Scorpio	Sagittarius	Capricorn	Aquarius	Pisces

	1	2	3	4	5	6	7	8	9
			1	2	3	4	5	6	7	8	9
A	Day	S.Time	Sun	Moon	Mercury	Venus	Mars		
B	1	17:00	09 ♋ 44'	26 ♈ 37'	18 ♊ 30'	17 ♌ 15'	22 ♉ 56'	1804	sand
C	29	23:16	08 ♈ 05'	25 ♑ 16'	14 ♓ 16'	11 ♈ 37'	28 ♈ 32'	1838	chopin
D	4	19:14	12 ♌ 12'	02 ♌ 45'	18 ♌ 13'	11 ♌ 17'	16 ♊ 24'	1838	sand
E	1	21:26	10 ♓ 14'	14 ♑ 36'	18 ♒ 20'	06 ♓ 45'	07 ♈ 35'	1810	chopin

Fig.39. Matrix showing the natal planetary positions of George Sand and Fredric Chopin, together with their progressed planetary positions for the year 1838.

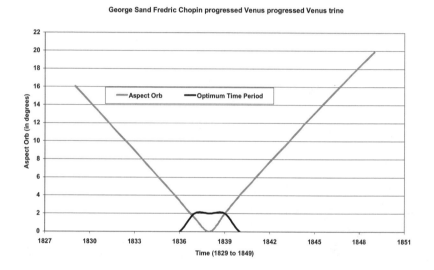

Fig.40. Graph showing the two degree window of opportunity 1837 to 1839 created by Sand and Chopin's progressed-Venus trine

The key factors in her relationship with Chopin include an exact progressed-Venus trine in fire signs. This aspect is one of gripping romanticism. It has the unerring capability of thrusting two people into a tryst that is characterised by deep and inspiring feelings of love, often replete with all the poetry that they can muster. In this instance, Sand's Venus is retrograde and Chopin's is direct. The brevity of the aspect is

♈	♉	♊	♋	♌	♍	♎	♏	♐	♑	♒	♓
Aries	Taurus	Gemini	Cancer	Leo	Virgo	Libra	Scorpio	Sagittarius	Capricorn	Aquarius	Pisces

increased because the 'velocity' of the two planets is increased like two vehicles travelling in opposite directions at roughly the same speed.

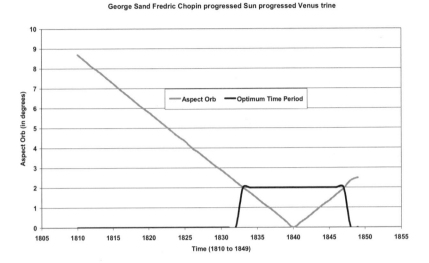

Fig.41. Graph showing the two degree window of opportunity 1833 to 1848 created by Sand and Chopin's progressed-Sun-Venus trine

Louis Blanc

In 1844, after both salient aspects in Sand and Chopin's relationship had begun to separate, she had an affair with Louis Blanc, a socialist politician of some note. It is clear that her allegiance was to Chopin, but that this relationship became less than exclusive as time went by.

With Louis Blanc there are a remarkable set of synastric aspects – perhaps too many. The most important is a progressed-Sun progressed-Venus trine which is applying within one degree in the year of their relationship – 1844. Also present is the popular natal-Sun-Venus trine (although this one is not included in the statistics upon which this book is based because this relationship came to light after the initial 1300 were compiled) this extraordinary complex of synastry could be the reason why

♈	♉	♊	♋	♌	♍	♎	♏	♐	♑	♒	♓
Aries	Taurus	Gemini	Cancer	Leo	Virgo	Libra	Scorpio	Sagittarius	Capricorn	Aquarius	Pisces

Sand could not resist Louis Blanc while in such an important relationship with Chopin[xcv].

	1	2	3	4	5	6	7	8	9
			Sun	Moon	Mercury	Venus	Mars		
A	Day	S.Time							
B	1	17:00	09 ♋ 44'	26 ♈ 37'	18 ♊ 30'	17 ♌ 15'	22 ♉ 56'	1804	sand
C	1	16:37	08 ♐ 27'	24 ♊ 52'	15 ♐ 22'	21 ♐ 00'	16 ♒ 32'	1844	blanc
D	10	19:37	17 ♌ 58'	20 ♎ 41'	29 ♌ 37'	07 ♌ 43'	20 ♊ 22'	1844	sand
E	29	14:27	05 ♏ 11'	04 ♈ 47'	22 ♎ 33'	09 ♏ 37'	22 ♑ 19'	1811	blanc

Fig.42. Matrix showing the natal planetary positions of George Sand and Louis Blanc, together with their progressed planetary positions for the year 1844.

♈	♉	♊	♋	♌	♍	♎	♏	♐	♑	♒	♓
Aries	Taurus	Gemini	Cancer	Leo	Virgo	Libra	Scorpio	Sagittarius	Capricorn	Aquarius	Pisces

Seven

Grace Kelly

*As an unmarried woman, I was thought to be
a danger*
Grace Kelly

In the mid 1950s the US film industry was changing, the old studio system was coming to an end and the long contracts and guaranteed work that had been the mainstay of the industry and which had created household names such as Humphrey Bogart, Clark Gable, Lana Turner and Ava Gardner, were giving way to individual initiatives and as such actors became sub contractors for individual projects rather than studios dreaming up scripts as vehicles for their stable of stars. The main reason for this was the burgeoning popularity of television, which was luring the audiences from the movie theatres across the US.

One of the last of these contract stars was Grace Kelly, a slim, blonde Philadelphian who wore white gloves. This portrayed something whole-some, virginal and eligible. Grace was a role model for Middle America. In the days of Eisenhower and McCarthy, of right-wing gossip columnists like Louella Parsons and Hedda Hopper, Grace Kelly was just what the studios needed: someone whose image – especially the white gloves – agreed with the policy of a nation.

Grace was a second generation Irish American. Her grandfather, John Kelly, emigrated from County Mayo in Ireland in the 1860s hopeful of a better life in the land of the free, eventually putting down roots in Philadelphia and taking a job in a textile mill. The youngest of his ten children with his wife Mary was Jack Kelly, Grace's father, who, despite his

♈	♉	♊	♋	♌	♍	♎	♏	♐	♑	♒	♓
Aries	Taurus	Gemini	Cancer	Leo	Virgo	Libra	Scorpio	Sagittarius	Capricorn	Aquarius	Pisces

humble beginnings made a great success of himself as both a world-class sportsman (his sport was rowing) and a very successful businessman.

Jack Kelly started his working life in the same textile mill where his father and siblings worked, but later became a bricklayer. His business *Kelly for Brickwork* became one of the most successful businesses in Philadelphia, and made him a millionaire.

Grace was born on 12 November 1929 and after graduating from Stevens High School in 1947 she went on to study acting at the American Academy of Dramatic Arts in New York. From 1948, and while studying in New York, she worked as both a model and actress. After signing with the MCA agency, she landed her first big film role in what was supposedly a low budget 'art' picture alongside Gary Cooper called *High Noon*. MGM's offer of a long contract was on the table almost immediately, but in 1950 she turned it down. Two years later there came a point where MGM, not hiring so many in the early fifties, bribed her into signing a long contract at a time when new MGM boss Dore Schary was introducing new measures of efficiency and in order to compete with TV, they could not afford a big stable of indentured professionals. Grace was special though, and an exception had to be made.

In the opinion of many of her industry contemporaries and at least three royal princes, Grace Kelly was one of the most beautiful actresses to appear on the silver screen. Her wholesome image, portrayed at the behest of the all-powerful and politically swayed studio system, belied a very sexually oriented person, fond of men and eager for romance.

Grace said that she was in love once in her young life, with a high school sweetheart, Harper Davis. They were an item in 1944 before he left for wartime service. Grace's father forced her to break it off before he embarked. When Harper returned he developed multiple sclerosis, dying young in 1953.

When asked by her fiancé Prince Rainier if she had ever been in love before she responded by telling him: 'Yes. I was in love with Harper Davis.

♈	♉	♊	♋	♌	♍	♎	♏	♐	♑	♒	♓
Aries	Taurus	Gemini	Cancer	Leo	Virgo	Libra	Scorpio	Sagittarius	Capricorn	Aquarius	Pisces

He died.'

She allegedly lost her virginity to a friend's husband. The salacious story says she was visiting a friend who wasn't home. She was made welcome by the friend's husband and they decided to sleep together. This was before she enrolled in the American Academy of Dramatic Arts in October 1947. She claimed later to have engineered the liaison, not wishing to arrive at college inexperienced in the ways of love.

Grace Kelly and Mark 'Herb' Miller

Herb Miller was a fellow student at the American Academy of Dramatic Art and describes his meeting with Grace Kelly in James Spada's book thus:

'We were turned on to each other from the first day we met. We were two young, vital, horny kids, and our relationship was very physical. It was a hot and heavy thing. There was a recreation room on the thirteenth floor of the Barbizon, and Grace used to bring me up there and we'd smooch. We were very much in love, and we had an awful lot of fun. Sometimes you can have a physical relationship with someone and not like them. But Grace and I really liked each other.' [xcvi]

	1	2	3	4	5	6	7	8	9
A	Day	S.Time	Sun	Moon	Mercury	Venus	Mars		
B	12	13:55	19 ♏ 34'	21 ♓ 50'	10 ♏ 42'	28 ♎ 51'	25 ♏ 37'	1929	kelly
C	12	17:22	19 ♐ 57'	06 ♏ 40'	17 ♐ 59'	06 ♒ 21'	19 ♏ 24'	1947	miller
D	30	15:06	07 ♐ 45'	29 ♏ 10'	09 ♐ 20'	21 ♏ 23'	08 ♐ 34'	1947	kelly
E	20	15:55	27 ♏ 39'	23 ♑ 33'	19 ♐ 26'	14 ♑ 41'	04 ♏ 36'	1925	miller

Fig.43. Matrix showing the natal planetary positions of Grace Kelly and Mark Miller together with their progressed planetary positions for the year 1947.

Analysis of the synastry between Kelly and Miller, reveals a close progressed-Venus (D6) Mars (C7) conjunction in Scorpio. This aspect is waning or separating and had been exact in 1943 – 44. It is still within the

♈	♉	♊	♋	♌	♍	♎	♏	♐	♑	♒	♓
Aries	Taurus	Gemini	Cancer	Leo	Virgo	Libra	Scorpio	Sagittarius	Capricorn	Aquarius	Pisces

limits of acceptability for progressed synastry, but within a couple of years, its effect would be diminished.[xcvii]

Grace Kelly and Alexander D'Arcy

A month long fling with an established actor who was over twenty years older than her, was the next of Grace's recorded affairs. It appears he was quite the gentleman and only touched her knee in the taxi they were sharing after a night out when she launched herself at him, taking him by surprise. He was surprised at her boldness, commenting that she seemed so demure, but that she also seemed so experienced.

	1	2	3	4	5	6	7	8	9
A	Day	S.Time	Sun	Moon	Mercury	Venus	Mars		
B	12	13:55	19 ♏ 34'	21 ♓ 50'	10 ♏ 42'	28 ♎ 51'	25 ♏ 37'	1929	kelly
C	19	11:51	26 ♍ 07'	19 ♋ 13'	17 ♎ 48'	10 ♌ 11'	16 ♏ 42'	1948	darcy
D	1	15:10	08 ♐ 45'	11 ♐ 25'	10 ♐ 54'	22 ♏ 38'	09 ♐ 17'	1948	kelly
E	10	9:14	17 ♌ 25'	23 ♑ 11'	06 ♌ 42'	08 ♋ 37'	21 ♌ 14'	1908	darcy

Fig.44. Matrix showing the natal planetary positions of Grace Kelly and Alex D'Arcy, together with their progressed planetary positions for the year 1948.

Their astrology is the usual sexual progression of progressing-Venus (D'Arcy) in a trine aspect with progressing-Mars (Kelly). Grace's progressed-Sun is also in trine to D'Arcy's progressing-Venus. These aspects are transient and the fact that they are present in so many relationships suggests that they contributed significantly to the fact of their one-month fling in 1948.

Grace Kelly and Don Richardson

In 1948 Grace started an affair with one of her tutors at the Academy. Don Richardson was eleven years older than her. He had rescued her from the class bully then taken her out for tea to comfort her without first checking

♈	♉	♊	♋	♌	♍	♎	♏	♐	♑	♒	♓
Aries	Taurus	Gemini	Cancer	Leo	Virgo	Libra	Scorpio	Sagittarius	Capricorn	Aquarius	Pisces

in his wallet. He realised he did not have enough cash so they dropped by his flat. He got the fire going and went to make coffee. On his return he found Grace in bed waiting for him. Richardson was stunned. He describes her as 'stunning', 'like something sculptured by Rodin'.

There was no introduction, no flirtation, no prelude beyond Richardson rescuing Grace, nothing. Grace went straight to the main event. Kelly and Richardson continued to see each other for a number of years until, that is, Richardson recognized a piece of jewellery that Prince Aly Khan presented to those women who had shared his bed.

He dropped the jewellery into Grace's fish tank and left.

	1	2	3	4	5	6	7	8	9
A	Day	S.Time	Sun	Moon	Mercury	Venus	Mars		
B	12	13:55	19 ♏ 34'	21 ♓ 50'	10 ♏ 42'	28 ♎ 51'	25 ♏ 37'	1929	kelly
C	30	4:28	08 ♊ 14'	03 ♒ 36'	14 ♉ 10'	25 ♈ 48'	20 ♍ 13'	1948	richardson
D	1	15:10	08 ♐ 45'	11 ♐ 25'	10 ♐ 54'	22 ♏ 38'	09 ♐ 17'	1948	kelly
E	30	2:30	09 ♉ 19'	27 ♐ 01'	03 ♉ 51'	23 ♓ 21'	13 ♍ 59'	1918	richardson

Fig.45. Matrix showing the natal planetary positions of Grace Kelly and Don Richardson, together with their progressed planetary positions for the year 1948.

Grace and Don encountered each other under the auspices of two interesting progressions, firstly her progressing-Venus (D6) makes a trine aspect to his natal-Venus (E6), and secondly, their progressing-Suns are in a permanent opposition (C3 – D3). Their age difference meant that although their Suns were ten degrees from opposition at birth, by the time Grace was born Don's progressing-Sun was in opposition to her Sun. When comparing Suns, I find that although they are not usually a great indicator of sexual attraction, they could often signal a mutual fascination, especially when in opposition. It should also be noted that Grace's Mars or her planet of sexual expression is 117 degrees from Don's Venus. Many astrologers would treat this as a close aspect and a primary relationship

♈	♉	♊	♋	♌	♍	♎	♏	♐	♑	♒	♓
Aries	Taurus	Gemini	Cancer	Leo	Virgo	Libra	Scorpio	Sagittarius	Capricorn	Aquarius	Pisces

indicator. My view is that their Venus – Venus trine is the primary indicator in this case. But if the wide Venus-Mars trine was absent, this affair may never have happened in the manner it did.

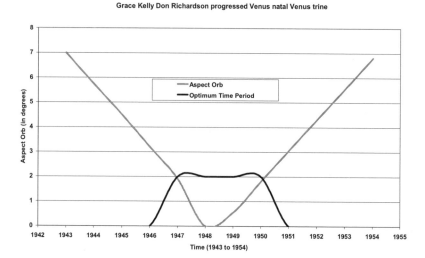

Grace Kelly Don Richardson progressed Venus natal Venus trine

Fig.46. Graph showing the two degree window of opportunity 1947 to 1950 created by Kelly's progressing-Venus in trine to Richardsons natal-Venus

Grace Kelly and Gene Lyons

The summer of 1951 saw Grace falling in love with Gene Lyons, again an older, theatrical type. Unlike many of her contemporaries, Lyons was a shy introverted individual when not on stage, sensitive and passionate about acting and Grace saw in him someone with whom she could identify and whom she could both love and work with.

Gene Lyons stimulated Grace Kelly and he again took on the role of mentor, the same role that Don Richardson had filled, inspiring her and making her want to achieve success and fame with him.

They made a TV drama together, *The Rich Boy*, the story of a woman who leaves her lover due to his drinking. This reflected the fate of their

♈	♉	♊	♋	♌	♍	♎	♏	♐	♑	♒	♓
Aries	Taurus	Gemini	Cancer	Leo	Virgo	Libra	Scorpio	Sagittarius	Capricorn	Aquarius	Pisces

off-screen relationship. The sensitive Lyons took to the bottle, and this caused their relationship to draw to a premature conclusion.

	1	2	3	4	5	6	7	8	9
A	Day	S.Time	Sun	Moon	Mercury	Venus	Mars		
B	12	13:55	19 ♏ 34'	21 ♓ 50'	10 ♏ 42'	28 ♎ 51'	25 ♏ 37'	1929	kelly
C	11	23:14	20 ♓ 23'	10 ♈ 33'	04 ♓ 43'	02 ♉ 48'	19 ♈ 48'	1951	lyons
D	4	15:22	11 ♐ 48'	17 ♑ 26'	15 ♐ 36'	26 ♏ 24'	11 ♐ 29'	1951	kelly
E	9	21:16	20 ♒ 13'	06 ♓ 32'	06 ♓ 37'	06 ♈ 58'	27 ♓ 09'	1921	lyons

Fig.47. Matrix showing the natal planetary positions of Grace Kelly and Gene Lyons, together with their progressed planetary positions for the year 1951.

Their mutual synastry is underlined by the intensely romantic window created by her progressing-Venus in trine to his natal-Mars (D6 – E7) during 1951 -1952. Their natal-Mars' (B7 – E7) are also in a harmonious trine, suggesting that they would have a complimentary working relationship.

Their relationship continued into mid-1952. James Spada remarks that she realised his problems were so deep-seated, she would never be able to 'reform' him.[xcviii] So although they remained an item, their days together were numbered simply because the selective and ambitious Grace no longer thought of him as a potential marriage partner.

I feel their Sun – Sun aspects are also of importance to the development of this relationship. Between 1949 and 1951 Gene Lyons' progressing-Sun (C3) was making a transient trine aspect to Grace's natal-Sun (B3). As we have noted, Sun aspects in synastry denote how in tune the life-paths or 'karmic agenda' of the individuals are. This is usually not an issue, as people can quite easily spend their lives in parallel with their partners if their personalities allow it. Issues only arise when the life-paths are at a tangent to each other and when the parties involved are both fixed and purposeful. Issues often arise when the harmonious transient progressions present at the beginning of the relationship recede, thus revealing the true

♈	♉	♊	♋	♌	♍	♎	♏	♐	♑	♒	♓
Aries	Taurus	Gemini	Cancer	Leo	Virgo	Libra	Scorpio	Sagittarius	Capricorn	Aquarius	Pisces

nature of the personal connection. This is the case with Grace Kelly and
Gene Lyons.

As is often the case with the natal or progressed-Sun square, the two
parties actually have different life-agendas that can be hidden or overlooked
during the period of courting which is so often ruled by the sex planets
Mars and Venus, but it is difficult to maintain a relationship, regardless of
their ability to work together, where the two parties have diverging
agendas. By 1952, Lyon's progressing-Sun has moved out of orb with
Grace's natal-Sun and the salient differences in the approach a Sun Scorpio
and a Sun Aquarius with an exact square between their natal-Suns take in
following their dreams are exposed.

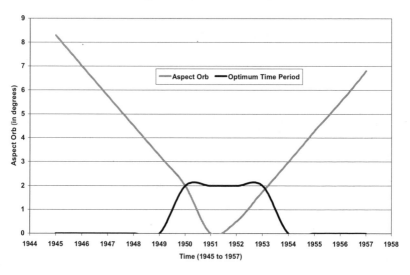

Progress of Kelly's Venus in trine to Lyons' natal Mars

**Fig.48. Graph showing the two degree window of opportunity 1950 to
1953 created by Kelly's progressing-Venus in trine to Lyons' natal-
Mars**

Grace Kelly and Gary Cooper

Grace's first big screen role was in *High Noon* with Gary Cooper. Although

♈	♉	♊	♋	♌	♍	♎	♏	♐	♑	♒	♓
Aries	Taurus	Gemini	Cancer	Leo	Virgo	Libra	Scorpio	Sagittarius	Capricorn	Aquarius	Pisces

much older than her he had always had the reputation of a 'stud'. In fact, the silent movie actress Clara Bow had given him the nickname Studs in the 1920s.

	1	2	3	4	5	6	7	8	9
A	Day	S.Time	Sun	Moon	Mercury	Venus	Mars		
B	12	13:55	19 ♏ 34'	21 ♓ 50'	10 ♏ 42'	28 ♎ 51'	25 ♏ 37'	1929	kelly
C	26	7:00	04 ♋ 11'	03 ♏ 12'	25 ♋ 30'	19 ♋ 21'	20 ♍ 32'	1951	cooper
D	4	15:22	11 ♐ 48'	17 ♑ 26'	15 ♐ 36'	26 ♏ 24'	11 ♐ 29'	1951	kelly
E	7	3:43	16 ♉ 14'	27 ♐ 52'	07 ♉ 53'	17 ♉ 57'	28 ♌ 47'	1901	cooper

Fig.49. Matrix showing the natal planetary positions of Grace Kelly and Gary Cooper, together with their progressed planetary positions for the year 1951.

In 1951 Gary Cooper's progressing-Venus was arriving in trine to Grace Kelly's natal-Sun. We have so far seen this carefully timed aspect in the

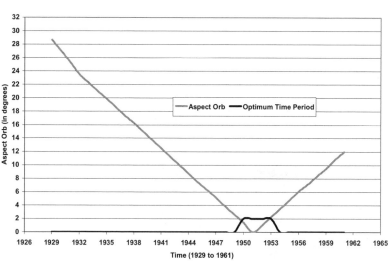

Grace Kelly Gary Cooper Natal Sun Progressed Venus Trine

Fig.50. Graph showing the two degree window of opportunity 1950 to 1953 created by Cooper's progressing-Venus in trine to Kelly's natal-Sun

♈	♉	♊	♋	♌	♍	♎	♏	♐	♑	♒	♓
Aries	Taurus	Gemini	Cancer	Leo	Virgo	Libra	Scorpio	Sagittarius	Capricorn	Aquarius	Pisces

relationship of George Sand and Prosper Merimee. Cooper was infatuated by Grace and she was in awe of him. This window of opportunity was only exact in 1951.

Grace Kelly and Clark Gable

Reading between the lines in commentaries about this relationship, which incidentally started in Africa where these two were filming *Mogambo*, it is obvious that there was a lot of tenderness, mutual respect and even a touch of requited love. Perhaps hand holding, hugging, kissing, spending time together, walking, reading poetry to each other and delight in each others company is not evidence of a full-blown sexual relationship, but there seems to have been something deep and meaningful, at least for a few months, between Clark Gable and Grace Kelly.

Of Grace's biographers, James Spada is probably one of the most diligent and his opinion is that a sexual affair did not take place, Jane Ellen Wayne, on the other hand, goes into much greater detail about their time together, suggesting from eye-witness accounts that Gable and Kelly were virtually inseparable and made up a foursome with Ava Gardner and Frank Sinatra on a romantic trip to the beach resort of Malindi.

	1	2	3	4	5	6	7	8	9
A	Day	S.Time	Sun	Moon	Mercury	Venus	Mars		
B	12	13:55	19 ♏ 34'	21 ♓ 50'	10 ♏ 42'	28 ♎ 51'	25 ♏ 37'	1929	kelly
C	25	23:38	04 ♈ 08'	12 ♊ 21'	09 ♓ 00'	24 ♓ 41'	23 ♌ 40'	1953	gable
D	6	15:29	13 ♐ 50'	11 ♒ 08'	18 ♐ 44'	28 ♏ 55'	12 ♐ 56'	1953	kelly
E	1	20:13	11 ♒ 57'	15 ♋ 55'	19 ♒ 24'	19 ♑ 56'	10 ♍ 07'	1901	gable

Fig.51. Matrix showing the natal planetary positions of Grace Kelly and Clark Gable, together with their progressed planetary positions for the year 1953.

Their astrology for 1953 is actually quite good. Their window of opportunity is defined by Gable's progressing-Venus (C6) in applying trine to Grace's natal-Mars. Effectively, in this case, it is a temporary love and

♈	♉	♊	♋	♌	♍	♎	♏	♐	♑	♒	♓
Aries	Taurus	Gemini	Cancer	Leo	Virgo	Libra	Scorpio	Sagittarius	Capricorn	Aquarius	Pisces

sex aspect. We observed this relationship aspect previously between Kelly and Lyons. As with all progressed to natal aspects it provides a chance for two people to encounter each other, what they do after the aspect has reached climax is their choice; often they move on. This couple were never going to do anything else, although there is speculation that they talked of marriage, but decided that their age difference was insurmountable. Gable was, at the time, quite footloose and fancy free. His Aquarian goal of freedom was about to become reality having recently separated from his wife Sylvia Fairbanks, he was also about to be freed from his film contract with MGM.

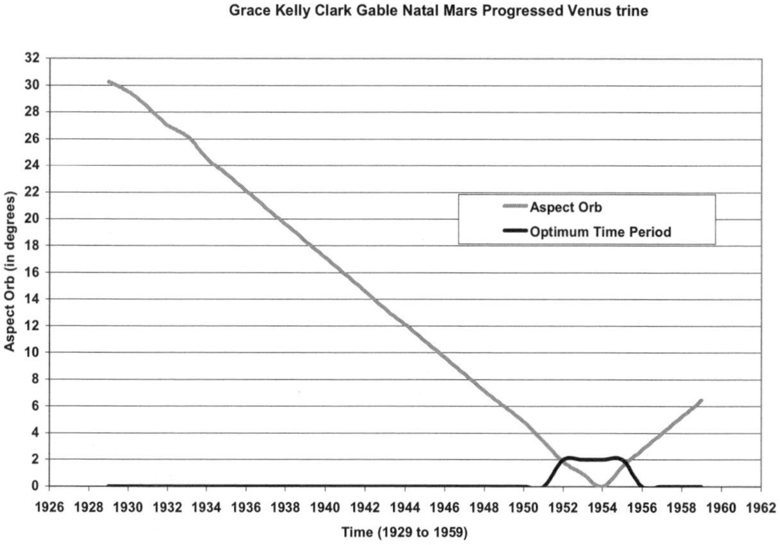

Grace Kelly Clark Gable Natal Mars Progressed Venus trine

Fig.52. Graph showing the two degree window of opportunity 1952 to 1955 created by Gable's progressing-Venus in trine to Kelly's natal-Mars

Grace Kelly and Jean-Pierre Aumont

After a formal start in 1953 while filming a TV drama, in which Grace insisted on calling him Mr Aumont, French actor Jean-Pierre Aumont

♈	♉	♊	♋	♌	♍	♎	♏	♐	♑	♒	♓
Aries	Taurus	Gemini	Cancer	Leo	Virgo	Libra	Scorpio	Sagittarius	Capricorn	Aquarius	Pisces

became Grace's lover. She showed him the sights of New York and he fell in love with her.

'I loved her because she was so lovely', was Aumont's simple summation of her allure.

Aumont was spotted kissing Grace at the 1955 Cannes film festival, so their relationship was quite friendly even two years later.

	1	2	3	4	5	6	7	8	9
A	Day	S.Time	Sun	Moon	Mercury	Venus	Mars		
B	12	13:55	19 ♏ 34'	21 ♓ 50'	10 ♏ 42'	28 ♎ 51'	25 ♏ 37'	1929	kelly
C	16	21:41	26 ♒ 42'	04 ♎ 39'	04 ♒ 34'	16 ♓ 12'	11 ♑ 17'	1953	aumont
D	6	15:29	13 ♐ 50'	11 ♒ 08'	18 ♐ 44'	28 ♏ 55'	12 ♐ 56'	1953	kelly
E	5	18:55	14 ♑ 03'	09 ♓ 49'	24 ♑ 42'	23 ♑ 38'	11 ♐ 11'	1911	aumont

Fig.53. Matrix showing the natal planetary positions of Grace Kelly and Jean-Pierre Aumont, together with their progressed planetary positions for the year 1953.

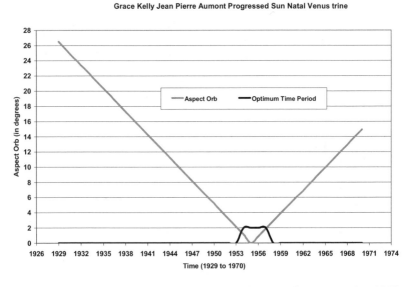

Grace Kelly Jean Pierre Aumont Progressed Sun Natal Venus trine

Fig.54. Graph showing the two degree window of opportunity 1953 to 1957 created by Aumont's progressing-Sun in trine to Kelly's natal-Venus

♈	♉	♊	♋	♌	♍	♎	♏	♐	♑	♒	♓
Aries	Taurus	Gemini	Cancer	Leo	Virgo	Libra	Scorpio	Sagittarius	Capricorn	Aquarius	Pisces

Their mutual astrology is typical. Aumont's progressing-Sun (C3) is applying to trine Grace's natal-Venus (B6). They also share a progressed-Mars (D7) natal-Mars (E7) conjunction that has just passed climax. Progressed-Sun natal-Venus trine aspects are common in affairs of the heart. As previously noted, they present a window of opportunity that lasts for a fixed period of five years.

Jean Pierre Aumont later married Marisa Pavan, twin sister of Pier Angeli.

Grace Kelly and Ray Milland

When *Hollywood Confidential* found out about Grace Kelly and Ray Milland it presented Milland with some problems. They were filming *Dial M for Murder* and, although Milland's thirty year marriage had weathered one or two storms in the past, it had never had to do so in public. He split with his wife after she found out he was not really going on a business trip, but was in fact seen boarding a plane with Grace Kelly. He fell hopelessly in love with Grace and would have left his wife for her but for the fact that everything he owned was in his wife's name and so, perhaps faced with financial ruin, he begrudgingly went back home.

	1	2	3	4	5	6	7	8	9
A	Day	S.Time	Sun	Moon	Mercury	Venus	Mars		
B	12	13:55	19 ♏ 34'	21 ♓ 50'	10 ♏ 42'	28 ♎ 51'	25 ♏ 37'	1929	kelly
C	19	21:53	29 ♒ 42'	22 ♉ 05'	12 ♓ 57'	13 ♑ 12'	08 ♐ 07'	1954	milland
D	7	15:33	14 ♐ 51'	23 ♒ 02'	20 ♐ 18'	00 ♐ 10'	13 ♐ 40'	1954	kelly
E	3	18:47	11 ♑ 58'	23 ♌ 07'	24 ♐ 48'	02 ♐ 57'	10 ♏ 22'	1907	milland

Fig.55. Matrix showing the natal planetary positions of Grace Kelly and Ray Milland, together with their progressed planetary positions for the year 1954.

Again – as in the case of Aumont-Kelly – the significant astrological factor is his progressed-Sun (C3) is in trine to her natal-Venus (B6). The window of opportunity is close to being shut in 1954 as his progressing-Sun has

♈	♉	♊	♋	♌	♍	♎	♏	♐	♑	♒	♓
Aries	Taurus	Gemini	Cancer	Leo	Virgo	Libra	Scorpio	Sagittarius	Capricorn	Aquarius	Pisces

already moved past exact aspect with her Venus, but nevertheless, the effect of the aspect would still be relevant and powerful, especially to someone approaching fifty, married thirty years and faced with a beauty such as Grace Kelly.

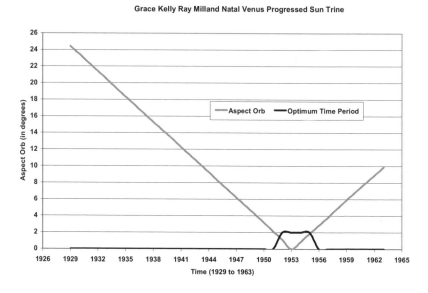

Grace Kelly Ray Milland Natal Venus Progressed Sun Trine

Fig.56. Graph showing the two degree window of opportunity 1951 to 1956 created by Milland's progressing-Sun in trine to Kelly's natal-Venus

Grace Kelly and Oleg Cassini

Grace was with Jean-Pierre Aumont, trying to get over the loss of Ray Milland, when she met Oleg Cassini. Cassini had seen Grace Kelly in *Mogambo* and was already besotted when he spied her in a restaurant in New York. She was with Aumont whom Oleg Cassini already knew as they had competed for the love of Gene Tierney in the past. Cassini was something of a Casanova; an 'accomplished seducer' as such he set his sights on winning Grace's heart and did so in typical fashion. 'It was to be

♈	♉	♊	♋	♌	♍	♎	♏	♐	♑	♒	♓
Aries	Taurus	Gemini	Cancer	Leo	Virgo	Libra	Scorpio	Sagittarius	Capricorn	Aquarius	Pisces

the greatest, most exhilarating campaign of my life.' Cassini set about developing a plan of seduction which involved sending a dozen red roses to Grace's home for ten days, he did not sign the card, instead he wrote 'from the friendly florist'. On the tenth day he called her saying he was the friendly florist. He got her laughing and got her to join him on a date (she was chaperoned by her sister on this occasion).

She told Oleg she was in love with Ray Milland. A silver-tongued and confident Aries, Oleg told her it was not a problem and that she would be engaged to him (Oleg Cassini that is) within a year.

Grace left for LA the next day, but Oleg made sure he was seen by gossip columnists in the company of beauties such as Pier Angeli and Anita Ekberg in order that he would be read about by Grace in their newspaper columns.

They eventually met up again on the French Riviera where they spent an evening together in what Oleg describes as a 'distressingly platonic' situation. He poured out his heart to Grace, declared the essence of his inner desires and that was it, his persistence paid off.

Oleg Cassini's biggest obstacle to life-long happiness with Grace Kelly was his past (he had been married before and linked with many beautiful women), which caused a problem for Grace's mother who considered Oleg a bad risk for a husband. Her father, who was old-fashioned in many respects, supposedly considered Cassini to be too much of a 'foreigner' for his daughter.

	1	2	3	4	5	6	7	8	9
A	Day	S.Time	Sun	Moon	Mercury	Venus	Mars		
B	12	13:55	19 ♏ 34'	21 ♓ 50'	10 ♏ 42'	28 ♎ 51'	25 ♏ 37'	1929	kelly
C	23	18:00	01 ♊ 19'	05 ♑ 50'	19 ♉ 44'	26 ♈ 54'	11 ♈ 23'	1955	cassini
D	8	15:37	15 ♐ 52'	05 ♓ 03'	21 ♐ 52'	01 ♐ 26'	14 ♐ 24'	1955	kelly
E	11	15:14	20 ♈ 35'	11 ♊ 05'	29 ♓ 32'	11 ♉ 25'	09 ♓ 09'	1913	cassini

Fig.57. Matrix showing the natal planetary positions of Grace Kelly and Oleg Cassini, together with their progressed planetary positions for the year 1955.

♈	♉	♊	♋	♌	♍	♎	♏	♐	♑	♒	♓
Aries	Taurus	Gemini	Cancer	Leo	Virgo	Libra	Scorpio	Sagittarius	Capricorn	Aquarius	Pisces

Their mutual astrology is influenced by a progressed-Venus (D6) progressed-Sun (C3) opposition. The opposition as we have seen causes great attraction, but, unlike the trine aspect does not make for smooth relations. Often with an opposition something gets in the way of the relationship, in this case it is Grace's parents. This effect is distinct from life circumstances getting in the way of romance. Circumstances such as poverty, fame or motherhood that require compromise for the couple to be together is often accompanied by progressed-Sun being square to progressed-Sun.

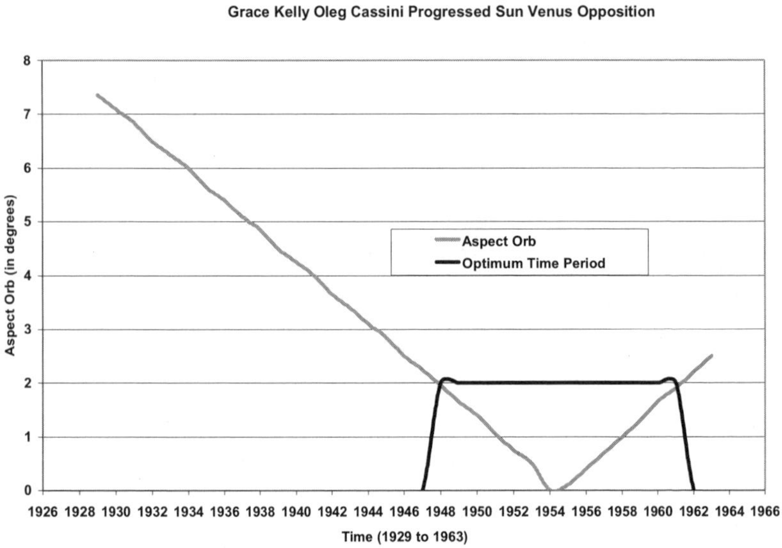

Grace Kelly Oleg Cassini Progressed Sun Venus Opposition

Fig.58. Graph showing the two degree window of opportunity 1947 to 1961 created by Cassini's progressing-Sun in opposition to Kelly's progressing-Venus

Grace Kelly and William Holden

Grace met William Holden when they made *The Bridges of Toko Ri* together in 1954. They had 'quite a fling' and a friend of Holden's remarked that he was crazy about her.

♈	♉	♊	♋	♌	♍	♎	♏	♐	♑	♒	♓
Aries	Taurus	Gemini	Cancer	Leo	Virgo	Libra	Scorpio	Sagittarius	Capricorn	Aquarius	Pisces

	1	2	3	4	5	6	7	8	9
A	Day	S.Time	Sun	Moon	Mercury	Venus	Mars		
B	12	13:55	19 ♏ 34'	21 ♓ 50'	10 ♏ 42'	28 ♎ 51'	25 ♏ 37'	1929	kelly
C	23	15:02	01 ♊ 58'	09 ♏ 18'	07 ♉ 00'	18 ♈ 30'	18 ♍ 12'	1954	holden
D	7	15:33	14 ♐ 51'	23 ♒ 02'	20 ♐ 18'	00 ♐ 10'	13 ♐ 40'	1954	kelly
E	17	12:41	27 ♈ 06'	24 ♋ 39'	10 ♉ 20'	10 ♓ 54'	14 ♍ 13'	1918	holden

Fig.59. Matrix showing the natal planetary positions of Grace Kelly and William Holden, together with their progressed planetary positions for the year 1954.

'*It was a heavy romance*' Robert Lacey quotes Mel Dellar, an assistant director on the *Bridges of Toko Ri.*[xcix]

Holden's psychiatrist Michael Jay Klassman has stated that Holden wished the world to know the detail of his alcoholism and so revealed some of the details of his therapy.

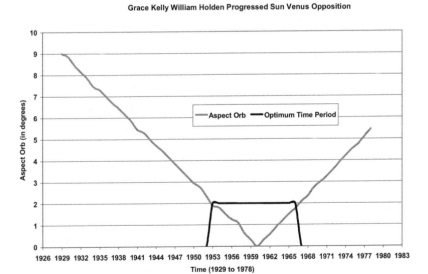

Fig.60. Graph showing the two degree window of opportunity 1953 to 1966 created by Holden's progressing-Sun in opposition to Kelly's progressing-Venus

♈	♉	♊	♋	♌	♍	♎	♏	♐	♑	♒	♓
Aries	Taurus	Gemini	Cancer	Leo	Virgo	Libra	Scorpio	Sagittarius	Capricorn	Aquarius	Pisces

Part of these revelations concerns Holden's relationship with Grace Kelly. It transpires that Holden and Grace were so serious that she took him home to meet her family. The reception he received was 'cold and hostile'.

'We fell head over heels in love with each other. We couldn't help our feelings.' [c]...But Bill Holden was a married man.

As in the case of Grace and Oleg Cassini, Grace shared with William Holden a progressing-Venus (D6) – progressing-Sun (C3) opposition. What is slightly different is that they also share this aspect natally and therefore a certain dynamic of their relationship is permanent. This is an aspect of intense attraction and is present in a number of long-lasting relationships. The progression is also a long-lived aspect and so this is less of a window of opportunity and more of a liaison waiting to happen. Again the obstacle to Grace and William marrying was Grace's father Jack. Cassini and Holden both faced the same opposition. Jack Kelly shook his fist in William Holden's face. Holden walked away.

HSH Princess Grace of Monaco and HSH Prince Rainier of Monaco

Something other than love brought this couple together and something other than love kept them together. For someone who chose her partners with such an eye for an astrological match, albeit unknowingly, Grace Kelly must have felt just a little bit uneasy when she woke up to realise what she was about to do. She told Oleg Cassini: 'I will learn to love him.' As you would expect from a couple who do not marry for love, they drifted apart, they stopped sharing the same bed then they moved into separate bedrooms. Later Grace spent most of her time in Paris while Rainier lived in Monte Carlo.

Jane Ellen Wayne writing in *The Golden Girls of MGM* states that in 1953 Aristotle Onassis had invested heavily in Monte Carlo and later spoke to Gardner Cowles, the publisher of *Look* magazine, about the sagging economy of Monaco and how they might lure the US dollar there. One

♈	♉	♊	♋	♌	♍	♎	♏	♐	♑	♒	♓
Aries	Taurus	Gemini	Cancer	Leo	Virgo	Libra	Scorpio	Sagittarius	Capricorn	Aquarius	Pisces

solution, writes Wayne, was to marry Prince Rainier off to a beautiful movie star; the first one that came to mind was Marilyn Monroe. Cowles offered to arrange a meeting with Norma Jean, who was only too happy to help, but by then Rainier was engaged to Grace Kelly.

	1	2	3	4	5	6	7	8	9
A	Day	S.Time	Sun	Moon	Mercury	Venus	Mars		
B	31	21:30	08 ♊ 43'	22 ♐ 27'	05 ♊ 33'	11 ♉ 32'	00 ♋ 12'	1923	ranier
C	9	15:41	16 ♐ 53'	17 ♓ 16'	23 ♐ 26'	02 ♐ 41'	15 ♐ 08'	1956	kelly
D	3	23:40	10 ♋ 14'	08 ♓ 09'	20 ♊ 55'	21 ♊ 29'	21 ♋ 43'	1956	ranier
E	12	13:55	19 ♏ 34'	21 ♓ 50'	10 ♏ 42'	28 ♎ 51'	25 ♏ 37'	1929	kelly

Fig.61. Matrix showing the natal planetary positions of Grace Kelly and HSH Prince Rainier of Monaco, together with their progressed planetary positions for the year 1956.

This story paints a none-too-romantic picture of the machinations of state that led Grace Kelly to Monaco's Cathedral of St Nicholas on 18 April 1956. Her synastric hit-rate among her leading men had been in the high 80% region, but each one was an encounter based on her preference: she was attracted to them. Her Royal Prince brought different qualities to her life and as such few of the conventional astrological patterns are detectable in their natal or progressed planetary positions for 1956. Even their Moons are square to one another. A dissociate trine between Rainier's Mars (B7) and Grace's Venus (E6) is the key attracting factor in this relationship. Dissociation happens when an aspect occurs at the cusp of two signs, in the case of the 120-degree trine this places the planets involved in signs of different (and incompatible) elements. Any progressed aspects that have formed in the past (for example Rainier's progressing-Mars has just passed the 2 degree separation mark from trine with natal Grace's Sun and would have been exact in 1953) are out of range and the next significant aspect between the two occurs in 1961 when Grace's Venus opposes Rainier's Sun. This can often mean attraction and can kick-start a new relationship. By 1961 this relationship would be five years old and this opposition is

♈	♉	♊	♋	♌	♍	♎	♏	♐	♑	♒	♓
Aries	Taurus	Gemini	Cancer	Leo	Virgo	Libra	Scorpio	Sagittarius	Capricorn	Aquarius	Pisces

more likely to signify a couple whose relationship becomes slightly strained.

HSH Prince Rainier of Monaco and Gisele Pascal

Before he met Grace Kelly, Prince Rainier was involved for six years with a French actress called Gisele Pascal. It was expected that any prospective bride of Rainier's would undergo a maternity test owing to the agreement that if Monaco was ever to be without a male heir, it would revert to French rule. Gisele Pascal underwent such a test and failed. This meant that Rainier had to break off their relationship. It is suggested that the prince's spiritual advisor, Father Francis Tucker, did not approve of Gisele. When he finished their relationship, the Prince said to Father Tucker, 'If you ever hear that my subjects think I do not love them, tell them what I have done today'.

	1	2	3	4	5	6	7	8	9
A	Day	S.Time	Sun	Moon	Mercury	Venus	Mars		
B	31	21:30	08 ♊ 43'	22 ♐ 27'	05 ♊ 33'	11 ♉ 32'	00 ♋ 12'	1923	ranier
C	13	13:24	19 ♎ 07'	04 ♐ 51'	01 ♎ 09'	27 ♎ 52'	27 ♍ 01'	1949	pascal
D	26	23:13	03 ♋ 34'	01 ♐ 58'	11 ♊ 30'	12 ♊ 59'	17 ♋ 11'	1949	ranier
E	17	11:41	23 ♍ 33'	23 ♐ 31'	13 ♎ 42'	25 ♍ 27'	10 ♍ 28'	1923	pascal

Fig.62. Matrix showing the natal planetary positions of Gisele Pascal and HSH Prince Rainier, together with their progressed planetary positions for the year 1949.

Gisele and Rainier shared a natal-Venus (B6) natal-Mars (E7) trine, which is the same aspect that Grace shared with Rainier (although it was Grace's Venus and Rainier's Mars in this case).

Gisele later married and bore a child, provoking the rumour that the results of her maternity test were falsified.

♈	♉	♊	♋	♌	♍	♎	♏	♐	♑	♒	♓
Aries	Taurus	Gemini	Cancer	Leo	Virgo	Libra	Scorpio	Sagittarius	Capricorn	Aquarius	Pisces

Eight

Elizabeth Taylor

What do you expect me to do? Sleep alone?
Elizabeth Taylor

Elizabeth Rosamund Taylor was born in London on 27 February 1932 at 02:15hrs. Her parents, Francis and Sara, were US citizens living in London. In 1939, with the threat of war approaching, the family moved from London to Los Angeles where young Elizabeth proceeded to test for both MGM and Universal, signing a deal with Universal for $200 a week and famously being rejected after a year for not being able to sing, dance or act (she couldn't cry on demand) and for having an overbearing mother.

MGM producer Sam Marx was unaware Elizabeth had already been rejected by MGM and reportedly would not have asked her along for an audition had he known, but he was taken with her, commenting that she was: 'the prettiest child I had ever seen'. Marx was casting for *Lassie Come Home* and Taylor was taken on signing a $100 a week contract with MGM.

She went on to star in *Jane Eyre, National Velvet* and *Little Women* before her first adult role in 1948's *The Conspirator,* when she was 16. Robert Taylor gave Elizabeth Taylor her first on-screen kiss in this film. It was released in 1950.

In 1949, Howard Hughes reportedly offered Francis Taylor $1m for his daughter's hand in marriage. Elizabeth was repulsed by Hughes and reportedly refused a box of jewels he presented her with.

A brief engagement to businessman William Pawley Jr. in 1949 was called off when Elizabeth refused to give up her career. There followed an infatuation and friendship with bisexual actor Montgomery Clift; the pair

♈	♉	♊	♋	♌	♍	♎	♏	♐	♑	♒	♓
Aries	Taurus	Gemini	Cancer	Leo	Virgo	Libra	Scorpio	Sagittarius	Capricorn	Aquarius	Pisces

remained close.

Nicky Hilton, heir to the $100 million plus hotel fortune, saw Elizabeth at a party and as is the way with such men of fortune, got his friend Peter Lawford to arrange an introduction. It was late 1949 and Hilton's eligibility interested both Sara and Elizabeth.

Elizabeth Taylor and Nicky Hilton

	1	2	3	4	5	6	7	8	9
			Sun	Moon	Mercury	Venus	Mars		
A	Day	S.Time							
B	27	12:37	07 ♓ 17'	15 ♏ 35'	07 ♓ 27'	17 ♈ 09'	01 ♓ 34'	1932	taylor
C	30	10:29	06 ♌ 37'	20 ♈ 49'	19 ♌ 48'	07 ♋ 32'	28 ♈ 59'	1950	hilton
D	16	13:48	25 ♓ 17'	01 ♋ 49'	11 ♈ 15'	08 ♉ 02'	15 ♓ 45'	1950	taylor
E	6	8:55	13 ♋ 43'	04 ♊ 22'	09 ♌ 40'	09 ♊ 02'	14 ♈ 24'	1926	hilton

Fig.63. Matrix showing the natal planetary positions of Elizabeth Taylor and Nicky Hilton, together with their progressed planetary positions for the year 1950.

Elizabeth's first marriage was a disaster. Nicky Hilton turned out to be a violent bully who was fundamentally incompatible with Taylor. Their honeymoon included a trip to Europe aboard the *Queen Mary*.

C. David Heymann recounts the following anecdote from socialite Martha Reed:

> '*I heard from Connie [Conrad Hilton – Nicky's father] that once they reached Europe, Nick and Liz engaged in a series of dramatic fights and altercations. They were obviously incompatible. At some point I crossed paths with them in Paris, and Elizabeth looked rather pained.* 'ci

Heymann also quotes a conversation Elizabeth Taylor had with director Larry Peerce on this issue:

> '*We had a very prim and proper courtship, a very fiftyish type of courtship where a woman didn't go to bed with a man prior to marriage. During the courtship, except on one or two occasions, Nicky was able*

♈	♉	♊	♋	♌	♏	♎	♏	♐	♑	♒	♓
Aries	Taurus	Gemini	Cancer	Leo	Virgo	Libra	Scorpio	Sagittarius	Capricorn	Aquarius	Pisces

to control what I later determined to be his violent nature. Once I discovered his problem, it was too late to do much about it. We were already married, and I was too ashamed to admit that I had made such a grievous error. ^{cii}

A trine aspect progression of Hilton's Venus (C6) to Elizabeth's natal-Sun (B3) during 1949 – 1951 provided some simulated compatibility that would be at its height for this relatively brief window. From the natal point of view, Taylor and Hilton shared a square aspect between *her* Sun and *his* Venus. Further to this, *his* Sun and *her* Venus were only 3 and a half degrees from exact square, basically the same difficult aspect occurs twice here.

The progressing-Venus in a trine to natal-Sun aspect is again encountered in a fleeting relationship. We have seen already that many intimate relationships are accompanied by a close shared contact of the Sun in one person's chart and Venus in the other and this is the case here. What is interesting here is that it temporarily masked a marked incompatibility between the bride and groom.

Hilton's natal-Mars is in one of its favorite places (the middle of Aries), while this position has a reputation for endowing the character and physique with positive masculine characteristics, it is complicated by the fact that the Sun and Mars are in another 90 degree square aspect to each other, this sometimes indicates a somewhat macho and aggressive egocentric, and this could impede his capacity for a close relationship at such a young age, especially to a star like Elizabeth Taylor. It was reported that Hilton stayed in the bar on his wedding night and that he had raised his hand to his wife within the first six months of marriage. The transient progressed-Venus – natal-Sun trine pulled them together, but other factors including a progressed-Sun – progressed-Venus square (meaning the way that they are changing and growing; from her point of view in relationships and from his point of view in his life-plan, were fundamentally at a tangent to each other) would have revealed in a short time that they were really only

♈	♉	♊	♋	♌	♍	♎	♏	♐	♑	♒	♓
Aries	Taurus	Gemini	Cancer	Leo	Virgo	Libra	Scorpio	Sagittarius	Capricorn	Aquarius	Pisces

meant to be together temporarily, to learn lessons perhaps, or just to fulfil the potential of their briefly compatible charts.

	1	2	3	4	5	6	7	8	9
			Sun						
A	Day	S.Time	Sun	Moon	Mercury	Venus	Mars		
B	27	12:37	07 ♓ 17'	15 ♏ 35'	07 ♓ 27'	17 ♈ 09'	01 ♓ 34'	1932	taylor
C	1	10:37	08 ♌ 32'	18 ♉ 14'	18 ♌ 42'	09 ♋ 56'	00 ♉ 06'	1952	hilton
D	18	13:56	27 ♓ 17'	27 ♋ 55'	14 ♈ 24'	10 ♉ 18'	17 ♓ 19'	1952	taylor
E	6	8:55	13 ♋ 43'	04 ♊ 22'	09 ♌ 40'	09 ♊ 02'	14 ♈ 24'	1926	hilton

Fig.64. Matrix showing the natal planetary positions of Elizabeth Taylor and Nicky Hilton, together with their progressed planetary positions for the year 1952.

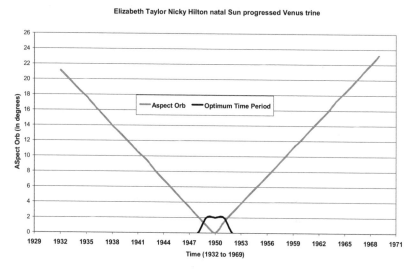

Elizabeth Taylor Nicky Hilton natal Sun progressed Venus trine

Fig.65. Graph showing the window of opportunity created by Nicky Hilton's progressed-Venus in trine to Elizabeth Taylor's natal-Sun from 1949 to 1951

Elizabeth Taylor and Stanley Donen

Heymann describes how Stanley Donen, although still married at the time, began to pursue Elizabeth around the time of her official separation from Nicky Hilton (1 December 1950). Donen was a director who had

♈	♉	♊	♋	♌	♍	♎	♏	♐	♑	♒	♓
Aries	Taurus	Gemini	Cancer	Leo	Virgo	Libra	Scorpio	Sagittarius	Capricorn	Aquarius	Pisces

	1	2	3	4	5	6	7	8	9
A	Day	S.Time	Sun	Moon	Mercury	Venus	Mars		
B	27	12:37	07 ♓ 17'	15 ♏ 35'	07 ♓ 27'	17 ♈ 09'	01 ♓ 34'	1932	taylor
C	9	3:08	18 ♉ 34'	19 ♋ 09'	16 ♉ 18'	02 ♋ 48'	08 ♒ 29'	1950	donen
D	16	13:48	25 ♓ 17'	01 ♋ 49'	11 ♈ 15'	08 ♉ 02'	15 ♓ 45'	1950	Taylor
E	13	1:25	23 ♈ 16'	05 ♌ 04'	12 ♉ 25'	08 ♊ 38'	23 ♑ 21'	1924	donen

Fig.66. Matrix showing the natal planetary positions of Elizabeth Taylor and Stanley Donen, together with their progressed planetary positions for the year 1950.

graduated from the Broadway chorus to directing Hollywood pictures. At 27 he was directing Elizabeth in a comedy called *Love is Better than Ever*.

Their short romance effectively ended in June 1951 when she left the US to film *Ivanhoe* in Britain. She was clearly not interested enough to pursue a long distance relationship, she never did like to be apart from her partners. Although they exchanged letters, their correspondence eventually stopped.

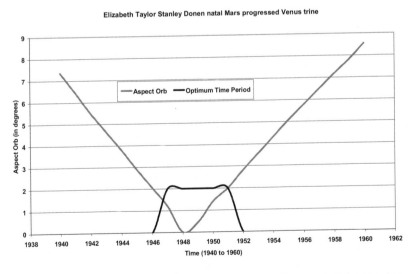

Fig.67. Graph showing the window of opportunity created by Stanley Donen's progressing-Venus in trine to Elizabeth Taylor's natal-Mars

♈	♉	♊	♋	♌	♍	♎	♏	♐	♑	♒	♓
Aries	Taurus	Gemini	Cancer	Leo	Virgo	Libra	Scorpio	Sagittarius	Capricorn	Aquarius	Pisces

This brief romance was blamed as the major contributory factor in the breakdown of Donen's marriage to Jeanne Coyne (who went on to marry Gene Kelly a decade later). The most significant single factor here is a progressed trine aspect between Taylor's Mars (B7) and Donen's Venus (C6). This is separating in 1950, but reaches the 2-degree barrier in 1951, the year their relationship ended.

Stanley's marriage to Jeanne Coyne contained two natal-Sun-Venus squares and an exact natal-Sun natal-Mars conjunction. He later partnered up with Yvette Mimeiux, also a relationship steeped in progressed synastry, this time mostly positive.

Elizabeth Taylor and Michael Wilding

	1	2	3	4	5	6	7	8	9
A	Day	S.Time	Sun	Moon	Mercury	Venus	Mars		
B	27	12:37	07 ♓ 17'	15 ♏ 35'	07 ♓ 27'	17 ♈ 09'	01 ♓ 34'	1932	taylor
C	1	10:41	08 ♍ 39'	01 ♉ 24'	23 ♌ 36'	24 ♍ 23'	29 ♍ 13'	1952	wilding
D	18	13:56	27 ♓ 17'	27 ♋ 55'	14 ♈ 24'	10 ♉ 18'	17 ♓ 19'	1952	taylor
E	23	8:03	00 ♌ 13'	27 ♏ 07'	27 ♌ 12'	05 ♌ 02'	03 ♍ 56'	1912	wilding

Fig.68. Matrix showing the natal planetary positions of Elizabeth Taylor and Michael Wilding, together with their progressed planetary positions for the year 1952.

In London, Elizabeth was drawn to much older and a lot less threatening Michael Wilding, who presents a slightly different, but no less expected astrological pattern. Elizabeth had met Wilding three years previously (1949) while filming *the Conspirator*, and developed something of a crush on him. He was 36 in 1949, while Elizabeth was only 17.

In 1951, although technically still married to Kay Young, Wilding had also fallen for Elizabeth. He did not appear in *Ivanhoe*, but he spent a lot of time on the set. It was partly due to Wilding's advice that Elizabeth signed a new seven-year contract with MGM.

In 1952, the year they married, his progressed-Sun (C3) was opposite

♈	♉	♊	♋	♌	♍	♎	♏	♐	♑	♒	♓
Aries	Taurus	Gemini	Cancer	Leo	Virgo	Libra	Scorpio	Sagittarius	Capricorn	Aquarius	Pisces

her natal-Sun (B3). His progressed-Mars (C7) was opposite her progressed-Sun (D3) and her progressed-Venus (D6) was slowly separating from a trine with his progressed-Sun.

There are lots of reasons why a relationship would form, lots of positive energy flowing between the two, but not much from the traditional astrological perspective that would keep them together, at least as far as the planetary aspects are concerned. Most of the significant astrological indicators here are separating progressed aspects which would have been most powerful a couple of years previously.

	1	2	3	4	5	6	7	8	9
A	Day	S.Time	Sun	Moon	Mercury	Venus	Mars		
B	27	12:37	07 ♓ 17'	15 ♏ 35'	07 ♓ 27'	17 ♈ 09'	01 ♓ 34'	1932	taylor
C	29	10:29	05 ♍ 45'	24 ♓ 14'	24 ♌ 03'	20 ♍ 41'	27 ♍ 17'	1949	wilding
D	15	13:44	24 ♓ 17'	19 ♊ 20'	09 ♈ 34'	06 ♉ 53'	14 ♓ 58'	1949	taylor
E	23	8:03	00 ♌ 13'	27 ♏ 07'	27 ♌ 12'	05 ♌ 02'	03 ♍ 56'	1912	wilding

Fig.69. Matrix showing the natal planetary positions of Elizabeth Taylor and Michael Wilding, together with their progressed planetary positions for the year 1949.

This is interesting because their progressed-Sun – Venus trine is closer together in 1949 and their Sun – Mars opposition has not yet become active. By 1956 this had ceased to be a significant factor and had been replaced by a series of 150-degree *Inconjunct* aspects (called by Linda Goodman **6:8** relationships), and their progressed-Sun-Mars opposition had changed

	1	2	3	4	5	6	7	8	9
A	Day	S.Time	Sun	Moon	Mercury	Venus	Mars		
B	27	12:37	07 ♓ 17'	15 ♏ 35'	07 ♓ 27'	17 ♈ 09'	01 ♓ 34'	1932	taylor
C	5	10:56	12 ♍ 31'	24 ♊ 39'	24 ♌ 59'	29 ♍ 20'	01 ♎ 48'	1956	wilding
D	22	14:12	01 ♈ 15'	25 ♍ 11'	19 ♈ 42'	14 ♉ 48'	20 ♓ 28'	1956	taylor
E	23	8:03	00 ♌ 13'	27 ♏ 07'	27 ♌ 12'	05 ♌ 02'	03 ♍ 56'	1912	wilding

Fig.70. Matrix showing the natal planetary positions of Elizabeth Taylor and Michael Wilding, together with their progressed planetary positions for the year 1956.

♈	♉	♊	♋	♌	♍	♎	♏	♐	♑	♒	♓
Aries	Taurus	Gemini	Cancer	Leo	Virgo	Libra	Scorpio	Sagittarius	Capricorn	Aquarius	Pisces

signs from adaptable Virgo-Pisces to direct and single-minded Libra-Aries:

In natal astrology we allow much wider orbs of influence for natal aspects and as such it is clear that the way these two people 'work' in private as well as in business were at two ends of the Pisces – Virgo scale, their natal-Mars' being just over 2 degrees from exact opposition, hers in Pisces and his in Virgo. Virgo Mars has a controlling nature, but it doesn't react violently to the intangible workings of Pisces, it more-than-likely accepts their differences and opts for a safer, more structured future.

Wilding is described by different commentators as 'a gentleman'; 'a gentle, placid man, whose charm prevented him from ever giving offence'; 'too passive to argue' and in describing himself he said: 'I'm the type who just can't stand a row of any kind'. This is a signature of Mars in uncompetitive Virgo. And probably more pertinently, his personality stands in marked contrast to that of Elizabeth Taylor.

This relationship appears to have been the passionate whim of a young, rich, Hollywood starlet who fell in love with, pursued and persuaded a man almost twice her age to marry her. She bought her own engagement ring and supposedly surprised her groom by announcing the wedding date. She was infatuated by Wilding, who was a safe and considerate option after her difficult time with Nicky Hilton.

Irene Selznick is quoted by C. David Heymann as saying:

'I sensed the relationship wouldn't last. He seemed too mild and staid for her. Her attraction to Michael could only have been a reaction to Nicky Hilton's recklessness.'[ciii]

They married on 21 February 1952 in Westminster's Caxton Hall. Elizabeth was not yet twenty years old.

Oppositions are sometimes difficult to live with as their main function is to cause conscious reflection. They can manifest as sexual attraction in many cases. Problems arise if and when the aspect starts to separate or its effect wears off. The relationship depends heavily on what it is replaced

♈	♉	♊	♋	♌	♍	♎	♏	♐	♑	♒	♓
Aries	Taurus	Gemini	Cancer	Leo	Virgo	Libra	Scorpio	Sagittarius	Capricorn	Aquarius	Pisces

with and how much the parties involved are prepared to compromise: this depends further on other factors such as age, value-system and other extraneous factors such as children.

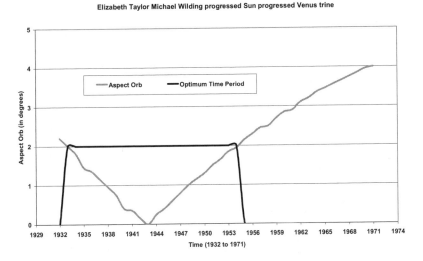

Elizabeth Taylor Michael Wilding progressed Sun progressed Venus trine

Fig.71. Graph showing the window of opportunity created by Elizabeth Taylor's Sun in trine to Michael Wilding's progressed-Venus open from 1933 to 1955

Taylor eventually tired of buying her own jewels (she picked out, and ultimately paid for, the ones Wilding bought her). She actually wanted a 'big strong guy' who would buy her jewels and furs and look after her.

Their relationship turned full circle in a kind of predictable way: she was dependant on Wilding when she was nineteen, made all the running and all the decisions and by the time she was twenty three, he was complaining that he hated 'following her around' and being 'left in a corner'.

They turned their relationship into a brother – sister arrangement. Wilding became her agent for a while.

♈	♉	♊	♋	♌	♍	♎	♏	♐	♑	♒	♓
Aries	Taurus	Gemini	Cancer	Leo	Virgo	Libra	Scorpio	Sagittarius	Capricorn	Aquarius	Pisces

Elizabeth Taylor and Mike Todd

The first rule of astrological research is to establish good data to an agreed standard of accuracy. The date on a birth certificate is generally agreed to be the second best kind of evidence of a person's date of birth. Unfortunately in some rare cases, what is written on a birth certificate is actually wrong. The case of Avrom Hirsch Goldbogen is one of these rare cases. Avrom changed his name to Mike Todd and then, according to both Eddie Fisher and Michael Todd Jr., he also changed his age. The date on his gravestone reads 22 June 1909, this came courtesy of a birth certificate provided by Hubert Humphrey when he was Mayor of Minneapolis. The date on another birth certificate, probably also provided by Humphrey, reads 19 June 1911. His son, Michael Todd Jr., gave a date of "on or about 22 June 1907".[civ] If his second birth certificate were true, his connection with Elizabeth Taylor in 1956 would look like this:

	1	2	3	4	5	6	7	8	9
A	Day	S.Time	Sun	Moon	Mercury	Venus	Mars		
B	27	12:37	07 ♓ 17'	15 ♏ 35'	07 ♓ 27'	17 ♈ 09'	01 ♓ 34'	1932	taylor
C	3	3:42	09 ♌ 49'	24 ♏ 22'	05 ♍ 12'	21 ♍ 41'	11 ♉ 55'	1956	todd (bc)
D	22	14:12	01 ♈ 15'	25 ♍ 11'	19 ♈ 42'	14 ♉ 48'	20 ♓ 28'	1956	taylor
E	19	0:45	26 ♊ 52'	19 ♓ 53'	10 ♊ 28'	11 ♌ 18'	11 ♈ 48'	1911	todd (bc)

Fig.72. Matrix showing the natal planetary positions of Elizabeth Taylor and Michael Todd, together with their progressed planetary positions for the year 1956 if he was born in 1911.

If we believe his son and most of his biographers then their connection for 1956 looks like this:

	1	2	3	4	5	6	7	8	9
A	Day	S.Time	Sun	Moon	Mercury	Venus	Mars		
B	27	12:37	07 ♓ 17'	15 ♏ 35'	07 ♓ 27'	17 ♈ 09'	01 ♓ 34'	1932	taylor
C	10	4:10	16 ♌ 29'	27 ♌ 49'	28 ♋ 10'	06 ♌ 45'	06 ♑ 59'	1956	todd (2)
D	22	14:12	01 ♈ 15'	25 ♍ 11'	19 ♈ 42'	14 ♉ 48'	20 ♓ 28'	1956	taylor
E	22	0:57	29 ♊ 42'	09 ♏ 34'	24 ♋ 28'	06 ♊ 56'	17 ♑ 06'	1907	todd (2)

Fig.73. Matrix showing the natal planetary positions of Elizabeth

♈	♉	♊	♋	♌	♍	♎	♏	♐	♑	♒	♓
Aries	Taurus	Gemini	Cancer	Leo	Virgo	Libra	Scorpio	Sagittarius	Capricorn	Aquarius	Pisces

Taylor and Michael Todd, together with their progressed planetary positions for the year 1956 if he was born in 1907.

The first pattern is similar in nature to a later relationship of Elizabeth Taylor's, a progressed-Venus (C6) progressed-Mars (D7) opposition; the second pattern similar to her earlier relationship with Nicky Hilton: a natal-Sun-Venus (B3 – E6) square *and* a natal-Venus-Mars (B6-E7) square are softened temporarily by a progressed-Sun (C3) natal-Venus (B6) trine.

I'm not sure what year Mike Todd was born. Three of his relationships were originally included in the 1300 relationships because of his birth certificate, but as I researched Eddie Fisher, the facts about Avrom Hirsch Goldbogen started to look wrong.

Despite this I have decided to include him here, it is an interesting fact that if he was born on 22 June 1907 or 19 June 1911 then he and Elizabeth Taylor have pertinent positive progressed synastry.

Elizabeth Taylor's first real meeting with Mike Todd took place on 30 June 1956 aboard a yacht. She and Michael Wilding had been invited to accompany Mike, his fiancée Evelyn Keyes and six other guests as Todd intended to finish the filming of *Around the World in 80 Days* with some footage of a Japanese schooner which was scheduled to sail past the coast of Santa Barbara.

The relationship and marriage that blossomed from these days afloat became the first of two great loves of Taylor's life. Mike Todd was a strong willed, successful man. He once said of Taylor:

> *'This gal's been cruising for trouble all her life and now she's found someone to give it to her. Trouble is everybody was too nice to fight back. Not me. When she flies into a tantrum, I fly into a bigger one. She's been on a milk-toast diet all her life with men. But me – I'm red meat.'*[CV]

One minute they would be photographed necking in public in the

♈	♉	♊	♋	♌	♍	♎	♏	♐	♑	♒	♓
Aries	Taurus	Gemini	Cancer	Leo	Virgo	Libra	Scorpio	Sagittarius	Capricorn	Aquarius	Pisces

company of the Australian Prime Minister, the next, photographs of them howling at one another and using universal hand gestures flashed around the globe.

These pendulous fluctuations between love and war are astrologically significant for Liz Taylor and she was to experience a similar relationship a few years later.

Their relationship was punctuated with violence, or at least extreme physicality, however, unlike Elizabeth's relationship with Hilton, she seemed to encourage and welcome most of Todd's rough horseplay. Eddie Fisher comments in his autobiography: '*I could never get used to the fact that she tolerated being hit, that maybe she even needed it to respect a man...she hit me all the time too and tried to goad me into hitting her back. I wouldn't do it.* 'cvi

What we can see developing here is a pattern that will continue and it concerns an oscillation between harmony and conflict.

Elizabeth Taylor and Eddie Fisher

Eddie Fisher was Mike Todd's best friend, a successful nightclub singer, he idolised Todd and at the time of Todd's death he was married to the whole-some Debbie Reynolds. The couple were known as America's Sweethearts. After Mike's death, Elizabeth Taylor started to rely heavily on Eddie Fisher. They spent a lot of time in shared grief and from this grief an intimate relationship evolved.

Eddie Fisher describes the time he fell in love with Elizabeth:

'*Endless songs have been written about the way love begins, but I don't know of any of them that got it right. The moment you fall in love, really fall in love, your life is forever divided into the time before that moment and the rest of your life.* 'cvii

Taylor later claimed that she had only married Eddie Fisher because Mike Todd had said:

♈	♉	♊	♋	♌	♍	♎	♏	♐	♑	♒	♓
Aries	Taurus	Gemini	Cancer	Leo	Virgo	Libra	Scorpio	Sagittarius	Capricorn	Aquarius	Pisces

'If anything happens to me I want Eddie to take care of you.'

This was probably not true, but the position of Venus in her birth chart gives her what may appear to be a butterfly temperament as far as love is concerned. When Venus is in a close conjunction with Uranus, (which it is in Elizabeth Taylor's chart) it can often lead to sudden and abrupt desires and uncontrollable spur-of-the-moment trysts. In the impulsive and self-oriented sign Aries this means that partnerships can often be an individual's undoing, to the puzzlement and regret of their series of lovers.

	1	2	3	4	5	6	7	8	9
A	Day	S.Time	Sun	Moon	Mercury	Venus	Mars		
B	27	12:37	07 ♓ 17'	15 ♏ 35'	07 ♓ 27'	17 ♈ 09'	01 ♓ 34'	1932	taylor
C	9	10:55	16 ♍ 31'	19 ♋ 36'	05 ♎ 54'	05 ♎ 34'	18 ♊ 37'	1958	fisher
D	24	14:20	03 ♈ 14'	25 ♎ 23'	21 ♈ 43'	17 ♉ 01'	22 ♓ 02'	1958	taylor
E	10	8:56	17 ♌ 34'	10 ♊ 50'	11 ♌ 22'	28 ♌ 34'	00 ♊ 50'	1928	fisher

Fig.74. Matrix showing the natal planetary positions of Elizabeth Taylor and Eddie Fisher, together with their progressed planetary positions for the year 1958.

Eddie Fisher was someone whom Liz Taylor could rely on, someone who undoubtedly loved her and someone who would do the things Liz Taylor liked for her.

This relationship is not typical of those who share a natal-Sun – Venus trine, but it is illustrative of the downside of this type of trine. Trines are all about ease of action; they facilitate harmony because they cause 'energy' to flow unhindered. People are drawn together by trines, and depending on the content of their character, they can often be the catalyst for a wonderful relationship based on mutual understanding and shared vision. But for people who have everything, trines are a run-of-the-mill thing. Harmonious communication, intuitive understanding and natural compatibility are expected by millionaires whose employees are paid to act as if they are impressed by their employer's wit, looks and taste in clothes.

♈	♉	♊	♋	♌	♍	♎	♏	♐	♑	♒	♓
Aries	Taurus	Gemini	Cancer	Leo	Virgo	Libra	Scorpio	Sagittarius	Capricorn	Aquarius	Pisces

One astrologer notes that the Titanic sank, very efficiently and completely unhindered, under the influence of a trine.

Eddie Fisher and Liz Taylor had good emotional compatibility together. While oppositions make you feel like you're in love for the first time and you want to make love all day and all night, trines can sometimes make you feel like you've been in love for years and you want to knit pullovers or plant a beautiful garden. This couple had the remnants of a progressing-Sun progressing-Venus opposition, which was on the wane by the time they married. Its effect would have been nominal in 1959, the year of their marriage, and non-existent by 1962, the year their marriage ended.

In 1958, Fisher's progressed-Sun (C3) was making an aspect to Taylor's natal and progressed-Venus (B6 and D6).

His progressing-Sun (C3) casts a wide 150-degree inconjunct aspect to her natal-Venus (B6), which gives a servile quality to the combination of the two principles. He, it would appear, made many compromises in order to make Taylor happy, not least of which, according to him, was to divorce Debbie Reynolds. His progressing-Sun (C3) also casts a trine aspect to Elizabeth's progressed-Venus (D6). This had already passed exact, but was still in orb for a few years and is the single most significant astrological factor in their marriage. By 1970 it was over two degrees out of orb.

Stewart Granger was present in Rome when Elizabeth and Eddie's marriage ended. He sums up a crucial and mysterious trait in her personality, which *'emasculated the old lover while making the transition to someone new'* cviii

Elizabeth Taylor was in Rome to shoot the epic Cleopatra. Her co-star was Welsh actor Richard Burton.

It was New Years Eve 1961, actor John Valva and Richard Burton's wife Sybil threw a party at the Burton Villa near Rome. Burton and Taylor were laughing and smooching.

This was the first evidence that something was going on between Burton and Taylor. Eddie Fisher tried to get Elizabeth to leave early, but she

♈	♉	♊	♋	♌	♍	♎	♏	♐	♑	♒	♓
Aries	Taurus	Gemini	Cancer	Leo	Virgo	Libra	Scorpio	Sagittarius	Capricorn	Aquarius	Pisces

became offensive towards him in front of the other guests.

	1	2	3	4	5	6	7	8	9
A	Day	S.Time	Sun	Moon	Mercury	Venus	Mars		
B	27	12:37	07 ♓ 17'	15 ♏ 35'	07 ♓ 27'	17 ♈ 09'	01 ♓ 34'	1932	taylor
C	13	11:10	20 ♍ 25'	13 ♍ 34'	11 ♎ 49'	10 ♎ 30'	20 ♊ 44'	1962	fisher
D	28	14:36	07 ♈ 11'	23 ♐ 45'	24 ♈ 21'	21 ♉ 26'	25 ♓ 09'	1962	taylor
E	10	8:56	17 ♌ 34'	10 ♊ 50'	11 ♌ 22'	28 ♌ 34'	00 ♊ 50'	1928	fisher

Fig.75. Matrix showing the natal planetary positions of Elizabeth Taylor and Michael Wilding, together with their progressed planetary positions for the year 1962.

Eddie Fisher loved Elizabeth Taylor. Unfortunately for Eddie Fisher, in a few areas a Venus-Mars opposition can trump a Sun-Venus trine. Sex is one of these areas. Sun-Venus trines promote nurturing, protection, love and feelings of well-being. But when one of the partners is confrontational and

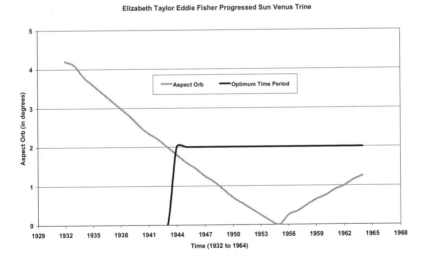

Elizabeth Taylor Eddie Fisher Progressed Sun Venus Trine

Fig.76. Graph showing the window of opportunity present in the Taylor Fisher relationship framed by a progressed-Sun progressed-Venus trine. In this case, its passage over the one-degree separation barrier happened the year that their marriage ended 1962

♈	♉	♊	♋	♌	♍	♎	♏	♐	♑	♒	♓
Aries	Taurus	Gemini	Cancer	Leo	Virgo	Libra	Scorpio	Sagittarius	Capricorn	Aquarius	Pisces

likes to fight with their lovers, oppositions are more appropriate. Elizabeth and Mike Todd would fight openly as part of their lovemaking. The connections she shared with Eddie Fisher, although conventionally more preferable, were useful to her only for a while.

Richard Burton

Richard Burton was born to act. His resonant voice, his stature, demeanour, love of poetry and literature and, it must also be added, his inherent lack of self-esteem, forced him onto the stage and from there to the infinitely more lucrative silver screen. He needed adulation, success and reward. His personality contained drama, romance and boldness, but it also contained a deeply ingrained self-loathing that was sometimes directed with venom, anger and spite at others, but this aggressive cynicism was often followed by a subsequent gesture of generosity and love. Burton, or Jenkins as he was known then, developed a taste for drink at an early age and drank alcohol almost every day for the rest of his life. He may have needed anything from mild stupor to outright inebriation to overcome his lack of inner confidence and as is the way with such a mixture of talent, self-doubt and alcoholic fuel, he wasted much of his career in pursuit of money and fame rather than harnessing the talent and letting the money and fame arrive (which was ostensibly the case with his rival Lord Olivier). He was one of those actors who was constantly in competition with others, and the benchmarks he used were both the gravity of his starring role in the picture (often measured by the gravitas of his co-stars in the picture) and the number of noughts on his paycheck. Bugger art, as it were... most of the time.

That said, to speak to anyone who witnessed his stage performances is to learn about a man who could captivate an audience, claim the stage like he was some emperor claiming a new land for his empire and leave the gathered throng in no doubt whatsoever that he was the greatest actor of his generation. When the three greatest actors of 20th-century British theatre,

♈	♉	♊	♋	♌	♍	♎	♏	♐	♑	♒	♓
Aries	Taurus	Gemini	Cancer	Leo	Virgo	Libra	Scorpio	Sagittarius	Capricorn	Aquarius	Pisces

Sir Ralph Richardson, Sir John Gielgud and Sir Laurence Olivier were gathered together on screen for their only appearance together, it was as supporting players to Richard Burton who played the title role in the TV epic *Wagner*.

Burton was good. The trouble with the Burton legacy was that his choice of film was not so good. He could recognise a potboiler a mile away, but he couldn't resist the paycheck at the end of the day.

Glance at the index of any book about Richard Burton and you will read a collection of unmemorable or forgotten films interspersed every once in a while with classics of the cinematic era. Misguided epics like *Alexander the Great, Cleopatra, Demetrius and the Gladiators* and *The Robe* and plain old awful films like *Hammersmith is Out, Exorcist II – The Heretic*, and *The Rains of Ranchipur*, rub shoulders with classics like *1984, Look Back in Anger, The Spy Who Came in From the Cold* and *Who's Afraid of Virginia Woolfe?* Burton regularly made mediocre films watchable.

He was also a very active lover whose pursuit of women was as legendary as the lengths he would go to to have them. He once took apart a Hollywood star's woodshed in order to sneak into her house and, while her husband slept upstairs, made love to her in front of an open fire in her living room.

He met his first wife Sybil Williams towards the end of 1948, they had similar backgrounds, both were brought up in Wales, and their marriage in February 1949 took place within months of their meeting.

During his marriage he had a number of affairs and two stand out in particular as being on record and undisputed. The first with actress Claire Bloom took place in 1953 and lasted for at least two years. The second with actress Susan Strasberg in 1955 was of shorter duration, but was perhaps as serious for a while. There were others including affairs with Dawn Addams during the making of *The Robe* and a reported dalliance with Jeans Simmons. All this time he held his marriage to Sybil in high regard and always returned to her. He was always careful to cover his tracks and

♈	♉	♊	♋	♌	♍	♎	♏	♐	♑	♒	♓
Aries	Taurus	Gemini	Cancer	Leo	Virgo	Libra	Scorpio	Sagittarius	Capricorn	Aquarius	Pisces

obtained the collusion of friends and family for his many affairs, their cooperation was guaranteed only because they did not wish to see Sybil hurt. She was well liked and popular with all of Burton's friends and family. She may have tolerated his behavior, knowing his desperate need for attention.cix

Richard Burton and Sybil Williams

	1	2	3	4	5	6	7	8	9
A	Day	S.Time	Sun	Moon	Mercury	Venus	Mars		
B	27	0:17	06 ♈ 19'	02 ♏ 11'	17 ♓ 15'	07 ♉ 54'	06 ♋ 43'	1929	williams
C	3	19:17	10 ♐ 55'	17 ♋ 44'	26 ♐ 57'	28 ♑ 02'	13 ♏ 23'	1948	burton
D	15	1:32	25 ♈ 01'	10 ♋ 40'	22 ♈ 36'	02 ♉ 49'	15 ♋ 37'	1948	williams
E	10	17:46	17 ♏ 40'	09 ♍ 13'	06 ♐ 48'	04 ♑ 02'	28 ♎ 01'	1925	burton

Fig.77. Matrix showing the natal planetary positions of Richard Burton and Sybil Williams, together with their progressed planetary positions for the year 1948. A wide natal-Venus (E6) natal-Mars (B7) opposition is joined in 1948 by an applying progressed-Venus (D6) natal-Venus (E6) trine.

Claire Bloom is said to have been cool about Richard Burton and when she discovered he was to play Hamlet to her Ophelia, she made a comment that somehow got back to Richard. She referred to him as *'that uncouth actor'*.

Burton's reputed response was one of quiet Scorpionic resolve:

'I'll make her pay... I'll have her, whichever way I like.'

And he did. For several years from the summer of 1953 Burton was close to Bloom. She, it is reported, fell deeply in love with Burton and would do anything for him. They first met in 1949 and, according to their progressed synastry, the progressed-Venus conjunction (C6 –D6) that was most likely to have been the attracting factor in their relationship, was much closer to exact in the 1940s than when their affair started, in 1953. It was, however, still within our 2-degree limit in 1953 and separated beyond that in 1956.

♈	♉	♊	♋	♌	♍	♎	♏	♐	♑	♒	♓
Aries	Taurus	Gemini	Cancer	Leo	Virgo	Libra	Scorpio	Sagittarius	Capricorn	Aquarius	Pisces

They were still seeing each other occasionally in 1957. In 1959 Claire Bloom married Rod Steiger.[cx]

Richard Burton and Claire Bloom

	1	2	3	4	5	6	7	8	9
			Sun	Moon	Mercury	Venus	Mars		
A	Day	S.Time	Sun	Moon	Mercury	Venus	Mars		
B	15	21:38	25 ≈ 51'	03 ≈ 24'	05 ≈ 43'	09 ♑ 32'	00 ♌ 17'	1931	bloom
C	8	19:37	16 ♐ 00'	17 ♏ 04'	23 ♐ 09'	02 ≈ 48'	16 ♏ 46'	1953	burton
D	9	23:04	17 ♓ 57'	26 ♏ 53'	12 ♓ 04'	04 ≈ 05'	27 ♋ 26'	1953	bloom
E	10	17:46	17 ♏ 40'	09 ♏ 13'	06 ♐ 48'	04 ♑ 02'	28 ♎ 01'	1925	burton

Fig.78. Matrix showing the natal planetary positions of Richard Burton and Claire Bloom, together with their progressed planetary positions for the year 1953.

Richard Burton and Susan Strasberg

Richard began an affair with Susan Strasberg while working in New York in 1957. His usual discretion was dropped in favor of having-a-good-time. He attended parties and restaurants with Susan and their relationship became somewhat obvious to many observers in New York at the time. When Sybil visited New York Richard reverted to his role as a devoted husband and Sybil seemed to support him, preferring to believe his side of the story. Susan, who was only nineteen at the time, thought Burton was just stalling and despite the fact that she saw him off at the airport, fully expected him to return to her. He, on the other hand, had told others that he was afraid she would throw a fit in front of photographers, had he brought their relationship to an end. He did not return, but Susan did visit him in London and it was there that she was given the news that her relationship was over. Some say Claire Bloom had to hide in Burton's bathroom when Susan visited him, but this tale is hallmarked 24 carat Burton anecdote, so facts might not actually be accurately reflected in this as much as his own sense of humour.

♈	♉	♊	♋	♌	♍	♎	♏	♐	♑	≈	♓
Aries	Taurus	Gemini	Cancer	Leo	Virgo	Libra	Scorpio	Sagittarius	Capricorn	Aquarius	Pisces

	1	2	3	4	5	6	7	8	9
A	Day	S.Time	Sun	Moon	Mercury	Venus	Mars		
B	22	7:28	00 ♊ 52'	02 ♓ 15'	05 ♉ 41'	27 ♊ 33'	19 ♊ 41'	1938	strasberg
C	12	19:53	20 ♐ 04'	08 ♏ 04'	17 ♐ 50'	06 ♒ 26'	19 ♏ 29'	1957	burton
D	10	8:43	19 ♊ 04'	23 ♏ 14'	04 ♊ 56'	20 ♋ 24'	02 ♋ 22'	1957	strasberg
E	10	17:46	17 ♏ 40'	09 ♍ 13'	06 ♐ 48'	04 ♑ 02'	28 ♎ 01'	1925	burton

Fig.79. Matrix showing the natal planetary positions of Richard Burton and Susan Strasberg, together with their progressed planetary positions for the year 1957.

The probable truth surrounding Burton and Strasberg's connective relationship is that they were sexually and physically suited, her natal-Venus was (B6) as receptive to his natal-Mars (E7) as anyone's could be, the trine aspect being present in Air signs. Their complimentarity was good, especially in the year in question, but with progressed-Venus (D6) and Mars (D7) both in cloying Cancer, compatible as they might have been to Burton's Capricorn Venus (E6) and Scorpio progressed-Mars (C7), they are unmanageable planets. Had he been a free agent this relationship would have been much more viable, as it was, he wasn't and it wasn't.[cxi]

Elizabeth Taylor and Richard Burton

The story of Elizabeth Taylor and Richard Burton is one of passion, desire and a Mars-Venus opposition that affected three marriages and created

	1	2	3	4	5	6	7	8	9
A	Day	S.Time	Sun	Moon	Mercury	Venus	Mars		
B	27	12:37	07 ♓ 17'	15 ♏ 35'	07 ♓ 27'	17 ♈ 09'	01 ♓ 34'	1932	taylor
C	17	20:12	25 ♐ 09'	20 ♑ 04'	12 ♐ 20'	10 ♒ 44'	22 ♏ 52'	1962	burton
D	28	14:36	07 ♈ 11'	23 ♐ 45'	24 ♈ 21'	21 ♉ 26'	25 ♓ 09'	1962	taylor
E	10	17:46	17 ♏ 40'	09 ♍ 13'	06 ♐ 48'	04 ♑ 02'	28 ♎ 01'	1925	burton

Fig.80. Matrix showing the natal planetary positions of Richard Burton and Elizabeth Taylor, together with their progressed planetary positions for the year 1962.

♈	♉	♊	♋	♌	♍	♎	♏	♐	♑	♒	♓
Aries	Taurus	Gemini	Cancer	Leo	Virgo	Libra	Scorpio	Sagittarius	Capricorn	Aquarius	Pisces

headlines all over the world for more than a decade.

Her progressing, feminine, Venus is embraced passionately by Burton's progressing, masculine, Mars.

In examining the psychological dynamics of their relationship – after it has begun – the Sun Moon opposition (B3-E4) and conjunction (E3-B4) are useful in delineating the way they were together. But like all natal placements, and particularly Sun Moon aspects, they define deep-rooted 'quanta' of the two personalities, essentially how they will blend with and react to each other. It can be said that the 'end is in the beginning': that the Taylor Sun – Burton Moon opposition would suggest a need for a certain element of role-reversal and as such would require a willingness on both sides to allow this to take place. A Sun-Saturn Scorpio like Burton (he has the Sun in the same place as Saturn in his birth chart) may have had some difficulty (maybe guilt) in accepting this arrangement even at secret, intimate moments. This Sun-Saturn conjunction is also in conjunction with Taylor's Moon, while she wished to be with him all the time and to tend to his needs, mop his brow and generally be his devoted wife, would also lead to an emotional power struggle and a conflict of his male ego versus her emotional nature.

So who needs any other astrological significators?

Well, in examining their progressed and natal planetary positions for 1962 we can see that Mars and Venus are already at work in this couple's day-for-a-year progressions. Taylor and Burton were hired in 1960 to film the epic *Cleopatra*, which took three years to film and literally employed a cast of thousands. Their first scenes together were in January 1962 and I have taken this date as the start date for their relationship. I don't have a date for their first kiss, and although the New Year's Eve party thrown by Valva and Sybil was obviously a precursor of things to come, Heymann suggests that Burton's conquest of Taylor took place in the third week of January 1962. Because this study is based upon the relatively slow-moving day-for-a-year progressions the exact date is not required. But the

♈	♉	♊	♋	♌	♍	♎	♏	♐	♑	♒	♓
Aries	Taurus	Gemini	Cancer	Leo	Virgo	Libra	Scorpio	Sagittarius	Capricorn	Aquarius	Pisces

	1	2	3	4	5	6	7	8	9
A	Day	S.Time	Sun	Moon	Mercury	Venus	Mars		
B	10	17:46	17 ♏ 40'	09 ♍ 13'	06 ♐ 48'	04 ♑ 02'	28 ♎ 01'	1925	burton
C	28	14:36	07 ♈ 11'	23 ♐ 45'	24 ♈ 21'	21 ♉ 26'	25 ♓ 09'	1962	taylor
D	17	20:12	25 ♐ 09'	20 ♑ 04'	12 ♐ 20'	10 ♒ 44'	22 ♏ 52'	1962	burton
E	27	12:37	07 ♓ 17'	15 ♏ 35'	07 ♓ 27'	17 ♈ 09'	01 ♓ 34'	1932	taylor
F	Day	S.Time	Sun	Moon	Mercury	Venus	Mars		
G	10	17:46	17 ♏ 40'	09 ♍ 13'	06 ♐ 48'	04 ♑ 02'	28 ♎ 01'	1925	burton
H	29	14:40	08 ♈ 11'	07 ♑ 25'	24 ♈ 42'	22 ♉ 32'	25 ♓ 56'	1963	taylor
I	18	20:16	26 ♐ 10'	04 ♒ 52'	11 ♐ 42'	11 ♒ 34'	23 ♏ 33'	1963	burton
J	27	12:37	07 ♓ 17'	15 ♏ 35'	07 ♓ 27'	17 ♈ 09'	01 ♓ 34'	1932	taylor
K	Day	S.Time	Sun	Moon	Mercury	Venus	Mars		
L	10	17:46	17 ♏ 40'	09 ♍ 13'	06 ♐ 48'	04 ♑ 02'	28 ♎ 01'	1925	burton
M	30	14:44	09 ♈ 10'	20 ♑ 41'	24 ♈ 56'	23 ♉ 37'	26 ♓ 43'	1964	taylor
N	19	20:20	27 ♐ 11'	19 ♒ 31'	11 ♐ 15'	12 ♒ 22'	24 ♏ 14'	1964	burton
O	27	12:37	07 ♓ 17'	15 ♏ 35'	07 ♓ 27'	17 ♈ 09'	01 ♓ 34'	1932	taylor
P	Day	S.Time	Sun	Moon	Mercury	Venus	Mars		
Q	10	17:46	17 ♏ 40'	09 ♍ 13'	06 ♐ 48'	04 ♑ 02'	28 ♎ 01'	1925	burton
R	31	14:47	10 ♈ 09'	03 ♒ 35'	25 ♈ 02'	24 ♉ 43'	27 ♓ 30'	1965	taylor
S	20	20:24	28 ♐ 12'	03 ♓ 58'	11 ♐ 00'	13 ♒ 10'	24 ♏ 55'	1965	burton
T	27	12:37	07 ♓ 17'	15 ♏ 35'	07 ♓ 27'	17 ♈ 09'	01 ♓ 34'	1932	taylor
U	Day	S.Time	Sun	Moon	Mercury	Venus	Mars		
V	10	17:46	17 ♏ 40'	09 ♍ 13'	06 ♐ 48'	04 ♑ 02'	28 ♎ 01'	1925	burton
W	1	14:51	11 ♈ 08'	16 ♒ 12'	25 ♈ 01'	25 ♉ 48'	28 ♓ 17'	1966	taylor
X	21	20:28	29 ♐ 13'	18 ♓ 08'	10 ♐ 54'	13 ♒ 56'	25 ♏ 36'	1966	burton
Y	27	12:37	07 ♓ 17'	15 ♏ 35'	07 ♓ 27'	17 ♈ 09'	01 ♓ 34'	1932	taylor
Z	Day	S.Time	Sun	Moon	Mercury	Venus	Mars		
AA	10	17:46	17 ♏ 40'	09 ♍ 13'	06 ♐ 48'	04 ♑ 02'	28 ♎ 01'	1925	burton
AB	2	14:55	12 ♈ 07'	28 ♒ 33'	24 ♈ 53'	26 ♉ 52'	29 ♓ 03'	1967	taylor
AC	22	20:32	00 ♑ 15'	02 ♈ 02'	10 ♐ 58'	14 ♒ 42'	26 ♏ 17'	1967	burton
AD	27	12:37	07 ♓ 17'	15 ♏ 35'	07 ♓ 27'	17 ♈ 09'	01 ♓ 34'	1932	taylor
AE	Day	S.Time	Sun	Moon	Mercury	Venus	Mars		
AF	10	17:46	17 ♏ 40'	09 ♍ 13'	06 ♐ 48'	04 ♑ 02'	28 ♎ 01'	1925	burton
AG	3	14:59	13 ♈ 07'	10 ♓ 43'	24 ♈ 38'	27 ♉ 57'	29 ♓ 50'	1968	taylor
AH	23	20:36	01 ♑ 16'	15 ♈ 37'	11 ♐ 12'	15 ♒ 27'	26 ♏ 58'	1968	burton
AI	27	12:37	07 ♓ 17'	15 ♏ 35'	07 ♓ 27'	17 ♈ 09'	01 ♓ 34'	1932	taylor

Fig.81. Matrix showing the natal planetary positions for Richard Burton and Elizabeth Taylor together with their progressed planetary positions for the years 1962 to 1968

following testimony suggests January is a safe bet:

Christopher Mankeiwicz remembers Burton striding briskly onto the set

♈	♉	♊	♋	♌	♍	♎	♏	♐	♑	♒	♓
Aries	Taurus	Gemini	Cancer	Leo	Virgo	Libra	Scorpio	Sagittarius	Capricorn	Aquarius	Pisces

one morning and informing a couple of dozen actors and crew members that he had made love to Elizabeth Taylor the night before in the back seat of his Cadillac.[cxii]

This is not the only piece of odd, or at least telling, behavior on record at the outset of their relationship. Eddie Fisher recalls a showdown with Burton where Burton insisted that Fisher didn't need Taylor as much as he (Burton) did because Eddie Fisher was already a big star, whereas Taylor would make Burton a big star. This odd, probably drunken, entreaty was perceived by Fisher to mean that Burton intended to use his affair with Elizabeth Taylor to increase his own level of stardom and inevitably his pricetag.

It is probably also true that Burton did not know at the time the extent to which Elizabeth Taylor could control her men and, believing he was in control, he may have underestimated his new partner's acquisitive nature. The Venus-Mars opposition is, however, important in their relationship.

Taylor's Venus, powerful in Taurus and Burton's Mars equally well placed in Scorpio are moving steadily to behold each other in a kind of medieval dance, as Venus begins to notice Mars, she becomes fascinated and they eye each other with interested half smiles and knowing glances. While the two actors' relationship is being watched by millions, they are beholding each other and marvelling in the sexuality of the moment, enraptured and transfixed. Their relationship became known in Italy, the scene of their first tryst, as Le Scandale.

It can be seen that this opposition is applying in 1962, becoming closer in 1963, closing in and at its most powerful in 1964 the year of their marriage and exact some time in 1965. From then on it separates and like any other couple who would experience such a powerfully passionate dynamic aspect, so do they. I imagine that – if the progression played the role it appears to have played at the time, between 1962 and 1972, when their relationship was strong – they must have hankered

♈	♉	♊	♋	♌	♍	♎	♏	♐	♑	♒	♓
Aries	Taurus	Gemini	Cancer	Leo	Virgo	Libra	Scorpio	Sagittarius	Capricorn	Aquarius	Pisces

	1	2	3	4	5	6	7	8	9
A	Day	S.Time	Sun	Moon	Mercury	Venus	Mars		
B	10	17:46	17 ♏ 40'	09 ♏ 13'	06 ♐ 48'	04 ♑ 02'	28 ♎ 01'	1925	burton
C	9	15:23	19 ♈ 01'	21 ♉ 57'	21 ♈ 21'	04 ♊ 17'	04 ♈ 30'	1974	taylor
D	29	21:00	07 ♑ 22'	02 ♋ 03'	14 ♐ 58'	19 ♒ 31'	01 ♐ 05'	1974	burton
E	27	12:37	07 ♓ 17'	15 ♏ 35'	07 ♓ 27'	17 ♈ 09'	01 ♓ 34'	1932	taylor

Fig.82. Matrix showing the natal planetary positions for Richard Burton and Elizabeth Taylor together with their progressed planetary positions for the year 1974.

after something that was lost and however hard they tried to recreate it, they would fail, as they did in 1975-76 when they re-married under a completely different set of auspices.

By 1974, the year of their divorce, their Venus – Mars opposition is now out of orb and has been replaced by other progressed aspects. Burton's Mars (D7) has progressed to a position where it exactly squares Taylor's Mars (E7) and her Mars (C7) has progressed to a position where it exactly squares his Venus (B6).

In conclusion it can be said that although there are factors that suggest a close personal relationship was possible between these two, the period their progressed-progressed opposition between Venus and Mars was in orb was the period that their relationship was most successful.

At the end both said they had worked hard to make their marriage work, but, astrologically, this is a misleading thing to say, like many relationships the brilliant beginning had provided enough incentive for them to work hard to preserve it.

In 1982 Richard said of their relationship:

'Elizabeth and I are like a pair of bookends. Other people may come between us but in the end the two of us are still there, **opposite** each other.'[cxiii] [my emphasis]

Here is a chart showing the event from the perspective of the orb of their

♈	♉	♊	♋	♌	♍	♎	♏	♐	♑	♒	♓
Aries	Taurus	Gemini	Cancer	Leo	Virgo	Libra	Scorpio	Sagittarius	Capricorn	Aquarius	Pisces

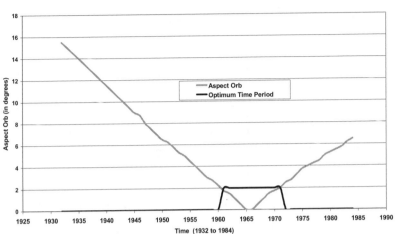

Fig.83. Graph showing the window of opportunity created by Elizabeth Taylor's progressing-Venus in opposition to Richard Burton's progressing-Mars 1962 to 1971

progressed-Venus-Mars opposition:

Two other notable relationships contained this progressed-Venus-Mars opposition across the sexual/sensual signs of Scorpio/Taurus. Lana Turner and Johnny Stomponato (who was accidentally killed by Lana's daughter Cheryl Crane) and the highly sexual relationship of DH Lawrence and Frieda Weekley (who is said to be the model upon whom Lawrence's character Lady Chatterley was based).

Richard Burton and Princess Elizabeth of Yugoslavia

On 17 October 1974, shortly after his divorce from Elizabeth Taylor, it was announced that Richard Burton had become engaged to Princess Elizabeth of Yugoslavia (the mother of actress Catherine Oxenberg). By February 1975, this relationship had run its course and Richard returned to his for-

♈	♉	♊	♋	♌	♍	♎	♏	♐	♑	♒	♓
Aries	Taurus	Gemini	Cancer	Leo	Virgo	Libra	Scorpio	Sagittarius	Capricorn	Aquarius	Pisces

mer wife Elizabeth Taylor.

Again Mars and Venus played an important role in Burton's relationship: the aspect is natal rather than progressed and this time it is a trine.

		1	2	3	4	5	6	7	8	9
A	Day		S.Time	Sun	Moon	Mercury	Venus	Mars		
B	10		17:46	17 ♏ 40'	09 ♍ 13'	06 ♐ 48'	04 ♑ 02'	28 ♎ 01'	1925	burton
C	16		3:36	25 ♉ 25'	25 ♓ 00'	13 ♊ 37'	13 ♉ 33'	02 ♊ 11'	1975	elizabeth y
D	30		21:04	08 ♑ 24'	14 ♋ 07'	15 ♐ 54'	20 ♒ 07'	01 ♐ 46'	1975	burton
E	7		1:02	17 ♈ 29'	23 ♎ 30'	14 ♈ 13'	25 ♓ 39'	04 ♉ 08'	1936	elizabeth y

Fig.84. Matrix showing the natal planetary positions for Richard Burton and Princess Elizabeth of Yugoslavia together with their progressed planetary positions for the year 1975.

Also on this occasion, it is Burton's Venus and Princess Elizabeth's Mars in aspect. At the end of their relationship she was said to be suffering somewhat poetically from a 'surfeit of Burton'. Their natal-Suns (B3 – E3) are in an exact Inconjunct and their progressing-Mars (C7 – D7) are opposed in 1975. Despite their physical attraction, their relationship was described at the time as volatile. The opposition of Mars in one person's chart to Mars in their partner's chart, you may recall, is described by Arroyo as ...*Very stimulating, very activating, but can you live with the other person?* And by the other astrologers as: *A clash of wills with both wishing to assert themselves in opposite ways at the same time or each may alternatively irritate the other.* Enough said, as they say.[cxiv]

Richard Burton and Sally Hay

Burton married on two more occasions, first to Susan Hunt, previously the wife of racing driver James Hunt. This marriage began to fail after six years, making way for his final marriage to Sally Hay, a film production assistant. Burton started to notice Sally in 1982 and although he saw her often on the set of *Wagner*, he did not get to know her until he spotted her

♈	♉	♊	♋	♌	♍	♎	♏	♐	♑	♒	♓
Aries	Taurus	Gemini	Cancer	Leo	Virgo	Libra	Scorpio	Sagittarius	Capricorn	Aquarius	Pisces

eating alone in a restaurant. They were introduced by Ron Berkeley who was also working on *Wagner*. They became close and were married in 1983. Burton died on 5 August 1984.

	1	2	3	4	5	6	7	8	9
A	Day	S.Time	Sun	Moon	Mercury	Venus	Mars		
B	10	17:46	17 ♏ 40'	09 ♍ 13'	06 ♐ 48'	04 ♑ 02'	28 ♎ 01'	1925	burton
C	25	22:17	05 ♓ 48'	16 ♍ 52'	24 ♒ 47'	16 ♈ 17'	24 ♌ 52'	1983	sally
D	7	21:35	16 ♑ 33'	19 ♎ 59'	25 ♐ 05'	24 ♒ 02'	07 ♐ 16'	1983	burton
E	21	19:59	00 ♒ 22'	24 ♉ 51'	11 ♒ 59'	04 ♓ 10'	06 ♍ 30'	1948	sally

Fig.85. Matrix showing the natal planetary positions for Richard Burton and Sally Hay together with their progressed planetary positions for the year 1983.

Again we find a progressed-Venus (D6) – Mars (C7) opposition that became exact in 1984, the year of Burton's death. This time, it is Richard's Venus progressing forward in Aquarius to oppose Sally's Mars in Leo that is moving backwards. Their embrace is passionate, but brief. It is exact in 1984.cxv

Elizabeth Taylor and John Warner

	1	2	3	4	5	6	7	8	9
A	Day	S.Time	Sun	Moon	Mercury	Venus	Mars		
B	27	12:37	07 ♓ 17'	15 ♏ 35'	07 ♓ 27'	17 ♈ 09'	01 ♓ 34'	1932	taylor
C	8	7:59	17 ♈ 56'	15 ♋ 17'	20 ♓ 19'	20 ♉ 23'	25 ♊ 12'	1976	warner
D	11	15:31	20 ♈ 59'	15 ♊ 56'	19 ♈ 51'	06 ♊ 22'	06 ♈ 03'	1976	taylor
E	18	4:45	29 ♒ 07'	22 ♍ 16'	14 ♓ 58'	20 ♓ 22'	28 ♉ 20'	1927	warner

Fig.86. Matrix showing the natal planetary positions for Elizabeth Taylor and Senator John Warner together with their progressed planetary positions for the year 1976

On paper, you might not expect a US Republican senator and the world's

♈	♉	♊	♋	♌	♍	♎	♏	♐	♑	♒	♓
Aries	Taurus	Gemini	Cancer	Leo	Virgo	Libra	Scorpio	Sagittarius	Capricorn	Aquarius	Pisces

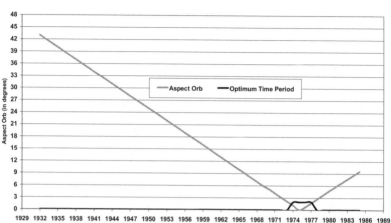

Elizabeth Taylor Senator John Warner natal Venus progressed Sun conjunction

Fig.87. The progressed-Sun natal-Venus conjunction that formed for John Warner and Elizabeth Taylor from 1974 to 1977 was 43 degrees from exact in 1932 the year Elizabeth Taylor was born

erstwhile no.1 AIDS campaigner to have much in common. You'd be wrong, but only partly wrong. In 1976 they had lots in common, including a progressing-Sun (C3) in conjunction with natal-Venus (B6). This was intense, current and relevant in 1976. As you have no doubt heard a week is a long time in politics, likewise a day for a year can be a long time in progressed astrology. Their window of opportunity symbolized by this conjunction opened around late 1974 and continued until about 1978, after this point the reason why they came together in the first place has changed and they have to find new common ground or split. They split in 1981 and divorced in 1982.

Elizabeth Taylor and George Hamilton

George Hamilton is a health conscious individual and he was a positive influence on Taylor during their six month romance in 1986. Their mutual

♈	♉	♊	♋	♌	♍	♎	♏	♐	♑	♒	♓
Aries	Taurus	Gemini	Cancer	Leo	Virgo	Libra	Scorpio	Sagittarius	Capricorn	Aquarius	Pisces

	1	2	3	4	5	6	7	8	9
A	Day	S.Time	Sun	Moon	Mercury	Venus	Mars		
B	12	5:10	18 ♌ 42'	08 ♋ 44'	15 ♌ 49'	11 ♌ 59'	24 ♑ 50'	1939	hamilton
C	21	16:10	00 ♉ 45'	03 ♏ 37'	14 ♈ 06'	16 ♊ 21'	13 ♈ 46'	1986	taylor
D	28	8:15	04 ♎ 17'	01 ♈ 14'	08 ♎ 51'	10 ♎ 19'	01 ♒ 38'	1986	hamilton
E	27	12:37	07 ♓ 17'	15 ♏ 35'	07 ♓ 27'	17 ♈ 09'	01 ♓ 34'	1932	Taylor

Fig.88. Matrix showing the natal planetary positions for Elizabeth Taylor and George Hamilton together with their progressed planetary positions for the year 1986

astrology for 1986 is textbook – a natal-Sun-Venus trine (B3 – E6) along with a natal-Venus progressed-Mars trine (B6 – C7) in fire signs. You would expect this relationship to involve mutual love and support with a passionate edge. For its short duration, all accounts concur that this is pretty close to the mark. It's worth contemplating that Liz Taylor always has some conventional Sun-Venus or Mars-Venus activity in her relationships. Here she has both. Is it that she has a refined eye for compatibility, or is it that the people who become close to her must overcome several obstacles including her wealth and fame to before they are actually considered? The former is obviously the case.

It may be of interest to note George Hamilton's marriage to Alana Stewart. The planetary dynamics are similar to those of his relationship with Liz Taylor – the natal-Sun-Venus trine (B3 – E6) is present in both relationships.

George Hamilton and Alana Stewart

	1	2	3	4	5	6	7	8	9
A	Day	S.Time	Sun	Moon	Mercury	Venus	Mars		
B	12	5:10	18 ♌ 42'	08 ♋ 44'	15 ♌ 49'	11 ♌ 59'	24 ♑ 50'	1939	hamilton
C	14	15:46	23 ♊ 27'	23 ♌ 14'	22 ♊ 07'	08 ♉ 09'	02 ♍ 32'	1972	alana
D	14	7:20	20 ♍ 36'	02 ♎ 37'	13 ♍ 14'	22 ♍ 53'	26 ♍ 53'	1972	hamilton
E	18	13:59	27 ♉ 34'	27 ♌ 36'	02 ♉ 53'	19 ♈ 47'	12 ♈ 18'	1945	alana

Fig.89. Matrix showing the natal planetary positions for George

♈	♉	♊	♋	♌	♍	♎	♏	♐	♑	♒	♓
Aries	Taurus	Gemini	Cancer	Leo	Virgo	Libra	Scorpio	Sagittarius	Capricorn	Aquarius	Pisces

Hamilton and Alana Stewart together with their progressed planetary positions for the year 1972

Elizabeth Taylor and Larry Fortensky

	1	2	3	4	5	6	7	8	9
	Day	S.Time	Sun	Moon	Mercury	Venus	Mars		
A	Day	S.Time	Sun	Moon	Mercury	Venus	Mars		
B	17	19:43	26 ♑ 19'	24 ♍ 10'	05 ♑ 33'	17 ♐ 40'	28 ♎ 48'	1952	fortensky
C	22	16:14	01 ♉ 44'	18 ♏ 52'	13 ♈ 54'	17 ♊ 19'	14 ♈ 32'	1987	taylor
D	21	22:01	01 ♈ 48'	07 ♑ 58'	01 ♈ 17'	00 ♒ 22'	12 ♏ 49'	1987	fortensky
E	27	12:37	07 ♓ 17'	15 ♏ 35'	07 ♓ 27'	17 ♈ 09'	01 ♓ 34'	1932	Taylor

Fig.90. Matrix showing the natal planetary positions for Elizabeth Taylor and Larry Fortensky together with their progressed planetary positions for the year 1987

Taylor met Larry Fortensky at the Betty Ford Clinic. They were at first considered to be a slightly odd couple, Taylor would wave Fortensky off to work in the morning (Fortensky was a construction worker) from their multi-million dollar home. Some say she packed his lunch for him. The ordinary life Fortensky did not wish to leave behind must have been interesting to Taylor, whose image as a cosseted MGM starlet is contradicted by those commentators who have known her and attest to her ability to adapt wholeheartedly and without complaint to any scenario.

	1	2	3	4	5	6	7	8	9
A	Day	S.Time	Sun	Moon	Mercury	Venus	Mars		
B	17	19:43	26 ♑ 19'	24 ♍ 10'	05 ♑ 33'	17 ♐ 40'	28 ♎ 48'	1952	fortensky
C	26	16:30	05 ♉ 37'	16 ♑ 45'	13 ♈ 55'	21 ♊ 04'	17 ♈ 35'	1991	taylor
D	25	22:17	05 ♈ 50'	07 ♓ 24'	08 ♈ 43'	05 ♒ 17'	14 ♏ 00'	1991	fortensky
E	27	12:37	07 ♓ 17'	15 ♏ 35'	07 ♓ 27'	17 ♈ 09'	01 ♓ 34'	1932	taylor

Fig.91. Matrix showing the natal planetary positions for Elizabeth Taylor and Larry Fortensky together with their progressed planetary positions for the year 1991

♈	♉	♊	♋	♌	♍	♎	♏	♐	♑	♒	♓
Aries	Taurus	Gemini	Cancer	Leo	Virgo	Libra	Scorpio	Sagittarius	Capricorn	Aquarius	Pisces

Their attraction is based upon a natal-Venus trine (B6 – E6), but their window of opportunity is formed by the progressing-Mars natal-Venus trine (C7 – B6) and was present for a couple of years. They married at Michael Jackson's Neverland ranch in 1991.

Fortensky and Taylor announced their separation in 1995.

♈	♉	♊	♋	♌	♍	♎	♏	♐	♑	♒	♓
Aries	Taurus	Gemini	Cancer	Leo	Virgo	Libra	Scorpio	Sagittarius	Capricorn	Aquarius	Pisces

Nine

Royal Relationships

To love is not to look at one another, But to look together in the same direction.
Antoine de Saint Exupery

Royal relationships last longer than most relationships purely because, like the relationships of politicians, marriage is a vital factor in public acceptance of individuals and institutions as a model by which society should live. The level of detectable conventional planetary synastry in a royal relationship does not depend entirely on the amount of freedom to choose of the parties involved, but there are examples of love matches in royal circles. Here are some interesting examples.

Arthur, Katherine and Henry

For a hundred years the royal houses of England and Spain were closely connected. Their connection is no longer close, but back in the days before the Reformation both were powerful Catholic kingdoms. King Henry VII, the man who vanquished Richard III at the battle of Bosworth Field, sought close ties with Spain and a marriage was negotiated between Henry's eldest son and heir, Prince Arthur, and the Spanish Infanta, Katherine of Aragon.

They were married in 1501, but a few months later the young Prince Arthur was dead.

With Arthur's death, the political marriage between Spain and England ended. This was in no one's interest and so a new alliance was decided upon which saw Katherine hastily betrothed to her dead husband's eleven-year-

♈	♉	♊	♋	♌	♍	♎	♏	♐	♑	♒	♓
Aries	Taurus	Gemini	Cancer	Leo	Virgo	Libra	Scorpio	Sagittarius	Capricorn	Aquarius	Pisces

old younger brother, the boy who was to become Henry VIII.

This marriage was only possible if Arthur and Katherine's short marriage had gone unconsummated. For the sake of politics, this was the story told by all those involved, including Katherine. Years later, Henry came to believe that his marriage was cursed, believing that to take his dead brother's wife was sinful and therefore the reason why he had not been delivered of a male heir by Katherine. He used this as a central argument to divorce Katherine and begin the English reformation, founding the Church of England in the process.

There is little doubt in my mind that Katherine and Arthur were, astrologically speaking, very compatible as marriage partners. Other royal arranged marriages in history have not been so notable, an example is the case of Louis XVI of France and his wife Marie Antionette who had to wait years before the King was able to consummate the marriage. This was probably not the case with Arthur and Katherine. A supremely sensuous natal-Sun-Venus trine (B3 – E6) is accompanied by two physically easy Mars-Venus trines and a progressed-Venus natal-Venus opposition, in their progressed charts for 1501. There is no reason why they would not be drawn to and in sympathy with each other's love and sex centres. There was certainly nothing astrological stopping them.

	1	2	3	4	5	6	7	8	9
			Sun	Moon	Mercury	Venus	Mars		
A	Day	S.Time							
B	29	12:32	06 ♎ 07'	03 ♋ 57'	23 ♎ 55'	23 ♌ 37'	22 ♊ 48'	1486	arthur
C	10	8:00	19 ♑ 52'	23 ♏ 13'	06 ♒ 58'	23 ♒ 54'	21 ♐ 37'	1501	katherine
D	14	13:31	20 ♎ 59'	15 ♑ 53'	14 ♏ 15'	11 ♍ 02'	27 ♊ 25'	1501	arthur
E	25	6:57	03 ♑ 34'	17 ♈ 32'	13 ♐ 39'	04 ♒ 13'	09 ♐ 57'	1485	katherine

Fig.92. Matrix showing the natal planetary positions for Prince Arthur and Katherine of Aragon together with their progressed planetary positions for the year 1501

Henry VIII and Katherine of Aragon

Prince Henry was the younger son of King Henry VII. Upon the death of

♈	♉	♊	♋	♌	♍	♎	♏	♐	♑	♒	♓
Aries	Taurus	Gemini	Cancer	Leo	Virgo	Libra	Scorpio	Sagittarius	Capricorn	Aquarius	Pisces

his brother Prince Arthur, he became heir to the throne of England. He was considered a devoutly religious young man who was destined for the church before becoming heir to the throne. His life story has been told many times, mainly because of consequences of his marital choices and the subsequent reformation of the church in England. Had he been blessed with a son from his marriage to Katherine of Aragon these events would not have taken place and perhaps the world would be a different place today. Where Prince Arthur and Katherine share a tender natural harmony in their Sun-Venus-Mars contacts, Henry and Katherine are less compatible. Although betrothed many years previously, by the time of their marriage in 1509 the couple were lacking in the natural synastry that Arthur and Katherine shared. On the horizon was an applying progressed-Sun (C3) natal-Venus (B6) trine, which would have sustained the first five years of the marriage; it is always useful in a relationship. (In fact, Henry and Katherine had been known to show great affection for each other publicly, and it should be noted that their natal-Venuses are in compatible positions.) But a separating progressed-Mars (D7) natal-Venus (E6) trine has already passed beyond the 2-degree demarcation point.

	1	2	3	4	5	6	7	8	9
	Day	S.Time	Sun	Moon	Mercury	Venus	Mars		
A									
B	7	3:44	14 ♋ 34'	10 ♈ 43'	06 ♌ 37'	00 ♊ 44'	26 ♍ 13'	1491	henry VIII
C	18	8:31	28 ♑ 01'	03 ♓ 32'	19 ♒ 35'	03 ♓ 40'	27 ♐ 30'	1509	katherine
D	25	4:55	01 ♌ 45'	24 ♏ 36'	28 ♌ 50'	20 ♊ 39'	06 ♎ 43'	1509	henry VIII
E	25	6:57	03 ♑ 34'	17 ♈ 32'	13 ♐ 39'	04 ♒ 13'	09 ♐ 57'	1485	katherine

Fig.93. Matrix showing the natal planetary positions for King Henry VIII and Katherine of Aragon together with their progressed planetary positions for the year 1509

After their progressed-Sun natal-Venus trine passed it was immediately replaced by a similar, though practically different progression. Katherine's Venus, progressing through Pisces started to form a trine aspect with Henry's natal-Sun. This, as we have seen already, is usually short lived,

♈	♉	♊	♋	♌	♍	♎	♏	♐	♑	♒	♓
Aries	Taurus	Gemini	Cancer	Leo	Virgo	Libra	Scorpio	Sagittarius	Capricorn	Aquarius	Pisces

almost always promising, but again never an aspect of certainty. As the progressed trine gained impetus in 1516 it entered within the two-degree window and a daughter was born, the future Queen Mary. By 1518 when the trine was exact, Katherine was again pregnant and the possibility that she was to deliver Henry of the male heir he so desired was at its most promising. Henry wrote to Cardinal Wolsey, his Archbishop and Lord Chancellor, that he was 'loath to repair to London,' as he wished to move her as little as possible during this pregnancy. This pregnancy was Katherine's last, at age 33 she gave birth to a stillborn son.

	1	2	3	4	5	6	7	8	9
A	Day	S.Time	Sun	Moon	Mercury	Venus	Mars		
B	7	3:44	14 ♋ 34'	10 ♈ 43'	06 ♌ 37'	00 ♊ 44'	26 ♍ 13'	1491	henry VIII
C	27	9:07	07 ♒ 09'	09 ♋ 49'	04 ♒ 34'	14 ♓ 34'	04 ♋ 11'	1518	katherine
D	3	5:31	10 ♌ 23'	06 ♈ 08'	03 ♍ 55'	00 ♋ 54'	12 ♎ 12'	1518	henry VIII
E	25	6:57	03 ♑ 34'	17 ♈ 32'	13 ♐ 39'	04 ♒ 13'	09 ♐ 57'	1485	katherine

Fig.94. Matrix showing the natal planetary positions for King Henry VIII and Katherine of Aragon together with their progressed planetary positions for the year 1518

After 1518, and the separation of this 'Cinderella' Sun-Venus trine aspect, their relationship began to suffer. One of Henry's mistresses gave birth to a son whom Henry titled the Duke of Richmond. It was clear therefore (to him) that although he could produce sons, his wife Katherine could not.

The events that led to the English reformation began in 1526, when Henry fell in love with Anne Boleyn. By now Henry's relationship with Katherine had become distant. He believed that a passage in the bible (Leviticus XX, 21) 'If a man shall take his brother's wife it is an unclean thing... they shall be childless', referred somehow to his lack of a male heir. Although Katherine had denied that her marriage with Arthur had been consummated, Henry believed that it had. He therefore sought a divorce and a chain of events was set in motion that has been told many times.

What has not been noted was the progressed synastry of Henry and

♈	♉	♊	♋	♌	♍	♎	♏	♐	♑	♒	♓
Aries	Taurus	Gemini	Cancer	Leo	Virgo	Libra	Scorpio	Sagittarius	Capricorn	Aquarius	Pisces

Katherine in the 1520s. Their remoteness after seventeen years of marriage is probably due to a progressed-Venus progressed-Mars opposition (D6 – C7). Although this aspect can and does arouse passion between lovers, it is more dependent upon the state of their relationship than any other aspect. Oppositions do not just attract, they also vie, challenge and compete. Such is the case here.

	1	2	3	4	5	6	7	8	9
	Day	S.Time	Sun	Moon	Mercury	Venus	Mars		
A	7	3:44	14 ♋ 34'	10 ♈ 43'	06 ♌ 37'	00 ♊ 44'	26 ♍ 13'	1491	henry VIII
B	4	9:39	15 ♒ 16'	25 ♎ 26'	18 ♒ 43'	24 ♓ 10'	10 ♑ 09'	1526	katherine
C	11	6:02	18 ♌ 04'	14 ♋ 02'	03 ♍ 02'	10 ♋ 08'	17 ♎ 13'	1526	henry VIII
D	25	6:57	03 ♑ 34'	17 ♈ 32'	13 ♐ 39'	04 ♒ 13'	09 ♐ 57'	1485	katherine

Fig.95. Matrix showing the natal planetary positions for King Henry VIII and Katherine of Aragon together with their progressed planetary positions for the year 1526

We find in 1526 that Henry's Venus (his relationship planet), is exactly opposed to Katherine's Mars (the planet of her assertiveness). Katherine did assert her opposition to the divorce and so did her family. The end of the Roman Catholic domination of the English Christian church can quite easily be seen in this opposition. Cancer, the sign of Henry's Venus is self-protecting and wants a child, Capricorn the sign of Katherine's Mars is traditional, authoritative and through its relationship with the planet Saturn it is associated with the 'old order' or the 'established authority'.

Henry VIII and Anne of Cleves

Of Henry's other five wives we only have a date of birth for Anne of Cleves, his fourth wife, and the one he was least attracted to. Anne was the most fortunate of the wives of Henry in that he married her for political reasons, then, with her cooperation, they quietly divorced. Henry allowed Anne to live in peace in the English countryside with many houses and a substantial income.

♈	♉	♊	♋	♌	♍	♎	♏	♐	♑	♒	♓
Aries	Taurus	Gemini	Cancer	Leo	Virgo	Libra	Scorpio	Sagittarius	Capricorn	Aquarius	Pisces

It is said that Henry's ambassadors had combed the aristocratic houses of Europe for an eligible marriage partner for Henry, but his reputation had preceded him. One royal princess said that if she had two heads the marriage might work out, but as she had only one, she would have to decline. Henry wanted to marry a Catholic princess, his reformation had changed supreme authority of the Church in England, in that it now lay with the King rather than the pope, but England had not embraced the Lutheran Protestantism of Northern Europe.

The King had been looking for a wife since the death of his favorite wife, Jane Seymour. She had died in childbirth in 1537 giving Henry his only son, the future King Edward VI. Henry had not mourned for long, but marriage negotiations took time, exacerpated by his reputation; one of the reasons why it took until December 1539 for Anne of Cleves to arrive in England.

Henry's only caveat to his ambassadors was that his next wife must be attractive and he would not allow any approach until he had approved of their looks. The marriage was arranged by the ill-fated Thomas Cromwell, who, anxious to secure a protestant bride for Henry, informed him of Anne's beauty and showed him a painting by Hans Holbein from which Henry agreed to the marriage. Upon meeting her in the flesh, however, Henry was not pleased. He did not find Anne in the least bit attractive, but 'went through the motions' for the sake of politics. He is said to have described Anne as the 'Flanders mare'. On his wedding day, Henry commented solemnly to Thomas Cromwell:

> 'My Lord, if it were not to satisfy the world, and My Realm, I would not do that I must do this day for none earthly thing.'

Their marriage remained unconsummated, and although Henry was repulsed by Anne, he did not wish her harm. Their marriage ended in May 1540 and was annulled without objection by Anne. This annulment was quite legal, as Anne had been engaged to a French duke some years before

♈	♉	♊	♋	♌	♍	♎	♏	♐	♑	♒	♓
Aries	Taurus	Gemini	Cancer	Leo	Virgo	Libra	Scorpio	Sagittarius	Capricorn	Aquarius	Pisces

and their engagement has not been annulled in the correct administrative manner. Anne was accorded a high rank in the English court, three thousand pounds a year and estates which included Anne Boleyn's childhood home, Hever Castle in Kent. She was to be known as the King's 'good sister'.

They were married in January 1540, a time when Anne's progressing-Venus (C6) was exactly 90 degrees from Henry's natal-Sun (B3). This is an extreme example of the type of progressed-Venus square that keeps a couple from appreciating each other. Indeed Anne was said to have commented later that she believed herself to be more attractive than Katherine Parr, Henry's sixth wife. So once more we witness the mystery of human attraction: it's not what you look like, but whether you resonate.

	1	2	3	4	5	6	7	8	9
	Day	S.Time	Sun	Moon	Mercury	Venus	Mars		
A									
B	7	3:44	14 ♋ 34'	10 ♈ 43'	06 ♌ 37'	00 ♊ 44'	26 ♍ 13'	1491	henry VIII
C	27	14:18	02 ♏ 57'	05 ♓ 22'	20 ♎ 02'	14 ♎ 30'	18 ♎ 06'	1540	cleves
D	25	6:57	01 ♍ 35'	17 ♍ 53'	22 ♌ 14'	26 ♋ 35'	26 ♎ 15'	1540	henry VIII
E	2	12:40	08 ♎ 04'	02 ♈ 09'	01 ♎ 33'	13 ♍ 26'	01 ♎ 38'	1515	cleves

Fig.96. Matrix showing the natal planetary positions for King Henry VIII and Anne of Cleves together with their progressed planetary positions for the year 1540

It should be noted that Henry's Venus is in good aspect to Anne's Mars, but this physical aspect is evidently not enough for Henry and I haven't found that this natal trine is as convincingly prevalent in the 1300 relationships as the progressed versions of the same aspect. The friendly sextile between Henry's natal-Sun (B3) and Anne's natal-Venus (E6) promotes brother-sister communication rather than grand passion. Anne's Sun opposes Henry's Moon: in modern times this aspect is not such a bad thing, but for a headstrong king like Henry it would have created an untenable relation-ship: Anne would have been too directorial for him and their roles would have conflicted with the social mores of Tudor times. Anne's Moon is not

♈	♉	♊	♋	♌	♍	♎	♏	♐	♑	♒	♓
Aries	Taurus	Gemini	Cancer	Leo	Virgo	Libra	Scorpio	Sagittarius	Capricorn	Aquarius	Pisces

well placed for Henry's Sun and as such the decision to separate was undoubtedly good for both parties.

King Henri II of France with Diane de Poitiers and Catherine de Medici

Henri of France and Catherine de Medici were just fourteen years old when they married on 28 October 1533 (OS). This political marriage is a useful example of astrology at work simply because Henri did not love Catherine, but was destined to marry her, yet his true love, Diane de Poitiers, a woman twenty years older than Henri, remained in his life and they carried on their affair despite the presence of Catherine in the French court.

Henri d'Orleans, second son of King Francis I, was destined to become Dauphin and then King of France after his elder brother Francis died. He was married to Catherine, who is described by some commentators as unattractive, by an arrangement between King Francis and Pope Clement VII, Catherine's relative and de-facto guardian.

Diane, the widow of the Grand Seneschal of Normandy, Louis de Breze, however, is acknowledged as a woman of great beauty. Her relationship with Henri supposedly began soon after the death of her husband in 1533.

It is said that Diane took a keen interest in politics and the governance of France and as such made sure that the King visited Catherine regularly (usually returning to Diane's bed the same evening after performing his 'royal duties').

Henri and Catherine therefore had a large family (ten children between 1544 and 1556), but Henri's loyalty, love and devotion was to Diane, who was said to have remained beautiful well into her fifties. Diane became the mother of one of Henri's children.

Such was Diane's influence over Henri that she often signed official documents for him using the cipher HenriDiane. Their initials formed a monogram that was officially recognised; inscribed even upon the palace doorknobs.

♈	♉	♊	♋	♌	♍	♎	♏	♐	♑	♒	♓
Aries	Taurus	Gemini	Cancer	Leo	Virgo	Libra	Scorpio	Sagittarius	Capricorn	Aquarius	Pisces

In 1533, the year of Henri and Catherine's marriage, a progressed-Venus natal-Venus conjunction is evident. Fatalists might suggests that this is suggestive of the nature of their marriage, Venus intertwined at the outset, but never truly present thereafter. On the other hand, Diane and Henri share a very close natal-Sun-Venus trine often found in idealistic unions, together with a progressed-Sun, natal-Venus opposition that spanned the years 1531 to 1536, exact in 1533.

Michel de Nostradame famously predicted the demise of Henri II in a joust. This prophecy was fulfilled in 1559, and from this point onwards Catherine came into her own, she banished Diane from court and purloined one of her homes. Three of Catherine's children occupied the French throne in succession and her daughter married the King of Spain. Her years spent in abeisance had given her time to study, plot and prepare for the power of her children, all of whom, however, died without heirs. Catherine outlived all but two of her ten children.

It is in cases like this where we see the mistress versus the wife that we can glimpse how astrology relates to compatibility in individual cases. Henri loved Diane, but could not marry her. He could, however, stay with her, protect her and love her while being married to his wife because he was King and had such power. Had he had ultimate choice, it is certain that he would have chosen Diane over Catherine.

Henri II of France and Catherine de Medici

	1	2	3	4	5	6	7	8	9
A	Day	S.Time	Sun	Moon	Mercury	Venus	Mars		
B	10	20:02	19 ♈ 12'	29 ♈ 01'	21 ♓ 46'	22 ♈ 35'	12 ♋ 09'	1519	henri II
C	7	19:59	15 ♉ 21'	22 ♈ 33'	01 ♉ 02'	25 ♉ 47'	25 ♋ 49'	1533	catherine
D	24	20:57	02 ♉ 51'	24 ♎ 12'	09 ♈ 06'	09 ♉ 52'	19 ♋ 05'	1533	henri II
E	23	19:04	01 ♉ 48'	10 ♎ 43'	07 ♈ 31'	08 ♉ 33'	18 ♋ 32'	1519	catherine

Fig.97. Matrix showing the natal planetary positions for King Henri II of France and Catherine de Medici together with their progressed planetary positions for the year 1533

♈	♉	♊	♋	♌	♍	♎	♏	♐	♑	♒	♓
Aries	Taurus	Gemini	Cancer	Leo	Virgo	Libra	Scorpio	Sagittarius	Capricorn	Aquarius	Pisces

Henri II of France and Diane de Poitiers

	1	2	3	4	5	6	7	8	9
A	Day	S.Time	Sun	Moon	Mercury	Venus	Mars		
B	10	20:02	19 ♈ 12'	29 ♈ 01'	21 ♓ 46'	22 ♈ 35'	12 ♋ 09'	1519	henri II
C	17	13:42	23 ♎ 50'	12 ♐ 34'	16 ♏ 52'	01 ♎ 57'	02 ♈ 02'	1534	poitiers
D	25	21:01	03 ♉ 49'	06 ♏ 59'	10 ♈ 36'	11 ♉ 06'	19 ♋ 35'	1534	henri II
E	12	11:24	19 ♍ 16'	23 ♌ 33'	24 ♍ 15'	18 ♌ 55'	11 ♈ 31'	1499	poitiers

Fig.98. Matrix showing the natal planetary positions for King Henri II of France and Diane de Poitiers together with their progressed planetary positions for the year 1534

Queen Victoria and Prince Albert

Victoria first met Albert in 1836 and she doesn't appear to have been that impressed at first. It's only when their progressing-Sun-Venus trine (C3 – D6) starts to become closer, and on their next meeting in 1839 that she falls deeply in love with him. This trine is at its strongest between 1836 and 1845. They married in 1840. This aspect is the same as that shared by Charles and Camilla.

	1	2	3	4	5	6	7	8	9
A	Day	S.Time	Sun	Moon	Mercury	Venus	Mars		
B	24	20:20	02 ♊ 07'	03 ♊ 42'	08 ♉ 56'	26 ♈ 35'	17 ♈ 40'	1819	victoria
C	15	4:49	21 ♍ 30'	03 ♌ 50'	08 ♍ 06'	14 ♍ 58'	05 ♋ 28'	1839	albert
D	13	21:39	21 ♊ 15'	28 ♒ 19'	01 ♊ 56'	20 ♉ 18'	02 ♉ 34'	1839	victoria
E	26	3:30	02 ♍ 05'	02 ♏ 26'	21 ♍ 53'	20 ♌ 11'	23 ♊ 27'	1819	albert

Fig.98a. Matrix showing the natal planetary positions for Queen Victoria and Prince Albert together with their progressed planetary positions for the year 1839

♈	♉	♊	♋	♌	♍	♎	♏	♐	♑	♒	♓
Aries	Taurus	Gemini	Cancer	Leo	Virgo	Libra	Scorpio	Sagittarius	Capricorn	Aquarius	Pisces

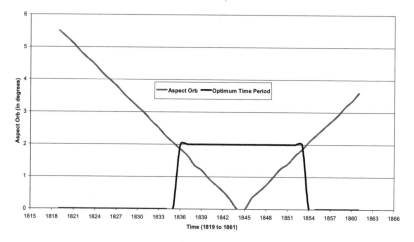

Fig.99. Graph showing the window of opportunity created by Queen Victoria's progressing-Venus in trine to Prince Albert's progressing-Venus 1836 to 1853

King George VI and Queen Elizabeth the Queen Mother

King George, then the Duke of York, first met the grown-up Elizabeth Bowes-Lyon in 1920. They had known each other as children, but their first meeting in adult life took place in either June or August of 1920. They were certainly together at Drummond Castle in Scotland on 14 August 1920.

The story goes that the young Elizabeth Bowes-Lyon initially rejected the advances of the man who was to become Britain's wartime King, but finally gave into him in 1923. She was a social creature and the duties associated with royal family life did not appeal. Despite this she consented at last to marry the Duke of York, who had been a persistent suitor. An examination of their progressed synastry shows us why. His progressing-Sun is opposite her progressing-Venus. This pattern can emerge quite quickly and relatively unexpectedly, but because of the motion of the Sun and Venus it can often remain close to exactness for a while. In any event

♈	♉	♊	♋	♌	♍	♎	♏	♐	♑	♒	♓
Aries	Taurus	Gemini	Cancer	Leo	Virgo	Libra	Scorpio	Sagittarius	Capricorn	Aquarius	Pisces

Sun-Venus oppositions cause attraction and fascination and here the roles are both conventional and apt.

Their natal-Venuses (B6 – E6) are also just over two degrees from an exact trine.

	1	2	3	4	5	6	7	8	9
A	Day	S.Time	Sun	Moon	Mercury	Venus	Mars		
B	4	21:18	11 ♌ 09'	14 ♏ 46'	06 ♌ 40'	07 ♋ 57'	25 ♊ 59'	1900	elizabeth
C	11	10:25	20 ♑ 26'	04 ♐ 46'	03 ♒ 24'	07 ♐ 44'	21 ♐ 20'	1923	george VI
D	27	22:49	03 ♍ 15'	23 ♍ 42'	17 ♌ 22'	19 ♋ 23'	11 ♋ 02'	1923	elizabeth
E	14	8:35	21 ♐ 54'	24 ♏ 51'	18 ♐ 14'	05 ♏ 45'	01 ♐ 21'	1895	george VI

Fig.100. Matrix showing the natal planetary positions for George, Duke of York (Later King George VI) and Elizabeth Bowes-Lyon (later Queen Elizabeth the Queen Mother) together with their progressed planetary positions for the year 1923

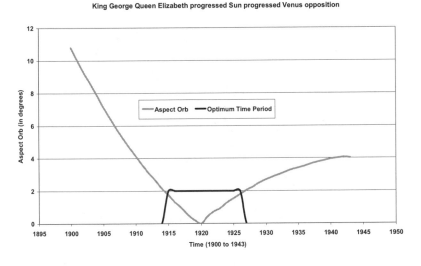

Fig.101. Graph showing the window of opportunity created by George Duke of York's (later King George VI) progressing-Sun in opposition to Elizabeth Bowes-Lyon's (later Queen Elizabeth the Queen Mother) progressing-Venus 1915 to 1927

♈	♉	♊	♋	♌	♍	♎	♏	♐	♑	♒	♓
Aries	Taurus	Gemini	Cancer	Leo	Virgo	Libra	Scorpio	Sagittarius	Capricorn	Aquarius	Pisces

The Duke and Duchess of Windsor

This is one of the great progressed synastry relationships: an exact progressed-Sun-Venus conjunction in the mid 1930s that precipitated a national crisis.

A not unrelated relationship to the previous one, instead we find that the relationship of Edward and Wallis was begun by a conjunction of the same planets rather than an opposition. The crown of England was affected by this relationship and Wallis Simpson's attraction for the future King Edward VIII was the reason he eventually abdicated. Love is a very powerful thing.

This aspect was over ten degrees apart in 1896, when Wallis Warfield was born; its steady progress over the years brought it closer to perfection. It eventually achieved exactness in 1934, the year these two became 'exclusive' partners.

They met in 1931 and married in 1937, soon after Edward had abdicated the British throne. The King was given the title Duke of Windsor, and although Wallis became the Duchess of Windsor, she was never given the title of Her Royal Highness, something of a contentious issue for years to come between the Duke and his brother, the new King George VI.

	1	2	3	4	5	6	7	8	9
A	Day	S.Time	Sun	Moon	Mercury	Venus	Mars		
B	23	16:03	02 ♋ 20'	03 ♓ 52'	27 ♋ 36'	23 ♉ 16'	00 ♈ 23'	1894	edward
C	24	23:43	02 ♌ 37'	07 ♒ 27'	25 ♋ 06'	06 ♌ 56'	16 ♉ 03'	1931	wallis
D	30	18:29	07 ♌ 39'	14 ♋ 45'	23 ♋ 34'	06 ♋ 41'	21 ♈ 44'	1931	edward
E	19	21:25	29 ♊ 14'	21 ♎ 15'	16 ♊ 04'	23 ♊ 54'	21 ♈ 42'	1896	wallis
F	Day	S.Time	Sun	Moon	Mercury	Venus	Mars		
G	23	16:03	02 ♋ 20'	03 ♓ 52'	27 ♋ 36'	23 ♉ 16'	00 ♈ 23'	1894	edward
H	27	23:55	05 ♌ 29'	14 ♓ 45'	01 ♌ 24'	10 ♌ 38'	18 ♉ 02'	1934	wallis
I	2	18:40	10 ♌ 31'	00 ♍ 14'	23 ♋ 51'	10 ♋ 16'	23 ♈ 11'	1934	edward
J	19	21:25	29 ♊ 14'	21 ♎ 15'	16 ♊ 04'	23 ♊ 54'	21 ♈ 42'	1896	wallis
K	Day	S.Time	Sun	Moon	Mercury	Venus	Mars		
L	23	16:03	02 ♋ 20'	03 ♓ 52'	27 ♋ 36'	23 ♉ 16'	00 ♈ 23'	1894	edward
M	30	0:07	08 ♌ 21'	20 ♈ 32'	07 ♌ 42'	14 ♌ 20'	19 ♉ 59'	1937	wallis
N	5	18:52	13 ♌ 23'	13 ♎ 03'	25 ♋ 06'	13 ♋ 52'	24 ♈ 35'	1937	edward
O	19	21:25	29 ♊ 14'	21 ♎ 15'	16 ♊ 04'	23 ♊ 54'	21 ♈ 42'	1896	wallis

Fig.102. Matrix showing the natal planetary positions for Edward,

♈	♉	♊	♋	♌	♍	♎	♏	♐	♑	♒	♓
Aries	Taurus	Gemini	Cancer	Leo	Virgo	Libra	Scorpio	Sagittarius	Capricorn	Aquarius	Pisces

Prince of Wales (later King Edward VIII and later still the Duke of Windsor) and Wallis Simpson together with their progressed planetary positions for the years 1931, 1934 and 1937

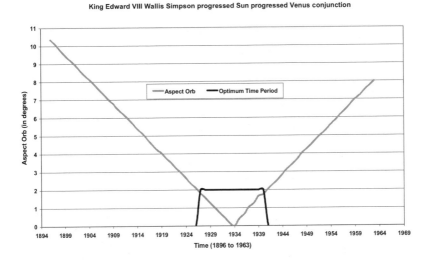

Fig.103. Graph showing the window of opportunity formed by Wallis Simpson's progressing-Venus in conjunction with Edward's progressing-Sun 1927 to 1940

Queen Elizabeth II and Prince Phillip

Her majesty the Queen began communicating with Phillip Mountbatten during the war when she was still a teenager and he a young naval officer in his twenties. Their friendship was encouraged and they eventually married in November 1947. As can be seen from their progressed synastry patterns for 1947, a trine from Phillip's progressing-Sun to HM's natal-Venus became exact shortly before this date.

♈	♉	♊	♋	♌	♍	♎	♏	♐	♑	♒	♓
Aries	Taurus	Gemini	Cancer	Leo	Virgo	Libra	Scorpio	Sagittarius	Capricorn	Aquarius	Pisces

	1	2	3	4	5	6	7	8	9
		Day	S.Time	Sun	Moon	Mercury	Venus	Mars	
A	Day	S.Time	Sun	Moon	Mercury	Venus	Mars		
B	21	15:33	00 ♉ 12'	12 ♌ 07'	04 ♈ 39'	13 ♓ 57'	20 ♒ 51'	1926	elizabeth2
C	6	14:42	14 ♋ 09'	02 ♌ 01'	16 ♋ 21'	28 ♉ 35'	11 ♋ 57'	1947	philip
D	12	16:56	20 ♉ 34'	22 ♉ 02'	27 ♈ 50'	05 ♈ 50'	06 ♓ 01'	1947	elizabeth2
E	10	13:00	19 ♊ 20'	22 ♌ 15'	13 ♋ 31'	05 ♉ 43'	24 ♊ 35'	1921	philip

Fig.104. Matrix showing the natal planetary positions for Princess Elizabeth (later Queen Elizabeth II) and Phillip Mountbatten (later Duke of Edinburgh) together with their progressed planetary positions for the year 1947

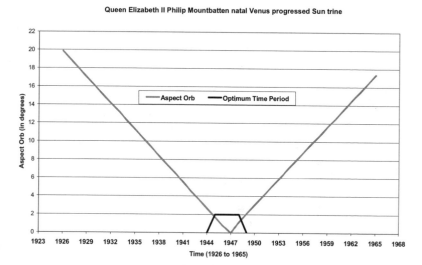

Queen Elizabeth II Philip Mountbatten natal Venus progressed Sun trine

Fig.105. Graph showing the window of opportunity created by Phillip Mountbatten's progressing-Sun in trine to Princess Elizabeth's natal-Venus 1945 to 1948

Princess Margaret and Anthony Armstrong-Jones (Lord Snowdon)

Too much of a good thing can be a problem, especially if it all comes at the start of a relationship.

The major aspects that occurred around the beginning of this

♈	♉	♊	♋	♌	♍	♎	♏	♐	♑	♒	♓
Aries	Taurus	Gemini	Cancer	Leo	Virgo	Libra	Scorpio	Sagittarius	Capricorn	Aquarius	Pisces

relationship include two Sun-Venus trines and a Sun-Venus opposition (all progressed – natal) together with a developing progressed-Venus – progressed-Mars trine.

The aspect that was a precursor to the relationship, and which probably plays the most obvious role is Snowdon's progressing-Venus (D6) in trine aspect to Margaret's natal-Sun (E3). This was applying to exact in 1959.

	1	2	3	4	5	6	7	8	9
A	Day	S.Time	Sun	Moon	Mercury	Venus	Mars		
B	7	17:11	15 ♓ 57'	04 ♊ 28'	25 ♒ 48'	22 ♓ 55'	22 ♒ 11'	1930	snowdon
C	19	20:14	26 ♍ 09'	19 ♌ 08'	00 ♎ 15'	12 ♏ 16'	13 ♋ 33'	1959	margaret
D	5	19:06	14 ♈ 44'	28 ♊ 52'	18 ♈ 44'	28 ♈ 56'	14 ♓ 52'	1959	snowdon
E	21	18:19	28 ♌ 01'	25 ♋ 14'	24 ♍ 55'	12 ♎ 56'	25 ♊ 46'	1930	margaret

Fig.106. Matrix showing the natal planetary positions for Princess Margaret and Anthony Armstrong-Jones (later Lord Snowdon) together with their progressed planetary positions for the year 1959

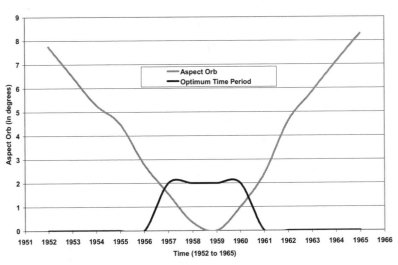

Princess Margaret Lord Snowdon natal Sun progressed Venus trine

Fig.107. Graph showing the window of opportunity created by Anthony Armstrong-Jones' progressing-Venus in trine to Princess Margaret's natal-Sun 1957 to 1960

♈	♉	♊	♋	♌	♍	♎	♏	♐	♑	♒	♓
Aries	Taurus	Gemini	Cancer	Leo	Virgo	Libra	Scorpio	Sagittarius	Capricorn	Aquarius	Pisces

Crown Prince Felipe of Spain and Letitzia Ortiz Rocasolano

Prince Felipe fell for this former news anchorwoman in 2003 and their relationship blossomed into an engagement. Letitzia became the first commoner in Spanish history in line to be Queen. She is also a divorcee.

	1	2	3	4	5	6	7	8	9
			Sun	Moon	Mercury	Venus	Mars		
A	Day	S.Time	**Sun**	Moon	Mercury	Venus	Mars		
B	30	20:35	09 ≈ 39'	19 ≈ 52'	28 ≈ 01'	04 ♑ 36'	16 ♓ 24'	1968	felipe
C	16	13:40	23 ♎ 13'	04 ≈ 16'	10 ♏ 35'	12 ♍ 54'	10 ♎ 03'	2003	ortiz
D	5	22:53	14 ♓ 59'	24 ♉ 26'	18 ≈ 56'	17 ≈ 36'	13 ♈ 12'	2003	felipe
E	15	11:38	22 ♍ 44'	19 ♐ 25'	18 ♍ 53'	07 ♌ 56'	20 ♍ 03'	1972	ortiz

Fig.108. Matrix showing the natal planetary positions for Crown Prince Felipe of Spain and Letitzia Ortiz Rocasolano together with their progressed planetary positions for the year 2003

This couple's primary synastry indicator is an applying Sun-Venus opposition that was present natally, but which has been playing catch-up since 1972. This progressed-Sun-Venus opposition will become closer and stronger over the next few years. Here is its position in 2005:

	1	2	3	4	5	6	7	8	9
A	Day	S.Time	**Sun**	Moon	Mercury	Venus	Mars		
B	30	20:35	09 ≈ 39'	19 ≈ 52'	28 ≈ 01'	04 ♑ 36'	16 ♓ 24'	1968	felipe
C	18	13:48	25 ♎ 12'	00 ♓ 26'	13 ♏ 29'	15 ♍ 15'	11 ♎ 21'	2005	ortiz
D	7	23:01	16 ♓ 59'	18 ♊ 12'	20 ≈ 13'	20 ≈ 03'	14 ♈ 43'	2005	felipe
E	15	11:38	22 ♍ 44'	19 ♐ 25'	18 ♍ 53'	07 ♌ 56'	20 ♍ 03'	1972	ortiz

Fig.109. Matrix showing the natal planetary positions for Crown Prince Felipe of Spain and Letitzia Ortiz Rocasolano together with their progressed planetary positions for the year 2005

For royalty, there are numerous extraneous constraints placed on relationships, as we have already noted in the case of Henri II of France and Diane de Poitiers. In the modern age, political interference and constitutional rules are the first obstacles, followed closely by protocol,

♈	♉	♊	♋	♌	♍	♎	♏	♐	♑	≈	♓
Aries	Taurus	Gemini	Cancer	Leo	Virgo	Libra	Scorpio	Sagittarius	Capricorn	Aquarius	Pisces

formality and psychological issues relating to self-knowledge. For example, it may be difficult, although by no means impossible, for anyone brought up to be *symbolically important* to have a true and equitable knowledge or sense of self, and this may be one of the most important factors in our ability to establish and form good, long-term relationships.

♈	♉	♊	♋	♌	♍	♎	♏	♐	♑	♒	♓
Aries	Taurus	Gemini	Cancer	Leo	Virgo	Libra	Scorpio	Sagittarius	Capricorn	Aquarius	Pisces

Ten

Love Vibrations

Try as we may to make a silence, we cannot.
John Cage

We are intrinsically bound up in a system of motion and change. We are trapped in time and of all the systems in which we live – some other examples of systems include socio-economic, ecological, cultural, legal and political – *time* is the most fundamental. It governs absolutely everything in our lives. We cannot escape from it, and all we can do is observe its passing: as humans it is the most significant thing in any of our lives. We realise that although the Earth is not the centre of the universe as was once believed, we can't help looking at it as if we are individually at its centre. This point of view is one of both personal and collective meaning: we each have a horoscope which develops at our personal rate, but we experience life collectively: sharing the system within which we live with 6 billion other entities (not including other animals) who also have a unique individual meaning described by their time and place of birth. How we interact with the other members of planet Earth depends on our horoscope/horoscopes. If astrology were simply a force that imprinted personality traits upon you, it would not logically follow that relationship astrology as it is practiced would be workable. It may be possible that Leos might appreciate the qualities of Sagittarian personalities, but that's not really how relationship astrology works in practice. It's not just about compatible personality traits: it's about mathematics, frequency, resonance, harmony and discord. It's about comparing the angles that planets form between separate birth charts. If astrology is supposed to work in a

♈	♉	♊	♋	♌	♍	♎	♏	♐	♑	♒	♓
Aries	Taurus	Gemini	Cancer	Leo	Virgo	Libra	Scorpio	Sagittarius	Capricorn	Aquarius	Pisces

physically causal way, then comparing birth charts mathematically is an abstract, and therefore a potentially unrealistic, idea. But there are models of the universe, into which astrology would fit quite happily.

Astrology is the study of correlations between the movements of the planets and life and events on Earth and is interpreted using a symbolic language. This language communicates information about who we are and where we are going. When we try to translate what astrology is and what astrological symbolism means, from its pure basis into the spoken or written word, we can use many words to define the individual elements of astrology. Astrological variables have lots of different, but congruent values. The ultimate purpose for an astrological language is to enable us to extract information about the significance and meaning of time. We do this by observing and applying meaning to the mathematical relationships of the local indicators of time – the Sun, Moon and planets.

There is a wide variety of dialects of the astrological language; each of them seeks to transmit the truth about the meaning of time. All languages are used and abused in a variety of different ways. Fairground fortune tellers who use astrology, if they are not the charlatans that many believe them to be, are merely singers of songs in the language of the stars: they use their knowledge of the language to hum you a tune and you pay them for it. The tune might make you feel good and its words might be meaningful. You will probably cross their palm with silver (or maybe it will be gold). There are others who use this language to write poetry, many do this in daily newspapers and magazines. They are paid to help you think positively and they are using a system of astrology (called mundane astrology) that when focused at individual targets (rather than a twelfth of the population) can yield tangible results. But these singers of songs and tellers of poetically positive stories are only doing to their language what pop stars and buskers do to the English, French, German, Italian, Spanish or Japanese languages. Remember that songs in any language can have meaning to some people and no meaning to others.

♈	♉	♊	♋	♌	♍	♎	♏	♐	♑	♒	♓
Aries	Taurus	Gemini	Cancer	Leo	Virgo	Libra	Scorpio	Sagittarius	Capricorn	Aquarius	Pisces

Carl Jung

It has been proposed that the key to astrology lies in archetypal symbols that are part and parcel of life on Earth and which the mind can intuitively recognise. For instance the psychologist Carl Jung saw astrology as the revelatory part of a connecting principle that operates at the level of the unconscious mind and which links everyone and everything. Rather than causing events, Jung's interpretation of astrology was basically that time itself has qualities that are linked to human life and events in the world. He called this idea *synchronicity*, observing that every moment in time has particular qualities and that events that take place in any given moment reflect these qualities. Jung described his idea of holistic interconnectivity as the *collective unconscious,* which in turn has been described by some as the DNA of the psyche. The collective unconscious can be envisaged as a system of underground (unconscious) networks and wires that connect human beings up on the (conscious) surface by different symbolic connectivity protocols (which are different depending on your psychological predisposition). Or, more simplistically, as a great sea that pervades all things, and we, like ships on this sea that float around on its surface, are free to chart our own course or be blown by the wind. We are connected to all the other ships in the world by the sea beneath our decks. Indeed in this model, the ships themselves have very deep hulls that stretch down into the depths, but our consciousness up on deck rarely goes down to these lower levels, except in our dreams, meditations and nightmares.

Assumptions and Misrepresentations

Many people misinterpret what astrology is on two broad levels. Some attempt to understand astrology by treating it as a literal science that is physically causal in nature. This approach is guaranteed to create a scenario that makes it easy to dismiss astrology as an early and unsuccessful attempt at understanding the relationship that we as humans have with the universe. It is therefore referred to perjoratively as a pseudoscience. In reality,

♈	♉	♊	♋	♌	♍	♎	♏	♐	♑	♒	♓
Aries	Taurus	Gemini	Cancer	Leo	Virgo	Libra	Scorpio	Sagittarius	Capricorn	Aquarius	Pisces

astrology is not regarded by many astrologers as a science, but as a much more fundamental subject that is closely related to our personal experience as human beings, rather than simply our clever ability to measure physical things. As Patrick Curry has remarked, modern science is naturally limited, by its very foundation, to be exactly what astrology is not.

> 'In any case, the very identity of modern science is founded, in part, on not being astrology; or rather, on being not-astrology. Why? Because in order for modern science and its programme of naturalism, mechanism and rationalism to succeed, the stars and planets - the source and object, ever since the Greek philosophers, of the most perfect truth available to human perception - had to be turned from spiritual and qualitatively distinct and unique agents, subjectivities, into fully 'natural', lifeless and quantitatively identical objects. (Note the change from an irreducibly plural pantheon to a single stuff.) So astrology had to be defeated, and for science it remains a heresy: embarrassing if not threatening, and those who still experience the heavens in the old way superstitious if not downright perverse.'[cxvi]

Ancient astronomers/astrologers regarded astrology as emanating from some kind of physical influence, although gravitation was unknown to the ancient and medieval astrologers and magnetism was not well understood, so the trend then was to attribute the effect either to an unknown force, or to a divine entity, (or both).[cxvii] The fact that the influence of early astrologers has pervaded astrology as far as structure and interpretation is concerned, makes it easy for literal minded thinkers to adopt the same standpoint, and with the benefit of recent developments in science, notably their ability to measure the forces of gravity, electromagnetism, and the two nuclear forces, which are regarded as the four fundamental forces of nature, they can reject the subject using the same literal criteria that the early astrologers *thought* they were dealing with: put simply they thought that the planets influence was causal, physical and literal. It is now clear that this is

♈	♉	♊	♋	♌	♍	♎	♏	♐	♑	♒	♓
Aries	Taurus	Gemini	Cancer	Leo	Virgo	Libra	Scorpio	Sagittarius	Capricorn	Aquarius	Pisces

not the case. Actually no astrologer, or anyone else for that matter, in the history of the subject, has ever been able to satisfactorily attribute any causal force or influence to astrology.

The Holographic Universe

A hologram is a three dimensional projected picture.

To make a hologram an object is first placed in front of a laser beam. Then a second laser beam is bounced off the reflected light of the first and the resulting interference pattern (the point where the two laser beams collide) is captured on film.

When the film is developed, it has no particular form. But as soon as another laser beam is aimed at the developed film a three-dimensional image of the original object appears.

The three-dimensionality of such images is not the only remarkable characteristic of holograms. If a hologram of an image is cut into two pieces and then illuminated by a laser, each piece will still be found to contain the entire image. In this sense a hologram does not behave in the same way as a photograph cut into two pieces. Whereas both of the fragments of the photograph would contain a jigsaw-piece of the picture, each half of the hologram would contain the whole of its original picture.

Indeed, even if the halves are divided again, each snippet of film will always be found to contain a smaller but intact version of the original image. Unlike normal photographs, every part of a hologram contains all the information possessed by the whole.

The theory that the universe is a giant hologram is founded upon the separate works of quantum physicist David Bohm and neurophysiologist Karl Pribram who developed the holonomic model of the brain. Working independently, they both concluded that the universe is a giant hologram, containing both matter and consciousness in a single field, created, at least in part, by the human mind. Pribram concluded that memory is not stored in cells in the brain, but in wave interference patterns. He has said that if

♈	♉	♊	♋	♌	♍	♎	♏	♐	♑	♒	♓
Aries	Taurus	Gemini	Cancer	Leo	Virgo	Libra	Scorpio	Sagittarius	Capricorn	Aquarius	Pisces

human psychological processes are quantum in nature, then this could explain spiritual experiences as these experiences parallel the descriptions of quantum physics. Bohm's concepts of order challenge the prevalent view that all things can be reduced to their constituent parts. Our notion of space and time (the 'reality' in which we live) is basically an abstraction that is derived from a deeper order (the universe is a giant hologram). The basic nature of reality in Bohm's model suggests that everything is interconnected at a deeper level and that the reality we perceive is not necessarily reflective of the true nature of the universe.

The nature of holograms is closely related to the concept of fractals in mathematics and, I believe, horoscopes. *As Above So Below* is just another way of saying 'what is in the universe or the macrocosm is mirrored in man, the microcosm'. This would be true if the universe were a giant hologram.

Multiverse

Victorian scholar Edwin Abbott published a book entitled *Flatland: A Romance in Many Dimensions*[cxviii] in 1884. This book is both a treatise on multi-dimensional space and a humorous allegory of life in Victorian England. The story is based in a world that exists in two dimensions (forwards and backwards); in Flatland there is no UP or DOWN. The inhabitants of Flatland are shaped differently; men are portrayed as polygons whose shape is directly proportional to their social status: the lower classes are triangles and the priestly classes are multi-sided polygons (circles represent perfection in Flatland). Women are not polygonal in Flatland, they are straight lines. The perception of 'Flatlanders' is that they only see their neighbour's plane: as there is no depth, everyone's perception is of straight lines (men) or points (women). Women are, however, required to sway from side to side when walking in Flatland!

The intrusion into Flatland of a three dimensional creature (a sphere, or after Carl Sagan, an apple), who spies a square and decides to introduce himself, is not understood by the square. He hears a voice, but the voice

♈	♉	♊	♋	♌	♍	♎	♏	♐	♑	♒	♓
Aries	Taurus	Gemini	Cancer	Leo	Virgo	Libra	Scorpio	Sagittarius	Capricorn	Aquarius	Pisces

sounds like it emanates from his own body. Madness perhaps? The square cannot look UP, so the three dimensional sphere descends into Flatland. It is only possible for a three dimensional creature to be perceived in Flatland in section or slice. The sphere would appear from nowhere, eventually becoming a wider slice of sphere until its equator is visible as a line.

The sphere is able to remove objects from locked containers; this is because in a theoretical 2D universe such as Flatland, all boxes would have sides, but no top or bottom. More interestingly, the sphere would be able to teleport 2D individuals via a third dimension without traversing space; it would do this by picking them 'UP', moving and then putting them back 'DOWN'. Of course, to the 2D perspective, this would be a process of dematerialization and re-appearance.

A number of commentators on this story have conjectured that if dimensions exist beyond the ones in which we live, (we apparently are three dimensional 'spatial' objects, existing in four dimensional time) then our perception of reality is limited. If we imagine time as a line and so therefore pretend it is one-dimensional we can attempt to understand the relationship of subsequent dimensions with time. Petr Ouspensky devoted a few pages of his book about the teachings of George Gurdjieff *In Search of the Miraculous* to this concept.

Gurdjieff simply stated that the fifth dimension being at right-angles to time crosses each point in time or 'stretches each moment of time into eternity', this suggests that every moment in time contains a finite number of choices for human beings dependent on the choices made at the previous point in time, it is therefore seen by some as a dimension of possibilities and is also a dimension where time as we know it does not exist. As it contains possibilities for the next moment in time, it is also a dimension containing the actualities of the previous moment. All of those possibilities that did not come to pass because of free choice remain unactualized and unactualizable. If human beings were simply three dimensional objects, existing in 'four dimensional time', then there would be no difference

♈	♉	♊	♋	♌	♍	♎	♏	♐	♑	♒	♓
Aries	Taurus	Gemini	Cancer	Leo	Virgo	Libra	Scorpio	Sagittarius	Capricorn	Aquarius	Pisces

between a human being and a rock or an apple or any other three dimensional object. The fact that human beings (and other animals for that matter) are capable of making choices suggests an 'extra' factor. Some people choose to label this extra factor the fifth dimension and in this analogy, the label suits. There is a small but significant implication here and it concerns logic. Logic, the essence of reductionist science, can be applied to three dimensional objects because their existence is predictable – the apple lacks the choice to fall from the tree and must wait for external factors to allow it to fall – most of the time this law does not apply to human beings unless they happen to be trapped inside a three dimensional object (like, say, an aeroplane whose engines have failed) where their options are limited by a previous choice (to board the plane). So, it appears arguable that most of the time human beings actually function within a fifth dimension made up of finite, but variable choices: fate is fan-shaped.

Physics tells us that the past is ordered and the future chaotic. Suggesting time can be envisaged as something like a zip fastener and that the past is 'zipped up'; the future is an open zipper.

Consciousness

The brain has been likened to a computer, wherein nerve cells act as simple switches. In a computer these switches are either 'on' or 'off', 'yes' or 'no'. There is no 'perhaps' or 'maybe' in this kind of model, suggesting that because there are no grey areas in computation, but there are in our experience of life, we don't actually have computer-like brains. Here again we find the contrast between human beings and three-dimensional logical objects. Our position in this scheme of dimensions appears to suggest that we are good at creating, understanding and maintaining logical processes (processes that are beneath us in dimensional terms), but when it comes to replicating intelligence artificially in our own image, we might be at a loss.

Professor Stuart Hameroff and Sir Roger Penrose have theorized that the brain does not process information in the way that modern physics

♈	♉	♊	♋	♌	♍	♎	♏	♐	♑	♒	♓
Aries	Taurus	Gemini	Cancer	Leo	Virgo	Libra	Scorpio	Sagittarius	Capricorn	Aquarius	Pisces

would suggest. Their theories suggest that microtubules in the brain process information related to consciousness like a quantum computer processes information, that is, instead of just being able to process 'yes' and 'no', a quantum computer can also process data that exists simultaneously as both 'yes' and 'no', with a numerical coefficient representing the probability for each state, this basically means a quantum computer can deal with 'grey areas'. Hameroff has also suggested that the information stored in the brain's microtubules can survive bodily death in an organised quantum state through a process known as quantum coherence. He is theorising that spirituality can be explained by the fact that our minds and our physical bodies operate according to different laws (quantum laws and physical laws respectively), which is closely related to Pribram and Bohm's holonomic model of the brain.[cxix] This is in line with the idea that the body is a three dimensional (logical) object, but the mind is a five dimensional (non-logical) thing.

The idea of the holographic universe suggests that the whole universe is connected at a deep and as yet inaccessible level: that the concepts of time and space as we understand them are not fundamental, they are merely there for our convenience as reference points, enabling us to experience life at this particular level of reality. The multiverse supposes that we don't experience the truth of reality from our position in the universe. Quantum consciousness suggests that our thoughts and feelings are governed by different rules to those that govern our physical existence.

Science today believes that astrology is not true. The experiments that have been carried out to arrive at this conclusion have been heavily weighted towards classical and modern physics. I believe that it is time to step out of the box and look at astrology from a different perspective.

It is only when we realize that all the constituent parts of the universe may contain information about the whole universe rather than vice versa that we can then understand how vibration, harmonics and resonance can play a role in human relationships.

♈	♉	♊	♋	♌	♍	♎	♏	♐	♑	♒	♓
Aries	Taurus	Gemini	Cancer	Leo	Virgo	Libra	Scorpio	Sagittarius	Capricorn	Aquarius	Pisces

Everything is noise. At the deepest quantum levels we are told that matter is not solid, but is made up of information. Atoms are more like thoughts than they are like solid objects. The universe is mainly empty space, indeed as John Hunt notes in *Bringing God Back to Earth*, if we were to extract the space from every human being on Earth, what remains would be enough to fill a matchbox.

The noise that surrounds us is not necessarily audible noise; we have senses that filter out information, but all matter is essentially information vibrating at a particular rate. Our 'collective consciousness' can agree that a table is a table or a cat is a cat, but the cat and the table are fundamentally physical only in an agreed sense. In fact, the two things are a mass of vibrating particles that have somehow been fashioned into a table and a cat. At our level of perception we do not experience the table as a vibration we experience it as something we can sit at and eat dinner.

If we are individuals in a universe which is in fact purely holographic then it is our individual vibrational rate that provides this uniqueness. This means that although we are a part of the whole (and we apparently each have access to information about the whole), we are also experiencing life as a discrete set of resonant factors: (energy patterns which we can also analogise as objects in a toolbox of life) these factors begin for us the moment we step into material life. I believe that we are surrounded by inaudible noise at all times and much of this noise is discordant. Our intimate relationships are often the parts of life where we conventionally seek to escape from the noise of life and as such we are attracted to people who vibrate in harmony with ourselves. We seek out harmonious resonance, but we cannot have perfection all of the time and so we compromise in some areas. Our future relationships are also influenced by our past relationships and if we are accustomed to harmony we are less likely to seek relationships that don't reflect our expectations. Attachment patterns and learned behaviour also tend to reflect the opposite – if you are

♈	♉	♊	♋	♌	♍	♎	♏	♐	♑	♒	♓
Aries	Taurus	Gemini	Cancer	Leo	Virgo	Libra	Scorpio	Sagittarius	Capricorn	Aquarius	Pisces

used to having discordant patterns in your relationships, you are more likely to accept them in future relationships.

The Solar System as a Concert Hall

Among the myths surrounding astrology is that the fact that there is no 'plausible physical explanation' for astrological effects is proof that therefore there must be no effect. Electromagnetic forces we receive from the Sun, Moon and planets are negligible. The force of gravity declines with distance, meaning that the gravitational effects of the Moon are so much stronger than those of Jupiter, but other local objects – for example a midwife – will exert more gravitation than Venus. Solar radiation is sometimes posited, but this is variable. So, according to physics, because there is no plausible physical explanation for astrology, it is simpler to posit no related effect. Here's how John Anthony West views this argument:

> *'Any system is inconceivable without a directing intelligence or consciousness. The more sophisticated the system, the subtler the manner in which physical forces are deployed, and the more inescapable – and mysterious – the conscious or volitional element. In a mainly physical system, the conscious element is concealed, while in a mainly conscious system, it is the physical element that eludes detection.*
>
> *To use a homely example, let us say we want to drive a nail into a block of wood. This represents a very simple and ephemeral system, lasting no longer than the act itself. It barely qualifies as a system in the usual sense of the word. Still, simple as it is, it is ineluctably metaphysical. A decision motivates it, and that decision has no physical measurable properties. But because it is so simple, calculating its dominant constituent physical factors – force, velocity, resistance – is a relatively straightforward procedure. There is an easily understood relationship between the effect (nail driven into wood) and its plausible physical explanation (hammer hitting nail). But if we want to move a*

♈	♉	♊	♋	♌	♍	♎	♏	♐	♑	♒	♓
Aries	Taurus	Gemini	Cancer	Leo	Virgo	Libra	Scorpio	Sagittarius	Capricorn	Aquarius	Pisces

ton of steel with a cup full of gasoline, a more sophisticated system is called for. The energy potential of the gasoline is finite and easily worked out. But if it is ignited on top of our ton of steel nothing much will happen. If, however, the ton of steel is organised into a Porsche, then the same cup of gas will send it from 0 to 60 mph in six seconds. Here the element of consciousness involved in organizing the system is much more intense and conspicuous. And the relationship between the amount of energy expended and the effect produced far more complex. The effect is purely mechanical, of course, traceable and comprehensible on the basis of known physical laws. Intention or consciousness plays no role in the operation of the completed system in this case. The element of consciousness stayed back in the factory in Stuttgart. But there would be no Porsche without it.

When we revert to [the] image of a concert hall, the consciousness or intention (Mozart's genius in this case) plays the commanding role while the physical forces involved become much more difficult to quantify and impossible to understand analytically. This is the opposite pole to our hammer/nail system.

The concert hall filled with people is also a system – once the music starts to play. The faintest quaver of the solo flute then becomes significant. Before the music started, the orchestra shuffling around and tuning up had no effect at all, though it made much more noise.

The concert hall also provides a useful model for countering a number of other anti-astrological arguments; chiefly: 1) that the planets are too far away to produce effects; 2) that the forces exerted by them are too small; 3) that astrologers do not take into account the variable distance of the planets in their orbits; and 4) that the planets vary enormously in size amongst themselves and also in their distances from earth, and astrologers take little or no note of these differences. But in the concert hall, as in astrology, there is no plausible physical explanation to account for the effect produced. The cause is meta-

♈	♉	♊	♋	♌	♍	♎	♏	♐	♑	♒	♓
Aries	Taurus	Gemini	Cancer	Leo	Virgo	Libra	Scorpio	Sagittarius	Capricorn	Aquarius	Pisces

physical (the genius of Mozart). Physical musical instruments act as a medium for transmitting the message. They cannot be called a plausible physical explanation of the music. And indeed, considered apart from the metaphysical cause, they are mere mechanisms, pieces of wood and brass. They exert no measurable force; they simply create disturbances within the self-contained air of the system, and like the planets, they act at a distance. Yet, the distance itself, and even the magnitude of the disturbance, that is to say the volume of the music, are of secondary importance...For if the concert hall is well designed, we will hear the music, and be moved by it, in the last row of the top balcony, and we will hear it even if there is a pillar blocking our line of vision to the orchestra, or if we happen to find ourselves sitting behind a team of sumo wrestlers. Along the same lines the massive tuba and thunderous tympani are no more or less important than the diminutive flute or violin. People are involved in the concert hall model, as they are in astrology. The primitive hammer/nail model of reality will not suffice. And that plausible physical explanation required to account for astrological effects (more accurately 'correspondences') no more depends upon large magnitudes of gravitational or magnetic force than the effects produced by Mozart's music depends upon soundwaves...

...There is today not the slightest possible doubt that the solar system is a system; interrelated, delicately balanced and dynamic; and curiously analogous to the system represented on the human scale by the concert hall...it is not implausible to suggest that we are inextricably bound up within that system. And from remotest pre-history, astrology has been the discipline devoted to studying our part in it. [cxx]

Harmonics and Resonance

It has been proposed that the aspects between planets work through a system of harmonic resonance, that is a conjunction of two planets is an aspect of the *first* harmonic, an opposition, where we divide the circle in

♈	♉	♊	♋	♌	♍	♎	♏	♐	♑	♒	♓
Aries	Taurus	Gemini	Cancer	Leo	Virgo	Libra	Scorpio	Sagittarius	Capricorn	Aquarius	Pisces

two is an aspect of the *second* harmonic, a trine where we divide the circle by three represents the *third* harmonic and a square, where we divide the circle by four is representative of the *fourth* harmonic. Astrology in essence is no different from music, which is also communicated in its own language and which to the uninitiated is written as just a series of lines, dots and squiggles on a page, but when interpreted correctly produces an ordered truth which can inspire meaning within us that is difficult to quantify.

Resonance

Resonance is the process in which oscillations in a system are produced, maintained or enhanced by means of periodic transfer of energy from another oscillating system whose frequency is identical to that of the first system. This means that if relationship astrology is true, that quite often the planets which symbolise our attracting qualities will harmonise with planets which symbolise reciprocal meanings in our partner's astrology charts, the charts in this case are an abstract representation of our inner potential.

The frequency of a piece of music, its *resonance with our own vibration*, is what attracts us to it. It harmonizes with our inner being. But some people prefer Beethoven to Mozart or the Beastie Boys to the Beatles. People are different and this difference, according to astrology, is created by the planetary positions in their birth chart.

Meta-Astrology

The astrological *meta-model* where human beings are subject to a system of meaningful time is possible in an interconnected universe where symbols and metaphorical ideas can be experienced collectively, but not really within a universe where planets only exert forces upon us, as there is no real-time relationship between you and the positions of the planets – say – thirty days after your birth affecting you in your thirtieth year. We must, therefore, regard something akin to the holographic model of the universe as an example of a universe that could produce the phenomenon of

♈	♉	♊	♋	♌	♍	♎	♏	♐	♑	♒	♓
Aries	Taurus	Gemini	Cancer	Leo	Virgo	Libra	Scorpio	Sagittarius	Capricorn	Aquarius	Pisces

progressions in astrology. Furthermore our experience of music is, I believe, analogous to the way we experience the result of the astrological process.

The phenomenon of being mutually attracted is often referred to as *chemistry*. It's not chemistry. It's music.

The human world is suffused with sound: music, and the oscillations and resonant harmonies that we produce when we place sound into some kind of order is a way of harnessing what appear to be chaotic rules and making them unchaotic. If astrology is true, it is evidence that someone else has already done this at a higher level than the human interpretation of music. Try as we may we will never silence the universe.

♈	♉	♊	♋	♌	♍	♎	♏	♐	♑	♒	♓
Aries	Taurus	Gemini	Cancer	Leo	Virgo	Libra	Scorpio	Sagittarius	Capricorn	Aquarius	Pisces

Eleven

Poet and Muse

Why have such scores of lovely, gifted girls,
married impossible men?
Robert Graves

The poet Dante Alghieri loved a woman named Beatrice Portinari. Although they met on only two occasions, Dante devoted a whole book to describing his love for her. He actually stalked Beatrice for about nine years, hanging out on street corners in Florence where he might see her pass by. He wrote the following in about the year 1293, which was, incidentally, three years after her death:

> *My Lady carries love within her eyes; All that she looks on is made pleasanter; Upon her path men turn to gaze at her; He whom she greeteth feels his heart rise.*[cxxi]

It strikes me that this is the thirteenth-century equivalent of a verse in Eddie Cochran's song 'Somethin' Else':

> *(A look a-there, here she comes, there comes that girl again, wanted to date her since I don't know when, but she don't notice me when I pass, she goes with all the guys from outa my class, but that can't stop me from a-thinkin' to myself, she's sure fine lookin' man, she's something else)*[cxxii]

The point I'm attempting to make, of course, is that desire is a direct cause of poetry and this has been the case for many centuries. Some poet-muse relationships are more obvious than others. This is the case with love poet

♈	♉	♊	♋	♌	♍	♎	♏	♐	♑	♒	♓
Aries	Taurus	Gemini	Cancer	Leo	Virgo	Libra	Scorpio	Sagittarius	Capricorn	Aquarius	Pisces

Robert Graves who explicitly referred to his partners as his muses. Infamous Black Magician Aleister Crowley needed to have a certain kind of woman to help him on his path to unworldly power and self-destruction and he referred to these muses as his 'scarlet women'. But there are others and here are a few.

Ike and Tina Turner

Tina Turner's story was told in the 1992 film *What's Love Got To Do With It?* with Angela Bassett playing the role of Tina. In this story, adapted from Tina's book *I Tina,* Ike's relationship with Tina is shown to be that of a Svengali whose controlling influence lacked tenderness. He is shown to be at best a clumsy lover with a satyr's appetite for women and sex; he was violently jealous, seeking attention and enrichment at the expense of others. At worst he was depicted as a violent bully who resorted to assault and rape. Tina's book also makes mention of Ike's gaudy taste in interior design and his need to have people around him whom he could control completely.

The position of Venus in Scorpio in Ike's birth chart is thought by astrological traditionalists to symbolise the type of lover for whom passion is paramount. When passion is of paramount importance the pursuit of self-satisfaction is also a strong possibility. When Venus is in one of Mars' two signs (Aries and Scorpio), there is a tendency to rush things, and to be emotionally intense. Occasionally this leads to an inability to contain the feelings and a lack of consideration for other's rights, a by-product of this can be jealousy as there is often some measure of self-knowledge that this type of behaviour is inadequate and unacceptable. The combination of the controlling Sun, also in Scorpio, can create a person who either rises above their impulses through self-control or gives in to them and seeks to control others. This certainly was the impression that Tina's book gave of Ike.

Their marriage and partnership lasted from 1959 until 1976 though it is worth noting that Tina appears to have come to terms with Ike after a

♈	♉	♊	♋	♌	♍	♎	♏	♐	♑	♒	♓
Aries	Taurus	Gemini	Cancer	Leo	Virgo	Libra	Scorpio	Sagittarius	Capricorn	Aquarius	Pisces

couple of years, and she states quite clearly she began to hate Ike around 1968-69 when she was 29 years old (this age is a turning point in most people's lives when an event known to astrologers as the Saturn return[cxxiii] takes place) then she learned to – in the main – contain his behaviour as she grew spiritually, and finally fled when she was sufficiently capable.

	1	2	3	4	5	6	7	8	9
A	Day	S.Time	Sun	Moon	Mercury	Venus	Mars		
B	5	14:55	12 ♏ 06'	10 ♍ 35'	22 ♏ 53'	27 ♏ 16'	04 ♐ 18'	1931	ike
C	16	9:49	24 ♐ 19'	05 ♓ 54'	03 ♐ 00'	19 ♑ 53'	17 ♓ 58'	1959	tina
D	3	16:45	10 ♐ 21'	20 ♍ 43'	01 ♑ 34'	02 ♑ 12'	24 ♐ 59'	1959	ike
E	26	8:30	04 ♐ 00'	07 ♊ 14'	07 ♐ 40'	24 ♐ 58'	04 ♓ 48'	1939	tina

Fig.110. Matrix showing the natal planetary positions of Ike and Tina Turner, together with their progressed planetary positions for the year 1959

Their mutual astrology has little to do with Venus, although she was present at the beginning of their relationship in 1959 – Ike's progressing-Mars (D7) has moved slowly forward to form a close conjunction with Tina's natal-Venus (E6). Mars-Venus conjunctions tend towards physical attractions and are often the signpost for a relationship that is based on the physical side of intimacy. Ike's masculine Mars in fiery Sagittarius leads Tina's feminine Venus in the same place. The conjunction aspect assures intensity and similarity. Ike claims that when he first made love to Tina it felt like he was making love to his sister, it didn't feel right.

As this is a progressed aspect the effect is limited to the time Ike's Mars stays near to Tina's Venus. 1959 is the culmination of this aspect. It's downhill after this point. Tina joined Ike's band a couple of years previously but was not intimately involved with him until 1959. In fact Tina had given birth to her first son Craig, whose father Raymond Hill was another band member, the year before. Tina's progressing-Sun is also part of the Mars-Venus conjunction in 1959 signifying that her aspirations at the time were tied in with loving Ike Turner and letting him love her. In fact all

♈	♉	♊	♋	♌	♍	♎	♏	♐	♑	♒	♓
Aries	Taurus	Gemini	Cancer	Leo	Virgo	Libra	Scorpio	Sagittarius	Capricorn	Aquarius	Pisces

Tina wanted to do was sing and Ike facilitated this, but in the long term this was at a heavy price.

Ike and Tina's natal planets are also significant – his Mars (B7) casts a square aspect to her Mars (E7) while conjoining her Sun (E3) thus signifying that although physically they need different things – he needs fiery and uncontrolled love (Sagittarius), she needs her physical encounters to be spiritual, dreamy and sensitive affairs (Pisces) – her aspirations are tied in with his ability to drive and direct. This aspect continues by progression (C3 – D7).

By the time their divorce comes about in 1976, progressed conjunctions have been replaced by squares. Her Mars (C7) has moved into a square aspect with his Sun (D3) while his Mars (D7) has moved out of conjunction with her Sun (C3). She no longer needs his Mars energy to create momentum for her to move forward. Her Venus (C6) is a year away from making an exact square to his Sun (B3). The square, remember, invokes conflict, its principle being to spark action through bringing two different perspectives into proximity. This often leads to the two parties getting their fingers burned and they then repel because in loving relation-ships conflict requires release and the release of the pent up energies the square produces often underlines the couples dissimilarity. In fixed signs the Sun-Venus square signifies two people with different ideas about the ideal relationship and who won't budge on the issue.

	1	2	3	4	5	6	7	8	9
A	Day	S.Time	Sun	Moon	Mercury	Venus	Mars		
B	5	14:55	12 ♏ 06'	10 ♍ 35'	22 ♏ 53'	27 ♏ 16'	04 ♐ 18'	1931	ike
C	2	10:56	11 ♑ 38'	24 ♎ 02'	25 ♐ 19'	10 ♒ 59'	29 ♓ 26'	1976	tina
D	20	17:52	27 ♐ 38'	06 ♉ 05'	29 ♐ 46'	23 ♑ 23'	07 ♑ 53'	1976	ike
E	26	8:30	04 ♐ 00'	07 ♊ 14'	07 ♐ 40'	24 ♐ 58'	04 ♓ 48'	1939	tina

Fig.111. Matrix showing the natal planetary positions of Ike and Tina Turner, together with their progressed planetary positions for the year 1959.

♈	♉	♊	♋	♌	♍	♎	♏	♐	♑	♒	♓
Aries	Taurus	Gemini	Cancer	Leo	Virgo	Libra	Scorpio	Sagittarius	Capricorn	Aquarius	Pisces

So which is poet, Ike or Tina? The answer is surely Ike Turner. Tina acted as much more than an inspiration. Ike built his whole act around his wife's talent to deliver his music and his nose was put out of joint when Phil Spector began working with Tina on *River Deep Mountain High*. Despite his musical talents, Ike was insufficiently emotionally capable to cope with the fact that he was reliant upon Tina for high success, but in the big scheme of things that is what she brought him: his finest hour.

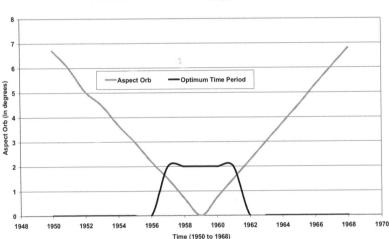

Tina Turner Ike Turner natal Venus progressed Mars conjunction

Fig.112. Graph showing the two degree window of opportunity 1957 to 1961 created by Ike and Tina's progressed-Mars natal-Venus conjunction

Sonny and Cher

Sonny Bono met 16-year-old Cherilyn LaPierre in 1963. He was in his late twenties, separated from his first wife and working on the fringes of the record industry; she was an experienced and precocious teenager whose experimentation had included an encounter with Warren Beatty. Although by Sonny's own admission they never had a good physical relationship, they started a relationship within a month or so, began living together, and

♈	♉	♊	♋	♌	♍	♎	♏	♐	♑	♒	♓
Aries	Taurus	Gemini	Cancer	Leo	Virgo	Libra	Scorpio	Sagittarius	Capricorn	Aquarius	Pisces

married in October 1964. They borrowed $168 to record their first single *Baby Don't Go*. Their second single *I Got You Babe* was a worldwide hit.

This marriage of Aquarius and Taurus (their natal-Suns in cells B3 and E3 below are *square* to one another meaning their ideals are different and their lives will probably diverge as they pursue different goals) is also possessed of the holy grail of relationship aspects: a natal-Sun (E3) Venus (B6) trine. At its birth Sonny's progressing-Venus (C6) is trine Cher's progressing-Mars (D7) and there is a wide (just over two degrees) progressed-Venus (D6) – natal-Venus (E6) trine which as we have noted in the relationship of David and Primmie Niven, tends to make the world stop turning temporarily.

	1	2	3	4	5	6	7	8	9
	Day	S.Time	Sun	Moon	Mercury	Venus	Mars		
A									
B	20	7:15	28 ♉ 59'	18 ♑ 17'	16 ♉ 28'	25 ♊ 45'	13 ♌ 20'	1946	cher
C	17	13:55	25 ♓ 34'	21 ♌ 23'	28 ♒ 01'	23 ♈ 28'	22 ♎ 38'	1963	sonny
D	6	8:22	15 ♊ 18'	14 ♍ 57'	22 ♊ 49'	16 ♋ 13'	22 ♌ 22'	1963	cher
E	16	12:05	27 ♒ 29'	12 ♌ 41'	27 ♒ 51'	18 ♓ 56'	23 ♎ 58'	1935	sonny

Fig.113. Matrix showing the natal planetary positions of Sonny and Cher, together with their progressed planetary positions for the year 1963.

After a successful recording career which culminated in the loss of about half a million dollars on the movie *Chastity*, they had evolved into a successful nightclub comedy act with Sonny as the straight man. A hit TV show began in 1971. Their daughter (also called Chastity) was born in 1969 and their romance ended in the early 70s. In late 1972 Cher had fallen in love with their guitarist Bill Hamm and Sonny fell for Connie Foreman.

At its end, Sonny and Cher were living in the same house with different partners. They got on okay, but separated and divorced in 1974.

Their Sun-Venus and Venus-Mars trines are in Air signs. They would always get on well, but would never be too intense. Cher's progressing-Venus (D6) may have interrupted their sexual compatibility around 1969 as

♈	♉	♊	♋	♌	♍	♎	♏	♐	♑	♒	♓
Aries	Taurus	Gemini	Cancer	Leo	Virgo	Libra	Scorpio	Sagittarius	Capricorn	Aquarius	Pisces

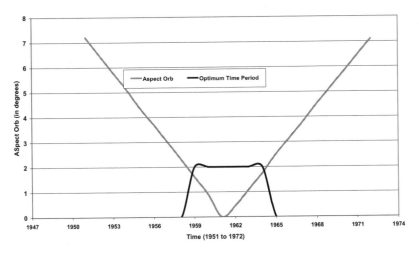

Fig.114. Graph showing the two-degree window of opportunity 1959 to 1964 created by Sonny and Cher's progressed-Mars progressed-Venus conjunction

it formed a square with Sonny's natal-Mars (E7). This is often a shock and in many relationships can often be resolved as the aspect very often wanes after a few years. In other relationships, usually those where there is a lot of opportunity to take comfort elsewhere, it can have a devisive and ultimately devastating effect.

Theirs was a great opportunity to come together and have a safe and happy loving relationship for a time. It took a few years before they admitted they had different and tangential goals, but in the end the time they spent together furnished them with the opportunity to pursue their different paths.

Cher became an Oscar winning actress and musical icon in her own right and Sonny became a congressman. Without a diploma or a degree he excelled as a politician in the same way he excelled at being a songwriter without even knowing three chords. I like that a lot in a person because it

♈	♉	♊	♋	♌	♍	♎	♏	♐	♑	♒	♓
Aries	Taurus	Gemini	Cancer	Leo	Virgo	Libra	Scorpio	Sagittarius	Capricorn	Aquarius	Pisces

summarizes what *potential* actually is, it is not a piece of paper, it is a combination of all the elements of the self, whether one is a genius or not.

Sonny Bono died in a skiing accident in 1998.

	1	2	3	4	5	6	7	8	9
	Day	S.Time	Sun	Moon	Mercury	Venus	Mars		
A									
B	20	7:15	28 ♉ 59'	18 ♑ 17'	16 ♉ 28'	25 ♊ 45'	13 ♌ 20'	1946	cher
C	26	14:31	04 ♈ 30'	12 ♐ 29'	08 ♓ 58'	04 ♉ 27'	20 ♎ 10'	1972	sonny
D	15	8:58	23 ♊ 54'	03 ♑ 21'	10 ♋ 44'	26 ♋ 57'	27 ♌ 20'	1972	cher
E	16	12:05	27 ♒ 29'	12 ♌ 41'	27 ♒ 51'	18 ♓ 56'	23 ♎ 58'	1935	sonny

Fig.115. Matrix showing the natal planetary positions of Sonny and Cher, together with their progressed planetary positions for the year 1972.

Again Sonny was the poet, Cher was his muse. For a while the magic worked and as is the case with all complex synastric relationships, when she left him, so to a great extent did his ability to channel his musical creativity. Iconic as they were of the youth of the sixties, Sonny and Cher were a modern example of this great poetic tradition.

Ted Hughes and Sylvia Plath

In a far more conventional sense can we relate the poet muse idea to Plath and Hughes, but it is now more difficult to define which was poet and which was muse, for they both played this role for each other. I would however, venture to suggest that Plath was more the muse to the poet Hughes than Hughes was to Plath.

Neil Spencer devoted a number of pages in his book about astrology, *True as the Stars Above* to Ted Hughes and Sylvia Plath; their shared interest in astrology and their ill-starred and tragic, yet obviously passionate relationship and the astrological synastry inherent in their union.

Ted Hughes eventually became poet laureate: the Queens official poet, and among the responsibilities of this post is the production of verse for Royal occasions, for example significant birthdays and weddings of

♈	♉	♊	♋	♌	♍	♎	♏	♐	♑	♒	♓
Aries	Taurus	Gemini	Cancer	Leo	Virgo	Libra	Scorpio	Sagittarius	Capricorn	Aquarius	Pisces

members of the Royal family and other such events and celebrations. It therefore surprised a few members of the establishment when he produced a book of poems titled *Birthday Letters*, which was full of odes to the passion of his life: Sylvia Plath, his late wife who was also an accomplished poet. Plath had committed suicide in 1962 by gassing herself. These poems were surprising because they were filled with astrological references and symbolism.

Hughes met Plath on 25 February 1956 at a party in Cambridge. Neil Spencer describes the event as:

*'A night which left the hulking poet bleeding from a love bite incised on his cheek by Plath '*cxxiv

Spencer goes on to suggest that Hughes, conscious of the planetary positions, considered their relationship ill-starred at their first encounter. *St Botolphs*, the poem that reveals this suggestion to be true has the following line within it:

That day the solar system married us whether we knew it or not.

Which also suggests Hughes considered the positions of the planets were important in their relationship and marriage.

Spencer goes on to ask the following question:

*'Was the stormy marriage between the two poets really made in heaven?' The Ill-matched combination of their Suns in the fixed signs of fiery Leo (Hughes) and watery Scorpio (Plath) would cause most astromatchmakers to blanch, but elsewhere the overlaps between the charts match their emotionally compulsive relationship. Most glaringly, Plath's Moon (feelings) falls exactly on Hughes's Venus (Love) in the romantic sign of Libra, while Hughes's Sun (self) is sited exactly with Plath's Mars (sexual energy).*cxxv

I concur with Neil Spencer. This is a useful pen picture of their natal synastry. Of course, using progressed synastry we can burrow a little

♈	♉	♊	♋	♌	♍	♎	♏	♐	♑	♒	♓
Aries	Taurus	Gemini	Cancer	Leo	Virgo	Libra	Scorpio	Sagittarius	Capricorn	Aquarius	Pisces

deeper to look at the changing elements of their relationship with remarkable accuracy.

In 1956, the fact that there are conflicting natal-Sun signs is actually being suppressed, or rather its effect is overshadowed by other aspects of easier or more favorable synastry and as is the case with progressed synastry, sharper astrological accuracy.

Ted and Sylvia married in June 1956. Although Sylvia wanted a career first, Ted wanted children and they were joined by Frieda in 1960 and Nicholas in 1962.

It can be seen in the table below that in 1956, this couple benefited from a progressing-Venus natal-Sun conjunction in the emotionally intense and deep-feeling sign Scorpio. This is not the aspect of passion that made their relationship so vital so quickly, but its presence is necessary to compliment the sexual combination of Plath's progressing-Venus in romantic Libra in an applying trine to Hughes' natal-Mars in wordy Gemini.

The fleeting nature of progressed aspects means that the window of opportunity that brought this couple together closes sooner than most, by 1957 the Sun-Venus aspect is history and the Venus-Mars aspect (similar in geometry and time-frame to the Venus-Mars trine in Chris Evans and Billie Piper's relationship) is separating or waning, and during this crucial time, what it leaves in its wake is a close natal, and therefore permanent, Venus-Mars square. This is slightly ameliorated by the presence of a progressing-Sun natal-Venus conjunction, but this is in the detail-conscious and slightly cooler sign of Virgo. By 1961 this conjunction is separating and soon after this Ted Hughes began an affair with Assia Wevill. Sylvia killed herself in 1962 by gassing. Interestingly Assia Wevill, the next woman in Ted's life, did the same thing in 1968.

♈	♉	♊	♋	♌	♍	♎	♏	♐	♑	♒	♓
Aries	Taurus	Gemini	Cancer	Leo	Virgo	Libra	Scorpio	Sagittarius	Capricorn	Aquarius	Pisces

	1	2	3	4	5	6	7	8	9
A	Day	S.Time	Sun	Moon	Mercury	Venus	Mars		
B	17	21:37	24 ♌ 19'	00 ♊ 38'	20 ♍ 19'	08 ♎ 45'	23 ♊ 17'	1930	hughes
C	20	22:58	28 ♏ 15'	21 ♌ 47'	19 ♌ 29'	22 ♎ 24'	03 ♏ 16'	1956	plath
D	12	23:20	19 ♍ 28'	14 ♉ 25'	05 ♎ 47'	05 ♏ 46'	09 ♋ 31'	1956	hughes
E	27	21:23	04 ♏ 09'	08 ♎ 24'	21 ♏ 27'	23 ♍ 38'	21 ♌ 13'	1932	plath
F	Day	S.Time	Sun	Moon	Mercury	Venus	Mars		
G	17	21:37	24 ♌ 19'	00 ♊ 38'	20 ♍ 19'	08 ♎ 45'	23 ♊ 17'	1930	hughes
H	21	23:02	29 ♏ 16'	04 ♍ 52'	19 ♐ 57'	23 ♎ 37'	03 ♍ 44'	1957	plath
I	13	23:23	20 ♍ 26'	27 ♉ 14'	05 ♎ 16'	06 ♏ 44'	10 ♋ 07'	1957	hughes
J	27	21:23	04 ♏ 09'	08 ♎ 24'	21 ♏ 27'	23 ♍ 38'	21 ♌ 13'	1932	plath
K	Day	S.Time	Sun	Moon	Mercury	Venus	Mars		
L	17	21:37	24 ♌ 19'	00 ♊ 38'	20 ♍ 19'	08 ♎ 45'	23 ♊ 17'	1930	hughes
M	22	23:06	00 ♐ 17'	18 ♍ 20'	20 ♐ 18'	24 ♎ 51'	04 ♍ 11'	1958	plath
N	14	23:27	21 ♍ 25'	10 ♊ 21'	04 ♎ 38'	07 ♏ 42'	10 ♋ 43'	1958	hughes
O	27	21:23	04 ♏ 09'	08 ♎ 24'	21 ♏ 27'	23 ♍ 38'	21 ♌ 13'	1932	plath
P	Day	S.Time	Sun	Moon	Mercury	Venus	Mars		
Q	17	21:37	24 ♌ 19'	00 ♊ 38'	20 ♍ 19'	08 ♎ 45'	23 ♊ 17'	1930	hughes
R	23	23:10	01 ♐ 17'	02 ♏ 16'	20 ♐ 31'	26 ♏ 04'	04 ♍ 39'	1959	plath
S	15	23:31	22 ♍ 23'	23 ♊ 49'	03 ♎ 53'	08 ♏ 39'	11 ♋ 18'	1959	hughes
T	27	21:23	04 ♏ 09'	08 ♎ 24'	21 ♏ 27'	23 ♍ 38'	21 ♌ 13'	1932	plath
U	Day	S.Time	Sun	Moon	Mercury	Venus	Mars		
V	17	21:37	24 ♌ 19'	00 ♊ 38'	20 ♍ 19'	08 ♎ 45'	23 ♊ 17'	1930	hughes
W	24	23:14	02 ♐ 18'	16 ♎ 39'	20 ♐ 35'	27 ♏ 17'	05 ♍ 06'	1960	plath
X	16	23:35	23 ♍ 22'	07 ♋ 40'	03 ♎ 03'	09 ♏ 36'	11 ♋ 53'	1960	hughes
Y	27	21:23	04 ♏ 09'	08 ♎ 24'	21 ♏ 27'	23 ♍ 38'	21 ♌ 13'	1932	plath
Z	Day	S.Time	Sun	Moon	Mercury	Venus	Mars		
AB	17	21:37	24 ♌ 19'	00 ♊ 38'	20 ♍ 19'	08 ♎ 45'	23 ♊ 17'	1930	hughes
AC	25	23:18	03 ♐ 19'	01 ♏ 28'	20 ♐ 29'	28 ♎ 30'	05 ♍ 32'	1961	plath
AD	17	23:39	24 ♍ 20'	21 ♋ 54'	02 ♎ 08'	10 ♏ 32'	12 ♋ 29'	1961	hughes
AE	27	21:23	04 ♏ 09'	08 ♎ 24'	21 ♏ 27'	23 ♍ 38'	21 ♌ 13'	1932	plath
AF	Day	S.Time	Sun	Moon	Mercury	Venus	Mars		
AG	17	21:37	24 ♌ 19'	00 ♊ 38'	20 ♍ 19'	08 ♎ 45'	23 ♊ 17'	1930	hughes
AH	26	23:21	04 ♐ 20'	16 ♏ 37'	20 ♐ 13'	29 ♎ 44'	05 ♍ 59'	1962	plath
AI	18	23:43	25 ♍ 19'	06 ♍ 29'	01 ♎ 08'	11 ♏ 28'	13 ♋ 04'	1962	hughes
AJ	27	21:23	04 ♏ 09'	08 ♎ 24'	21 ♏ 27'	23 ♍ 38'	21 ♌ 13'	1932	plath

Fig.116. Matrix showing the natal planetary positions of Ted Hughes and Sylvia Plath, together with their progressed planetary positions for the years 1956 to 1962.

♈	♉	♊	♋	♌	♍	♎	♏	♐	♑	♒	♓
Aries	Taurus	Gemini	Cancer	Leo	Virgo	Libra	Scorpio	Sagittarius	Capricorn	Aquarius	Pisces

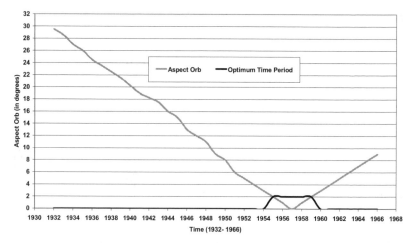

Ted Hughes Sylvia Plath natal Mars progressed Venus trine

Fig.117. Graph showing the two-degree window of opportunity 1955 to 1959 created by Plath and Hughes' progressed-Venus natal-Mars trine

Robert Graves

The poet finds inspiration from actually being in love; the experience is fuel for the output of creativity and verse.

One of the most remarkable love poets of modern times was Robert Graves. His obituary described him as 'the greatest love poet in English since Donne' and this is at least fair. His remarkable literary output is of the highest quality. His understanding of both antiquity and the symbolic language of the past is unrivalled by any other modern poet. He is most commonly remembered as the writer of *I Claudius* and as one of the more famous 'War Poets' of the Great War.

Graves worked through his 'muses' or his lovers. He had seven significant female muses during his life, Nancy, his first wife, followed by poetess Laura Riding, then Beryl Pritchard who became his second wife and finally four woman known as Judith, Margot, Laracuen and Julie, who became kind of surrogate muses (with the full knowledge of his wife Beryl). It is interesting to me that Graves' idea of the White Goddess, a

religiouslike ideal that he thought was the feminine predecessor to the masculine religions that arose from the Judaic seed, is closely associated with both the Moon and Venus. Graves proposed the idea of Solar and Lunar knowledge to describe the two worlds in which the poet must inhabit: the Solar world being the masculine, scientific consciousness that seeks mastery over the universe; the Lunar world being the one inhabited by those whose method of thought is more feminal in origin – the type of consciouness that can appreciate the subtleties of life from an intuitive point of view. The poet must live in the conscious, masculine world, but must regularly visit the Lunar world in order to function as a poet to gain and use inspiration. Graves evidently got his inspiration from the feeling of *being in love* together with all the disparate feelings of joy and pain that accompany this altered state. Graves symbolically attributed being in love and the arrival of his muses upon the White Goddess; my view is that he was describing the arrival or presence of Venus.

In both natal and progressed synastry we can give dates and facts to these intuitive ideas. It would be interesting to see what role Venus plays in Graves' relationships and by extension, his poetry.

We have sufficient birth data for both Laura Riding and Beryl Pritchard to test whether there was a Venus connection, we also know when these relationships began. Graves met Laura Riding on 2 January 1926, their relationship was sexual until 1932 and thereafter, although she cast a kind of spell upon Graves, he eventually threw it off and fell in love with Beryl Pritchard some time in 1938, marrying her twelve years later in 1950.

Laura was an idealist feminist, whose influence absorbed Graves as a person, but not as a poet. His muses all brought out the poet and allowed the man to become acquiescent, submissive and strangely subdued by domesticity. This domesticity included anything from doing housework to making jam, in between writing some of the most important pieces of English literature of the twentieth century.

His submission to Riding was total, and despite the fact that his talent

♈	♉	♊	♋	♌	♍	♎	♏	♐	♑	♒	♓
Aries	Taurus	Gemini	Cancer	Leo	Virgo	Libra	Scorpio	Sagittarius	Capricorn	Aquarius	Pisces

totally eclipsed hers (although she was a good poet) Graves labored long and hard to ensure her creative needs were met, often at the expense of his own work.

	1	2	3	4	5	6	7	8	9
A	Day	S.Time	Sun	Moon	Mercury	Venus	Mars		
B	24	0:32	00 ♌ 59'	28 ♌ 24'	11 ♋ 07'	15 ♍ 49'	26 ♌ 55'	1895	graves
C	10	2:20	21 ♒ 17'	09 ♏ 52'	05 ♓ 39'	01 ♒ 26'	07 ♍ 21'	1926	riding
D	24	2:34	00 ♍ 43'	21 ♎ 38'	06 ♍ 59'	03 ♎ 32'	16 ♍ 29'	1926	graves
E	16	0:41	25 ♑ 54'	08 ♐ 24'	22 ♑ 26'	00 ♑ 17'	12 ♍ 28'	1901	riding

Fig.118. Matrix showing the natal planetary positions of Robert Graves and Laura Riding, together with their progressed planetary positions for the year 1926.

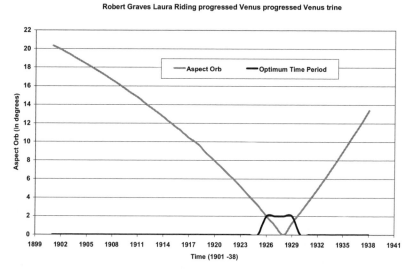

Fig.119. Graph showing the two-degree window of opportunity 1926 to 1929 created by Graves and Riding's progressed-Venus trine.

Laura and Robert's relationship involved three popular progressed planetary aspects, between the Sun and Venus and, importantly progressing-Venus in a trine with progressing-Venus (C6-D6). The graph above shows how this progressing-Venus trine opened a window that

♈	♉	♊	♋	♌	♍	♎	♏	♐	♑	♒	♓
Aries	Taurus	Gemini	Cancer	Leo	Virgo	Libra	Scorpio	Sagittarius	Capricorn	Aquarius	Pisces

included the sexual years of their relationship. Venus visited Graves in the form of the muse for a brief, but prolific period of time. Laura's desire to lose the sexual side of their relationship (for the sake of their true natures) occurred after the aspect began to separate.

There is a note in Robert Graves's diary for 11 August 1938 (he was still 'with' Laura at the time) in which he states *'We are getting very fond of Beryl.'*[cxxvi] Beryl was working ostensibly as their typist at the time and when he says *we*, he means *I*.

Beryl was unlike any of the other loves in Graves' life. Martin Seymour-Smith, Graves biographer, states that Graves:

'...Who had had no woman to turn to for human sympathy for the whole of his life, was now turning irresistibly and with natural ease, astonishing to him, to Beryl.'[cxxvii]

The couple were together from this point onwards, although their complex relationship was not finally legalised until 11 May 1950. They had two children, Lucia born in 1943 and Juan born in 1944.

Seymour-Smith has this to say about their relationship, in reference to a poem of Graves' entitled 'Assumption Day'.

'The poem Assumption Day is not important as a poem, but rather as an indicator of how he felt as he awaited Nemesis – whatever form that may take – in that summer in Brittany. For he dared not acknowledge to himself that he had fallen in love for the first (and only) time in his life, with a person – rather than someone who represented something he needed, such as a wife, or a Muse.'[cxxviii]

Beryl shares with Graves a close *natal*-Venus trine. This aspect is exactly the same as the one present in the relationships of Cassavetes and Rowlands and Polanski and Seigner. A natural aspect for romance and love, but as previously mentioned, not always a dynamic aspect, that while it gives a drawing together and a commonality as far as relationships are concerned,

♈	♉	♊	♋	♌	♍	♎	♏	♐	♑	♒	♓
Aries	Taurus	Gemini	Cancer	Leo	Virgo	Libra	Scorpio	Sagittarius	Capricorn	Aquarius	Pisces

	1	2	3	4	5	6	7	8	9
A	Day	S.Time	Sun	Moon	Mercury	Venus	Mars		
B	24	0:32	00 ♌ 59'	28 ♌ 24'	11 ♋ 07'	15 ♍ 49'	26 ♌ 55'	1895	graves
C	17	23:35	25 ♓ 49'	14 ♈ 59'	28 ♒ 19'	12 ♒ 27'	06 ♓ 15'	1938	beryl
D	5	3:22	12 ♍ 20'	22 ♓ 30'	28 ♍ 00'	03 ♎ 00'	24 ♍ 10'	1938	graves
E	22	22:05	02 ♓ 47'	06 ♊ 54'	01 ♓ 14'	16 ♑ 39'	18 ♒ 10'	1915	beryl

Fig.120. Matrix showing the natal planetary positions of Robert Graves and Beryl Pritchard, together with their progressed planetary positions for the year 1938.

doesn't always spur them into being. This is simply because Venus has the tendency to wait for another person to make the first move. In synastry this often requires a third planet to kick the relationship off. Robert's progressing-Sun is four degrees from a trine to Beryl's Venus in 1938, but it is applying and 'moving ever forward'. This aspect would be at its height in 1942 – 1943 around the time of the birth of Lucia. The muse seems to have appeared to Graves in the form of a Venus trine once more, but this time, instead of the trine being ephemeral or temporary, it was fixed and therefore a permanent dynamic in their synastry complex.

Aleister Crowley

The case of Aleister Crowley is of similar interest. Crowley considered himself a poet, as well as being a black magician, the beast 666, the wickedest man in the world and a host of other libertine, rebellious and, it has to be said, quite unpleasant epithets. His muses were many and varied, but he referred to them as his *Scarlet Women* demanding that they swear an oath of fealty to him which included the declaration that they would prostitute themselves freely and willingly for other 'creatures', which included, it would appear, goats. A disproportionate number of Crowley's associates either went mad or died prematurely. It seems that it was something of a hazard of knowing this extraordinary man. The first of his scarlet women, Rose Kelly, became his wife in 1903. Crowley married Rose the

♈	♉	♊	♋	♌	♍	♎	♏	♐	♑	♒	♓
Aries	Taurus	Gemini	Cancer	Leo	Virgo	Libra	Scorpio	Sagittarius	Capricorn	Aquarius	Pisces

day after he met her and they honeymooned in Egypt, spending part of their time in the Great Pyramid where Crowley invoked demons. He describes fully the details of their intimate life. The following sentence says it all:

'The honeymoon was a period of uninterrupted debauchery.'

Their honeymoon in Egypt was also a period of profound change in Crowley's life. A Black Magic ritual (the preliminary invocation of the Goetia, a ceremony designed to conjure up demons), carried out in the Kings Chamber of the Great Pyramid had an unexpected result. Rose began to have visions that brought forth a discarnate entity, which proceeded to dictate Crowley's extreme, blasphemous and above all completely self-defining, *Book of the Law*. From this point Crowley started to embrace the evil, uncaring character that has become the larger part of his public image and he gradually became the vehicle for dark rebellion that found its highest point in the free love generation of the 1960s.

In his relationship with Rose Kelly we witness an exact progressed aspect of her Venus and his Mars, this time in a trine, which hides or temporarily overshadows a natal Square between these her Mars and his Venus.

Crowley and Rose had a daughter together, and, after Crowley abandoned them in South East Asia to seek out a certain prostitute in Shanghai the child contracted Typhoid and died in Rangoon. Crowley, somewhat unfairly and typically, blamed Rose for her death and left her. She reportedly went mad.

	1	2	3	4	5	6	7	8	9
A	Day	S.Time	Sun	Moon	Mercury	Venus	Mars		
B	12	1:06	19 ♎ 14'	22 ♓ 48'	13 ♏ 21'	24 ♎ 24'	22 ♑ 52'	1875	crowley
C	21	9:58	28 ♌ 12'	11 ♐ 49'	12 ♌ 14'	11 ♎ 06'	13 ♌ 39'	1903	rose
D	9	2:56	17 ♏ 11'	00 ♈ 39'	29 ♎ 37'	29 ♏ 26'	11 ♒ 32'	1903	crowley
E	23	8:04	00 ♌ 23'	21 ♏ 38'	04 ♌ 39'	07 ♍ 43'	24 ♋ 59'	1874	rose

Fig.121. Matrix showing the natal planetary positions of Aleister Crowley and Rose Kelly, together with their progressed planetary positions for the year 1903.

♈	♉	♊	♋	♌	♍	♎	♏	♐	♑	♒	♓
Aries	Taurus	Gemini	Cancer	Leo	Virgo	Libra	Scorpio	Sagittarius	Capricorn	Aquarius	Pisces

Leah Hirsig entered Crowley's life in the spring of 1918. Crowley was at the time living in Greenwich Village, NY and Leah, a student of the occult, sought him out. It is said that Crowley and Leah felt an immediate and instinctive connection.

Colin Wilson, one of Crowley's biographers, writes:

'Towards the end of his American period, Crowley discovered yet another 'scarlet woman'. A woman named Renata Faesi called on him with her younger sister Leah, a thin girl with a broad mouth, sharp teeth and flat breasts. Apparently 'something clicked' as soon as they saw one another, and Crowley seized her and began to kiss her violently, to Renata's astonishment. "It was sheer instinct," says Crowley. 'cxxix

This is unsurprising as their progressed synastry for 1918 attests.

	1	2	3	4	5	6	7	8	9
A	Day	S.Time	Sun	Moon	Mercury	Venus	Mars		
B	12	1:06	19 ♎ 14'	22 ♓ 48'	13 ♏ 21'	24 ♎ 24'	22 ♑ 52'	1875	crowley
C	14	3:27	23 ♉ 19'	29 ♌ 30'	15 ♊ 06'	19 ♈ 41'	18 ♈ 10'	1918	hirsig
D	24	3:56	02 ♐ 19'	29 ♎ 34'	15 ♏ 40'	18 ♐ 12'	22 ♒ 03'	1918	crowley
E	9	1:09	19 ♈ 17'	16 ♉ 34'	11 ♈ 52'	08 ♓ 23'	21 ♓ 11'	1883	hirsig

Fig.122. Matrix showing the natal planetary positions of Aleister Crowley and Leah Hirsig, together with their progressed planetary positions for the year 1918.

It includes examples of all the Sun-Venus-Mars trines as well as a Sun-Sun opposition and a Sun-Venus opposition. An astonishing combination of progressed synastry based around the same degree of the signs Aries, Sagittarius and Libra.

Of course, progressed synastry changes and so did their relationship. Crowley moved on in the mid 1920s to other women, although Leah remained in his service at least until 1925.

She died in 1975, one hundred years after Crowley's birth.

♈	♉	♊	♋	♌	♍	♎	♏	♐	♑	♒	♓
Aries	Taurus	Gemini	Cancer	Leo	Virgo	Libra	Scorpio	Sagittarius	Capricorn	Aquarius	Pisces

Twelve

With The Beatles

Venus and Mars are fine tonight
Paul McCartney

The phenomenon known as Beatlemania came about by an Act of the British Parliament.

The British Government abolished National Military Service on 31 December 1960 and because of the timing of this change in legislation, two twenty-one year old lads from Liverpool narrowly missed military call up and were given the freedom to collaborate in the invention of pop music as we know it today. One of these young men was Richard Starkey, the other John Lennon, who together with Paul McCartney and George Harrison, defined the sound and techniques that were to influence much of the music that was to follow. And so, instead of doing their basic training in military camps, they learned their art in the clubs of Liverpool and Hamburg. It is arguable that no piece of British legislation has ever had such a profound social and cultural impact.

John Winston Lennon was born in Liverpool on 9 October 1940 to Julia and Freddie Lennon. His early life was blighted by his parents' separation; Freddie Lennon was a roving merchant seaman whose relationship with Julia was weakened by the time he spent at sea. By the time John was five years old Julia had given him up to her sister Mimi who became the significant female role model in John's early life. Julia died in 1958, a point in John's life when he was just getting to know her.

♈	♉	♊	♋	♌	♍	♎	♏	♐	♑	♒	♓
Aries	Taurus	Gemini	Cancer	Leo	Virgo	Libra	Scorpio	Sagittarius	Capricorn	Aquarius	Pisces

John Lennon and Cynthia Powell
and Yoko Ono and May Pang

John met first wife Cynthia Powell in 1957, they were both students at
Liverpool College of Art at the time and Cynthia's first impressions of John
were not good. He was disruptive, scruffy and rough around the edges.
After his mother Julia was killed in a road accident he said that he spent two
years being either drunk or angry. It was under the auspices of such a life
tragedy that his relationship with Cynthia Powell began.

Lennon appears to those who study him to have been a highly dependent character, and one who, like many people, sought love and approval in
his relationships. It was in his nature to collaborate and socialise: others
helped him channel his enormous creative force, which was heavily influenced by new ideas. The inspiration for his songs often came from stories
he saw on TV, newspaper articles, and on one occasion from a circus poster.
This reliance on new, fresh ideas brought him into collaboration with Paul
McCartney, the creative artist Yoko Ono and to adopt gurus as diverse as
the Maharishi Mahesh Yogi and "Magic" Alex Mardas, a TV repairman
who convinced John he could invent such things as audio wallpaper and
flying saucers. Although John could work alone, he seemed to prefer to
work with a partner; this suggests he believed himself to be dependent on
others for form and function.

Cynthia mothered John. She was an archetypal housewife, whose devotion to the hearth and home was good for John as long as his insecurities

	1	2	3	4	5	6	7	8	9
A	Day	S.Time	Sun	Moon	Mercury	Venus	Mars		
B	9	18:42	16 ♎ 16'	03 ♒ 32'	08 ♏ 33'	03 ♍ 12'	02 ♎ 39'	1940	lennon
C	28	12:25	04 ♎ 27'	03 ♈ 19'	09 ♎ 09'	10 ♎ 31'	01 ♒ 42'	1957	cynthia
D	26	19:49	03 ♏ 09'	04 ♍ 57'	26 ♏ 23'	22 ♍ 53'	13 ♎ 39'	1957	lennon
E	10	11:14	16 ♍ 52'	04 ♌ 48'	06 ♍ 00'	18 ♍ 07'	25 ♑ 57'	1939	cynthia

**Fig.123. Matrix showing the natal planetary positions for John Lennon
and Cynthia Powell together with their progressed planetary positions
for the year 1957**

♈	♉	♊	♋	♌	♍	♎	♏	♐	♑	♒	♓
Aries	Taurus	Gemini	Cancer	Leo	Virgo	Libra	Scorpio	Sagittarius	Capricorn	Aquarius	Pisces

kept him in the frame of mind that needed this type of relationship.

Often our progressed planets will reveal what we are prepared to do at a particular point in time. Over a period of time, these things will change until we appear to be totally different people.

In 1957, the most striking applying aspect occurs between John's progressing-Mars and Cynthia's progressing-Venus. This is a progressed conjunction. There is familiarity and role conventionality here, but in the years in which their relationship developed, so does this aspect. It began at just over three degrees from exact, but reached exact in 1962, the year of their marriage and around the time their son Julian was conceived. Over the same time period 1958 to 1962, a trine from John's progressed-Venus (D6) to Cynthia's progressed-Mars (E7) also forms and fades.

	1	2	3	4	5	6	7	8	9
			Sun	Moon	Mercury	Venus	Mars		
A	Day	S.Time	16 ♎ 16'	03 ♒ 32'	08 ♏ 33'	03 ♍ 12'	02 ♎ 39'	1940	lennon
B	9	18:42							
C	3	12:45	09 ♎ 22'	05 ♊ 34'	17 ♎ 36'	16 ♎ 45'	03 ♒ 48'	1962	cynthia
D	31	20:09	08 ♏ 09'	19 ♏ 32'	28 ♏ 06'	28 ♍ 48'	16 ♎ 55'	1962	lennon
E	10	11:14	16 ♍ 52'	04 ♌ 48'	06 ♍ 00'	18 ♍ 07'	25 ♑ 57'	1939	cynthia

Fig.124. Matrix showing the natal planetary positions for John Lennon and Cynthia Powell together with their progressed planetary positions for the year 1962

By 1966, it has passed the two-degree mark once more and Cynthia's progressing-Venus mirror's her encounter with her husband John symbolically. 1966 was the year that John met the love of his life, Yoko Ono.

By the time John met Yoko Ono in 1966 he was a lonely, flirtatious figure. His numerous affairs and one night stands in the years leading up to his divorce from Cynthia attest to the fact that he wanted to capitalise on his fame in the same way his fellow Beatles, who were all single men, had done. Cynthia was his wife and as the only married Beatle during the phenomenon of Beatlemania, he did not want to miss out on the attention he had, in part, created. As is the case with most people who explore in this

♈	♉	♊	♋	♌	♍	♎	♏	♐	♑	♒	♓
Aries	Taurus	Gemini	Cancer	Leo	Virgo	Libra	Scorpio	Sagittarius	Capricorn	Aquarius	Pisces

	1	2	3	4	5	6	7	8	9
A	Day	S.Time	Sun	Moon	Mercury	Venus	Mars		
B	9	18:42	16 ♎ 16'	03 ♒ 32'	08 ♏ 33'	03 ♍ 12'	02 ♎ 39'	1940	lennon
C	7	13:00	13 ♎ 18'	29 ♋ 54'	24 ♎ 07'	21 ♎ 45'	05 ♒ 37'	1966	cynthia
D	4	20:25	12 ♏ 09'	16 ♑ 33'	27 ♏ 06'	03 ♎ 35'	19 ♎ 31'	1966	lennon
E	10	11:14	16 ♍ 52'	04 ♌ 48'	06 ♍ 00'	18 ♍ 07'	25 ♑ 57'	1939	cynthia

Fig.125. Matrix showing the natal planetary positions for John Lennon and Cynthia Powell together with their progressed planetary positions for the year 1966

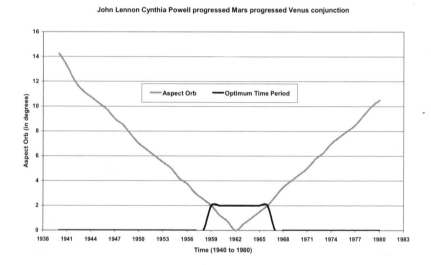

John Lennon Cynthia Powell progressed Mars progressed Venus conjunction

[Legend: —— Aspect Orb   —— Optimum Time Period]

Y-axis: Aspect Orb (in degrees)
X-axis: Time (1940 to 1980)

Fig.126. Graph showing the window of opportunity created by John Lennon's progressing-Mars in conjunction with Cynthia Powell's progressing-Venus 1958 to 1965

way, they are likely to stumble upon someone else whose planets (or as Noel Coward eloquently put it, their *cosmic thingummys*) are 'fused more perfectly' with their own.

John Dunbar, owner of the Indica Gallery in London, invited Lennon to an exhibition of conceptual art by Japanese artist Yoko Ono. John famously climbed a ladder at the top of which was a magnifying glass. Holding the

♈	♉	♊	♋	♌	♍	♎	♏	♐	♑	♒	♓
Aries	Taurus	Gemini	Cancer	Leo	Virgo	Libra	Scorpio	Sagittarius	Capricorn	Aquarius	Pisces

magnifying glass up to a placard on the ceiling revealed a single word "Yes". John later remarked that if it had been any other word he might not have been so impressed. Yoko is said to have asked John for five shillings to hammer an imaginary nail into the wall. John offered an imaginary five shillings.

Yoko and John have remarkable progressed planetary positions for 1966. They met on the 9th of November. On the day before Lennon and Ono met, Saturn and Uranus were in exact opposition creating a signature that more than adequately sums up their unconventional style of rebellion against the establishment. John Lennon shared a (wide-ish at just over two degrees) natal-Sun-Venus trine with his second wife.

Their relationship was friendly at first, but as Yoko sought John out more and more, it became difficult for John to ignore the fascination and attraction that Yoko inspired in him. Intrigued, and with one foot outside his relationship with Cynthia, John and Yoko spent 1967 and 1968 becoming more closely acquainted. John and Cynthia's marriage ended in May 1968 when Cynthia returned from holiday to find Yoko's slippers outside her bedroom door. They were divorced on 8 November 1968. John and Yoko married in Gibraltar on 20 March 1969.

		1	2	3	4	5	6	7	8	9
		Day	S.Time	Sun	Moon	Mercury	Venus	Mars		
A										
B		9	18:42	16 ♎ 16'	03 ♒ 32'	08 ♏ 33'	03 ♍ 12'	02 ♎ 39'	1940	lennon
C		23	23:32	02 ♈ 23'	00 ♓ 40'	02 ♈ 08'	24 ♓ 54'	03 ♍ 19'	1966	ono
D		4	20:25	12 ♏ 09'	16 ♑ 33'	27 ♏ 06'	03 ♎ 35'	19 ♎ 31'	1966	lennon
E		18	21:21	29 ♒ 22'	11 ♐ 07'	07 ♓ 53'	13 ♒ 47'	15 ♏ 07'	1933	ono

Fig.127. Matrix showing the natal planetary positions for John Lennon and Yoko Ono together with their progressed planetary positions for the year 1966

The primary indicator in this relationship is a conjunction between his natal-Venus (B6) and her progressing-Mars (C7), which is moving backwards and applying, along with an opposition between her progressing-Sun

♈	♉	♊	♋	♌	♍	♎	♏	♐	♑	♒	♓
Aries	Taurus	Gemini	Cancer	Leo	Virgo	Libra	Scorpio	Sagittarius	Capricorn	Aquarius	Pisces

(C3) and his progressing-Venus (D6), which was within two degrees from about 1949 to 1970, exact in 1960. In addition to these aspects John's natal-Mars (B7) is also opposed by her progressing-Sun (C3). All of these factors suggest that all their mutual needs and desires will be satisfied in order for a relationship to begin, – love, desire, attraction, the creative will and the urge to make something happen are present – nothing else is required to start a relationship. Keeping it alive depends on many other factors, but the beginning of one relationship here means the end of another. Cynthia's planetary positions suggest her relationship with John has moved to another level, she can't compete with Yoko's timing.

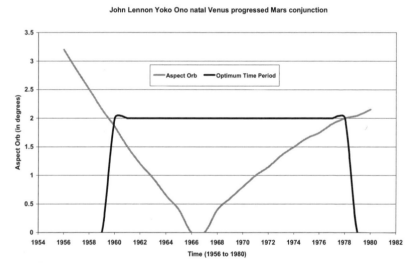

John Lennon Yoko Ono natal Venus progressed Mars conjunction

Fig.128. Graph showing the window of opportunity created by Yoko Ono's progressing-Mars in conjunction with John Lennon's natal-Venus

Although John and Yoko spent many happy years together until his tragic murder in 1980, there was one interruption to their relationship when Lennon had a brief affair with his personal assistant May Pang.

May comments on this arrangement:

♈	♉	♊	♋	♌	♍	♎	♏	♐	♑	♒	♓
Aries	Taurus	Gemini	Cancer	Leo	Virgo	Libra	Scorpio	Sagittarius	Capricorn	Aquarius	Pisces

"One day in June 1973, Yoko approached me in my office at the Dakota. She explained that she and John needed a break from each other — which was obvious to everyone around them. She also decided that I would be his 'companion' — effective immediately. By now, nothing could really come as a shock in the zany world of John and Yoko. But this...this was beyond the pale, even for them."

So began an 18-month relationship that has become known misleadingly as "Lennon's Lost Weekend"... In February of 1975, John and Yoko were reunited."[cxxx]

Their progressed synastry tells an interesting story. May Pang's natal-Venus (E6) was about to be conjoined by Lennon's progressing-Mars (D7).

	1	2	3	4	5	6	7	8	9
A	Day	S.Time	Sun	Moon	Mercury	Venus	Mars		
B	9	18:42	16 ♎ 16'	03 ♒ 32'	08 ♏ 33'	03 ♍ 12'	02 ♎ 39'	1940	lennon
C	16	16:15	23 ♏ 35'	22 ♒ 18'	02 ♐ 09'	24 ♏ 13'	07 ♑ 44'	1973	maypang
D	11	20:52	19 ♏ 11'	12 ♈ 24'	19 ♏ 46'	11 ♎ 59'	24 ♎ 06'	1973	lennon
E	24	14:44	00 ♏ 31'	15 ♈ 38'	25 ♎ 05'	25 ♎ 21'	20 ♐ 31'	1950	maypang

Fig.129. Matrix showing the natal planetary positions for John Lennon and May Pang together with their progressed planetary positions for the year 1973

In 1975 this aspect began to separate. Another useful anecdotal relationship event, but again, only significant because of the frequency of this aspect in relationships and because of the astrological meaning of natal-Venus – progressed-Mars both in Libra is the equivalent of a beautiful damsel being forced by an errant knight to visit his room late at night. However May Pang may have wanted Lennon (and a Venus-Mars conjunction will almost always imply some kind of physical familiarity), the fact remains that the situation was in some sense required of her *"She also decided that I would be his 'companion' — effective immediately"* suggests May Pang had two choices.

♈	♉	♊	♋	♌	♍	♎	♏	♐	♑	♒	♓
Aries	Taurus	Gemini	Cancer	Leo	Virgo	Libra	Scorpio	Sagittarius	Capricorn	Aquarius	Pisces

	1	2	3	4	5	6	7	8	9
A	Day	S.Time	Sun	Moon	Mercury	Venus	Mars		
B	9	18:42	16 ♎ 16'	03 ♒ 32'	08 ♏ 33'	03 ♏ 12'	02 ♎ 39'	1940	lennon
C	18	16:22	25 ♏ 36'	18 ♓ 03'	05 ♐ 14'	26 ♏ 43'	09 ♑ 15'	1975	maypang
D	13	21:00	21 ♏ 12'	06 ♉ 05'	17 ♏ 09'	14 ♎ 24'	25 ♎ 24'	1975	lennon
E	24	14:44	00 ♏ 31'	15 ♈ 38'	25 ♎ 05'	25 ♎ 21'	20 ♐ 31'	1950	maypang

Fig.130. Matrix showing the natal planetary positions for John Lennon and May Pang together with their progressed planetary positions for the year 1975

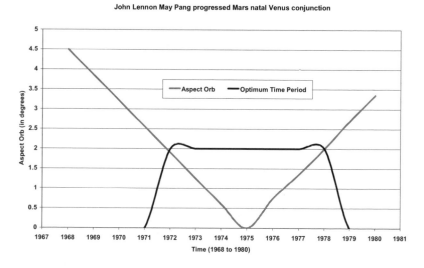

John Lennon May Pang progressed Mars natal Venus conjunction

Fig.131. Graph showing the window of opportunity created by John Lennon's progressing-Mars in conjunction with May Pang's natal-Venus

George Harrison with Pattie Boyd and Olivia Arias; Patti with Eric Clapton

Here we witness one of the great examples of the power of progressed planetary aspects. Beatle George met model/actress Pattie Boyd in 1964 on the set of the Beatles film *A Hard Days Night* and they were married in January 1966.

♈	♉	♊	♋	♌	♍	♎	♏	♐	♑	♒	♓
Aries	Taurus	Gemini	Cancer	Leo	Virgo	Libra	Scorpio	Sagittarius	Capricorn	Aquarius	Pisces

	1	2	3	4	5	6	7	8	9
A	Day	S.Time	Sun	Moon	Mercury	Venus	Mars		
B	24	8:57	05 ♓ 27'	00 m, 09'	09 ≈ 52'	29 ♓ 18'	21 ♑ 23'	1943	harrison
C	8	1:06	18 ♈ 31'	16 ♎ 00'	07 ♉ 15'	27 ♓ 31'	05 ♋ 40'	1966	boyd
D	19	10:28	28 ♓ 27'	05 ♍ 36'	14 ♓ 24'	27 ♈ 34'	08 ≈ 32'	1966	harrison
E	17	23:39	26 ♓ 46'	22 ♐ 36'	26 ♓ 23'	00 ♓ 28'	24 ♊ 41'	1944	boyd

Fig.132. Matrix showing the natal planetary positions for George Harrison and Patti Boyd together with their progressed planetary positions for the year 1966 - Patti's progressed-Venus is behind George's progressed-Sun.

At first glance the pair appear to be quite well matched sharing a wide natal-Sun (Boyd) natal-Venus (Harrison) conjunction.

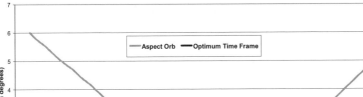

Fig.133. Graph showing the window of opportunity created by Pattie Boyd's Venus in conjunction with George Harrison's progressed-Sun 1962 to 1978

It's difficult to date the exact breakdown of their relationship as it appears that Pattie was besotted with George and vice versa – at first – then

♈	♉	♊	♋	♌	♍	♎	♏	♐	♑	♒	♓
Aries	Taurus	Gemini	Cancer	Leo	Virgo	Libra	Scorpio	Sagittarius	Capricorn	Aquarius	Pisces

George's behaviour began to include extra-marital affairs and regular
meditation, which is best done in solitude. Pattie felt rejected and
according to Eric Clapton used a brief affair with him to try to re-engage
Harrison and win back his attention, the effect of this was to make Clapton
fall hopelessly in love with Pattie and so he began to pursue her. In 1970
Clapton gave Pattie an ultimatum. He showed her a bag of heroin and told
her that if she didn't leave her husband for him, he would take the heroin.
Pattie felt anger and guilt. Eric became a recluse for four years finally
succeeding in his pursuit of Pattie in 1974 after kicking his heroin habit. At
about this point, Pattie's progressing-Venus begins to closely conjoin his
natal-Sun. This conjunction became exact in 1976.

	1	2	3	4	5	6	7	8	9
	Day	S.Time	Sun	Moon	Mercury	Venus	Mars		
A									
B	30	8:16	09 ♈ 44'	02 ♏ 26'	27 ♈ 07'	02 ♉ 59'	04 ♓ 24'	1945	clapton
C	18	1:45	28 ♈ 19'	28 ♒ 30'	15 ♉ 48'	09 ♈ 49'	10 ♋ 58'	1976	boyd
D	30	10:18	10 ♉ 04'	17 ♐ 40'	17 ♈ 23'	17 ♈ 55'	28 ♓ 26'	1976	clapton
E	17	23:39	26 ♓ 46'	22 ♐ 36'	26 ♓ 23'	00 ♓ 28'	24 ♊ 41'	1944	boyd

**Fig.134. Matrix showing the natal planetary positions for Eric Clapton
and Patti Boyd together with their progressed planetary positions for
the year 1976**

George and Pattie's relationship came to an end in 1974, the same year he
met his future wife, Olivia Arias, who was working for George's record
company at the time. The Clapton's married in 1979. Their marriage ended
in 1988.

Pattie's planets follow a path that is reflected elsewhere with great
regularity and it illustrates the difference between Sun and Venus:

Theoretically it shouldn't matter whose Venus is in conjunction
with whose Sun, it should just matter that there is a conjunction. In actual
fact it matters very much. In the Boyd Harrison case, it is Harrison's
progressed-Sun (broadly speaking: *the attracted*) that is leading Pattie's
progressed-Venus (broadly speaking: *the attractor*) down the aisle in 1966.

♈	♉	♊	♋	♌	♍	♎	♏	♐	♑	♒	♓
Aries	Taurus	Gemini	Cancer	Leo	Virgo	Libra	Scorpio	Sagittarius	Capricorn	Aquarius	Pisces

In reality though, their relationship consists of her natal-Sun leading his natal-Venus: she will have to metaphorically wine him and dine him to keep the flame alive. Her Sun (her aspirations) is wooing his Venus (his romantic impulse) because she believes she needs him more than he needs her.

When Pattie tries to get George's attention she does so by using *creative action* (this is one of the Sun's functions in astrology). Then she falls for a man whose natal-Sun will temporarily entertain her progressing-Venus. It is often the case that people choose partners from within their immediate circle. It may be that often one's immediate circle of friends may not contain anyone who is suited to you, but in this case the suit is strong, if temporary.

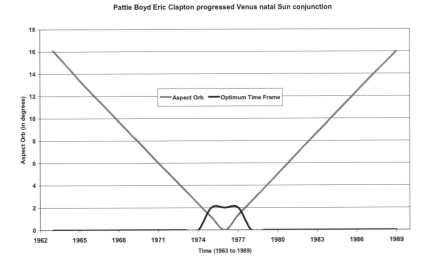

Pattie Boyd Eric Clapton progressed Venus natal Sun conjunction

Fig.135. Graph showing the window of opportunity created by Pattie Boyd's progressing-Venus in conjunction with Eric Clapton's natal-Sun 1974 to 1977

♈	♉	♊	♋	♌	♍	♎	♏	♐	♑	♒	♓
Aries	Taurus	Gemini	Cancer	Leo	Virgo	Libra	Scorpio	Sagittarius	Capricorn	Aquarius	Pisces

Eric and Patti in 1988

	1	2	3	4	5	6	7	8	9
A	Day	S.Time	Sun	Moon	Mercury	Venus	Mars		
B	30	8:16	09 ♈ 44'	02 ♏ 26'	27 ♈ 07'	02 ♉ 59'	04 ♓ 24'	1945	clapton
C	30	2:33	10 ♉ 00'	12 ♌ 41'	13 ♉ 31'	24 ♈ 34'	17 ♋ 31'	1988	boyd
D	12	11:05	21 ♉ 41'	05 ♊ 17'	25 ♈ 42'	17 ♈ 51'	07 ♈ 38'	1988	clapton
E	17	23:39	26 ♓ 46'	22 ♐ 36'	26 ♓ 23'	00 ♓ 28'	24 ♊ 41'	1944	boyd

Fig.136. Matrix showing the natal planetary positions for Eric Clapton and Patti Boyd together with their progressed planetary positions for the year 1988

George and Olivia in 1974

	1	2	3	4	5	6	7	8	9
A	Day	S.Time	Sun	Moon	Mercury	Venus	Mars		
B	24	8:57	05 ♓ 27'	00 ♏ 09'	09 ♒ 52'	29 ♓ 18'	21 ♑ 23'	1943	harrison
C	13	5:26	22 ♊ 21'	12 ♍ 38'	07 ♋ 07'	09 ♋ 00'	11 ♏ 42'	1974	olivia
D	27	10:59	06 ♈ 23'	21 ♐ 35'	28 ♓ 59'	07 ♉ 18'	14 ♒ 33'	1974	harrison
E	18	3:44	27 ♉ 26'	29 ♍ 55'	17 ♊ 00'	06 ♋ 56'	29 ♌ 50'	1948	olivia

Fig.137. Matrix showing the natal planetary positions for George Harrison and Olivia Arias together with their progressed planetary positions for the year 1974

George and Olivia in 1978

	1	2	3	4	5	6	7	8	9
A	Day	S.Time	Sun	Moon	Mercury	Venus	Mars		
B	24	8:57	05 ♓ 27'	00 ♏ 09'	09 ♒ 52'	29 ♓ 18'	21 ♑ 23'	1943	harrison
C	17	5:42	26 ♊ 10'	07 ♏ 47'	05 ♋ 59'	07 ♋ 07'	13 ♍ 43'	1978	olivia
D	31	11:15	10 ♈ 20'	18 ♒ 15'	06 ♈ 47'	12 ♉ 08'	17 ♒ 33'	1978	harrison
E	18	3:44	27 ♉ 26'	29 ♍ 55'	17 ♊ 00'	06 ♋ 56'	29 ♌ 50'	1948	olivia

Fig.138. Matrix showing the natal planetary positions for George Harrison and Olivia Arias together with their progressed planetary positions for the year 1978

♈	♉	♊	♋	♌	♍	♎	♏	♐	♑	♒	♓
Aries	Taurus	Gemini	Cancer	Leo	Virgo	Libra	Scorpio	Sagittarius	Capricorn	Aquarius	Pisces

Sir Paul McCartney and Linda Eastman

Paul McCartney's relationship with Linda Eastman is included here for consistency's sake, but unlike many of the relationships in this study, their's has other qualities that are beyond the usual attraction-recognition qualities of progressed synastry. Every so often I encounter a relationship that does not include the conventional Sun-Venus-Mars connections that I believe draw people together. This requires me to dig a little deeper. In doing so for this case, I found a relationship based very much on the angles of their birth charts rather than just the interaction of the planet Venus, her tantalising qualities are elsewhere in this book, but not here. Here we have two people whose lives were so interwoven they did not need an exact Venus aspect to get them to notice each other. In fact there is a common connection between their natal-Venuses (they are in opposite signs) and without it I'm sure their relationship would have been different, but the primary relationship indicator in their mutual astrology is actually Linda's Sun being in close conjunction with Paul's Descendant. This is the point opposite the Ascendant (or the beginning of the chart) and is actually also the cusp of the 7th house, which is also called the house of relationships. In real terms this is similar to a Sun-Venus conjunction, but the actual relationship acts in terms as if the couple belong together, despite all things. There does not have to be electricity before there is light.

In addition to this Paul's Venus is opposite Linda's Moon, while Paul's Moon is square to Linda's Moon. This couple work together and support

	1	2	3	4	5	6	7	8	9
A	Day	S.Time	Sun	Moon	Mercury	Venus	Mars		
B	24	14:12	01 ♎ 07'	17 ♏ 33'	25 ♎ 23'	11 ♏ 06'	21 ♈ 28'	1941	linda
C	13	7:22	20 ♋ 27'	20 ♋ 25'	00 ♋ 55'	18 ♊ 22'	18 ♌ 11'	1967	paul
D	20	15:54	26 ♎ 47'	26 ♎ 35'	10 ♏ 22'	11 ♐ 11'	13 ♈ 53'	1967	linda
E	18	5:44	26 ♊ 36'	17 ♌ 26'	18 ♊ 21'	18 ♉ 59'	02 ♌ 40'	1942	paul

Fig.139. Matrix showing the natal planetary positions for Paul McCartney and Linda Eastman together with their progressed planetary positions for the year 1967

♈	♉	♊	♋	♌	♍	♎	♏	♐	♑	♒	♓
Aries	Taurus	Gemini	Cancer	Leo	Virgo	Libra	Scorpio	Sagittarius	Capricorn	Aquarius	Pisces

each other's work.

When they met on 15th May 1967, Linda's progressed-Sun was in an exact trine with Paul's natal-Sun. This has the effect of making two people very at home with each other at the start of their relationship.

Sir Paul McCartney and Heather Mills

This couple met at the *Mirror Pride of Britain* awards in May 1999. They became lovers when Sir Paul invited Heather Mills around to his office to talk about a charity initiative (Heather Mills lost part of her leg in August 1993 when she was hit by a police motorcycle, and is now deeply involved with Land Mine clearance and prosthetic limb provision charities).

Although his time of birth is available, hers is not.. I have therefore used his time of birth of 2:30am 18 June 1942 and midday GMT on 12 January 1968 for Heather's natal planetary positions. The first thing that strikes me is the fact that they have a wide natal-Sun-Venus Trine at between 2 and 3 degrees from exact, an aspect I have found to be the most prevalent in long lasting relationships and at just about the same distance as that of John Lennon and Yoko Ono, but not quite as close as the one between George and Olivia. I do not count this aspect in this study at more than two degrees, though I accept this view is conservative.

What it shows us is that he is the romantic one in this relationship: there will be a sharing in many areas including love of art, music and culture. They will also work well together. There is every reason to believe that any couple with this planetary contact natally have a good chance of staying the course, of course this aspect does not give guarantees, nor does it affect the length of the relationship in any other way than make those involved feel very easy in each other's romantic company. It does give warmth and heart to a relationship, but not fireworks. That is the remit of Venus with Mars, and for this couple, Venus and Mars are key to the foundation of their relationship.

Heather's progressing-Mars and Sir Paul's progressing-Venus achieved

♈	♉	♊	♋	♌	♍	♎	♏	♐	♑	♒	♓
Aries	Taurus	Gemini	Cancer	Leo	Virgo	Libra	Scorpio	Sagittarius	Capricorn	Aquarius	Pisces

exact trine around 1999 at the start of their relationship, the effects of this progressed trine will start to fade as his progressing-Venus moves away from her progressing-Mars. From 2006 the honeymoon period will be over. Heather's progressing-Mars will temporarily square Paul's natal-Venus when he's sixty-four. This will test their natal-Sun-Venus trine, but this type of natal aspect is reasonably resilient.

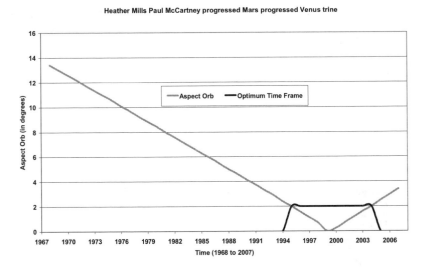

Fig.140. Graph showing the window of opportunity created by Paul McCartney's progressed-Venus in trine to Heather Mills' progressing-Mars 1995 to 2005

♈	♉	♊	♋	♌	♍	♎	♏	♐	♑	♒	♓
Aries	Taurus	Gemini	Cancer	Leo	Virgo	Libra	Scorpio	Sagittarius	Capricorn	Aquarius	Pisces

	1	2	3	4	5	6	7	8	9
A	Day	S.Time	Sun	Moon	Mercury	Venus	Mars		
B	18	18:12	26 ♊ 09'	11 ♌ 37'	18 ♊ 33'	18 ♉ 26'	02 ♌ 23'	1942	macca
C	12	21:26	22 ♒ 50'	00 ♌ 38'	29 ♒ 21'	20 ♑ 31'	26 ♓ 26'	1999	mills
D	14	21:57	20 ♌ 35'	12 ♍ 49'	01 ♍ 44'	26 ♋ 13'	07 ♍ 59'	1999	macca
E	12	19:24	21 ♑ 21'	14 ♊ 37'	00 ♒ 19'	12 ♐ 42'	02 ♓ 24'	1968	mills
F	Day	S.Time	Sun	Moon	Mercury	Venus	Mars		
G	18	18:12	26 ♊ 09'	11 ♌ 37'	18 ♊ 33'	18 ♉ 26'	02 ♌ 23'	1942	macca
H	13	21:30	23 ♒ 51'	14 ♌ 00'	28 ♒ 22'	21 ♑ 45'	27 ♓ 12'	2000	mills
I	15	22:01	21 ♌ 33'	25 ♍ 39'	03 ♍ 34'	27 ♋ 26'	08 ♍ 37'	2000	macca
J	12	19:24	21 ♑ 21'	14 ♊ 37'	00 ♒ 19'	12 ♐ 42'	02 ♓ 24'	1968	mills
K	Day	S.Time	Sun	Moon	Mercury	Venus	Mars		
L	18	18:12	26 ♊ 09'	11 ♌ 37'	18 ♊ 33'	18 ♉ 26'	02 ♌ 23'	1942	macca
M	14	21:34	24 ♒ 51'	27 ♌ 40'	27 ♒ 17'	22 ♑ 59'	27 ♓ 58'	2001	mills
N	16	22:05	22 ♌ 31'	08 ♎ 44'	05 ♍ 22'	28 ♋ 39'	09 ♍ 15'	2001	macca
O	12	19:24	21 ♑ 21'	14 ♊ 37'	00 ♒ 19'	12 ♐ 42'	02 ♓ 24'	1968	mills
P	Day	S.Time	Sun	Moon	Mercury	Venus	Mars		
Q	18	18:12	26 ♊ 09'	11 ♌ 37'	18 ♊ 33'	18 ♉ 26'	02 ♌ 23'	1942	macca
R	15	21:38	25 ♒ 52'	11 ♍ 34'	26 ♒ 09'	24 ♑ 12'	28 ♓ 44'	2002	mills
S	17	22:09	23 ♌ 28'	22 ♎ 02'	07 ♍ 08'	29 ♋ 52'	09 ♍ 53'	2002	macca
T	12	19:24	21 ♑ 21'	14 ♊ 37'	00 ♒ 19'	12 ♐ 42'	02 ♓ 24'	1968	mills
U	Day	S.Time	Sun	Moon	Mercury	Venus	Mars		
V	18	18:12	26 ♊ 09'	11 ♌ 37'	18 ♊ 33'	18 ♉ 26'	02 ♌ 23'	1942	macca
W	16	21:42	26 ♒ 52'	25 ♍ 39'	25 ♒ 00'	25 ♑ 26'	29 ♓ 30'	2003	mills
X	18	22:12	24 ♌ 26'	05 ♏ 36'	08 ♍ 53'	01 ♌ 05'	10 ♍ 31'	2003	macca
Y	12	19:24	21 ♑ 21'	14 ♊ 37'	00 ♒ 19'	12 ♐ 42'	02 ♓ 24'	1968	mills
Z	Day	S.Time	Sun	Moon	Mercury	Venus	Mars		
AA	18	18:12	26 ♊ 09'	11 ♌ 37'	18 ♊ 33'	18 ♉ 26'	02 ♌ 23'	1942	macca
AB	17	21:46	27 ♒ 53'	09 ♎ 50'	23 ♒ 52'	26 ♑ 40'	00 ♈ 16'	2004	mills
AC	19	22:16	25 ♌ 24'	19 ♏ 25'	10 ♍ 37'	02 ♌ 18'	11 ♍ 09'	2004	macca
AD	12	19:24	21 ♑ 21'	14 ♊ 37'	00 ♒ 19'	12 ♐ 42'	02 ♓ 24'	1968	mills
AE	Day	S.Time	Sun	Moon	Mercury	Venus	Mars		
AF	18	18:12	26 ♊ 09'	11 ♌ 37'	18 ♊ 33'	18 ♉ 26'	02 ♌ 23'	1942	macca
AG	18	21:50	28 ♒ 54'	24 ♎ 04'	22 ♒ 45'	27 ♑ 54'	01 ♈ 02'	2005	mills
AH	20	22:20	26 ♌ 22'	03 ♐ 29'	12 ♍ 19'	03 ♌ 31'	11 ♍ 47'	2005	macca
AI	12	19:24	21 ♑ 21'	14 ♊ 37'	00 ♒ 19'	12 ♐ 42'	02 ♓ 24'	1968	mills
AJ	Day	S.Time	Sun	Moon	Mercury	Venus	Mars		
AK	18	18:12	26 ♊ 09'	11 ♌ 37'	18 ♊ 33'	18 ♉ 26'	02 ♌ 23'	1942	macca
AL	19	9:52	29 ♒ 24'	01 ♏ 11'	22 ♒ 13'	28 ♑ 31'	01 ♈ 25'	2006	mills
AM	21	22:24	27 ♌ 19'	17 ♐ 47'	14 ♍ 00'	04 ♌ 44'	12 ♍ 25'	2006	macca
AN	12	19:24	21 ♑ 21'	14 ♊ 37'	00 ♒ 19'	12 ♐ 42'	02 ♓ 24'	1968	mills

Fig.141. Matrix showing the natal planetary positions for Paul McCartney and Heather Mills together with their progressed planetary positions for the years 1999 to 2006

♈	♉	♊	♋	♌	♍	♎	♏	♐	♑	♒	♓
Aries	Taurus	Gemini	Cancer	Leo	Virgo	Libra	Scorpio	Sagittarius	Capricorn	Aquarius	Pisces

All of the Beatles married twice. Two of them, John and George, married on the second occasion a partner whose Venus was close to 120 degrees from their natal-Sun, a third, Paul chose someone whose Sun was close to 120 degrees from his Venus.

So what about Ringo?

Well, Ringo is the odd one out. He seems to have been one of those people who prefers the excitement and unpredictability of the 90-degree square aspect. He has always been seen as slightly unconventional, and both of his marriages have a mix of what astrologers see as the slightly harmonious coupled with the intensely exciting. Couples with square aspects in their relationships can often live on the edge (Ava Gardner and Frank Sinatra are one example). I don't believe these relationships were particular exceptions to that rule. But what Ringo's first marriage had instead of trines was sextiles. This·aspect has not been emphasised in this book because it muddies the issue, the sextile is traditionally harmonious, but is more friendly than it is passionate or idealistic.

Ringo with Maureen Cox

The progressing-Venus (C6) – natal-Sun (B3) square has just separated in 1965, a separating square is far more favourable than an applying square, and although Maureen's time of birth is unavailable. This is an accurate picture of their marriage year. The progressed-Venus (D6) – progressed-Sun (C3) sextile is good, useful, fun, communicative and happy. It is supported by another exact aspect from Ringo's natal-Venus (B6) to Maureen's progressing-Sun. As I've already stated, sextile aspects are good, their only problem is they can be improved upon. Ringo and Maureen divorced in 1975. I have a rule of thumb in cases where harmonious Venus aspects natally and by progression are absent, because I don't view sextile aspects as particularly powerful or passionate, I look to the Moon and her aspect to the Sun or Venus. This is only possible where a time of birth is available.

♈	♉	♊	♋	♌	♍	♎	♏	♐	♑	♒	♓
Aries	Taurus	Gemini	Cancer	Leo	Virgo	Libra	Scorpio	Sagittarius	Capricorn	Aquarius	Pisces

In this case no time is available for Maureen, but we can see that her Moon is in Scorpio (and therefore in a sign compatible to his Cancerian Sun) and his Moon is in the same sign as her Sun, Leo. What is certain is that with Venus in their natal charts being in incompatible signs (Gemini and Virgo), the likelihood that they shared the same view of what a relationship should be like is slim. But that's easy to say now that they're divorced[cxxxi].

	1	2	3	4	5	6	7	8	9
A	Day	S.Time	Sun	Moon	Mercury	Venus	Mars		
B	7	18:04	14 ♋ 40'	04 ♌ 03'	05 ♌ 12'	29 ♊ 24'	02 ♌ 14'	1940	starr
C	23	10:04	29 ♌ 44'	15 ♋ 23'	11 ♌ 35'	15 ♎ 13'	08 ♎ 49'	1965	cox
D	1	19:42	08 ♌ 32'	00 ♋ 52'	24 ♋ 40'	29 ♊ 56'	18 ♌ 07'	1965	starr
E	4	8:49	11 ♌ 29'	07 ♏ 22'	08 ♌ 17'	24 ♍ 37'	26 ♍ 50'	1946	cox

Fig.142. Matrix showing the natal planetary positions for Ringo Starr and Maureen Cox together with their progressed planetary positions for the year 1965

Ringo with Barbara Bach

Ringo and Barbara met on the set of the 1980 film *The Caveman*. Their marriage has been close and it appears happy, reports that they both attended rehab for alcoholism are typical of the square aspect in a close relationship. There is often the necessity to work hard to overcome an obstacle with these 90-degree complexes (there are some natal squares in their synastry). Venus in both natal charts sits in compatible signs, but without any angular

	1	2	3	4	5	6	7	8	9
A	Day	S.Time	Sun	Moon	Mercury	Venus	Mars		
B	7	18:04	14 ♋ 40'	04 ♌ 03'	05 ♌ 12'	29 ♊ 24'	02 ♌ 14'	1940	starr
C	1	8:07	07 ♎ 31'	14 ♐ 46'	19 ♎ 46'	21 ♏ 11'	04 ♏ 29'	1980	bach
D	16	20:41	22 ♌ 55'	29 ♑ 58'	05 ♌ 25'	09 ♋ 02'	27 ♌ 38'	1980	starr
E	28	5:53	04 ♍ 23'	22 ♍ 25'	18 ♌ 34'	20 ♎ 14'	11 ♎ 55'	1946	bach

Fig.143. Matrix showing the natal planetary positions for Ringo Starr and Barbara Bach together with their progressed planetary positions for the year 1980

♈	♉	♊	♋	♌	♍	♎	♏	♐	♑	♒	♓
Aries	Taurus	Gemini	Cancer	Leo	Virgo	Libra	Scorpio	Sagittarius	Capricorn	Aquarius	Pisces

proximity. Of the greatest importance for any couple is the distance between their chart angles and in this case, their Ascendants (based on the times and places they were born) are in an exact trine from Scorpio – Pisces. Theoretically this is useful in a close relationship. Barbara's Moon also sits close to Ringo's Descendant – the sign of a protecting, nurturing and supportive partner.

...and not forgetting **Stuart Sutcliffe and Astrid Kirschherr**, whose relationship blossomed as the Beatles played Hamburg in late 1960. Astrid was the photographer who chronicled the Beatles' German adventure. It is said that Astrid was responsible for their characteristic mop top haircuts. Her relationship with Stuart saw him stay with Astrid when the other four Beatles headed back to the Cavern club and subsequent glory. Stuart married Astrid in 1961 and he died in Hamburg of a brain haemorrhage in April 1962, shortly before the Beatles hit the big time.

Stu's relationship with Astrid appears to have been accompanied by a close conjunction between his progressed-Sun (C3) and her progressed-Venus (D6) in Cancer. This is identical to the conjunction in George and Pattie's relationship.

Astrid's progressing-Venus also makes a conjunction with Stu's natal-Mars (E7) in 1962.[cxxxii]

	1	2	3	4	5	6	7	8	9
			Sun	Moon	Mercury	**Venus**	Mars		
A	Day	S.Time	Sun	Moon	Mercury	Venus	Mars		
B	20	3:49	28 ♉ 48'	06 ♒ 09'	03 ♉ 24'	24 ♊ 57'	18 ♊ 14'	1938	kirschherr
C	13	7:24	20 ♋ 54'	06 ♏ 54'	04 ♌ 22'	27 ♊ 17'	06 ♌ 23'	1960	sutcliffe
D	11	5:16	19 ♊ 53'	03 ♐ 31'	06 ♊ 36'	21 ♋ 25'	02 ♋ 56'	1960	kirschherr
E	23	6:06	01 ♋ 50'	14 ♒ 38'	27 ♋ 06'	07 ♋ 09'	23 ♋ 40'	1940	sutcliffe

Fig.144. Matrix showing the natal planetary positions for Stuart Sutcliffe and Astrid Kirscherr together with their progressed planetary positions for the year 1960

Three of the Beatles experienced a natal-Sun-Venus trine in their relationship, but it's not just Beatles who experience these very common aspects in

♈	♉	♊	♋	♌	♍	♎	♏	♐	♑	♒	♓
Aries	Taurus	Gemini	Cancer	Leo	Virgo	Libra	Scorpio	Sagittarius	Capricorn	Aquarius	Pisces

their relationships. Mick and Bianca Jagger also shared this aspect natally:

And when news reports romantically linked John Lennon's son Sean with Mick Jagger's daughter Elizabeth, you might be forgiven for thinking that it would be extraordinary if they happened to share a natal-Sun-Venus trine, but they do.

And just to make the point that close natal-Sun-Venus *trines* are extremely prevalent in the relationships of British Rock icons it's worth mentioning that David Bowie also shares this aspect – within two degrees – with his wife Iman Abdulmajid... and what's more interesting is that he probably also shared one with Mary Angela Barnett, better known as Angie Bowie, his first wife.[cxxxiii] While I'm on this subject I should also mention Australian musical icons are not immune: Kylie Minogue has had two relationships that contained natal-Sun-Venus trines within two degrees, with actor Rupert Penry-Jones,[cxxxiv] whom she dated in 1999 and with another Australian Rock icon, Michael Hutchence. On the subject of Michael Hutchence...

♈	♉	♊	♋	♌	♍	♎	♏	♐	♑	♒	♓
Aries	Taurus	Gemini	Cancer	Leo	Virgo	Libra	Scorpio	Sagittarius	Capricorn	Aquarius	Pisces

Thirteen

Bob Geldof and Paula Yates and Michael Hutchence

Ever has it been that love knows not its own depth until the hour of separation.
Kahlil Gibran

…Natal-Sun-Venus trines also happen in the relationships of Irish Rock icons, but progressed-Sun-Venus trines can present much more telling information.

Bob Geldof and Paula Yates' relationship is a lesson in how people and situations change. And perhaps more importantly for students of astrology this relationship gives an insight into how too many trines can cause destructive complacency.

Bob and Paula had *two* close natal-Sun – Venus trines, this, as you may have gathered by now, is a very popular aspect among couples and their astrologers, both theoretically and actually, but in its natal state it is most useful when considering how people will react to each other when they are in a relationship.

To actually get the relationship underway we often need mutual progressed aspects to play catalytic roles. Astrology is a very complex subject and it is fortunate that progressed synastry is a system that allows us to tap into a type of astrology that works with conventions. That is: there are very few fixed rules in relationship astrology, but there are a few patterns that

♈	♉	♊	♋	♌	♍	♎	♏	♐	♑	♒	♓
Aries	Taurus	Gemini	Cancer	Leo	Virgo	Libra	Scorpio	Sagittarius	Capricorn	Aquarius	Pisces

recur often enough to allow us to gain insight. In 1977 and indeed through-out their relationship this couple had one of these catalytic progressions. Paula's progressing-Sun is in a consistent trine with Bob's progressing-Venus. Again, this trine came inside a *one*-degree orb in 1977, and remained in 'step', that is, both planets were progressing at the same rate, and in the same direction, for the rest of their relationship. It's as if the time was right in 1977 for them to meet and begin a relationship. In fact, from 1977 through to 1995, this aspect was within one degree.

Paula Yates and Bob Geldof 1977 – the year they met

Around Christmas 1977, Bob was sitting in the Boomtown Rats' promoter's office in Dublin when a waif-like, platinum blonde walked in. She was about 17 years old, had just finished her 'A levels' and was work-ing in London as a charlady. Bob introduced himself and Paula informed him that they had already met. Bob didn't remember. Bob invited her to a concert that night and in the back of a chauffeur driven Daimler, Paula unzipped Bob's trousers. Bob half-heartedly tried to stop her. She after-wards defended her actions by saying she thought that was what all rock stars expected.

Later that evening Bono intoduced himself to Paula.

'Hi I'm Bono. I'm the singer in a band called U2.'

'So what.' said Paula.

At the end of the evening, Bob said to Paula: *'Well, are you coming back with me or not?'*

And so their relationship began.[cxxxv]

Paula was given the nickname 'the Limpet' by the other members of Bob's band, presumably because of her stickability.

At the time the Boomtown Rats shared a house in Chessington, UK. Bob invited Paula to stay and they became something of a regular couple. Paula would make an effort to cook and clean for Bob and later in 1978

♈	♉	♊	♋	♌	♍	♎	♏	♐	♑	♒	♓
Aries	Taurus	Gemini	Cancer	Leo	Virgo	Libra	Scorpio	Sagittarius	Capricorn	Aquarius	Pisces

	1	2	3	4	5	6	7	8	9
A	Day	S.Time	Sun	Moon	Mercury	Venus	Mars		
B	24	13:30	03 ♉ 03'	13 ♏ 50'	06 ♈ 07'	10 ♊ 43'	07 ♋ 41'	1959	yates
C	31	15:56	07 ♏ 18'	20 ♏ 19'	18 ♏ 27'	21 ♍ 25'	16 ♍ 06'	1977	geldof
D	12	14:40	20 ♉ 30'	05 ♋ 46'	28 ♈ 38'	01 ♋ 30'	18 ♋ 06'	1977	yates
E	5	14:13	11 ♎ 29'	09 ♐ 10'	05 ♎ 18'	04 ♍ 08'	00 ♍ 20'	1951	geldof

Fig.145. Matrix showing the natal planetary positions for Bob Geldof and Paula Yates together with their progressed planetary positions for the year 1977

they went on holiday together to Barbados. This was the first 'proper' holiday of Bob's life.

Paula made a living from writing – journalism mainly to start with, but she later became a prolific book writer – as well as TV presenting. In the early 1980s together with Jools Holland she presented Channel Four's seminal Friday night pop music programme *The Tube*... And Bob continued to pursue his career as a recording artist with the Boomtown Rats.

As Paula's star found its ascendancy, so Bob's began to fall. By 1984, Paula was the main breadwinner in the family (into which the charmingly named Fifi Trixibelle was born, also in 1984) as the 'Rats' became yesterday's news.

A moment of inspired realisation changed the course of Bob's life in 1984. Enraged by the helplessness he felt while witnessing a TV news report of the plight of famine victims in Ethiopia, he mobilised the pop music world into one and began a quest to abolish hunger. Bob succeeded in producing *Live Aid*, the most phenomenal concert ever staged, and raised tens of millions of dollars to feed the world's hungry.

Paula and Bob's relationship, although slightly unconventional in some people's eyes, was seemingly stable, wholesome and supportive. This couple were for many years the model of a successful celebrity relationship. Bob Geldof received an honorary knighthood from the Queen in 1986 and married Paula the same year. Some astrologers believe that a marriage

♈	♉	♊	♋	♌	♍	♎	♏	♐	♑	♒	♓
Aries	Taurus	Gemini	Cancer	Leo	Virgo	Libra	Scorpio	Sagittarius	Capricorn	Aquarius	Pisces

changes the starting point of a relationship, and therefore gives the relationship itself a new horoscope. A consequence of this is that it changes the relationship dynamics. Others simply believe that marriage is a different proposition from a de facto relationship and that changes in perception take place on the part of both partners. My assessment of this instance is slightly different. By 1993, their relationship was rocky. Paula was dissatisfied with her role, possibly depressed and although Bob clearly loved Paula, she seemed to blame him for her woes.

Paula Yates and Bob Geldof 1986 – the year they married

	1	2	3	4	5	6	7	8	9
			Sun	Moon	Mercury	Venus	Mars		
A	Day	S.Time	Sun	Moon	Mercury	Venus	Mars		
B	24	13:30	03 ♉ 03'	13 ♏ 50'	06 ♈ 07'	10 ♊ 43'	07 ♋ 41'	1959	yates
C	9	16:31	16 ♏ 20'	27 ♓ 29'	01 ♐ 59'	29 ♍ 46'	21 ♏ 26'	1986	geldof
D	21	15:16	29 ♉ 11'	06 ♏ 54'	14 ♉ 19'	11 ♋ 37'	23 ♋ 24'	1986	yates
E	5	14:13	11 ♎ 29'	09 ♐ 10'	05 ♎ 18'	04 ♍ 08'	00 ♏ 20'	1951	geldof

Fig.146. Matrix showing the natal planetary positions for Bob Geldof and Paula Yates together with their progressed planetary positions for the year 1986

This progressing-Sun (D3) – progressing-Venus (C6) trine never actually achieved perfection during their 18-year relationship; it was always within a degree. In 1986 (the year they got married) it was nearer to half a degree, by 1995, it stretched to a full degree from exactitude. This was a significant year in Paula and Bob's life.

According to most reports 1995 was the year Paula began a relationship with Australian singer Michael Hutchence. In fact their relationship probably began at least two years earlier in late autumn 1993.[cxxxvi] They met originally in 1985 when Paula interviewed Michael on *The Tube* this is remembered by some as an occasion when she flirted with him unabashedly. That was her style though, so no one thought twice about it at

♈	♉	♊	♋	♌	♍	♎	♏	♐	♑	♒	♓
Aries	Taurus	Gemini	Cancer	Leo	Virgo	Libra	Scorpio	Sagittarius	Capricorn	Aquarius	Pisces

	1	2	3	4	5	6	7	8	9
A	Day	S.Time	Sun	Moon	Mercury	Venus	Mars		
B	24	13:30	03 ♉ 03'	13 ♏ 50'	06 ♈ 07'	10 ♊ 43'	07 ♋ 41'	1959	yates
C	16	4:39	26 ♒ 06'	02 ♎ 48'	11 ♓ 06'	23 ♑ 58'	24 ♑ 23'	1985	hutchence
D	20	15:12	28 ♉ 13'	21 ♎ 56'	12 ♉ 26'	10 ♋ 30'	22 ♋ 48'	1985	yates
E	22	3:00	00 ♒ 45'	02 ♏ 52'	27 ♑ 33'	23 ♐ 25'	05 ♑ 37'	1960	hutchence

Fig.147. Matrix showing the natal planetary positions for Michael Hutchence and Paula Yates together with their progressed planetary positions for the year 1985

the time. Their appearance together in a regular interview slot called *'On the Bed with Paula'* in an edition of *The Big Breakfast*, a morning TV show produced by Bob's company in October 1994, was, according to biographer Gerry Agar, simply a continuation of a date the previous night:

'On the morning of 31st October, I flicked on the TV for my customary background viewing of the Big Breakfast, while I got the children ready for school. But I had to stop everything when Paula's interview slot came up – she was on the bed with Michael. I hooted with amazement at her shameless audacity: not content to conduct her affair in the safety of hotel rooms, she was flaunting it to the nation as they ate their cornflakes. And while everyone choked on their toast at the sexual chemistry that oozed from their screens, as if the two of them had just stumbled upon a soulmate for the first time, I was in fits, because Paula had told me the day before that she was staying with Michael that night.'[cxxxvii]

	1	2	3	4	5	6	7	8	9
A	Day	S.Time	Sun	Moon	Mercury	Venus	Mars		
B	24	13:30	03 ♉ 03'	13 ♏ 50'	06 ♈ 07'	10 ♊ 43'	07 ♋ 41'	1959	yates
C	24	5:10	04 ♓ 10'	24 ♑ 52'	22 ♓ 15'	03 ♒ 48'	00 ♒ 28'	1993	hutchence
D	28	15:44	05 ♊ 54'	19 ♒ 27'	28 ♉ 23'	19 ♋ 19'	27 ♋ 32'	1993	yates
E	22	3:00	00 ♒ 45'	02 ♏ 52'	27 ♑ 33'	23 ♐ 25'	05 ♑ 37'	1960	hutchence

Fig.148. Matrix showing the natal planetary positions for Michael Hutchence and Paula Yates together with their progressed planetary positions for the year 1993

♈	♉	♊	♋	♌	♍	♎	♏	♐	♑	♒	♓
Aries	Taurus	Gemini	Cancer	Leo	Virgo	Libra	Scorpio	Sagittarius	Capricorn	Aquarius	Pisces

Michael was in a relationship with Helena Christensen at this point, but on 11 February 1995 the story of Paula and Michael's affair was made public. Michael had wanted to let Helena down gently (or maybe not tell her). Paula was afraid of Bob's reaction, but Bob, although he was distraught, was as selfless as ever and put her mind at rest while also professing a deep love for her. He was willing to forgive. For Paula it was too late. She was entranced.

Michael and Paula's affair was an intense and fateful relationship, Paula obviously liked to be in love and she found it with the man she called 'God's gift to women'. Paula's natal-Sun was in exact opposition to Hutchence's natal Moon. Michael's progressing-Venus was applying in trine with her progressing-Sun.

Paula had effectively swapped a *separating* progressed-Sun-Venus trine for an identical *applying* one. This is very similar to the change Prince Charles had made in 1986 when he swapped Diana for Camilla. The difference here is that Paula was the 'Sun' person in both relationships.

After their first meeting in 1985 Paula is said to have carried a torch for the Australian rocker. She even kept a picture of him on her fridge door surrounded by fairy lights. Bob would pass the fridge every now and again and deface the picture, which Paula would then replace. This apparently went on for years.

In 1985 their progressed synastry was very different to later when they began their affair. There is a progressed-Venus-Mars opposition like the one experienced by Taylor and Burton, except that Paula Yates is the Mars person – the pursuer, while Hutchence is the Venus person – the pursued.

Paula Yates and Bob Geldof 1995 – the year of their public split

It was evident from her later behaviour and comments that she was rebelling against what she saw as drudgery: Bob Geldof's point of view was that sexual passion burns out, he is quoted as saying: *"To live your life*

♈	♉	♊	♋	♌	♍	♎	♏	♐	♑	♒	♓
Aries	Taurus	Gemini	Cancer	Leo	Virgo	Libra	Scorpio	Sagittarius	Capricorn	Aquarius	Pisces

in a state of passion would be tedious because everything is distorted. It is extremely dull and limiting.," whereas Yates is quoted as saying*: [I could be]* "a steaming Jezebel given half an opportunity. Why can't I be? Why can I only be this great lactating person?"

The relationship dynamics in Paula and Michael's charts suggest Mars (here meaning sex) was playing a significant, though peripheral role: Michael's progressing-Sun (C3) was progressing through a trine with Paula's natal-Mars (B7). Paula Yates said of their first assignation: *'Michael did six things to me I was convinced were illegal.'*

	1	2	3	4	5	6	7	8	9
A	Day	S.Time	Sun	Moon	Mercury	Venus	Mars		
B	24	13:30	03 ♉ 03'	13 ♏ 50'	06 ♈ 07'	10 ♊ 43'	07 ♋ 41'	1959	yates
C	26	5:18	06 ♓ 11'	23 ♒ 30'	24 ♓ 01'	06 ♒ 15'	01 ♒ 59'	1995	hutchence
D	30	15:51	07 ♊ 49'	15 ♓ 11'	02 ♊ 39'	21 ♋ 29'	28 ♋ 44'	1995	yates
E	22	3:00	00 ♒ 45'	02 ♏ 52'	27 ♑ 33'	23 ♐ 25'	05 ♑ 37'	1960	hutchence

Fig.149. Matrix showing the natal planetary positions for Michael Hutchence and Paula Yates together with their progressed planetary positions for the year 1995

There is also a wide natal-Mars-natal-Mars (B7 - E7) opposition suggesting that their 'methods of doing things' might be at odds with each other. By 1997 their progressing-Sun – natal-Mars trine has reached exactitude and started to separate. Also, Michael and Paula's progressed-Suns (C3 – D3) were moving at the same speed in a permanent square. They could well have felt that they were sexually and romantically the most compatible couple in the world (at least in 1995), but despite this their lives were not entwined in a mutually progressive path. The Sun in synastry denotes the individual's will and aspirations: their wishes for themselves as individuals or their wishes for others in relation to themselves. When two Suns are in square aspect by progression they should be read as: two wills (or wishes) wanting different things or, because of differing situations that they have grown into (stardom, marriage, motherhood, imprisonment, poverty,

♈	♉	♊	♋	♌	♍	♎	♏	♐	♑	♒	♓
Aries	Taurus	Gemini	Cancer	Leo	Virgo	Libra	Scorpio	Sagittarius	Capricorn	Aquarius	Pisces

lifestyle); demand a compromise from the other party. The Sun is not a significator of compromise, although it does seek to negotiate deals for us by asserting what we want from a situation. Indeed compromise is the domain of Venus and there would always be some mutual difficulty to overcome for them to be together. In an interview in 1997, Michael said of the press coverage he and Paula had received since she left Bob:

*"The press, especially in England, makes a construct of a human, and then they either do two things with that person. They make them beyond human, or they dehumanise them. Bob was taken beyond human to sainthood, and if you left him, that leaves one choice. You are bad, you are wrong, it's as simple as that."*cxxxviii

Hutchence was touring Australia with his band INXS in 1997 and enjoined in a battle of wills with Geldof over where Yates' children would spend Christmas when he was found hanged in a Sydney hotel.

	1	2	3	4	5	6	7	8	9
	Day	S.Time	**Sun**	Moon	Mercury	**Venus**	**Mars**		
A	24	13:30	03 ♉ 03'	13 ♏ 50'	06 ♈ 07'	10 ♊ 43'	07 ♋ 41'	1959	yates
B	28	5:26	08 ♓ 12'	21 ♓ 14'	25 ♓ 13'	08 ♒ 43'	03 ♒ 31'	1997	hutchence
C	1	15:59	09 ♊ 44'	09 ♈ 36'	07 ♊ 00'	23 ♋ 39'	29 ♋ 55'	1997	yates
D	22	3:00	00 ♒ 45'	02 ♏ 52'	27 ♏ 33'	23 ♐ 25'	05 ♑ 37'	1960	hutchence

Fig.150. Matrix showing the natal planetary positions for Michael Hutchence and Paula Yates together with their progressed planetary positions for the year 1997

Paula Yates died of a non-dependant heroin overdose on 17 September 2000.

Bob Geldof now cares for their three daughters, Fifi, Pixie and Peaches as well as Yates' and Hutchence's daughter Tiger Lily.

'It will never go away. It just will never go away. I mean, I lived with this person who I was in love with for 20 years, and she the same and then she wasn't. That's understandable of course, but beyond that, why?

♈	♉	♊	♋	♌	♍	♎	♏	♐	♑	♒	♓
Aries	Taurus	Gemini	Cancer	Leo	Virgo	Libra	Scorpio	Sagittarius	Capricorn	Aquarius	Pisces

There's loads of reasons, but anyone who went through that sort of thing will ask themselves that. People say 'Hey, you get on with it,' but you don't. You're utterly changed. It's a cliché, but you're very bruised.'

'Time does not heal, it only accommodates. [seeking peace of mind] is a neurotic pursuit, people who practise yoga and lock themselves away on mountain fasts and in caves and shit – it's a pathological condition!. It's just a life. A soap opera. It all just happens to you and you have no control over what comes next. [but] It's random, it's chaos and it's fantastic that it's that. You can only control it by saying it doesn't matter. 'cxxxix

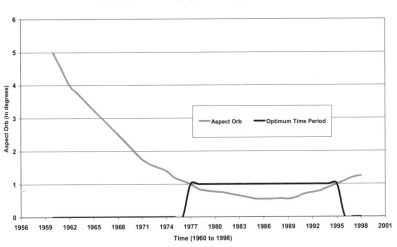

Paula Yates Bob Geldof progressed Sun progressed Venus trine

Fig.151. Graph showing the one-degree window of opportunity created by Bob Geldof and Paula Yates' progressed-Sun-Venus trine that co-incidentally demarcated the years of their relationship 1977 to 1995

This graph shows the progress of Paula and Bob's progressed-Sun-Venus trine. It was five degrees apart in 1960 the year after Paula was born, but closed to within a degree in 1977. It continued within a degree for 18 years never actually reaching perfection. It came closest in the mid 1980s when

♈	♉	♊	♋	♌	♍	♎	♏	♐	♑	♒	♓
Aries	Taurus	Gemini	Cancer	Leo	Virgo	Libra	Scorpio	Sagittarius	Capricorn	Aquarius	Pisces

it was just over half a degree from exact. By 1995 it had separated to be one degree apart for the first time since 1977. So the graph accurately shows that, for this couple, the 18 years of their relationship happened while this progressed-Sun-Venus aspect was within one degree.

The graph below shows Paula and Michael's progressed-Sun-Venus trine. This aspect's pace was far quicker than the Geldof-Yates trine and manifested within a shorter period of time.

It would have achieved exactitude in 2001 – the year after Paula died. After this point it separates as Michael's Venus is moving much more rapidly than Paula's Sun.

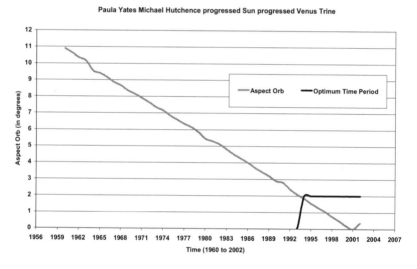

Fig.152. Graph showing the window of opportunity created by Paula Yates progressed-Sun in a trine aspect to Michael Hutchence's Venus from 1993

♈	♉	♊	♋	♌	♍	♎	♏	♐	♑	♒	♓
Aries	Taurus	Gemini	Cancer	Leo	Virgo	Libra	Scorpio	Sagittarius	Capricorn	Aquarius	Pisces

Fourteen

Selected Relationships

There is love of course. And then there's life,
its enemy.
Jean Anouilh

By now my point has been made, progressed and natal aspects of Venus do seem to coincide with relationships, at least in those that become part of the public record. The following chapter rounds up a few relationships of historic and general interest.

A Scandal: Christine Keeler and John Profumo

In July 1961 John Profumo, the British Minister for War, was visiting Cliveden, home of Lord and Lady Astor. A friend of Lord Astor, Stephen Ward, was also present. He had brought along a young friend, Christine Keeler, a girl of nineteen over whom he had something of a Svengali influence. Christine was sleeping with a Russian Military attaché, Eugene Ivanov at the time, but as Profumo became infatuated with her, she also began a relationship with him. This was a fleeting relationship, friendly at first, but which led to sex. The situation, scandalous in itself, was made more complex by the fact that Profumo was sharing Christine's affection with the Ivanov, presumed to be a spy.

When the scandal erupted in 1962, Profumo lied to the House of Commons about his involvement with Christine and when it became clear this was a mistake, he retracted his denial and resigned. A subsequent court case brought against Stephen Ward on charges of living off immoral earnings saw Christine Keeler and her fellow good-time girl Mandy Rice-

♈	♉	♊	♋	♌	♍	♎	♏	♐	♑	♒	♓
Aries	Taurus	Gemini	Cancer	Leo	Virgo	Libra	Scorpio	Sagittarius	Capricorn	Aquarius	Pisces

Davies becoming household names due their performances in the witness box. Stephen Ward committed suicide.

In the political melee that followed, Harold MacMillan resigned as Prime Minister in late 1963 and the conservative government fell at a General Election in 1964, probably as a direct result of the Profumo–Keeler scandal.

	1	2	3	4	5	6	7	8	9
A	Day	S.Time	Sun	Moon	Mercury	Venus	Mars		
B	30	20:34	09 ≈ 31'	01 ♌ 07'	25 ≈ 40'	22 ♐ 57'	00 ≈ 11'	1915	profumo
C	13	21:36	22 ♓ 12'	07 ≈ 55'	25 ≈ 28'	11 ≈ 15'	03 ♊ 35'	1961	keeler
D	17	23:35	25 ♓ 49'	14 ♈ 59'	28 ≈ 19'	12 ≈ 27'	06 ♓ 15'	1961	profumo
E	22	20:21	03 ♓ 10'	25 ♉ 16'	11 ≈ 36'	05 ≈ 31'	22 ♉ 28'	1942	keeler

Fig.153. Matrix showing the natal planetary positions for John Profumo and Christine Keeler together with their progressed planetary positions for the year 1961

Here we witness two favorable Venus conjunctions taking place in 1961. First Keeler's progressing-Venus (C6) is still within touching distance of Profumo's natal-Sun (B3), having moved past conjunction some years before they met, its effect would still be noticeable. The second aspect is a far more important indicator of their relationship. This was not a meeting of minds and the conjunction between Profumo's progressing-Venus (D6) and Keeler's progressing-Venus (C6) creates a romantic scene in 1961. It should also be noted that Profumo's natal-Sun (B3) and Keeler's natal-Venus (E6) are only four degrees from conjunction.

Yet there is another, altogether less favorable aspect also forming with culmination around the same time. Keeler's progressing-Sun (C3) is forming a Square aspect with Profumo's natal-Venus (B6). This aspect creates difficulties and separations. It brings differences into sharp focus and at the time there was a definite contrast between the lives of Keeler and Profumo. He was enchanted by and infatuated with her, but his desire was largely physical. It is my opinion that it is this square aspect is the most congruent indicator of the difficult period that followed, but that without the earlier

♈	♉	♊	♋	♌	♍	♎	♏	♐	♑	≈	♓
Aries	Taurus	Gemini	Cancer	Leo	Virgo	Libra	Scorpio	Sagittarius	Capricorn	Aquarius	Pisces

Fig.154. Graph showing window of opportunity 1955 to 1963 created by Profumo and Keeler's progressed-Venus conjunction

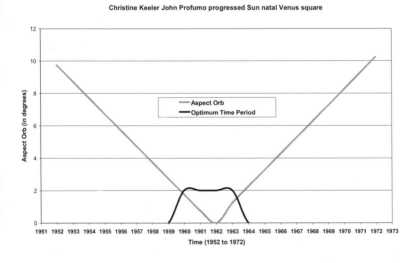

Fig.155. Graph showing the progress of Christine Keeler's Sun in square aspect to John Profumo's natal-Venus which was within two degrees from 1960 to 1963

♈	♉	♊	♋	♌	♍	♎	♏	♐	♑	♒	♓
Aries	Taurus	Gemini	Cancer	Leo	Virgo	Libra	Scorpio	Sagittarius	Capricorn	Aquarius	Pisces

Venus conjunction, this relationship would not have taken place.

John Profumo was married at the time to British actress Valerie Hobson with whom he shared the archetypal relationship aspect, the natal-Sun-Venus trine.

	1	2	3	4	5	6	7	8	9
A	Day	S.Time	Sun	Moon	Mercury	Venus	Mars		
B	30	20:34	09 ≈ 31'	01 ♌ 07'	25 ≈ 40'	22 ♐ 57'	00 ≈ 11'	1915	profumo
C	22	3:58	00 ♊ 48'	18 ♊ 29'	22 ♉ 16'	07 ♊ 43'	13 ♉ 03'	1955	hobson
D	11	23:12	19 ♓ 50'	27 ♑ 56'	24 ≈ 22'	05 ≈ 35'	01 ♓ 32'	1955	profumo
E	14	1:28	23 ♈ 57'	19 ♑ 31'	09 ♉ 55'	20 ♈ 51'	14 ♈ 29'	1917	hobson

Fig.156. Matrix showing the natal planetary positions for John Profumo and Valerie Hobson together with their progressed planetary positions for the year 1955

Their wedding was announced in October 1954 and as can be seen in the synastry matrix, their natal-Sun (E3) Venus (B6) trine is accompanied by a progressed – natal trine of the same variety (C6 – B3). The two-degree window is a fast moving aspect, which opens towards the end of 1954 and becomes exact in 1956.

The graph opposite shows that despite their natal-Sun-Venus trine, the progressed version of this aspect is at its most intense in the years before the Keeler Profumo affair. By 1961 it is over four degrees from exact, which may give us an insight into the reason's why Profumo's roving eye was captured briefly by Christine Keeler. It is certain, however, that Profumo learned from this mistake and realised very quickly where his loyalty and love were most appreciated.[cxl]

Valerie Hobson stood by her husband and supported him as he withdrew from politics. They worked together for charities in the East End of London from 1963 onwards. In 1975, a politically rehabilitated John Profumo was awarded a CBE by Queen Elizabeth.

♈	♉	♊	♋	♌	♍	♎	♏	♐	♑	♒	♓
Aries	Taurus	Gemini	Cancer	Leo	Virgo	Libra	Scorpio	Sagittarius	Capricorn	Aquarius	Pisces

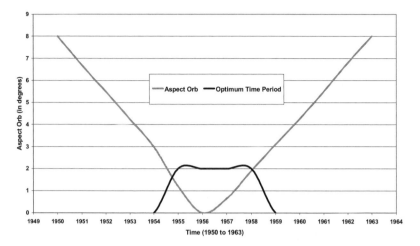

John Profumo Valerie Hobson natal Sun progressed Venus trine

Fig.157. Graph showing the window of opportunity 1955 to 1958 created by Valerie Hobson's Venus in trine to John Profumo's natal-Sun

A Secret Affair: John Mortimer and Wendy Craig

In September 2004 it was revealed that British actress Wendy Craig's youngest son, Ross Bentley, was the born after an extramarital liaison she had with barrister and playwright John Mortimer, writer of *Rumpole of the Bailey* and whose adaptation for television of Evelyn Waugh's novel *Brideshead Revisited* became an international success.

Mortimer was unaware that he was Ross' father until Wendy Craig informed him in 2004, although Ross had actually known the identity of his biological father for twenty years.

It appears that biographers had latched on to the facts and Craig was concerned that Mortimer should find out from her rather than from a book.

Their affair began in 1960 when Wendy was cast in Mortimer's play *The Wrong Side of the Park*, a play dealing with the subject of infidelity. Their relationship continued through another play, *Lunch Hour*, again deal-

♈	♉	♊	♋	♌	♍	♎	♏	♐	♑	♒	♓
Aries	Taurus	Gemini	Cancer	Leo	Virgo	Libra	Scorpio	Sagittarius	Capricorn	Aquarius	Pisces

ing with the same theme, but ended in 1961. In November, after their affair had ended, Ross was born.

Wendy was married to Jack Bentley and when she became pregnant with Mortimer's child she told Bentley the truth and he accepted the situation and brought Ross up as his own.

	1	2	3	4	5	6	7	8	9
A	Day	S.Time	Sun	Moon	Mercury	Venus	Mars		
B	21	1:54	00 ♉ 21'	28 ♊ 12'	14 ♉ 06'	23 ♓ 58'	03 ♊ 39'	1923	mortimer
C	16	7:34	23 ♋ 15'	15 ♍ 23'	15 ♋ 36'	21 ♊ 20'	00 ♋ 24'	1960	craig
D	28	4:20	06 ♊ 07'	12 ♏ 06'	07 ♊ 04'	08 ♉ 16'	28 ♊ 25'	1960	mortimer
E	20	5:52	28 ♊ 27'	01 ♎ 03'	21 ♋ 45'	20 ♉ 47'	12 ♊ 34'	1934	craig

Fig.158. Matrix showing the natal planetary positions for John Mortimer and Wendy Craig together with their progressed planetary positions for the year 1960

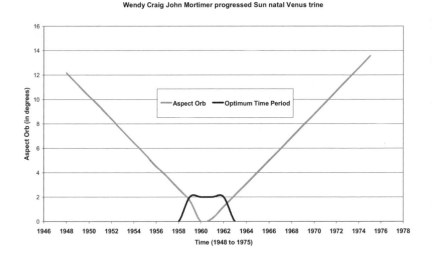

Fig.159. Graph showing the window of opportunity 1959 to 1962 created by Wendy Craig's progressing-Sun in trine to John Mortimer's natal-Venus

♈	♉	♊	♋	♌	♍	♎	♏	♐	♑	♒	♓
Aries	Taurus	Gemini	Cancer	Leo	Virgo	Libra	Scorpio	Sagittarius	Capricorn	Aquarius	Pisces

The timing of this affair sees a progressed-Sun (C3) natal-Venus (B6) trine
that is exact at the height of the affair in 1960. The aspect begins to separate quite rapidly in 1961 and the affair comes to a conclusion.[cxli]

At the time of his affair with Wendy Craig, John Mortimer had been
happily married for eleven years to writer Penelope Fletcher. Their natal
and progressed synastry is based upon Mortimer's natal-Venus (B6) being
in close opposition to Fletcher's natal-Sun (E3). This aspect is also present
by progression. The course of this progression also gives us some evidence
that suggests that the idea that the distance in orb of the applying aspect
mirrors itself in the negative in the separation of a 'primary' aspect. With
Geldof and Yates' progressed trine, they met at one degree applying and
separated at one degree separating. Olivier and Leigh met during a progressed-Sun-Venus opposition that was applying at a distance of 1.25
degrees in 1936; she declared that she didn't love him anymore in 1949
when the same aspect was at 1.25 degrees separating. Mortimer and
Fletcher marry at just over one degree applying and his affair with Wendy
Craig coincides with the aspect waning to one degree.

John Mortimer and Penelope Fletcher

	1	2	3	4	5	6	7	8	9
	Day	S.Time	Sun	Moon	Mercury	Venus	Mars		
A									
B	21	1:54	00 ♉ 21'	28 ♊ 12'	14 ♉ 06'	23 ♓ 58'	03 ♊ 39'	1923	mortimer
C	20	13:52	26 ♎ 17'	04 ♉ 52'	29 ♎ 40'	17 ♎ 35'	13 ♐ 43'	1949	penelope
D	17	3:36	25 ♉ 33'	12 ♊ 58'	10 ♊ 53'	25 ♈ 03'	21 ♊ 08'	1949	mortimer
E	15	11:50	25 ♍ 43'	10 ♓ 55'	07 ♍ 57'	08 ♍ 59'	21 ♏ 48'	1918	penelope

**Fig.160. Matrix showing the natal planetary positions for John
Mortimer and Penelope Fletcher together with their progressed planetary positions for the year 1949**

The progress of John Mortimer and Penelope Fletcher's Sun-Venus opposition is applying within one degree from 1950 reaching exactitude in 1955.

♈	♉	♊	♋	♌	♍	♎	♏	♐	♑	♒	♓
Aries	Taurus	Gemini	Cancer	Leo	Virgo	Libra	Scorpio	Sagittarius	Capricorn	Aquarius	Pisces

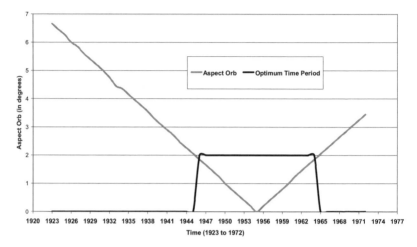

John Mortimer Penelope Fletcher progressed Venus progressed Sun opposition

Fig.161. Graph showing the window of opportunity 1946 to 1965 created by John Mortimer's progressing-Venus in opposition to Penelope Fletcher's progressing-Sun

It again passes the one-degree waning point in 1960, the year of his affair with Wendy Craig. This is a good example of what happens when a very strongly attracting progressed aspect such as a Sun-Venus opposition starts to separate.

This couple divorced in 1971, six years after the two-degree window of opportunity closed. John Mortimer married Penelope Gollop in 1972. They are still together.[cxlii]

Modern Hollywood: Brad Pitt and Jennifer Aniston

Another good illustrative example of natal-Sun progressed-Venus trine aspect resulting in marriage and then separation is in the relationship of Brad Pitt and Jennifer Aniston. In this case, however, because the motion of Venus after Jennifer Aniston's birth involved a period of

♈	♉	♊	♋	♌	♍	♎	♏	♐	♑	♒	♓
Aries	Taurus	Gemini	Cancer	Leo	Virgo	Libra	Scorpio	Sagittarius	Capricorn	Aquarius	Pisces

Retrogradation (Venus appears to move backwards from our vantage point on Earth), the window of opportunity created by the Sun-Venus trine is uncharacteristically extended beyond its usual five-year cycle. In George Sand and Michel de Bourges' case, this window was created by progressing-Sun in a trine to natal-Venus. As the Sun never undergoes periods of Retrogradation, this type of aspect always lasts for five years. With the slightly more common progressed-Venus - natal-Sun trine aspect, this would normally be an approximate five-year process, but only if Venus is in forward motion. In Brad and Jennifer's case this two-degree window is extended to about twenty-eight years from 1989 to 2017.

	1	2	3	4	5	6	7	8	9
			Sun	Moon	Mercury	Venus	Mars		
A	Day	S.Time							
B	18	17:45	25 ♐ 50'	22 ♑ 34'	16 ♑ 05'	23 ♑ 26'	10 ♑ 00'	1963	pitt
C	12	17:44	22 ♓ 30'	18 ♑ 14'	00 ♓ 56'	26 ♈ 17'	06 ♐ 44'	1998	aniston
D	22	20:03	01 ♒ 29'	05 ♉ 02'	07 ♑ 23'	06 ♓ 34'	07 ♒ 15'	1998	pitt
E	11	15:50	23 ♒ 22'	23 ♐ 16'	00 ♒ 27'	09 ♈ 13'	23 ♏ 50'	1969	aniston

Fig.162. Matrix showing the relative positions of the planets in Brad Pitt and Jennifer Aniston's natal horoscopes together with progressed planetary positions for the year 1998

But Brad and Jen announced their separation in 2005, so what happened to their compatibility?

This type of progressed aspect presents compatibility in the form of attraction and therefore creates a foundation upon which a relationship can begin. A relationship is more than just attraction and the symbolic Sun and Venus are in effect striking what is a romantic deal.

Their separation may not have been because they fell out of love or at least fell out of attraction to one another, but that the natal-Sun – progressing-Venus trine, although facilitative in that it gets people together, is not a panacea for love. Underlying this is a natal-Venus (E6) Mars (B7) square suggesting a tangential difference in some areas of the relationship.

♈	♉	♊	♋	♌	♍	♎	♏	♐	♑	♒	♓
Aries	Taurus	Gemini	Cancer	Leo	Virgo	Libra	Scorpio	Sagittarius	Capricorn	Aquarius	Pisces

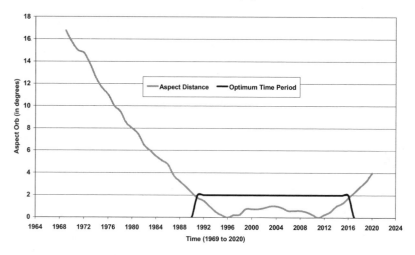

Fig.163. Graph showing Brad Pitt and Jennifer Aniston's extended window of opportunity (1989 to 2017)

Brad Pitt has shared positive Venus synastry with other partners and close friends. His close connection to Angelina Jolie[cxliii] also includes a trine between her progressed-Venus (C6) in Leo and his natal-Sun (B3) in Sagittarius, which is exact between 2004-2005, (this is an identical angle to that of Brad and Jennifer) together with a "Romeo-Juliet" progressed-Venus (Pitt - D6) natal-Sun (Jolie - E3) square, a wide separating progressed-Sun (C3) progressed-Venus (D6) trine is also present.

He shared a similar Venus – Sun relationship with Juliette Lewis, albeit one that developed from being about four degrees from exact in 1989. This trine between Brad's progressing-Venus and Juliette's natal-Sun was exact in 1992. He also shared a wide (four degrees from exact) natal-Sun natal-Venus trine with Gwyneth Paltrow.[cxliv]

♈	♉	♊	♋	♌	♍	♎	♏	♐	♑	♒	♓
Aries	Taurus	Gemini	Cancer	Leo	Virgo	Libra	Scorpio	Sagittarius	Capricorn	Aquarius	Pisces

	1	2	3	4	5	6	7	8	9
A	Day	S.Time	Sun	Moon	Mercury	Venus	Mars		
B	18	17:45	25 ♐ 50'	22 ♑ 34'	16 ♑ 05'	23 ♑ 26'	10 ♑ 00'	1963	pitt
C	3	10:53	11 ♋ 06'	03 ♉ 11'	19 ♊ 47'	25 ♌ 31'	01 ♉ 47'	2004	jolie
D	28	20:27	07 ♒ 35'	01 ♌ 20'	12 ♑ 56'	13 ♓ 52'	11 ♒ 58'	2004	pitt
E	4	8:58	13 ♊ 25'	13 ♈ 05'	22 ♊ 19'	28 ♋ 09'	10 ♈ 42'	1975	jolie

Fig.164. Matrix showing the relative positions of the planets in Brad Pitt and Angelina Jolie's natal horoscopes together with progressed planetary positions for the year 2004

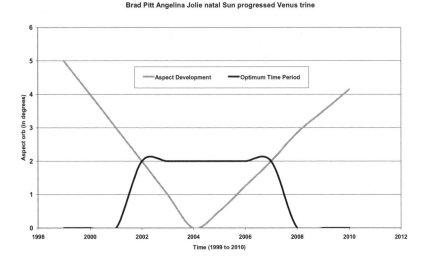

Brad Pitt Angelina Jolie natal Sun progressed Venus trine

Fig.165. Graph showing the window of time formed by Angelina Jolie's progressing-Venus in trine aspect to Brad Pitt's natal-Sun

♈	♉	♊	♋	♌	♍	♎	♏	♐	♑	♒	♓
Aries	Taurus	Gemini	Cancer	Leo	Virgo	Libra	Scorpio	Sagittarius	Capricorn	Aquarius	Pisces

Jessica Simpson and Nick Lachey

'Newlyweds' Nick Lachey and Jessica Simpson share a progressing-Sun natal-Venus *opposition* that was exact in the year they married – 2002.

	1	2	3	4	5	6	7	8	9
A	Day	S.Time	Sun	Moon	Mercury	Venus	Mars		
B	9	15:14	16 ♏ 56'	02 ♉ 07'	19 ♏ 08'	04 ♑ 00'	27 ♈ 08'	1973	lachey
C	1	8:40	09 ♌ 22'	12 ♈ 43'	19 ♋ 57'	26 ♊ 14'	12 ♎ 37'	2002	jessica
D	8	17:08	16 ♐ 15'	24 ♉ 29'	29 ♏ 25'	00 ♒ 26'	26 ♈ 18'	2002	lachey
E	10	7:14	18 ♋ 21'	26 ♊ 10'	20 ♋ 24'	16 ♊ 18'	29 ♍ 51'	1980	jessica

Fig.166. Matrix showing the relative positions of the planets in Nick Lachey and Jessica Simpson's natal horoscopes together with progressed planetary positions for the year 2002

The progress of this aspect can be seen in the following graph:

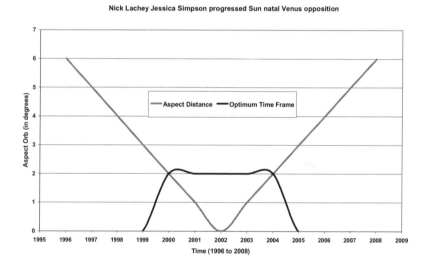

Fig.167. Graph showing the window of opportunity (1996 to 2008) created by Nick Lachey's progressing-Sun in opposition to Jessica Simpson's natal-Venus

♈	♉	♊	♋	♌	♍	♎	♏	♐	♑	♒	♓
Aries	Taurus	Gemini	Cancer	Leo	Virgo	Libra	Scorpio	Sagittarius	Capricorn	Aquarius	Pisces

Bryan McFadden and Kerry Katona

Another couple in the news in Great Britain and Australia in 2004, and who experienced a similar fate to Brad Pitt and Jennifer Aniston, are Kerry Katona and Bryan McFadden. Kerry is a singer and TV celebrity, while Brian is a successful solo artist and former member of record-breaking Irish band Westlife. They met in 1999 and married in 2001. They enjoyed three years of married life and have two daughters. In 2004 Kerry emerged as the winner of a British TV show *I'm a Celebrity Get Me Out of Here*.[cxlv] The same year, Bryan left his band Westlife to begin a solo career. After a number one hit record he approached Australian singer and actor Delta Goodrem to record a duet and they subsequently became a couple. Shortly before this, he told his wife Kerry that he no longer loved her and moved out of the family home.

	1	2	3	4	5	6	7	8	9
A	Day	S.Time	Sun	Moon	Mercury	Venus	Mars		
B	6	11:02	14 ♍ 02'	11 ♌ 17'	23 ♍ 51'	28 ♋ 41'	05 ♏ 24'	1980	katona
C	3	2:46	13 ♉ 11'	19 ♐ 44'	02 ♉ 02'	25 ♊ 04'	29 ♌ 50'	2001	mcfadden
D	27	12:25	04 ♎ 31'	16 ♉ 57'	26 ♎ 34'	21 ♌ 30'	19 ♏ 38'	2001	katona
E	12	1:23	22 ♈ 43'	15 ♓ 13'	26 ♓ 58'	08 ♊ 19'	26 ♌ 05'	1980	mcfadden

Fig.168. Matrix showing the relative positions of the planets in Kerry Katona and Bryan McFadden's natal horoscopes together with progressed planetary positions for the year 2001

Again, as in the case of Brad and Jen, we find a couple with a progressed-Venus natal-Sun trine.

The progress of this trine is not extended by Retrogradation and as such its trajectory is a familiar collision. The separation of the aspect past the two-degree barrier arrives on cue in mid 2004.

This story does not end here, however, (although it is illustrative of the length of time the common natal-Sun progressed-Venus trine will last), because Bryan's new choice of partner is the Australian singer Delta Goodrem, we can take a look at their mutual astrology.

♈	♉	♊	♋	♌	♍	♎	♏	♐	♑	♒	♓
Aries	Taurus	Gemini	Cancer	Leo	Virgo	Libra	Scorpio	Sagittarius	Capricorn	Aquarius	Pisces

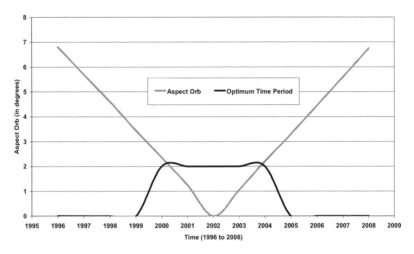

Kerry Katona Bryan McFadden progressed Venus natal Sun trine

Fig.169. Graph showing Katona and McFadden's window of opportunity (2000 to 2004)

Bryan McFadden and Delta Goodrem

	1	2	3	4	5	6	7	8	9
			Sun	Moon	Mercury	Venus	Mars		
A	Day	S.Time	Sun	Moon	Mercury	Venus	Mars		
B	12	1:23	22 ♈ 43'	15 ♓ 13'	26 ♓ 58'	08 ♊ 19'	26 ♌ 05'	1980	mcfadden
C	29	16:34	07 ♐ 27'	28 ♒ 11'	28 ♐ 40'	18 ♑ 34'	10 ♒ 21'	2004	goodrem
D	6	2:57	16 ♉ 05'	28 ♑ 51'	08 ♉ 05'	26 ♊ 52'	00 ♍ 40'	2004	mcfadden
E	9	15:15	17 ♏ 16'	25 ♉ 48'	04 ♐ 21'	24 ♐ 34'	25 ♑ 20'	1984	goodrem

Fig.170. Matrix showing the relative positions of the planets in Delta Goodrem and Bryan McFadden's natal horoscopes together with progressed planetary positions for the year 2004

Not only do Bryan and Delta have a natal-Sun (B3) Venus (E6) trine (this time Delta's Venus is close to 120 degrees from Bryan's Sun because it is at 24 degrees 34 minutes Sagittarius, whereas Kerry's progressed-Venus

♈	♉	♊	♋	♌	♍	♎	♏	♐	♑	♒	♓
Aries	Taurus	Gemini	Cancer	Leo	Virgo	Libra	Scorpio	Sagittarius	Capricorn	Aquarius	Pisces

was moving through the last ten degrees of Leo, the other fire sign), they also have a natal-Mars (B7) Venus (E6) trine within two degrees. There are also a number of progressed planetary aspects that are in various stages of development.[cxlvi]

So in Bryan McFadden's case we have a switch from the progressing or temporary version of the Sun-Venus trine to the natal or permanent version. Although there are no guarantees that a relationship will last, even with the natal-Sun-Venus trine aspect, it does mean that potentially there will be fewer surprises as the relationship develops over time.

Kim Novak and Sammy Davis Jr

Doomed from the start, the love affair between Kim Novak and Sammy Davis was destined to end cruelly for political reasons because he was a black man and she a white woman who also happened to be Columbia Picture's number one female star at the time.

Studio head and notorious dictator Harry Cohn apparently used contacts with 'the mob' to put pressure on the Rat Packer to end his relationship with his prized asset.

Kim Novak had arrived in LA from her home city Chicago in 1953 as a model on a promotional tour of refrigerators for Thor appliances. She liked the climate and so decided to stay. Novak never regarded herself as a good actor, though she considered herself an expert at opening fridge doors.

It was a semi-legendary accident that supposedly brought Novak her film contract. At the time Harry Cohn wanted to teach Rita Hayworth a lesson. Hayworth had married singer Dick Haymes, by many accounts a difficult character, who had taken to managing all of her affairs. She was to appear in Frank Capra's *Joseph and His Brethren* when Dick Haymes marched into Cohn's office demanding that he play Joseph or he would pull his wife from the picture.

Cohn's responded by saying *'Pull her out, I don't give a damn. The next girl that comes through the door will be the queen of the lot'.*[cxlvii]

♈	♉	♊	♋	♌	♍	♎	♏	♐	♑	♒	♓
Aries	Taurus	Gemini	Cancer	Leo	Virgo	Libra	Scorpio	Sagittarius	Capricorn	Aquarius	Pisces

The next girl that walked in the door was Kim Novak.

Cohn was one of the most controlling dictators who ever owned a film studio, which is saying a lot as the owners of the studios (Louis B Mayer, Jack L. Warner, Darryl Zanuck, Joe Schenck and Sam Goldwyn) were very powerful men indeed (they were all men). He groomed Kim Novak to be the successor to Rita Hayworth and effectively turned her into one of Hollywood's biggest stars. At one point she was receiving over three thousand fan letters a week.

Kim Novak's Sun in Aquarius suggests that fundamentally she is either a rebel or a maverick. In any event she was not burdened by the prejudices that seeped through Western society in the 1950s. According to one journalist it may have only been rebellion against the controlling 'King' Cohn that made her go out with Sammy Davis, however, their mutual planetary progressions tell another story.

In their book *The Bad and the Beautiful*, writers Sam Kashner and Jennifer MacNair write:

> *'The Cosmic Connection of the reluctant movie star and the star struck entertainer at first seems unlikely. But by the late 1950's both Novak and Davis deeply resented their circumscribed worlds, his defined by racism and hers by sexism and Harry Cohn* [cxlviii]

Tony Curtis introduced the couple at a party he and wife Janet Leigh gave in 1957. They spent the evening talking. This was reported by gossip columnists the next day. When Davis phoned to apologize, Novak invited him around for dinner. At first they established a careful routine where he would visit her in disguise. Later they rented a house by the sea together.

This relationship defied convention and to many commentators the relationship was an act of rebellion in itself.

In 1957 (and only in 1957) Sammy Davis' progressing-Venus (C6) is in exact conjunction with Kim Novak's natal-Sun (B3). This is the most significant single astrological factor in their relationship. When they met at the

♈	♉	♊	♋	♌	♍	♎	♏	♐	♑	♒	♓
Aries	Taurus	Gemini	Cancer	Leo	Virgo	Libra	Scorpio	Sagittarius	Capricorn	Aquarius	Pisces

party in 1957 the universe was poised and waiting for them to be together, albeit for a brief encounter.

	1	2	3	4	5	6	7	8	9
			Sun	Moon	Mercury	Venus	Mars		
A	Day	S.Time	Sun	Moon	Mercury	Venus	Mars		
B	13	21:45	24 ≈ 21'	01 ♎ 16'	28 ≈ 42'	07 ≈ 34'	16 ♍ 43'	1933	novak
C	9	1:34	18 ♑ 45'	18 ♏ 10'	27 ♐ 54'	24 ≈ 46'	08 ♐ 46'	1957	davis
D	9	23:19	18 ♓ 29'	15 ♌ 58'	06 ♈ 06'	07 ♓ 31'	07 ♍ 50'	1957	novak
E	8	23:27	16 ♐ 09'	19 ♍ 00'	22 ♐ 58'	02 ≈ 57'	16 ♏ 52'	1925	davis

Fig.171. Matrix showing the natal planetary positions for Kim Novak and Sammy Davis Jr. together with their progressed planetary positions for the year 1957

Out on a Limb – Shirley Maclaine with Andrew Peacock

Known to the mysticism-reading and TV-movie-watching public as Gerry Stamford, Australian politician Andrew Peacock was Shirley's karmic love interest in *Out on a Limb*. Although the start-date of their relationship may have been prior to 1978, a delightful Venus progression which slipped inside two degrees in 1977 is present. Using noon GMT for Andrew's birth data (not brilliantly accurate with Australian births) Shirley's natal-Sun in Taurus is just over three degrees from an exact trine to Andrew's natal-Venus in Capricorn. But if we move the time to midday Australian time Venus moves closer by 22 minutes of arc. This trine could actually be inside

	1	2	3	4	5	6	7	8	9
A	Day	S.Time	Sun	Moon	Mercury	Venus	Mars		
B	24	11:05	03 ♉ 58'	06 ♍ 58'	15 ♈ 25'	17 ♓ 55'	01 ♉ 39'	1934	maclaine
C	24	19:53	02 ♈ 47'	10 ♉ 38'	17 ♈ 35'	21 ≈ 44'	01 ♑ 40'	1978	peacock
D	7	13:59	16 ♊ 23'	27 ♈ 40'	09 ♋ 37'	06 ♉ 13'	03 ♊ 41'	1978	maclaine
E	13	17:19	23 ≈ 43'	18 ♐ 04'	19 ≈ 15'	07 ♑ 24'	09 ♐ 01'	1939	peacock

Fig.172. Matrix showing the natal planetary positions of Shirley Maclaine and Andrew Peacock, together with their progressed planetary positions for the year 1978.

♈	♉	♊	♋	♌	♍	♎	♏	♐	♑	≈	♓
Aries	Taurus	Gemini	Cancer	Leo	Virgo	Libra	Scorpio	Sagittarius	Capricorn	Aquarius	Pisces

three degrees if Andrew was born in the early morning in Melbourne, Australia.cxlix

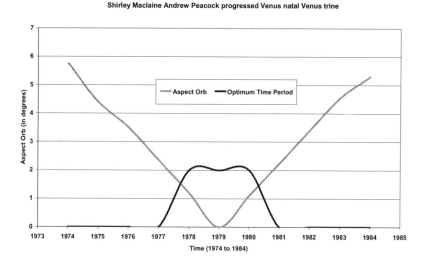

Fig.173. Graph showing the window of opportunity created by Shirley Maclaine's progressing-Venus in trine to Andrew Peacock's natal-Venus 1974 to 1984

The Battling Sinatras

Ava Gardner came from a poor background in North Carolina. She was born in the descriptively named Grabtown and grew up in the nearby Boon Hill Township. The youngest of seven children raised in the midst of the tobacco fields she rolled her first cigarette aged five and when the depression hit town in 1929, the family sold up and moved, first to Newport News in Virginia and then to Rock Ridge North Carolina.

Such a depressed upbringing often sows the seeds of a positive outlook and Ava was not afraid of getting her hands dirty, unlike some of her future colleagues.

Ava's eldest sister Bappie married a New York photographer, Larry Tarr

♈	♉	♊	♋	♌	♍	♎	♏	♐	♑	♒	♓
Aries	Taurus	Gemini	Cancer	Leo	Virgo	Libra	Scorpio	Sagittarius	Capricorn	Aquarius	Pisces

and it was through photographs taken by her brother-in-law that Ava was first noticed. A messenger boy working for Loew's legal department (Loew's was the parent company of MGM) who had seen her picture in the window of Tarr's photo studio took a fancy to Ava and posing as a talent scout got the photos sent to the MGM offices. After it became clear Ava was not a local girl (she was still living in North Carolina) the messenger, Barney Duhan, passed the photographs on to Marvin Schenck, the man in charge of talent at MGM. MGM then offered Ava a job at fifty dollars a week and in due course she set off for Hollywood. She was coached, shaped, modelled and educated into being a film star by MGM. In 1941 she married Mickey Rooney who was then the number one box office draw at MGM. Their 14-month marriage ended in divorce and the straight talking, yet insecure Ava later married the intellectual jazz band leader Artie Shaw. When that marriage ended (because of Shaw's overly critical behaviour), Ava divorced him and embarked on a close relationship with Howard Hughes. She was seeing Howard Duff in 1949 when she bumped into Frank Sinatra, a man whom she had dated on one occasion in 1948.

Frank Sinatra was born in Hoboken. His grandparents had migrated from Sicily in the late nineteenth century, settling in this working class town in New Jersey.

Sinatra's ambitions to be a singer were realised while he was still a teenager. He would sing all night for a couple of dollars or a few packs of cigarettes anywhere that would let him. He was learning his trade; practising for a future he could half-see.

His big break came in the form of Amateur Hour on a New York radio show which made him team up with three musicians from his home town. The Hoboken Four, as they were christened, stayed together for a while in 1930, but Frank didn't want to be the member of a group and ego prevailed.

His steady rise to fame through the 1930s is well documented, as is his 1939 marriage to Nancy Barbato, the wife who had promised not to get in his way in his rise to the top.

♈	♉	♊	♋	♌	♍	♎	♏	♐	♑	♒	♓
Aries	Taurus	Gemini	Cancer	Leo	Virgo	Libra	Scorpio	Sagittarius	Capricorn	Aquarius	Pisces

By the 1940s Sinatra was challenging Bing Crosby for the title of US number one singing star. His style owed something to Crosby's crooning, but not everything. Sinatra had melded Crosby's use of the microphone with a more upbeat vocal texture that was to create a stir among the teenagers of the 1940s. Sinatra's fans actually came to blows with Crosby's fans and their comic rivalry, conducted via their radio broadcasts, was toned down after a serious assault took place between two of their fans.

An MGM contract followed that made Sinatra a star in two mediums, music and film. His late 1940s musicals with Gene Kelly gave Sinatra an opportunity to show that he could also dance.

By 1949, however, the wheel had started to come off for Frank. In his third picture with Kelly he was given second billing and it looked like MGM were thinking hard about his future.

An affair with one of their biggest stars, while he was still in a very serious Catholic marriage to Nancy was probably the worst course of action for Frank, but having told a friend in 1944 after seeing Ava Gardner on the front of Photoplay *'I'm going to marry that broad'*, his fate, luck and underlying optimism conspired to change the status quo and, although he had never been faithful to Nancy, there was something serious about his pursuit of Ava Gardner.

Their date in 1948 revealed they had much in common, the common ground upon which they met may have been related to their poor beginnings. Ava was very sensitive and found it difficult to ignore the contrast between her early life, barefoot in the tobacco fields, and her current life as the icon of glamour, success and the aspirations of others. Like many stars whose beginnings were of such a contrast there was always the fear of being found out or exposed as a fraud. Although Frank may not have shared these insecurities, he will surely have been sensitive to the fact that others had it easier than he did and that certain of these 'others' looked down their noses at 'people like him'.

So their initial date had allowed them to open up to each other and this

♈	♉	♊	♋	♌	♍	♎	♏	♐	♑	♒	♓
Aries	Taurus	Gemini	Cancer	Leo	Virgo	Libra	Scorpio	Sagittarius	Capricorn	Aquarius	Pisces

common bond of communication is often the link that enables individuals to engage in an intellectual relationship.

In late 1949 Frank and Ava met again at a Palm Springs party, where the sparks that would later fly at each other flew between them and they drank, laughed, talked and fell in love.

On their second date Ava quizzed Frank about his marriage. He told her his marriage was over, but that he was committed to his children. This seems to have been enough for Ava and that night they made love for the first time. Ava is quoted as saying:

'Oh, God, it was magic. We became lovers forever. [cl]

Ava broke off her relationship with Howard Duff and became Frank's girl-friend. Frank thought hard about his situation. It is clear that Ava was now the most important woman in Frank's life, but he still had a wife and kids back home, and Nancy was used to his philandering ways. She knew he was easy to tempt, but she had also managed to keep him despite all the affairs he had had during the 1940s, which included trysts with stars like Lana Turner and Marilyn Maxwell.

Lana Turner was a good friend of Ava's and counselled her about Frank in no uncertain terms. She wanted to warn Ava that Frank had been a 'son of a bitch' towards her and a host of other big female stars. Ava told Lana that they were in love and that he would leave Nancy for good. Ava would not compromise on this issue. [cli]

Nancy reacted in typical fashion when she found out, she decided on a trial separation so that Frank could get Ava out of his system. Ava could not understand Nancy's attitude. [clii]

The course of their courtship and marriage did not run smoothly at any point and many casualties were left in their wake. The first of these was Frank's film career, the second his music career, another was his publicist George Evans whom Frank fired after Ava questioned the fact that he (Frank) followed all of Evans' advice to the letter. She thought Evans

♈	♉	♊	♋	♌	♍	♎	♏	♐	♑	♒	♓
Aries	Taurus	Gemini	Cancer	Leo	Virgo	Libra	Scorpio	Sagittarius	Capricorn	Aquarius	Pisces

pushed Frank around and by firing him, Frank was proving a point. Problems followed. Frank's singing career took a nosedive, his records stopped selling, a stupid joke he told about Louis B Mayer saw him ejected from MGM and his contract cancelled. Consequently, over the next two years, Frank's stock started to drop. His concerts weren't well received, partly due to a problem with his voice and partly to do with the negative publicity he garnered following his romance with Ava. Many of Frank's other infidelities started to become public knowledge and in the early 1950s that was very bad news indeed.

The couple were married, eventually, after Frank's divorce from Nancy was granted and also after many fights, wedding postponements and engagement-ring-throwing, in November 1951. Frank was not financially stable at the time and Ava paid for everything. Their honeymoon, at least, appears to have been fight-free. Shortly after their marriage they were dubbed the 'Battling Sinatra's' because of both their public and well-attested private fall outs.

Jealousy played a big part in their shared problems. Frank was jealous of Ava's continuing platonic relationship with her ex-husband Artie Shaw. On one occasion in New York Ava was visiting Artie and his girlfriend at the time, Ruth Cosgrove, at their apartment. Frank found out and went after her. When he saw her in Shaw's apartment with a drink in her hand he said goodbye, returned to their hotel and staged a fake suicide. It was not the first time or the last he would cry out to Ava in such a way.

Just prior to their marriage, Ava had been sent to Spain by MGM (ostensibly to get her out of the way) to shoot *Pandora and the Flying Dutchman*, with James Mason. While there she had a brief one-night-stand with bullfighter-turned-actor, Mario Cabre (Ava had a soft spot for bullfighters). Cabre used his relationship with Ava to further his own career and word got back to Frank who was dying (not literally, but almost) on stage at the Copacabana club in New York due to a submucosal throat haemorrhage. Frank made off for Spain at the earliest opportunity to confront Ava. Frank

♈	♉	♊	♋	♌	♍	♎	♏	♐	♑	♒	♓
Aries	Taurus	Gemini	Cancer	Leo	Virgo	Libra	Scorpio	Sagittarius	Capricorn	Aquarius	Pisces

was dependent upon pills at the time, mainly for sleeping, and was quite sick, but he eventually confronted Ava about the affair.

According to Randy Taraborelli, Frank shook Ava violently and pleaded:

> 'Why are you doing this? Don't you know how I feel about you? Don't you know what you're doing to me, lady? Help me. Help us. I'm begging you Ava. ᶜliii

Ava's response was headstrong and unsympathetic. She told Frank to fuck off. She insisted that she and Cabre were 'just friends'. She was lying. But she was asserting herself. She knew that Frank needed her more than she needed him and she was treating Frank the same way that he had treated so many women in the past. If Frank had done the same to her, she would not have put up with it and through this self-confident attitude Ava was able to control all of her relationships. Shortly after this interlude, Frank flew to Paris and Mario Cabre returned to Spain after shooting some location scenes in Italy. The demonstrative Cabre was also declaring his undying love for 'Senorita Ava' in front of reporters.

Senorita Ava did more or less the same thing to Senor Cabre as she had done to Senor Sinatra. She used him, kicked him out of her room and then stopped off in Paris to rekindle her relationship with Frank en-route to London.

Ava Gardner had the upper hand throughout her relationship with Frank Sinatra, mainly because of the fact that for the few years they were together she was the bigger star. Their constant cycle of bickering, fighting and then making up began to wear thin after a while and after an attempted reconciliation in Africa where Ava was filming *Mogambo* with Clark Gable and Grace Kelly, things started to look up for Frank. He landed the part of Private Maggio in *From Here to Eternity* (allegedly after Ava had exerted influence on Columbia pictures boss Harry Cohn, through her friendship with his wife), which led to an Oscar winning performance. In contrast to

♈	♉	♊	♋	♌	♍	♎	♏	♐	♑	♒	♓
Aries	Taurus	Gemini	Cancer	Leo	Virgo	Libra	Scorpio	Sagittarius	Capricorn	Aquarius	Pisces

this, Ava had two pregnancy terminations, signalling the beginning of the end for their relationship.

The synastry between Ava and Frank is complex and interesting and enables us to see the contrast between harmonious Venus synastry and conflicting Venus synastry.

Their actual relationship was filled with jealousy, disagreements, drinking, petty arguments and making-up. Although it was passionate and sexual, there are conflicting reports of just how good it was in this area.

Sinatra's biographer Randy Taraborelli suggests the following:

'The extraordinary passion that burned between them was undeniable. It fused them together in a magical and as it would turn out – damaging way.'[cliv]

	1	2	3	4	5	6	7	8	9
A	Day	S.Time	Sun	Moon	Mercury	Venus	Mars		
B	12	13:19	19 ♐ 13'	05 ♓ 07'	17 ♐ 09'	11 ♑ 55'	27 ♌ 34'	1915	sinatra
C	20	8:07	29 ♑ 56'	14 ♓ 50'	14 ♒ 56'	14 ♐ 01'	29 ♓ 41'	1949	gardner
D	15	15:33	23 ♑ 51'	29 ♉ 21'	11 ♒ 13'	24 ♒ 09'	28 ♌ 26'	1949	sinatra
E	24	6:20	02 ♑ 25'	19 ♓ 02'	12 ♑ 42'	26 ♏ 09'	09 ♓ 53'	1922	gardner

Fig.174. Matrix showing the natal planetary positions for Ava Gardner and Frank Sinatra together with their progressed planetary positions for the year 1949

Ava and Frank shared a natal-Venus (Ava) Mars (Frank) Square (E6-B7). This most conflicting of angles is more of a problem because it is in fixed signs. It is present in both the natal and natal – progressed states in their relationship. During their courtship and marriage another square between Frank's progressed-Venus and Ava's natal-Venus (D6-E6) also forms and separates. Frank's progressing-Mars (D7) is Retrograde and so, moving backwards, it begins to underline and amplify their natal-Mars-Venus Square in about 1950.

In contrast to this relationship, which would mean nothing if this couple hadn't had the capacity for a different type of relationship with

♈	♉	♊	♋	♌	♍	♎	♏	♐	♑	♒	♓
Aries	Taurus	Gemini	Cancer	Leo	Virgo	Libra	Scorpio	Sagittarius	Capricorn	Aquarius	Pisces

different person, stands Sinatra's marriage to Barbara Marx and Ava's relationship with Artie Shaw, whom Taraborelli describes as the love of her life.

Shaw and Gardner share two significant progressions in 1945. Shaw's progressing-Venus is temporarily opposite Gardner's natal-Venus, while her progressing-Sun is separating from a trine to his progressing-Venus.

	1	2	3	4	5	6	7	8	9
A	Day	S.Time	Sun	Moon	Mercury	Venus	Mars		
B	24	6:20	02 ♑ 25'	19 ♓ 02'	12 ♑ 42'	26 ♏ 09'	09 ♓ 53'	1922	gardner
C	27	6:18	04 ♋ 56'	00 ♓ 34'	13 ♊ 57'	27 ♉ 18'	05 ♌ 12'	1945	shaw
D	16	7:51	25 ♑ 52'	24 ♑ 36'	14 ♒ 03'	10 ♐ 34'	26 ♓ 46'	1945	gardner
E	23	4:00	01 ♊ 27'	23 ♏ 25'	04 ♊ 49'	17 ♈ 37'	13 ♋ 25'	1910	shaw

Fig.175. Matrix showing the natal planetary positions for Ava Gardner and Artie Shaw together with their progressed planetary positions for the year 1945

Sinatra was married on a further two occasions. First to Mia Farrow, thirty years his junior, Frank was fifty when they married. The lovely attracting progressed-Venus progressed-Mars trine is key to their relationship.

	1	2	3	4	5	6	7	8	9
A	Day	S.Time	Sun	Moon	Mercury	Venus	Mars		
B	12	13:19	19 ♐ 13'	05 ♓ 07'	17 ♐ 09'	11 ♑ 55'	27 ♌ 34'	1915	sinatra
C	28	5:59	09 ♓ 51'	29 ♍ 45'	09 ♓ 47'	23 ♈ 33'	11 ♒ 06'	1964	farrow
D	30	16:32	09 ♒ 06'	09 ♐ 25'	20 ♒ 58'	12 ♓ 35'	24 ♌ 12'	1964	sinatra
E	9	4:45	20 ♒ 42'	12 ♑ 14'	06 ♒ 54'	07 ♈ 23'	26 ♑ 27'	1945	farrow

Fig.176. Matrix showing the natal planetary positions for Frank Sinatra and Mia Farrow together with their progressed planetary positions for the year 1964

Again we have an example of a progressed aspect becoming exact at the crucial time in a relationship.

♈	♉	♊	♋	♌	♍	♎	♏	♐	♑	♒	♓
Aries	Taurus	Gemini	Cancer	Leo	Virgo	Libra	Scorpio	Sagittarius	Capricorn	Aquarius	Pisces

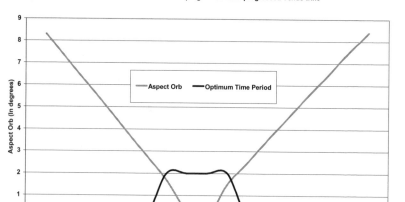

Fig.177. Graph showing the window of opportunity created by Farrow and Sinatra progressed-Venus-Mars trine within two degrees from 1963 to 1966

Mia was relaxing on the 20th Century Fox lot in October 1964 when she wandered on to the set of Sinatra's film, *Von Ryan's Express*. Mia was taking a break from acting in *Peyton Place* at the time and the clumsy 19 year old was invited to sit down by Frank after nearly ruining a scene by getting into the shot. They had met eight years previously when Mia was eleven, but Frank may not have remembered.

The contents of Mia's shoulder bag emptied onto the floor at Frank's feet as she sat and he helped her pick them up. Her dental brace (retainer), jars of baby food for her cat, tampons, parts of a green doughnut and her chapstick. She apologised profusely and no doubt felt like a klutz. She said of the incident:

'I thought the only thing I could do now is get out of here and with any shred of dignity that might remain. And as I stood up to leave, his eyes met mine, and my heart stopped, you know? Everything came together.

♈	♉	♊	♋	♌	♍	♎	♏	♐	♑	♒	♓
Aries	Taurus	Gemini	Cancer	Leo	Virgo	Libra	Scorpio	Sagittarius	Capricorn	Aquarius	Pisces

I was just so alive at that moment, whole parts of me that I had never used before. [clv]

In her autobiography, she describes the feelings further:

'I felt a column of light rising inside me, pulling particles from dark dead corners. I was a little dazed when I headed back to work.'

Frank invited Mia to a private screening of his first directorial effort *None But The Brave* in a Warner Brothers screening room. He held her hand.

Afterwards he invited Mia to his home is Palm Springs, sending a private plane for Mia and her cat. [clvi]

The enchanting beginning of Mia and Frank's relationship led to marriage in 1966, a marriage that was at least happy for a time. Cracks started to appear in 1967 after Mia was photographed dancing with Frank's arch enemy Bobby Kennedy. Frank's reaction was typically an over reaction to an innocent issue. Mia had meant no harm, but Frank hated Bobby for banning him from the White House after John Kennedy's victory. Frank felt betrayed by Mia.

After things calmed down a little, (and after a heated showdown with Mia) Frank decided that they should act in a movie together and decided upon *The Detective*. Mia protested that she preferred to do her own thing, but eventually agreed, but first she would do Polanski's *Rosemary's Baby*.

When shooting on the Polanski film over ran, Frank tried to pull Mia from the film, something she would not countenance.

Frank cast Jacqueline Bisset in an abbreviated version of Mia's role and commenced to have an affair with Lee Remick who also appeared in the picture.

It was October 1967 and the Sinatra Farrow marriage was over.

Doris Sinatra, Frank's mother, counselled him, asking if he was still happy. He responded in the negative. She advised divorce.

Divorce papers were filed on Mia on the set of *Rosemary's Baby* on the

♈	♉	♊	♋	♌	♍	♎	♏	♐	♑	♒	♓
Aries	Taurus	Gemini	Cancer	Leo	Virgo	Libra	Scorpio	Sagittarius	Capricorn	Aquarius	Pisces

day before Thanksgiving 1967.

Although Frank and Mia were briefly reunited over the Christmas holidays, their relationship had ended. Frank knew that Mia needed him in the same way he had needed Ava and although he loved her, he was tough. His decision was made

Laurence Olivier and Vivien Leigh

Vivian Leigh was born near Darjeeling, India on 5 November 1913. Her father was an exchange broker in Calcutta. Her first film role was in the British production *Things are Looking Up* in 1934. She went on to work with the popular Gracie Fields in *Look up and Laugh* in 1935.

Both Olivier and Leigh were in marriages when their affair began. They had been introduced by a mutual friend at the Savoy Grill in London and Leigh, whose husband was the lawyer, Leigh Holman, got on famously well with both Olivier and his wife Jill Esmond.

A 1937 engagement in Elsinore, Denmark, the setting for Shakespeare's *Hamlet*, saw them become close and their relationship began. They decided to come clean to their respective spouses, who both hoped that the affair would burn out quickly. Olivier's child was only weeks old when he took up with Vivien Leigh.

They married on 31 August 1940, soon after Olivier's divorce from Jill became final. They had by now spent three years as lovers and during this period Vivien had become an even bigger star than Olivier by clinching the role of Scarlett O'Hara in *Gone With The Wind*, the most sought after part in Hollywood history.

The picture painted by both the press and the couple was that they were so divinely lucky and happy together; that their love was totally unselfish – that each wanted the best for the other – and that their romance was not tarnished by rivalry. But there was an unfortunate fly on their apple pie in the shape of Vivien's mental health. She suffered gradually and quite seriously from a manic depressive illness that made her moods swing from complete

♈	♉	♊	♋	♌	♍	♎	♏	♐	♑	♒	♓
Aries	Taurus	Gemini	Cancer	Leo	Virgo	Libra	Scorpio	Sagittarius	Capricorn	Aquarius	Pisces

euphoria to abject depression and there was little anyone, least of all Olivier, could do about it. He was obviously and seriously besotted with Vivien as she was with him, but as the years went by he found it increasingly difficult to keep their marriage afloat. Vivien's unpredictable behaviour wore him down and although sympathetic to her illness in the extreme, the love that they shared was gradually undermined. It was a characteristic of her illness that she could not remember the darkest episodes.

The couple kept up the façade that everything was perfect due their theatrical genius, and Vivien's illness was always referred to as a 'nervous breakdown'. It is obvious that her emotional volatility, while adding greatly to her dramatic presence, was not something she could easily control.

Across the back cover of Jesse Lasky Jnr's book about their relationship *Love Scene* are the words *Star-Crossed Lovers*. Again this phrase is actually apt, for if it means anything in astrology it means two of the planets related to relationships, this time Mars and Venus, are at an angle of 90 degrees, which in astrology provides a quarter of the configuration known as the Grand Cross. Olivier's natal-Mars and Leigh's natal-Venus are indeed 90 degrees apart and this aspect although not particularly harmonious, does tend to provide a relationship with very passionate and exciting sexual dynamics. It is not the primary indicator in this union, but it is a very relevant factor that adequately describes the manner in which their relationship began (it was not the easy glide from bachelorhood/spinsterhoood into a marriage of love, light and flowers) and how it ended. So what heavenly

	1	2	3	4	5	6	7	8	9
A	Day	S.Time	Sun	Moon	Mercury	Venus	Mars		
B	22	20:54	29 ♉ 57'	19 ♍ 08'	27 ♉ 18'	29 ♈ 29'	17 ♑ 43'	1907	olivier
C	29	15:54	06 ♐ 39'	24 ♐ 57'	23 ♏ 36'	18 ♏ 51'	24 ♋ 31'	1937	leigh
D	21	22:52	28 ♊ 40'	24 ♎ 23'	23 ♋ 08'	05 ♊ 37'	17 ♑ 19'	1937	olivier
E	5	14:20	12 ♏ 27'	09 ♒ 06'	05 ♐ 32'	18 ♎ 51'	21 ♋ 42'	1913	leigh

Fig.178. Matrix showing the natal planetary positions for Laurence Olivier and Vivien Leigh together with their progressed planetary positions for the year 1937

♈	♉	♊	♋	♌	♍	♎	♏	♐	♑	♒	♓
Aries	Taurus	Gemini	Cancer	Leo	Virgo	Libra	Scorpio	Sagittarius	Capricorn	Aquarius	Pisces

aspect can be seen to have brought them together and kept them together, at least until their divorce in 1961? Again it is a connection between the Sun and Venus, but this time it is the opposition – another powerful and passionate astrological dynamic. In every Grand Cross there are two oppositions and four squares, so again star-crossed is an accurate descriptive term for the astrological element that almost certainly brought these two together.

In 1937 Leigh's progressing-Sun was moving more slowly than Olivier's progressing-Venus, but the two progressing planets were just about one degree from opposition. It took a few years for Olivier's Venus to catch up with Leigh's Sun and it did so sometime between 1942 and 1943. If the factor that brought them together *was* their progressing-Sun-Venus opposition, then this point in time is the culmination of their relationship. After 1943 the aspect separates, perhaps imperceptibly at first, but as it separates, the distance between the lovers becomes wider.

	1	2	3	4	5	6	7	8	9
A	Day	S.Time	Sun	Moon	Mercury	Venus	Mars		
B	22	20:54	29 ♉ 57'	19 ♍ 08'	27 ♉ 18'	29 ♈ 29'	17 ♑ 43'	1907	olivier
C	2	16:06	09 ♐ 42'	04 ♒ 35'	22 ♏ 39'	22 ♏ 36'	24 ♋ 20'	1940	leigh
D	24	23:04	01 ♋ 32'	07 ♐ 37'	26 ♋ 43'	09 ♊ 15'	16 ♑ 41'	1940	olivier
E	5	14:20	12 ♏ 27'	09 ♒ 06'	05 ♐ 32'	18 ♎ 51'	21 ♋ 42'	1913	leigh

Fig.179. Matrix showing the natal planetary positions for Laurence Olivier and Vivien Leigh together with their progressed planetary positions for the year 1940

	1	2	3	4	5	6	7	8	9
A	Day	S.Time	Sun	Moon	Mercury	Venus	Mars		
B	22	20:54	29 ♉ 57'	19 ♍ 08'	27 ♉ 18'	29 ♈ 29'	17 ♑ 43'	1907	olivier
C	11	16:42	18 ♐ 50'	23 ♉ 15'	27 ♏ 56'	03 ♐ 54'	23 ♋ 04'	1949	leigh
D	3	23:40	10 ♋ 06'	17 ♈ 20'	04 ♌ 38'	20 ♊ 10'	14 ♑ 23'	1949	olivier
E	5	14:20	12 ♏ 27'	09 ♒ 06'	05 ♐ 32'	18 ♎ 51'	21 ♋ 42'	1913	leigh

Fig.180. Matrix showing the natal planetary positions for Laurence Olivier and Vivien Leigh together with their progressed planetary positions for the year 1949

♈	♉	♊	♋	♌	♍	♎	♏	♐	♑	♒	♓
Aries	Taurus	Gemini	Cancer	Leo	Virgo	Libra	Scorpio	Sagittarius	Capricorn	Aquarius	Pisces

By 1949 the progressed-Sun-Venus opposition that I would highlight as the primary factor that brought this couple into each other's arms, has reached a distance of 1.25 degrees of separation. This was the same distance it had been apart when their affair began (but in 1937 it was applying and therefore would create a feeling of optimistic, passionate anticipation).

In spring 1949 Leigh delivered a blow of mighty proportions to Olivier by declaring *'I don't love you any more'*.clvii In fact she said that she saw their relationship more as that of a brother and sister (even though 'incest' was still encouraged). It appears then, that in this particular case the window of opportunity is almost exactly equal in length of applying (1935 to 1942) and separating (1943 to 1950) and even though this couple stayed together for ten more years, or more precisely acted their relationship out on the public stage, their love was at its height during the window created by their Sun-Venus opposition.

Progressed-Sun progressed-Venus aspects can last a reasonable length of time and while present they give the impression of deep and meaningful love. On passing they leave a feeling of confusion, doubt and sometimes frustration.

	1	2	3	4	5	6	7	8	9
			Sun	Moon	Mercury	**Venus**	Mars		
A	Day	S.Time	Sun	Moon	Mercury	Venus	Mars		
B	22	20:54	29 ♉ 57'	19 ♍ 08'	27 ♉ 18'	29 ♈ 29'	17 ♑ 43'	1907	olivier
C	21	17:21	29 ♐ 00'	09 ♎ 26'	10 ♐ 26'	16 ♐ 28'	20 ♋ 23'	1959	leigh
D	13	0:19	19 ♋ 39'	17 ♌ 42'	07 ♌ 07'	02 ♋ 21'	11 ♑ 27'	1959	olivier
E	5	14:20	12 ♏ 27'	09 ♒ 06'	05 ♐ 32'	18 ♎ 51'	21 ♋ 42'	1913	leigh

Fig.181. Matrix showing the natal planetary positions for Laurence Olivier and Vivien Leigh together with their progressed planetary positions for the year 1959

♈	♉	♊	♋	♌	♍	♎	♏	♐	♑	♒	♓
Aries	Taurus	Gemini	Cancer	Leo	Virgo	Libra	Scorpio	Sagittarius	Capricorn	Aquarius	Pisces

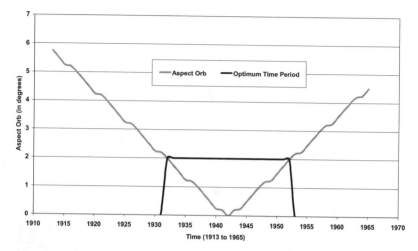

Laurence Olivier Vivian Leigh progressed Venus progressed Sun opposition

Fig.182. Graph showing the window of opportunity created by Laurence Olivier's progressing-Venus in opposition to Vivien Leigh's progressing-Sun 1931 to 1953

Vivien Leigh and Peter Finch

One of the reasons for the failure of their marriage was Vivien's very strong sex-drive, exascerpated by her illness. She is supposed to have had sex with strangers in public places while in her manic depressive state.

The Oliviers had 'discovered' Peter Finch in Sydney during their Australian tour in 1948. They invited him to come to London, signed him to a contract and kickstarted his career.

It is said that both Olivier and Leigh were fascinated by Peter Finch, but that Vivien's affair with Finch began in 1953 when they travelled to Ceylon to film *Elephant Walk*. Their affair was not discreet and coincided with one of Vivien's more difficult periods of illness.

Her behaviour was such that the film's director, Irving Asher, contacted Olivier who flew out from London (not an easy or safe flight in those days) to try to help bring the film, and its stars, back on track. Finch was warned

♈	♉	♊	♋	♌	♍	♎	♏	♐	♑	♒	♓
Aries	Taurus	Gemini	Cancer	Leo	Virgo	Libra	Scorpio	Sagittarius	Capricorn	Aquarius	Pisces

of Olivier's arrival and moved out of Vivien's rooms. He had contributed to Vivien's state by encouraging her to drink. Her difficult behaviour and demands led to her re-writing scenes with dialogue that made no sense.

Olivier arrived and assessing the situation, was told that the couple had not slept together, at least not in a bed, this was not true, but he may have known that. They had spent nights sleeping together under the stars and judging from reports of her later behaviour, Vivien would not have seen the bedroom as the only place to make love.

	1	2	3	4	5	6	7	8	9
A	Day	S.Time	Sun	Moon	Mercury	Venus	Mars		
B	28	13:27	05 ♎ 03'	19 ♎ 51'	18 ♎ 47'	19 ♌ 47'	13 ♏ 24'	1916	finch
C	15	16:58	22 ♐ 54'	15 ♋ 52'	02 ♐ 30'	08 ♐ 56'	22 ♋ 08'	1953	leigh
D	4	15:53	11 ♏ 47'	05 ♓ 11'	00 ♏ 02'	01 ♎ 46'	09 ♐ 43'	1953	finch
E	5	14:20	12 ♏ 27'	09 ♒ 06'	05 ♐ 32'	18 ♎ 51'	21 ♋ 42'	1913	leigh

Fig.183. Matrix showing the natal planetary positions for Peter Finch and Vivien Leigh together with their progressed planetary positions for the year 1953

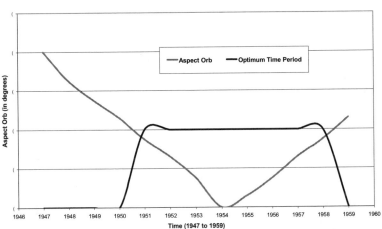

Vivien Leigh Peter Finch progressed Venus progressed Mars conjunction

Fig.184. Graph showing the window of opportunity created by Vivien Leigh's progressing-Venus in conjunction with Peter Finch's progressing-Mars 1947 to 1959

♈	♉	♊	♋	♌	♍	♎	♏	♐	♑	♒	♓
Aries	Taurus	Gemini	Cancer	Leo	Virgo	Libra	Scorpio	Sagittarius	Capricorn	Aquarius	Pisces

Vivien Leigh shared a progressing-Venus (C6) progressing-Mars (D7) conjunction that was at its height in 1953 becoming exact in 1954.[i]

In 1959 Peter married Yolande Turner with whom he shared a natal-Sun-Venus trine within two degrees.

Although the marriage of Vivien Leigh and Laurence Olivier did not end immediately after her affair with peter Finch, there were simply too many problems for it to continue. Vivien's illness was the worst of them. In public, the couple continued to present a united front. By 1958 their marriage was no longer relevant to their relationship.

Single Gender Relationships

As stated earlier, there is no difference between the synastry of same-sex relationships and that of gender-conventional relationships. Astrology describes the human condition and as such it would be illogical to claim that the feeling of intimate love, and therefore the reason why a couple is together, is tangibly different in relationships where both partners are of the same gender.

Ellen Degeneres and Anne Heche

Actress and comedian Ellen Degeneres began a close relationship with Anne Heche in 1997. They met at the Academy Awards presentation in March 1997. Heche later wrote: *"I became oblivious to everything the*

	1	2	3	4	5	6	7	8	9
A	Day	S.Time	Sun	Moon	Mercury	Venus	Mars		
B	25	13:04	04 ♊ 26'	20 ♍ 09'	09 ♊ 45'	21 ♈ 09'	11 ♐ 53'	1969	heche
C	6	20:24	15 ♓ 18'	24 ♍ 14'	17 ♓ 38'	05 ♒ 17'	22 ♑ 02'	1997	degeneres
D	22	14:54	01 ♋ 13'	28 ♍ 49'	08 ♊ 59'	15 ♉ 36'	03 ♐ 19'	1997	heche
E	26	17:50	05 ♒ 56'	17 ♈ 25'	13 ♑ 55'	09 ♒ 53'	24 ♐ 01'	1958	degeneres

Fig.185. Matrix showing the natal planetary positions for Anne Heche and Ellen Degeneres together with their progressed planetary positions for the year 1997

♈	♉	♊	♋	♌	♍	♎	♏	♐	♑	♒	♓
Aries	Taurus	Gemini	Cancer	Leo	Virgo	Libra	Scorpio	Sagittarius	Capricorn	Aquarius	Pisces

second I saw Ellen. I'd never been attracted to a woman before. I mean, I loved women, but not at all physically. Within seconds of meeting Ellen, I had my hands on her". This was Anne's first relationship with a woman. She had previously been involved with Steve Martin (with whom she shares a natal-Sun-Venus trine within two degrees), their two year relationship came to an end in 1995.

As can be seen from the above matrix, a progressed trine from Ellen's Venus in unconventional Aquarius (C6) has just formed a trine aspect with Anne's Sun in Gemini (B3). This transient aspect is separating in 1997, but still close to being exact. Ellen's Venus is in forward motion and traversed the two-degree barrier around 1999. This type of aspect, as we have seen, is common in gender conventional relationships and demonstrates here that the same type of connectivity is present in same gender relationships.

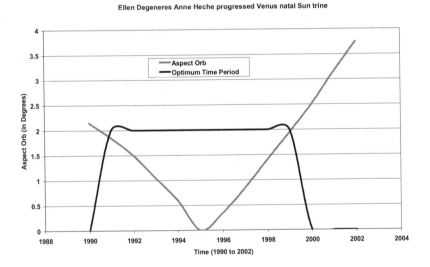

Fig.186. Graph showing the window of opportunity 1990 to 2000 created by Ellen Degeneres progressed-Venus in trine aspect to Anne Heche's natal-Sun

♈	♉	♊	♋	♌	♍	♎	♏	♐	♑	♒	♓
Aries	Taurus	Gemini	Cancer	Leo	Virgo	Libra	Scorpio	Sagittarius	Capricorn	Aquarius	Pisces

Ellen Degeneres and Portia de Rossi

More recently Ellen began a relationship with the actress Portia de Rossi. Again we find the same Sun (B3) Venus (C6) connection, but this time the aspect is the conjunction.

		1	2	3	4	5	6	7	8	9
A	Day	S.Time	Sun	Moon	Mercury	Venus	Mars			
B	31	20:42	11 ≈ 29'	08 ♑ 34'	13 ≈ 22'	24 ♑ 38'	21 ♐ 50'		1973	de rossi
C	14	20:55	23 ♓ 17'	16 ♑ 29'	03 ♈ 14'	10 ≈ 12'	27 ♑ 52'		2005	degeneres
D	4	22:48	13 ♓ 46'	07 ♓ 28'	28 ♓ 35'	04 ♓ 38'	14 ♑ 11'		2005	de rossi
E	26	17:50	05 ≈ 56'	17 ♈ 25'	13 ♑ 55'	09 ≈ 53'	24 ♐ 01'		1958	degeneres

Fig.187. Matrix showing the natal planetary positions for Portia de Rossi and Ellen Degeneres together with their progressed planetary positions for the year 2005

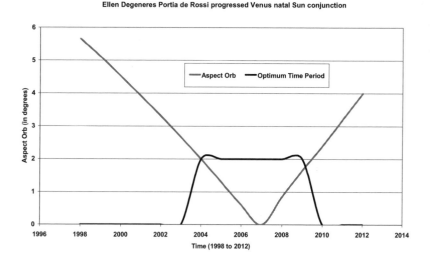

Fig.188. Graph showing the window of opportunity 1998 to 2012 created by Ellen Degeneres progressed-Venus in conjunction with Portia de Rossi's natal-Sun

♈	♉	♊	♋	♌	♍	♎	♏	♐	♑	≈	♓
Aries	Taurus	Gemini	Cancer	Leo	Virgo	Libra	Scorpio	Sagittarius	Capricorn	Aquarius	Pisces

Also of note in this relationship is the natal version of the aspect between Ellen's natal-Venus (E6) and Portia's natal-Sun (B3). The progress of Ellen's Venus maps out the window of opportunity for a relationship to begin, while the natal aspect provides the cushion of similarity in their potential charts.[clix]

Romaine Brooks and Natalie Barney

This lesbian couple were avowed in their non-monogamy, both taking a series of lovers, but from 1915 onwards they enjoyed a love affair that ended in 1970 with painter Brook's death aged 96. Barney, a celebrated turn of the century salonist, died two years later having reached the same age.

	1	2	3	4	5	6	7	8	9
A	Day	S.Time	Sun	Moon	Mercury	Venus	Mars		
B	31	14:40	08 ♏ 26'	19 ♈ 28'	20 ♎ 15'	25 ♍ 46'	11 ♎ 16'	1876	barney
C	11	5:18	20 ♊ 19'	13 ♉ 02'	09 ♋ 12'	17 ♋ 42'	27 ♊ 18'	1915	brooks
D	9	17:14	17 ♐ 49'	05 ♎ 14'	20 ♐ 36'	12 ♏ 24'	06 ♏ 27'	1915	barney
E	1	2:36	10 ♉ 54'	08 ♏ 59'	18 ♈ 27'	27 ♉ 48'	29 ♉ 15'	1874	brooks

Fig.189. Matrix showing the natal planetary positions for Natalie Barney and Romain Brooks together with their progressed planetary positions for the year 1915

They met in wartime London. Brooks and Barney have opposite Suns, Venuses in wide-ish trine and a progressed-Venus (D6) natal-Sun (E3) opposition, separating from exact in 1915.[clx]

Gertrude Stein and Alice B Toklas

The feminist poet and playwright Gertrude Stein met her life partner Alice Toklas, (whose famous cook book contains a recipe for Hashish Fudge), in 1907. Ernest Hemingway suggested that Stein treated Toklas as her 'wife'.

Their natal synastry includes a natal-Sun (E3) Venus (B6) square, but in 1907 when they met, they experienced two important Sun-Venus

♈	♉	♊	♋	♌	♍	♎	♏	♐	♑	♒	♓
Aries	Taurus	Gemini	Cancer	Leo	Virgo	Libra	Scorpio	Sagittarius	Capricorn	Aquarius	Pisces

	1	2	3	4	5	6	7	8	9
A	Day	S.Time	Sun	Moon	Mercury	Venus	Mars		
B	3	20:53	14 ♒ 32'	07 ♍ 09'	14 ♒ 28'	09 ♒ 40'	25 ♓ 36'	1874	stein
C	30	4:32	09 ♊ 07'	17 ♑ 34'	03 ♊ 35'	15 ♊ 24'	25 ♒ 52'	1907	toklas
D	8	23:04	17 ♓ 46'	15 ♏ 02'	03 ♈ 30'	20 ♓ 58'	20 ♈ 24'	1907	stein
E	30	2:34	10 ♉ 13'	14 ♐ 35'	00 ♊ 48'	08 ♉ 28'	08 ♒ 16'	1877	toklas

Fig.190. Matrix showing the natal planetary positions for Gertrude Stein and Alcie B. Toklas together with their progressed planetary positions for the year 1907

progressions, the first a trine between Stein's natal-Sun (B3) and Toklas' progressing-Venus was separating in 1907, but a second trine between Toklas' progressing-Sun (C3) and Stein's natal-Venus (B6) was applying to perfection at this time. They also share a physically congruent natal-Mars (E7) natal-Venus (B6) conjunction in unconventional Aquarius. The majority of these aspects, being focused on Stein's Venus suggest that in all-female relationships Venus may be the dominant planet.

WH Auden and Chester Kallman

	1	2	3	4	5	6	7	8	9
A	Day	S.Time	Sun	Moon	Mercury	Venus	Mars		
B	8	9:38	17 ♑ 17'	05 ♑ 07'	11 ♑ 59'	01 ♓ 26'	02 ♈ 09'	1921	kallman
C	25	18:51	03 ♈ 28'	08 ♌ 56'	20 ♓ 47'	20 ♒ 58'	26 ♐ 19'	1939	auden
D	26	10:49	05 ♒ 37'	05 ♍ 50'	12 ♒ 00'	21 ♓ 44'	16 ♓ 05'	1939	kallman
E	21	16:45	01 ♓ 30'	13 ♊ 22'	16 ♓ 02'	15 ♑ 06'	09 ♐ 07'	1907	auden

Fig.191. Matrix showing the natal planetary positions for WH Auden and Chester Kallman together with their progressed planetary positions for the year 1939

The poets WH Auden and Chester Kallman met early in 1939.

Although they remained companions for the rest of their lives, their intimate physical relationship was only a small part of their life together. Notwithstanding this, their mutual synastry is worthy of comment. Auden's

♈	♉	♊	♋	♌	♍	♎	♏	♐	♑	♒	♓
Aries	Taurus	Gemini	Cancer	Leo	Virgo	Libra	Scorpio	Sagittarius	Capricorn	Aquarius	Pisces

natal-Venus (E6) is just outside two degrees from conjunction with Kallman's natal-Sun (B3) and conversely, Kallman's natal-Venus (B6) is almost exactly in conjunction with Auden's natal-Sun (E3). Again this is demonstrative of the similarity of harmony being played by these astrological planets. The fact that this couple were together intimately for a while corresponds with the astrological reason why many couples find the similarity of the Sun-Venus conjunction harmonious and again demonstrates the nature of Venus synastry and that it is not specific to different gender relationships.

Benjamin Britten and Peter Pears

	1	2	3	4	5	6	7	8	9
			Sun	Moon	Mercury	**Venus**	**Mars**		
A	Day	S.Time							
B	22	5:59	00 ♋ 09'	26 ♐ 16'	07 ♊ 45'	21 ♉ 31'	02 ♌ 05'	1910	pears
C	15	17:34	22 ♐ 56'	16 ♋ 12'	02 ♐ 32'	08 ♐ 58'	22 ♋ 08'	1936	britten
D	18	7:41	24 ♋ 57'	10 ♐ 16'	23 ♋ 34'	21 ♊ 56'	18 ♌ 20'	1936	pears
E	22	16:03	29 ♏ 35'	14 ♍ 50'	01 ♐ 23'	10 ♏ 06'	24 ♋ 26'	1913	britten

Fig.192. Matrix showing the natal planetary positions for Benjamin Britten and Peter Pears together with their progressed planetary positions for the year 1936

Benjamin Britten and Peter Pears spent forty years together. Their relationship began under the auspices of a progressed-Sun (C3) progressed-Venus (D6) opposition sometime between 1934 and 1936. This aspect was of a long duration, coming into two degree orb around 1930 to one degree in 1936 and perfecting in 1942.[clxi]

Christopher Isherwood and Don Bachardy

Writer Isherwood and painter Bachardy were together for 32 years from 1952, but there at the beginning was a progressed-Venus (D6) natal-Sun (E3) trine. The window created by this aspect was open at two degrees from 1950 to 1954 and exact in late 1952.[clxii]

♈	♉	♊	♋	♌	♍	♎	♏	♐	♑	♒	♓
Aries	Taurus	Gemini	Cancer	Leo	Virgo	Libra	Scorpio	Sagittarius	Capricorn	Aquarius	Pisces

	1	2	3	4	5	6	7	8	9
			Sun	Moon	Mercury	Venus	Mars		
A	Day	S.Time	Sun	Moon	Mercury	Venus	Mars		
B	18	3:41	26 ♉ 50'	22 ♋ 40'	03 ♊ 16'	13 ♈ 14'	19 ♉ 04'	1934	bachardy
C	14	13:30	20 ♎ 42'	00 ♑ 15'	08 ♎ 58'	16 ♏ 47'	07 ♍ 57'	1952	isherwood
D	5	4:52	14 ♊ 07'	26 ♓ 20'	06 ♋ 22'	03 ♉ 30'	02 ♊ 00'	1952	bachardy
E	27	10:21	03 ♍ 45'	19 ♓ 32'	29 ♍ 34'	17 ♍ 33'	07 ♌ 55'	1904	isherwood

Fig.193. **Matrix showing the natal planetary positions for Don Bachardy and Christopher Isherwood together with their progressed planetary positions for the year 1952**

♈	♉	♊	♋	♌	♍	♎	♏	♐	♑	♒	♓
Aries	Taurus	Gemini	Cancer	Leo	Virgo	Libra	Scorpio	Sagittarius	Capricorn	Aquarius	Pisces

Part Three
Conclusions

♈	♉	♊	♋	♌	♍	♎	♏	♐	♑	♒	♓
Aries	Taurus	Gemini	Cancer	Leo	Virgo	Libra	Scorpio	Sagittarius	Capricorn	Aquarius	Pisces

Fifteen

Reflections on Synastry

Who has not been lifted high by love? Who has not felt the world change in a moment of secret tenderness? And who has not been ripped open by love and left bleeding and alone, wide-eyed at four in the morning?
Jodie and Steven Forrest

The complexity of relationship astrology is easy to understate. Whenever a commentator goes into print on the subject they have to hedge their bets. This is because astrology is such a convoluted mass of interconnected potentials and actuals that to declare absolute truth is to ask for trouble.

It doesn't necessarily make good sense to regard the attraction of two people via their natal horoscope in the same light as the attraction of two people because of aspects involving a progressed or dynamic factor. Perhaps the natural conclusion that we would jump to is that aspects between the natal chart – being permanent features in our relationship – are enough to keep us together for life, where progressed aspects are temporary and therefore people who experience them are experiencing illusion or at least a temporary or casual state of compatibility. Our first step to resolving this could be to look at the length of relationships involving permanent features of compatibility and compare – say - the average length of those relationships based on – say – a natal-Sun *natal-Venus* trine with those based on a natal-Sun *progressed-Venus* trine.

In the 1300 relationships analysed, we find the first group – those with natal-Sun natal-Venus trines – together for 10.77 years, while the second

♈	♉	♊	♋	♌	♍	♎	♏	♐	♑	♒	♓
Aries	Taurus	Gemini	Cancer	Leo	Virgo	Libra	Scorpio	Sagittarius	Capricorn	Aquarius	Pisces

group – those with natal-Sun progressed-Venus trines – are together for 11.28 years. Both groups have a similar number of 'failed' relationships (47 and 52 respectively) from samples of 75 and 82.

54 of the natal-Sun natal-Venus trines got married, staying together an average of 12.33 years. 55 of the natal-Sun progressed-Venus trines also married, staying together an average of 14.78 years.

From these figures it looks like it's better to have a temporary natal-Sun progressed-Venus trine than a permanent natal Sun natal Venus trine. So am I making a mistake to over-emphasise the failure of certain relationships based on progressions involving Venus?

The visible evidence that a relationship has changed is that it ceased. But the evidence of change may not always be visible, simply because different people have different levels of tolerance. There is also the question of values: whether a relationship ends 'on the outside' because it has changed 'on the inside' is often dependent on the value systems held by the couple, individually and as a unit. The problem with marriages and astrology is that there are too many invisible, hard-to-get-to secrets to be able to draw concrete conclusions from such things as the length of time a couple stay together. Where affairs between unmarried partners are concerned we can perceive that it is easier to end such a relationship, often there are no children to consider, no wedding presents to return, less loss of face, fewer legal concerns. We therefore have precisely what astrological research needs: a fairer field from which to infer the influence of the planets. So it might not be surprising that we find that of the non-married pairs with these two aspects, the natal-Sun *natal*-Venus trines stayed together 6.3 years, where the natal-Sun *progressed*-Venus trines stayed together for 3.53 years.

When we look at the difference between the number of marriages and unmarried affairs, we see the number of natal aspects fall compared to progressed aspects. In this study there are 365 affairs (or non-marriages) to 935 marriages. Despite this disparity in numbers, it is still interesting to note that in the group of 365 affairs we find 28 progressed-Venus progressed-

♈	♉	♊	♋	♌	♍	♎	♏	♐	♑	♒	♓
Aries	Taurus	Gemini	Cancer	Leo	Virgo	Libra	Scorpio	Sagittarius	Capricorn	Aquarius	Pisces

Mars trines, (an aspect that has connotations of positive sexual attraction in its nature), that is *twice as many* as we would expect. Conventional progressed-Venus aspects occur at a higher rate in the affairs group across the board, but when we look solely at marriages, natal aspects start to occur at a more comparable frequency to progressed aspects. We can infer from this that progressed trines and conjunctions occur more often in affairs than natal aspects because of their fleeting nature: an inference here could be that they cause the relationship to be an affair rather than allow it to develop into a marriage. All this actually does is fortify the idea that progressed aspects play a role, it does not 'prove' they are the reason the affair has to end, but the visible product of change is easier to see in an affair than in a marriage and so my leaning is towards the idea that if an affair is obviously based upon a progressed aspect, then the affair will change as the progressed aspect wanes and in some cases, <u>but certainly not all cases</u>, that can mean the end of the affair.

Should we be looking at natal aspects in the same study as progressed aspects? Or, should we be assigning the same type of role to both styles of aspect?

The difference in my mind is that people probably respond in different ways to what we are forced to call the 'frequencies' of other people. Sexually, both men and women respond to the sexual planets of their opposite number, similarly they respond mentally to the 'frequencies' of each other's intellectual planets. Whether these 'frequencies' emanate from their natal chart or their progressed chart is immaterial. We are aeons away from understanding in detail how the natal chart works, let alone the progressed chart, yet it is the progressed chart with its critical accuracy, that in many cases convinces astrologers to keep on working. Arthur M. Young, the inventor of the Bell Helicopter, was a thoughtful and clearly intelligent man. His view appears to have been that if astrology is to be accepted as a non-pseudo-science it would be because of symbolic progressions, which may demonstrate a correspondent connection in time; rather than through

♈	♉	♊	♋	♌	♍	♎	♏	♐	♑	♒	♓
Aries	Taurus	Gemini	Cancer	Leo	Virgo	Libra	Scorpio	Sagittarius	Capricorn	Aquarius	Pisces

experimentation with the ideas that planets cause events with some kind of unknown spatial force that we cannot yet measure.[clxiii] If we are to construct experiments that measure how astrology really works, we should bear these significant facts is mind.

Synastry in Context

A common, modern idea is that the type of person you are and the type of person you are looking for are dictated by your social and religious background, parenting, (basically childhood generally) and a host of other second level indicators. Astrology is a lower level indicator that plays a part in all of the above and more. It could be called a very low level indicator and as such it is harder to examine the reasons behind the development of the self from an astrological perspective than it is from a psychological or sociological perspective because we just don't have access to such fundamental questions as: *What is the meaning of time?* Because of this inability to get the core of what astrology actually is it can only really be examined forensically – as a series of effects with only a symbolic cause (the motions of the planets). This does not stop the esoterically minded from putting forward ideas and theories for what astrology is and it is in this realm of metaphysical conjecture that we can try to understand why synastry might work.

Some astrologers of the scientific school suggest a kind of symbiosis between life and the universe, so that life developed in harmony with the alignments of the system within which we live (we obviously view life 'from the inside' or from a mundane perspective, but our solar system and existence could actually be viewed 'from the outside' as a very unusual 'event' indeed).

Another perspective suggests that we can actually project our consciousness onto seemingly inanimate objects and processes, through some ability of the unconscious mind. Alternatively our consciousness is bound up in a single network at the quantum level that actually creates

♈	♉	♊	♋	♌	♍	♎	♏	♐	♑	♒	♓
Aries	Taurus	Gemini	Cancer	Leo	Virgo	Libra	Scorpio	Sagittarius	Capricorn	Aquarius	Pisces

reality and is not regulated by time, but produces time as a means by which we can experience meaningful events and consequences. Astrology could be part and parcel of this mechanism, but its importance in this process is confined to the physical world. Some esoterically minded scientists suggest that there is only one 'soul' and that we are all discrete extrusions of this single dream-like consciousness into what is, essentially, a 'dramaworld' (or a place where the soul or spirit gets to undergo dramatic experiences). This perspective does not usually include astrology, but as a *regulatory process* in this type of dreamworld/dramaworld universe I cannot think of any other better suited mechanism than the astrological concept. By this I mean that it is possible – if there really is a rebirth process – that astrology is an intricate way to control and monitor the 'game' being played.

At a subtly different level, more esoterically-minded and 'evolutionary' astrologers (also called 'karmic' astrologers) see the process of life on Earth mirroring another process of life that takes place beyond our perception, which may be related to the other ideas mentioned, but which is more person-centred than event-centred. Again this is the process of reincarnation or rebirth through many lives, but instead of positing one soul, we consider all of the conscious extrusions as individual souls who retain, at least for a period of 'time', a semblage of individuality. This idea includes within its wide brief the idea that these singular souls live many lives in succession, during which they have a series of new encounters with unfamiliar souls and re-encounters with souls with whom they have become familiar throughout their successive lives. At the root of this idea is the principle of the soul mate and the twin soul; the latter are souls who can work to achieve something in life; for this soul pattern, the square and opposition would   be most appropriate type of aspect as they constitute challenging and dynamic conditions. The former are souls who search for each other through successive lives, like iterative *Romeo et Juliets*, constantly seeking the familiarity of that which has gone before.

In order for a soul to retain some kind of individuality through

♈	♉	♊	♋	♌	♍	♎	♏	♐	♑	♒	♓
Aries	Taurus	Gemini	Cancer	Leo	Virgo	Libra	Scorpio	Sagittarius	Capricorn	Aquarius	Pisces

successive incarnations it is necessary for this individuality to be measured against something else – as we don't remember previous incarnations it is feasible to assume whoever we were 'last time around' is now dead or at least hidden. But if we have a twin-soul, a soul mate or a group of soul mates with whom we share successive lives, then the individuality of our consciousness can be equated to 'something that is not us' – a support system if you like. It is possible that our continuing individuality can only really be measured against something that is exterior to our 'self'.

It is tempting to oversimplify or overcomplicate this issue and as such I'll concentrate on the possibility of soul mates and astrology.

Soul mates

As a phrase this one is surely misunderstood. The only people who seem to be able to make authoritative statements on the issue are generally those who are in touch with a spirit guide or who have some revelatory relationship with another level of existence, but from the astrological perspective, there seem to be some implications and some possibilities that synastry may reflect this type of life view.

Jodie and Steven Forrest continue their discussion on this subject:

'Just what does it mean to keep company with a soulmate? The first step is to forget that the seconds, months, and decades you spend with such a person are some kind of blissful orgasmic dream. That may be part of it sometimes, but the core of the idea is that in a soulmate we are capable of meeting someone who is capable of altering our fundamental natures, helping us alter our souls, in other words. And that process can make a ride on a roller coaster look like teatime with your maiden aunt. ·clxiv

It appears that there is more than one explanation of what soul mates might be. Firstly there is the idea that there is more than one person walking the Earth attached to the same soul or over-being, suggesting that individuals

♈	♉	♊	♋	♌	♍	♎	♏	♐	♑	♒	♓
Aries	Taurus	Gemini	Cancer	Leo	Virgo	Libra	Scorpio	Sagittarius	Capricorn	Aquarius	Pisces

are, at their core, not actually individuals, but divisions of a higher self, which is itself a division of the single 'true' soul.

Soul mates according to this idea are simply people who are attached by a different invisible cord to the same higher self. Why the soul would want to bring two parts of 'itself' together rather than explore the many other options available is a moot, but nevertheless interesting point.

Another theory (actually a conjecture) suggests that souls decide upon their life (and horoscope) before birth, the intention being to experience a particular life path, which although predestined in many ways also allows for the developing and difficult-to-predict context that is human life on Earth (the mathematics of 6 billion people each with a different life plan which could theoretically overlap or influence any of the other 5,999,999,999 are vast enough to give the impression of life and all of its people-related events being completely accidental while some or all may not be). The possibility that souls get together on 'the other side' and decide to meet up on 'this side' is also an interesting idea that some esotericists maintain is plain fact. I find this idea attractive; pencilling in an appointment at a particular stage in your life journey makes the whole thing seem like much more of an adventure. That doesn't make it true, but it's an interesting thought.

A third instance is the idea that life is a karmic process: one that demands payment and gives reward through successive incarnations. That people (souls) encounter each other during life because they are drawn together as a process of learning, teaching and experiencing certain events and situations. It is possible that soul mates are just people who have business with each other (and by implication this could be unfinished business). Or it could just be that certain souls really do love certain other souls so much that their purpose has become the constant encounter that reincarnation avails them. Maybe the karma of these cosmic twins is so intertwined that they are in fact allowed by providence, the powers that be, God or whatever is in control of the process, to spend successive lifetimes

♈	♉	♊	♋	♌	♍	♎	♏	♐	♑	♒	♓
Aries	Taurus	Gemini	Cancer	Leo	Virgo	Libra	Scorpio	Sagittarius	Capricorn	Aquarius	Pisces

together. Who knows? The concensus, if that is the right word, seems to be that most soul mates are together for a reason and a purpose that is completely related to their soul-development.

Astrology and Religion

Other religious views deal with astrology differently. The advanced culture of Islam sheltered and cradled astrology, along with many other examples of classical knowledge, throughout the European dark ages, preserving the works of Claudius Ptolemy and, as a culture, producing great astrologers the like of Al Biruni, Masha Allah, Alkindi and Abu Mashar and the Jewish astrologer Abraham Ibn Ezra, who was born in Toledo in a Spain at a time when it was ruled by the Muslim Moors. The works of these Arab and Judaic astrologers were eventually used by Christian theologians in the late middle ages to learn, practice and comment upon astrology. Contemporary Islamic scholars are more guarded about the practice of astrology, but as is the case with all clerics, astrology can provide competition to faith and is therefore seen as unwelcome in some quarters.

The views of the medieval Christian astrologers were not taken serious-ly by the majority of later Christians and despite the superstitious nature of many Christian practitioners, the mechanism of astrology has often been seen as a challenge to Christian ideas about the omnipotence of God. It seems to me to be a matter of detail that a God who created heaven and earth could quite easily have included astrology in the process and still be omnipotent, in fact astrology, if true, actually demonstrates the omnipotency of God. It's just His way of keeping tabs on you. The fact that astrology challenges the teachings of some Churches is a mundane issue which has nothing to do with God.

Some Christians believe that the fact that astrology appears to be true, is because it is the product of demons. I do not believe that this is true. Billy Graham and his wife Ruth Bell met under a progressing-Sun natal-Venus trine in 1940 and married under no less than three conventional Venus

♈	♉	♊	♋	♌	♍	♎	♏	♐	♑	♒	♓
Aries	Taurus	Gemini	Cancer	Leo	Virgo	Libra	Scorpio	Sagittarius	Capricorn	Aquarius	Pisces

aspects in 1943. If it works for the Graham's, surely synastry can't be the work of demons.[clxv] Mormons also believe that astrology is evil:[clxvi] yet their relationships are not devoid of the model of conventional synastry that I have proposed. George and Olive Osmond, parents of the Osmond Brothers, are an example of two people whose relationship began under two progressed-Sun – natal-Venus oppositions. Joseph Smith, founder of the Mormon religion shared a close natal-Venus opposition with his wife Emma similar to that of Shah Jahan and Mumtaz Mahal. Brigham Young and Eliza Snow shared a natal-Sun-Venus trine (again this was inside two degrees). Eliza was also married to Joseph Smith and in the year they married, 1842, her Mars conjoined his Venus in Aquarius. Of course, they weren't aware of this at the time, but that is just the point – you don't have to be aware of it to respond to astrological attraction.[clxvii] My conclusion can only be this: Whatever force of nature brought forward love also brought forward astrology.

My understanding of synastry suggests that the windows of opportunity that we can often see in progressed synastry act more as entrances than exits. Temperament, circumstances, expectation, status and above all the inherent capacity of individuals to actually *relate* to others, all have a role to play in the ending of relationships. Astrology scaffolds relationships and helps them to happen. It is a nice thought, but it is impossible to prove that these progressions develop in order to optimise the chances of two souls to encounter each other by creating a window in time where their attraction is most powerful.

We always have free will simply because this mechanism exists within human life. If two people agree to meet on the corner of two streets in Manhattan at 5.30pm next Friday they have established the scientific co-ordinates for a meeting to take place. The difference between fate and free will is that the criterion for the encounter to happen requires the will of both parties to turn up to the meeting. Love is like this: astrology provides the means for attraction, and the framework for a host of extraneous factors,

♈	♉	♊	♋	♌	♍	♎	♏	♐	♑	♒	♓
Aries	Taurus	Gemini	Cancer	Leo	Virgo	Libra	Scorpio	Sagittarius	Capricorn	Aquarius	Pisces

but the relationship only happens if both parties agree. Often relationships that appear to be fated appear so because these extraneous factors do not hinder progress. The will to love was there all along.

Planning Synastry

Because astrology is so bound up with prediction, it might occur to the reader that it would be possible to pre-empt the traditional scenarios of finding love and use astrology to predict who you will be more compatible with.

In theory it should be possible to plan your relationships using progressed and natal synastry, but as with astrology generally, synastry suggests – either – a higher order playing a role in human life or too large a set of variables in play to make this approach useful. Synastry suggests either a natural process in the accidental universe that we can neither conceive nor understand or it suggests that there is meaning in the exterior universe; taken to the extreme synastry suggests 'extra terrestrial intelligence' (in that something not of this world is influencing the behaviour of its inhabitants), and so if synastry *is* true, it is not necessarily there for you to pre-empt. Occultists and esotericists have always maintained that in order to get the best results from their magical and oracular systems, they must treat them with respect. Some Tarot readers and Horary astrologers will not ask more than one question for themselves or any other individual per week. This approach is a kind of religious view that suggests the oracle will only respond on its terms.

With this in mind the implications of knowing about something like progressed synastry are still useful in some respects. For example, in this age of internet and telephone dating it may be interesting to know in advance if you have a chance to 'hit it off' as it were. I'm not sure using astrology as a time-saving device is a good idea, and as everyone has a unique horoscope and the vast majority have a bundle of unresolved issues which they have picked up from childhood onwards, it would be virtually

♈	♉	♊	♋	♌	♍	♎	♏	♐	♑	♒	♓
Aries	Taurus	Gemini	Cancer	Leo	Virgo	Libra	Scorpio	Sagittarius	Capricorn	Aquarius	Pisces

impossible to guarantee a perfect relationship as far as quality-over-time is concerned. But it is possible to give yourself a better chance of attraction, at least in the short term. Synastry can highlight those factors in potential partners that suggest you will have certain things in common and as astrology tells us which combinations are the most potent for love, sex, creative passion, nurturing, support and overall complimentarity, it should also be possible to predict who will have the more favorable share of these qualities together. With progressed synastry it is also now possible to say when couples will share these qualities and for how long. As for how long any couple's relationship will last, it always depends on them and the feelings and lessons they learn in the time they spend together whether they consider themselves to be 'soul mates' or not. An argument against this type of approach is that it could be folly to reject the usefulness of aspects such as the square or the inconjunct just because they are not conventional in relationships and this is a valid objection. Many people have personalities that respond well to the hard work and friction that squares imbue, just as some people prefer the passion of oppositions to the relatively quiet harmony of trines (Elizabeth Taylor springs to mind). In some senses a relationship with Mars-Mars squares, where one partner is constantly encouraging the other to keep fit, will be much more exciting and vigorous than one with Sun-Venus trines, which can encourage complacency and laziness. There is always a pay-off in a relationship and every case is unique. All progressed synastry can do is partially show what worked for other people's relationships and often more fully *when* it worked. If all you want from a relationship is a brief encounter with no strings, then the progressed-Venus progressed-Mars trine appears to have been the preferred option in the past more often than chance would expect.

Women are from Venus

In observing the progressed and natal synastry of George Sand, Elizabeth Taylor and Grace Kelly (and if you wish to research further, I suggest Merle

♈	♉	♊	♋	♌	♍	♎	♏	♐	♑	♒	♓
Aries	Taurus	Gemini	Cancer	Leo	Virgo	Libra	Scorpio	Sagittarius	Capricorn	Aquarius	Pisces

Oberon, Brigitte Bardot, Shirley Maclaine, Marilyn Monroe, Rita Hayworth and Jeanne Moreau are women whose relationships mirror the three examples here): these were women with some measure of control over their lives. The point is that these icons made their own choices: they did not, in the main, sit like wallflowers at the side of a dance floor waiting for Mr Right to ask them to dance. It is therefore a consideration that the fact that *most* of their relationships have progressed synastry signatures may be because they had the increased personal agency that iconic beauty, fame or money provides and this allowed them to choose a series of partners with a definite element of selectivity. It is certainly quite interesting and possibly quite a rare event to obtain the birth details of so many relationships involving the same individual, or in this case the same influential and iconic women. It is therefore clear that there are significant aspects of Venus that recur for people who have a series of relationships.

Some Men are from Venus too

So, is there a gender consideration involved in synastry? Do men prefer Mars and Woman prefer Venus aspects in relationships? You might recall the relationships of Richard Burton were primarily connections between Mars and Venus. This is also the case with Clark Gable and Errol Flynn's relationships. Those of the actresses Grace Kelly and Merle Oberon, however, were primarily connections between the Sun and Venus. Having looked at some of the relationships of men like Howard Hughes, Errol Flynn, Prince Aly Khan, David Niven and some of the conquests of Warren Beatty I have come to the conclusion that the charming bon viveurs of recent history often respond to factors other than those presented by the softer Venus aspects, which are preferred by the female counterparts. This does not mean that those, perhaps we should call them more *serious* men, do not respond to Venus – they do, but if their purpose is just to go to bed with beautiful women and nothing more, then it doesn't really matter what type of Venus connection is made between the two. In fact it is

♈	♉	♊	♋	♌	♍	♎	♏	♐	♑	♒	♓
Aries	Taurus	Gemini	Cancer	Leo	Virgo	Libra	Scorpio	Sagittarius	Capricorn	Aquarius	Pisces

theoretically far more important for a Mars connection to be present, making the connection strictly physical with no romantic baggage; or perhaps a Venus sextile aspect where communication is good, but not too intense and distracting. Where David Niven's relationships with Primula Rollo, Rita Hayworth and Evelyn Keyes contain conventional Venus synastry, his relationships with Merle Oberon and Anne Todd do not. Errol Flynn was well known as a womaniser, but his three *marriages* to Lili Damita, Nora Eddington and Patrice Wymore all contain conventional Venus synastry. Perhaps the only relationship of Warren Beatty's that was out of *his* control was his 15-month affair with Madonna. In this relationship *his* progressing-Venus made a trine to *her* natal-Sun. This aspect became exact in 1991.

For billionaire Howard Hughes the statistical peaks are with Sun-Venus oppositions, he has four – one of each style – in 17 relationships and natal-Sun-Venus sextiles – he has six in 17 relationships (an aspect of friendly, facilitative communication between the goals of one partner and the relationship centre of the other partner). He also has five progressed-Venus – progressed-Venus trines in 17 relationships. The conjuror, escapologist and noted sceptic Harry Houdini shared this aspect with his wife Wilhelmina Rahner – he met and married her in the space of three weeks in 1893. Indeed it can also appear out of nowhere to people who already know each other and propel them into a serious relationship as if they just realised all of a sudden that they were actually 'right' for each other. Progressed-Venus – Venus trines provide the weakest of the three Venus trine combinations, but they consistently appear to embody meaning in the relationships in which they appear despite the fact that individually they do not constitute any particular proof, they still occur twice as often as progressed-Venus squares (the actual frequency ratio of this type of trine to square being 37:18).

Talk of which brings me nicely to the results of the study.

For the mathematically minded, the following totals are the results of

♈	♉	♊	♋	♌	♍	♎	♏	♐	♑	♒	♓
Aries	Taurus	Gemini	Cancer	Leo	Virgo	Libra	Scorpio	Sagittarius	Capricorn	Aquarius	Pisces

this survey of progressed and natal aspects in the 1300 relationships:

	Sun-Venus	Venus-Mars	Sun-Mars	Venus-Venus	Sun-Sun	Mars-Mars
Trine	307	261	237	138	108	69
Conjunction	163 (326)	120 (240)	103 (206)	61 (122)	59 (118)	65 (130)
Opposition	152 (304)	122 (244)	118 (236)	59 (118)	53 (106)	58 (116)
Square	228	232	263	98	117	107
Sextile	229	242	213	105	102	116
Inconjunct	260	250	210	121	104	129
Semi-sextile	243	211	212	105	85	116

Table of two-degree Aspect Frequencies in 1300 Relationships (includes all natal aspects together with progressed aspects for the start-year/marriage year of the relationship)

This table shows that there is a > **30%** difference (**79** actual occurrences) between the **228** instances of two-degree Sun-Venus squares and the **307** instances of two-degree Sun-Venus trines in the 1300 relationships analysed in this study.

More importantly, the progressed-Venus natal-Sun trine occurs **82** times giving a chi-square value of $p=0.003$. While this is only suggestive of the fact that this figure is significant, since it could be due to some anomaly or artefact in the sample, it does mean that we are **99.7%** certain that this figure is not due to chance.[i]

The Sun-Venus, Venus-Mars and Sun-Mars trines, squares, inconjuncts, sextiles and semi-sextiles should occur about **234.96** times if chance were the only factor. The conjunctions and oppositions of these planets should occur about **117.481** times. For single planet connections, such as Venus aspecting Venus, we should see **117.481** trines, squares, inconjuncts, sextiles and semi-sextiles and about **58.740** conjunctions and oppositions.

Since there are only four degrees in every 360 when a conjunction or opposition can form whereas there are eight degrees in any 360 when any of the other aspects can form, I have simply doubled the final figure for

♈	♉	♊	♋	♌	♍	♎	♏	♐	♑	♒	♓
Aries	Taurus	Gemini	Cancer	Leo	Virgo	Libra	Scorpio	Sagittarius	Capricorn	Aquarius	Pisces

conjunctions and oppositions (shown in brackets) in order for the reader to easily compare these frequencies with the frequencies of the other aspects.

In theory, squares should happen just as often as trines between random birth charts. But where Venus is concerned, they don't. So in respect of Sun-Venus aspects we may have a good case for astrology.

In the case of Venus-Mars aspects the case is weaker, but an interestingly similar pattern of numeric superiority is observed for trines. For Venus-Venus, we still observe a numeric superiority for trines, but we appear to lose superiority and significance for conjunctions and oppositions.

In my view, nothing, other than astrology, can account for the high incidence of natal-Sun – progressed-Venus trines and conjunctions (which occur at a rate of 82 and 46 respectively).

For example, Merle Oberon was particularly sensitive to Sun-Venus trines: she has nine Sun-Venus trines of different styles in 14 relationships; one Sun-Venus conjunction and 0 Sun-Venus oppositions. She chose at least three husbands whose natal-Venus was in a trine aspect to her natal-Sun, whereas Grace Kelly never experienced this natal aspect in a relationship (at least none that I have examined). Elizabeth Taylor had two relationships with the natal-Sun-Venus trine present and another with a progressed-Sun-Venus trine, but they were not her most passionate and neither were they particularly long-lived partnerships (Eddie Fisher, George Hamilton and Michael Wilding). But these relationships did have very different qualities to those relationships that were loaded with oppositions and squares: her three 'fighting' marriages, to Hilton, Todd (probably) and Burton. While the Hilton marriage included a brief progressed-Venus natal-Sun trine, it was also filled with squares and the marriage ended after Hilton was violent towards her. Hilton's violence differed from the love-fights she enjoyed with Todd and Burton. The salient point here, however, is not to show the difference between the square (unwelcome violence) and the opposition (participative rough stuff), but to

♈	♉	♊	♋	♌	♍	♎	♏	♐	♑	♒	♓
Aries	Taurus	Gemini	Cancer	Leo	Virgo	Libra	Scorpio	Sagittarius	Capricorn	Aquarius	Pisces

show that the trine can engender a genuinely selfless love; a caring and protective regard. Fisher, Hamilton and Wilding did Elizabeth Taylor no harm and these may have been relationships that could have done her a lot of good. In the case of Fisher, he adored her in a different way to the regard Burton gave her. Fisher, it could be argued, was the one man that Elizabeth Taylor married in her earlier life who put her interests before his own, and this can only really be argued because he admits it was the one relationship – in a life packed with failed relationships – in which he actually was selfless because he was in love.[clxviii] Hamilton was also reportedly someone who urged Elizabeth to take care of her health. We can't say that Eddie Fisher loved Elizabeth Taylor more than Mike Todd or Richard Burton loved her, but we can propose that his motivation was different from Burton's (and probably different from Todd's) at the outset of the relationship and that his regard for her was consummate. Trines are soft, oppositions and squares are hard (yet different). We also saw with Elizabeth Taylor, at least earlier in her life, that she oscillated between softness and toughness. For her marriages, she followed each conflicting relationship with a placid one. Hilton – Wilding – Todd – Fisher – Burton – Warner and we also saw that as far as the placid relationships are concerned, we see trines and conjunctions of the Sun and Venus. The rough relationships contained more edgy aspects.

While the Sun-Venus trine didn't work for Elizabeth Taylor, it is one of the most important of the major natal astrological connections between the Sun and Venus (the natal-Sun-Venus conjunction and opposition both occur at a proportionately more prevalent rate). This suggests that for some people, the natal-Sun-Venus trine works very well, whereas for others it is not as useful. Elizabeth Taylor, for instance, rejected softness in favor of passion, others (Merle Oberon for example) tended to do the opposite. Disregarding the fact that individuals with choice will tend to make a choice based on their taste and their values (both words associated with Venus), it would appear that although this connection provides a positive

♈	♉	♊	♋	♌	♍	♎	♏	♐	♑	♒	♓
Aries	Taurus	Gemini	Cancer	Leo	Virgo	Libra	Scorpio	Sagittarius	Capricorn	Aquarius	Pisces

backdrop to a potentially successful relationship, it must also be noted that it makes no promises, at least in celebrity relationships, that the relationship will last.

This brings me to an important point. Celebrity relationships could reveal one of two things: they could be a reflection of the human ideal – where freedom and choice allow an individual to act the way they would if they were completely unfettered, or alternatively, they could provide an artificial experimental situation – where celebrity relationships are not reflective of real relationships simply because the people involved appear to have this extra measure of freedom, but in fact their fame stops them from experiencing real life and real relationships the way us ordinary folk do.

Perhaps both interpretations are true, but in my astrological practice I see conventional two-degree synastry patterns involving Venus in seven out of 10 relationships, and I see progressed synastry patterns involving Venus (within two degrees) at the start of relationships in more than 50% so I tend to believe the former to be the case. In fact 920 out of the 1300 relationships I have examined for this book have at least one trine, conjunction or opposition of Venus to the Sun, Venus or Mars either natally or by progression within two degrees. Of course, if I were to expand this orb to three degrees this percentage would rise, but so would the distribution of all the other aspects. The further apart the 'orb', the more 'noise' would be encountered. The deviation of the aspect-to-orb ratio (where the numeric frequency of aspects flatten out) is a fact that has not yet been established.

Independent Influence, Numerical Superiority and Proportionate Superiority

In order to define the astrological aspects that can be ascribed as conventional relationship indicators, I have used three criteria

1. Numerical Superiority – as in the case of the Sun-Venus trines we find they occur at consistent levels and these levels are numerically

♈	♉	♊	♋	♌	♍	♎	♏	♐	♑	♒	♓
Aries	Taurus	Gemini	Cancer	Leo	Virgo	Libra	Scorpio	Sagittarius	Capricorn	Aquarius	Pisces

greater than the other aspect types.

2. Proportionate Superiority – as in the case of Sun-Venus conjunctions and oppositions, we expect half as many but actually observe their frequency to be proportionately greater than half the other aspect types and in the case of the Sun-Venus conjunctions, they occur at proportionately greater levels than any other aspect

3. Independent Influence - in order to eliminate 'noise' created by odd aspect types which occur at high rates, we must compare all those aspect types with 'established relationship indicators' (Sun-Venus trines, conjunctions and oppositions) to see if we are observing an aspect type that occurs independently (on its own) or if its high frequency is a by-product of another aspect type or another artefact. We do this by removing all the established relationship indicators from the sample and observing the frequency of the remaining aspect types.

Progressed-Sun-Venus Semi-Sextiles

The natal-Sun natal-Venus semi-sextile (30 degree) aspect is interesting in this study. It occurs very often.

The types of *progressed-Sun-Venus* aspects experienced in a relationship are dependant upon the types of *natal* aspects between the Sun and Venus, which are in turn dependant upon the couple's birth dates. This dependency is noticeable in progressed synastry most often in the case of aspects types that are thirty degrees apart. There are thirty degrees between the conjunction and the semi-sextile, then thirty degrees between the semi-sextile and the sextile. Thirty more degrees separates the sextile from the square, thirty more separates the square and the trine. Add thirty degrees to a trine and you get an inconjunct and add a further thirty and you arrive at the opposition. If you carry on adding thirty degrees you start to go backwards again arriving at the inconjunct, then the trine, the square, sextile, semi-sextile and finally back to the conjunction having completed a circle.

♈	♉	♊	♋	♌	♍	♎	♏	♐	♑	♒	♓
Aries	Taurus	Gemini	Cancer	Leo	Virgo	Libra	Scorpio	Sagittarius	Capricorn	Aquarius	Pisces

While natal-Sun-Venus semi-sextiles occur with great regularity, progressed-Sun progressed-Venus semi-sextiles do not occur often: only 46 times (in 44 relationships[clxix]) in the 1300 relationships, suggesting that the frequency of Sun-Venus semi-sextiles is inconsistent.

There are two directions in which a natal-Sun-Venus semi-sextile can develop or progress over a lifetime – backwards, or moving from 30 degrees to 0 degrees: here the separating semi-sextile will eventually become an applying conjunction; or forwards from 30 to 60 degrees and in this instance the separating semi-sextile eventually becomes an applying 60 degree sextile. If a couple are born with the Sun and Venus 30 degrees apart, it is possible, but not certain, that this aspect will progress to become a progressed conjunction or sextile over the following 30 or so years. If we examine how many of the relationships have both a natal-Sun-Venus semi-sextile and some kind of progressed-Sun-Venus sextile we find that there are 16 relationships. If we examine the same for conjunctions we find there are 31 progressed-Sun-Venus conjunctions (in a total of 29 relationships) that also have a natal-Sun-Venus semi-sextile. This suggests to me that because people choose relationships under the influence of progressed-Sun-Venus conjunctions, then the presence of natal-Sun-Venus semi-sextiles in great numbers is *because progressing conjunctions involving the Sun and Venus happen so often in relationships*. The high frequency of natal-Sun-Venus semi-sextiles can therefore be described as a statistical artefact.

There are 39 Sun-Venus trines, conjunctions and oppositions in the 74 relationships with a natal-Sun-Venus semi-sextile. If we do the same test on the natal-Sun-Venus trine, we find that they happen in relationships along with 21 progressed squares (30 degrees backwards) and 23 progressed inconjuncts (30 degrees forwards). This suggests that the natal-Sun-Venus trine has a greater level of independence than the natal-Sun-Venus semi-sextile. It is clear therefore that while the conjunction is responsible for the high number of natal-Sun-Venus semi-sextiles, I cannot say that

♈	♉	♊	♋	♌	♍	♎	♏	♐	♑	♒	♓
Aries	Taurus	Gemini	Cancer	Leo	Virgo	Libra	Scorpio	Sagittarius	Capricorn	Aquarius	Pisces

progressed squares or progressed inconjuncts are responsible for the high number of natal-Sun-Venus trines, making the latter an independent parameter having a major influence on why relationships form and fade.

Progressed-Sun-Venus Inconjuncts

The inconjunct symbolises an element of stress in that there is often a pay-off of sorts in this aspect. It seems probable that this aspect would not be the conventional choice in relationships between, say, progressed-Sun and progressed-Venus. Again we find that it occurs with quite interesting regularity: 70 times in 1300 relationships (chance would suggest it might occur 59 times). After digging a little deeper to see if we could find something resembling an effect with regards to Sun-Venus inconjuncts, we find that although they undoubtedly have as much of an effect on the quality of the relationship as any other aspect, their high incidence is also something of a red herring. Again this is because 150-degree aspects either develop from trines or into oppositions. From the 70 relationships in this category, if we remove all the Sun-Venus trines, conjunctions and oppositions, all the Venus-Mars trines, conjunctions and oppositions and all the Venus-Venus trines, conjunctions and oppositions we are left with only 10 relationships, including John Major and Edwina Currie and Henry VIII and Katherine of Aragon. One of these is regarded as a strange affair and the other something of a marriage of convenience and therefore outside my expectations for Venus synastry. This leaves eight relationships out of 1300. If I do the same in reverse, by removing all those relationships with Sun-Venus, Venus-Mars and Venus-Venus semi-sextiles and inconjuncts (remember oppositions and conjunctions should occur half as often as the other aspects, so if it looks like an unfair test to remove only two aspect types to compare them with Sun-Venus trines, conjunctions and oppositions it is in fact, the same thing), I have 35 progressed-Sun progressed-Venus trines remaining compared to 10 for the inconjunct.

With progressed-Sun progressed-Venus semi-sextiles, we fare a

♈	♉	♊	♋	♌	♍	♎	♏	♐	♑	♒	♓
Aries	Taurus	Gemini	Cancer	Leo	Virgo	Libra	Scorpio	Sagittarius	Capricorn	Aquarius	Pisces

little better. We have 13 relationships in this category. Searching for meaning in Sun-Venus inconjuncts and semi-sextiles requires subtlety: they don't make relationships happen.

Progressed-Sun-Venus Squares

As for the progressed-Sun - progressed-Venus square, this occurs in 59 relationships within two degrees. If we again remove the relationships with Venus related trines, conjunctions and oppositions, we are left with 17 relationships.

If we try another test by removing all relationships with any kind of two-degree Sun-Venus square from the sample, we have a sample of 1086 relationships and we are still left with occurrences of Sun-Venus trines at above the level of chance in all categories.

Sun-Venus	Natal	Natal-Sun Progressed-Venus	Progressed-Sun Natal-Venus	Progressed
Trine	52	58	61	59
Conjunctions	36 (72)	38 (76)	33 (66)	38 (74)
Oppositions	39 (78)	36 (72)	36 (72)	30 (60)

Sun-Venus trines, conjunctions and oppositions when all relationships with a Sun-Venus square within two degrees have been removed from the sample

Conventional Relationship Indicators

This establishes that Sun-Venus trines, conjunctions and oppositions are the most frequently found aspects in the sample. This does not contradict the expectations of conventional astrological ideas. We can therefore ascribe to them the label 'conventional relationship indicators'. If we then remove all the relationships that contain any of the 'conventional relationship indicators', we can test other aspect sets to see if we can also ascribe this label to them.

♈	♉	♊	♋	♌	♍	♎	♏	♐	♑	♒	♓
Aries	Taurus	Gemini	Cancer	Leo	Virgo	Libra	Scorpio	Sagittarius	Capricorn	Aquarius	Pisces

If we test the natal-Sun progressed-Venus Inconjunct, which occurs frequently, we find that it occurs 36 times in relationships without the conventional Sun-Venus trines, conjunctions and oppositions, but that it occurs 37 times in relationships with these aspects. This means it occurs with the same regularity with and without the 'conventional relationship indicators'.

If we compare it to the natal-Venus natal-Mars trine (which occurs less frequently), we find that it occurs 18 times in relationships with Sun-Venus trines, conjunctions and oppositions, but 33 times in relationships without these aspects, suggesting that it is a more *independent* relationship indicator than the Sun-Venus inconjunct. The natal-Venus natal-Mars trine might therefore be referred to as a relationship indicator because it can 'stand on its own' and catalyse attraction whereas the Sun-Venus inconjunct cannot.

If we do the same test with the progressed-Sun progressed-Venus inconjunct, we find a similar state of affairs. It occurs 34 times with the 'conventional relationship indicators' and 34 times without them, whereas the progressed-Venus progressed-Mars trine occurs 30 times with the conventional aspects and 41 times without them.

Can you see a pattern emerging here?

If we compare all four styles of Venus-Mars conjunctions against all four styles of Venus-Mars inconjuncts using this same principle, we find that the numerically inferior conjunctions occur only 120 times (240 comparatively), to the 250 instances of the inconjunct. If we now compare them with and without Sun-Venus trines, conjunctions and oppositions we find that for Venus-Mars conjunctions, there are 34 more relationships that do not contain a Sun-Venus trine, conjunction or opposition, than those that do contain such an aspect. For Venus-Mars inconjuncts this difference is only 28 relationships that do not include a conventional Sun-Venus aspect. In real terms this means that Venus-Mars conjunctions are more than twice as independent as Venus-Mars inconjuncts because we should see half as

♈	♉	♊	♋	♌	♍	♎	♏	♐	♑	♒	♓
Aries	Taurus	Gemini	Cancer	Leo	Virgo	Libra	Scorpio	Sagittarius	Capricorn	Aquarius	Pisces

332 WHEN STARS COLLIDE

many conjunctions as inconjuncts and because we actually observe seven more occasions where they act independently, we can assume that they are a more likely cause of relationships.

For these reasons, I can't assign conventionality to Venus-Mars inconjuncts, because although I am sure they play a role; it is not the same role as the conventional Venus aspects and they don't make relationships happen.

The progressed-Venus progressed-Mars opposition noted in the Burton Taylor relationship occurs 27 times. It does so with obvious independence from Sun-Venus aspects. Only five of these relationships happen with a conventional Sun-Venus aspect, all the rest are independent suggesting that this particular aspect does possess the attracting qualities I have ascribed to it.

As for the Venus-Venus inconjuncts, comparing them with Venus-Venus trines reveals the following:

58 relationships contain a two-degree natal-Venus progressed-Venus inconjunct aspect: 28 of these relationships do not have a conventional Sun-Venus aspect, the other 30 do.

If we look at natal-Venus progressed-Venus trines, we find 67 relationships, 22 of which include a conventional Sun-Venus aspect and 45 do not. This suggests the natal-Venus progressed-Venus trine is a relationship indicator in the conventional sense. The opposition version of this aspect style occurs only 30 times, but it manages to do so independently 17 times and 13 times with conventional Sun-Venus aspects. The progressed-Venus   progressed-Venus opposition occurs rarely in this study and is numerically the weakest of all the Venus oppositions, but is still a Venus opposition and therefore we would expect a certain level of independence and we find that it occurs seven times without conventional Sun-Venus synastry and five times with it. The progressed-Venus-Venus inconjunct occurs 32 times, but 16 times with 'conventional relationship indicators' and 16 times   without. Indeed if we remove all the

♈	♉	♊	♋	♌	♍	♎	♏	♐	♑	♒	♓
Aries	Taurus	Gemini	Cancer	Leo	Virgo	Libra	Scorpio	Sagittarius	Capricorn	Aquarius	Pisces

Venus-Mars and Venus-Venus trines conjunctions and oppositions from this set we are left with only five relationships. If we do the reverse with the Venus-Venus oppositions and remove all the Sun-Venus, Venus-Venus and Venus-Mars inconjuncts and semi-sextiles from the progressed-Venus oppositions set, we are left with four relationships, but of course, we only started with 12 relationships in this category so we still have a third of our sample, compared to less than a sixth of our 32 progressed-Venus inconjuncts.

So, apart from the numerical superiority of conventional Sun-Venus aspects, there are other ways to dig deeper and establish the independent power of the other Venus aspects.

♈	♉	♊	♋	♌	♍	♎	♏	♐	♑	♒	♓
Aries	Taurus	Gemini	Cancer	Leo	Virgo	Libra	Scorpio	Sagittarius	Capricorn	Aquarius	Pisces

Sixteen

I could go on...

Love is a perky elf dancing a merry little jig and then suddenly he turns on you with a miniature machine gun.
Matt Groening

So what have we shown, and what does it mean for you?

First of all it is important to reiterate that positive Venus synastry is not required for a relationship to be successful, it is just a conventional factor that re-occurs often enough naturally for us to observe and comment upon.

This book began by looking at some seemingly anomalous factors in some public relationships: those of the Prince and Princess of Wales, Evans and Piper, and a number of other couples. The planetary co-relationships of these couples did not always validate the ideas of natal astrology, but when we add the progressed charts to the mix, the aspects that astrology supposes were not only present, they also seemed to make some sense in the timing of these relationships.

We then looked at Colman and Hume, the liberated George Sand, Sonny and Cher, Ike and Tina, Graves and Riding, and Plath and Hughes and again we saw Venus playing an extraordinarily apt role. We saw how Grace Kelly, before she became a royal princess, picked her beaux with such an eye for progressed synastry that almost all of them fit a conventional Venus pattern. How Elizabeth Taylor's relationships, although unspectacular at the level of natal astrology, almost always involved a progressed synastry pattern with Venus involved.

We saw that in three Beatles marriages there is a natal-Sun-Venus trine.

♈	♉	♊	♋	♌	♍	♎	♏	♐	♑	♒	♓
Aries	Taurus	Gemini	Cancer	Leo	Virgo	Libra	Scorpio	Sagittarius	Capricorn	Aquarius	Pisces

That five of George Sand's relationships had a Sun-Venus trine of one sort or another. We could actually see what happens sometimes when a progressing aspect starts to separate: if the relationship had been founded on the feelings or dynamics that this aspect creates then we can see, for example, that the separating Sun-Venus aspect in Geldof and Yates' chart reflected a turmoil of frustration and how the aspect spanned their relationship. We saw the same thing in the relationships of Katona and McFadden, Burton and Taylor and many others.

Not every relationship that begins under exact or applying progressed-Venus aspects or aspects to natal-Venus peters out or ends abruptly. Many becalmed relationships drift towards idealistic perfection. Some people are better equipped to deal with difficult periods, and for others the problem (if there is a problem), of a separating progressed aspect is either replaced because another progressed aspect takes its place, or the qualities of their natal-Sun Moon connection comes to the fore (in theory, this should be an important astrological connection for long-term relationships). Or they may sublimate relationship change because of devotion: simply being 'in love', a state for which there is no singular astrological explanation and a state that transcends the *attraction* that gets people together in the first instance. Everyone changes and everyone experiences changes in other people. It is often our level of understanding as to why change happens that determines our response to it.

If there is such a thing as synastry, and I think this study is convincing in this respect, then we can be pretty sure Venus is the astrological factor that plays the biggest role in bringing people together in intimate relationships. It is also obvious that progressions play a real role in relationships and to illustrate this point I'll return again to some of the 'numbers' that support this view:

Sun-Venus Squares and Trines

In this survey of 1300 relationships, natal-Sun-Venus trines within two

♈	♉	♊	♋	♌	♍	♎	♏	♐	♑	♒	♓
Aries	Taurus	Gemini	Cancer	Leo	Virgo	Libra	Scorpio	Sagittarius	Capricorn	Aquarius	Pisces

degrees occur almost *twice as often* as natal-Sun-Venus squares within the same orb. In the 1300 relationships there are **75** trines and only **41** squares. There is no mathematical or astrometric reason for this difference.[clxx]

Sun-Venus Conjunctions and Oppositions

There are **38** natal-Sun-Venus conjunctions and **40** natal-Sun-Venus oppositions in my sample of 1300 relationships with the two-degree orb. Because these aspects only occur once in any circle and the 90 degree and 120 degree aspect occurs twice, we need to examine them using different criteria or to make this simple we can either double them or add their totals together to compare results and once again, regardless of probability, they occur at a similar frequency to natal-Sun-Venus trines which is almost twice that of the natal-Sun-Venus square. Again this validates the astrological worldview that Venus, feminine and fond of harmony, would avoid the conflict inherent in the 90-degree aspect. Put simply this means that as far as initial attraction is concerned, certain 90-degree aspects suggest some level of avoidance or incompatibility and 0, 120 and 180-degree aspects suggest the opposite.

But what of progressed aspects?

Progressing-Venus aspecting Natal-Sun

Progressed-Venus aspects to the natal-Sun makes a marginally more impressive relationship indicator than aspects from progressed-Sun to natal-Venus.

There are 82 trines under this heading, 46 conjunctions, 40 oppositions and 62 squares. Further to these aspects there are 46 sextiles, 73 inconjuncts and 55 semi-sextiles.

Remember conjunctions and oppositions occur only once in a circle, all the others occur twice. This suggests that progressing-Venus in *conjunction* with natal-Sun is the single most significant progressed relationship aspect in this study while the trine combination is numerically speaking the most prevalent.

♈	♉	♊	♋	♌	♍	♎	♏	♐	♑	♒	♓
Aries	Taurus	Gemini	Cancer	Leo	Virgo	Libra	Scorpio	Sagittarius	Capricorn	Aquarius	Pisces

Progressing-Sun aspecting Natal-Venus

There are 74 trines, 38 conjunctions, 38 oppositions, 66 squares, 56 sextiles, 53 Inconjuncts and 65 semi-sextiles in this category.

Progressing-Venus aspecting the Progressed-Sun

Progressed-Sun progressed-Venus aspects occur with the following frequency:

There are 76 trines, 41 conjunctions, 34 oppositions, 59 squares, 62 sextiles, 70 inconjuncts and 46 semi-sextiles.

	Sun-Venus
Trine	307
Conjunction	163 (326)
Opposition	152 (304)
Square	228
Sextile	229
Inconjunct	260
Semi-sextile	243

The 41 natal-Sun-Venus squares

The relationship of Jeanne Coyne and Stanley Donen included two natal-Sun-Venus squares. This means that only 40 relationships include a natal-Sun-Venus square. If we look at the **40** relationships that include a 90-degree aspect between Natal-Sun and Natal-Venus within two degrees, we find **16** also have some sort of Sun-Venus trine, conjunction or opposition within two degrees. This leaves **24** relationships. Of these relationships **11** have a Venus-Mars trine, conjunction or opposition within two degrees. This leaves **13** relationships. Of these **4** have a Venus-Venus trine, conjunction or opposition, leaving **9** relationships. These relationships are those of Bruce Willis and Demi Moore, Bruce Paltrow and Blythe Danner, John D Rockefeller and Abby Rockefeller, Rod and Alana Stewart, Loretta

♈	♉	♊	♋	♌	♍	♎	♏	♐	♑	♒	♓
Aries	Taurus	Gemini	Cancer	Leo	Virgo	Libra	Scorpio	Sagittarius	Capricorn	Aquarius	Pisces

Young and Jean-Louis Berthault, Romina Power and Al Bano, Joyce Matthews and Billy Rose, Lady Antonia Fraser and Harold Pinter and Adolph Hitler and Eva Braun.

In the case of Willis and Moore a progressed-Venus natal-Mars opposition is applying in 1987 and just over two degrees. Bruce Paltrow and Blythe Danner have a natal-Sun-Venus trine at just over three degrees (about the same distance as McCartney and Mills and Lennon and Ono), John D Rockefeller's Moon is in a trine to Abby's Sun, as is Rod Stewart's Moon to Alana Stewart's Sun. Loretta Young and Jean-Louis Berthault married late in life (she was 80, he was 86), but her Sun and his Moon are in compatible signs, and possibly in trine. Romina Power and Al Bano have a close Mars-Venus sextile aspect, leaving Joyce Matthews and Billy Rose, Lady Antonia Fraser and Harold Pinter and Adolph Hitler and Eva Braun as the only Sun-Venus square relationships without the conventional planetary synastric indicators that I have ascribed. Well that's not entirely true as Hitler and Braun have some obvious Sun-Mars synastry in 1932 and Hitler's Moon is in a trine aspect to Braun's Venus. And, as is the case with astrology, squares may not be a conventional choice for most people's Venus, that doesn't mean that some people don't prefer to have a relationship that is in some senses conflicting. Remember, we are assessing conventionality here, not judging the way people who do not respond to conventionality conduct their relationships. The salient point is not who is theoretically astrologically incompatible, but just how few Sun-Venus squares there are in number compared with trines, conjunctions and oppositions.

There are almost as many natal-Sun-Venus conjunctions and oppositions as there are natal-Sun-Venus squares (38, 40 and 41 respectively). There should be twice as many squares as conjunctions and oppositions.

♈	♉	♊	♋	♌	♍	♎	♏	♐	♑	♒	♓
Aries	Taurus	Gemini	Cancer	Leo	Virgo	Libra	Scorpio	Sagittarius	Capricorn	Aquarius	Pisces

The 59 progressed-Sun progressed-Venus squares

Of the **59** progressed-Sun-Venus squares, there are **14** without a 'favorable' Venus aspect. Included in this group are the relationships of Naomi Campbell and Adam Clayton, Catherine Zeta Jones and Mick Hucknall, and Joan Collins and Sydney Chaplin.

Venus aspecting Mars

As for Venus and Mars together, there is a slight difference in the aspect type and frequency.

	Venus-Mars
Trine	261
Conjunction	120 (240)
Opposition	122 (244)
Square	232
Sextile	242
Inconjunct	250
Semi-sextile	211

Natal-Venus aspecting Natal-Mars

Although overall there are **261** trines against **232** squares, there are fewer *natal-Venus-Mars* trines compared to *natal-Venus-Mars* squares, **52** to **58** respectively.[clxxi]

The natal-Venus-Mars square sample includes some successful relationships, but the presence of such relationships as Lex Barker and Lana Turner (she divorced him after he abused her daughter), Rod Stewart and Britt Ekland, Rock Hudson and Phyllis Gates (he allegedly married her to avoid accusations of homosexuality), the Battling Sinatras, JFK and Jackie, Paul McCartney and Jane Asher, Olivier and Leigh, Pitt and Aniston, Aleister

♈	♉	♊	♋	♌	♍	♎	♏	♐	♑	♒	♓
Aries	Taurus	Gemini	Cancer	Leo	Virgo	Libra	Scorpio	Sagittarius	Capricorn	Aquarius	Pisces

Crowley and Rose Kelly (Crowley abandoned Kelly in Rangoon) and Plath and Hughes (Plath killed herself) does not do a great deal to recommend it as an indicator of conventional harmony. In fact there are 40 failed relationships in this category compared to only 25 failed relationships in the natal-Venus-Mars trine category, which also includes some far more sedate relationships including Grace and Rainier, Sonny and Cher, Frankie Laine and Nan Grey, Kylie Minogue and Olivier Martinez, John and Bo Derek and Beyonce Knowles and Jay Z.[clxxii]

Progressed-Venus and natal-Mars

Progressing-Venus (as opposed to static Venus) looks strong in the Sun-Venus sample, and in the case of progressed-Venus natal-Mars, this pattern is continued for conjunctions and oppositions, but not for trines where both categories are high, but natal-Venus progressed-Mars trines are slightly higher in number than progressed-Venus natal-Mars.

Progressed-Venus squares to Mars are also low in number (48 observed: 58.74 expected), compared to 38 and 39 conjunctions and oppositions (we would expect 29.37) demonstrating that progressing-Venus avoids squares but not conjunctions and oppositions.

Progressed-Venus aspecting Progressed-Mars

The main difference in the Venus-Mars set occurs with progressed aspects of the same planets, for example there are **73** progressed-Venus progressed-Mars trines compared with **60** progressed-Venus progressed-Mars squares, **38** of these 'square' relationships are without a supporting Venus-Mars trine conjunction or opposition, of these only **21** do not have a supporting Sun-Venus trine, conjunction or opposition. This means that out of the **60** progressed-Venus-Mars squares that were present at the start of the relationship, only **21** did not have a more recognisable two-degree aspect of astrological harmony. If we then remove the harmonious Venus-Venus aspects we are left with **17** from the original **60** relationships.

♈	♉	♊	♋	♌	♍	♎	♏	♐	♑	♒	♓
Aries	Taurus	Gemini	Cancer	Leo	Virgo	Libra	Scorpio	Sagittarius	Capricorn	Aquarius	Pisces

Sun-Venus aspects versus Venus-Mars aspects

Because Sun-Venus trines, conjunctions and oppositions are so obviously indicative of relationships, Venus and Mars appear to become less so. If we remove the noise created by the Sun-Venus trines, conjunctions and oppositions we can get a better idea of the efficacy of Venus and Mars together. We should do this because we may already have a 'reason' for the relationship in the form of the Sun with Venus and our results are now effectively skewed by the presence of the conventional Sun-Venus aspects and all of the 'noise' that surrounds these relationships in the form of the other aspects that happen within them.

If we remove the conventional Sun-Venus indicators we uncover the following numbers:

As this sample now only contains 770 relationships, we would expect

	Venus-Mars
Trine	163
Conjunction	77 (154)
Opposition	82 (164)
Square	135
Sextile	137
Inconjunct	138
Semi-sextile	132

to see 139 two-degree trines, squares, sextiles, inconjuncts and semi-sextiles and 69 conjunctions and oppositions. ...Which leads me to believe that Venus-Mars trines, conjunctions and oppositions are also relationship-forming aspects.

♈	♉	♊	♋	♌	♍	♎	♏	♐	♑	♒	♓
Aries	Taurus	Gemini	Cancer	Leo	Virgo	Libra	Scorpio	Sagittarius	Capricorn	Aquarius	Pisces

Venus in aspect to Venus

	Venus-Venus
Trine	138
Conjunction	61 (122)
Opposition	59 (118)
Square	98
Sextile	105
Inconjunct	121
Semi-sextile	105

...the peaks in this category are largely progressed aspects, for example there are **67** natal-Venus progressed-Venus trines compared with **53** natal-Venus progressed-Venus squares while there are **37** progressed-Venus progressed-Venus trines (if you recall this style of aspect was the one I noticed in my own relationship back in 1997, in effect it was the aspect style that began this study) compared to only **18** progressed-Venus progressed-Venus squares.

It should be noted that oppositions involving Venus are different to oppositions involving Mars. Most astrological textbooks would say that a Venus opposition is a lot easier to deal with than a Mars opposition.

Venus trine Venus

Venus-Venus trines occur more often than the other Venus-Venus aspects, but they occur less often than the Venus-Mars and Sun-Venus aspects. If we look at how many Venus-Venus trines happen independent of the conventional Sun-Venus aspects, using the Venus-Venus inconjuncts as a comparison we get the following results:

♈	♉	♊	♋	♌	♍	♎	♏	♐	♑	♒	♓
Aries	Taurus	Gemini	Cancer	Leo	Virgo	Libra	Scorpio	Sagittarius	Capricorn	Aquarius	Pisces

	With two-degree Sun-Venus trines, conjunctions or oppositions	Without two-degree Sun-Venus trines, conjunctions or oppositions
Natal-Venus trines	10	24
Natal-Venus progressed-Venus trines	22	45
Progressed-Venus progressed-Venus trines	12	25
Natal-Venus inconjuncts	15	15
Natal-Venus progressed-Venus inconjuncts	30	28
Progressed-Venus progressed-Venus inconjuncts	16	16

The Venus-Venus trines, therefore, do not appear to require the presence of a Sun-Venus trine, conjunction or opposition to get a relationship underway. This is not the case for the Venus-Venus inconjuncts.

If we do the same test with the Venus-Venus conjunctions and oppositions we see less pronounced, but consistent results:

	With two-degree Sun-Venus trines, conjunctions or oppositions	Without two-degree Sun-Venus trines, conjunctions or oppositions
Natal-Venus conjunctions	8	11
Natal-Venus progressed-Venus conjunctions	7	19
Progressed-Venus progressed-Venus conjunctions	5	10
Natal-Venus oppositions	8	9
Natal-Venus progressed-Venus oppositions	13	17
Progressed-Venus progressed-Venus oppositions	5	7

This pattern of more trines and conjunction/oppositions only occurs when Venus is involved. If we look at Sun – Mars for example we get the

♈	♉	♊	♋	♌	♍	♎	♏	♐	♑	♒	♓
Aries	Taurus	Gemini	Cancer	Leo	Virgo	Libra	Scorpio	Sagittarius	Capricorn	Aquarius	Pisces

following results:

	Sun-Mars
Trine	237
Conjunction	103 (206)
Opposition	118 (236)
Square	263
Sextile	213
Inconjunct	210
Semi-sextile	212

Sun aspects to Mars

Progressed-progressed squares (**72**) and oppositions (**38**) occur more often than progressed trines (**52**) and conjunctions (**24**)

Mars aspecting Mars

For Mars-Mars aspects we get the following results:

	Mars-Mars
Trine	69
Conjunction	65 (130)
Opposition	58 (116)
Square	107
Sextile	116
Inconjunct	129
Semi-sextile	116

There are only **13** natal-Mars-Mars trines, **21** conjunctions, **14** oppositions and **27** squares in the 1300 relationships. This is in contrast to natal-Sun-Venus aspects where trines occur twice as often as squares, Mars seems to avoid trines in relationships in the same way that Venus avoids squares.

♈	♉	♊	♋	♌	♍	♎	♏	♐	♑	♒	♓
Aries	Taurus	Gemini	Cancer	Leo	Virgo	Libra	Scorpio	Sagittarius	Capricorn	Aquarius	Pisces

Sun aspecting Sun

If we look at Sun-Sun aspects we get the following results:

	Sun-Sun
Trine	108
Conjunction	59 (118)
Opposition	53 (106)
Square	117
Sextile	102
Inconjunct	104
Semi-sextile	85

So if we relied solely on Sun-Sun aspects within two degrees we would find little validation for any theory except perhaps that progressed-Sun semi-sextile aspects (**18**) occur much less in relationships than progressed-Sun-Sun squares (**32**), which rather invalidates the premise of many books based on Sun Sign compatibilities, but only as far as two-degree aspects are concerned.

Venus avoids Conflict – Mars likes Friction

My conclusion, from an astrological point of view, is that Venus in synastry conventionally avoids conflict in relationships and prefers the harmonious complimentarity of the trine, the familiar 'we have so much in common' of the conjunction or the intrajection inherent in the polarising, attracting opposition. Exceptions include when Mars is involved and then there is a slight propensity towards the excitement and conflict delivered by the square aspect, but nevertheless there is still a preference for harmony in this planetary complex.

Of course, if we drill a little deeper into those relationships that have conflicting aspects, we can be certain of finding many that also contain harmonious aspects that cause the 'rose-coloured-scenario'. This scenario

♈	♉	♊	♋	♌	♍	♎	♏	♐	♑	♒	♓
Aries	Taurus	Gemini	Cancer	Leo	Virgo	Libra	Scorpio	Sagittarius	Capricorn	Aquarius	Pisces

actually does away with the necessity for numerical superiority. Although I have arrived at my conclusions by counting aspects, then by filtering and manipulating the aspect groups, the idea that only one harmonious aspect can be so overpowering in effect that it drowns out the discordant aspects in a couple's synastry, means that only one trine or conjunction among half a dozen squares could actually make a relationship happen. If we take two relationships at random – Clapton and Boyd and Harrison and Boyd – we can count 14 two-degree aspects. Only two of these are Sun-Venus conjunctions. If it is true that the Sun-Venus conjunctions are the aspects that form the relationship, it means that the astrological indicators that help relationships to happen do not necessarily have to be statistically noticeable and this is why we need qualitative studies rather than quantitative studies in astrology. It just happens that we also have numerical superiority as well. Which is why astrologers do astrology – they pay a lot of attention to what they do. So, as many relationship astrologers believe it's good to have a bit of both harmony and conflict (or excitement) in relationships, this seems to make some sense. There is always a greater frequency of relationships with Venus trines than squares because, at least in the modern age, that is what people conventionally demand from their relationships – harmony, ease and the feeling that they haven't compromised too much. Yet it also appears that Mars may prefer a bit of conflict, friction, excitement or danger, if the frequency of squares and oppositions in Mars-Mars and Mars-Sun aspects is anything to go by. It may be that I have stumbled upon a universal stereotype in this respect and while all women may not be from Venus and all men may not be from Mars, perhaps the well-used stereotype of Mars and Venus is poking through the clouds of doubt that lurk around astrology just enough to tell us something valid about human relationships, human behaviour and even astrology itself.

As for progressed synastry, we have seen in the relationships of the 'stars' many occasions when progressing planets 'collide' with natal and progressed planets and these collisions or progressions have made an

♈	♉	♊	♋	♌	♍	♎	♏	♐	♑	♒	♓
Aries	Taurus	Gemini	Cancer	Leo	Virgo	Libra	Scorpio	Sagittarius	Capricorn	Aquarius	Pisces

obvious difference in the analysis of the *quality* of the relationship as an event.

There can be little doubt that in the case of Burton and Taylor or Geldof and Yates or Charles and Diana or... you know how I could go on... that the progressed planets that I maintain were the important indicators in their relationship can be shown to do just what astrology would expect of them, on many occasions applying – becoming exact – then separating in tune with the facts of the relationship.

The fact that the horoscope changes has been underplayed, and in the case of synastry I have been able to align one of the systems used by astrologers – the day for a year system of secondary progressions – with a psychological process that the majority of people go through – the intimate relationship event. And only when it is realised that we have a dynamic or changing horoscope (or horoscopes) will we be able to design experiments that will show how astrology really works. This means we actually have a complex of horoscopes working together – one of which symbolises our potential in the same way that an acorn symbolises a potential oak tree and another showing how these potentials unfold through time. They all suggest fatalism, but because of the number of possible paths this is only theoretical fate or 'soft' determinism. Skeptical commentators have a different view, they propose that astrology = fatalism. It doesn't and never has. Astrologers have misinterpreted their subject as often as objective commentators have, but then again so have geologists, geographers, physicists, biologists, anthropologists, palaeontologists – you know how I could go on here....

Astrology works. It has some shortcomings, but these shortcomings lie with astrologers rather than astrology. Generally speaking, the way human life and events on Earth interact with time seems to be reflected accurately enough to capture the imagination and intellect of a significant percentage of those who become aware of it in passing or who study it in depth.

The results of this survey of the planetary positions in celebrity

♈	♉	♊	♋	♌	♍	♎	♏	♐	♑	♒	♓
Aries	Taurus	Gemini	Cancer	Leo	Virgo	Libra	Scorpio	Sagittarius	Capricorn	Aquarius	Pisces

relationships has caused me to concur with another astrologer, Robert Blaschke, who proposed in 1997 that day-for-a-year progressions create windows of opportunity for relationships of all kinds to happen. These windows in time reflect our growth and in the case of Venus project and reflect our compatibilities and, to an extent, our changes in taste, attraction and above all our expectations of intimacy.

There is a subtlety in astrology that takes years to accept and more years to grasp, but within this subtle subject lies a glimpse at the workings of order amongst chaos.

I've allowed my understanding of astrology to be illuminated by statistics, without being shackled by them, which is the best way to use statistics, at least with a subject like astrology. Statistics will never decisively settle any astrological question, but it can sometimes be used to illuminate and guide the astrologer towards a more clearly defined astrological question.

Carl Sagan once said that extraordinary claims require extraordinary proofs. It is worth considering that using the word 'extraordinary' in the context of astrology can be clearly seen to be related to a psychological state based upon the education and belief systems of individuals, which in turn is subject to the zeitgeist of the age in which they live. Extraordinary or not, all of Carl Sagan's three marriages[clxxiii] contain obvious Venus synastric indicators (his first marriage was to Lynn Margulis, whose Sun in Pisces is in an exact 120 degree trine to Sagan's Venus in Scorpio while his second marriage to Linda Saltzman was accompanied by a progressed-Venus progressed-Mars trine which was exact in 1967), and even, if I must make the point, Charles Darwin's relationship with Emma Wedgwood began under an exact progressed-Venus synastry pattern (a progressed-Venus natal-Mars conjunction exact in 1839 and applying within one degree in 1838; Darwin proposed marriage on 11 November 1838).[clxxiv] Also worthy of note is the marriage of one of astrology's most vocal detractors, the late Bart J. Bok, the man who co-authored the 1975 work

♈	♉	♊	♋	♌	♍	♎	♏	♐	♑	♒	♓
Aries	Taurus	Gemini	Cancer	Leo	Virgo	Libra	Scorpio	Sagittarius	Capricorn	Aquarius	Pisces

Objections to Astrology. His marriage to Priscilla Fairfield began when his progressing-Sun made a conjunction with her natal-Venus in Taurus.[clxxv] In the case of Carl Sagan and Ann Druyan, it was a progressed-Venus natal-Venus opposition within two degrees in 1977 (they met at a dinner party three years before, incidentally during a progressed-Sun natal-Venus trine). I could go on to detail sceptical humanists and political thinkers such as Karl Marx and his wife Jenny von Westphalen or Lenin and Krupskaya who also married under precise progressed synastry. I might then go on to mention Mikhail and Raisa Gorbachev,[clxxvi] or sceptics like the science fiction writer L.Sprague de Camp[clxxvii] and his wife Catherine or the sceptical humorist Steve Allen and his wife Jayne Meadows. Four of Bertrand Russell's relationships contained positive progressed-Venus synastry at the time of their formation.[clxxviii] I fear Lord Russell was right and we may be being 'kept stupid', not by astrology, but by our lack of willingness to investigate what astrology really is.[clxxix] As we saw in an introductory chapter, even the relationship of the existentialists Jean-Paul Sartre and Simone de Beauvoir was subject to obvious Venus synastry. Indeed it appears that even those who criticise or deny astrology cannot avoid proving it when they fall in love.

The extraordinariness of an idea, like both treason and astrological attraction, is a matter of dates.

Many people find synastry useful. A problem might arise if we make it as the sole consideration in decisions about relationships. I have encountered people who will not consider a relationship with people born under certain Sun signs. I believe that while astrology can possibly impart information in unusual ways, it is an error to believe that a close, intimate relationship can be governed by the position of the Sun in one horoscope and its angle to the Sun in a potential partner's horoscope. It is a better idea to use astrology merely as a positive guide to include rather than a negative one to exclude people from your life. I don't believe that answers to questions about relationships can be satisfactorily given by Sun Sign

♈	♉	♊	♋	♌	♍	♎	♏	♐	♑	♒	♓
Aries	Taurus	Gemini	Cancer	Leo	Virgo	Libra	Scorpio	Sagittarius	Capricorn	Aquarius	Pisces

astrology. Synastry works best as a complimentary method of understanding relationships. Because it is complex, and, unless you are highly
skilled or gifted and pay a great deal of attention to detail, you can never be
certain you have considered all the facts. It follows that I only recommend
using astrology to enhance the decision making process, rather than as the
only criterion for the decision. All of the planets in the natal and progressed
charts play a role in the quality of our relationships, the focus of this book
has been narrow, in reality, life experience and the experience of being in
relationships is much wider.

It's also a good idea to remember that the experience of meeting your
soul mate is not an end in itself, but a step in a process. People who live
happily ever after also have some living to do…Life may be the enemy of
love, but effort is a great ally in any relationship.

I hope that this book has shown one thing: the reason why many
astrologers do astrology is not because they have some intuitive feeling that
perhaps many Leos really do need to be the centre of attention, or that the
salient characteristic of every Gemini they have ever met is that they do a
lot of talking, and so therefore there must be 'something in astrology', but
for another reason that is difficult to communicate or pin down. That, for
example, three out of nine Beatles marriages contained natal-Sun-Venus
trines, although only one of these trines was within two degrees (and so
only one is included in the 75 trines mentioned above) the others are certainly close enough for any astrologer to 'count' them as being effective and
to delight at their presence in a relationship, but they have fallen by the
wayside in this study because of the two-degree rule.

The same goes for the closer of the *two* natal-Sun-Venus conjunctions
in George Harrison and Pattie Boyd's relationship. Another two Beatles
relationships had a progressed-Sun-Venus conjunction and another had a
progressed-Venus-Mars conjunction, although this Venus-Mars conjunction
was exact when Lennon married Powell, it was not within two degrees
when they met, and, in not meeting my strict criteria, it is also not

♈	♉	♊	♋	♌	♍	♎	♏	♐	♑	♒	♓
Aries	Taurus	Gemini	Cancer	Leo	Virgo	Libra	Scorpio	Sagittarius	Capricorn	Aquarius	Pisces

included in the statistics. This number of common relationship indicators is not a bad trawl for so few relationships. In the case of Prince Charles and Camilla, Duchess of Cornwall, I have been able to show the relevancy of a progressing-Sun-Venus trine, but as I have to use a start date for their relationship of 1972 I cannot include this aspect in the statistics for progressed-Sun-Venus trines, and as can be seen from these necessary exclusions, statistical rules can hide information and therefore cause gullibility as often as they might illuminate the truth.

Astrology may be an impossible subject to prove scientifically, but that does not mean it is not true and if time is taken to look in the right places with the right knowledge the simple patterns that lie beneath the veil can be seen in the experiences of real people.

It is certain that those people who have rejected astrology publicly in the past, did so without the information contained in this book, and it is also certain that they are unlikely to change their beliefs based on these facts, and that's OK, (the world needs different points of view), but facts they are. It is also certain that astrology will never be science. Not in the current sense. As Patrick Curry says, modern science was founded on being not-astrology. But future science could be quite different to modern science.

Synastry is about the closest thing we will ever get to a scientific under-standing of love, in this sense astrology is a *sacred* science, and there are those who might infer from this that when science tries to answer such questions as why we fall in love, it becomes pseudo-astrology. Now there's a thought.

One other thing is also certain. We will always have the agency, the control and the free-choice to attempt to make our relationships work.

Contrary to what some believe, your horoscope makes you *different*, not *the same as a twelfth of the population of the world*. Astrology's role is one of *individuation* rather than *compartmentalisation*. There are no dump-bins or pigeon holes in real astrology, only in the imaginations of those who abuse or criticise it. In fact every experience you have is unique to you, both

♈	♉	♊	♋	♌	♍	♎	♏	♐	♑	♒	♓
Aries	Taurus	Gemini	Cancer	Leo	Virgo	Libra	Scorpio	Sagittarius	Capricorn	Aquarius	Pisces

astrologically and 'practically'. Woody Allen is quoted as saying that "Time is nature's way of keeping everything from happening at once", this joke illuminates the reason why astrology works in the way that it does, and if it worked in the same way as, say, geology or computer programming, which would make it possible to fathom scientifically, then being human would be a different experience; life would not contain the wondrous variety that it does. Every day would be the same. It may be because of whatever is behind astrology (what it is that astrology illuminates) that every day is a different experience along a series of collective themes reflected in the events, encounters and personal growth that develop in line with the process of life.

Astrology, according to one of history's most rigorous observational astronomers, Tycho Brahe, is *really more reliable than one would think'*.

I have had to dig a little to get 'underneath the stars', but any astrologer or researcher who does this kind of research does so to get closer to the *seam of gold* that we believe lies at the core of astrological tradition. We won't know for certain if the facts relayed in this book are revelatory of astrology or just of this astrologer until someone else looks at this idea, but I believe that we have only glimpsed a fraction of the bottom corner of the big picture of astrology at work. And we can only get glimpses of it because there are events in life where we have *similarities* of experience and *the beginning of* intimate relationships fall within this criterion more than most other areas of human experience.

Although the quality of your relationship is, above all, a matter for yourself and in most cases its success is directly related to the effort you expend to make it good, strong, happy and long, it appears that the astrological Venus will often have a say not only in *who* you will be attracted to, but, it appears, also *when* this attraction will manifest, whether you know about it or not.

♈	♉	♊	♋	♌	♍	♎	♏	♐	♑	♒	♓
Aries	Taurus	Gemini	Cancer	Leo	Virgo	Libra	Scorpio	Sagittarius	Capricorn	Aquarius	Pisces

Appendices

i *Private Lives* by Noel Coward, A study guide prepared by Martin Andrucki, Charles A. Dana Professor of Theater Bates College http://www.thepublictheatre.org/stdygds/private_lives_study_guide_03_04.htm

ii People born between 23rd May and 21st June have the Sun is in Gemini, while those born between 24th July and 23rd August have the Sun in Leo. Depending in the year in question, the start and end dates of all the Sun signs varies slightly, but there is no such thing as "being born on the cusp so you're a bit of both" – you are either one or the other.

iii 920 out of 1300 relationships have a close trine, conjunction or opposition of the planet Venus to either the Sun, Venus or Mars in their partner's natal or progressed chart

iv See Chapters Fifteen and Sixteen for more on this issue.

v I later found that another astrologer was writing about the same idea at about the same time. Robert Blaschke wrote about synastric progressions in 1997 in *Astrology: A Language of Life Volume 1- Progressions,* Earthwalk School of Astrology, 1997, p79

vi Interestingly, two squares between the Sun and Venus formed between the progressed and natal horoscopes of Princess Margaret and Peter Townshend between 1950 and 1956.

vii Many of the celebrities dates and times of birth included in this study are also included in Astrodatabank, it is difficult, however, to always match couples whose times of birth are known for certain. In this respect I have had to find a large number of individual dates from other sources, these have included online resources including IMDB.com, findagrave.com, the Encyclopedia Britannica, internet newsgroups and other miscellaneous web pages. The accuracy of

dates of birth in IMDB.com is questionable in some cases, but it is
very useful as a resource to find out who individual celebrities were
married to and when these marriages took place. There is however a
point at which IMDB becomes the only resource for relatively
obscure individuals dates of birth and so this is possibly the
weakest (while also one of the most useful) links in this study.
Every date of birth has been checked for dispute or inaccuracy.
Those that are under dispute have been rejected.

viii Lois Haines Sargent, *How to Handle your Human Relationships*,
AFA, 1958, p11

ix *ibid* p11

x *ibid* p11

xi *ibid* p11

xii Garth Fletcher, *The New Science of Intimate Relationships*,
Blackwell, 2002, p101

xiii It should be noted that there are many harmonic aspects (divisions
of the zodiacal circle) other than the seven mentioned in this book
and as such aspects of 36, 40, 45, 51, 72, 80, 102, 135 and 144
degrees and others may also have important roles to play in the
intimate connections of the Sun, Venus and Mars.

xiv Ronald Davison, *Synastry – Understanding Human Relations
through Astrology*, Aurora, 1983, p7

xv *ibid*, p8

xvi David Plant *Johannes Kepler And the Music of the Spheres*,
Traditional Astrologer magazine, summer 1995

xvii *ibid*

xviii John Anthony West, *The Case for Astrology*, Viking, 1991, p171

xix David Plant *Johannes Kepler And the Music of the Spheres*,
Traditional Astrologer magazine, summer 1995
(Of these Keplerian aspects, I have come to regard the 72° Quintile
as a favourable relationship indicator, but I have not yet subjected

this aspect to large-scale quantitative scrutiny)

xx   Arthur M Young (1905 – 1995) was the inventor of the Bell Helicopter.

xxi   Nancy Hastings, *Secondary Progressions* Weiser, 1984, foreword by Rob Hand, p ix

xxii   Bernadette Brady, *Predictive Astrology, The Eagle and the Lark*, Weiser, 1999, p100-101

xxiii   Stephen Arroyo, *Astrology, Karma and Transformation*, CRCS, 1992, p167

xxiv   Charles E.O Carter, *The Principles of Astrology*

xxv   Robert P Blaschke, *Astrology: A Language of Life Volume 1- Progressions,* Earthwalk School of Astrology, 1997, p5

xxvi   Martin Freeman, *Forecasting by Astrology*, Aquarian Press, 1982, p35

xxvii   Eric Francis quoted from an article here: http://www.cainer.com/ericfrancis/aug20.html

xxviii   Dane Rudhyar, *The Astrology of Personality*, Aurora, 1991, p336

xxix   Laurie Efrein, *How to Rectify a Birth Chart*, Aquarian Press, 1987, p166

xxx   Placidus de Titus' book Primum Mobile was originally published in 1657 and translated (1994) by Michael Baigent. Garry Phillipson also quotes Henry Coley from a manuscript in the British Library Sloan Ms2280 p.5, in the context of a chart interpretation which begins 'The nativity of Madam Eliz. Hope don by Dr Oznoy anno 1690'… 'and the Ascend to the square of Mercury at the very same time according to (?) this (?) way of Direction us'd by Placidus de Titus a monk, about the year 1655'

xxxi   On page 164 of his book, *A History of Horoscopic Astrology* (AFA). James Holden writes:

"[Kepler] is also said to have considered that the number of days after birth that the Sun took to reach a natal planet was equivalent to the number of years of the native's life that would lapse before the indicated influence would manifest itself. This is the earliest instance I have encountered of the use of what we would call a secondary direction"

xxxii The modern Western use of progressed aspects demands that they have a limited influence in terms of time based on the type of aspect. Traditionalists apply different orbs depending on the planets involved.

xxxiii Eric Francis, quoted from an article here: http://www.cainer.com/ericfrancis/aug20.html

xxxiv Adrian Duncan, *Doing Time on Planet Earth*, Element, 1990, p39

xxxv Robert Hand, *Horoscope Symbols*, Whitford Press, 1981

xxxvi Lois Haines Sargent, *How to Handle your Human Relationships*, AFA, 1997

xxxvii Ronald Davison, *Synastry – Understanding Human Relations Through Astrology*, Aurora Press, 1983

xxxviii Frances Sakoian and Louis S. Acker, *The Astrology of Human Relationships*, Peter Davies, 1976

xxxix Stephen Arroyo, *Relationships and Life Cycles*, CRCS, 1993

xl Lois Haines Sargent, *How to Handle your Human Relationships*, AFA, 1997, p49

xli *ibid* p49

xlii Ronald Davison, *Synastry – Understanding Human Relations Through Astrology*, Aurora Press, 1983, p101

xliii Stephen Arroyo, *Relationships and Life Cycles*, CRCS, 1993, p90

xliv Lois Haines Sargent, *How to Handle your Human Relationships*, AFA, 1997, p50

xlv *ibid* p50

xlvi *ibid* p69

xlvii Ronald Davison, *Synastry – Understanding Human Relations Through Astrology*, Aurora Press, 1983, p127

xlviii Sheridan Morley, *The Other Side of the Moon*, Coronet, 1986, p162

xlix   David Niven and Primula Rollo's relationship is not included in the 1300 relationships

l   Lois Haines Sargent, *How to Handle your Human Relationships*, AFA, 1997, p70

li   The relationship of Shah Jahan and Mumtaz Mahal is not included in the 1300 relationships

lii   Lois Haines Sargent, *How to Handle your Human Relationships*, AFA, 1997, p69

liii   Mia Farrow, *What Falls Away*, Doubleday, 1997, p120

liv   *ibid* p70

lv   *ibid* p74

lvi   *ibid* p75

lvii   Stephen Arroyo, *Relationships and Life Cycles*, CRCS, 1993, p91-92

lviii   Lois Haines Sargent, *How to Handle your Human Relationships*, AFA, 1997, p69

lix   *ibid* p51

lx   Ronald Davison, *Synastry – Understanding Human Relations Through Astrology*, Aurora Press, 1983, p105

lxi   Lois Haines Sargent, *How to Handle your Human Relationships*, AFA, 1997, p52

lxii   *ibid* p52

lxiii   *ibid* p52

lxiv   *ibid* p52

lxv   *ibid* p52-53

lxvi   *ibid* p52

lxvii   *ibid* p53

lxviii   *ibid* p70

lxix   Frances Sakoian and Louis S. Acker, *The Astrology of Human Relationships*, Peter Davies, 1976, p170

lxx   Ronald Davison, *Synastry – Understanding Human Relations Through Astrology*, Aurora Press, 1983, p127-129

lxxi   Lois Haines Sargent, *How to Handle your Human Relationships*, AFA, 1997, p70

lxxii   *ibid* p70

lxxiii   Frances Sakoian and Louis S. Acker, *The Astrology of Human Relationships*, Peter Davies, 1976, p184

lxxiv   Ronald Davison, *Synastry – Understanding Human Relations Through Astrology*, Aurora Press, 1983, p127-129

lxxv   Stephen Arroyo, *Relationships and Life Cycles*, CRCS, 1993, p87

lxxvi   Barry Norman, *The Hollywood Greats*, BBC Books, 1980, p180

lxxvii   Mary Wollstonecraft, *A Vindication of the Rights of Women*, The full Etext can be found on this web site: http://womenshistory.about.com/library/etext/bl_vindication000.htm

lxxviii   The relationship of George Sand and Casimir Dudevant is not included in the 1300 relationships

lxxix   Belinda Jack, *George Sand A Women's Life Writ Large*, Vintage, 2001, p110

lxxx   George Sand, *Deuvres autobiographique* vol II (ed George Lubin), p27

lxxxi   Belinda Jack, *George Sand A Women's Life Writ Large*, Vintage, 2001, p113

lxxxii   *ibid*, p117

lxxxiii   *ibid*, p157

lxxxiv   George Sand, Correspondence, quoted in Jack, p157

lxxxv   Belinda Jack, *George Sand A Women's Life Writ Large*, Vintage, 2001, p212

lxxxvi   *ibid, p217*

lxxxvii   The relationship of George Sand and Marie Dorval is not included in the 1300 relationships

lxxxviii   George Sand, Correspondence, quoted in Jack, p220

lxxxix   Belinda Jack, *George Sand A Women's Life Writ Large*, Vintage, 2001, p221

xc   Alfred de Musset, quoted in Rene Doumic, *Biography of George*

Sand, http://www.worldwideschool.org/library/books/hst/biogra
phy/BiographyofGeorgeSand/chap6.html

xci Belinda Jack, *George Sand A Women's Life Writ Large*, Vintage,
2001, p248

xcii George Sand, *Deuvres autobiographique* vol II (ed George Lubin),
p322

xciii http://perso.wanadoo.fr/negrel/hommes/michel_de_bourges.htm

xciv Marion D March and Joan McEvers, *The Only Way to Learn About
Relationships*, ACS, 1992, p94

xcv The relationship of George Sand and Louis Blanc is not included in
the 1300 relationships

xcvi James Spada, *Grace, The Secret Lives of a Princess*, Penguin, 1988,
p48

xcvii The relationship of Grace Kelly and Mark Miller is not included in
the 1300 relationships

xcviii James Spada, *Grace, The Secret Lives of a Princess*, Penguin, 1988,
p76

xcix Robert Lacey, *Grace*, G.P. Putnam & Sons, 1994, p157

c *ibid,* p157

ci C. David Heymann, *Liz - An Intimate Biography of Elizabeth
Taylor*, Mandarin, 1996, p108-109

cii *ibid,* p109

ciii *ibid, p132*

civ Michael Todd Jr. and Susan McCarthy Todd, *A Valuable Property –
The Life Story of Michael Todd,* Arbor House, 1983, p13

cv Kitty Kelley, *Elizabeth Taylor – The Last Star*, BCA, 1981, p101

cvi Eddie Fisher with David Fisher, *Been There, Done That*, Arrow,
1999, p158-159

cvii *ibid,* p180

cviii C. David Heymann, *Liz - An Intimate Biography of Elizabeth
Taylor*, Mandarin, 1996, p279

cix   The relationship of Richard Burton and Sybil Williams is not included in the 1300 relationships

cx   The relationship of Richard Burton and Claire Bloom is not included in the 1300 relationships

cxi   The relationship of Richard Burton and Susan Strasberg is not included in the 1300 relationships

cxii   C. David Heymann, *Liz - An Intimate Biography of Elizabeth Taylor*, Mandarin, 1996, p279 *(the actual word used in this declaration was 'nailed' not 'made love to')*

cxiii   Graham Jenkins, *Richard Burton My Brother*, Sphere Books, 1988, p304-305

cxiv   The relationship of Richard Burton and Princess Elizabeth of Yugoslavia is not included in the 1300 relationships

cxv   The relationship of Richard Burton and Sally Hay is not included in the 1300 relationships

cxvi   the 2004 Carter Memorial Lecture delivered by Dr. Patrick Curry http://www.skyscript.co.uk/enchantment.html

cxvii   Chapter two of the first tractate of Guido Bonatti's Liber Astronomiae (written in the thirteenth Century CE) is entitled *That the Stars Imprint [their influences] on Inferior Bodies and that the Mutations Which Happen in This World Happen by the Motion of the Stars*. In this chapter, Bonatti explains that the circular motion of the heavens causes change on Earth and that because the Sun and Moon are closer to the Earth, their presence is felt more than the impressions made by the other planets and stars. Of course, Bonatti firstly ascribed cause to the divinity of God and secondly to the motion of heavenly objects. In essence he is describing physical causality subject to a divine will.

cxviii   Edwin Abbott, *Flatland, A Romance in Many Dimensions*, Penguin, 1999

cxix   For further information see Roger Penrose, *Shadows of the Mind*,

Vintage, 1995

cxx   John Anthony West, *The Case for Astrology*, Viking, 1991, p173 - 175

cxxi   Dante Alghieri, La Vita Nuova, XXI, translated by Dante Gabriel Rossetti

cxxii   Eddie Cochran and Sharon Sheeley, *Somethin' Else*

cxxiii   The Saturn return takes place between the ages of 29 and 31 years depending on the motion of Saturn. It happens when the planet of responsibility and achievement returns to the position in the chart it occupied when the subject was born. Many people change jobs, relationship or lifestyle at this point in their lives as Saturn holds a proverbial mirror up to their life and asks them whether the direction in which they are travelling is the right one for them.

cxxiv   Neil Spencer, *True As The Stars Above*, Orion, 2000, p230

cxxv   *ibid*, p231

cxxvi   Martin Seymour-Smith, *Robert Graves - His Life and Work*, , 1983, p314

cxxvii   *ibid* p317

cxxviii   *ibid* p317

cxxix   Colin Wilson, *The Occult*, Grafton, 1979, p477

cxxx   http://www.maypang.com/bio.html

cxxxi   The relationship of Ringo Starr and Maureen Cox is not included in the 1300 relationships

cxxxii   The relationship of Stuart Sutcliffe and Astrid Kirscherr is not included in the 1300 relationships

cxxxiii   The relationship of David and Angie Bowie is not included in the 1300 relationships. Angie's date of birth is not readily accessible in the public domain, but it is known that she celebrated her 25th birthday on August 9th 1974.

cxxxiv   The relationship of Kylie Minogue and Rupert Penry-Jones is not included in the 1300 relationships

cxxxv   Bob Geldof, *Is That It?*, Penguin, 1986, p153

cxxxvi   Gerry Agar - *Paula Michael and Bob – Everything You Know is Wrong*, Michael O'Mara Books, 2003, p35

cxxxvii   *ibid*, p51-52

cxxxviii   Sharon Krum *The Manhattan Interview*, Sept 1997 available to view online at: http://www.thei.aust.com/music3/hutch9.html

cxxxix   http://www.bobgeldof.info/interviews.htm

cxl   The relationship of John Profumo and Valerie Hobson is not included in the 1300 relationships

cxli   The relationship of John Mortimer and Wendy Craig is not included in the 1300 relationships

cxlii   The relationship of John Mortimer and Penelope Fletcher is not included in the 1300 relationships

cxliii   The relationship of Brad Pitt and Angelina Jolie is not included in the 1300 relationships

cxliv   Jennifer Aniston has recently been linked with Vince Vaughan. They share a natal Sun natal Venus conjunction within two degrees.

cxlv   This was the TV show which brought Katie Price (AKA Jordan) together with singer Peter Andre. They share a progressed-Venus progressed-Mars opposition.

cxlvi   The relationship of Bryan McFadden and Delta Goodrem is not included in the 1300 relationships

cxlvii   Sam Kashner and Jennifer MacNair, *The Bad and the Beautiful*, WW Norton and Co, 2002, p199

cxlviii   *ibid* p206

cxlix   The relationship of Shirley Maclaine and Andrew Peacock is not included in the 1300 relationships

cl   J.Randall Taraborelli, *Sinatra, The Man Behind the Myth*, Mainstream Publishing, 2001, p140

cli   *ibid*, p146

clii   *ibid*, p155

cliii   *ibid*, p167

cliv   *ibid*, p144

clv   J Randall Taraborelli, Sinatra, the Man behind the Myth, Mainstream, p435

clvi   *ibid*, p436

clvii   Laurence Olivier, *Confessions of an Actor*, Coronet, 1983, p172

clviii   The relationship of Vivien Leigh and Peter Finch is not included in the 1300 relationships

clix   The relationship of Ellen Degeneres and Portia de Rossi is not included in the 1300 relationships

clx   The relationship of Romaine Brooks and Natalie Barney is not included in the 1300 relationships

clxi   The relationship of Benjamin Britten and Peter Pears is not included in the 1300 relationships

clxii   The relationship of Christopher Isherwood and Don Bachardy is not included in the 1300 relationships

clxiii   See this web page for an introduction to Arthur Young's ideas about progressions: http://www.arthuryoung.com/3time.html

clxiv   Jodie and Steven Forrest, *Skymates- Love Sex and Evolutionary Astrology*, Seven Paws Press, 2002, p4

clxv   The relationship of Rev. Billy Graham and Ruth Bell is not included in the 1300 relationships

clxvi   Mormon Elder Bruce R.McConkie has this to say:[Astrology is a] form of divination and fortune telling akin to sorcery, astrology is a pseudo science that pretends to divulge the influence of the stars upon human affairs; it is a false science that claims to foretell earthly events by means of the positions and aspects of these heavenly luminaries. It is, of course, one of Satan's substitutes for the true science of astronomy and for the true principle of receiving revelation of future events from divine sources.

Ancient uninspired peoples were frequently deluded by the snares

of the astrologers among them (Isa. 47; Dan. 1:20; 2:27; 4:7; 5:7),
but it is difficult to understand why people in modern and
supposedly enlightened and civilized nations should submit to these
same stargazing absurdities. Enlightened people in and out of the
Church shun them for the abominations they are. *Mormon Doctrine,
p.56 http://www.lightplanet.com/mormons/daily/prayer/improper
_channels.htm*

clxvii   The relationships of Joseph Smith and Emma, Joseph Smith and
Eliza Snow and Brigham Young and Eliza Snow are not included in
the 1300 relationships.

clxviii   Eddie Fisher with David Fisher, *Been There, Done That*, Arrow,
1999, p217-296

clxix   It occurs twice in two relationships

clxx   Of course, the other side of the coin is that this survey is in itself,
incomplete. I have tested only the major astrological aspects. I
acknowledge that most scientists would not accept my view as plain
fact without considering all the other possible angles between planets.

clxxi   The natal Venus natal Mars trine aspect hasn't featured - in isolation
- in many of the relationships in this book. See the relationships of
Burton and Elizabeth of Yugoslavia, Grace and Rainier, Rainier and
Gisele Pascal and Grace and Cary Grant. It is present, although not
in isolation, in the relationship of Prince William of Wales and Kate
Middleton.

clxxii   The progressed Venus progressed Mars trine was also present in the
relationship of Elton John and David Furnish in 1993 when they
met. This is not included in the 1300 relationships.

clxxiii   The relationships of Carl Sagan with Lynn Margulis, Linda
Saltzman and Anne Druyan are not included in the 1300 relationships

clxxiv   The relationship of Charles Darwin and Emma Wedgwood is not
included in the 1300 relationships. The progressed-Venus natal
Mars conjunction occurs 38 times in this survey.

clxxv The relationship of Bart J. Bok and Priscilla Fairfield is not included in the 1300 relationships. For more information about *Objections to Astrology* see John Anthony West's *The Case for Astrology.*

clxxvi None of the following relationships are included in the 1300 relationships: Lenin and Krupskaya, Marx and von Westphalen or the Gorbachev's.

clxxvii The relationship of L. Sprague de Camp and Catherine Crook is not included in the 1300 relationships (progressed-Sun conjunction progressed-Venus)

clxxviii The relationships of Bertrand Russell with Ottoline Morrell, Constance Malleson, Dora Black, Edith Finch and Vivienne Eliot are not included in the 1300 relationships. His relationship with Constance Malleson contains a *natal* Venus *progressed-Mars* opposition, within one degree in 1915, this aspect does not occur enough times in the survey to be described as a *strong* indicator, whereas *progressed-Venus* opposite *natal* Mars does.

clxxix Bertrand Russell wrote the following in 1932: '*That [astrologers proliferation] should be possible is creditable to them but very discreditable to our educational system. In schools and universities information of all sorts is ladled out, but no one is taught to reason, or to consider what is evidence for what. To any person with even the vaguest idea of the nature of scientific evidence, such beliefs as those of astrologers are of course impossible. But so are most of the beliefs upon which governments are based, such as the peculiar merit of persons living in a certain area, or of persons whose income exceeds a certain sum. It would not do to teach people to reason correctly, since the result would be to undermine these beliefs. If these beliefs were to fade, mankind might escape disaster, but politicians could not. At all costs, therefore, we must be kept stupid.*'

Appendix A - The 1300 Relationships

NO.	Forename	Surname	DOB	Forename	Surname	DOB	Start Year	Marriage	End Date
1	Elizabeth	Taylor	27 Feb 1932	Richard	Burton	10 Nov 1925	1962	15 Mar 1964	26 Jun 1974
2	Tom	Baker	20 Jan 1934	Lalla	Ward	28 Jun 1951	1979	13 Dec 1980	Jun 1981
3	Vivien	Leigh	05 Nov 1913	Laurence	Olivier	22 May 1907	1937	31 Aug 1940	02 Dec 1960
4	Spencer	Tracy	05 Apr 1900	Katherine	Hepburn	12 May 1907	1942		10 Jun 1967
5	George	Harrison	24 Feb 1943	Patti	Boyd	17 Mar 1944	1964	21 Jan 1966	1977
6	Eric	Clapton	30 Mar 1945	Patti	Boyd	17 Mar 1944	1974	1979	01 Jun 1988
7	Audrey	Hepburn	04 May 1929	Mel	Ferrer	25 Aug 1917		25 Sep 1954	1968
8	John	Lennon	09 Oct 1940	Yoko	Ono	18 Feb 1933	9 Nov 1966	1969	1980
9	Marilyn	Monroe	01 Jun 1926	Joe	Dimaggio	25 Nov 1914		14 Jan 1954	27 Oct 1954
10	Marilyn	Monroe	01 Jun 1926	Arthur	Miller	17 Oct 1915		29 Jun 1956	20 Jan 1961
11	Marilyn	Monroe	01 Jun 1926	John F	Kennedy	29 May 1917	1960		1960
12	Elizabeth	Taylor	27 Feb 1932	Michael	Wilding	23 Aug 1912		21 Feb 1952	30 Jan 1957
13	Barbara	Stanwyck	16 Jul 1907	Robert	Wagner	10 Feb 1930	1953		1957
14	Elizabeth	Taylor	27 Feb 1932	Eddie	Fisher	10 Aug 1928		12 May 1959	01 Jan 1964
15	Elizabeth	Taylor	27 Feb 1932	John W	Warner	18 Feb 1927		04 Dec 1976	07 Nov 1982
16	Charlie	Chaplin	16 Apr 1889	Mildred	Harris	29 Nov 1901		23 Oct 1918	1920
17	Charles	Boyer	28 Aug 1899	Pat	Paterson	07 Apr 1910		1934	23 Aug 1978
18	Dorothy	Brett	10 Nov 1883	DH	Lawrence	11 Sep 1885	1923		1933
19	Charlie	Chaplin	16 Apr 1889	Oona	Chaplin	13 May 1926		16 Jun 1943	25 Dec 1977
20	Humphrey	Bogart	25 Dec 1899	Lauren	Bacall	16 Sep 1924		1945	14 Jan 1957
21	Bob	Geldof	05 Oct 1951	Paula	Yates	24 Apr 1959	25 Dec 1977	1986	1995
22	Paula	Yates	24 Apr 1959	Michael	Hutchence	22 Jan 1960	1995	1996	1997
23	Evelyn	Keyes	20 Nov 1919	John	Huston	05 Aug 1906		1946	1950
24	Evelyn	Keyes	20 Nov 1919	Artie	Shaw	23 May 1910		1957	1964
25	Roman	Polanski	18 Aug 1933	Nastassia	Kinski	24 Jan 1961	Oct 1976		1979

NO.	Forename	Surname	DOB	Forename	Surname	DOB	Start Year	Marriage	End Date
26	Evelyn	Keyes	20 Nov 1919	Charles	Vidor	27 Jul 1900	1940	1943	1945
27	Frank	Sinatra	12 Dec 1915	Ava	Gardner	24 Dec 1922		07 Nov 1951	05 Jul 1957
28	Frank	Sinatra	12 Dec 1915	Mia	Farrow	09 Feb 1945		1966	1968
29	Frank	Sinatra	12 Dec 1915	Barbara	Marx	16 Oct 1930		1976	14 May 1998
30	Prince	Charles	14 Nov 1948	Diana	Spencer	01 Jul 1961		1981	1992
31	Mia	Farrow	09 Feb 1945	Woody	Allen	01 Dec 1935	1982		1996
32	Mia	Farrow	09 Feb 1945	Andre	Previn	09 Apr 1929		1970	1978
33	Demi	Moore	11 Nov 1962	Ashton	Kutcher	07 Feb 1978	2003		none
34	Madonna	Ciccone	16 Aug 1958	Sean	Penn	17 Aug 1960	1985	Aug 1985	01 Sep 1989
35	Madonna	Ciccone	16 Aug 1958	Warren	Beatty	30 Mar 1937	1989		Mar 1990
36	Madonna	Ciccone	16 Aug 1958	Guy	Ritchie	10 Sep 1968	1998	2000	none
37	Warren	Beatty	30 Mar 1937	Annette	Bening	29 May 1958		1992	none
38	Elvis	Presley	08 Jan 1935	Priscilla	Beaulieu	24 May 1945	1957	1967	1972
39	Prince	Rainier	31 May 1923	Grace	Kelly	12 Nov 1929		1956	1982
40	Clark	Gable	01 Feb 1901	Carole	Lombard	06 Oct 1908		29 Mar 1939	16 Jan 1942
41	Francesca	Annis	14 May 1944	Ralph	Fiennes	22 Dec 1962	1995		none
42	David	Bowie	08 Jan 1947	Iman	Abdulmajid	25 Jul 1955		24 Apr 92	none
43	Judy	Garland	10 Jun 1922	Vincente	Minelli	28 Feb 1903		1945	1951
44	Errol	Flynn	20 Jun 1909	Patrice	Wymore	17 Dec 1926		Oct 1950	14 Oct 1959
45	Errol	Flynn	20 Jun 1909	Nora	Eddington	25 Feb 1924		Aug 1943	07 Jul 1948
46	Errol	Flynn	20 Jun 1909	Lili	Damita	19 Jul 1901		Jun 1935	Apr 1942
47	Goldie	Hawn	21 Nov 1945	Kurt	Russell	17 Mar 1951		1983	none
48	Kirk	Douglas	09 Dec 1916	Diana	Dill	22 Jan 1923		02 Nov 1943	1951
49	Robert	Browning	07 May 1812	Elizabeth	Barrett	06 Mar 1806	1845	12 Sep 1846	29 Jun 1861
50	Bruce	Paltrow	26 Nov 1943	Blythe	Danner	03 Feb 1943		1970	2002
51	Bruce	Willis	19 Mar 1955	Demi	Moore	11 Nov 1962		21 Nov 1987	18 Oct 2000
52	Tom	Cruise	03 Jul 1962	Penelope	Cruz	28 Apr 1974		2001	2004
53	Michael	Douglas	25 Sep 1944	Catherine	Zeta-Jones	25 Sep 1969	1999	2000	none
54	Brad	Pitt	18 Dec 1963	Jennifer	Aniston	11 Feb 1969		1998	2005
55	Diana	Dors	23 Oct 1931	Alan	Lake	24 Nov 1940		1968	1984

NO.	Forename	Surname	DOB	Forename	Surname	DOB	Start Year	Marriage	End Date
56	Angelica	Huston	08 Jul 1951	Jack	Nicholson	22 Apr 1937	1973		1989
57	Joan	Collins	23 May 1933	Anthony	Newley	24 Sep 1931		1963	1971
58	Cary	Grant	18 Jan 1904	Dyan	Cannon	04 Jan 1937	1962	22 Jul 1965	21 Mar 1968
59	Tyrone	Power	05 May 1914	Linda	Christian	13 Nov 1924		27 Jan 1949	07 Aug 1956
60	Peter	Sellers	08 Sep 1925	Britt	Ekland	06 Oct 1942		19 Feb 1964	1968
61	Rod	Stewart	10 Jan 1945	Britt	Ekland	06 Oct 1942		1976	1977
62	Roger	Moore	14 Oct 1927	Dorothy	Squires	25 Mar 1915		06 Jul 1953	1968
63	Mick	Jagger	26 Jul 1943	Jerry	Hall	02 Jul 1956	1979	1991	09 Jul 1999
64	Mick	Jagger	26 Jul 1943	Bianca	Jagger	02 May 1945		1969	1978
65	Ali	McGraw	01 Apr 1938	Robert	Evans	29 Jun 1930		24 Oct 1969	1972
66	Steve	McQueen	24 Mar 1930	Ali	McGraw	01 Apr 1938		1973	1978
67	Steve	McQueen	24 Mar 1930	Neile	Adams	10 Jul 1932		1957	1972
68	Sonny	Bono	16 Feb 1935	Cher		20 May 1946	1963		26 Jun 1975
69	Prince	Michael of Kent	04 Jul 1942	Marie-Christine	Reibnitz	15 Jan 1945	1978	1978	none
70	James	Mason	15 May 1909	Pamela	Mason	10 Mar 1918		01 Feb 1941	1964
71	Paul	McCartney	18 Jun 1942	Linda	McCartney	24 Sep 1941	1968	12 Mar 1969	17 Apr 1998
72	Kenneth	Branagh	10 Dec 1960	Emma	Thompson	15 Apr 1959	1988	20 Aug 1989	30 Sep 1995
73	Julia	Roberts	28 Oct 1967	Benjamin	Bratt	16 Dec 1963	1998		2001
74	Yul	Brynner	07 Jul 1915	Virginia	Gilmore	26 Jul 1919		1944	1960
75	Stewart	Granger	06 May 1913	Elspeth	March	05 Mar 1911		1938	1948
76	Jean	Simmons	31 Jan 1929	Richard	Brooks	18 May 1912		1960	1977
77	Jean	Simmons	31 Jan 1929	Stewart	Granger	06 May 1913		1950	1960
78	Paul	Simon	13 Oct 1941	Edie	Brickell	10 Mar 1966		1992	none
79	Carrie	Fisher	21 Oct 1956	Paul	Simon	13 Oct 1941		16 Aug 1983	1983
80	Maggie	Smith	28 Dec 1934	Beverley	Cross	13 Apr 1931		1975	20 Mar 1998
81	Maggie	Smith	28 Dec 1934	Robert	Stephens	14 Jul 1931		1967	1974
82	Robert	Wagner	10 Feb 1930	Jill	StJohn	19 Aug 1940	1981	1991	none
83	Robert	Wagner	10 Feb 1930	Natalie	Wood	20 Jul 1938		1957 & 1971	29 Nov 1981
84	Jane	Fonda	21 Dec 1937	Roger	Vadim	26 Jan 1928		14 Aug 1965	16 Jan 1973
85	Jane	Fonda	21 Dec 1937	Tom	Hayden	11 Dec 1939		1973	1989

NO.	Forename	Surname	DOB	Forename	Surname	DOB	Start Year	Marriage	End Date
86	Jane	Fonda	21 Dec 1937	Ted	Turner	19 Nov 1938		21 Dec 1991	22 May 2001
87	Cyd	Charisse	08 Mar 1921	Tony	Martin	25 Dec 1912		1948	none
88	Tom	Hanks	09 Jul 1956	Rita	Wilson	26 Oct 1958		1988	none
89	Holly	Hunter	20 Mar 1958	Janusz	Kaminsky	27 Jun 1959		20 May 1995	Oct 2001
90	Michelle	Pfieffer	29 Apr 1958	Peter	Horton	20 Jul 1953		1981	1989
91	Michelle	Pfieffer	29 Apr 1958	David E	Kelley	04 Apr 1956		1993	none
92	James	Cameron	16 Aug 1954	Gale-Anne	Hurd	25 Oct 1955		1985	1989
93	Dennis	Quaid	09 Apr 1954	Meg	Ryan	19 Nov 1961		1991	2000
94	Chris	Evans	01 Apr 1966	Billie	Piper	22 Sep 1982	2000	2001	2004
95	Sophia	Loren	20 Sep 1934	Carlo	Ponti	11 Dec 1912		1957	none
96	Yves	Montand	13 Oct 1921	Marilyn	Monroe	01 Jun 1926	1960		1960
97	Lucille	Ball	06 Aug 1911	Gary	Morton	19 Dec 1924		19 Nov 1961	26 Apr 1969
98	Greer	Garson	29 Sep 1904	Richard	Ney	12 Nov 1915		1943	1947
99	William	Friedkin	29 Aug 1939	Lesley-Anne	Down	17 Mar 1954		1982	1985
100	Mark	Harmon	02 Sep 1951	Pam	Dawber	18 Oct 1951	1985		none
101	Nelson	Mandela	18 Jul 1918	Winnie	Mandela	26 Sep 1936		1958	1996
102	FDR	Roosevelt	30 Jan 1882	Eleanor	Roosevelt	11 Oct 1884		17 Mar 1905	12 Apr 1945
103	George	Bush	12 Jun 1924	Barbara	Bush	08 Jun 1925		1945	none
104	Ronald	Reagan	06 Feb 1911	Jane	Wyman	04 Jan 1914		26 Jan 1940	1948
105	Ronald	Reagan	06 Feb 1911	Nancy	Reagan	06 Jul 1921		1952	05 Jun 2004
106	JF	Kennedy	29 May 1917	Jacquie	Kennedy	28 Jul 1929		1953	1963
107	Leslie	Caron	01 Jul 1931	Peter	Hall	22 Nov 1930		1956	1966
108	Betty	Grable	18 Dec 1916	Jackie	Coogan	26 Oct 1914		1937	1940
109	Betty	Grable	18 Dec 1916	Harry	James	15 Mar 1916		1943	1965
110	John	Malkovich	09 Dec 1953	Glenne	Headly	13 Mar 1955		1982	1988
111	Sylvester	Stallone	06 Jul 1946	Jennifer	Flavin	14 Aug 1968		17 May 1997	none
112	Sylvester	Stallone	06 Jul 1946	Brigitte	Neilson	15 Jul 1963		15 Dec 1985	1987
113	Mickey	Rooney	23 Sep 1920	Ava	Gardner	24 Dec 1922		10 Jan 1942	21 May 1943
114	Mickey	Rooney	23 Sep 1920	Martha	Vickers	28 May 1925		1948	1951
115	Gene	Kelly	23 Aug 1912	Betsy	Blair	11 Dec 1923		1940	1957

NO.	Forename	Surname	DOB	Forename	Surname	DOB	Start Year	Marriage	End Date
116	Gene	Kelly	23 Aug 1912	Jeanne	Coyne	28 Feb 1923		1960	1973
117	Jeanne	Coyne	28 Feb 1923	Stanley	Donen	13 Apr 1924		1948	1949
118	Ginger	Rogers	16 Jul 1911	Lew	Ayres	28 Dec 1908		13 Nov 1934	13 Mar 1940
119	Ginger	Rogers	16 Jul 1911	Jacques	Bergerac	26 May 1917		07 Feb 1953	07 Jul 1957
120	Ginger	Rogers	16 Jul 1911	William	Marshall	02 Oct 1917		16 Mar 1961	1970
121	Isabel	Adjani	27 Jun 1955	Daniel	Day-Lewis	29 Apr 1957	1989		1994
122	Ralph	Bellamy	17 Jun 1904	Ethel	Smith	22 Nov 1910		1945	1947
123	Richard	Briers	14 Jan 1934	Ann	Davies	25 Dec 1934	1958		none
124	Doris	Day	03 Apr 1922	Martin	Melcher	01 Jul 1915		03 Apr 1951	20 Apr 1968
125	Doris	Day	03 Apr 1922	George	Weidler	11 Jul 1926		30 Mar 1946	31 May 1949
126	Josh	Brolin	12 Feb 1968	Minnie	Driver	31 Jan 1970	01 Oct 1999		01 Oct 2001
127	Dawn	French	11 Oct 1957	Lenny	Henry	29 Aug 1958		1984	none
128	Sheila	Hancock	22 Feb 1933	John	Thaw	03 Jan 1942		24 Dec 1973	21 Feb 2002
129	Trey	Farley	01 Jul 1975	Katy	Hill	15 Apr 1971		2001	none
130	Dennis	Hopper	17 May 1936	Michelle	Phillips	04 Jun 1944		1970	1970
131	Chrissie	Hynde	07 Sep 1951	Ray	Davies	21 Jun 1944	1978		1983
132	Jim	Kerr	09 Jul 1959	Chrissie	Hynde	07 Sep 1951		1984	1990
133	Patsy	Kensit	04 Mar 1968	Jim	Kerr	09 Jul 1959		1992	1996
134	Patsy	Kensit	04 Mar 1968	Liam	Gallagher	12 Sep 1972		1997	22 Sep 2000
135	Deborah	Kerr	30 Sep 1921	Peter	Viertel	16 Nov 1920		1962	none
136	Kevin	Kline	24 Oct 1947	Phoebe	Cates	16 Jul 1963		1989	none
137	Vivien	Leigh	05 Nov 1913	John	Merivale	01 Dec 1917	1959		1967
138	Richard	Nixon	09 Jan 1913	Pat	Nixon	16 Mar 1912		21 Jun 1940	22 Jun 1993
139	Laurence	Olivier	22 May 1907	Jill	Esmond	26 Feb 1908		25 Jul 1930	29 Jan 1940
140	Laurence	Olivier	22 May 1907	Joan	Plowright	28 Oct 1929	1960	17 Mar 1961	11 Jul 1989
141	Peter	O'Toole	02 Aug 1932	Sian	Phillips	14 May 1934		1959	1979
142	Oliver	Reed	13 Feb 1938	Josephine	Burge	16 Apr 1964	1980	1985	02 May 1999
143	Ringo	Starr	07 Jul 1940	Barbara	Bach	28 Aug 1946		1981	none
144	Jessica	Tandy	07 Jun 1909	Hume	Cronyn	18 Jul 1911		1942	11 Sep 1994
145	Jessica	Tandy	07 Jun 1909	Jack	Hawkins	14 Sep 1910		1932	1942

NO.	Forename	Surname	DOB	Forename	Surname	DOB	Start Year	Marriage	End Date
146	Jamie	Theakston	21 Dec 1970	Joely	Richardson	09 Jan 1965	2001		2002
147	Dan	Ackroyd	01 Jul 1952	Donna	Dixon	20 Jul 1957		1983	none
148	Roseanne	Barr	03 Nov 1952	Tom	Arnold	06 Mar 1959		20 Jan 1990	1994
149	David	Lynch	20 Jan 1946	Isabella	Rossellini	18 Jun 1952		1985	17 Dec 1990
150	Charles	Bronson	03 Nov 1921	Jill	Ireland	24 Apr 1936	1968	05 Oct 1968	18 May 1990
151	David	McCallum	19 Sep 1933	Jill	Ireland	24 Apr 1936		1957	1967
152	Tia	Carrere	02 Jan 1967	Elie	Samaha	10 May 1956		22 Nov 1992	01 Feb 2000
153	Arlene	Dahl	11 Aug 1925	Lex	Barker	08 May 1919		1951	1952
154	Fernando	Lamas	09 Jan 1915	Arlene	Dahl	11 Aug 1925		1954	1960
155	Fernando	Lamas	09 Jan 1915	Esther	Williams	08 Aug 1921		1969	1982
156	Johnny	Depp	09 Jun 1963	Vanessa	Paradis	22 Dec 1972		1998	none
157	Johnny	Depp	09 Jun 1963	Winona	Ryder	29 Oct 1971	1988		1993
158	Drew	Barrymore	22 Feb 1975	Tom	Green	30 Jul 1971		07 Jul 2001	17 Dec 2001
159	Duke of	Gloucester	26 Aug 1944	Brigitte	van Deurs	20 Jun 1946		08 Jul 1972	none
160	Steve	Martin	14 Aug 1945	Victoria	Tennent	30 Sep 1950		20 Nov 1986	1994
161	Sarah-Jessica	Parker	25 Mar 1965	Mathew	Broderick	21 Mar 1962		1997	none
162	Sarah-Jessica	Parker	25 Mar 1965	Robert	Downey Jnr	04 Apr 1965	1983		1990
163	Kelly	Preston	13 Sep 1962	John	Travolta	18 Feb 1954		1991	none
164	Arnold	Schwarzenegger	30 Jul 1947	Maria	Shriver	06 Nov 1955		26 Apr 1986	none
165	James	Brolin	18 Jul 1940	Barbara	Streisand	24 Apr 1942	1996	01 Jul 1998	none
166	Michael	Caine	14 Mar 1933	Shakira	Caine	23 Feb 1947		1973	none
167	Mimi	Rogers	27 Jan 1956	Tom	Cruise	03 Jul 1962		09 May 1987	1990
168	Nicole	Kidman	20 Jun 1967	Tom	Cruise	03 Jul 1962	1989	1990	2001
169	Gloria	Estefan	01 Sep 1957	Emilio	Estefan	04 Mar 1953	1976	1978	none
170	Barbara	Streisand	24 Apr 1942	Elliot	Gould	29 Aug 1938		21 Mar 1963	09 Jul 1971
171	Julie	Andrews	01 Oct 1935	Blake	Edwards	26 Jul 1922		12 Nov 1969	none
172	Julie	Andrews	01 Oct 1935	Tony	Walton	24 Oct 1934		10 May 1959	1967
173	Dwight	Eisenhower	14 Oct 1890	Mamie	Eisenhower	14 Nov 1896		01 Jul 1916	28 Mar 1969
174	Jeff	Goldblum	22 Oct 1952	Geena	Davis	21 Jan 1956		01 Nov 1987	Oct 1990
175	Jeff	Goldblum	22 Oct 1952	Laura	Dern	10 Feb 1967		1995	1997

NO.	Forename	Surname	DOB	Forename	Surname	DOB	Start Year	Marriage	End Date
176	Herbert	Hoover	10 Aug 1874	Lou	Hoover	29 Mar 1874		10 Feb 1899	07 Feb 1944
177	Lyndon	Johnson	27 Aug 1908	Lady Bird	Johnson	22 Dec 1912		17 Nov 1934	22 Jan 1973
178	Harry	Truman	08 May 1884	Bess	Truman	13 Feb 1885		28 Jun 1919	26 Dec 1972
179	Frances	McDormand	23 Jun 1957	Joel	Coen	29 Nov 1954		1984	none
180	Chandra	Levy	14 Apr 1977	Gary	Condit	21 Apr 1948	2001		2001
181	Mme	DuBarry	19 Aug 1743	Louis	XV	15 Feb 1710	1768		1774
182	Mme	Pompadour	29 Dec 1721	Louis	XV	15 Feb 1710	1745		1764
183	Bette	Davis	05 Apr 1908	Gary	Merrill	02 Aug 1915		1950	1960
184	Franchot	Tone	27 Feb 1905	Barbara	Payton	17 Nov 1927		1951	1952
185	Franchot	Tone	27 Feb 1905	Jean	Wallace	12 Oct 1923		1941	1948
186	Billy Bob	Thornton	04 Aug 1955	Angelina	Jolie	04 Jun 1975		05 May 2000	18 Jul 2002
187	Prince	Andrew	19 Feb 1960	Sarah	Ferguson	15 Oct 1959	1985	1986	1992
188	Paul	Newman	26 Jan 1925	Joanne	Woodward	27 Feb 1930		1958	none
189	Matt	Damon	08 Oct 1970	Winona	Ryder	29 Oct 1971	31 Dec 1997		01 May 2000
190	Joseph	Fiennes	27 May 1970	Cath	McCormack	01 Jun 1972	1998		2000
191	Ben	Affleck	15 Aug 1972	Gwyneth	Paltrow	28 Sep 1972	1998		01 Jan 1999
192	Gwyneth	Paltrow	28 Sep 1972	Brad	Pitt	18 Dec 1963	1996		1997
193	Gwyneth	Paltrow	28 Sep 1972	Luke	Wilson	21 Sep 1971	2001		2001
194	Dame Judi	Dench	09 Dec 1934	Michael	Williams	09 Jul 1935		05 Feb 1971	11 Jan 2001
195	Ryan	O'Neal	20 Apr 1941	Farrah	Fawcett	02 Feb 1947	1980		1997
196	Nancy	Sinatra	08 Jun 1940	Tommy	Sands	27 Aug 1937		12 Sep 1960	1965
197	Herbert	Wilcox	19 Apr 1890	Anna	Neagle	20 Oct 1904	1932	09 Aug 1943	15 May 1977
198	Glen	Ford	01 May 1916	Eleanor	Powell	21 Nov 1912		1943	1959
199	Jack	Lemmon	08 Feb 1925	Felicia	Farr	04 Oct 1932		1962	27 Jul 2001
200	John	Carradine	05 Feb 1906	Doris	Rich	03 May 1919		1957	1971
201	Sean	Connery	25 Aug 1930	Diane	Cilento	05 Oct 1933		1962	1974
202	Richard	Cromwell	08 Jan 1910	Angela	Lansbury	16 Oct 1925		1945	1946
203	David	Duchovny	07 Aug 1960	Tea	Leoni	25 Feb 1966		1997	none
204	Mary Beth	Supinger	26 Sep 1948	William	Hurt	20 Mar 1950		1971	1981
205	Hedy	Lamarr	09 Nov 1913	John	Loder	03 Jan 1898		1943	1947

NO.	Forename	Surname	DOB	Forename	Surname	DOB	Start Year	Marriage	End Date
206	Hedy	Lamarr	09 Nov 1913	Gene	Markey	11 Dec 1895		1939	1940
207	King	Abdullah of Jordan		30 Jan 1962	Queen	Rania	31 Aug 1970		10 Jun 1993
none									
208	Ally	Sheedy	13 Jun 1962	David	Lansbury	25 Feb 1961		10 Oct 1992	none
209	Robert	Taylor	05 Aug 1911	Ursula	Theiss	15 May 1924		1954	08 Jun 1969
210	Robert	Taylor	05 Aug 1911	Barbara	Stanwyck	16 Jul 1907	1937	1939	1951
211	Barbara	Stanwyck	16 Jul 1907	Frank	Fay	17 Nov 1897		1928	1935
212	George	Sanders	03 Jul 1906	Benita	Hume	14 Oct 1906		10 Feb 1959	01 Nov 1967
213	Albert	Finney	09 May 1936	Anouk	Aimee	27 Apr 1932		1970	1978
214	Mary	Shelley	30 Aug 1797	Percy	Shelley	04 Aug 1792	28 Jul 1814	30 Dec 1816	08 Jul 1822
215	George	Scott	18 Oct 1927	Colleen	Dewhurst	03 Jun 1924		1960	1965
216	George	Scott	18 Oct 1927	Trish	VanDevere	09 Mar 1943		14 Sep 1972	22 Sep 1999
217	Michael	Jackson	29 Aug 1958	Lisa-Marie	Presley	01 Feb 1968		18 May 1994	18 Jan 1996
218	Jane	Seymour	15 Feb 1951	James	Keach	07 Dec 1948		1993	none
219	Halle	Berry	14 Aug 1968	Eric	Benet	15 Oct 1970		24 Jan 2001	15 Sep 2003
220	Michel	Gauquelin	13 Nov 1928	Francoise	Gauquelin	19 Jun 1929	1954		1982
221	Ted	Hughes	17 Aug 1930	Sylvia	Plath	27 Oct 1932	1956		1962
222	Judy	Loe	06 Mar 1947	Richard	Beckinsale	06 Jul 1947	1972	1977	19 Mar 1979
223	Nicolas	Cage	07 Jan 1964	Patricia	Arquette	08 Apr 1968		8 Apr 1995	18 May 2001
224	Eric	Clapton	30 Mar 1945	Lori	DelSanto	28 Sep 1958		1985	1986
225	Roald	Dahl	13 Sep 1916	Patricia	Neal	20 Jan 1926		2 Jul 1953	17 Nov 1983
226	Les	Dennis	12 Oct 1953	Amanda	Holden	16 Feb 1971	1993	1995	26 Dec 2002
227	Helen	Mirren	26 Jul 1945	Taylor	Hackford	31 Dec 1945		1967	none
228	Courtney	Love	09 Jul 1964	Kurt	Cobain	20 Feb 1967		24 Feb 1992	05 Apr 1994
229	Benjamin	Bratt	16 Dec 1963	Talisa	Soto	27 Mar 1967	2001	13 Apr 2002	none
230	Rod	Steiger	14 Apr 1925	Claire	Bloom	15 Feb 1931		1959	1969
231	Courteney	Cox	15 Jun 1964	David	Arquette	08 Sep 1971		12 Jun 1999	none
232	Helena	Bonham-Carter	26 May 1966	Kenneth	Branagh	10 Dec 1960	1994		1999
233	Helena	Bonham-Carter	26 May 1966	Tim	Burton	25 Aug 1958	01 Oct 2001		none
234	Jim	Carrey	17 Jan 1962	Lauren	Holly	28 Oct 1963		23 Sep 1996	29 Jul 1997

NO.	Forename	Surname	DOB	Forename	Surname	DOB	Start Year	Marriage	End Date
235	Jim	Carrey	17 Jan 1962	Rene	Zellweger	25 Apr 1969	1999		2001
236	Joan	Fontaine	22 Oct 1917	Brian	Aherne	02 May 1902		20 Aug 1939	1945
237	Joan	Fontaine	22 Oct 1917	William	Dozier	13 Feb 1908		02 May 1946	1951
238	Joan	Fontaine	22 Oct 1917	Collier	Young	19 Aug 1908		01 Nov 1952	1961
239	Jean	Harlow	03 Mar 1911	Paul	Bern	03 Dec 1889		1932	1932
240	Jean	Harlow	03 Mar 1911	Hal	Rossen	06 Apr 1895		1933	1935
241	Anne	Heche	25 May 1969	Ellen	Degeneres	26 Jan 1958		1997	2000
242	Simon	LeBon	27 Oct 1958	Yasmin	Parvanah	29 Oct 1964		1985	none
243	Ryan	Phillipe	10 Sep 1974	Reese	Witherspoon	22 Mar 1976	1999		none
244	Liv	Tyler	01 Jul 1977	Joaquin	Phoenix	28 Oct 1974	1995		1998
245	Liv	Tyler	01 Jul 1977	Johnny	Whitworth	31 Oct 1975	1994		1995
246	Omar	Sharif	10 Apr 1932	Faten	Hamama	27 May 1931	1952	1953	1974
247	Clark	Gable	01 Feb 1901	Loretta	Young	06 Jan 1913		1935	1936
248	Jane	Wyman	04 Jan 1914	Fred	Karger	13 Feb 1916		1952	1954
249	Jean	Harlow	03 Mar 1911	William	Powell	29 Jul 1892		1935	1937
250	William	Powell	29 Jul 1892	Carole	Lombard	06 Oct 1908		1931	1933
251	William	Powell	29 Jul 1892	Diana	Lewis	18 Sep 1919		06 Jan 1940	1984
252	Humphrey	Bogart	25 Dec 1899	Mayo	Methot	03 Mar 1904		1938	1945
253	Humphrey	Bogart	25 Dec 1899	Mary	Philips	23 Jan 1901		1928	1938
254	Yves	Montand	13 Oct 1921	Edith	Piaf	19 Dec 1915	1944		1946
255	Marlene	Dietrich	27 Dec 1901	Rudolph	Sieber	20 Feb 1897		17 May 1924	24 Jun 1976
256	Anthony	Armstrong-Jones	07 Mar 1930	Princess	Margaret	21 Aug 1930	1959	1960	11 Jul 1978
257	Peter	Sellers	08 Sep 1925	Lynne	Frederick	25 Jul 1954		1977	1980
258	Judy	Garland	10 Jun 1922	Mark	Herron	08 Jul 1928		12 Jun 1964	1967
259	Judy	Garland	10 Jun 1922	David	Rose	24 Jun 1909		1941	1945
260	Dean	Goodman	02 Jul 1920	Maria	Riva	13 Dec 1924		23 Aug 1943	1947
261	John	McEnroe	16 Feb 1959	Tatum	O'Neal	05 Nov 1963		1986	1994
262	Liza	Minnelli	12 Mar 1946	Peter	Allen	10 Feb 1944		3 Mar 1967	1972
263	Ike	Turner	05 Nov 1931	Tina	Turner	26 Nov 1939	1956	1958	1977
264	Helena	Christensen	25 Dec 1968	Norman	Reedus	06 Jan 1969	1998		2003

NO.	Forename	Surname	DOB	Forename	Surname	DOB	Start Year	Marriage	End Date
265	Michael	Hutchence	22 Jan 1960	Helena	Christensen	25 Dec 1968	1990		1995
266	Kylie	Minogue	28 May 1968	Michael	Hutchence	22 Jan 1960	1989		1990
267	Jared	Leto	26 Dec 1971	Cameron	Diaz	30 Aug 1972	2000		2003
268	Pauline	Collins	03 Sep 1940	John	Alderton	27 Nov 1940	1969		none
269	Ernest	Borgnine	24 Jan 1917	Katy	Jurado	16 Jan 1924	1959	1963	
270	Errol	Flynn	20 Jun 1909	Beverly	Aadland	16 Sep 1942	1958		1959
271	Stephanie	Powers	02 Nov 1942	William	Holden	17 Apr 1918	1974		16 Nov 1981
272	Cecil B	Demille	12 Aug 1881	Constance	Adams	27 Apr 1874		16 Aug 1902	21 Jan 1959
273	John	Derek	12 Aug 1926	Ursula	Andress	19 Mar 1936		1957	1966
274	John	Derek	12 Aug 1926	Linda	Evans	18 Nov 1942		1968	1974
275	John	Derek	12 Aug 1926	Bo	Derek	20 Nov 1956		1977	22 May 1998
276	Danny	Devito	17 Nov 1944	Rhea	Perlman	31 Mar 1948		28 Jan 1982	none
277	Shannen	Doherty	12 Apr 1971	Ashley	Hamilton	30 Sep 1974		24 Sep 1993	Apr 1994
278	Richard	Gere	31 Aug 1949	Cindy	Crawford	20 Feb 1966		12 Dec 1991	1995
279	Kenneth	Hawks	12 Aug 1898	Mary	Astor	03 May 1906		1928	1930
280	Olivia	Hussey	17 Apr 1951	Dean Paul	Martin	17 Nov 1951		17 Apr 1971	1978
281	Olivia	Hussey	17 Apr 1951	Akira	Fuse	18 Dec 1947		1980	1987
282	Gary	Oldman	21 Mar 1958	Uma	Thurman	29 Apr 1970		Oct 1990	1992
283	Uma	Thurman	29 Apr 1970	Ethan	Hawke	06 Nov 1970		1997	2003
284	Fernando	Rey	20 Sep 1917	Mabel	Karr	07 Oct 1934		1960	09 Mar 1994
285	John	Ritter	17 Sep 1948	Amy	Yasbeck	12 Sep 1963	1997	1999	11 Sep 2003
286	Rudolph	Valentino	06 May 1895	Jean	Acker	23 Oct 1893		1919	1922
287	Rudolph	Valentino	06 May 1895	Natacha	Rambova	19 Jan 1897		1923	19 Jan 1926
288	Angela	Bassett	16 Aug 1958	Courtney	Vance	12 Mar 1960	1997	12 Oct 1997	none
289	Duke of	Windsor	23 Jun 1894	Duchess of	Windsor	19 Jun 1896	1931	03 Jun 1937	28 May 1972
290	Phillip	Mountbatten	10 Jun 1921	Queen	Elizabeth II	21 Apr 1926		20 Nov 1947	none
291	Sinead	Cusack	18 Feb 1948	Jeremy	Irons	19 Sep 1948		28 Mar 1978	none
292	Queen	Elizabeth QM	04 Aug 1900	King	George VI	14 Dec 1895	1920	1923	1952
293	David	Beckham	02 May 1975	Victoria	Adams	17 Apr 1974	1997	04 Jul 1999	none
294	Charles	Laughton	01 Jul 1899	Elsa	Lanchester	28 Oct 1902	1929		15 Dec 1962

NO.	Forename	Surname	DOB	Forename	Surname	DOB	Start Year	Marriage	End Date
295	Buster	Keaton	04 Oct 1895	Natalie	Talmadge	29 Apr 1899		1921	1932
296	Rod	Stewart	10 Jan 1945	Alana	Stewart	18 May 1945	1978	04 Jun 1979	1983
297	Howard	Hughes	24 Dec 1905	Jean	Peters	15 Oct 1926	1946	1957	1971
298	Ian	Holm	12 Sep 1931	Penelope	Wilton	03 Jun 1946		1991	none
299	Raymond	Massey	30 Aug 1896	Adrianne	Allen	07 Feb 1907		1929	1939
300	Emilio	Estevez	12 May 1962	Paula	Abdul	19 Jun 1962		01 Apr 1992	01 May 1994
301	Danny	Kaye	18 Jan 1911	Gwen	Verdon	13 Jan 1925	1950		1952
302	Jimmy	Carter	01 Oct 1924	Rosalyn	Carter	18 Aug 1927		1946	none
303	Cary	Grant	18 Jan 1904	Betsy	Drake	11 Sep 1923		25 Dec 1949	14 Aug 1962
304	Hugh	Grant	09 Sep 1960	Elizabeth	Hurley	10 Jun 1965	1988		2000
305	Ashley	Hamilton	30 Sep 1974	Angie	Everhart	07 Sep 1969		01 Dec 1996	Mar 1997
306	Athole	Shearer	20 Nov 1900	Howard	Hawks	30 May 1896		28 May 1928	1940
307	Julia	Roberts	28 Oct 1967	Lyle	Lovett	01 Nov 1957		25 Jun 1993	22 Mar 1995
308	Liam	Neeson	07 Jun 1952	Julia	Roberts	28 Oct 1967	1988		1990
309	Rod	Stewart	10 Jan 1945	Rachel	Hunter	09 Sep 1969		1990	1999
310	Ben	Stiller	30 Nov 1965	Christine	Taylor	30 Jul 1971		13 May 2000	none
311	Brook	Yeaton	13 Feb 1968	Traci	Lords	07 May 1968		20 Sep 1990	1995
312	Cary	Grant	18 Jan 1904	Virginia	Cherrill	12 Apr 1908		10 Feb 1934	26 Mar 1935
313	Paul	Hogan	08 Oct 1939	Linda	Koslowski	07 Jan 1958	1986		none
314	Johnny Lee	Miller	15 Nov 1972	Angelina	Jolie	04 Jun 1975		1995	03 Feb 1999
315	Nicolas	Cage	07 Jan 1964	Lisa-Marie	Presley	01 Feb 1968		10 Aug 2002	25 Nov 2002
316	Cher		20 May 1946	Gregg	Allman	08 Dec 1947		1975	1978
317	Alex	Kingston	11 Mar 1963	Ralph	Fiennes	22 Dec 1962		1993	28 Oct 1997
318	Daniel	Day-Lewis	29 Apr 1957	Rebecca	Miller	15 Sep 1962		13 Nov 1996	none
319	Jean	Peters	15 Oct 1926	Stanley	Hough	23 Jul 1918		1971	23 Feb 1990
320	Jean-Michel	Jarre	24 Aug 1948	Isabelle	Adjani	27 Jun 1955		01 Jul 2002	none
321	Jean-Michel	Jarre	24 Aug 1948	Charlotte	Rampling	05 Feb 1945		08 Oct 1976	1996
322	Alan	Davies	06 Mar 1966	Julia	Sawalha	09 Sep 1968	2002		none
323	Naomi	Campbell	22 May 1970	Adam	Clayton	13 Mar 1960	Feb 1993		Apr 1994
324	Kate	Winslet	05 Oct 1975	Sam	Mendes	01 Aug 1965	Sep 2001		none

NO.	Forename	Surname	DOB	Forename	Surname	DOB	Start Year	Marriage	End Date
325	Julia	Roberts	28 Oct 1967	Kiefer	Sutherland	21 Dec 1966	1989		1991
326	Julia	Roberts	28 Oct 1967	Jason	Patric	17 Jun 1966	Jun 1991		May 1992
327	Julia	Roberts	28 Oct 1967	Daniel	Moder	31 Jan 1969	2000	4 Jul 2002	none
328	Catherine Zeta	Jones	25 Sep 1969	Mick	Hucknall	08 Jun 1960	Mar 1998		Jul-98
329	Catherine Zeta	Jones	25 Sep 1969	Angus	Macfadyen	21 Oct 1963	Aug 1993		May 1996
330	Paul	McCartney	18 Jun 1942	Heather	Mills	12 Jan 1968	2000	11 Jun 2002	none
331	Tony	Blackburn	29 Jan 1943	Tessa	Wyatt	23 Apr 1948	1972		1979
332	Betty	Grable	18 Dec 1916	George	Raft	26 Sep 1895	1940		1943
333	Anthony	Quinn	21 Apr 1915	Katherine	Demille	29 Jun 1911		05 Oct 1937	1963
334	Billy	Joel	09 May 1949	Christie	Brinkley	02 Feb 1954	1983	23 Mar 1985	24 Aug 1994
335	Farrah	Fawcett	02 Feb 1947	Lee	Majors	23 Apr 1939	1968	28 Jul 1973	1979
336	Liam	Neeson	07 Jun 1952	Natasha	Richardson	11 May 1963		03 Jul 1994	none
337	Robbie	Williams	13 Feb 1974	Rachel	Hunter	09 Sep 1969	2002		2003
338	Liam	Gallagher	12 Sep 1972	Nicole	Appleton	07 Dec 1974	2000		none
339	Harpo	Marx	23 Nov 1888	Susan	Fleming	19 Feb 1908		28 Sep 1936	28 Sep 1964
340	Rex	Harrison	05 Mar 1908	Lilli	Palmer	24 May 1914	1943		1957
341	Rex	Harrison	05 Mar 1908	Kay	Kendal	21 May 1926		1957	06 Sep 1959
342	Rex	Harrison	05 Mar 1908	Rachel	Roberts	20 Sep 1927		1962	1971
343	Gene	Wilder	11 Jun 1933	Gilda	Radner	28 Jun 1946		18 Sep 1984	20 May 1989
344	Merle	Oberon	19 Feb 1911	Alexander	Korda	16 Sep 1893		03 Jun 1939	1945
345	Merle	Oberon	19 Feb 1911	Lucien	Ballard	06 May 1908		26 Jun 1945	01 Aug 1949
346	Merle	Oberon	19 Feb 1911	Robert	Wolders	28 Sep 1936	1970	31 Jan 1975	26 Nov 1979
347	Audrey	Hepburn	04 May 1929	Robert	Wolders	28 Sep 1936	1980		20 Jan 1993
348	Kim	Basinger	08 Dec 1963	Alec	Baldwin	03 Apr 1958		19 Aug 1993	12 Jan 2001
349	Kevin	Bacon	08 Jul 1958	Kyra	Sedgwick	19 Aug 1965		03 Sep 1988	none
350	Faye	Dunaway	14 Jan 1941	Peter	Wolf	07 Mar 1946		07 Aug 1974	1979
351	Brigitte	Bardot	28 Sep 1934	Jacques	Charrier	06 Nov 1936		18 Jun 1959	20 Nov 1962
352	Melanie	Griffith	09 Aug 1957	Antonio	Banderas	10 Aug 1960		14 May 1996	none
353	Melanie	Griffith	09 Aug 1957	Don	Johnson	15 Dec 1949		29 Jun 1989	1996
354	Catherine	Deneuve	22 Oct 1943	David	Bailey	02 Jan 1938		1965	1972

NO.	Forename	Surname	DOB	Forename	Surname	DOB	Start Year	Marriage	End Date
355	Jean	Cocteau	05 Jul 1889	Jean	Marais	11 Dec 1913	1937		11 Oct 1963
356	Brigitte	Bardot	28 Sep 1934	Roger	Vadim	26 Jan 1928		20 Dec 1952	06 Dec 1957
357	Sting		02 Oct 1951	Trudie	Styler	06 Jan 1955	1982	20 Aug 1992	none
358	William	Friedkin	29 Aug1935	Jeanne	Moreau	23 Jan 1928		1977	1979
359	Catherine	Deneuve	22 Oct 1943	Marcello	Mastroianni	26 Sep 1924	1971	1972	1975
360	Mel	Brooks	28 Jun 1926	Anne	Bancroft	17 Sep 1931	1961	05 Aug 1964	06 Jun 2005
361	Roger	Vadim	26 Jan 1928	Catherine	Deneuve	22 Oct 1943	1961	1962	1964
362	Jayne	Mansfield	19 Apr 1933	Mickey	Hargitay	13 Jan 1934		13 Jan 1958	26 Aug 1964
363	Kirstie	Alley	12 Jan 1955	Parker	Stevenson	04 Jun 1952		22 Dec 1983	01 Dec 1997
364	Michael	Douglas	25 Sep 1944	Brenda	Vacarro	18 Nov 1939	1969		1975
365	Joan	Blondell	30 Aug 1914	Dick	Powell	14 Nov 1904		1936	1945
366	Joan	Blondell	30 Aug 1914	George	Barnes	16 Oct 1892		1932	1936
367	Zara	Phillips	15 May 1981	Mike	Tindall	18 Oct 1978	2004		none
368	Pier	Angeli	19 Jun 1932	Vic	Damone	12 Jun 1928		1954	1958
369	Ann	Margret	28 Apr 1941	Roger	Smith	18 Dec 1932	1962	08 May 1967	none
370	Victoria	Shaw	25 May 1935	Roger	Smith	18 Dec 1932		1956	1965
371	Jose	Ferrer	08 Jan 1912	Rosemary	Clooney	23 May 1928		1953	1967
372	Loretta	Young	06 Jan 1913	Tom	Lewis	08 Jul 1901		1940	1969
373	Richard	Gere	31 Aug 1949	Carey	Lowell	11 Feb 1961		1995	none
374	Ingrid	Bergman	29 Aug 1915	Roberto	Rossellini	08 May 1906		24 May 1950	07 Nov 1957
375	Genevieve	Bujold	01 Jul 1942	Paul	Almond	26 Apr 1931		1967	1973
376	George	Burns	20 Jan 1896	Gracie	Allen	26 Jul 1902	1922	07 Jan 1926	27 Aug 1964
377	Peter	Finch	28 Sep 1916	Yolande	Turner	12 Dec 1935		04 Jul 1959	11 Nov 1965
378	Diahann	Carroll	17 Jul 1935	Vic	Damone	12 Jun 1928		1987	1996
379	Judith	Rawlins	24 Jun 1936	Vic	Damone	12 Jun 1928		1963	1971
380	Pier	Angeli	19 Jun 1932	Armando	Trovajoli	02 Sep 1917		1962	1969
381	Keir	Dullea	30 May 1936	Mia	Dillon	09 Jul 1955		1999	none
382	Matthew	Perry	19 Aug 1969	Renee	Zellweger	25 Apr 1969	2002		2002
383	Dorothy	Gish	11 Mar 1898	James	Rennie	18 Apr 1890		26 Dec 1920	1935
384	Virginia	Mayo	30 Nov 1920	Michael	O'Shea	17 Mar 1906		1947	04 Dec 1973

NO.	Forename	Surname	DOB	Forename	Surname	DOB	Start Year	Marriage	End Date
385	Danny	Kaye	18 Jan 1913	Sylvia	Fine	29 Aug 1913		1940	30 Mar 1987
386	Tex	Ritter	12 Jan 1905	Dorothy	Fay	04 Apr 1915		14 Jun 1941	02 Jan 1974
387	Michael	Redgrave	20 Mar 1908	Rachel	Kempson	28 May 1910		1935	21 Mar 1985
388	Susan	Sarandon	04 Oct 1946	Chris	Sarandon	24 Jul 1942		1968	1979
389	Susan	Sarandon	04 Oct 1946	Tim	Robbins	16 Oct 1958		1988	none
390	Bryan	Forbes	22 Jul 1926	Constance	Smith	22 Jan 1928		1951	1955
391	Bryan	Forbes	22 Jul 1926	Nanette	Newman	29 May 1934		1955	none
392	Mary	Steenburgen	08 Feb 1953	Malcolm	Macdowell	13 Jun 1943		1980	1990
393	Susan	George	26 Jul 1950	Simon	Maccorkindale	12 Feb 1952		05 Oct 1984	none
394	Michael J	Fox	09 Jun 1961	Tracey	Pollan	22 Jun 1960		06 Jul 1988	none
395	Will	Smith	25 Sep 1968	Jada	Pinkett	18 Sep 1971		31 Dec 1997	none
396	Will	Smith	25 Sep 1968	Sheree	Smith	16 Nov 1967		09 May 1992	1995
397	Steven	Seagal	10 Apr 1951	Kelly	LeBrock	24 Mar 1960		1987	1996
398	Mary	Martin	01 Dec 1913	Richard	Halliday	03 Apr 1905		05 May 1940	03 Mar 1973
399	Ted	Danson	29 Dec 1947	Mary	Steenburgen	08 Feb1953		07 Oct 1995	none
400	Princess	Anne	15 Aug 1950	Tim	Lawrence	01 Mar 1955		1992	none
401	Bebe	Buell	14 Jul 1953	Todd	Rundgren	22 Jun 1948	1971		1979
402	Bebe	Buell	14 Jul 1953	Steve	Tyler	26 Mar 1948	1976		1976
403	Andre	Agassi	29 Apr 1970	Brooke	Shields	31 May 1965		19 Apr 1997	09 Apr 1999
404	Andre	Agassi	29 Apr 1970	Steffi	Graf	14 Jun 1969		22 Oct 2001	none
405	William	Wyler	01 Jul 1902	Margaret	Tallichet	13 Mar 1914		23 Oct 1938	27 Jul 1981
406	Roger	Vadim	26 Jan 1928	Marie-Christian	Barrault	21 Mar 1944		1990	11 Feb 2000
407	Enrique	Iglesias	08 May 1975	Anna	Kournikova	07 Jun 1981	2002		none
408	Britt	Ekland	06 Oct 1942	Slim-Jim	Phantom	20 Mar 1961		20 Mar 1984	1992
409	Diana	Dors	23 Oct 1931	Rod	Stieger	14 Apr 1925	1957		1957
410	Eric	Stoltz	30 Sep 1961	Bridget	Fonda	27 Jan 1964	1990		1998
411	Meg	Ryan	19 Nov 1961	Russell	Crowe	07 Apr 1964	2001		2001
412	Sean	Penn	17 Aug 1960	Robyn	Wright	08 Apr 1966		27 Apr 1996	none
413	Roger	Vadim	26 Jan 1928	Annette	Vadim	07 Dec 1936		1958	1960
414	Eric	Stoltz	30 Sep 1961	Ally	Sheedy	13 Jun 1962	1980		1983

NO.	Forename	Surname	DOB	Forename	Surname	DOB	Start Year	Marriage	End Date
415	Eric	Stoltz	30 Sep 1961	Jennifer	Jason-Lee	05 Feb 1962	1985		1989
416	Rod	Steiger	14 Apr 1925	Sally	Gracie	31 Dec 1920		1952	1958
417	Ronald	Colman	09 Feb 1892	Benita	Hume	14 Sep 1906	1934	30 Sep 1938	19 May 1958
418	Joan	Bennett	27 Feb 1910	Walter	Wanger	11 Jul 1894		12 Jan 1940	01 Sep 1965
419	Sean	Bean	17 Apr 1959	Melanie	Hill	11 Jan 1962	1981	1991	1997
420	Brian	Depalma	11 Sep 1940	Nancy	Allen	24 Jun 1950	1978	12 Jan 1979	1983
421	Virginia	Bruce	29 Sep 1910	J-Walter	Ruben	14 Aug 1899		1937	1942
422	James	Brolin	18 Jul 1940	Jan	Smithers	03 Jul 1949		1986	1995
423	Ann	Dvorak	02 Aug 1912	Leslie	Fenton	12 Mar 1902		1932	1945
424	Ann	Dvorak	02 Aug 1912	Igor	Dega	09 Jan 1916		1947	1951
425	Princess	Diana	01 Jul 1961	Dodi	Alfayed	15 Apr 1955	1997		1997
426	Loretta	Young	06 Jan 1913	Jean-Louis	Berthault	05 Oct 1907		1991	20 Apr 1997
427	Ava	Gardner	24 Dec 1922	Artie	Shaw	23 May 1910		17 Oct 1945	25 Oct 1946
428	Lynne	Frederick	25 Jul 1954	David	Frost	07 Apr 1939		1981	1982
429	John	Lennon	09 Oct 1940	May	Pang	24 Oct 1950	1973		1978
430	Serge	Gainsbourg	02 Apr 1928	Jane	Birkin	14 Dec 1946		1968	1980
431	Louise	Lasser	11 Apr 1939	Woody	Allen	01 Dec 1935		1966	1969
432	King	H. of Jordan	14 Nov 1935	Lisa	Halaby	23 Aug 1951	1978	15 Jul 1978	1999
433	Christopher	Lambert	29 Mar 1957	Diane	Lane	22 Jan 1965		Oct 1988	Mar 1994
434	Hedy	Lamarr	09 Nov 1913	Teddy	Stauffer	02 May 1909		1951	1952
435	Gene	Markey	11 Dec 1895	Myrna	Loy	02 Aug 1905		1946	1950
436	Nelson	Mandela	18 Jul 1918	Graca	Machel	17 Oct 1945		18 Jul 1998	none
437	Gene	Markey	11 Dec 1895	Joan	Bennett	27 Feb 1910		12 Mar 1932	1938
438	Owen	Moore	12 Dec 1886	Katherine	Perry	05 Jan 1897		1921	3 Jun 1939
439	Burgess	Meredith	16 Nov 1908	Margaret	Perry	23 Feb 1913		10 Jan 1936	Jul 1938
440	John	Carroll	17 Jul 1906	Steffi	Duna	08 Feb 1910		1935	1936
441	Lee	Remick	14 Dec 1935	Bill	Colleran	16 Apr 1923		1957	1968
442	Lana	Turner	08 Feb 1921	Fernando	Lamas	09 Jan 1915	1952		1953
443	Lana	Turner	08 Feb 1921	Lex	Barker	08 May 1919		08 Sep 1953	22 Jul 1957
444	Eric	Stoltz	30 Sep 1961	Laura	Linney	05 Feb 1964	2001		2002

NO.	Forename	Surname	DOB	Forename	Surname	DOB	Start Year	Marriage	End Date
445	Brooke	Shields	31 May 1965	Chris	Henchy	23 Mar 1964		04 Apr 2001	none
446	Walter	Wanger	11 Jul 1894	Justine	Johnstone	31 Jan 1895		01 Sep 1919	1938
447	Charles	Vidor	27 Jul 1900	Karen	Morley	12 Dec 1909		1932	1943
448	Lana	Turner	08 Feb 1921	Artie	Shaw	23 May 1910		Feb 1940	Sep 1940
449	Nancy	Allen	24 Jun 1950	Craig	Shoemaker	15 Nov 1962		1992	1998
450	Jane	Wyman	04 Jan 1914	Lew	Ayres	28 Dec 1908	1948		1949
451	Van	Heflin	13 Dec 1910	Frances	Neal	27 Jun 1921		1942	1967
452	Claudia	Schiffer	25 Aug 1970	Matthew	Vaughn	07 Mar 1971		25 May 2002	none
453	Freddie	Prinze	08 Mar 1976	Sarah-Michelle	Gellar	14 Apr 1977	Feb-02	01 Sep 2002	none
454	Roman	Polanski	18 Aug 1933	Sharon	Tate	24 Jan 1943		20 Jan 1968	09 Aug 1969
455	Roman	Polanski	18 Aug 1933	Emmanuelle	Seigner	22 Jun 1966		1989	none
456	Stanley	Donen	13 Apr 1924	Yvette	Mimieux	08 Jan 1942		1972	1982
457	Gordon	Jackson	19 Dec 1923	Rona	Anderson	03 Aug 1926		02 Jun 1951	15 Jan 1990
458	Jack	Ryder	21 Sep 1981	Kym	Marsh	13 Jun 1976	2001	10 Aug 2002	None
459	Louis	Malle	30 Oct 1932	Candice	Bergen	09 May 1946		1981	23 Nov 1995
460	Amy	Madigan	11 Sep 1950	Ed	Harris	28 Nov 1950	1981	1982	none
461	Mark	Wahlberg	05 Jun 1971	Jordana	Brewster	26 Apr 1980	2000		Jun 2001
462	Burt	Reynolds	11 Feb 1936	Judy	Carne	27 Apr 1939		1963	1965
463	Burt	Reynolds	11 Feb 1936	Loni	Anderson	05 Aug 1946		29 Apr 1988	1993
464	Clint	Eastwood	31 May 1930	Frances	Fisher	11 May 1952	1992		1993
465	Clint	Eastwood	31 May 1930	Sondra	Locke	28 May 1947	1975		1988
466	Steve	McFadden	20 Mar 1959	Lucy	Benjamin	25 Jun 1970	2001		2003
467	Dervla	Kirwan	24 Oct 1971	Stephen	Tompkinson	15 Oct 1966	1995		1999
468	Ozzy	Osbourne	03 Dec 1948	Sharon	Osbourne	10 Oct 1953	1979	04 Jul 1982	none
469	Lorraine	Bracco	02 Oct 1955	Harvey	Keitel	13 May 1939		1982	1993
470	Shirley	Temple	23 Apr 1947	John	Agar	31 Jan 1921		19 Sep 1945	1950
471	Jennifer	Saunders	06 Jul 1958	Adrian	Edmondson	24 Jan 1957		11 May 1985	none
472	Rik	Mayall	07 Mar 1958	Lise	Meyer	29 Nov 1957	1979		1986
473	Debbie	Harry	01 Jul 1945	Chris	Stein	05 Jan 1950	1973		none
474	John	Taylor	20 Jun 1960	Amanda	de Cadenet	19 May 1972		1990	1997

NO.	Forename	Surname	DOB	Forename	Surname	DOB	Start Year	Marriage	End Date
475	Keanu	Reeves	02 Sep 1964	Amanda	de Cadenet	19 May 1972	1996		1998
476	Keanu	Reeves	02 Sep 1964	Jennifer	Syme	07 Dec 1972	1998		2000
477	Sophie	Marceau	17 Nov 1966	Andrez	Zulawski	22 Nov 1940	1994		none
478	Milla	Jovovich	17 Dec 1975	Luc	Besson	18 Mar 1959		1997	none
479	Neil	Hamilton	13 Mar 1949	Christine	Hamilton	10 Nov 1949		1983	none
480	Jeremy	Edwards	17 Feb 1971	Rachel	Stevens	09 Apr 1978	2000		2004
481	Jamie	Redknapp	25 Jun 1973	Louise	Nurding	04 Nov 1974	1996		none
482	Nigella	Lawson	06 Jan 1960	John	Diamond	10 May 1953	1986	1989	02 Mar 2002
483	Nigella	Lawson	06 Jan 1960	Charles	Saatchi	09 Jun 1943	2002		none
484	Juan	Carlos	05 Jan 1938	Queen	Sofia	02 Nov 1938		14 May 1962	none
485	Bill	Clinton	19 Aug 1946	Hillary	Clinton	26 Oct 1947	1970	11 Oct 1975	none
486	Gerard	Depardieu	27 Dec 1948	Elizabeth	Guignot	05 Aug 1941	1969	1970	1996
487	Britney	Spears	02 Dec 1981	Justin	Timberlake	31 Jan 1981	Jan 1999		Mar 2002
488	Ivana	Trump	20 Feb 1949	Donald	Trump	14 Jun 1946		1977	1990
489	Marla	Maples	27 Oct 1963	Donald	Trump	14 Jun 1946		Dec 1993	08 Jun 1999
490	Adolph	Hitler	20 Apr 1889	Eva	Braun	06 Feb 1912	1932	29 Apr 1945	30 Apr 1945
491	Claude	Rains	10 Nov 1889	Isabel	Jeans	16 Sep 1891		1913	1915
492	Kaija	Keel-Olmos	14 Jan 1950	James	Olmos	24 Feb 1947	1967	29 Dec 1971	01 Apr 1990
493	Nastassja	Kinski	24 Jan 1959	Quincy	Jones	14 Mar 1933	1991		1997
494	Peggy	Lipton	30 Aug 1946	Quincy	Jones	14 Mar 1933		Sep 1974	1990
495	Debbie	Reynolds	01 Apr 1932	Eddie	Fisher	10 Aug 1928		18 Sep 1955	1959
496	Christine	Kaufman	11 Jan 1945	Tony	Curtis	03 Jun 1925		1963	1967
497	Janet	Leigh	06 Jul 1927	Tony	Curtis	03 Jun 1925	1950	1951	1962
498	Tony	Blair	06 May 1953	Cherie	Booth	23 Sep 1954	1976	1980	none
499	Caroline	Aherne	24 Dec 1963	Peter	Hook	13 Feb 1956	1994		1997
500	Charlotte	Gainsbourg	22 Jul 1971	Yvan	Attal	04 Jan 1965		1996	none
501	Gwen	Verdon	13 Jan 1925	Bob	Fosse	23 Jun 1927		1960	1987
502	Lily	Tomlin	01 Sep 1939	Jane	Wagner	2 Feb 1935	1971		none
503	Quentin	Tarantino	27 Mar 1963	Mira	Sorvino	28 Sep 1967	1996		Feb 1998
504	Eddie	Sutherland	05 Dec 1895	Louise	Brooks	14 Nov 1906		Jul 1926	Jun 1928

NO.	Forename	Surname	DOB	Forename	Surname	DOB	Start Year	Marriage	End Date
505	William A	Seiter	10 Jun 1890	Marian	Nixon	20 Oct 1904		1934	Jul 1964
506	William A	Seiter	10 Jun 1890	Laura	Laplante	01 Nov 1904		1926	1934
507	Edward G	Robinson	12 Dec 1893	Gladys	Lloyd	11 Oct 1895		1927	1956
508	Paul	Robeson	09 Apr 1898	Eslanda	Goode	15 Dec 1895		17 Aug 1921	13 Dec 1965
509	Christopher	Plummer	13 Dec 1927	Tammy	Grimes	30 Jan 1934		1956	1960
510	Dudley	Moore	19 Apr 1935	Tuesday	Weld	27 Aug 1943		20 Sep 1975	1980
511	Tom	Mix	06 Jan 1880	Olive	Stoke	10 Apr 1887		1907	1917
512	Tom	Mix	06 Jan 1880	Victoria	Forde	21 Apr 1896		1918	1931
513	Princess	Margaret	21 Aug 1930	Peter	Townsend	22 Nov 1914	1950		1955
514	John	Major	29 Mar 1943	Edwina	Currie	13 Oct 1946	1984		1988
515	Ben	Lyon	06 Feb 1901	Marian	Nixon	20 Oct 1904		1971	22 Mar 1979
516	Ben	Lyon	06 Feb 1901	Bebe	Daniels	14 Jan 1901		1930	1971
517	Andrew	Lloyd-Webber	22 Mar 1948	Sarah	Brightman	14 Aug 1960		1984	1990
518	Harold	Lloyd	20 Apr 1893	Mildred	Davis	22 Feb 1901		10 Feb 1923	18 Aug 1969
519	David	Niven	01 Mar 1910	Evelyn	Keyes	20 Nov 1919	1947		1947
520	Laura	Laplante	01 Nov 1904	Irving	Asher	16 Sep 1903		1934	1985
521	Harry	Langdon	15 Jun 1884	Rose	Mensolf	04 Dec 1882		1903	1929
522	Frankie	Laine	30 Mar 1913	Nan	Grey	25 Jul 1918		1950	25 Jul 1993
523	Jaclyn	Smith	26 Oct 1947	Anthony B	Richmond	07 Jul 1942		1981	1989
524	Jaclyn	Smith	26 Oct 1947	Roger	Davis	05 Apr 1939		1972	1975
525	Jaclyn	Smith	26 Oct 1947	Dennis	Cole	19 Jul 1940		1978	1981
526	Alfred	Hitchcock	13 Aug 1899	Alma	Reville	14 Aug1899		02 Dec 1926	29 Apr 1980
527	Susan	Hampshire	12 May 1938	Pierre	Granier-Deferre		22 Jul 1927	1967	1974
528	Zoe	Wanamaker	13 May 1949	Gawn	Grainger	12 Oct 1940		1994	none
529	Melissa	Gilbert	08 May 1964	Bo	Brinkman	17 Sep 1956		21 Feb 1988	1992
530	Melissa	Gilbert	08 May 1964	Bruce	Boxleitner	12 May 1950		01 Jan 1995	none
531	Brendan	Fraser	03 Dec 1968	Afton	Smith	03 Dec 1967	1993	27 Sep 1998	none
532	Michele	Dotrice	27 Sep 1948	Edward	Woodward	01 Jun 1930		1987	none
533	Walt	Disney	05 Dec 1901	Lillian	Disney	15 Feb 1899		13 Jul 1925	15 Dec 1966
534	Miles	Davis	26 May 1926	Cicely	Tyson	19 Dec 1933		28 Nov 1981	1988

NO.	Forename	Surname	DOB	Forename	Surname	DOB	Start Year	Marriage	End Date
535	Peter	Davison	13 Apr 1951	Sandra	Dickinson	20 Oct 1948		26 Dec 1978	1994
536	Billy	Connolly	24 Nov 1942	Pamela	Stephenson	04 Dec 1949		20 Dec 1989	none
537	Michael	Brandon	20 Apr 1945	Glynis	Barber	25 Oct 1955		18 Nov 1989	none
538	Marlon	Brando	03 Apr 1924	Movita	Castenada	04 Dec 1917		04 Jun 1960	1968
539	Marlon	Brando	03 Apr 1924	Anna	Kashfi	30 Sep 1934		11 Oct 1957	22 Apr 1959
540	Clara	Bow	29 Jul 1905	Rex	Bell	16 Oct 1903		03 Dec 1931	04 Jul 1962
541	Steve	Allen	26 Dec 1921	Jayne	Meadows	27 Sep 1924		1953	2000
542	Franco	Nero	23 Nov 1941	Vanessa	Redgrave	30 Jan 1937		1967	1971
543	Val	Kilmer	31 Dec 1959	Joanne	Whalley	25 Aug 1964		Mar 1988	Feb 1996
544	Michael	Weatherly	08 Jul 1968	Amelia	Heinle	17 Mar 1973		1995	1997
545	Michael	Weatherly	08 Jul 1968	Jessica	Alba	28 Apr 1981	May 2001		2003
546	Mike	Tyson	30 Jun 1966	Robin	Givens	27 Nov 1964		07 Feb 1988	14 Feb 1989
547	Jeanne	Tripplehorn	10 Jun 1963	Ben	Stiller	30 Nov 1965	1993		1997
548	David	Thewlis	20 Mar 1963	Anna	Friel	12 Jul 1976	2001		none
549	Eric	Stoltz	30 Sep 1961	Helen	Hunt	15 Jun 1963	1992		1992
550	Ben	Stiller	30 Nov 1965	Clare	Forlani	01 Jul 1972	1998		1999
551	Cybill	Shepherd	18 Feb 1950	Peter	Bogdanovich	30 Jul 1939	1971		1978
552	Edmund	Purdom	19 Dec 1924	Linda	Christian	13 Nov 1924		1962	1963
553	Prince	Rogers-Nelson	07 Jun 1958	Mayte	Garcia	12 Nov 1973	1993	14 Feb 1996	1999
554	David	Price	17 Nov 1961	Lysette	Anthony	26 Sep 1963		10 Apr 1999	21 Aug 2001
555	Jane	Powell	01 Apr 1929	Dickie	Moore	12 Sep 1925		21 May 1988	none
556	Adrian	Pasdar	30 Apr 1965	Natalie	Maines	14 Oct 1974		24 Jun 2000	none
557	Edward	Norton	18 Aug 1969	Courtney	Love	09 Jul 1964		1996	1998
558	Edward	Norton	18 Aug 1969	Selma	Hayek	02 Sep 1966		1999	2003
559	Jack	Nicholson	22 Apr 1937	Lara	Flynn-Boyle	24 Mar 1970	1999		2001
560	Audie	Murphy	20 Jun 1924	Wanda	Hendrix	03 Nov 1928		08 Feb 1949	14 Apr 1950
561	Viggo	Mortensen	20 Oct 1958	Exene	Cervenka	01 Feb 1956		1987	1997
562	Elizabeth	McGovern	18 Jul 1961	Simon	Curtis	11 Mar 1960		12 Dec 1992	none
563	Heather	Locklear	25 Sep 1961	Richie	Sambora	11 Jul 1959		17 Dec 1994	none
564	James	Cameron	16 Aug 1954	Kathryn	Bigelow	27 Nov 1951		17 Aug 1989	1991

NO.	Forename	Surname	DOB	Forename	Surname	DOB	Start Year	Marriage	End Date
565	Juliette	Lewis	23 Jun 1973	Stephen	Berra	10 May 1973		09 Sep 1999	2003
566	Jessica	Lange	20 Apr 1949	Sam	Shepard	05 Nov 1943		1982	none
567	James	Cameron	16 Aug 1954	Suzy	Amis	05 Jan 1962		04 Jun 2000	none
568	Veronica	Lake	14 Nov 1919	Andre	De Toth	15 May 1912		13 Dec 1944	Jun 1952
569	Kris	Kristofferson	22 Jun 1936	Rita	Coolidge	01 May 1945		1973	1980
570	Ashley	Judd	19 Apr 1968	Dario	Franchitti	19 May 1973	1999	21 Dec 2001	none
571	Mick	Jagger	26 Jul 1943	Marianne	Faithfull	29 Dec 1946	1965		22 Sep 1970
572	Rance	Howard	17 Nov 1928	Jean	Speegle	31 Jan 1927		1949	02 Sep 2000
573	Whitney	Houston	09 Aug 1963	Bobby	Brown	05 Feb 1969		18 Jul 1992	none
574	Natasha	Henstridge	15 Aug 1974	Damian	Chapa	29 Oct 1963		1995	1996
575	Teri	Hatcher	08 Dec 1964	Jon	Tenney	16 Dec 1961		27 May 1994	none
576	Daryl	Hannah	03 Dec 1960	John F	Kennedy Jnr	25 Dec 1960	1989		1994
577	Daryl	Hannah	03 Dec 1960	Jackson	Browne	09 Oct 1948	1982		1992
578	Milos	Forman	18 Feb 1932	Jana	Brejchova	20 Jan 1940		1951	1956
579	Jessica	Simpson	10 Jul 1980	Nick	Lachey	09 Nov 1973	2001	26 Oct 2002	none
580	Carmen	Electra	20 Apr 1972	Dennis	Rodman	13 May 1961		14 Nov 1998	06 Apr 1999
581	Anita	Ekberg	29 Sep 1931	Anthony	Steel	21 May 1920		22 May 1956	14 May 1959
582	Olympia	Dukakis	20 Jun 1931	Louis	Zorich	12 Feb 1924		1962	none
583	Angie	Dickinson	30 Sep 1931	Burt	Bacharach	12 May 1928		May 1965	1980
584	Dom	Deluise	01 Aug 1931	Carol	Deluise	04 Aug 1935		23 Nov 1965	none
585	Judy	Davis	23 Apr 1955	Colin	Friels	25 Sep 1952		1984	none
586	Gisele	Bundchen	20 Jul 1980	Leonardo	Dicaprio	11 Nov 1974	2002		2002
587	Juliette	Binoche	09 Mar 1964	Benoit	Magimel	11 May 1974		1999	none
588	Ellen	Barkin	16 Apr 1954	Gabriel	Byrne	12 May 1950		1988	1993
589	Carol	Bayer-Sager	08 Mar 1947	Burt	Bacharach	12 May 1928		1982	1990
590	Hank	Azaria	25 Apr 1964	Helen	Hunt	15 Jun 1963	1997	17 Aug 1999	18 Dec 2000
591	Christina	Applegate	25 Nov 1971	Johnathan	Schaech	10 Sep 1969		20 Oct 2001	none
592	Annabella		14 Jul 1904	Jean	Murat	13 Jul 1888		1931	1938
593	Pamela	Anderson	01 Jul 1967	Kid	Rock	17 Jan 1971	2002		2004
594	Karen	Allen	05 Oct 1951	Kale	Browne	16 Jun 1950		01 May 1988	1997

NO.	Forename	Surname	DOB	Forename	Surname	DOB	Start Year	Marriage	End Date
595	Norman	Cook	16 Jul 1963	Zoe	Ball	23 Nov 1970		20 Aug 1999	01 Dec 2002
596	Declan	Donnelly	25 Sep 1975	Clare	Buckfield	10 Apr 1976	1993		2003
597	Celine	Dion	30 Mar 1968	Rene	Angelil	16 Jan 1942		17 Dec 1994	none
598	Claudia	Schiffer	25 Aug 1970	David	Copperfield	16 Sep 1956	1994		1999
599	Christy	Turlington	02 Jan 1969	Edward	Burns	29 Jan 1968	2001		2002
600	Bill	Wyman	24 Oct 1936	Mandy	Smith	17 Jul 1970	1983	1989	1991
601	Lorraine	Bracco	02 Oct 1955	James	Olmos	24 Feb 1947		1994	01 Mar 2002
602	Alfred	Molina	24 May 1953	Jill	Gascoine	11 Apr 1937		1985	none
603	Lindsay	Wagner	22 Jun 1949	Michael	Brandon	20 Apr 1945		1976	1979
604	Annabella		14 Jul 1904	Tyrone	Power	05 May 1914		23 Apr 1939	26 Jan 1948
605	Princess	Anne	15 Aug 1950	Mark	Phillips	22 Sep 1948		14 Nov 1973	1992
606	Brian	May	19 Jul 1947	Anita	Dobson	29 Apr 1949	1987	18 Nov 2000	none
607	Alain	Delon	08 Nov 1935	Mireile	Darc	15 May 1938	1968	1970	1983
608	Alain	Delon	08 Nov 1935	Nathalie	Canovas	01 Aug 1941		1964	1969
609	Jean	Seberg	13 Nov 1938	Romain	Gary	08 May 1914		1962	1979
610	Meg	Tilly	14 Feb 1960	Colin	Firth	10 Sep 1960		1989	1993
611	Maiwen	Le Besco	17 Apr 1976	Luc	Besson	18 Mar 1959		1993	1995
612	Anne	Parillaud	16 May 1960	Luc	Besson	18 Mar 1959		1986	1988
613	Tom	Selleck	29 Feb 1945	Jillie	Mack	25 Dec 1957	1983	07 Aug 1987	none
614	Barbara	Dana	28 Dec 1940	Alan	Arkin	26 Mar 1934		1964	none
615	Maeve	Quinlan	16 Nov 1969	Tom	Sizemore	29 Sep 1964		01 Sep 1996	19 Nov 1999
616	Curt	Jurgens	13 Dec 1915	Judith	Holzmeister	14 Feb 1920		16 Oct 1947	1955
617	Cedric	Hardwicke	19 Feb 1893	Helena	Pickard	13 Oct 1900		1928	1948
618	Horst	Buccholz	04 Dec 1933	Myriam	Bru	20 Apr 1932		07 Dec 1958	03 Mar 03
619	Claudette	Colbert	13 Sep 1903	Norman	Foster	13 Dec 1900		1928	1935
620	Sally	Blane	11 Jul 1910	Norman	Foster	13 Dec 1900		1937	1976
621	Georgiana	Young	30 Sep 1923	Ricardo	Montalban	25 Nov 1920		1945	none
622	Shelley	Winters	18 Aug 1922	Vittorio	Gassman	01 Sep 1922		1952	1954
623	Shelley	Winters	18 Aug 1922	Anthony	Franciosa	25 Oct 1928		1957	1960
624	Nora	Ricci	19 Jul 1924	Vittorio	Gassman	01 Sep 1922		1944	1952

NO.	Forename	Surname	DOB	Forename	Surname	DOB	Start Year	Marriage	End Date
625	Richard	Madeley	13 May 1956	Judy	Finnigan	16 May 1948		1986	none
626	Robert	Montgomery	21 May 1904	Elizabeth	Allen	09 Apr 1908		04 Apr 1928	1950
627	Elizabeth	Montgomery	15 Apr 1933	Robert	Foxworth	01 Nov 1941	1974	28 Jan 1993	18 May 1995
628	Elizabeth	Montgomery	15 Apr 1933	William	Asher	08 Aug 1921		1963	1973
629	Elizabeth	Montgomery	15 Apr 1933	Gig	Young	04 Nov 1913		28 Dec 1956	1963
630	Romy	Schneider	23 Sep 1938	Alain	Delon	08 Nov 1935	1959		1963
631	Romy	Schneider	23 Sep 1938	Harry	Meyen	31 Aug 1924		1966	1972
632	William	Shatner	22 Mar 1931	Nerine	Kidd	13 Jul 1959		15 Nov 1997	08 Aug 1999
633	Keith	Richards	18 Dec 1943	Anita	Pallenberg	25 Jan 1944	1967		1969
634	Callista	Flockhart	11 Nov 1964	Harrison	Ford	13 Jul 1942	2002		none
635	Jacquie	Bouvier	28 Jul 1929	Aristotle	Onassis	20 Jan 1906		20 Oct 1968	15 Mar 1975
636	Maria	Callas	02 Dec 1923	Aristotle	Onassis	20 Jan 1906	1960		1965
637	Harry	Connick Jr	11 Sep 1967	Jill	Goodacre	29 Mar 1965		1994	none
638	Anne	Baxter	07 May 1923	John	Hodiak	16 Apr 1914		07 Jul 1946	27 Jan 1953
639	Dean	Stockwell	05 Mar 1936	Millie	Perkins	12 May 1936		April 1960	1962
640	Sterling	Hayden	26 Mar 1916	Madeleine	Carroll	26 Feb 1906		1942	1945
641	Bruce	Dern	04 Jun 1936	Diane	Ladd	29 Nov 1935		1960	1969
642	Cameron	Diaz	30 Aug 1972	Justin	Timberlake	31 Jan 1981	2003		none
643	Coral	Browne	23 Jul 1913	Vincent	Price	27 May 1911		1974	1991
644	Mary	Grant	20 Feb 1917	Vincent	Price	27 May 1911		1949	1973
645	Edith	Barrett	19 Jan 1907	Vincent	Price	27 May 1911		1938	1948
646	Ursula	Andress	19 Mar 1936	Harry	Hamlin	30 Oct 1951	1978		1982
647	Laura	Johnson	01 Aug 1957	Harry	Hamlin	30 Oct 1951		09 Mar 1985	1989
648	Nicolette	Sheridan	21 Nov 1963	Harry	Hamlin	30 Oct 1951		07 Sep 1991	1994
649	Lisa	Rinna	11 Jul 1965	Harry	Hamlin	30 Oct 1951		20 Mar 1997	none
650	Nicolette	Sheridan	21 Nov 1963	Leif	Garrett	08 Nov 1961	1979		1985
651	William	Holden	17 Apr 1918	Brenda	Marshall	29 Sep 1915		1941	1971
652	Boris	Becker	22 Nov 1967	Barbara	Feltus	01 Nov 1966		17 Dec 1993	15 Jan 2001
653	Jane	Russell	21 Jun 1921	Bob	Waterfield	26 Jul 1920		1943	1968
654	Jean-Luc	Godard	03 Dec 1930	Anna	Karina	22 Sep 1940		03 Mar 1961	1965

NO.	Forename	Surname	DOB	Forename	Surname	DOB	Start Year	Marriage	End Date
655	Jean-Luc	Godard	03 Dec 1930	Anne	Wiazemsky	14 May 1947		22 Jul 1967	1979
656	Yves	Montand	13 Oct 1921	Simone	Signoret	25 Mar 1921		1951	1985
657	Yves	Allegret	13 Oct 1905	Simone	Signoret	25 Mar 1921		1944	1949
658	Francois	Truffaut	06 Feb 1932	Fanny	Ardant	22 Mar 1949		1981	1984
659	King	Vidor	08 Feb 1894	Florence	Vidor	23 Jul 1895		1915	1925
660	King	Vidor	08 Feb 1894	Eleanor	Boardman	19 Aug 1898		1926	1931
661	Cloris	Leachman	30 Apr 1926	George	Englund	22 Jun 1926		1953	1979
662	Fredric	March	31 Aug 1897	Florence	Eldridge	05 Sep 1901		30 May 1927	14 Apr 1975
663	Jason	Robards	26 Jul 1922	Lauren	Bacall	16 Sep 1924		04 Jul 1961	10 Sep 1969
664	John	Lennon	09 Oct 1940	Cynthia	Powell	10 Sep 1939	1957	23 Aug 1962	08 Nov 1968
665	Sean	Lennon	09 Oct 1975	Bijou	Phillips	01 Apr 1980	2001		2003
666	Martin	Balsam	04 Nov 1914	Joyce	Van Patten	09 Mar 1934		1959	1962
667	Paul Thomas	Anderson	26 Jun 1970	Fiona	Apple	13 Sep 1977		2001	none
668	Desmond	Wilcox	21 May 1931	Esther	Rantzen	22 Jun 1940	1968	1978	06 Sep 2000
669	Catherine	Zeta-Jones	25 Sep 1969	John	Leslie	20 Feb 1965	1991		1993
670	Jacques	Villeneuve	09 Apr 1971	Dannii	Minogue	20 Oct 1971	1999		2001
671	Queen	Victoria	24 May 1819	Prince	Albert	26 Aug 1819	1839	11 Feb 1840	1861
672	Sid	Vicious	10 May 1957	Nancy	Spungen	27 Feb 1958	1977		1978
673	Eddie	Van Halen	26 Jan 1955	Valerie	Bertinelli	30 Apr 1960	1980	1981	none
674	Ulrika	Jonsson	16 Aug 1967	Sven Goran	Eriksson	05 Feb 1948	2001		2002
675	Catherine	Oxenberg	22 Sep 1961	Robert	Evans	29 Jun 1930		12 Jul 1998	21 Jul 1998
676	Shannon	Tweed	10 Mar 1957	Gene	Simmons	25 Aug 1949	1984		none
677	Catherine	Oxenberg	22 Sep 1961	Caspar	Van Dien	18 Dec 1968		08 May 1999	none
678	Gwen	Stefani	03 Oct 1969	Gavin	Rossdale	30 Oct 1967	1996	14 Sep 2002	none
679	Robert	Evans	29 Jun 1930	Sharon	Hugueny	29 Feb 1944		28 May 1961	1962
680	James	Cameron	16 Aug 1954	Linda	Hamilton	26 Sep 1956		26 Jul 1997	1999
681	Phil	Silvers	11 May 1911	Jo-Carroll	Dennison	16 Dec 1923		1945	1950
682	Gerald	Scarfe	01 Jun 1936	Jane	Asher	05 Apr 1946	1970	1981	none
683	Mickey	Rourke	16 Sep 1950	Carre	Otis	28 Sep 1968	1990	1992	1998
684	John	Stamos	19 Aug 1963	Rebecca	Romijn	06 Nov 1972	24 Dec 1997	19 Sep 1998	none

NO.	Forename	Surname	DOB	Forename	Surname	DOB	Start Year	Marriage	End Date
685	Caroline	Quentin	11 Jun 1961	Paul	Merton	17 Jan 1957	1989	1990	1997
686	Neil	Morrisey	04 Jul 1962	Rachel	Weisz	07 Mar 1971	1998		1998
687	Neil	Morrisey	04 Jul 1962	Amanda	Holden	16 Feb 1971	2000		2000
688	Tim	McGraw	01 May 1967	Faith	Hill	21 Sep 1967		06 Oct 1996	none
689	Paul	McCartney	18 Jun 1942	Jane	Asher	05 Apr 1946	1963		1968
690	Malcolm	X	19 May 1925	Betty	Shabazz	28 May 1936		14 Jan 1958	21 Feb 1965
691	Martin Luther	King	15 Jan 1929	Coretta Scott	King	27 Apr 1927		18 Jun 1953	04 Apr 1968
692	Caspar	Van Dien	18 Dec 1968	Carrie	Mitchum	15 Jun 1965	1993		1997
693	Kerry	Katona	06 Sep 1980	Bryan	McFadden	12 Apr 1980	2000		2004
694	George	Jones	12 Sep 1931	Tammy	Wynette	05 May 1942	1968		1975
695	Elizabeth	Taylor	27 Feb 1932	Nicky	Hilton	06 Jul 1926	1950		1951
696	Prince	Edward	10 Mar 1964	Sophie	Rhys Jones	20 Jan 1965		29 Jun 1999	none
697	Jane	Danson	08 Nov 1978	Robert	Beck	01 Aug 1970	May 1999		none
698	Marie	Curie	07 Nov 1867	Pierre	Curie	15 May 1859	1894	1895	19 Apr 1906
699	Prince	Charles	14 Nov 1948	Camilla	Parker-Bowles	17 Jul 1947	1970		none
700	Chris	Guest	05 Feb 1948	Jamie Lee	Curtis	22 Nov 1958		18 Dec 1984	none
701	Russell	Crowe	07 Apr 1964	Danielle	Spencer	29 Sep 1970	2002	2003	none
702	Barbara	Hershey	05 Feb 1948	David	Carradine	08 Dec 1936	1968		1975
703	Dannii	Minogue	20 Oct 1971	Julian	McMahon	27 Jul 1968		1994	1995
704	Grace	Kelly	12 Nov 1929	Don	Richardson	30 Apr 1918	1948		1953
705	Diane	Lane	22 Jan 1965	Josh	Brolin	12 Feb 1968	2002		none
706	Grace	Kelly	12 Nov 1929	Bing	Crosby	03 May 1903	1955		1955
707	Grace	Kelly	12 Nov 1929	Gene	Lyons	09 Feb 1921	1951		1954
708	Grace	Kelly	12 Nov 1929	Oleg	Cassini	11 Apr 1913	1955		1956
709	Grace	Kelly	12 Nov 1929	Clark	Gable	01 Feb 1901	1953		1954
710	Grace	Kelly	12 Nov 1929	Gary	Cooper	07 May 1901	1951		1951
711	Grace	Kelly	12 Nov 1929	William	Holden	17 Apr 1918	1955		1955
712	Grace	Kelly	12 Nov 1929	Ray	Milland	03 Jan 1907	1954		1955
713	Grace	Kelly	12 Nov 1929	Jean-Pierre	Aumont	05 Jan 1911	1953		1955
714	Marisa	Pavan	19 Jun 1932	Jean-Pierre	Aumont	05 Jan 1911		1956	2001

NO.	Forename	Surname	DOB	Forename	Surname	DOB	Start Year	Marriage	End Date
715	Pier	Angeli	19 Jun 1932	James	Dean	08 Feb 1931	1954		1954
716	Rita	Hayworth	17 Oct 1918	Orson	Welles	06 May 1915	1942	07 Sep 1943	01 Dec 1948
717	Rita	Hayworth	17 Oct 1918	Aly	Khan	13 Jun 1911		27 May 1949	26 Jan 1953
718	Rita	Hayworth	17 Oct 1918	Dick	Haymes	13 Sep 1916		24 Sep 1953	12 Dec 1955
719	Rita	Hayworth	17 Oct 1918	James	Hill	01 Aug 1916		02 Feb 1958	1 Sep 1961
720	Frederico	Fellini	20 Jan 1920	Guilietta	Masina	22 Feb 1921		1943	1993
721	Julia	Roberts	28 Oct 1967	Dylan	McDermott	16 Oct 1961	1988		1989
722	Gwyneth	Paltrow	28 Sep 1972	Chris	Martin	02 Mar 1977	2002		none
723	Sian	Lloyd	03 Jul 1958	Lembit	Opik	02 Mar 1965	2002		none
724	Eric	Stoltz	30 Sep 1961	Lili	Taylor	20 Feb 1967	1989		1990
725	Eric	Stoltz	30 Sep 1961	Rachel	Griffiths	20 Feb 1968	1999		2000
726	Margaret	Whigham	01 Dec 1912	Duke of	Argyll	18 Jun 1903		21 Mar 1951	1963
727	Liv	Tyler	01 Jul 1977	Royston	Langdon	01 May 1972		2003	none
728	Prince	Rainier	31 May 1923	Gisele	Pascal	17 Sep 1923	1949		1955
729	Bridget	Fonda	27 Jan 1964	Danny	Elfman	29 May 1953	2003		none
730	Milla	Jovovich	17 Dec 1975	Paul	Anderson	04 Mar 1965	2003		none
731	Rudolph	Valentino	06 May 1895	Pola	Negri	03 Jan 1897	1926		1926
732	Steven	Spielberg	18 Dec 1946	Amy	Irving	10 Sep 1953	1975	1985	1989
733	Steven	Spielberg	18 Dec 1946	Kate	Capshaw	03 Nov 1953	1989	1991	none
734	Jemima	Goldsmith	30 Jan 1974	Imran	Khan	25 Nov 1952		1995	none
735	William	Baldwin	21 Feb 1963	Chynna	Phillips	12 Feb 1968		09 Sep 1995	none
736	Kathryn	Grant	25 Nov 1933	Bing	Crosby	03 May 1903		1957	14 Oct 1977
737	Dixie	Lee	04 Nov 1911	Bing	Crosby	03 May 1903		1930	1952
738	Gene	Tierney	19 Nov 1920	Oleg	Cassini	11 Apr 1913		1941	1952
739	Bruno	Bareto	16 Mar 1955	Amy	Irving	10 Sep 1953	1990		none
740	Brigitte	Bardot	28 Sep 1934	Jean Louis	Trintignant	11 Dec 1930	1957		1957
741	Brigitte	Bardot	28 Sep 1934	Sacha	Distel	29 Jan 1933	1958		1958
742	Daniel	Gelin	19 May 1921	Daniele	Delorme	09 Oct 1926	1943	1945	1955
743	Kim	Novak	13 Feb 1933	Sammy	Davis	08 Dec 1925	1957		1957
744	Kim	Novak	13 Feb 1933	Richard	Johnson	30 Jul 1927		15 Mar 1965	1966

NO.	Forename	Surname	DOB	Forename	Surname	DOB	Start Year	Marriage	End Date
745	Gloria	Swanson	27 Mar 1897	Wallace	Beery	01 Apr 1885		1916	1919
746	Gloria	Swanson	27 Mar 1897	Joseph	Kennedy	06 Sep 1888	1928		1930
747	Gloria	Swanson	27 Mar 1897	Michael	Farmer	09 May 1902		1931	1934
748	Yves	Robert	21 Jun 1920	Daniele	Delorme	09 Oct 1926		1956	10 May 2001
749	Rita	Hayworth	17 Oct 1918	Gary	Merrill	02 Aug 1915	1961		1962
750	Brooke	Hayward	05 Jul 1937	Dennis	Hopper	17 May 1936	1960	1961	1969
751	Brooke	Hayward	05 Jul 1937	Buck	Henry	09 Dec 1930	1971		1976
752	Brooke	Hayward	05 Jul 1937	Peter	Duchin	28 Jul 1937	.	1985	none
753	Jennifer	Jones	02 Mar 1919	Robert	Walker	13 Oct 1919		1939	1944
754	Daniel	Baldwin	05 Oct 1960	Isabella	Hoffmann	11 Dec 1958		1994	none
755	Ingmar	Bergman	14 Jul 1918	Liv	Ullmann	16 Dec 1938	1965		1971
756	Ingmar	Bergman	14 Jul 1918	Kabi	Laretei	14 Jul 1922		1959	1965
757	Carey	Lowell	11 Feb 1961	Griffin	Dunne	08 Jun 1955	1989		1995
758	Ida	Lupino	04 Feb 1918	Collier	Young	19 Aug 1908		1948	1951
759	Ida	Lupino	04 Feb 1918	Louis	Hayward	19 Mar 1909		16 Nov 1938	11 May 1945
760	Ida	Lupino	04 Feb 1918	Howard	Duff	24 Nov 1913		1951	1973
761	Joseph L	Mankiewicz	11 Feb 1909	Rose	Stradner	31 Jul 1913		28 Jul 1939	27 Sep 1958
762	Mai	Zetterling	24 May 1924	Tutte	Lemkow	28 Aug 1918		1944	1953
763	Lisa	Loeb	11 Mar 1968	Dweezil	Zappa	05 Sep 1969	1999		none
764	Richard D	Zanuck	13 Dec 1932	Linda	Harrison	26 Jul 1945		01 Nov 1969	1978
765	Richard D	Zanuck	13 Dec 1934	Lili	Fini	02 Apr 1954	06 May 1978		none
766	Darryl F	Zanuck	05 Sep 1902	Virginia	Fox	19 Apr 1902		24 Jan 1924	1956
767	Darryl F	Zanuck	05 Sep 1902	Bella	Darvi	23 Oct 1928	1955		1956
768	Richard	Widmark	26 Dec 1914	Jean	Hazlewood	04 Aug 1916		05 Apr 1942	1997
769	Rainer	Fassbinder	31 May 1945	Ingrid	Cavan	03 Aug 1938		26 Aug 1970	27 Sep 1972
770	Frank	Sinatra	12 Dec 1915	Lana	Turner	08 Feb 1921	1946		1946
771	Cary	Grant	18 Jan 1904	Barbara	Hutton	14 Nov 1912		08 Jul 1942	30 Aug 45
772	Bobbe	Arnst	11 Oct 1903	Johnny	Weissmuller	02 Jun 1904		28 Feb 1931	1932
773	Lupe	Velez	18 Jul 1908	Johnny	Weissmuller	02 Jun 1904	1933		1939
774	Joan	Blair	08 Jun 1903	Victor	Fleming	23 Feb 1883	1931		1932

NO.	Forename	Surname	DOB	Forename	Surname	DOB	Start Year	Marriage	End Date
775	Clara	Bow	29 Jul 1905	Victor	Fleming	23 Feb 1883	1925		1925
776	Lupe	Velez	18 Jul 1908	Victor	Fleming	23 Feb 1883	1929		1929
777	Clara	Bow	29 Jul 1905	Gary	Cooper	07 May 1901	1926		1926
778	Hope	Lange	28 Nov 1931	Don	Murray	31 Jul 1929		1956	1961
779	Hope	Lange	28 Nov 1931	Alan J	Pakula	07 Apr 1928		1963	1969
780	John	Frankenheimer	19 Feb 1930	Evans	Evans	26 Nov 1936		1961	2002
781	Rip	Torn	06 Feb 1931	Anne	Wedgeworth	21 Jan 1935		1956	1961
782	Rip	Torn	06 Feb 1931	Geraldine	Page	22 Dec 1924		1961	1987
783	Cornel	Wilde	13 Oct 1915	Patricia	Knight	28 Apr 1920		21 Sep 1937	1951
784	Cornel	Wilde	13 Oct 1915	Jean	Wallace	12 Oct 1923		1951	1981
785	Gena	Rowlands	19 Jun 1934	John	Cassavetes	09 Dec 1929		1954	03 Feb 1989
786	Richard	Basehart	31 Aug 1914	Valentina	Cortese	01 Jan 1923		24 Mar 1951	1960
787	Jim	Backus	25 Feb 1913	Henny	Backus	21 Mar 1911		1941	03 Jul 1989
788	Sam	Jaffe	10 Mar 1891	Bettye	Ackerman	28 Feb 1928		1956	1984
789	Dina	Merrill	09 Dec 1925	Cliff	Robertson	09 Sep 1923		22 Dec 1966	1986
790	Dina	Merrill	09 Dec 1925	Ted	Hartley	06 Nov 1935		1989	none
791	Carole	Burnett	26 Apr 1933	Joe	Hamilton	06 Jan 1929		01 May 1963	1982
792	Carole	Burnett	26 Apr 1933	Don	Saroyan	04 Oct 1928		1955	1962
793	Deanna	Durbin	04 Dec 1921	Felix	Jackson	05 Jun 1902		13 Jun 1945	27 Oct 1949
794	James	Farentino	24 Feb 1938	Debrah	Farentino	30 Sep 1959		1985	1988
795	James	Farentino	24 Feb 1938	Michele	Lee	24 Jun 1942		1967	1982
796	James	Farentino	24 Feb 1938	Elizabeth	Ashley	30 Aug 1939		01 Sep 1962	1965
797	George	Peppard	01 Oct 1928	Elizabeth	Ashley	30 Aug 1939		1966	1972
798	Bruce	Cabot	20 Apr 1904	Adrienne	Ames	03 Aug 1907		1933	1937
799	George	Osmond	13 Oct 1917	Olive	Osmond	04 May 1925		01 Dec 1944	09 May 1904
800	Busby	Berkeley	29 Dec 1895	Esther	Muir	11 Mar 1903		1930	1931
801	Busby	Berkeley	29 Dec 1895	Merna	Kennedy	07 Sep 1908		1934	1935
802	Fritz	Lang	05 Dec 1890	Thea	von Harbou	27 Dec 1888		1922	1933
803	William R	Hearst	29 Apr 1863	Marion	Davies	03 Jan 1897	1924		1951
804	Barry	Levinson	06 Apr 1942	Valerie	Curtin	31 Mar 1945		1975	1982

NO.	Forename	Surname	DOB	Forename	Surname	DOB	Start Year	Marriage	End Date
805	Lana	Turner	08 Feb 1921	Johnny	Stomponato	19 Oct 1925	1957		1958
806	Norma	Shearer	10 Aug 1902	George	Raft	26 Sep 1895	1938		1941
807	Jeanette	Macdonald	18 Jun 1903	Nelson	Eddy	29 Jun 1901	1933		1938
808	Judy	Garland	10 Jun 1922	Joseph L	Mankiewicz	11 Feb 1909	1943		1943
809	Judy	Garland	10 Jun 1922	Tyrone	Power	05 May 1914	1943		1944
810	Judy	Garland	10 Jun 1922	Artie	Shaw	23 May 1910	1939		1939
811	Lana	Turner	08 Feb 1921	Tyrone	Power	05 May 1914	1946		1946
812	Lana	Turner	08 Feb 1921	Mickey	Rooney	23 Sep 1920	1939		1939
813	Robert	Graves	24 Jul 1895	Laura	Riding	16 Jan 1901	02 Jan 1926		1938
814	Robert	Graves	24 Jul 1895	Beryl	Pritchard	22 Feb 1915	1938	1950	1985
815	Charlize	Theron	07 Aug 1975	Stuart	Townsend	15 Dec 1972	2002		none
816	Crown Prince	Haakon	20 Jul 1973	Mette-Marit	Tjessem-Hoisby		19 Aug 1973	25 Aug 2001	none
817	George	Raft	26 Sep 1895	Virginia	Pine	11 Aug 1911	1932		1938
818	Frank	Sinatra	12 Dec 1915	Nancy	Barbato	25 Mar 1917	1934	04 Feb 1939	1951
819	Frank	Sinatra	12 Dec 1915	Marilyn	Maxwell	03 Aug 1921	1946	1946	
820	John	Conte	15 Sep 1915	Marilyn	Maxwell	03 Aug 1921	1944	1946	
821	Juliet	Mills	21 Nov 1941	Maxwell	Caulfield	23 Nov 1959	1980	none	
822	Hayley	Mills	18 Apr 1946	Roy	Boulting	21 Nov 1913	1971	1976	
823	Fay	Wray	10 Sep 1907	Robert	Riskin	30 Mar 1897	23 Aug 1942	20 Sep 1955	
824	Fay	Wray	10 Sep 1907	John Monk	Saunders	22 Dec 1895	15 Jun 1928	1939	
825	Gordon	Macrae	12 Mar 1921	Sheila	Macrae	24 Sep 1924	21 May 1941	15 Apr 1967	
826	Boots	Mallory	22 Oct 1913	Herbert	Marshall	23 May 1890		1947	1958
827	Edna	Best	3 Mar 1900	Herbert	Marshall	23 May 1890		1928	1940
828	Marilyn	Monroe	01 Jun 1926	Joseph M	Schenck	25 Dec 1878	1947		1947
829	Daniel	Massey	10 Oct 1933	Penelope	Wilton	03 Jun 1946		1975	1984
830	Daniel	Massey	10 Oct 1933	Adrienne	Corri	13 Nov 1933		1961	1967
831	Anna	Massey	11 Aug 1937	Jeremy	Brett	03 Nov 1933		May 1958	1962
832	Dean Paul	Martin	17 Nov 1951	Dorothy	Hamill	26 Jul 1956		17 Nov 1951	26 Jul 1956
833	Marsha	Mason	03 Apr 1942	Neil	Simon	04 Jul 1927		25 Oct 1973	1981
834	Elaine	Joyce	19 Dec 1945	Neil	Simon	04 Jul 1927		11 Sep 1999	none

NO.	Forename	Surname	DOB	Forename	Surname	DOB	Start Year	Marriage	End Date
835	Elaine	Joyce	19 Dec 1945	Bobby	Van	06 Dec 1928		1968	1980
836	Joyce	Mathews	06 Dec 1919	Billy	Rose	09 Sep 1899		02 Jun 1956	1966
837	Joyce	Mathews	06 Dec 1919	Don	Beddoe	01 Jul 1903		1974	none
838	Joyce	Mathews	06 Dec 1919	Milton	Berle	12 Jul 1908		1941	1947
839	Fanny	Brice	29 Oct 1891	Billy	Rose	09 Sep 1899		1929	1938
840	Eleanor	Holm	06 Dec 1913	Billy	Rose	09 Sep 1899		1939	1954
841	Eleanor	Holm	06 Dec 1913	Arthur	Jarrett	20 Jul 1907		1933	09 Jun 1938
842	Patty	Smyth	26 Jun 1957	John	McEnroe	16 Feb 1959		1997	none
843	Prince	Arthur Tudor	29 Sep 1486	Katherine	of Aragon	25 Dec 1485		1501	1502
844	Virginia	McKenna	07 Jun 1931	Bill	Travers	03 Jan 1922		1957	1994
845	Virginia	McKenna	07 Jun 1931	Denholm	Elliott	31 May 1922		1954	1954
846	Lee	Meriwether	27 May 1935	Frank	Aletter	14 Jan 1926		1958	1974
847	Reza	Pahlavi	26 Oct 1919	Soraya	Pahlavi	22 Jun 1932		1951	1957
848	Esther	Williams	08 Aug 1921	Jeff	Chandler	15 Dec 1918	1958		1959
849	Kylie	Minogue	28 May 1968	Olivier	Martinez	12 Jan 1966	2003		none
850	Marisa	Tomei	04 Dec 1964	Dana	Ashbrook	27 May 1967	1999		none
851	Linda	Darnell	16 Oct 1923	J Peverall	Marley	14 Aug 1901		1944	1952
852	Lina	Basquette	19 Apr 1907	J Peverall	Marley	14 Aug 1901		Jan 1929	11 Sep 1930
853	Lina	Basquette	19 Apr 1907	Sam	Warner	10 Aug 1887		04 Jul 1925	05 Oct 1927
854	Lina	Basquette	19 Apr 1907	Teddy	Hayes	07 Sep 1888		19 Oct 1931	1932
855	Margo		10 May 1917	Eddie	Albert	22 Apr 1908		05 Dec 1945	17 Jul 1985
856	Margo		10 May 1917	Francis	Lederer	06 Nov 1899		1937	1940
857	Alice	Faye	05 May 1912	Tony	Martin	25 Dec 1912		1936	1940
858	Alice	Faye	05 May 1912	Rudi	Vallee	28 Jul 1901	1934		1934
859	Alice	Faye	05 May 1912	Phil	Harris	24 Jun 1904		1941	1995
860	June	Greer	09 Sep 1924	Rudi	Vallee	28 Jul 1901		1943	1944
861	John	Gilbert	10 Jul 1899	Leatrice	Joy	07 Nov 1893		1923	1924
862	John	Gilbert	10 Jul 1899	Greta	Garbo	18 Sep 1905	1926		1928
863	John	Gilbert	10 Jul 1899	Virginia	Bruce	29 Sep 1910		1932	1934
864	John	Gilbert	10 Jul 1899	Ina	Claire	15 Oct 1893		1929	1931

NO.	Forename	Surname	DOB	Forename	Surname	DOB	Start Year	Marriage	End Date
865	Norma	Shearer	10 Aug 1902	Irving	Thalberg	30 May 1899		1927	1936
866	Susan	Hayward	30 Jun 1918	Jess	Barker	04 Jun 1912		1944	1954
867	Laurence	Harvey	01 Oct 1928	Joan	Perry	07 Jul 1911		1968	1972
868	Laurence	Harvey	01 Oct 1928	Margaret	Leighton	26 Feb 1922		1957	1961
869	Harry	Cohn	23 Jul 1891	Joan	Perry	07 Jul 1911		1941	27 Feb 1958
870	Michael	Wilding	23 Jul 1912	Margaret	Leighton	26 Feb 1922		1964	14 Jan 1976
871	Michelle	Pfieffer	29 Apr 1958	Fisher	Stevens	27 Nov 1963	1989		1990
872	Elizabeth	Taylor	27 Feb 1932	George	Hamilton	12 Aug 1939	1986		1986
873	Elizabeth	Taylor	27 Feb 1932	Larry	Fortensky	17 Jan 1952	1991	06 Oct 1991	1996
874	Ava	Gardner	24 Dec 1922	Robert	Taylor	05 Aug 1911	1949		1949
875	Ava	Gardner	24 Dec 1922	Robert	Walker	13 Oct 1919	1948		1948
876	Ava	Gardner	24 Dec 1922	Howard	Duff	24 Nov 1913	1947		1947
877	Ava	Gardner	24 Dec 1922	Mario	Cabre	06 Jan 1916	1950		1950
878	Jean-Louis	Trintignant	11 Dec 1930	Nadine	Marquand	06 Feb 1935		1960	none
879	Tina	Aumont	14 Feb 1946	Christian	Marquand	15 Mar 1927		1963	2000
880	Ava	Gardner	24 Dec 1922	George C	Scott	18 Oct 1927	1966		1966
881	Artie	Shaw	25 May 1935	Kathryn	Windsor	16 Oct 1919		Aug 1946	1948
882	Howard	Hughes	24 Dec 1905	Kathryn	Grayson	09 Feb 1922	1951		1953
883	Howard	Hughes	24 Dec 1905	Terry	Moore	07 Jan 1929	1949		1951
884	John	Shelton	18 May 1915	Kathryn	Grayson	09 Feb 1922		1940	1947
885	Johnny	Johnston	01 Dec 1915	Kathryn	Grayson	09 Feb 1922		1947	1949
886	Bob	Hope	29 May 1903	Delores	Reade	27 May 1909		1933	27 Jul 2003
887	Bob	Hope	29 May 1903	Barbara	Payton	17 Nov 1927	1949		1949
888	Glenn	Davis	26 Dec 1824	Terry	Moore	07 Jan 1929	1951		1951
889	Charles	Chaplin	16 Apr 1889	Thelma	Todd	29 Jul 1906	1936		1936
890	Stewart	Granger	06 May 1913	Deborah	Kerr	30 Sep 1921	1945		1945
891	George	Hamilton	12 Aug 1939	Alana	Hamilton	18 May 1945		1970	1975
892	Alice B	Toklas	30 Apr 1877	Gertrude	Stein	03 Feb 1874	1907		07 Jun 1927
893	Gloria	Grahame	28 Nov 1923	Cy	Howard	27 Sep 1915		15 Aug 1954	31 Oct 1957
894	Gloria	Grahame	28 Nov 1923	Nicholas	Ray	07 Aug 1911		01 Jun 1948	14 Aug 1952

NO.	Forename	Surname	DOB	Forename	Surname	DOB	Start Year	Marriage	End Date
895	Gloria	Grahame	28 Nov 1923	Stanley	Clements	16 Jul 1926		29 Aug 1945	01 Jun 1948
896	Norma	Talmadge	06 May 1893	Joseph M	Schenck	25 Dec 1878	1916	1917	1934
897	Howard	Hughes	24 Dec 1905	Marion	Marsh	17 Oct 1913	1932		1932
898	Howard	Hughes	24 Dec 1905	Billie	Dove	14 May 1903	1929		1929
899	Howard	Hughes	24 Dec 1905	Bette	Davis	05 Apr 1908	1938		1939
900	Howard	Hughes	24 Dec 1905	Ginger	Rogers	16 Jul 1911	1938		1938
901	Howard	Hughes	24 Dec 1905	Linda	Darnell	16 Oct 1921	1946		1946
902	Howard	Hughes	24 Dec 1905	Katherine	Hepburn	12 May 1907	1935		1936
903	Howard	Hughes	24 Dec 1905	Gloria	Vanderbilt	20 Feb 1924	1941		1941
904	Howard	Hughes	24 Dec 1905	Ava	Gardner	24 Dec 1922	1943		1945
905	Howard	Hughes	24 Dec 1905	Lana	Turner	08 Feb 1921	1945		1945
906	Howard	Hughes	24 Dec 1905	Rita	Hayworth	17 Oct 1918	1947		1947
907	Howard	Hughes	24 Dec 1905	Olivia	De Havilland	01 Jul 1916	1939		1939
908	Howard	Hughes	24 Dec 1905	Yvonne	De Carlo	01 Sep 1922	1945		1945
909	Howard	Hughes	24 Dec 1905	Jane	Greer	09 Sep 1924	1943		1943
910	Howard	Hughes	24 Dec 1905	Faith	Domergue	16 Jun 1924	1941		1946
911	Gloria	Vanderbilt	20 Feb 1924	Sidney	Lumet	25 Jun 1924		27 Aug 1956	1963
912	Gloria	Vanderbilt	20 Feb 1924	Leopold	Stowkowski	18 April 1882		1945	1955
913	Gloria	Vanderbilt	20 Feb 1924	Pat	DeCicco	14 Feb 1909		1941	1945
914	Gloria	Vanderbilt	20 Feb 1924	Wyatt	Cooper	01 Sep 1927		1963	05 Jan 1978
915	Thelma	Todd	29 Jul 1906	Pat	DeCicco	14 Feb 1909		1932	1934
916	Joan	Collins	23 May 1933	Maxwell	Reed	02 Apr 1919		24 May 1952	1956
917	Joan	Collins	23 May 1923	Sydney	Chaplin	31 Mar 1926	1954		1954
918	Betty	Grable	18 Dec 1916	Artie	Shaw	23 May 1910	1940		1940
919	Joan	Cooper	27 May 1923	Arthur	Lowe	22 Sep 1915		10 Jan 1948	15 Apr 1982
920	Jennifer	Jones	02 Mar 1919	David O	Selznick	10 May 1902		13 Jul 1949	23 Jun 1965
921	Stevie	Wonder	13 May 1950	Syreeta		28 Feb 1946		14 Sep 1970	1972
922	Liza	Minnelli	12 Mar 1946	Jack	Haley Jnr	25 Oct 1933		1974	1979
923	Maria	Ewing	27 Mar 1950	Peter	Hall	22 Nov 1930		1982	1990
924	Robert	Sterling	13 Nov 1917	Ann	Sothern	22 Jan 1909		1943	1949

NO.	Forename	Surname	DOB	Forename	Surname	DOB	Start Year	Marriage	End Date
925	Robert	Sterling	13 Nov 1917	Anne	Jeffreys	26 Jan 1923		1951	none
926	Roger	Pryor	27 Aug 1901	Ann	Sothern	22 Jan 1909		27 Sep 1936	1942
927	James	Stewart	20 May 1908	Gloria	Stewart	10 Mar 1918		09 Aug 1949	16 Feb 1994
928	David	Niven	01 Mar 1910	Anne	Todd	24 Jan 1909	1931		1931
929	David	Niven	01 Mar 1910	Merle	Oberon	19 Feb 1911	1935		1936
930	David	Niven	01 Mar 1910	Rita	Hayworth	17 Oct 1918	1946		1946
931	Oskar	Schindler	28 Apr 1908	Emilie	Schindler	22 Oct 1907		03 Mar 1928	09 Oct 1974
932	Michael	Powell	30 Sep 1905	Thelma	Schoonmaker	03 Jan 1940		17 May 1984	19 Feb 1990
933	Martin	Scorsese	17 Nov 1942	Isabella	Rossellini	18 Jun 1952		19 Sep 1978	1983
934	Emilio	Estevez	12 May 1962	Demi	Moore	11 Nov 1962	1983		1987
935	Corinne	Calvet	30 Apr 1925	John	Bromfield	11 Jun 1922		1948	17 Mar 1954
936	Alison	Steadman	26 Aug 1946	Mike	Leigh	20 Feb 1943	1973	2001	
937	Diane	Cilento	05 Oct 1933	Anthony	Shaffer	15 May 1926		1985	06 Nov 2001
938	Sheila	Sim	05 Jun 1922	Richard	Attenborough	29 Aug 1923		22 Jan 1945	none
939	Steven	Soderbergh	14 Jan 1963	Jules	Asner	14 Feb 1968		12 May 1903	none
940	David	Soul	28 Aug 1943	Lynne	Marta	30 Oct 1946	1976		1979
941	David	Soul	28 Aug 1943	Karen	Carlson	15 Jan 1945		1968	1977
942	Paul Michael	Glaser	25 Mar 1943	Tracy	Barone	01 Nov 1962		24 Nov 1996	none
943	Anthony	Booth	09 Oct 1931	Pat	Phoenix	26 Nov 1923	1981	1986	1986
944	Alan	Browning	23 Mar 1926	Pat	Phoenix	26 Nov 1923		23 Dec 1972	07 Sep 1979
945	Edith	Piaf	19 Dec 1915	Theo	Sarapo	26 Jan 1936		09 Oct 1962	11 Oct 1963
946	John	Pertwee	07 Jul 1919	Jean	Marsh	01 Jul 1934		02 Apr 1955	1960
947	Mandy	Patinkin	30 Nov 1952	Kathryn	Grody	06 Nov 1946		1980	none
948	Harold	Pinter	10 Oct 1930	Antonia	Fraser	27 Aug 1932		27 Nov 1980	none
949	Paulina	Poriskova	09 Apr 1965	Ric	Ocasek	23 Mar 1949		23 Aug 1989	none
950	Vernon	Presley	10 Apr 1916	Gladys	Presley	25 Apr 1912		17 Jun 1933	14 Aug 1958
951	Dwight	Yorke	03 Nov 1971	Jordan		22 May 1978	2001		2001
952	Rachel	Ward	12 Sep 1957	Bryan	Brown	23 Jun 1947		1983	none
953	Lena	Horne	30 Jun 1917	Lennie	Hayton	13 Feb 1908		1947	24 Apr 1971
954	Kimberley	Conrad	06 Aug 1963	Hugh	Hefner	09 Apr 1926		01 Jul 1989	Sep 1999

NO.	Forename	Surname	DOB	Forename	Surname	DOB	Start Year	Marriage	End Date
955	Lena	Olin	22 Mar 1956	Lasse	Halstrom	02 Jun 1946		1994	none
956	David	Hasselhoff	17 Jul 1952	Catherine	Hickland	11 Feb 1956		24 Mar 1984	01 Mar 1989
957	David	Hasselhoff	17 Jul 1952	Pamela	Bach	16 Oct 1963		08 Dec 1989	none
958	Michael E	Knight	07 May 1959	Catherine	Hickland	11 Feb 1956		27 Jun 1992	none
959	Goldie	Hawn	21 Nov 1945	Bruno	Wintzell	23 Mar 1944		1973	1975
960	Dick	Haymes	13 Sep 1916	Nora	Eddington	25 Feb 1924		1949	1953
961	Dick	Haymes	13 Sep 1916	Joanne	Dru	31 Jan 1922		1941	1949
962	Dick	Haymes	13 Sep 1916	Fran	Jeffries	18 May 1937		1956	Jan 1965
963	John	Ireland	31 Jan 1914	Joanne	Dru	31 Jan 1922		1949	1956
964	Richard	Quine	12 Nov 1920	Fran	Jeffries	18 May 1937		1965	1989
965	Jose	Ferrer	08 Jan 1912	Uta	Hagen	12 Jun 1919		1938	1948
966	Herbert	Berghof	13 Sep 1909	Uta	Hagen	12 Jun 1919		25 Jan 1957	1990
967	Jose	Ferrer	08 Jan 1912	Phyllis	Hill	27 Oct 1920		1948	1953
968	Frank	Overton	12 Mar 1918	Phyllis	Hill	27 Oct 1920		1962	24 Apr 1967
969	Kay	Kendal	21 May 1926	Sydney	Chaplin	31 Mar 1926	1954		1954
970	Ava	Gardner	24 Dec 1922	Walter	Chiari	02 Mar 1924	1956		1957
971	Ava	Gardner	24 Dec 1922	Luis Miguel	Dominguin	09 Dec 1926	1954		1954
972	Lucia	Bose	28 Jan 1931	Luis Miguel	Dominguin	09 Dec 1926		1954	1968
973	Michael	Learned	09 Apr 1939	Peter	Donat	20 Jan 1928		08 Sep 1956	14 Feb 1972
974	Carlos	Thompson	07 Jun1923	Lili	Palmer	24 May 1914		1958	27 Jan 1986
975	Ty	Hardin	01 Jun 1930	Andra	Martin	15 Jul 1935		30 Aug 1957	1961
976	Mickey	Rooney	23 Sep 1920	Carolyn	Mitchell	25 Jan 1937		01 Dec 1957	31 Jan 1966
977	Troy	Donahue	27 Jan 1936	Suzanne	Pleshette	31 Jan 1937		1964	1964
978	Tom	Poston	17 Oct 1921	Jean	Sullivan	26 May 1923		1955	1968
979	John	Profumo	30 Jan 1915	Christine	Keeler	22 Feb 1942	1961		1963
980	Rula	Lenska	30 Sep 1947	Dennis	Waterman	24 Aug 1945		03 Jan 1986	31 Mar 1998
981	Rula	Lenska	30 Sep 1947	Brian	Deacon	13 Feb 1949		1977	1981
982	Wim	Wenders	14 Aug 1945	Ronee	Blakley	24 Aug 1945		1979	1981
983	Wim	Wenders	14 Aug 1945	Lisa	Kreuzer	02 Dec 1945		1974	1978
984	Paul	Weston	12 Mar 1912	Jo	Stafford	12 Nov 1917		1952	1996

NO.	Forename	Surname	DOB	Forename	Surname	DOB	Start Year	Marriage	End Date
985	Heath	Ledger	04 Apr 1979	Heather	Graham	29 Jan 1970		Oct 2000	Jun 2001
986	Tom	Poston	17 Oct 1921	Suzanne	Pleshette	31 Jan 1937		11 May 01	none
987	Miriam	Hopkins	18 Oct 1902	Anatole	Litvak	10 May 1902		04 Sep 1937	11 Oct 1939
988	Miriam	Hopkins	18 Oct 1902	Austin	Parker	10 Sep 1892		1931	1932
989	Silvana	Mangano	23 Apr 1930	Dino	DiLaurentiis	08 Aug 1919		17 Jul 1949	16 Dec 1989
990	Robert	Kennedy	20 Nov 1925	Ethel	Kennedy	11 Apr 1928		17 Jun 1950	06 Jun 1968
991	Barbara	Rush	04 Jan 1927	Jeffrey	Hunter	25 Nov 1927		01 Dec 1950	29 Mar 1955
992	Joan	Bartlett	11 Oct 1929	Jeffrey	Hunter	25 Nov 1927		07 Jul 1957	28 Feb 1967
993	Emily	McLaughlin	01 Dec 1928	Jeffrey	Hunter	25 Nov 1927		04 Feb 1969	27 May 1969
994	Emily	McLaughlin	01 Dec 1928	Robert	Lansing	05 Jun 1928		1956	1969
995	David	Lean	25 Mar 1908	Anne	Todd	24 Jan 1909		1949	1957
996	David	Lean	25 Mar 1908	Kay	Walsh	27 Aug 1914		1940	1949
997	Bjorn	Ulvaeus	25 Apr 1945	Agnetha	Faltskog	05 Apr 1950	1969	06 Jul 1971	1979
998	Benny	Andersson	16 Dec 1946	Anni Frid	Lingstadt	15 Nov 1945	1969	06 Oct 1978	Feb 1981
999	Colin	Farrell	31 May 1976	Amelia	Warner	04 Jun 1982	17 Jul 2001		Nov 2001
1000	Winston	Churchill	30 Nov 1874	Clementine	Churchill	01 April 1885		21 Sep 1908	24 Jan 1965
1001	George	Sand	01 Jul 1804	Alfred	de Musset	11 Dec 1810	Jun 1833		Jun 1835
1002	George	Sand	01 Jul 1804	Fredric	Chopin	01 Mar 1810	May 1838		1846
1003	George	Sand	01 Jul 1804	Jules	Sandeau	19 Feb 1811	1830		1833
1004	Robert	Mapplethorpe	04 Nov 1946	Patti	Smith	30 Dec 1946	1967		1968
1005	Barbra	Streisand	24 Apr 1942	Jon	Peters	03 Jun 1945	1975		1983
1006	Amandine	Nicolem	01 Oct 1981	Patrick	Bresson	19 Jan 1970	1994		1995
1007	Andreas	Baader	06 May 1943	Ulrike	Meinhof	07 Oct 1934	1969		1977
1008	Andreas	Baader	06 May 1943	Gudrun	Enslin	15 Aug 1940	1967		1977
1009	Simone	de Beauvoir	09 Jan 1908	Jean-Paul	Sartre	21 Jun 1905	1929		1980
1010	Mistinguette		03 Apr 1875	Maurice	Chevalier	12 Sep 1888	1905		1909
1011	Nicoletta	Mantovani	23 Nov 1969	Luciano	Pavarotti	12 Oct 1935	1995		none
1012	Gabriele	d'Annunzio	12 Mar 1863	Eleanore	Duse	03 Oct 1858	1897		1902
1013	Marcel	Cerdan	22 Jul 1916	Edith	Piaf	19 Dec 1915	1947		27 Oct 1949
1014	Naomi	Campbell	22 May 1970	Flavio	Briatore	12 Apr 1950	1999		2001

NO.	Forename	Surname	DOB	Forename	Surname	DOB	Start Year	Marriage	End Date
1015	Bill	Clinton	19 Aug 1946	Gennifer	Flowers	24 Jan 1950	1977		1991
1016	Jennifer	Connelly	12 Dec 1970	Paul	Bettany	27 May 1971		01 Jan 2003	none
1017	Oprah	Winfrey	29 Jan 1954	Stedman	Graham	06 Mar 1951	May 1986		none
1018	Barbara	Villiers	22 May 1641	Charles	II	08 Jun 1630	1660		1673
1019	Archduke	Rudolph	21 Aug 1858	Maire	Vetsera	19 Mar 1870	1889		1889
1020	Jean	Cocteau	05 Jul 1889	Raymond	Radiguet	18 Jun 1903	1918		1923
1021	Rebecca	West	21 Dec 1892	HG	Wells	21 Sep 1866	1913		1923
1022	Glen	Campbell	22 Apr 1936	Tanya	Tucker	10 Oct 1958	1980		1981
1023	Whoopi	Goldberg	13 Nov 1955	Frank	Langella	01 Jan 1938	1995		2000
1024	Pele		21 Oct 1940	Xuxa		27 Mar 1963	1982		1992
1025	Luciano	Szafir	31 Dec 1968	Xuxa		27 Mar 1963	1997		none
1026	Deborah	Allen	03 Jan 1967	Charles	Stuart	18 Dec 1959	Jul 1989		01 Apr 1990
1027	Juliette	Greco	07 Feb 1927	Sacha	Distel	29 Jan 1933	1955		1957
1028	Edmond	O'Brien	10 Sep 1915	Nancy	Kelly	25 Mar 1921		Feb 1941	Feb 1942
1029	Edmond	O'Brien	10 Sep 1915	Olga	San Juan	16 Mar 1927		29 Jun 1948	1976
1030	George	O'Brien	19 Apr 1900	Marguerite	O'Brien	25 Dec 1910		15 Jul 1933	1948
1031	Dennis	O'Keefe	29 Mar 1908	Steffi	Duna	08 Feb 1910		1940	1968
1032	George Bernard	Shaw	26 Jul 1856	Florence	Farr	07 Jul 1860	1890		1898
1033	Lynn	Rodden	14 Mar 1951	Mark	McTague	01 Mar 1960	1986		1990
1034	Bryan	Adams	05 Nov 1959	Cecilie	Thomsen	29 Oct 1974	1992		2002
1035	Gavin	Macleod	28 Feb 1931	Terry	Cole-Whittaker	03 Dec 1939	1981		1981
1036	Phillipe	Le Friant	14 Jul 1948	Marie	Arbant	08 Nov 1951	1988		none
1037	Rob	Camiletti	01 Aug 1964	Cher		20 May 1946	1986		1989
1038	Jim	Morrison	08 Dec 1943	Pamela	Courson	22 Dec 1946	1965		1971
1039	Burt	Reynolds	11 Feb 1936	Dinah	Shore	29 Feb 1916	1971		1975
1040	Loni	Anderson	05 Aug 1945	Gary	Sandy	25 Dec 1945	1981		1981
1041	Alfred	Douglas	22 Oct 1870	Oscar	Wilde	16 Oct 1854	1891		1891
1042	Dorothy	Stratten	28 Feb 1960	Peter	Bogdanovich	30 Jul 1939	1979		1980
1043	Stefanie	Grimaldi	01 Feb 1965	Daniel	Ducruet	27 Nov 1964	1991	01 Jul 1995	1996
1044	Fili	Houtteman	07 May 1972	Daniel	Ducruet	27 Nov 1964	1996		1996

NO.	Forename	Surname	DOB	Forename	Surname	DOB	Start Year	Marriage	End Date
1045	Pablo	Picasso	25 Oct 1881	Francoise	Gilot	26 Nov 1921	Mar 1946		1953
1046	Pablo	Picasso	25 Oct 1881	Dora	Maar	22 Nov 1907	1936		1945
1047	Eric	Halphen	05 Oct 1959	Helene	Halphen	31 Dec 1958		07 Jul 1984	23 Oct 1995
1048	Evelyn	Nesbitt	25 Dec 1884	Stanford	White	09 Nov 1853	1901		1901
1049	Sheena	Easton	27 Apr 1959	Don	Johnson	15 Dec 1949	1988		1988
1050	Maurizio	Gucci	26 Sep 1948	Paola	Franchi	17 Nov 1953	1985		1995
1051	Marcelle	Auclair	11 Nov 1899	Jean-Paul	Prevost	13 Jun 1901	28 Apr 1926		01 Aug 1944
1052	WH	Auden	21 Feb 1907	Chester	Kallman	07 Jan 1921	08 Apr 1939		1973
1053	Romina	Power	02 Oct 1951	Al Bano		20 May 1943		26 Jul 1970	none
1054	Joy	Dirksen	10 Feb 1929	Howard	Baker	15 Nov 1925		22 Dec 1951	1993
1055	Corazon	Aquino	25 Jan 1933	Benigno	Aquino	27 Nov 1932	1953	11 Oct 1954	21 Aug 1983
1056	Jim	Bakker	02 Jan 1940	Tammy Faye	LaValley	07 Mar 1942	1960	1960	Feb 1992
1057	Claus	Amsberg	06 Sep 1926	Queen	Beatrix	31 Jan 1938		10 Mar 1966	none
1058	Guy	Ballard	28 Jul 1878	Edna	Ballard	25 Jun 1886		1916	1939
1059	David	Arien	07 Apr 1941	Jonelle	Arien	09 Aug 1945		1976	1982
1060	Jean-Louis	Barrault	08 Sep 1910	Madeleine	Renaud	21 Feb 1900		05 Sep 1940	22 Jan 1994
1061	Fred	Astaire	10 May 1899	Robyn	Astaire	14 Aug 1944	1976	24 Jun 1980	22 Jun 1987
1062	Alessandro	Benetton	02 Mar 1964	Debora	Compagnoni	04 Jun 1970	1999		none
1063	Harvey	Beeferman	23 Apr 1942	Bonnie	Beeferman	10 Aug 1942		Jun-64	none
1064	Bob	Dole	22 Jul 1923	Elizabeth	Dole	29 Jul 1936	1972	06 Dec 1975	none
1065	Linda	Ronstadt	15 Jul 1946	Jerry	Brown	07 Apr 1938	1979		1981
1066	Rupert	Murdoch	11 Mar 1931	Anna	Torv	30 Jun 1944		28 Mar 1967	1998
1067	Emperor	Akihito	23 Dec 1933	Empress	Michiko	20 Oct 1934	Aug-57	10 Mar 1959	none
1068	William	Allaria	06 Aug 1954	Nadine	Pillet	18 Mar 1957		27 Mar 1976	18 Dec 1984
1069	Jose	Menendez	06 May 1944	Kitty	Menendez	14 Oct 1941		1963	20 Aug 1989
1070	Jacqueline	Du Pre	26 Jan 1945	Daniel	Barenboim	15 Nov 1942		18 Jun 1967	19 Oct 1987
1071	Daryl	Dragon	27 Aug 1942	Toni	Tennille	08 May 1940	1971	14 Feb 1974	none
1072	Donald	Sutherland	17 Jul 1935	Shirley	Douglas	02 Apr 1934	1965	1966	1970
1073	Jack	Jones	14 Jan 1938	Jill	St John	19 Aug 1940		14 Oct 1967	1969
1074	Victor	Hugo	26 Feb 1802	Juliette	Drouet	10 Apr 1806	1833		11 May 1883

NO.	Forename	Surname	DOB	Forename	Surname	DOB	Start Year	Marriage	End Date
1075	Diane	Coulerie	21 Mar 1951	Phillipe de	Dieuleveut	04 Jul 1951		28 May 1977	1985
1076	Bobby	Darin	14 May 1936	Sandra	Dee	23 Apr 1942	1960	01 Dec 1960	23 Apr 1966
1077	Charles	De Gaulle	22 Nov 1890	Yvonne	De Gaulle	22 May 1900		06 Apr 1921	09 Nov 1970
1078	Princess	Alexandra	25 Dec 1936	Angus	Ogilvy	14 Sep 1928		24 Apr 1963	none
1079	John	Dukakis	09 Jun 1958	Lisa	Thurmond	23 Jan 1956		Jul 1987	none
1080	Chaing	Kai Shek	31 Oct 1887	Soong	May Ling	04 Jun 1898		01 Dec 1927	05 Apr 1975
1081	Emile	Zola	02 Apr 1840	Alexandrine	Meley	23 Mar 1839		1870	28 Sep 1902
1082	Tony	Peck	24 Oct 1956	Cheryl	Tiegs	25 Sep 1947	1983	22 Nov 1990	Jan 1995
1083	Luciano	Pavarotti	12 Oct 1935	Adua	Pavarotti	21 Feb 1936		Sep 1961	1996
1084	Gill	Paquet	08 Mar 1938	Huguette	Meusnier	08 Dec 1940		17 Jul 1968	26 Jan 1996
1085	Dimitra	Papandreou	29 Apr 1955	Andreas	Papandreou	05 Feb 1919	1986	13 Jul 1989	23 Jun 1996
1086	Mary	McCreary	8 Feb 1951	Leon	Russell	02 Apr 1942		1976	1978
1087	Thierry	Roussell	16 Feb 1953	Christina	Onassis	11 Dec 1950		17 Mar 1984	19 Nov 1988
1088	Carl	Wilson	21 Dec 1946	Annie	Wilson	27 Dec 1949		1965	04 Jul 1978
1089	Phillip	Crane	03 Nov 1930	Arlene	Crane	23 Jul 1937		14 Feb 1959	none
1090	Nessim	Boutboul	02 Oct 1912	Marie	Cons	10 Jun 1924		30 Apr 1958	21 Nov 1990
1091	Roberto	Benigni	27 Oct 1952	Nicoletta	Braschi	19 Apr 1960	1982	1990	none
1092	Jojo	Starbuck	14 Feb 1951	Terry	Bradshaw	12 Sep 1948		Jun 1976	1983
1093	Marc	Matz	28 Nov 1949	Maritha	Pottenger	21 May 1952		1982	none
1094	King	Henri II of France	10 Apr 1519	Diane	de Poitiers	03 Sep 1499	1534		10 Jul 1559
1095	Louis	Gaste	18 Mar 1908	Line	Renaud	02 Jul 1928		18 Dec 1950	08 Jan 1995
1096	Shelley	Fabares	19 Jan 1944	Mike	Farrell	06 Feb 1939		1984	none
1097	Michael	Dukakis	03 Nov 1933	Kitty	Dukakis	26 Dec 1936		20 Jun 1963	none
1098	Federico	Fachinetti	11 Nov 1946	Ornella	Muti	09 Mar 1955		25 Jun 1988	1998
1099	Salvatore	Ferragamo	05 Jun 1898	Wanda	Ferragamo	18 Dec 1921		09 Nov 1940	07 Aug 1960
1100	F Scott	Fitzgerald	24 Sep 1896	Zelda	Fitzgerald	24 Jul 1900	01 Jul 1918	04 Mar 1920	21 Dec 1940
1101	Larry	Flynt	01 Nov 1942	Althea	Flynt	06 Nov 1953	1974		27 Jun 1987
1102	Henry	Ford Jr	04 Sep 1917	Kathy	Ford	11 Feb 1940	1970	01 Oct 1980	29 Sep 1987
1103	Steven	Forrest	06 Jan 1949	Jodie	Forrest	08 Feb 1956	16 Dec 1981	07 Jan 1984	none
1104	Gerald	Gallego	17 Jul 1946	Charlene	Gallego	19 Oct 1956	10 Sep 1977	30 Sep 1978	1981

NO.	Forename	Surname	DOB	Forename	Surname	DOB	Start Year	Marriage	End Date
1105	Rajiv	Gandhi	20 Aug 1944	Sonia	Gandhi	09 Dec 1946	Jan 1965	25 Feb 1968	31 Oct 1984
1106	Paola	Gassman	28 Jun 1945	Luciano	Virgilio	06 Jan 1943		1967	1973
1107	Darryl F	Zanuck	05 Sep 1902	Juliette	Greco	07 Feb 1927	1957		1958
1108	Marilyn	Horne	16 Jan 1934	Henry	Lewis	16 Oct 1932		02 Jul 1960	1974
1109	John	Gates	09 Sep 1942	Heather	Gates	08 Jan 1955	1992	14 Feb 1993	none
1110	Strawberry	Gatts	08 Oct 1945	Marshall	Ho'o	06 May 1910	1984		02 Oct 1993
1111	Barry	Gibb	01 Sep 1946	Linda	Gibb	11 May 1950		01 Sep 1970	none
1112	Frank	Gifford	16 Aug 1930	Kathie-Lee	Gifford	16 Aug 1953		1986	none
1113	Johann Von	Goethe	28 Aug 1749	Christiane	Goethe	01 Jun 1765	1788	1806	06 Jun 1816
1114	Paul	Gourvennac	16 Jun 1938	Nicole	Gourvennac	10 Jan 1937		22 Dec 1969	none
1115	Suzanne	Grossman	24 Dec 1945	Jim	Perilman	13 Feb 1939	1992		none
1116	Eva	Duarte	07 May 1908	Juan	Peron	08 Oct 1895	1943	21 Oct 1945	26 Jul 1952
1117	Gregory	Harrison	31 May 1950	Randi	Oakes	19 Aug 1951	1980		none
1118	Gary	Hart	28 Nov 1936	Lee	Ludwig	20 Feb 1936		1958	none
1119	Ko	Hashiuchi	15 Jul 1955	Juli	Hashiguchi	14 Jul 1965	Apr 1992	20 Sep 1993	none
1120	Ernest	Hemingway	21 Jul 1899	Mary	Welsh	05 Apr 1908	1944	1946	02 Jul 1961
1121	King	Henry VIII	07 Jul 1491	Katherine	of Aragon	25 Dec 1485		1509	1527
1122	Karla	Homolka	4 May 1970	Paul	Bernardo	27 Aug 1964		Jun 1990	1993
1123	David	Helfgott	19 May 1947	Gillian	Helfgott	10 Dec 1931	30 Nov 1983	26 Aug 1984	none
1124	Rock	Hudson	17 Nov 1925	Phyllis	Gates	09 Dec 1925		09 Nov 1955	1957
1125	Daniel	Toscan	07 Apr 1941	Marie-Christine	Barrault	21 Mar 1944		22 Apr 1965	13 Dec 1978
1126	Daniel	Toscan	07 Apr 1941	Sophie	Bouniol	28 Jul 1957		18 Jun 1991	20 Dec 1996
1127	Christa	Mcauliffe	02 Sep 1948	Steven	Mcauliffe	03 Mar 1948		23 Aug 1970	27 Jan 1986
1128	Pascual	Maragall	23 Jan 1941	Diana	Maragall	10 Nov 1944		18 Dec 1965	none
1129	Marie	Antionette	02 Nov 1755	King	Louis XVI	23 Aug 1754		1770	21 Jan 1793
1130	Michael	Jackson(II)	16 Apr 1934	Alana	Ladd	21 Apr 1943		1965	none
1131	Joseph P	Kennedy	06 Sep 1888	Rose	Kennedy	22 Jul 1890		07 Oct 1914	08 Nov 1969
1132	William	Masters	27 Dec 1915	Virginia	Johnson	11 Feb 1925		07 Jan 1971	1992
1133	Carolyn	Bressette	07 Jan 1966	John F	Kennedy Jnr	25 Dec 1960	1995	21 Sep 1996	16 Jul 1999
1134	Dirk	Matheson	05 Jun 1959	Susan	Matheson	13 Mar 1958		Jan 1993	none

NO.	Forename	Surname	DOB	Forename	Surname	DOB	Start Year	Marriage	End Date
1135	Lucien	Kouassi	08 Jan 1963	Diana	Kouassi	24 Sep 1962		07 Nov 1991	none
1136	Brigitte	Nielson	15 Jul 1963	Raoul	Meyer	28 May 1960		17 Dec 1993	none
1137	Andrew	Parker-Bowles	27 Dec 1939	Camilla	Parker-Bowles	17 Jul 1947	1965	04 Jul 1973	1992
1138	Andrew	Parker-Bowles	27 Dec 1939	Rosemary	Pitman	19 Jan 1940		1996	none
1139	Gerard	Pigny	21 Sep 1946	Colette	Lacaisse	15 Mar 1953		1971	none
1140	Princess	Caroline	23 Jan 1957	Stefano	Casiraghi	08 Sep 1960		29 Dec 1983	03 Oct 1990
1141	Princess	Caroline	23 Jan 1957	Phillipe	Junot	19 Apr 1940	Dec 1975	Jun 1978	1980
1142	Julie	London	26 Sep 1926	Jack	Webb	02 Apr 1920		1947	Nov 1953
1143	Lois	Fast	22 May 1928	George	Rodden	16 Sep 1916	31 Mar 1948	13 Feb 1949	03 Aug 1965
1144	Robert	Schumann	08 Jun 1810	Clara	Schumann	13 Sep 1819		Sep 1840	29 Jul 1857
1145	Marc	Singer	04 Sep 1949	Amy	Rodden	23 Nov 1949		1980	Aug 1986
1146	Ben	Thomas	07 Oct 1966	Roseanne	Barr	03 Nov 1952	1994	Feb 1995	04 Mar 2002
1147	McLean	Stevenson	14 Nov 1927	Ginny	Stevenson	22 Mar 1945		22 Jan 1982	15 Feb 1996
1148	Jennifer	Jones	02 Mar 1919	Norton	Simon	05 Feb 1907		29 May 1981	01 Jun 1993
1149	Clint	Eastwood	31 May 1930	Dina	Ruiz	11 Jul 1965		Mar1996	none
1150	Bridget	Fonda	27 Jan 1964	Dwight	Yoakam	23 Oct 1956	1997		1998
1151	Eddie	Fisher	10 Aug 1928	Terry	Richard	30 Jul 1954		1975	1981
1152	Jean-Francois	Revel	19 Jan 1924	Claude	Sarraute	24 Jul 1927		07 Jul 1967	none
1153	Jill	St John	19 Aug 1940	Lance	Reventlow	24 Feb 1936		1959	1963
1154	Paula	Prentice	04 Mar 1938	Richard	Benjamine	22 May 1938	1958	1961	none
1155	Matthew	McConaughey	04 Nov 1969	Sandra	Bullock	26 Jul 1964	2003		2003
1156	Tate	Donovan	25 Sep 1963	Sandra	Bullock	26 Jul 1964	1992		1993
1157	Ryan	Gosling	12 Nov 1980	Sandra	Bullock	26 Jul 1964	2002		2003
1158	Tsar	Nicholas II	19 May 1868	Tsarina	Alexandra	06 Jun 1872		26 Nov 1894	17 Jul 1918
1159	Emperor	Hirohito	29 Apr 1901	Empress	Nagako	06 Mar 1905		26 Jan 1924	07 Jan 1989
1160	Melvin	Belli	29 Jul 1907	Pat	Montandon	26 Dec 1928		May 1969	Jun 1969
1161	Rex	Harrison	05 Mar 1908	Carole	Landis	01 Jan 1919	1947		1948
1162	Whoopi	Goldberg	13 Nov 1955	David	Claessen	06 Mar 1959		01 Sep 1986	Oct-88
1163	Elizabeth	Taylor	27 Feb 1932	Stanley	Donen	13 Apr 1924	1951		1952
1164	Vanessa	Redgrave	30 Jan 1937	Tony	Richardson	05 Jun 1928		1962	1967

NO.	Forename	Surname	DOB	Forename	Surname	DOB	Start Year	Marriage	End Date
1165	Vanessa	Redgrave	30 Jan 1937	Timothy	Dalton	21 Mar 1946	1980		1994
1166	Steve	Martin	14 Aug 1945	Anne	Heche	25 May 1969	1993		1996
1167	Jeanne	Moreau	23 Jan 1928	Pierre	Cardin	02 Jul 1922	1962		1974
1168	Jeanne	Moreau	23 Jan 1928	Marcello	Mastroianni	26 Sep 1924	1961		1962
1169	Jeanne	Moreau	23 Jan 1928	Louis	Malle	30 Oct 1932	1958		1958
1170	Joan	Collins	23 May 1933	George	Englund	22 Jun 1926	1957		1957
1171	Joan	Collins	23 May 1933	Harry	Belafonte	01 Mar 1927	1956		1956
1172	Joan	Collins	23 May 1933	Nicky	Hilton	06 Jul 1926	1955		1955
1173	William	Marshall	02 Oct 1917	Michele	Morgan	29 Feb 1920		1942	1948
1174	William	Marshall	02 Oct 1917	Micheline	Presle	22 Aug 1922		1950	1954
1175	Henri	Vidal	26 Nov 1919	Michele	Morgan	29 Feb 1920		1950	1959
1176	Lee	Davey	30 May 1980	Sophie	Pritchard	09 Jun 1977		2003	none
1177	George	Sand	01 Jul 1804	Prosper	Merimee	28 Sep 1803	1833		1833
1178	Gower	Champion	23 Jul 1921	Marge	Champion	02 Sep 1919	1947		1972
1179	Harry	Houdini	24 Mar 1874	Wilhelmina	Rahner	22 Jan 1875		22 Jun 1894	31 Oct 1926
1180	Kurt	Russell	17 Mar 1951	Season	Hubley	14 Mar 1951		1979	1983
1181	Lotte	Lenya	18 Oct 1898	Kurt	Weill	02 Mar 1900	1924	1925	03 Apr 1950
1182	Freida	Weekley	11 Aug 1879	DH	Lawrence	11 Sep 1885	1912	1914	02 Mar 1930
1183	Marg	Helgenberger	16 Nov 1958	Alan	Rosenberg	04 Oct 1950		09 Sep 1989	none
1184	Debra	Winger	16 May 1955	Timothy	Hutton	16 Aug 1960		16 Mar 1989	1990
1185	George	Sand	01 Jul 1804	Michel	De Bourges	30 Oct 1797	1835		1837
1186	Deborah	Sheridan	18 Aug 1956	Bill	Sheridan	16 Jun 1954		14 Feb 1976	none
1187	Marcia	Moore	22 May 1928	Howard	Alltounian,	13 Jun 1937		1977	1979
1188	Dave	Stewart	09 Sep 1952	Siobhan	Fahey	10 Sep 1958		01 Aug 1987	1996
1189	Tony	Visconti	24 Apr 1944	May	Pang	24 Oct 1950	1988	1988	2001
1190	Robert	Urich	19 Dec 1946	Heather	Menzies	03 Dec 1949		21 Nov 1975	16 Apr 2002
1191	Midge	Ure	10 Oct 1953	Annabel	Giles	20 May 1959		30 Dec 1985	none
1192	Miguel	Ferrer	07 Feb 1955	Leilani	Sarelle	28 Sep 1966		1991	2003
1193	Katie	Price	22 May 1978	Gareth	Gates	12 Jul 1984	2002		2002
1194	Shane	Richie	11 Mar 1964	Colleen	Nolan	12 Mar 1965		1989	2002

NO.	Forename	Surname	DOB	Forename	Surname	DOB	Start Year	Marriage	End Date
1195	John	Dee	23 Jul 1527	Jane	Fremonds	02 May 1555		1578	1608
1196	Michelle	Martin	15 Jan 1960	Marc	Dutroux	06 Nov 1956	1982	16 Dec 1988	Aug 1994
1197	Marc	Rich	18 Dec 1934	Denise	Rich	26 Jan 1944		Oct 1966	1996
1198	Nelson	Rockefeller	08 Jul 1908	Happy	Rockefeller	09 Jun 1926	1962	1963	26 Jan 1979
1199	John D	Rockefeller	29 Jan 1874	Abby	Rockefeller	26 Oct 1874	1894	09 Oct 1901	11 May 1960
1200	Franz	Liszt	22 Oct 1811	Marie	d'Agoult	31 Dec 1805	1834		1844
1201	King	Edward VII	09 Nov 1841	Queen	Alexandra	01 Dec 1844		10 Mar 1863	06 May 1910
1202	Debra	Winger	16 May 1955	Robert	Kerrey	27 Aug 1943	1983		1985
1203	Jay	Kay	30 Dec 1969	Denise	Van Outen	27 May 1974	1999		2001
1204	Viveca	Lindfors	29 Dec 1920	Don	Siegal	26 Oct 1912		1948	1953
1205	Viveca	Lindfors	29 Dec 1920	George	Tabori	24 Apr 1914		1953	1970
1206	Margot	Kidder	17 Oct 1934	John	Heard	07 Mar 1945		1979	1979
1207	Margot	Kidder	17 Oct 1934	Phillipe	De Broca	15 Mar 1933		1983	1984
1208	Doe	Avedon	07 Apr 1928	Don	Siegal	26 Oct 1912		1957	none
1209	Milla	Jovovich	17 Dec 1975	Stuart	Zender	18 Mar 1974	1999		2001
1210	Cilla	Black	27 May 1943	Bobby	Willis	25 Jan 1942	1958		2001
1211	Shirley	Maclaine	24 Apr 1934	Robert	Mitchum	06 Aug 1917	1961		1962
1212	Shirley	Maclaine	24 Apr 1934	Yves	Montand	13 Oct 1921	1962		1962
1213	Sarah	Greene	24 Oct 1958	Mike	Smith	23 Apr 1955	1982	1988	none
1214	Audrey	Hepburn	04 May 1929	William	Holden	17 Apr 1918	1954		1954
1215	Jonathan	Ross	17 Nov 1960	Jane	Goldman	11 Jun 1970	1989	1990	none
1216	Joanna	Taylor	24 Jul 1978	Danny	Murphy	18 Mar 1977	2002		none
1217	Jude	Law	29 Dec 1972	Sienna	Miller	28 Dec 1981	2003		none
1218	Jane	Seymour	15 Feb 1951	Michael	Attenborough	13 Feb 1950	1969	1971	1973
1219	Jane	Seymour	15 Feb 1951	Peter	Cetera	13 Sep 1944	1991		1992
1220	Rod	Stewart	10 Jan 1945	Joanna	Lumley	01 May 1946	1972		1972
1221	Rod	Stewart	10 Jan 1945	Bebe	Buell	14 Jul 1953	1977		1978
1222	Rod	Stewart	10 Jan 1945	Marcy	Hanson	22 Dec 1952	1977		1977
1223	Rod	Stewart	10 Jan 1945	Vicki	Hodge	17 Oct 1946	1972		1973
1224	Rod	Stewart	10 Jan 1945	Teri	Copley	10 May 1961	1984		1990

NO.	Forename	Surname	DOB	Forename	Surname	DOB	Start Year	Marriage	End Date
1225	Charles	Lindbergh	04 Feb 1902	Anne	Morrow	22 Jun 1906	1927	May 1929	26 Aug 1974
1226	Mick	Jagger	26 Jul 1 943	Luciana	Morad	03 Nov 1969	1998		1998
1227	Beyonce	Knowles	04 Sep 1981	Jay	Z	04 Dec 1969	2002		none
1228	Nadia	Comaneci	12 Nov 1961	Bart	Conner	27 Mar 1958	1991	1992	none
1229	Prince	Felipe	30 Jan 1968	Letitzia	Ortiz-Rocasolano		13 Sep 1972	2003	none
1230	Gail	Porter	23 Mar 1971	Dan	Hipgrave	05 Aug 1975	2000	2001	none
1231	Paula	Yates	24 Apr 1959	Finlay	Quaye	25 Mar 1974	1999		1999
1232	River	Phoenix	23 Aug 1970	Samantha	Mathis	12 May 1970	1993		1993
1233	River	Phoenix	23 Aug 1970	Martha	Plimpton	16 Nov 1970	1988		1988
1234	Nicole	Kidman	20 Jun 1967	Lenny	Kravitz	26 May 1964	2003		none
1235	Adriana	Lima	12 Jun 1981	Lenny	Kravitz	26 May 1964	2002		2003
1236	Kian	Egan	29 Apr 1980	Jodi	Albert	22 Jul 1983	2003		none
1237	King	Edward VII	23 Jun 1894	Lilly	Langtry	13 Oct 1853	1877		1890
1238	Lisa	Bonet	16 Nov 1967	Lenny	Kravitz	26 May 1964	1987		1993
1239	Rod	Stewart	10 Jan 1945	Kimberley	Conrad	06 Aug 1963	1999		1999
1240	Rod	Stewart	10 Jan 1945	Penny	Lancaster	15 Mar 1971	1999		none
1241	Tom	Neal	28 Jan 1914	Barbara	Payton	16 Nov 1927		1952	1952
1242	Tom	Neal	28 Jan 1914	Vicky	Lane	05 May 1926		1948	1950
1243	Peter	Candoli	28 Jun 1923	Vicky	Lane	05 May 1926		1953	1958
1244	Aleister	Crowley	12 Oct 1875	Leah	Hirsig	09 Apr 1883	1918		1925
1245	Peter	Candoli	28 Jun 1923	Betty	Hutton	26 Feb 1921		1960	1964
1246	Charles	O'Curran	05 Apr 1913	Betty	Hutton	26 Feb 1921		1952	1955
1247	Aleister	Crowley	12 Oct 1875	Rose	Kelly	23 Jul 1874	1903	12 Aug 2003	1905
1248	Louis	Calhern	19 Feb 1895	Ilka	Chase	08 Apr 1905		Jun 1926	Feb 1927
1249	Louis	Calhern	19 Feb 1895	Julia	Hoyt	15 Sep 1897		17 Sep 1927	06 Aug 1932
1250	Louis	Calhern	19 Feb 1895	Natalie	Schafer	05 Nov 1900		20 Apr 1933	1942
1251	Katie	Price	22 May 1978	Dane	Bowers	29 Dec 1979	2000		2002
1252	Katie	Price	22 May 1978	Peter	Andre	27 Feb 1973	2004		none
1253	Imogen	Stubbs	20 Feb 1961	Trevor	Nunn	14 Jan 1940		1994	none
1254	George	Harrison	24 Feb 1943	Olivia	Arias	18 May 1948	1974	1978	29 Nov 2001

NO.	Forename	Surname	DOB	Forename	Surname	DOB	Start Year	Marriage	End Date
1255	Sean	Lennon	09 Oct 1975	Elizabeth	Jagger	02 Mar 1984	2004		2004
1256	Brigitte	Bardot	28 Sep 1934	Serge	Gainsbourg	02 Apr 1928	1967		1969
1257	Elvis	Costello	25 Aug 1954	Diane	Krall	16 Nov 1964		06 Dec 2003	none
1258	Mira	Sorvino	28 Sep 1967	Olivier	Martinez	12 Jan 1966	1999		2002
1259	Brook	Burns	16 Mar 1978	Bruce	Willis	19 Mar 1955	2003		2004
1260	Brook	Burns	16 Mar 1978	Julian	McMahon	27 Jul 1968	1999		2002
1261	Drew	Barrymore	22 Feb 1975	Fabrizio	Moretti	02 Jun 1980	2002		none
1262	Phil	Spector	25 Dec 1940	Lana	Clarkson	05 Apr 1962	2002		2003
1263	Phil	Spector	25 Dec 1940	Veronica	Bennett	10 Aug 1943		1968	1974
1264	Dudley	Moore	19 Apr 1935	Brogan	Lane	01 Oct 1955	1985	1988	1990
1265	Dudley	Moore	19 Apr 1935	Susan	Anton	12 Oct 1950	1980		1985
1266	Piper	Laurie	22 Jan 1932	Gene	Nelson	24 Mar 1920	Apr 1956		May 1957
1267	Tuesday	Weld	27 Aug 1943	Gary	Lockwood	21 Feb 1937	1961		1962
1268	Tuesday	Weld	27 Aug 1943	Elvis	Presley	08 Jan 1935	1960		1961
1269	Natalie	Wood	20 Jul 1938	Elvis	Presley	08 Jan 1935	1956		1957
1270	Gary	Lockwood	21 Feb 1937	Stefanie	Powers	02 Nov 1942	1966		1966
1271	John Drew	Barrymore	04 Jun 1932	Tuesday	Weld	27 Aug 1943	1960		1960
1272	Julia	Roberts	28 Oct 1967	Daniel	Day-Lewis	29 Apr 1957	1994		1995
1273	Natasha	Richardson	11 May 1963	Robert	Fox	25 Mar 1952	1984		1992
1274	Tyrone	Power Jnr	22 Jan 1959	Delane	Matthews	07 Aug 1962		1994	none
1275	Cherie	Lunghi	04 Apr 1945	Roland	Joffe	17 Nov 1945	1985		none
1276	Merle	Oberon	19 Feb 1911	Richard	Hillary	20 Apr 1919	1941		1942
1277	Merle	Oberon	19 Feb 1911	Robert	Ryan	11 Nov 1909	1947		1948
1278	Merle	Oberon	19 Feb 1911	George	Brent	15 Mar 1899	1938		1938
1279	Merle	Oberon	19 Feb 1911	Rod	Taylor	11 Jan 1930	1962		1962
1280	Merle	Oberon	19 Feb 1911	Leslie	Hutchinson	07 Mar 1900	1930		1931
1281	Merle	Oberon	19 Feb 1911	Miles	Mander	14 May 1888	1930		1930
1282	Merle	Oberon	19 Feb 1911	David	Beatty	22 Feb 1905	1950		1951
1283	Merle	Oberon	19 Feb 1911	Joseph M	Schenck	25 Dec 1878	1933		1934
1284	Merle	Oberon	19 Feb 1911	Leslie	Howard	03 Apr 1893	1934		1935

NO.	Forename	Surname	DOB	Forename	Surname	DOB	Start Year	Marriage	End Date
1285	Ruth	Chatterton	24 Dec 1893	George	Brent	15 Mar 1899		1932	1934
1286	Ruth	Chatterton	24 Dec 1893	Ralph	Forbes	30 Sep 1896		1924	1932
1287	Ann	Sheridan	21 Feb 1919	George	Brent	15 Mar 1899		05 Jan 1942	05 Jan 1943
1288	Ann	Sheridan	21 Feb 1919	Edward	Norris	10 Mar 1911		16 Aug 1936	06 Oct 1939
1289	Ann	Sheridan	21 Feb 1919	Scott	Mackay	28 May 1922		1966	1967
1290	Heather	Angel	09 Feb 1909	Ralph	Forbes	30 Sep 1896		1934	1937
1291	Heather	Angel	09 Feb 1909	Robert B	Sinclair	24 May 1905		15 Apr 1944	04 Jan 1970
1292	Constance	Worth	19 Aug 1912	George	Brent	15 Mar 1899		1937	1937
1293	Merle	Oberon	19 Feb 1911	Turhan	Bey	30 Mar 1922	1946		1946
1294	Greta	Garbo	18 Sep 1905	George	Brent	15 Mar 1899	1934		1935
1295	Douglas	Fairbanks Sr	23 May 1883	Sylvia	Ashley	01 Apr 1904	1933	1936	12 Dec 1939
1296	Clark	Gable	01 Feb 1901	Sylvia	Ashley	01 Apr 1904		1949	1950
1297	John Drew	Barrymore	04 Jun 1932	Jaid	Mako	08 May 1946	1974		1975
1298	Olivia	Newton-John	26 Sep 1948	Matt	Lattanzi	01 Feb 1959		1984	1995
1299	Merle	Oberon	19 Feb 1911	Giorgio	Cini	26 Nov 1918	Feb1948		30 Aug 1949
1300	Heath	Ledger	04 Apr 1979	Naomi	Watts	28 Sep 1968	2003		2004

Appendix B - Research

Intellectually, Arthur M. Young was no slouch. He was a mathematician, engineer and inventor who turned his attention to astrology. Many deep thinking people have done this. Most have dabbled, skim-read and dipped their toes. Some stay the course.

Those in business who use astrology to make money tend to keep it quiet. J P Morgan suggested that millionaires don't use astrology, but billionaires do. Billionaires may use astrology, but they aren't going to let on if they do, and of course, we can never be sure that they use astrology because it works, or because, being billionaires, they can do whatever they like.

Arthur Young's interest in astrology was not limited to the usual introductory texts, he actually became an astrologer. Carl Jung did this as well, but Jung's focus was upon the natal chart. Young's focus was upon advanced astrology and in particular he seems to have developed an interest in progressions – the subject of this book.

What Young appears to have believed is that in order for astrology to be taken seriously – as a subject – the association between birth charts and their symbolic progressions would need to be explained, accepted and then tested.

Perhaps anyone who considers astrology and learns about progressions is presented with a difficult choice. Many cannot accept an abstraction (which the progressed chart appears to be) to be anything other than a wishful or artistic diversion from the real-time astrology of the natal chart and the transiting chart, which could – just possibly – be the products of a *causal* explanation for astrology. If I had been asked in – say – 1987 to design an experiment to demonstrate astrology using progressions, I would not have considered synastry to be a possible option as my choice of subject. I would have probably suggested collecting data for people who

♈	♉	♊	♋	♌	♍	♎	♏	♐	♑	♒	♓
Aries	Taurus	Gemini	Cancer	Leo	Virgo	Libra	Scorpio	Sagittarius	Capricorn	Aquarius	Pisces

moved house, or changed jobs or possibly got married, then looked at the positions of Jupiter and Venus progressing in aspect to the 4th, 10th and 7th house cusps of the chart. I would probably have located some really good examples, but, statistically speaking, I might not have had any success because astrology really does function on so many levels it's unlikely I would have been able to boil the subject down to a reasonably simple and testable question and answer that includes the heart of what astrology is – finitely variable, but very variable. The idea that progressions and synastry might work together consistently, which they appear to do, is surprising, but also completely congruent with astrological ideas.

No one appears to have ever worked out a way to demonstrate simply how advanced astrology techniques such as progressions can be utilized to show how astrology works.

This study started out as a personal astrological study, that is: I was curious to obtain a number of examples to test my own ideas and to help me develop a good model of relationship astrology. After a while I expanded this study to look in greater detail at the simple statistics of certain aspects in relationships. This approach is not ideal. The arbitrary collection of celebrity relationship data has been useful, but it does not look or sound like good method even if it actually is. I collected as many examples of relationships as I could in order to assess the common astrological properties of each relationship. Initially for my own curiosity and to improve my own approach to relationship astrology, only later (in Autumn 2002) did the idea for a book about the subject concretise. So in essence this study is the result of just one astrologer calculating the aspects of Sun Venus and Mars in his (large) collection of horoscopes. Other astrologers could do the same thing with possibly even larger collections.

Although the world of statistics is a cold and uncompromising place for any astrologer to inhabit, even for a while (astrology is centred upon individuals, statistics must be applied to groups), it is also a worthwhile way of establishing if the isolated patterns we see when we look at many

♈	♉	♊	♋	♌	♍	♎	♏	♐	♑	♒	♓
Aries	Taurus	Gemini	Cancer	Leo	Virgo	Libra	Scorpio	Sagittarius	Capricorn	Aquarius	Pisces

horoscopes have any singular significance beyond our own artistic reason, or if we are experiencing *apophenia* and only seeing 'patterns in smoke'. I have therefore had to abandon any unscientific illogic in favor of headway. Many astrologers consider this subject to be so complex that statistical method is unsuitable to fathom the truth in astrology and I agree with them most of the time. Any portion of the astrology chart cannot be considered without reference to the whole, and if we do so, we lose sight of the holistic truth. It follows that because all human experience is unique, any investigation of astrological effects in people has to focus on a human experience or characteristic that is shared by a particular division of the population. We could say that receiving a promotion at work is the same for everyone who has ever received a promotion. The problem here is that the experience of getting promoted is a different experience for all concerned. For instance, it might involve taking on more work or less work depending on the level you are promoted to. It depends on the job and the industry what level of responsibility the promotion will entail. Furthermore if you seek promotion *because* you have a large mortgage it is a tangibly different experience (one of relief perhaps) than if you achieve a promotion and then buy a bigger house because you have more money, although the outcome may actually be the same (a big house and a large mortgage). The same goes for other human experiences such as grief, winning the lottery or gaining a professional qualification. The difference in personal experience here will skew astrological data and it would be a very complex exercise to control such a data sample without unduly influencing the result.

Angles other than the seven major aspects were not included simply because at the start of this study this was a manual exercise and as you will have already seen from the matrices I produce, manual calculation of aspects is fairly easy to do with round-numbers, but not so easy for angles such as 72, 45, 36, 135 or 51 degrees or the higher harmonic aspects. As 5200 individual chart-entities needed to be calculated (two per person per relationship) extending the study would have been impossible given my

♈	♉	♊	♋	♌	♍	♎	♏	♐	♑	♒	♓
Aries	Taurus	Gemini	Cancer	Leo	Virgo	Libra	Scorpio	Sagittarius	Capricorn	Aquarius	Pisces

own limitations of time. This is one of the reasons why this study cannot be described as conclusive or 'scientifically' valid in any strict sense, but I do contend it is more revealing of the facts that underpin relationship astrology than any previous study.

I have tried to resolve disputes with regard to dates of birth or dates of relationship through research; those that could not be resolved to my reasonable satisfaction have been excluded and replaced. At the time of writing the main sample contains 1300 relationships, the exclusions list includes 64 relationships with unresolved data. I have 934 public record relationships that have not yet been processed (most of the aspect styles have not been calculated) or verified, and a further 50 or so unprocessed non-celebrity relationships. Included in the new relationships are many marriages of the European aristocracy, but at this time I am purely collecting this information rather than processing. As this study is ongoing, by the time you read this, more examples will have been found, processed, rejected and included. The seemingly arbitrary figure of 1300 was arrived at simply because this was the number I had arrived at when I started to write this book. It would have been an overly complicated exercise to keep updating statistics as the book was written, so although I have continued to gather further relationship data, I have not calculated the collective significance of any new data, I have however, included some of these newly found relationships in the book if they came to light after the sample was completed and if they are relevant to the text. On occasion I have been able to correct dates of birth and dates of relationship in the sample. As noted in the book, when a date of relationship is corrected, (the case of Ronald Colman and Benita Hume is used as an example) the progressed aspects of the relationship change. When this happens with a date of *birth*, both the natal and progressed aspects change. This was the case with the relationships of Humphrey Bogart. Bogie was born on Christmas Day 1899 and according to all sources did not particularly appreciate having a birthday on such a day.[i] His 'other' birthday is 23 January 1899.

♈	♉	♊	♋	♌	♍	♎	♏	♐	♑	♒	♓
Aries	Taurus	Gemini	Cancer	Leo	Virgo	Libra	Scorpio	Sagittarius	Capricorn	Aquarius	Pisces

	1	2	3	4	5	6	7	8	9
A	Day	S.Time	Sun	Moon	Mercury	Venus	Mars		
B	16	5:39	23 ♍ 04'	28 ♈ 36'	14 ♍ 18'	07 ♌ 13'	25 ♒ 34'	1924	bacall
C	9	23:07	18 ♓ 43'	16 ♒ 31'	27 ♓ 51'	03 ♒ 44'	20 ♋ 02'	1944	bogart
D	6	6:58	12 ♎ 42'	21 ♑ 07'	28 ♍ 27'	28 ♌ 30'	26 ♒ 35'	1944	bacall
E	23	8:08	02 ♒ 48'	21 ♊ 35'	11 ♑ 21'	17 ♐ 37'	27 ♋ 07'	1899	bogart

If he was born on 23 January 1899, as some claimed, then his meeting with Lauren Bacall in 1944 was without conventional synastric incident (above).

	1	2	3	4	5	6	7	8	9
A	Day	S.Time	Sun	Moon	Mercury	Venus	Mars		
B	16	5:39	23 ♍ 04'	28 ♈ 36'	14 ♍ 18'	07 ♌ 13'	25 ♒ 34'	1924	bacall
C	8	3:43	19 ♒ 35'	14 ♊ 40'	18 ♒ 45'	24 ♓ 09'	14 ♒ 06'	1944	bogart
D	6	6:58	12 ♎ 42'	21 ♑ 07'	28 ♍ 27'	28 ♌ 30'	26 ♒ 35'	1944	bacall
E	25	0:46	03 ♑ 48'	10 ♎ 30'	11 ♐ 43'	28 ♑ 37'	09 ♑ 04'	1899	bogart

Replacing the false date of birth with the true date produces a progressed Venus natal Sun opposition that was exact between 1943 and 1944. (Because this aspect style happens so often, it suggests that it is pertinent – in calculating aspect frequency, the statistics provide us with a primer.)

What I mean to show with this example is, although my method (investigating and rectifying false data rather than rejecting the data and replacing it with solid new data, as well as using data from secondary sources) is not the preferred model for statisticians, I believe it has been a good way to approach celebrity relationships. There have been numerous occasions when the rectification of false data has allowed me to test my hypothesis; the Bogart Bacall example is just one case, and as the purpose of this study is to locate the main players in relationship astrology rather than to prove the subject, then this approach is valid.

I have, however, tried to be completely objective as far as the selection of subjects is concerned, that is, I have used only the following criteria: that the relationship was real and intimate (this is defined in Part One of the book), that the start date or marriage date is available and not under dispute and that the dates of birth of both parties are available and either

♈	♉	♊	♋	♌	♍	♎	♏	♐	♑	♒	♓
Aries	Taurus	Gemini	Cancer	Leo	Virgo	Libra	Scorpio	Sagittarius	Capricorn	Aquarius	Pisces

undisputed or verifiable within reason.[ii] And although data quality is of great importance, I have preferred to use this opportunity to look at relationships that would not ordinarily have been assessed. Astrological researchers, often wishing to pre-empt any criticism from scientific quarters, generally require their data sample to contain the times and places of birth of those included in order to be able to erect valid birth chart for each individual. They also prefer a primary data source, for example a birth certificate or a biographical citation. (For a data sample of this size primary sources in most cases would be impossible to obtain). Because the subject of this study is planetary synastry, I have not found it necessary to use times of birth in all cases, and, although tracking down celebrity birth data is possible, the serendipitous event where one celebrity whose birth time is known gets together with another whose birth time is also recorded is actually not that common (about a third of my sample includes such relationships). I am able to use dates without times because the daily motion of the Sun, Venus and Mars is such that, in the progressed chart, a difference of 24 hours for these planets will not cause much more than a degree of error. We can therefore be assured that any planetary aspects formed by natal and progressed planets in such charts will be close enough to observe and it is likely that if any aspects that are in reality wide of my accurate criteria (two degrees for each planetary aspect), then just as many that are inside two degrees will fall outside it in the study. The vast majority of natal and progressed charts *that do not include a time of birth* have been calculated for 12:00:00hrs (Noon) GMT. This, I believe, gives a fair result for both natal and progressed planetary positions, independent of the birth place. It should also be noted that I have included all the relationships that fell within my 'relationship' criteria and then I have then decided to reject those whose dates were spurious. This means I have been unselective in the first instance. I have then calculated the aspects in the relationships in the following gradual process.

As mentioned previously I have focused on three 'planets' Venus, Mars

♈	♉	♊	♋	♌	♍	♎	♏	♐	♑	♒	♓
Aries	Taurus	Gemini	Cancer	Leo	Virgo	Libra	Scorpio	Sagittarius	Capricorn	Aquarius	Pisces

and the Sun (the Sun is treated as a 'planet' for astrological purposes). The quantitative data put forward in this book is based upon the dates of the first 1300 public (or celebrity) relationships I gathered minus those that proved to contain false or disputed birth data. The start date is much more important than the actual marriage date, but having said that, I have presumed that where a clear date for the commencement of the relationship is not available (first meeting with an immediate subsequent relationship, first date, first kiss) that whatever astrological factors brought a couple together should in theory still be present at the time of marriage. This assumption is not a particularly reliable one. I can emphasise this point by giving examples of couples whose synastry at the time their relationship commenced was radically different to their synastry at the time of their marriage. But this is a line I had to draw in order to move forward because many relationship dates are, by their very nature, secrets that the people involved must always keep.

In the movie world of the 1930s and 40s when many of the couples in this study got together, courtships were generally quite short in duration as the studio heads did not tend to tolerate unmarried co-habitation.

Colman and Hume, mentioned in the main text, were an exception. Ronald Colman suffered a painful divorce in the early 1930s and preferred not to marry his lover Benita Hume straight away. Benita lived next door, so they had a door constructed in one of the walls of Ronald's house that allowed her to come and go in the strictest secrecy.

It is, however, often possible to research a relationship to an accurate year. An example is that of movie people who meet and begin a relationship while working on a particular film. The basic assumption is, therefore, that the relationship began the same year the film was made (which is sometimes, but not always, different from the year the film was released, usually in the previous year). I have used biographical sources as far as possible and in most cases more than one reference point in deciding upon a start date for a relationship.

♈	♉	♊	♋	♌	♍	♎	♏	♐	♑	♒	♓
Aries	Taurus	Gemini	Cancer	Leo	Virgo	Libra	Scorpio	Sagittarius	Capricorn	Aquarius	Pisces

Using the Kepler astrology program it is fairly easy to generate a large control group to test whether an aspect between the Sun in one chart and Venus in another chart occurs in – say – the trine aspect of 118 to 122 degrees, at levels above chance. This type of control is not really suitable to test the results of this study, which requires a Monte Carlo type of test (where we move all the dates forwards or backwards and then re-check the results. We would have to do this about a million times to really be sure of an effect). A method I could have employed would have involved pairing the individuals in this study together in false relationships. This was the method adopted by Carl Jung for his marriage experiment. In this case, I could have chosen, for example, to marry Charlie Chaplin off to Queen Victoria. The problem would lie in deciding which year they would have met and/or married. Queen Victoria, of course, died when Charlie was twelve years old. So although we can easily compare *natal* Sun Venus and Mars aspects, we can't do it for progressions with the same degree of satisfaction.

The point of the book has not really been to prove astrology, but to produce a work that describes my view as to the role played by astrology in relationships and as such the purpose of the statistical study (which I refer to as a pilot study, but is in fact the state of play at a certain point in an ongoing personal study) has been purely to enable me to focus on areas that appear to be significant. I have used the statistics gathered to point me in the right direction, but the results were not particularly surprising.

♈	♉	♊	♋	♌	♍	♎	♏	♐	♑	♒	♓
Aries	Taurus	Gemini	Cancer	Leo	Virgo	Libra	Scorpio	Sagittarius	Capricorn	Aquarius	Pisces

Table of Aspects Observed and Expected in 1300 Relationships

	nSun – nVenus		nSun – pVenus		pSun – nVenus		pSun – p Venus		Total	
	Obs	Exp	Obs	Exp	Obs	Exp	Obs	Exp	Obs	Exp
Trines	75	58.740	82	58.740	74	58.740	76	58.740	307	234.96
Conjunctions	38	29.370	46	29.370	38	29.370	41	29.370	163	117.481
Oppositions	40	29.370	40	29.370	38	29.370	34	29.370	152	117.481
Squares	41	58.740	62	58.740	66	58.740	59	58.740	228	234.96
Sextiles	65	58.740	46	58.740	56	58.740	62	58.740	229	234.96
Inconjuncts	64	58.740	73	58.740	53	58.740	70	58.740	260	234.96
Semi-sextiles	77	58.740	55	58.740	65	58.740	46	58.740	243	234.96
	nVenus – nMars		nVenus – pMars		pVenus – nMars		pVenus – pMars		Obs	Exp
Trines	52	58.740	71	58.740	65	58.740	73	58.740	261	234.96
Conjunctions	35	29.370	23	29.370	38	29.370	24	29.370	120	117.481
Oppositions	30	29.370	26	29.370	39	29.370	27	29.370	122	117.481
Squares	58	58.740	66	58.740	48	58.740	60	58.740	232	234.96
Sextiles	62	58.740	62	58.740	61	58.740	57	58.740	242	234.96
Inconjuncts	65	58.740	69	58.740	56	58.740	60	58.740	250	234.96
Semi-sextiles	50	58.740	55	58.740	55	58.740	55	58.740	211	234.96
	nSun – nMars		nSun – pMars		pSun – nMars		pSun – pMars		Obs	Exp
Trines	55	58.740	68	58.740	62	58.740	52	58.740	237	234.96
Conjunctions	24	29.370	25	29.370	30	29.370	24	29.370	103	117.481
Oppositions	22	29.370	31	29.370	27	29.370	38	29.370	118	117.481
Squares	59	58.740	63	58.740	69	58.740	72	58.740	263	234.96
Sextiles	42	58.740	52	58.740	62	58.740	57	58.740	213	234.96
Inconjuncts	54	58.740	51	58.740	56	58.740	49	58.740	210	234.96
Semi-sextiles	52	58.740	52	58.740	45	58.740	63	58.740	212	234.96
	nVenus – nVenus		nVenus – pVenus		pVenus – pVenus				Obs	Exp
Trines	34	29.370	67	58.740	37	29.370			138	117.481
Conjunctions	19	14.685	27	29.370	15	14.685			61	58.740
Oppositions	17	14.685	30	29.370	12	14.685			59	58.740
Squares	27	29.370	53	58.740	18	29.370			98	117.481
Sextiles	21	29.370	57	58.740	27	29.370			105	117.481
Inconjuncts	30	29.370	59	58.740	32	29.370			121	117.481
Semi-sextiles	32	29.370	51	58.740	22	29.370			105	117.481
	nMars – nMars		nMars – pMars		pMars – pMars				Obs	Exp
Trines	13	29.370	39	58.740	17	29.370			69	117.481
Conjunctions	21	14.685	33	29.370	11	14.685			65	58.740
Oppositions	15	14.685	30	29.370	15	14.685			58	58.740
Squares	27	29.370	50	58.740	30	29.370			107	117.481
Sextiles	23	29.370	64	58.740	29	29.370			116	117.481
Inconjuncts	35	29.370	61	58.740	33	29.370			129	117.481
Semi-sextiles	24	29.370	63	58.740	29	29.370			116	117.481
	nSun – nSun		nSun – pSun		pSun – pSun				Obs	Exp
Trines	26	29.370	58	58.740	23	29.370			107	117.481
Conjunctions	16	14.685	29	29.370	14	14.685			59	58.740
Oppositions	18	14.685	25	29.370	10	14.685			53	58.740
Squares	25	29.370	60	58.740	32	29.370			117	117.481
Sextiles	23	29.370	50	58.740	29	29.370			102	117.481
Inconjuncts	24	29.370	56	58.740	24	29.370			104	117.481
Semi-sextiles	22	29.370	46	58.740	18	29.370			86	117.481

If you wish to test other aspect types you can work out the significance of other aspects for yourself using the following test as a guide.

If we have 1300 relationships and 360 degrees in a circle and we use a two-degree orb we would expect to use the following calculation to arrive at the number of expected conjunctions and oppositions of the Sun and Venus. (The example used here is progressed Venus conjunct natal Sun):

♈	♉	♊	♋	♌	♍	♎	♏	♐	♑	♒	♓
Aries	Taurus	Gemini	Cancer	Leo	Virgo	Libra	Scorpio	Sagittarius	Capricorn	Aquarius	Pisces

1300 (relationships) divided by **360** (degrees) multiplied by **8.133333333** (possible degrees in a circle where a conjunction can occur[iii]) (Note: if these were trines, squares, sextiles, inconjuncts or semi-sextiles we would multiply this figure by **2**)

= **29.370**

Observed conjunctions (**46**) minus expected conjunctions (**29.370**) = **16.63**

Subtract .5 as a continuity correction = **16.13**

16.13 x 16.13 = 260.1769

260.1769/29.370 = 8.8585938

x2 (chi square) = **8.8585938**

Df (degrees of freedom) = **1**

p = 0.0029

This *p* value suggests there is less than a **0.2%** chance that this result is insignificant or a **99.81%** probability that this result is *not* due to chance.

Those of you who are sceptical because of my lack of a control group might feel more at ease if I mention that the distribution is constant for natal Sun progressed Venus conjunctions in both the first 650 and the second 650 relationships in the study. There are 22 in the first 650 (expected is 14.685) and 24 in the second 650.

It doesn't tell us whether the results of the study are watertight, just that if they are true, then they are significant. It should also be noted that this is only a pilot study. A more thorough Monte Carlo test is required to test the relevancy of the anomalies encountered.

Any post hoc attributions in this study have been with regard to the detail in which progressions play a role in synastry, not in the planets involved. Although I did at first suspect that I might see some kind of a correlation, however small, between the Sun in one person's progressed horoscope and the Sun or Mars in either of their partner's two horoscopes, there is no obvious statistical correlation on the same lines as there is with Venus (although it only takes a keen eye for astrological detail to often see

♈	♉	♊	♋	♌	♍	♎	♏	♐	♑	♒	♓
Aries	Taurus	Gemini	Cancer	Leo	Virgo	Libra	Scorpio	Sagittarius	Capricorn	Aquarius	Pisces

when Sun Mars aspects are individually pertinent): this has been both logically and factually dealt with during this course of the book. When we cut through the 'noise' we tend to reveal 'music'.

Background Arguments

The metaphysical view of astrology suggests that astrology is beyond or above science, another way of describing this proposition is that astrology (or in simple terms, the *meaning* inherent in *time* itself) acts in a way that includes science within its boundaries. And science; the human attempt to understand universal laws of nature lies within this system of meaningful time and is therefore at a disadvantage in coming to terms with the meaning that may underpin the purpose of the universe. A simple analogy will help me to explain this perspective. Imagine a human civilisation that develops in a room with no windows to enable a view of whatever is outside and no doors to enable excursions to measure the outer-world. Let us propose one member of this civilisation has the intellect of Galileo and that they have the mathematical ability to weigh and measure, and also that scientific enquiry is one mode of thought that is inherent in humanness. It would be perfectly possible for this person of great genius to measure whatever is inside this room and to formulate a mathematical theory of its dimensions and physical attributes, despite his imprisonment. He/she could then even begin to formulate theories of motion (though this may take a lot of theoretical serendipity). It would also be theoretically possible for this individual to account for the room's material beginnings (of course it may have come about by some natural accident, and our imprisoned Galileo may be forgiven for hypothesising either design by accident or design by some other unknown intelligence. It is certain that any philosophical hypothesis will be coloured by the information, legends and stories passed on by previous generations occupying the room). In the end all of the theories that emanate from this remarkable individual, whether testable or not, are subject to one all consuming problem: they are based on conditions inside

♈	♉	♊	♋	♌	♍	♎	♏	♐	♑	♒	♓
Aries	Taurus	Gemini	Cancer	Leo	Virgo	Libra	Scorpio	Sagittarius	Capricorn	Aquarius	Pisces

the room. If the room is shaped like a cube, the worldview has to be that everyone in the room lives in a cube-shaped world. This is because the shape of the cubic room can be measured to perfection from the inside, but unfortunately for the inhabitants of the cubic room, they cannot get outside to measure its exterior dimensions, which may in fact be globe shaped, star-shaped or it may in fact be shaped like a cup cake and have a large flashing neon sign attached to its roof. Science has the same problem, it can measure and solve any problem within its jurisdiction, but astrology, because it is apparently a system that describes the meaning inherent in moments in time, may actually be outside this jurisdiction and still be true. As I have already stated, science is subject to time, but time is not necessarily subject to science.[iv]

The idea that astrology is part of the occult, it is supernatural and that it is therefore implausible seems to me to be an assumption made by those who don't want to make any effort to define it or what kind of qualities it would have if it happened to be true.

In my opinion, if astrology is true, then it simply *has to be hard to fathom* for it to have been developed (or for it to have developed naturally) in the first instance.

Of course, if we accept astrology is true and if we recognise it as more than an organising principle, we are also accepting a universe imbued with *meaning* and we are also probably accepting some kind of god-force, as the existence of an astrological phenomenon suggests that there is some kind of intelligent design to the world in which we live. We would probably be forced to accept that it is there for a *purpose* of some sort, although there is no guarantee that we can ever know its purpose. This perspective is not popular with most scientists as it undermines their *raison d'etre*. A universe that can never be completely understood empirically is one that ultimately relegates the work of the scientist to a more limited and therefore seemingly less important level. Astrology suggests that we can never be masters of the universe and scientists don't want to hear any kind of talk

♈	♉	♊	♋	♌	♍	♎	♏	♐	♑	♒	♓
Aries	Taurus	Gemini	Cancer	Leo	Virgo	Libra	Scorpio	Sagittarius	Capricorn	Aquarius	Pisces

that might impact on their status and funding, and they have a very practical point here. There is no better reason to ignore, refute and ridicule astrology than the fact that if astrology were true, it would be inconvenient.

Science, in general terms, has reached a point where it no longer requires the presence of a god or gods to explain the origin of physical life and the universe. This is by no means a permanent solution to the various imponderable riddles and questions that observation of the universe throws up, but it makes some sense at this moment in time: it is as if primitive human beings posit God as the creator until they become able to question and analyse in some critical depth, they then spend some time embarking on useful scepticism at which point they disposit God in favor of Nature, a word which can reliably describe the physical laws of the universe – an impersonal God – then, I would venture to suggest, after an appropriate amount of time, it will become clear that in order to rationalise the many observable truths of life, the idea of God, an intelligent universe, or perhaps quantum consciousness with all its implications of an afterlife, must be reappraised. I think therefore that the current scientific trend of treating our experience of the world rationally is a useful part of a development process. I also have some sympathy with the views of people who are sceptical about astrology. After all, at this moment in the evolution of civilisation, I would rather rely on well measured, well researched, balanced pragmatism than be subject to the inquisition. Air travel is also far more useful to most people than astral travel…at this point in time.

At present astrology is making useful progress, as are many other fringe subjects (subjects that are not seen as worthy enough at present to attract large numbers of prodigious thinkers). Astrology is simply where it should be at this point in time. Although people who champion the use of astrology have to develop thick skins, they can do without ill-informed, unnecessary criticism and bad-mouthing by professional conjurors and comics, but at the moment most are free to practice and make a living doing something they love and importantly their services are well received by

♈	♉	♊	♋	♌	♍	♎	♏	♐	♑	♒	♓
Aries	Taurus	Gemini	Cancer	Leo	Virgo	Libra	Scorpio	Sagittarius	Capricorn	Aquarius	Pisces

their clientele. They can study for a diploma, a degree or a PhD in the subject, and they're getting happier and better at what they do. Eventually, astrology will probably earn some respectability. Slippery or not, astrology – the James Dean of subjects – a rebel and an outsider in many respects and above all of them *a result without a cause* – really is more reliable than one would think.

♈	♉	♊	♋	♌	♍	♎	♏	♐	♑	♒	♓
Aries	Taurus	Gemini	Cancer	Leo	Virgo	Libra	Scorpio	Sagittarius	Capricorn	Aquarius	Pisces

Appendix C – Understanding the Ephemeris

In order to understand the tables used in this book to illustrate progressed synastry aspects, the tables of planetary positions from which each line in these synastry matrices that are used throughout the book, are drawn. These planetary location tables are called ephemeredes. The singular is ephemeris.

The Ephemeris

				Ephemeris for May 1917						
				Time=20:00:00 UT						
Day	S.Time	Sun	Moon	Mercury	Venus	Mars	Jupiter	Saturn	Uranus	Neptune	Pluto
1	10:36	10 ♉ 51'	09 ♍ 17'	28 ♉ 51'	12 ♉ 16'	27 ♈ 40'	16 ♉ 25'	24 ♋ 51'	23 ♒ 24'	02 ♌ 11'	02 ♋ 43'
2	10:40	11 ♉ 49'	21 ♍ 22'	29 ♉ 08'	13 ♉ 30'	28 ♈ 25'	16 ♉ 40'	24 ♋ 55'	23 ♒ 26'	02 ♌ 11'	02 ♋ 44'
3	10:44	12 ♉ 47'	03 ♎ 41'	29 ♉ 21'	14 ♉ 44'	29 ♈ 10'	16 ♉ 54'	24 ♋ 59'	23 ♒ 27'	02 ♌ 12'	02 ♋ 45'
4	10:48	13 ♉ 45'	16 ♎ 15'	29 ♉ 28'	15 ♉ 58'	29 ♈ 55'	17 ♉ 08'	25 ♋ 03'	23 ♒ 28'	02 ♌ 13'	02 ♋ 46'
5	10:52	14 ♉ 43'	29 ♎ 06'	29 ♉ 29'	17 ♉ 12'	00 ♉ 40'	17 ♉ 22'	25 ♋ 07'	23 ♒ 29'	02 ♌ 13'	02 ♋ 47'
6	10:56	15 ♉ 41'	12 ♏ 14'	29 ♉ 26'	18 ♉ 26'	01 ♉ 25'	17 ♉ 37'	25 ♋ 11'	23 ♒ 30'	02 ♌ 14'	02 ♋ 48'
7	11:00	16 ♉ 39'	25 ♏ 38'	29 ♉ 17'	19 ♉ 40'	02 ♉ 10'	17 ♉ 51'	25 ♋ 15'	23 ♒ 31'	02 ♌ 15'	02 ♋ 49'
8	11:04	17 ♉ 37'	09 ♐ 15'	29 ♉ 04'	20 ♉ 54'	02 ♉ 55'	18 ♉ 05'	25 ♋ 20'	23 ♒ 32'	02 ♌ 16'	02 ♋ 50'
9	11:08	18 ♉ 35'	23 ♐ 03'	28 ♉ 47'	22 ♉ 08'	03 ♉ 40'	18 ♉ 19'	25 ♋ 24'	23 ♒ 33'	02 ♌ 17'	02 ♋ 51'
10	11:12	19 ♉ 33'	06 ♑ 59'	28 ♉ 26'	23 ♉ 22'	04 ♉ 25'	18 ♉ 34'	25 ♋ 29'	23 ♒ 34'	02 ♌ 17'	02 ♋ 52'
11	11:16	20 ♉ 31'	21 ♑ 01'	28 ♉ 01'	24 ♉ 36'	05 ♉ 09'	18 ♉ 48'	25 ♋ 33'	23 ♒ 35'	02 ♌ 18'	02 ♋ 53'
12	11:20	21 ♉ 29'	05 ♒ 07'	27 ♉ 33'	25 ♉ 50'	05 ♉ 54'	19 ♉ 02'	25 ♋ 38'	23 ♒ 36'	02 ♌ 19'	02 ♋ 54'
13	11:24	22 ♉ 27'	19 ♒ 16'	27 ♉ 02'	27 ♉ 04'	06 ♉ 39'	19 ♉ 16'	25 ♋ 43'	23 ♒ 37'	02 ♌ 20'	02 ♋ 55'
14	11:27	23 ♉ 25'	03 ♓ 26'	26 ♉ 30'	28 ♉ 18'	07 ♉ 23'	19 ♉ 31'	25 ♋ 48'	23 ♒ 38'	02 ♌ 21'	02 ♋ 57'
15	11:31	24 ♉ 23'	17 ♓ 36'	25 ♉ 56'	29 ♉ 31'	08 ♉ 08'	19 ♉ 45'	25 ♋ 53'	23 ♒ 38'	02 ♌ 22'	02 ♋ 58'
16	11:35	25 ♉ 20'	01 ♈ 43'	25 ♉ 21'	00 ♊ 45'	08 ♉ 52'	19 ♉ 59'	25 ♋ 58'	23 ♒ 39'	02 ♌ 23'	02 ♋ 59'
17	11:39	26 ♉ 18'	15 ♈ 45'	24 ♉ 46'	01 ♊ 59'	09 ♉ 37'	20 ♉ 13'	26 ♋ 03'	23 ♒ 39'	02 ♌ 24'	03 ♋ 00'
18	11:43	27 ♉ 16'	29 ♈ 38'	24 ♉ 11'	03 ♊ 13'	10 ♉ 21'	20 ♉ 27'	26 ♋ 08'	23 ♒ 40'	02 ♌ 26'	03 ♋ 01'
19	11:47	28 ♉ 14'	13 ♉ 19'	23 ♉ 37'	04 ♊ 27'	11 ♉ 05'	20 ♉ 42'	26 ♋ 13'	23 ♒ 40'	02 ♌ 27'	03 ♋ 03'
20	11:51	29 ♉ 11'	26 ♉ 45'	23 ♉ 05'	05 ♊ 40'	11 ♉ 50'	20 ♉ 56'	26 ♋ 18'	23 ♒ 41'	02 ♌ 28'	03 ♋ 04'
21	11:55	00 ♊ 09'	09 ♊ 53'	22 ♉ 35'	06 ♊ 54'	12 ♉ 34'	21 ♉ 10'	26 ♋ 24'	23 ♒ 41'	02 ♌ 29'	03 ♋ 05'
22	11:59	01 ♊ 07'	22 ♊ 44'	22 ♉ 07'	08 ♊ 08'	13 ♉ 18'	21 ♉ 24'	26 ♋ 29'	23 ♒ 42'	02 ♌ 30'	03 ♋ 06'
23	12:03	02 ♊ 05'	05 ♋ 17'	21 ♉ 43'	09 ♊ 22'	14 ♉ 02'	21 ♉ 38'	26 ♋ 35'	23 ♒ 42'	02 ♌ 32'	03 ♋ 08'
24	12:07	03 ♊ 02'	17 ♋ 34'	21 ♉ 22'	10 ♊ 36'	14 ♉ 46'	21 ♉ 52'	26 ♋ 40'	23 ♒ 42'	02 ♌ 33'	03 ♋ 09'
25	12:11	04 ♊ 00'	29 ♋ 38'	21 ♉ 04'	11 ♊ 49'	15 ♉ 30'	22 ♉ 06'	26 ♋ 46'	23 ♒ 42'	02 ♌ 34'	03 ♋ 10'
26	12:15	04 ♊ 57'	11 ♌ 34'	20 ♉ 51'	13 ♊ 03'	16 ♉ 14'	22 ♉ 20'	26 ♋ 52'	23 ♒ 43'	02 ♌ 36'	03 ♋ 12'
27	12:19	05 ♊ 55'	23 ♌ 24'	20 ♉ 41'	14 ♊ 17'	16 ♉ 58'	22 ♉ 34'	26 ♋ 57'	23 ♒ 43'	02 ♌ 37'	03 ♋ 13'
28	12:23	06 ♊ 53'	05 ♍ 16'	20 ♉ 36'	15 ♊ 31'	17 ♉ 42'	22 ♉ 48'	27 ♋ 03'	23 ♒ 43'	02 ♌ 38'	03 ♋ 14'
29	12:27	07 ♊ 50'	17 ♍ 12'	20 ♉ 35'	16 ♊ 44'	18 ♉ 25'	23 ♉ 02'	27 ♋ 09'	23 ♒ 43'	02 ♌ 40'	03 ♋ 16'
30	12:31	08 ♊ 48'	29 ♍ 19'	20 ♉ 39'	17 ♊ 58'	19 ♉ 09'	23 ♉ 16'	27 ♋ 15'	23 ♒ 43'	02 ♌ 41'	03 ♋ 17'
31	12:34	09 ♊ 45'	11 ♎ 40'	20 ♉ 47'	19 ♊ 12'	19 ♉ 53'	23 ♉ 30'	27 ♋ 21'	23 ♒ 42'	02 ♌ 43'	03 ♋ 18'

The above example is of a page in the ephemeris taken from the Astrodienst

♈	♉	♊	♋	♌	♍	♎	♏	♐	♑	♒	♓
Aries	Taurus	Gemini	Cancer	Leo	Virgo	Libra	Scorpio	Sagittarius	Capricorn	Aquarius	Pisces

Swiss ephemeris and comprises the planets positions during May 1917 for each day at 8pm GMT.

On 1 May 1917 at 8pm in London, the Sun was at 10 degrees 51 minutes of the astrological sign Taurus[V] and on the 31st it has moved approximately one degree a day to 9 degrees 45 minutes of the astrological sign Gemini. From 1 May to 2 May the Sun moved from 10 degrees 51 minutes of Taurus to 11 degrees 49 minutes of Taurus, a distance of 58 minutes of arc. The daily motion of the Sun on 1 May between these times was therefore 58 minutes of arc. The distance covered between 30 May and 31 May was 57 minutes of arc, so the daily motion of the Sun between these dates is 57 minutes of arc.

The ephemeris also gives the relative positions of the moon and the other major planets, Mercury through to Pluto. Note how quickly the moon changes sign, in this case from Virgo (♍) on the 1st, into Libra (♎) by the 3rd, Scorpio (♏) by the 6th and into Sagittarius (♐) by the 8th. The moon position, along with all the other planets in this picture, is timed at 8pm Universal Time or GMT, so we are observing their positions in the zodiacal circle at 8pm for each of the days from 1 to 31 May 1917. Meanwhile Mercury is retrograde (it appears to be moving backwards) in Taurus (♉) while Venus moved from Taurus (♉) to Gemini (♊) around the 16th and Mars changes from Aries (♈) to Taurus (♉) around the 5th and the slow movers Jupiter in Taurus (♉), Saturn in Cancer (♋), Uranus in Aquarius (♒), Neptune in Leo (♌) and Pluto also in Cancer (♋), progress steadily in their wider and prolonged orbits.

The daily motion of Venus is about 1 degree 14 minutes of arc on every day in May 1917. This rate of motion can change due to the phenomenon of Retrogradation, which slows Venus' daily motion down to a standstill and reverses her direction.

The daily motion of Mars in May 1917 is between 45 and 46 minutes of arc per day. Mars also undergoes the phenomenon of Retrogradation.

The Sun does not undergo any period of Retrogradation.

♈	♉	♊	♋	♌	♍	♎	♏	♐	♑	♒	♓
Aries	Taurus	Gemini	Cancer	Leo	Virgo	Libra	Scorpio	Sagittarius	Capricorn	Aquarius	Pisces

For anyone born on 1 May 1917, their progressed planets for their tenth year can be found by counting forward 10 days. The positions of the planets from 11 May would be the progressed planetary positions for their 10th year. In 1932, when this person was 15 years old, their natal Venus would move from Taurus into Gemini (this corresponds with the change of sign for Venus on 16 May. In 1937, their Sun would also move from Taurus to Gemini, as it does on 21 May.

Appendix D - Birth Data

Paul Westran 8th Nov 1966, 00:20hrs, Totley, Sheffield, UK, (53N17 1W32), A: from family members.

Sarah Crawford 3rd Mar 1969, 02:06hrs, Sleaford, Lincolnshire, UK (53N00, 0W24), A: from family members.

Chris Evans, 1st Apr 1966, Warrington, UK, no time, noon GMT used, X: date only. Source his marriage certificate printed in UK Newspaper *The Mirror* May 2001

Billie Piper, 22nd Sep 1982, Swindon, UK, no time, noon GMT used, X – date only. Source her marriage certificate printed in UK Newspaper *The Mirror* May 2001

Cary Grant 18th Jan 1904, 01:07hrs, Bristol, UK, (51N27 2W35), B: Lois Rodden quotes the biography "Conversations with Cary Grant," p.1. Reference: AstroDatabank, www.astrodatabank.com

Dyan Cannon 4th Jan 1937, 09:34hrs, Tacoma, Washington, (47N14 122W26), AA: Steinbrecher quotes B.C. Reference: AstroDatabank, www.astrodatabank.com

Charles Prince of Wales, 14th Nov 1948, 21:14hrs, London, England, (51N30 0W10), A: news report, Judith Gee in AFA, 4/1973, news at the time. Reference: AstroDatabank, www.astrodatabank.com

Diana   Princess of Wales, 1st Jul 1961, 19:45hrs, Sandringham,

♈	♉	♊	♋	♌	♍	♎	♏	♐	♑	♒	♓
Aries	Taurus	Gemini	Cancer	Leo	Virgo	Libra	Scorpio	Sagittarius	Capricorn	Aquarius	Pisces

England (52N50 0E30) A: Charles Harvey quotes data from her mother
(Penny Thornton gives 2:00 PM, "just before the start of play at Wimbledon." The Princess has employed several astrologers; separate and various reports have confirmed the time of 7:45 PM) (In Nov/Dec 1997 Astrological Journal, Vol. 39, No. 5, Nick Campion writes, "When Diana's engagement to Charles was announced her birth time was given as 2.00 pm on 1 Jul 1961, Sandringham. The time was then corrected to 7.45 pm and confirmed in a letter to Charles Harvey from the Queen's assistant press secretary as being from Diana's mother (note 15, p 168). This is the time used by Debbie Frank, Diana's astrologer for the last eight years, and I would recommend that it remain the Princess's officially recognized birth time...Debbie Frank told me that in the eighteen months before Diana died she raised the question of Diana's birth time with her, and Diana was insistent that she was born in the evening.") Biography: Sally Bedell Smith, "Diana in Search of Herself," published Aug 1999

Nicholas Campion, 'Diana Princess of Wales', Astrological Journal, Vol. 39. no 6. Reference: AstroDatabank, www.astrodatabank.com.

Camilla, Duchess of Cornwall 17th Jul 1947, 07:10am GDWT, London, UK, (51N30, 0W10), B: LMR quotes Caroline Graham, "Camilla, The King's Mistress," p.1, "just after 7:00 AM." Reference: AstroDatabank, www.astrodatabank.com

Brad Pitt 18th Dec 1963, 06:31am, Shawnee, Oklahoma (35N19 96W55), A: LMR quotes a trusted colleague from Pitt. Reference: AstroDatabank, www.astrodatabank.com

Jennifer Aniston 11th Feb 1969, 10:22pm, Los Angeles, California (34N03 118W14), AA: Marc Penfield quotes B.C. #7097-017113 viewed at Norwalk Records Bureau 7/2001. She was born at Hollywood Community Hospital on DeLongpre but given on the B.C. as Los Angeles, the daughter of John Anthony Aniston and Nancy Ellen Dow. Thought the family name was originally Anistonopolous (or Anistissakis), her dad apparently had legally changed his name prior to her birth.

♈	♉	♊	♋	♌	♍	♎	♏	♐	♑	♒	♓
Aries	Taurus	Gemini	Cancer	Leo	Virgo	Libra	Scorpio	Sagittarius	Capricorn	Aquarius	Pisces

Same data from Sue   Jorgenson 7/2001. Reference: AstroDatabank, www.astrodatabank.com

Angelina Jolie 4th Jun 1975, 9:09am, Los Angeles, California, (34N03, 118W14), AA: Marc Penfield quotes B.C. #0190-046359, B.C. viewed at Norwalk Records Dept, CA (Daughter of Mar eline Bertrand and Jon Voight, born at Cedars in Los Angeles). Same data confirmed by Sue Jorgenson 7/2001. Reference: AstroDatabank, www.astrodatabank.com

Kerry Katona 6th Sep 1980, no time - noon GMT used, Warrington, Cheshire, UK, X: numerous online sources including http://en.wikipedia.org/wiki/Kerry_Katona

Bryan Nicholas McFadden 12th Apr 1980, no time noon GMT used, Dublin, Eire, X: sources include http://www.westlife.org/about.shtml

Delta Lea Goodrem 9th Nov 1984, no time – noon GMT used, Sydney. NSW, X: biography.ms: http://delta-goodrem.biography.ms/

Nick Lachey 9th Nov 1973, Harlan, KN, no time Noon GMT used, X: nick-lachey.net

Jessica Simpson 10th Jul 1980, Abilene, TX, no time Noon GMT used, XX: IMDB.com

Shah Jahan I 15th Jan 1592, Lahore, India, no time, Noon LMT used, X: http://www.uq.net.au/~zzhsoszy/ips/misc/mughal.html

Begum Mumtaz Mahal 25th Apr 1593, Agra, India, no time, Noon LMT used, X: http://www.uq.net.au/~zzhsoszy/ips/misc/mughal.html

Primula Susan Rollo, 21st Feb 1918, no time, Huish, UK Noon GMT used,

http://worldroots.com/gitte/famous/m02/maryenglanddesc1496-130.htm

Gwyneth Paltrow 27th Sep 1972, 05:25pm, PDT, Los Angeles, CA, (34N03, 118W14), AA: LMR quotes B.C. in hand 3/2001. Reference: AstroDatabank, www.astrodatabank.com

Chris Martin 2nd Mar 1977, Exeter, UK no time Noon GMT used, X: www.exetermemories.co.uk/EM/ExeterPeople.html

♈	♉	♊	♋	♌	♍	♎	♏	♐	♑	♒	♓
Aries	Taurus	Gemini	Cancer	Leo	Virgo	Libra	Scorpio	Sagittarius	Capricorn	Aquarius	Pisces

Jean Paul Sartre 21st Jun 1905, 06:45pm LMT, Paris, France, (48N52, 2E20), Francoise Gauquelin quotes B.R. in correction of Gauquelin Vol. 6/727, which gives 3:15 PM. Reference: AstroDatabank, www.astrodatabank.com

Simone de Beauvoir 9th Jan 1908, 04:00am LMT, Paris, France, (48N52, 2E20), AA: Gauquelin Vol. 6/72. Same in "Memoirs of a Dutiful Daughter," 1959. Reference: AstroDatabank, www.astrodatabank.com

Will Smith 25th Sep 1968, Philadelphia, PA, no time Noon GMT used, X: LMR quotes media for date; time unknown. Reference: AstroDatabank, www.astrodatabank.com

Jada Pinkett 18th Sep 1971, Baltimore, Maryland, no time Noon GMT used, X: IMDB.com

Darryl Zanuck 5th Sep 1902, Wahoo, Nebraska, no time Noon GMT used, X: Zanuck - The Rise and Fall of Hollywoods Last Tycoon - Leonard Mosley

Virginia Fox 19th Apr 1902, Wheeling, West Virginia, no time Noon GMT used, X: IMDB.com

Michael Jackson 29th Aug 1958, Gary, IN, no time Noon GMT used, X: Michael Jackson, "Moonwalk," Doubleday, 1988. . Reference: AstroDatabank, www.astrodatabank.com

Lisa Marie Presley 1st Feb 1968, 05:01pm CST, Memphis, TN, (35N08, 90W03), A: Church of Light quotes the L.A. Times on date. Reference: AstroDatabank, www.astrodatabank.com

Emma Thompson 15th Apr 1959, no time Noon GMT used, London, UK, X: LMR quotes Biography magazine 7/2001 for date; time unknown. Reference: AstroDatabank, www.astrodatabank.com

Kenneth Branagh 10th Dec 1960, 04:40pm, GMT, Belfast, NI, (54N35, 5W55), B: MR quotes his autobiography, "Beginnings," Chatto & Windus 1989, p.11, "In the late afternoon . . . about ten minutes to five . . just in time for the football results." . Reference: AstroDatabank, www.astrodatabank.com

♈	♉	♊	♋	♌	♍	♎	♏	♐	♑	♒	♓
Aries	Taurus	Gemini	Cancer	Leo	Virgo	Libra	Scorpio	Sagittarius	Capricorn	Aquarius	Pisces

Rod Stewart 10th Jan 1945, 01:17am, GWT, Highgate, UK, (51N34, 0W09), A: Dana Haynes quotes his wife, Kimberly Stewart, data from him as "just after the pubs closed."

(Debbi Kempton-Smith quoted him for 1:17 AM, rectified by a close friend of his.)

(Angela Thomas misquotes Kempton-Smith for 1946, given in the AFI Journal/1999. Reference books all give 1945.) Reference: AstroDatabank, www.astrodatabank.com

Britt Ekland, 6th Oct 1942, 12:20am, MET, Stockholm, Sweden, (59N20, 18E03) AA: Roscoe Hope quotes hospital records from Jan Gejrot in the Stockholm Dept of Records, AA 12/86. Reference: AstroDatabank, www.astrodatabank.com

Ronald Colman 9th Feb 1891, 06:00pm, Richmond, England (54N24 1W44), DD: Sabian Symbols No.214. PC quotes Sabian Symbols for 6:00 AM. Church of Light had 5:45 AM spec. from Miss Whitney. Grave stone states 1891. Reference: AstroDatabank, www.astrodatabank.com

Benita Hume 14th Oct 1906, no time noon GMT used, London, UK, XX: IMDB.com and other online sources, here are no apparent alternative dates for Benita's birth.

Robert Graves 24th Jul 1895, 04:26am, Wimbledon, UK, (51N25 0W13), B: David Fisher quotes Martin Seymour-Smith, an astrologer and personal friend of Graves in his biography "Robert Graves: His Life and Work." "Good-Bye to All That: An Autobiography," Anchor Books 1988. Reference: AstroDatabank, www.astrodatabank.com

Laura Riding 16th Jan 1901, no time Noon GMT used, New York City, NY, X: Martin Seymour-Smith, "Robert Graves: His Life and Work" p122

Beryl Pritchard 22nd Feb 1915, no time Noon GMT used, Hampstead, London, UK, X: Martin Seymour-Smith, "Robert Graves: His Life and Work" p313

Aleister Crowley 12th Oct 1875, 11:42pm, Leamington Spa, UK, (52N18 1W31), B: Jim Eshelman quotes his autobiography, "Confessions

♈	♉	♊	♋	♌	♍	♎	♏	♐	♑	♒	♓
Aries	Taurus	Gemini	Cancer	Leo	Virgo	Libra	Scorpio	Sagittarius	Capricorn	Aquarius	Pisces

of Aleister Crowley," in which he gives a time of "11:00 PM to Midnight," rectified by Eshelman. Crowley did, however, publish a chart in "Equinox of the Gods" that is set for 10:50 PM LMT. LeGros gave 10:58 PM in AA. Penfield quotes the chart in "Equinox" for 10:32 PM in Mercury Hour Ext., 1/1980. Steinbrecher rectified to 11:04 PM. Reference: AstroDatabank, www.astrodatabank.com

Rose Edith Kelly 23rd Jul 1874, no time, British Isles, place Unknown, Noon GMT used, XX: www.thelemapedia.org

Leah Hirsig 9th Apr 1883, no time, Noon GMT used, Trachselwald, Bern, Switzerland X:source: http://pages.sbcglobal.net/jmaxit/hirsig/pafg06.htm#133 A web site listing "All the Hirsigs on planet Earth"

Ike Turner 5th Nov 1931, no time, noon GMT used, Clarksdale, MS, X: B.C. in hand from Frank C. Clifford; no time. Reference: AstroDatabank, www.astrodatabank.com

Tina Turner 26th Nov 1939, 10:10pm, Nutbush, TN (35N41, 89W24), AA: B.C. in hand from Frank C. Clifford. Reference: AstroDatabank, www.astrodatabank.com

Sonny Bono 16th Feb 1935, 09:21pm, Detroit, MI, (42N20, 83W03), AA: Contemporary American Horoscopes (He told Linda Clark 12:01 PM, but she said that he hesitated. He gave 9:21 PM to another colleague). Reference: AstroDatabank, www.astrodatabank.com

Cherilyn Lapierre 20th May 1946, 07:25am, El Centro, CA, (32N48, 115W34), AA: Contemporary American Horoscopes. Reference: AstroDatabank, www.astrodatabank.com

Ted Hughes 17th Aug 1930, 11:55pm, Mytholmroyd, Yorkshire, UK, (53N44, 1E59), C: Lois Rodden speculative chart, deduced from his poem which refers to his date of meeting Sylvia Plath.

"Our magazine was merely an overture

To the night and the party. I had predicted

Disastrous expense: a planetary

Certainty, according to Prospero's book.

♈	♉	♊	♋	♌	♍	♎	♏	♐	♑	♒	♓
Aries	Taurus	Gemini	Cancer	Leo	Virgo	Libra	Scorpio	Sagittarius	Capricorn	Aquarius	Pisces

Jupiter and the full moon conjunct
Opposed Venus, Disastrous expense
According to that book. Especially for me.
The conjunction combust my natal Sun,
Venus pinned exact on my mid-heaven."

....

"That conjunction, conjunct my Sun, conjunct
With your ruling Mars. And Chaucer
Would have pointed to that day's Sun in the Fish
Conjunct your Ascendant exactly
Opposite my Neptune and fixed
In my tenth House of good and evil fame.
......That day the solar system married us
Whether we knew it or not."

Using wide orbs, on the date they met, Jupiter at 25 Leo conjunct the full Moon at 4 Virgo were conjunct his Sun at 24 Leo and Neptune at 3 Virgo; conjunct her Mars at 21 Leo. "That day's Sun in the Fish .... in my Tenth House," puts his Neptune in the 4th house.

The only planet that does not fit is "Venus pinned exactly on my mid-heaven" as transit Venus was at 17 Aries. The Astrological Journal 5/1988, "time estimated as 3:30 AM" gives an MC of 17 Aries.

Biography: Emma Tennant, "Sylvia and Ted," Holt, 2001. Reference: AstroDatabank, www.astrodatabank.com

Sylvia Plath 27th Oct 1932, 02:10pm, Boston, MA, (42N22, 71W04), A: R.H. Oliver quotes AA 10/1977, from her mother. (PC gives same data as B.C., Massachusetts certificates did not record B.C. before 1940.)

These data give an ASC of 29 Aquarius; Hughes in his letters refers to "that day's Sun in the Fish conjunct your Ascendant exactly opposite my Neptune," with his Neptune at 3 Virgo. Reference: AstroDatabank, www.astrodatabank.com

Grace Kelly 12th Nov 1929, 05:31am EST, Philadelphia, PA, (39N57,

♈	♉	♊	♋	♌	♍	♎	♏	♐	♑	♒	♓
Aries	Taurus	Gemini	Cancer	Leo	Virgo	Libra	Scorpio	Sagittarius	Capricorn	Aquarius	Pisces

75W10), AA: birth certificate in hand. Reference: AstroDatabank, www.astrodatabank.com

Alex D'Arcy 10th Aug 1908, no time noon GMT used, Cairo, Egypt, XX: IMDB.com

Don Richardson 30th Apr 1918, no time, noon GMT used, New York, NY, (40N42 74W00), XX: source is IMDB.com

Mark 'Herb' Miller 20th Nov 1925, no time noon GMT used, Houston, TX, XX: IMDB.com

Prince Aly Khan 13th Jun 1911, 02:00pm MET, Turin, Italy (45N03 7E40) AA: Leonard Slater, "Aly," copy of B.C. printed. Reference: AstroDatabank, www.astrodatabank.com

Gary Cooper 7th May 1901, 05:45am MST, Helena, MT, (46N36, 112W02), DD: Church of Light, 1961. Judy Johns has a time of 7:40 AM. Reference: AstroDatabank, www.astrodatabank.com

Gene Lyons 9th Feb 1921, no time, noon GMT used, Pittsburgh Pennsylvania (40N26 79W59), XX: source is IMDB.com

Clark Gable 1st Feb 1901, 05:30am CST, Cadiz, OH, (40N16, 81W00), DD: Lois Rodden quotes biographer Jean Garceau, "Dear Mr. Gable", 1961, p.18. Reference: AstroDatabank, www.astrodatabank.com

Oriana Fallaci interviewed Gable in the 1940's. His response to her question 'When were you born?' was this:

"February 1st 1901, mademoiselle"

Then he added, with a smile "And I was registered as a girl"

"What?"

"As a girl. But they found it out and corrected it immediately" he concluded seriously. He wasn't amused by the thing. It had happened, that was all, and he said it.

William Holden 17th Apr 1918, 05:00pm CST, O'Fallon, IL (38N36, 89W54), AA: B.R. in hand from Steinbrecher . Reference: AstroDatabank, www.astrodatabank.com

Ray Milland 3rd Jan 1911, no time, noon GMT used, Neath, Wales

♈	♉	♊	♋	♌	♍	♎	♏	♐	♑	♒	♓
Aries	Taurus	Gemini	Cancer	Leo	Virgo	Libra	Scorpio	Sagittarius	Capricorn	Aquarius	Pisces

(51N40 3W48) XX, source is Leonard Maltin's Movie Encyclopedia

Jean Pierre Aumont 5th Jan 1911, no time, noon GMT used, Paris, France (48N52, 2E20), XX, Source is IMDB.com

Oleg Cassini 11th Apr 1913, 02:00am, Paris, France, (48N52, 2E20), B: Autobiography "In My Own Fashion," 1987, p.16. Reference: AstroDatabank, www.astrodatabank.com

David Niven 1st Mar 1910, no time, noon GMT used, Belgrave Mansions, London, UK (51N30 00W10)) X: *The Other Side of the Moon,* Sheridan Morley

HSH Prince Rainier 31st May 1923, 06:00am GDT, Monte Carlo, Monaco, (43N45, 7E25), DD: Church of Light quotes World Astrology. AQR Winter/1958 gives 1:15 AM. Reference: AstroDatabank, www.astrodatabank.com

Gisele Pascal 17th Sep 1923, no time, noon GMT used, Cannes, France (43N33 7E01) XX: IMDB.com

Shirley Maclaine 24th Apr 1934, 03:57am EST, Richmond, VA, (37N33 77W27), AA: Church of Light quotes B.C. Reference: AstroDatabank, www.astrodatabank.com

Andrew Peacock 13th Feb 1939, no time Noon GMT used, Melbourne, Australia, XX: http://en.wikipedia.org/wiki/Andrew_Peacock

Liz Taylor 27th Feb 1932; 2:15 a.m. GMT; London, England (51°N30', 00°W10'); A: excerpt from *My Daughter Elizabeth,* where her mother states: "She was born around 2:00 a.m." Reference: AstroDatabank, www.astrodatabank.com

Nicky Hilton 6th Jul 1926, 08:00am, Dallas, TX, (32N47, 96W49), C: Church of Light quotes Nell Botterill, 1958. Reference: AstroDatabank, www.astrodatabank.com

Stanley Donen 13th Apr 1924, no time, noon GMT used, Columbia, SC (34N00 81W02) X: source is Leonard Maltin's Movie Encyclopedia

Michael Wilding 23rd Apr 1912, no time, noon GMT used, Westcliffe-on-Sea, UK (51N32 00E41) X: source is Leonard Maltin's Movie

♈	♉	♊	♋	♌	♍	♎	♏	♐	♑	♒	♓
Aries	Taurus	Gemini	Cancer	Leo	Virgo	Libra	Scorpio	Sagittarius	Capricorn	Aquarius	Pisces

Encyclopedia

Mike Todd 19th Jun 1911, 01:00am CST, Minneapolis, MN, (44N59 93W16), A: Date on B.C. in hand, no time, Steinbrecher. Time from Gunther Menzer given from a German magazine "from him." Reference: AstroDatabank, www.astrodatabank.com

According to Eddie Fisher and Mike Todd Jr, Todd changed his Birth Certificate.

Eddie Fisher 10th Aug 1928, 07:42am EDT, Philadelphia, PA, (39N57 75W09), AA: Contemporary American Horoscopes

Biography: Myra Greene, "The Eddie Fisher Story," p.24 gives 7:45 AM. Reference: AstroDatabank, www.astrodatabank.com

Richard Burton 10th Nov 1925; 2:30 p.m. GMT; Pontrhydyfen, Wales (52°N17', 03°W51'); DD: conflicting/unverified data for birth time (place and date are not under dispute). I am using the time quoted in *British Entertainers: The Astrological Profiles,* by Frank Clifford: (according to Burton's brother) "midafternoon, just before his siblings came home from school."

John W Warner 18th Feb 1927, 01:55pm EST, Washington DC (38N53 77W02), AA: Contemporary American Horoscopes Quoted BC/BR. Reference: AstroDatabank, www.astrodatabank.com

George Hamilton 12th Aug 1939, 01:51am CST, Memphis, TN, (35N08 90W02), DD: Dana Haynes quotes him, 1997, after insisting that he check with his mom for the correct time, inasmuch as he had given out various times. Linda Clark quotes him for 9:51 AM, written in his own hand, 10/1996. Lynne Palmer quotes him (prior to 1995) for 1:05 PM CST. Reference: AstroDatabank, www.astrodatabank.com

Larry Fortensky 17th Jan 1952, no time noon GMT used, no place, X: source is a biographical note for Liz Taylor in Astrodatabank. Reference: AstroDatabank, www.astrodatabank.com

Alana Hamilton 18th May 1945, 03:15pm PWT, San Diego, CA, (32N42 117W09), A: Lynne Palmer quotes her; same from Dana Haynes

♈	♉	♊	♋	♌	♍	♎	♏	♐	♑	♒	♓
Aries	Taurus	Gemini	Cancer	Leo	Virgo	Libra	Scorpio	Sagittarius	Capricorn	Aquarius	Pisces

quoting her. Reference: AstroDatabank, www.astrodatabank.com

Sybil Williams 27th Mar 1929, Tylorstown, South Africa, no time Noon GMT used, X: IMDB.com

Susan Strasberg 22nd May 1938, 11:30am, New York, NY, (40N42 74W00), A: Robert Jansky "from her personally." Tom Csere quotes her for the same data. In her autobiography "Bittersweet," Putnam, 1980, p.5, she gives 12:00 PM EST.

(Tom Csere quotes Strasberg, "Blanca Holmes rectified the time to 10:19 AM on events that my mother gave to her. I've had it done for 10:30 also; the degrees differ slightly but all the times work out."). Reference: AstroDatabank, www.astrodatabank.com

Claire Bloom 15th Feb 1931, London, UK, no time Noon GMT used, X Source: Leonard Maltin's Movie Encyclopedia

Princess Elizabeth of Yugoslavia 7th Apr 1936, Belgrade, Yugoslavia, no time Noon GMT used, X Source: http://en.wikipedia.org/wiki/Princess_Elizabeth_of_Yugoslavia

Sally Hay 21st Jan 1948, 10:30pm, Braintree, Essex, UK (51N53, 0E32), A: Lenore Canter quotes her, a client c. 1985. Reference: AstroDatabank, www.astrodatabank.com

George Sand 1st Jul 1804, 10:30pm LMT, Paris, France, (48N52, 2E20), AA: Luc de Marre quotes Choisnard, B.C. (Sabian Symbols No.818 gives 10:25 PM. Biographies give "evening."). Reference: AstroDatabank, www.astrodatabank.com

Jules Sandeau 19th Feb 1811, 07:00am LMT, Aubusson, France (45N57, 2E11), AA: Gauquelin Vol 6/724. Reference: AstroDatabank, www.astrodatabank.com

Marie Dorval 6th Jan 1798, 08:00pm LMT, Lorient, France (47N45, 3W22), AA: Gauquelin Vol 5/265 (Lescaut quotes B.R. for 1 Jul 1798). Reference: AstroDatabank, www.astrodatabank.com

Prosper Merimee 28th Sep 1803, 10:00pm, Paris, France (48N52, 2E20), AA: Petitallot quotes B.C., Cadran No.31, 6/1996. Reference:

♈	♉	♊	♋	♌	♍	♎	♏	♐	♑	♒	♓
Aries	Taurus	Gemini	Cancer	Leo	Virgo	Libra	Scorpio	Sagittarius	Capricorn	Aquarius	Pisces

AstroDatabank, www.astrodatabank.com

Alfred de Musset 11th Dec 1810, 11:00am LMT, Paris, France (48N52, 2E20), AA: Gauquelin Vol. 6/593. Reference: AstroDatabank, www.astro-databank.com

Michel De Bourges (Louis-Chrysostome Michel) 30th Oct 1797, Pourrieres, France, no time Noon GMT used, X: http://perso.wanadoo.fr/negrel/hommes/michel_de_bourges.htm

Fredric Chopin 1st Mar 1810, 06:00pm LMT, Zelazowa Wola, Poland (52N14, 20E40), DD: Mar 1, 1810: David Fisher quotes Valerie Matthews letter from Dariusz Proskurnicki in Poland. Reference: AstroDatabank, www.astrodatabank.com

Louis Blanc 29th Oct 1811, no time Noon GMT used, Madrid, Spain, X: http://en.wikipedia.org/wiki/Louis_Blanc

Frank Sinatra 12th Dec 1915, 03:00am EST, Hoboken, NJ, (40N44, 74W02), A: Lynne Palmer quotes his dad. Reference: AstroDatabank, www.astrodatabank.com

Ava Gardner 24th Dec 1922, 07:10pm, Boon Hill Township, NC (35N28, 78W11), AA: Ruth Hale Oliver quotes B.C. (Same in Gauquelin Book of American Charts) (Gardner herself gave 10:00 PM in a Times interview 7 Jun 1975). Reference: AstroDatabank, www.astrodatabank.com

Mia Farrow 9th Feb 1945, 11:27am, PWT, Los Angeles, CA, (34N03, 118W14), AA: B.C. in hand, LMR, same in Gauquelin Book of American Charts and Contemporary American Horoscopes. Reference: AstroDatabank, www.astrodatabank.com

King Henri II of France 10th Apr 1519, 06:00am, LMT, St.Germain-En-Laye, France, (48N54, 2E05), DD Martin Harvey quotes Latin records. Reference: AstroDatabank, www.astrodatabank.com

Diane de Poitiers 3rd Sep 1499, no time Noon GMT used, St Vallier, France, X: http://en.wikipedia.org/wiki/Diane_de_Poitiers. Reference: AstroDatabank, www.astrodatabank.com

Queen Catherine de Medici 23rd Apr 1519, 05:04am LMT, Florence,

♈	♉	♊	♋	♌	♍	♎	♏	♐	♑	♒	♓
Aries	Taurus	Gemini	Cancer	Leo	Virgo	Libra	Scorpio	Sagittarius	Capricorn	Aquarius	Pisces

Italy (43N46, 11E15), DD: agan in AA 2/70 gives "recorded as sunrise." Martin Harvey in Nativitas I says, "No historic evidence has been found." Garicus gave 4:38 AM and Giuntini, 5:23 AM. NN No.537 gives 4:30 AM. PC Q. NN No.537 for 4:00 AM. Holliday quotes two different biographies for 11:00 AM. Reference: AstroDatabank, www.astrodatabank.com

King Henry VIII of England 28th Jun 1491, 08:45am, LMT, Greenwich, England, (51N29, 0W00), AA: Martin Harvey in AJ, Summer/1972, quotes B.R. (In "Nativitas I" he states that Jun 28, 1491 OS is authentic with precision, 8:45 AM. The ASC he prints is 7 Virgo, which computes to 8:45 AM GMT, not LAT). Reference: AstroDatabank, www.astrodatabank.com

Prince Arthur Tudor 29th Sep 1486, no time, Noon GMT used, Winchester, England, X: http://www.thepeerage.com/p10142.htm#i101420

Catherine of Aragon 25th Dec 1485, 12:30am LMT, Alcala, Spain (40N29, 3W22), C: Frances McEvoy writes (4/1993) that Alison Weir in "The Six Wives of Henry VIII" tells of the birth "on the night of 15-16 Dec 1485 in the palace of the Bishop of Toledo at Alcala de Henares in the midst of war." The queen, Isabella, had been in the saddle all day before the birth and rose the next day after delivery to go back on the March , consigning the child to nurses. (She had suffered many miscarriages and lost five infants.)

As Catherine's birth is usually given as Dec 16 OS, she was probably born in the early morning, soon after midnight."

(Penfield Collection gives 2:30 PM, "from royal records which simply state "mid-afternoon." Alleged records not confirmed). Reference: AstroDatabank, www.astrodatabank.com

Anne of Cleves 2nd Oct 1515, Augsburg, Bavaria, no time Noon used, X: Encyclopedia Britannica - www.britannica.com/eb/article%3Feu=7780

Edward Duke of Windsor 23rd Jun 1894, 09:55pm GMT, Richmond, Surrey, England, (54N24, 1W44), AA: Fagan quotes official news release in AA, 11/1976. Reference: AstroDatabank, www.astrodatabank.com

♈	♉	♊	♋	♌	♍	♎	♏	♐	♑	♒	♓
Aries	Taurus	Gemini	Cancer	Leo	Virgo	Libra	Scorpio	Sagittarius	Capricorn	Aquarius	Pisces

Wallis Warfield Simpson 19th Jun 1896, 10:30pm EST, Blue Ridge Summit, PA (39N43, 77W28), DD: .H. Oliver quotes the attending physician in a letter in AA 1/1937, as "he recalled the unusual circumstances of her birth." AA 4/1945 wrote, "The physician, Dr. Allen, said she was born between 9:00 to 11:00 AM." In Wynn magazine 10/1944, Blanca Holmes wrote, "In a letter from her, she gave 6:00 to 7:00 AM, rectified by Homes to 7:00 AM."

(Sabian Symbols No.982 gives 7:00 AM. AA 4/1950 has "between 9:00 and 11:00 AM." AA 11/1957 gives 5:30 AM. PC quotes AA 8/1945 for 6:00 to 7:00 AM. AQ Srping 1937 stated, "We have unimpeachable information of 5:30 AM, Baltimore." Reference: AstroDatabank, www.astrodatabank.com

Queen Elizabeth II of England 21st Apr 1926, 02:40am GDT, London, UK (51N30, 0W10), AA: Fagan quotes official announcement AA 3/l976. Reference: AstroDatabank, www.astrodatabank.com

Prince Phillip, Duke of Edinburgh 10th Jun 1921, 09:46pm EET, Corfu, Greece (39N40, 19E42), AA: British Astrological Association quotes official bulletin, 11/1972. Reference: AstroDatabank, www.astrodatabank.com

Princess Margaret 21st Aug 1930, 09:22pm, Glamis Castle, Scotland, (56N36, 3W00), AA: Joanne Clancy in AA June 1956 quotes British Registrar. (Holliday had 8:14 AM GDT. Penfield Collection gave 9:30 PM GDT "from news." Tucker wrote in AA Jan 1956 that official records are always given in standard time, a statement that has not been confirmed. Fagan in AA Jan 1961 gave 9:22 PM GDT) Reference: AstroDatabank, www.astrodatabank.com

Anthony Armstrong-Jones (Lord Snowdon) 7th Mar 1930, 06:15am GMT, London, UK, (51N30, 0W10), A: Gleadow quotes him, time from his mom in AA, 8/1960. Reference: AstroDatabank, www.astrodatabank.com

HM Queen Elizabeth the Queen Mother 4th Aug 1900, 12:30am GMT, London, England, (51N30, 0W10), DD: Dana Holliday quotes

♈	♉	♊	♋	♌	♍	♎	♏	♐	♑	♒	♓
Aries	Taurus	Gemini	Cancer	Leo	Virgo	Libra	Scorpio	Sagittarius	Capricorn	Aquarius	Pisces

"official bulletin" given in AA Journal for 11:31 AM, Waldenbury, England. Reference: AstroDatabank, www.astrodatabank.com

King George VI of England 14th Dec 1895, 03:05am GMT, Sandringham, UK (52N50 0E30), AA: Fagan quotes official record in AA, 9/1940. (It would seem that Fagan was giving London time of 3:05 AM GMT, as in Sandringham, the time was a half hour later, which would make the birth at 3:35 AM Sandringham time). Reference: AstroDatabank, www.astrodatabank.com

Crown Prince Felipe Borbon of Spain 30th Jan 1968, 12:45pm MET, Madrid, Spain (40N24 3W41), A: Nuria Lopez quotes Madrid newspaper.

Felipe Juan Pablo Alfonso de Todos los Santos Borbon Schleswig-Holstein Borbon Sonderberg Glucksburg . Reference: AstroDatabank, www.astrodatabank.com

Letizia Ortiz Rocasolano 15th Sep 1972, Oviedo, Spain, no time Noon GMT used, X: numerous online biographies give the same date including: http://www.nationmaster.com/encyclopedia/Letizia%2C-Princess-of-Asturias

Paula Yates 24th Apr 1959, 12:10pm GDT, Colwyn Bay, Wales (53N18, 3W43), AA: Frank Clifford quotes a photocopy of the Daily Mail 1/24/1998, p.42 in which Paula's mother was quoted as saying she was born at 12.25 in the morning, assumed to be 00:25 AM. Now, in The Sunday Times Magazine (11/2/01), a new article on Paula's childhood states that her mother recorded her birth in a fancy baby book: "Paula was born on Apr 24, 1959, at 12.10 PM. Elaine recorded the details in "The First Seven Years: a Record Book for Mother and Child"; weight, 7lb 3oz; eyes, blue; hair, blonde; brows, blonde; lashes, blonde; complexion, fair." Reference: AstroDatabank, www.astrodatabank.com

Bob Geldof 5th Oct 1951, 02:20pm, GDT, Dublin, Eire, (53N20 6W15), A: David Fisher quotes a letter from Jo Logan, editor of "Prediction" on 5/14/1986 quoting Geldof verbally, and his press agent. Reference: AstroDatabank, www.astrodatabank.com

♈	♉	♊	♋	♌	♍	♎	♏	♐	♑	♒	♓
Aries	Taurus	Gemini	Cancer	Leo	Virgo	Libra	Scorpio	Sagittarius	Capricorn	Aquarius	Pisces

Michael Hutchence 22nd Jan 1960, 05:00am AEST, Sydney, Australia (33S52 151E13), B: Data UK quotes Toby Cresswell's interview in Juice Magazine, "A Life Lived INXS." Reference: AstroDatabank, www.astro-databank.com

Laurence Olivier 22nd May 1907, 05:00am GMT, Dorking, UK (51N14 0W20), AA: Dana Holliday quotes J. Cottrel, "Laurence Olivier," 1975. Reference: AstroDatabank, www.astrodatabank.com

Vivien Leigh 5th Nov 1913, 05:16pm LMT, Darjeeling, India (27N02 88E16), B: Dana Holliday quotes Cottrell, "Lawrence Olivier," 1975, for Leigh's time of birth as, "sunset" (Sunset time given by courtesy of the Los Angeles Library Science Dept. PC gives sunset as 5:30 PM IST, adding that Sabian Symbols gives 3:00 AM. Sabian Symbols No.563 has no time specified.)

Data given as LMT. Reference: AstroDatabank, www.astrodatabank.com

John Lennon 9th Oct 1940, 06:30pm GDT, Liverpool, UK, (53N25 2W55), A: LMR quotes his step-mom, Pauline Stone, by correspondence, "from Lennon's aunt who was present at the birth." Reference: AstroDatabank, www.astrodatabank.com

Cynthia Powell 10th Sep 1939 no time Noon GMT used, Blackpool, UK, X: media reports and "Lennon the definitive Biography".

Yoko Ono 18th Feb 1933 08:30pm JST, Tokyo, Japan (35N42 139E46), A: Roger Elliott quotes her, client (Church of Light gives the same from Don Singleton in NY Daily News 11/22/71). Reference: AstroDatabank, www.astrodatabank.com

May Pang 24th Oct 1950, 07:35am EST, Manhattan, NY (40N46 73W59), A: Shelley Ackerman quotes her, a friend: www.maypang.com. Reference: AstroDatabank, www.astrodatabank.com

Paul McCartney 18th Jun 1942, 2pm, Liverpool, UK (53N25 2W55), Source Astrodatabank RR A: Nalini Kanta Das (Tom Hopke) quotes Linda McCartney for the data of Paul and her, presented in an article printed in

♈	♉	♊	♋	♌	♍	♎	♏	♐	♑	♒	♓
Aries	Taurus	Gemini	Cancer	Leo	Virgo	Libra	Scorpio	Sagittarius	Capricorn	Aquarius	Pisces

ACVA Journal Summer 1998, Vol 4 No.1. Dean DeLucia quotes Nalini for the data in 1994. David Goldstein confirms the data by email in Jan 1999. Reference: AstroDatabank, www.astrodatabank.com

Linda Eastman 24th Sep 1941, 10:00am EDT, New York, NY (40N42 74W00), A: David Goldstein quotes Nalini Kanta Das (Tom Hopke) for data from her, given in an article in ACVA Journal Summer 1998 Vol 4 No.1. Reference: AstroDatabank, www.astrodatabank.com

Heather Mills McCartney 12th Jan 1968 no time RR X. Midday used. Source: Heather Mills McCartney and Pamela Cockerill, *A Single Step,* Warner Books, 2002 quote: Chapter 1. Reference: AstroDatabank, www.astrodatabank.com

George Harrison 24th Feb 1943, 11:42pm GDT, Liverpool, UK (53N25 2W55), A: Mercury Hour, 4/1993, p.1, "Janice Giles of New Zealand sent us some interesting news from George Harrison who wrote, "For instance, I only learned recently after all these years that the date and time of my own birth have always been off by one calendar day and about a half hour on the clock," reported in Billboard magazine, 12/1992." On a prior ocassion, he had given out Feb 25, 1943, 00:05 AM GDT, (23 minutes later). Tashi Grady met Harrison in 7/1993 and he said that he and his astrologer had rectified the time to 11:52:19 PM.

On 2/24/2002, Jayj Jacobs wrote, "Early this morning I was listening to a Westwood One broadcast syndicated on SF's fabled KFRC. The show, 'Beatle Brunch' was on George Harrison, a bio & music compilation, in which they interviewed George's sister, on the air.

She said she was confused by her brother's statements concerning the change in his birth date & time *Because* she had a birth record in hand — in her mother's handwriting — saying he was born at 12:10 am on the 25th. She also said that her mother was awake and aware of the birth.

She commented that in those days, "before digital clocks an all that" that spoken remarks re time were approximated to the nearest 5 minutes or so, "'ten of' or 'a quarter after' and such". That should make 12:10 accu-

♈	♉	♊	♋	♌	♍	♎	♏	♐	♑	♒	♓
Aries	Taurus	Gemini	Cancer	Leo	Virgo	Libra	Scorpio	Sagittarius	Capricorn	Aquarius	Pisces

rate within 2-3 minutes either way, about as close as we ever get — without a stopwatch holding astrologer on the premises. Reference: AstroDatabank, www.astrodatabank.com

Patricia Anne Boyd 17th Mar 1944 in Taunton, Somerset, no time Noon GMT used. X: Her *year* of birth has been miscalculated in some publications, but according to her marriage certificate she was 21 years old on 21st Jan 1966 and was therefore born in 1944. Source: Geoffrey Giuliano *The Illustrated George Harrison*, Chartwell Books, Inc. 1993, p.28. She wrote this in the Jul 1965 edition of 16 Magazine: *My birthday,* Pat Heidenfelder of St Louis, Mo, *was on March 17th, and I was 21 - or, as we say here, I "got a key to the door."*

Olivia Arias Harrison 18th May 1948, no time Noon GMT used, Mexico City, Mexico, XX: IMDB.com

Eric Clapton 30th Mar 1945, 20:45hrs was born in Ripley, Surrey, UK, 51N19, 00W34,DD:Source: Astrodatabank, the Kepler database and a quote from an online biography at this address:

http://www.sing365.com/music/lyric.nsf/singerUnid/FD96AB79BED4 598248256877002C0DAE noting quite specifically: 'Eric Patrick Clapton was born on Mar 30, 1945, in his grandparent's house at 1, The Green, Ripley, Surrey, England.' RR DD

Kim Novak 13th Feb 1933, 06:13am CST, Chicago, IL (41N52 87W39), AA: B.C. in hand from the Wilsons. Reference: AstroDatabank, www.astrodatabank.com

Sammy Davis Jnr 8th Dec 1925, 01:20pm EST, New York City, NY, (40N42 74W00), DD: LeGros in AA 10/1957. Old-file has 1:11 PM. Reference: AstroDatabank, www.astrodatabank.com

John Profumo Although there is a dispute as to Profumo's date of birth, I am satisfied that his true date of birth is 30th Jan 1915 in Lemsfort, UK. Profumo has worked for the Toynbee Hall charitable foundation since falling from grace in 1963. He is still working for them at the time of writing in 2004 and a biography on their web site http://www.beaconfel-

♈	♉	♊	♋	♌	♍	♎	♏	♐	♑	♒	♓
Aries	Taurus	Gemini	Cancer	Leo	Virgo	Libra	Scorpio	Sagittarius	Capricorn	Aquarius	Pisces

lowship.org.uk/biography2003_15.asp written in 2003/04 states he still working for them aged 88. If his other claimed date of birth were true (19 Oct 1912), he would be 92 years old. I feel the emphasis placed upon his age in this 'semi-official' biography is significant enough for me to conclude his 1915 birth date, given in Who's Who in 1971; in records that attest to him being one of the youngest MP's in the commons, elected for Northamptonshire, Kettering at the age of 25 years and 36 days for parliament on 6th Mar 1940 (a leap year) and in other biographical material.

Christine Keeler, 22nd Feb 1942, 11:15am, London, UK, A: Abayakoon in AQ 12/1963 vouches for the accuracy of the data. Reference: AstroDatabank, www.astrodatabank.com

Ellen Degeneres 26th Jan 1958, 03:30am, Metairie, LA, (29N59, 90W09), C: LMR quotes date from her autobiography 1995, Bantam Books, NY, p.3. On Access Hollywood 9/20/99, she said, "Now I have another label. I'm a lesbian Aquarian Sagittarian." With 15 Sag rising, this comes out to 3:30 AM. Reference: AstroDatabank, www.astrodatabank.com

Anne Heche 25th Jun 1969, 04:51pm, Cleveland, OH, (41N29, 81W41), AA: B.C. in hand, LMR. Reference: AstroDatabank, www.astrodatabank.com

Portia de Rossi, 31st Jan 1973, Geelong, Australia, no time Noon GMT used, X: sources include IMDB.com

Wystan Hugh Auden, 21st Feb 1907, 06:45am, York, England (53N58, 1W05), DD: Penfield Collection spec. Dave Hayward finds this time to work well with progressions and transits.

Fowlers gives 11:00 PM LMT, no source. Reference: AstroDatabank, www.astrodatabank.com

Chester Kallman, 7th Jan 1921, 09:30pm, Brooklyn, NY, (40N38, 73W56), B: Sy Scholfield quotes Dorothy J. Farnan, "Auden in Love," Longon: Faber & Faber, p.44. (Note: Farnan was one of Kallman's stepmothers). Reference: AstroDatabank, www.astrodatabank.com

♈	♉	♊	♋	♌	♍	♎	♏	♐	♑	♒	♓
Aries	Taurus	Gemini	Cancer	Leo	Virgo	Libra	Scorpio	Sagittarius	Capricorn	Aquarius	Pisces

Christopher Isherwood, 26th Aug 1904, 11:45pm, Disley, England, (53N21, 2W02), B: Penfield Collection quotes his autobiography, "Kathleen and Frank," p.271, verified by LMR. Reference: AstroDatabank, www.astrodatabank.com

Gertrude Stein, 3rd Feb 1874, 08:00am, Allegheny Co, PA, (40N30, 79W50), B: LMR quotes James R. Mellow "Charmed Circle," which relates that she was informed by her dad that her birth was "about 8:00 AM." Reference: AstroDatabank, www.astrodatabank.com

Alice B. Toklas, 30th Apr 1877, San Francisco, CA, no time Noon GMT used, X: Sources include http://en.wikipedia. org/wiki/Alice_B._Toklas

Romaine Brooks, 1st May 1874, Rome, Italy, no time Noon GMT used, X: Sources include http://home.earthlink.net/~bigsismedia/brooks-bio.html

Natalie Barney, 31st Oct 1876, Dayton, OH, no time Noon GMT used, X: sources include http://en.wikipedia.org/wiki/Natalie_Clifford_Barney

Benjamin Britten, 22nd Nov 1913, 07:00pm, Lowestoft, England, (52N29, 1E45), A: Astrology Quarterly quotes his personal friend, Spring/1952. Reference: AstroDatabank, www.astrodatabank.com

Peter Pears, 22nd Jun 1910, Fanham, Surrey, England, no time Noon GMT used, X: sources include http://en.wikipedia.org/wiki/Peter_Pears

Don Bachardy, 18th May 1934, Los Angeles, CA, no time Noon GMT used, X: sources include http://www.glbtq.com/arts/bachardy_d.html

All dates prior to 1752, which were not already converted, have been converted to New System (NS) dates using Cosmic Patterns Kepler astrological software.

♈	♉	♊	♋	♌	♍	♎	♏	♐	♑	♒	♓
Aries	Taurus	Gemini	Cancer	Leo	Virgo	Libra	Scorpio	Sagittarius	Capricorn	Aquarius	Pisces

Bibliography

Source Biographies:

Grace – The Secret Lives of a Princess, James Spada, Penguin, 1988

Grace - Robert Lacey, GP Putnams, 1994

Grace Kelly's Men – Jane Ellen Wayne, SMP, 1991

Merle – A Biography of Merle Oberon, Charles Higham and Roy Moseley, NEL, 1984

Ginger – My Story, Ginger Rogers, Headline, 1991

Zanuck –The Rise and Fall of Hollywood's Last Tycoon, Leonard Mosley, Granada, 1984

The Other Side of the Moon – The Life of David Niven, Sheridan Morley, Coronet, 1986

Liz - An Intimate Biography of Elizabeth Taylor - C. David Heymann, Mandarin, 1996

Elizabeth Taylor – A Celebration – Sheridan Morley, Pavilion Books, 1989

Been There, Done That – Eddie Fisher, Arrow, 1999

Joan Collins - Second Act, Joan Collins, Boxtree, 1996

Joan Collins - Past Imperfect, Joan Collins, Coronet, 1979

Scarlet O'Hara's Younger Sister, Evelyn Keyes, Lyle Stuart, 1977

I'll Think About That Tomorrow, Evelyn Keyes, Dutton, 1991

Warren Beatty – The Sexiest Man Alive, Ellis Amburn, Virgin, 2002

The Times We Had –Marion Davies, Ballantine Books, 1990

Charlie Chaplin and his Times, Kenneth S Lynn, Aurum Books, 2002

La Moreau – A Biography of Jeanne Moreau, Marianne Gray, Warner Books, 1995

Bardot, Deneuve and Fonda – The Memoirs of Roger Vadim, Roger Vadim, Weidenfeld and Nicolson, 1986

Memoirs of the Devil – Roger Vadim, Hutchinson, 1976

♈	♉	♊	♋	♌	♍	♎	♏	♐	♑	♒	♓
Aries	Taurus	Gemini	Cancer	Leo	Virgo	Libra	Scorpio	Sagittarius	Capricorn	Aquarius	Pisces

Detour – My Life with Lana Turner, My Mother, Cheryl Crane/Cliff Jahr, Sphere, 1989

The Golden Girls of MGM, Jane Ellen Wayne, Robson Books, 2002

The Bad and the Beautiful – Hollywood in the Fifties, Sam Kashner and Jennifer MacNair, Norton, 2002

Sinatra – The Man Behind the Myth, J. Randall Taraborrelli, Mainstream, 1999

Rat Pack Confidential, Shawn Levy, Fourth Estate, 1999

The Hollywood Greats, Barry Norman, BBC, 1979

Marilyn Monroe The Biography – Donald Spoto, Arrow, 1994

Norma Jean – The Story of Marilyn Monroe - Fred Lawrence Guiles, Granada, 1984

Sex Lives of the Hollywood Goddesses, Nigel Cawthorne, Prion, 1997

Sex Lives of the Hollywood Idols, Nigel Cawthorne, Prion, 1997

Rita – The Life of Rita Hayworth, Edward Z. Epstein and Joseph Morella, W H Allen, 1983

What Falls Away – Mia Farrow, Doubleday, 1997

Howard Hughes – The Untold Story, Peter Harry Brown and Pat H. Broeske, Warner Books, 1997

Among the Porcupines, Carol Matthau, Orion, 1993

Depardieu – A Biography, Marianne Gray, Warner Books, 1992

Churchill, Roy Jenkins, MacMillan, 2001

Brando – The Biography, Peter Manso, Hyperion, 1994

Who on Earth is Tom Baker, Tom Baker, Harper Collins, 1997

Cary Grant – A Class Apart, Graham McCann, Fourth Estate, 1997

The Trouble with Cinderella – An Outline of Identity, Artie Shaw, Fithian Press, 1992

Nobody's Fool – The Lives of Danny Kaye, Bob Gottfried, Simon & Schuster, 1994

Bob Hope – The Road Well Travelled, Lawrence J. Quirk, Applause, 2000

♈	♉	♊	♋	♌	♍	♎	♏	♐	♑	♒	♓
Aries	Taurus	Gemini	Cancer	Leo	Virgo	Libra	Scorpio	Sagittarius	Capricorn	Aquarius	Pisces

Notorious Divorces, Edward Z. Epstein, Lyle Stuart, 1976

Evil Spirits – The Life of Oliver Reed, Cliff Goodwin, Virgin, 2000

Gossip 1920 – 1970, Andrew Barrow, Hamish Hamilton, 1978

My Lucky Stars, Shirley Maclaine, Bantam 1996

The Incomparable Rex, Patrick Garland, Pan, 1999

Lawrence's Women – The Intimate Life of DH Lawrence, Elaine Feinstein, Flamingo, 1994

I Tina – Tina Tuner with Kurt Loder, Penguin, 1987

Rod Stewart – The New Biography – Tim Ewbank and Stafford Hildred, Portrait, 2003

The Real Life of Laurence Olivier – Roger Lewis, Arrow, 1996

Love Scene – The Romance of Laurence Olivier and Vivien Leigh – Jesse Lansky Jr, Sphere, 1980

Olivier – Anthony Holden, Sphere, 1988

Paul McCartney Many Years from Now Barry Miles, Vintage, 1997

Lennon - The Definitive Biography – Ray Coleman, Pan, 2000

Richard Burton – My Brother – Graham Jenkins with Barry Turner, Sphere, 1988

Burton - The Man Behind the Myth – Penny Junor, Sphere, 1986

The Moon's a Balloon – David Niven, Coronet, 1973

Robert Graves His Life and Works – Martin Seymour-Smith, Abacus, 1983

Peter Ustinov The Gift of Laughter - John Miller, Orion, 2004

Charles Boyer – Larry Swindell, Weidenfield and Nicolson, 1983

Is That It? - Bob Geldof, Penguin, 1986

Paula, Michael and Bob – Everything You Know is Wrong – Gerry Agar, Michael O'Mara Books, 2003

Just a Man The Real Michael Hutchence - Tina Hutchence and Patricia Glassop, Pan, 2001

Roman by Polanski – Roman Polanski, Pan, 1985

Bogart – In Search of My Father – Stephen Bogart with Gary Provost,

♈	♉	♊	♋	♌	♍	♎	♏	♐	♑	♒	♓
Aries	Taurus	Gemini	Cancer	Leo	Virgo	Libra	Scorpio	Sagittarius	Capricorn	Aquarius	Pisces

Pan, 1996

The Strange Loves of Adolph Hitler – Gerald McKnight, Sphere, 1978

Tony Curtis – The Autobiography – Tony Curtis and Barry Paris, Mandarin, 1995

Yul – The Man Who Would Be King – Rock Brynner, Fontana, 1990

George Sand – A Womans Life Writ Large – Belinda Jack, Vintage, 2001

Citizen Jane – Christopher Andersen, Dell, 1991

Jane Fonda – An Intimate Biography – Bill Davidson, Signet, 1991

Sparks Fly Upward – Stewart Granger, Granada, 1981

Elizabeth and Phillip The Untold Story – Charles Higham and Roy Moseley, Pan, 1991

Niv - Graham Lord, Orion, 2004

The Moon's a Balloon – David Niven, Coronet, 1971

Bring on the Dancing Horses – David Niven, Coronet, 1973

My Wicked, Wicked Ways – Errol Flynn, Aurum Press, 2002

A Valuable Property – The Life Story of Michael Todd – Michael Todd Jr. and Susan McCarthy Todd, Arbor House, 1983

Books about Astrology:

The Mars Venus Affair – Wendell Perry and Linda Perry, Llewellyn, 2000

Love Signs – Linda Goodman, Pan, 1978

Synchronicity an Acausal Connecting Principle – Carl Jung, Princeton, 1973

Born to be Together – Terry Lamb, Hay House, 1998

Astrology: A Language of Life Volume 1 Progressions – Robert Blaschke, Earthwalk School of Astrology, 1997

Astrology: A Language of Life Volume 4 Relationship Analysis – Robert Blaschke, Earthwalk School of Astrology, 2004

Secondary Progressions – A Time to Remember, Nancy Hastings, Weiser, 1984

Predictive Astrology – The Eagle and The Lark, Bernadette Brady,

♈	♉	♊	♋	♌	♍	♎	♏	♐	♑	♒	♓
Aries	Taurus	Gemini	Cancer	Leo	Virgo	Libra	Scorpio	Sagittarius	Capricorn	Aquarius	Pisces

Weiser, 1999

Predictive Astrology – Christine Shaw, Llewellyn, 2001

Planets in Love – John Townley, Whitford Press, 1978

How to Handle your Human Relationships – Lois Sargent, AFA, 1958

Skymates, Love Sex and Evolutionary Astrology – Jodie and Steven Forrest, Seven Paws Press, 2002

Relationships and Life Cycles – Stephen Arroyo, CRCS, 1993

Astrology, Karma and Transformation – Stephen Arroyo, CRCS, 1992

Astrology, Psychology and the Four Elements - Stephen Arroyo, CRCS, 1975

The Chart Interpretation Handbook – Stephen Arroyo, CRCS, 1989

Synastry - Ronald Davison, Aurora Press, 1983

The Astrology of Human Relationships – Frances Sakoian and Louis S Acker, Peter Davies, 1976

The Combination of Stellar Influences – Reinhold Ebertin, AFA, 1997

Astrology for Lovers – Liz Greene, Thorsons, 1999

Horoscope Symbols – Robert Hand, Whitford Press, 1980

Tetrabiblos – Claudius Ptolemy, Harvard University Press, 1998

Primum Mobile – Placidus de Titus, Institute for the Study of Cycles in World Affairs, 1983

Planets in Youth – Robert Hand, Whitford Press, 1977

Planets in Aspect – Robert Pelletier, Whitford Press, 1974

Astrological Aspects – A Process Oriented Approach - Leyla Rael and Dane Rudhyar, Aurora Press, 1980

The Astrology of Personality – Dane Rudhyar, Aurora Press, 1991

How to Rectify a Birth Chart – Laurie Efrein, Aquarian Press, 1987

The Twelve Houses – Howard Sasportas, Aquarian Press, 1985

Synthesis and Counselling in Astrology – Noel Tyl, Llewellyn, 2004

Harmonics in Astrology – John Addey, Urania Trust, 1996

The Astrologers Handbook - Frances Sakoian and Louis S Acker, Harper Collins, 1987

♈	♉	♊	♋	♌	♍	♎	♏	♐	♑	♒	♓
Aries	Taurus	Gemini	Cancer	Leo	Virgo	Libra	Scorpio	Sagittarius	Capricorn	Aquarius	Pisces

Comment on Astrology

The Moment of Astrology – Geoffrey Cornelius, The Wessex Astrologer, 2002

Astrology in the Year Zero – Garry Phillipson, Flare, 2000

True as the Stars Above – Neil Spencer, Orion, 2000

The Cosmic Loom – Dennis Elwell, Urania Trust, 1999

The Case for Astrology – John Anthony West, Viking, 1991

The Night Speaks, a Meditation on the Astrological Worldview – Steven Forrest, ACS, 1993

Doing Time on Planet Earth – Adrian Duncan, Element, 1990

Web sites:

Arthur Young - www.arthuryoung.com

Astrology in Academia

Faculty of Astrological Studies - www.astrology.org.uk

Avalon School of Astrology - www.avalonastrology.com

Kepler College - www.kepler.edu

Bath Spa University College - www.bathspa.ac.uk/schools/historical-and-cultural-studies/sophia/

RGCSA - www.astrology-research.net/noasp/rgcsa.htm

Mayo School of Astrology - www.astrology-world.com/mayo.html

Astrological Organisations

The Astrological Association of Great Britain - www.astrologer.com/aanet/

International Society for Astrological Research - www.isarastrology.com/

Company of Astrologers - coa.hubcom.net/

American Federation of Astrologers - www.astrologers.com/

Association of Professional Astrologers - www.professionalastrologers.org/

♈	♉	♊	♋	♌	♍	♎	♏	♐	♑	♒	♓
Aries	Taurus	Gemini	Cancer	Leo	Virgo	Libra	Scorpio	Sagittarius	Capricorn	Aquarius	Pisces

Visit the author's website: http://www.positiveastrology.com

[i] Stephen Bogart writes that his father was born on Christmas Day 1899. Bogie told Stephen on his birthday: 'I hope you enjoy it. I never had a birthday of my own to celebrate. I got cheated out of a birthday.' Stephen Bogart, *Bogart – In Search of My Father,* Pan Books, 1995, p17

[ii] There may be some relationships in the 1300 that contain wrong data, it is impossible to deal with completely accurate birth data. I was not present at any of the births and so cannot claim accuracy, over and above, my self-imposed criteria.

[iii] For ease of calculation I have counted an aspect in orb when one planet is at 0 degrees 00 minutes and another is at 2 degrees 00 minutes, this actually means the orbs used are 2 degrees and 1 minute of arc, this when multiplied by 8 equates to the decimal 8.13333333333333333333 degrees.

[iv] I must recognise Plato's Cave in the formulation of this scenario.

[v] The astrological sign of Taurus is a static division of the ecliptic and is no longer coterminous with the constellation Taurus which is an astronomical constellation.

♈	♉	♊	♋	♌	♍	♎	♏	♐	♑	♒	♓
Aries	Taurus	Gemini	Cancer	Leo	Virgo	Libra	Scorpio	Sagittarius	Capricorn	Aquarius	Pisces

O

is a symbol of the world,
of oneness and unity. O Books
explores the many paths of wholeness
and spiritual understanding which
different traditions have developed down
the ages. It aims to bring this knowledge
in accessible form, to a general readership,
providing practical spirituality to today's seekers.

For the full list of over 200 titles covering:

- CHILDREN'S PRAYER, NOVELTY AND GIFT BOOKS
- CHILDREN'S CHRISTIAN AND SPIRITUALITY
- CHRISTMAS AND EASTER
- RELIGION/PHILOSOPHY
- SCHOOL TITLES
- ANGELS/CHANNELLING
- HEALING/MEDITATION
- SELF-HELP/RELATIONSHIPS
- ASTROLOGY/NUMEROLOGY
- SPIRITUAL ENQUIRY
- CHRISTIANITY, EVANGELICAL
AND LIBERAL/RADICAL
- CURRENT AFFAIRS
- HISTORY/BIOGRAPHY
- INSPIRATIONAL/DEVOTIONAL
- WORLD RELIGIONS/INTERFAITH
- BIOGRAPHY AND FICTION
- BIBLE AND REFERENCE
- SCIENCE/PSYCHOLOGY

Please visit our website,
www.O-books.net

The Instant Astrologer

Lyn Birkbeck

A revolutionary new book and software package for the astrological seeker.

With 628pages in full colour, large format, cased, with CD Software, *The Instant Astrologer* is the most comprehensive astrology package available for astrologers everywhere at a readily affordable price, uniquely including a software package of the kind that generally costs at least £200 to use separately. An in-depth analysis is offered for each astrological configuration that an individual chart contains, including the Sign and House positions of the Sun, Moon and Planets, the five major aspects between them, and the Ascendant and Midheaven. In addition to thoroughly interpreting the natal chart, The Instant Astrologer also calculates and interprets Transits (planetary influences through time) for any month or year period, and the Synastry of any two individuals' charts (the chemistry between them).

The Instant Astrologer is divided into three sections, covering the Personality Profile, the Timeline Profile, and the Relationship Profile. The CD similarly consists of three modules that calculate the basic astrological data and then gives the page numbers in the book where the interpretations are given. Complete reports can be shown on screen but not printed. Sit at home and instantly work out your own charts for partners, parents, colleagues, friends as well as yourself!

Lyn is one of those rare astrologers who combines profound personal information with an accessible style designed to empower his readers to do it for themselves. This ground-breaking combination of software and book will enable people to look deeply into themselves and their relationships with others. Lyn knows the magic that comes from giving people the freedom to follow their own investigations.
RICHARD BEAUMONT, *Kindred Spirit*

The brilliant Lyn Birkbeck's new book and CD package, The Instant Astrologer, combines modern technology and the wisdom of the ancients, creating an invitation to enlightenment for the masses, just when we need it most!
Astrologer JENNY LYNCH, Host of NYC's StarPower Astrology Television Show

Lyn Birkbeck manages to provide a self-contained package of "do it yourself" psychological astrology for the novice in a remarkably comprehensive and practical way. It is also a useful resource to aid chart interpretation and research for the more experienced astrologer. It goes beyond the "instant astrologer" approach of its title, most notably by giving practical guidance on how to synthesise all the information gathered. Impressive in its scope and detail, and good value too. LIGHT

Lyn Birkbeck began his working life as a musician and record producer and has now been a widely-consulted astrologer for over 20 years.

1-903816-49-1
£39.00 $69.00

Divine Astrology: the Cosmic Religion

Enlisting the Aid of the Planetary Powers
Lyn Birkbeck

Most of what has been written in the name of astrology refers to personality and prediction. *Divine Astrology* presents Astrology in its true sense as a spiritual rather than predictive system. It sees personality as being an expression of Spirit, and life as being a journey of Spirit driven by cosmic forces and governed by definite laws. Seen in this way the user is no longer simply a hapless puppet of the astrological influences prevailing at birth and through life. He or she is seen as an entity who can become en rapport with the very energies that are the stuff of astrology, the Planetary Powers. It relates these to the nature of God, to other religions and to modern cosmology and physics. We are co-creators with God, and by communing with the Hands of God, the Planetary Powers, we can change our destiny for the better.

To this end, *Divine Astrology* first equips the reader with the "Scriptures", the planets, Signs and Houses that tell what forces we are all subject to. But we are direct expressions of these Powers and Conditions, and so are able to commune with them. This paves the way for the esoteric teaching that we are able to become as Gods. It leads onto the "Rituals" that are the Practice of Astrology, the Cosmic Religion. Like any religion, this involves prayer and ceremony, but more precisely "Invocation". The "equipment" of these Rituals are the 40 Cards that come with the book. The seeker is shown ways to resolve problems, have questions answered, attain support and security, receive enlightenment, become empowered.

The book closes with "God's Skywriting" which demonstrates in simple tabular form how all the major events of the 20th and early 21st Century are correlated to the Cycles of various Planetary Pairs. It shows us how we are all caught up in something far greater and more universal than we usually believe.

For *The Instant Astrologer*

Lyn is one of those rare astrologers who combines profound personal information with an accessible style designed to empower his readers to do it for themselves. This ground-breaking combination of software and book will enable people to look deeply into themselves and their relationships with others. Lyn knows the magic that comes from giving people the freedom to follow their own investigations.
RICHARD BEAUMONT, *Kindred Spirit*

The brilliant Lyn Birkbeck's new book and CD package, The Instant Astrologer, *combines modern technology with the wisdom of the ancients, creating an invitation to enlightenment for the masses, just when we need it most!*
JENNY LYNCH, *Host of NYC's StarPower Astrology Television Show*

Lyn Birkbeck began his working life as a musician and record producer and has now been a widely-consulted astrologer for over 20 years. He is the best-selling author of *Do It Yourself Astrology, The Astrological Oracle, The Instant Astrologer*, and *Astro-Wisdom,* and lives in the Lake District, England.

1 90547 03 7

£14.99/$24.95

The Goddess, the Grail and the Lodge

Alan Butler

We're only just beginning to realize that Bronze Age people knew far more about astronomy and engineering than we have given them credit for, that the Goddess religion continued in various forms through Christianity in the worship of the Virgin Mary down to our own time, that small groups of families and brotherhoods of knights have been highly influential throughout European history. In the essentials of knowledge nothing is new, and the icon of this knowledge has been the Grail.

Reading like a thriller, *The Goddess, the Grail and the Lodge* explains why it was adopted and used, how it existed on different levels to different people, and shows what "Grail Knowledge" really was and is.

Alan Butler is a qualified engineer and an expert on Megalithic cultures and the Knights Templar.

1-903816-69-6

£12.99 $15.95

Savage Breast

One Man's Search for the Goddess
Tim Ward

We think of God as male, but the most common representation of the divine through our history has been as female, as the Goddess. When did this major change happen, and why? More importantly, what did it do to our psyches, and what does it mean for present day relationships between men and women?

Facing the Goddess unleashes turbulent emotions for Ward. With frank honesty he describes the traumas that erupt in his relationship with the woman he loves, who accompanied him on many of his journeys. He weaves travelogue, archaeology, history, art, autobiography into a fascinating and gripping journey through the depths of our history and minds.

An epic, elegant, scholarly search for the goddess, weaving together travel, Greek mythology, and personal autobiographic relationships into a remarkable exploration of the Western World's culture and sexual history. It is also entertainingly human, as we listen and learn from this accomplished person and the challenging mate he wooed. If you ever travel to Greece, take Savage Breast along with you. **HAROLD SCHULMAN**, Professor of Gynaecology at Winthrop University Hospital, and author of *An Intimate History of the Vagina.*

Few male writers except theologians have dared to interpret the goddess movement but Tim Ward in his frank, intrepid way, has given us a thoughtful, personal account of one man's look at the goddess and why many men have been so angry at women. **SUSAN SWAN**, author of *What Cassanova Told Me.*

Ward's book is a kind of archaeology of the soul. He digs through the layers of his own male psyche and cultural conditioning, and does not flinch at what he finds buried underneath. He brings ancient rituals to life as he re-imagines what it must have been like to be a man living in the time of the Goddess. His vivid account cuts to the heart of man's relationship with the feminine divine – and, even more important, to men's relationships with flesh-and-blood women.
WADE DAVIS, author of *One River,* and *The Serpent and the Rainbow.*

Weaving the mythic into the everyday, this book is a fascinating and honest exploration of one man's venture into the realms of the divine feminine. A modern-day Odyssey, a rich travelogue of interior and exterior dimensions, *Savage Breast* is a valuable contribution to not only understanding but experiencing the spirit of unity.
LUCINDA VARDEY, author of *God in All Worlds,* and *The Flowering of the Soul.*

A brutally honest and passionate account of one man's odyssey as he searches to reconcile himself with the goddess, ie; the mysterious yet all powerful feminine principle so deeply rooted in each of us.
Tom Harpur, author of *The Pagan Christ*.

Savage Breast is a powerful account of one man's relationship with the ancient goddesses of Europe. Tim Ward's personal encounters with the goddesses' statues, frescos, temples and sacred sites remind us that these artefacts are not sterile stones but the touchstones to a still living world of human experience.
Richard Rudgley, author of *Lost Civilizations of the Stone Age*.

Savage Breast is ballsy, entertaining, adventuresome, wild, scholarly, sexy, and deep. **Helen Knode**, author of *The Ticket Out*.

A fascinating and fearless exploration of the Goddess and her attributes, for men and women alike. Tim Ward's bold exploration of sexuality in all its guises is an inspiration—frightening, funny, intoxicating (sexy!), always illuminating.
James O'Reilly, publisher, *Travelers' Tales*.

Tim Ward studied philosophy at the University of British Columbia and lived in Asia for six years. He wrote three books about his experiences in the Far East, including the best selling *What the Buddha Never Taught*. He now teaches communications courses based in Maryland, and continues to travel globally.

1 905047 58 4
£12.99 $20.95

Everyday Buddha

A contemporary rendering of the Buddhist classic, The Dhammapada
Karma Yonten Senge

These quintessential sayings of the Buddha offer a rich tapestry of spiritual teachings and reflections on the spiritual path. More than just a collection of Buddhist sayings, *The Dhammapada's* message is timeless and crosses all cultural boundaries. It offers the reader a constant source of inspiration, reflection and companionship. It is a treasure trove of pure wisdom that has something to offer to everyone.

Everyday Buddha brings the original teaching and traditional text of *The Dhammapada* into our 21st century lifestyle, with a contemporary context. Without straying far from the Pali text it renders it in a fresh and modern idiom, with a universal appeal. An introduction provides a background to the life and times of the historical Buddha, and his teachings on the four noble truths and eight fold noble path.

Foreword by H.H. The Dalai Lama, with his seal of approval.

Karma Yonten Senge is a Dharma practitioner of the Karma Kagyu tradition of Tibetan Buddhism. He is an avid follower of Buddha Dharma, and currently lives in Australia.

1 905047 30 4

£9.99/$19.95

In the Light of Meditation

Mike George

In the Light of Meditation offers an introduction to the art and practice of meditation while laying down the foundations for ongoing spiritual development. A series of ten lessons provide specific insights into Raja Yoga, with practical exercises to complement and to help your understanding of the method and underlying teachings.

Accessible, powerful and challenging, this book shows how meditation is more an experience than something that you do, more a process than an achievement, more an ongoing inner journey than a destination. Take your time, be patient with yourself and always be ready to go back to basics, to lesson one, the true identity of the self, which is the foundation of everything.

Beautifully illustrated in full colour, it comes with a CD.

Mike George is a spiritual teacher, motivational speaker, retreat leader and management development facilitator. He brings together the three key strands of his millennium-spiritual and emotional intelligence, leadership development, and continuous learning. His previous books include *Discover Inner Peace, Learn to Relax* and *The 7 Aha!s.*

Is There An Afterlife?

David Fontana

The question whether or not we survive physical death has occupied the minds of men and women since the dawn of recorded history. The spiritual traditions of both West and East have taught that death is not the end, but modern science generally dismisses such teachings.

The fruit of a lifetime's research and experience by a world expert in the field, *Is There An Afterlife?* presents the most complete survey to date of the evidence, both historical and contemporary, for survival of physical death. It looks at the question of what survives-personality, memory, emotions and body image in particular exploring the question of consciousness as primary to and not dependent on matter in the light of recent brain research and quantum physics. It discusses the possible nature of the afterlife, the common threads in Western and Eastern traditions, the common features of "many levels," group souls and reincarnation.

As well a providing the broadest overview of the question, giving due weight to the claims both of science and religion, *Is There An Afterlife?* brings it into personal perspective. It asks how we should live in this life as if death is not the end, and suggests how we should change our behaviour accordingly.

David Fontana is a Fellow of the British Psychological Society (BPS), Founder Chair of the BPS Transpersonal Psychology Section, Past President and current

Vice President of the Society for Psychical Research, and Chair of the SPR Survival Research Committee. He is Distinguished Visiting Fellow at Cardiff University, and Professor of Transpersonal Psychology at Liverpool John Moores University. His many books on spiritual themes have been translated into 25 languages.

1 903816 90 4

£11.99/$16.95

The Fall

The Evidence of a Golden Age, 6,000 Years of Insanity and the Dawning of a New Era

Steve Taylor

The Fall is a major work that overturns mainstream current thinking on the nature of civilization and human nature. It draws on the increasing evidence accumulated over recent decades that pre-literate humanity was relatively peaceful and egalitarian, rather than war-like and crude. It is not "natural" for human beings to kill each other, for men to oppress women, for individuals to accumulate massive wealth and power, or to abuse nature. The worldwide myths of a Golden Age or an original paradise have a factual, archaeological basis.

Taylor's ideas are provocative, and never fail to captivate the reader. It is my fervent wish that this important book will have a wide audience and reach the individuals and institutions that mould public opinion and behaviour. In a world where the very existence of humanity is threatened, Steve Taylor offers a visionary yet practical path out of the morass that distorts human nature.
DR STANLEY KRIPPNER, Professor of Psychology, Saybrooke Graduate School, California.

The Fall *is an astonishing work, full of amazing erudition, all brilliantly organized and argued. The argument that human beings have not always been - and do not have to be - such a psychological mess is presented with a beautiful inevitability and logic. The book is a remarkable feat.* COLIN WILSON

The Fall *is a fascinating heretical work which demonstrates that the myth of the golden age reflects an archaic social reality. Read it and be cured.*
RICHARD RUDGLEY, author of *Lost Civilizations of the Stone Age*

A fascinating, enlightening and inspiring investigation into the roots of human consciousness and a much needed proscription for a truly human future.
GARY LACHMANN, author of *A Secret History of Consciousness*

A thought-provoking diagnosis of the causes of warfare, patriarchy and materialism which holds potential for bringing humans more in harmony with each other, nature, and themselves.
TIM KASSER, author of *The High Price of Materialism*

Well-argued, thoughtful, provocative and a pleasure to read.
CHRISTOPHER RYAN, Institute of Advanced Medicine and Advanced Behavioral Technology, Juarez, Mexico

Steve Taylor is a university and college lecturer in Manchester, England, and spent seven years researching and writing this book. He has written many articles and essays on psychology and spirituality for mainstream magazines and academic journals.

1 905047 20 7
£12.99 $24.95